Introduction to Social and Political Philosophy

To Marjan & Tara
and Stefan & Beren

Introduction to Social and Political Philosophy
Texts and Cases

EDITED BY OMID PAYROW SHABANI AND MONIQUE DEVEAUX

OXFORD
UNIVERSITY PRESS

OXFORD
UNIVERSITY PRESS

Oxford University Press is a department of the University of Oxford.
It furthers the University's objective of excellence in research, scholarship,
and education by publishing worldwide. Oxford is a registered trade mark of
Oxford University Press in the UK and in certain other countries.

Published in Canada by
Oxford University Press
8 Sampson Mews, Suite 204,
Don Mills, Ontario M3C 0H5 Canada

www.oupcanada.com

Library and Archives Canada Cataloguing in Publication

Introduction to social and political philososphy : texts and cases /
edited by Omid Payrow Shabani, and Monique Deveaux.

Includes index.
ISBN 978-0-19-543131-5 (bound)

1. Political science—Philosophy—Textbooks. 2. Social sciences—
Philosophy—Textbooks. I. Payrow Shabani, Omid, editor of
compilation II. Deveaux, Monique, editor of compilation

JA71.I58 2014   320.01   C2013-908211-5

Cover image: Jean Heguy/First Light/Getty Images

Oxford University Press is committed to our environment.
Wherever possible, our books are printed on paper which comes from
responsible sources.

Printed and bound in the United States of America

1 2 3 4 — 17 16 15 14

Contents

XVIII Charles Taylor 469

Preface

The current textbook came about as a result of a particular gap in this area. Existing textbooks in social and political philosophy introduce students to this field of study through a familiar selection of canonical—mainly historical—readings. Some also offer brief introductory explanations or notes to accompany each reading. Few, however, connect these writings with a discussion of particular social and political issues or events that demonstrate the enduring relevance of these theoretical texts for the non-specialist reader. Of the small subset that do, none focuses on examples important to Canadian history and politics. By contrast, our textbook pairs key readings by philosophers with a "case" from Canadian social, legal, or political contexts. From the British Columbia Supreme Court's testing of laws against polygamy in 2011, to a Quebec bill aimed at ending the province's student strikes of 2012, to the question of First Nations' self-determination, the cases presented here are topical and timely. Controversies drawn from one's own social and political context are, we believe, of more immediate interest and relevance to many readers; thus, a textbook that relates social and political philosophy to questions and controversies that have arisen in Canadian society should help to better engage students in Canadian universities.

In our experience as instructors of introductory courses in social and political philosophy, the prose of the classic texts in this area can be challenging for many students, and their significance sometimes opaque. Students appreciate any contextualization and "translation" of these texts; they also seek an account of why *these* texts are still read, and what insights they hold for us today. For many students, what ultimately enables them to grasp the gist of these texts is to see them in terms of events or contexts that are somewhat familiar and which seem to *matter*. So, as teachers, we often find ourselves supplying this context by drawing on contemporary examples to illustrate the continued significance of these writings. For instance, the insights of John Locke's *A Letter Concerning Toleration* strikes many first-year students as obvious and uncontentious until they see it made relevant through the discussion of such issues as public funding for religious schools in Ontario, the banning of religious garments and symbols in the public service in Quebec, or the ordination of women priests. The goal of this textbook, therefore, is to help instructors and students make these sorts of connections between classic readings and contemporary problems more easily and explicitly. This is the unique feature of the textbook that we hope will prove a useful tool for teaching and learning classic and contemporary readings in social and political philosophy.

The addition of introductory notes giving an overview of the life and thought of each philosopher makes the primary readings more accessible to undergraduate readers. We also supply commentary that explains the background and context of the event or legal decision under discussion, indicating how the reading and the text relate to one another. Finally, study questions for both the classic texts and the cases are provided in order to help students to engage more closely and critically with the readings.

A Note to Instructors

All textbooks in social and political philosophy comprise a distinctive, and partial, selection of readings from this field of study. The present collection is no exception. We do not attempt to provide a comprehensive selection of the history of social and political philosophy. Instead, we begin with selections from the canonical writings of Plato and Aristotle and end with readings by several of the most significant authors in contemporary social and political philosophy, with an eye toward the practical relevance of these texts for today's students. In part, this relevance is decided by how well a particular philosophical text lends itself to a discussion of a concrete issue (or legal case) drawn from the Canadian context. The selection, however, is in the end, just that: a selection. We have tried to include thinkers that instructors of introductory courses in social and political philosophy in Canada frequently teach, and have thus left out philosophers that many of us reserve for upper-level courses (hence, Hegel, a notoriously difficult thinker, is notably absent). There are more chapters on contemporary thinkers than is usual for textbooks of this sort, a decision we think is warranted by both the case-pairing format and our desire to encourage students to find connections between their moral and political worlds and the concepts and problems explored by philosophical texts. Demands of space prevented us from including all the thinkers and periods we would like to have covered; medieval thinkers are not represented in this volume, for instance. But because this textbook is not intended as a comprehensive overview of the history of political thought, but rather, as a topical introduction to classic readings explored through contemporary controversies in social and political philosophy, selectivity was especially essential.

While the particular array of readings and thinkers included here is not comprehensive, then, we believe it is large enough to allow instructors to pick what works best for their purposes. Instructors will notice that while the chapters on historical figures are ordered chronologically (according to the date of birth of the thinker), the chapters on twentieth- and twenty-first-century philosophers are organized more thematically, to better chart the trajectory of philosophical discussion about particular socio-political issues in recent thought—notably, inequality, gender justice, social power, religious pluralism, and multiculturalism.

A final important note concerns the matching of cases with readings: no particular example from Canadian social, legal, or political history fully reflects all of the main insights of its companion reading. The cases are merely meant as a tool to enable instructors and readers to delve more deeply into one (or a few) aspects of a classic text, by raising an issue that is important to the argument of the reading. For example, in the chapter on Locke, the case we have chosen explores the right of parents to refuse secular ethics instruction for their school-aged children; this example brings into focus Locke's idea of the separation of church and state in *A Letter Concerning Toleration*, but leaves out any discussion of the *Second Treatise of Government* (also included here). The instructor, therefore, should remind the students that the readings are always much richer in theoretical substance than what the discussion of a case might reveal.

Acknowledgements

The idea for this textbook emerged from Payrow Shabani's experience of teaching an introductory course in social and political philosophy at the University of Guelph over several years. He would like to thank his students in these classes for their enthusiasm, interest, and enlightening curiosity; their feedback has been invaluable for preparing this book. Payrow Shabani is also grateful to colleagues at Guelph who offered comments, encouragement, and guidance on this project, especially Peter Lopston, Andrew Bailey, Karen Wendling, and John Lundy. He also expresses gratitude to Deveaux for her significant contribution to this project. Finally, he thanks his family—his wife Marjan and daughter Tara—who not only bore the chaos associated with his working on the book at home, but also provided love and support so that he could see this project through.

Deveaux joined this project after it was already launched, and is grateful to Payrow Shabani for conceiving of the textbook, as well as for his perseverance and patience. She also thanks the students in her introductory courses in social and political philosophy at Williams College in Massachusetts (1998–2009), who inspired her to draw connections between classic texts and current socio-political problems.

Both authors are grateful to the editorial staff at Oxford University Press Canada, particularly Jodi Lewchuk, Stephen Kotowych, and Lisa Ball for their guidance and support, and to Tara Tovell for her excellent copy-editing work.

Introduction

This textbook consists of selected writings by 18 historical and contemporary thinkers of central importance to the study of Western social and political philosophy today. What distinguishes this volume from similar collections is that it pairs each reading with a specific issue or event drawn from the Canadian social, legal, or political context. These "cases" are carefully chosen to illuminate some of the key concepts and problems explored by the philosophical text. In this way, we aim to bring social and political theory to life for students by helping them to see the relevance of these writings to their own political and legal landscape. Although students and instructors will not likely be familiar with all of the controversies or cases presented here, we think that they will agree that these examples serve not only to illustrate the themes in the primary reading, but also to provide an invitation for deeper explorations of the arguments of their authors.

The format of this textbook reflects the editors' view of social and political philosophy as first and foremost the study of problems and questions that concern our collective social and political life. It is often said that the first question of political theory (or philosophy) is simply "How should I live?," a question that philosophers of antiquity in particular addressed extensively. But as the readings in this textbook show, parsing this question quickly leads us to questions about the form that our political world should take: "How should we organize our political society?," "Who should rule, and *why*?," and "Why should I obey?" These questions about political authority and governance are arguably deeply enmeshed with questions of value: "What does a good life consist of?," "What do human beings *need* in order to flourish?," and "*How* should these needs be met—and which social and political arrangements can best facilitate this?" As these questions suggest, at its broadest, social and political philosophy stretches far beyond questions concerning the organization of political society, intersecting at times with the closely related fields of normative ethics, the philosophy of law, and moral philosophy. Some contemporary social and political philosophy also draws on—and contributes to—such emerging fields of study as critical race theory, feminist thought, and development ethics (concerned with questions of North–South inequality, poverty, and development).

Although "social and political philosophy" is frequently treated as a single area of study, it is worth noting the subtle distinctions between these two branches. Political philosophy, while arguably including many of the topics associated with social philosophy, attends more directly to questions regarding our collective institutional arrangements. Thus, for example, the topics of political authority, obligation, legitimacy, and sovereignty are of central concern to political philosophy; so are, relatedly, inquiries into the proper relationship between the state and citizens, as well as between fellow citizens and private individuals. Many of the normative frameworks and institutional arrangements for political life proposed by political theorists since Plato have emerged as responses to these questions and issues (or as responses to other thinkers' reflections on these matters). For example, social contract-type and contractarian justifications for the state, Marxist and anarchist critiques of state power, and proposals for democratic models of political power can be seen as responses to the perennial problems of political obligation, political legitimacy, the proper scope and limits of personal freedom, the nature and justification of rights, and the fairness—or injustice—of particular systems of social and economic distribution and property ownership.

By contrast, social philosophy, while not necessarily uninterested in the state or political power, tends to foreground the social relations, structures, and arrangements of a given society. It asks, for instance, about the dynamics of power that underpin—and sometimes follow from—particular social institutions, forms of political authority, and social practices. Among the topics of concern to social (and some moral) philosophers are the family and parenting; love, sexuality, and friendship; racism and sexual oppression; and war and violence. Michel Foucault's explorations of the social practices and modes of subjectivity associated with modern institutions such as the public school, the prison, and the mental hospital illustrate social philosophy's interest in questions that stretch beyond the core institutions and problems of political life. Feminist philosophers and thinkers who address race show how our social institutions, practices, and relationships deeply affect, and in turn are shaped by, the content and character of our legal and political institutions. The norms and practices in the traditional family in Western society, for instance, have a deep impact on the social equality—or inequality—of the sexes, and so the justice—or injustice—of our collective life.

Increasingly, contemporary political philosophers have begun to expand their study of problems of politics far beyond the classic problems of political authority and obligation, or related topics, such as personal freedom, citizenship, and the just distribution of social and economic goods and opportunities. Notably, political thinkers that address the ramifications of race, ethnicity, class, and gender are especially keen to explore the connections between the social and political aspects of life. The view that social and ethical institutions and practices are important to politics is of course not new; it has characterized many pivotal periods of political thought (ancient Greek and Roman, for example). Its re-emergence as a valid perspective in contemporary political theory nonetheless signals an important—and, we argue, welcome—shift. Scholars of political philosophy can bring much-needed insights to the study of social life because they are usually careful to ask about its institutional and legal dimensions, and their implications. This focus in turn is partly explained by the influence of some areas of the discipline of political science on political philosophy: at least in North America, scholars of political theory are trained in departments of political science, where a premium is placed on analyses of the institutional forms—actual or possible—that solutions may take.

The subtle distinctions between social and political philosophy, then, have begun to give way to an expanded view of "the social," and especially, "the political," insofar as philosophical study is concerned. The breadth of social and political philosophy and its focus on issues of direct relevance to our daily lives as private individuals, members of families and communities, and citizens (domestic and global), gives it a special place of prominence within philosophy as a whole. It is no coincidence that many of the best-known thinkers in the history of philosophy have written extensively in social or political philosophy (Plato, Aristotle, Aquinas, Augustine, Machiavelli, Kant, Locke, Hume, Hegel, Mill). While at times the problems they take up can seem rather abstract, in reality, they bear directly on many aspects of our everyday lives: indeed, they speak to our roles as members of particular polities; to our status as citizens or holders of liberties; to our standing as members of cultural and social groups, and even to our experiences as members of the global community.

To underscore the relevance of the study of social and political thought, the present collection of readings not only foregrounds concepts that have long been of central importance to this branch of philosophy, but also includes topics that have emerged more recently—such as sexual inequality, racism, and cultural justice. Still, it makes sense, we think, for newcomers to begin with the foundational questions of political philosophy. Readers will see that the selections from Plato's *Republic* and Aristotle's *Nicomachean Ethics* encourage us to contemplate the best form of political society and the many elements, individual as well as collective, of which it is comprised. Plato's thoughts on knowledge and political power, moreover, serve as a cautionary note to those engaged in imagining the ideal state. Selections from *The Republic* are followed by a discussion of the Senate in Canada, which many critics have argued departs in practice from the original (Platonic) justification for this kind of institution: namely, that its leaders (appointed senators) would be highly knowledgeable and not have vested political interests. Next, in *Nicomachean Ethics*, Aristotle addresses the topic of "Justice," which gets divided into distributive justice—the share that people acquire from the state or each other by way of contract—and corrective justice—a compensatory measure to balance what has been distributed. Readers will see how a Canadian Supreme Court case that concerns proportionality in criminal sentencing (*R. v. Ipeelee*, 2012) invites us to consider Aristotle's insights on justice.

Niccolò Machiavelli's *The Prince* and Thomas Hobbes' *Leviathan* direct our attention to problems of political power and obligation. Whether we are inclined to read *The Prince* as a how-to manual for princes seeking to maintain power, or as a clever critique of princely rule coupled with a veiled argument for republican freedoms, this text squarely focuses our attention on the problems of political power and political morality. A consideration of the legacy of renowned Quebec politician Maurice Duplessis provides an opportunity to reflect on the concrete manifestation of Machiavelli's advice to princes. Hobbes' treatise is also concerned with these themes but takes a different tack, famously framing the problem of political obligation in terms of the need for absolute obedience in order to establish the security of the state. Unlike other thinkers associated with the social contract tradition, for Hobbes the prospect of political resistance is deeply undermining of the political covenant. We invite readers to contemplate this issue through a discussion of legislation introduced in 2012 by the Quebec legislature to end widespread public (especially student) protests over the government's proposed tuition fee increases.

If Hobbes is credited with focusing attention on the nature and scope of political authority and obligation, John Locke and Jean-Jacques Rousseau deepen this inquiry by including a more systematic analysis of the basis of political legitimacy. Locke's *Second Treatise of Government*, included in this volume, advances a compelling argument in favour of limited representative government, all the while challenging feudal and absolutist conceptions of political power. His *Letter Concerning Toleration* fleshes out what was for Locke a very immediate and pressing problem, namely, religious intolerance. The accompanying 2012 Supreme Court decision (*S.L. v. Commission scolaire des Chênes*) illustrates that the issue of religious toleration remains important to Canadians today: in this case, parents of Quebec schoolchildren claimed that their (and their children's) Charter rights to freedom of religion and expression are violated by the introduction of a mandatory—and secular— Ethics and Religious Culture course in schools, replacing the previously religious content of similar courses.

Rousseau's *Social Contract* also asks about the basis of political legitimacy and the scope of political obligation, but gives quite different answers from those of Hobbes or Locke. Indeed, the anti-Enlightenment tone of Rousseau's treatise demands that we think hard about some of the negative implications of systems of political representation and reconsider the requirements of popular sovereignty. The enduring relevance of these topics is illustrated through a discussion of the constitutionality of Quebec's secessionist aspirations (*Reference re Secession of Quebec*, 1998).

Immanuel Kant, John Stuart Mill, and Karl Marx are the final thinkers studied in the historical section of the reader. Kant's essay "On the Common Saying: 'This May Be True in Theory but It Does Not Apply in Practice,'" stands as an important refutation of the view— held by Hobbes, among others—that political philosophy ought only to be concerned with pragmatic matters and not questions of abstract right. Contemporary charters of rights, such as the Canadian Charter of Rights and Freedoms, are a testament to Kant's insistence that principles of right are an essential element of practical political governance. Kant's classic essay is paired with the Charter as a way of encouraging students to delve more deeply into questions surrounding the interface of political principles with practical legal rights and duties.

Mill, alarmed at the worsening social and work conditions in his society, and a noted social reformer, nonetheless held fast to the ideal of representative liberal government as a solution to society's many injustices and ailments. At its best, such a government could and should protect the widest possible scope of personal and group liberty—as he argues in "On Liberty"—as well as enhancing the overall happiness or utility of individuals—as he insists in "Utilitarianism". Yet as Mill himself well understood, sometimes the ideals of social utility and personal freedom in matters of lifestyle and conscience stand in tension; the British Columbia Supreme Court's testing of the constitutionality of Canada's law against polygamy in 2011 provides an excellent illustration of this tension, echoing Mill's own discussion of the practice in "On Liberty".

Questions concerning the political legitimacy of the state, raised so sharply by Rousseau, are revisited by Marx in his *Communist Manifesto* (co-authored with Friedrich Engels), but with still more radical implications. Impugning the exploitative labour and property relations of mid-nineteenth-century Europe, Marx speculated that the cyclical crises of capitalism, together with worker solidarity and communist leadership, would eventually hasten the end of the misery caused by unfettered capitalism. A discussion of the Winnipeg General Strike of 1919 brings to light some important aspects of this history of social class struggle in the Canadian context.

The questions and problems that preoccupy the contemporary thinkers represented here are many and varied; they both overlap with and, in some cases, depart significantly from those taken up by the historical figures. We have chosen to cluster contemporary thinkers together according to the theoretical traditions—and sometimes topics—with which they are most closely associated, rather than order them chronologically. John Rawls and Robert Nozick invoke the social contract tradition by inviting readers to imagine hypothetical choice situations that function in much the same way as earlier thinkers' metaphorical states of nature. Unlike these earlier authors, however, Rawls and Nozick are concerned not only with political legitimacy and ideal political arrangements, but also with questions of justice in property, as well as the distribution of social and economic benefits and advantages. To illustrate the relevance of issues of socio-economic justice for us today, we have included an excerpt from the landmark document that affirms universal health care in Canada: the Canada Health Act. This 1984 legislation explains why access to publicly funded health services is not only a right of citizens and residents, but also conducive to a good life and a well-functioning society. By contrast, the challenges that Nozick directs at the liberal social welfare state, particularly what he perceives as restrictions on personal liberty, are nicely highlighted by the Canadian Supreme Court's decision in *R. v. Oakes* (1986). This case, which explores the presumption of innocence and the burden of proof in Canadian criminal law, ultimately deals with the justifiable and unjustifiable limitations on state power.

Among the most trenchant critics of the social contract tradition of liberalism are feminist theorists and philosophers of race. In a selection from her paradigm-shifting 1989 book *Justice, Gender, and the Family*, Susan Moller Okin argues that liberal thinkers have traditionally only been concerned with voluntary, contractual relationships (seen as the basis for government), while ignoring the indispensible role played by involuntary relationships and practices, such as nurturing and raising children. This blind spot in turn means that liberal thinkers have not paid attention to sexual inequality in the private and social spheres, including, most importantly, in the family. Okin insists that this inequality jeopardizes political justice in myriad ways, chiefly because it undermines the norms of fairness and equal treatment (and opportunity) in social, economic, and political life. To secure liberal justice, we need to see and address actual gender inequalities in society. The Supreme Court case of *R. v. Lavallee* (1990)—which deals with what has come to be known as the "battered woman syndrome"—demonstrates that there are background social conditions that may impair female citizens' equal access to justice in the legal and political realms.

Charles Mills also explores some troubling features of liberalism in his essay "Racial Liberalism." In this article, Mills suggests that the liberal social contract that undergirds liberal democratic societies depends upon the historical denial of the personhood of non-white persons. As such, it cannot deliver the universal rights and individual equality taken to be the hallmarks of liberalism. To help students explore the nature of this charge and its relevance to the Canadian context, we have paired Mill's article with a Canadian Human Rights Tribunal hearing that commenced in 2012. In this case, First Nations groups claim that the federal government discriminates against Aboriginal children on reserves by giving significantly less funding to their child welfare services than to non-Aboriginal child services.

The view that liberalism, at least in its unamended form, cannot make good on its myriad promises is one that is broadly shared by three otherwise quite divergent thinkers: Martha Nussbaum, Jürgen Habermas, and Michel Foucault. Nussbaum draws on Aristotelian and Marxian conceptions of human flourishing to advance a conception of "human capabilities" that she argues ought to be supported by modern liberal democratic governments. These capabilities flesh out, in essence, the goods and capacities to which human rights declarations typically refer. Yet Nussbaum's contention that laws and practices that prevent the full development of women's capabilities ought not to be permitted in liberal societies stands uneasily with her claim that the capabilities approach is culturally universal, and not specific to Western societies. This tension is illuminated by the proposal to introduce shari'a (Islamic law) arbitration into the family court system in Ontario in 2004, and the various responses to this prospect by feminists, Muslim groups, and advocates of religious pluralism.

Habermas and Foucault further examine the vexed relationship between the social, political, and legal arrangements of contemporary societies. While both thinkers situate themselves within the Kantian tradition of critical theory, they pursue the ideal of emancipation in very different ways. For Habermas, emancipation results from unfettered communication aimed at understanding. In order to reach this goal in politics, citizens' communicative action ought to be protected against external influences such as power, money, and any coercion in general. The principle of democratic inclusion, critical to Habermas's normative thought, is explored by looking at the establishment, and subsequent dismantling, of a federal program that enabled Canadians to test the Charter's protection of their equality rights.

For Foucault, emancipation, and freedom in general, is complicated by the omnipresence of relations of social and political power, which continually shape us and our institutions on multiple levels. Once we begin to look at these relationships of power more closely, we see that concepts such as consent, choice, and autonomy take on ever-greater complexity. In the Supreme Court case of *Norberg v. Wynrib* (1992), Foucauldian ideas can help us to better understand the relationship between Norberg (a female patient) and Wynrib (a male doctor) not as a zero sum power relation, but rather, as a site in which complex subjectivities are produced by social norms, practices, and institutions.

Finally, we come to the issues of cultural belonging, group identity and membership, and sovereignty, all of which figure centrally in the Canadian social and political landscape. All of these themes are highlighted by Charles Taylor's essay, "Why Do Nations Have to Become States?," and Will Kymlicka's pivotal book on justice for cultural groups in liberal democratic states, *Multicultural Citizenship*. Readers will easily recognize in these selections the familiar dilemma of how a modern multicultural society can accommodate diverse religious, ethnic, linguistic, and cultural groups without fracturing common political ideals and institutions. Excerpts from the final report of the Bouchard-Taylor Commission on the accommodation of religious and cultural minorities in Quebec, which Charles Taylor co-authored, provide an unusual opportunity to place this thinker's ideas in historical context. To help students critically reflect on Kymlicka's arguments concerning the special status and rights claims of national minority groups, we have included an excerpt from the landmark final agreement between the Maa-nulth First Nations people of Vancouver island (2011) and the federal and B.C. governments.

While no textbook in social and political theory can possibly hope to provide a complete overview of all of the significant themes in this expansive area of philosophy, the present volume aims to introduce most of the key concepts and questions that are of unquestionable relevance for Canadian students today. The introductions to the readings in social and political thought serve as a roadmap to these sometimes difficult texts, situating each piece historically and alerting the reader to its main ideas. The contemporary "case" that follows each classic reading provides a current and topical context for exploring the (sometimes conflicting) claims, principles, or ideals that emerge in the primary text. Together, these classic and contemporary readings, juxtaposed with legal or political controversies drawn from the Canadian context, present readers with an opportunity to reflect critically—and anew—on key problems and questions in social and political philosophy.

CHAPTER
1

Plato

Introduction

Plato was a Greek philosopher, born in Athens around 427 BCE into an aristocratic family. Socrates was a friend of Plato's family and his teacher from early childhood. Because of the influence of Socrates' teaching, Plato did not go into politics and instead pursued philosophy. But Socrates never wrote any of his ideas down, which is why Plato actively defended and elaborated on Socrates' ideas in a series of books. Many of these, like the present text, take the form of a dialogue between Socrates and various interlocutors. Plato also develops his own ideas in some of these texts.

Plato

After the execution of Socrates (399 BCE), Plato left Athens. But he returned in 387 BCE and founded the Academy, a school of higher learning and education that endured for centuries. Plato lived a long life and died at the age of 81 in 347 BCE.

The excerpts provided here are from *The Republic*, probably the most influential book in the history of philosophy. The reason for this degree of influence is simple: Plato's *Republic* offers the first in-depth treatment of some of the most fundamental philosophical questions in philosophy, such as the nature of justice and truth, and the character of the just city. Scholars disagree about the extent to which *The Republic* should be read as a prescription for the just society; some argue that it is best approached as a thought exercise in ethics rather than a blueprint for political justice. It is composed of 10 books and the present textbook includes substantial parts of Books III, IV, V, and VII. This selection of *The Republic* starts as a conversation among Socrates and Plato's two older brothers, Glaucon and Adeimantus, on the comparison between a just man and an unjust man—as a way of determining whether justice is better than injustice. Socrates suggests that they begin with something easier than comparing the two individual men, and theorizes a bigger context in which the ideal of justice can be seen more clearly. He proposes to first look at what makes a city just and then, by way of analogy, to extend the conclusion to the individual men.

Early on in the dialogue, Socrates establishes that there are different classes of citizens in a city, who by their nature are suited for specific tasks. He names three such classes as the ruling class of guardians, the auxiliary class of warriors, and the producer class, made up of artisans, farmers, and merchants. It is from the guardian class that philosopher kings emerge, ruling the city based on their knowledge and experience. The job of the auxiliary class of warriors is to protect and assist the rulers by enforcing their rule. The job of the producer class is to provide basic goods and services, and to obey the rule of the guardians.

According to the Greek doctrine of the four cardinal virtues, in a good city we will have wisdom, courage, moderation, and justice. Now, given that we have found the first three virtues respectively in the conduct of the guardians, the warriors, and the producer class, justice, according to Socrates, is to be found in the attributes of the city that allow for the first three qualities to come to the fore. Justice, therefore, is each part doing what it does best—that is, each class doing the task for which it is suited. This is only possible when wisdom, courage, and moderation work together in harmony.

Socrates moves on to define the just person. He argues that in the same way that there are three classes of person in the city, so too is the soul of an individual made up of three parts: the calculating or rational part, the spirited part, and the desiring or appetitive part. In the just soul, and, by extension, just person, it is important that reason rules the appetite, with the spirit assisting in this. The just person is thus revealed not so much by his or her external acts but by the degree to which these three parts are in a harmonious relationship (with reason playing the guiding role). Similarly, in the just city, the different classes do not meddle with each other or interfere with one another's distinctive tasks. The virtue of justice, then, seems to express the health, beauty, and good condition of a soul. The meandering route that Socrates takes to reach these and other conclusions starts, in the following excerpt, with a conversation with Glaucon on the subject of the best training for a good judge.

Further Readings

Annas, J. (1981). *An Introduction to Plato's Republic*. Oxford: Clarendon Press.

Annas, J. (2003). *Plato: A Very Short Introduction*. Oxford: Oxford University Press.

Kraut, R. (ed.) (1992). *The Cambridge Companion to Plato*. Cambridge: Cambridge University Press.

Kraut, R. (1997). *Plato's Republic: Critical Essays*. Lanham: Rowman and Littlefield.

Smith, N.D. (2000). *The Philosophy of Socrates*. Boulder: Westview Press.

White, N. (1979). *A Companion to Plato's Republic*. Indianapolis: Hackett.

Plato, From *The Republic*

Plato's Republic, *translated by G.M.A. Grube*
(Indianapolis: Hackett Publishing Company, 1974).

Book III, 409a–417b
Socrates/Glaucon

409   As for the judge,[1] my friend, it is with his soul that he rules another soul, and it is not possible for a soul to be nurtured among evil souls, associate with them, indulge itself in all kinds of wrongdoing, and come through in the end so as to be able to judge other people's crimes from its own experience as it can with physical diseases. It must itself remain pure and without experience of vice when it is young, if it is to be beautiful and good itself and have a healthy judgment of just actions. That is why b good people, when young, appear simple-minded and easily deceived, because they do not have within themselves any model of evil feelings. —They certainly have that experience.

Therefore, I said, a good judge must not be a young but an old man, who has learned late the nature of injustice. He cannot recognize it as anything of his own, he must have studied it as something alien, present in other people. It is only after a long time that he fully recognizes c its nature, intellectually, and not from his own experience.

Such a judge, he said, is likely to be a very noble character.

And good too, which was what you asked, for he who has a good soul is good. That other character, the clever and suspicious one who has committed many wrongs himself, the rascal who thinks himself wise, appears clever in the company of his like because of his caution and because he refers things to a model within himself, but when he meets with good, older people, he is seen to be foolish, distrustful at the wrong time, d and ignorant of moral health, as he has no model of this within himself. Too often, however, whether the people he meets are good or bad, he is thought to be wise rather than ignorant by others as well as by himself. —That is altogether true.

It is not such a man that we must seek to be a good and wise judge, but the former type. Wickedness could never know either itself or virtue, whereas virtue, as one's nature is being educated, will at the same time acquire the knowledge of itself and of wickedness. It is that man e who becomes wise, as I believe, not the bad man. —I agree with you.

Therefore you will legislate in our city for the kind of medicine we have mentioned and for this kind of judicial system. Together they will look after the well endowed in 410 body and soul. Those not so endowed physically will be allowed to die, and those who are incurably evil in their soul will be executed.

That seems to be best, he said, both for the victims and for the city.

The young, I said, will obviously be wary of coming into court because theirs is that simple culture in the arts which we said engenders modesty. —Quite so.

And will not the cultured man if he is willing to pur- b sue physical culture in the same way, choose to have no need of medicine except when unavoidable? —I think so.

He will labour at physical exercises in order to arouse the spirited part of his nature rather than to acquire that physical strength for the sake of which the other athletes diet and exercise. —Quite right.

And I said: Those, Glaucon, who establish education in the arts and physical training do not do so with the c aim that people attribute to them, namely to take care of the body by means of the one, and of the soul by means of the other. —What then?

They may well, I said, establish both in large part to look after the soul. —How so?

Do you not realize, I said, the state of mind of those who practise physical culture throughout their life but do not touch the arts, and of those in the opposite case? —What are you talking about?

I am talking of harshness and rigidity, I said, and d also of softness and gentleness.

I get the point, he said. You mean that those who devote themselves exclusively to physical culture turn out to be harsher than they should be, while those who devote themselves to the arts become softer than is good for them.

And further, said I, it is the spirited part of one's nature which provides the harshness; rightly nurtured it becomes courageous, but if strained too far it would be likely to become rigid and harsh to deal with. —I think so.

e　　And is it not the wisdom-loving nature which provides the gentleness, and, if relaxed too far, becomes softer than it should, though if properly nurtured it is gentle and orderly? —That is so.

We said that our guardians must have both these natures. —They must.

These must then be harmonized with each other? —Of course.

411　　If this harmony is achieved the soul is both moderate and brave? —Certainly.

If not, it becomes cowardly and boorish? —Yes indeed.

Therefore, when a man gives music an opportunity to charm his soul with the flute, and to pour through his ears as through a funnel those sweet, soft, and plaintive tunes we have mentioned, when he spends his whole life humming them and delighting in them, then at fast, if he b　has any spirit, it is softened as iron is tempered and, from being hard and useless, is made useful. But if he keeps on, does not desist, but is beguiled by this music, after a time his spirit is melted and dissolved until it vanishes, cut out of his soul like a tendon, and he becomes "a feeble warrior."[2] —Quite so.

And if, I said, he had a spiritless nature from the first, this process is soon accomplished. If he had a spirited nature, this spirit becomes weak and unstable, flaring c　up for trifles and as quickly quenched. So men become quick-tempered and prone to anger instead of spirited, and they are full of peevishness. —That is certainly true.

What if a man labours much at physical exercises and lives well but is quite out of touch with the arts and philosophy? Is he not in good physical condition at first, full of resolution and spirit, and becomes braver than he was before? — Certainly.

But if he does nothing else and never associates with d　the Muse? He never has a taste of any learning or any investigation; he has no share in any reasoned discussion or any other form of culture; even if he had some love of learning in his soul it soon becomes enfeebled, deaf, and blind as it is not aroused or nurtured; and even his senses are not sharpened. —That is so, he said.

I believe that such a man comes to hate reasoned discussion and the arts; he makes no further use of pere　suasion but bulls his way through every situation by force and fierceness like a wild beast; he lives in ignorance and ineptitude [sic] with a total lack of harmony and grace. —That is most certainly the case.

It seems then that a god has given men these two means, artistic and physical education, to deal with these two parts of themselves, not the body and the soul except

incidentally but the spirited and the wisdom-loving parts, in order that these be in harmony with each other,　412 each being stretched and relaxed to the proper point. —It seems so.

We should then quite correctly call the man who achieves the most beautiful blend of physical and artistic culture, and in due measure impresses this upon his soul, the completely Muse-inspired and harmonious man, far more so than the musician who harmonizes the strings of his instrument. —That is very likely, Socrates.

Therefore in our city too, Glaucon, we shall always need this kind of man as an overseer, if our community　b is to be preserved? —We shall certainly have the greatest need of him.

These then are the outlines of our education and upbringing, but why should one enumerate the dances of our youth, their hunts and chases with hounds, their gymnastic and horse-riding contests? These must pretty clearly follow our outlines and are no longer hard to discover. —Perhaps not.

Very well, I said. Shall we choose as our next topic of discussion which of these same men shall rule,[3] and　c which be ruled? —Why not?

Now it is obvious that the rulers must be older men and that the younger must be ruled. —Obviously.

And that the rulers must be the best of them? —That too.

The best farmers are those who have to the highest degree the qualities required for farming? —Yes.

Now as the rulers must be the best among the guardians, they must have to the highest degree the qualities required to guard the city? —Yes.

And for this they must be intelligent, able, and also care for the city? —That is so.　　d

Now one cares most for that which one loves. —Necessarily.

And one loves something most when one believes that what is good for it is good for oneself, and that when it is doing well the same is true of oneself, and so with the opposite. —Quite so, he said.

We must therefore select from among our guardians those who, as we test them, hold throughout their lives to the belief that it is right to pursue eagerly what they believe to be to the advantage of the city, and who are　e in no way willing to do what is not. —Yes, for they are good men.

I think we must observe them at all ages to see whether they are guardians of this principle, and make sure that they cannot be tempted or forced to discard or forget the belief that they must do what is best for the city. —What, he said, do you mean by discarding?

I will tell you, I said. I think the discarding of a belief

is either voluntary or involuntary; voluntary when the belief is false, and as a result of learning one changes one's mind, involuntary when the belief is true. —I understand the voluntary discarding, but not the involuntary.

Really? Do you not think that men are unwilling to be deprived of good things, but willingly deprived of bad things? Is not untruth and missing the truth a bad thing, while to be truthful is good? And is not to have a true opinion to be truthful? —You are right, he said, and people are unwilling to be deprived of a true opinion.

But they can be so deprived by theft, or compulsion, or under a spell? —I do not understand even now.

I fear I must be talking like a tragic poet! I apply the word "theft" to those who change their mind or those who forget, not realizing that time or argument has robbed them of their belief. Do you understand now? —Yes.

By compulsion I mean those whom pain or suffering causes to change their mind. —That too I understand and you are right.

Those under a spell I think you would agree are those who change their mind because they are bewitched by pleasure or fear. —It seems to me, he said, that anything which deceives bewitches.

As I said just now, we must find out who are the best guardians of their belief that they must always do whatever they think to be in the best interest of the city. We must keep them under observation from childhood and set them tasks which would most easily lead one to forget this belief, or to be deceived. We must select the one who keeps on remembering and is not easily deceived, the other we will reject. Do you agree? —Yes.

We must also subject them to labours, sufferings, and contests in which to observe this. —Right.

Then, I said, for the third kind we must observe how they face bewitchment. Like those who lead colts into noise and tumult to see if they are fearful, so we must expose our young to fears and pleasures to test them, much more thoroughly than one tests gold in fire, and see whether a guardian is hard to bewitch and behaves well in all circumstances as a good guardian of himself and of the cultural education he has received, always showing himself a gracious and harmonious personality, the best man for himself and for the city. The one who is thus tested as a child, as a youth, and as an adult, and comes out of it untainted, is to be made a ruler as well as a guardian. He is to be honoured both in life and after death and receive the most esteemed rewards in the form of tombs and memorials. The one who does not prove himself in this way is to be rejected. It seems to me, Glaucon, I said, that rulers and guardians must be selected and established in some such way as this, to speak in a general way and not in exact detail. —I also think it must be done in some such way.

These are the men whom it is most correct to call proper guardians, so that the enemies without shall not have the power, and their friends within shall not have the desire, to harm the city. Those young men whom we have called guardians hitherto we shall call auxiliaries to help the rulers in their decisions. —I agree.

What device could we find to make our rulers, or at any rate the rest of the city, believe us if we told them a noble fiction, one of those necessary untruths of which we have spoken? —What kind of fiction?

Nothing new, I said, but a Phoenician story which the poets say has happened in many places and made people believe them; it has not happened among us, though it might, and it will take a great deal of persuasion to have it believed.

You seem hesitant to tell your story, he said.

When you hear it you will realize that I have every reason to hesitate. Speak without fear.

This is the story—yet I don't know that I am bold enough to tell it or what words I shall use. I shall first try to persuade the rulers and the soldiers, and then the rest of the city, that the upbringing and the education we gave them, and the experience that went with them, were a dream as it were, that in fact they were then being fashioned and nurtured inside the earth, themselves and their weapons and their apparel. Then, when they were quite finished, the earth, being their mother, brought them out into the world. So even now they must take counsel for, and defend, the land in which they live as their mother and nurse, if someone attacks it, and they must think of their fellow-citizens as their earth-born brothers.

It is not for nothing that you were shy, he said, of telling your story.

Yes, I said, I had very good reason. Nevertheless, hear the rest of the tale. "All of you in the city are brothers" we shall tell them as we tell our story, "but the god who fashioned you mixed some gold in the nature of those capable of ruling because they are to be honoured most. In those who are auxiliaries he has put silver, and iron and bronze in those who are farmers and other workers. You will for the most part produce children like yourselves but, as you are all related, a silver child will occasionally be born from a golden parent, and vice versa, and all the others from each other. So the first and most important command of the god to the rulers is that there is nothing they must guard better or watch more carefully than the mixture in the souls of the next generation. If their own offspring should be found to have iron or bronze in his nature, they must not pity him in any way, but give him the esteem appropriate to his nature;

they must drive him out to join the workers and farmers. Then again, if an offspring of these is found to have gold or silver in his nature they will honour him and bring him up to join the rulers or guardians, for there is an oracle that the city will be ruined if ever it has an iron or bronze guardian." Can you suggest any device which will make our citizens believe this story?

d   I cannot see any way, he said, to make them believe it themselves, but the sons and later generations might, both theirs and those of other men.

Even that, I said, would help to make them care more for their city and each other, for I do understand what you mean. But let us leave this matter to later tradition. Let us now arm our earthborn and lead them forth with their rulers in charge. And as they march let them look for the best place in the city to have their camp, a site from which they could most easily control those

e   within, if anyone is unwilling to obey the laws, and ward off any outside enemy who came like a wolf upon the flock. When they had established their camp and made the right sacrifices, let them see to their sleeping quarters, or what do you suggest? —I agree.

These must protect them adequately both in winter and summer.

Of course, he said, you mean their dwellings.

Yes, I said, dwellings for soldiers, not for money-makers.

416   What would you say is the difference? he asked.

I will try to tell you, I said. The most terrible and shameful thing for a shepherd is to train his dogs, who should help the flocks, in such a way that, through lack of discipline or hunger or bad habit, those very dogs maltreat the animals and behave like wolves rather than dogs. —Quite true.

b   We must therefore take every precaution to see that our auxiliaries, since they are the stronger, do not behave like that toward the citizens, and become cruel masters instead of kindly allies. —We must watch this.

And a really good education would endow them with the greatest caution in this regard? —But surely they have had that.

And I said: Perhaps we should not assert this dogmatically, my dear Glaucon. What we can assert is what we were saying just now, that they must have the correct

c   education, whatever that is, in order to attain the greatest degree of gentleness toward each other and toward those whom they are protecting. —Right.

Besides this education, an intelligent man might say that they must have the amount of housing and of other property which would not prevent them from being the

d   best guardians and would not encourage them to maltreat the other citizens. —That would be true.

Consider then, said I, whether they should live in some such way as this if they are to be the kind of men we described: First, not one of them must possess any private property beyond what is essential. Further, none of them should have a house or a storeroom which anyone who wishes is not permitted to enter. Whatever moderate and courageous warrior-athletes require will   e be provided by taxation upon the other citizens as a salary for their guardianship, no more and no less than they need over the year. They will have common messes and live together as soldiers in a camp. We shall tell them that the gold and silver they always have in their nature as a gift from the gods makes the possession of human gold unnecessary, indeed that it is impious for them to defile this divine possession by any admixture of the human kind of gold, because many an impious deed is commit-   417 ted in connection with the currency of the majority, and their own must remain pure. For them alone among the city's population it is unlawful to touch or handle gold or silver; they must not be under the same roof with it, or wear any, or drink from gold or silver goblets; in this way they may preserve themselves and the city. If they themselves acquire private land and houses and currency, they will be household managers and farmers instead of guardians, hostile masters of the other citi-   b zens instead of their allies; they will spend their whole life hating and being hated, plotting and being plotted against; they will be much more afraid of internal than of external enemies, and they will rush themselves and their city very close to ruin. For all these reasons, I said, let us say that the guardians must be provided with housing and other matters in this way, and these are the laws we shall establish.

Certainly, said Glaucon.

Book IV, 419a–421c; 422a–428a; 432b–432c; 433a–435c; 441c–441e; 443c–444a
Socrates/Adeimantus

Adeimantus took up the argument and said: What de-   419 fence, Socrates, would you offer against the charge that you are not making your guardians very happy, and that through their own fault? The city is really in their power, yet they derive no good from this. Others own land, build grand and beautiful houses, acquire furnishings appropriate to them, make their own private sacrifices to the gods, entertain, also, as you mentioned just now, have gold and silver and all the possessions which are thought to belong to people who will be happy. One might well say that your guardians are simply settled in the city like paid mercenaries, with nothing to do but to watch over it.

Yes, said I. Moreover, they work for their keep and   420

get no extra wages as the others do, so that if they want to leave the city privately they cannot do so; they have nothing to give their mistresses, nothing to spend in whatever other way they wish, as men do who are considered happy. You have omitted these and other such things from the charge. —Let these accusations be added, he said.

b   Now you ask what defence we shall offer? —Yes.

I think we shall discover what to say if we follow the same path as before, I said. We shall say that it would not be at all surprising if these men too were very happy. In any case, in establishing our city, we are not aiming to make anyone group outstandingly happy, but to make the whole city so, as far as possible. We thought that in such a city we would most easily find justice, find injustice in a badly governed one, and then decide what we

c   have been looking for all the time. Now we think we are fashioning the happy city not by separating a few people in it and making them happy, but by making the whole city so. We shall look at the opposite kind of city presently. If someone came to us while we were painting a statue[4] and objected because we did not apply the finest colours to the finest parts of the body, for the eyes are the most beautiful part, and they are not made purple but black, we should appear to offer a reasonable defence if

d   we said: "My good sir, do not think that we must make the eyes so beautiful that they no longer appear to be eyes at all, and so with the other parts, but look to see whether by dealing with each part appropriately we are making the whole statue beautiful." And so now, do not force us to give our guardians the kind of happiness which would make them anything but guardians.

e   We know how to clothe our farmers too in purple robes, surround them with gold and tell them to work the land at their pleasure, and how to settle our potters on couches by the fire, feasting and passing the wine, put their wheel by them and tell them to make pots as much as they want; we know how to make all the others also happy in the same way, so that the whole city is happy. Do not

421   exhort us to do this, however. If we do, the farmer will not be a farmer, nor the potter a potter; nor would anyone else fulfill any of the functions which make up the state. For the others this is less important: if shoemakers become inferior and corrupt, and claim to be what they are not, the state is not in peril, but, if the guardians of our laws and city only appear to be guardians and are not, you surely see that they destroy the city utterly, as they alone have the opportunity to govern it well and to make it happy.

b   If then we are making true guardians who are least likely to work wickedness upon the city, whereas our accuser makes some farmers into banqueters, happy as at some festival but not in a city, he would be talking about something else than a city. We should examine then,

with this in mind, whether our aim in establishing our guardians should be to give them the greatest happiness, or whether we should in this matter look to the whole city and see how its greatest happiness can be secured.

c   We must compel and persuade the auxiliaries and the guardians to be excellent performers of their own task, and so with all the others. As the whole city grows and is well governed, we must leave it to nature to provide each group with its share of happiness.

I think, he said, that you put that very well.

. . .

We have, it seems, found other dangers against which our guardians must guard most carefully, lest these should penetrate the city unnoticed. —What are these?

Both wealth and poverty, I said. The former makes   422 for luxury, idleness, and political change, the latter for meanness, bad work, and change as well.

That is certainly true, he said, but please consider this point, Socrates: how will our city be able to fight a war, since it has not acquired wealth, especially if it has to fight against a mighty and wealthy opponent?

Obviously, I said, it will be harder to fight one such   b city than two. —How do you mean? said he.

First of all, said I, if they must fight, will they not be fighting as warrior-athletes against rich men? —As far as that goes, yes.

Well then, Adeimantus, I said, do you not think that one boxer who has had the best possible training could easily fight two rich and fat non-boxers? —Perhaps not at the same time.

Not even, said I, if he could run off and then turn round and hit the one close to him, and did this again   c and again in the stifling heat of the sun? Would he not be able, in his condition, to tackle even more than two? —That would certainly not be surprising.

And do you not think that the rich have more knowledge and experience of boxing than of fighting in war? —I do.

Our athletes would then most likely be able to fight with ease twice or three times their own numbers. —I will agree with you, for I think you are talking sense.

What if they sent envoys to the other city and said,   d which is the truth: "We have no use for gold or silver and it is not lawful for us to possess them, but you can. So join us in this war and make the other side's possessions your own." Do you think that any people on hearing this would choose to fight against hardened and spare dogs rather than, with the dogs on their side, fight against sleek and soft sheep?

No, I do not think so, he said, but if the wealth of the others came to be gathered together in one city, take care   e that this does not imperil your non-wealthy city.

You are fortunate, I said, if you think that any other city than the kind we are founding deserves the name. —What do you mean?

We must find a grander name for the others, as each of them is a cluster of cities, not one city, as they say in the game.[5] Each of them, in any case, consists of two hostile cities, that of the poor and that of the rich, and each of these contains many. It would be a grave mistake to approach them as one, but if you approach them as many and give the possessions of one to the other, their wealth, their power, and even their persons, you will always have many allies and few enemies. As long as our city is governed with moderation as we have just established it, it will itself have greatness. I do not mean great repute but true greatness, even if it have only one thousand men to fight for it. You will not easily find one great city in this sense either among Greeks or barbarians, though you will find a very large number that are thought to be great. Do you think differently? —By Zeus no.

This then would be the best limitation which our guardians should put upon the size of the city; they should then mark off the amount of land required for its size, and let the rest go. —What is this limitation?

I think, I said, that it is this: to let the city grow as long as it is willing to retain its unity, but not beyond that point. —Quite right.

This then is another order we shall give our guardians: to watch most carefully that the city should not appear either small or big, but sufficient, and remain one. —This, he said, is indeed an easy order we shall give them!

Even easier than that, I said, is the one we mentioned before when we said that, if an offspring of the guardians is inferior, he must be sent off to join the other citizens, and if the others have an able offspring, he must be taken into the guardian group. This was meant to make clear that the other citizens must each be directed to the one task for which each is naturally fitted, so that he should pursue that one task which is his own and be himself one person and not many, and the city itself be a unity and not a plurality. —That is an even easier order than the other!

These orders we give them, my good Adeimantus, I said, are not, as one might think, either numerous or important; they are all secondary, provided that they guard the one great thing, as people say, though rather than great I would call it sufficient. —What is that?

Their education and their upbringing, I said. If they become cultured, moderate men, they will easily see these things for themselves, and other things too which we are now omitting, the acquiring of wives and children which must all accord with the old proverb, that the possessions of friends must be held in common. —That would be the best way.[6]

Surely, I said, once our city gets a good start, it would go on growing in a circle. Good education and upbringing, if preserved, will lead to men of a better nature, and these in turn, if they cling to their education, will improve with each generation both in other respects and also in their children, just like other animals. —Quite likely.

To put it briefly, those in charge of our city must cling to this and see that education is not corrupted without their noticing it, guard above all else that there should be no innovations in physical and artistic education as established, and be as careful as they can. They should be fearful when they hear anyone say:

> Men care most for the song,
> which is newest to the singer,[7]

lest anyone should praise this, thinking that the poet meant not new songs but new ways of singing. One should not praise such a thing nor take it up; one should be cautious in adopting a new kind of poetry and music, for this endangers the whole system. The ways of poetry and music are not changed anywhere without change in the most important laws of a city, as Damon affirms and I believe. —You can count me too among the believers.

It is here, said I, in music and the arts, that our guardians must build their bulwark against change.

Yes, he said, for lawlessness easily creeps in there unawares.

Yes, said I, as if it was just play and did no harm at all.

Nor does it, he said, except that, after establishing itself there, lawlessness quietly flows over into the character and pursuits of men. Then, greatly increased, it steps out into private contracts, and from private contracts it makes its way insolently into the laws and the government, until in the end it upsets everything public and private.

Very well, I said, is that how it works? —I think so.

Then, as we said at the beginning, our children's games must be more law-abiding, for if their games become lawless and the children follow suit, it is impossible for them to grow up into good and law-abiding men. —How could they?

When children play the right games from the first, they absorb obedience to the law through their training in the arts, quite the opposite of what happens to those who play lawless games. This lawfulness follows them in everything, fosters their growth, and can correct anything that has gone wrong before in the city. —This is indeed true.

They then discover those conventions which seem unimportant, all of which those who came before them have destroyed. —What conventions?

b Things like this: when it is proper for the young to be silent in the company of their elders, how they should sit at table, when to give up their seat, care for their parents, hair styles, what clothes and shoes to wear, deportment, and the other things of that kind. Do you not think so? —I do.

I think it is foolish to legislate about such things. Verbal or written decrees will never make them come about or last. —How could they?

c They are likely to follow as necessary consequences from the direction one's education takes. Does not like always call to like? —Quite so.

And we might say that it ends in one complete and vigorous product which is itself either good or the opposite. —Quite so.

For these reasons, I said, I would not go on to attempt legislation about such things. —That seems right.

d Then by the gods what about market business, the private contracts which they make with one another in the market place; add, if you wish, cases of insulting behaviour, ill treatment, the bringing of lawsuits, the establishment of juries, the payment and assessment of dues that may be necessary in markets or harbours, and all the regulations in the market, the city, or the harbour, and all other such—shall we venture to legislate for any of these?

It is not worthwhile, he said, to make orders about these for good men and true; they will easily discover e most of those which need legislation.

Yes, my friend, I said, if a god grant the preservation of the laws which we have already described.

And if not, he said, they will spend their lives enacting many laws and amending them, believing that they are thus attaining what is best.

You mean, I said, that they will live the same sort of life as those sick people who, through lack of self-control, cannot give up their bad diet? —Quite so.

426 They too live a pleasant life! Their treatment achieves nothing, except that their complaints become worse and more varied; they are always hoping, when someone advises a new medicine, that this will cure them. —That is certainly the experience of that kind of sick people, he said.

Further, I said, is this not charming of them, that they consider as their worst enemy the man who tells them the truth, namely that until they give up drunk-b enness, overeating, lechery, and idleness, no medicine, cautery, or surgery, no charms or amulets or anything of the kind will do them any good.

Not charming at all, for to quarrel with one who is saying the right thing has no charm.

You do not approve, it seems, of such men, I said. —By Zeus, I certainly do not.

Nor will you approve if, as we said, a whole city behaves in this way. Don't you think that those which are badly governed behave like this when they warn their citizens not to disturb the whole political establishment c on pain of death? Thus governed, people will consider as good and wise in important matters, and greatly honour, the man who serves them most pleasantly, who indulges them, flatters them, anticipates their wishes, and is clever at fulfilling them.

Certainly they seem to behave in the same way, he said, and I do not approve at all.

What about those who are willing and eager to d serve such cities? Do you not admire their courage and complaisance?

I do, he said, except for those who are deceived by the approval of the majority into believing that they are true statesmen.

How do you mean, I asked, do you not forgive them? or do you think it possible for a man ignorant of measurement not to believe it himself when many other ignorant people tell him that he is six feet tall? —No, I do e not think that either.

Do not be hard on them; they are of all men the most engaging. They pass laws on those subjects which we were just enumerating, and amend them, and they always think they will find a way to put a stop to cheating on contracts and the other things I was mentioning. They do not realize that this is, in fact, like cutting off a 427 hydra's head.[8] —That is surely what they are doing.

I should have thought, said I, that the true lawgiver must not bother with that kind of law and administration either in a well governed or in a badly governed city—in the latter, because it is useless and accomplishes nothing, in the former, because anyone at all could discover some of these laws for himself, while other laws follow automatically from the pursuits we laid down earlier.

What, he asked, is now left for us to deal with under b the heading of legislation?

I answered: For us nothing, but for the Delphic Apollo the greatest, the finest, and the first enactments. —What are these?

The establishing of temples, sacrifices, and other forms of service to the gods, spirits, and heroes; then again the burials of the dead and the services which ensure their favour. We have no knowledge of these things and in establishing our city we shall not, if we are wise, c accept any other advice or use any other than our ancestral guide. This god is the ancestral interpreter of these things for all men as he sits upon the rock which is the center of the earth.[9] —You are quite right, he said, and we must do so.

d   Well, son of Ariston, I said, your city might now be said to be established. The next step is for you to look inside it with what light you can procure, to call upon your brother and Polemarchus and the others, if we can somehow see where justice resides in it, and where injustice, what the difference is between them, and which of the two the man who intends to be happy should possess, whether gods and men recognize it or not.

Nonsense, said Glaucon. You promised to look for them yourself because you said it was impious for you
e   not to come to the rescue of justice in every way you could.

True, I said, as you remind me; I must do so, but you must help. —We will, he said.

I hope to find it. I said, in this way. I think our city, if it is rightly founded, is completely good. —Necessarily so, he said.

Clearly then it is wise, brave, moderate, and just.[10] —Clearly.

Therefore whichever of these we find in the city, the rest will be what we have not found? —You mean?

428   As with any four things, if we were looking for anyone of them in anything, if we first recognize it, that would be enough, but if we recognize the other three first, then by that very fact we recognize what we are looking for. For clearly it can be no other than what is left. —Correct, he said.

. . .

Socrates/Glaucon

432b   Very well, I said. We have now found three of the four in the city, as far as our present discussion takes us. What would the remaining kind be which still makes the city share in virtue? Or is it clear that this is justice? —Quite clear.

So now we must concentrate our attention like hunters surrounding a coppice, lest justice escape us and vanish without our seeing it, for obviously it is somewhere
c   around here. Look eagerly, now, in case you see it before I do, and tell me.

I wish I could, he said, but you will make a more sensible use of me if you take me to be a follower who can see things when you point them out.

Follow then, I said, and join me in a prayer. —I will do that, but you lead.

Indeed, I said, the place seems impenetrable and full of shadows; it is certainly dark and hard to hunt in. However, go on we must. —We must indeed.

. . .

Well, I said, listen whether I am talking sense. I   433
think that justice is the very thing, or some form of the thing which, when we were beginning to found our city, we said had to be established throughout. We stated, and often repeated, if you remember, that everyone must pursue one occupation of those in the city, that for which his nature best fitted him. —Yes, we kept saying that.

Further, we have heard many people say, and have often said ourselves, that justice is to perform one's own task and not to meddle with that of others. —We have   b
said that.

This then, my friend, I said, when it happens, is in some way justice, to do one's own job. And do you know what I take to be a proof of this? —No, tell me.

I think what is left over of those things we have been investigating, after moderation and courage and wisdom have been found, was that which made it possible for those three qualities to appear in the city and to continue as long as it is present. We also said that what remained   c
after we found the other three was justice. —It had to be.

And surely, I said, if we had to decide which of the four will make the city good by its presence, it would be hard to judge whether it is a common belief among the rulers and the ruled, or the preservation among the soldiers of a law-inspired belief as to the nature of what is, and what is not, to be feared, or the knowledge and   d
guardianship of the rulers, or whether it is, above all, the presence of this fourth in child and woman, slave and free, artisan, ruler and subject, namely that each man, a unity in himself, performed his own task and was not meddling with that of others. —How could this not be hard to judge?

It seems then that the capacity for each in the city   e
to perform his own task rivals wisdom, moderation, and courage as a source of excellence for the city. —It certainly does.

You would then describe justice as a rival to them for excellence in the city? —Most certainly.

Look at it this way and see whether you agree: you will order your rulers to act as judges in the courts of the city? —Surely.

And will their exclusive aim in delivering judgment not be that no citizen should have what belongs to another or be deprived of what is his own? —That would be their aim.

That being just? —Yes.

In some way then possession of one's own and the performance of one's own task could be agreed to be jus-   434
tice.[11] —That is so.

Consider then whether you agree with me in this: if a carpenter attempts to do the work of a cobbler, or a cobbler that of a carpenter, and they exchange their tools and the esteem that goes with the job, or the same man tries to do both, and all the other exchanges are made, do you think that this does any great harm to the city? —No.

b But I think that when one who is by nature a worker or some other kind of moneymaker is puffed up by wealth, or by the mob, or by his own strength, or some other such thing, and attempts to enter the warrior class, or one of the soldiers tries to enter the group of counsellors and guardians, though he is unworthy of it, and these exchange their tools and the public esteem, or when the same man tries to perform all these jobs together, then I think you will agree that these exchanges and this meddling bring the city to ruin. —They certainly do.

The meddling and exchange between the three established orders does very great harm to the city and c would most correctly be called wickedness. —Very definitely.

And you would call the greatest wickedness worked against one's own city injustice? —Of course.

That then is injustice. And let us repeat that the doing of one's own job by the moneymaking, auxiliary, and guardian groups, when each group is performing its own task in the city, is the opposite, it is justice and makes the d city just. —I agree with you that this is so.

Do not let us, I said, take this as quite final yet. If we find that this quality, when existing in each individual man, is agreed there too to be justice, then we can assent to this—for what can we say?—but if not, we must look for something else. For the present, let us complete that examination which we thought we should make, that if we tried to observe justice in something larger which contains it, this would make it easier to observe it in the e individual. We thought that this larger thing was a city, and so we established the best city we could, knowing well that justice would be present in the good city. It has now appeared to us there, so let us now transfer it to the individual and, if it corresponds, all will be well. But if it is seen to be something different in the individual, then we must go back to the city and examine this new no-435 tion of justice. By thus comparing and testing the two, we might make justice light up like fire from the rubbing of firesticks, and when it has become clear, we shall fix it firmly in our own minds. —You are following the path we set, and we must do so.

Well now, when you apply the same name to a thing whether it is big or small, are these two instances of it like or unlike with regard to that to which the same name applies? —They are alike in that, he said.

b So the just man and the just city will be no different but alike as regards the very form of justice. —Yes, they will be.

Now the city was thought to be just when the three kinds of men within it each performed their own task, and it was moderate and brave and wise because of some other qualities and attitudes of the same groups. —True.

And we shall therefore deem it right, my friend, that c the individual have the same parts in his own soul, and through the same qualities in those parts will correctly be given the same names. —That must be so.

Once again, my good man, I said, we have come upon an easy inquiry whether the soul has these three parts or not!

It does not look easy to me, he said. Perhaps the old saying is true, that all fine things are difficult.

. . .   441

We have now made our difficult way through a sea of argument to reach this point, and we have fairly agreed that the same kinds of parts, and the same number of parts, exist in the soul of each individual as in our city. —That is so.

It necessarily follows that the individual is wise in the same way, and in the same part of himself, as the city. —Quite so.

And the part which makes the individual brave is d the same as that which makes the city brave, and in the same manner, and everything which makes for virtue[12] is the same in both? —That necessarily follows.

Moreover, Glaucon, I think we shall say that a man is just in the same way as the city is just. —That too is inevitable.

We have surely not forgotten that the city was just because each of the three classes in it was fulfilling its own task. —I do not think, he said, that we have forgotten that.

We must remember then that each one of us within whom each part is fulfilling its own task will himself be e just and do his own work. —We must certainly remember this.

. . .   443

We have then completely realized the dream we had when we suspected[13] that, by the grace of god, we came c upon a principle and mould of justice right at the beginning of the founding of our city. —Very definitely.

Indeed, Glaucon—and this is why it is useful—it was a sort of image of justice, namely that it was right for one who is by nature a cobbler to cobble and to do nothing else, and for the carpenter to carpenter, and so with the others. —Apparently.

And justice was in truth, it appears, something like this. It does not lie in a man's external actions, but in the d way he acts within himself, really concerned with himself and his inner parts. He does not allow each part of himself to perform the work of another, or the sections of his soul to meddle with one another. He orders what are in the true sense of the word his own affairs well; he is master of himself, puts things in order, is his own friend, harmonizes the three parts like the limiting notes of a musical scale, the high, the low, and the middle, and any others there may be between. He binds them all together, and himself from a plurality becomes a unity. Being thus moderate and harmonious, he now performs any action, be it about the acquisition of wealth, the care of his body, some public actions, or private contract.[14] In all these fields he thinks the just and beautiful action, which he names as such, to be that which preserves this inner harmony and indeed helps to achieve it, wisdom to be the knowledge which oversees this action, an unjust action to be that which always destroys it, and ignorance the belief which oversees that. —Socrates you are altogether right.

Very well, I said, we would then not be thought to be lying if we claim that we have found the just man, the just city, and the justice that is in them. —No by Zeus, we would not.

. . .

Book V, 449a–457c; 471c–473e
Socrates/Adeimantus/Glaucon/
Thrasymachus

. . .

This then is the kind of city and government which I call good and right, and so too this kind of man. And if this is the right kind, then the others are bad and wrong, both in the management of the cities and the manner of life of the individual soul. Their badness is of four kinds. —What are these?

I was going to enumerate them and say how I thought they developed out of one another,[15] but Polemarchus—he was sitting a little further away than Adeimantus—extended his hand and took hold of the other's cloak from above at the shoulder, drew him toward himself while he leaned forward and said something to him of which I only heard the words "Shall we let it pass, or what shall we do?"

Certainly not, said Adeimantus, now speaking aloud.

And I asked: What is it which you won't let pass? —You, he said.

Why in particular? I asked.

We think that you are getting slack, he said, and that you have filched away a whole section of the argument and one of some importance, in order to avoid dealing with it. You thought we would not notice when you said casually that as regards wives and children

anyone could see that the possessions of friends should be held in common.[16] —Was that not right Adeimantus? said I.

Yes, he said, but that "right," like the other things, requires explanation as to the manner of this holding in common, for there could be many ways; so do not fail to tell us which you mean. We have been waiting for some time for you to mention how they will beget children and bring them up, and this whole subject of the holding in common of wives and children. We believe that the right or the wrong way of it makes a considerable difference, indeed all the difference, to the government of your city. At this point, since you are going on to deal with another kind of government before you have adequately dealt with these matters, we thought, as you heard, that we would not let you off until you deal fully with all this as you have with the other matters.

And Glaucon said: Count me as associating myself with this proposal. In fact, added Thrasymachus, consider this, Socrates, as the vote of us all.

What a thing you have done, I said, in stopping me! What an argument you have started up again as if from the beginning about the administration of our city! I joyfully thought I had completed this, and I was quite glad that anyone would accept what was then said on the subject and let me go on. You do not realize what a swarm of arguments you have stirred up by now calling me to account. I was aware of this when I passed it by, for fear it might give us much trouble.

Come now, said Thrasymachus, do you think these men have come here to smelt ore for gold[17] and not to hear a discussion?

They have come for discussion, I said, but discussion within reason.

It is within reason, Socrates, said Glaucon, for intelligent men to listen to a discussion of this kind their whole life long. So never mind about us, but do not weary of telling us at length what your thoughts are on the subject about which we enquired, namely what this common ownership of wives and children will be for the guardians, and how the children will be brought up while they are small, from the time of their birth until they begin their education, which seems the most difficult period. Try to tell us what the manner of this upbringing must be.

It is not, my dear friend, said I, an easy subject to explain for it raises even more doubts than the subjects we have expounded before. People may not believe that what we say is possible or that, if it should come to pass, it would be for the best. Hence my hesitation in broaching the subject, lest our discussion should seem to be mere wishful thinking.

Do not hesitate, he said, for your audience is neither inconsiderate, nor incredulous, nor ill-disposed.

And I said: Do you wish to encourage me by saying this? —I do.

Well, I said, you are doing the opposite. Your encouragement would be fine if I trusted myself to speak with knowledge, for one can feel both safe and bold if one speaks among intelligent friends about the most important and cherished subjects with knowledge of the truth, but to speak at a time when one is still in doubt and searching, which is what I am doing, is both frightening and unsafe. I am not afraid of being laughed at—that indeed would be childish—but I fear that I may not only miss my footing in my search for the truth, but also drag down my friends in my fall where a false step should least occur. So I bow to Adrasteia[18] for what I am going to say, as I expect it is a lesser crime to kill someone involuntarily than to deceive people about beautiful, good, and just institutions. It is better then to run that risk among enemies than among friends, so you do indeed encourage me!

Glaucon laughed and said: Well, Socrates, if we suffer anything untoward as a result of this conversation, then, as if it were murder, we free you of any guilt; we declare you pure and no deceiver. So speak boldly.

Surely, I said, as the law declares a man to be pure who is freed from guilt in the case of homicide, this is likely to apply here also. —As far as that goes speak then, he said.

We must now, said I, go back to what should have been said earlier in sequence. However, this may well be the right way: after we have completed the parts that men must play, we turn to those of women, especially as you call on me to do so.

For men of such a nature and education as we have described there is, in my opinion, no other right way to deal with wives and children than following the road upon which we started them. We attempted, in our argument, to establish the men as guardians of the flock. —Yes.

Let us then give them for the birth and upbringing of children a system appropriate to that function and see whether it suits us or not. —How?

Like this: do we think that the wives of our guardian watchdogs should join in whatever guardian duties the men fulfill, join them in the hunt, and do everything else in common, or should we keep the women at home as unable to do so because they must bear and rear their young, and leave to the men the labour and the whole care of the flock?

All things, he said, should be done in common, except that the women are physically weaker and the men stronger.

And is it possible, I asked, to make use of living creatures for the same purposes unless you give them the same upbringing and education? —It is not possible.

So if we use the women for the same tasks as the men, they must be taught the same things. —Yes.

Now we gave the men artistic and physical culture. —Yes.

So we must give both also to the women, as well as training in war, and use them for the same tasks. —That seems to follow from what you say.

Perhaps, I said, many of the things we are saying, being contrary to custom, would stir up ridicule, if carried out in practice in the way we are telling them. —They certainly would, he said.

What, I asked, is the most ridiculous feature you see in this? Or is it obviously that women should exercise naked in the palaestra along with the men, not only the young women but the older women too, as the old men do in the gymnasia when their bodies are wrinkled and not pleasant to look at and yet they are fond of physical exercise? —Yes, by Zeus, he said, it would appear ridiculous as things stand now.

Surely, I said, now that we have started on this argument, we must not be afraid of all the jokes of the kind that the wits will make about such a change in physical and artistic culture, and not least about the women carrying arms and riding horses. —You are right, he said.

As we have begun this discussion we must go on to the tougher part of the law and beg these people not to practise their own trade of comedy at our expense but to be serious and to remember that it is not very long since the Greeks thought it ugly and ridiculous, as the majority of barbarians still do, for men to be seen naked. When first the Cretans and then the Lacedaemonians started their physical training, the wits of those days could have ridiculed it all, or do you not think so? —I do.

But I think that after it was found in practice to be better to strip than to cover up all those parts, then the spectacle ceased to be looked on as ridiculous because reasonable argument had shown that it was best. This showed that it is foolish to think anything ridiculous except what is bad, or to try to raise a laugh at any other spectacle than that of ignorance and evil as being ridiculous, as it is foolish to be in earnest about any other standard of beauty than that of the good. —Most certainly.

Must we not lust agree whether our proposals are possible or not? And we must grant an opportunity for discussion to anyone who, in jest or seriously, wishes to argue the point whether female human nature can share all the tasks of the male sex, or none at all, or some but not others, and to which of the two waging war belongs.

Would this not be the best beginning and likely to lead to the best conclusion? —Certainly.

Do you then want us to dispute among ourselves on behalf of those others, lest the other side of the argument fall by default? —There is nothing to stop us.

b

Let us then speak on their behalf: "Socrates and Glaucon, there is no need for others to argue with you. You yourselves, when you began to found your city, agreed that each person must pursue the one task for which he is fitted by nature." I think we did agree to this, of course. —"Can you deny that a woman is by nature very different from a man?" —Of course not. "And is it not proper to assign a different task to each according to their nature?" —Certainly. "How then are you not wrong and contradicting yourselves when you say that men and women must do the same things, when they have quite separate natures?" Do you have any defence against that argument, my good friend?

c

That is not very easy offhand, he said, but I ask and beg you to explain the argument on our side, whatever it is.

It is these and many other difficulties that I foresaw, Glaucon, I said, when I was afraid and hesitated to tackle the law concerning the acquiring of wives and the upbringing of children. —By Zeus, he said, it does not seem at all easy.

d

It is not, said I, but the fact is that whether a man falls into a small swimming pool or in the middle of the ocean, he must swim all the same. —Certainly.

So then we must swim too and try to save ourselves from the sea of our argument, hoping that a dolphin will pick us up or we may find some other miraculous deliverance. —It seems so.

e

Come now, said I, let us see if we can find a way out. We have agreed that a different nature must follow a different occupation and that the nature of man and woman is different, and we now say that different natures must follow the same pursuits. This is the accusation brought against us. —Surely.

How grand is the power of disputation, Glaucon. —Why?

454

Because, I said, many people fall into it unwittingly and think they are not disputing but conversing because they cannot analyze their subject into its parts, but they pursue mere verbal contradictions of what has been said, thus engaging in a dispute rather than in a conversation.

Many people, he said, have that experience, but does this also apply to us at the present moment?

It most certainly does, I said. I am afraid we have indeed unwittingly fallen into disputation. —How?

b

We are bravely, but in a disputatious and verbal fashion, pursuing the principle that a nature which is not the same must not engage in the same pursuits, but when we assigned different tasks to a different nature and the same to the same nature, we did not examine at all what kind of difference and sameness of nature we had in mind and in what regard we were distinguishing them. —No, we did not look into that.

We might therefore just as well, it seems, ask ourselves whether the nature of bald men and long-haired men is the same and not opposite, and then, agreeing that they are opposite, if we allow bald men to be cobblers, not allow long-haired men to be, or again if long-haired men are cobblers, not allow the others to be. —That would indeed be ridiculous.

c

Is it ridiculous for any other reason than because we did not fully consider their same or different natures in every respect but we were only watching the kind of difference and sameness which applied to those particular pursuits? For example, a male and a female physician, we said, have the same nature of soul, or do you not think so? —I do.

d

But a physician and a carpenter have a different nature? —Surely.

Therefore, I said, if the male and the female are seen to be different as regards a particular craft or other pursuit we shall say this must be assigned to one or the other. But if they seem to differ in this particular only, that the female bears children while the male begets them, we shall say that there has been no kind of proof that a woman is different from a man as regards the duties we are talking about, and we shall still believe that our guardians and their wives should follow the same pursuits. —And rightly so.

e

Next we shall bid anyone who holds the contrary view to instruct us in this: with regard to what craft or pursuit concerned with the establishment of the city is the nature of man and woman not the same but different? —That is right.

455

Someone else might very well say what you said a short time ago, that it is not easy to give an immediate reply, but that it would not be at all difficult after considering the question. —He might say that.

Do you then want us to beg the one who raises these objections to follow us to see whether we can show him that no pursuit connected with the management of the city belongs in particular to a woman? —Certainly.

b

Come now, we shall say to him, give us an answer: did you mean that one person had a natural ability for a certain pursuit, while another had not, when the first learned it easily, the latter with difficulty? The one, after a brief period of instruction, was able to find things out for himself from what he had learned, while the other, after much instruction, could not even remember what he had learned; the former's body adequately served his mind, while the other's physical reactions opposed his. Are there any other ways in which you distinguished the naturally gifted in each case from those who were not? —No one will say anything else.

Do you know of any occupation practised by mankind in which the male sex is not superior to the female in all these respects? Or shall we pursue the argument at length by mentioning weaving, baking cakes, cooking vegetables, tasks in which the female sex certainly seems to distinguish itself, and in which it is most laughable of all for women to be inferior to men?

What you say is true, he said, namely that one sex is much superior to the other in almost everything, yet many women are better than many men in many things, but on the whole it is as you say.

There is therefore no pursuit connected with city management which belongs to woman because she is a woman, or to a man because he is a man, but various natures are scattered in the same way among both kinds of persons. Woman by nature shares all pursuits, and so does man, but in all of them woman is a physically weaker creature than man. —Certainly.

Shall we then assign them all to men, and none to a woman? —How can we?

One woman, we shall say, is a physician, another is not, one is by nature artistic, another is not. —Quite so.

One may be athletic or warlike, while another is not warlike and has no love of athletics. —I think so.

Further, may not one woman love wisdom, another hate it, or one may be high-spirited, another be without spirit? —That too.

So one woman may have a guardian nature, the other not. Was it not a nature with these qualities which we selected among men for our male guardians too? —We did.

Therefore the nature of man and woman is the same as regards guarding the city, except in so far as she is physically weaker, and the man's nature stronger. —So it seems.

Such women must then be chosen along with such men to live with them and share their guardianship, since they are qualified and akin to them by nature. —Certainly.

Must we not assign the same pursuits to the same natures? —The same.

We have come round then to what we said before, and we agree that it is not against nature to give to the wives of the guardians an education in the arts and physical culture. —Definitely not.

We are not legislating against nature or indulging in mere wishful thinking since the law we established is in accord with nature. It is rather the contrary present practice which is against nature as it seems. —It appears so.

Now we were to examine whether our proposals were possible and the best. —We were.

That they are possible is now agreed? —Yes.

After this we must seek agreement whether they are the best. —Clearly.

With a view to having women guardians, we should not have one kind of education to fashion the men, and another for the women, especially as they have the same nature to begin with. —No, not another.

What is your opinion of this kind of thing? —Of what?

About thinking to yourself that one man is better and another worse, or do you think that they are all alike? —Certainly not.

In the city we were establishing, do you think the guardians are made better men by the education they have received, or the cobblers who were educated for their craft? —Your question is ridiculous.

I know, said I. Well, are these guardians not the best of all the citizens? —By far.

Will then these women guardians not be the best of women? —That too by far.

Is there anything better for a city than to have the best possible men and women? —Nothing.

And it is the arts and physical culture, as we have described them, which will achieve this? —Of course.

So the institution we have established is not only possible but also the best. —That is so.

The women then must strip for their physical training, since they will be clothed in excellence. They must share in war and the other duties of the guardians about the city, and have no other occupation; the lighter duties will be assigned to them because of the weakness of their sex. The man who laughs at the sight of naked women exercising for the best of reasons is "plucking the unripe fruit of laughter,"[19] he understands nothing of what he is laughing at, it seems, nor what he is doing. For it is and always will be a fine saying that what is beneficial is beautiful, what is harmful is ugly. —Very definitely.

Let us say then that we have escaped from one wave of criticism in our discussion of the law about women, and we have not been altogether swamped when we laid it down that male and female guardians must share all their duties in common, and our argument is consistent when it states that this is both possible and beneficial.

—It is, he said, certainly no small wave from which you are escaping.

. . .

Socrates/Glaucon

471c   Let us then make this a law for our guardians, neither to ravage the country nor to burn the houses.

Let us, he said, and let us also say that these things are well, as is what went before. But I think, Socrates, that if one lets you talk on these subjects, you will never remember the subject you postponed before you said all this, namely, that it is possible for this city to exist and how it can be brought about. I agree that, if it existed, all the things we have mentioned would be good for the city in which they occurred, including things you are leaving

d   out: they would be excellent fighters against an enemy because they would be least likely to desert each other, since they know each other as, and call each other by the name of, brothers, fathers, sons. Moreover, if their women joined their campaigns, whether in the same ranks or drawn up behind as reserves, either to frighten the enemy or as reinforcements, should they ever be needed, I know that this would make them quite unbeatable. I also see that a number of good things would ensue for them at home which have not been mentioned. Take it

e   that I agree that all these things would happen as well as innumerable others, if this kind of government were to exist. Say no more on this subject but let us now try to convince ourselves of this, namely that it is possible and how it is possible. Let the rest go.

472   This is a sudden attack you have made upon my argument, I said, and you show no leniency toward my loitering. You may not realize that I have barely escaped from the first two waves of objections as you bring the third upon me, the biggest and most difficult to deal with. When you hear and see it you will surely be more lenient toward my natural hesitation and my fear to state, and attempt thoroughly to examine, such a paradox.

The more you speak like this, he said, the less we

b   shall let you off from telling us how this city is possible. So speak and do not waste time.

Well then, I said, we must first remember that we have come to this point while we were searching for the natures of justice and injustice. —We must, but what of it?

Nothing, but if we find out what justice is, shall we require that the just man be in no way different from that

c   justice itself, and be like justice in every respect, or shall we be satisfied if he comes as close to it as possible, and share in it far more than others? —That will satisfy us.

It was then to have a model, I said, that we were seeking the nature of justice itself, and of the completely just

man, if he should exist, and what kind of man he would be if he did, and so with injustice and the most unjust man. Our purpose was, with these models before us, to see how they turned out as regards happiness and its opposite. Thus we would be forced to come to an agreement about ourselves, that he who was as like them as possible would   d also have a life most like theirs. It was not our purpose to prove that these could exist. —What you say is true.

Do you think a man is any less a good painter if, having painted a model of what the most beautiful man would be, and having rendered all the details satisfactorily in his picture, he could not prove that such a man can come into being? —By Zeus. I do not.

Well then, do we not also say that we were making a model of a good city in our argument? —Certainly.   e

Do you think our discussion less worthwhile if we cannot prove that it is possible to found a city such as we described? —Not at all.

And indeed, I said, that is the truth. But if we must, to please you, exert ourselves to pursue this topic, namely to show how and in what respect this might best be possible, then you in turn should agree that the same thing applies to this demonstration. —What thing?

Is it possible to realize anything in practice as it can   473 be formulated in words or is it natural for practice to have a lesser grip on truth than theory,[20] even if some people do not think so? Will you first agree to this or not? —I agree.

Then do not compel me to show that the things we have described in theory can exist precisely in practice. If we are able to discover how the administration of a city can come closest to our theories, shall we say that we have found that those things are possible which you told us to   b prove so? Or will you not be satisfied with that measure of success? For I would be satisfied. —So would I.

Next, it seems, we should try to find out and to show what is now badly done in the cities which prevents them from being governed in this way, and what is the smallest change which would enable a city to reach our type of government—one change if possible, or, if not one, then two, or at any rate as few changes and as insignificant in their effects as possible. —By all means.   c

There is one change to which I think we could point which would accomplish this. It is certainly neither small nor easy, but it is possible. —What is it?

I have now come, I said, to what we likened to the greatest wave. However, it shall be said even if, like a wave of laughter, it will simply drown me in ridicule and contempt. —Say on.

And I said: Cities will have no respite from evil, my dear Glaucon, nor will the human race, I think, unless philosophers[21] rule as kings in the cities, or those whom   d we now call kings and rulers genuinely and adequately study philosophy, until, that is, political power and philosophy coalesce, and the various natures of those who now pursue the one to the exclusion of the other are forcibly debarred from doing so. Otherwise the city we have been describing will never grow into a possibility or see the light of day. It is because I saw how very paradoxical this statement would be that I have for some time hesitated to make it. It is hard to realize that there can be no happiness, public or private, in any other city. . . .

e

Book VII, 514a–521a; 532a–534d
Socrates/Glaucon

514 Next, I said, compare the effect of education and the lack of it upon our human nature to a situation like this: imagine men to be living in an underground cave-like dwelling place, which has a way up to the light along its whole width, but the entrance is a long way up. The men have been there from childhood, with their neck and legs in fetters, so that they remain in the same place and can only see ahead of them, as their bonds prevent them turning their heads. Light is provided by a fire burning some way behind and above them. Between the fire and the prisoners, some way behind them and on a higher ground, there is a path across the cave and along this a low wall has been built, like the screen at a puppet show in front of the performers who show their puppets above it. —I see it.

b

See then also men carrying along that wall, so that they overtop it, all kinds of artifacts, statues of men, reproductions of other animals in stone or wood fashioned in all sorts of ways, and, as is likely, some of the carriers are talking while others are silent. —This is a strange picture, and strange prisoners.

c

515

They are like us, I said. Do you think, in the first place, that such men could see anything of themselves and each other[22] except the shadows which the fire casts upon the wall of the cave in front of them? —How could they, if they have to keep their heads still throughout life?

b

And is not the same true of the objects carried along the wall? —Quite.

If they could converse with one another, do you not think that they would consider these shadows to be the real things? —Necessarily.

What if their prison had an echo which reached them from in front of them? Whenever one of the carriers passing behind the wall spoke, would they not think that it was the shadow passing in front of them which was talking? Do you agree? —By Zeus I do.

c

Altogether then, I said, such men would believe the truth to be nothing else than the shadows of the artifacts? —They must believe that.

Consider then what deliverance from their bonds and the curing of their ignorance would be if something like this naturally happened to them. Whenever one of them was freed, had to stand up suddenly, turn his head, walk, and look up toward the light, doing all that would give him pain, the flash of the fire would make it impossible for him to see the objects of which he had earlier seen the shadows. What do you think he would say if he was told that what he saw then was foolishness, that he was now somewhat closer to reality and turned to things that existed more fully, that he saw more correctly? If one then pointed to each of the objects passing by, asked him what each was, and forced him to answer, do you not think he would be at a loss and believe that the things which he saw earlier were truer than the things now pointed out to him? —Much truer.

d

If one then compelled him to look at the fire itself, his eyes would hurt, he would turn round and flee toward those things which he could see, and think that they were in fact clearer than those now shown to him. —Quite so.

e

And if one were to drag him thence by force up the rough and steep path, and did not let him go before he was dragged into the sunlight, would he not be in physical pain and angry as he was dragged along? When he came into the light, with the sunlight filling his eyes, he would not be able to see a single one of the things which are now said to be true. —Not at once, certainly.

516

I think he would need time to get adjusted before he could see things in the world above; at first he would see shadows most easily, then reflections of men and other things in water, then the things themselves. After this he would see objects in the sky and the sky itself more easily at night, the light of the stars and the moon more easily than the sun and the light of the sun during the day. —Of course.

b

Then, at last, he would be able to see the sun, not images of it in water or in some alien place, but the sun itself in its own place, and be able to contemplate it. —That must be so.

After this he would reflect that it is the sun which provides the seasons and the years, which governs everything in the visible world, and is also in some way the cause of those other things which he used to see. —Clearly that would be the next stage.

c

What then? As he reminds himself of his first dwelling place, of the wisdom there and of his fellow prisoners, would he not reckon himself happy for the change, and pity them? —Surely.

And if the men below had praise and honours from each other, and prizes for the man who saw most clearly the shadows that passed before them, and who could best remember which usually came earlier and which later, and which came together and thus could most ably prophesy the future, do you think our man would desire those rewards and envy those who were honoured and held power among the prisoners, or would he feel, as Homer put it, that he certainly wished to be "serf to another man without possessions upon the earth"[23] and go through any suffering, rather than share their opinions and live as they do? —Quite so, he said, I think he would rather suffer anything.

Reflect on this too, I said. If this man went down into the cave again and sat down in the same seat, would his eyes not be filled with darkness, coming suddenly out of the sunlight? —They certainly would.

And if he had to contend again with those who had remained prisoners in recognizing those shadows while his sight was affected and his eyes had not settled down—and the time for this adjustment would not be short—would he not be ridiculed? Would it not be said that he had returned from his upward journey with his eyesight spoiled, and that it was not worthwhile even to attempt to travel upward? As for the man who tried to free them and lead them upward, if they could somehow lay their hands on him and kill him, they would do so. —They certainly would.

This whole image, my dear Glaucon, I said, must be related to what we said before. The realm of the visible should be compared to the prison dwelling, and the fire inside it to the power of the sun. If you interpret the upward journey and the contemplation of things above as the upward journey of the soul to the intelligible realm, you will grasp what I surmise since you were keen to hear it. Whether it is true or not only the god knows, but this is how I see it, namely that in the intelligible world the Form of the Good is the last to be seen, and with difficulty; when seen it must be reckoned to be for all the cause of all that is right and beautiful, to have produced in the visible world both light and the fount of light, while in the intelligible world it is itself that which produces and controls truth and intelligence, and he who is to act intelligently in public or in private must see it. —I share your thought as far as I am able.

Come then, share with me this thought also: do not be surprised that those who have reached this point are unwilling to occupy themselves with human affairs, and that their souls are always pressing upward to spend their time there, for this is natural if things are as our parable indicates. —That is very likely.

Further, I said, do you think it at all surprising that anyone coming to the evils of human life from the contemplation of the divine behaves awkwardly and appears very ridiculous while his eyes are still dazzled and before he is sufficiently adjusted to the darkness around him, if he is compelled to contend in court or some other place about the shadows of justice or the objects of which they are shadows, and to carry through the contest about these in the way these things are understood by those who have never seen Justice itself? —That is not surprising at all.

Anyone with intelligence, I said, would remember that the eyes may be confused in two ways and from two causes, coming from light into darkness as well as from darkness into light. Realizing that the same applies to the soul, whenever he sees a soul disturbed and unable to see something, he will not laugh mindlessly but will consider whether it has come from a brighter life and is dimmed because unadjusted, or has come from greater ignorance into greater light and is filled with a brighter dazzlement. The former he would declare happy in its life and experience, the latter he would pity, and if he should wish to laugh at it, his laughter would be less ridiculous than if he laughed at a soul that has come from the light above. —What you say is very reasonable.

We must then, I said, if these things are true, think something like this about them, namely that education is not what some declare it to be; they say that knowledge is not present in the soul and that they put it in, like putting sight into blind eyes. —They surely say that.

Our present argument shows, I said, that the capacity to learn and the organ with which to do so are present in every person's soul. It is as if it were not possible to turn the eye from darkness to light without turning the whole body; so one must turn one's whole soul from the world of becoming until it can endure to contemplate reality, and the brightest of realities, which we say is the Good. —Yes.

Education then is the art of doing this very thing, this turning around, the knowledge of how the soul can most easily and most effectively be turned around; it is not the art of putting the capacity of sight into the soul; the soul possesses that already but it is not turned the right way or looking where it should. This is what education has to deal with. —That seems likely.

Now the other so-called virtues of the soul seem to be very close to those of the body—they really do not exist before and are added later by habit and practice—but the virtue of intelligence belongs above all to something more divine, it seems, which never loses its capacity but, according to which way it is turned, becomes useful and beneficial or useless and harmful. Have you never noticed in men who are said to be wicked but clever, how sharply their little soul looks into things to which it turns its attention? Its capacity for sight is not inferior, but it is compelled to serve evil ends, so that the more sharply it looks the more evils it works. —Quite so.

Yet if a soul of this kind had been hammered at from childhood and those excrescences had been knocked off it which belong to the world of becoming and have been fastened upon it by feasting, gluttony, and similar pleasures, and which like leaden weights draw the soul to look downward—if, being rid of these, it turned to look at things that are true, then the same soul of the same man would see these just as sharply as it now sees the things toward which it is directed. —That seems likely.

Further, is it not likely, I said, indeed it follows inevitably from what was said before, that the uneducated who have no experience of truth would never govern a city satisfactorily, nor would those who are allowed to spend their whole life in the process of educating themselves; the former would fail because they do not have a single goal at which all their actions, public and private, must aim; the latter because they would refuse to act, thinking that they have settled, while still alive, in the faraway islands of the blessed. —True.

It is then our task as founders, I said, to compel the best natures to reach the study which we have previously said to be the most important, to see the Good and to follow that upward journey. When they have accomplished their journey and seen it sufficiently, we must not allow them to do what they are allowed to do today. —What is that?

To stay there, I said, and to refuse to go down again to the prisoners in the cave, there to share both their labours and their honours, whether these be of little or of greater worth.[24]

Are we then, he said, to do them an injustice by making them live a worse life when they could live a better one?

You are again forgetting, my friend, I said, that it is not the law's concern to make some one group in the city outstandingly happy but to contrive to spread happiness throughout the city, by bringing the citizens into harmony with each other by persuasion or compulsion, and to make them share with each other the benefits which each group can confer upon the community. The law has not made men of this kind in the city in order to allow each to turn in any direction they wish but to make use of them to bind the city together. —You are right, I had forgotten.

Consider then, Glaucon, I said, that we shall not be doing an injustice to those who have become philosophers in our city, and that what we shall say to them, when we compel them to care for and to guard the others, is just. For we shall say: "Those who become philosophers in other cities are justified in not sharing the city's labours, for they have grown into philosophy of their own accord, against the will of the government in each of those cities, and it is right that what grows of its own accord, as it owes no debt to anyone for its upbringing, should not be keen to pay it to anyone. But we have made you in our city kings and leaders of the swarm, as it were, both to your own advantage and to that of the rest of the city; you are better and more completely educated than those others, and you are better able to share in both kinds of life. Therefore you must each in turn go down to live with other men and grow accustomed to seeing in the dark. When you are used to it you will see infinitely better than the dwellers below; you will know what each image is and of what it is an image, because you have seen the truth of things beautiful and just and good, and so, for you as for us, the city will be governed as a waking reality and not as in a dream, as the majority of cities are now governed by men who are fighting shadows and striving against each other in order to rule as if this were a great good." For this is the truth: a city in which the prospective rulers are least keen to rule must of necessity be governed best and be most free from civil strife, whereas a city with the opposite kind of rulers is governed in the opposite way. —Quite so.

Do you think that those we have nurtured will disobey us and refuse to share the labours of the city, each group in turn, though they may spend the greater part of their time dwelling with each other in a pure atmosphere?

They cannot, he said, for we shall be giving just orders to just men, but each of them will certainly go to rule as to something that must be done, the opposite attitude from that of the present rulers in every city.

That is how it is, my friend, I said. If you can find a way of life which is better than governing for the prospective governors, then a well-governed city can exist for you. Only in that city will the truly rich rule, not rich in gold but in the wealth which the happy man must have, a life with goodness and intelligence. If beggars hungry for private goods go into public life, thinking that they must snatch their good from it, the well-governed city cannot exist, for then office is fought for, and such a war at home inside the city destroys them and the city as well. —Very true.

. . .

Socrates/Glaucon

This now, Glaucon, I said, is the law which dialectic fulfills. The law is intelligible, and the power of sight would be imitating it when we described it as attempting to look at actual living creatures, then at the actual stars, and finally at the actual sun. So whenever one tries through dialectic, and without any help from the senses but by means of reason, to set out to find each true reality and does not give up before apprehending the Good itself with reason alone, one reaches the final goal of the intelligible as the prisoner escaping from the cave reached the final goal of the visible. —That is altogether so.

Well then, do you not call this journey dialectic? —I do.

The deliverance from bonds and the turning around from the shadows to the images and the firelight, and then the way up out of the cave to the sunlight, and there the continuing inability to look at living creatures and plants and the light of the sun but only at divine[25] images of them in water and shadows of actual things—no longer at shadows of images thrown by another source of light which is itself an image as compared the sun—the practice of every study we have described has this power to rouse the best part of the soul and lead it upward to the contemplation of that which is the best among the existents, just as then the clearest sense in the body was driven to the contemplation of the brightest thing in the physical and visible world.

I accept that it is so, he said, and yet these things seem hard to accept, but then in another way they are hard to reject. Nevertheless—for we must hear this not only at the present moment but must return often to the subject again—assuming them to be as you now say, let us turn to the law itself and discuss it in the same way as we did the prelude. Tell us the way in which the power of dialectic works, what its parts are, and what paths it follows. For these, it would seem, lead to the very place arriving where a man may find rest from travelling and the end and purpose of his journey.

Not yet, my dear Glaucon, I said, will you be able to follow—it is not that keenness is lacking on my part—for you would no longer be seeing an image of what we are discussing but the truth itself, or so it seems to me. It is not worthwhile insisting that it is so in fact, but we must maintain that one would see something of this kind. Is that not so? —It surely is.

And that the power of dialectic will only appear to one who is experienced in the studies we have described, and cannot ever appear otherwise. —That too is worth insisting on.

No one will dispute with us when we say that dialectic is a different study which attempts to apprehend methodically, with regard to each thing, what each really is. All the other crafts are concerned with the opinions of men and their passions, or with the process of generation and composition, or the care of plants and composite things. The remainder which we said grasp at reality to some extent, namely geometry and those which follow it, we see as dreaming about reality, unable to have a waking view of it so long as they make use of hypotheses and leave them undisturbed and cannot give a reasoned account of them. What begins with an unknown has its conclusion and the steps in between put together from the unknown, so how could any agreed conclusion it comes to ever become knowledge? —It cannot.

Now dialectic is the only subject which travels this road, doing away with hypotheses[26] and proceeding to the first principle where it will find certainty. It gently draws the eye of the soul, which is really buried in a kind of barbaric mire, and leads it upwards, using the sciences we have described as assistants and helpers in the process of turning the soul around. We have often called these by the name of science through force of habit, but they need another name, clearer than opinion and more obscure than science—we described it as reasoning somewhere before—but it seems to me that people who have as many things to investigate as we have do not dispute about a name. —Certainly not.

It will therefore be enough, I said, as before, to call the first section knowledge, the second reasoning, the third belief, and the fourth imagination. The last two together we call opinion, the other two intelligence.[27] Opinion is concerned with the process of generation while intelligence is concerned with being. As being is to generation, so intelligence is to opinion, and as intelligence is to opinion, so knowledge is to belief and reasoning to imagination. We pass over the proportions between the objects to which they apply, and the division of either section, the opinable and the knowable, into two, Glaucon, lest it involve us in a great many more arguments than those which went before. —I agree, he said, with the rest, in so far as I am able to follow.

And you also call a dialectician the man who can give a reasoned account of the reality of each thing? To the man who can give no such account, either to himself or another, you will to that extent deny knowledge of his subject? —How could I say he had it?

And the same applies to the Good. The man who cannot by reason distinguish the Form of the Good from all others, who does not, as in a battle, survive all refutations, eager to argue according to reality and not according to opinion, and who does not come through all the tests without faltering in reasoned discourse—such a man you will say does not know the Good itself, nor any kind of good. If he gets hold of some image of it, it is by opinion, not knowledge; he is dreaming and asleep throughout his present life, and, before he wakes up here, he will arrive in Hades and go to sleep forever. —Yes, by Zeus, I will declare all this to be true.

Post-Reading Questions

1. What is the point of Socrates' controversial discussion of gold, silver, and bronze types of persons in Book III?
2. What definition of justice emerges in Book IV of *The Republic*?
3. How are women guardians to be trained in the hypothetical republic (Book V), and are there different expectations of them?
4. In what sense is knowledge a journey, and how does the dialogic style of *The Republic* illustrate this?
5. What is the allegory of the cave, in Book VII, and what purpose does it serve?

CASE STUDY
THE CANADIAN SENATE

Introduction

The Senate of Canada, established by the Constitution Act of 1867, is the upper house of Parliament. Its 105 members are appointed by the governor general on the advice of the prime minister; in practice, the prime minister typically appoints individuals loyal to or in some way affiliated with his or her political party. Senate positions are allocated according to region, but with the intention of balancing the interests of the provinces and territories rather than reflecting their relative populations. Until 1965, senators were appointed for life, but the Constitution Act of 1965—formerly the British North America Act—introduced a mandatory retirement age of 75.

The purpose of the Senate is to serve as a body of "sober second thought": senators are to give careful scrutiny to certain bills introduced into the House of Commons, suggesting amendments where necessary, and proposing the reform of existing legislation. The Senate has a number of standing committees devoted to specific areas of importance— such as national finance, agriculture and forestry, and human rights—and these sometimes conduct special studies on issues within their domain. Ideally, then, the Senate provides a check on the power of the House of Commons by providing careful and critical scrutiny of legislation, and may even initiate needed bills that the House has overlooked. However, the appointed status of the Senate's members and their close affiliation with the party of the prime minister that appointed them have led many critics to question the supposed independence of the Senate. Some parties, such as the New Democratic Party (NDP) and the Bloc Québécois, have called for the abolition of the institution, characterizing it as an elitist and outdated body. Numerous efforts to reform the Senate have been proposed by the government over the years. These have mostly focused on changing the appointment process for senators (including proposals to move toward an elected Senate), altering the limits to the terms senators may serve, and changing the regional allocation of Senate seats.

Like Plato's Guardians in his ideal city, senators are expected to possess the qualities of wisdom, equanimity, and good judgment. The appointed—unelected—status of the senators means that they do not represent the citizenry in the way that members of the House of Commons do, but rather act as a safeguard on the elected, democratic body of the House. While, unlike Plato's Guardians, senators are not perceived as "rulers" per se, they are similarly thought to be advisors who can be trusted to use wisdom and judgment. They are also expected, in principle, to exercise independence from the prevailing system of political governance.

Readers of Plato's *Republic* sometimes express concern about the elitism and essentialism in Socrates' account of the Guardian class, as well as its undemocratic character. Similar qualms have been voiced in connection with the Senate in Canada. Justifications of this institution emphasize the benefits to a well-functioning democracy of a body of appointed persons believed to have greater powers of reflection and judgment than ordinary citizens. This bears some similarity to the reasoning behind the wise Guardians in Plato's *Republic*. In particular, it may be interesting to compare the ideals behind the Senate with the "Myth of the Metals" described in Book III, which stipulates that the city is made up of the three main (hierarchically ordered) groups corresponding to the bronze, silver, and gold metals: the merchants, warriors, and rulers/advisors.

As the following opinion piece indicates, there have been numerous legislative initiatives to reform Canada's Senate over the years. In 2008, the year in which this article appeared, the House of Commons considered several pieces of legislation aimed at Senate reform. These proposals, like others before it and in the years since, have tended to focus on more incremental changes. Significant changes to the Senate would require constitutional amendments, which are only possible with the agreement of seven of the country's provinces, totalling at least 50 per cent of the population. Although some polls show that a slight majority of Canadians favour abolishing the Senate, there has not yet been a serious attempt to do so, despite the fact that some provinces (Ontario, Nova Scotia, and British Columbia) advocate this course of action. A major 2013 scandal involving three Conservative senators who made fraudulent expense claims totalling hundreds of thousands of dollars may, however, have increased the public's opposition to this institution.

Sarah Barmak, "Why the Senate Deserves Props"

*Sarah Barmak, "Why the Senate Deserves Props," Toronto Star, 9 March 2008.
www.thestar.com/news/2008/03/09/why_the_senate_deserves_props.html*

It is the place where Canada's lawmakers go for sober second thought.

Or, as one senator likes to call it, "the pause that refreshes."

Or, as the public imagines it, the place where nothing important ever happens.

Go on. Think about the Senate, and try hard to stifle a yawn.

Who knew that in 1991, a Senate vote kept abortion legal in Canada? Or that its research in 1971 led to important national poverty reform? Or that it battled to ensure NAFTA was supported by the public? That it has a greater representation of women and minorities than the House of Commons?

In a time when Senate reform has become a multipartisan issue, Canadians seem just as confused about the issue as ever. Our upper house of Parliament is one of Canada's most powerful, maligned, and yet least understood public bodies.

Even the pro-reform Harper Tories inadvertently showed they need the Senate when they vowed Thursday to block Liberal legislation providing a $5,000 education tax shelter to parents—a bill that quietly passed through the House of Commons.

The musty old Senate is wrestling with Bill C-10 as well. The omnibus tax bill, that proposes cutting off federal tax breaks to artistic productions deemed inconsistent with public policy, has been called a censorship measure. According to Progressive Conservative senator Elaine McCoy—the only senator to keep a regularly updated blog on senate issues—that bill "flew through the House of Commons in about 60 seconds flat. . . . No discussion, no committee study, nothing."

Celine Hervieux-Payette, Liberal leader of the upper chamber, vowed Wednesday that the body would protect artistic freedoms, amending the bill if necessary.

The Senate . . . to the rescue?

It is certainly becoming clearer that the Tories' ire on the education tax break, or the protests of a reportedly 28,000-strong Facebook group opposed to Bill C-10, might come to nothing were it not for the Senate affording a chance to revisit laws passed in a hurry.

In today's climate of Senate reform, at least five separate motions and bills—plus a Special Committee chaired by Calgary senator Dan Hays—are proposing ways to fix the upper chamber. This includes Harper's Bill S-4, which would amend the constitution to limit senate terms to eight years, and his Bill C-43, which proposes that senators run as candidates for election.

Last fall, an Ipsos-Reid poll reported that two-thirds of Canadians would support a referendum on the future of the Senate, with a majority (52 per cent) favouring reform over outright abolition. Yet despite desire for change, most Canadians don't really know much about the Senate.

Senator McCoy is forming a new section on her website, titled Braintrust, to address the problem.

"We're going through all the reports on the senate and pulling out what we think are significant ones over the last 14 years, so it makes it more accessible to people," McCoy says.

"Among the more recent ones is the Kirby Report on Mental Health Care, put together by a committee. It led to the allotment of $55 million in federal funding to pursue mental health issues. It's the epitome of what the Senate does well. It takes subjects that are somewhat awkward for elected politicians and drills down into them deeply."

The Senate's policy reviews have reckoned with everything from corporate ownership of media and freedom of speech to the historic committee on poverty in 1971, to improving the legislation that created CSIS, according to Peter H. Russell, a professor of political science at the University of Toronto. His new book, *Two Cheers for Minority Government: The Evolution of Canadian Parliamentary Democracy*, has a chapter on the Senate.

Yet with all that work, the word "Senate" conjures up a caricature of old, white men with toga-like robes, sleepily rubberstamping documents, crossing T's and dotting I's.

That image was bolstered in 1998, when Ontario Liberal senator Andrew Thompson was notoriously found in contempt of the upper chamber and suspended for failing to explain his 2.2 per cent attendance record in the 1990s the worst of any senator.

Revelations that he had lived in Mexico for much of the time while drawing a $64,400 salary seemed to show up the Senate as a pasture for the patronage of worn-out politicians. . . .

There is a Senate catch-22 that is difficult to escape. When it passes legislation quickly and cleanly, which it mostly does, the Senate seems pointless. When it spends a long time debating a bill—as it did with the federal crime bill in recent weeks, sparking the ire of Prime Minister Harper, who threatened to call an election if the legislation wasn't passed quickly—it is deemed an impediment to the democratic process.

But that process, slow and bumbling though it may sometimes be, is essential to democracy, not an obstacle, according to Russell.

"Democracy is not just a matter of an election and government, it's debate and discussion of policy. We have a phrase for it: government by discussion."

"This phrase obstruction of democracy is rhetoric," agrees McCoy. "Democracy doesn't mean rushing pell-mell just because you have a majority. Indeed, when I speak of constraining the executive power, I mean the value of the senate is ensuring the tyranny of the majority doesn't carry us down the wrong path. When you look at some of the emerging democracies and some of the troubles they're having now, it often comes down to minorities and how do you let everyone have a role."

Russell, who discusses the Senate in his classes, says the upper chamber was founded as a check on the power of the house. Having it be elected wasn't a serious consideration in an age when secret ballots didn't even exist, he says.

"It would be inaccurate to say well, the fathers of Confederation didn't give a sh-t about democracy," he laughs. "They were comfortable with the possibility that this second chamber, though not elected, would debate and examine everything the government was doing. It turns out to have done that not so badly, but the problem is our culture has changed. We're way more democratic. The senate doesn't have legitimacy with the people."

"The notion that had I been appointed at the age of 35 I could have served for 40 years makes parts of the Soviet Union look democratic," quips Tory senator Hugh Segal, who has introduced a motion in the Senate to call a referendum on whether to abolish the body entirely. He also supports the prime minister's two reform bills.

"We've had over 20 efforts at Senate reform over the years and none have really gone anywhere, and I think it's because the public hasn't really been involved in the equation," he argues.

One obstacle to Senate reform is the fact that deep change would involve amending the constitution, like any change to the four core elements of Parliament—the five-year electoral cycle, the Crown, the House of Commons, or the Senate.

Yet the British, whose House of Lords numbers 738 to our Senate's 103, have managed reforms, Segal says.

"We have a powerful institution without any democratic legitimacy and I think we can do better than that in a world where we're supposed to be a proponent of democratization."

Equal representation, especially for the West, is one of the biggest issues driving Senate reform.

"If you've only got six from Alberta out of 103, there are fewer of us to carry our message to the other 97," McCoy argues.

But there are hidden traps in the push to make the Senate an elected body, warns Russell.

"Perhaps the majority of my students and colleagues want an elected Senate or none at all," he says. "But we're not going to have an elected Senate. Quebec would never, never, never accept being equal to the other provinces."

He cites a solution floated by David E. Smith, professor emeritus of the University of Saskatchewan: the prime minister should appoint people to the Senate on the advice of a non-political body representing the arts and letters of Canada, business and labour, sports, and science.

"Have people in the Senate who are accomplished in every endeavour. Getting there won't require that you are a good member of my party. It's going to have to do with talent, and ability, and experience. I think the Canadian people would say 'go for it.' This is what a lot of us are saying. Get the party hacks out and put in outstanding Canadians."

The NDP has long favoured abolishing the Senate, which the party sees as unaccountable. They even run an official-looking website called Senatehalloffame.ca, that trashes the Senate for influence peddling, corporate kowtowing, partisanship, and inaction.

In a 2005 statement Ed Broadbent repeated that the government should "do away with this trough once and for all."

Yet for better or for worse, the "trough" is often the only thing standing between faulty legislation and the law books.

In the nearly 30 years he has been in the Senate, senator Lowell Murray remembers the Senate's role in improving legislation, and even defeating the occasional bad bill. And where the Senate has failed, in his opinion—lately in the passage of Harper's crime bill under threat of calling an election, for instance ("We should have called his bluff!")—it can also succeed, as in the case of Bill C-10.

"I guarantee you we'll find other stuff in this budget (Bill C-10) that we didn't know about and has been slipped in. They do it all the time," he says in a slightly weathered tone. . . .

Says Murray "Many governments, having got legislation through too fast, recognize that a change had to be made and depended on us to make it."

Post-Case-Reading Questions

1. Can an analogy be usefully drawn between the appointed members of Canada's Senate and the Guardians in Plato's "ideal republic"?
2. Defenders of the Senate urge its reform rather than its abolition. How might an advocate defend this institution using some of Plato's arguments in *The Republic*?

CHAPTER 11

Aristotle

Introduction

Aristotle was the second-most prominent philosopher in ancient Greece. He was born in 384 BCE, in the city of Stagira, which he left when he was very young in order to enrol in Plato's Academy in Athens. Aristotle remained at the Academy for 20 years—until Plato's death—at which time he went to Macedonia to take up the job of tutoring the young Alexander the Great. As head of the royal academy at Macedon, he also tutored other future political leaders.

Aristotle returned to Athens in 335 BCE to establish his own school of higher education, called the Lyceum. After the death of Alexander, and with the growing prevalence of anti-Macedonian feelings, Aristotle was forced to leave Athens for Chalcis, where he died in 322 BCE.

Unlike Plato, Aristotle's interest was not limited to political and philosophical questions but included a wide array of inquiries concerning the natural world, notably in the fields of botany, biology, and physics.

Aristotle

© iStockphoto.com/Philip Sigin-Lavdanski

Aristotle's work established the foundation of many disciplines, from biology to formal logic and from ethics to literary criticism. His influence on later thinkers was such that, from the Middle Ages onward, he was simply known as "the philosopher." It is estimated that more than half of his work was destroyed with the decline of the Roman Empire. What has survived roughly amounts to almost 2,500 pages of writing. These are not necessarily finished and polished texts; they include lecture and research notes as well as encyclopedic references.

A major contribution of Aristotle to philosophy and science was his idea of scientific method, which stressed, first, the importance of observation and sense perception as the starting point of any natural inquiry; second, the need to examine complex things first by studying their parts (though the whole is, for Aristotle, logically and ontologically prior to the parts); and third, the value of deductive reasoning. Aristotle hoped that his scientific method could lead us to discover the causes and principles of things, and enable us to see how these in turn fit into the scheme of nature. Today, we call Aristotle's distinctive approach to reasoning "teleological," meaning that the perceived end purpose of a thing is used to explain its nature or development.

Aristotle also formalized logic as a science that is concerned with arguments. Logic is the study of the relation between statements in an argument. It helps us to evaluate how good an argument is. He worked out the theory of syllogism, or categorical logic, which describes the relation among categories of real things. For Aristotle, categorical logic included all of logic. Aristotle's detailed work on logic should not, however, give us the wrong impression of him as uninterested in emotion; indeed, he believed that "Reason by itself produces nothing," and very much emphasized the role of emotion.

Aristotle's moral theory is laid out in his *Nicomachean Ethics*—excerpted below—which was named after his son, Nicomachus. Ethics, according to this text, is not aimed at knowing but rather at doing, a mode of acting that is the pursuit of living a virtuous and flourishing life. With respect to this pursuit, character becomes the central aspect of the individual's development. This activity is aimed at the human good, which is happiness or *eudaimonia*, as the foremost goal of human pursuits. A virtuous person achieves happiness when he or she masters the skill of avoiding excess and deficiency in all acts. For Aristotle, it is only by living a political life—that is, living in a city, with fellow citizens—that we have the opportunity to foster such skill by engaging in deliberations concerning the affairs of the state.

Aristotle thinks that the most general science of the good is politics because the good life cannot be lived if social arrangements do not make it possible. Aristotle's *Politics* is thus concerned with the proper form and structure of human communities in terms of their organization and governance, and his distinctively teleological approach to these matters is important to note. A city-state like Athens, one of the cities he wrote about, was a community in which many citizens knew one another and could deliberate about their concerns collectively. In *Politics*, Aristotle argues that this form of association—i.e., a city-state—is a natural form of association that makes human development and flourishing possible. The state exists not for people's mere coexistence, but rather in order to make the good life possible for its citizens.

The excerpts that follow are taken from Book V of the *Nicomachean Ethics*, in which Aristotle discusses the principle of "equity" as a way of correcting the rigidity of the law and so facilitating the aim of justice.

Further Readings

Ackrill, J.L. (1981). *Aristotle the Philosopher*. New York: Oxford University Press.

Barnes, J. (ed.) (1995). *The Cambridge Companion to Aristotle*. Cambridge: Cambridge University Press.

Barnes, J. (2001). *Aristotle: A Very Short Introduction*. Oxford: Oxford University Press.

Miller, F. Jr. (1995). *Nature, Justice and Rights in Aristotle's Politics*. Oxford: Clarendon Press.

Yack, B. (1993). *The Problems of a Political Animal*. Berkeley: University of California.

Aristotle, From *Nicomachean Ethics*

Excerpted from The Ethics of Artistotle: The Nicomachean Ethics, *translated by J.A.K. Thomson, revised with Notes and Appendices by Hugh Tredennick (London: Penguin Books, 1953 [translation], 1976 [revised translation]).*

Book V: Justice

What do we mean by justice and injustice?

i. In treating of justice and injustice we have to consider with what sort of actions they are actually concerned, what sort of a mean justice is, and what the extremes are between which justice lies. Let us conduct our inquiry on the same lines as our foregoing account.[1]

Well, when people speak of justice we see that they all mean that kind of state of character that disposes them to perform just acts, and behave in a just manner, and wish for what is just; and in the same way they mean by injustice the state that makes them act unjustly and wish for unjust things. So we too may begin by making these assumptions as a basis for our discussion. For in fact the case is not the same with states as it is with sciences and faculties, because whereas both members of a pair of contraries are held to be the concern of the same science or faculty,[2] a *state* that has a contrary does not cause results that are contrary to itself: e.g., health causes only healthy actions and not the contrary kind, for we say that a person walks healthily when he walks as a healthy man would.[3]

The nature of a contrary state is often recognized from its contrary, and states are often recognized from the subjects to which they belong, for if we know what is meant by a sound condition of the body, we get to know also what is meant by an unsound condition; and we recognize sound bodily condition from our knowledge of bodies in that condition, and vice versa. For instance, if bodily soundness is firmness of flesh, then bodily unsoundness must be flabbiness of flesh, and what conduces to soundness must be that which is productive of firmness in flesh. Also if one contrary is ambiguous, it follows for the most part[4] that the other is also; e.g., that if "just" is ambiguous, "unjust" will be too.

. . .

Distributive justice employs geometrical proportion

iii. Both the unjust man and the unjust act are unfair or unequal, and clearly in each case of inequality there is something intermediate, viz., that which is equal; because in any action that admits degrees of more and less there is also an equal. Then if what is unjust is unequal, what is just is equal; as is universally accepted even without the support of argument. And since what is equal is a mean, what is just will be a sort of mean. But an instance of equality involves two terms at least. Therefore what is just must be a mean, and equal, and relative (i.e., just for certain persons[5]); and *qua* mean, it must be between extremes (i.e., a greater and a less); and *qua* equal, it must involve two things; and *qua* just, it affects certain persons. So a just act necessarily involves at least four terms: two persons for whom it is in fact just, and two shares in which its justice is exhibited. And there will be the same equality between the shares as between the persons, because the shares will be in the same ratio to one another as the persons; for if the persons are not equal, they will not have equal shares; and it is when equals have or are assigned unequal shares, or people who are not equal, equal shares, that quarrels and complaints break out.

This is also clear from the principle of assignment according to merit. Everyone agrees that justice in distribution must be in accordance with merit in some sense, but they do not all mean the same kind of merit: the democratic view is that the criterion is free birth; the oligarchic that it is wealth or good family; the aristocratic that it is excellence.

So justice is a sort of proportion; for proportion is a property not only of number as composed of abstract units, but of number in general; for proportion is an equality of ratios, and involves four terms at least (that a discrete proportion[6] involves four terms is obvious, but so does a continuous proportion, because it treats one term as two, i.e., states it twice: e.g., A:B = B:C. Thus B has been stated twice. So if B is taken twice there will be four proportionals). Justice too involves at least four terms, and the ratio is the same <between the first two and the last two>; for the persons and the shares have been divided in the same ratio,[7] so the third term will be to the fourth as the first is to the second, and so by alternation the second will be to the fourth as the first to the third. And so also the sum <of the first and third> is to the sum <of the second and fourth>. This is the combination produced by the allocation of shares; and if it is made up in this way it is a just combination. Therefore justice in distribution consists in conjunction of the first with the third term, and of the second with the fourth; and what is just in this sense is a mean, whereas what is unjust violates the proportion, because the proportional is a mean, and what is just is proportional. (This kind of proportion is called geometrical by mathematicians, because in geometrical proportion the effect is that the ratio of whole to whole is the same as that of each part to each corresponding part.) But this proportion[8] is not continuous, because in it we do not get one and the same term representing both a person and a share.

What is just in this sense, then, is what is proportional, and what is unjust is what violates the proportion. So one share becomes too large and the other too small. This is exactly what happens in practice: the man who acts unjustly gets too much and the victim of injustice too little of what is good. In the case of an evil the position is reversed, for in comparison with the greater the lesser evil is reckoned as a good, because the lesser evil is more to be chosen than the greater, and what is to be chosen is a good, and what is more to be chosen is a greater good.

This, then, is one kind of justice.

. . .

Political justice: its conditions

vi. The relation of reciprocity to justice has been discussed already.[9] But we must not overlook the fact that the subject of our inquiry is not only justice in general but *political* justice. Political justice obtains between those who share a life for the satisfaction of their needs as persons free and equal, either arithmetically or proportionately.[10] Hence in associations where these conditions are not present there is no political justice between the members, but only a sort of approximation to justice. For justice is only found among those whose mutual relations are controlled by law, and law is only found among those who are liable to injustice; for legal justice consists in distinguishing between what is just and what is unjust. But injustice implies unjust conduct (although unjust conduct does not always imply injustice[11]); and this consists in assigning to oneself too much of what is generally good and too little of what is generally bad. That is why we do not allow a man to rule, but the principle of law;[12] because a man does so for his own advantage, and becomes a despot, whereas the ruler is the upholder of justice, and if of justice, of equality. And since it is agreed that if he is a just man he derives no advantage (because he does not assign himself a larger share of what is generally good, unless the share is proportionate to his merits, so that his labours are altruistic: hence the saying, already mentioned,[13] that justice is the good of others): it follows that he ought to be given some reward, viz. honour and dignity. It is those who are not satisfied with these rewards that develop into despots.

. . .

Political justice may be based upon natural or upon civil law

vii. There are two sorts of political justice, one natural and the other legal. The natural is that which has the same validity everywhere and does not depend upon acceptance; the legal is that which in the first place can take one form or another indifferently, but which, once laid down, is decisive: e.g., that the ransom for a prisoner of war shall be one mina,[14] or that a goat shall be sacrificed and not two sheep; and also any enactments for particular circumstances, such as the sacrifices in honour of Brasidas, and decisions made by special resolution. Some hold the view that all regulations are of this kind, on the ground that whereas natural laws are immutable and have the same validity everywhere (as fire burns both here and in Persia), they can see that notions of justice are variable. But this contention[15] is not true as stated, although it is true in a sense. Among the gods, indeed, justice presumably never changes at all; but in our world, although there is such a thing as natural law, everything is subject to change;[16] but still some things are so by nature and some are not, and it is easy to see what sort of thing, among those that admit of being otherwise, is so by nature and what is not, but is legal and conventional, assuming that both alike are changeable. And the same distinction will apply in all other cases; for the right hand is by nature the stronger, and yet it is possible for everyone to become ambidextrous.

Rules of justice established by convention and on the ground of expediency may be compared to standard measures; because the measures used in the wine and corn trades are not everywhere equal: they are larger[17] in the wholesale and smaller in the retail trade. Similarly laws that are not natural but man-made are not the same everywhere, because forms of government are not the same either; but everywhere there is only one natural form of government, namely that which is best.

The several rules of law and justice are related to the actions performed in conformity with them as the universal is to the particular, because the latter are many, but each of the former is only one, being universal.

. . .

Voluntary and involuntary acts: the importance of intention

viii. Since just and unjust acts are as we have described them, it is only when a person acts voluntarily that he does a just or unjust act. When he acts involuntarily his action is neither just nor unjust, except incidentally; because people do perform actions to which justice and injustice are incidental.[18] Thus just and unjust conduct are distinguished by being voluntary or involuntary, because it is when an act is voluntary that it is blamed, and then also that it becomes an unjust act. So there can be something that is unjust, but stops short of being an unjust act, unless voluntariness is present too. By a voluntary act I mean (as has been said above[19]) any act lying in the agent's power that he does knowingly, i.e., not being ignorant either of the person affected or of the instrument used or of the result (e.g., *whom* he is striking, or *with what*, or *to what effect*), no particular being due to accident or compulsion. Thus if a man were to seize the hand of another and with it strike a third party, the second man would not be a voluntary agent, because he could not help himself. It is possible for the person struck to be the agent's father, although the agent is only aware that he is a human being, or one of the company, and not that he is his father. The same sort of distinction may be similarly assumed with regard to the result and the action as a whole. An involuntary act, then, is an act done in ignorance, or if not in ignorance, outside the agent's control, or under compulsion (for there are actually a number of the natural processes that we carry out or experience, none of which are either voluntary or involuntary, although we are fully conscious of them: e.g., growing old or dying). In the case of just and unjust acts alike there is also an accidental factor. For example, a man may return a deposit unwillingly and through fear; then we must not say that he is acting justly, or doing a right action, except incidentally. Similarly we must admit that a man who fails to return a deposit only under compulsion and against his will is only incidentally acting unjustly or doing a wrong action. Some of our voluntary acts we do from choice, and some we do not; those which are the result of deliberation are chosen, and those which are not the result of deliberation are not chosen.

. . .

To be just is not easy, because just conduct presupposes a virtuous moral state

ix. People suppose that it is in their power to act unjustly, and that therefore it is easy to be just; but this is not so. To go to bed with your neighbour's wife, to strike the man next to you, to slip money into somebody's hand—this is easy and lies in their power; but it is not easy, nor in their power, to do these things as the outcome of a certain state of character. Similarly they assume that it takes no special wisdom to recognize what is just and unjust, because it is not difficult to understand the instructions that the law gives us (although the acts that it prescribes are just only incidentally[20]); but how actions are to be performed and distributions made in order to be just—to know that is a harder task than to know what one's health requires; because in medicine too, although it is easy to know what honey and wine and hellebore[21] and cautery and surgery are, to know *how* and *to whom* and *when* they should be applied to produce health is no less a task than to be a qualified doctor. It is for this very reason[22] that people actually suppose that a just man is as capable of unjust as of just behaviour, on the ground that he could do any unjust act not less well but even better than a just one:[23] commit adultery or assault; and the brave man could throw away his shield, turn and run in either direction.[24] But to be a coward, or to act unjustly, is not merely to do these acts (except incidentally[25]), but to do them from a certain <moral> state; just as being a doctor or curing a patient is a matter not merely of using or not using surgery or medication, but of using them in a particular way.

. . .

A digression on equity, which corrects the deficiencies of legal justice

x. Our next task is to say something about equity and the equitable: what is the relation of equity to justice, and of what is equitable to what is just? When we look into the matter we find that justice and equity are neither absolutely identical nor generically different.[26] Sometimes we commend what is equitable and the equitable man, to the extent of transferring the word to other contexts as a term of approbation instead of "good," thus showing that what is more equitable is better. At other times, however, when we follow out the line of argument it seems odd that what is equitable should be commendable if it does not coincide with what is just; because if it is something different, then either what is just or what is equitable is not good; or alternatively if both are good, they are identical.

These, broadly speaking, are the arguments that raise the difficulty about what is equitable: yet there is a sense in which they are all correct, and there is no inconsistency between them. For equity, though superior to one kind of justice,[27] is still just, it is not superior to justice as being a different genus. Thus justice and equity coincide, and although both are good, equity is superior. What causes the difficulty is the fact that equity is just, but not what is legally just: it is a rectification of legal justice. The explanation of this is that all law is universal,[28] and there are some things about which it is not possible to pronounce rightly in general terms; therefore in cases where it is necessary to make a general pronouncement, but impossible to do so rightly, the law takes account of the majority of cases, though not unaware that in this way errors are made. And the law is none the less right; because the error lies not in the law nor in the legislator, but in the nature of the case; for the raw material of human behaviour is essentially of this kind.[29] So when the law states a general rule, and a case arises under this that is exceptional, then it is right, where the legislator owing to the generality of his language has erred in not covering that case, to correct the omission by a ruling such as the legislator himself would have given if he had been present there, and as he would have enacted if he had been aware of the circumstances.

This is why equity, although just, and better than a kind of justice, is not better than absolute justice—only

than the error due to generalization. This is the essential nature of equity; it is a rectification of law in so far as law is defective on account of its generality. This in fact is also the reason why everything is not regulated by law: it is because there are some cases that no law can be framed to cover, so that they require a special ordinance. An irregular object has a rule of irregular shape, like the leaden rule of Lesbian architecture:[30] just as this rule is not rigid but is adapted to the shape of the stone, so the ordinance is framed to fit the circumstances.

It is now clear what equity is, and that it is just, and superior to one kind of justice. This also makes plain what the equitable man is. He is one who chooses and does equitable acts, and is not unduly insistent upon his rights, but accepts less than his share, although he has the law on his side. Such a disposition is equity: it is a kind of justice, and not a distinct state of character.

Post-Reading Questions

1. How are justice and virtue related, for Aristotle?
2. In what sense is an unjust act also an unequal and unfair one, according to Aristotle?
3. Why does Aristotle say that an unjust act presupposes voluntary or intentional action? Do you agree?
4. According to Aristotle, what is equity, and why is it important?

CASE STUDY
PROPORTIONAL JUSTICE: R. v. IPEELEE

Introduction

This 2012 Supreme Court case concerns legal appeals made by two Aboriginal men, Manasie Ipeelee and Frank Ralph Ladue, who sought reductions to sentences that they received after breaching their long-term supervision orders (LTSOs). Both had incurred LTSOs following multiple convictions, for which they received, and served, prison sentences. In addition to long criminal records and a history of alcohol and drug abuse, however, both men had suffered from poverty, neglect, and extensive abuse. [In the excerpt included here, the case of Ladue has been omitted.] The central issue before the Court, according to the final judgment, was "how to determine a fit sentence for a breach of an LTSO in the case of an Aboriginal offender in particular." Crucial to this question was whether the 1999 Supreme Court case decision *Gladue*, which held that the distinctive abuse and cultural oppression suffered by Aboriginal offenders should be taken into consideration in sentencing, should be applied here.

The Court in *R. v. Ipeelee* based its ruling on the following sections of Canadian Criminal Code:

718.1 A sentence must be proportionate to the gravity of the offence and the degree of responsibility of the offender.

718.2 A court that imposes a sentence shall also take into consideration the following principles:

(e) all available sanctions other than imprisonment that are reasonable in the circumstances should be considered for all offenders, with particular attention to the circumstances of aboriginal offenders.

The case thus highlights the question of how to determine a "fit" sentence for Aboriginal offenders. In so doing, it illuminates the Aristotelian insights that principles of equity and fairness should be used to correct the rigidity of a rule or law in the context of concrete practical demands. Here, equity is an attempt to "correct" the generality of the law—which Aristotle thought rendered many laws defective—in light of the particularity of a situation. The Court's deliberation is a clear instance of using equity as a gauge for discovering the right or just fit between the general and the particular.

In Book V of the *Nicomachean Ethics*, Aristotle argues that justice and injustice are properly understood in the light of the different contexts in which they arise. He stresses the futility of attempting to define justice in a purely general (and therefore overly simple) way. That is, justice has different dimensions that ought not to be collapsed: for example, there is a distributive aspect, not to be confused with the rectificatory aspect of justice. Importantly, he also discusses the importance of proportionality to justice, which requires a sound and thorough understanding of the context of the action, or person, that is considered unjust.

As we can see from this short description, Aristotle's thoughts arguably have implications for the issue of sentencing: what is a just response to one person's wrongdoing may not be fit or equitable in the case of another. Although Aristotle did not consider the matter of sentencing in any detail—nor, of course, did he consider the situation of oppressed cultural or racial minorities in society—his contextualist approach to matters of justice and injustice remains relevant to discussions of equality and fairness. In particular, Aristotle's insight that equality or equity requires treating *like* cases alike, and *different* cases differently, challenges a more simplistic conception of equality as requiring identical treatment. Moreover, Aristotle's emphasis on the importance of examining the background circumstances in which an unjust action occurs, the intention of the perpetrator, and the particular harms (and profits) that result, provide an early conceptual roadmap to the vexed problem of equitable criminal sentencing in an unequal society.

From *R. v. Ipeelee*, [2012] 1 S.C.R. 433

R. v. Ipeelee, *2012 SCC 13, [2012] 1 S.C.R. 433.*
http://scc.lexum.org/decisia-scc-csc/scc-csc/scc-csc/en/item/8000/index.do

[The majority decision was delivered by LeBel J.]

I. Introduction

[This appeal raises] the issue of the principles governing the sentencing of Aboriginal offenders for breaches of long-term supervision orders ("LTSOs"). [The appeal concerns] Aboriginal offenders with long criminal records. [It provides] an opportunity to revisit and reaffirm the judgment of this Court in *R. v. Gladue*, [1999]. I propose to allow the offender's appeal in *Ipeelee* . . . .

II. Manasie Ipeelee

A. Background and Criminal History

Mr. Manasie Ipeelee is an Inuk man who was born and raised in Iqaluit, Nunavut. His life story is far removed from the experience of most Canadians. His mother was an alcoholic. She froze to death when Manasie Ipeelee was five years old. He was raised by his maternal grandmother and grandfather, both of whom are now deceased. Mr. Ipeelee began consuming alcohol when he was 11 years old and quickly developed a serious alcohol addiction. He dropped out of school shortly thereafter. His involvement with the criminal justice system began in 1985, when he was only 12 years old.

Mr. Ipeelee is presently 39 years old. He has spent a significant proportion of his life in custody or under some form of community supervision. His youth record contains approximately three dozen convictions. The majority of those offences were property-related, including breaking and entering, theft, and taking a vehicle without consent (joyriding). There were also convictions for failure to comply with an undertaking, breach of probation, and being unlawfully at large. Mr. Ipeelee's adult record contains another 24 convictions, many of which are for similar types of offences. He has also committed violent crimes. His record includes two convictions for assault causing bodily harm and one conviction each for aggravated assault, sexual assault, and sexual assault causing bodily harm. I will describe these offences in greater detail, as they provided the basis for his eventual designation as a long-term offender.

In December 1992, Mr. Ipeelee pleaded guilty to assault causing bodily harm. He and a friend assaulted a man who was refusing them entry to his home. Mr. Ipeelee was intoxicated at the time. During the fight, he hit the victim over the head with an ashtray and with a chair. He was sentenced to 21 days' imprisonment and one year's probation.

In December 1993, Mr. Ipeelee again pleaded guilty to assault causing bodily harm. The incident took place outside a bar in Iqaluit and both Mr. Ipeelee and the victim were intoxicated. Witnesses saw Mr. Ipeelee kicking the victim in the face at least 10 times, and the assault continued after the victim lost consciousness. The victim was hospitalized for his injuries. At the time of the offence, Mr. Ipeelee was on probation. He received a sentence of five months' imprisonment.

In November 1994, Mr. Ipeelee pleaded guilty to aggravated assault. The incident involved another altercation outside the same bar in Iqaluit. Once more, both Mr. Ipeelee and the victim were intoxicated. During the fight, Mr. Ipeelee hit and kicked the victim. After the victim lost consciousness, Mr. Ipeelee continued to hit him and stomp on his face. The victim suffered a broken jaw and had to be sent to Montréal for treatment. Mr. Ipeelee was once again on probation at the time of the offence. He was sentenced to 14 months' imprisonment.

Mr. Ipeelee received an early release from that sentence in the fall of 1995. Approximately three weeks later, while still technically serving his sentence, he committed a sexual assault. The female victim had been drinking in her apartment in Iqaluit with Mr. Ipeelee and others, and was passed out from intoxication. Witnesses observed Mr. Ipeelee and another man carrying the victim into her room. Mr. Ipeelee was later seen having sex with the unconscious woman on her bed. Mr. Ipeelee was sentenced to two years' imprisonment. He remained in custody until his warrant expiry date in February 1999, as Corrections Canada officials deemed him to be a high risk to reoffend.

After serving his sentence, Mr. Ipeelee moved to Yellowknife. He began drinking within one half-hour of his arrival and was arrested for public intoxication that evening, and again 24 hours later. In the six months leading up to his next conviction, he was arrested at least nine more times for public intoxication.

On August 21, 1999, Mr. Ipeelee committed another sexual assault, this one causing bodily harm, which led to his designation as a long-term offender. Mr. Ipeelee, while intoxicated, entered an abandoned van that homeless persons frequented. Inside, a 50-year-old woman was sleeping. She awoke to find Mr. Ipeelee removing her pants. She struggled and Mr. Ipeelee began punching her in the face. When she called out for help, he told her to shut up or he would kill her. He then sexually assaulted her. The victim was finally able to escape when Mr. Ipeelee fell asleep. He was arrested and the victim was taken to the hospital to be treated for her injuries.

At the sentencing hearing for this offence, Richard J. of the Northwest Territories Supreme Court noted that Mr. Ipeelee's criminal record "shows a consistent pattern of Mr. Ipeelee administering gratuitous violence against vulnerable, helpless people while he is in a state of intoxication" (*R. v. Ipeelee* at para. 34). The expert evidence produced at the sentencing hearing indicated that Mr. Ipeelee did not suffer from any major mental illness and had average to above average intelligence. However, he was diagnosed as having both an antisocial personality disorder and a severe alcohol abuse disorder. The expert evidence also indicated that Mr. Ipeelee presented a high-moderate to high risk for violent reoffence, and a high-moderate risk for sexual reoffence. After evaluating all of the evidence, Richard J. concluded that there was a substantial risk that Mr. Ipeelee would reoffend and designated him a long-term offender under s. 753.1(1) of the Criminal Code, R.S.C. 1985, c. C-46. Mr. Ipeelee was sentenced to six years' imprisonment for the sexual assault, to be followed by a 10-year LTSO.

B. The Current Offence

Mr. Ipeelee was detained until his warrant expiry date for the 1999 sexual assault causing bodily harm. His LTSO came into effect on March 14, 2007, when he was released from Kingston Penitentiary to the Portsmouth Community Correctional Centre in Kingston. One of the conditions of Mr. Ipeelee's LTSO is that he abstain from using alcohol.

Mr. Ipeelee's LTSO was suspended on four occasions: from June 13 to July 5, 2007, for deteriorating performance and behaviour, and attitude problems; from July 23 to September 14, 2007, for sleeping in the living room and the kitchen, contrary to house rules; from September 24 to October 24, 2007, for being agitated and noncompliant, and for refusing urinalysis; and from October 25, 2007, to May 20, 2008, as a result of a fraud charge being laid against him (the charge was subsequently withdrawn). Mr. Ipeelee served those periods of suspension at the Kingston Penitentiary.

On August 20, 2008, the police found Mr. Ipeelee riding his bicycle erratically in downtown Kingston. He was obviously intoxicated and had two bottles of alcohol in his possession. He was charged with breaching a condition of his LTSO. . . . Mr. Ipeelee pleaded guilty to that offence on November 14, 2008.

. . .

IV. Issues

[This appeal raises] issues concerning the application of the principles and objectives of sentencing set out in Part XXIII of the Criminal Code. Specifically, the Court must determine the principles governing the sentencing of Aboriginal offenders, including the proper interpretation and application of this Court's judgment in *Gladue*, and the application of those principles to the breach of an LTSO. Finally, given those principles, the Court must determine whether either of the decisions under appeal contains an error in principle or imposes an unfit sentence warranting appellate intervention.

V. Analysis

A. The Principles of Sentencing

The central issue in these appeals is how to determine a fit sentence for a breach of an LTSO in the case of an Aboriginal offender. In particular, the Court must address whether, and how, the *Gladue* principles apply to these sentencing decisions. But first, it is important to review the principles that guide sentencing under Canadian law generally. . . .

The fundamental principle of sentencing (i.e., proportionality) is intimately tied to the fundamental purpose of sentencing—the maintenance of a just, peaceful, and safe society through the imposition of just sanctions. Whatever weight a judge may wish to accord to the various objectives and other principles listed in the Code, the resulting sentence must respect the fundamental principle of proportionality. Proportionality is the *sine qua non* of a just sanction. First, the principle ensures that a sentence reflects the gravity of the offence. This is closely tied to the objective of denunciation. It promotes justice for victims and ensures public confidence in the justice system.

. . .

Second, the principle of proportionality ensures that a sentence does not exceed what is appropriate, given the moral blameworthiness of the offender. In this sense, the principle serves a limiting or restraining function and ensures justice for the offender. In the Canadian criminal justice system, a just sanction is one that reflects both perspectives on proportionality and does not elevate one at the expense of the other.

. . .

B. The Offence—Sentencing for Breach of a Long-Term Supervision Order

[The appeal involves persons] designated as long-term offenders who are charged with breaching a condition of their LTSOs. This is the first time the Court has had the opportunity to discuss this particular offence.

. . .

Section 753.1(1) of the Criminal Code now directs when a court may designate an offender as a long-term offender. The section states,

> 753.1 (1) The court may, on application made under this Part following the filing of an assessment report under subsection 752.1(2), find an offender to be a long-term offender if it is satisfied that
> (a) it would be appropriate to impose a sentence of imprisonment of two years or more for the offence for which the offender has been convicted;
> (b) there is a substantial risk that the offender will reoffend; and
> (c) there is a reasonable possibility of eventual control of the risk in the community.

If the court finds an offender to be a long-term offender, it must impose a sentence of two years or more for the predicate offence and order that the offender be subject to long-term supervision for a period not exceeding 10 years (Criminal Code, s. 753.1(3)).

. . .

. . . The purpose of an LTSO is two-fold: to protect the public *and* to rehabilitate offenders and reintegrate them into the community. In fact, s. 100 of the CCRA [Corrections and Criminal Release Act] singles out rehabilitation and reintegration as the purpose of community supervision including LTSOs. As this Court indicated in *L.M.*, rehabilitation is the key feature of the long-term offender regime that distinguishes it from the dangerous offender regime. To suggest, therefore, that rehabilitation has been determined to be impossible to achieve in the long-term offender context is simply wrong. Given this context, it would be contrary to reason to conclude that rehabilitation is not an appropriate sentencing objective. . . .

. . .

C. The Offender—Sentencing Aboriginal Offenders

Section 718.2(e) of the Criminal Code directs that "all available sanctions other than imprisonment that are reasonable in the circumstances should be considered for all offenders, with particular attention to the circumstances of aboriginal offenders." This provision was introduced into the Code as part of the 1996 Bill C-41 amendments to codify the purpose and principles of sentencing. According to the then-minister of justice, Allan Rock, "the reason we referred specifically there to aboriginal persons is that they are sadly overrepresented in the prison populations of Canada" (House of Commons, *Minutes of Proceedings and Evidence of the Standing Committee on Justice and Legal Affairs*, No. 62, 1st Sess., 35th Parl., November 17, 1994, at p. 15).

Aboriginal persons were sadly overrepresented indeed. Government figures from 1988 indicated that Aboriginal persons accounted for 10 per cent of federal prison inmates, while making up only 2 per cent of the national population. The figures were even more stark in the Prairie provinces, where Aboriginal persons accounted for 32 per cent of prison inmates compared to 5 per cent of the population. The situation was generally worse in provincial institutions. . . . The foregoing statistics led the Royal Commission on Aboriginal Peoples ("RCAP") to conclude, at p. 309 of its Report, *Bridging the Cultural Divide: A Report on Aboriginal People and Criminal Justice in Canada* (1996):

> The Canadian criminal justice system has failed the Aboriginal peoples of Canada—First Nations,

Inuit and Métis people, on-reserve and off-reserve, urban and rural—in all territorial and governmental jurisdictions. The principal reason for this crushing failure is the fundamentally different world views of Aboriginal and non-Aboriginal people with respect to such elemental issues as the substantive content of justice and the process of achieving justice.

The overrepresentation of Aboriginal people in the Canadian criminal justice system was the impetus for including the specific reference to Aboriginal people in s. 718.2(e). It was not at all clear, however, what exactly the provision required or how it would affect the sentencing of Aboriginal offenders. In 1999, this Court had the opportunity to address these questions in *Gladue*. Cory and Iacobucci JJ., writing for the unanimous Court, reviewed the statistics and concluded, at para. 64:

> These findings cry out for recognition of the magnitude and gravity of the problem, and for responses to alleviate it. The figures are stark and reflect what may fairly be termed a crisis in the Canadian criminal justice system. The drastic overrepresentation of aboriginal peoples within both the Canadian prison population and the criminal justice system reveals a sad and pressing social problem. It is reasonable to assume that Parliament, in singling out aboriginal offenders for distinct sentencing treatment in s. 718.2(e), intended to attempt to redress this social problem to some degree. The provision may properly be seen as Parliament's direction to members of the judiciary to inquire into the causes of the problem and to endeavour to remedy it, to the extent that a remedy is possible through the sentencing process.

The Court held, therefore, that s. 718.2(e) of the Code is a remedial provision designed to ameliorate the serious problem of overrepresentation of Aboriginal people in Canadian prisons, and to encourage sentencing judges to have recourse to a restorative approach to sentencing (*Gladue*, at para. 93). It does more than affirm existing principles of sentencing; it calls upon judges to use a different method of analysis in determining a fit sentence for Aboriginal offenders. Section 718.2(e) directs sentencing judges to pay particular attention to the circumstances of Aboriginal offenders because those circumstances are unique and different from those of non-Aboriginal offenders (*Gladue*, at para. 37). When sentencing an Aboriginal offender, a judge must consider: (a) the unique systemic or background factors which may have played a part in bringing the particular Aboriginal offender before the courts; and (b) the types of sentencing procedures and sanctions which may be appropriate in the circumstances for the offender because of his or her particular Aboriginal heritage or connection (*Gladue*, at para. 66). Judges may take judicial notice of the broad systemic and background factors affecting Aboriginal people generally, but additional case-specific information will have to come from counsel and from the pre-sentence report (*Gladue*, at paras. 83–84).

. . .

Over a decade has passed since this Court issued its judgment in *Gladue*. As the statistics indicate, s. 718.2(e) of the Criminal Code has not had a discernible impact on the overrepresentation of Aboriginal people in the criminal justice system. Granted, the *Gladue* principles were never expected to provide a panacea. There is some indication, however, from both the academic commentary and the jurisprudence, that the failure can be attributed to some extent to a fundamental misunderstanding and misapplication of both s. 718.2(e) and this Court's decision in *Gladue*. The following is an attempt to resolve these misunderstandings, clarify certain ambiguities, and provide additional guidance so that courts can properly implement this sentencing provision.

1. Making Sense of Aboriginal Sentencing

Section 718.2(e) of the Criminal Code and this Court's decision in *Gladue* were not universally well received. Three interrelated criticisms have been advanced: (1) sentencing is not an appropriate means of addressing overrepresentation; (2) the *Gladue* principles provide what is essentially a race-based discount for Aboriginal offenders; and (3) providing special treatment and lesser sentences to Aboriginal offenders is inherently unfair as it creates unjustified distinctions between offenders who are similarly situated, thus violating the principle of sentence parity. In my view, these criticisms are based on a fundamental misunderstanding of the operation of s. 718.2(e) of the Criminal Code.

. . .

First, sentencing judges can endeavour to reduce crime rates in Aboriginal communities by imposing sentences that effectively deter criminality and rehabilitate offenders. These are codified objectives of sentencing. To the extent that current sentencing practices do not further these objectives, those practices must change so as to meet the needs of Aboriginal offenders and their communities.

. . .

Second, judges can ensure that systemic factors do not lead inadvertently to discrimination in sentencing. Professor Quigley aptly describes how this occurs:

> Socioeconomic factors such as employment status, level of education, family situation, etc., appear on the surface as neutral criteria. They are considered as such by the legal system. Yet they can conceal an extremely strong bias in the sentencing process. Convicted persons with steady employment and stability in their lives, or at least prospects of the same, are much less likely to be sent to jail for offences that are borderline imprisonment offences. The unemployed, transients, the poorly educated are all better candidates for imprisonment. When the social, political and economic aspects of our society place Aboriginal people disproportionately within the ranks of the latter, our society literally sentences more of them to jail. This is systemic discrimination.

Sentencing judges, as front-line workers in the criminal justice system, are in the best position to re-evaluate these criteria to ensure that they are not contributing to ongoing systemic racial discrimination.

Section 718.2(e) is therefore properly seen as a "direction to members of the judiciary to inquire into the causes of the problem and to endeavour to remedy it, *to the extent that a remedy is possible through the sentencing process*" (*Gladue*, at para. 64 (emphasis added)). Applying the provision does not amount to "hijacking the sentencing process in the pursuit of other goals" (Stenning and Roberts, at p. 160). The purpose of sentencing is to promote a just, peaceful and safe society through the imposition of just sanctions that, among other things, deter criminality and rehabilitate offenders, all in accordance with the fundamental principle of proportionality. Just sanctions are those that do not operate in a discriminatory manner. Parliament, in enacting s. 718.2(e), evidently concluded that nothing short of a specific direction to pay particular attention to the circumstances of Aboriginal offenders would suffice to ensure that judges undertook their duties properly.

. . .

The sentencing process is therefore an appropriate forum for addressing Aboriginal overrepresentation in Canada's prisons. Despite being theoretically sound, critics still insist that, in practice, the direction to pay particular attention to the circumstances of Aboriginal offenders invites sentencing judges to impose more lenient sentences simply because an offender is Aboriginal. In short, s. 718.2(e) is seen as a race-based discount on sentencing, devoid of any legitimate tie to traditional principles of sentencing.

. . .

First, systemic and background factors may bear on the culpability of the offender, to the extent that they shed light on his or her level of moral blameworthiness. This is perhaps more evident in *Wells* where Iacobucci J. described these circumstances as "the unique systemic or background factors *that are mitigating in nature* in that they may have played a part in the aboriginal offender's conduct" (para. 38 (emphasis added)). Canadian criminal law is based on the premise that criminal liability only follows from voluntary conduct. Many Aboriginal offenders find themselves in situations of social and economic deprivation with a lack of opportunities and limited options for positive development. While this rarely—if ever—attains a level where one could properly say that their actions were not *voluntary* and therefore not deserving of criminal sanction, the reality is that their constrained circumstances may diminish their moral culpability.

. . .

The second set of circumstances—the types of sanctions which may be appropriate—bears not on the degree of culpability of the offender, but on the effectiveness of the sentence itself. As Cory and Iacobucci JJ. point out, at para. 73 of *Gladue*: "What is important to recognize is that, for many if not most aboriginal offenders, the current concepts of sentencing are inappropriate because they have frequently not responded to the needs, experiences, and perspectives of aboriginal people or aboriginal communities." As the RCAP indicates, at p. 309, the "crushing failure" of the Canadian criminal justice system vis-à-vis Aboriginal peoples is due to "the fundamentally different world views of Aboriginal and non-Aboriginal people with respect to such elemental issues as the substantive content of justice and the process of achieving justice." The *Gladue* principles direct sentencing judges to abandon the presumption that all offenders and all communities share the same values when it comes to sentencing and to recognize that, given these fundamentally different world views, different or alternative sanctions may more effectively achieve the objectives of sentencing in a particular community.

. . .

A third criticism, intimately related to the last, is that the Court's direction to utilize a method of analysis when sentencing Aboriginal offenders is inherently unfair as it creates unjustified distinctions between offenders who are otherwise similarly situated. This, in turn, violates the principle of sentence parity. This criticism

is premised on the argument that the circumstances of Aboriginal offenders are not, in fact, unique.

. . .

VI. Application

A. Manasie Ipeelee

Megginson J. sentenced Mr. Ipeelee to three years' imprisonment, less credit for pre-sentence custody. The Court of Appeal upheld that sentence. Both courts emphasized the serious nature of the breach, given the documented link between Mr. Ipeelee's use of alcohol and his propensity to engage in violence. As a result, both courts emphasized the objectives of denunciation, deterrence, and protection of the public.

In my view, the courts below made several errors in principle warranting appellate intervention. First, the courts reached the erroneous conclusion that protection of the public is the paramount objective when sentencing for breach of an LTSO and that rehabilitation plays only a small role. As discussed, while protection of the public is important, the legislative purpose of an LTSO as a form of conditional release set out in s. 10f the CCRA is to rehabilitate offenders and reintegrate them into society. The courts therefore erred in concluding that rehabilitation was not a relevant sentencing objective.

As a result of this error, the courts below gave only attenuated consideration to Mr. Ipeelee's circumstances as an Aboriginal offender. Relying on *Carrière*, the Court of Appeal concluded that this was the kind of offence where the sentence will not differ as between Aboriginal and non-Aboriginal offenders, and relying on *W. (H.P.)*, held that features of Aboriginal sentencing play little or no role when sentencing long-term offenders. Given certain trends in the jurisprudence discussed above, it is easy to see how the court reached this conclusion. Nonetheless, they erred in doing so. These errors justify the Court's intervention.

It is therefore necessary to consider what sentence is warranted in the circumstances. Mr. Ipeelee breached the alcohol abstention condition of his LTSO. His history indicates a strong correlation between alcohol use and violent offending. As a result, abstaining from alcohol is critical to managing his risk in the community. That being said, the conduct constituting the breach was becoming intoxicated, not becoming intoxicated and engaging in violence. The Court must focus on the actual incident giving rise to the breach. A fit sentence should seek to manage the risk of reoffence he continues to pose to the community in a manner that addresses his alcohol abuse, rather than punish him for what might have been.

To engage in the latter would certainly run afoul of the principles of fundamental justice.

At the time of the offence, Mr. Ipeelee was 18 months into his LTSO. He was living in Kingston, where there were few culturally relevant support systems in place. There is no evidence, other than one isolated instance of refusing urinalysis, that he consumed alcohol on any occasion prior to this breach. Mr. Ipeelee's history indicates that he has been drinking heavily since the age of 11. Relapse is to be expected as he continues to address his addiction.

Taking into account the relevant sentencing principles, the fact that this is Mr. Ipeelee's first breach of his LTSO and that he pleaded guilty to the offence, I would substitute a sentence of one year's imprisonment. Given the circumstances of his previous convictions, abstaining from alcohol is crucial to Mr. Ipeelee's rehabilitation under the long-term offender regime. Consequently, this sentence is designed to denounce Mr. Ipeelee's conduct and deter him from consuming alcohol in the future. In addition, it provides a sufficient period of time without access to alcohol so that Mr. Ipeelee can get back on track with his alcohol treatment. Finally, the sentence is not so harsh as to suggest to Mr. Ipeelee that success under the long-term offender regime is simply not possible.

. . .

VII. Conclusion

For the foregoing reasons, I would allow the offender's appeal in *Ipeelee* and substitute a sentence of one year's imprisonment. . . .

Post-Case-Reading Questions

1. How might Aristotle's notions of equity and proportionality in law apply in considering whether judges should be permitted to give different (more lenient) sentences, and/or culturally specific sanctions, to Aboriginal offenders in Canada?
2. Do the background social conditions of Aboriginal people in Canada—particularly the context of racism and poverty, associated with high rates of alcoholism and abuse—make the actions of criminal offenders like Manasie Ipeelee less "voluntary," in Aristotle's sense? If so, should this background context diminish judgments of individual culpability, and therefore impact sentencing?

Niccolò Machiavelli

Introduction

Niccolò Machiavelli was born in 1469 into a well-established family of meager means in the city-state of Florence. His father was a lawyer who took his son's education very seriously. Niccolò was rigorously trained in the sciences of the day, as well as in the humanistic disciplines, such as grammar, rhetoric, poetry, and Latin.

Shortly after the fall of the puritanical regime of Savanorola in 1498, Machiavelli landed a position as a high-ranking civil servant in the government of the Florentine Republic, at the impressively young age of 29. During his service, he acquired extensive understanding of the arts of governance, diplomacy, and military strategy. Machiavelli travelled widely while he held this position; most notably, his ambassadorial-like duties included a three-and-a-half month stint at the court of Cesare Borgia. Machiavelli's observations of the formidable duke's political and military strategizing helped to shape the political realism we now associate with his writings.

Nicolo Machiavelli

When the Medici family regained control over Florence in 1512, Machiavelli became *persona non grata*, and was stripped of his post, imprisoned, and tortured. After his release, he went into exile at his home in San Casciano in rural Tuscany. It was there that he penned *The Prince* (in 1513–14) and *The Discourses on Livy* (1518 or 1519). Machiavelli, truly a man of the Italian Renaissance, also wrote works in other genres: he is the author of *Mandragola*, an important work of comedy (1518); *The Art of War*, a dialogue on military strategy and practices (1521); *Florentine Histories* (1525); a poem entitled *The Golden Ass* (1517); and a short novel, *Belfagor* (1517).

Among his many works, the most celebrated and influential are *The Prince* and *The Discourses*, which are often considered to be the beginning of "modern" political thought. While both are concerned with political life, they differ significantly in their orientation and direction. *The Discourses* endorses the Roman Republic and emphasizes ideas of self-government and liberty, while *The Prince* argues for the need for strong princely rule and is more concerned with statecraft than with ethics or politics. This apparent contradiction is a source of considerable confusion among Machiavelli's readers. Some scholars of Machiavelli's writings argue that the tension between the two texts can be resolved when we realize that his sober and realist views in *The Prince* were rational given the political climate of the day—namely, the rise to power of the Medici family and the subsequent demise of democratic and republican institutions. Machiavelli's advice on how to develop princely *virtù* (i.e., the capacities of an effective, strong ruler) and his seeming endorsement of ruthless tactics of statecraft may have reflected his desire to secure a position in the new Medici administration. Recently fired from his senior post in the Florentine Republic, Machiavelli hoped that by writing *The Prince* and engaging the help of his friend Francesco Vettori (the new Florentine ambassador to Rome), he might be appointed by Lorenzo di Piero de' Medici (ruler of Florence) to a post in Rome. Despite dedicating the book to the latter, however, this position never materialized.

Machiavelli lived in a volatile time, when Italy was fragmented into five main states (the Republic of Florence, the Republic of Venice, the kingdom of Naples, the Papal State, and the Duchy of Milan) and several independent cities (notably Genoa, Bologna, Ferrara, Siena, and Lucca). During his lifetime, the government of Florence changed hands several times. He had first-hand experience of what it took for these changes to be brought about in terms of political, military, and diplomatic means. It is against this backdrop that *The Prince* advocates that a wise and strong ruler must learn "how not to be good": skilled in the art of deception, he must not be bound by conventional moral principles, particularly those dictated by Christian ethics. Religion could help maintain peace and stability among the people, according to Machiavelli, but it should not hinder the prince by constraining his actions where effective rule is needed.

Since its publication, reaction to and assessment of *The Prince* has varied greatly. Readers in France and England initially dismissed it as a handbook of cynical rules for tyrants. The text was denounced by the Church as a work of the devil, and Machiavelli branded an atheist; in 1559, the Vatican put the book on its index of banned books. It took a century for the negative and polemical critique of *The Prince* to dissipate and give way to more sober (though by no means uniform) interpretations of the book by such readers as Hume, Rousseau, and Montesquieu. Today, *The Prince* may be viewed, arguably, as offering a rejection of conventional (especially Christian and Platonic) views of politics, as well as of the aristocratic (Medicean) approach to the art of the state as a system of patronage employed to control the republic's institutions. Read this way, the path-breaking advice that Machiavelli offers to new rulers in *The Prince* might even be understood as an ambitious attempt to provide the basis for a new political order that could unify Italy.

Following excerpts from *The Prince*, we explore the legacy of the former Quebec premier Maurice Duplessis, whose rule was branded as *la Grande Noirceur* (the Great Darkness) due to his Machiavellian approach to obtaining, maintaining, and using political power.

Further Readings

Dietz, M. (1980). "Trapping the Prince: Machiavelli and the Politics of Deception," *American Political Science Review* 86 (3): 777–99.

King, R. (2007). *Machiavelli*. New York: Harper-Collins Publishers.

Ridolfi, R. (1963). *The Life of Niccolò Machiavelli*. Trans. Cecil Grayson. Chicago: University of Chicago Press.

Skinner, Q. (2000). *Machiavelli: A Very Short Introduction*. Oxford: Oxford University Press.

Strauss, L. (1958). *Thoughts on Machiavelli*. Glencoe: Free Press.

Niccolò Machiavelli, From *The Prince*

Niccolò Machiavelli, The Prince, *translated and edited by Peter Bondanella*
(Oxford: Oxford University Press, 2005).

III Of mixed principalities
[*De principatibus mixtis*]

But it is in the new principality that difficulties arise. In the first place, if it is not completely new but is like an added appendage (so that the two parts together may be called mixed), its difficulties derive first from one natural problem inherent in all new principalities: that men gladly change their ruler, thinking to better themselves. This belief causes them to take up arms against their ruler, but they fool themselves in this, since they then see through experience that matters have become worse. This stems from another natural and ordinary necessity, which is that a new prince must always harm his new subjects, both with his soldiers as well as with countless other injuries involved in his new conquest. Thus, you have made enemies of all those you harmed in occupying the principality, and you are unable to maintain as friends those who helped you to rise to power, since you cannot satisfy them in the way that they had supposed. Nor can you use strong medicines[1] against them, for you are in their debt: this is so because, although someone may have the most powerful of armies, he always needs the support of the inhabitants to seize a region. For these reasons, Louis XII, King of France, quickly occupied Milan and just as quickly lost it.[2] The first time, the troops of Ludovico alone were needed to retake it from him, because those citizens who had opened the gates of the city to the King, finding themselves deceived in their beliefs and in that future improvement they had anticipated, could not support the vexations of the new prince.

It is indeed true that when lands that have rebelled once are taken a second time it is more difficult to lose them; for the ruler, taking advantage of the rebellion, is less reticent about punishing offenders, ferreting out suspects, and shoring up weak positions. And so, if only a Duke Ludovico[3] creating a border disturbance sufficed for France to lose Milan the first time, the whole world[4] had to oppose her and destroy her armies or chase them from Italy to cause her to lose it the second time. This occurred for the reasons mentioned above. Nevertheless, it was taken from her both the first and the second time.

The general explanations for the first loss have been discussed. Now it remains to specify those for the second, and to see what remedies the King of France had, and those that someone in the same situation could have, so as to be able to maintain a stronger grip on his conquest than France did.

I say, therefore, that those dominions, upon being conquered and added to the long-established state of the one who acquires them, are either of the same region and language or they are not. When they are it is easier to hold them, especially when they are unaccustomed to freedom. To possess them securely it is sufficient only to have wiped out the family line of the prince who ruled them, because so far as other things are concerned, men live peacefully as long as their old way of life is maintained and there is no change in customs. We have seen what happened in the case of Burgundy, Brittany, Gascony, and Normandy,[5] which have been part of France for such a long time; and although there are some linguistic differences, nevertheless the customs are similar, and they have been able to get along together easily. Anyone who acquires these lands and wishes to hold on to them must keep two things in mind: first, that the family line of the old prince must be wiped out; second, that neither their laws nor their taxes be altered. As a result, in a very short time they will become one body with the old principality.

But when dominions are acquired in a region that is not similar in language, customs, and institutions, it is here that difficulties arise; and it is here that one needs much good luck and much diligence to hold on to them. One of the best and most efficacious remedies would be for the person who has taken possession of them to go there to live. This would make that possession more secure and durable; as happened with the Turk in Greece;[6] for despite all the other methods he employed to retain that dominion, if he had not gone to live there it would have been impossible for him to hold on to it. By being on the spot, troubles are seen at their birth and can be quickly remedied; not being there, they are heard about after they have grown up and there is no longer any remedy. Moreover, the region would not be plundered by your own officers; the subjects would be pleased to have direct recourse to their prince; thus, those wishing to be good subjects have more reason to love him, and those wanting to be otherwise, more reason to fear him. Anyone who might wish to invade that dominion from abroad would be more hesitant; so that living right there, it is only with the greatest difficulty that the prince can lose it.

The other and better solution is to send colonies into one or two places, that will act as shackles[7] on that state; for it is necessary that the prince either do this or maintain a large number of cavalry and infantry. Colonies do not cost much, and with little or no expense a prince can send and maintain them. In so doing he injures only those whose fields and houses have been taken away and given to the new inhabitants, who are only a small part of that dominion. Those he injures, finding themselves scattered and poor, can never be a threat to him; and all the others remain uninjured on the one hand, and because of this they should remain peaceful, and on the other hand are afraid of making a mistake, for fear that what happened to those who were dispossessed might happen to them. I conclude that these colonies are not expensive, they are more loyal, they are less injurious, and the offended can do no harm since they are poor and scattered (as I have said). Concerning this, it should be noted that men must be either caressed or wiped out; because they will avenge minor injuries, but cannot do so for grave ones. Any harm done to a man must be of the kind that removes any fear of revenge. But by garrisoning troops there instead of colonies, one spends much more, being obliged to consume all the revenues of the state in standing guard, so that the gain turns into a loss; and far greater injury is committed, since the entire state is harmed by the army changing quarters from one place to another. Everybody resents this inconvenience, and everyone becomes the ruler's enemy; and these are enemies that can be harmful, since, although conquered, they remain in their own homes. And so, in every respect, this form of protection is as useless as the other kind, colonization, is useful.

Moreover, anyone who is in a region that is unlike his own in the ways mentioned above should make himself the leader and defender of his less powerful neighbours, and do all he can to weaken those who are more powerful; and he should be careful that, for whatever reason, no foreigner equal to himself in strength should enter there. And it will always happen that the outsider will be brought in by those who are dissatisfied, either because of too much ambition or because of fear, as was once seen when the Aetolians brought the Romans into Greece.[8] In every other province that the Romans entered, the native inhabitants brought them in. The order of things is such that, as soon as a powerful foreigner enters a region, all who are less powerful cling to him, moved by the envy they have against the ruler who has ruled over them. And so, concerning these weaker powers, the invader has no trouble whatsoever in winning them over, since all of them will immediately and willingly become part of the state he has acquired. He need only be careful that they do not seize too much military power and authority. With his own military power and their support, he can very easily put down those who are powerful, and remain complete arbiter of that region. Anyone who does not follow this procedure will quickly lose what he has taken, and while he holds it, he will find it full of infinite difficulties and troubles.

. . .

IV Why the kingdom of Darius, occupied by Alexander, did not rebel against his successors after the death of Alexander [*Cur Darii regnum, quod Alexander occupaverat, a successoribus suis post Alexandri mortem non defecit*]

Considering the difficulties one has in maintaining a newly acquired territory, one might wonder how it happened that when Alexander the Great died, having become ruler of Asia in a few years and having hardly occupied it, Alexander's successors[9] nevertheless managed to hold on to it, although it would have seemed reasonable for the whole region to revolt. And in keeping it, they had no other difficulty than that which arose among themselves from their own ambition. Let me reply that all principalities known to us are governed in two different ways: either by a prince with all the others his servants, who as ministers (through his favour and permission) assist in governing that kingdom; or by a prince and by barons, who hold that rank not because of any favour of their master but because of the antiquity of their bloodline. Such barons as these have their own dominions and subjects, who recognize them as masters and have natural affection for them. In those states that are governed by a prince and his servants, the prince has greater authority, for in all his territories there is no one else recognized as superior to him; and if the people do obey any other persons, it is because they are his ministers and officials; and they harbour a special affection for him.

Contemporary examples of these two different kinds of governments are the Turk and the King of France. One ruler governs the entire kingdom of the Turk; the others are his servants; and dividing his kingdom into sanjaks,[10] he sends various administrators there, and he moves them and changes them around as he pleases. But the King of France is placed among a group of hereditary nobles who are recognized in that state by their subjects and who are loved by them; they have their hereditary privileges, which the King cannot take away without endangering himself. Anyone, then, who considers the one and the other of these two states will find that for the Turk the difficulty lies in taking possession of the state, but once it has been conquered it is very simple to hold on to it. And so (on the other hand), you will find that in some respects it is easier to occupy the Kingdom of France, but extremely difficult to hold on to it.

The reasons for the difficulty in being able to occupy the kingdom of the Turk are because it is not possible to be summoned there by the princes of that kingdom, or to hope, through the rebellion of those the ruler has around him, to make your enterprise easier. This is because of the reasons mentioned above: since they are all his slaves and bound to him, it is more difficult to corrupt them; and even if they could be corrupted, little profit can be hoped for, since they will not be followed by the people for the reasons already discussed. Therefore, anyone who attacks the Turk must realize that he will find him completely united, and he must rely more on his own forces than on the disunity of his opponent. But once beaten and broken in battle so that he cannot regroup his troops, there is nothing else to be feared than the ruler's family. Once it has been wiped out, there remains no one else to be feared, for the others have no credit with the people. And just as, before the victory, the victor could place no hope in them, so afterwards he should not fear them.

The opposite occurs in kingdoms governed like that of France, because you can invade them with ease once you have won to your side some barons of the kingdom, since you can always find malcontents and men who desire a change. These people, for the reasons already given, can open the way to that dominion and facilitate your victory. However, when you wish to hold on to it this is accompanied by endless problems, both with those who have helped you and with those you have suppressed. Nor is it sufficient for you to wipe out the ruling family, since the nobles who make themselves heads of new insurrections still remain. And since you are neither able to make them happy nor to wipe them out, you lose that dominion whenever the opportunity arises.

Now, if you will consider the type of government Darius had, you will find it similar to the kingdom of the Turk; and therefore Alexander had first to overwhelm it totally and defeat it in battle. After this victory, Darius being dead, that state remained securely in Alexander's hands for the reasons discussed above. And had his successors been united they would have enjoyed it at their leisure, for in that kingdom no disorders arose other than those they stirred up themselves. But in states organized like that of France, it is impossible to hold them with such tranquillity. Because of this there arose the frequent rebellions in Spain, France, and Greece against the Romans, all because of the numerous principalities that existed in those regions. So long as the memory of them lasted, Rome was always uncertain of those possessions; but once this memory had been wiped out because of their long and powerful rule, the Romans became sure possessors. Afterwards, when the Romans fought among themselves, each Roman leader was able to draw a following from those regions, according to the authority he enjoyed there, and since the bloodlines of their former rulers had been wiped out, these regions acknowledged only the Romans. Taking all these things into account therefore, no one should be at all surprised by the ease with which Alexander held on to the region of Asia, or by the problems others encountered in preserving the territory they acquired, such as Pyrrhus and many others. This is not caused by the greater or lesser virtue of the conqueror, but rather by the different characteristics of the conquered territories.

V How cities or principalities should be governed that lived by their own laws before they were occupied [*Quodmodo administrande sunt civitates vel principatus qui ante quam occuparentur suis legibus vivebant*]

When those states that are acquired, as I have said, are accustomed to living under their Own laws and in freedom, there are three methods of holding on to them: the first is to destroy them; the second is to go there in person to live; the third is to allow them to live with their own laws, forcing them to pay a tribute and creating an oligarchy there that will keep the state friendly toward you.[11] For since such a government, having been set up by that prince, knows it cannot last without his friendship and power, it must do everything possible to maintain them. A city accustomed to living in freedom is more easily maintained through the means of its own citizens than in any other way, if you decide to preserve it.

As examples, there are the Spartans and the Romans. The Spartans held Athens and Thebes by establishing oligarchies there;[12] yet they lost them both. In order to hold Capua, Carthage, and Numantia, the Romans destroyed them and did not lose them.[13] They wished to hold Greece in almost the same manner as the Spartans held it, making it free and leaving it under its own laws, and they did not succeed. Thus, they were obliged to destroy many of the cities in that region in order to retain it.[14] For in fact, there is no secure means of holding on to cities except by destroying them. Anyone who becomes master of a city accustomed to living in liberty and does not destroy it may expect to be destroyed by it, because such a city always has as a refuge in any rebellion the name of liberty and its ancient institutions, neither of which is ever forgotten either because of the passing of time or because of the bestowal of benefits. And it matters very little what one does or foresees, since if one does not separate or scatter the inhabitants, they will not forget that name or those institutions. Immediately, and in every instance, they will return to them, just as Pisa did[15] after 100 years of being held in servitude by the Florentines. However, when cities or regions are accustomed to living under a prince and his bloodline has been wiped out, being on the one hand accustomed to obedience and, on the other, not having their old prince and not being able to agree upon choosing another one from among themselves—yet not knowing how to live as free men—they are, as a result, hesitant in taking up arms, and a prince can win them over and assure himself of their support with greater ease. But in republics, greater vitality, greater hatred, and greater desire for revenge exist. The memory of ancient liberty does not and cannot allow them to rest, so that the most secure course is either to wipe them out or to go to live there.

VI Of new principalities acquired by one's own troops and virtue [*De principatibus novis qui armis propriis et virtute acquiruntur*]

No one should wonder if, in speaking of principalities that are completely new as to their ruler and form of government, I cite the greatest examples. Since men almost always follow the paths trod by others, and proceed in their affairs by imitation,[16] although they are not fully able to stay on the path of others, nor to equal the virtue of those they imitate, a wise man should always enter those paths trodden by great men, and imitate those who have been most excellent, so that if one's own virtue does not match theirs, at least it will have the smell of it. He should do as those prudent archers do[17] who, aware of the strength of their bow when the target at which they are aiming seems too distant, set their sights much higher than the designated target, not in order to reach such a height with their arrow, but instead to be able, by aiming so high, to strike their target.

I say, therefore, that in completely new principalities, where there is a new prince, greater or lesser difficulty in maintaining them exists according to the greater or lesser virtue of the person who acquires them. Because for a private citizen to become a prince presupposes virtue or Fortune, it appears that either the one or the other of these two things should partially mitigate many of the problems. Nevertheless, he who relies less upon Fortune has maintained his position best. Matters are also facilitated when the prince, having no other dominions to govern, is constrained to come to live there in person.

However, to come to those who have become princes by means of their own virtue and not because of Fortune, I say that the most outstanding are Moses, Cyrus, Romulus, Theseus, and others of their kind.[18] Although we should not discuss Moses, since he was a mere executor of things he was ordered to do by God, nevertheless he must be admired at least for the grace that made him worthy of speaking with God. Let us then consider Cyrus and the others who have acquired or founded kingdoms. You will find them all admirable; and if their deeds and their particular methods are considered, they will not appear different from those of Moses, who had so great a teacher. In examining their deeds and their lives, one can see that they received nothing from Fortune except opportunity, which gave them the material they could mould into whatever form they liked.[19] Without that opportunity the strength of their spirit would have been exhausted, and without that strength, their opportunity would have come in vain.

It was therefore necessary for Moses to find the people of Israel slaves in Egypt and oppressed by the Egyptians, in order that they might be disposed to follow him to escape this servitude. It was necessary for Romulus not to stay in Alba, and that he be exposed at birth, so that he might become king of Rome and founder of that nation. It was necessary for Cyrus to find the Persians unhappy about the rule of the Medes, and the Medes rendered soft and effeminate after a lengthy peace. Theseus could not have demonstrated his ability if he had not found the Athenians dispersed. These opportunities, therefore, made these men successful, and their outstanding virtue enabled them to recognize that opportunity,[20] whereby their nation was ennobled and became extremely happy.

Those who, like these men, become princes through their virtue acquire the principality with difficulty, but they hold on to it easily. The difficulties they encounter in acquiring the principality grow, in part, out of the new institutions and methods[21] they are forced to introduce in order to establish their state and their security. One should bear in mind that there is nothing more difficult to execute, nor more dubious of success, nor more dangerous to administer, than to introduce new political orders. For the one who introduces them has as his enemies all those who profit from the old order, and he has only lukewarm defenders in all those who might profit from the new order. This lukewarmness partly arises from fear of the adversaries who have the law on their side, and partly from the incredulity of men, who do not truly believe in new things unless they have actually had personal experience of them. Therefore, it happens that whenever those who are enemies have the chance to attack, they do so with partisan zeal, whereas those others defend hesitantly, so that they, together with the prince, run the risk of grave danger.

However, if we desire to examine this argument thoroughly, it is necessary to consider whether these innovators act on their own or are dependent on others: that is, if they are forced to beg for help or are able to employ force in conducting their affairs. In the first case, they always come to a bad end and never accomplish anything. But when they depend on their own resources and can use force, then only seldom do they run the risk of grave danger. From this comes the fact that all armed prophets were victorious and the unarmed came to ruin. For, besides what has been said, people are fickle by nature: it is easy to convince them of something, but difficult to hold them in that conviction. Therefore, affairs should be managed in such a way that when they no longer believe, they can be made to believe by force. Moses, Cyrus, Theseus, and Romulus could not have made their institutions respected for long if they had been unarmed; as in our times happened to Brother Girolamo Savonarola,[22] who was ruined in his new institutions when the populace began to believe in them no longer, since he had no way of holding steady those who had believed, nor of making the unbelievers believe.

Therefore, such men encounter serious problems in conducting their affairs, and meet all their dangers as they proceed, and must overcome them with their virtue. However, once they have overcome them and have begun to be venerated, having wiped out all those who were envious of their accomplishments, they remain powerful, secure, honoured, and successful.

To such lofty examples I should like to add a lesser one; but it will have some relation to the others, and I should like it to suffice for all similar cases: and this is Hiero of Syracuse. From a private citizen, this man became the ruler of Syracuse. He received nothing from Fortune but the opportunity, for as the Citizens of Syracuse were oppressed, they elected him as their captain, and from that rank he proved himself worthy of becoming their prince. He had so much virtue while still a private citizen that someone who wrote about him said: "quod nihil illi deerat ad regnandum praeter regnum" ["that he lacked nothing to reign but a kingdom"].[23] He did away with the old army and established a new one; he abandoned old alliances and forged new ones; since he possessed allies and soldiers of his own, he was able to construct whatever he desired on such a foundation; so that it cost him great effort to acquire, but little to maintain.

VII Of new principalities acquired with the arms of others and by Fortune [*De principatibus novis qui alienis armis et fortuna acquiruntur*]

Those private citizens who become princes through Fortune alone do so with little effort, but to maintain their position they need a great deal. They encounter no obstacles along their way, since they fly there, but all their problems arise once they have arrived. And these are the men who have been granted a state either because they have money, or because they enjoy the favour of him who grants it. This occurred to many in Greece, in the cities of Ionia and the Hellespont, where Darius set up rulers in order to hold these cities for his own security and glory. The same thing happened to those emperors who came to power from being private citizens by corrupting the soldiers.

Such men depend solely upon two very uncertain and unstable things: the will and the Fortune of him who granted them the state. But they do not know how, and are unable, to maintain their position. They do not know how to hold their state, since if men are not of great intelligence and virtue, it is not reasonable that they should know how to command, having always lived as private citizens. They are unable to do so, since they do not have forces that are faithful and loyal to them. Besides, states that arise quickly, just like all the other natural things that are born and grow rapidly, cannot have roots and branches and will be wiped out by the first adverse weather. This occurs unless the men who have suddenly become princes (as I have noted) possess such virtue that they know how to prepare themselves rapidly to preserve what Fortune has dropped into their laps, and to construct afterwards those foundations others have laid before becoming princes.

. . .

VIII Of those who have become princes through wickedness [*De his qui per scelera ad principatum pervenere*]

Because there still remain two additional methods for an ordinary citizen to become a prince that cannot be attributed completely to either Fortune or virtue, I believe they should not be omitted, although one of them will be discussed at greater length in a treatise on republics.[24] These two methods are when one becomes prince through some wicked and nefarious means; or when a private citizen becomes prince of his native city[25] through the favour of his fellow citizens. In discussing the first way, I shall cite two examples, one from ancient times and the other from modern times, without otherwise entering into the merits of this method, since I consider them sufficient for anyone who finds it necessary to imitate them.

Agathocles the Sicilian, who became King of Syracuse, was not only an ordinary citizen but also of the lowest and most abject condition. A potter's son, this man lived a wicked life at every stage of his career. Yet he joined to his wickedness such strength of mind and body, that when he entered upon a military career, he rose through the ranks to become praetor of Syracuse. Once placed in such a position, having decided to become prince and to hold with violence and without any obligations to others what had been conferred upon him by universal consent, and having informed Hamilcar the Carthaginian (who was waging war with his armies in Sicily), one morning he called together the people and the senate of Syracuse as if he were going to discuss some matters concerning the republic. At a prearranged signal he had his troops kill all the senators and the richest citizens; and when they were dead he seized and held the rule of the city without any opposition from the citizenry. Although he was twice defeated by the Carthaginians and finally besieged, not only was he able to defend his city, but, leaving part of his troops for the defence of the siege, with his other forces he attacked Africa, and in a short time he freed Syracuse from the siege and forced the Carthaginians into dire straits. They were obliged to make peace with him and to be content with dominion over Africa, leaving Sicily to Agathocles.[26]

Anyone, therefore, who examines the deeds and the life of this man will observe nothing (or very little) that can be attributed to Fortune. Not with the assistance of others (as was mentioned before), but by rising through the ranks, which involved a thousand hardships and dangers, did he come to rule the principality that he then maintained by many brave and dangerous actions. Still,

it cannot be called virtue to kill one's fellow citizens, to betray allies, to be without faith, without pity, without religion; by these means one can acquire power, but not glory.[27] If one were to consider Agathocles' virtue in getting into and out of dangers, and his greatness of spirit in bearing up under and overcoming adversities, one can see no reason why he should be judged inferior to any most excellent commander. Nevertheless, his vicious cruelty and inhumanity, along with numerous wicked deeds, do not permit us to honour him among the most excellent of men. One cannot, therefore, attribute either to Fortune or to virtue what he accomplished without either the one or the other.

In our own days (during the reign of Alexander VI), Oliverotto of Fermo, who many years before had been left as a little child without a father, was brought up by his maternal uncle named Giovanni Fogliani. In the early days of his youth he was sent to serve as a soldier under Paulo Vitelli, so that, once he was versed in that discipline, he might attain some outstanding military rank. Then, after Paulo died,[28] he soldiered under Paulo's brother Vitellozzo. In a very short time, because of his skill and his boldness of body and mind, he became the first man of Vitellozzo's troops. However, since he felt it was demeaning to serve under others, he decided, with Vitellozzo's help and with the assistance of some of its citizens (those who preferred servitude to the liberty of their native city), to take over Fermo. He wrote to Giovanni Fogliani that, since he had been away from home for so long, he wanted both to come to see him and his city and to check his inheritance. Since he had exerted himself for no other reason than to acquire honour, he wanted to arrive in honourable fashion, accompanied by an escort of 100 horsemen from among his friends and servants, so that his fellow citizens might see that he had not spent his time in vain. In addition, he begged his uncle to arrange for an honourable reception from the people of Fermo, one that might bring honour not only to Giovanni but also to himself as his pupil.

Therefore, Giovanni in no way failed in his duty toward his nephew: he had him received in honourable fashion by the people of Fermo, and he gave him rooms in his own dwellings. After a few days had passed and he had secretly made the preparations necessary for his forthcoming wickedness, Oliverotto gave a magnificent solemn banquet,[29] to which he invited Giovanni Fogliani and all of the first citizens of Fermo. When the meal and all the other entertainments customary at such banquets were completed, Oliverotto artfully began to discuss serious matters speaking of the greatness of Pope Alexander and his son Cesare, and of their undertakings.

After Giovanni and the others had replied to his arguments, he suddenly arose, declaring that these were matters to be discussed in a more secluded place, and withdrew into another room. Giovanni and all the other citizens followed him. No sooner were they seated than, from secret places in the room, soldiers emerged who killed Giovanni and all the others.[30] After this murder Oliverotto mounted his horse, paraded through the town, and besieged the chief officials in the government palace. They were forced to obey him out of fear, and to constitute a government of which he made himself prince. After he killed all those who might have harmed him because they were unhappy with the situation, he strengthened his power by instituting new civil and military institutions. As a result, in the space of the year that he held the principality, not only was he secure in the city of Fermo, but he had become feared by all its neighbours. His expulsion would have been as difficult as that of Agathocles, if he had not let himself be tricked by Cesare Borgia (as was noted above), when the Duke captured the Orsini and the Vitelli at Senigallia. There Oliverotto too was captured, a year after he committed his parricide,[31] and together with Vittellozzo, who had been his teacher in his virtues and wickedness, he was strangled.

One might well wonder how, after so many betrayals and cruelties, Agathocles and others like him could live for such a long time secure in their native cities and defend themselves from foreign enemies without being plotted against by their own citizens. Many others, employing cruel means, were unable to hold on to their state even in peaceful times, not to speak of the uncertain times of war. I believe that this depends on whether cruelty be badly or well used.[32] Those cruelties are well used (if it is permitted to speak well of evil) that are carried out in a single stroke, done out of necessity to protect oneself, and then are not continued, but are instead converted into the greatest possible benefits for the subjects. Those cruelties are badly used that, although few at the outset, increase with the passing of time instead of disappearing. Those who follow the first method can remedy their standing, both with God and with men, as Agathocles did; the others cannot possibly maintain their positions.

Hence it should be noted that, in conquering a state, its conqueror should weigh all the injurious things he must do and commit them all at once, so as not to have to repeat them every day. By not repeating them, he will be able to make men feel secure and win them over with the benefits he bestows upon them. Anyone who does otherwise, either out of timidity or because of bad advice, is always obliged to keep his knife in his hand.

Nor can he ever count upon his subjects, who, because of their recent and continuous injuries, cannot feel secure with him. Therefore, injuries should be inflicted all at once, for the less they are tasted, the less harm they do. However, benefits should be distributed a little at a time, so that they may be fully savoured. Above all, a prince should live with his subjects in such a way that no unforeseen event, either bad or good, may cause him to alter his course; for when difficulties arise in adverse conditions, you do not have time to resort to cruelty, and the good that you do will help you very little, since it will be judged a forced measure, and you will earn from it no gratitude whatsoever.

IX Of the civil principality
[*De principatu civili*]

But let us come to the second instance, when a private citizen becomes prince of his native city not through wickedness or any other intolerable violence, but with the favour of his fellow citizens. This can be called a civil principality, the acquisition of which neither depends completely upon virtue nor upon Fortune, but instead upon a fortunate astuteness. I maintain that one reaches this princedom either with the favour of the common people or with that of the nobility, since these two different humours[33] are found in every body politic. They arise from the fact that the people do not wish to be commanded or oppressed by the nobles, while the nobles do desire to command and to oppress the people. From these two opposed appetites, there arises in cities one of three effects: a principality, liberty, or licence. A principality is brought about either by the common people or by the nobility, depending on which of the two parties has the opportunity. When the nobles see that they cannot resist the populace, they begin to support someone from among themselves, and make him prince in order to be able to satisfy their appetites under his protection. The common people as well, seeing that they cannot resist the nobility, give their support to one man so as to be defended by his authority. He who attains the principality with the help of the nobility maintains it with more difficulty than he who becomes prince with the help of the common people, for he finds himself a prince amidst many who feel themselves to be his equals, and because of this he can neither govern nor manage them as he wishes. But he who attains the principality through popular favour finds himself alone, and has around him either no one or very few who are not ready to obey him. Besides this, one cannot honestly satisfy the nobles without harming others, but the common people can certainly be satisfied. Their desire is more just than that of the nobles—the former want not to be oppressed, while the latter want to oppress. In addition, a prince can never make himself secure when the people are his enemy, because there are so many of them; he can make himself secure against the nobles, because they are so few. The worst that a prince can expect from a hostile people is to be abandoned by them; but with a hostile nobility, not only does he have to fear being abandoned, but also that they will oppose him. Since the nobles are more perceptive and cunning, they always have time to save themselves, seeking the favours of the side they believe will prevail. Furthermore, a prince must always live with the same common people, but he can easily do without the same nobles, having the power every day to make and unmake them, or to take away and restore their power as he sees fit.

In order better to clarify this point, let me say that the nobles should be considered chiefly in two ways: either they conduct themselves in such a way that they commit themselves completely to your cause, or they do not. Those who commit themselves and are not rapacious should be honoured and loved. Those who do not commit themselves can be evaluated in two ways. If they act in this manner out of pusillanimity and a natural lack of courage, you should make use of them, especially those who are wise advisers, since in prosperous times they will gain you honour, and in adverse times you need not fear them. But when, cunningly and influenced by ambition, they refrain from committing themselves to you, this is a sign that they think more of themselves than of you. The prince should be on guard against them and fear them as if they were declared enemies, because they will always help to bring about his downfall in adverse times.

Therefore, one who becomes prince with the support of the common people must keep them well disposed. This is easy for him, since the only thing they ask of him is not to be oppressed. But one who becomes prince with the help of the nobility against the will of the common people must, before all else, seek to win the people's support, which should be easy if he takes them under his protection. Because men who are well treated by those from whom they expected harm are more obliged to their benefactor, the common people quickly become better disposed toward him than if he had become prince with their support. A prince can gain their favour in various ways, but because these vary according to the situation, no fixed rules can be given for them, and therefore I shall not discuss them. I shall conclude by saying only that a prince must have the friendship of the common people. Otherwise, he will have no support in times of adversity. Nabis, Prince of the Spartans, withstood a siege by all of Greece and by one of Rome's most

victorious armies, and he defended his native city and his own state against them. When danger suddenly approached, he needed only to protect himself from a few of his subjects, but if he had had the common people hostile, this would not have been sufficient.

Let no one contradict my opinion by citing that trite proverb, claiming he who builds upon the people builds upon mud; for that is true when a private citizen makes them his foundation, and allows himself to believe that the common people will free him if he is oppressed by enemies or by the public officials. In such a case, a man might often find himself deceived, as were the Gracchi in Rome or as Messer Giorgio Scali was in Florence. When the prince who builds his foundations on the people is a man able to command and of spirit, is not bewildered by adversities, does not fail to make other preparations, and is a leader who keeps up the spirits of the populace through his courage and his institutions, he will never find himself deceived by the common people, and he will discover that he has laid his foundations well.

Principalities of this type are usually endangered when they are about to change from a civil government into an absolute form of government. For these princes rule either by themselves or by means of public magistrates. In the latter case, their status is weaker and more dangerous, since they depend entirely upon the will of those citizens who are appointed as magistrates. These men can very easily (especially in adverse times) seize the state, either by abandoning him or by opposing him. And in such periods of danger the prince has no time for seizing absolute authority, since the citizens and subjects[34] who are used to receiving their orders from the magistrates are not willing to obey his orders in these crises. And in doubtful times he will always find a scarcity of men in whom he can trust. Such a prince cannot rely upon what he sees during periods of calm when the citizens need his rule, because then everyone comes running, everyone makes promises, and each person is willing to die for him, since death is remote. But in times of adversity, when the state needs its citizens, then few are to be found. And this experiment is all the more dangerous since it can be tried but once. Therefore, a wise prince must think of a method by which his citizens will need the state and himself at all times and in every circumstance. Then they will always be loyal to him.

X How the strength of all principalities should be measured [*Quomodo omnium principatuum vires perpendi debeant*]

In examining the qualities of these principalities, another consideration arises: that is, whether the prince has so much power that he can (if necessary) stand up on his own, or whether he always needs the protection of others. In order to clarify this matter, let me say that I judge those princes self-sufficient who, either through abundance of troops or of money, are capable of gathering together a suitable army and of fighting a battle against whoever might attack them. I consider men who always need the protection of others to be those who cannot meet their enemy in the field, but must seek refuge behind their city walls and defend them. The first case has already been treated,[35] and later on I shall say whatever else is necessary on the subject. Nothing more can be added to the second case than to encourage such princes to fortify and provision their own cities, and not to concern themselves with the surrounding countryside. Anyone who has fortified his city well, and has managed his affairs well with his subjects in the manner I discussed above and discuss below, will be attacked only with great hesitation, for men are always enemies of undertakings in which they foresee difficulties, and it cannot seem easy to attack someone whose city is well fortified and who is not hated by his people.

The cities of Germany are completely independent, they control little surrounding territory, they obey the emperor when they please, and they fear neither him nor any other nearby power. For they are fortified in such a manner that everyone considers their capture to be a tedious and difficult affair. They all have appropriate moats and walls; they have enough artillery; they always store in their public warehouses enough drink, food, and fuel for a year. Besides all this, in order to be able to keep the lower classes fed without loss of public funds, they always keep in reserve a year's supply of raw materials sufficient to give these people work at those trades that are the nerves and lifeblood of that city and of the industries from which the people earn their living. Moreover, they hold the military arts in high regard, and they have many regulations for maintaining them.

Therefore, a prince who has a city organized in this fashion and who does not make himself hated cannot be attacked. Even if he were to be attacked, the enemy would have to retreat in shame, for the affairs of this world are so changeable that it is almost impossible for anyone to sustain a siege for a year with his troops idle. And if it is objected that when the people have their possessions outside the city, and see them destroyed, they will lose patience, and that the long siege and self-interest will cause them to forget their love for their prince, let me reply that a prudent and spirited prince will always overcome all such difficulties, inspiring his subjects now with hope that the evil will not last long, now with fear of the enemy's cruelty, now by protecting

himself with clever manoeuvres against those who seem too outspoken. Besides this, the enemy will in all likelihood burn and lay waste to the surrounding country upon their arrival, just when the spirits of the defenders are still ardent and determined on the city's defence. And thus the prince has so much the less to fear, because after a few days, when their spirits have cooled down somewhat, the damage has already been inflicted and the evils suffered, and there is no longer any remedy for them. Now the people will rally around their prince even more, for it would appear that he is bound to them by obligations, since their homes were burned and their possessions destroyed in his defence. The nature of men is such that they find themselves obligated as much for the benefits they confer as for those they receive. Thus, if everything is taken into consideration, it will not be difficult for a prudent prince to keep the spirits of his citizens firm during the siege before and after this destruction, so long as he does not lack sufficient food and weapons for his defence.

. . .

XII Of the various kinds of troops and mercenary soldiers [*Quot sunt genera militiae et de mercenaries militibus*]

Having treated in detail all the characteristics of those principalities that I proposed to discuss at the beginning, and having considered, to some extent, the reasons for their success or failure, and having demonstrated the methods by which many have tried to acquire them and to maintain them, it remains for me now to speak in general terms of the kinds of offence and defence that can be adopted by each of the previously mentioned principalities.

We have said above that a prince must have laid firm foundations; otherwise he will necessarily come to ruin. And the principal foundations of all states, the new as well as the old or the mixed, are good laws and good armies. Since good laws cannot exist where there are no good armies, and where good armies exist there must be good laws, I shall leave aside the arguments about laws and shall discuss the armed forces.

I say, then, that the armies with which a prince defends his state are made up of his own troops, or mercenaries, or auxiliaries, or of mixed troops. Mercenaries and auxiliaries are useless and dangerous. If a prince holds on to his state by means of mercenary armies, he will never be stable or secure. Mercenaries are disunited, ambitious, undisciplined, and disloyal. They are brave with their friends; with their enemies, they are cowards. They have no fear of God, and they keep no faith with men. Their ruin is deferred only so long as an attack is deferred. In peacetime you are plundered by them, in war by your enemies. The reason for this is that they have no other love nor other motive to keep them in the field than a meagre salary, which is not enough to make them want to die for you. They love being your soldiers when you are not waging war, but when war comes, they either flee or desert. This would require little effort to demonstrate, since the present ruin of Italy is caused by nothing other than its having relied on mercenary troops for a period of many years. These forces did, on occasion, help some to get ahead, and they appeared courageous in combat with other mercenaries. But when the invasion of the foreigner came,[36] they showed themselves for what they were, and thus Charles, King of France, was permitted to take Italy with a piece of chalk.[37] The man who said that our sins were the cause of this disaster spoke the truth;[38] but they were not at all those sins he had in mind, but rather these I have recounted; and because they were the sins of princes, the princes in turn have suffered the punishment for them.

I wish to demonstrate more fully the failure of such armies. Mercenary captains are either excellent men or they are not. If they are, you cannot trust them, since they will always aspire to their own greatness, either by oppressing you, who are their masters, or by oppressing others against your intent; but if the captain is without ability, he usually ruins you. If someone were to reply that anyone who bears arms will act in this manner, mercenary or not, I would answer that armies have to be commanded either by a prince or by a republic. The prince must go in person and perform the office of captain himself. A republic must send its own citizens, and when it sends one who does not turn out to be an able man, it must replace him. If he is capable, the republic must restrain him with laws so that he does not exceed his authority. We see from experience that only princes and republics armed with their own troops make very great progress, and that mercenaries cause nothing but damage. A republic armed with its own citizens is less likely to come under the rule of one of its citizens than a city armed with foreign soldiers.

Rome and Sparta for many centuries stood armed and free. The Swiss are extremely well armed and are very free. An example from antiquity of the use of mercenary troops is the Carthaginians. They were almost overcome by their own mercenary soldiers after the first war with the Romans, even though the Carthaginians had their own citizens as officers. Philip of Macedon was made captain of their army by the Thebans after the death of Epaminondas, and after the victory he took their liberty away from them. After the death of

Duke Filippo, the Milanese employed Francesco Sforza to wage war against the Venetians; having defeated the enemy at Caravaggio,[39] he joined with them to oppress the Milanese, his employers. Sforza, his father,[40] being in the employ of Queen Giovanna of Naples, all at once left her without defences. Because of this, so as not to lose her kingdom, she was forced to throw herself into the lap of the King of Aragon. And if the Venetians and the Florentines have in the past increased their dominion with such soldiers, and their captains have not yet made themselves princes but have, instead, defended them, I answer that the Florentines have been favoured in this matter by luck. Among their able captains whom they could have had reason to fear, some did not win, others met with opposition, and others turned their ambition elsewhere. The one who did not win was John Hawkwood, whose loyalty will never be known since he did not win. But anyone will admit that, had he succeeded, the Florentines would have been at his mercy. Sforza always had Braccio's soldiers as enemies, so that each checked the other. Francesco turned his ambition to Lombardy, Braccio against the Church and the Kingdom of Naples.

But let us come to what has occurred just recently. The Florentines made Paulo Vitelli their captain, a very able man and one who rose from being a private citizen to achieve great prestige. If he had captured Pisa, no one would deny that the Florentines would have had to become his ally. If he had become employed by their enemies, they would have had no defence, and if they had kept him on, they would have been obliged to obey him. As for the Venetians, if we examine the course they followed, we see that they operated securely and gloriously as long as they fought with their own troops (this was before they began to fight on the mainland); with their nobles and their common people armed, they fought courageously [at sea]. But when they began to fight on land, they abandoned this successful strategy and followed the usual practices of waging war in Italy. As they first began to expand their territory on the mainland, since they did not have much to control there and enjoyed great prestige, they had little to fear from their captains. When their territory increased, which happened under Carmagnola, the Venetians had a taste of this mistake. Having found him very able (since under his command they had defeated the Duke of Milan), and knowing, on the other hand, that he had cooled off in waging war, they judged that they could no longer conquer under him, for he had no wish to do so. Yet they could not dismiss him, for fear of losing what they had acquired. So, in order to secure themselves against him, they were forced to execute him. Then they had as their captains Bartolomeo da Bergamo,

Roberto da San Severino, the Count of Pitigliano, and the like. With men such as these they had to fear their losses, not their acquisitions, as occurred later at Vaila,[41] where, in a single day,[42] they lost what had cost them 800 years of exhausting effort to acquire.[43] From these kinds of soldiers, therefore, come only slow, tardy, and weak conquests but sudden and astonishing losses.

And since with these examples I have begun to treat of Italy, which for many years has been ruled by mercenary soldiers, I should like to discuss them in greater depth, so that once their origins and developments are uncovered they can be more easily corrected. You must, then, understand how in recent times, when the Empire began to be driven out of Italy and the Pope began to win more prestige in temporal affairs, Italy was divided into many states. Many of the large cities took up arms against their nobles, who (at first backed by the Emperor) had kept them under their control. The Church supported these cities to increase its temporal power; in many other cities, citizens became princes. Hence, after Italy came almost entirely into the hands of the Church and of several republics, those priests and other citizens who were not accustomed to bearing arms began to hire foreigners. The first to give prestige to such troops was Alberigo of Conio from the Romagna. From this man's training emerged, among others, Braccio and Sforza, who in their day were the arbiters of Italy. After them came all the others who have commanded these soldiers until the present day. The result of their skills has been that Italy has been overrun by Charles, plundered by Louis, violated by Ferdinand, and insulted by the Swiss.

Their method was, first, to increase the prestige of their own soldiers by taking away the prestige of the infantry. They did so because they were men without a state of their own, who lived by their profession; a small number of foot-soldiers could not give them prestige, and they could not afford to hire a large number of them. So they relied completely upon cavalry, since for possessing only a reasonable number of horsemen they were provided for and honoured. They reduced matters to such a state that in an army of 20,000 troops, one could hardly find 2,000 foot-soldiers. Besides this, they had used every means to spare themselves and their soldiers fear and hardship, not killing each other in their scuffles, but instead taking each other prisoner without demanding ransom. They would not attack cities at night. Those in the cities would not attack the tents of the besiegers. They built neither stockades nor trenches around their camps. They did not campaign in the winter. And all these things were permitted by their military institutions and gave them a means of escaping hardships and dangers, as was mentioned. As a result, these *condottieri* have conducted Italy into slavery and disgrace.[44]

. . .

XV Of those things for which men, and particularly princes, are praised or blamed [*De his rebus quibus homines et presertim principes laudantur aut vituperantur*]

Now, it remains to be considered what should be the methods and principles of a prince in dealing with his subjects and allies. Because I know that many have written about this,[45] I am afraid that by writing about it again I shall be considered presumptuous, especially since in discussing this material I depart from the procedures of others. But since my intention is to write something useful for anyone who understands it, it seemed more suitable for me to search after the effectual truth of the matter rather than its imagined one. Many writers have imagined republics and principalities that have never been seen nor known to exist in reality. For there is such a distance between how one lives and how one ought to live, that anyone who abandons what is done for what ought to be done achieves his downfall rather than his preservation. A man who wishes to profess goodness at all times will come to ruin among so many who are not good. Therefore, it is necessary for a prince who wishes to maintain himself to learn how not to be good, and to use this knowledge or not to use it according to necessity.

Leaving aside, therefore, matters concerning an imaginary prince, and taking into account those that are true, let me say that all men, when they are spoken of—and especially princes, since they are placed on a higher level—are judged by some of those qualities that bring them either blame or praise. And this is why one is considered generous, another miserly (to use a Tuscan word, since "avaricious" in our language is still used to mean one who wishes to acquire by means of theft; we call "miserly" one who is excessive in avoiding using what he has). One is considered a giver, the other rapacious; one cruel, the other merciful; one a breaker of faith, the other faithful; one effeminate and cowardly, the other fierce and courageous; one humane, the other proud; one lascivious, the other chaste; one trustworthy, the other shrewd; one hard, the other easygoing; one serious, the other frivolous; one religious, the other unbelieving; and the like. And I know that everyone will admit it would be a very praiseworthy thing to find in a prince those qualities mentioned above that are held to be good. But since it is neither possible to have them nor to observe them all completely, because the human condition does not permit it, a prince must be prudent enough to know how to escape the infamy of those vices that would take the state away from him, and be on guard against those vices that will not take it from him, whenever possible. But if he cannot, he need not concern himself unduly if he ignores these less serious vices. Moreover, he need not worry about incurring the infamy of those vices without which it would be difficult to save the state. Because, carefully taking everything into account, he will discover that something which appears to be a virtue,[46] if pursued, will result in his ruin; while some other thing which seems to be a vice, if pursued, will secure his safety and his well-being.

XVI Of generosity and miserliness
[*De liberalitate et parsimonia*]

Beginning, therefore, with the first of the above-mentioned qualities, I say that it would be good to be considered generous. Nevertheless, generosity employed in such a way as to give you a reputation for it will injure you, because if it is employed virtuously[47] and as one should employ it, it will not be recognized, and you will not avoid the infamy of its opposite. And so, if a prince wants to maintain his reputation for generosity among men, it is necessary for him not to neglect any possible means of sumptuous display; in so doing, such a prince will always use up all his resources in such displays, and will eventually be obliged, if he wishes to maintain his reputation for generosity, to burden the people with excessive taxes and to do all those things one does to procure money. This will begin to make him hateful to his subjects and, if he becomes impoverished, he will be held in low regard by everyone. As a consequence of this generosity of his, having injured the many and rewarded the few, he will feel the effects of any discontent and will vacillate at the first sign of danger; recognizing this and wishing to change his ways, he immediately incurs the infamy of being a miser. Therefore, a prince, being unable to use this virtue of generosity in a manner that will not harm himself if he is known for it, should, if he is wise, not concern himself about the reputation of being miserly. With time he will come to be considered more generous, once it is evident that, as a result of his parsimony, his income is sufficient, he can defend himself from anyone who wages war against him, and he can undertake enterprises without overburdening his people. In this way he appears as generous to all those from whom he takes nothing, who are countless, and as miserly to all those to whom he gives nothing, who are few.

In our times we have not seen great deeds accomplished except by those who were considered miserly; the others were all wiped out. Although he made use of his reputation for generosity in order to gain the papacy,[48] Pope Julius II then decided not to maintain this reputation, in order to be able to wage war. The present King of France[49] has waged many wars without imposing extraordinary taxes on his subjects, only because his habitual parsimony has provided for the additional expenditures. If he had been considered generous, the present King of Spain[50] would not have engaged in or successfully carried out so many enterprises. Therefore—in order not to have to rob his subjects, to be able to defend himself, not to become poor and contemptible, and not to be forced to become rapacious—a prince must consider it of little account if he incurs the reputation of being a miser, for this is one of those vices that enables him to rule. And if someone were to say: "Caesar with his generosity achieved imperial power, and many others, because they were generous and known to be so, achieved very high positions," I would reply: You are either already a prince, or you are on the way to becoming one. In the first case such generosity is damaging; in the second, it is indeed necessary to be thought generous. Caesar was one of those who wanted to gain the principality of Rome; but if he had survived and had not moderated his expenditures after doing so, he would have destroyed the power he acquired.[51] And if someone were to reply: "There have existed many princes who have accomplished great deeds with their armies who have been considered generous," I would answer you: A prince either spends his own money and that of his subjects, or that of others. In the first case he must be economical; in the second, he must not hold back any part of his generosity. For the prince who goes out with his armies and lives by looting, sacking, and ransoms, and who lays hands on the property of others, such generosity is necessary; otherwise he would not be followed by his soldiers. Of what is not yours or your subjects, you can be a more generous donor, as were Cyrus, Caesar, and Alexander: spending the wealth of others does not lessen your reputation, but only adds to it. Only the spending of your own is what does you harm. There is nothing that uses itself up faster than generosity; for as you employ it, you lose the means of employing it, and you become either poor or despised or else, to escape poverty, you become rapacious and hated. And above all things, a prince must guard himself against being despised and hated. Generosity leads you both to one and to the other. So it is wiser to live with the reputation of a miser, which gives birth to an infamy without hatred, than to be forced to incur the reputation of rapacity because you want to be considered generous, which gives birth to an infamy with hatred.

XVII Of cruelty and mercy, and whether it is better to be loved than to be feared or the contrary [*De crudelitate et pietate; et an sit melius amari quam timeri, vel e contra*]

Turning to the other qualities mentioned above, let me say that every prince must desire to be considered merciful and not cruel; nevertheless, he must take care not to use such mercy badly. Cesare Borgia was considered cruel; nonetheless, this cruelty of his brought order to the Romagna,[52] united it, and restored it to peace and loyalty. If we examine this carefully, we shall see that he was more merciful than the Florentine people, who allowed the destruction of Pistoia in order to avoid being considered cruel.[53] Therefore, a prince must not worry about the infamy of being considered cruel when it is a matter of keeping his subjects united and loyal. With a very few examples of cruelty, he will prove more compassionate than those who, out of excessive mercy, permit disorders to continue from which arise murders and plundering, for these usually injure the entire community, while the executions ordered by the prince injure specific individuals. Of all the types of princes, the new prince cannot escape the reputation for cruelty, since new states are full of dangers. Thus Virgil, through the mouth of Dido, declares: "*Res dura et regni novitas me talia cogunt moliri et late fines custode tueri*"[54] ["The harshness of things and the newness of my rule make me act in such a manner, and to set guards over my land on all sides"]. Nevertheless, a prince must be cautious in believing accusations and in acting against individuals, nor should he be afraid of his own shadow. He should proceed in such a manner, tempered by prudence and humanity, that too much trust may not render him incautious, nor too much suspicion render him insufferable.

From this arises an argument: whether it is better to be loved than to be feared, or the contrary. The answer is that one would like to be both one and the other. But since it is difficult to be both together, it is much safer to be feared than to be loved, when one of the two must be lacking. For one can generally say this about men: they are ungrateful, fickle, simulators and deceivers, avoiders of danger, and greedy for gain. While you work for their benefit they are completely yours, offering you their blood, their property, their lives, and their sons, as I said above, when the need to do so is far away. But when it draws nearer to you, they turn away. The prince who relies entirely upon their words comes to ruin, finding himself stripped naked of other preparations. For friendships acquired by a price and not by greatness and nobility of spirit are purchased but are not owned, and at the proper time cannot be spent. Men are less hesitant about injuring someone who makes himself loved than one who makes himself feared, because love is held together by a chain of obligation that, since men are a wretched lot, is broken on every occasion for their own self-interest; but fear is sustained by a dread of punishment that will never abandon you.

A prince must nevertheless make himself feared in such a way that he will avoid hatred, even if he does not acquire love; since one can very easily be feared and yet not hated. This will always be the case when he abstains from the property of his citizens and subjects, and from their women. If he must spill someone's blood, he should do this when there is proper justification and manifest cause. But above all else, he should abstain from seizing the property of others; for men forget the death of their father more quickly than the loss of their patrimony. Moreover, reasons for taking their property are never lacking, and he who begins to live by stealing always finds a reason for taking what belongs to others; reasons for spilling blood, on the other hand, are rarer and more fleeting.

But when the prince is with his armies and has a multitude of soldiers under his command, then it is absolutely necessary that he should not worry about being considered cruel, for without that reputation he will never keep an army united or prepared for any action. Numbered among the remarkable deeds of Hannibal is this: that while he had a very large army made up of all kinds of men that he commanded in foreign lands, there never arose the slightest dissension, either among themselves or against their leader, both during his periods of good and bad luck.[55] This could not have arisen from anything other than his inhuman cruelty, which, along with his many other virtues, made him always venerable and terrifying in the eyes of his soldiers. Without that quality, his other virtues would not have sufficed to attain the same effect. Having considered this matter very superficially, historians on the one hand admire these deeds of his, and on the other condemn the main cause of them.

That it is true that his other virtues would not have been sufficient can be seen from the case of Scipio, a most extraordinary man, not only in his time but in all of recorded history, whose armies in Spain rebelled against him. This came about from nothing other than his excessive compassion, which gave his soldiers more licence than is suitable to military discipline. For this he was censured in the Senate by Fabius Maximus, who called him the corruptor of the Roman army. When Locri was destroyed by one of his legates,[56] the Locrians were not avenged by him, nor was the arrogance of that legate corrected, all this arising from his easygoing nature. Someone in the Senate who tried to excuse him declared that there were many men who knew how not to err better than they knew how to correct their mistakes. In time such a character[57] would have damaged Scipio's fame and glory if he had long continued to command armies, but, living under the control of the Senate, this harmful quality of his was not only concealed but also contributed to his glory.

Let me conclude, then—returning to the issue of being feared and loved—that since men love at their own pleasure and fear at the pleasure of the prince, the wise prince should build his foundation upon that which is his own, not upon that which belongs to others: only he must seek to avoid being hated, as I have said.

XVIII How a prince should keep his word
[*Quomodo fides a principibus sit servanda*]

How praiseworthy it is for a prince to keep his word and to live with integrity and not by cunning, everyone knows. Nevertheless, one sees from experience in our times that the princes who have accomplished great deeds are those who have thought little about keeping faith and who have known how cunningly to manipulate men's minds; and in the end they have surpassed those who laid their foundations upon sincerity.

Therefore, you must know that there are two modes of fighting: one in accordance with the laws, the other with force.[58] The first is proper to man, the second to beasts. But because the first, in many cases, is not sufficient, it becomes necessary to have recourse to the second: therefore, a prince must know how to make good use of the natures of both the beast and the man. This rule was taught to princes symbolically by the writers of antiquity: they recounted how Achilles and many others of those ancient princes were given to Chiron the centaur to be raised and cared for under his discipline. This can only mean[59] that, having a half-beast and half-man as a teacher, a prince must know how to employ the nature of the one and the other; for the one without the other is not lasting.

Since, then, a prince must know how to make use of the nature of the beast, he should choose from among the beasts the fox and the lion;[60] for the lion cannot defend itself from traps, while the fox cannot protect itself from the wolves. It is therefore necessary to be a fox, in order to recognize the traps, and a lion, in order to frighten the wolves: those who base their behaviour only on the bon

do not understand things. A wise ruler, therefore, cannot and should not keep his word when such an observance would be to his disadvantage, and when the reasons that caused him to make a promise are removed. If men were all good, this precept would not be good. But since men are a wicked lot and will not keep their promises to you, you likewise need not keep yours to them. A prince never lacks legitimate reasons to colour over his failure to keep his word.[61] Of this, one could cite an endless number of modern examples to show how many pacts and how many promises have been made null and void because of the faithlessness of princes; and he who has known best how to use the ways of the fox has come out best. But it is necessary to know how to colour over this nature effectively, and to be a great pretender and dissembler. Men are so simple-minded and so controlled by their immediate needs that he who deceives will always find someone who will let himself be deceived.

I do not wish to remain silent about one of these recent examples. Alexander VI never did anything else, nor thought about anything else, than to deceive men, and he always found someone to whom he could do this. There never has been a man who asserted anything with more effectiveness, nor whose affirmations rested upon greater oaths, who observed them less. Nevertheless, his deceptions always succeeded to his heart's desire, since he knew this aspect of the world very well.

Therefore, it is not necessary for a prince to possess all of the above-mentioned qualities, but it is very necessary for him to appear to possess them. Furthermore, I shall dare to assert this: that having them and always observing them is harmful, but appearing to observe them is useful: for instance, to appear merciful, faithful, humane, trustworthy, religious, and to be so; but with his mind disposed in such a way that, should it become necessary not to be so, he will be able and know how to change to the opposite. One must understand this: a prince, and especially a new prince, cannot observe all those things for which men are considered good, because in order to maintain the state he must often act against his faith, against charity, against humanity, and against religion. And so it is necessary that he should have a mind ready to turn itself according to the way the winds of Fortune and the changing circumstances command him. And, as I said above, he should not depart from the good if it is possible to do so, but he should know how to enter into evil when forced by necessity.

Therefore, a prince must be very careful never to let anything fall from his lips that is not imbued with the five qualities mentioned above; to those seeing and hearing him, he should appear to be all mercy, all faithfulness, all integrity, all humanity, and all religion. And there is nothing more necessary than to seem to possess this last quality. Men in general judge more by their eyes than their hands: everyone can see, but few can feel. Everyone sees what you seem to be, few touch upon what you are, and those few do not dare to contradict the opinion of the many who have the majesty of the state to defend them. In the actions of all men, and especially of princes, where there is no tribunal to which to appeal, one must consider the final result.[62] Therefore, let a prince conquer and maintain the state, and his methods will always be judged honourable and praised by all. For ordinary people are always taken in by appearances and by the outcome of an event. And in the world there are only ordinary people; and the few have no place, while the many have a spot on which to lean. A certain prince of the present times, whom it is best not to name,[63] preaches nothing but peace and faith, and to both one and the other he is extremely hostile. If he had observed both peace and faith, he would have had either his reputation or his state taken away from him many times over.

XIX Of avoiding being despised and hated [*De contemptu et odio fugiendo*]

But since I have spoken about the most important of the qualities mentioned above, I should like to discuss the others briefly under this general rule: that the prince, as was noted above, should concentrate upon avoiding those things that make him hated and contemptible. When he has avoided this, he will have carried out his duties, and none of his other infamous deeds will cause him any danger at all. As I have said, what makes him hated above all else is being rapacious and a usurper of the property and the women of his subjects. He must refrain from this. In most cases, so long as you do not deprive them of either their honour or their property, most men live content, and you only have to contend with the ambition of the few, who can be restrained without difficulty and by many means. What makes him despised is being considered changeable, frivolous, effeminate, cowardly, and irresolute. From these qualities, a prince must guard himself as if from a reef, and he must strive to make everyone recognize in his actions greatness, spirit, dignity, and strength. Concerning the private affairs of his subjects, he must insist that his decisions be irrevocable. And he should maintain this reputation in such a way that no man can imagine he is able to deceive or trick him.

That prince who creates such an opinion of himself has a great reputation; and it is difficult to conspire against a man with such a reputation and difficult to attack him, provided that he is understood to be of great ability and revered by his subjects. For a prince should have two fears: one internal, concerning his subjects; the other external, concerning foreign powers. From the latter, he can defend himself by his effective arms and his effective allies, and he will always have effective allies if he has effective arms. Internal affairs will always be stable when external affairs are stable, provided that they are not already disturbed by a conspiracy. And even if external conditions change, if he is properly organized and lives as I have said, and does not lose control of himself, he will always be able to withstand every attack, just as I said that Nabis the Spartan did.

But concerning his subjects, when external affairs do not change, he has to fear that they may be plotting in secret. The prince will protect himself against this danger by avoiding being either hated or despised and by keeping the people satisfied with him.

. . .

XXI How a prince should act to acquire esteem [*Quod principem deceat ut egregious habeatur*]

Nothing makes a prince more esteemed than great undertakings and showing himself to be extraordinary. In our own times we have Ferdinand of Aragon, the present King of Spain. This man can be called almost a new prince, since from being a weak ruler, through fame and glory he became the first king of Christendom. If you consider his deeds you will find them all very grand, and some even extraordinary. In the beginning of his reign he attacked Granada,[64] and that enterprise was the basis of his state. First, he acted while things were peaceful and when he had no fear of opposition. He kept the minds of the barons of Castile occupied with this, so that, concentrating on that war, they did not consider rebellion. In this way he acquired reputation and dominion over them without their noticing it. He was able to maintain armies with money from the Church and the people, and through that long war he laid a basis for his own army, which has since brought him honour.[65] Besides this, in order to be able to undertake great enterprises, he had recourse to a pious cruelty, always employing religion for his own purposes,[66] chasing the Marranos out of his kingdom and seizing their property.[67] No example of his actions could be more pathetic or more extraordinary than this. He attacked Africa[68] under the same cloak of religion. He undertook the invasion of Italy.[69] Lately, he attacked France.[70] And thus he has always accomplished and organized great deeds, that have always kept the minds of his subjects surprised, amazed, and occupied with their outcome. One action of his would spring from another in such a way that, between one and the other, he would never give men enough time to be able to work calmly against him.

It also helps a prince a great deal to show himself to be extraordinary in dealing with internal affairs, as in the reports about Messer Bernabò Visconti of Milan.[71] When the occasion arises that a person in public life performs some extraordinary act, be it good or evil, the prince should find a way of rewarding or punishing him that will provoke a great deal of discussion. And above all a prince should strive in all of his actions to achieve the reputation of a great man of outstanding intelligence.

A prince is also respected when he is a true friend and a true enemy: that is, when he declares himself to be on the side of one prince against another, without reserve. Such a policy will always be more useful than remaining neutral, for if two powerful neighbours of yours come to blows, they will be of the kind that, when one has emerged victorious, you will either have cause to fear the victor or you will not. In either of these two cases, it will always be more useful for you to declare yourself and to wage open warfare. In the first case, if you do not disclose your intentions you will always be the prey of whoever wins, to the delight and satisfaction of whoever loses, and you will have no reason at all why anyone should come to your assistance or take you in. Because whoever wins does not want reluctant allies who would not assist him in times of adversity; whoever loses will not give you refuge, since you were unwilling to run the risk of sharing his fortune.

Antiochus came into Greece, sent there by the Aetolians to drive out the Romans. Antiochus sent ambassadors to the Achaeans, who were allies of the Romans, to encourage them to remain neutral. On the other hand, the Romans urged them to take up arms with them. This matter came up for debate in the council of the Achaeans where the legate of Antiochus persuaded them to remain neutral. To this the Roman legate replied: "*Quod autem isti dicunt, non interponendi vos bello, nihil magis alienum rebus vestries est: sine gratia, sine dignitate premium vitoris eritis*"[72] ["The counsel these men give you about not entering the war is indeed contrary to your interests: without respect and dignity, you will be the prey of the victors"]. It will always happen that he who is not your friend will request your neutrality, and he who is your friend will ask you to disclose your intentions by taking up arms. In order to avoid present dangers, irresolute princes follow the neutral path most of the time, and most of the time they come to ruin. But when the prince declares himself energetically in favour of one side, if the one with whom you have joined wins, he has an obligation toward you and there exists a bond

of affection between you, although he may be powerful and you may be left in his power. Men are never so dishonest that they will repress an ally with such a flagrant display of ingratitude. Nor are victories ever so clear-cut that the victor can be completely free of concern, especially for justice. But if the one with whom you join loses, you can be given refuge by him, and while he is able to do so, he can help you, and you will become the comrade of a fortune that may flourish again.

In the second case, when those who fight together are such that you need not fear the one who wins, it is even more prudent to take sides; since you achieve the downfall of one prince with the aid of another, who should have saved him if he had been wise; and who, once he has won, remains at your discretion—and it is impossible for him not to win, with your help. Here it is to be noted that a prince must avoid ever joining forces with one more powerful than himself to injure others, unless necessity compels you, as was mentioned above. For if you win you remain his prisoner, and princes should avoid being left at the discretion of others as much as possible. The Venetians allied themselves with France against the Duke of Milan,[73] and they could have avoided that alliance: it resulted in their downfall.[74] But when such an alliance cannot be avoided, as happened to the Florentines when the Pope and Spain went with their armies to attack Lombardy,[75] then a prince should join for the reasons given above. Nor should any state ever believe that it can always choose safe courses of action. On the contrary, it should recognize that they will all be risky, for we find this to be in the order of things: that whenever we try to avoid one disadvantage, we run into another. Prudence consists in knowing how to recognize the nature of disadvantages, and how to choose the least sorry one as good.

A prince should also demonstrate that he is a lover of the virtues,[76] by giving hospitality to virtuous men and by honouring those who excel in a particular skill.[77] Furthermore, he should encourage his subjects to pursue their trades in tranquility, whether in commerce, agriculture, or in any other human pursuit. No one should be afraid to increase his property for fear that it will be taken away from him, while no one should shrink from undertaking any business through fear of taxes. Instead, the prince must establish rewards for those who wish to do these things, and for anyone who seeks in any way to enrich his city or state.[78] Besides this, at the appropriate times of the year he should keep the populace occupied with festivals and spectacles. And because each city is divided into guilds[79] or neighbourhoods,[80] he should take account of these groups, meet with them on occasion, and offer himself as an example of humanity and munificence while always, nevertheless, firmly maintaining the majesty of his dignity.

. . .

XXV Of Fortune's power in human affairs and how she can be resisted [*Quantum Fortuna in rebus humanis posit et quomodo illi sit occurrendum*]

I am not unaware that many have held, and do still hold, the opinion that the affairs of this world are controlled by Fortune and by God, that men cannot control them with their prudence, and that, on the contrary, men can have no remedy whatsoever for them. For this reason, they might judge that it is useless to lose much sweat over such matters, and let them be controlled by fate. This opinion has been held all the more in our own times because of the enormous upheavals that have been observed and are being observed every day—events beyond human conjecture. When I have thought about it, sometimes I am inclined to a certain degree toward their opinion. Nevertheless, in order not to wipe out our free will, I consider it to be true that Fortune is the arbiter of one half of our actions, but that she still leaves the control of the other half, or almost that, to us.[81] I compare her to one of those destructive rivers that, when they become enraged, flood the plains, ruin the trees and buildings, raising the earth from one spot and dropping it onto another. Everyone flees before it; everyone yields to its impetus, unable to oppose it in any way. But although rivers are like this, it does not mean that we cannot take precautions with dikes and dams when the weather is calm, so that when they rise up again either the waters will be channelled off or their force will be neither so damaging nor so out of control. The same things occur where Fortune is concerned. She shows her power where there is no well-ordered virtue[82] to resist her, and therefore turns her impetus toward where she knows no dikes and dams have been constructed to hold her in. If you consider Italy, the seat of these upheavals and the area which has set them in motion, you will see a countryside without dikes and without a single dam: if Italy had been protected with proper virtue, as is the case in Germany, Spain, and France, either this flood would not have produced the enormous upheavals that it has, or it would not have struck here at all. And with this I consider I have said enough about resisting Fortune in general.

Restricting myself more to particulars, let me say that one sees a prince prospering today and coming to ruin tomorrow without having seen him change his nature or his qualities. I believe this happens first because of the causes that have been discussed at length earlier. That is, that the prince who relies completely upon Fortune will come to ruin as soon as she changes. I also believe that the man who adapts his method of procedure to the nature of the times will prosper, and likewise, that the man who establishes his procedures out of tune with the times will come to grief. We can observe in the affairs that lead them to the end they seek—that is, toward glory and wealth—that men proceed in different ways: one man with caution, another with impetuousness; one with violence, another with astuteness; one with patience, another with its opposite. Each may achieve his goals with these different means. In the case of two cautious men, we also see that one reaches his goal while the other does not. And likewise, two men prosper equally employing two different means, one being cautious and the other impetuous. This occurs from nothing other than from the quality of the times, that either match or do not match their procedures. This follows from what I said: two men acting differently can reach the same result; and of two men acting identically, one reaches his goal and the other does not. On this also depends the variation of the good,[83] for if a man governs himself with caution and patience, while the times and circumstances are turning in such a way that his conduct is appropriate, he will prosper. But if the times and circumstances change he will be ruined, because he does not change his method of procedure. No man is so prudent that he knows how to adapt himself to this fact, both because he cannot deviate from that to which he is by nature inclined, and also because he cannot be persuaded to depart from a path after having always prospered by following it. And therefore, when it is time to act impetuously the cautious man does not know how to do so, and is ruined as a result; for if he had changed his conduct with the times, Fortune would not have changed.

Pope Julius II acted impetuously in all his affairs, and he found the times and circumstances so suitable to this method of procedure that he always achieved felicitous results. Consider the first campaign he waged against Bologna while Messer Giovanni Bentivoglio was still alive.[84] The Venetians were unhappy about it and so was the King of Spain. Julius still had negotiations going on about it with France. Nevertheless, he started personally on this expedition with his usual ferocity and impetuosity. Such a move astonished Spain and the Venetians and stopped them in their tracks, the latter out of fear and the former out of a desire to recover the entire Kingdom of Naples. On the other hand, Julius involved the King of France, for when the King saw him move, and wishing to make him his ally in order to defeat the Venetians, the King decided that he could not deny the Pope the use of his troops without openly injuring him. Therefore, with his impetuous move, Julius accomplished what no other pontiff would ever have achieved with the greatest of human prudence. For if he had waited until he could leave Rome with agreements settled and everything in order, as any other pontiff would have done, he would never have succeeded, because the King of France would have found a thousand excuses and the others would have aroused in him a thousand fears. I wish to leave unmentioned the other deeds of his, since all were similar and all succeeded well. The brevity of his life[85] did not allow him to experience the contrary; since if times that required proceeding with caution had arrived, his ruin would have followed, for he would never have deviated from those methods to which his nature inclined him.

I therefore conclude that, since Fortune varies and men remain obstinate in their ways, men prosper when the two are in harmony[86] and fail to prosper when they are not in accord. I certainly believe this: that it is better to be impetuous than cautious, because Fortune is a woman, and if you want to keep her under it is necessary to beat her and force her down. It is clear that she more often allows herself to be won over by impetuous men than by those who proceed coldly. And so, like a woman, Fortune is always the friend of young men, for they are less cautious, more ferocious, and command her with more audacity.

Post-Reading Questions

1. Machiavelli favours the concentration of political power. Why? And how does it figure in his account of a strong ruler?
2. Machiavelli suggests that there are no absolutes in matters of virtue and vice. Is his moral relativism persuasive?
3. Why is it better to be feared than loved, according to Machiavelli?
4. Why, given his views about the compatibility of fear and effective rule, would Machiavelli state that rulers must take care not to become the object of contempt or hate?
5. What does Machiavelli mean when he writes that "Fortune is a woman"?

CASE STUDY
CANADA'S MACHIAVELLI: MAURICE DUPLESSIS

Introduction

In the Canadian context, it is hard to think of Machiavelli and his philosophy without thinking of Maurice Duplessis. For 18 years—first from 1935 to 1939 and then from 1944 to 1949—Duplessis ruled unchallenged as Quebec's premier. Born in Trois Rivières in 1890 to a politician father, Maurice attended the Séminaire Saint-Joseph de Trois-Rivières and went on to earn a law degree from Laval University. After a few years of practising law in his hometown, in 1927 he was elected to the Quebec House of Assembly. In 1933, Duplessis became the leader of the Conservative Party of Quebec, which shortly thereafter joined forces with the Action libéral nationale party to form the ultra-conservative Union

Maurice Duplessis

Nationale party. For the next 20 years—starting in 1936—Duplessis won every election, except one in 1939. In addition to his position as the premier, he also held the position of attorney general within his government.

Like Machiavelli's ideal ruler, Duplessis was very much a power broker, playing different provincial powers (the federal government, the Catholic Church, political parties, etc.) against each other in order to strengthen his own political position. His actions led to greater centralization of power at the provincial level and laid the groundwork for greater autonomy for Quebec as a whole. Despite campaigning on a progressive platform in 1936, Duplessis quickly became known for his autocratic style and for successive administrations marked by corruption and scandal. The Duplessis Orphans scandal was a particular low point: Duplessis and the Catholic Church, it emerged, had engaged in a scheme to defraud the federal government by branding orphan children as mentally ill and in need of care in order to obtain funds from the government. It would seem that Duplessis heeded Machiavelli's advice in *The Prince* (Chapter 18) that a ruler should be *seen* to have positive qualities (such as compassion, generosity, charity, and faith) yet always be willing to set these aside and engage in deception should expedience demand it.

Duplessis governed Quebec and conducted his affairs in a Machiavellian manner in the sense that he did not see himself bound by the rules and laws that governed ordinary citizens; for him, the end justified the means, even where those means involved unscrupulous behaviour. This attitude can be seen in the Supreme Court case of *Roncarelli v. Duplessis* (1959), which considered whether, in administering justice, the discretion of a government official is ever absolute, as Dupplessis assumed it was. The case concerned Mr. Roncarelli, a restaurant owner and Jehovah's Witness. In the 1940s, the Jehovah's Witnesses' activity in Quebec brought them into conflict with the Catholic Church. As a result of the Church's close ties to the provincial government, police interfered with the Witnesses' proselytizing by arresting them for distributing "seditious pamphlets." Mr. Roncarelli posted bail for the arrested Witnesses, whose number reached into the hundreds. When this was brought to the attention of Mr. Duplessis in his capacity as the attorney general, Duplessis, acting as the premier, instructed the chair of the Quebec Liquor Commission to revoke the liquor license for Roncarelli's restaurant—an action that ultimately resulted in the closure of the restaurant. Mr. Roncarelli sued for financial damages, but the real significance of the case lies in its challenge to the use of autocratic decision making in the administration of justice, and the concentration of power more generally. As such, the case might be seen as a challenge to a Machiavellian approach to political governance.

From *Roncarelli v. Duplessis*, [1959] S.C.R. 121

Roncarelli v. Duplessis, *[1959] S.C.R. 121.*
http://scc.lexum.org/decisia-scc-csc/scc-csc/scc-csc/en/item/2751/index.do

[The majority opinion was delivered by Justice Martland J.]

This is an appeal from a judgment of the Court of Queen's Bench, Appeal Side, for the Province of Quebec,[87] District of Montreal, rendered on 12 April 1956, overruling the judgment of the Superior Court rendered on 2 May

1951, under the terms of which the appellant had been awarded damages in the sum of $8,123.53 and costs.

The appellant had appealed from the judgment of the Superior Court in respect of the amount of damages awarded. This appeal was dismissed.

The facts which give rise to this appeal are as follows:
The appellant, on 4 December, 1946, was the owner

of a restaurant and café situated at 1429 Crescent Street in the City of Montreal. At that time he was the holder of a liquor permit, no. 68, granted to him on 1 May 1946, pursuant to the provisions of the Alcoholic Liquor Act of the Province of Quebec and which permitted the sale of alcoholic liquors in the restaurant and café. The permit was valid until 30 April 1947, subject to possible cancellation by the Quebec Liquor Commission (hereinafter sometimes referred to as "the Commission") in accordance with the provisions of s. 35 of that Act. The business operated by the appellant had been founded by his father in the year 1912 and it had been continuously licensed until 4 December 1946. The evidence is that prior to that date the appellant had complied with the requirements of the Alcoholic Liquor Act and had conducted a high-class restaurant business.

The appellant was an adherent of the Witnesses of Jehovah. From some time in 1944 until 12 November 1946, he had, on numerous occasions, given security for Witnesses of Jehovah who had been prosecuted under City of Montreal by-laws numbered 270 and 1643 for minor offences of distributing, peddling and canvassing without a licence. The maximum penalty for these offences was a fine of $40 and costs, or imprisonment for 60 days. The total number of bonds furnished by the appellant was 390. These security bonds were accepted by the City attorney and the Recorder of the City of Montreal without remuneration to the appellant. None of the accused who had been bonded ever defaulted. Subsequently the appellant was released from these bonds at his own request and new security was furnished by others.

As a result of a change of procedure in the Recorder's Court in Montreal by the attorney in chief of that court, the appellant was not accepted as a bondsman in any cases before that court after 12 November 1946.

. . .

The appellant commenced action against the respondent on 3 June 1947, claiming damages in the total sum of $118,741. He alleged that the respondent, without legal or statutory authority, had caused the cancellation of his liquor permit as an act of reprisal because of his having acted as surety or bondsman for the Witnesses of Jehovah in connection with the charges above mentioned. He alleged that the permit had been arbitrarily and unlawfully cancelled and that, as a result, he had sustained the damages claimed.

. . . He alleged that in his capacity as attorney-general of the Province of Quebec, after becoming cognizant of the conduct of the appellant and of the fact that he held a permit issued by the Quebec Liquor Commission, he had decided, after careful reflection, that it was contrary to public order to permit the appellant to

enjoy the benefit of the privileges of this permit and that he, the respondent, had recommended to the manager of the Quebec Liquor Commission the cancellation of that permit. It was alleged that the permit did not give any right, but constituted a privilege available only during the pleasure of the Commission. He alleged that in the matter he had acted in his quality of prime minister and attorney-general of the Province of Quebec and, accordingly, could not incur any personal responsibility. He further pleaded the provisions of art. 88 of the Code of Civil Procedure and alleged that he had not received notice of the action as required by the provisions of that article.

. . .

. . . [A]fter reviewing the evidence, I am satisfied that there was ample evidence to sustain the finding of the trial judge that the cancellation of the appellant's permit was the result of instructions given by the respondent to the manager of the Commission.

. . .

The Attorney-General's Department Act, R.S.Q. 1941, c. 46

. . .

3. The attorney-general is the official legal adviser of the lieutenant-governor, and the legal member of the Executive Council of the Province of Quebec.

4. The duties of the attorney-general are the following:

1. To see that the administration of public affairs is in accordance with the law;
2. To exercise a general superintendence over all matters connected with the administration of justice in the Province.

5. The function and powers of the attorney-general are the following:

1. He has the functions and powers which belong to the office of attorney-general of England, respectively, by law or usage, insofar as the same are applicable to this Province, and also the functions and powers, which, up to the Union, belonged to such offices in the late Province of Canada, and which, under the provisions of the British North America Act, 1867, are within the powers of the government of this Province;
2. He advises the heads of the several departments of the government of the Province upon all matters of law concerning such departments, or arising in the administration thereof;

. . .

7. He is charged with superintending the administration or the execution, as the case may be, of the laws respecting police.

The Executive Power Act, R.S.Q. 1941, c. 7

. . .

5. The lieutenant-governor may appoint, under the Great Seal, from among the members of the Executive Council, the following officials, who shall remain in office during pleasure:

1. A prime minister who shall, ex-officio, be president of the Council.

The Alcoholic Liquor Act, R.S.Q. 1941, c. 255 Division XII: Investigation and Prosecution of Offences

148. The attorney-general shall be charged with:

1. Assuring the observance of this act and of the Alcoholic Liquor Possession and Transportation Act (Chap. 256), and investigating, preventing and suppressing the infringements of such acts, in every way authorized thereby;
2. Conducting the suits or prosecutions for infringements of this act or of the said Alcoholic Liquor Possession and Transportation Act.

I do not find, in any of these provisions, authority to enable the respondent, either as attorney-general or prime minister, to direct the cancellation of a permit under the Alcoholic Liquor Act. On the contrary, the intent and purpose of that Act appears to be to place the complete control over the liquor traffic in Quebec in the hands of an independent commission. The only function of the attorney-general under that statute is in relation to the assuring of the observance of its provisions. There is no evidence of any breach of that Act by the appellant.

. . .

In my view, the respondent was not acting in the exercise of any official powers which he possessed in doing what he did in this matter.

The third point to be considered is as to whether the appellant's permit was lawfully cancelled by the Commission under the provisions of the Alcoholic Liquor Act. Section 35 of that Act makes provision for the cancellation of a permit in the following terms:

35. 1. Whatever be the date of issue of any permit granted by the Commission, such permit shall expire on 30 April following, unless it be cancelled by the Commission before such date, or unless the date at which it must expire be prior to 30 April following.

The Commission may cancel permit at its discretion.

. . .

With respect to [the allegation that there was a breach of violation of the rules of natural justice], it would appear to be somewhat doubtful whether the appellant had a right to a personal hearing, in view of the judgment of Lord Radcliffe in *Nakkuda Ali v. Jayaratne*.[88] However, regardless of this, it is my view that the discretionary power to cancel a permit given to the Commission by the Alcoholic Liquor Act must be related to the administration and enforcement of that statute. It is not proper to exercise the power of cancellation for reasons which are unrelated to the carrying into effect of the intent and purpose of the Act. The association of the appellant with the Witnesses of Jehovah and his furnishing of bail for members of that sect, which were admitted to be the reasons for the cancellation of his permit and which were entirely lawful, had no relationship to the intent and purposes of the Alcoholic Liquor Act.

Furthermore, it should be borne in mind that the right of cancellation of a permit under that Act is a substantial power conferred upon what the statute contemplated as an independent commission. That power must be exercised solely by that corporation. It must not and cannot be exercised by anyone else.

. . .

In the present case it is my view, for the reasons already given, that the power was not, in fact, exercised by the Commission, but was exercised by the respondent, acting through the manager of the Commission. Cancellation of a permit by the Commission at the request or upon the direction of a third party, whoever he may be, is not a proper and valid exercise of the power conferred upon the Commission by s. 35 of the Act. The Commission cannot abdicate its own functions and powers and act upon such direction.

Finally, there is the question as to the giving of notice of the action by the appellant to the respondent pursuant to art. 88 of the Code of Civil Procedure, which reads as follows:

Action Against Public Officers
88. No public officer or other person fulfilling any public function or duty can be sued for damages by reason of any act done by him in the exercise of his functions, nor can any verdict or judgment be

rendered against him, unless notice of such action has been given him at least one month before the issue of the writ of summons.

Such notice must be in writing; it must state the grounds of the action, and the name of the plaintiff's attorney or agent, and indicate his office; and must be served upon him personally or at his domicile.

. . .

. . . For the reasons already given in dealing with the second of the four points under discussion, I do not think that it was a function either of the prime minister or of the attorney-general to interfere with the administration of the Commission by causing the cancellation of a liquor permit. That was something entirely outside his legal functions. It involved the exercise of powers which, in law, he did not possess at all.

. . .

[However], there was nothing on which the respondent could found the belief that he was entitled to deprive the appellant of his liquor permit.

On the issue of liability, I have, for the foregoing reasons, reached the conclusion that the respondent, by acts not justifiable in law, wrongfully caused the cancellation of the appellant's permit and thus cause damage to the appellant. The respondent intentionally inflicted damage upon the appellant and, therefore, in the absence of lawful justification, which I do not find, he is liable to the appellant for the commission of a fault under art. 1053 of the Civil Code.

I now turn to the matter of damages.

. . .

. . . [I]n all the circumstances, the amount of these damages must be determined in a somewhat arbitrary fashion. I consider that $25,000 should be allowed as damages for the diminution of the value of the good will and for the loss of future profits.

I would allow both appeals, with costs here and below, and order the respondent to pay to the appellant damages in the total amount of $33,123.53, with interest from the date of the judgment in the Superior Court, and costs.

Post-Case-Reading Questions

1. In what ways did Maurice Duplessis' actions with respect to Mr. Roncarelli and the Jehovah's Witnesses in Quebec echo Machiavelli's advice to political rulers? In what ways did it depart from this advice?

2. Does the judgment in the case of *Roncarelli v. Duplessis* vindicate Machiavelli's view—as developed in *The Prince*—that the end justifies the means? Or does it challenge this view?

CHAPTER
IV

Thomas Hobbes

Introduction

Thomas Hobbes was born in Malmesbury, England, in 1588, and lived until the age of 91. His father, a vicar with a violent temper, abandoned the family following an altercation with another clergyman while Hobbes was still young. An intelligent boy, Thomas was sent by his uncle to Magdalen College, Oxford, to study in 1602 or 1603. Shortly after his graduation in 1608, Hobbes became the tutor—and eventually secretary, advisor, and travel companion—to William Cavendish, who later became the second Earl of Devonshire.

His position with the Cavendish family lasted for many years, affording Hobbes the opportunity to travel widely throughout Europe and associate with some of the leading intellectuals and scientists of his time. After the death of William Cavendish, Hobbes accompanied

Thomas Hobbes

© iStockphoto.com/Denis Kozlenko

the earl's eldest son, the young third Earl of Devonshire, on a tour of Europe from 1634 to 1636. In Italy, Hobbes met Galileo, and in Paris, he made the acquaintance of Mersenne and also interacted with followers and detractors of Descartes. Captivated by the emerging sciences of the day, and more convinced than ever of the importance of observation and deductive reasoning, Hobbes resolved to write on physical nature, human nature, and the nature of human society. He developed this plan into a three-volume work entitled *The Elements of Philosophy*, which included *De Cive* (on the citizen) in 1642, *De Corpore* (on the body) in 1655, and *De Homine* (of man) in 1658. A prolific thinker and author throughout his life, Hobbes was also a translator: of particular note are his translations (into English) of *The Odyssey* and the *Iliad*, as well as Thucydides' *History of the Peloponnesian War*. Later in life, he also authored a history of civil wars in England (*Behemoth*), which was published posthumously.

The book Hobbes is best known for today is *Leviathan*, widely regarded as one of the most important texts in political philosophy in the English language. Written against the backdrop of the English Civil War, *Leviathan* was published in 1651, upon Hobbes' return to England after a long period of exile on the Continent. Well known for his royalist views and controversial opinions on religion, the ever-fearful Hobbes fled to Paris in 1640, where he continued to write and associate with intellectuals and scientists. *Leviathan* is very much a product of this turbulent period, concerned as it is with the problem of how to maintain absolute political authority and avoid civil war. Highly learned in the sciences, Hobbes also drew on his understanding of logic, geometry, and physics to explore central questions concerning human nature and the establishment of the state. From a materialist perspective, he argues that social and physical events are nothing but bodies in motion, and that human behaviour can be categorized into two sorts of motions: voluntary and vital (i.e., involuntary bodily processes). Human action, he asserts, is motivated by the impulses of appetite (love) and aversion (hate). Moreover, human beings are roughly equal in their capacities and strength, and so remain vulnerable to attack by one another in the "state of nature." This equality, coupled with the inevitability of competition for the same scarce goods in the world, leads us to a condition of constant insecurity, and at times, a "war of all against all." But because human beings fear death and desire comfort, safety, and peace, they have an incentive to leave this state of nature behind and form a society.

It is rational, Hobbes argues, for individuals to devise an arrangement to protect themselves from each other. This arrangement is the creation of a political state, and Hobbes thought it could be achieved by people's voluntary transfer of their rights to a common body (the sovereign) in an act he called a "covenant." As part of this covenant, or social contract, everyone is to transfer their "right of nature" into the hands of a sovereign, the Leviathan. This all-powerful sovereign agrees to protect the lives of his subjects from civil war and foreign aggression, and tries to cultivate peace and prosperity in his Commonwealth. In return, he demands strict obedience: the sovereign's power is absolute and undivided, and rebellion against him is a crime. Only if the sovereign fails to protect (or directly threatens) our life is resistance rational and justified. The sovereign also has sole authority over the laws of the land, and determines what form of religious practice is permissible (i.e., what church or churches are to be permitted, and whether public, or only private, worship is prudent).

After considering excerpts from *Leviathan*, we will examine legislation introduced in 2012 by the provincial Liberal government in Quebec that aimed to restrict the right to engage in public protest. Bill 78, which was a direct response to the widespread demonstrations and student boycotts of institutions of higher education in 2012, provides a concrete context in which to consider Hobbes' insistence on the importance of an absolute prohibition on revolt. Given his emphasis on peace and political stability, Hobbes' preference for absolute sovereignty may seem sensible: peace is best preserved, he thought, when law is the exclusive command of the sovereign. But, more controversially, Hobbes argued that in civil society there is no such thing as unjust laws, since the sovereign is the author of all laws as well as justice. While to the modern reader such claims may sound dangerous, to Hobbes, who was concerned with security above all else, preventing subjects from questioning the justice of particular laws was essential. Although his proposals regarding governance are unsuited to advanced liberal democracies, Hobbes' insights on political authority and obedience remain provocative and compelling even today.

Further Readings

Dietz, M. (1986). *Thomas Hobbes and Political Theory*. Oxford: Oxford University Press.

Hampton, J. (1986). *Hobbes and the Social Contract Tradition*. Cambridge: Cambridge University Press.

Skinner, Q. (1996). *Reason and Rhetoric in the Philosophy of Hobbes*. Cambridge: Cambridge University Press.

Sorell, T. (2001). "Hobbes and the Morality Beyond Justice," *Pacific Philosophical Quarterly* 82 (3–4): 227–42.

Tuck, R. (2002). *Hobbes: A Very Short Introduction*. Oxford: Oxford University Press.

Thomas Hobbes, From *Leviathan*

Thomas Hobbes, Leviathan, *edited by J.C.A. Gaskin
(Oxford: Oxford University Press, 1996, reissued 2008).*

Part 1 Of Man

Chapter V Of Reason and Science

1. When a man *reasoneth*, he does nothing else but conceive a sum total, from *addition* of parcels; or conceive a
remainder, from *subtraction* of one sum from another:
which (if it be done by words,) is conceiving of the consequence from the names of all the parts, to the name
of the whole; or from the names of the whole and one
part, to the name of the other part. And though in some
things, (as in numbers,) besides adding and subtracting,
men name other operations, as *multiplying* and *dividing*;
yet they are the same; for multiplication, is but adding
together of things equal; and division, but subtracting
of one thing, as often as we can. These operations are
not incident to numbers only, but to all manner of things
that can be added together, and taken one out of another.
For as arithmeticians teach to add and subtract in *numbers*; so the geometricians teach the same in *lines, figures*
(solid and superficial,) *angles, proportions, times,* degrees
of *swiftness, force, power,* and the like; the logicians teach
the same in *consequences of words*; adding together two
names, to make an *affirmation*; and two *affirmations*, to
make a *syllogism*; and *many syllogisms* to make a *demonstration*; and from the *sum*, or *conclusion* of a *syllogism*,
they subtract one *proposition*, to find the other. Writers
of politics, add together *pactions* [contracts] to find men's
duties; and lawyers, *laws*, and *facts*, to find what is *right*
and *wrong* in the actions of private men. In sum, in what
matter soever there is place for *addition* and *subtraction*,
there also is place for *reason*; and where these have no
place, there *reason* has nothing at all to do.

2. Out of all which we may define, (that is to say
determine,) what that is, which is meant by this word
reason, when we reckon it amongst the faculties of the
mind. For REASON, in this sense, is nothing but *reckoning* (that is, adding and subtracting) of the consequences
of general names agreed upon, for the *marking* and signifying of our thoughts; I say *marking* them, when we

reckon by ourselves; and *signifying*, when we demonstrate, or approve our reckonings to other men.

3. And as in arithmetic, unpractised men must, and
professors themselves may often err, and cast up false; so
also in any other subject of reasoning, the ablest, most
attentive, and most practised men, may deceive themselves, and infer false conclusions; not but that reason
itself is always right reason, as well as arithmetic is a certain and infallible art: but no one man's reason, nor the
reason of anyone number of men, makes the certainty;
no more than an account is therefore well cast up, because a great many men have unanimously approved it.
And therefore, as when there is a controversy in an account, the parties must by their own accord, set up for
right reason, the reason of some arbitrator, or judge, to
whose sentence they will both stand, or their controversy must either come to blows, or be undecided, for
want of a right reason constituted by nature; so is it also
in all debates of what kind soever: and when men that
think themselves wiser than all others, clamour and demand right reason for judge; yet seek no more, but that
things should be determined, by no other men's reason
but their own, it is as intolerable in the society of men,
as it is in play after trump is turned, to use for trump
on every occasion, that suite whereof they have most in
their hand. For they do nothing else, that will have every
of their passions, as it comes to bear sway in them, to be
taken for right reason, and that in their own controversies: bewraying [revealing] their want of right reason, by
the claim they lay to it.

4. The use and end of reason, is not the finding of
the sum, and truth of one, or a few consequences, remote from the first definitions, and settled significations
of names; but to begin at these; and proceed from one
consequence to another. For there can be no certainty
of the last conclusion, without a certainty of all those affirmations and negations, on which it was grounded, and
inferred. As when a master of a family, in taking an account, casteth up the sums of all the bills of expense, into
one sum; and not regarding how each bill is summed up,
by those that give them in account; nor what it is he pays

for; he advantages himself no more, than if he allowed the account in gross, trusting to every of the accountants' skill and honesty: so also in reasoning of all other things, he that takes up conclusions on the trust of authors, and doth not fetch them from the first items in every reckoning, (which are the significations of names settled by definitions), loses his labour; and does not know any thing; but only believeth.

5. When a man reckons without the use of words, which may be done in particular things (as when upon the sight of anyone thing, we conjecture what was likely to have preceded, or is likely to follow upon it;) if that which he thought likely to follow, follows not; or that which he thought likely to have preceded it, hath not preceded it, this is called ERROR; to which even the most prudent men are subject. But when we reason in words of general signification, and fall upon a general inference which is false, though it be commonly called *error*, it is indeed an ABSURDITY, or senseless speech. For error is but a deception, in presuming that somewhat is past, or to come; of which, though it were not past, or not to come; yet there was no impossibility discoverable. But when we make a general assertion, unless it be a true one, the possibility of it is inconceivable. And words whereby we conceive nothing but the sound, are those we call *absurd, insignificant,* and *nonsense.* And therefore if a man should talk to me of a *round quadrangle;* or *accidents of bread in cheese;* or, *immaterial substances;* or of *a free subject; a free will;* or any *free,* but free from being hindered by opposition,[8] I should not say he were in an error, but that his words were without meaning; that is to say, absurd.

6. I have said before, (in the second chapter,) that a man did excel all other animals in this faculty, that when he conceived any thing whatsoever, he was apt to inquire the consequences of it, and what effects he could do with it. And now I add this other degree of the same excellence, that he can by words reduce the consequences he finds to general rules, called *theorems,* or *aphorisms;* that is, he can reason, or reckon, not only in number, but in all other things, whereof one may be added unto, or subtracted from another.

7. But this privilege, is allayed by another; and that is, by the privilege of absurdity; to which no living creature is subject, but man only. And of men, those are of all most subject to it, that profess philosophy. For it is most true that Cicero saith of them somewhere; that there can be nothing so absurd, but may be found in the books of philosophers.[9] And the reason is manifest. For there is not one of them that begins his ratiocination from the definitions, or explications of the names they are to use; which is a method that hath been used

only in geometry; whose conclusions have thereby been made indisputable.

8. The first cause of absurd conclusions I ascribe to the want of method; in that they begin not their ratiocination from definitions; that is, from settled significations of their words: as if they could cast account, without knowing the value of the numeral words, *one, two,* and *three.*

9. And whereas all bodies enter into account upon divers considerations, (which I have mentioned in the precedent chapter;) these considerations being diversely named, divers absurdities proceed from the confusion, and unfit connection of their names into assertions. And therefore

10. The second cause of absurd assertions, I ascribe to the giving of names of *bodies,* to *accidents;* or of *accidents* to *bodies;* as they do, that say, *faith is infused,* or *inspired;* when nothing can be *poured,* or *breathed* into anything, but body; and that, *extension is body;* that *phantasms* are *spirits,* etc.

11. The third I ascribe to the giving of the names of the *accidents* of *bodies without us,* to the *accidents* of our *own bodies;* as they do that say the *colour is in the body; the sound is in the air,* etc.

12. The fourth, to the giving of the names of *bodies,* to *names,* or *speeches;* as they do that say, that *there be things universal;* that *a living creature is genus,* or *a general thing,* etc.

13. The fifth, to the giving of the names of *accidents,* to *names* and *speeches;* as they do that say, *the nature of a thing is its definition; a man's command is his will;* and the like.

14. The sixth, to the use of metaphors, tropes, and other rhetorical figures, instead of words proper. For though it be lawful to say (for example) in common speech, *the way goeth, or leadeth hither, or thither, the proverb says this or that* (whereas ways cannot go, nor proverbs speak;) yet in reckoning, and seeking of truth, such speeches are not to be admitted.

15. The seventh, to names that signify nothing;[10] but are taken up, and learned by rote from the schools, as *hypostatical, transubstantiate, consubstantiate, eternal-now,* and the like canting of Schoolmen.

16. To him that can avoid these things, it is not easy to fall into any absurdity, unless it be by the length of an account; wherein he may perhaps forget what went before. For all men by nature reason alike, and well, when they have good principles. For who is so stupid, as both to mistake in geometry, and also to persist in it, when another detects his error to him?

17. By this it appears that reason is not as sense, and memory, born with us; nor gotten by experience only, as

prudence is; but attained by industry; first in apt imposing of names; and secondly by getting a good and orderly method in proceeding from the elements, which are names, to assertions made by connection of one of them to another; and so to syllogisms, which are the connections of one assertion to another, till we come to a knowledge of all the consequences of names appertaining to the subject in hand; and that is it, men call SCIENCE. And whereas sense and memory are but knowledge of fact, which is a thing past, and irrevocable; *Science* is the knowledge of consequences, and dependence of one fact upon another: by which, out of that we can presently do, we know how to do something else when we will, or the like, another time: because when we see how any thing comes about, upon what causes, and by what manner; when the like causes come into our power, we see how to make it produce the like effects.

18. Children therefore are not endued with reason at all, till they have attained the use of speech; but are called reasonable creatures, for the possibility apparent of having the use of reason in time to come. And the most part of men, though they have the use of reasoning a little way, as in numbering to some degree; yet it serves them to little use in common life; in which they govern themselves, some better, some worse, according to their differences of experience, quickness of memory, and inclinations to several ends; but specially according to good or evil fortune, and the errors of one another. For as for *science*, or certain rules of their actions, they are so far from it, that they know not what it is. Geometry they have thought conjuring: but for other sciences, they who have not been taught the beginnings, and some progress in them, that they may see how they be acquired and generated, are in this point like children, that having no thought of generation, are made believe by the women, that their brothers and sisters are not born, but found in the garden.

19. But yet they that have no *science*, are in better, and nobler condition, with their natural prudence; than men, that by mis-reasoning, or by trusting them that reason wrong, fall upon false and absurd general rules. For ignorance of causes, and of rules, does not set men so far out of their way, as relying on false rules, and taking for causes of what they aspire to, those that are not so, but rather causes of the contrary.

20. To conclude, the light of human minds is perspicuous words, but by exact definitions first snuffed, and purged from ambiguity; *reason* is the *pace*; increase of *science*, the *way*; and the benefit of mankind, the *end*. And on the contrary, metaphors, and senseless and ambiguous words, are like *ignes fatui*;[11] and reasoning upon them, is wandering amongst innumerable absurdities;

and their end, contention, and sedition, or contempt [indifference].

21. As, much experience, is *prudence*; so, is much science, *sapience*. For though we usually have one name of wisdom for them both; yet the Latins did always distinguish between *prudentia* and *sapientia*; ascribing the former to experience, the latter to science. But to make their difference appear more clearly, let us suppose one man endued with an excellent natural use, and dexterity in handling his arms; and another to have added to that dexterity, an acquired science, of where he can offend, or be offended by his adversary, in every possible posture, or guard: the ability of the former, would be to the ability of the latter, as prudence to sapience; both useful; but the latter infallible. But they that trusting only to the authority of books, follow the blind blindly, are like him that, trusting to the false rules of a master of fence, ventures presumptuously upon an adversary, that either kills or disgraces him.

22. The signs of science, are some, certain and infallible; some, uncertain. Certain, when he that pretendeth the science of any thing, can teach the same; that is to say, demonstrate the truth thereof perspicuously to another; uncertain, when only some particular events answer to his pretence, and upon many occasions prove so as he says they must. Signs of prudence are all uncertain; because to observe by experience, and remember all circumstances that may alter the success, is impossible. But in any business, whereof a man has not infallible science to proceed by; to forsake his own natural judgment, and be guided by general sentences read in authors, and subject to many exceptions, is a sign of folly, and generally scorned by the name of pedantry. And even of those men themselves, that in councils of the commonwealth, love to show their reading of politics and history, very few do it in their domestic affairs, where their particular interest is concerned; having prudence enough for their private affairs: but in public they study more the reputation of their own wit, than the success of another's business.

Chapter VI Of the Interior Beginnings of Voluntary Motions; Commonly Called the Passions. And the Speeches by Which They Are Expressed

1.[12] There be in animals, two sorts of *motions* peculiar to them: one called *vital*; begun in generation, and continued without interruption through their whole life; such as are the *course* of the *blood*, the *pulse*, the *breathing*, the *concoction* [digestion], *nutrition*, *excretion*, etc.; to which motions there needs no help of imagination: the other is *animal motion*, otherwise called *voluntary motion*; as to *go*, to *speak*, to *move* any of our limbs, in such manner as first fancied in our minds. That sense, is motion in the organs and interior parts of man's body, caused by the action of the things we see, hear, etc.; and that fancy is but the relics of the same motion, remaining after sense, has been already said in the first and second chapters. And because *going*, *speaking*, and the like voluntary motions, depend always upon a precedent thought of *whither*, *which way*, and *what*; it is evident, that the imagination is the first internal beginning of all voluntary motion. And although unstudied men, do not conceive any motion at all to be there, where the thing moved is invisible; or the space it is moved in, is (for the shortness of it) insensible; yet that doth not hinder, but that such motions are. For let a space be never so little, that which is moved over a greater space, whereof that little one is part, must first be moved over that. These small beginnings of motion, within the body of man, before they appear in walking, speaking, striking, and other visible actions, are commonly called ENDEAVOUR.[13]

2. This endeavour, when it is toward something which causes it, is called APPETITE, or DESIRE; the latter, being the general name; and the other oftentimes restrained to signify the desire of food, namely *hunger* and *thirst*. And when the endeavour is fromward something, it is generally called AVERSION. These words *appetite*, and *aversion* we have from the Latins; and they both of them signify the motions, one of approaching, the other of retiring. So also do the Greek words for the same, which are ὁρμή and ἀφορμή. For nature itself does often press upon men those truths, which afterwards, when they look for somewhat beyond nature, they stumble at. For the Schools find in mere appetite to go, or move, no actual motion at all: but because some motion they must acknowledge, they call it metaphorical motion; which is but an absurd speech: for though words may be called metaphorical; bodies, and motions can not.

3. That which men desire, they are also said to LOVE: and to HATE those things, for which they have aversion. So that desire, and love, are the same thing; save that by desire, we always signify the absence of the object; by love, most commonly the presence of the same. So also by aversion, we signify the absence; and by hate, the presence of the object.

4. Of appetites and aversions, some are born with men; as appetite of food, appetite of excretion, and exoneration,[14] (which may also and more properly be called aversions, from somewhat they feel in their bodies;) and some other appetites, not many. The rest, which are appetites of particular things, proceed from experience, and trial of their effects upon themselves, or other men.

For of things we know not at all, or believe not to be, we can have no further desire, than to taste and try. But aversion we have for things, not only which we know have hurt us; but also that we do not know whether they will hurt us, or not.

5. Those things which we neither desire, nor hate, we are said to *contemn*: CONTEMPT being nothing else but an immobility, or contumacy [obstinacy] of the heart, in resisting the action of certain things; and proceeding from that the heart is already moved otherwise, by other more potent objects; or from want of experience of them.

6.[15] And because the constitution of a man's body is in continual mutation; it is impossible that all the same things should always cause in him the same appetites, and aversions: much less can all men consent, in the desire of almost any one and the same object.

. . .

Chapter X Of Power, Worth, Dignity, Honour, and Worthiness

1. The power *of a man*, (to take it universally,) is his present means, to obtain some future apparent good. And is either *original* or *instrumental*.

2. *Natural power*, is the eminence of the faculties of body, or mind: as extraordinary strength, form, prudence, arts, eloquence, liberality, nobility. *Instrumental* are those powers, which acquired by these, or by fortune, are means and instruments to acquire more: as riches, reputation, friends, and the secret working of God, which men call good luck. For the nature of power, is in this point, like to fame, increasing as it proceeds; or like the motion of heavy bodies, which the further they go, make still the more haste.

3. The greatest of human powers, is that which is compounded of the powers of most men, united by consent, in one person, natural, or civil, that has the use of all their powers depending on his will; such as is the power of a commonwealth: or depending on the wills of each Particular; such as is the power of a faction or of divers factions leagued. Therefore to have servants, is power; to have friends, is power: for they are strengths united.

4. Also riches joined with liberality, is power; because it procureth friends, and servants: without liberality, not so; because in this case they defend not; but expose men to envy, as a prey.

5. Reputation of power, is power; because it draweth with it the adherence of those that need protection.

6. So is reputation of love of a man's country, (called popularity,) for the same reason.

7. Also, what quality soever maketh a man beloved, or feared of many; or the reputation of such quality, is

power; because it is a means to have the assistance, and service of many.

8. Good success is power; because it maketh reputation of wisdom, or good fortune; which makes men either fear him, or rely on him.

9. Affability of men already in power, is increase of power; because it gaineth love.

10. Reputation of prudence in the conduct of peace or war, is power; because to prudent men, we commit the government of ourselves, more willingly than to others.

11. Nobility is power, not in all places, but only in those commonwealths, where it has privileges: for in such privileges consisteth their power.

12. Eloquence is power; because it is seeming prudence.

13. Form is power; because being a promise of good, it recommendeth men to the favour of women and strangers.

14. The sciences, are small power; because not eminent; and therefore, not acknowledged in any man; nor are at all, but in a few; and in them, but of a few things. For science is of that nature, as none can understand it to be, but such as in a good measure have attained it.

15. Arts of public use, as fortification, making of engines, and other instruments of war; because they confer to defence, and victory, are power: and though the true mother of them, be science, namely the mathematics; yet, because they are brought into the light, by the hand of the artificer, they be esteemed (the midwife passing with the vulgar for the mother,) as his issue.

16. The *value*, or WORTH of a man, is as of all other things, his price; that is to say, so much as would be given for the use of his power: and therefore is not absolute; but a thing dependent on the need and judgment of another. An able conductor of soldiers, is of great price in time of war present, or imminent; but in peace not so. A learned and uncorrupt judge, is much worth in time of peace; but not so much in war. And as in other things, so in men, not the seller, but the buyer determines the price. For let a man (as most men do,) rate themselves at the highest value they can; yet their true value is no more than it is esteemed by others.

17. The manifestation of the value we set on one another, is that which is commonly called honouring, and dishonouring. To value a man at a high rate, is to *honour* him; at a low rate, is to *dishonour* him. But high, and low, in this case, is to be understood by comparison to the rate that each man setteth on himself.

18. The public worth of a man, which is the value set on him by the commonwealth, is that which men commonly call DIGNITY. And this value of him by the commonwealth, is understood, by offices of command, judicature, public employment; or by names and titles, introduced for distinction of such value.

. . .

53. WORTHINESS, is a thing different from the worth, or value of a man; and also from his merit, or desert, and consisteth in a particular power, or ability for that, whereof he is said to be worthy: which particular ability, is usually named FITNESS, or *aptitude*.

54. For he is worthiest to be a commander, to be a judge, or to have any other charge, that is best fitted, with the qualities required to the well discharging of it; and worthiest of riches, that has the qualities most requisite for the well using of them: any of which qualities being absent, one may nevertheless be a worthy man, and valuable for something else. Again, a man may be worthy of riches, office, and employment, that nevertheless, can plead no right to have it before another; and therefore cannot be said to merit or deserve it. For merit, presupposeth a right, and that the thing deserved is due by promise: of which I shall say more hereafter, when I shall speak of contracts.

Chapter XI Of the Difference of Manners

1. By MANNERS, I mean not here, decency of behaviour; as how one should salute another, or how a man should wash his mouth, or pick his teeth before company, and such other points of the *small morals*; but those qualities of mankind, that concern their living together in peace, and unity. To which end we are to consider, that the felicity of this life, consisteth not in the repose of a mind satisfied. For there is no such *finis ultimus*, (utmost aim,) nor *summum bonum*, (greatest good,) as is spoken of in the books of the old moral philosophers. Nor can a man any more live,[16] whose desires are at an end, than he, whose senses and imaginations are at a stand. Felicity is a continual progress of the desire, from one object to another; the attaining of the former, being still but the way to the latter. The cause whereof is, that the object of man's desire, is not to enjoy once only, and for one instant of time; but to assure for ever, the way of his future desire. And therefore the voluntary actions, and inclinations of all men, tend, not only to the procuring, but also to the assuring of a contented life; and differ only in the way: which ariseth partly from the diversity of passions, in divers men; and partly from the difference of the knowledge, or opinion each one has of the causes, which produce the effect desired.

2. So that in the first place, I put for a general inclination of all mankind, a perpetual and restless desire

of power after power, that ceaseth only in death. And the cause of this, is not always that a man hopes for a more intensive delight, than he has already attained to; or that he cannot be content with a moderate power: but because he cannot assure the power and means to live well, which he hath present, without the acquisition of more. And from hence it is, that kings, whose power is greatest, turn their endeavours to the assuring it at home by laws, or abroad by wars: and when that is done, there succeedeth a new desire; in some, of fame from new conquest; in others, of ease and sensual pleasure; in others, of admiration, or being flattered for excellence in some art, or other ability of the mind.

3. Competition of riches, honour, command, or other power, inclineth to contention, enmity, and war: because the way of one competitor, to the attaining of his desire, is to kill, subdue, supplant, or repel the other. Particularly, competition of praise, inclineth to a reverence of antiquity. For men contend with the living, not with the dead; to these ascribing more than due, that they may obscure the glory of the other.

4. Desire of ease, and sensual delight, disposeth men to obey a common power: because by such desires, a man doth abandon the protection that might be hoped for from his own industry, and labour. Fear of death, and wounds, disposeth to the same; and for the same reason. On the contrary, needy men, and hardy, not contented with their present condition; as also, all men that are ambitious of military command, are inclined to continue the causes of war; and to stir up trouble and sedition: for there is no honour military but by war; nor any such hope to mend an ill game, as by causing a new shuffle.

5. Desire of knowledge, and arts of peace, inclineth men to obey a common power: for such desire, containeth a desire of leisure; and consequently protection from some other power than their own.

6. Desire of praise, disposeth to laudable actions, such as please them whose judgment they value; for of those men whom we contemn, we contemn also the praises. Desire of fame after death does the same. And though after death, there be no sense of the praise given us on earth, as being joys, that are either swallowed up in the unspeakable joys of Heaven, or extinguished in the extreme torments of hell: yet is not such fame vain; because men have a present delight therein, from the foresight of it, and of the benefit that may redound thereby to their posterity: which though they now see not, yet they imagine; and any thing that is pleasure to the sense, the same also is pleasure in the imagination.[17]

. . .

Chapter XIII Of the Natural Condition of Mankind as Concerning Their Felicity, and Misery

1. NATURE hath made men so equal, in the faculties of the body, and mind; as that though there be found one man sometimes manifestly stronger in body, or of quicker mind than another; yet when all is reckoned together, the difference between man, and man, is not so considerable, as that one man can thereupon claim to himself any benefit, to which another may not pretend, as well as he. For as to the strength of body, the weakest has strength enough to kill the strongest, either by secret machination, or by confederacy with others, that are in the same danger with himself.

2. And as to the faculties of the mind, (setting aside the arts grounded upon words, and especially that skill of proceeding upon general, and infallible rules, called science; which very few have, and but in few things; as being not a native faculty, born with us; nor attained (as prudence,) while we look after somewhat else,) I find yet a greater equality amongst men, than that of strength. For prudence, is but experience; which equal time, equally bestows on all men, in those things they equally apply themselves unto. That which may perhaps make such equality incredible, is but a vain conceit of one's own wisdom, which almost all men think they have in a greater degree, than the vulgar; that is, than all men but themselves, and a few others, whom by fame, or for concurring with themselves, they approve. For such is the nature of men, that howsoever they may acknowledge many others to be more witty, or more eloquent, or more learned; yet they will hardly believe there be many so wise as themselves; for they see their own wit at hand, and other men's at a distance. But this proveth rather that men are in that point equal, than unequal. For there is not ordinarily a greater sign of the equal distribution of any thing, than that every man is contented with his share.

3. From this equality of ability, ariseth equality of hope in the attaining of our ends. And therefore if any two men desire the same thing, which nevertheless they cannot both enjoy, they become enemies; and in the way to their end, (which is principally their own conservation, and sometimes their delectation only,) endeavour to destroy, or subdue one another. And from hence it comes to pass, that where an invader hath no more to fear, than another man's single power; if one plant, sow, build, or possess a convenient seat, others may probably be expected to come prepared with forces united, to dispossess, and deprive him, not only of the fruit of

his labour, but also of his life, or liberty. And the invader again is in the like danger of another.

4. And from this diffidence of one another, there is no way for any man to secure himself, so reasonable, as anticipation; that is, by force, or wiles, to master the persons of all men he can, so long, till he see no other power great enough to endanger him: and this is no more than his own conservation requireth, and is generally allowed. Also because there be some, that taking pleasure in contemplating their own power in the acts of conquest, which they pursue farther than their security requires; if others, that otherwise would be glad to be at ease within modest bounds, should not by invasion increase their power, they would not be able, long time, by standing only on their defence, to subsist. And by consequence, such augmentation of dominion over men, being necessary to a man's conservation, it ought to be allowed him.

5. Again, men have no pleasure, (but on the contrary a great deal of grief) in keeping company, where there is no power able to over-awe them all. For every man looketh that his companion should value him, at the same rate he sets upon himself: and upon all signs of contempt, or undervaluing, naturally endeavours, as far as he dares (which amongst them that have no common power to keep them in quiet, is far enough to make them destroy each other,) to extort a greater value from his contemners, by damage; and from others, by the example.

6. So that in the nature of man, we find three principal causes of quarrel. First, competition; secondly, diffidence; thirdly, glory.

7. The first, maketh men invade for gain; the second, for safety; and the third, for reputation. The first use violence, to make themselves masters of other men's persons, wives, children, and cattle; the second, to defend them; the third, for trifles, as a word, a smile, a different opinion, and any other sign of undervalue, either direct in their persons, or by reflection in their kindred, their friends, their nation, their profession, or their name.

8.[18] Hereby it is manifest, that during the time men live without a common power to keep them all in awe, they are in that condition which is called war; and such a war, as is of every man, against every man. For WAR, consisteth not in battle only, or the act of fighting; but in a tract of time, wherein the will to contend by battle is sufficiently known: and therefore the notion of *time*, is to be considered in the nature of war; as it is in the nature of weather. For as the nature of foul weather, lieth not in a shower or two of rain; but in an inclination thereto of many days together: so the nature of war, consisteth not in actual fighting; but in the known disposition thereto,

during all the time there is no assurance to the contrary. All other time is PEACE.

9. Whatsoever therefore is consequent to a time of war, where every man is enemy to every man; the same is consequent to the time, wherein men live without other security, than what their own strength, and their own invention shall furnish them withal. In such condition, there is no place for industry; because the fruit thereof is uncertain: and consequently no culture of the earth; no navigation, nor use of the commodities that may be imported by sea; no commodious building; no instruments of moving, and removing such things as require much force; no knowledge of the face of the earth; no account of time; no arts; no letters; no society; and which is worst of all, continual fear, and danger of violent death; and the life of man, solitary, poor, nasty, brutish, and short.

10. It may seem strange to some man, that has not well weighed these things; that nature should thus dissociate, and render men apt to invade, and destroy one another: and he may therefore, not trusting to this inference, made from the passions, desire perhaps to have the same confirmed by experience. Let him therefore consider[19] with himself, when taking a journey, he arms himself, and seeks to go well accompanied; when going to sleep, he locks his doors; when even in his house he locks his chests; and this when he knows there be laws, and public officers, armed, to revenge all injuries shall be done him; what opinion he has of his fellow-subjects, when he rides armed; of his fellow citizens, when he locks his doors; and of his children, and servants, when he locks his chests. Does he not there as much accuse mankind by his actions, as I do by my words? But neither of us accuse man's nature in it. The desires, and other passions of man, are in themselves no sin. No more are the actions, that proceed from those passions, till they know a law that forbids them: which till laws be made they cannot know: nor can any law be made, till they have agreed upon the person that shall make it.

11. It may peradventure be thought, there was never such a time, nor condition of war as this;[20] and I believe it was never generally so, over all the world: but there are many places, where they live so now. For the savage people in many places of America, except the government of small families, the concord whereof dependeth on natural lust, have no government at all; and live at this day in that brutish manner, as I said before. Howsoever, it may be perceived what manner of life there would be, where there were no common power to fear; by the manner of life, which men that have formerly lived under a peaceful government, use to degenerate into, in a civil war.

12. But though there had never been any time, wherein particular men were in a condition of war one

against another; yet in all times, kings, and persons of sovereign authority, because of their independency, are in continual jealousies, and in the state and posture of gladiators; having their weapons pointing, and their eyes fixed on one another; that is, their forts, garrisons, and guns upon the frontiers of their kingdoms; and continual spies upon their neighbours; which is a posture of war. But because they uphold thereby, the industry of their subjects; there does not follow from it, that misery, which accompanies the liberty of particular men.

13. To this war of every man against every man, this also is consequent; that nothing can be unjust. The notions of right and wrong, justice and injustice have there no place. Where there is no common power, there is no law: where no law, no injustice. Force, and fraud, are in war the two cardinal virtues. Justice, and injustice are none of the faculties neither of the body, nor mind. If they were, they might be in a man that were alone in the world, as well as his senses, and passions. They are qualities, that relate to men in society, not in solitude. It is consequent also to the same condition, that there be no propriety, no dominion, no *mine* and *thine* distinct; but only that to be every man's, that he can get; and for so long, as he can keep it. And thus much for the ill condition, which man by mere nature is actually placed in; though with a possibility to come out of it, consisting partly in the passions, partly in his reason.

14. The passions that incline men to peace, are fear of death; desire of such things as are necessary to commodious living; and a hope by their industry to obtain them. And reason suggesteth convenient articles of peace, upon which men may be drawn to agreement. These articles, are they, which otherwise are called the Laws of Nature: whereof I shall speak more particularly, in the two following chapters.

Chapter XIV Of the First and Second Natural Laws, and of Contracts

1. THE RIGHT OF NATURE, which writers commonly call *jus naturale*, is the liberty each man hath, to use his own power, as he will himself, for the preservation of his own nature; that is to say, of his own life; and consequently, of doing any thing, which in his own judgment, and reason, he shall conceive to be the aptest means thereunto.

2. By LIBERTY, is understood, according to the proper signification of the word, the absence of external impediments: which impediments, may oft take away part of a man's power to do what he would; but cannot hinder him from using the power left him, according as his judgment, and reason shall dictate to him.

3. A LAW OF NATURE, (*lex naturalis*,) is a precept, or general rule, found out by reason, by which a man is forbidden to do, that, which is destructive of his life, or taketh away the means of preserving the same; and to omit, that, by which he thinketh it may be best preserved. For though they that speak of this subject, use to confound *jus*, and *lex*, *right* and *law*; yet they ought to be distinguished; because RIGHT, consisteth in liberty to do, or to forbear: whereas LAW, determineth, and bindeth to one of them: so that law, and right, differ as much, as obligation, and liberty; which in one and the same matter are inconsistent.

4. And because the condition of man, (as hath been declared in the precedent chapter) is a condition of war of every one against every one; in which case every one is governed by his own reason; and there is nothing he can make use of, that may not be a help unto him, in preserving his life against his enemies; it followeth, that in such a condition, every man has a right to every thing; even to one another's body. And therefore, as long as this natural right of every man to every thing endureth, there can be no security to any man, (how strong or wise soever he be,) of living out the time, which nature ordinarily alloweth men to live. And consequently it is a precept, or general rule of reason,[21] *that every man, ought to endeavour peace, as for as he has hope of obtaining it; and when he cannot obtain it, that he may seek, and use, all helps, and advantages of war.* The first branch of which rule, containeth the first, and fundamental law of nature; which is, *to seek peace, and follow it.* The second, the sum of the right of nature; which is, *by all means me can, to defend ourselves.*

5. From this fundamental law of nature, by which men are commanded to endeavour peace, is derived this second law; *that a man be willing, when others are so too, as far-forth, as for peace, and defence of himself he shall think it necessary, to lay down this right to all things; and be contented with so much liberty against other men, as he would allow other men against himself.* For as long as every man holdeth this right, of doing any thing he liketh; so long are all men in the condition of war. But if other men will not lay down their right, as well as he; then there is no reason for anyone, to divest himself of his: for that were to expose himself to prey, (which no man is bound to) rather than to dipose himself to peace. This is that law of the Gospel; *whatsoever you require that others should do to you, that do ye to them.* And that law of all men, *quod tibi fieri non vis, alteri ne feceris.*[22]

6. To *lay down* a man's *right* to any thing, is to *divest* himself of the *liberty*, of hindering another of the benefit of his own right to the same. For he that renounceth, or passeth away his right, giveth not to any other man

a right which he had not before; because there is nothing to which every man had not right by nature: but only standeth out of his way, that he may enjoy his own original right, without hindrance from him; not without hindrance from another. So that the effect which redoundeth to one man, by another man's defect of right, is but so much diminution of impediments to the use of his own right original.

7. Right is laid aside, either by simply renouncing it; or by transferring it to another. By *simply* RENOUNCING; when he cares not to whom the benefit thereof redoundeth. By TRANSFERRING; when he intendeth the benefit thereof to some certain person, or persons. And when a man hath in either manner abandoned, or granted away his right; then he is said to be OBLIGED, or BOUND, not to hinder those, to whom such right is granted, or abandoned, from the benefit of it: and that he *ought*, and it is his DUTY, not to make void that voluntary act of his own: and that such hindrance is INJUSTICE, and INJURY, as being *sine jure*; the right being before renounced, or transferred. So that *injury*, or *injustice*, in the controversies of the world, is somewhat like to that, which in the disputations of scholars is called *absurdity*. For as it is there called an absurdity, to contradict what one maintained in the beginning: so in the world, it is called injustice, and injury, voluntarily to undo that, which from the beginning he had voluntarily done. The way by which a man either simply renounceth, or transferreth his right, is a declaration, or signification, by some voluntary and sufficient sign, or signs, that be doth so renounce, or transfer; or hath so renounced, or transferred the same, to him that accepteth it. And these signs are either words only, or actions only; or (as it happeneth most often) both words, and actions. And the same are the BONDS, by which men are bound, and obliged: bonds, that have their strength, not from their own nature, (for nothing is more easily broken than a man's word,) but from fear of some evil consequence upon the rupture.

8. Whensoever a man transferreth his right, or renounceth it; it is either in consideration of some right reciprocally transferred to himself; or for some other good he hopeth for thereby. For it is a voluntary act:[23] and of the voluntary acts of every man, the object is some *good to himself*. And therefore there be some rights, which no man can be understood by any words, or other signs, to have abandoned, or transferred. As first a man cannot lay down the right of resisting them, that assault him by force, to take away his life; because he cannot be understood to aim thereby, at any good to himself. The same may be said of wounds, and chains, and imprisonment; both because there is no benefit consequent to such

patience; as there is to the patience of suffering another to be wounded, or imprisoned: as also because a man cannot tell, when he seeth men proceed against him by violence, whether they intend his death or not. And lastly the motive, and end for which this renouncing, and transferring of right is introduced, is nothing else but the security of a man's person, in his life, and in the means of so preserving life, as not to be weary of it. And therefore if a man by words, or other signs, seem to despoil himself of the end, for which those signs were intended; he is not to be understood as if he meant it, or that it was his will; but that he was ignorant of how such words and actions were to be interpreted.

9. The mutual transferring of right, is that which men call CONTRACT.

10. There is difference, between transferring of right to the thing; and transferring, or tradition, that is, delivery of the thing itself. For the thing may be delivered together with the translation of the right; as in buying and selling with ready-money; or exchange of goods, or lands: and it may be delivered some time after.

11. Again, one of the contractors, may deliver the thing contracted for on his part, and leave the other to perform his part at some determinate time after, and in the mean time be trusted; and then the contract on his part, is called PACT, or COVENANT: or both parts may contract now, to perform hereafter: in which cases, he that is to perform in time to come, being trusted, his performance is called *keeping of promise*, or faith; and the failing of performance (if it be voluntary) *violation of faith*.

12. When the transferring of right, is not mutual; but one of the parties transferreth, in hope to gain thereby friendship, or service from another, or from his friends; or in hope to gain the reputation of charity, or magnanimity; or to deliver his mind from the pain of compassion; or in hope of reward in heaven; this is not contract, but GIFT, FREE-GIFT, GRACE: which words signify one and the same thing.

13. Signs of contract, are either *express*, or *by inference*. Express, are words spoken with understanding of what they signify: and such words are either of the time *present*, or *past*; as, *I give, I grant, I have given, I have granted, I will that this be yours*: or of the future; as, *I will give, I will grant*: which words of the future are called PROMISE.

14. Signs by inference, are sometimes the consequence of words; sometimes the consequence of silence; sometimes the consequence of actions; sometimes the consequence of forbearing an action: and generally a sign by inference, of any contract, is whatsoever sufficiently argues the will of the contractor.

15. Words alone, if they be of the time to come, and contain a bare promise, are an insufficient sign of a free-gift, and therefore not obligatory. For if they be of the time to come, as, *tomorrow I will give*, they are a sign I have not given yet, and consequently that my right is not transferred, but remaineth till I transfer it by some other act. But if the words be of the time present, or past, as, *I have given*, or *do give to be delivered tomorrow*, then is my morrow's right given away to-day; and that by the virtue of the words, though there were no other argument of my will. And there is a great difference in the significa-tion of these words, *volo hoc tuum esse cras dabo*; that is, between *I will that this be thine tomorrow*, and, *I will give it thee tomorrow*: for the word *I will*, in the former manner of speech, signifies an act of the will present; but in the latter, it signifies a promise of an act of the will to come: and therefore the former words, being of the present, transfer a future right; the latter, that be of the future, transfer nothing. But if there be other signs of the will to transfer a right, besides words; then, though the gift be free, yet may the right be understood to pass by words of the future: as if a man propound a prize to him that comes first to the end of a race, the gift *is* free; and though the words be of the future, yet the right passeth: for if he would not have his words so be understood, be should not have let them run.

16. In contracts, the right passeth, not *only* where the words are of the time present, or past; but also where they are of the future: because all contract *is* mu-tual translation, or change of right; and therefore he that promiseth only, because he hath already received the benefit for which he promiseth, is to be understood as if he intended the right should pass: for unless he had been content to have his words so understood, the other would not have performed his part first. And for that cause, in buying, and selling, and other acts of contract, a promise is equivalent to a covenant; and therefore obligatory.

17. He that performeth first in the case of a contract, is said to MERIT that which he is to receive by the per-formance of the other; and he hath it as *due*. Also when a prize is propounded to many, which is to be given to him only that winneth; or money *is* thrown amongst many, to be enjoyed by them that catch it; though this be a free gift; yet so to win, or so to catch, is to *merit*, and to have it as DUE. For the right is transferred in the pro-pounding of the prize, and in throwing down the money; though it be not determined to whom, but by the event of the contention. But there is between these two sorts of merit, this difference, that in contract, I merit by virtue of my own power, and the contractor's need; but in this case of free gift, I am enabled to merit only by the benig-nity of the giver: in contract, I merit at the contractor's

hand that he should depart with his right; in this case of gift, I merit not that the giver should part with his right; but that when he has parted with it, it should be mine, rather than another's. And this I think to be the mean-ing of that distinction of the Schools, between *meritum congrui*, and *meritum condigni*.[24] For God Almighty, hav-ing promised Paradise to those men (hoodwinked with carnal desires,) that can walk through this world accord-ing to the precepts, and limits prescribed by him; they say, he that shall so walk, shall merit Paradise *ex congruo*. But because no man can demand a right to it, by his own righteousness, or any other power in himself, but by the free grace of God only; they say, no man can merit Paradise *ex condigno*. This I say, I think is the meaning of that distinction; but because disputers do not agree upon the signification of their own terms of art, longer than it serves their turn; I will not affirm any thing of their meaning: only this I say; when a gift *is* given indefinitely, as a prize to be contended for, be that winneth meriteth, and may claim the prize as due.

18. If a covenant be made, wherein neither of the parties perform presently, but trust one another; in the condition of mere nature, (which is a condition of war of every man against every man,) upon any reasonable suspicion, it is void: but if there be a common power set over them both, with right and force sufficient to com-pel performance, it is not void. For he that performeth first, has no assurance the other will perform after; be-cause the bonds of words are too weak to bridle men's ambition, avarice, anger, and other passions, without the fear of some coercive power; which in the condition of mere nature, where all men are equal, and judges of the justness of their own fears, cannot possibly be supposed. And therefore he which performeth first, does but betray himself to his enemy; contrary to the right (he can never abandon) of defending his life, and means of living.

19. But in a civil estate, where there is a power set up to constrain those that would otherwise violate their faith, that fear is no more reasonable; and for that cause, he which by the covenant is to perform first, is obliged so to do.

20. The cause of fear, which maketh such a covenant invalid, must be always something arising after the cov-enant made; as some new fact, or other sign of the will not to perform: else it cannot make the covenant void. For that which could not hinder a man from promising, ought not to be admitted as a hindrance of performing.

21. He that transferreth any right, transferreth the means of enjoying it, as far as lieth in his power. As he that selleth land, is understood to transfer the herbage, and whatsoever grows upon it; nor can he that sells a mill turn away the stream that drives it. And they that

give to a man the right of government in sovereignty, are understood to give him the right of levying money to maintain soldiers; and of appointing magistrates for the administration of justice.

22. To make covenants with brute beasts, is impossible; because not understanding our speech, they understand not, nor accept of any translation of right; nor can translate any right to another: and without mutual acceptation, there is no covenant.

23. To make covenant with God,[25] is impossible, but by mediation of such as God speaketh to, either by revelation supernatural, or by his lieutenants that govern under him, and in his name: for otherwise we know not whether our covenants be accepted, or not. And therefore they that vow anything contrary to any law of nature, vow in vain; as being a thing unjust to pay such vow. And if it be a thing commanded by the law of nature, it is not the vow, but the law that binds them.

24. The matter, or subject of a covenant, is always something that falleth under deliberation; (for to covenant, is an act of the will; that is to say an act, and the last act, of deliberation;) and is therefore always understood to be something to come; and which is judged possible for him that covenanteth, to perform.

25. And therefore, to promise that which is known to be impossible, is no covenant. But if that prove impossible afterwards, which before was thought possible, the covenant is valid, and bindeth, (though not to the thing itself,) yet to the value; or, if that also be impossible, to the unfeigned endeavour of performing as much as is possible: for to more no man can be obliged.

26. Men are freed of their covenants two ways; by performing; or by being forgiven. For performance, is the natural end of obligation; and forgiveness, the restitution of liberty; as being a retransferring of that right, in which the obligation consisted.

27. Covenants entered into by fear, in the condition of mere nature, are obligatory. For example, in covenant to pay a ransom, or service for my life, to an enemy; I am bound by it. For it is a contract, wherein one receiveth the benefit of life; the other is to receive money, or service for it; and consequently, where no other law (as in the condition, of mere nature) forbiddeth the performance, the covenant is valid. Therefore prisoners of war, if trusted with the payment of their ransom, are obliged to pay it: and if a weaker prince, make a disadvantageous peace with a stronger, for fear; he is bound to keep it; unless (as hath been said before) there ariseth some new, and just cause of fear, to renew the war. And even in commonwealths, if I be forced to redeem myself from a thief by promising him money, I am bound to pay it, till the civil law discharge me. For whatsoever I may lawfully do

without obligation, the same I may lawfully covenant to do through fear: and what I lawfully covenant, I cannot lawfully break.

28. A former covenant, makes void a later. For a man that hath passed away his right to one man to-day, hath it not to pass tomorrow to another: and therefore the later promise passeth no right, but is null.

29.[26] A covenant not to defend myself from force, by force, is always void. For (as I have showed before) no man can transfer, or lay down his right to save himself from death, wounds, and imprisonment, (the avoiding whereof is the only end of laying down any right;) and therefore the promise of not resisting force, in no covenant transferreth any right; nor is obliging. For though a man may covenant thus, *unless I do so, or so, kill me*; he cannot covenant thus, *unless I do so, or so, I will not resist you, when you come to kill me*. For man by nature chooseth the lesser evil, which is danger of death in resisting; rather than the greater, which is certain and present death in not resisting. And this is granted to be true by all men, in that they lead criminals to execution, and prison, with armed men, notwithstanding that such criminals have consented to the law, by which they are condemned.

30. A covenant to accuse oneself, without assurance of pardon, is likewise invalid. For in the condition of nature, where every man is judge, there is no place for accusation: and in the civil state, the accusation is followed with punishment; which being force, a man is not obliged not to resist. The same is also true, of the accusation of those, by whose condemnation a man falls into misery; as of a father, wife, or benefactor. For the testimony of such an accuser, if it be not willingly given, is presumed to be corrupted by nature: and therefore not to be received: and where a man's testimony is not to be credited, he is not bound to give it. Also accusations upon torture, are not to be reputed as testimonies. For torture is to be used but as means of conjecture, and light, in the further examination, and search of truth: and what is in that case confessed, tendeth to the ease of him that is tortured; not to the informing of the torturers: and therefore ought not to have the credit of a sufficient testimony: for whether he deliver himself by true, or false accusation, he does it by the right of preserving his own life.

. . .

Chapter XV Of Other Laws of Nature

1. From that law of nature, by which we are obliged to transfer to another, such rights, as being retained, hinder the peace of mankind, there followeth a third; which

is this, *that men perform their covenants made*: without which, covenants are in vain, and but empty words; and the right of all men to all things remaining, we are still in the condition of war.

2. And in this law of nature, consisteth the fountain and original of JUSTICE. For where no covenant hath preceded, there hath no right been transferred, and every man has right to every thing; and consequently, no action can be unjust. But when a covenant is made, then to break it is *unjust*: and the definition of INJUSTICE, is no other than *the not performance of covenant*. And whatsoever is not unjust, is *just*.

3. But because covenants of mutual trust, where there is a fear of not performance on either part, (as hath been said in the former chapter,) are invalid; though the original of justice be the making of covenants; yet injustice actually there can be none, till the cause of such fear be taken away; which while men are in the natural condition of war, cannot be done. Therefore before the names of just, and unjust can have place, there must be some coercive power, to compel men equally to the performance of their covenants, by the terror of some punishment, greater than the benefit they expect by the breach of their covenant; and to make good that propriety, which by mutual contract men acquire, in recompense of the universal right they abandon: and such power there is none before the erection of a commonwealth. And this is also to be gathered out of the ordinary definition of justice in the Schools: for they say, that *justice is the constant will of giving to every man his own*.[27] And therefore where there is no *own*, that is, no propriety, there is no injustice; and where there is no coercive power erected, that is, where there is no commonwealth, there is no propriety; all men having right to all things: therefore where there is no commonwealth, there nothing is unjust. So that the nature of justice, consisteth in keeping of valid covenants: but the validity of covenants begins not but with the constitution of a civil power, sufficient to compel men to keep them: and then it is also that propriety begins.

4. The fool hath said in his heart, there is no such thing as justice;[28] and sometimes also with his tongue; seriously alleging, that every man's conservation, and contentment, being committed to his own care, there could be no reason, why every man might not do what he thought conduced thereunto: and therefore also to make, or not make; keep, or not keep covenants, was not against reason, when it conduced to one's benefit. He does not therein deny, that there be covenants; and that they are sometimes broken, sometimes kept; and that such breach of them may be called injustice, and the observance of them justice: but he questioneth,

whether injustice, taking away the fear of God, (for the same fool hath said in his heart there is no God,) may not sometimes stand with that reason, which dictateth to every man his own good; and Particularly then, when it conduceth to such a benefit, as shall put a man in a condition, to neglect not only the dispraise, and revilings, but also the power of other men. The kingdom of God is gotten by violence:[29] but what if it could be gotten by unjust violence? were it against reason so to get it, when it is impossible to receive hurt by it? and if it be not against reason, it is not against justice: or else justice is not to be approved for good. From such reasoning as this, successful wickedness hath obtained the name of virtue: and some that in all other things have disallowed the violation of faith; yet have allowed it, when it is for the getting of a kingdom. And the heathen that believed, that Saturn was deposed by his son Jupiter, believed nevertheless the same Jupiter to be the avenger of injustice: somewhat like to a piece of law in Coke's[30] *Commentaries on Littleton*; where he says, if the right heir of the crown be attainted of treason; yet the crown shall descend to him, and *eo instante* the attainder be void: from which instances a man will be very prone to infer; that when the heir apparent of a kingdom, shall kill him that is in possession, though his father; you may call it injustice, or by what other name you will; yet it can never be against reason, seeing all the voluntary actions of men tend to the benefit of themselves; and those actions are most reasonable, that conduce most to their ends. This specious reasoning is nevertheless false.

5. For the question is not of promises mutual, where there is no security of performance on either side; as when there is no civil power erected over the parties promising; for such promises are no covenants: but either where one of the parties has performed already; or where there is a power to make him perform; there is the question whether it be against reason, that is, against the benefit of the other to perform, or not. And I say it is not against reason. For the manifestation whereof, we are to consider; first, that when a man doth a thing, which notwithstanding any thing can be foreseen, and reckoned on, tendeth to his own destruction, howsoever some accident which he could not expect, arriving may turn it to his benefit; yet such events do not make it reasonably or wisely done. Secondly, that in a condition of war, wherein every man to every man, for want of a common power to keep them all in awe, is an enemy, there is no man can hope by his own strength, or wit, to defend himself from destruction, without the help of confederates; where every one expects the same defence by the confederation, that anyone else does: and therefore he which declares he thinks it reason to deceive those that help him, can in

reason expect no other means of safety, than what can be had from his own single power. He therefore that breaketh his covenant, and consequently declareth that he thinks he may with reason do so, cannot be received into any society, that unite themselves for peace and defence, but by the error of them that receive him; nor when he is received, be retained in it, without seeing the danger of their error; which errors a man cannot reasonably reckon upon as the means of his security: and therefore if he be left, or cast out of society, he perisheth; and if he live in society, it is by the errors of other men, which he could not foresee, nor reckon upon; and consequently against the reason of his preservation; and so, as all men that contribute not to his destruction, forbear him only out of ignorance of what is good for themselves.

6.[31] As for the instance of gaining the secure and perpetual felicity of heaven, by any way; it is frivolous: there being but one way imaginable; and that is not breaking, but keeping of covenant.

7. And for the other instance of attaining sovereignty by rebellion; it is manifest, that though the event follow, yet because it cannot reasonably be expected, but rather the contrary; and because by gaining it so, others are taught to gain the same in like manner, the attempt thereof is against reason. Justice therefore, that is to say, keeping of covenant, is a rule of reason, by which we are forbidden to do any thing destructive to our life; and consequently a law of nature.

8. There be some that proceed further; and will not have the law of nature, to be those rules which conduce to the preservation of man's life on earth; but to the attaining of an eternal felicity after death; to which they think the breach of covenant may conduce; and consequently to just and reasonable; (such are they that think it a work of merit to kill, or depose, or rebel against, the sovereign power constituted over them by their own consent.) But because there is no natural knowledge of man's estate after death; much less of the reward that is then to be given to breach of faith; but only a belief grounded upon other men's saying that they know it supernaturally, or that they know those, that knew them, that knew others, that knew it supernaturally; breach of faith cannot be called a precept of reason, or nature.

. . .

Part 2 Of Commonwealth

Chapter XVII Of the Causes, Generation, and Definition of a Commonwealth[32]

1. The final cause, end, or design of men, (who naturally love liberty, and dominion over others,) in the introduction of that restraint upon themselves, (in which we see them live in commonwealths) is the foresight of their own preservation, and of a more contented life thereby; that is to say, of getting themselves out from that miserable condition of war, which is necessarily consequent (as hath been shown, Chapter XIII) to the natural passions of men, when there is no visible power to keep them in awe, and tie them by fear of punishment to the performance of their covenants, and observation of those laws of nature set down in the fourteenth and fifteenth chapters.

2. For the laws of nature (as *justice*, *equity*, *modesty*, *mercy*, and (in sum) *doing to others, as we would be done to*,) of themselves, without the terror of some power to cause them to be observed are contrary to our natural passions, that carry us to partiality, pride, revenge, and the like. And covenants, without the sword, are but words, and of no strength to secure a man at all. Therefore notwithstanding the laws of nature (which every one hath then kept, when he has the will to keep them, when he can do it safely) if there be no power erected, or not great enough for our security; every man will, and may lawfully rely on his own strength and art, for caution against all other men. And in all places, where men have lived by small families, to rob and spoil one another, has been a trade, and so far from being reputed against the law of nature, that the greater spoils they gained, the greater was their honour;[33] and men observed no other laws therein, but the laws of honour; that is, to abstain from cruelty, leaving to men their lives, and instruments of husbandry. And as small families did then; so now do cities and kingdoms which are but greater families (for their own security) enlarge their dominions, upon all pretences of danger, and fear of invasion, or assistance that may be given to invaders, and endeavour as much as they can, to subdue, or weaken their neighbours, by open force, and secret arts, for want of other caution, justly; and are remembered for it in after ages with honour.

3. Nor is it the joining together of a small number of men, that gives them this security; because in small numbers, small additions on the one side or the other, make the advantage of strength so great, as is sufficient to carry the victory; and therefore gives encouragement to an invasion. The multitude sufficient to confide in for our security, is not determined by any certain number, but by comparison with the enemy we fear; and is then sufficient, when the odds of the enemy is not of so visible and conspicuous moment, to determine the event of war, as to move him to attempt.

. . .

13. The only way to erect such a common power, as may be able to defend them from the invasion of

foreigners, and the injuries of one another, and thereby to secure them in such sort, as that by their own industry, and by the fruits of the earth, they may nourish themselves and live contentedly; is, to confer all their power and strength upon one man, or upon one assembly of men, that may reduce all their wills, by plurality of voices, unto one will: which is as much as to say, to appoint one man, or assembly of men, to bear their person; and every one to own, and acknowledge himself to be author of whatsoever he that so beareth their person, shall act, or cause to be acted, in those things which concern the common peace and safety; and therein to submit their wills, every one to his will, and their judgments, to his judgment. This is more than consent, or concord; it is a real unity of them all, in one and the same person, made by covenant of every man with every man, in such manner, as if every man should say to every man, *I authorize and give up my right of governing myself, to this man, or to this assembly of men, on this condition, that thou give up thy right to him, and authorize all his actions in like manner.* This done, the multitude so united in one person, is called a COMMONWEALTH, in Latin CIVITAS. This is the generation of that great LEVIATHAN, or rather (to speak more reverently) of that *Mortal God*, to which we owe under the *Immortal God*, our peace and defence. For by this authority, given him by every particular man in the commonwealth, he hath the use of so much power and strength conferred on him, that by terror thereof, he is enabled to conform the wills of them all, to peace at home, and mutual aid against their enemies abroad. And in him consisteth the essence of the commonwealth; which (to define it,) is *one person, of whose acts a great multitude, by mutual covenants one with another, have made themselves every one the author, to the end he may use the strength and means of them all, as he shall think expedient, for their peace and common defence.*

14. And he that carrieth this person, is called SOVEREIGN, and said to have *sovereign power*, and every one besides, his SUBJECT.

15. The attaining to this sovereign power, is by two ways. One, by natural force; as when a man maketh his children, to submit themselves, and their children to his government, as being able to destroy them if they refuse; or by war subdueth his enemies to his will, giving them their lives on that condition. The other, is when men agree amongst themselves, to submit to some man, or assembly of men, voluntarily, on confidence to be protected by him against all others. This latter, may be called a political commonwealth, or commonwealth by *institution*; and the former, a commonwealth by *acquisition*. And first, I shall speak of a commonwealth by institution.

Chapter XVIII Of the Rights of Sovereigns by Institution[34]

1. A *commonwealth* is said to be *instituted*, when a *multitude* of men do agree, and *covenant, every one, with every one*, that to whatsoever *man*, or *assembly of men*, shall be given by the major part, the *right* to *present* the person of them all (that is to say, to be their *representative*;) every one, as well he that *voted for it*, as he that *voted against it*, shall *authorize* all the actions and judgments, of that man, or assembly of men, in the same manner, as if they were his own, to the end, to live peaceably amongst themselves, and be protected against other men.

2. From this institution of a commonwealth are derived all the *rights*, and *faculties* of him, or them, on whom the sovereign power is conferred by the consent of the people assembled.

3. First, because they covenant, it is to be understood, they are not obliged by former covenant to any thing repugnant hereunto. And consequently they that have already instituted a commonwealth, being thereby bound by covenant, to own the actions, and judgments of one, cannot lawfully make a new covenant, amongst themselves, to be obedient to any other, in any thing whatsoever, without his permission. And therefore, they that are subjects to a monarch, cannot without his leave cast off monarchy, and return to the confusion of a disunited multitude; nor transfer their person from him that beareth it, to another man, or other assembly of men: for they are bound, every man to every man, to own, and be reputed author of all, that he that already is their sovereign, shall do, and judge fit to be done: so that anyone man dissenting, all the rest should break their covenant made to that man, which is injustice: and they have also every man given the sovereignty to him that beareth their person; and therefore if they depose him, they take from him that which is his own, and so again it is injustice. Besides, if he that attempteth to depose his sovereign, be killed, or punished by him for such attempt, he is author of his own punishment, as being by the institution, author of all his sovereign shall do: and because it is injustice for a man to do any thing, for which he may be punished by his own authority, he is also upon that title, unjust. And whereas some men have pretended for their disobedience to their sovereign, a new covenant, made, not with men, but with God; this also is unjust: for there is no covenant with God,[35] but by mediation of somebody that representeth God's person; which none doth but God's lieutenant, who bath the sovereignty under God. But this pretence of covenant with God, is so evident a lie, even in the pretenders' own consciences, that it is not only an act of an unjust, but also of

a vile, and unmanly disposition.

4. Secondly, because the right of bearing the person of them all, is given to him they make sovereign, by covenant only of one to another, and not of him to any of them; there can happen no breach of covenant on the part of the sovereign; and consequently none of his subjects, by any pretence of forfeiture, can be freed from his subjection. That he which is made sovereign maketh no covenant with his subjects beforehand, is manifest; because either he must make it with the whole multitude, as one party to the covenant; or be must make a several covenant with every man. With the whole, as one party, it is impossible; because as yet they are not one person: and if he make so many several covenants as there be men, those covenants after he hath the sovereignty are void; because what act soever can be pretended by anyone of them for breach thereof, is the act both of himself, and of all the rest, because done in the person, and by the right of every one of them in particular. Besides, if any one, or more of them, pretend a breach of the covenant made by the sovereign at his institution; and others, or one other of his subjects, or himself alone, pretend there was no such breach, there is in this case, no judge to decide the controversy; it returns therefore to the sword again; and every man recovereth the right of protecting himself by his own strength, contrary to the design they bad in the institution. It is therefore in vain to grant sovereignty by way of precedent covenant. The opinion that any monarch receiveth his power by covenant, that is to say on condition, proceedeth from want of understanding this easy truth, that covenants being but words, and breath, have no force to oblige, contain, constrain, or protect any man, but what it has from the public sword; that is, from the untied hands of that man, or assembly of men that hath the sovereignty, and whose actions are avouched by them all, and performed by the strength of them all, in him united. But when an assembly of men is made sovereign; then no man imagineth any such covenant to have passed in the institution; for no man is so dull as to say, for example, the people of Rome, made a covenant with the Romans, to hold the sovereignty on such or such conditions; which not performed, the Romans might lawfully depose the Roman people. That men see not the reason to be alike in a monarchy, and in a popular government, proceedeth from the ambition of some, that are kinder to the government of an assembly, whereof they may hope to participate, than of monarchy, which they despair to enjoy.

5. Thirdly, because the major part hath by consenting voices declared a sovereign; he that dissented must now consent with the rest; that is, be contented to avow all the actions he shall do, or else justly be destroyed by the rest. For if he voluntarily entered into the congregation of them that were assembled, he sufficiently declared thereby his will (and therefore tacitly covenanted) to stand to what the major part should ordain: and therefore if he refuse to stand thereto, or make protestation against any of their decrees, he does contrary to his covenant, and therefore unjustly. And whether he be of the congregation, or not; and whether his consent be asked, or not, he must either submit to their decrees, or be left in the condition of war he was in before; wherein he might without injustice be destroyed by any man whatsoever.

6. Fourthly, because every subject is by this institution author of all the actions, and judgments of the sovereign instituted; it follows, that whatsoever he doth, it can be no injury to any of his subjects; nor ought he to be by any of them accused of injustice. For he that doth anything by authority from another, doth therein no injury to him by whose authority he acteth: but by this institution of a commonwealth, every particular man is author of all the sovereign doth: and consequently he that complaineth of injury from his sovereign, complaineth of that whereof he himself is author; and therefore ought not to accuse any man but himself; no nor himself of injury; because to do injury to one's self, is impossible. It is true that they that have sovereign power, may commit iniquity; but not injustice, or injury in the proper signification.

7. Fifthly, and consequently to that which was said last, no man that hath sovereign power can justly be put to death, or otherwise in any manner by his subjects punished. For seeing every subject is author of the actions of his sovereign; he punisheth another, for the actions committed by himself.

8. And because the end of this institution, is the peace and defence of them all; and whosoever has right to the end, has right to the means; it belongeth of right, to whatsoever man, or assembly that hath the sovereignty, to be judge both of the means of peace and defence; and also of the hindrances, and disturbances of the same; and to do whatsoever he shall think necessary to be done, both beforehand, for the preserving of peace and security, by prevention of discord at home, and hostility from abroad; and, when peace and security are lost, for the recovery of the same. . . .

. . .

20. But a man may here object, that the condition of subjects is very miserable; as being obnoxious to the lusts, and other irregular passions of him, or them that have so unlimited a power in their hands. And commonly they that live under a monarch, think it the fault of monarchy; and they that live under the government of democracy, or other sovereign assembly, attribute all the

inconvenience to that form of commonwealth; whereas the power in all forms, if they be perfect enough to protect them, is the same; not considering that the state of man can never be without some incommodity or other; and that the greatest, that in any form of government can possibly happen to the people in general, is scarce sensible, in respect of the miseries, and horrible calamities, that accompany a civil war; or that dissolute condition of masterless men, without subjection to laws, and a coercive power to tie their hands from rapine and revenge: nor considering that the greatest pressure of sovereign governors, proceedeth not from any delight, or profit they can expect in the damage, or weakening of their subjects, in whose vigour, consisteth their own strength and glory; but in the restiveness of themselves, that unwillingly contributing to their own defence, make it necessary for their governors to draw from them what they can in time of peace, that they may have means on any emergent occasion, or sudden need, to resist, or take advantage on their enemies. For all men are by nature provided of notable multiplying glasses (that is their passions and self-love,) through which, every little payment appeareth a great grievance; but are destitute of those prospective glasses, (namely moral and civil science,) to see afar off the miseries that hang over them, and cannot without such payments be avoided.

. . .

Chapter XXI Of the Liberty of Subjects

1. LIBERTY,[36] or FREEDOM, signifieth (properly) the absence of opposition; (by opposition, I mean external impediments of motion;) and may be applied no less to irrational, and inanimate creatures, than to rational. For whatsoever is so tied, or environed, as it cannot move, but within a certain space, which space is determined by the opposition of some external body, we say it hath not liberty to go further. And so of all living creatures, whilst they are imprisoned, or restrained, with walls, or chains; and of the water whilst it is kept in by banks, or vessels, that otherwise would spread itself into a larger space, we use to say, they are not at liberty, to move in such manner, as without those external impediments they would. But when the impediment of motion, is in the constitution of the thing itself, we use not to say, it wants the liberty; but the power to move; as when a stone lieth still, or a man is fastened to his bed by sickness.

2. And according to this proper, and generally received meaning of the word, a FREEMAN, *is he, that in those things, which by his strength and wit he is able to do, is not hindered to do what he has a will to.* But when the words *free*, and *liberty*, are applied to any thing but *bodies*,

they are abused; for that which is not subject to motion, is not subject to impediment: and therefore, when 'tis said (for example) the way is free, no liberty of the way is signified, but of those that walk in it without stop. And when we say a gift is free, there is not meant any liberty of the gift, but of the giver, that was not bound by any law, or covenant to give it. So when we *speak freely*, it is not the liberty of voice, or pronunciation, but of the man, whom no law hath obliged to speak otherwise than he did. Lastly, from the use of the word *free-will*, no liberty can be inferred of the will, desire, or inclination, but the liberty of the man; which consisteth in this, that he finds no stop, in doing what he has the will, desire, or inclination to do.[37]

3. Fear and liberty are consistent; as when a man throweth his goods into the sea for *fear* the ship should sink,[38] he doth it nevertheless very willingly, and may refuse to do it if he will: it is therefore the action, of one that was *free*: so a man sometimes pays his debt, only for *fear* of imprisonment, which because nobody hindered him from detaining, was the action of a man at *liberty*. And generally all actions which men do in commonwealths, for *fear* of the law, are actions, which the doers had *liberty* to omit.

4. *Liberty*, and *necessity* are consistent: as in the water, that hath not only *liberty*, but a *necessity* of descending by the channel; so likewise in the actions which men voluntarily do: which, because they proceed from their will, proceed from *liberty*; and yet, because every act of man's will, and every desire, and inclination proceedeth from some cause, and that from another cause, in a continual chain, (whose first link is in the hand of God the first of all causes,) they proceed from *necessity*. So that to him that could see the connection of those causes, the *necessity* of all men's voluntary actions, would appear manifest. And therefore God, that seeth, and disposeth all things, seeth also that the *liberty* of man in doing what he will, is accompanied with the *necessity* of doing that which God will, and no more, nor less.[39] For though men may do many things, which God does not command, nor is therefore author of them; yet they can have no passion, nor appetite to any thing, of which appetite God's will is not the cause. And did not his will assure the *necessity* of man's will, and consequently of all that on man's will dependeth, the *liberty* of men would be a contradiction, and impediment to the omnipotence and *liberty* of God. And this shall suffice, (as to the matter in hand) of that natural *liberty*, which only is properly called *liberty*.

5. But as men, for the attaining of peace, and conservation of themselves thereby, have made an artificial man, which we call a commonwealth; so also have they

made artificial chains, called *civil laws*, which they themselves, by mutual covenants, have fastened at one end, to the lips of that man, or assembly, to whom they have given the sovereign power; and at the other end to their own ears. These bonds in their own nature but weak, may nevertheless be made to hold, by the danger, though not by the difficulty of breaking them.

6. In relation to these bonds only it is, that I am to speak now, of the *liberty of subjects*. For seeing there is no commonwealth in the world, wherein there be rules enough to set down, for the regulating of all the actions, and words of men; (as being a thing impossible): it followeth necessarily, that in all kinds of actions, by the laws praetermitted [passed over], men have the liberty, of doing what their own reasons shall suggest, for the most profitable to themselves. For if we take liberty in the proper sense, for corporal liberty; that is to say, freedom from chains, and prison, it were very absurd for men to clamour as they do, for the liberty they so manifestly enjoy. Again, if we take liberty, for an exemption from laws, it is no less absurd, for men to demand as they do, that liberty, by which all other men may be masters of their lives. And yet as absurd as it is, this is it they demand; not knowing that the laws are of no power to protect them, without a sword in the hands of a man, or men, to cause those laws to be put in execution. The liberty of a subject, lieth therefore only in those things, which in regulating their actions, the sovereign hath praetermitted: such as is the liberty to buy, and sell, and otherwise contract with one another; to choose their own abode, their own diet, their own trade of life, and institute their children as they themselves think fit; and the like.

. . .

9. But it is an easy thing, for men to be deceived, by the specious name of liberty; and for want of judgment to distinguish, mistake that for their private inheritance, and birth-right, which is the right of the public only. And when the same error is confirmed by the authority of men in reputation for their writings on this subject, it is no wonder if it produce sedition, and change of government. In these western parts of the world, we are made to receive our opinions concerning the institution, and rights of commonwealths, from Aristotle, Cicero, and other men, Greeks and Romans, that living under popular states, derived those rights, not from the principles of nature, but transcribed them into their books, out of the practice of their own commonwealths, which were popular; as the grammarians describe the rules of language, out of the practice of the time; or the rules of poetry, out of the poems of Homer and Virgil. And because the Athenians were taught, (to keep them from desire of changing their government,) that they were freemen,

and all that lived under monarchy were slaves; therefore Aristotle puts it down in his *Politics* (lib. 6. cap. 2.): "In democracy, LIBERTY is to be supposed: for it is commonly held, that no man is FREE in any other government". And as Aristotle; so Cicero, and other writers have grounded their civil doctrine, on the opinions of the Romans, who were taught to hate monarchy, at first, by them that having deposed their sovereign, shared amongst them the sovereignty of Rome; and afterwards by their successors. And by reading of these Greek, and Latin authors, men from their childhood have gotten a habit (under a false show of liberty,) of favouring tumults, and of licentious controlling the actions of their sovereigns; and again of controlling those controllers; with the effusion of so much blood; as I think I may truly say, there was never any thing so dearly bought, as these western parts have bought the learning of the Greek and Latin tongues.

10. To come now to the particulars of the true liberty of a subject; that is to say, what are the things, which though commanded by the sovereign, he may nevertheless, without injustice, refuse to do; we are to consider, what rights we pass away, when we make a commonwealth; or (which is all one) what liberty we deny ourselves, by owning all the actions (without exception) of the man, or assembly we make our sovereign. For in the act of our *submission*, consisteth both our *obligation*, and our *liberty*; which must therefore be inferred by arguments taken from thence; there being no obligation on any man, which ariseth not from some act of his own; for all men equally, are by nature free. And because such arguments, must either be drawn from the express words, *I authorize all his actions*, or from the intention of him that submitteth himself to his power, (which intention is to be understood by the end for which he so submitteth;) the obligation, and liberty of the subject, is to be derived, either from those words, (or others equivalent;) or else from the end of the institution of sovereignty; namely, the peace of the subjects within themselves, and their defence against a common enemy.

11. First therefore, seeing sovereignty by institution, is by covenant of every one to every one; and sovereignty by acquisition, by covenants of the vanquished to the victor, or child to the parent; it is manifest, that every subject has liberty in all those things, the right whereof cannot by covenant be transferred. I have shewn before in the fourteenth chapter, that covenants, not to defend a man's own body, are void. Therefore,

12. If the sovereign command a man (though justly condemned,) to kill, wound, or maim himself; or not to resist those that assault him; or to abstain from the use of food, air, medicine, or any other thing, without which he cannot live; yet hath that man the liberty to disobey.

13. If a man be interrogated by the sovereign, or his authority, concerning a crime done by himself, he is not bound (without assurance of pardon) to confess it; because no man (as I have shown in the same chapter) can be obliged by covenant to accuse himself.

14. Again, the consent of a subject to sovereign power, is contained in these words, *I authorize, or take upon me, all his actions*; in which there is no restriction at all, of his own former natural liberty: for by allowing him to *kill me*, I am not bound to kill myself when he commands me. It is one thing to say, *kill me, or my fellow, if you please*; another thing to say, *I will kill myself, or my fellow*. It followeth therefore, that

15. No man is bound by the words themselves, either to kill himself, or any other man; and consequently, that the obligation a man may sometimes have, upon the command of the sovereign to execute any dangerous, or dishonourable office, dependeth not on the words of our submission; but on the intention, which is to be understood by the end thereof. When therefore our refusal to obey, frustrates the end for which the sovereignty was ordained; then there is no liberty to refuse: otherwise there is.[40]

16. Upon this ground, a man that is commanded as a soldier to fight against the enemy, though his sovereign have right enough to punish his refusal with death, may nevertheless in many cases refuse, without injustice; as when he substituteth a sufficient solider in his place: for in this case he deserteth not the service of the commonwealth. And there is allowance to be made for natural timorousness; not only to women, (of whom no such dangerous duty is expected,) but also to men of feminine courage. When armies fight, there is on one side, or both, a running away; yet when they do it not out of treachery, but fear, they are not esteemed to do it unjustly, but dishonourably. For the same reason, to avoid battle, is not injustice, but cowardice. But he that enrolleth himself a soldier, or taketh impressed money [advance payment], taketh away the excuse of a timorous nature; and is obliged, not only to go to the battle, but also not to run from it, without his captain's leave. And when the defence of the commonwealth, requireth at once the help of all that are able to bear arms, every one is obliged; because otherwise the institution of the commonwealth, which they have not the purpose, or courage to preserve, was in vain.

17. To resist the sword of the commonwealth, in defence of another man, guilty, or innocent, no man hath liberty; because such liberty, takes away from the sovereign, the means of protecting us; and is therefore destructive of the very essence of government. But in case a great many men together, have already resisted the sovereign power unjustly, or committed some capital crime, for which every one of them expecteth death, whether have they not the liberty then to join together, and assist, and defend one another? Certainly they have: for they but defend their lives, which the guilty man may as well do, as the innocent. There was indeed injustice in the first breach of their duty; their bearing of arms subsequent to it, though it be to maintain what they have done, is no new unjust act. And if it be only to defend their persons, it is not unjust at all. But the offer of pardon taketh from them, to whom it is offered, the plea of self-defence, and maketh their perseverance in assisting, or defending the rest, unlawful.

18. As for other liberties, they depend on the silence of the law. In cases where the sovereign has prescribed no rule, there the subject hath the liberty to do, or forbear, according to his own discretion. And therefore such liberty is in some places more, and in some less; and in some times more, in other times less, according as they that have the sovereignty shall think most convenient. As for example, there was a time, when in England a man might enter into his own land, (and dispossess such as wrongfully possessed it,) by force. But in aftertimes, that liberty of forcible entry, was taken away by a statute made (by the king) in parliament. And in some places of the world, men have the liberty of many wives: in other places, such liberty is not allowed.

19. If a subject have a controversy with his sovereign, of debt, or of right of possession of lands or goods, or concerning any service required at his hands, or concerning any penalty, corporal, or pecuniary, grounded on a precedent law; he hath the same liberty to sue for his right, as if it were against a subject; and before such judges, as are appointed by the sovereign. For seeing the sovereign demandeth by force of a former law, and not by virtue of his power; he declareth thereby, that he requireth no more, than shall appear to be due by that law. The suit therefore is not contrary to the will of the sovereign; and consequently the subject hath the liberty to demand the hearing of his cause; and sentence, according to that law. But if he demand, or take any thing by pretence of his power; there lieth, in that case, no action of law; for all that is done by him in virtue of his power, is done by the authority of every subject, and consequently he that brings an action against the sovereign, brings it against himself.

20. If a monarch, or sovereign assembly, grant a liberty to all, or any of his subjects, which grant standing, he is disabled to provide for their safety, the grant is void; unless he directly renounce, or transfer the sovereignty to another. For in that he might openly, (if it had been his will,) and in plain terms, have renounced,

or transferred it, and did not; it is to be understood it was not his will; but that the grant proceeded from ignorance of the repugnancy between such a liberty and the sovereign power: and therefore the sovereignty is still retained; and consequently all those powers, which are necessary to the exercising thereof; such as are the power of war, and peace, of judicature, of appointing officers, and councillors, of levying money, and the rest named in the eighteenth chapter.

21. The obligation of subjects to the sovereign, is understood to last as long, and no longer, than the power lasteth, by which he is able to protect them. For the right men have by nature to protect themselves, when none else can protect them, can by no covenant be relinquished. The sovereignty is the soul of the commonwealth; which once departed from the body, the members do no more receive their motion from it. The end of obedience is protection; which, wheresoever a man seeth it, either in his own, or in another's sword, nature applieth his obedience to it, and his endeavour to maintain it. And though sovereignty, in the intention of them that make it, be immortal; yet is it in its own nature, not only subject to violent death, by foreign war; but also through the ignorance, and passions of men, it hath in it, from the very institution, many seeds of a natural mortality, by intestine discord.

22. If a subject be taken prisoner in war; or his person, or his means of life be within the guards of the enemy, and hath his life and corporal liberty given him, on condition to be subject to the victor, he bath liberty to accept the condition; and having accepted it, is the subject of him that took him; because he had no other way to preserve himself. The case is the same, if he be detained on the same terms, in a foreign country. But if a man be held in prison, or bonds, or is not trusted with the liberty of his body; he cannot be understood to be bound by covenant to subjection; and therefore may, if be can, make his escape by any means whatsoever.

23. If a monarch shall relinquish the sovereignty, both for himself and his heirs; his subjects return to the absolute liberty of nature; because, though nature may declare who are his sons, and who are the nearest of his kin; yet it dependeth on his own will, (as hath been said in the precedent chapter,) who shall be his heir. If therefore he will have no heir, there is no sovereignty, nor subjection. The case is the same, if he die without known kindred, and without declaration of his heir. For then there can no heir be known, and consequently no subjection be due.

24. If the sovereign banish his subject; during the banishment, he is not subject. But he that is sent on a message, or hath leave to travel, is still subject; but it is, by contract between sovereigns, not by virtue of the covenant of subjection. For whosoever entereth into another's dominion, is subject to all the laws thereof; unless he have a privilege by the amity of the sovereigns, or by special licence.

25. If a monarch subdued by war, render himself subject to the victor; his subjects are delivered from their former obligation, and become obliged to the victor. But if he be held prisoner, or have not the liberty of his own body; he is not understood to have given away the right of sovereignty; and therefore his subjects are obliged to yield obedience to the magistrates formerly placed, governing not in their own name, but in his. For, his right remaining, the question is only of the administration; that is to say, of the magistrates and officers; which, if he have not means to name, he is supposed to approve those, which he himself had formerly appointed.

Post-Reading Questions

1. How does Hobbes understand reason and reasoning?
2. What is Hobbes' account of our natural condition in the state of nature, and our relationship to one another outside of political society? Does it seem plausible to you?
3. Why do we seek to leave the state of nature and form a society, according to Hobbes?
4. What is Hobbes' definition of power? Do you agree with it?
5. What is Hobbes' understanding of liberty, or freedom? Is it satisfactory?

CASE STUDY
THE QUEBEC STUDENT PROTEST AND BILL 78

Introduction

In the spring of 2012, large numbers of students in Quebec began a boycott of university and CÉGEP[41] classes in response to the announcement by Premier Jean Charest's government that university tuition would rise dramatically over the next several years. Although tuition would remain low in comparison to that charged in other provinces in Canada, public support for wide accessibility to higher education meant that the proposed increase met with strong disapproval in Quebec. That support, coupled with the steepness of the announced hike (75 per cent over five years), fuelled the strike by about a third of post-secondary students in the province. At its height, nearly 250,000 students boycotted classes (as well as preventing other students from attending); the largest public demonstrations in Montreal reached similar numbers.

In May 2012, the Charest government brought forth two pieces of emergency legislation that might be characterized as Hobbesian in spirit. First, a law was passed mandating the immediate suspension of the semester at those schools affected by the strike, in an attempt to end the boycott. Next, more dramatically, Bill 78 was passed by the Quebec National Assembly, placing significant restrictions on the right to demonstrate in public, as well as on the right to strike of those employed in the education sector. This emergency legislation declared illegal any strikes or gatherings within 50 metres of the outside perimeter of higher educational institutions. It further required that protestors give advance notice of proposed demonstrations and details of the venue or route, in order to receive police approval. Once in force, the law quickly led to a surge of arrests and steep fines.

Interestingly, opposition to the introduction of Bill 78 caused the student protest movement to grow into a still broader social movement: inspired by public demonstrations in Latin America, students and other citizens in Montreal and several cities in Quebec marched in the streets and banged pots and pans to register their opposition to the legislation. While some Quebecers had been prepared to accept—and even supported—a rise in tuition, the government's crackdown against protesters was much less well received. Ultimately, the furor surrounding Bill 78 led to an early election, and Premier Charest's government was soundly defeated.

Widely criticized at home and abroad for restricting the civil liberties of Quebecers, the emergency legislation enacted by the provincial government was arguably consistent with Hobbes' insistence that there can be no rights of protest or rebellion in a secure state. The liberal idea that political legitimacy depends crucially upon the right of subjects (or, later, citizens) to question the actions of the government was quite simply foreign to Hobbes' way of thinking. A viable state, for Hobbes, is one in which the sovereign enjoys uncontested political authority and absolute power, subject only to the condition that he ensure the security of his people. While Bill 78 was the act of a democratically elected government, and not the decree of a single ruler, its defence by the Charest administration was broadly consistent with three of Hobbes' core ideas: the belief that the sovereign may legitimately introduce any laws he deems consistent with the maintenance of security; the belief that such security is always more important than what we moderns would call the freedom of subjects or citizens; and the view that the sovereign (or government) cannot rightly be accused of injustice by subjects since they have consented to his authority (via the Covenant).

Andy Blatchford, "Bill 78: Quebec Student Protest Legislation 'Worst Law' Since War Measures Act, Law Professor Says"

Andy Blatchford, "Bill 78: Quebec Student Protest Legislation 'Worst Law'
Since War Measures Act, Law Professor Says," Canadian Press.
Used with permission.

There were warnings Friday from Quebec's legal community that the government's strict legislation aimed at ending the student crisis has gone too far.

One law professor even compared the controversial Bill 78 to the now-defunct War Measures Act. Other observers, meanwhile, supported the law as a way to bring calm after months of unrest.

The emergency legislation lays out stern regulations governing demonstrations and contains provisions for heavy fines for students and their federations.

Lucie Lemonde, a law professor at Université du Québec à Montréal, said Friday that she was stunned by how far the bill reaches.

"It's the worst law that I've ever seen, except for the War Measures Act," said Lemonde, referring to the notorious federal law imposed in Quebec during the 1970 FLQ crisis.

"We knew something was coming, but I didn't think they would use it to change the rules of the game in terms of the rights to demonstrate."

The legislation, set to expire after a year, is designed to deal with an immediate problem.

Tens of thousands of Quebec students have been on strike for more than three months to oppose the government's plan to hike tuition fees. Some demonstrations have led to vandalism and violent exchanges with riot police, and some students have been blocked while attempting to return to class.

While Lemonde doesn't support the tuition increases, she has found herself stuck in the middle of the occasionally aggressive dispute.

She was forced to cancel a class Wednesday when dozens of chanting, masked protesters stormed into her UQAM classroom. The school invasion, which made international headlines, left her shaken up.

Still, Lemonde said Bill 78 attacks an individual's rights to freedom of expression, association and conscience.

Other experts also questioned the bill's legality Friday.

Louis Masson, head of the provincial bar association, said in a statement that the bill violates constitutional rights. However, there were grumblings from some members of the bar that not all Quebec lawyers are quite that opposed to the law.

One Quebec lawyer said in an email to The Canadian Press that some members of the association were upset that Masson spoke on their behalf.

Also Pierre Marc Johnson, a former Parti Québécois premier, criticized an earlier statement by the association recommending mediation between the government and students.

In a letter published Friday in Montreal newspaper *La Presse*, Johnson urged the government to have the courage to take a strong stand to protect the democratic rights of law-abiding citizens. Johnson, a lawyer, warned against "improvised approaches."

Bill 78 quickly earned praise Friday from some pro-business institutions.

Michel Leblanc, president and chief executive of the Board of Trade of Metropolitan Montreal, welcomed it as a way to protect downtown businesses. Many have complained that they are suffering because of the frequent demonstrations.

Leblanc noted that fewer people have been heading to stores and restaurants in the business district since the protests started.

"The objective was to pause the troubles," he said of the bill in an interview.

"It was important to find a way to calm the city."

Leblanc also hoped the legislation would enable students who want to complete their semester to do so.

The director of an association that represents 8,000 businesses in downtown Montreal was pleased with Bill 78, but wondered what took so long for the Charest government to act.

Andre Poulin of Destination Centre-Ville said business owners have been "taken hostage" by protesters for more than three months.

"It makes no sense to let something go for that long," said Poulin. "The impact has been enormous."

But even some people who disagree with the student strike think Bill 78's measures are too repressive.

Celina Toia, a first-year UQAM law student, was physically shaken up by a protester when they rushed into her school Wednesday to disrupt the classes.

The invaders also hurled insults at her in an incident she described as "completely shocking."

While Toia believes protesters have no right acting aggressively and blocking others from going to class, she thinks the government has come down too hard on their rights.

"It goes against the principles that I abide by, which is the supremacy of law," said Toia, who doesn't support the tuition increases, either.

"Because if I were to accept this piece of legislation, I'm also denying a democratic right to someone else."

Under the Constitution's Charter of Rights and Freedoms, everyone has the right to free expression and peaceful assembly—within reasonable limits prescribed by law.

Some are arguing that Bill 78 doesn't pass the test.

The law lays out strict regulations governing demonstrations, including having to give eight hours' notice for details such as the itinerary, the duration and the time at which they are being held.

Simply offering encouragement for someone to protest at a school—either tacitly or otherwise—is subject to punishment.

Remarks from the education minister fuelled some of the confusion about the bill's potential reach.

Michelle Courchesne, less than a week in her new position, raised more than a few eyebrows by mentioning that tweets from the social network website Twitter could also be considered as encouragement to protest.

When asked to clarify, she said she would leave it up to the police's discretion to deem what was within the limits of the law. It remains unknown whether "re-tweeting" a potentially illegal message could also land others in hot water.

Toia and Lemonde both predicted the law will heighten tensions and confuse people—students and teachers.

Lemonde said some faculty members are now wondering whether it's still safe to wear red squares pinned to their clothes—a symbol of support for the anti-tuition-increase movement.

"I think people are scared," she said.

"They say, 'Just by wearing the red square, could I be charged?'"

From Bill 78: An Act to Enable Students to Receive Instruction from the Post-secondary Institutions They Attend

Bill 78: An Act to Enable Students to Receive Instruction from the Post-secondary Institutions They Attend. Introduced 18 May 2012, passed in principle 18 May 2012. Quebec. National Assembly. Bill 78. 39th Legislature, 2nd Session (18 May 2012). Quebec Official Publisher, 2012.

Explanatory Notes

The purpose of this Act is to enable students to receive instruction from the post-secondary institutions they attend. The Act suspends academic terms in progress as regards all classes interrupted and still interrupted on its coming into force. It provides for when and how classes are to resume and includes measures to ensure the validity of the 2012 winter and fall terms and the 2013 winter term. Other provisions in the Act are aimed at ensuring the continuity of instructional services as regards all other classes. The Act contains further provisions to maintain peace, order and public security as well as various administrative, civil and penal measures to ensure enforcement of the law.

The Parliament of Quebec Enacts as Follows:

Division I
Interpretation
1. In this Act . . . "federation of associations" means a body bringing together various student associations such as the Association pour une solidarité syndicale étudiante (ASSÉ), the Fédération étudiante collégiale du Québec (FECQ), the Fédération étudiante universitaire du Québec (FEUQ), and the Table de concertation étudiante du Québec as well as any coalition to which any of those student associations belong, including the CLASSE (Coalition large de l'Association pour une solidarité syndicale étudiante).

. . .

Division II
Continuity of Instructional Services
2. The 2012 winter term and, in universities, the 2012 summer term, are suspended in institutions as regards all classes interrupted during such a term and still interrupted 18 May 2012. Classes at all colleges must resume not later than 7:00 a.m. on 17 August 2012, except at CÉGEP de Maisonneuve, where classes must resume not later than 7:00 a.m. on 22 August 2012, and at CÉGEP d'Ahuntsic, where classes must resume not later than 7:00 a.m. on 30 August 2012. As for all other institutions, the suspension under the first paragraph is effective until the resumption date set by each institution, unless it cancels or has cancelled the interrupted classes.

. . .

3. Every institution and its officers and representatives must employ appropriate means to ensure that instructional services are delivered or continue to be delivered to all students having a right to such services. . . .

Division III
Provisions to Maintain Peace, Order and Public Security
16. A person, a body or a group that is the organizer of a demonstration involving 10 people or more to take place in a venue accessible to the public must, not less than eight hours before the beginning of the demonstration, provide the following information in writing to the police force serving the territory where the demonstration is to take place:

(1) the date, time, duration and venue of the demonstration as well as its route, if applicable; and

(2) the means of transportation to be used for those purposes.

The police force serving the territory where the demonstration is to take place may, before the demonstration and to maintain peace, order and public security, order a change of venue or route; the organizer must comply with the change ordered and inform the participants.

17. A person, a body or a group that is the organizer of a demonstration and a student association or a federation of associations taking part in the demonstration without being its organizer must employ appropriate means to ensure that the demonstration takes place in compliance with the information provided under subparagraph 1 of the first paragraph of section 16. . . .

Division IV
Administrative and Civil Measures
1.—Assessments, premises, and furniture
18. On noting that it is unable to deliver instructional services to all or some of the students having a right to such services, an institution must, without delay, report the situation to the minister of education, recreation and sports, including the circumstances that caused the situation, the groups of students affected and, for each of those groups, the student association to which it belongs as well as any other information that may be useful for the purposes of this Act. If the minister notes that the institution is unable to deliver instructional services as a result of a failure by a student association to comply with an obligation imposed by this Act, the minister may, despite any provision to the contrary, order the institution to cease collecting the assessment established by the student association or any successor student association and to cease providing premises, furniture, notice boards and display stands to the student association or any successor student association free of charge.

. . .

Division V
Penal Provisions
25. Anyone who contravenes section 3, the first paragraph of section 10, section 11, the second paragraph of section 12 or section 13, 14, 15, 16 or 17 is guilty of an offence and is liable, for each day or part of a day during which the contravention continues, to a fine of $1,000 to $5,000.

However, the fine is (1) $7,000 to $35,000 if the offence is committed by a senior officer, an employee or a representative, including a spokesperson, of a student association, a federation of associations or an association of employees, by a senior officer or a representative of an institution, or by a natural person who is the organizer of a demonstration; and (2) $25,000 to $125,000 if the offence is committed by a student association, a federation of associations, an association of employees or an institution, or by a legal person, a body or a group that is the organizer of a demonstration. The fines prescribed by this section are doubled for a second or subsequent offence.

26. An institution that contravenes the first paragraph of section 18 or fails to comply with an order made under that section is guilty of an offence and is liable to the fine prescribed by subparagraph 2 of the second paragraph of section 25.

27. A student association that fails to comply with an order made under section 20 is guilty of an offence and is liable to the fine prescribed by subparagraph 2 of the second paragraph of section 25.

28. An institution that fails to comply with a request made under section 34 is guilty of an offence and is liable to the fine prescribed by subparagraph 2 of the second paragraph of section 25.

29. Anyone who, by an act or omission, helps or, by encouragement, advice, consent, authorization or command, induces a person to commit an offence under this Act is guilty of the same offence and is liable to the fine prescribed by the first paragraph of section 25 or by subparagraph 1 or 2 of the second paragraph of that section if either subparagraph applies.

30. The amounts of fines set out in this Act apply in all cases and despite article 233 of the Code of Penal Procedure (R.S.Q., chapter C-25.1).

Division VI
Final Provisions

31. Judicial proceedings, including applications for an injunction, instituted before 18 May 2012 seeking an order for the delivery of instructional services to students having a right to such services may not be continued as of that date. Moreover, any judgment rendered or order issued for that purpose on the basis of such proceedings ceases to have effect on that date. This section does not prevent the institution or continuance of proceedings for contempt of court after 18 May 2012 in relation to contraventions of a judgment rendered or an order issued before that date.

32. An institution, the student association of the institution and the associations representing the employees of the institution may enter into an agreement so that students who, following a judgment or an order, including an injunction, received, before 18 May 2012, instructional services to which they had a right and are still receiving them on that date may continue receiving them.

33. An institution must provide any information the minister of education, recreation and sports requests for the purposes of this Act within the time limit the minister specifies.

34. The minister of education, recreation and sports is responsible for the administration of this Act, except Division III, the administration of which is under the responsibility of the minister of public security.

35. The provisions of this Act cease to have effect on 1 July 2013 or on any earlier date or dates set by the government.

36. This Act comes into force on 18 May 2012.

Post-Case-Reading Questions

1. Do the emergency measures enacted by Bill 78 reflect Hobbes' views on how the sovereign should respond to challenges to his political authority?
2. What values and principles might the Quebec government have been seeking to balance by introducing this emergency law? How do these compare with the political values Hobbes thought were most important?

CHAPTER V

John Locke

Introduction

John Locke is widely regarded as the most important thinker of early modern liberalism. Born in Somerset, England, in 1632, he grew up during the time of the English Civil War (1642–1651), a conflict between the Parliament and King Charles. His father, a country lawyer, served on the side of the parliamentary army during the war. Through connections forged by his service, Locke senior was able to secure a spot for his son at the top school in England (Westminster).

In 1652, Locke entered Christ Church College at Oxford, where he mastered the classics and earned bachelor and master of arts degrees. Offered a position as tutor at the college in 1661, Locke stayed on, and eventually held other positions there. He had a wide-ranging appetite for learning: as a result of his association with

John Locke

© iStockphoto.com/pictore

some prominent scientists such as Robert Boyle, Isaac Newton, and Thomas Sydenham, he developed an interest in modern sciences and began to train in medicine. Locke's early writings are surprisingly illiberal, but his ideas began to change this through his association with Lord Ashley, who became the first Earl of Shaftesbury. As Shaftesbury's personal physician and advisor from 1667, Locke was very influenced by—and soon became embroiled in—the Earl's Whig politics. When the Whig plot to assassinate King Charles II and his brother James (in the famous Rye House plot) came to light in 1683, Locke fled to Holland.

In seventeenth-century Europe, the limits on religious freedom were considerable. Holland was the only country where a person could express whichever religious creed he or she wished without fear of persecution. In 1689—after the Glorious Revolution of the previous year, the overthrow of King James II by Parliamentarians, and the installation of the Dutch prince William as King of England (William III)—Locke returned to England. Soon thereafter, he published his major works, including *Two Treatises of Government* (1689), *A Letter Concerning Toleration* (1689), and *An Essay Concerning Human Understanding* (1690). Although the latter book broadly explores the basis of human knowledge and defends an empirical epistemology, the other works deal squarely with politics and political philosophy. The *Two Treatises*, Locke's most extended discussion of the problem of political authority, is divided into two parts: the First Treatise rejects the traditional view of the legitimacy of political power as a divinely ordained right, especially as advocated by Sir Robert Filmer; and the Second Treatise goes further and famously argues—in stark contrast to Hobbes' view—that when the holders of political power fail to protect their subjects, or gravely violate their trust, the people have the right to rebel and dissolve the government.

Locke's version of social contract theory as developed in the Second Treatise is distinctive in a few respects: unlike Hobbes' highly conflictual state of nature, Locke thinks of pre-political society as a state of men living together relatively peacefully yet without a common civil authority. Reason teaches us that we all are free, equal, and independent and that no one should violate another "in his life, health, liberty or possessions." But this reason is not infallible, and disputes do arise; lacking a legitimate political authority to arbitrate these, our property is not secure. While, for Hobbes, a right to property could exist only after civil society has been established, Locke argues that the right to private property precedes civil society, for it is grounded in natural moral law. Specifically, the labour we put into cultivating that which is necessary to our own survival in the state of nature provides the basis for private ownership. Eventually, the escalation of conflicts between those laying claim to goods in the state of nature leads us to seek out the protection of a civil government that can establish impartial rules, thereby making our property (in both our person and our goods) secure. Contrary to Hobbes' absolutist view, Locke argues that since the justification for civil society is the preservation of property, when the legislative or monarch fails to do so it forfeits its power and people have the right to change the government.

A Letter Concerning Toleration was written in Latin and published as *Epistola de la Tolerantia* in Holland in 1685. It was translated into English in 1689 by Popple, a critic who argued against it. Locke's reply came in the form of two additional texts, *A Second Letter Concerning Toleration* (1690) and *A Third Letter Concerning Toleration* (1692). While he was a defender of religious toleration, prudence requires limits to this; Locke was concerned about the power of the Catholic Church and skeptical about the obedience of Catholic subjects (as well as atheists) to a civil government. The proper use of civil power, however, does not and ought not extend to the salvation of the citizens' soul. In the *Letter*, Locke argues that the power of government does not include establishing an official faith by the force of law, for law requires enforcement by penalties, and religious belief is not something that can be compelled. Locke's text defended clear limitations on, and boundaries for, the authority of both church and state. In this way, he showed how the emerging democratic apparatus of government might come to grow independent of the influence of religion, as well as how religious pluralism could exist without state persecution. The principle of separation, however, was not meant—and not understood by Locke himself—to confine all religious expressions to the private realm.

Except for *An Essay Concerning Human Understanding*, Locke published his work anonymously and only admitted authorship in his will upon his death. He died in 1704 at the age of 72.

The case that follows the reading concerns the Quebec government's decision to change the province's high school curriculum by replacing Catholic and Protestant school courses in religion and morals with a secular Ethics and Religious Culture (ERC) course. The case provides an opportunity to explore Locke's argument for separating the domains of civil authority and religion.

Further Readings

Dunn, J. (1969). *The Political Thought of John Locke*. Cambridge: Cambridge University Press.

Dunn, J. (2003). *Locke: A Very Short Introduction*. New York: Oxford University Press.

Marshall, J. (1994). *John Locke: Resistance, Religion and Responsibility*. Cambridge: Cambridge University Press.

Tully, J. (1993). *An Approach to Political Philosophy: Locke in Context*. Cambridge: Cambridge University Press.

Woolhouse, R. (2007). *Locke: A Biography*. Cambridge: Cambridge University Press.

John Locke, From *The Two Treatises of Civil Government*

John Locke, The Two Treatises of Civil Government, *edited by Thomas Hollis (London: A. Millar et al., 1764). Retrieved from the Online Library of Liberty: http://oll.libertyfund.org/?option=com_staticxt&staticfile=show.php%3Ftitle=222*

Chapter II Of the State of Nature

. . .

4. To understand political power right, and derive it from its original, we must consider, what state all men are naturally in, and that is, a *state of perfect freedom* to order their actions, and dispose of their possessions and persons, as they think fit, within the bounds of the law of nature, without asking leave, or depending upon the will of any other man.

A *state* also *of equality*, wherein all the power and jurisdiction is reciprocal, no one having more than another; there being nothing more evident, than that creatures of the same species and rank, promiscuously born to all the same advantages of nature, and the use of the same faculties, should also be equal one among another without subordination or subjection, unless the lord and master of them all should, by any manifest declaration of his will, set one above another, and confer on him, by an evident and clear appointment, an undoubted right to dominion and sovereignty.

5. This *equality* of men by nature, the judicious *Hooker* looks upon as so evident in itself, and beyond all question, that he makes it the foundation of that obligation to mutual love among men, on which he builds the duties they owe one another, and from whence he derives the great maxims *of justice* and *charity*. His words are,

> The like natural inducement hath brought men to know that it is no less their duty, to love others than themselves; for seeing those things which are equal, must needs all have one measure; if I cannot but wish to receive good, even as much at every man's hands, as any man can wish unto his own soul, how should I look to have any part of my desire herein satisfied, unless myself be careful to satisfy the like desire, which is undoubtedly in other men, being of one and the same nature? To have any thing offered them repugnant to this desire, must needs in all respects grieve them as much as me; so that if I do harm, I must look to suffer, there being no reason that others should show greater measure of love to me, than they have by me showed unto them: my desire therefore to be loved of my equals in nature, as much as possible may be, imposeth upon me a natural duty of bearing to them-wardfully the like affection; from which relation of equality between ourselves and them that are as ourselves, what several rules and canons natural reason hath drawn, for direction of life, no man is ignorant. *Eccl. Pol. Lib. 1.*

6. But though this be *a state of liberty*, yet *it is not a state of licence*: though man in that state have an uncontroulable liberty to dispose of his person or possessions, yet he has not liberty to destroy himself, or so much as any creature in his possession, but where some nobler use than its bare preservation calls for it. The *state of nature* has a law of nature to govern it, which obliges every one: and reason, which is that law, teaches all mankind, who will but consult it, that being all *equal and independent*, no one ought to harm another in his life, health, liberty, or possessions: for men being all the workmanship of one omnipotent, and infinitely wise maker; all the servants of one sovereign master, sent into the world by his order, and about his business; they are his property,

whose workmanship they are, made to last during his, not one another's pleasure: and being furnished with like faculties, sharing all in one community of nature, there cannot be supposed any such *subordination* among us, that may authorize us to destroy one another, as if we were made for one another's uses, as the inferior ranks of creatures are for ours. Every one, as he is *bound to preserve himself*, and not to quit his station wilfully, so by the like reason, when his own preservation comes not in competition, ought he, as much as he can, *to preserve the rest of mankind*, and may not, unless it be to do justice on an offender, take away, or impair the life, or what tends to the preservation of the life, the liberty, health, limb, or goods of another.

7. And that all men may be restrained from invading others rights, and from doing hurt to one another, and the law of nature be observed, which willeth the peace and *preservation of all mankind*, the *execution* of the law of nature is, in that state, put into every man's hands, whereby every one has a right to punish the transgressors of that law to such a degree, as may hinder its violation: for the *law of nature* would, as all other laws that concern men in this world, be in vain, if there were no body that in the state of nature had a *power to execute* that law, and thereby preserve the innocent and restrain offenders. And if any one in the state of nature may punish another for any evil he has done, every one may do so: for in that *state of perfect equality*, where naturally there is no superiority or jurisdiction of one over another, what any may do in prosecution of that law, every one must needs have a right to do.

8. And thus, in the state of nature, *one man comes by a power over another*; but yet no absolute or arbitrary power, to use a criminal, when he has got him in his hands, according to the passionate heats, or boundless extravagancy of his own will; but only to retribute to him, so far as calm reason and conscience dictate, what is proportionate to his transgression, which is so much as may serve for *reparation* and *restraint*: for these two are the only reasons, why one man may lawfully do harm to another, which is that we call *punishment*. In transgressing the law of nature, the offender declares himself to live by another rule than that of reason and common equity, which is that measure God has set to the actions of men, for their mutual security; and so he becomes dangerous to mankind, the tie, which is to secure them from injury and violence, being slighted and broken by him. Which being a trespass against the whole species, and the peace and safety of it, provided for by the law of nature, every man upon this score, by the right he hath to preserve mankind in general, may restrain, or where it is necessary, destroy things noxious to them, and so may bring

such evil on anyone, who hath transgressed that law, as may make him repent the doing of it, and thereby deter him, and by his example others, from doing the like mischief. And in this case, and upon this ground, *every man hath a right to punish the offender, and be executioner of the law of nature.*

. . .

11. From these *two distinct rights*, the one of *punishing* the crime *for restraint*, and preventing the like offence, which right of punishing is in every body; the other of taking *reparation*, which belongs only to the injured party, comes it to pass that the magistrate, who by being magistrate hath the common right of punishing put into his hands, can often, where the public good demands not the execution of the law, *remit* the punishment of criminal offences by his own authority, but yet cannot *remit* the satisfaction due to any private man for the damage he has received. That, he who has suffered the damage has a right to demand in his own name, and he alone can remit: the damnified person has this power of appropriating to himself the goods or service of the offender, *by right of self-preservation*, as every man has a power to punish the crime, to prevent its being committed again, *by the right he has of preserving all mankind*, and doing all reasonable things he can in order to that end: and thus it is, that every man, in the state of nature, has a power to kill a murderer, both to *deter* others from doing the like injury, which no reparation can compensate, by the example of the punishment that attends it from every body, and also to secure men from the attempts of a criminal, who having renounced reason, the common rule and measure God hath given to mankind, hath, by the unjust violence and slaughter he hath committed upon one, declared war against all mankind, and therefore may be destroyed as a *lion* or a *tiger*, one of those wild savage beasts, with whom men can have no society nor security: and upon this is grounded that great law of nature, *Whoso sheddeth man's blood, by man shall his blood be shed.* And *Cain* was so fully convinced, that every one had a right to destroy such a criminal, that after the murder of his brother, he cries out, *Every one that findeth me, shall slay me;* so plain was it writ in the hearts of all mankind.

. . .

13. To this strange doctrine, *viz.* That *in the state of nature every one has the executive power* of the law of nature, I doubt not but it will be objected, that it is unreasonable for men to be judges in their own cases, that self-love will make men partial to themselves and their friends: and on the other side, that ill nature, passion and revenge will carry them too far in punishing others; and hence nothing but confusion and disorder will follow, and that therefore God hath certainly appointed government to

restrain the partiality and violence of men. I easily grant, that *civil government* is the proper remedy for the inconveniencies of the state of nature, which must certainly be great, where men may be judges in their own case, since it is easy to be imagined, that he who was so unjust as to do his brother an injury, will scarce be so just as to condemn himself for it: but I shall desire those who make this objection, to remember, that *absolute monarchs* are but men; and if government is to be the remedy of those evils, which necessarily follow from men's being judges in their own cases, and the state of nature is therefore not to be endured, I desire to know what kind of government that is, and how much better it is than the state of nature, where one man, commanding a multitude, has the liberty to be judge in his own case, and may do to all his subjects whatever he pleases, without the least liberty to anyone to question or control those who execute his pleasure? and in whatsoever he doth, whether led by reason, mistake or passion, must be submitted to? Much better it is in the state of nature, wherein men are not bound to submit to the unjust will of another: and if he that judges, judges amiss in his own, or any other case, he is answerable for it to the rest of mankind.

14. It is often asked as a mighty objection, *where are, or ever were there any men in such a state of nature?* To which it may suffice as an answer at present, that since all princes and rulers of *independent* governments all through the world, are in a state of nature, it is plain the world never was, nor ever will be, without numbers of men in that state. I have named all governors of *independent communities*, whether they are, or are not, in league with others: for it is not every compact that puts an end to the state of nature between men, but only this one of agreeing together mutually to enter into one community, and make one body politic; other promises, and compacts, men may make one with another, and yet still be in the state of nature. The promises and bargains for truck, etc. between the two men in the desert island, mentioned by *Garcilasso de la Vega*, in his history of *Peru*; or between a *Swiss* and an *Indian*, in the woods of *America*, are binding to them, though they are perfectly in a state of nature, in reference to one another: for truth and keeping of faith belongs to men, as men, and not as members of society.

. . .

Chapter V Of Property

25. Whether we consider natural *reason*, which tells us, that men, being once born, have a right to their preservation, and consequently to meat and drink, and such other things as nature affords for their subsistence: or

revelation, which gives us an account of those grants God made of the world to *Adam*, and to *Noah*, and his sons, it is very clear, that God, as king *David* says (*Psal.* CXV. 16) *has given the earth to the children of men*; given it to mankind in common. But this being supposed, it seems to some a very great difficulty, how anyone should ever come to have a *property* in any thing: I will not content myself to answer, that if it be difficult to make out *property*, upon a supposition that God gave the world to *Adam*, and his posterity in common, it is impossible that any man, but one universal monarch, should have any *property* upon a supposition, that God gave the world to *Adam*, and his heirs in succession, exclusive of all the rest of his posterity. But I shall endeavour to show, how men might come to have a *property* in several parts of that which God gave to mankind in common, and that without any express compact of all the commoners.

26. God, who hath given the world to men in common, hath also given them reason to make use of it to the best advantage of life, and convenience. The earth, and all that is therein, is given to men for the support and comfort of their being. And though all the fruits it naturally produces, and beasts it feeds, belong to mankind in common, as they are produced by the spontaneous hand of nature; and no body has originally a private dominion, exclusive of the rest of mankind, in any of them, as they are thus in their natural state: yet being given for the use of men, there must of necessity be a *means* to *appropriate* them some way or other, before they can be of any use, or at all beneficial to any particular man. The fruit, or venison, which nourishes the wild *Indian*, who knows no enclosure, and is still a tenant in common, must be his, and so his—i.e., a part of him—that another can no longer have any right to it, before it can do him any good for the support of his life.

27. Though the earth, and all inferior creatures, be common to all men, yet every man has a *property* in his own *person*: this no body has any right to but himself. The *labour* of his body, and the *work* of his hands, we may say, are properly his. Whatsoever then he removes out of the state that nature hath provided, and left it in, he hath mixed his *labour* with, and joined to it something that is his own, and thereby makes it his *property*. It being by him removed from the common state nature hath placed it in, it hath by this *labour* something annexed to it, that excludes the common right of other men: for this *labour* being the unquestionable property of the labourer, no man but he can have a right to what that is once joined to, at least where there is enough, and as good, left in common for others.

28. He that is nourished by the acorns he picked up under an oak, or the apples he gathered from the trees

in the wood, has certainly appropriated them to himself. No body can deny but the nourishment is his. I ask then, when did they begin to be his? when he digested? or when he ate? or when he boiled? or when he brought them home? or when he picked them up? and it is plain, if the first gathering made them not his, nothing else could. That *labour* put a distinction between them and common: that added something to them more than nature, the common mother of all, had done; and so they became his private right. And will anyone say, he had no right to those acorns or apples, he thus appropriated, because he had not the consent of all mankind to make them his? Was it a robbery thus to assume to himself what belonged to all in common? If such a consent as that was necessary, man had starved, notwithstanding the plenty God had given him. We see in *commons*, which remain so by compact, that it is the taking any part of what is common, and removing it out of the state nature leaves it in, which *begins the property*; without which the common is of no use. And the taking of this or that part, does not depend on the express consent of all the commoners. Thus the grass my horse has bit; the turfs my servant has cut; and the ore I have dug in any place, where I have a right to them in common with others, become my *property*, without the assignation or consent of any body. The *labour* that was mine, removing them out of that common state they were in, hath *fixed* my *property* in them.

. . .

31. It will perhaps be objected to this, that if gathering the acorns, or other fruits of the earth, etc. makes a right to them, then anyone may *ingross* [claim possession of] as much as he will. To which I answer, Not so. The same law of nature, that does by this means give us property, does also *bound* that *property* too. *God has given us all things richly* (1 Tim. vi. 12) is the voice of reason confirmed by inspiration. But how far has he given it us? *To enjoy.* As much as anyone can make use of to any advantage of life before it spoils, so much he may by his labour fix a property in: whatever is beyond this, is more than his share, and belongs to others. Nothing was made by God for man to spoil or destroy. And thus, considering the plenty of natural provisions there was a long time in the world, and the few spenders; and to how small a part of that provision the industry of one man could extend itself, and ingross it to the prejudice of others; especially keeping within the *bounds*, set by reason, of what might serve for his *use*; there could be then little room for quarrels or contentions about property so established.

32. But the *chief matter of property* being now not the fruits of the earth, and the beasts that subsist on it, but *the earth itself*; as that which takes in and carries with it all the rest; I think it is plain, that *property* in that too is acquired as the former. *As much land* as a man tills, plants, improves, cultivates, and can use the product of, so much is his *property*. He by his labour does, as it were, enclose it from the common. Nor will it invalidate his right, to say every body else has an equal title to it; and therefore he cannot appropriate, he cannot enclose, without the consent of all his fellow-commoners, all mankind. God, when he gave the world in common to all mankind, commanded man also to labour, and the penury of his condition required it of him. God and his reason commanded him to subdue the earth, i. e. improve it for the benefit of life, and therein layout something upon it that was his own, his labour. He that in obedience to this command of God, subdued, tilled and sowed any part of it, thereby annexed to it something that was his *property*, which another had no title to, nor could without injury take from him.

. . .

33. Nor was this appropriation of any parcel of land, by improving it, any prejudice to any other man, since there was still enough, and as good left; and more than the yet unprovided could use. So that, in effect, there was never the less left for others because of his inclosure for himself: for he that leaves as much as another can make use of, does as good as take nothing at all. No body could think himself injured by the drinking of another man, though he took a good draught, who had a whole river of the same water left him to quench his thirst: and the case of land and water, where there is enough of both, is perfectly the same.

. . .

42. To make this a little clearer, let us but trace some of the ordinary provisions of life, through their several progresses, before they come to our use, and see how much they receive of their *value from human industry*. Bread, wine, and cloth are things of daily use, and great plenty; yet notwithstanding, acorns, water and leaves, or skins, must be our bread, drink, and clothing, did not *labour* furnish us with these more useful commodities: for whatever *bread* is more worth than acorns, wine than water, and *cloth* or *silk*, than leaves, skins or moss, that is wholly *owing to labour* and *industry*; the one of these being the food and raiment which unassisted nature furnishes us with; the other, provisions which our industry and pains prepare for us, which how much they exceed the other in value, when anyone hath computed, he will then see how much *labour makes the far greatest part of the value* of things we enjoy in this world: and the ground which produces the materials, is scarce to be reckoned in, as any, or at most, but a very small part of it; so little, that even among

us, land that is left wholly to nature, that hath no improvement of pasturage, tillage, or planting, is called, as indeed it is, *waste*; and we shall find the benefit of it amount to little more than nothing.

This shows how much numbers of men are to be preferred to largeness of dominions; and that the increase of lands, and the right employing of them, is the great art of government: and that prince, who shall be so wise and godlike, as by established laws of liberty to secure protection and encouragement to the honest industry of mankind, against the oppression of power and narrowness of party, will quickly be too hard for his neighbours: but this by the by. . . .

Chapter VI Of Paternal Power

. . .

54. Though I have said above, Chap. II, *That all men by nature are equal*, I cannot be supposed to understand all sorts of *equality*: *age* or *virtue* may give men a just precedency: *excellency of parts* and merit may place others above the common level: *birth* may subject some, and *alliance* or *benefits* others, to pay an observance to those to whom nature, gratitude, or other respects, may have made it due: and yet all this consists with the *equality*, which all men are in, in respect of jurisdiction or dominion one over another; which was the *equality* I there spoke of, as proper to the business in hand, being that *equal right*, that every man hath, to *his natural freedom*, without being subjected to the will or authority of any other man.

55. *Children*, I confess, are not born in this full state of *equality*, though they are born to it. Their parents have a sort of rule and jurisdiction over them, when they come into the world, and for some time after; but it is but a temporary one. The bonds of this subjection are like the swaddling clothes they art wrapt up in, and supported by, in the weakness of their infancy: age and reason as they grow up, loosen them, till at length they drop quite off, and leave a man at his own free disposal.

. . .

57. The law, that was to govern *Adam*, was the same that was to govern all his posterity, the *law of reason*. But his offspring having another way of entrance into the world, different from him, by a natural birth, that produced them ignorant and without the use of *reason*, they were not presently *under that law*; for no body can be under a law, which is not promulgated to him; and this law being promulgated or made known by *reason* only, he that is not come to the use of his *reason*, cannot be said to be *under this law*; and *Adam's* children, being not presently as soon as born *under this law of reason*, were not

presently *free*: for *law*, in its true notion, is not so much the limitation as *the direction of a free and intelligent agent* to his proper interest, and prescribes no farther than is for the general good of those under that law: could they be happier without it, the *law*, as an useless thing, would of itself vanish; and that ill deserves the name of confinement which hedges us in only from bogs and precipices. So that, however it may be mistaken, *the end of law* is not to abolish or restrain, but to *preserve and enlarge freedom*: for in all the states of created beings capable of laws, *where there is no law, there is no freedom*: for *liberty* is, to be free from restraint and violence from others; which cannot be, where there is no law: but freedom is not, as we are told, *a liberty for every man to do what he lists*: (for who could be free, when every other man's humour might domineer over him?) but a *liberty* to dispose, and order as he lists, his person, actions, possessions, and his whole property, within the allowance of those laws under which he is, and therein not to be subject to the arbitrary will of another, but freely follow his own.

58. The *power*, then, *that parents have* over their children, arises from that duty which is incumbent on them, to take care of their offspring, during the imperfect state of childhood. To inform the mind, and govern the actions of their yet ignorant nonage, till reason shall take its place, and ease them of that trouble, is what the children want, and the parents are bound to: for God having given man an understanding to direct his actions, has allowed him a freedom of will, and liberty of acting, as properly belonging thereunto, within the bounds of that law he is under. But whilst he is in an estate, wherein he has not *understanding* of his own to direct his *will*, he is not to have any *will* of his own to follow: he that *understands* for him, must *will* for him too; he must prescribe to his will, and regulate his actions; but when he comes to the estate that made his *father* a *freeman*, the *son is a freeman* too.

. . .

61. Thus we are *born free*, as we are born rational; not that we have actually the exercise of either: age, that brings one, brings with it the other too. And thus we see how *natural freedom and subjection to parents* may consist together, and are both founded on the same principle. A *child* is *free* by his father's title, by his father's understanding, which is to govern him till he hath it of his own. The *freedom of a man at years of discretion*, and the *subjection* of a child *to his parents*, whilst yet short of that age, are so consistent, and so distinguishable, that the most blinded contenders for monarchy, *by right of fatherhood*, cannot miss this *difference*; the most obstinate cannot but allow their consistency: for were their doctrine all true, were the right heir of *Adam* now known, and by that title settled a monarch in his throne, invested with

all the absolute unlimited power Sir *Robert Filmer* talks of; if he should die as soon as his heir were born, must not the *child*, notwithstanding he were never so free, never so much sovereign, be in subjection to his mother and nurse, to tutors and governors, till age and education brought him reason and ability to govern himself and others? The necessities of his life, the health of his body, and the information of his mind, would require him to be directed by the will of others, and not his own; and yet will anyone think, that this restraint and subjection were inconsistent with, or spoiled him of that liberty or sovereignty he had a right to, or gave away his empire to those who had the government of his nonage? This government over him only prepared him the better and sooner for it. If any body should ask me, when my son is *of age to be free*? I shall answer, just when his monarch is of age to govern. *But at what time,* says the judicious *Hooker,* (*Eccl Pol. 1.* i. sect. 6) *a man may be said to have attained so far forth the use of reason, as sufficeth to make him capable of those laws whereby he is then bound to guide his actions: this is a great deal more easy for sense to discern, than for anyone by skill and learning to determine.*

62. Commonwealths themselves take notice of, and allow, that there is a *time when men* are to *begin to act like free men*, and therefore till that time require not oaths of fealty, or allegiance, or other public owning of, or submission to the government of their countries.

63. The *freedom* then of man, and liberty of acting according to his own will, is *grounded* on his having *reason*, which is able to instruct him in that law he is to govern himself by, and make him know how far he is left to the freedom of his own will. To turn him loose to an unrestrained liberty, before he has reason to guide him, is not the allowing him the privilege of his nature to be free; but to thrust him out among brutes, and abandon him to a state as wretched, and as much beneath that of a man, as theirs. This is that which puts the *authority* into the *parents* hands to govern the *minority* of their children. God hath made it their business to employ this care on their offspring, and hath placed in them suitable inclinations of tenderness and concern to temper this power, to apply it, as his wisdom designed it, to the children's good, as long as they should need to be under it.

. . .

Chapter VII Of Political or Civil Society

77. God having made man such a creature, that in his own judgment, it was not good for him to be alone, put him under strong obligations of necessity, convenience, and inclination to drive him into *society*, as well as fitted him with understanding and language to continue and enjoy it. The *first society* was between man and wife, which gave beginning to that between parents and children; to which, in time, that between master and servant came to be added: and though all these might, and commonly did meet together, and make up but one family, wherein the master or mistress of it had some sort of rule proper to a family; each of these, or all together, came short of *political society*, as we shall see, if we consider the different ends, ties, and bounds of each of these.

78. *Conjugal society* is made by a voluntary compact between man and woman; and though it consist chiefly in such a communion and right in one another's bodies as is necessary to its chief end, procreation; yet it draws with it mutual support and assistance, and a communion of interests too, as necessary not only to unite their care and affection, but also necessary to their common offspring, who have a right to be nourished, and maintained by them, till they are able to provide for themselves.

79. For the end of *conjunction, between male and female*, being not barely procreation, but the continuation of the species; this conjunction betwixt male and female ought to last, even after procreation, so long as is necessary to the nourishment and support of the young ones, who are to be sustained by those that got them, till they are able to shift and provide for themselves. This rule, which the infinite wise maker hath set to the works of his hands, we find the inferior creatures steadily obey. In those viviparous animals which feed on grass, the *conjunction between male and female* lasts no longer than the very act of copulation; because the teat of the dam being sufficient to nourish the young, till it be able to feed on grass, the male only begets, but concerns not himself for the female or young, to whose sustenance he can contribute nothing. But in beasts of prey the *conjunction* lasts longer: because the dam not being able well to subsist herself, and nourish her numerous offspring by her own prey alone, a more laborious, as well as more dangerous way of living, than by feeding on grass, the assistance of the male is necessary to the maintenance of their common family, which cannot subsist till they are able to prey for themselves, but by the joint care of male and female. The same is to be observed in all birds, (except some domestic ones, where plenty of food excuses the cock from feeding, and taking care of the young brood) whose young needing food in the nest, the cock and hen continue mates, till the young are able to use their wing, and provide for themselves.

80. And herein I think lies the chief, if not the only reason, *why the male and female in mankind are tied to a longer conjunction* than other creatures, *viz.* because the female is capable of conceiving, and *de facto* is commonly with child again, and brings forth too a new birth, long

before the former is out of a dependency for support on his parents help, and able to shift for himself, and has all the assistance is due to him from his parents: whereby the father, who is bound to take care for those he hath begot, is under obligation to continue in conjugal society with the same woman longer than other creatures, whose young being able to subsist of themselves, before the time of procreation returns again, the conjugal bond dissolves of itself, and they are at liberty, till *Hymen* at his usual anniversary season summons them again to choose new mates. Wherein one cannot but admire the wisdom of the great Creator, who having given to man foresight, and an ability to lay up for the future, as well as to supply the present necessity, hath made it necessary, that *society of man and wife should be more lasting*, than of male and female among other creatures; that so their industry might be encouraged, and their interest better united, to make provision and lay up goods for their common issue, which uncertain mixture, or easy and frequent solutions of conjugal society would mightily disturb.

81. But though these are ties upon *mankind*, which make the *conjugal bonds* more firm and lasting in man, than the other species of animals; yet it would give one reason to enquire, why this *compact*, where procreation and education are secured, and inheritance taken care for, may not be made determinable, either by consent, or at a certain time, or upon certain conditions, as well as any other voluntary compacts, there being no necessity in the nature of the thing, nor to the ends of it, that it should always be for life; I mean, to such as are under no restraint of any positive law, which ordains all such contracts to be perpetual.

82. But the husband and wife, though they have but one common concern, yet having different understandings, will unavoidably sometimes have different wills too; it therefore being necessary that the last determination— i.e., the rule—should be placed somewhere; it naturally falls to the man's share, as the abler and the stronger. But this reaching but to the things of their common interest and property, leaves the wife in the full and free possession of what by contract is her peculiar right, and gives the husband no more power over her life than she has over his; the *power of the husband* being so far from that of an absolute monarch, that the *wife* has in many cases a liberty to separate from him, where natural right, or their contract allows it; whether that contract be made by themselves in the state of nature, or by the customs or laws of the country they live in; and the children upon such separation fall to the father or mother's lot, as such contract does determine.

83. For all the ends of marriage being to be obtained under politic government, as well as in the state of nature, the civil magistrate doth not abridge the right or power of either naturally necessary to those ends, *viz.* procreation and mutual support and assistance while they are together; but only decides any controversy that may arise between man and wife about them. If it were otherwise, and that absolute *sovereignty* and power of life and death naturally belonged to the husband, and were *necessary to the society between man and wife*, there could be no matrimony in any of those countries where the husband is allowed no such absolute authority. But the ends of matrimony requiring no such power in the husband, the condition of *conjugal society* put it not in him, it being not at all necessary to that state. *Conjugal society* could subsist and attain its ends without it; nay, community of goods, and the power over them, mutual assistance and maintenance, and other things belonging to *conjugal society*, might be varied and regulated by that contract which unites man and wife in that society, as far as may consist with procreation and the bringing up of children till they could shift for themselves; nothing being necessary to any society, that is not necessary to the ends for which it is made.

. . .

85. *Master* and *servant* are names as old as history, but given to those of far different condition; for a freeman makes himself a servant to another, by selling him, for a certain time, the service he undertakes to do, in exchange for wages he is to receive: and though this commonly puts him into the family of his master, and under the ordinary discipline thereof; yet it gives the master but a temporary power over him, and no greater than what is contained in the *contract* between them. But there is another sort of servants, which by a peculiar name we call *slaves*, who being captives taken in a just war, are by the right of nature subjected to the absolute dominion and arbitrary power of their masters. These men having, as I say, forfeited their lives, and with it their liberties, and lost their estates; and being in the *state of slavery*, not capable of any property, cannot in that state be considered as any part of *civil society*; the chief end whereof is the preservation of property.

86. Let us therefore consider a *master of a family* with all these subordinate relations of *wife, children, servants,* and *slaves*, united under the domestic rule of a family; which, what resemblance soever it may have in its order, offices, and number too, with a little commonwealth, yet is very far from it, both in its constitution, power and end: or if it must be thought a monarchy, and the *paterfamilias* the absolute monarch in it, absolute monarchy will have but a very shattered and short power, when it is plain, by what has been said before, that the *master of the family* has a very distinct and differently limited *power*,

both as to time and extent, over those several persons that are in it; for excepting the slave (and the family is as much a family, and his power as *paterfamilias* as great, whether there be any slaves in his family or no) he has no legislative power of life and death over any of them, and none too but what a *mistress of a family* may have as well as he. And he certainly can have no absolute power over the whole *family*, who has but a very limited one over every individual in it. But how *a family*, or any other society of men, differ from that which is properly *political society*, we shall best see, by considering wherein *political society* itself consists.

87. Man being born, as has been proved, with a title to perfect freedom, and an uncontrolled enjoyment of all the rights and privileges of the law of nature, equally with any other man, or number of men in the world, hath by nature a power, not only to preserve his property, that is, his life, liberty and estate, against the injuries and attempts of other men; but to judge of, and punish the breaches of that law in others, as he is persuaded the offence deserves, even with death itself, in crimes where the heinousness of the fact, in his opinion, requires it. But because no *political* society can be, nor subsist, without having in itself the power to preserve the property, and in order thereunto, punish the offences of all those of that society; there, and there only is *political society*, where every one of the members hath quitted this natural power, resigned it up into the hands of the community in all cases that exclude him not from appealing for protection to the law established by it. And thus all private judgment of every particular member being excluded, the community comes to be umpire, by settled standing rules, indifferent, and the same to all parties; and by men having authority from the community, for the execution of those rules, decides all the differences that may happen between any members of that society concerning any matter of right; and punishes those offences which any member hath committed against the society, with such penalties as the law has established: whereby it is easy to discern, who are, and who are not, in *political society* together. Those who are united into one body, and have a common established law and judicature to appeal to, with authority to decide controversies between them, and punish offenders, are in *civil society* one with another: but those who have no such common people, I mean on earth, are still in the state of nature, each being, where there is no other, judge for himself, and executioner; which is, as I have before showed it, the perfect *state of nature*.

88. And thus the commonwealth comes by a power to set down what punishment shall belong to the several transgressions which they think worthy of it, committed among the members of that society, (which is the *power of making laws*) as well as it has the power to punish any injury done unto any of its members, by anyone that is not of it, (which is the *power of war and peace*;) and all this for the preservation of the property of all the members of that society, as far as is possible. But though every man who has entered into civil society, and is become a member of any commonwealth, has thereby quitted his power to punish offences, against the law of *nature*, in prosecution of his own private judgment, yet with the judgment of offences, which he has given up to the legislative in all cases, where he can appeal to the magistrate, he has given a right to the commonwealth to employ his force, for the execution of the judgments of the commonwealth, whenever he shall be called to it; which indeed are his own judgments, they being made by himself, or his representative. And herein we have the original of the *legislative* and *executive power* of civil society, which is to judge by standing laws, how far offences are to be punished, when committed within the commonwealth; and also to determine, by occasional judgments founded on the present circumstances of the fact, how far injuries from without are to be vindicated; and in both these to employ all the force of all the members, when there shall be need.

89. Wherever therefore any number of men are so united into one society, as to quit every one his executive power of the law of nature, and to resign it to the public, there and there only is a *political*, or *civil society*. And this is done, whereever any number of men, in the state of nature, enter into society to make one people, one body politic, under one supreme government; or else when anyone joins himself to, and incorporates with any government already made: for hereby he authorizes the society, or which is all one, the legislative thereof, to make laws for him, as the public good of the society shall require; to the execution whereof, his own assistance (as to his own decrees) is due. And this *puts men* out of a state of nature *into* that of a *commonwealth*, by setting up a judge on earth, with authority to determine all the controversies, and redress the injuries that may happen to any member of the commonwealth; which judge is the legislative, or magistrates appointed by it. And wherever there are any number of men, however associated, that have no such decisive power to appeal to, there they are still in *the state of nature*.

90. Hence it is evident, that *absolute monarchy*, which by some men is counted the only government in the world, is indeed *inconsistent with civil society*, and so can be no form of civil government at all: for the end *of civil society*, being to avoid, and remedy those inconveniencies of the state of nature, which necessarily follow from every man's being judge in his own case, by setting

up a known authority, to which every one of that society may appeal upon any injury received, or controversy that may arise, and which every one of the society ought to obey; wherever any persons are, who have not such an authority to appeal to, for the decision of any difference between them, there those persons are still in *the state of nature*; and so is every *absolute prince*, in respect of those who are under his *dominion*.

Chapter VIII Of the Beginning of Political Societies

95. Men being, as has been said, by nature, all free, equal, and independent, no one can be put out of this estate, and subjected to the political power of another, without his own consent. The only way whereby anyone divests himself of his natural liberty, and puts on the *bonds of civil society*, is by agreeing with other men to join and unite into a community, for their comfortable, safe, and peaceable living one among another, in a secure enjoyment of their properties, and a greater security against any, that are not of it. This any number of men may do, because it injures not the freedom of the rest; they are left as they were in the liberty of the state of nature. When any number of men have so *consented to make one community* or *government*, they are thereby presently incorporated and make *one body politic*, wherein the *majority* have a right to act and conclude the rest.

96. For when any number of men have, by the consent of every individual, made a *community*, they have thereby made that *community* one body, with a power to act as one body, which is only by the will and determination of the *majority*: for that which acts any community, being only the consent of the individuals of it, and it being necessary to that which is one body to move one way; it is necessary the body should move that way whither the greater force carries it, which is the *consent of the majority*: or else it is impossible it should act or continue one body, *one community*, which the consent of every individual that united into it, agreed that it should; and so every one is bound by that consent to be concluded by the *majority*. And therefore we see, that in assemblies, empowered to act by positive laws, where no number is set by that positive law which empowers them, the *act of the majority* passes for the act of the whole, and of course determines, as having, by the law of nature and reason, the power of the whole.

97. And thus every man, by consenting with others to make one body politic under one government, puts himself under an obligation, to every one of that society, to submit to the determination of the *majority*, and to be concluded by it; or else this *original compact*, whereby he with others incorporates into *one society*, would signify nothing, and be no compact, if he be left free, and under no other ties than he was in before in the state of nature. For what appearance would there be of any compact? what new engagement if he were no farther tied by any decrees of the society, than he himself thought fit, and did actually consent to? This would be still as great a liberty, as he himself had before his compact, or anyone else in the state of nature hath, who may submit himself, and consent to any acts of it if he thinks fit.

98. For if *the consent of the majority* shall not, in reason, be received as *the act of the whole*, and conclude every individual; nothing but the consent of every individual can make any thing to be the act of the whole: but such a consent is next to impossible ever to be had, if we consider the infirmities of health, and avocations of business, which in a number, though much less than that of a commonwealth, will necessarily keep many away from the public assembly. To which if we add the variety of opinions, and contrariety of interests, which unavoidably happen in all collections of men, the coming into society upon such terms would be only like *Cato's* coming into the theatre, only to go out again. Such a constitution as this would make the mighty *Leviathan* of a shorter duration, than the feeblest creatures, and not let it outlast the day it was born in: which cannot be supposed, till we can think, that rational creatures should desire and constitute societies only to be dissolved: for where the *majority* cannot conclude the rest, there they cannot act as one body, and consequently will be immediately dissolved again.

99. Whosoever therefore out of a state of nature unite into a *community*, must be understood to give up all the power, necessary to the ends for which they unite into society, to the *majority* of the community, unless they expressly agreed in any number greater than the majority. And this is done by barely agreeing to *unite into one political society*, which is *all the compact* that is, or needs be, between the individuals, that enter into, or make up a *commonwealth*. And thus that, which begins and actually *constitutes any political society*, is nothing but the consent of any number of freemen capable of a majority to unite and incorporate into such a society. And this is that, and that only, which did, or could give beginning to any *lawful government* in the world.

. . .

104. But to conclude, reason being plain on our side, that men are naturally free, and the examples of history showing, that the *governments* of the world, that were begun in peace, had their beginning laid on that foundation, and were *made by the consent of the people*; there

can be little room for doubt, either where the right is, or what has been the opinion, or practice of mankind, about the *first erecting of government*.

. . .

106. Thus, though looking back as far as records give us any account of peopling the world, and the history of nations, we commonly find the government to be in one hand; yet it destroys not that which I affirm, *viz.* that they beginning of politic society depends upon the consent of the individuals, to join into, and make one society; who, when they are thus incorporated, might set up what form of government they thought fit. But this having given occasion to men to mistake, and think, that by nature government was monarchical, and belonged to the father, it may not be amiss here to consider, why people in the beginning generally pitched upon this form, which though perhaps the father's pre-eminence might, in the first institution of some commonwealths, give a rise to, and place in the beginning, the power in one hand; yet it is plain that the reason, that continued the form of *government in a single person*, was not any regard, or respect to paternal authority; since all petty *monarchies*, that is, almost all monarchies, near their original, have been commonly, at least upon occasion, *elective*.

. . .

116. This has been the practice of the world from its first beginning to this day; nor is it now any more hindrance to the freedom of mankind, that they are *born under constituted and ancient polities*, that have established laws, and set forms of government, than if they were born in the woods, among the unconfined inhabitants, that run loose in them: for those, who would persuade us, that *by being born under any government, we are naturally subjects* to it, and have no more any title or pretence to the freedom of the state of nature, have no other reason (bating that of paternal power, which we have already answered) to produce for it, but only, because our fathers or progenitors passed away their natural liberty, and thereby bound up themselves and their posterity to a perpetual subjection to the government, which they themselves submitted to. It is true, that whatever engagements or promises anyone has made for himself, he is under the obligation of them, but *cannot*, by any *compact* whatsoever, *bind his children* or *posterity*: for his son, when a man, being altogether as free as the father, any *act of the father can no more give away the liberty of the son*, than it can of any body else: he may indeed annex such conditions to the land, he enjoyed as a subject of any commonwealth, as may oblige his son to be of that community, if he will enjoy those possessions which were his father's; because that estate being his father's property, he may dispose, or settle it, as he pleases.

. . .

119. *Every man* being, as has been shown, *naturally free*, and nothing being able to put him into subjection to any earthly power, but only his own *consent*; it is to be considered, what shall be understood to be a *sufficient declaration* of a man's *consent*, to *make him subject* to the laws of any government. There is a common distinction of an express and a tacit consent, which will concern our present case. No body doubts but an express *consent*, of any man entering into any society, makes him a perfect member of that society, a subject of that government. The difficulty is, what ought to be looked upon as a *tacit consent*, and how far it binds, i.e. how far anyone shall be looked on to have consented, and thereby submitted to any government, where he has made no expressions of it at all. And to this I say, that every man, that hath any possessions, or enjoyment, of any part of the dominions of any government, doth thereby give his *tacit consent*, and is as far forth obliged to obedience to the laws of that government, during such enjoyment, as anyone under it; whether this his possession be of land, to him and his heirs for ever, or a lodging only for a week; or whether it be barely travelling freely on the highway; and in effect, it reaches as far as the very being of anyone within the territories of that government.

. . .

121. But since the government has a direct jurisdiction only over the land, and reaches the possessor of it, (before he has actually incorporated himself in the society) only as he dwells upon, and enjoys that; the obligation anyone is under, by virtue of such enjoyment, to *submit to the government, begins and ends with the enjoyment*; so that whenever the owner, who has given nothing but such a *tacit consent* to the government, will, by donation, sale, or otherwise, quit the said possession, he is at liberty to go and incorporate himself into any other commonwealth; or to agree with others to begin a new one, *in vacuis locis*, in any part of the world, they can find free and unpossessed: whereas he, that has once, by actual agreement, and any *express* declaration, given his *consent* to be of any commonwealth, is, perpetually and indispensibly obliged to be, and remain unalterably a subject to it, and can never be again in the liberty of the state of nature; unless, by any calamity, the government he was under comes to be dissolved; or else by some public act cuts him off from being any longer a member of it.

122. But submitting to the laws of any country, living quietly, and enjoying privileges and protection under them, *makes not a man a member of that society*: this is only a local protection and homage due to and from all those, who, not being in a state of war, come within the territories belonging to any government, to all parts whereof

the force of its laws extends. But this no more *makes a man a member of that society*, a perpetual subject of that commonwealth, than it would make a man a subject to another, in whose family he found it convenient to abide for some time; though, whilst he continued in it, he were obliged to comply with the laws, and submit to the government he found there. And thus we see, that *foreigners*, by living all their lives under another government, and enjoying the privileges and protection of it, though they are bound, even in conscience, to submit to its administration, as far forth as any denison; yet do not thereby come to be *subjects* or *members of that commonwealth*. Nothing can make any man so, but his actually entering into it by positive engagement, and express promise and compact. This is that, which I think, concerning the beginning of political societies, and that consent *which makes anyone a member* of any commonwealth.

. . .

Chapter IX Of the Ends of Political Society and Government

123. If man in the state of nature be so free, as has been said; if he be absolute lord of his own person and possessions, equal to the greatest, and subject to no body, why will he part with his freedom? why will he give up this empire, and subject himself to the dominion and control of any other power? To which it is obvious to answer, that though in the state of nature he hath such a right, yet the enjoyment of it is very uncertain, and constantly exposed to the invasion of others: for all being kings as much as he, every man his equal, and the greater part no strict observers of equity and justice, the enjoyment of the property he has in this state is very unsafe, very unsecure. This makes him willing to quit a condition, which, however free, is full of fears and continual dangers: and it is not without reason, that he seeks out, and is willing to join in society with others, who are already united, or have a mind to unite, for the mutual *preservation* of their lives, liberties and estates, which I call by the general name, *property*.

124. The great and *chief end*, therefore, of men's uniting into commonwealths, and putting themselves under government, is *the preservation of their property*. To which in the state of nature there are many things wanting.

First, there wants an *established*, settled, known *law*, received and allowed by common consent to be the standard of right and wrong, and the common measure to decide all controversies between them: for though the law of nature be plain and intelligible to all rational creatures; yet men being biased by their interest, as well as ignorant for want of study of it, are not apt to allow of it

as a law binding to them in the application of it to their particular cases.

125. *Secondly*, in the state of nature there wants a *known and indifferent judge*, with authority to determine all differences according to the established law: for every one in that state being both judge and executioner of the law of nature, men being partial to themselves, passion and revenge is very apt to carry them too far, and with too much heat, in their own cases; as well as negligence, and unconcernedness, to make them too remiss in other men's.

126. *Thirdly*, in the state of nature there often wants *power* to back and support the sentence when right, and to *give* it due *execution*. They who by any injustice offended, will seldom fail, where they are able, by force to make good their injustice; such resistance many times makes the punishment dangerous, and frequently destructive, to those who attempt it.

127. Thus mankind, notwithstanding all the privileges of the state of nature, being but in an ill condition, while they remain in it, are quickly driven into society. Hence it comes to pass, that we seldom find any number of men live any time together in this state. The inconveniencies that they are therein exposed to, by the irregular and uncertain exercise of the power every man has of punishing the transgressions of others, make them take sanctuary under the established laws of government, and therein seek *the preservation of their property*. It is this makes them so willingly give up every one his single power of punishing, to be exercised by such alone, as shall be appointed to it among them; and by such rules as the community, or those authorized by them to that purpose, shall agree on. And in this we have the original *right and rise of both the legislative and executive power*, as well as of the governments and societies themselves.

. . .

131. But though men, when they enter into society, give up the equality, liberty, and executive power they had in the state of nature, into the hands of the society, to be so far disposed of by the legislative, as the good of the society shall require; yet it being only with an intention in every one the better to preserve himself, his liberty and property; (for no rational creature can be supposed to change his condition with an intention to be worse) the power of the society, or *legislative* constituted by them, can *never be supposed to extend farther, than the common good*; but is obliged to secure every one's property, by providing against those three defects above mentioned, that made the state of nature so unsafe and uneasy. And so whoever has the legislative or supreme power of any commonwealth, is bound to govern by established *standing laws*, promulgated and known to the

people, and not by extemporary decrees; by *indifferent and upright judges*, who are to decide controversies by those laws; and to employ the force of the community at home, *only in the execution of such laws*, or abroad to prevent or redress foreign injuries, and secure the community from inroads and invasion. And all this to be directed to no other *end*, but the *peace, safety*, and *public good* of the people.

. . .

Chapter XI Of the Extent of the Legislative Power

134. The great end of men's entering into society, being the enjoyment of their properties in peace and safety, and the great instrument and means of that being the laws established in that society; the *first and fundamental positive law* of all commonwealths *is the establishing of the legislative* power; as the *first and fundamental natural law*, which is to govern even the legislative itself, *is the preservation of the society*, and (as far as will consist with the public good) of every person in it. This *legislative* is not only *the supreme power* of the commonwealth, but sacred and unalterable in the hands where the community have once placed it; nor can any edict of any body else, in what form soever conceived, or by what power soever backed, have the force and obligation of a *law*, which has not its *sanction from* that *legislative* which the public has chosen and appointed: for without this the law could not have that, which is absolutely necessary to its being a *law*,[1] *the consent of the society*, over whom no body can have a power to make laws, but by their own consent, and by authority received from them; and therefore all the *obedience*, which by the most solemn ties anyone can be obliged *to* pay, ultimately terminates in this *supreme power*, and is directed by those laws which it enacts: nor can any oaths to any foreign power whatsoever, or any domestic subordinate power, discharge any member of the society from his *obedience to the legislative*, acting pursuant to their trust; nor oblige him to any obedience contrary to the laws so enacted, or farther than they do allow; it being ridiculous to imagine one can be tied ultimately to *obey* any *power* in the society, which is not the *supreme*.

135. Though the *legislative*, whether placed in one or more, whether it be always in being, or only by intervals, though it be the *supreme* power in every commonwealth; yet,

First, it is *not*, nor can possibly be absolutely *arbitrary* over the lives and fortunes of the people: for it being but the joint power of every member of the society given up to that person, or assembly, which is legislator; it can be no more than those persons had in a state of nature before they entered into society, and gave up to the community: for no body can transfer to another more power than he has in himself; and no body has an absolute arbitrary power over himself, or over any other, to destroy his own life, or take away the life or property of another. A man, as has been proved, cannot subject himself to the arbitrary power of another; and having in the state of nature no arbitrary power over the life, liberty, or possession of another, but only so much as the law of nature gave him for the preservation of himself, and the rest of mankind; this is all he doth, or can give up to the commonwealth, and by it to the *legislative power*, so that the legislative can have no more than this. Their power, in the utmost bounds of it, is *limited* to *the public good* of the society. It is a power, that hath no other end but preservation, and therefore can never[2] have a right to destroy, enslave, or designedly to impoverish the subjects. The obligations of the law of nature cease not in society, but only in many cases are drawn closer, and have by human laws known penalties annexed to them, to enforce their observation. Thus the law of nature stands as an eternal rule to all men, *legislators* as well as others. The *rules* that they make for other men's actions, must, as well as their own and other men's actions, be conformable to the law of nature, i.e., to the will of God, of which that is a declaration, and the *fundamental law of nature being the preservation of mankind*, no human sanction can be good, or valid against it.

136. *Secondly*,[3] the *legislative*, or supreme authority, cannot assume to its self a power to rule by extemporary arbitrary decrees, but *is bound to dispense justice*, and decide the rights of the subject *by promulgated standing laws, and known authorized judges*: for the law of nature being unwritten, and so no where to be found but in the minds of men, they who through passion or interest shall miscite, or misapply it, cannot so easily be convinced of their mistake where there is no established judge: and so it serves not, as it ought, to determine the rights, and fence the properties of those that live under it, especially where every one is judge, interpreter, and executioner of it too, and that in his own case: and he that has right on his side, having ordinarily but his own single strength, hath not force enough to defend himself from injuries, or to punish delinquents. To avoid these inconveniencies, which disorder men's properties in the state of nature, men unite into societies, that they may have the united strength of the whole society to secure and defend their properties, and may have *standing rules* to bound it, by which every one may know what is his. To this end it is that men give up all their natural power to the society which they enter into, and the community put the legislative power into such hands as they think

fit, with this trust, that they shall be governed by *declared laws*, or else their peace, quiet, and property will still be at the same uncertainty, as it was in the state of nature.

137. Absolute arbitrary power, or governing without *settled standing laws*, can neither of them consist with the ends of society and government, which men would not quit the freedom of the state of nature for, and tie themselves up under, were it not to preserve their lives, liberties and fortunes, and by *stated rules* of right and property to secure their peace and quiet. It cannot be supposed that they should intend, had they a power so to do, to give to anyone, or more, an *absolute arbitrary power* over their persons and estates, and put a force into the magistrate's hand to execute his unlimited will arbitrarily upon them. This were to put themselves into a worse condition than the state of nature, wherein they had a liberty to defend their right against the injuries of others, and were upon equal terms of force to maintain it, whether invaded by a single man, or many in combination. Whereas by supposing they have given up themselves to the *absolute arbitrary power* and will of a legislator, they have disarmed themselves, and armed him, to make a prey of them when he pleases; he being in a much worse condition, who is exposed to the arbitrary power of one man, who has the command of 100,000, than he that is exposed to the arbitrary power of 100,000 single men; no body being secure, that his will, who has such a command, is better than that of other men, though his force be 100,000 times stronger. And therefore, whatever form the commonwealth is under, the ruling power ought to govern by *declared* and *received laws*, and nor by extemporary dictates and undetermined resolutions: for then mankind will be in a far worse condition than in the state of nature, if they shall have armed one, or a few men with the joint power of a multitude, to force them to obey at pleasure the exorbitant and unlimited decrees of their sudden thoughts, or unrestrained, and till that moment unknown wills, without having any measures set down which may guide and justify their actions: for all the power the government has, being only for the good of the society, as it ought not to be *arbitrary* and at pleasure, so it ought to be exercised by *established and promulgated laws*; that both the people may know their duty, and be safe and secure within the limits of the law; and the rulers too kept within their bounds, and not be tempted, by the power they have in their hands, to employ it to such purposes, and by such measures, as they would not have known, and own not willingly.

. . .

139. But *government*, into whatsoever hands it is put, being, as I have before shown, entrusted with this condition, *and for this end*, that men might have and secure their *properties*; the prince, or senate, however it may have power to make laws, for the regulating of *property* between the subjects one among another, yet can never have a power to take to themselves the whole, or any part of the subjects *property*, without their own consent: for this would be in effect to leave them no *property* at all. And to let us see, that even *absolute power*, where it is necessary, is *not arbitrary* by being absolute, but is still limited by that reason, and confined to those ends, which required it in some cases to be absolute, we need look no further than the common practice of martial discipline: for the preservation of the army, and in it of the whole commonwealth, requires an *absolute obedience* to the command of every superior officer, and it is justly death to disobey or dispute the most dangerous or unreasonable of them; but yet we see, that neither the sergeant, that could command a soldier to march up to the mouth of a cannon, or stand in a breach, where he is almost sure to perish, can command that soldier to give him one penny of his money; nor the *general*, that can condemn him to death for deserting his post, or for not obeying the most desperate orders, can yet, with all his *absolute power* of life and death, dispose of one farthing of that soldier's estate, or seize one jot of his goods; whom yet he can command any thing, and hang for the least disobedience; because such a blind obedience is necessary to that end, for which the commander has his power, *viz.* the preservation of the rest; but the disposing of his goods has nothing to do with it.

140. It is true, governments cannot be supported without great charge, and it is fit every one who enjoys his share of the protection, should payout of his estate his proportion for the maintenance of it. But still it must be with his own consent, i.e., the consent of the majority, giving it either by themselves, or their representatives chosen by them: for if anyone shall claim a *power* to *lay* and levy *taxes* on the people, by his own authority, and without such consent of the people, he thereby invades the *fundamental law of property*, and subverts the end of government: for what property have I in that, which another may by right take, when he pleases, to himself?

141. *Fourthly*, the *legislative cannot transfer the power of making laws* to any other hands: for it being but a delegated power from the people, they who have it cannot pass it over to others. The people alone can appoint the form of the commonwealth, which is by constituting the legislative, and appointing in whose hands that shall be. And when the people have said, We will submit to rules, and be governed by *laws* made by such men, and in such forms, no body else can say other men shall make *laws* for them; nor can the people be bound by any *laws*, but such as are enacted by those whom they have chosen, and authorized to make *laws* for them. The power of the

legislative, being derived from the people by a positive voluntary grant and institution, can be no other than what that positive grant conveyed, which being only to make *laws*, and not to make *legislators*, the *legislative* can have no power to transfer their authority of making laws, and place it in other hands.

142. These are the *bounds* which the trust, that is put in them by the society, and the law of God and nature, have *set to the legislative* power of every commonwealth, in all forms of government.

First, they are to govern by *promulgated established laws*, not to be varied in particular cases, but to have one rule for rich and poor, for the favourite at court, and the country man at plough.

Secondly, these *laws* also ought to be designed *for* no other end ultimately, but *the good of the people*.

Thirdly, they must *not raise taxes* on the *property of the people, without the consent of the people*, given by themselves, or their deputies. And this properly concerns only such governments where the *legislative* is always in being, or at least where the people have not reserved any part of the legislative to deputies, to be from time to time chosen by themselves.

Fourthly, the *legislative* neither must *nor can transfer the power of making laws* to any body else, or place it any where, but where the people have.

. . .

Chapter XIX Of the Dissolution of Government

211. He that will with any clearness speak of the *dissolution of government*, ought in the first place to distinguish between the *dissolution of the society* and the *dissolution of the government*. That which makes the community, and brings men out of the loose state of nature, into *one politic society*, is the agreement which every one has with the rest to incorporate, and act as one body, and so be one distinct commonwealth. The usual, and almost only way whereby *this union is dissolved*, is the inroad of foreign force making a conquest upon them: for in that case, (not being able to maintain and support themselves, as *one entire* and *independent body*) the union belonging to that body which consisted therein, must necessarily cease, and so every one return to the state he was in before, with a liberty to shift for himself, and provide for his own safety, as he thinks fit, in some other society. Whenever the *society is dissolved*, it is certain the government of that society cannot remain. Thus conquerors swords often cut up governments by the roots, and mangle societies to pieces, separating the subdued or scattered multitude from the protection of, and dependence on, that society

which ought to have preserved them from violence. The world is too well instructed in, and too forward to allow of, this way of dissolving of governments, to need any more to be said of it; and there wants not much argument to prove, that where the *society is dissolved*, the government cannot remain; that being as impossible, as for the frame of an house to subsist when the materials of it are scattered and dissipated by a whirl-wind, or jumbled into a confused heap by an earthquake.

212. Besides this over-turning from without, *governments are dissolved from within*,

First, when the *legislative* is *altered*. Civil society being a state of peace, among those who are of it, from whom the state of war is excluded by the umpirage, which they have provided in their legislative, for the ending all differences that may arise among any of them, it is in their *legislative*, that the members of a commonwealth are united, and combined together into one coherent living body. This is *the soul that gives form, life, and unity*, to the commonwealth: from hence the several members have their mutual influence, sympathy, and connexion: and therefore, when the *legislative* is broken, or *dissolved*, dissolution and death follows: for the *essence and union of the society* consisting in having one will, the legislative, when once established by the majority, has the declaring, and as it were keeping of that will. The *constitution of the legislative* is the first and fundamental act of society, whereby provision is made for the *continuation of their union*, under the direction of persons, and bonds of laws, made by persons authorized thereunto, by the consent and appointment of the people, without which no one man, or number of men, among them, can have authority of making laws that shall be binding to the rest. When anyone, or more, shall take upon them to make laws, whom the people have not appointed so to do, they make laws without authority, which the people are not therefore bound to obey; by which means they come again to be out of subjection, and may constitute to themselves a *new legislative*, as they think best, being in full liberty to resist the force of those, who without authority would impose any thing upon them. Everyone is at the disposure of his own will, when those who had, by the delegation of the society, the declaring of the public will, are excluded from it, and others usurp the place, who have no such authority or delegation.

. . .

221. There is therefore, secondly, another way whereby *governments are dissolved*, and that is, when the legislative, or the prince, either of them, act contrary to their trust.

First, the *legislative acts against the trust* reposed in them, when they endeavour to invade the property of the subject, and to make themselves, or any part of the community, masters, or arbitrary disposers of the lives, liberties, or fortunes of the people.

222. The reason why men enter into society, is the preservation of their property; and the end why they choose and authorize a legislative, is, that there may be laws made, and rules set, as guards and fences to the properties of all the members of the society, to limit the power, and moderate the dominion, of every part and member of the society: for since it can never be supposed to be the will of the society, that the legislative should have a power to destroy that which every one designs to secure, by entering into society, and for which the people submitted themselves to legislators of their own making; whenever the *legislators endeavour to take away, and destroy the property of the people*, or to reduce them to slavery under arbitrary power, they put themselves into a state of war with the people, who are thereupon absolved from any farther obedience, and are left to the common refuge, which God hath provided for all men, against force and violence. Whensoever therefore the *legislative* shall transgress this fundamental rule of society; and either by ambition, fear, folly or corruption, *endeavour to grasp* themselves, or *put into the hands of any other, an absolute power* over the lives, liberties, and estates of the people; by this breach of trust they forfeit *the power* the people had put into their hands for quite contrary ends, and it devolves to the people, who have a right to resume their original liberty, and, by the establishment of a new legislative, (such as they shall think fit) provide for their own safety and security, which is the end for which they are in society. What I have said here, concerning the legislative in general, holds true also concerning the supreme executor, who having a double trust put in him, both to have a part in the legislative, and the supreme execution of the law, acts against both, when he goes about to set up his own arbitrary will as the law of the society. He *acts* also *contrary to his trust*, when he either employs the force, treasure, and offices of the society, to corrupt the *representatives*, and gain them to his purposes; or openly pre-engages the *electors*, and prescribes to their choice, such, whom he has, by solicitations, threats, promises, or otherwise, won to his designs; and employs them to bring in such, who have promised beforehand what to vote, and what to enact. Thus to regulate candidates and electors, and new-model the ways of election, what is it but to cut up the government by the roots, and poison the very fountain of public security? For the people having reserved to themselves the choice of their *representatives*, as the fence to their properties, could do it for no other end, but that they might always be freely chosen, and

so chosen, freely act, and advise, as the necessity of the commonwealth, and the public good should, upon examination, and mature debate, be judged to require. This, those who give their votes before they hear the debate, and have weighed the reasons on all sides, are not capable of doing. To prepare such an assembly as this, and endeavour to set up the declared abettors of his own will, for the true *representatives* of the people, and the lawmakers of the society, is certainly as great a *breach of trust*, and as perfect a declaration of a design to subvert the government, as is possible to be met with. To which, if one shall add rewards and punishments visibly employed to the same end, and all the arts of perverted law made use of, to take off and destroy all that stand in the way of such a design, and will not comply and consent to betray the liberties of their country, it will be past doubt what is doing. What power they ought to have in the society, who thus employ it contrary to the trust went along with it in its first institution, is easy to determine; and one cannot but see, that he, who has once attempted any such thing as this, cannot any longer be trusted.

223. To this perhaps it will be said, that the people being ignorant, and always disconnected, to lay the foundation of government in the unsteady opinion an uncertain humour of the people, is to expose it to certain ruin; and *no government will be able long to subsist*, if the people may set up a new legislative, whenever they take offence at the old one. To this I answer, Quite the contrary. People are not so easily got out of their old forms, as some are apt to suggest. . . .

. . .

225. *Secondly*, I answer, such *revolutions happen* not upon every little mismanagement in public affairs. *Great mistakes* in the ruling part, many wrong and inconvenient laws, and all the *slips* of human frailty, will be *born by the people* without mutiny or murmur. But if a long train of abuses, prevarications and artifices, all tending the same way, make the design visible to the people, and they cannot but feel what they lie under, and see whither they are going; it is not to be wondered, that they should then rouse themselves, and endeavour to put the rule into such hands which may secure to them the ends for which government was at first erected; and without which, ancient names, and specious forms, are so far from being better, that they are much worse, than the state of nature, or pure anarchy; the inconveniencies being all as great and as near, but the remedy farther off and more difficult.

. . .

229. The end of government is the good of mankind; and which is *best for mankind*, that the people should be

always exposed to the boundless will of tyranny, or that the rulers should be sometimes liable to be opposed, when they grow exorbitant in the use of their power, and employ it for the destruction, and not the preservation of the properties of their people?

. . .

232. Whosoever uses *force without right*, as every one does in society, who does it without law, puts himself into a *state of war* with those against whom he so uses it; and in that state all former ties are cancelled, all other rights cease, and every one has a right to defend himself, and to *resist the aggressor*. . . .

. . .

240. Here, it is like, the common question will be made, *Who shall be judge*, whether the prince or legislative act contrary to their trust? This, perhaps, ill-affected and factious men may spread among the people, when the prince only makes use of his due prerogative. To this I reply, *The people shall be judge*; for who shall be *judge* whether his trustee or deputy acts well, and according to the trust reposed in him, but he who deputes him, and must, by having deputed him, have still a power to discard him, when he fails in his trust? If this be reasonable in particular cases of private men, why should it be otherwise in that of the greatest moment, where the welfare of millions is concerned, and also where the evil, if not prevented, is greater, and the redress very difficult, dear, and dangerous?

241. But further, this question, (*Who shall be judge?*) cannot mean, that there is no judge at all: for where there is no judicature on earth, to decide controversies among men, *God* in heaven is *judge*. He alone, it is true, is judge of the right. But *every man* is *judge* for himself, as in all other cases, so in this, whether another hath put himself into a state of war with him, and whether he should appeal to the Supreme Judge, as *Jeptha* did.

242. If a controversy arise betwixt a prince and some of the people, in a matter where the law is silent, or doubtful, and the thing be of great consequence, I should think the proper *umpire*, in such a case, should be the body of the *people*: for in cases where the prince hath a trust reposed in him, and is dispense from the common ordinary rules of the law; there, if any men find themselves aggrieved, and think the prince acts contrary to, or beyond that trust, who so proper to *judge* as the body of the *people*, (who, at first, lodged that trust in him) how far they meant it should extend? But if the prince, or whoever they be in the administration, decline that way of determination, the appeal then lies no where but to heaven; force between either persons, who have no known superior on earth, or which permits no appeal to a judge on earth, being properly a state of war, wherein the appeal lies only to heaven; and in that state the *injured party must judge* for himself, when he will think fit to make use of that appeal, and put himself upon it.

243. To conclude, The *power that every individual gave the society*, when he entered into it, can never revert to the individuals again, as long as the society lasts, but will always remain in the community; because without this there can be no community, no commonwealth, which is contrary to the original agreement: so also when the society hath placed the legislative in any assembly to men, to continue in them and their successors, with direction and authority for providing such successors, *the legislative can never revert to the people* whilst that government lasts; because having provided a legislative with power to continue for ever, they have given up their political power to continue for ever, they have given up their political power to the legislative, and cannot resume it. But if they have set limits to the duration of their legislative, and made this supreme power in any person, or assembly, only temporary; or else, when by the miscarriages of those in authority, it is forfeited; upon the forfeiture, or at the determination of the time set, *it reverts to the society*, and the people have a right to act as supreme, and continue the legislative in themselves; or erect a new form, or under the old form place it in new hands, as they think good.

FINIS

John Locke, *A Letter Concerning Toleration*

John Locke, A Letter Concerning Toleration, *edited by James Tully*
(Indianapolis: Hackett, 1983).

A Letter Concerning Toleration

Honoured Sir,

Since you are pleased to inquire what are my thoughts about the mutual toleration of Christians in their different professions of religion, I must needs answer you freely, that I esteem that toleration to be the chief characteristic mark of the true church. For whatsoever some people boast of the antiquity of places and names, or of the pomp of their outward worship; others, of the reformation of their discipline; all, of the orthodoxy of their faith; (for every one is orthodox to himself). These things, and all others of this nature, are much rather marks of men striving for power and empire over one another, than of the Church of Christ. Let any one have never so true a claim to all these things, yet if he be destitute of charity, meekness, and goodwill in general toward all mankind, even to those that are not Christians, he is certainly yet short of being a true Christian himself. *The Kings of the Gentiles exercise Lordship over them,* said our Saviour to his Disciples, *but ye shall not be so.*[4] The business of true religion is quite another thing. It is not instituted in order to the erecting of an external pomp, not to the obtaining of ecclesiastical dominion, nor to the exercising of compulsive forces; but to the regulating of men's loves according to the rules of virtue and piety. Whosoever will lift himself under the banner of Christ, must in the first place, and above all things, make war upon his own lusts and vices. It is in vain for any man to usurp the name of Christian, without holiness of life, purity of manners, and benignity and meekness of spirit. *Let every one that nameth the name of Christ, depart from iniquity.*[5] *Thou, when thou art converted, strengthen thy brethren,*[6] said our *Lord* to *Peter.* It would indeed be very hard for one that appears careless about his own salvation, to persuade me that he were extremely concerned for mine. For it is impossible that those should sincerely and heartily apply themselves to make other people Christians, who have not really embraced the Christian religion in their own hearts. If the gospel and the apostles may be credited, no man can be

a Christian without *charity*, and without *that faith which works*, not by force, but by *love.* Now I appeal to the consciences of those that persecute, torment, destroy, and kill other men upon pretence of religion, whether they do it out of friendship and kindness toward them, or no: and I shall then indeed, and not till then, believe they do so, when I shall see those fiery zealots correcting, in the same manner, their friends and familiar acquaintance, for the manifest sins they commit against the precepts of the gospel; when I shall see them prosecute with fire and sword the members of their own communion that are tainted with enormous vices, and without amendment are in danger of eternal perdition; and when I shall see them thus express their love and desire of the salvation of their souls, by the infliction of torments, and exercise of all manner of cruelties. For if it be out of a principle of charity, as they pretend, and love to men's souls, that they deprive them of their estates, maim them with corporal punishments, starve and torment them in noisome prisons, and in the end even take away their lives; I say, if all this be done merely to make men christians, and procure their salvation, why then do they suffer *whoredom, fraud, malice, and such like enormities,*[7] which (according to the apostle) manifestly relish of heathenish corruption, to predominate so much and abound among their flocks and people? These, and such like things, are certainly more contrary to the glory of God, to the purity of the church, and to the salvation of souls, than any conscientious dissent from ecclesiastical decisions, or separation from public worship, whilst accompanied with innocence of life. Why then does this burning zeal for God, for the church, and for the salvation of souls; burning, I say, literally, with fire and faggot; pass by those moral vices and wickednesses, without any chastisement, which are acknowledged by all men to be diametrically opposite to the profession of Christianity; and bend all its nerves either to the introducing of ceremonies, or to the establishment of opinions, which for the most part are about nice and intricate matters, that exceed the capacity of ordinary understandings? Which of the parties contending about these things is in the right, which of them is guilty of schism or heresy, whether those that domineer or those that suffer, will then at last be manifest, when the cause of their separation comes to be judged of. He certainly that follows Christ, embraces his doctrine, and bears his yoke, though he forsake both father and mother, separate from the public assemblies and ceremonies of his country, or whomsoever, or whatsoever else he relinquishes, will not then be judged a heretic.

Now, though the divisions that are among sects should be allowed to be never so obstructive of the salvation of souls, yet nevertheless *adultery, fornication, uncleanness, lasciviousness, idolatry, and such like things, cannot be denied to be works of the flesh*; concerning which the apostle has expressly declared, that *they who do them shall not inherit the kingdom of God.*[8] Whosoever therefore is sincerely solicitous about the kingdom of God, and think it his duty to endeavour the enlargement of it among men, ought to apply himself with no less care and industry to the rooting out of these immoralities, than to the extirpation of sects. But if and one do otherwise, and whilst he is cruel and implacable toward those that differ from him in opinion, he be indulgent to such iniquities and immoralities as are unbecoming the name of a Christian, let such a one talk never so much of the church, he plainly demonstrates by his actions, that 'tis another kingdom he aims at, and not the advancement of the kingdom of God.

That any man should think fit to cause another man whose salvation he heartily desires, to expire in torment and that even in an unconverted estate, would, I confess, seem very strange to me, and, I think, to any other also. But nobody, surely, will ever believe that such a carriage can proceed from charity, love, or goodwill. If anyone maintain that men ought to be compelled by fire and sword to profess certain doctrines, and conform to this or that exterior worship, without any regard had unto their morals; if anyone endeavour to convert them that are erroneous unto the faith, by forcing them to profess things that they do not believe, and allowing them to practise things that the gospel does not permit; it can not be doubted indeed but such a one is desirous to have a numerous assembly joined in the same profession with himself; but that he principally intends by those men to compose a truly Christian church, is altogether incredible. It is not therefore to be wondered at, if those do not really contend for the advancement of the true religion, and of the Church of Christ, make use of arms that do not belong to the Christian warfare. If, like the captain of our salvation, they sincerely desired the good of souls, they would tread in the steps, and follow the perfect example of that prince of peace, who sent out his soldiers to the subduing of nations, and gathering them into his church, not armed with the sword, or other instruments of force, but prepared with the gospel of peace, and with the exemplary holiness of their conversation. This was his method. Though if infidels were to be converted by force, if those that are either blind or obstinate were to be drawn off from their errors by armed soldiers, we know very well that it was much more easy for him to do it with armies of heavenly legions, than for any son of the church, how potent soever, with all his dragoons.

The toleration of those that differ from others in matters of religion, is so agreeable to the gospel of Jesus Christ, and to the genuine reason of mankind, that it seems monstrous for men to be so blind, as not here tax the pride and ambition of some, the passion and uncharitable zeal of others. These are faults from which humane affairs can perhaps scarce ever be perfectly freed; but yet such as no body will bear the plain imputation of, without covering them with some specious colour; and so pretend to commendation, whilst they are carried away by their own irregular passions. But however, that some may not colour their spirit of persecution and unchristian cruelty with a pretence of care of the public weal, and observation of the laws; and that others, under pretence of religion, may not seek impunity for their libertinism and licentiousness; in a word, that none may impose either upon himself or others, by the pretences of loyalty and obedience to the prince, or of tenderness and sincerity in the worship of God; I esteem it above all things necessary to distinguish exactly the business of civil government from that of religion, and to settle the just bounds that lie between the one and the other. If this be not done, there can be no end put to the controversies that will be always arising, between those that have, or at least pretend to have, on the one side, a concernment for the interest of men's souls, and on the other side, a care of the commonwealth.

The commonwealth seems to me to be a society of men constituted only for the procuring, preserving, and advancing of their own *civil interests*.

Civil interests I call life, liberty, health, and indolence of body; and the possession of outward things, such as money, lands, houses, furniture, and the like.

It is the duty of the civil magistrate, by the impartial execution of equal laws, to secure unto all the people in general, and to every one of his subjects in particular, the just possession of these things belonging to this life. If any one presume to violate the laws of public justice and equity, established for the preservation of those things, his presumption is to be checked by the fear of punishment, consisting of the deprivation or diminution of those civil interests, or goods, which otherwise he might and ought to enjoy. But seeing no man does willingly suffer himself to be punished by the deprivation of any part of his goods, and much less his liberty or life, therefore is the magistrate armed with the force and strength of all his subjects, in order to the punishment of those that violate any other man's rights.

Now that the whole jurisdiction of the magistrate reaches only to these civil concernments; and that all civil power, right and dominion, is bounded and confined to the only care of promoting these things; and that it neither can no ought in any manner to be extended to the salvation of souls, these following considerations seem unto me abundantly to demonstrate.

First, because the care of souls is not committed to the civil magistrate, any more than to other men. It is not committed unto him, I say, by God; because it appears not that God has ever given any such authority to one man over another, as to compel any one to his religion. Nor can such power be vested in the magistrate by the *consent of the people*; because no man can so far abandon the care of his own salvation, as blindly to leave it to the choice of any other, whether prince or subject, to prescribe to him what faith or worship he shall embrace. For no man can, if he would, conform his faith to the dictates of another. All the life and power of true religion consists in the inward and full persuasion of the mind; and faith is not faith without believing. Whatever profession we make, to whatever outward worship we conform, if we are not fully satisfied in our own mind that the one it true, and the other well pleasing unto God, such profession and such practice, far from being any furtherance, are indeed great obstacles to our salvation. For in this manner, instead of expiating other sins by the exercise of religion, I say in offering thus unto God almighty such a worship as we esteem to be displeasing unto him, we add unto the number of our other sins, those also of hypocrisy, and contempt of his divine majesty.

In the second place, the care of souls cannot belong to the civil magistrate, because his power consists only in outward force; but true and saving religion consists in the inward persuasion of the mind, without which nothing can be acceptable to God. And such is the nature if the understanding, that it cannot be compelled to the belief of any thing by outward force. Confiscation of estate, imprisonment, torments, nothing of that nature can have any such efficacy as to make men change the inward judgment that they have framed of things.

It may indeed be alleged, that the magistrate may make use of arguments, and thereby draw the heterodox into the way of truth, and procure their salvation. I grant it; but this is common to him with other men. In teaching, instructing, and redressing the erroneous by reason, he may certainly do what becomes any good man to do.

Magistracy does not oblige him to put off either humanity or christianity. But it is one thing to persuade, another to command; one thing to press with arguments, another with penalties. The civil power alone has a right to do; to the other goodwill is authority enough. Every man has commission to admonish, exhort, convince another of error, and by reasoning to draw him into truth: but to give laws, receive obedience, and compel with the sword, belongs to none but the magistrate. And upon this ground I affirm, that the magistrate's power extends not to the establishing of any articles of faith, or forms of worship, by the force of his laws. For laws are of no force at all without penalties, and penalties in this case are absolutely impertinent; because they are not proper to convince the mind. Neither the profession of any articles of faith, nor the conformity to any outward form of worship (as has already been said) can be available to the salvation of souls, unless the truth of the one, and the acceptableness of the other unto God, be thoroughly believed by those that so profess and practise. But penalties are no ways capable to produce such belief. It is only light and evidence that can work a change on men's opinions; which light can in no manner proceed from corporal sufferings, or any other outward penalties.

In the third place, the care of the salvation of mens' souls cannot belong to the magistrate; because, though the rigour of laws and the force of penalties were capable to convince and change men's minds, yet would not that help at all to the salvation of their souls. For there being but one truth, one way to heaven; what hopes is there that more men would be led into it, if they had no rule but the religion of the court, and were put under a necessity to quit the light of their own reason, and oppose the dictates of their own consciences, and blindly to resign up themselves to the will of their governors, and to the religion, which either ignorance, ambition, or superstition had chanced to establish in the countries where they were born? In the variety and contradiction of opinions in religion, wherein the princes of the world are as much divided as in their secular interests, the narrow way would be much straitened; one country alone would be in the right, and all the rest of the world put under an obligation of following their princes in the ways that lead to destruction; and that which heightens the absurdity, and very ill suits the notion of a deity, men would owe their eternal happiness or misery to the places of their nativity.

These considerations, to omit many others that might have been urged to the same purpose, seem unto me sufficient to conclude that all the power of civil government relates only to men's civil interests, is confined to the care of the things of this world, and hath nothing to do with the world to come.

Let us now consider what a church is. A church then I take to be a voluntary society of men, joining themselves together of their own accord, in order to the public worshipping of God, in such a manner as they judge acceptable to him, and effectual to the salvation of their souls.

I say it is a free and voluntary society. No body is born a member of any church; otherwise the religion of parents would descend unto children, by the same right of inheritance as their temporal estates, and everyone would hold his faith by the same tenure he does his lands; than which nothing can be imagined more absurd. Thus therefore that matter stands. No man by nature is bound unto any particular church or sect, but every one joins himself voluntarily to that society in which he believes he has found that profession and worship which is truly acceptable to God. The hopes of salvation, as it was the only cause of his entrance into that communion, so it can be the only reason of his stay there. For if afterwards he discover any thing either erroneous in the doctrine, or incongruous in the worship of that society to which he has joined himself, why should it not be as free for him to go out as it was to enter? No member of a religious society can be tied with any other bonds but what proceed from the certain expectation of eternal life. A church then is a society of members voluntarily uniting to this end.

It follows now that we consider what is the power of this church, and unto what laws it is subject.

Forasmuch as no society, how free soever, or upon whatsoever slight occasion instituted, (whether of philosophers for learning, of merchants for commerce, or of men of leisure for mutual conversation and discourse,) no church or company, I say, can in the least subsist and hold together, but will presently dissolve and break to pieces, unless it be regulated by some laws, and the members all consent to observe some order. Place, and time of meeting must be agreed on; rules for admitting and excluding members must be establisht; distinction of officers, and putting things into a regular course, and such like, cannot be omitted. But since the joining together of several members into this church-society, as has already been demonstrated, is absolutely free and spontaneous, it necessarily follows, that the right of making its laws can belong to none but the society it self, or at least (which is the same thing) to those whom the society by common consent has authorized thereunto.

Some perhaps may object, that no such society can be said to be a true church, unless it have in it a bishop, or presbyter, with ruling authority derived from the very apostles, and continued down unto the present times by an uninterrupted succession.

To these I answer. *In the first place*, let them show me the edict by which Christ has imposed that law upon his church. And let not any man think me impertinent if, in a thing of this consequence, I require that the terms of that edict be very express and positive. For the promise he has made us, that *wheresoever two or three are gathered together in his name, he will be in the midst of them,*[9] seems to imply the contrary. Whether such an assembly want any thing necessary to a true church, pray do you consider. Certain I am, that nothing can be there wanting unto the salvation of souls; which is sufficient to our purpose.

Next, pray observe how great have always been the divisions among even those who lay so much stress upon the divine institution, and continued succession of a certain order of rulers in the church. Now their very dissention unavoidably puts us upon a necessity of deliberating, and consequently allows a liberty of choosing that, which upon consideration, we prefer.

And in the last place, I consent that these men have a ruler of their church, established by such a long series of succession as they judge necessary; provided I may have liberty at the same time to join my self to that society, in which I am persuaded those things are to be found which are necessary to the salvation of my soul. In this manner ecclesiastical liberty will be preserved on all sides, and no man will have a legislator imposed upon him, but whom himself has chosen.

But since men are so solicitous about the true church, I would only ask them, here by the way, if it be not more agreeable to the Church of Christ, to make the conditions of her communion consist in such things, and such things only, as the holy spirit has in the holy scriptures declared, in express words, to be necessary to salvation; I ask, I say, whether this be not more agreeable to the Church of Christ, than for men to impose their own inventions and interpretations upon others, as if they were of divine authority, and to establish by ecclesiastical laws, as absolutely necessary to the profession of Christianity, such things as the holy scriptures do either not mention, or at least not expressly command. Whosoever requires those things in order to ecclesiastical communion, which Christ does not require in order to life eternal, he may perhaps indeed constitute a society accommodated to his own opinion and his own advantage, but how that can be called the Church of Christ, which is established upon laws that are not his, and which excludes such persons from its communion as he will one day receive into the kingdom of heaven, I understand not. But this being not a proper place to enquire into the marks of the true church, I will only mind those that contend so earnestly for the decrees of their own society, and that cry out continually the church, the church, with as much noise, and perhaps upon the same principle, as the *Ephesian* silversmiths did for their *Diana*: this, I say, I desire to mind them of, that the gospel frequently declares that the true disciples of Christ must suffer persecution; but that the Church of Christ should persecute others, and force others by fire and sword, to embrace her faith and doctrine, I could never yet find in any of the books of the new testament.

The end of a religious society (as has already been said) is the public worship of God, and by means thereof the acquisition of eternal life. All discipline ought therefore to tend to that end, and all ecclesiastical laws to be thereunto confined. Nothing ought, nor can be transacted in this society, relating to the possession of civil and worldly goods. No force is here to be made use of, upon any occasion whatsoever: for force belongs wholly to the civil magistrate, and the possession of all outward goods is subject to his jurisdiction.

But it may be asked, by what means then shall ecclesiastical laws be established, if they must be thus destitute of all compulsive power? I answer, they must be established by means suitable to the nature of such things, whereof the external profession and observation, if not proceeding from a thorough conviction and approbation of the mind, is altogether useless and unprofitable. The arms by which the members of this society are to be kept within their duty, are exhortations, admonitions, and advices. If by these means the offenders will not be reclaimed, and the erroneous convinced, there remains nothing farther to be done, but that such stubborn and obstinate persons, who give no ground to hope for their reformation, should be cast out and separated from the society. This is the last and utmost force of ecclesiastical authority: no other punishment can thereby be inflicted, than that the relation ceasing between the body and the member which is cut off, the person so condemned ceases to be a part of the church.

These things being thus determined, let us inquire in the next place, how far the duty of toleration extends, and what is required from every one by it.

And first, I hold, that no church is bound by the duty of toleration to retain any such person in her bosom, as, after admonition, continues obstinately to offend against the laws of the society. For these being the condition of communion, and the bond of the society, if the breach of them were permitted without any animadversion, the society would immediately be thereby dissolved. But nevertheless, in all such cases care is to be taken that the sentence of excommunication, and the execution thereof, carry with it no rough usage, of word or action, whereby the ejected person may any wise be damnified in body or estate. For all force (as has often been said) belongs only to the magistrate, nor ought any private persons, at any time, to use force; unless it be in self-defence against unjust violence. Excommunication

neither does, nor can, deprive the excommunicated person of any of those civil goods that he formerly possessed. All those things belong to the civil government, and are under the magistrate's protection. The whole force of excommunication consists only in this that, the resolution of the society in that respect being declared, the union that was between the body and some member comes thereby to be dissolved, and that relation ceasing, the participation of some certain things, which the society communicated to is members, and unto which no man has any civil right, comes also to cease. For there is no civil injury done unto the excommunicated person, by the church-minister's refusing him bread and wine, in the celebration of the lord's supper, which was not bought with his, but other men's money.

Secondly, no private person has any right, in any manner, to prejudice another person in his civil enjoyments, because he is of another church or religion. All the rights and franchises that belong to him as a man, or as a denison, are inviolably to be preserved to him. These are not the business of religion. No violence nor injury is to be offered him, whether he be Christian or pagan. Nay, we must not content our selves with the narrow measures of bare justice: charity, bounty, and liberality must be added to it. This the gospel enjoins, this reason directs, and this that natural fellowship we are born into requires of us. If any man err from the right way, it is his own misfortune, no injury to thee: nor therefore art thou to punish him in the things of this life, because thou supposes he will be miserable in that which is to come.

What I say concerning the mutual toleration of private persons differing from one another in religion, I understand also of particular churches; which stand as it were in the same relation to each other as private persons among themselves, nor has any one of them any manner of jurisdiction over any other, no not even when the civil magistrate (as it sometimes happens) comes to be of this or the other communion. For the civil government can give no new right to the church, nor the church to the civil government. So that whether the magistrate join himself to any church, or separate from it, the church remains always as it was before, a free and voluntary society. It neither acquires the power of the sword by the magistrate's coming to it, nor does it lose the right of instruction and excommunication by his going from it. This is the fundamental and immutable right of a spontaneous society, that is has power to remove any of its members who transgress the rules of its institution: but it cannot, by the accession of any new members, acquire any right of jurisdiction over those that are not joined with it. And therefore peace, equity, and friendship, are always mutually to be observed by particular churches, in the same manner as by private persons, without any pretence of superiority or jurisdiction over one another.

That the thing may be made yet clearer by an example: let us suppose two churches, the one of *Armenians*, the other of *Calvinists*, residing in the city of *Constantinople*. Will anyone say, that either of these churches has right to deprive the members of the other of their estates and liberty, (as we see practised elsewhere) because of their differing from it in some doctrines or ceremonies; whilst the *Turks* in the mean while silently stand by, and laugh to see with what inhumane cruelty Christians thus rage against Christians? But if one of these churches hath this power of treating the other ill, I ask which of them it is to whom that power belongs, and by what right? It will be answered, undoubtedly, that it is the orthodox church which has the right of authority over the erroneous or heretical. This is, in great and specious words, to say just nothing at all. For every church is orthodox to it self; to others, erroneous or heretical. For whatsoever any church believes, it believes to be true; and the contrary unto those things, it pronounces to be error. So that the controversy between these churches about the truth of their doctrines, and the purity of their worship, is on both sides equal; nor is there any judge, either at *Constantinople*, or elsewhere upon earth, by whose sentence it can be determined. The decision of that question belongs only to the supreme judge of all men, to whom also alone belongs the punishment of the erroneous. In the mean while, let those men consider how heinously they sin, who, adding injustice, if not to their error yet certainly to their pride, do rashly and arrogantly take upon them to misuse the servants of another master, who are not at all accountable to them.

Nay, further: if it could be manifest which of these two dissenting churches were in the right, there would not accrue thereby unto the orthodox any right of destroying the other. For churches have neither any jurisdiction in worldly matters, nor are fire and sword any proper instruments wherewith to convince men's minds of error, and inform them of the truth. Let us suppose, nevertheless, that the civil magistrate inclined to favour one of them, and to put his sword into their hands, that (by his consent) they might chastise the dissenters as they pleased. Will any man say, that any right can be derived unto a Christian church, over its brethren, from a Turkish emperor? An infidel, who has himself no authority to punish Christians for the articles of their faith, cannot confer such an authority upon any society of Christians, nor give unto them a right which he has not himself. This would be the case at *Constantinople*. And the reason of the thing is the same in any Christian kingdom. The civil power is the same in every place: nor can

that power, in the hands of a Christian prince, confer any greater authority upon the church, than in the hands of a heathen; which is to say, just none at all.

Nevertheless, it is worthy to be observed, and lamented, that the most violent of these defenders of the truth, the opposers of errors, the exclaimers against schism, do hardly ever let loose this their zeal for God, with which they are so warmed and inflamed, unless where they have the civil magistrate on their side. But so soon as ever court favour has given them the better end of the staff, and they begin to feel themselves the stronger, then presently peace and charity are to be laid aside: otherwise, they are religiously to be observed. Where they have not the power to carry on persecution, and to become masters, there they desire to live upon fair terms, and preach up toleration. When they are not strengthened with the civil power, then they can bear most patiently, and unmovedly, the contagion of idolatry, superstition, and heresy, in their neighbourhood; of which, in other occasions, the interest of religion makes them to be extremely apprehensive. They do not forwardly attack those errors which are in fashion at court, or are countenanced by the government. Here they can be content to spare their arguments: which yet (with their leave) is the only right method of propagating truth, which has no such way of prevailing, as when strong arguments and good reason, are joined with the softness of civility and good usage.

Nobody therefore, in fine, neither single persons, nor churches. Nay, nor even commonwealths, have any just title to invade the civil rights and worldly goods of each other, upon pretence of religion. Those that are of another opinion would do well to consider with themselves how pernicious a seed of discord and war, how powerful a provocation to endless hatreds, rapines, and slaughters, they thereby furnish unto mankind. No peace and security, no not so much as common friendship, can ever be established or preserved among men, so long as this opinion prevails, that *dominion is founded in grace*, and that religion is to be propagated by force of arms.

In the third place, let us see what the duty of toleration requires from those who are distinguished from the rest of mankind, (from the laity, as they please to call us) by some ecclesiastical character, and office; whether they be bishops, priests, presbyters, ministers, or however else dignified or distinguished. It is not my business to inquire here into the original of the power or dignity of the clergy. This only I say, that whence-soever their authority be sprung, since it is ecclesiastical, it ought to be confined within the bounds of the church, nor can it in any manner be extended to civil affairs; because the church it self is a thing absolutely separate and distinct from the commonwealth. The boundaries on both sides are fixed and immovable. He jumbles heaven and earth together, the things most remote and opposite, who mixes these two societies; which are in their original, end, business, and in every thing, perfectly distinct, and infinitely different from each other. No man, therefore, with whatsoever ecclesiastical office he be dignified, can deprive another man that is not of his church and faith, either of liberty, or of any part of his worldly goods, upon the account of that difference between them in religion. For whatsoever is not lawful to the whole church, cannot, by any ecclesiastical right, become lawful to any of its members.

But this is not all. It is not enough that ecclesiastical men abstain from violence and rapine, and all manner of persecution. He that pretends to be a successor of the apostles, and takes upon him the office of teaching, is obliged also to admonish his hearers of the duties of peace, and goodwill toward all men; as well toward the erroneous as the orthodox; toward those that differ from them in faith and worship, as well as toward those that agree with them therein: and he ought industriously to exhort all men, whether private persons or magistrates, (if any such there be in his church) to charity, meekness, and toleration; and diligently endeavour to allay and temper all that heat, and unreasonable averseness of mind, which either any mans fiery zeal for his own sect, or the craft of others, has kindled against dissenters. I will not undertake to represent how happy and how great would be the fruit, both in church and state, if the pulpits everywhere founded with this doctrine of peace and toleration; lest I should seem to reflect too severely upon those men whose dignity I desire not to detract from, nor would have it diminished either by others or themselves. But this I say, that thus it ought to be. And if any one that professes himself to be a minister of the word of God, a preacher of the gospel of peace, teach otherwise, he either understands not, or neglects the business of his calling, and shall one day give account thereof unto the prince of peace. If Christians are to be admonished that they abstain from all manner of revenge, even after repeated provocations and multiplied injuries, how much more ought they who suffer nothing, who have had no harm done them, forbear violence, and abstain from all manner of ill usage toward those from whom they have received none. This caution and temper they ought certainly to use toward those who mind only their own business, and are solicitous for nothing but that (whatever men think of them) they may worship God in that manner which they are persuaded is acceptable to him, and in which they have the strongest hopes of eternal salvation. In private domestic affairs, in the management of estates, in the conservation of bodily health, every man may consider what suits his own convenience, and follow what course he likes best. No man complains of the ill management of his neighbour's affairs. No man is angry with another for an error committed in sowing his land, or in marrying his daughter. Nobody corrects a spendthrift for consuming his substance in taverns. Let any man pull down, or build, or make whatsoever expenses he pleases, nobody murmurs, nobody controls him; he has his liberty. But if any man do not frequent the church, if he do not there conform his behaviour exactly to the accustomed ceremonies, or if he brings not his children to be initiated in the sacred mysteries of this or the other congregation; this immediately causes an uproar. The neighbourhood is filled with noise and clamour. Everyone is ready to be the avenger of so great a crime. And the zealots hardly have the patience to refrain from violence and rapine, so long till the cause be heard, and the poor man be, according to form, condemned to the loss of liberty, goods, or life. Oh that our ecclesiastical orators, of every sect, would apply themselves with all the strength of arguments that they are able, to the confounding of men's errors! But let them spare their persons. Let them not supply their want of reasons with the instruments of force, which belong to another jurisdiction, and do ill become a churchman's hands. Let them not call in the magistrate's authority to the aid of their eloquence, or learning; lest, perhaps, whilst they pretend only love for the truth, this their intemperate zeal, breathing nothing but fire and sword, betray their ambition, and show that what they desire is temporal dominion. For it will be very difficult to persuade men of sense, that he, who with dry eyes, and satisfaction of mind, can deliver his brother unto the executioner, to be burnt alive, does sincerely and heartily concern himself to save that brother from the flames of hell in the world to come.

In the last place, let us now consider what is the magistrate's duty in the business of toleration: which certainly is very considerable.

We have already proved, that the care of souls does not belong to the magistrate: not a magisterial care, I mean, (if I may so call it) which consists in prescribing by laws, and compelling by punishments. But a charitable care, which consists in teaching, admonishing, and persuading, cannot be denied unto any man. The care therefore of every man's soul belongs unto himself, and is to be left unto himself. But what if he neglect the care of his soul? I answer, what if he neglect the care of his health, or of his estate, which things are nearlier related to the government of the magistrate than the other? Will the magistrate provide by an express law, that such a one shall not become poor or sick? Laws provide, as much as is possible, that the goods and health of subjects be not injured by the fraud or violence of others; they do not guard them from the negligence or ill-husbandry of the possessors themselves. No man can be forced to be rich or healthful, whether he will or no. Nay, God himself will not save men against their wills. Let us suppose, however, that some prince were desirous to force his subjects to accumulate riches, or to preserve the health and strength of their bodies. Shall it be provided by law, that they must consult none but *Roman* physicians, and shall every one be bound to live according to their prescriptions? What, shall no potion, no broth, be taken, but what is prepared either in the *Vatican*, suppose, or in a *Geneva* shop? Or, to make these subjects rich, shall they all be obliged by law to become merchants, or musicians? Or, shall everyone turn victualler, or smith, because there are some that maintain their families plentifully, and grow rich in those professions? But it may be said, there are a thousand ways to wealth, but one only way to heaven. 'Tis well said indeed, especially by those that plead for compelling men into this or the other way. For if there were several ways that lead thither, there would not be so much as a pretence left for compulsion. But now if I be marching on with my utmost vigour, in that way which, according to the sacred geography, leads straight to *Jerusalem*; why am I beaten and ill used by others, because, perhaps, I wear not buskins; because my hair is not of the right cut; because perhaps I have not been dipped in the right fashion; because I eat flesh upon the road, or some other food which agrees with my stomach; because I avoid certain byways, which seem unto me to lead into briars or precipices; because among the several paths that are in the same road, I choose that to walk in which seems to be the straightest and cleanest; because I avoid to keep company with some travellers that are less grave, and others that are more sour than they ought to be; or in fine, because I follow a guide that either is, or is not, clothed in white, and crowned with a mitre? Certainly, if we consider right, we shall find that for the most part they are such frivolous things as these, that (without any prejudice to religion or the salvation of souls, if not accompanied with superstition or hypocrisy) might either be observed or omitted; I say they are such like things as these, which breed implacable enmities among Christian brethren, who are all agreed in the substantial and truly fundamental part of religion.

But let us grant unto these zealots, who condemn all things that are not of their mode, that from these circumstances arise different ends. What shall we conclude from thence? There is only one of these which is the true way to eternal happiness. But in this great variety of ways that men follow, it is still doubted which is this right one. Now neither the care of the commonwealth, nor the right of enacting laws, does discover this way that leads to heaven more certainly to the magistrate, than every private man's search and study discovers it unto himself. I have a weak body, sunk under a languishing disease, for which (I suppose) there is one only remedy, but that unknown. Does it therefore belong unto the magistrate to prescribe me a remedy, because there is but one, and because it is unknown? Because there is but one way for me to escape death, will it therefore be safe for me to do whatsoever the magistrate ordains? Those things that every man ought sincerely to enquire into himself, and by meditation, study, search, and his own endeavours, attain the knowledge of, cannot be looked upon as the peculiar possession of anyone sort of men. Princes indeed are born superior unto other men in power, but in nature equal. Neither the right, nor the art of ruling, does necessarily carry along with it the certain knowledge of other things; and least of all of the true religion. For if it were so, how could it come to pass that the lords of the earth should differ so vastly as they do in religious matters? But let us grant that it is probable the way to eternal life may be better known by a prince than by his subjects; or at least, that in this incertitude of things, the safest and most commodious way for private persons is to follow his dictates. You will say, what then? If he should bid you follow merchandise for your livelihood, would you decline that course for fear it should not succeed? I answer: I would turn merchant upon the princes command, because in case I should have ill success in trade, he is abundantly able to make up my loss some other way. If it be true, as he pretends, that he desires I should thrive and grow rich, he can set me up again when unsuccessful voyages have broke me. But this is not the case, in the things that regard the life to come. If there I take a wrong course, if in that respect I am once undone, it is not in the magistrate's power to repair my loss, to ease my suffering, nor to restore me in any measure, much less entirely, to a good estate. What security can be given for the kingdom of heaven?

Perhaps some will say that they do not suppose this infallible judgment, that all men are bound to follow in the affairs of religion, to be in the civil magistrate, but in the church. What the church has determined, that the civil magistrate orders to be observed; and he provides by his authority that no body shall either act or believe, in the business of religion, otherwise than the church teaches. So that the judgment of those things is in the church. The magistrate himself yields obedience thereunto, and requires the like obedience from others. I answer: Who sees not how frequently the name of the church which was so venerable in the time of the apostles has been made use of to throw dust in peoples eyes, in following ages? But however, in the present case it helps us not. The one only narrow way which leads to heaven is not better known to the magistrate than to private persons, and therefore I cannot safely take him for my guide, who may probably be as ignorant of the way as my self, and who certainly is less concerned for my salvation than I my self am. Among so many kings of the *Jews*, how many of them were there whom any *Israelite*, thus blindly following, had not fallen into idolatry, and thereby into destruction? Yet nevertheless, you bid me be of good courage, and tell me that all is now safe and secure, because the magistrate does not now enjoin the observance of his own decrees in matters of religion, but only the decrees of the church. Of what church I beseech you? Of that certainly which likes him best. As if he that compels me by laws and penalties to enter into this or the other church, did not interpose his own judgment in the matter. What difference is there whether he lead me himself, or deliver me over to be led by others? I depend both ways upon his will, and it is he that determines both ways of my eternal state. Would an *Israelite*, that had worshipped *Baal* upon the command of his king, have been in any better condition, because some body had told him that the king ordered nothing in religion upon his own head, nor commanded any thing to be done by his subjects in divine worship, but what was approved by the counsel of priests, and declared to be of divine right by the doctors of their church? If the religion of any church become therefore true and saving, because the head of that sect, the prelates and priests, and those of that tribe, do all of them, with their might, extol and praise it; what religion can ever be accounted erroneous, false, and destructive? I am doubtful concerning the doctrine of the *Socinians*. I am suspicious of the way of worship practised by the *Papists*, or *Lutherans*; will it be ever a jot the safer for me to join either unto the one or the other of those churches, upon the magistrates command, because he commands nothing in religion but by the authority and counsel of the doctors of that church?

But to speak the truth, we must acknowledge that the church (if a convention of clergymen, making canons, must be called by that name) is for the most part more apt to be influenced by the court, than the court by the church. How the church was under the vicissitude of orthodox and Arian emperors is very well known. Or if those things be too remote, our modem *English* history affords us fresh examples, in the reign of *Henry the 8th*, *Edward the 6th*, *Mary*, and *Elizabeth*, how easily and smoothly the clergy changed their decrees, their articles of faith, their form of worship, everything, according to the inclination of those kings and queens. Yet were those kings and queens of such different minds, in point of religion, and enjoined thereupon such different things, that no man in his wits (I had almost said one but an atheist) will presume to say that any sincere and upright worshipper of God could, with a safe conscience, obey their several decrees. To conclude, it is the same thing whether a king that prescribes laws to another mans religion pretend to do it by his own judgment, or by the ecclesiastical authority and advice of others. The decisions of churchmen, whose differences and disputes are sufficiently known, cannot be any sounder, or safe than his: nor can all their suffrages joined together add any new strength unto the civil power. Though this also must be taken notice of, that princes seldom have any regard to the suffrages of ecclesiastics that are not favourers of their own faith and way of worship.

But after all, the *principal consideration*, and which absolutely determines this controversy, is this. Although the magistrates opinion in religion be sound, and the way that he appoints be truly evangelical, yet if I be not thoroughly persuaded thereof in my own mind, there will be no safety for me in following it. No way whatsoever that I shall walk in, against the dictates of my conscience, will ever bring me to the mansions of the blessed. I may grow rich by an art that I take not delight in; I may be cured of some disease by remedies that I have not faith in; but I cannot be saved by a religion that I distrust, and by a worship that I abhor. It is in vain for an unbeliever to take up the outward show of another man's profession. Faith only, and inward sincerity, are the things that procure acceptance with God. The most likely and most approved remedy can have no effect upon the patient, if his stomach reject it as soon taken. And you will in vain cram a medicine down a sick mans throat, which his particular constitution will be sure to turn into poison. In a word, whatsoever may be doubtful in religion, yet this at least is certain, that no religion, which I believe not to be true, can be either true, or profitable unto me. In vain therefore do princes compel their subjects to come into their church communion under pretence of saving their souls. If they believe, they will come of their own accord; if they believe not, their coming will nothing avail them. How great soever, in fine, may be the pretence of goodwill, and charity, and concern for the salvation of men's souls, men cannot be forced to be saved whether they will or no. And therefore, when all is done, they must be left to their own consciences.

Having thus at length freed men from all dominion over one another in matters of religion, let us now consider what they are to do. All men know and acknowledge that God ought to be publicly worshipped. Why otherwise do they compel one another unto the public assemblies? Men therefore constituted in this liberty are to enter into some religious society, that they may meet together, not only for mutual edification, but to own to the world that they worship God, and offer unto his divine majesty such service as they themselves are not ashamed of, and such as they think not unworthy of him, nor unacceptable to him; and finally that by the purity of doctrine, holiness of life, and decent form of worship, they may draw others unto the love of the true religion, and perform such other things in religion as cannot be done by each private man apart.

These religious societies I call churches: and these I say the magistrate ought to tolerate. For the business of these assemblies of the people is nothing but what is lawful for every man in particular to take care of; I mean the salvation of their souls: nor in this case is there any difference between the national church, and other separated congregations.

But as in every church there are two things especially to be considered; the outward form and rites of worship, and the doctrines and articles of faith; these things must be handled each distinctly; that so the whole matter of toleration may the more clearly be understood.

Concerning outward worship, I say (in the first place) that the magistrate has no power to enforce by law, either in his own church, or much less in another, the use of any rites or ceremonies whatsoever in the worship of God. And this, not only because these churches are free societies, but because whatsoever is practised in the worship of God, is only so far justifiable as it is believed by those that practise it to be acceptable unto him. Whatsoever is not done with that assurance of faith, is neither well in it self, nor can it be acceptable to God. To impose such things therefore upon any people, contrary to their own judgment, is in effect to command them to offend God; which, considering that the end of all religion is to please him, and that liberty is essentially necessary to that end, appears to be absurd beyond expression.

But perhaps it may be concluded from hence, that I deny unto the magistrate all manner of power about indifferent things; which if it be not granted, the whole subject matter of law-making is taken away. No, I readily grant that indifferent things and perhaps none but such, are subjected to the legislative power. But it does not therefore follow, that the magistrate may ordain whatsoever he pleases concerning any thing that is indifferent. The public good is the rule and measure of all lawmaking. If a thing be not useful to the commonwealth, though it be never so indifferent, it may not presently be established by law.

And further, things never so indifferent in their own nature, when they are brought into the church and worship of God, are removed out of the reach of the magistrate's jurisdiction; because in that use they have no connection at all with civil affairs. The only business of the church is the salvation of souls: and it no ways concerns the commonwealth, or any member of it, that this, or the other ceremony be there made use of. Neither the use, nor the omission of any ceremonies, in those religious assemblies, does either advantage or prejudice the life, liberty, or estate of any man. For example: let it be granted, that the washing of an infant with water is in it self an indifferent thing. Let it be granted also, that if the magistrate understand such washing to be profitable to the curing or preventing of any disease that children are subject unto, and esteem the matter weighty enough to be taken care of by a law, in that case he may order it to be done. But will anyone therefore say, that a magistrate has the same right to ordain, by law, that all children shall be baptized by priests, in the sacred font, in order to the purification of their souls? The extreme difference of these two cases is visible to every one at first sight. Or let us apply the last case to the child of a *Jew*, and the things speaks itself. For what hinders but a Christian magistrate may have subjects that are *Jews*? Now if we acknowledge that such an inquiry may not be done unto a *Jew*, as to compel him, against his own opinion, to practise in his religion a thing that is in its nature indifferent; how can we maintain that anything of this kind may be done to a Christian?

Again, things in their own nature indifferent cannot, by any human authority, be made any part of the worship of God; for this very reason; because they are indifferent. For since indifferent things are not capable, by any virtue of their own, to propitiate the deity; no human power or authority can confer on them so much dignity and excellence as to enable them to do it. In the common affairs of life, that use of indifferent things which God has not forbidden, is free and lawful: and therefore in those things human authority has place. But it is not so in matters of religion. Things indifferent are not otherwise lawful in the worship of God than as they are instituted by God himself; and as he, by some positive command, has ordained them to be made a part of that worship which he will vouchsafe to accept of at the hands of poor sinful men. Nor when an incensed deity shall ask us, *Who has required these, or such like things at our hands?* will it be enough to answer him, that the magistrate commanded them. If civil jurisdiction extended thus far, what might not lawfully be introduced into religion? What hodge-podge of ceremonies, what superstitious inventions, built upon the magistrate's authority, might not (against conscience) be imposed upon the worshippers of God? For the greatest part of these ceremonies and superstitions consists in the religious use of such things as are in their own nature indifferent: nor are they sinful upon any other account than because God is not the author of them. The sprinkling of water, and the use of bread and wine, are both in their own nature, and in the ordinary occasions of life, altogether indifferent. Will any man therefore say that these things could have been introduced into religion, and made a part of divine worship, if not by divine institution? If any human authority or civil power could have done this, why might it not also enjoin the eating of fish, the drinking of ale, in the holy banquet, as a part of divine worship? Why not the sprinkling of the blood of beasts in churches, and expiations by water or fire, and abundance more of this kind? But these things, how indifferent soever they be in common uses, when they come to be annexed unto divine worship, without divine authority, they are as abominable to God, as the sacrifice of a dog. And why a dog so abominable? What difference is there between a dog and a goat, in respect of the divine nature, equally and infinitely distant from all affinity with matter; unless it be that God required the use of the one in his worship, and not of the other? We see therefore that indifferent things how much soever they be under the power of the civil magistrate, yet cannot upon that pretence be introduced into religion, and imposed upon religious assemblies; because in the worship of God they wholly cease to be indifferent. He that worships God does it with design to please him and procure his favour. But that cannot be done by him, who, upon the command of another, offers unto God that which he knows will be displeasing to him, because not commanded by himself. This is not to please God, or appease his wrath, but willingly and knowingly to provoke him, by a manifest contempt; which is a thing absolutely repugnant to the nature and end of worship.

But it will here be asked: if nothing belonging to divine worship be left to human discretion, how is it then that churches themselves have the power of ordering any thing about the time and place of worship, and the like? To this I answer; that in religious worship we must distinguish between what is part of the worship it self. And what is but a circumstance. That is a part of the worship which is believed to be appointed by God; and to be well-pleasing to him; and therefore that is necessary. Circumstances are such things which, though in general they cannot be separated from worship, yet the particular instances or modifications of them are not determined; and therefore they are indifferent. Of this sort are the time and place of worship, the habit and posture of him that worships. These are circumstances, and perfectly indifferent, where God has not given any express command about them. For example: among the *Jews* the time and place of their worship, and the habits of those that officiated in it, were not mere circumstances, but

a part of the worship it self; in which if any thing were defective, or different from that institution, they could not hope that it would be accepted by God. But these, to Christians under the liberty of the gospel, are mere circumstances of worship, which the prudence of every church may bring into such use as shall be judged most subservient to the end of order, decency, and edification. But, even under the gospel, those who believe the first, or the seventh day to be set apart by God, and consecrated still to his worship, to them that portion of time is not a simple circumstance, but a real part of divine worship, which can neither be changed or neglected.

In the next place, as the magistrate has no power to *impose* by his laws, the use of any rites and ceremonies in any church, so neither has he any power to *forbid* the use of such rites and ceremonies as are already received, approved, and practised by any church: because if he did so, he would destroy the church itself; the end of whose institution is only to worship God with freedom, after its own manner.

You will say, by this rule, if some congregations should have a mind to sacrifice infants, or (as the primitive Christians were falsely accused) lustfully pollute themselves in promiscuous uncleanness, or practise any other such heinous enormities, is the magistrate obliged to tolerate them, because they are committed in a religious assembly? I answer, no. These things are not lawful in the ordinary course of life, nor in *any* private house; and therefore neither are they so in the worship of God, or in any religious meeting. But indeed if any people congregated upon account of religion, should be desirous to sacrifice a calf, I deny that that ought to be prohibited by a law. *Melibaeus*, whose calf it is, may lawfully kill his calf at home and burn any part of it that he thinks fit. For no injury is thereby done to anyone, no prejudice to another mans goods. And for the same reason he may kill his calf also in a religious meeting. Whether the doing so be well-pleasing to God or no, it is their part to consider that do it. The part of the magistrate is only to take care that the commonwealth receive no prejudice, and that there be no injury done to any man, either in life or estate. And thus what may be spent on a feast, may be spent on a sacrifice. But if peradventure such were the state of things, that the interest of the commonwealth required all slaughter of beasts should be forborn for some while, in order to the increasing of the stock of cattle, that had been destroyed by some extraordinary murrain; who sees not that the magistrate, in such a case, may forbid all his subjects to kill any calves for any use whatsoever? Only 'tis to be observed, that in this case the law is not made about a religious, but a political matter: nor is the sacrifice, but the slaughter of calves thereby prohibited.

By this we see what difference there is between the church and the commonwealth. Whatsoever is lawful in the commonwealth, cannot be prohibited by the magistrate in the church. Whatsoever is permitted unto any of his subjects for their ordinary use, neither can nor ought to be forbidden by him to any sect of people for their religious uses. If any man may lawfully take bread or wine, either sitting or kneeling, in his own house, the law ought not to abridge him of the same liberty in his religious worship; though in the church the use of bread and wine be very different, and be there applied to the mysteries of faith, and rites of divine worship. But those things that are prejudicial to the commonweal of a people in their ordinary use, and are therefore forbidden by laws, those things ought not to be permitted to churches in their sacred rites. Only the magistrate ought always to be very careful that he do not misuse his authority, to the oppression of any church, under pretence of public good.

It may be said; what if a church be *idolatrous*, is that also to be tolerated by the magistrate? I answer, What power can be given to the magistrate for the suppression of an idolatrous church, which may not, in time and place, be made use of to the ruin of an orthodox one? For it must be remembered that the civil power is the same everywhere and the religion of every prince is orthodox to himself. If therefore such a power be granted unto the civil magistrate in spirituals, as that at *Geneva* (for example) he may extirpate, by violence and blood, the religion which is there reputed idolatrous; by the same rule another magistrate, in some neighbouring country, may oppress the reformed religion; and, in *India*, the Christian. The civil power can either change every thing in religion according to the prince's pleasure, or it can change nothing, if it be once permitted to introduce any thing into religion, by the means of laws and penalties, there can be no bounds put to it; but it will in the same manner be lawful to alter every thing, according to that rule of truth which the magistrate has framed unto himself. No man whatsoever ought therefore to be deprived of his terrestrial enjoyments, upon account of his religion. Not even *Americans*, subjected unto a Christian prince, are to be punished either in body or goods, for not embracing our faith and worship. If they are persuaded that they please God in observing the rites of their own country, and that they shall obtain happiness by that means, they are to be left unto God and themselves. Let us trace this matter to the bottom. Thus it is. An inconsiderable and weak number of Christians, destitute of every thing, arrive in a pagan country: these foreigners beseech the inhabitants, by the bowels of humanity, that they would succour them with the necessaries of life: those necessaries are given them; habitations are granted; and they all join together,

and grow up into one body of people. The Christian religion by this means takes root in that country, and spreads itself; but does not suddenly grow the strongest. While things are in this condition, peace, friendship, faith, and equal justice are preserved among them. At length the magistrate becomes a Christian, and by that means their party becomes the most powerful. Then immediately all compacts are to be broken, all civil rights to be violated, that idolatry may be extirpated: and unless these innocent pagans, strict observers of the rules of equity and the law of nature, and no ways offending against the laws of the society, I say unless they will forsake their ancient religion, and embrace a new and strange one, they are to be turned out of the lands and possessions of their forefathers, and perhaps deprived of life it self. Then at last it appears what zeal for the church, joined with the desire of dominion, is capable to produce; and how easily the pretence of religion, and of the care of souls, serves for a cloak to covetousness, rapine, and ambition.

Now whosoever maintains that idolatry is to be rooted out of any place by laws, punishments, fire, and sword, may apply this story to himself. For the reason of the thing is equal, both in *America* and *Europe*. And neither pagans there, nor any dissenting Christians here, can with any right be deprived of their worldly goods, by the predominating faction of a court-church: nor are any civil rights to be either changed or violated upon account of religion in one place more than another.

But *idolatry* (say some) is a sin, and therefore not to be tolerated. If they said it were therefore to be avoided, the inference were good. But it does not follow, that because it is a sin it ought therefore to be punished by the magistrate. For it does not belong unto the magistrate to make use of his sword in punishing everything, indifferently, that he takes to be a sin against God. Covetousness, uncharitableness, idleness, and many other things are sins, by the consent of all men, which yet no man ever said were to be punished by the magistrate. The reason is, because they are not prejudicial to other men's rights, nor do they break the public peace of societies. Nay, even the sins of lying and perjury, are no where punishable by laws; unless in certain cases, in which the real turpitude of the thing, and the offence against God, are not considered, but only the injury done unto men's neighbours, and to the commonwealth. And what if in another country, to a Mahumetan or a pagan prince, the Christian religion seem false and offensive to God; may not the Christians for the same reason, and after the same manner, be extirpated there?

But it may be urged further, that by the law of *Moses* idolaters were to be rooted out. True indeed, by the law of *Moses*. But that is not obligatory to us Christians. No body pretends that every thing, generally, enjoined by the law of *Moses*, ought to be practised by Christians. But there is nothing more frivolous than that common distinction of moral, judicial, and ceremonial law, which men ordinarily make use of. For no positive law whatsoever can oblige any people but those to whom it is given. *Hear O Israel*; sufficiently restrains the obligation of the law of *Moses* only to that people. And this consideration alone is answer enough unto those that urge the authority of the law of *Moses;* for the inflicting of capital punishments upon idolaters. But however, I will examine this argument a little more particularly.

The case of idolaters, in respect of the *Jewish* commonwealth, falls under a double consideration. The first is of those who, being initiated in the *Mosaical* rites, and made citizens of that commonwealth, did afterwards apostatise from the worship of the God of *Israel*. These were proceeded against as traitors and rebels, guilt of no less than high treason. For the commonwealth of the *Jews*, different in that from all others, was an absolute theocracy: nor was there, or could there be, any difference between that commonwealth and the church. The laws established there concerning the worship of one invisible deity, were the civil laws of that people, and a part of their political government; in which God himself was the legislator. Now if anyone can show me where there is a commonwealth, at this time, constituted upon that foundation, I will acknowledge that the ecclesiastical laws do there unavoidably become a part of the civil; and that the subjects of that government both may, and ought to be kept in strict conformity with that church, by the civil power. But there is absolutely no such thing, under the gospel, as a Christian commonwealth. There are, indeed, many cities and kingdoms that have embraced the faith of Christ; but they have retained their ancient form of government; with which the law of Christ hath not at all meddled. He, indeed, hath taught men how, by faith and good works, they may attain eternal life. But he instituted no commonwealth. He prescribed unto his followers no new and peculiar form of government; nor put he the sword into any magistrate's hand, with commission to make use of it in forcing men to forsake their former religion, and receive his.

Secondly, foreigners, and such as were strangers to the commonwealth of *Israel*, were not compelled by force to observe the rites of the *Mosaical* law. But, on the contrary, in the very same place where it is ordered that *an Israelite that was an idolater should be put to death*, there it is provided that *strangers should not be vexed nor oppressed.*[10] I confess that the seven nations that possessed the land which was promised to the *Israelites*, were utterly to be cut off. But this was not singly because they were

idolaters. For, if that had been the reason, why were the *Moabites* and other nations to be spared? No; the reason is this. God being in a peculiar manner the king of the *Jews*, he could not suffer the adoration of any other deity (which was properly an act of high treason against himself) in the land of *Canaan*, which was his kingdom. For such a manifest revolt could no ways consist with his dominion, which was perfectly political, in that country. All idolatry was therefore to be rooted out of the bounds of his kingdom; because it was an acknowledgment of anotherGod, that is to say, another king; against the laws of empire. The inhabitants were also to be driven out, that the entire possession of the land might be given to the *Israelites*. And for the like reason the *emims* and the *Horims* were driven out of their countries, by the children of *Esau* and *Lot*;[11] and their lands, upon the same grounds, given by God to the invaders. But though all idolatry was thus rooted out of the land of *Canaan*, yet every idolater was not brought to execution. The whole family of *Rahab*, the whole nation of the *Gibeonites*, articled with *Josuah*, and were allowed by treaty: and there were many captives among the *Jews*, who were idolaters. *David and Solomon* subdued many countries without the confines of the land of promise, and carried their conquests as far as *Euphrates*. Among so many captives taken, so many nations reduced under their obedience, we find not one man forced into the Jewish religion, and the worship of the true God, and punished for idolatry, though all of them were certainly guilty of it. If anyone indeed, becoming a proselyte, desired to be made a denison of their commonwealth, he was obliged to submit unto their laws; that is, to embrace their religion. But this he did willingly, on his own accord, not by constraint. He did not unwillingly submit, to show his obedience; but he sought and solicited for it, as a privilege. And as soon as he was admitted, he became subject to the laws of the commonwealth, by which all idolatry was forbidden within the borders of the land of *Canaan*. But that law (as I have said) did not reach to any of those regions, however subjected unto the *Jews*, that were situated without those bounds.

Thus far concerning outward worship. Let us now consider *articles of faith*.

The *articles* of religion are some of them *practical*, and some *speculative*. Now, though both sorts consist in the knowledge of truth, yet these terminate simply in the understanding, those influence the will and manners. Speculative opinions, therefore, and *articles of faith* (as they are called) which are required only to be believed, cannot be imposed on any church by the law of the land. For it is absurd that things should be enjoined by laws, which are not in men's power to perform. And to believe this or that to be true, does not depend upon our will.

But of this enough has been said already. But (will some say) let men at least profess that they believe. A sweet religion indeed, that obliges men to dissemble, and tell lies both to God and man, for the salvation of their souls! If the magistrate thinks to save men thus, he seems to understand little of the way of salvation. And if he does it not in order to save them, why is he so solicitous about the articles of faith as to enact them by a law?

Further, the magistrate ought not to forbid the preaching or professing of any speculative opinions in any church, because they have no manner of relation to the civil rights of the subjects. If a *Roman Catholic* believe that to be really the body of Christ, which another man calls bread, he does no injury thereby to his neighbour. If a *Jew* do not believe the new testament to be the word of God, he does not thereby alter any thing in men's civil rights. If a heathen doubt of both testaments, he is not therefore to be punished as a pernicious citizen. The power of the magistrate, and the estates of the people, may be equally secure, whether any man believe these things or no. I readily grant, that these opinions are false and absurd. But the business of laws is not to provide for the truth of opinions but for the safety and security of the commonwealth, and of every particular mans goods and person. And so it ought to be. For truth certainly would do well enough, if she were once left to shift for her self. She seldom has received, and I fear never will receive much assistance from the power of great men, to whom she is but rarely known, and more rarely welcome. She is not taught by laws, nor has she any need of force to procure her entrance into the minds of men. Errors indeed prevail by the assistance of foreign and borrowed succours. But if truth makes not her way into the understanding by her own light she will be but the weaker for any borrowed force violence can add to her. Thus much for speculative opinions. Let us now proceed to *practical* ones.

A good life, in which consists not the least part of religion and true piety, concerns also the civil government: and in it lies the safety both of men's souls, and of the commonwealth. Moral actions belong therefore to the jurisdiction both of the outward and inward court; both of the civil and domestic governor; I mean, both of the magistrate and conscience. Here therefore is great danger, least one of these jurisdictions entrench upon the other, and discord arise between the keeper of the public peace and the overseers of souls. But if what has been already said concerning the limits of both these governments be rightly considered, it will easily remove all difficulty in this matter.

Every man has an immortal soul, capable of eternal happiness or misery; whose happiness depending upon his believing and doing those things in this life, which are necessary to the obtaining of Gods favour, and are prescribed by God to that end; it follows from thence, *first*, that the observance of these things is the highest obligation that lies upon mankind, and that our utmost care, application, and diligence, ought to be exercised in the search and performance of them; because there is nothing in this world that is of any consideration in comparison with eternity. *Secondly*, that seeing one man does not violate the right of another, by his erroneous opinions, and undue manner of worship, nor is his perdition any prejudice to another man's affairs; therefore the care of each man's salvation belongs only to himself. But I would not have this understood, as if I meant hereby to condemn all charitable admonitions, and affectionate endeavours to reduce men from errors; which are indeed the greatest duty of a Christian. Any one many employ as many exhortations and arguments as he pleases, toward the promoting of another man's salvation. But all force and compulsion are to be forborn. Nothing is to be done imperiously. Nobody is obliged in that matter to yield obedience unto the admonitions or injunctions of another, further than he himself is persuaded. Every man, in that, has the supreme and absolute authority of judging for himself. And the reason is, because nobody else is concerned in it, nor can receive any prejudice from his conduct therein.

But besides their souls, which are immortal, men have also their temporal lives here upon earth; the state whereof being frail and fleeting, and the duration uncertain; they have need of several outward conveniences to the support thereof, which are to be procured or preserved by pains and industry. For those things that are necessary to the comfortable support of our lives are not the spontaneous products of nature, nor do offer themselves fit and prepared for our use. This part therefore draws on another care, and necessarily gives another employment. But the pravity of mankind being such, that they had rather injuriously prey upon the fruits of other men's labours, than take pains to provide for themselves; the necessity of preserving men in the possession of what honest industry has already acquired, and also of preserving their liberty and strength, whereby they may acquire what they further want; obliges men to enter into society with one another; that by mutual assistance, and joint force, they may secure unto each other their proprieties in the things that contribute to the comfort and happiness of this life; leaving in the meanwhile to every man the care of his own eternal happiness, the attainment whereof can neither be facilitated by another mans industry, nor can the loss of it turn to another mans prejudice, nor the hope of it be forced from him by any external violence. But forasmuch as men thus entering into societies, grounded upon their mutual compacts of assistance, for the defence of their temporal goods, may nevertheless be deprived of them, either by the rapine and fraud of their fellow citizens, or by the hostile violence of foreigners; the remedy of this evil consists in arms, riches, and multitude of citizens; the remedy of the other in laws; and the care of all things relating both to the one and the other, is committed by the society to the civil magistrate. This is the original, this is the use, and these are the bounds of the legislative (which is the supreme) power, in every commonwealth. I mean, that provision may be made for the security of each mans private possessions; for the peace, riches, and public commodities of the whole people; and, as much as possible, for the increase of their inward strength, against foreign invasions.

These things being thus explained, it is easy to understand to what end the legislative power ought to be directed, and by what measures regulated; and that is the temporal good and outward prosperity of the society; which is the sole reason of men's entering into society, and the only thing they seek and aim at in it. And it is also evident what liberty remains to men in reference to their eternal salvation, and that is, that everyone should do what he in his conscience is persuaded to be acceptable to the almighty, on whose good pleasure and acceptance depends their eternal happiness. For obedience is due in the first place to God, and afterwards to the laws.

But some may ask, *What if the magistrate should enjoin any thing by his authority that appears unlawful to the conscience of a private person?* I answer, that if government be faithfully administered, and the counsels of the magistrate be indeed directed to the public good, this will seldom happen. But if perhaps it do so fall out; I say, that such a private person is to abstain from the action that he judges unlawful; and he is to undergo the punishment, which it is not unlawful for him to bear. For the private judgment of any person concerning a law enacted in political matters, for the public good, does not take away the obligation of that law, nor deserve a dispensation. But if the law indeed concerning things that lie not within the verge of the magistrate's authority; (as for example, that the people, or any party among them, should be compelled to embrace a strange religion, and join in the worship and ceremonies of another church,) men are not in these cases obliged by that law, against their consciences. For the political society is instituted for no other end but only to secure every mans possession of the things of this life. The care of each mans soul, and of the things of heaven, which neither does belong to the commonwealth, nor can be subjected to it, is left entirely to every mans self. Thus the safeguard of men's lives, and of the things that belong unto this life, is the business of

the commonwealth; and the preserving of those things unto their owners is the duty of the magistrate. And therefore the magistrate cannot take away these worldly things from this man, or party, and give them to that; nor change propriety among fellow subjects, (no not even by a law) for a cause that has no relation to the end of civil government; I mean, for their religion; which whether it be true or false, does no prejudice to the worldly concerns of their fellow subjects, which are the things that only belong unto the care of the commonwealth.

But what if the magistrate believe such a law as this to be for the public good? I answer: As the private judgment of any particular person, if erroneous, does not exempt him from the obligation of law, so the private judgment (as I may call it) of the magistrate does not give him any new right of imposing laws upon his subjects, which neither was in the constitution of the government granted him, nor ever was in the power of the people to grant: much less, if he make it his business to enrich and advance his followers and fellow sectaries, with the spoils of others. But what if the magistrate believe that he has the right to make such laws, and that they are for the public good; and his subjects believe the contrary? Who shall be judge between them? I answer, God alone. For there is no judge upon earth between the supreme magistrate and the people. God, I say, is the only judge in this case, who will retribute unto every one at the last day according to his deserts; that is, according to his sincerity and uprightness in endeavouring to promote piety, and the public weal and peace of mankind. But what shall be done in the mean while? I answer: the principal and chief care of every one ought to be of his own soul first, and in the next place of the public peace: though yet there are very few will think 'tis peace there, where they see all laid waste.

There are two sorts of contests among men; the one managed by law, the other by force: and these are of that nature, that where the one ends, the other always begins. But it is not my business to inquire into the power of the magistrate in the different constitutions of nations. I only know what usually happens where controversies arise, without a judge to determine them. You will say then the magistrate being the stronger will have his will, and carry his point. Without doubt. But the question is not here concerning the doubtfulness of the event, but the rule of right.

But to come to particulars. I say, *first*, no opinions contrary to human society, or to those moral rules which are necessary to the reservation of civil society, are to be tolerated by the magistrate. But of these examples in any church are rare. For no sect can easily arrive to such a degree of madness, as that it should think fit to teach, for doctrines of religion, such things as manifestly undermine the foundations of society, and are therefore condemned by the judgment of all mankind: because their own interest, peace, reputation, every thing, would be thereby endangered.

Another more secret evil, but more dangerous to the commonwealth, is, when men arrogate to themselves, and to those of their own sect, some peculiar prerogative, covered over with a specious show of deceitful words, but in effect opposite to the civil right of the community. For example, we cannot find any sect that teaches expressly, and openly, that men are not obliged to keep their promise; that princes may be dethroned by those that differ from them in religion; or that the dominion of all things belongs only to themselves. For these things, proposed thus nakedly and plainly, would soon draw on them the eye and hand of the magistrate, and awaken all the care of the commonwealth to a watchfulness against the spreading of so dangerous an evil. But nevertheless, we find those that say the same things, in other words. What else do they mean, who teach that *faith is not to be kept with heretics*? Their meaning, forsooth, is that the privilege of breaking faith belongs unto themselves: for they declare all that are not of their communion to be heretics, or at least may declare them so whensoever they think fit. What can be the meaning of their asserting that *kings excommunicated forfeit their crowns and kingdoms*? It is evident that they thereby arrogate unto themselves the power of deposing kings: because they challenge the power of excommunication, as the peculiar right of their hierarchy. That *dominion is founded in grace*, is also an assertion by which those that maintain it do plainly lay claim to the possession of all things. For they are not so wanting to themselves as not to believe, or at least as not to profess, themselves to be the truly pious and faithful. These therefore, and the like, who attribute unto the faithful, religious and orthodox, that is, in plain terms, unto themselves, any peculiar privilege of power above other mortals, in civil concernments; or who, upon pretence of religion, do challenge any manner of authority over such, as are not associated with them in the ecclesiastical communion; I say these have no right to be tolerated by the magistrate; as neither those that will not own and teach the duty of tolerating all men in matters of mere religion. For what do all these and the like doctrines signify, but that they may, and are ready upon any occasion to seize the government, and possess themselves of the estates and fortunes of their fellow subjects; and that they only ask leave to be tolerated by the magistrate so long until they find themselves strong enough to effect it?

Again: that church can have no right to be tolerated by the magistrate, which is constituted upon such a bottom, that all those who enter into it, do thereby, *ipso facto*, deliver themselves up to the protection and service of another prince. For by this means the magistrate would give way to the settling of a foreign jurisdiction in his own country, and suffer his own people to be listed, as it were, for soldiers against his own government. Nor does the frivolous and fallacious distinction between the court and the church afford any remedy to this inconvenience; especially when both the one and the other are equally subject to the absolute authority of the same person; who has not only power to persuade the members of his church to whatsoever he lists, either as purely religious, or in order thereunto, but can also enjoin it them on pain of eternal fire. It is ridiculous for anyone to profess himself to be a *Mahumetan* only in his religion, but in every thing else a faithful subject to a Christian magistrate, whilst at the same time he acknowledges himself bound to yield blind obedience to the *mufti* of *Constantinople*; who himself is entirely obedient to the *Ottoman* emperor, and frames the feigned oracles of that religion according to his pleasure. But this Mahumetan living among Christians, would yet more apparently renounce their government, if he acknowledged the same person to be head of his church who is the supreme magistrate in the state.

Lastly, those are not at all to be tolerated who deny the being of a God. Promises, covenants, and oaths, which are the bonds of humane society, can have no hold upon an atheist. The taking away of God, though but even in thought, dissolves all. Besides also, those that by their atheism undermine and destroy all religion, can have no pretence of religion whereupon to challenge the privilege of a toleration. As for other practical opinions, though not absolutely free from all error, if they do not tend to establish domination over others, or civil impunity to the church in which they are taught, there can be no reason why they should not be tolerated.

It remains that I say something concerning those assemblies, which being vulgarly called, and perhaps having sometimes been *conventicles*, and nurseries of factions and seditions, are thought to afford the strongest matter of objection against this doctrine of toleration. But this has not happened by anything peculiar unto the genius of such assemblies, but by the unhappy circumstances of an oppressed or ill-settled liberty. These accusations would soon cease, if the law of toleration were once so settled, that all churches were obliged to lay down toleration as the foundation of their own liberty; and teach that liberty of conscience is every mans natural right, equally belonging to dissenters as to themselves; and that nobody ought to be compelled in matters of religion, either by law or force. The establishment of this one thing would take away all ground of complaints and tumults upon account of conscience. And these causes of discontents and animosities being once removed, there would remain nothing in these assemblies that were not more peaceable, and less apt to produce disturbance of state, than in any other meetings whatsoever. But let us examine particularly the heads of these accusations.

You'll say, that *assemblies and meetings endanger the public peace, and threaten the commonwealth*. I answer: If this be so, why are there daily such numerous meetings in markets, and courts of judicature? Why are crowds upon the exchange, and a concourse of people in cities suffered? You'll reply; Those are civil assemblies; but these we object against, are ecclesiastical. I answer: 'Tis a likely thing indeed, that such assemblies as are altogether remote from civil affairs, should be most apt to embroil them. O, but civil assemblies are composed of men that differ from one another in matters of religion; but these ecclesiastical meetings are of persons that are all of one opinion. As if an agreement in matters of religion, were in effect a conspiracy against the commonwealth; or as if men would not be so much the more warmly unanimous in religion, the less liberty they had of assembling. But it will be urged still, that civil assemblies are open, and free for anyone to enter into; whereas religious conventicles are more private, and thereby give opportunity to clandestine machinations. I answer, that this is not strictly true: for many civil assemblies are not open to every one. And if some religious meetings be private, who are they (I beseech you) that are to be blamed for it? Those that desire, or those that forbid their being public? Again; you'll say, that religious communion does exceedingly unite men's minds and affections to one another, and is therefore the more dangerous. But if this be so, why is not the magistrate afraid of his own church; and why does he not forbid their assemblies, as things dangerous to his government? You'll say, because he himself is a part, and even the head of them. As if he were not also a part of the commonwealth, and the head of the whole people.

Let us therefore deal plainly. The magistrate is afraid of other churches, but not of his own; because he is kind and favourable to the one, but severe and cruel to the other. These he treats like children, and indulges them even to wantonness. Those he uses as slaves; and how blamelessly soever they demean themselves, recompenses them no otherwise than by galleys, prisons, confiscations, and death. These he cherishes and defends: those he continually scourges and oppresses. Let him turn the tables: or let those dissenters enjoy but the same privileges in civils as his other subjects, and he will quickly find that these religious meetings will be no longer dangerous. For if men enter into seditious

conspiracies, 'tis not religion that inspires them to it in their meetings; but their sufferings and oppressions that make them willing to ease themselves. Just and moderate governments are every where quiet, everywhere safe. But oppression raises ferments, and makes men struggle to cast off an uneasy and tyrannical yoke. I know that seditions are very frequently raised, upon pretence of religion. But 'tis as true that, for religion, subjects are frequently ill treated, and live miserably. Believe me, the stirs that are made, proceed not from any peculiar temper of this or that church or religious society; but from the common disposition of all mankind, who when they groan under any heavy burthen, endeavour naturally to shake off the yoke that galls their necks. Suppose this business of religion were let alone, and that there were some other distinction made between men and men, upon account of their different complexions, shapes, and features, so that those who have black hair (for example) or grey eyes, should not enjoy the same privileges as other citizens; that they should not be permitted either to buy or sell, or live by their callings; that parents should not have the government and education of their own children; that all should either be excluded from the benefit of the laws, or meet with partial judges; can it be doubted but these persons, thus distinguished from others by the colour of their hair and eyes, and united together by one common persecution, would be as dangerous to the magistrate, as any others that had associated themselves merely upon the account of religion? Some enter into company for trade and profit: others, for want of business, have their clubs for claret. Neighbourhood joins some, and religion others. But there is one only thing which gathers people into seditious commotions, and that is oppression.

You'll say; what, will you have people to meet at divine service *against the magistrate's will*? I answer; why, I pray, against his will? Is it not both lawful and necessary that they should meet? Against his will, do you say? That's what I complain of. That is the very root of all the mischief. Why are assemblies less sufferable in a church than in a theatre or market? Those that meet there are not either more vicious, or more turbulent, than those that meet elsewhere. The business in that is, that they are ill used, and therefore they are not to be suffered. Take away the partiality that is used toward them in matters of common right; change the laws, take away the penalties unto which they are subjected, and all things will immediately become safe and peaceable; nay, those that are averse to the religion of the magistrate, will think themselves so much the more bound to maintain the peace of the commonwealth, as their condition is better in that place than elsewhere; and all the several separate congregations, like so many guardians of the public peace, will watch one another, that nothing may be innovated or changed in the form of the government: because they can hope for nothing better than what they already enjoy; that is, an equal condition with their fellow subjects, under a just and moderate government. Now if that church, which agrees in religion with the prince, be esteemed the chief support of any civil government, and that for no other reason (as has already been shown) than because the prince is kind, and the laws are favourable to it; how much greater will be the security of a government, where all good subjects, of whatsoever church they be, without any distinction upon account of religion, enjoying the same favour of the prince, and the same benefit of the laws, shall become the common support and guard of it; and where none will have any occasion to fear the severity of the laws, but those that do injuries to their neighbours, and offend against the civil peace?

That we may draw toward a conclusion. The *sum of all* we drive at is, *that every man may enjoy the same rights that are granted to others*. Is it permitted to worship God in the *Roman* manner? Let it be permitted to do it in the *Geneva* form also. Is it permitted to speak *Latin* in the marketplace? Let those that have a mind to it, be permitted to do it also in the church. Is it lawful for any man in his own house, to kneel, stand, sit, or use any other posture; and to clothe himself in white or black, in short or in long garments? Let it not be made unlawful to eat bread, drink wine, or wash with water, in the church. In a word: Whatsoever things are left free by law in the common occasions of life, let them remain free unto every church in divine worship. Let no mans life, or body, or house, or estate, suffer any manner of prejudice upon these accounts. Can you allow of the *Presbyterian* discipline? Why should not the *Episcopal* also have what they like? Ecclesiastical authority, whether it be administered by the hands of a single person, or many, is every where the same; an neither has any jurisdiction in things civil, nor any manner of power of compulsion, nor any thing at all to do with riches and revenues.

Ecclesiastical assemblies, and sermons, are justified by daily experience, and public allowance. These are allowed to people of some one persuasion: why not to all? If any thing pass in a religious meeting seditiously, and contrary to the public peace, it is to be punished in the same manner, and no otherwise, than as if it had happened in a fair or market. These meetings ought not to be sanctuaries for factious and flagitious fellows: nor ought it to be less lawful for men to meet in churches than in halls: nor are one part of the subjects to be esteemed more blameable, for their meeting together, than others. Every one is to be accountable for his own actions; and no man is to be laid under a suspicion, or odium, for the fault of another. Those that are seditious, murderers, thieves, robbers, adulterers, slanderers, etc. of whatsoever church, whether national or not, ought to be punished and suppressed. But those whose doctrine is peaceable, and whose manners are pure and blameless ought to be upon equal terms with their fellow subjects. Thus if solemn assemblies, observations of festivals, public worship, be permitted to any one sort of professors; all these things ought to be permitted to the *Presbyterians*, *Independents*, *Anabaptists*, *Armenians*, *Quakers*, and others, with the same liberty. Nay, if we may openly speak the truth, and as becomes man to another, neither *pagan*, nor *Mahumetan*, nor *Jew*, ought to be excluded from the civil rights of the commonwealth, because of his religion. The gospel commands no such thing. The church, which *judges not those that are without*, wants it not.[12] And the commonwealth, which embraces indifferently all men that are honest, peaceable, and industrious, requires it not. Shall we suffer a *pagan* to deal and trade with us, and shall we not suffer him to pray unto and worship God? If we allow the *Jews* to have private houses and dwellings among us, why should we not allow them to have synagogues? Is their doctrine more false, their worship more abominable, or is the civil peace more endangered, by their meeting in public than in their private houses? But if these things may be granted to *Jews* and *pagans*, surely the condition of any Christians ought not to be worse than theirs in a Christian commonwealth.

You'll say, perhaps, yes, it ought to be: because they are inclinable to factions, tumults, and civil wars. I answer: Is this the fault of the Christian religion? If it be so, truly the Christian religion is the worst of all religions, and ought neither to be embraced by any particular person, nor tolerated by any commonwealth. For if this be the genius, this the nature of the Christian religion, to be turbulent, and destructive to the civil peace, that church it self which the magistrate indulges will not always be innocent. But far be it from us to say any such thing of that religion, which carries the greatest opposition to covetousness, ambition, discord, contention, and all manner of inordinate desires; and is the most modest and peaceable religion that ever was. We must therefore seek another cause of those evils that are charged upon religion. And if we consider right, we shall find it to consist wholly in the subject that I am treating of. It is not the diversity of opinions (which can pot be avoided) but the refusal of toleration to those that are of different opinions, (which might have been granted) that. Has produced all the bustles and wars, that have been in the Christian world, upon account of religion. The heads and leaders of the church, moved by avarice and insatiable desire of dominion, making use of the immoderate ambition of magistrates, and the credulous superstition of the giddy multitude, have incensed and animated them against those that dissent from themselves; by preaching unto them, contrary to the laws of the gospel and to the precepts of charity, that schismatics and heretics are to be outed of their possessions, and destroyed. And thus have they mixed together and confounded two things that are in themselves most different, the church and the commonwealth. Now as it is very difficult for men patiently to suffer themselves to be stripped of the goods, which they have got by their honest industry; and contrary to all the laws of equity, both humane and divine, to be delivered up for a prey to other men's violence and rapine; especially when they are otherwise altogether blameless; and that the occasion for which they are thus treated does not at all belong to the jurisdiction of the magistrate; but entirely to the conscience of every particular man; for the conduct of which he is accountable to God only; what else can be expected, but that these men, growing weary of the evils under which they labour, should in the end think it lawful for them to resist force with force, and to defend their natural rights (which are not forfeitable upon account of religion) with arms as well as they can? That this has been hitherto the ordinary course of things, is abundantly evident in history: and that it will continue to be so hereafter, is but too apparent in reason. It cannot indeed be otherwise, so long as the principle of persecution for religion shall prevail, as it has done hitherto, with magistrate and people; and so long as those that ought to be the preachers of peace and concord, shall continue, with all their art and strength, to excite men to arms, and sound the trumpet of war. But that magistrates should thus suffer these incendiaries, and disturbers of the public peace, might justly be wondered at; if it did not appear that they have been invited by them unto a participation of the spoil, and have therefore thought fit to make use of their covetousness and pride as means whereby to increase their own power. For who does not see that *these good men* are indeed more ministers of the government, than ministers of the gospel; and that by flattering the ambition, and favouring the dominion of princes and men in authority, they endeavour with all their might to promote that tyranny in the commonwealth, which otherwise they should not be able to establish in the church? This is the unhappy agreement that we see between the church and state. Whereas if each of them would contain it self within its own bounds, the one attending to the worldly welfare of the commonwealth, the other to the salvation of souls, it is impossible that any discord should ever have happened between them. *Sed, pudet haec approbria, etc.* God almighty grant, I beseech him, that the gospel of peace

may at length be preached, and that civil magistrates growing more careful to conform their own consciences to the law of God, and less solicitous about the binding of other men's consciences by humane laws, may, like fathers of their country, direct all their counsels and endeavours to promote universally the civil welfare of all their children; except only of such as are arrogant, ungovernable, and injurious to their brethren; and that all ecclesiastical men, who boast themselves to be the successors of the apostles, walking peaceably and modestly in the apostles steps, without intermeddling with state affairs, may apply themselves wholly to promote the salvation of souls.

Farewell.

Perhaps it may not be amiss to add a few things concerning *heresy* and *schism*. A *Turk* is not, nor can be, either heretic or schismatic, to a *Christian*: and if any man fall off from the Christian faith to Mahumetism, he does not thereby become a heretic or schismatic, but an apostate and an infidel. This no body doubts of. And by this it appears that men of different religions cannot be heretics or schismatics to one another.

We are to inquire therefore, what men are of the same religion. Concerning which, it is manifest that those who have one and the same rule of faith and worship, are of the same religion: and those who have not the same rule of faith and worship are of different religions. For since all things that belong unto that religion are contained in that rule, it follows necessarily that those who agree in one rule are of one and the same religion: and *vice versa.* Thus Turks and Christians are of different religions: because these take the *holy scriptures* to be the rule of their religion, and those the *Alcoran.* And for the same reason, there may be different religions also even among Christians. The *Papists* and the *Lutherans*, though both of them profess faith in Christ, and are therefore called Christians, yet are not both of the same religion: because these acknowledge nothing but the holy scriptures to be the rule and foundation of their religion; those take in also traditions and the decrees of popes, and of these together make the rule of their religion. And thus the Christians of St. *John* (as they are called) and the Christians of *Geneva* are of different religions: because these also take only the scriptures; and those I know not what traditions, for the rule of their religion.

This being settled, it follows; *first*, that heresy is a separation made in ecclesiastical communion between men of the same religion, for some opinions no way contained in the rule it self. And *secondly*, that among those who acknowledge nothing but the holy scriptures to be their rule of faith, heresy is a separation made in their Christian communion, for opinions not contained in the express words of scripture. Now this separation may be made in a twofold manner.

1. When the greater part, or (by the magistrate's patronage) the stronger part, of the church separates it self from others, by excluding them out of her communion, because they will not profess their belief of certain opinions which are not the express words of the scripture. For it is not the paucity of those that are separated, nor the authority of the magistrate, that can make any man guilty of heresy. But he only is a heretic who divides the church into parts, introduces names and marks of distinction, and voluntarily makes a separation because of such opinions.

2. When anyone separates himself from the communion of a church, because that church does not publicly profess some certain opinions which the holy scriptures do not expressly teach.

Both these are *heretics: because they err in fundamentals, and they err obstinately against knowledge.* For when they have determined the holy scriptures to be the only foundation of faith, they nevertheless lay down certain propositions as fundamental, which are not in the scripture; and because others will not acknowledge these additional opinions of theirs, nor build upon them as if they were necessary and fundamental, they therefore make a separation in the church; either by withdrawing themselves from the others, or expelling the others from them. Nor does it signify any thing for them to say that their confessions and symbols are agreeable to scripture, and to the analogy of faith. For if they be conceived in the express words of scripture, there can be no question about them; because those things are acknowledged by all Christians to be of divine inspiration, and therefore fundamental. But if they say that the articles which they require to be professed, are consequences deduced from the scripture; it is undoubtedly well done of them who believe and profess such things as seem unto them so agreeable to the rule of faith. But it would be very ill done to obtrude those things upon others, unto whom they do not seem to be the indubitable doctrines of the scripture. And to make a separation for such things as these, which neither are nor can be fundamental, is to become heretics. For I do not think there is any man arrived to that degree of madness, as that he dare give out his consequences and interpretations of scripture as divine inspirations, and compare the articles of faith that he has framed according to his own fancy with the authority of the scripture. I know there are some

propositions so evidently agreeable to scripture, that no body can deny them to be drawn from thence: but about those therefore there can be no difference. This only I say, that however clearly we may think this or the other doctrine to be deduced from scripture, we ought not therefore to impose it upon others, as a necessary article of faith, because we believe it to be agreeable to the rule of faith; unless we would be content also that other doctrines should be imposed upon us in the same manner; and that we should be compelled to receive and profess all the different and contradictory opinions of *Lutherans, Calvinists, Remonstrants, Anabaptists,* and other sects, which the contrivers of symbols, systems and confessions, are accustomed to deliver unto their followers as genuine and necessary deductions from the holy scripture. I cannot but wonder at the extravagant arrogance of those men who think that they themselves can explain things necessary to salvation more clearly than the holy ghost, the eternal and infinite wisdom of God.

Thus much concerning *heresy*; which word in common use is applied only to the doctrinal part of religion. Let us now consider *schism*, which is a crime near akin to it. For both those words seem unto me to signify an *ill-grounded separation in ecclesiastical communion, made about things not necessary.* But since use, which is the supreme law in matter of language, has determined that heresy relates to errors in faith, and schism to those in worship or discipline, we must consider them under that distinction.

Schism then, for the same reasons that have already been alleged, is nothing else but a separation made in the communion of the church, upon account of something in divine worship, or ecclesiastical discipline, that is not any necessary part of it. Now nothing in worship or discipline can be necessary to Christian communion, but what Christ our legislator, or the apostles, by inspiration of the holy spirit, have commanded in express words.

In a word: he that denies not any thing that the holy scriptures teach in express words, nor makes a separation upon occasion of any thing that is not manifestly contained in the sacred text; however he may be nicknamed by any sect of Christians, and declared by some, or all of them to be utterly void of true Christianity, yet indeed and in truth this man cannot be either a heretic or schismatic.

These things might have been explained more largely, and more advantageously: but it is enough to have hinted at them, thus briefly, to a person of your parts.

FINIS

Post-Reading Questions

Second Treatise
1. What is Locke's argument against absolute sovereignty?
2. How and why do we enter political society, for Locke? Is his account persuasive?
3. What role does property play in Locke's theory of why we seek to leave the state of nature?
4. What forms of government might satisfy Locke's criteria for political legitimacy (consent, mutual obligation, social contract)?

A Letter Concerning Toleration
1. What is Locke's argument for the separation of church and state?
2. What reasons does Locke give for state toleration of religious pluralism, and what limits to toleration does he propose?

CASE STUDY
QUEBEC'S ETHICS AND RELIGIOUS CULTURE COURSE

Introduction

In February 2012, the Supreme Court of Canada handed down a decision in *S.L. v. Commission scolaire des Chênes* (the School Board of Chênes, in Quebec). The case was brought against the school board by parents, L. and J., who claimed that the mandatory Ethics and Religious Culture (ERC) course in Quebec schools violated their and their children's rights to freedom of religion and conscience. The course, introduced in 2008, replaced the more narrowly religious (Catholic and Protestant) content of moral and religious instruction in the province's schools. The parents who filed suit were seeking a ruling affirming that their (and their children's) Charter rights had been violated, and hoped to overturn a lower court decision rejecting their request to exempt their children from the mandatory course.

In rejecting their appeal, the Supreme Court decision emphasized that freedom of religion and conscience is not violated by merely exposing persons (in this case, children) to a diverse range of religious and ethical beliefs. L. and J. were still free to raise their children in the Catholic faith; nothing abridged this fundamental freedom. The argument in favour of religious freedom made in John Locke's pivotal text, *A Letter Concerning Toleration*, would seem to support this conclusion. Locke was chiefly concerned with the dangers of state-imposed religion and the persecution of minority faiths that was widespread in Locke's own day (Locke himself was affiliated with the Dissenters, who were Christians of minority sects, such as the Quakers). In response to the view that the religious strife of the day was caused by the presence of minority Christian groups, Locke argued forcefully that the problem was not religious pluralism, but rather, religious *intolerance*. As Locke wrote, "It is not the diversity of opinions (which cannot be avoided) but the refusal of toleration to those that are of different opinions . . . that has produced all the bustles and wars that have been in the Christian world upon account of religion" (p. 55).

Whether Locke would have approved of something like Quebec's ERC course is of course not something we can know for sure. But there are reasons to suspect that he might well have endorsed it. The criteria for genuine violations of freedom of religion and conscience to which the Supreme Court's decision alludes are surely in the spirit of Locke's polemic against religious intolerance. The ERC course, the justices reasoned, did not attempt to instill a particular set of religious belief in the pupils, nor did it in any way suggest the inferiority (much less impermissibility) of particular faiths. For Locke, this is as it should be. Faith, he argued, cannot be compelled by force; religion is voluntary, just as all belief is voluntary. Locke was in one sense in agreement with the parents in this case, then, for he agreed that exposing religious views to rational scrutiny and open debate could indeed cause us to change our beliefs. Unlike many of the parents seeking to exempt their children from the ERC course, however, he welcomed this possibility. Indeed, Locke observed that the majority of people in his own time lived and worked in circumstances that, regrettably, prevented them from examining their own belief systems, for they lacked access to education and free public exchange of religious ideas.

While the Court's decision is mainly a rejection of the appellants' claim that their Charter right to freedom of conscience and religion had been violated, the judgment also notes the rise of religious diversity in Quebec as in Canada as a whole and appears to endorse the ideal of religious and ethical pluralism that inspired the introduction of the ERC course into the school curriculum.

From *S.L. v. Commission scolaire des Chênes*, [2012] 1 S.C.R. 235

S.L. v. Commission scolaire des Chênes, *2012 SCC 7, [2012] 1 S.C.R. 235.*
http://scc.lexum.org/decisia-scc-csc/scc-csc/scc-csc/en/7992/1/document.do

English version of the judgment of McLachlin C.J. and Binnie, Deschamps, Abella, Charron, Rothstein and Cromwell JJ.
[The majority decision was delivered by Deschamps J.]

. . .

I. Facts

On 12 May 2008, the appellants requested that the school board exempt their children from the ERC course, putting forward the existence of serious harm to the children within the meaning of the second paragraph of s. 222 of the Education Act.

On 20 May 2008, the director of educational resources for young students denied the exemptions. On 26 May 2008, the appellants requested that the school board's council of commissioners reconsider that decision. On 25 June 2008, after a hearing at which the appellants presented their position, the council of commissioners upheld the director's decision. The appellants contested the decisions of 20 May and 25 June at the Superior Court, arguing that they had been made at the dictate of a third party, the ministère de l'education, du loisir et du sport ("ministère"). They sought both a declaration that the ERC program infringed their and their children's right to freedom of conscience and religion, and judicial review of the decision of the director and that of the council of commissioners, denying their requests for exemption from the ERC course. . . .

III. Issues

To begin, this Court must decide whether the trial judge erred in holding that the school board's refusal to exempt the appellants' children from the ERC course did not infringe the appellants' freedom of conscience and religion. This issue turns on whether the trial judge erred in finding that the appellants had not proven that the ERC program itself infringed their freedom of religion.

Then, the Court must decide whether the trial judge erred in holding that the school board's decision had not been made at the dictate of a third party and whether the

Court of Appeal erred in law in holding that the appeal had become moot.

. . .

VI. Application

The appellants sincerely believe that they have an obligation to pass on the precepts of the Catholic religion to their children (A.F., at para. 66). The sincerity of their belief in this practice is not challenged by the respondents in this case. The only question at issue is whether the appellants' ability to observe the practice has been interfered with.

To discharge their burden at the stage of proving an infringement, the appellants had to show that, from an objective standpoint, the ERC program interfered with their ability to pass their faith on to their children. This is not the approach they took. Instead, they argued that it was enough for them to say that the program infringed their right (A.F., at para. 126). As I have already explained, it is not enough for the appellants to say that they had religious reasons for objecting to their children's participation in the ERC course. Dubois J. of the Superior Court was therefore correct in rejecting that interpretation. He stated the following: [TRANSLATION] "To claim that the general presentation of various religions may have an adverse effect on the religion one practices, it is not enough to state with sincerity that one is a practising Catholic."

In their requests for exemption made to the school board on 12 May 2008, the appellants had alleged that the ERC course was liable to cause the following harm: [TRANSLATION]

1. Losing the right to choose an education consistent with one's own moral and religious principles; interfering with the fundamental freedom of religion, conscience, opinion and expression of children and their parents by forcing children to take a course that does not reflect the religious and philosophical beliefs with which their parents have the right and duty to bring them up.
2. Being put in the situation of learning from a teacher who is not adequately trained in the subject matter and who has been deprived of freedom of conscience by being forced to perform this task.
3. Upsetting children by exposing them at too young an age to convictions and beliefs that differ from the ones favoured by their parents.
4. Dealing with the phenomenon of religion in a course that claims to be "neutral."
5. Being exposed, through this mandatory course, to the philosophical trend advocated by the state, namely relativism.
6. Interfering with children's faith.

The principal argument that emerges from the reasons given by the appellants in their requests for an exemption is that the obligation they believe they have, namely to pass on their faith to their children, has been interfered with. In this regard, the freedom of religion asserted by the appellants is their own freedom, not that of the children. The common theme that runs through the appellants' objections is that the ERC program is not in fact neutral. According to the appellants, students following the ERC course would be exposed to a form of relativism, which would interfere with the appellants' ability to pass their faith on to their children. Insofar as certain of the appellants' complaints focus on the children's freedom of religion by referring to the "disruption" that would result from exposing them to different religious facts, I will discuss this in my analysis of the alleged infringement of the appellants' freedom of religion.

. . .

Therefore, following a realistic and non-absolutist approach, state neutrality is assured when the state neither favours nor hinders any particular religious belief, that is, when it shows respect for all postures toward religion, including that of having no religious beliefs whatsoever, while taking into account the competing constitutional rights of the individuals affected.

. . .

The ERC program has two components: instruction in ethics and instruction in religious culture. Its purpose is set out in the preamble found in each of the documents entitled "Ethics and Religious Culture" prepared by the ministère (online), one for the elementary level and the other for the secondary level:

For the purposes of this program, instruction in ethics is aimed at developing an understanding of ethical questions that allows students to make judicious choices based on knowledge of the values and references present in society. The objective is not to propose or impose moral rules, nor to study philosophical doctrines and systems in an exhaustive manner. Instruction in religious culture, for its part, is aimed at fostering an understanding of several religious traditions whose influence has been felt and is still felt in our society today. In this regard, emphasis will be placed on Quebec's religious heritage. The historical and cultural importance of

Catholicism and Protestantism will be given particular prominence. The goal is neither to accompany students in a spiritual quest, nor to present the history of doctrines and religions, nor to promote some new common religious doctrine aimed at replacing specific beliefs.

The ministère's formal purpose thus does not appear to have been to transmit a philosophy based on relativism or to influence young people's specific beliefs.

Regarding the program itself, Dubois J. reviewed the documentary evidence, heard the witnesses and drew the following conclusions,

> [TRANSLATION] Under the new program, the school will present the range of different religions and get children to talk about self-recognition and the common good. Subsequently, therefore, the additional work that must be done for religious practice is up to the parents and the pastors of the Church to which the parents and children belong.
>
> In light of all the evidence adduced, the Court does not see how the ERC course interferes with the applicants' freedom of conscience and religion for their children when what is done is to make a comprehensive presentation of various religions without forcing the children to join them.

After reviewing the record, I see no error in the trial judge's assessment. Having adopted a policy of neutrality, the Quebec government cannot set up an education system that favours or hinders any one religion or a particular vision of religion. Nevertheless, it is up to the government to choose educational programs within its constitutional framework. In light of this context, I cannot conclude that exposing children to "a comprehensive presentation of various religions without forcing the children to join them" constitutes in itself an indoctrination of students that would infringe the appellants' freedom of religion.

The appellants also maintain that exposing children to various religious facts is confusing for them. The confusion or "vacuum" allegedly results from the fact that different beliefs are presented on an equal footing.

. . .

Parents are free to pass their personal beliefs on to their children if they so wish. However, the early exposure of children to realities that differ from those in their immediate family environment is a fact of life in society. The suggestion that exposing children to a variety of religious facts in itself infringes their religious freedom or that of their parents amounts to a rejection of the multicultural reality of Canadian society and ignores the Quebec government's obligations with regard to public education. Although such exposure can be a source of friction, it does not in itself constitute an infringement of s. 2(a) of the Canadian Charter and of s. 3 of the Quebec Charter.

The appellants have not proven that the ERC program infringed their freedom of religion. Therefore, the trial judge did not err in holding that the school board's refusal to exempt their children from the ERC course did not violate their constitutional right.

Moreover, the appellants have shown no error that would justify setting aside the trial judge's conclusion that the school board's decision was not made at the dictate of a third party. As for the Court of Appeal's decision to dismiss the appeal for mootness, suffice it to say that the question before this Court was important and that it justified hearing the appeal even though the appellants' children were no longer subject to the obligation to take the ERC course.

The Court of Appeal was therefore right to uphold the conclusions of the Superior Court. For these reasons, the appeal is dismissed with costs.

. . .

Post-Case-Reading Questions

1. In light of Locke's views in his *Letter Concerning Toleration*, how might he respond to parents' claim that their and their children's rights to freedom of conscience and religion are violated by the mandatory Ethics and Religious Culture course?
2. If he were living today, would Locke endorse the Ethics and Religious Culture course as a means to promote toleration for religious pluralism, or would he prefer that no instruction on religion, however ecumenical, be given?

CHAPTER VI

Jean-Jacques Rousseau

Introduction

Jean-Jacques Rousseau was born in Geneva in 1712. His mother died shortly after his birth, he was raised by his father until the age of 10. At that time, Rousseau's father fled Geneva to avoid arrest—the result of a fight—and Rousseau was left in the care of an uncle. Soon he was sent (along with his cousin) to a local boarding school run by a pastor, where he reamained for 2 years. Upon leaving the school, he was apprenticed to an engraver in Geneva. There, the regular beatings he received motivated him to flee Geneva, as he tells us in his autobiography, *The Confessions*. In nearby Savoy, Rousseau received shelter from a Catholic priest, who soon transferred him to the care of a woman (Baronne de Warens) who converted young Protestants to Catholicism. After his own conversion, Rousseau worked as a domestic servant, teacher, and musician, and briefly trained to become a priest. In

Jean-Jacques Rousseau

© iStockphoto.com/Georgios Kollidas

1731 he moved into Mme. de Warens' house in Chamberly, where he remained—as her pupil, and later lover—for the remainder of the decade. Rousseau was a bright student and managed to digest a large amount of classical literature and philosophy during his time in Lyons.

In 1742, when he was 30 years old, Rousseau arrived in Paris. This was the time of the French Enlightenment: Paris was inflamed by the challenge that the *philosophes* of the *Encyclopédie project*—notably, Voltaire, Montesquieu, Diderot, d'Alembert and Condorcet—posed to traditional thinking about religion, morality, and government. They ushered in a new faith, one grounded in the emancipatory power of reason to offer us reliable knowledge. With little formal education, Rousseau joined the lively and creative atmosphere of the Age of Reason in Paris. While his association with the circle of the *philosophes* allowed him to socialize with higher classes of French society, he remained rather timid and diffident by nature and eventually rejected the airs of Parisian society. In 1746, he met Thérèse Levasseur, an uneducated laundress girl. They had five children together, all of whom were given away to an orphanage soon after birth.

In 1749, the Academy of Dijon announced an essay competition on the question "Has the restoration of the sciences and the arts contributed to the purification of morals?" Rousseau's reaction to this question was quite passionate, and he expressed his ideas in his prize-winning essay *Discourse on the Arts and Science* (1750). Opposing the spirit of the Age of Reason, Rousseau argued that the replacement of religion by science, and of feeling, by logic, had led to a corruption of morals. Human beings, he insisted, are by nature good and only get corrupted by bad institutions. Rousseau went on to write many important essays, including *Discourse on the Origins of Inequality* and *Discourse on Political Economy*, which similarly take issue with Enlightenment notions of reason and progress. These latter essays were followed by two very popular novels, *Julie, or the New Héloïse* (1761) and *Emile, or On Education* (1762). Rousseau is most widely read today for his contributions to political philosophy, which include the aforementioned two discourses, *The Social Contract, or Principles of Political Right* (1762), *Constitutional Project for Corsica* (1765), and *Considerations on the Government of Poland* (1772).

The social contract, according to Rousseau, is the solution to a problem of political community: how "to find a form of association which will defend and protect . . . the person and property of each associate, and under which each of them, uniting himself to all, will obey himself alone, and remain as free as before" (*The Social Contract*, book I, ch. vi). In contrast to Hobbes' view of human nature, and more in line with Locke's vision, Rousseau defended a positive view of humanity as essentially good. Also like Locke, he believed that we are born free with the ability for self-determination, but need to find a balance between personal freedom and political obedience. There is an obvious tension between these constituting aspects of community, however. Rousseau proposes to resolve the tension by introducing his notion of the "general will," which expresses the idea of political obedience to laws that one makes oneself, in concert with one's fellow citizens. Importantly, this idea requires that we view one another as social and political equals within a democratic republic. Democratic governance is not simply a matter of aggregating citizens' individual preferences, but rather of forming a political community united by common interests. Indeed, Rousseau took care to distinguish what he called the general will—which is concerned with the common interest—from the will of all, which simply is the sum of people's private interests.

To realize and maintain such a model of political association, Rousseau does not envision a representative form of government; rather, he proposes a model of direct democracy much like that associated with ancient Rome, where citizens met regularly to deliberate on issues concerning the common good. Not surprisingly, Rousseau advocated the formation of smaller polities with homogeneous populations, which he believed could facilitate this kind of democratic will formation. But in today's increasingly diverse liberal democracies, it is arguably more difficult to discover values and goods shared by all citizens. Rousseau's emphasis on the idea of developing "civic virtues" that would foster patriotism has caused some to characterize his theory as being hostile to value pluralism, and even as having totalitarian overtones.

Rousseau's political ideas did not find much support during his own lifetime. His educational treatise, *Emile*, attracted the opposition of Church officials, which led to its banning (and public burning) in Paris and Geneva in 1762. Rousseau fled France, returning to his native Switzerland, and later moved to England at the invitation of philosopher David Hume. Eventually suffering from acute paranoia, Rousseau became convinced that Hume was plotting to kill him and returned to France in 1767, still in the grips of mental illness. Before his death in 1778, he wrote several additional texts—in botany, music, and politics—and completed his lengthy *Confessions*.

The case to be considered in conjunction with Rousseau's thought is the *Reference Regarding the Secession of Quebec*, in which the Supreme Court was asked to rule on the question of Quebec's right to secede unilaterally from Canada. The Court gives an account of Canadian constitutionalism and its main principles, which call to mind the Rousseauian idea of the general will.

Further Readings

Cassirer, E. (1989). *The Question of Jean-Jacques Rousseau* (2nd edition). New Haven: Yale University Press.

Fralin, R. (1978). *Rousseau and Representation*. New York: Columbia University Press.

Miller, J. (1984). *Rousseau: Dreamer of Democracy*. New Haven: Yale University Press.

Riley, P. (1986). *The General Will Before Rousseau: Transformation of the Divine into the Civil*. Princeton: Princeton University Press.

Wokler, R. (2003). *Rousseau: A Very Short Introduction*. Oxford: Oxford University Press.

Jean-Jacques Rousseau, From *The Social Contract*

Jean-Jacques Rousseau, The Social Contract, *translated by Christopher Betts (New York: Oxford University Press, 1994).*

Book I

I intend to examine whether, in the ordering of society, there can be any reliable and legitimate rule of administration, taking men as they are, and laws as they can be. I shall try, throughout my enquiry, to combine what is allowed by right[1] with what is prescribed by self-interest, in order that justice and utility should not be separated.

I begin my discussion without proving the importance of my subject. People will ask me whether I write on politics because I am a ruler or a legislator. I answer that I am not; and that is the reason why I write on politics. If I were a ruler or legislator, I should not waste my time saying what ought to be done; I should do it, or hold my peace.

I was born a citizen of a free state and a member of its sovereign body,[2] and however weak may be the influence of my voice in public affairs, my right to vote on them suffices to impose on me the duty of studying them. How happy I am, each time that I reflect on governments, always to find new reasons, in my researches, to cherish the government of my country!

Chapter I The Subject of the First Book

Man was born free,[3] and everywhere he is in chains. There are some who may believe themselves masters of others, and are no less enslaved than they. How has this change come about? I do not know. How can it be made legitimate? That is a question which I believe I can resolve.

If I were to consider force alone, and the effects that it produces, I should say: for so long as a nation is constrained to obey, and does so, it does well; as soon as it is able to throw off its servitude, and does so, it does better; for since it regains freedom by the same right that was exercised when its freedom was seized, either the nation was justified in taking freedom back or else those who took it away were unjustified in doing so. Whereas the social order is a sacred right, and provides a foundation for all other rights. Yet it is a right that does not come from nature; therefore it is based on agreed conventions. Our business is to find out what those conventions are. Before we come to that, I must make good the assertion that I have just put forward.

Chapter II The First Societies

The most ancient of all societies, and the only one that is natural, is the family. Even in this case, the bond between children and father persists only so long as they have need of him for their conservation. As soon as this need ceases, the natural bond is dissolved. The children are released from the obedience they owe to their father, the father is released from the duty of care to the children, and all become equally independent. If they continue to remain living together, it is not by nature but voluntarily, and the family itself is maintained only through convention.[4]

This shared freedom is a result of man's nature. His first law is his own conservation, his first cares are owed to himself; as soon as he reaches the age of reason, he alone is the judge of how best to look after himself, and thus he becomes his own master.

If we wish, then, the family may be regarded as the first model of political society: the leader corresponds to the father, the people to the children, and all being born free and equal, none alienates his freedom except for reasons of utility. The sole difference is that, in the family, the father is paid for the care he takes of his children by the love he bears them, while in the state this love is replaced by the pleasure of being in command, the chief having no love for his people.

Grotius denies that all human power is instituted for the benefit of the governed.[5] He cites slavery as an example; his commonest mode of reasoning is to base a right on a fact.[6] A more logical method could be employed, but not one that is more favourable to tyrants.

It is therefore doubtful, following Grotius, whether the human race belongs to a hundred or so men, or whether these hundred men belong to the human race, and he seems inclined, throughout his book, toward the former opinion. This is Hobbes's view also.[7] Behold then the human race divided into herds of cattle, each with its chief, who preserves it in order to devour it.

"As a shepherd is of a nature superior to that of his flock, so too the shepherds of men, their chiefs, are of a nature superior to their peoples"—this argument, according to Philo, was used by the Emperor Caligula;[8] who would conclude (correctly enough, given his analogy) either that kings were gods or that the people were animals.

The reasoning employed by this Caligula amounts to the same as that of Hobbes and Grotius. Aristotle[9] too had said, earlier than any of them, that men are not naturally equal, but that some are born for slavery and some for mastery.

Aristotle was right, but he took the effect for the cause. Any man who is born in slavery is born for slavery; there is nothing surer. Slaves in their chains lose everything, even the desire to be rid of them; they love their servitude, like the companions of Odysseus, who loved their brutishness.[10] If there are slaves by nature, it is because slaves have been made against nature. The first slaves were made by force, and they remained so through cowardice.

I have said nothing of King Adam or of the Emperor Noah, the father of three great monarchs who shared the universe among themselves, like the children of Saturn, with whom they have been identified.[11] I hope that my restraint in this respect will be appreciated; for, being descended directly from one or other of these princes, and maybe from the senior branch of the family, who

knows but that, if my entitlement were verified, I might not find that I am the legitimate king of the human race? However that may be, it cannot be denied that Adam was sovereign over the world, like Crusoe on his island, for so long as he was the sole inhabitant; and the advantage of this form of rule was that the monarch, firm on his throne, had neither rebellions, nor wars, nor conspirators to fear.

Chapter III The Right of the Strongest

The stronger party is never strong enough to remain the master for ever, unless he transforms his strength into right, and obedience into duty. This is the source of the "right of the strongest," a right which people treat with apparent irony[12] and which in reality is an established principle. But can anyone ever explain the phrase? Force is a physical power; I do not see how any morality can be based on its effects. To yield to force is an act of necessity, not of consent; at best it is an act of prudence. In what sense can it be a duty?

Let us suppose for a moment that this alleged right is valid. I say that the result would be completely senseless. For as soon as right is founded on force, the effect will alter with its cause; any force that is stronger than the first must have right on its side in its turn. As soon as anyone is able to disobey with impunity he may do so legitimately, and since the strongest is always right the only question is how to ensure that one is the strongest. But what kind of a right is it that is extinguished when that strength is lost? If we must obey because of force we have no need to obey out of duty, and if we are no longer forced to obey we no longer have any obligation to do so. It can be seen therefore that the word "right" adds nothing to force; it has no meaning at all here.

"Obey the powers that be."[13] If this means: "Yield to force," it is a sound precept, but superfluous; I can guarantee that it will never be violated. All power is from God, I admit; but all disease is from God also. Does that mean we are forbidden to call the doctor? If a highwayman ambushes me on a road by a wood, I must give him my money by force, but if I can keep it away from him am I obliged in conscience to give it up? After all, the pistol that he holds is also a power.

Let us agree then that might is not right, and that we are obliged to obey only legitimate powers. Thus we return to my original question.

Chapter IV Slavery

Since no man has a natural authority over his fellow, and since strength does not confer any right, it follows that the basis remaining for all legitimate authority among men must be agreed convention.[14]

If, says Grotius, an individual is able to transfer[15] his liberty, and become the slave of a master, why should an entire nation not transfer its liberty and become subject to a king?[16] Here we have several equivocal words that need elucidation, but let us keep to the term *transfer*. To transfer is to give or to sell. Now a man who becomes the slave of another does not give himself: he sells himself, in exchange, at the very least, for his subsistence. But in exchange for what does a nation sell itself? A king, far from providing subsistence to his subjects, takes it all from them, and as Rabelais says, a king doesn't live cheaply. So will his subjects give him their persons on condition that he will take their property also? I cannot see what they still have to keep.

It will be objected that a despot ensures civil peace for his subjects. Very well; but what do they gain thereby, if the wars that his ambition brings down on them, his insatiable greed, and the troubles inflicted by his administrators, plague them more sorely than their dissensions would? What do they gain thereby, if civil peace itself is a source of misery? Prisoners live peacefully in their dungeons; is that enough for them to feel comfortable there? The Greek captives in the cave of the Cyclops[17] lived there peacefully, while awaiting their turn to be devoured.

To say that a man gives himself for nothing is an absurd and incomprehensible statement; such an action is illegitimate and void, simply because anyone who does it is not in his right mind. To say the same about an entire people is to imagine a nation of madmen, and madness does not make rights.

Even if each person could transfer himself, he could not transfer his children; they are born men, and free; their freedom belongs to them, and nobody except them has the right to dispose of it. Until they reach the age of reason, their father can stipulate, in their name, the conditions for their conservation and well-being, but he cannot make a gift of them, irrevocably and without condition; such a gift is contrary to the purposes of nature and exceeds the rights of fatherhood. In order, then, for an arbitrary government to be legitimate, it would be necessary for the people, at every new generation, to have the power to accept it or reject it; but in that case the government would no longer be arbitrary.

To renounce our freedom is to renounce our character as men, the rights, and even the duties, of humanity. No compensation is possible for anyone who renounces everything. It is incompatible with the nature of man; to remove the will's freedom is to remove all morality from our actions. Finally, a convention is vain and

contradictory if it stipulates absolute authority on one side and limitless obedience on the other. Is it not obvious that we have no obligations towards a person from whom we can demand anything, and that this condition, requiring nothing in return or exchange, is enough to render the covenant null? For what right can my slave have against me, since everything he has belongs to me? His rights being mine, a right of mine against myself is a word without a meaning.

Grotius and the others take war to be another origin of the so-called right of slavery.[18] The conqueror having the right, according to them, to kill the conquered, the latter may redeem his life at the expense of his freedom; an agreement that is the more legitimate because it is to the advantage of both parties.

But it is clear that this so-called right to kill the conquered does not derive in any way from the state of war. For the simple reason that men who are living in their original continuous relationship with each other for a state either of peace or war to exist, they are not naturally enemies.[19] It is the relationship of things, not of men, that constitutes a state of war, and since the state of war cannot be engendered merely be personal relationships but only be relationships between things,[20] a private war between man and man cannot exist—either in the state of nature, in which there is no permanent possession of property, or in the social state, in which everything is controlled by laws.

Single combat, duels, and chance encounters are actions which do not produce a state of affairs; and with respect to private wars, which were authorized by the Establishments of Louis IX of France and abrogated by the Peace of God,[21] they were an abuse due to feudal government, an absurd system if ever there was one, contrary both to the principles of natural law and all good polity.[22]

War is not, therefore, a relationship between man and man, but between state and state, in which individuals become enemies only by accident, not as men, nor even as citizens,[23] but as soldiers; not even as members of their own nation, but as its defenders. Furthermore each state can be enemy only to other states, and not to men, given that between things diverse in nature no true relationship can be established.

The principle involved conforms, moreover, to maxims accepted in every age, and to the constant practice of every politically organized nation. Declarations of war are notices given less to national powers than to their subjects.[24] A foreign king, or private individual, or people, who pillages, kills or detains a ruler's subjects, without declaring war on the ruler, is not an enemy, but a brigand. Even in war proper, a just ruler will indeed take possession, when he is in enemy territory, of anything belonging to the public, but will respect the person and property of individuals; he is respecting the rights on which his own are founded. The purpose of war being to destroy the enemy state, its defenders may rightfully be killed so long as they are carrying arms; but as soon as they lay them down and surrender, ceasing to be enemies or agents of the enemy, they become simply men again, and there is no longer any right over their lives. On occasion it is possible to kill the state without killing any of its members; war confers no rights that are not necessary to its purpose. These are not Grotius's principles; they are not based on the authority of poets, but derive from the nature of things, and are based on reason.[25]

As regards the right of conquest, its only foundation is the right of the strongest. If war does not give the victor the right to massacre the vanquished people, this right that he does not possess cannot create the right to enslave them. One has the right to kill an enemy only when it is impossible to make a slave of him: therefore the right to enslave him does not come from the right to kill him; therefore it is an iniquitous exchange to make him pay with his freedom for his life, over which one has no right. Is it not plain that there is a vicious circle in basing the right of life and death on the right to enslave, and the right to enslave on the right of life and death?

Even if we were to admit this terrible right of massacre, I say that men enslaved in war, or a conquered people, have no obligation at all to their masters, beyond obeying them to the extent that they are forced to do so. The conqueror has not spared the slave's life when he has taken the equivalent of life: instead of killing him without profit he has killed him usefully. So far from any authority having been added to the power that the one has over the other, the state of war continues between them, and their relation is the consequence of it. The enforcement of a right of war does not create the assumption that a peace treaty has been made. An agreement has indeed been reached, but this covenant is far from destroying the state of war, and makes the assumption that it still continues.

From whatever angle the question is considered, then, the right of slavery is void, not only because it is illegitimate, but because of its absurdity and meaninglessness. The words *slavery* and *right* contradict each other; they are mutually exclusive. Whether made by one man addressing another, or by a man addressing a nation, this statement will always be equally senseless: "I make a covenant between us which is entirely at your expense and entirely for my good, which I will observe as long as I please, and which you will observe as long as I please."

Chapter V That It Is Always Necessary to Go Back to an Original Convention

Even if I were to grant the truth of everything that I have refuted up to now, the instigators of despotism would be no further forward. There will always be a great difference between subjugating a multitude of men and ruling a society. If a series of men, in succession, are made to submit to one other man, all I can see in them is a master with his slaves, however many of them there may be; I cannot see a people and its leader. It could be said to be an aggregation, but it is not an association; there is no public good, no body politic. The one man, even if he were to have subjugated half the world, is still only an individual; his self-interest, separate from that of the rest, is still only a private interest. If this same man comes to his end, his empire after him is scattered and dissolved, as an oak breaks up and falls into a heap of ashes after being consumed by fire.

A people, says Grotius, can give itself to a king.[26] A people is a people, therefore, according to Grotius, before it gives itself to a king. The gift itself is a civil act, and assumes some public deliberation. Hence it would be as well, before we examine the act by which a people elects a king, to examine the act by which a people is a people. For this act is necessarily anterior to the other, and is the true foundation of society.

For if there were no prior covenant, where would the obligation be (if the election were not unanimous) for the minority to submit to the choice of the majority, and how could it be right for the votes of 100 who wanted a master to be binding on 10 who did not? The law of the majority vote itself establishes a covenant, and assumes that on one occasion at least there has been unanimity.[27]

Chapter VI The Social Pact

I make the assumption that there is a point in the development of mankind[28] at which the obstacles to men's self-preservation in the state of nature are too great to be overcome by the strength that any one individual can exert in order to maintain himself in this state. The original state can then subsist no longer, and the human race would perish if it did not change its mode of existence.

Now as men cannot generate new strength, but only unify and control the forces already existing, the sole means that they still have of preserving themselves is to create, by combination, a totality of forces sufficient to overcome the obstacles resisting them, to direct their operation by a single impulse, and make them act in unison.

The totality of forces can be formed only by the collaboration of a number of persons; but each man's strength and freedom being the main instruments of his preservation, how can he commit them to others without harming himself, and without neglecting the duty of care to himself? The difficulty as it relates to my subject may be defined in the following terms:

"Find a form of association which will defend and protect, with the whole of its joint strength, the person and property of each associate, and under which each of them, uniting himself to all, will obey himself alone, and remain as free as before." This is the fundamental problem to which the social contract gives the answer.

The clauses of this contract are so closely determined by the nature of the act in question that the slightest modification would make them empty and ineffectual; whence it is that, although they may perhaps never have been formally pronounced, they are the same everywhere, and everywhere tacitly recognized and accepted, until, should the social pact be violated, each associate thereupon recovers his original rights and takes back his natural freedom, while losing the freedom of convention for which he gave it up.

Properly understood, the clauses can all be reduced to one alone, namely, the complete transfer of each associate, with all his rights, to the whole community. For in the first place, each giving himself completely, the condition is the same for all; and the condition being the same for all, none has any interest in making it burdensome to the others.

Further, the transfer being carried out unreservedly, the union between the associates is as perfect as it can be, and none of them has any further requirements to add. For if individuals retained some rights, there being no common superior to give judgment between them and the public, each would make his own judgment on certain points, and would soon aspire to do so on all of them: the state of nature would remain in force, and the association would become, necessarily, either tyrannical or meaningless.

Finally, each in giving himself to all gives himself to none, and since there are no associates over whom he does not acquire the same rights as he cedes, he gains the equivalent of all that he loses, and greater strength for the conservation of what he possesses.

If therefore we set aside everything that is not essential to the social pact, we shall find that it may be reduced to the following terms. *Each of us puts his person and all his power in common under the supreme direction of the general will; and we as a body receive each member as an indivisible part of the whole.*[29]

Immediately, this act of association produces, in place of the individual persons of every contracting party, a moral and collective body, which is composed of as many members as there are votes in the assembly, and which, by the same act, is endowed with its unity, its common self, its life, and its will. The public person that is formed in this way by the union of all the others once bore the name *city*,[30] I and now bears that of *republic* or *body politic*; its members call it *the state* when it is passive, *the sovereign* when it is active, and a *power* when comparing it to its like. As regards the associates, they collectively take the name of *people*, and are individually called *citizens* as being participants in sovereign authority, and *subjects* as being bound by the laws of the state. But these terms are often confused, and one is taken for another; it is enough to know how to distinguish between them on the occasions when they are applied with complete precision.

Chapter VII The Sovereign

It will be seen from the formulation above that the act of association involves a reciprocal commitment between public and private persons; each individual enters on a contract with himself, so to speak, and becomes bound in a double capacity, namely, toward other individuals inasmuch as he is a member of the sovereign, and towards the sovereign inasmuch as he is a member of the state.[31] But the maxim used in civil law, that none is held to an undertaking made with himself, cannot be applied here, for to have an obligation towards oneself is quite different from having an obligation toward a whole of which one is a member.

We must note also that public decisions can put each subject under an obligation towards the sovereign, because he may be considered in his two different capacities, but, for the opposite reason, they cannot put the sovereign under any obligation towards itself; and in consequence, it is contrary to the nature of the body politic that the sovereign should impose on itself a law that it cannot infringe. Since it can be considered only in one capacity, it is in the situation of an individual contracting with himself; whence it will be seen that there is no kind of fundamental law, and cannot be any, not even the social contract, which is binding on the people as a body.[32] This does not mean that, in any matter not affecting the contract, the people cannot have a binding obligation towards others; for in respect of foreign nations it becomes a single being, an individual.

But since the body politic or the sovereign derives its being solely from the sanctity of the contract,[33] it cannot oblige itself to do anything that derogates from this original deed; for instance, to alienate some portion of itself or to submit to some other sovereign. To violate the act through which it exists would be to destroy itself, and that which is nothing can give rise to nothing.

As soon as the multitude is united thus in one body, it is impossible to injure one of its members without attacking the body, and still less to injure the body without its members being affected. Hence duty and self-interest oblige both contracting parties equally to give each other mutual assistance, and the same individuals must seek, in their double capacity, to take advantage of all the benefits which depend on it.

The sovereign, then, consisting solely of the individual persons which form it, has and can have no self-interest that is contrary to theirs; as a result, it does not need to give any form of guarantee to its subjects,[34] because it is impossible that the body should want to harm all its members; and as we shall see later,[35] it cannot harm any one individually. Simply by virtue of its existence, the sovereign is always what it should be.

But the position is different for the sovereign in relation to the subjects, because, despite the common interests of the two, nothing guarantees their commitment to it unless it can find a means of ensuring their fidelity.

For each individual can have, as a man, a personal will that is contrary or dissimilar to the general will that he has as a citizen. His personal interest can speak to him quite differently from the common interest: his mode of existence, absolute and independent, can make him regard what he owes to the common cause as a gratuitous contribution, the loss of which will be less onerous to others than its payment is for him; and envisaging the artificial person, in which the state consists, as an abstract being, on the grounds that it is not a man, he would thus enjoy the rights of a citizen while declining to fulfil the duties of a subject, an example of injustice which, if it were to spread, would bring the ruin of the body politic.

In order therefore that the social pact should not be an empty formula, it contains an implicit obligation which alone can give force to the others, that if anyone refuses to obey the general will he will be compelled to do so by the whole body; which means nothing else than that he will be forced to be free;[36] for such is the condition which, giving each citizen to his country, guarantees that he will not depend on any person.[37] This condition is the device that ensures the operation of the political machine; it alone legitimizes civil obligations, which without it would be absurd and tyrannical, and subject to the most terrible abuses.

Chapter VIII The Civil State[38]

This passage from the state of nature to the civil state produces in man a very remarkable change, replacing instinct by justice in his behaviour, and conferring on his actions the moral quality that they had lacked before. It is only now, as the voice of duty succeeds to physical impulse and right to appetite, that man, who had previously thought of nothing but himself, is compelled to act on other principles, and to consult his reason before he attends to his inclinations. Although, in the civil state, he deprives himself of a number of advantages which he has by nature, the others that he acquires are so great, so greatly are his faculties exercised and improved, his ideas amplified, his feelings ennobled, and his entire soul raised so much higher, that if the abuses that occur in his new condition did not frequently reduce him to a state lower than the one he has just left, he ought constantly to bless the happy moment when he was taken from it for ever, and which made of him, not a limited and stupid animal, but an intelligent being and a man.

Let us convert the balance of gains and losses into terms that are easy to compare. What man loses by the social contract is his natural freedom and an unlimited right to anything by which he is tempted and can obtain; what he gains is civil freedom and the right of property over everything that he possesses.

In order not to be misled over the compensating advantages, we must clearly distinguish natural freedom, which is limited only by the strength of the individual, from civil freedom, which is limited by the general will; and possession, which is merely the effect of force or the right of the first occupant, from property, which can be founded only on positive entitlement.

To the acquisition of moral status could be added, on the basis of what has just been said, the acquisition of moral liberty, this being the only thing that makes man truly the master of himself; for to be driven by our appetites alone is slavery, while to obey a law that we have imposed on ourselves is freedom. But I have already said more than enough on this point, and the philosophical sense of the word *freedom* is not my subject here.

Chapter IX Property[39]

Each member of the community, at the moment of its formation, gives himself to it as he then is, together with all his resources, of which the goods he possesses are part. It is not that, by this act, possessions change their nature as the possessor changes, so as to become property in the hands of the sovereign. But, just as the resources of the state are incomparably greater than those of one individual, so too public possession is, in fact, stronger and more irrevocable, although—at least for foreigners—it is no more legitimate. For the state, as regards its members, is master of all their property through the social contract, which in the state acts as the basis of all rights; but as regards other powers it is master only by the right of the first occupant, which passes to it from private individuals.

The right of the first occupant is more real than the right of the strongest, but does not become a true right until the right of property has been established. Every man has naturally a right to everything that is necessary to him; but by the positive legal act which makes him the owner of certain goods he is excluded from all the rest. He has his share, and must keep to it; he no longer has any rights over the community's goods. Here we have the reason why the right of first occupancy, which in the state of nature is so fragile, is respected by all in the civil state. Under this right, it is not so much property belonging to others, but rather property not belonging to us, that we respect.

In general, the following conditions are required in order to justify the right of first occupancy for a given piece of land. First, the land must as yet be uninhabited; secondly, no more must be occupied than is needed for subsistence; and in the third place, possession must be taken not by empty ceremonies, but by work and cultivation, the only mark of ownership which ought, in default of juridical title, to be respected by others.

For if we grant that the needs of the first occupier, and the work he does, create a right, have we not extended this right as far as it can go? How can it not be limited? Does putting one's foot on a piece of land suffice as a claim to ownership? If we have enough strength to keep other men out of it for a while, does that suffice to deprive them of their right ever to return? If a man, or a nation, lays hold of huge territories and denies them to the whole human race, what else is it but an act of usurpation deserving punishment, since it takes from the rest of mankind the dwelling-place and the sustenance which nature gives them in common? When, in the name of the kingdom of Castile, Nuñez Balboa[40] took possession, on the sea-shore, of the southern seas and the whole of southern America, did that suffice to dispossess all the inhabitants and to keep out all the world's rulers? If things stand thus, there was little purpose in his adding to the ceremonies he performed: all his Most Catholic Majesty had to do was to stay in his cabinet and take possession, all at once, of the whole universe; provided that he then

removed from his empire everything already in the possession of other rulers.

It is easy to understand how adjacent pieces of land belonging to individuals become, when combined, public territory, and how the right of sovereignty over subjects is extended to the terrain that they occupy, so covering both things and persons. This places the possessors of property in a further degree of dependence, so that even their resources become guarantors of their fidelity—an advantage which does not appear to have been fully appreciated by ancient monarchs, who by calling themselves kings of the Persians, of the Scythians, or of the Macedonians, seem to have considered themselves as commanders of men rather than masters of countries. Today's monarchs more cleverly call themselves kings of France, of Spain, of England, etc.; they well know that by keeping hold of their territories they will keep their hold on the inhabitants.

The remarkable thing about this transfer of ownership is that when the community receives the possessions of individuals it does not in any way despoil them, but instead ensures that their ownership is legitimate, changing usurpation into genuine right, and enjoyment of use into property. Those having possession being thenceforward considered as persons entrusted with public property, and their rights being respected by all members of the state and maintained against foreigners with all its power, their act of ceding ownership to the state has benefited not only the public but, even more, themselves, and they have as it were acquired everything they have given—a paradox which is easily explained if we distinguish between the rights that the sovereign and the owner have over the same piece of property, as we shall see in due course.[41]

It can also happen that men begin to form a community before having any property, and that later, as they take possession of land enough for all, they enjoy its use in common or share it between themselves, either in equal proportions, or according to those decided by the sovereign. In whatever manner the acquisition of ownership is carried out, the right that each individual has over his property is always subordinate to the right that the community has over everyone; otherwise, the social bond would be lacking in firmness and the exercise of sovereignty would lack true power.

I end this chapter, and this book, by a remark upon which the entire social system should be based: it is that, instead of destroying natural equality, the fundamental contract substitutes moral and legal equality for whatever degree of physical inequality nature has put among men; they may be unequal in strength or intelligence, but all become equal through agreed convention and by right.[42]

Book II

Chapter I That Sovereignty Cannot Be Transferred[43]

The first and most important consequence of the principles laid down hitherto is that only the general will can direct the powers of the state in accordance with the purpose for which it was instituted, which is the common good; for if the establishment of societies was made necessary because individual interests were in opposition, it was made possible because those interests concur. The social bond is formed by what these interests have in common; if there were no point at which every interest met, no society could exist. And it is solely on the basis of this common interest that society must be governed.

I therefore assert that sovereignty, being only the exercise of the general will,[44] can never be transferred, and that the sovereign, which cannot be other than a collective entity, cannot be represented except by itself;[45] power can be delegated, but the will cannot.

For although it is not impossible that an individual's will[46] may in some matter be in agreement with the general will, it is certainly not possible for the agreement to be firm and durable; since the tendency of an individual will is by nature towards making preferences, while that of the general will is towards equality. It is even less possible for any person to guarantee the agreement, even if it were to be permanent, for it would not be due to policy, but chance. What the sovereign can say is: "What I want at present is what this or that individual wants, or at least what he says he wants"; but it cannot say: "Tomorrow I shall still want what that individual wants," because it is absurd that the will should bind itself for the future, and it is beyond any will to consent to something contrary to the good of the being whose will it is. If therefore the people simply promises to obey, it dissolves itself by this very act, and loses its character as a people. From the moment that there is a master, sovereign authority ceases, and the body politic is thenceforward destroyed.

This is not to say that a chief's orders cannot pass for acts of the general will, so long as the sovereign authority, while free to reject them, refrains from doing so. In such a case the universal silence implies that the people has consented. I shall explain this at greater length.

Chapter II That Sovereignty Cannot Be Divided

Sovereignty is indivisible for the same reason that it is untransferable: a will is either general, or it is not; it is the will of the body of the people, or of a part only. In the first case, this will, once declared, is an act of sovereignty and has legal authority. In the second, it is only a particular act of will, or an administrative decision; at most it is a decree.

Our political theorists,[47] however, being unable to divide sovereignty in principle, have divided it according to its object: they separate power from will, legislature from executive, the right to raise taxes from the right to administer justice or declare war, and internal administration from the capacity to negotiate with foreign countries. Sometimes all the separate parts are mixed up, sometimes they are distinguished. The sovereign is made into a fantastic patchwork; it is as if they had made a man composed of more than one body, one having eyes, another arms, another feet, and nothing else. In Japan, it is said, magicians dismember a child before the audience's eyes, and then, throwing all its limbs one after another into the air, they bring it down alive again, all in one piece. Of the same kind, more or less, are the conjuring tricks done by our theorists; they have chopped up the body social by a sleight of hand worthy of a fairground showman, and you cannot tell how they reassemble the pieces.

The cause of their error is that they have no correct idea of the sovereign, and take manifestations of its authority to be parts of it. Thus the acts of declaring war and making peace, for instance, have been regarded as acts of sovereignty, which is wrong, because neither of these acts is in any way a law, but only an application of law, a particular decision determining that the law should take effect, as we shall see clearly when the idea associated with the word *law*[48] is defined.

If the theorists' other distinctions were examined in the same way, it would be found that whenever we believe sovereignty to be divided we are in error, and that the rights that are taken to be parts of the sovereign authority are all subordinate to it, supreme acts of will always being presupposed, and only the power to execute them being bestowed by these rights.

This lack of exactitude has caused an incalculable degree of obscurity in our authors' judgments on political theory when, following the principles they have laid down, they have tried to decide on the respective rights of kings and peoples. Anyone can see, in the third and fourth chapters of Grotius's Book I, how this learned man and his translator Barbeyrac[49] become confused and entangle themselves in their own sophistries, for fear of going too far or not far enough for what they had in mind, and of offending those interests to which they wished to be conciliatory. Grotius, dissatisfied with his own country, having sought refuge in France and wishing to win favour with Louis XIII, to whom he dedicated his book, spares nothing in order to despoil the people of all their rights and to make them over to the king, which he does with the greatest skill. Barbeyrac too, who dedicated his translation to the King of England, George I, would certainly have liked to do the same. But unfortunately the expulsion of James II, which he calls an abdication, forced him to be reticent, to distort and misrepresent, in order not to portray William as a usurper. If these two writers had adopted true principles, all their difficulties would have been removed, and they would have been consistent throughout; but they would have been telling unwelcome truths and winning favour only with the people. Truth does not lead to success, and the people does not appoint ambassadors or professors or give state salaries.

Chapter III Whether the General Will Can Err

It follows from what precedes that the general will is always in the right,[50] and always tends to the public welfare; but it does not follow that decisions made by the people have equal rightness. One always desires one's own good, but one does not always see what it is; the people can never be corrupted, but it can often be led into error, and it is only in this case that it seems to desire the bad.

There is often a difference between the will of everyone and the general will; the latter is concerned only with the common interest, while the former is concerned with private interests, and is the sum total of individual wants: but if you take away from these desires their excesses and insufficiencies, the common element remaining from the different desires is the general will.[51]

If, when properly informed, the people were to come to its decisions without any communication between its members the general will would always emerge from the large number of small differences, and the decision would always be good. But when there are intrigues, and partial associations arise at the expense of the greater one, the will of each of these associations becomes general in relation to its members and particular in relation to the state: it can then be said that the number of voters is no longer the same as the number of men, but only the same as the number of associations. The differences become fewer and give a less general result. Eventually, when one of the associations is big enough to triumph over all the others, the outcome is no longer the sum total of small differences, but a single difference; then there is no longer any general will, and the opinion that prevails is only a particular opinion.

It is therefore important, if the general will is to be properly ascertained, that there should be no partial society within the state, and that each citizen should decide according to his own opinion;[52] this sublime institution was due uniquely to Lycurgus.[53] If there are partial associations, their number should be increased and inequalities between them prevented, as was done by Solon, Numa, and Servius.[54] These are the only effective precautions if the general will is always to be enlightened and the people is not to fall into error.

Chapter IV The Limits of Sovereign Power

If the state or city is solely a collective person which exists through the union of its members, and if its fundamental concern is its own conservation, it must have a coercive force of universal scope, in order to move and control each part in the manner most advantageous to the whole. Just as nature gives each man absolute power over all his limbs, the social pact gives the body politic absolute power over its members; and as I have said, it is this same power, directed by the general will, that bears the name of sovereignty.

But besides the public self we have to consider the private persons of whom it consists, and whose life and freedom are independent of it by nature. The question is how to distinguish clearly between the respective rights of sovereign and citizen,[55] and between the duties that citizens have to perform as subjects, and the natural rights which they enjoy as men.

It is agreed that what each person transfers, in accordance with the social pact, as regards his power, his goods, and his freedom, amounts at most to the portion of these things that it is important for the community to use;[56] but it must also be agreed that the sovereign authority alone judges the degree of importance that is involved.

A citizen owes the state all the services that he can offer it whenever the sovereign asks for them; but the sovereign for its part cannot impose on its subjects any burden which is useless to the community: it cannot even want to impose it; for under the law of reason, as under the law of nature, nothing can be done without a cause.

The undertakings that unite us to the body of society are binding only because they are mutual, and their nature is such that in fulfilling them our efforts for others are efforts on our own behalf also. Why is it that the general will is always in the right, and why is the happiness of each the constant wish of all, unless it is because there is no one who does not apply the word *each* to himself, and is not thinking of himself when he votes for all? And this proves that equality as of right, and the notion of justice to which it gives rise, derive from the preference that each gives to himself, and consequently from the nature of man; that the general will, in order to be truly general, must be so not only in essence but also in respect of its object;[57] that it must issue from everyone in order that it should apply to everyone; and that it loses its natural rightfulness when it is directed towards some specific, individual object, since in this case we are making a judgment about something foreign to us, and have no true principle of equity to guide us.

For whenever a particular action or right is in question, relating to a point that has not been decided by prior general agreement, the matter becomes contentious.[58] It is like a case at law, in which the individuals concerned are on one side and the public on the other; but here I can see no law to be followed, nor a judge to decide. In such circumstances it would be ridiculous to want to refer to an explicit decision made by the general will: it would be simply the claim submitted by one side in the lawsuit. For the other side, therefore, it would be only the wish of a particular external body, inclined on this occasion to injustice and subject to error. Thus, in the same way as a particular will cannot represent the general will, so too, if what it is concerned with is particular, the general will changes its nature. Inasmuch as it is general, it cannot pronounce on a man or an act. When the Athenian people, for example, chose and dismissed its chiefs, or decreed honours for one man and punishment for another, and through a multitude of particular decrees exercised indiscriminately all the functions of a government, it did not then have a general will in the proper sense of the term; it was not acting as the sovereign authority, but as the government. This will seem contrary to the usual view; but I must be given time to put mine.[59]

From this it will be understood that the factor which makes the will general is not so much the number of persons voting, but rather the common interest that unites them, for under this system everyone necessarily submits to the conditions that he imposes on the others; self-interest and justice are in marvellous harmony, bestowing on communal decisions an impression of equity which is notably absent from any discussion on a particular matter, because of the lack of a common interest to unify and integrate the judge's criterion with that of the interested party.

By whichever method we go back to our principle, we always arrive at the same conclusion, namely, that the social pact establishes so great a degree of equality between citizens that they all commit themselves to the same conditions and ought all to enjoy the same rights. Thus by the nature of the pact every act of sovereignty, that is to say every authentic act of the general will, creates an obligation or a benefit for all the citizens equally, so that the sovereign authority has jurisdiction[60] exclusively over the body of the nation, without giving special treatment to any of its members. What then is an act of sovereignty, properly speaking? It is not an agreement made between superior and inferior, but an agreement between the body and each of its members. The agreement is legitimate, because it is based on the social contract; it is equitable, because it applies to all; beneficial, because its object can only be the general good; and firmly based, because it is guaranteed by communal strength and the supreme power. As long as subjects of the state submit only to such conventions as this, they are not obeying anyone except their own will; and to ask the extent of the respective rights of subjects and citizens is to ask how far the citizens' obligations extend towards themselves, each one towards all, and all towards each one.

We therefore see that the sovereign power, absolute as it is, sacred and inviolable as it is, does not and cannot go beyond the limits of general agreements, and that any man can make full use of that share of his goods and liberty that is left him by these agreements. Consequently the sovereign authority never has the right to place a heavier burden on one subject than on another, because the matter would then become a particular decision, and be outside the sovereign's jurisdiction.

If these distinctions are accepted, nothing is truly renounced by private individuals under the social contract; but instead their situation becomes preferable, in reality, as a result of the contract, to what it was before.[61] Instead of abandoning anything they have simply made a beneficial transfer, exchanging an uncertain and precarious mode of existence for a better and more secure one, natural independence for liberty, the power of hurting others for their own safety, and reliance on their own strength, which others might overcome, for a position of right that social unity makes invincible. Even their lives, which they have surrendered to the state, are continually protected by it, and when risking life in its defence what are they doing but paying back what it has given them? All have to fight for their country in case of need, it is true; but also, no one ever has to fight for himself. Is it not an advantage to face, for the sake of security, some part of the dangers that we should have to face for ourselves if that security were removed?

. . .

Chapter VI The Law[62]

By the social pact we have given existence and life to the body politic; we must now, by legislation, give it the ability to will and move. For the act by which this body is originally formed and unified does nothing to determine what it must do so as to preserve itself.

That which is good, and in conformity with order, is such by the nature of things, independently of human convention. All justice comes from God, he alone is its source; and if we knew how to attain it at so great a height, we should need neither government nor laws. Undoubtedly, absolute justice exists, emanating from reason alone; but in order for it to be accepted among men, it has to be reciprocal. To consider things in human terms, the laws of justice, if lacking any natural sanction, are without effect among men. They merely benefit the wicked and harm the just when the just man observes them toward everyone while no one observes them toward him. Conventions and laws are necessary, therefore, in order to combine rights with duties, and to enable justice to fulfil its object. In the state of nature, in which everything is common property, I owe nothing to others, having promised them nothing; the only things that I recognize as belonging to others are those that are no use to me. It is not the same in the civil state, where all rights are defined by law.

What then, finally, is a law? As long as we are content to define the word in metaphysical terms alone,[63] we shall go on failing to understand what we are arguing about, and even when we have defined a law of nature we shall be no closer to knowing what a law of the state is.

I have already said[64] that the general will cannot relate to a particular object. For any particular object of will is either inside the state, or outside. If it is outside the state, a will foreign to it is not general with respect to it; and if it is a thing inside the state, it forms part of it, and in that case, the relationship created between the whole and its part is such that they are two separate things, one being the part and the other the whole minus that part. But a whole lacking a part is not a whole, and as long as this relationship subsists there is no longer a whole, but two unequal parts; whence it follows also that the will of the one is no longer general with respect to the other.

But when the whole people makes a ruling for the whole people it is concerned with itself alone, and the relationship, if created, is between the whole object from one point of view and the whole object from another, the whole remaining undivided. Then the matter on which the ruling is made is general, as is the will that makes it. It is this act that I call a law.

When I say that the objects of laws are always general, I mean that the law considers the subjects of the state as a collectivity and actions in the abstract, but never a man as an individual, nor any particular action. Thus the law can rule that privileges will exist, but it cannot

bestow them on any person by name; the law can create different classes of citizen, or even define the qualifications for membership of these classes, but it cannot name this man or that man as members; it can establish a monarchical government and hereditary succession, but cannot elect a king or name a royal family. In a word, no function relating to an individual object belongs to the legislative power.[65]

It is at once clear, from this principle, that we must no longer ask who has the right to make the laws, since they are acts of the general will; nor whether the ruler is above the law, since he is a member of the state; nor whether the law can be unjust, since no one can be unjust towards himself; nor how it is possible to be free and subject to the laws, since they are nothing but the record of our acts of will.

We can see also, since the law combines universality in its object with universality of will, that anything ordained by a man on his own account, whatever his position, is not a law. Even what the sovereign ordains concerning a particular object is not a law, but a decree; nor is it an act of sovereignty, but of administration.

Consequently I call *republic* any state ruled by laws,[66] whatever the form of its administration: for it is only thus that the public interest governs, and that all things public count for something. All legitimate governments are republican:[67] I shall explain what is meant by *government* later.

Laws properly speaking are no more than a society's conditions of association. The people, being subject to the laws, must create them; it is the associates who have the right to determine the conditions of society. But how are they to determine them? By sudden inspiration bringing common agreement? Has the body politic some organ by which to articulate its wishes? Who will give it the foresight it needs to produce acts of will and publicize them in advance, or how, in time of need, will it make them known? How can the blind multitude, often ignorant of what it wants, because it seldom knows what is good for it, accomplish by itself so large and difficult an enterprise as a system of legislation? The people, of itself, always wants the good, but does not, of itself, always see it. The general will is always in the right, but the judgment guiding it is not always enlightened. The general will needs to be shown things as they are, and sometimes as they ought to appear, to be taught which path is the right one for it to follow, to be preserved from the seductiveness of particular wills, to have comparisons of times and places made for it, and be told of those remote and hidden dangers which counterbalance the attractions of visible, present advantages. Individuals can see the good and reject it; the public desires the good and cannot see it. All equally need guides. The one side must be obliged to shape their wills to their reason, the other must be taught the knowledge of what it wants. It is then that, from public enlightenment, comes the union of understanding and will in the social body; the parts are then in precise concordance, which results in the greater strength of the whole. This is why it is necessary to have a legislator.

Chapter VII The Legislator

In order to discover which rules of society suit nations best, a mind of a superior kind would be required, able to see all human emotions, while feeling none; without relationship to our nature, but knowing it to its depths; enjoying its own happiness independently of us, but prepared to be concerned with ours; a mind, in sum, which while preparing distant glory for itself in the fullness of time, could carry out its work in one century and enjoy its achievement in another.[68] It is gods that are needed to give laws to men.

The argument put by Caligula[69] as regards fact was put by Plato as regards right, in discussing the political leader or man of state, whom he seeks to define in his *Statesman*.[70] But if it is true that a great ruler is rare, what of a great legislator? The one has only to follow a pattern, the other must devise it; the legislator is the inventor of the machine, the ruler is the mechanic who sets it up and makes it work. "When societies are born," says Montesquieu,[71] "it is the leaders of republics who create their institutions, and afterwards it is the institutions that produce the leaders of the state."

The man who dares to undertake the establishment of a people has to feel himself capable of changing, so to speak, the nature of man; of transforming each individual, who in himself is a perfect, isolated whole, into a part of a larger whole from which the individual, as it were, receives his life and being; of altering man's constitution in order to strengthen it; of substituting a morally dependent existence for the physically independent existence that we have all received from nature. In a word, he must deprive man of his own strength so as to give him strength from outside, which he cannot use without the help of others. The more completely these natural strengths are destroyed and reduced to nothing, the more powerful and durable are those which replace them, and the firmer and more perfect, too, the society that is constituted: so that, when each citizen is nothing and can do nothing except through others, and when the strength given by the whole is equal or superior to the natural strength of all the individuals together, it may be said that legislation has reached the nearest point to perfection that it can.

Within the state, the legislator is a man extraordinary in every respect. If he is so by genius, he is no less so by function. His office is not a public office, and it is not sovereignty. The function of constituting the republic does not form part of its constitution, but is specific and superior, having nothing in common with human authority; if he who has control of men ought not to control the laws, then he who controls the laws ought not to control men: otherwise his laws would minister to his passions, often doing no more than perpetuate his unjust actions; and he would never be able to prevent his interests as an individual from impairing the sanctity of the work.

When Lycurgus gave laws to his country, he began by abdicating the throne. In most Greek towns, it was the custom to entrust the establishment of their laws to foreigners. The modern Italian republics have often imitated this habit; the republic of Geneva did the same and did well.[72] At Rome's finest period, the city witnessed in its midst the rebirth of all the crimes of tyranny, and came close to destruction, because legislative authority and sovereign power had been combined in the same persons.[73]

Yet even the decemvirs never arrogated to themselves the right to enact laws on their authority alone. "None of our proposals," they told the people, "can become law without your consent. Romans, you must yourselves authorize the laws that will ensure your happiness."

He who frames the laws, therefore, has not, or should not have, any rights of making law; the people cannot, even if it wished to, divest itself of these incommunicable rights, because, according to the fundamental pact, only the general will can be binding on individuals, and it can never be certain that something willed by a particular person is in conformity with the general will until it has been submitted to the free vote of the people. I have already said this, but it is worth repeating.[74]

We find in the business of legislation, then, two things that seem incompatible: an enterprise seemingly beyond human ability, and nothing, by way of authority, with which to carry it out.

There is another difficulty that deserves notice. Wise men who try to address the common people not in its own language, but in theirs, cannot make themselves understood. But there are innumerable ideas which cannot be translated into the language of the people. Projects of too great generality and concerns that are too remote are equally beyond its reach: each individual, disapproving of any plan for government except the one that suits his own particular interest, has difficulty in perceiving the advantages he must gain from the deprivations that are continually imposed on him by good laws. In order that a people in the process of formation should be capable of appreciating the principles of sound policy and follow the fundamental rules of reasons of state,[75] it would be necessary for the effect to become the cause; the spirit of community, which should be the result of the constitution, would have to have guided the constitution itself; before the existence of laws, men would have to be what the laws have made them. Thus the legislator is unable to employ either force or argument, and has to have recourse to another order of authority, which can compel without violence and win assent without arguing.

That is why the founders of nations have been forced in every period to resort to divine authority and attribute their own wisdom to the gods,[76] in order that their peoples, who are subject both to the laws of the state and those of nature, should recognize the same power in the creator of man and in the creator of society, obeying freely and submitting meekly to the enforcement of public felicity.

It is the decisions of this higher reason, beyond the scope of average men, that the legislator ascribes to the Immortals, so that those who cannot be moved by human prudence will be led by divine authority.[77] But it does not lie in every man to make the gods speak, nor to be believed when he proclaims himself to be their spokesman. The great soul of the legislator is the true miracle by which his mission is proved. Any man can write on tablets of stone, or pay for an oracle, or pretend to be in secret communication with some divinity, or train a bird to speak in his ear, or find other crude methods of deceiving the people. A man who knows no more than this may even, perhaps, be able to gather together a band of demented followers; but he will never found an empire, and his wild work will soon perish with him. The bond formed by empty marvels is ephemeral; only wisdom makes it endure. The Jewish law that still subsists, and the law of the child of Ishmael,[78] which has governed half the world for 10 centuries, demonstrate even today the greatness of the men who decreed them; and while arrogant philosophers or blind partisanship[79] see them merely as fortunate impostors, the true statesman is awed, seeing what they have established, by that greatness and power of mind which presides over lasting creations.

From all this, we should not conclude like Warburton that politics and religion have for us the same objective,[80] but that when nations are formed the one serves as instrument to the other.

. . .

Chapter IX The Same Continued

Just as nature has put limits to the size of a well-formed man, and outside these limits produces only dwarfs or giants, so too, when it is a question of the best constitution for a state, there are limits to the size that it can have, in order that it should neither be too large to be well governed, nor too small to continue to exist on its own. In every political body there is a maximum strength which it cannot exceed, and which it often loses by becoming larger. The further the social bond is stretched, the weaker it gets; and in general a small state is proportionately stronger than a large one.[81]

There are innumerable reasons for this principle. In the first place, administration is more difficult over large distances, just as a weight becomes heavier at the end of a longer bar, and it also becomes more onerous as the hierarchy of divisions increases; each town, to start with, has its administration, paid for by the inhabitants; each district too has its own, also paid for by the inhabitants; then each province; then the greater administrative areas, satrapies or vice-royalties, the cost of which increases from one level to the next, but still at the expense of the unhappy inhabitants; finally comes the supreme administration that crushes everything underneath.[82] All these added burdens are a continual drain on the subjects' resources: far from having a better administration at the different levels, they are less well governed than if there were only one above them. There are scarcely any reserves left for emergencies, and when it is necessary to resort to them the state is always on the brink of ruin.

Nor is this all. Not only is the government less swift and vigorous in seeing that the laws are observed, in preventing exactions, redressing abuses, and forestalling the attempts at sedition that can arise in distant places, but the people has less affection for its leaders, whom it never sees, for its country, which it regards as the whole world, and for its fellow citizens, most of whom are strangers. The same laws cannot be appropriate for all the various provinces, which have different customs and are situated in different climates; while a diversity of law can only engender conflict and confusion among peoples who, having the same leaders and in continual communication, move from one area to another and marry there, never knowing, as they become subject to other customary laws,[83] whether their heritage is really theirs. Talents are hidden, virtues ignored, and vice goes unpunished among all the multitude of men, unknown to each other, who are gathered together in one place because it is the seat of the supreme administration. The rulers, overburdened by the amount of business, see nothing for themselves, and their clerks govern the state. Finally, the measures necessary in order to maintain the central authority, which so many of its distant representatives try to evade or deceive, absorb all the energies of the public officers; what remains for the welfare of the people is insufficient, and there is scarcely enough for defence in case of need; in this way, a body too large for its own constitution declines and perishes, collapsing under its own weight.

. . .

Chapter XI The Various Systems of Legislation

If we seek to define precisely the greatest good of all, the necessary goal of every system of legislation, we shall find that the main objectives are limited to two only: *liberty* and *equality*; liberty, because any form of particular subordination[84] means that the body of the state loses some degree of strength; and equality because liberty cannot subsist without it.

I have already explained civil liberty;[85] as for equality, the word must not be taken to mean that the degrees of power and wealth should be exactly the same, but that, as regards personal power, it should not be so great as to make violence possible, and should be exercised only in accordance with social position and the law; and as regards wealth, that no citizen should be rich enough to be able to buy another, and none so poor that he has to sell himself:[86] and this depends on those of high position exercising restraint concerning property and influence, and on the common people restraining their greed and envy.

Equality, it is said, is a theorists' vision, which cannot exist in practice. But if an abuse is inevitable, does it follow that it should not at least be controlled? It is precisely because the force of things always tends to destroy equality that the force of law should tend always to conserve it.

But these general aims for any good scheme of legislation must be modified in every country by the relationships that arise both from its geographical situation and from the character of the inhabitants, and it is on the basis of these relationships that a particular system of laws must be devised for each people, a system which may not, perhaps, be the best in itself, but will be the best for the state for which it is intended. For example, suppose that the soil is hard to work and barren, or the country too cramped for its inhabitants—encourage crafts and industry, the products of which can be exchanged for the commodities that you lack. If on the contrary you live in rich plains and on fertile slopes, or if, on good land, you lack people, devote yourself wholly to agriculture, which causes the population to multiply, and expel crafts

and industry, since all they would do is to depopulate the country entirely, by crowding together the country's few inhabitants in a small number of locations.[87] Do you have a long shoreline, easily approached?—cover the sea with ships, apply yourself to trade and navigation, and your existence will be brilliant and short. Do the waves around your coasts beat on almost inaccessible rocks?—then remain primitive and make fish your diet; your life will be more peaceful, perhaps better, and certainly happier. In a word, besides the principles that apply to every nation, there is in each people some cause why they should be applied in a particular manner, making its legislation suitable for it alone. Thus the Hebrews in ancient times, and the Arabs recently, have made religion their primary concern; the Athenians, culture; Carthage and Tyre, trade; Rhodes, its navy; Sparta, war; and Rome virtue. The author of *The Spirit of Laws* has given a multitude of examples showing the skill with which a legislator directs a system of law towards each of these aims.[88]

. . .

Book III

Before discussing the various forms of government, let me try to define the exact sense of the word, which has not yet been very fully explained.

Chapter I Government in General

I should warn my readers that this chapter must be read without haste, and that I am ignorant of the art of making myself clear to those who do not wish to concentrate.

Every free act has two causes, which cooperate in order to produce it. The one, which is moral,[89] is the will that decides on the act, and the other, which is physical, is the force that carries it out. When I walk towards a thing, it is necessary in the first place that I should want to go towards it, and in the second that my feet should take me there. If a paralyzed man wants to run, and if an able-bodied man does not want to, both will stay where they are. The body politic has the same causes of action, and in it we likewise discern force and will, the former under the name of *executive power* and the latter under that of *legislative power*. Nothing is done, or should be done, unless they are in accordance.

We have seen that legislative power belongs to the people, and can belong to it alone.[90] It is easy to see, on the other hand, following the principles established above, that executive power cannot belong to the generality of the citizens in their legislative or sovereign capacity, because this power consists only in particular decisions, which fall outside the domain of law, and in consequence outside that of the sovereign, every act of which can only be a law.

Public force must therefore have its own agent, to unify it and give it effect following the directions of the general will, to provide the means of communication between state and sovereign, and to fulfil in the political entity the function that is performed in a man by the union of body and soul. This is the reason, in a state, for government, which has been inappropriately confused with the sovereign, of which it is only the minister.

What, then, is government? It is an intermediate body set up between subjects and sovereign to ensure their mutual correspondence, and is entrusted with the execution of laws and with the maintenance of liberty, both social and political.

The members of this body are called *officers* or *kings*,[91] that is to say *governors*, and the body as a whole has the name of *ruler*.[92][93] Hence those who maintain that the act by which a people submits to the authority of chiefs is not a contract[94] are perfectly correct. Government taken absolutely is only a function or employment, in which the agents of the sovereign exercise in its name the power which it has deposited with them, and which it may limit, modify, or take back when it pleases, the transfer of its rights in these respects being incompatible with the nature of the social body and contrary to the purpose of association.

What I call *government*, then, or supreme administration, is the legitimate exercise of the executive power, and I call *ruler* or principal officer[95] the man or body of men entrusted with this administration.

It is in government that are located those intermediate forces the relationship between which constitutes the relationship of all to all, or of sovereign to state. The latter may be expressed as the relationship which obtains between the two outside terms of a geometric proportion, the middle term being the government.[96] The government receives commands from the sovereign and gives them to the people, and for the state to be properly in balance it is necessary, when all the appropriate adjustments have been made, that equivalence should be maintained between the power of the government, or of the middle term multiplied by itself, and the power of the citizens, or of the product of their power as sovereign on one side, multiplied by their power as subjects on the other.

Further, it is impossible to alter any of the three terms without immediately destroying the proportion. If the sovereign insists on governing, or the officers of government insist on making laws, or the subjects refuse to obey, control is replaced by disorder, will and force no longer act in harmony, and the state disintegrates, falling into despotism or anarchy. Lastly, since any three-term proportion can have only one middle term so too in a state only one good government is possible; but since innumerable eventualities can alter relationships within a nation, different forms of government may not only suit different nations, but may suit the same nation at different times.

In order to try to illustrate the various relationships which may exist between the extremes, I shall take as an example the figures for population, as being the easiest to express as a proportion.

Let us suppose that the state is composed of tell thousand citizens. The sovereign can be thought of only collectively, as a single entity. Yet each particular person, in his capacity as subject, is considered as an individual. Thus the relationship of sovereign to subject is as ten thousand to one. In other words, each member of the state has only one ten-thousandth share of the sovereign authority, although he is entirely subject to it. If the population consists of a hundred thousand men, the position of the subject stays unaltered, each submitting equally to the whole authority of the laws, while the power of his vote is reduced to one hundred-thousandth, and his influence over the creation of law is ten times less. The subject remaining a single unit, then, the relationship between the sovereign and himself grows wider in proportion to the number of citizens. Whence it follows that the larger the state becomes, the more liberty decreases.

When I say that the relationship grows wider, I mean that it moves further away from equivalence. Thus the proportion in mathematical terminology is greater, but in ordinary language the relationship becomes less;[97] in the former case the relationship is considered quantitatively, and is measured by the division of the last term by the first, while in the latter it is considered according to the nature of the things involved, and is measured by the degree of resemblance.

Accordingly, the smaller the relationship between the wills of individuals and the general will, that is, between moral standards and the law, the greater the force of restraint should be. If, therefore, the government is to be a good one, it must be proportionately stronger according as the size of the population increases.

From another point of view, since any increase in the size of a state gives those who are entrusted with public authority greater temptation, and greater opportunities, to abuse their power, it follows that the greater the strength possessed by the government for the restraint of the people, the greater should be the strength that is possessed by the sovereign in its turn in order to restrain the government. I am not speaking here of strength in absolute terms, but of the relative strength of the various elements in the state.

The existence of this double relationship means that the concept of a proportion connecting sovereign, ruler, and people is not arbitrary, but a necessary consequence of the nature of political society. Further, since one of the outside terms of the proportion, namely the people considered as subject, is fixed, and represented by a single unit, it also means that whenever the ratio of the outside terms increases or diminishes, the ratio of each to the middle term increases or diminishes similarly, with the result that the middle term alters. This shows that there is no uniquely valid form of government, but that there may be as many governments of different natures as there are states of different sizes.

If it were to be said, turning my theory to ridicule, that in order to find the middle term of the proportion all that is required, in my view, is to take the square root of the population figure, I should reply that I take this number only as an example, and that the relationships which I am discussing cannot be measured solely in terms of numbers of men, but more generally by the quantity of action, which is generated by a multitude of causes; and besides, that although I have borrowed from the terminology of mathematics, in order to express myself in fewer words, I am nonetheless aware that mathematical precision is out of place in the measurement of moral behaviour.

A government is the same on a small scale as the body politic containing it is on a larger scale: a moral agent[98] endowed with certain faculties, being active like the sovereign and passive like the state, and subsuming, when analysed, other similar relationships. Whence is derived in consequence a new proportional relation, and within this another, as we rise through the ranks of government, until we arrive at a middle term that is not susceptible to further analysis, that is, at a single leader or supreme ruler, who may be represented as unity, at the centre of this progression, situated between the series of fractions and that of whole numbers.

Without becoming involved with this multiplicity of terms, let us be content to consider the government as a new body within the state, distinct from, and intermediate between, people and sovereign. There is an essential distinction between these bodies: the state exists of itself, while the government exists only through the sovereign. Thus the dominant will of the ruling body is only, or should only be, the general will or the law, its power is only the public power concentrated in it, and as soon as it has the desire to do some absolute and independent act of its own, the cohesiveness of the whole begins to be weakened. If at last it were to

happen that the ruling body's particular will were more vigorous than the sovereign's, and if, to obey this particular will, it resorted to the public power deposited with it, so that there were to be two sovereigns, so to speak, one by right and the other in fact, then social union would at once disappear, and political society would disintegrate.

However, in order that the body composing the government should have its own existence, a genuine life of its own, making it distinct from the body of the state, in order that all its members may act in concert and fulfil the purpose for which it is established, it needs to possess an individual self, a common sensibility among its members, its own will and force tending to self-conservation. It is a condition of this single mode of existence that there should be assemblies, councils, the power to deliberate and decide, rights, titles, and privileges belonging exclusively to the ruler, which will bring the greater honour to the position of ruling officer in proportion as his post is more burdensome. Difficulties arise in settling how, within the whole, this subordinate whole should be ordered, so as to ensure that it does not weaken the general constitution in strengthening its own, that it always distinguishes between its own power, meant for its conservation, and the public power meant for the conservation of the state, and in a word that it is always ready to sacrifice the government to the people, and not the people to the government.

However, although the government is an artificial body, and created by another artificial body, living as it were a borrowed and subordinate life, that does not prevent it from acting with greater or less energy and speed, or from enjoying, so to speak, more or less robust health. Finally, without completely neglecting the purpose for which it was established, it may diverge from it more or less, according to the way in which it is organized.

It is from all these differences that arise the diverse relations into which the government enters necessarily with the body of the state, according to the contingent and specific relationships which affect the state itself. For it can often happen that intrinsically the best government becomes the most defective, if its relationships are not modified in accordance with the deficiencies of the political body to which it belongs.

Chapter II The Constituent Principle of the Various Forms of Government

In order to explain the general cause of these differences, a distinction must now be made between ruler and government, in the same way as I distinguished previously between state and sovereign.

The body of government officers can consist of a larger or smaller number of members. We have stated[99] that the relationship of the sovereign authority to the subjects is a ratio that grows wider in proportion as the population is larger, and we can say the same about the government in relation to its members, the parallel being evident.

Further, the total strength of the government, always being the same as the state's, does not vary. From this it follows that the more strength it expends on its own members, the less remains to act on the people as a whole.

Consequently, the larger the number of officers of government, the weaker the government is. Since this principle is fundamental, let us attempt to elucidate it.

In the person of an officer of government, we can discern three essentially different wills: first, the will pertaining to the individual, which tends only to his particular advantage; secondly, the will common to the members of the government, which relates solely to the advantage of the ruling body, and which can be called a corporate will, being general in respect of the government and particular in respect of the state, the government being a part of the state; and in the third place, the will of the people or the sovereign will, which is general both as regards the state considered as a whole, and as regards the government considered as part of the whole.

Under an ideal legislation, the individual or particular will should count for nothing, the corporate will pertaining to the government for very little, and consequently the general or sovereign will should always dominate, and be the rule that uniquely determines the others.

In the natural way of things, however, these different kinds of will become more vigorous in proportion as they are more concentrated. Thus the general will is always weakest, the corporate will has second place, and the particular will comes first of all; so that, in the government, each person is primarily himself, then a member of government, and then a citizen—an order of priorities which is the exact contrary of the one demanded by the social order.

Let us suppose that all government is in the hands of a single man: then we have the individual's will and the corporate will perfectly combined, and the second is at the highest degree of concentration possible. Since it is on the degree of will that the use of force depends, and since the government's power does not vary, it follows that the most vigorous form of government is government by one person.

To get the contrary case, let us unite government and legislative authority; let the sovereign be ruler, and all the citizens be so many members of government. Then the corporate will is indistinguishable from the general will, and its degree of vigour will also be the same, leaving the strength of individual wills undiminished. In this case the activity or relative power of the government, which still has the same power absolutely speaking, is at a minimum.

These relationships are indisputable, and other considerations will also serve to confirm them. It is clear, for instance, that each officer of government is more active within it than the citizen is within the community as a whole, and consequently that a particular will has much more influence in acts of government than in acts of sovereignty; for a member of government is almost always responsible for some governmental function, whereas a citizen, taken singly, has no separate function within the sovereign. Moreover, the further the state expands, the more its real power increases, although power does not increase in proportion to extent; but when the state remains the same size, there is no point in increasing the size of the government, since it does not thereby acquire any greater real power, its power being that of the state and remaining a constant value. In this case the government's relative strength or activity diminishes and it cannot increase its real or absolute strength.

It is certain, moreover, that business is dealt with less expeditiously as the number of people responsible for it increases: that relying too much on prudence means relying too little on chance, that opportunities are not taken, and that the fruits of decision are often lost in the process of deciding.

What I have just demonstrated is that government becomes less effective in proportion as the officers of government multiply, and I have demonstrated previously[100] that the greater the population is, the more the force of containment ought to be increased. Whence it follows that the ratio between the government and its members should be the inverse of that between the sovereign and its subjects: that is to say, that the more the state expands, the more the government should contract, so that the number of those governing is reduced as the population rises.

I should add that I am speaking here only of the government's relative strength, not of its rightfulness:[101] for in the opposite case, the greater the number of officers of government, the closer their corporate will approaches to the general will; whereas, when a single person governs, that same corporate will is no more than a particular will, as I have said. Thus a loss on one side can be a gain on the other, and the legislator's skill consists in knowing how to define the point where the government's strength and will, still in reciprocal proportion, are combined in the most advantageous ratio for the state.

Chapter III The Classification of Governments[102]

The reasons for distinguishing governments into various kinds or forms according to the number of members composing them have been given in the preceding chapter; it remains to see in this how the various governments are created.

In the first place, the sovereign can entrust the responsibility of government to all the people or to the greater part of the people, so that more citizens will be members of the government than are simply individual citizens. The name given to this form of government is *democracy*.[103]

Or it can restrict government to a small number, so that more will be simply citizens than are members of the government; and this form bears the name of *aristocracy*.

Finally it can concentrate the whole of government in the hands of a single officer, from whom all the others take their power. This third form is the commonest, and is called *monarchy*, or royal government.

It should be observed that all these forms, or at least the first two, can occur in varying degrees, and within quite wide limits; for democracy can comprise the entire people, or no more than half. Aristocracy in turn can cover anything from half of the people down to the smallest possible number. Even royalty is capable of being shared to some extent. Sparta, under its constitution, always had two kings, and in the Roman Empire up to eight emperors at once were known, without it being possible to say that the empire was divided. Thus there comes a point at which each form of government is indistinguishable from the next, which shows that in reality, though there are only three denominations of government, it is capable of having as many different forms as the state has citizens.

Not only this, but since it is possible for the same government to be split up, in certain respects, into further divisions one arranged in one way and another in another, the three forms in combination can produce a multitude of mixed forms, and each one can be multiplied by all the simple forms.

At all times there has been much debate about the best form of government, without regard to the fact that each of them is the best in certain cases, and the worst in others.

If in the different states the number of officers of the supreme government must be in inverse ratio to the number of citizens it follows that in general the democratic form of government; will suit small states, the aristocratic form states of moderate size, and the monarchic form large states. This rule is derived directly from the principle above; but how are we to assess the multitude of circumstances which may create exceptions?

Chapter IV Democracy

The person who makes a law knows better than anyone else how it ought to be executed and interpreted. It would therefore seem that the best constitution would be one in which the executive power is united with the legislative; but it is just this that makes such a government deficient in certain respects, because things that ought to be distinct are not, and the ruling body and sovereign, being personally the same, produce nothing more, so to speak, than a government which is without government.

It is not good that the person who makes laws should execute them, nor that the body of the people should turn its attention from general considerations towards particular matters. Nothing is more dangerous than the influence of private interests in public affairs, and the abuse of law by the government is a lesser evil than the corruption of the legislative body, to which particular considerations inevitably lead. The substance of the state will be changed, with no possibility of reform. If a people were never to misuse government it would never misuse independence; a people that always governed well would not need to be governed.

If the term is taken in its strict sense, true democracy has never existed and never will. It is against the natural order that the majority should govern and the minority be governed. It is impossible to imagine the people permanently in session in order to deal with public affairs, and it is easy to see that it could not set up commissions for the purpose without the form of administration being altered.

I believe furthermore that we can state as a principle that, when the functions of government are divided between a number of bodies, the greatest authority passes sooner or later to those with the fewest members, if only because their facility in transacting business naturally brings matters before them.

Besides, what an unusual combination of circumstances is presupposed for this government to exist! First, a very small state, such that the people can be assembled without difficulty, and it is easy for every citizen to know all tile others; secondly, great simplicity of manners, in order to avoid a great quantity of business and tiresome discussions; further, a considerable degree of equality in rank and fortune, without which equality in rights and power cannot last long; and finally, little or no luxury, for luxury either derives from wealth or makes it necessary; it corrupts both rich and poor at once, one through possession, the other through covetousness; it puts the country on sale to vanity and soft living; it deprives the state of all its citizens, making each of them subject to the other, and all of them to public opinion.

This is why a famous author made virtue the principle of republics,[104] for these circumstances cannot all be present without virtue; but not having made the necessary distinctions, despite his genius, he often lacks precision and sometimes clarity, and did not see that, the sovereign authority being the same everywhere, the same principle should apply in every properly constituted state, though in greater or less degree, it is true, according to the form of its government.

It should be added that no government is so liable to civil war and internal disturbance than the democratic or popular type, for none has so strong and continual a tendency for its form to change, and none calls for so much vigilance and courage if its form is to be maintained. Under this constitution, more than any other, the citizen must arm himself with strength and constancy, and repeat every day in the depths of his heart the observation made by a virtuous lord palatine[105] in the Polish Diet: "I prefer freedom with all its dangers to tranquillity with servitude."[106]

If there were a nation of gods it would be governed democratically. So perfect a government is not suitable for men.

Chapter V Aristocracy

Here we have two very distinct corporate moral agents, namely the government and the sovereign; and in consequence two general wills, one relating to all the citizens, the other only to the members of the administration. Hence, although this government can regulate its internal organization as it wishes, it can never speak to the people unless it is in the name of the sovereign, which means in the name of the people themselves; a point that must never be forgotten.

The first societies were governed aristocratically. The heads of families debated public affairs among themselves, and the young yielded without difficulty to the authority of experience. Hence come the words *priest, elders, senate, gerontes.*[107] The savages of North America are still governed in this way today, and are governed very well.

But, as the inequalities of society become more important than natural inequalities, wealth or power[108] came to be preferred to age, and aristocracy became

elective. Finally, along with property, power was transmitted from father to son, which by creating patrician families made the government hereditary, and senators were seen who were 20 years old.

Aristocracy is therefore of three kinds: natural, elective, and hereditary. The first is only suited to simple societies; the third is the worst of all forms of government.[109] The second is the best; it is aristocracy in the true sense of the word.[110]

It has the advantage not only that it separates the two powers,[111] but that its members are selected; for with popular government all citizens are members of it by birth; but membership of aristocratic government is limited to a few, and is obtained by election:[112] by which means integrity, intelligence, experience, and all the other reasons for preference and public esteem, are so many additional guarantees of wise government.

Furthermore, assemblies of government are more easily arranged, its business is better debated and transacted with greater order and diligence, and respected senators will uphold the state's reputation abroad better than an unknown or despised populace.

In a word, the best and most natural order of things is that the wisest should govern the multitude, so long as it is certain that they will govern it for its advantage and not for theirs. The means of action ought not to be needlessly increased, nor 20,000 men made to do a task that 100 selected men can do better. But it must be noted that corporate interest here begins to follow less closely the rule of the general will in directing public power, and that by another inevitable process some part of the executive power is no longer available to the law.[113]

As regards the particular suitability of aristocracy, the state should not be so small, nor its people so simple and upright, that the execution of laws immediately follows the public will, as in a good democracy. Nor should the nation be so large that, those governing it being far distant from each other, each can set himself up as sovereign in his area, and begin by making himself independent in order to end up as master.

But if aristocracy requires slightly fewer virtues than democratic government it also requires some of its own, for instance that the rich should use their wealth moderately and the poor be content with their lot; for it would seem that strict equality would be out of place; even in Sparta it was not maintained.

Moreover, if this government entails some financial inequalities, it is certainly in order that the administration of public business should generally be entrusted to those who can most easily devote all their time to it, and not, as Aristotle claims, in order that the preference should always fall on the wealthy.[114] On the contrary, it is important that the opposite choice should sometimes teach the people that a man's worth can include more important causes of preference than money.

Chapter VI Monarchy[115]

Hitherto we have considered the ruling body as a collective artificial person, made a unity by force of law, and entrusted within the state with executive power.[116] We have now to consider this power when it is entirely in the hands of a natural person, a real man, so that he alone has the right to exercise it according to the laws. He is called a monarch or king.

Reversing the position under other administrations, where a collective being is seen as[117] an individual, here an individual is seen as a collective being, so that the artificial unity constituting the ruling body is at the same time a physical unity, in which all the faculties that the law takes such trouble to combine in the other types of government are associated naturally.

Thus the will of the people, the will of the ruler, the public strength of the state, the private strength of the government, all respond to a single impulse, all the energy of the mechanism is under single control, everything serves the same purpose; there are no opposing forces that nullify each other, and under no other constitution that can be imagined does less effort produce greater action. Archimedes, calmly sitting on the shore and drawing a great ship over the water,[118] is for me the image of a skilful monarch, governing his huge territories from his study, and making everything move while seeming to be immobile.

But if there is no other government that has so much vigour, there is also none in which a particular will has so much influence and so easily dominates the others: everything serves the same purpose, it is true; but that purpose is not public felicity, and the very strength of the administration constantly operates to the detriment of the state.

Kings want absolute rule, and the cry reaches them from afar that the best way to get it is to make their people love them. It is a fine maxim, and even, in some respects, very true. Unfortunately, among courtiers it will always be derided. The power that comes from the love of the people is certainly the strongest; but it is precarious and conditional; it will never satisfy a ruler. The best of kings want the power to do harm if they wish, without ceasing to be masters. The preacher of political sermons can tell them as often as he likes that, since their strength lies in the strength of their people, their own best interest is that the people should multiply, prosper, and be feared; kings know very well that this is not true. Their personal interest is primarily that the people should be weak and wretched, and that it should never be capable of resistance. I admit that, supposing that his subjects were always perfectly submissive, the ruler's interest might then supposedly be that the people should be powerful, so that their power, being his, would make him formidable to his neighbours; but since this interest is only secondary and subordinate, and the two suppositions I have made are incompatible, it is natural that rulers should always give preference to the maxim which is of most immediate use to them. It was strongly argued by Samuel addressing the Hebrews; it was demonstrated with the utmost clarity by Machiavelli,[119] who, while he pretended to give instruction to kings, gave valuable lessons to their peoples. Machiavelli's *Prince* is a book for republicans.[120]

We have established[121] by abstract reasoning that monarchy is suitable only for large states, and if we examine it in itself we shall find the same thing. The more numerous those responsible for government, the less the numerical difference between ruling body and subjects, and the more nearly equal their relationship becomes, so that in a democracy the relationship is unity, or true equivalence. This relationship widens according as the government contracts in numbers, and is at its maximum when the government is in one man's hands. The distance between ruler and people is then too great, and the state loses cohesion. In order that it should be restored, intermediate orders are therefore necessary:[122] and in order that they should be filled, royal princes, great lords, a nobility. None of this, however, is suitable for a small state, which is ruined by all these graded ranks.

But if it is difficult for a large state to be well governed, it is much more so for it to be well governed by a single man, and everyone knows what happens when a king chooses others to act in his place.[123]

An intrinsic and unavoidable defect in monarchical government, which will always make it inferior to a republic,[124] is that in a democratic government those who are put into high office by public vote are almost always enlightened, capable men, who perform their duties with honour; whereas in a monarchy the ones who succeed are petty incompetents, petty scoundrels, petty intriguers, whose trivial talents, those that bring great success at a court, serve only to show the public their owners' ineptitude as soon as they gain office. In making its choices the public errs much less than a king; and it is almost as uncommon to find a minister of genuine ability under a monarchy as a fool at the head of a republican government. As a result, when by some happy chance one of those men who are born for government takes charge of administration in a monarchy almost ruined by a collection of smart jacks-in-office, his resourceful-ness is a matter of astonishment, and marks a new epoch in the country's history.[125]

For a monarchical state to be well governed, its size or extent would need to be calculated so as to suit the abilities of the person governing. It is easier to conquer than to administer. If you had the world at the end of a long enough lever, you could move it with your finger; but to support the world on your shoulders you would need to be Hercules. For a state of any size, the ruler is almost always too small. When the contrary happens, and the state is too small for its ruler, which is very rare, it is still not well governed, because its leader, his mighty projects constantly in mind, forgets the interests of his people, and renders them no less unhappy by misusing his superfluous talents than does an incompetent leader through his lack of capacity. It would be desirable if, so to speak, the kingdom expanded or shrank with each reign, according to the abilities of the new monarch; whereas under a senate, with its more stable range of talent, the state can have fixed limits and the administration will be carried on equally well.

The most evident drawback of government by a single person is the absence of the successive replace-ments which, in the two other forms, ensure uninter-rupted continuity. A king dies, another is required; his selection leaves a dangerous interval; troubles can de-velop, and unless the citizens show a degree of disinter-estedness and integrity that this form of government hardly encourages, plots and corruption play their part. It is rare for someone to whom the state has sold itself not to sell it again in his turn, extorting money from the weak in compensation for the payments he made to the powerful. All things are for sale, sooner or later, under a government of this kind, and the peace en-joyed under such a king is worse than the disorder of an interregnum.

What remedies have been devised for these ills? The crown has been made hereditary within particular fami-lies; and an order of succession has been drawn up which eliminates any dispute when a king dies: which means that, the inconveniences of a regency having been sub-stituted for those of an election the risks of being ruled by children, monsters or imbeciles have been preferred to the necessity of debating the choice of a good king.[126] What has been lost to sight is that, given the risks in the contrary possibility, the odds are against a favourable outcome. The young Dionysius made a very shrewd re-mark when his father said, reproaching him for a shame-ful action: "Was it I who set you that example?' Said his son: "Ah! but your father wasn't a king."[127]

All things combine to prevent the man who is brought up to command others from possessing justice and reason. Much trouble is taken, so it is said, to teach young princes the art of ruling, but it does not appear that they derive any advantage from their education. It would be better to begin by teaching them the art of obeying. The great kings most celebrated in history were not brought up to rule; it is a form of knowledge that is known least well by those who have studied it most, and which is better acquired by obedience than by giv-ing orders. "For the quickest and best way of deciding between good things and bad is to ask what you would have wanted and would not have wanted if someone else had been ruler."[128]

One consequence of this discontinuity is the in-constancy of royal government, which first follows one plan, then another, according to the king's character, or the character of those who rule for him, and cannot long maintain stability of purpose or consistency in policy: its changeableness makes the state veer from principle to principle and from project to project, something that does not occur with other forms of government, where the ruler remains the same. Moreover, it is noticeable that in general, if greater cunning is to be found at court, there is more wisdom in a senate, and that republics achieve their purposes through steadier and more coher-ent policies; by contrast, every change of minister under a monarch produces an upheaval in the state, since the principle that is common to all ministers, and to almost all kings, is to do the opposite from their predecessors in everything.

The same lack of continuity is the key to refuting a sophism well known to apologists for royalty: it consists not only in comparing the government of a country to that of a household, and the ruler to the head of a family, an error that I have already disproved,[129] but also in gen-erously giving their officer of government every virtue that he might need, and forever assuming that a king is what he ought to be: on this assumption, royal govern-ment is evidently preferable to any other, since it is un-doubtedly the strongest, so that, in order to be also the best, the only thing lacking is a governmental will more in conformity with the general will.

But if, as Plato says,[130] it is so rare to find a man who is a king by nature, how often will nature and chance combine to put one on the throne? And if the education given to royalty necessarily corrupts its re-cipients, what is to be expected from a succession of men brought up to reign? To confuse royal government with government by a good king, therefore, is deliber-ate self-deception. In order to see what royal govern-ment is in itself, it has to be studied in the persons of kings who are without ability or ill-disposed; for either that is what they are on reaching the throne, or else what they become once there.

These problems have not been overlooked by the theorists, but they have not troubled them. The remedy, they say, is to obey without dissent: God in his wrath gives us bad kings, and they must be endured as a punishment from Heaven.[131] This is certainly an edifying way to talk, but it may be thought more suitable for the pulpit than for a book on politics. What would we think of a doctor who promised miracles, and whose only treatment was to exhort the sick to patience? Everyone knows that when we have a bad government we must put up with it; the question is how to find a good one.

Chapter VII Mixed Forms of Government

Strictly speaking, no simple form of government exists. A single leader must have subordinate officers; a government of the people must have a leader. Thus in the distribution of executive power there is always a gradation, going from the larger number to the smaller, the variation being that sometimes the larger number depends on the smaller, and sometimes the smaller on the larger.

On occasion the distribution is equal, either when the component parts are mutually dependent, as with the English constitution, or when the authority of each part is independent, but incomplete, as in Poland.[132] This last form is bad, because there is no unity in the government, and the state lacks cohesion.

Which is better, a simple or a mixed form of government? The question is much debated among theorists, and calls for the same answer as I gave above when discussing governments in general.[133]

Simple government is best in itself, precisely because it is simple. But when the dependence of the executive power on the legislative is not great enough, that is to say when the relative dominance of ruler over sovereign is greater than that of the people over the ruler, the disproportion must be remedied by making a division in government; for when it is divided each of the parts has no less authority over the subjects, while the division between them makes them together less powerful with respect to the sovereign.

The same disadvantage can also be avoided by creating intermediate officers, whose only purpose, the government remaining undivided, is to maintain the balance between the two powers and preserve their respective rights. The government is then not mixed, but modified.[134]

Similar means can be used as a remedy for the contrary failing: when the government is too weak, commissions[135] can be established in order to reinforce it; this is what is done in all democracies. In the previous case the government was divided in order to weaken it, and in this one in order to strengthen it; for the maximum amounts both of strength and weakness are to be found in the simple governments, and average amounts in the mixed forms.

. . .

Chapter X The Abuse of Government and Its Tendency to Degenerate

Just as a particular will constantly acts against the general will, so too the government exerts itself continually against the sovereign. The greater its efforts, the more the constitution deteriorates; and since there is no other corporate will to resist the ruling will, it must sooner or later come about that the ruler will dominate the sovereign authority and break the social contract. This is an inherent and unavoidable defect which, as soon as the body politic is born, tends ceaselessly to its destruction, in the same way as old age and death eventually destroy the human body.

Generally speaking there are two ways in which government degenerates: either when it contracts in size, or when the state is dissolved.

A government contracts when it passes from the hands of a larger number into those of a smaller: that is to say, from democracy to aristocracy, and from aristocracy to royalty. That is its natural tendency.[136] If it were to return from the smaller number to the larger, it could be said to expand: but this reverse movement is impossible.

For in fact a government never changes form unless the mainspring of its power wears out, leaving it too weak to preserve its own form. Then, if by expanding it were to grow slacker still, its power would diminish to nothing, and its life would be even shorter. The spring must therefore be wound up and tightened before it loses power: otherwise the state that depends on it will fall into ruins.

The case of the dissolution of the state can occur in one of two ways.

First, when the ruling body no longer administers the state in accordance with the laws, and usurps sovereign authority. The change that then takes place deserves notice: it is that the state, not the government, contracts in size; I mean that the greater state is dissolved, and that within it another is created, consisting only of the members of the government, which in relation to the rest of the people is no more than its master and tyrant. So that, as soon as the government usurps sovereignty, the social pact is broken; and every ordinary citizen, restored by right to his natural liberty, is forced, but not obliged, to obey.[137]

The same case also occurs when members of the government separately usurp the power that they ought only to exercise as a body: which is no less an infringement of the laws and produces even greater disorder. There is then, as it were, the same number of rulers as there are members of the government; and the state, being no less divided than the government perishes or changes its form.

When the state is dissolved, a wrongful government of any type is given the general name of *anarchy*.[138] To distinguish: democracy degenerates into *ochlocracy*, aristocracy into *oligarchy*; I might add that monarchy degenerates into *tyranny*; but the word is ambiguous and requires explanation.[139]

In the ordinary sense, a tyrant is a king who governs with violence, and without regard for justice and law. In the exact sense, a tyrant is a private individual who takes royal power for himself without having any right to it. This is the way in which the Greeks understood the word *tyrant*; they bestowed it on good and bad rulers alike if their authority was not legitimate.[140] Thus the words *tyrant* and *usurper* are exact synonyms.

In order to give different things different names, I shall call the man who usurps royal power a tyrant, and the man who usurps the sovereign power a despot. The tyrant is one who sets himself up against the law in order to govern according to law; the despot, one who puts himself even above the law. So the tyrant need not be a despot, but the despot is always a tyrant.

. . .

Chapter XV Deputies or Representatives

As soon as serving the public is no longer the main concern of the citizens, and they prefer not to give service themselves, but to use their purses, the state is already near to ruin. Is there a battle to be fought?—they pay for troops and stay at home; are public decisions to be made?—they choose deputies and stay at home. Through being lazy and having money, they end up with soldiers to oppress their country and representatives to sell it.

Service done in person is changed into money because people are busy with their trade or craft, greedily self-interested for profit, lovers of comfort and material possessions. They surrender a part of their earnings so as to be at leisure to increase them. Pay out money, and soon you will be in chains. The word *finance* is for slaves, it is unknown in a real state. In a truly free state, the citizens do everything with their own hands, and nothing with money: far from paying in order to be exempted from their duties, they would pay in order to carry them out themselves. I do not share the ordinary view at all: I believe that taxes are more contrary to freedom than the enforced labour of the *corvée*.[141]

The better a state is constituted, the higher is the priority given, in citizens' minds, to public rather than private business. There is even a reduction in the amount of private business, because, when the total sum of public happiness contributes a larger portion to the happiness of each individual, there remains less for him to gain from his own efforts. In a well-ordered republic, everyone hurries to the assemblies; under a bad government, no one is willing to stir a step in order to be there, because no one is interested in what goes on there, nor believes that the general will will dominate, and finally because domestic affairs monopolize everything. Good laws make for better ones, bad laws bring worse. As soon as anyone says, about the affairs of the state, "What does it matter to me?", the state must be regarded as lost.

The weakening love of country, the energy spent on private interests, the immense size of the state, conquests, and the abuse of government, have suggested the idea of having deputies or representatives of the people in national assemblies. They are what some countries dare to call the Third Estate.[142] Thus the private interests of two orders are ranked first and second; the public interest comes third.

Sovereignty cannot be represented, for the same reason that it cannot be transferred; it consists essentially in the general will, and the will cannot be represented; it is itself or it is something else; there is no other possibility. The people's deputies are not its representatives, therefore, nor can they be, but are only its agents; they cannot make definitive decisions. Any law that the people in person has not ratified is void; it is not a law. The people of England believes itself to be free; it is quite wrong: it is free only during the elections of Members of Parliament. Once they are elected, the people is enslaved, it is nothing.[143] Seeing the use it makes of liberty during its brief moments of possession, it deserves to lose it.

The idea of representation is modern: it came from feudalism, that unjust and absurd form of government which degrades the human race, and under which the name of man was dishonourable.[144] In the ancient republics, and even monarchies, the people never had representatives: the word itself was unknown. It is a most remarkable thing that in Rome, where the tribunes were so sacred, no one ever imagined that they might usurp the functions of the people, and that, even surrounded as they were by so great a multitude, they never once tried to hold a plebiscite on their own authority. Yet the problems sometimes caused by the throngs of people may be gauged by what happened at the time of the Gracchi, when a number of citizens cast their votes from the rooftops.

When right and liberty count above everything, inconvenience is nothing.[145] The wisdom of the Roman people put a true value on everything: it allowed its lictors to do what the tribunes would not have dared to;[146] it was not afraid that the lictors would try to represent it.

In order to explain the way in which the tribunes did sometimes represent it, however, it is enough to understand how the government represents the sovereign. Law being no more than the declaration of the general will, it is clear that as regards the legislative power the people cannot be represented; but it can and must be as regards executive power, this power being no more than the application of force to law. This shows that, if a careful analysis were made, it would be found that very few nations have laws. However that may be, it is certain that the tribunes, who had no part in the executive power, were never entitled to represent the Roman people by virtue of their office, but only by usurping the rights of the Senate.

Among the Greeks the people did for itself all that it needed to do: it was constantly in assembly in the town square. The Greeks lived in a mild climate; they were not avaricious; slaves did their work; their great concern was liberty. If these advantages are now lacking, how can the same rights be retained? Because of your harsher climate you have greater needs:[147] during six months of the year meetings cannot be held in the public squares; your indistinct tongues cannot be understood in the open air; you are more interested in profit than in freedom, and are less afraid of servitude than of being poor.

So can liberty be preserved only with the help of slaves? Maybe. The one extreme meets the other. Everything that is not natural has its disadvantages, and civil society more than anything else. There are some unhappy situations in which one's liberty can be kept only at the expense of another's, and the citizen can be perfectly free only if the slave is in complete servitude. Such was the position in Sparta. As for you, the modern nations, you have no slaves, but are enslaved; you are paying for their freedom with yours. It is all very well to boast that this is an improvement; I find it cowardly rather than humane.

I do not mean that it is necessary to have slaves, nor that there is a legitimate right to enslave, since I have proved the contrary:[148] I am simply giving the reasons why modern peoples that believe themselves free have representatives, and why the ancient peoples did not. Be that as it may, the moment that a people provides itself with representatives, it is no longer free; it no longer exists.

All things rightly considered, I cannot see how it is henceforward possible among us for the sovereign to retain the exercise of its rights unless the state is very small.

But if it is very small, will it be subjugated? No. I shall show later[149] how the exterior power of a great nation can be combined with the good order and ease of administration found in a small state.

Chapter XVII The Institution of a Government

How then should we conceive the act by which a government is instituted? I note first that this act is complex, that is, it consists in two parts, namely the establishment of the law and the execution of the law.

By the first act, the sovereign lays down that a governing body will be established, taking such and such a form; and this act is clearly a law.

By the second, the people appoints the chiefs to whom the government that has been established will be committed; and their appointment, being a particular act, is not a further law, but a consequence of the first, or a function of government.

The problem is to understand how an act of government can occur before the government exists, and how the people, which can be only the sovereign or the subjects, can in certain circumstances become ruler or officer of government.

Here once again is displayed one of those astonishing features of the political body, enabling it to carry out operations which, in appearance, are contradictory; for what happens in this case is the instantaneous conversion of sovereignty into democracy, so that, without any change being visible, but only because of the new relationship between all and all, the citizens become officers of government, and their acts pass from the general to the particular, from making a law to its execution.[150]

This change in relationship is not a mere subtlety of theory, to which nothing corresponds in practice; it takes place as a matter of course in the English parliament, where on certain occasions the Lower Chamber sits as a committee, for the more efficient discussion of business, and thus becomes merely a branch of government instead of a sovereign body, which it had been a moment earlier; so that it can later report to itself, as House of Commons, on what it has just decided in grand committee, and resumes the debate, in one capacity, of matters that it has already settled in another.

It is thus an advantage inherent in democratic government that it may be established in fact by a simple act of the general will. After which the provisional government will either retain its authority, if democracy is the form of government which has been adopted, or else it will set up, in the name of the sovereign, the form that has been prescribed by law; and so everything is in order. Any other manner of instituting the government cannot be legitimate and will be a renunciation of the principles set out above.

Book IV

Chapter 1 That the General Will Is Indestructible

So long as a number of men gathered together consider themselves as a single body, they have a single will also, which is directed to their common conservation and to the general welfare. All the mechanisms of the state are strong and simple, and its maxims clear and luminous; there is no tangle of contradictory interests; the common good is obvious everywhere, and all that is required to perceive it is good sense. Peace, unity, and equality are the enemies of political subtlety. Simple, upright men are difficult to deceive because of their simplicity: elaborate pretexts and allurements fail to impress them; they are not sophisticated enough to be dupes. When, among the world's most fortunate nation,[151] groups of peasants are to be seen under an oak tree, deciding on matters of state and governing with unfailing wisdom, how can we not despise the refinements found among other peoples, who gain themselves glory and unhappiness with such ingenuity and such an air of mystery?

The state which is thus governed needs very few laws; and when it comes necessary to promulgate new ones, the necessity for them is universally understood. The first man to propose them merely puts into words something that all have felt already. There is never any question of vote-catching or speech-making in order to make it a law to do what everyone has already resolved that he will do himself, once he is sure that others will do the same.

What misleads the theorists is that, since all the states they have seen were wrongly constituted from the beginning, they cannot believe in the possibility of maintaining a political system of this kind. They laugh as they think of all the foolish ideas that some clever rascal or eloquent flatterer could put into the heads of the crowd in London or Paris. They are not aware that in Berne the people would have sent Cromwell, with a bell round his neck, to do hard labour, and that the Genevans would have put the Duc de Beaufort in a reformatory.[152]

But when the social tie begins to loosen, and the state to weaken, when particular interests begin to make themselves felt, and smaller groupings influence the greater one, then the common interest no longer remains unaltered, but is met with opposition, the votes are no longer unanimous, and the general will no longer the will of all;[153] contradiction and argument arise, and the best opinion is not accepted without dispute.

Finally, when the state is close to ruin and subsists only through empty and deluding forms, when in each man's heart the social bond is broken, when the crudest self-interest insolently adorns itself with the sacred name of the public good, then the general will falls silent; the motives of all are kept secret, their votes are no more the votes of citizens than if the state bad never existed, and the decrees that are falsely passed, under the name of laws, have private interests as their only aim.

Does this mean that the general will is annihilated or corrupt? No: it remains constant, unalterable, and pure; but it is subordinated to others which have vanquished it. Each man, while detaching his own interests from the common interest, sees clearly that he cannot separate them entirely; but his share of the wrong done to the public seems nothing to him when compared to the exclusive advantage that he intends to take for himself. Except for this private advantage, he has on his own behalf as strong a desire as anyone else for the public good. Even if he sells his vote for money, he does not extinguish the general will that is in him, but eludes it. The mistake he makes is to change the state of the question, giving an answer foreign to what is asked; so that instead of saying, by his vote: "It is beneficial to the state," he says: "It is beneficial to this man, or that party, for such-and-such a view to prevail." Thus in assemblies the law of public order is not so much that the general will must be maintained, but rather to ensure that it is always consulted, and its response always made clear.

At this point there are many reflections that I could make the simple right of voting in any act of sovereignty, a right of which the citizens can never be deprived; and on the rights of giving an opinion, proposing, distinguishing, and debating, which governments always take great care to reserve to their members;[154] but this important subject would require a separate treatise, and I cannot say everything here.

Chapter II Voting

It will be seen from the preceding chapter that the manner in which matters of general concern are treated can give a fairly reliable guide to the current state of moral attitudes and the health of the body politic. The greater the degree of concord that prevails in public assemblies, that is to say the more nearly unanimous the decisions are, the more general interest dominates; but long debates, dissension, and disorder are a sign that particular interests are in the ascendant and the state in decline.

This argument will seem less evident when two or more orders of society constitute the state, as in Rome with the patricians and plebeians, whose disagreements often disrupted the *comitia*, even during the best period of the Republic. But the exception is more apparent than real, for in such cases, because of an inherent defect in the body politic, we have as it were two states in one. What is untrue of the two together is true as regards each separately, for in fact, when the Senate was not involved, the plebiscites of the people[155] went through calmly and with large majorities, even during the most tempestuous times: when citizens had a single interest, the people had a single will.

Unanimity returns at the other extreme, when the citizens fall into servitude and no longer have either freedom or will. Then, by flattery, voting is changed into acclamation; no longer is there any discussion, but only worship or imprecation. Such was the Senate's degraded way of taking votes under the Emperors; and ridiculous precautions were sometimes taken. Tacitus observes[156] that, under Otho, the senators would rain down curses on Vitellius, but took care at the same time to make an appalling noise, in order that if Vitellius chanced to become their master, he would not know what each of them had said.

It is these general considerations that give rise to the principles to be followed in regulating methods of counting votes and comparing opinions, according as the general will is more or less easily perceptible and the state more or less in decline.

There is one sole law that by its nature demands unanimous consent: it is the social pact. For civil association is the most completely voluntary of acts; each man having been born free and master of himself, no one, under any pretext at all, may enslave him without his consent. To conclude that the son of a slave is born into slavery is to conclude that he is not born a man.[157]

If therefore when the social pact is agreed there are those who oppose it, their opposition does not invalidate the contract, but merely prevents it from being applied to them: they are foreigners among citizens. Once the state has been constituted, consent lies in residing in it; to live within its boundaries is to submit to its sovereignty.[158]

Except for this original contract, a majority vote is always binding on all the others; that is a direct consequence of the contract. But the question is how a man can be free and forced to conform to the will of others than himself. How can those who are in opposition be free and subject to laws to which they have not consented?

My reply is that the question is wrongly put. The citizen consents to every law, even those that are passed against his opposition, and even those which punish him when he dares to violate one of them. The constant will of all the citizens of the state is the general will: it is through the general will that they are citizens and have freedom.[159] When a law is proposed in the assembly of the people, what they are asked is not precisely whether they accept or reject the proposal, but whether it is or is not in conformity with the general will, which is their will; everyone, by voting, gives his opinion on the question· and counting the votes makes the general will manifest. When an opinion contrary to mine prevails, therefore, it proves only that I had been mistaken, and that the general will was not what I had believed it to be. If my particular will had prevailed, I should have done otherwise than I wished; and then I should not have been free.

This argument, it is true, presupposes that all the characteristics of the general will are present also in majority decisions; when they cease to be, whatever view may be adopted liberty exists no longer.

Having explained previously how particular wills could replace the general will in the deliberations of the people, I have made sufficiently clear what means to adopt so as to forestall this abuse; I shall return to the subject later.[160] As regards what proportion of the vote suffices to affirm the general will I have also laid down the principles by which it may be determined. A difference of one breaks a tie, and one opposing voice destroys unanimity; but between unanimity and a tied vote there are various degrees of inequality, each of which can be taken for the proportion in question, according to the condition and needs of the body politic.

Two maxims can be used to determine these relationships: one is that the more important and serious the issue the closer the deciding vote should be to unanimity; the other, that the greater the urgency of the matter, the smaller the majority required should be. When a debate has to be concluded immediately, it must suffice to decide by a difference of one vote. Of these maxims, the first appears more appropriate for law-making, and the second for the dispatch of business. However that may be, it is by using them in combination that the most suitable proportions for majority decisions are established.

. . .

Chapter VII The Office of Censor[161]

As the declaration of the general will is made through the law, so the declaration of public judgment is made through the censorship. Public opinion is that kind of law of which the censor is the minister, and which, in the same way as the ruler, he applies to particular cases.

A board of censors, then, is in no way the arbitrator of public opinion, but is simply the mouthpiece for it; as soon as they depart from it, their decisions are empty and ineffectual. It is of no avail to treat a nation's moral conduct separately from the objects of its esteem; for all these things depend on the same principle, and are necessarily associated. Amongst every nation in the world, it is not nature but opinion which determines the choice of pleasures. Put men's opinions to rights, and their behaviour will improve spontaneously. Men always prize what is beautiful or what they find beautiful; but it is in their judgement of beauty that they err; therefore it is their judgements that have to be guided. In judging behaviour we judge honour, and in judging honour we take public opinion for law.

A nation's opinions are engendered by its constitution. Although the law does not control moral standards, it is legislation that gives them birth: when laws grow weak, standards of behaviour degenerate; but the censors' judgment will not then succeed, if the strength of the laws has failed.

From this it follows that the office of censor may be useful in preserving morality, but never in reintroducing it. Establish a censorship when the laws are in their full vigour; as soon as they lose it, the case is desperate; nothing lawful can remain strong when the laws no longer have their strength.

The censorship maintains standards of conduct by preventing the debasement of public opinion, preserving its integrity by applying it wisely, and sometimes even by giving it a fixed form when it is still doubtful. The custom of having seconds in duels, which was taken to crazy lengths in the kingdom of France, was abolished simply by these words, appearing in a royal edict: "As for those who are cowardly enough to call on seconds." This expression of opinion anticipated that of the public and fixed it immediately. Yet when other royal edicts tried to establish that it was also cowardly to fight a duel, which is very true but contrary to the usual opinion,[162] their judgment was derided by the public, which had already made up its mind on the point.

I have argued elsewhere[163] that, since public opinion cannot be constrained, even the slightest trace of constraint should be absent from the court set up to represent it. It is impossible to praise too highly the skill with which this means of influencing behaviour, which we moderns have entirely lost, was practised among the Romans, or, better still, among the Lacedaemonians.

In Sparta, a man of bad character made a valuable suggestion in council; the ephors took no notice, but had the same suggestion made by a man of virtue. What an honour for him, and what disgrace for the other, without praise or blame being given to either! Some drunkards from Samos[164] defiled the court of the ephors: the next day a public edict gave leave to the Samians to be filthy. A real punishment would have been less severe than a reprieve of this sort. When Sparta has decided on what is and is not honourable, Greece does not appeal against its judgments.

Chapter VIII   The Civil Religion[165]

Originally men had no kings except their gods, and no government except theocracy. Their argument was the same as Caligula's;[166] and in those days it was correct. Ideas and sentiments must go through a long period of development before men can bring themselves to accept one of their own kind as king, and flatter themselves that they will benefit from it.

Simply from the fact that God was put at the head of every civil society, it followed that there was the same number of gods as of nations. Two nations foreign to each other, and almost always enemies, could not keep the same master for long: two armies opposing each other in battle cannot obey the same leader. Thus the division between nations gave rise to polytheism, and subsequently to theological and political intolerance, which are the same in nature, as I shall explain later.

. . .

Among us, the Kings of England have put themselves at the head of the Church; and the Czars have gone to the same lengths.[158] But by taking the tide they have made themselves less the masters of the Church than its ministers; they have not so much acquired the right to change it as the power to maintain it; within it they are not its legislators, but only its rulers.[168] Wherever the clergy forms one body,[169] it is master and lawgiver on its own ground. In England and Russia, therefore, there are two powers, two sovereigns, just as in other countries.

Among all the Christian writers, only Hobbes, the philosopher, has clearly perceived both the disease and its remedy, and dared to suggest the reunion of the two heads of the eagle,[170] making everything tend towards political unity, without which neither state nor government will ever be properly constituted.[171] But he must have seen that Christianity's urge to dominate was incompatible with his system, and that the interest of the priesthood would always be stronger than the interest of the state. What made his political theory obnoxious was not so much that some of it was false and abhorrent, but rather that some was right and true.[172]

. . .

Chapter IX Conclusion

Having set down the true principles of political right and attempted to lay the basis for the foundation of the state, it remains for me to give it stability in its external relationships. This would involve international law, trade, the law of warfare and conquest, public law, federations, negotiation, treaties, etc.[173] But all these form a new subject which extends too far for my weak sight; I should always have kept it fixed on things closer to me.

Post-Reading Questions

1. If we are free and noble in the state of nature, as Rousseau claims, why does he think we seek to form civil society at all?
2. Rousseau distinguishes between the *will of all* and the *general will*. What is this distinction, and why is it important?
3. What is Rousseau's critique of representative democracy, and why does he urge more direct forms of democracy that eliminate the need for representatives?
4. Rousseau insists that "all legitimate governments are republican." What does he mean by this?
5. Rousseau thinks it is essential that the state shape men's values and opinions. Why? How does he propose the state should do this?

CASE STUDY
DOES QUEBEC HAVE A RIGHT TO SECEDE?

Introduction

In 1998, the Supreme Court of Canada was asked to determine whether it would be legal, according to the Canadian constitution, for Quebec to unilaterally secede from the rest of the country. The court was prompted to consider this question by the governor general of Canada, acting on the advice of the federal cabinet. In addition to the question of the legality of unilateral secession, the Court considered whether such an action would be supported by international law, and how to proceed in the case of a conflict between international and domestic law on this issue.

Although the ruling in this case did not suggest a decisive victory for either the pro- or anti-secession sides, it did explore—in an unusually direct way—the topics of democracy, sovereignty, federalism, rule of law, and self-government in the Canadian context. These topics are of central importance to the democratic republican thinker Jean-Jacques Rousseau. Like Rousseau's *Social Contract*, the decision in *Reference re Secession of Quebec* stresses that democracy is fundamentally about the self-determination of a people bound together by shared political values, as well as by social, cultural, and economic ties.

This account of democracy cuts both ways, as the *Reference* acknowledges. On the one hand, it might lend credence to the democratic self-determination of Quebec following a referendum by Quebecers in favour of secession. On the other hand, given that Quebec is part of the federation of Canada—which itself is bound by a democratic constitution and the rule of law—it could be asserted that any decision by Quebec to secede must be negotiated with the other parties within that federation.

It is interesting to note that the *Reference* emphasizes ideas championed by republican defenders of democracy such as Rousseau. These include the importance of the sovereign will of the people, the rule of law as the mechanism through which this will is identified and expressed, and the need for political processes such as deliberation and referenda to ensure that the "consent of the governed" (sect. 67) is faithfully secured.

Ironically, anti-federalist supporters of Quebec sovereignty could just as easily draw from Rousseau's *Social Contract* a number of rhetorical points to support their case for the right of unilateral secession. Rousseau argues in that text that large-scale modern states are inevitably places of inequality and domination, and do not support the democratic liberty of their members. These states are simply too large in scale to be capable of acting faithfully in the interests of citizens, or to allow genuine self-governance. As a consequence, in such states the ends of government are not genuinely aligned with the good of the community they serve. Despite the *Reference*'s endorsement of many Rousseauian principles, then, it is likely that were he alive today, Rousseau—both as an advocate of direct, not representative, democracy, and as a deep critic of social and economic inequality—would have doubted the robustness of Canadian democracy.

From Reference re Secession of Quebec, *[1998] 2 S.C.R. 217*

Reference re Secession of Quebec, [1998] 2 S.C.R. 217.
http://scc.lexum.org/decisia-scc-csc/scc-csc/scc-csc/en/item/1643/index.do

In the Matter of Section 53 of the Supreme Court Act, R.S.C., 1985, c. S-26;

And in the Matter of a Reference by the Governor in Council concerning certain questions relating to the secession of Quebec from Canada, as set out in Order in Council P.C. 1996–1497, dated the 30th day of September, 1996

Pursuant to s. 53 of the *Supreme Court Act*, the Governor in Council referred the following questions to this Court:

1. Under the Constitution of Canada, can the National Assembly, legislature or government of Quebec effect the secession of Quebec from Canada unilaterally?

. . .

(1) Supreme Court's Reference Jurisdiction

. . .

The reference questions are justiciable and should

be answered. They do not ask the Court to usurp any democratic decision that the people of Quebec may be called upon to make. The questions, as interpreted by the Court, are strictly limited to aspects of the legal framework in which that democratic decision is to be taken. Since the reference questions may clearly be interpreted as directed to legal issues, the Court is in a position to answer them. The Court cannot exercise its discretion to refuse to answer the questions on a pragmatic basis. The questions raise issues of fundamental public importance and they are not too imprecise or ambiguous to permit a proper legal answer. Nor has the Court been provided with insufficient information regarding the present context in which the questions arise. Finally, the Court may deal on a reference with issues that might otherwise be considered not yet "ripe" for decision.

. . .

I. Introduction

This Reference requires us to consider momentous questions that go to the heart of our system of constitutional government. The observation we made more than a decade ago in *Reference re Manitoba Language Rights,* [1985]

1 S.C.R. 721 (*Manitoba Language Rights Reference*), at p. 728, applies with equal force here: as in that case, the present one "combines legal and constitutional questions of the utmost subtlety and complexity with political questions of great sensitivity." In our view, it is not possible to answer the questions that have been put to us without a consideration of a number of underlying principles. An exploration of the meaning and nature of these underlying principles is not merely of academic interest. On the contrary, such an exploration is of immense practical utility. Only once those underlying principles have been examined and delineated may a considered response to the questions we are required to answer emerge.

. . .

(3) Analysis of the Constitutional Principles
(a) Nature of the Principles

What are those underlying principles? Our Constitution is primarily a written one, the product of 131 years of evolution. Behind the written word is a historical lineage stretching back through the ages, which aids in the consideration of the underlying constitutional principles. These principles inform and sustain the constitutional text: they are the vital unstated assumptions upon which the text is based. The following discussion addresses the four foundational constitutional principles that are most germane for resolution of this Reference: federalism, democracy, constitutionalism and the rule of law, and respect for minority rights. These defining principles function in symbiosis. No single principle can be defined in isolation from the others, nor does any one principle trump or exclude the operation of any other.

. . .

(b) Federalism

It is undisputed that Canada is a federal state. . . .

In a federal system of government such as ours, political power is shared by two orders of government: the federal government on the one hand, and the provinces on the other. Each is assigned respective spheres of jurisdiction by the Constitution Act, 1867. . . . In interpreting our constitution, the courts have always been concerned with the federalism principle, inherent in the structure of our constitutional arrangements, which has from the beginning been the lodestar by which the courts have been guided.

. . .

The principle of federalism recognizes the diversity of the component parts of Confederation, and the autonomy of provincial governments to develop their societies within their respective spheres of jurisdiction. The federal structure of our country also facilitates democratic participation by distributing power to the government thought to be most suited to achieving the particular societal objective having regard to this diversity.

. . .

(c) Democracy

Democracy is a fundamental value in our constitutional law and political culture. While it has both an institutional and an individual aspect, the democratic principle was also argued before us in the sense of the supremacy of the sovereign will of a people, in this case potentially to be expressed by Quebecers in support of unilateral secession. It is useful to explore in a summary way these different aspects of the democratic principle.

. . .

Democracy is not simply concerned with the process of government. On the contrary, as suggested in *Switzman v. Elbling*, *supra*, at p. 306, democracy is fundamentally connected to substantive goals, most importantly, the promotion of self-government. Democracy accommodates cultural and group identities. . . . Put another way, a sovereign people exercises its right to self-government through the democratic process. In considering the scope and purpose of the Charter, the Court in *R. v. Oakes* articulated some of the values inherent in the notion of democracy:

> The Court must be guided by the values and principles essential to a free and democratic society which I believe to embody, to name but a few, respect for the inherent dignity of the human person, commitment to social justice and equality, accommodation of a wide variety of beliefs, respect for cultural and group identity, and faith in social and political institutions which enhance the participation of individuals and groups in society.

In institutional terms, democracy means that each of the provincial legislatures and the federal Parliament is elected by popular franchise. These legislatures, we have said, are "at the core of the system of representative government." . . .

It is, of course, true that democracy expresses the sovereign will of the people. Yet this expression, too, must be taken in the context of the other institutional values we have identified as pertinent to this Reference. The relationship between democracy and federalism means, for example, that in Canada there may be different and equally legitimate majorities in different provinces and territories and at the federal level. No one majority is more or less "legitimate" than the others as an expression of democratic opinion, although, of course, the consequences will vary with the subject matter. A federal system of government enables different provinces to pursue policies responsive to the particular concerns and interests of people in that province. At the same time, Canada as a whole is also a democratic community in which citizens construct and achieve goals on a national scale through a federal government acting within the limits of its jurisdiction. The function of federalism is to enable citizens to participate concurrently in different collectivities and to pursue goals at both a provincial and a federal level.

The consent of the governed is a value that is basic to our understanding of a free and democratic society. Yet democracy in any real sense of the word cannot exist without the rule of law. It is the law that creates the framework within which the "sovereign will" is to be ascertained and implemented. To be accorded legitimacy, democratic institutions must rest, ultimately, on a legal foundation. That is, they must allow for the participation of, and accountability to, the people, through public institutions created under the constitution. Equally, however, a system of government cannot survive through adherence to the law alone. A political system must also possess legitimacy, and in our political culture, that requires an interaction between the rule of law and the democratic principle. The system must be capable of reflecting the aspirations of the people. But there is more. Our law's claim to legitimacy also rests on an appeal to moral values, many of which are imbedded in our constitutional structure. It would be a grave mistake to equate legitimacy with the "sovereign will" or majority rule alone, to the exclusion of other constitutional values.

Finally, we highlight that a functioning democracy requires a continuous process of discussion. The constitution mandates government by democratic legislatures, and an executive accountable to them, "resting ultimately on public opinion reached by discussion and the interplay of ideas" (*Saumur v. City of Quebec, supra*, at p. 330). At both the federal and provincial level, by its very nature, the need to build majorities necessitates compromise, negotiation, and deliberation. No one has a monopoly on truth, and our system is predicated on the faith that in the marketplace of ideas, the best solutions to public problems will rise to the top. Inevitably, there will be dissenting voices. A democratic system of government is committed to considering those dissenting voices, and seeking to acknowledge and address those voices in the laws by which all in the community must live.

. . .

(d) Constitutionalism and the Rule of Law

The principles of constitutionalism and the rule of law lie at the root of our system of government. . . . At its most basic level, the rule of law vouchsafes to the citizens and residents of the country a stable, predictable and ordered society in which to conduct their affairs. It provides a shield for individuals from arbitrary state action.

In the *Manitoba Language Rights Reference*, this Court outlined the elements of the rule of law. We emphasized, first, that the rule of law provides that the law is supreme over the acts of both government and private persons. There is, in short, one law for all. Second, we explained, that "the rule of law requires the creation and maintenance of an actual order of positive laws which preserves and embodies the more general principle of normative order." It was this second aspect of the rule of law that was primarily at issue in the *Manitoba Language Rights Reference* itself. A third aspect of the rule of law is, as recently confirmed in the *Provincial Judges Reference, supra*, at para. 10, that "the exercise of all public power must find its ultimate source in a legal rule." Put another way, the relationship between the state and the individual must be regulated by law. Taken together, these three considerations make up a principle of profound constitutional and political significance.

The constitutionalism principle bears considerable similarity to the rule of law, although they are not identical. The essence of constitutionalism in Canada is embodied in s. 52(1) of the Constitution Act, 1982, which provides that "[t]he Constitution of Canada is the supreme law of Canada, and any law that is inconsistent with the provisions of the Constitution is, to the extent of the inconsistency, of no force or effect." Simply put, the constitutionalism principle requires that all government action comply with the constitution. The rule of law principle requires that all government action must comply with the law, including the constitution. . . .

An understanding of the scope and importance of the principles of the rule of law and constitutionalism is aided by acknowledging explicitly why a constitution is entrenched beyond the reach of simple majority rule. There are three overlapping reasons.

First, a constitution may provide an added safeguard for fundamental human rights and individual freedoms which might otherwise be susceptible to government interference. Although democratic government is generally solicitous of those rights, there are occasions when the majority will be tempted to ignore fundamental rights in order to accomplish collective goals more easily or effectively. Constitutional entrenchment ensures that those rights will be given due regard and protection. Second, a constitution may seek to ensure that vulnerable minority groups are endowed with the institutions and rights necessary to maintain and promote their identities against the assimilative pressures of the majority. And third, a constitution may provide for a division of political power that allocates political power amongst different levels of government. That purpose would be defeated if one of those democratically elected levels of government could usurp the powers of the other simply by exercising its legislative power to allocate additional political power to itself unilaterally.

The argument that the Constitution may be legitimately circumvented by resort to a majority vote in a province-wide referendum is superficially persuasive, in large measure because it seems to appeal to some of the same principles that underlie the legitimacy of the Constitution itself, namely, democracy and self-government. In short, it is suggested that as the notion of popular sovereignty underlies the legitimacy of our existing constitutional arrangements, so the same popular sovereignty that originally led to the present Constitution must (it is argued) also permit "the people" in their exercise of popular sovereignty to secede by majority vote alone. However, closer analysis reveals that this argument is unsound, because it misunderstands the meaning of popular sovereignty and the essence of a constitutional democracy.

Canadians have never accepted that ours is a system of simple majority rule. Our principle of democracy, taken in conjunction with the other constitutional principles discussed here, is richer. Constitutional government is necessarily predicated on the idea that the political representatives of the people of a province have the capacity and the power to commit the province to be bound into the future by the constitutional rules being adopted. These rules are "binding" not in the sense of frustrating the will of a majority of a province, but as defining the majority which must be consulted in order to alter the fundamental balances of political power (including the spheres of autonomy guaranteed by the principle of federalism), individual rights, and minority rights in our society. Of course, those constitutional rules are themselves amenable to amendment, but only through a process of negotiation which ensures that there is an opportunity for the constitutionally defined rights of all the parties to be respected and reconciled.

In this way, our belief in democracy may be harmonized with our belief in constitutionalism. Constitutional amendment often requires some form of substantial consensus precisely because the content of the underlying principles of our constitution demand it. By requiring broad support in the form of an "enhanced majority" to achieve constitutional change, the constitution ensures that minority interests must be addressed before proposed changes which would affect them may be enacted.

. . .

(e) Protection of Minorities

The fourth underlying constitutional principle we address here concerns the protection of minorities. There are a number of specific constitutional provisions protecting minority language, religion and education rights. Some of those provisions are, as we have recognized on a number of occasions, the product of historical compromises. As this Court observed . . . the protection of minority religious education rights was a central consideration in the negotiations leading to Confederation. In the absence of such protection, it was felt that the minorities in what was then Canada East and Canada West would be submerged and assimilated. . . .

However, we highlight that even though those provisions were the product of negotiation and political compromise, that does not render them unprincipled. Rather, such a concern reflects a broader principle related to the protection of minority rights. Undoubtedly, the three other constitutional principles inform the scope and operation of the specific provisions that protect the rights of minorities. We emphasize that the protection of minority rights is itself an independent principle underlying our constitutional order. . . .

The concern of our courts and governments to protect minorities has been prominent in recent years, particularly following the enactment of the Charter. Undoubtedly, one of the key considerations motivating the enactment of the Charter, and the process of constitutional judicial review that it entails, is the protection of minorities. However, it should not be forgotten that the protection of minority rights had a long history before the enactment of the Charter. Indeed, the protection of minority rights was clearly an essential consideration in the design of our constitutional structure even at the time of Confederation: *Senate Reference, supra*, at p. 71. Although Canada's record of upholding the rights of minorities is not a spotless one, that goal is one toward which Canadians have been striving since Confederation, and the process has not been without successes. The principle of protecting minority rights continues to exercise influence in the operation and interpretation of our constitution.

(4) The Operation of the Constitutional Principles in the Secession Context

. . . We hold that Quebec could not purport to invoke a right of self-determination such as to dictate the terms of a proposed secession to the other parties: that would not be a negotiation at all. As well, it would be naive to expect that the substantive goal of secession could readily be distinguished from the practical details of secession. The devil would be in the details. The democracy principle, as we have emphasized, cannot be invoked to trump the principles of federalism and rule of law, the rights of individuals and minorities, or the operation of democracy in the other provinces or in Canada as a whole. No negotiations could be effective if their ultimate outcome, secession, is cast as an absolute legal entitlement based upon an obligation to give effect to that act of secession in the Constitution. Such a foregone conclusion would actually undermine the obligation to negotiate and render it hollow.

However, we are equally unable to accept the reverse proposition, that a clear expression of self-determination by the people of Quebec would impose no obligations upon the other provinces or the federal government. The continued existence and operation of the Canadian constitutional order cannot remain indifferent to the clear expression of a clear majority of Quebecers that they no longer wish to remain in Canada. This would amount to the assertion that other constitutionally recognized principles necessarily trump the clearly expressed democratic will of the people of Quebec. Such a proposition fails to give sufficient weight to the underlying constitutional principles that must inform the amendment process, including the principles of democracy and federalism. The rights of other provinces and the federal government cannot deny the right of the government of Quebec to pursue secession, should a clear majority of the people of Quebec choose that goal, so long as in doing so, Quebec respects the rights of others. Negotiations would be necessary to address the interests of the federal government, of Quebec and the other provinces, and other participants, as well as the rights of all Canadians both within and outside Quebec.

Is the rejection of both of these propositions reconcilable? Yes, once it is realized that none of the rights or principles under discussion is absolute to the exclusion of the others. This observation suggests that other parties cannot exercise their rights in such a way as to amount to an absolute denial of Quebec's rights, and similarly, that so long as Quebec exercises its rights while respecting the rights of others, it may propose secession and seek to achieve it through negotiation.

The negotiation process precipitated by a decision of a clear majority of the population of Quebec on a clear question to pursue secession would require the reconciliation of various rights and obligations by the representatives of two legitimate majorities, namely, the clear majority of the population of Quebec, and the clear majority of Canada as a whole, whatever that may be. There can be no suggestion that either of these majorities "trumps" the other. A political majority that does not act in accordance with the underlying constitutional principles we have identified puts at risk the legitimacy of the exercise of its rights.

IV. Summary of Conclusions

. . .

The Reference requires us to consider whether Quebec has a right to *unilateral* secession. Those who support the existence of such a right found their case primarily on the principle of democracy. Democracy, however, means more than simple majority rule. As reflected in our constitutional jurisprudence, democracy exists in the larger context of other constitutional values such as those already mentioned. In the 131 years since Confederation, the people of the provinces and territories have created close ties of interdependence (economically, socially, politically, and culturally) based on shared values that include federalism, democracy, constitutionalism and the rule of law, and respect for minorities. A democratic decision of Quebecers in favour of secession would put those relationships at risk. The constitution vouchsafes order and stability, and accordingly secession of a province "under the Constitution" could not be achieved unilaterally, that is, without principled negotiation with other participants in Confederation within the existing constitutional framework.

The constitution is not a straitjacket. Even a brief review of our constitutional history demonstrates periods of momentous and dramatic change. Our democratic institutions necessarily accommodate a continuous process of discussion and evolution, which is reflected in the constitutional right of each participant in the federation to initiate constitutional change. This right implies a reciprocal duty on the other participants to engage in discussions to address any legitimate initiative to change the constitutional order. While it is true that some attempts at constitutional amendment in recent years have faltered, a clear majority vote in Quebec on a clear question in favour of secession would confer democratic legitimacy on the secession initiative which all of the other participants in Confederation would have to recognize.

Quebec could not, despite a clear referendum result, purport to invoke a right of self-determination to dictate the terms of a proposed secession to the other parties to the federation. The democratic vote, by however strong a majority, would have no legal effect on its own and could not push aside the principles of federalism and the rule of law, the rights of individuals and minorities, or the operation of democracy in the other provinces or in Canada as a whole. Democratic rights under the constitution cannot be divorced from constitutional obligations. Nor, however, can the reverse proposition be accepted. The continued existence and operation of the Canadian constitutional order could not be indifferent to a clear expression of a clear majority of Quebecers that they no longer wish to remain in Canada. The other provinces and the federal government would have no basis to deny the right of the government of Quebec to pursue secession, should a clear majority of the people of Quebec choose that goal, so long as in doing so, Quebec respects the rights of others. The negotiations that followed such a vote would address the potential act of secession as well as its possible terms should in fact secession proceed. There would be no conclusions predetermined by law on any issue. Negotiations would need to address the interests of the other provinces, the federal government, Quebec and indeed the rights of all Canadians both within and outside Quebec, and specifically the rights of minorities. No one suggests that it would be an easy set of negotiations.

The negotiation process would require the reconciliation of various rights and obligations by negotiation between two legitimate majorities, namely, the majority of the population of Quebec, and that of Canada as a whole. A political majority at either level that does not act in accordance with the underlying constitutional principles we have mentioned puts at risk the legitimacy of its exercise of its rights, and the ultimate acceptance of the result by the international community.

The task of the Court has been to clarify the legal framework within which political decisions are to be taken "under the Constitution," not to usurp the prerogatives of the political forces that operate within that framework. The obligations we have identified are binding obligations under the Constitution of Canada.

However, it will be for the political actors to determine what constitutes "a clear majority on a clear question" in the circumstances under which a future referendum vote may be taken. Equally, in the event of demonstrated majority support for Quebec secession, the content and process of the negotiations will be for the political actors to settle. The reconciliation of the various legitimate constitutional interests is necessarily committed to the political rather than the judicial realm precisely because that reconciliation can only be achieved through the give and take of political negotiations. To the extent issues addressed in the course of negotiation are political, the courts, appreciating their proper role in the constitutional scheme, would have no supervisory role. . . .

. . . A state whose government represents the whole of the people or peoples resident within its territory, on a basis of equality and without discrimination, and respects the principles of self-determination in its internal arrangements, is entitled to maintain its territorial integrity under international law and to have that territorial integrity recognized by other states. Quebec does not meet the threshold of a colonial people or an oppressed people, nor can it be suggested that Quebecers have been denied meaningful access to government to pursue their political, economic, cultural, and social development. In the circumstances, the National Assembly, the legislature, or the government of Quebec do not enjoy a right at international law to effect the secession of Quebec from Canada unilaterally.

Although there is no right, under the constitution or at international law, to unilateral secession—that is secession without negotiation on the basis just discussed—this does not rule out the possibility of an unconstitutional declaration of secession leading to a de facto secession. The ultimate success of such a secession would be dependent on recognition by the international community, which is likely to consider the legality and legitimacy of secession having regard to, amongst other facts, the conduct of Quebec and Canada, in determining whether to grant or withhold recognition. Such recognition, even if granted, would not, however, provide any retroactive justification for the act of secession, either under the Constitutionw of Canada or at international law. . . .

Post-Case-Reading Questions

1. How does this legal discussion by the Supreme Court reconcile the principles of federalism and political self-determination?
2. This "reference" says that "a functioning democracy requires a continuous process of discussion." What is meant by this, and does Rousseau's republican vision of democracy have a similar requirement?

Immanuel Kant

Introduction

Immanuel Kant is arguably the foremost philosopher of the Enlightenment—the "Age of Reason"—in that he gave the most powerful and systematic expression to its ideals. He was born in 1724 in the East Prussian city of Königsberg (renamed Kaliningrad in 1946), the eldest of five surviving children. His parents were religious followers of Pietism, a branch of Lutheranism that emphasized individual piety and simplicity in matters of worship. Though his family was not well off—his father was a saddler whose business steadily declined—Kant's mother, Anna, arranged for him to be educated at the local Pietist school. Later, at the age of 16, Kant entered the University of Königsberg as a theological student. There, he not only studied the classics and philosophy but, encouraged by a favourite professor—Martin Knutzen—became interested in mathematics and Newtonian physics as well. In 1755, he became a lecturer at the University of Königsberg, and was later (in 1770) appointed professor of logic and metaphysics. Kant did not marry, and lived his entire life in Königsberg until his death in 1804.

Immanuel Kant

© iStockphoto.com/Steven Wynn

Kant was a philosopher of enormous breadth, and his many works include major contributions to various fields in philosophy: *Critique of Pure Reason* (1781), *Groundwork of the Metaphysics of Morals* (1785), *Critique of Practical Reason* (1788), *Critique of Judgment* (1790), *Religion within the Limits of Reason Alone* (1793), *Perpetual Peace: A Philosophical Sketch* (1795), and *Metaphysics of Morals* (1797). An important theme in several of Kant's works is the concept of autonomy, or freedom, which he saw as central to both morality and politics. Kant did not think that we should aspire to unfettered freedom, however, arguing that "if freedom is not restricted by objective rules, the result is much savage disorder" (*Lectures on Ethics*).[1] To maintain the unconditional value of human autonomy and also to explain how we can regulate our freedom, Kant insisted that we have to understand it in relation to reason—that is, to see it as "freedom according to reason."

To show the rational limit of freedom in morality, Kant begins by making a distinction between moral maxims and practical maxims. He calls practical maxims of action *hypothetical imperatives*, which are motivated by particular needs and desires. They take the following form: "if you want so and so then you ought to do such and such." The "ought" in a hypothetical imperative loses its force as soon as the needs or desires that motivate the maxim are satisfied.

In contrast with a hypothetical imperative, moral maxims, which Kant calls *categorical imperatives*, are not motivated by any particular needs and interests but only by duty, or the necessity to act out of reverence for the law. Their form is "you ought to do so and so, without qualification," such as the maxim that one ought never to tell a lie.

The categorical imperative dictates that you should "act only according to that maxim by which you can at the same time will that it should become a universal law" (*Groundwork of the Metaphysics of Morals*).[2] It is easy to understand the motivation of hypothetical imperatives because we see the force of "ought" in our desires. It is not so easy to grasp the reason for categorical imperatives. Kant accepts that the will needs to have motives, and argues that the force of the categorical "ought" is derived from our rationality. Categorical "oughts" are binding because they derive their force from a universal principle—reason—that any rational agent would recognize as valid.

For Kant, acting morally cannot be understood except through the formulation of a theoretical maxim—namely, that of a categorical imperative. In practice, this works by asking us whether, in considering an action, we would judge it acceptable if everybody in the world did the same thing. If we think that the action can become a universal maxim without contradiction (as Kant put it), then it is morally admissible. Kant views this as proof that in morality, everything that is true in theory must also be valid in practice.

As for the political sphere, Kant takes the basic problem of politics to be the transition from the state of war to the state of peace and security: how can different individuals with different capacities and interests live peacefully together? The application of the categorical imperative enables Kant to approach this problem in terms of the reconciliation of the freedom of one individual with that of others.

In the essay included here, "On the Common Saying: 'This May Be True in Theory, but It Does Not Apply in Practice'" (1793), Kant considers the relation between theory and practice. He thinks that we need mediation between our understanding and our acts of judgment so that our theoretical insights can inform our practical life and vice versa. This dependency should be enough to prevent those who want to dismiss the value of theory out of hand. But there are many who insist that theoretical work is unnecessary. Kant, by contrast, considered this opposition dangerous, particularly when it comes to the theories founded on the concept of duty, such as those relating to morality, law, and politics. Theory's importance, he insisted, must be defended against charges of ideality and uselessness. Kant set himself the task of examining this maxim in three separate areas: (1) in morality in general, with regard to the welfare of each individual man; (2) in politics, with regard to the welfare of states; and (3) in the cosmopolitan sphere, or international law, with regard to the welfare of the human species.

Human beings' rational nature enables them to come together under a contract in order to make laws that would govern their common life. This contract, which Kant calls a civil constitution, is an association of free and equal men who are bearers of individual rights and subject to coercive laws. Kant defines "right" as that which enables the freedom of each individual to coexist with the freedom of everyone else in accordance with a universal law. The contract is motivated not by any particular end such as happiness or the instinct of self-preservation but by the idea of reason, which binds us, as rational beings, by an absolute duty in our mutual external relationship. This, for Kant, shows that what is valid in theory must hold in practice as well.

The case that follows Kant's essay, and which provides an example of Kantian constitution-making, is the Canadian Charter of Rights and Freedoms. The Charter may be viewed as an attempt to lay out a design that allows for the greatest individual freedom consistent with the equal freedom of other Canadians.

Further Readings

Beiner, R. and J. Booth. (1993). *Kant and Political Philosophy: The Contemporary Legacy.* New Haven: Yale University Press.

Bohman, J. and M. Lutz-Bachmann (eds.). (1997). *Perpetual Peace: Essays on Kant's Cosmopolitan Ideal.* Cambridge: MIT Press.

Mulholland, L. (1990). *Kant's System of Rights.* New York: Columbia University Press.

Rosen, A. (1993). *Kant's Theory of Justice.* Ithaca: Cornell University Press.

Scruton, R. (2001). *Kant: A Very Short Introduction.* Oxford: Oxford University Press.

Williams, H. (1986). *Kant's Political Philosophy.* New York: St. Martin's Press.

Immanuel Kant, "On the Common Saying: 'This May Be True in Theory, but It Does Not Apply in Practice'"[3]

Immanuel Kant, "On the Common Saying: 'This May Be True in Theory, but It Does Not Apply in Practice,'" in Kant: Political Writings, *edited by H.S. Reiss, translated by H.B. Nisbet (Cambridge: Cambridge University Press, 1970 [1991]).*

A collection of rules, even of practical rules, is termed a *theory* if the rules concerned are envisaged as principles of a fairly general nature, and if they are abstracted from numerous conditions which, nonetheless, necessarily influence their practical application. Conversely, not all activities are called *practice*, but only those realizations of a particular purpose which are considered to comply with certain generally conceived principles of procedure.

It is obvious that no matter how complete the theory may be, a middle term is required between theory and practice, providing a link and a transition from one to the other. For a concept of the understanding, which contains the general rule, must be supplemented by an act of judgment whereby the practitioner distinguishes instances where the rule applies from those where it does not. And since rules cannot in turn be provided on every occasion to direct the judgment in subsuming each instance under the previous rule (for this would involve an infinite regress), theoreticians will be found who can never in all their lives become practical, since they lack judgment. There are, for example, doctors or lawyers who did well during their schooling but who do not know how to act when asked to give advice. But even where a natural talent for judgment is present, there may still be a lack of premises. In other words, the theory may be incomplete, and can perhaps be perfected only by future experiments and experiences from which the newly qualified doctor, agriculturalist or economist can and ought to abstract new rules for himself to complete his theory. It is therefore not the fault of the theory if it is of little practical use in such cases. The fault is that there is *not enough* theory; the person concerned ought to have learnt from experience. What he learnt from experience might well be true theory, even if he were unable to impart it to others and to expound it as a teacher in systematic general propositions, and were consequently unable to claim the title of a theoretical physician, agriculturalist or the like. Thus no one can pretend to be practically versed in a branch of knowledge and yet treat theory with scorn, without exposing the fact that he is an ignoramus in his subject. He no doubt imagines that he can get further than he could through theory if he gropes around in experiments and experiences, without collecting certain principles (which in fact amount to what we term theory) and without relating his activities to an integral whole (which, if treated methodically, is what we call a system).

Yet it is easier to excuse an ignoramus who claims that theory is unnecessary and superfluous in his supposed practice than a would-be expert who admits the value of theory for teaching purposes, for example as a mental exercise, but at the same time maintains that it is quite different in practice, and that anyone leaving his studies to go out into the world will realize he has been pursuing empty ideals and philosopher's dreams—in short, that whatever sounds good in theory has no practical validity. (This doctrine is often expressed as: "this or that proposition is valid *in thesi*, but not *in hypothesi*.") Now all of us would merely ridicule the empirical engineer who criticized general mechanics or the artilleryman who criticized the mathematical theory of ballistics by declaring that, while the theory is ingeniously conceived, it is not valid in practice, since experience in applying it gives results quite different from those predicted theoretically. For if mechanics were supplemented by the theory of friction and ballistics by the theory of air resistance, in other words if only more theory were added, these theoretical disciplines would harmonize very well with practice. But a theory which concerns objects of perception[4] is quite different from one in which such objects are represented only through concepts, as with objects of mathematics and of philosophy. The latter objects can perhaps quite legitimately be *thought* of by reason, yet it may be impossible for them to be *given*. They may merely exist as empty ideas which either cannot be used at all in practice or only with some practical disadvantages. This would mean that the aforesaid common saying might well be correct in such cases.

But in a theory founded on the *concept of duty*, any worries about the empty ideality of the concept completely disappear. For it would not be a duty to strive after a certain effect of our will if this effect were impossible in experience (whether we envisage the experience as complete or as progressively approximating to completion). And it is with theory of this kind that the present essay is exclusively concerned. For to the shame of philosophy, it is not uncommonly alleged of such theory that whatever may be correct in it is in fact invalid in practice. We usually hear this said in an arrogant, disdainful tone, which comes of presuming to use experience to reform reason itself in the very attributes which do it most credit. Such illusory wisdom imagines it can see further and more clearly with its mole-like gaze fixed on experience than with the eyes which were bestowed on a being designed to stand upright and to scan the heavens.

This maxim, so very common in our sententious, inactive times, does very great harm if applied to matters of morality, i.e., to moral or legal duty. For in such cases, the canon of reason is related to practice in such a way that the value of the practice depends entirely upon its appropriateness to the theory it is based on; all is lost if the empirical (hence contingent) conditions governing the execution of the law are made into conditions of the law itself, so that a practice calculated to produce a result which *previous* experience makes probable is given the right to dominate a theory which is in fact self-sufficient.

I shall divide up this essay in terms of three points of view which the worthy gentleman[5] who so boldly criticizes theories and systems adopts in judging his objects. The three attitudes are those of the private individual or *man of affairs*, the *statesman*, and the *man of the world* or cosmopolitan. These three individuals are united in attacking the *academic*, who works for them all, for their own good, on matters of theory. Since they fancy that they understand this better than he does, they seek to relegate him to his classroom (*illa se iactet in aula!*)[6] as a pedant who, unfitted for practical affairs, merely stands in the way of their experienced wisdom.

We shall therefore deal with the relationship of theory to practice in three separate areas: firstly in *morality* in general, with regard to the welfare of each *individual man*, secondly in *politics*, with regard to the welfare of *states*, and thirdly in the *cosmopolitical* sphere, with regard to the welfare of the *human race* as a whole, in so far as the welfare of mankind is increasing within a series of developments extending into all future ages. The titles of the sections, for reasons arising out of the essay itself will express the relationship of theory to practice in *morality*, in *political right* [Staatsrecht], and in *international right* [Völkerrecht].[7]

I. On the Relationship of Theory to Practice in Morality in General

(*In Reply to Some Objections by Professor Garve*[8])[9]

Before I proceed to the actual controversy over what is valid in theory and practice in the application of one and the same concept, I must compare my theory, as I have myself presented it elsewhere, with the picture which Professor Garve presents of it. We may thus see in advance whether we have understood one another.

A. I had provisionally designated the study of morals as the introduction to a discipline which would teach us not how to be happy, but how we should become worthy of happiness.[10] Nor had I omitted to point out at the same time that man is not thereby expected to *renounce* his natural aim of attaining happiness as soon as the question of following his duty arises; for like any finite rational being, he simply cannot do so. Instead, he must completely *abstract* from such considerations as soon as the imperative of duty supervenes, and must on no account make them a *condition* of his obeying the law prescribed to him by reason. He must indeed make every possible conscious effort to ensure that no *motive* derived from the desire for happiness imperceptibly infiltrates his conceptions of duty. To do this, he should think rather of the sacrifices which obedience to duty (i.e., virtue) entails than of the benefits he might reap from it, so that he will comprehend the imperative of duty in its full authority as a self-sufficient law, independent of all other influences, which requires unconditional obedience.

a. This proposition of mine is expressed by Garve as follows: I had asserted "that adherence to the moral law, regardless of happiness, is *the one and only ultimate end* for man, and that it must be considered as the creator's unique intention." (My theory is that the creator's unique intention is neither human morality in itself nor happiness in itself, but the highest good possible on earth, the union and harmony of them both.)

B. I had further noted that this concept of duty does not need to be based on any particular end, but rather itself *occasions* a new end for the human will, that of striving with all one's power towards the highest good possible on earth, towards the universal happiness of the whole world, combined with and in keeping with the purest morality. Since the attainment of this good lies within our power in one of its two aspects, but not in both taken together, it elicits from our reason a faith, *for practical purposes*, in a moral being who governs the world, and in a future existence. This does not mean that faith in both of these is a necessary condition lending "support and stability" (i.e., a solid foundation and enough strength to constitute a *motive*) to the general concept of duty. It merely ensures that this concept acquires an *object* in the shape of an ideal of pure reason.[11] For in itself, duty is nothing more than a *limitation* of the will within a universal legislation which was made possible by an initially accepted maxim. The object or aim of the will can be of any kind whatsoever (even including happiness). But in this case, we completely abstract from whatever particular end is adopted. Thus so far as the *principle* of morality is concerned, the doctrine of the *highest good* as the ultimate end of a will which is determined by this doctrine and which conforms to its laws can be bypassed and set aside as incidental. And it will emerge from what follows that the actual controversy is not in fact concerned with this at all, but only with morality in general.

b. Garve expresses the above propositions as follows: "The virtuous man cannot and may not ever lose sight of this consideration (i.e., that of his own happiness), since he would otherwise be completely without access to the invisible world and to belief in the existence of God and of immortality. Such belief, according to this theory, is absolutely necessary *to lend support and stability to the moral system.*" He concludes by briefly summing up as follows the statements he ascribes to me: "The virtuous man, according to these principles, constantly strives to be worthy of happiness, but never, *in so far as* he is truly virtuous, to be actually happy." (The words *in so far as* create an ambiguity which must be eliminated before we go any further. They can signify *in the act* of submitting, as a virtuous man, to one's duty—in which case the sentence is perfectly compatible with my theory—or they could imply that if he is never anything but virtuous, the virtuous man should not take happiness into consideration at all, even where the question of duty does not arise and where there is no conflict with duty—in which case the sentence is totally at variance with my statements.)

These objections are therefore nothing but misunderstandings (for I have no wish to see them as misrepresentations). Their very possibility would astonish us, if it were not that such phenomena can be adequately explained by the human tendency to follow a habitual train of thought, even in judging the thoughts of others, and thus to carry the former over into the latter.

Garve follows up this polemical account of the above moral principle with a dogmatic exposition of its direct opposite. By analytical methods, he comes to the following conclusion: "In the ordering of *concepts*, the states which entitle us to give *preference* to one rather than others must first be recognized and distinguished before we choose anyone of them and thus decide in advance what aim we shall pursue. But a state which a being who is aware of himself and of his own state would *prefer* to other ways of existence as soon as he saw it before him, is a *good* state; and a series of good states is the most general notion expressed by the word *happiness.*" He continues: "A law presupposes motives, but motives presuppose that a difference has already been recognized between a worse state and a better one. This recognized difference is the element of the concept of happiness," and so on. And again: "*Happiness*, in the most general sense of the word, *is the source of the motives behind every effort*, including obedience to the moral law. I must first of all know whether something is good before I can ask whether the fulfillment of moral duties belongs to the category of good things. Man must have an *incentive* to set him in motion *before* he can be given a *goal*[12] towards which this motion should be directed."

This argument is nothing more than a play upon the ambiguity of the word *good*. For it can be taken to mean something absolutely good in itself, as opposed to that which is evil in itself, or something only relatively good, as opposed to something more or less good than itself. In the latter case, the preferred state may be only comparatively better, yet nonetheless evil in itself. The maxim of absolute obedience to a categorically binding law of the free will (i.e., of duty), without reference to any ulterior end, is essentially different (i.e., different *in kind*) from the maxim of pursuing, as a motive for a certain way of acting, the end which nature itself has imposed upon us and which is generally known as happiness. For the first maxim is good in itself, but the second is not. The second may, if it conflicts with duty, be thoroughly evil. But if a certain end is made basic, so that no law is absolutely binding but always relative to the end adopted, two opposing actions might both be relatively good, with one better than the other, which would then count as comparatively evil. For they would differ only in *degree*, not in *kind*. And it is the same with all actions whose motive is not the absolute law of reason (duty), but an end which we have arbitrarily taken as a basis. For this end will be a part of the total of ends whose attainment we call happiness, and one action may contribute more, and another less to my happiness, so that one will be better or worse than the other. But to *give preference* to one state rather than another as a determinant of the will is merely an act of freedom (*res merae facultatis*,[13] as the lawyers say) which takes no account of whether the particular determinant is good or evil in itself, and is thus neutral in both respects.

A state of being bound by a certain *given end* which I have preferred to all others *of the same kind*, is a comparatively better state in terms of happiness (which *reason* never recognizes as more than *relatively good*, according to the extent to which a person is worthy of it). But that state of consciously preferring the moral law of duty in cases where it conflicts with certain of my ends is not just a better state, but the only state which is good in itself. It is good in a completely different sense, in that it takes no account whatsoever of any ends that may present themselves (including their sum total, which is happiness). The determinant in this case is not the content of the will (i.e., a particular basic object) but the pure form of universal lawfulness embodied in its maxim.—Thus it can by no means be said that I class as happiness every state which I *prefer* to all other modes of existence. For I must first be certain that I am not acting against my duty. Only then am I entitled to look round for happiness, in so far as I can reconcile it with the state I know to be morally (not physically) good.[14]

The will, however, must have *motives*. But these are not objects of *physical feeling* as predetermined ends in themselves. They are none other than the absolute *law* itself, and the will's receptivity to it as an absolute compulsion is known as *moral feeling*. This feeling is therefore not the cause but the effect of the will's determinant, and we should not have the least awareness of it within ourselves if such compulsion were not already present in us. Thus the old refrain that this feeling, i.e., a desire which we take as our end, is the first cause determining the will, so that happiness (of which that desire is an element) is the basis of all objective necessity of action and thus of all moral obligations, is a piece of *trivial sophistry*. For if we go on asking even after we know the cause of a given event, we end up by making an effect the cause of itself.

I have now reached the point which really concerns us here, the task of testing and illustrating with examples the supposedly conflicting interest of theory and practice in philosophy. Garve's above-quoted essay furnishes the best possible illustration. He first says (with reference to the distinction I make between a doctrine of how to be *happy* and one of how to be *worthy* of happiness): "For my own part, I admit that while I well understand this distinction among ideas in my *mind*, I do not find any such distinction among the desires and aspirations in my *heart*, so that I fail even to comprehend how anyone can be aware of having neatly set apart his actual desire for happiness and thus of having fulfilled his duty completely unselfishly."

I shall answer the last point first. I willingly concede that no one can have certain awareness of *having fulfilled* his duty completely unselfishly. For this is part of inward experience, and such awareness of one's psychological state would involve an absolutely clear conception of all the secondary notions and considerations which, through imagination, habit and inclination, accompany the concept of duty. And this is too much to ask for. Besides, the non-existence of something (including that of an unconsciously intended advantage) can never be an object of experience. But man is aware with the utmost clarity that he *ought to fulfill* his duty completely unselfishly, and *must* totally separate his desire for happiness from the concept of duty, in order to preserve the latter's purity. For if anyone thought he did not have this clear awareness, he could reasonably be asked to acquire it, so far as his powers might permit. And he must be able to do so, for the true value of morality consists precisely in the purity of its concept. Perhaps no recognized and respected duty has ever been carried out by anyone without some selfishness or interference from other motives; perhaps no one will ever succeed in doing so, however hard he tries. But by careful self-examination, we can perceive a certain amount. We can be aware not so much of any accompanying motives, but rather of our own self-denial with respect to many motives which conflict with the idea of duty. In other words, we can be aware of the maxim of striving towards moral purity. And this is sufficient for us to observe our duty. On the other hand, it is the death of all morality if we make it our maxim to foster such motives, on the pretext that human nature does not permit moral purity (which no one can say with certainty in any case).

As for Garve's above confession that he cannot find such a distinction (more correctly a separation) in his *heart*, I have no hesitation in contradicting his self-accusation outright and in championing his heart against his mind. For as an honest man, he has in fact always found this separation in his heart, i.e., in the determinants of his will. But even for the purposes of speculative thinking and of comprehending that which is incomprehensible or inexplicable (i.e., the possibility of categorical imperatives such as those of duty), he was unable in his own mind to reconcile this separation with the usual principles of psychological explanation, which are all based on the mechanism of natural necessity.[15]

But I must loudly and resolutely disagree with Garve when he concludes by saying: "Such subtle distinctions between ideas become *obscure* even when we *think* about particular objects; but they *vanish completely* when it comes to *action*, when they are supposed to apply to desires and intentions. The more simple, rapid and *devoid of clear ideas* the step from consideration of motives to actual action is, the less possible it is to determine exactly and unerringly the precise momentum which each motive has contributed in guiding the step in this and in no other direction."

The concept of duty in its complete purity is incomparably simpler, clearer and more natural and easily comprehensible to everyone than any motive derived from, combined with, or influenced by happiness, for motives involving happiness always require a great deal of resourcefulness and deliberation. Besides, the concept of duty, if it is presented to the exclusive judgment of even the most ordinary human reason, and confronts the human will separately and in actual opposition to other motives, is far *more powerful*, incisive and likely to promote success than all incentives borrowed from the latter selfish principle. Let us take, for example, the case of someone who has under his trust an endowment (*depositum*), the owner of which is deceased, while the heirs are ignorant of and could never discover its existence. Let us also suppose that the trustee of this deposit, through no fault of his own, has at this very time suffered a complete collapse in his financial circumstances, and has around him a miserable family of wife and children, oppressed by want, and knows that he could at once relieve this distress if he appropriated the pledge entrusted to him. He is also benevolent and philanthropic, while the heirs are rich, uncharitable, thoroughly extravagant

and luxurious, so that it would make little difference if the aforesaid addition to their property were thrown into the sea. Now if this case is explained even to a child of around eight or nine years old, and it is asked whether it might be permissible under the circumstances to devote the deposit to one's own use, the reply will undoubtedly be negative. Whoever we ask will merely answer, without further ado, that *it is wrong*, i.e., that it conflicts with duty. Nothing can be clearer than this, while it is genuinely not the case that the trustee would be furthering his own *happiness* if he surrendered the deposit. For if he expected his decision to be dictated by such considerations, he might for instance reason as follows: "If I give up unasked to the real owners the property I have here, they will presumably reward me for my honesty. Or if they do not, I will still acquire a good reputation at large, and this could prove very remunerative. But all this is most uncertain. Yet various doubts can also be raised in support of this argument. For if I were to embezzle the deposit to relieve my depressed circumstances at one stroke, I should incur suspicion, if I made quick use of it, as to how and by what means I had so soon bettered my circumstances. But if I used it slowly, my poverty would meanwhile increase so greatly that it would become impossible to alleviate it at all." Thus a will which follows the maxim of happiness vacillates between various motives in trying to reach a decision. For it considers the possible results of its decision, and these are highly uncertain; and it takes a good head to find a way out of the host of arguments and counter-arguments without miscalculating the total effect. On the other hand, if we ask what duty requires, there is no confusion whatsoever about the answer, and we are at once certain what action to take. We even feel, if the concept of duty means anything to us, a revulsion at the very idea of calculating the advantages we might gain through violating our duty, just as if the choice were still a real one.

When Garve says that these distinctions (which, as we have shown, are not so subtle as he thinks, but are inscribed in the soul of man in the plainest and most legible characters) *vanish completely when it comes to action*, this contradicts even his own experience. Admittedly, it does not contradict the experience which the *history* of maxims derived from various principles provides. Such experience, alas, proves that most of them are based on selfishness. But it does contradict our (necessarily inward) experience that no idea can so greatly elevate the human mind and inspire it with such enthusiasm as that of a pure moral conviction, respecting duty above all else, struggling with countless evils of existence and even with their most seductive temptations, and yet overcoming them-for we may rightly assume that man can do so. The fact that man is aware that he can do this just because he ought to discloses within him an ample store of divine capabilities and inspires him, so to speak, with a holy awe at the greatness and sublimity of his true vocation. And if man were frequently enough reminded so that it became a habit for him to purge virtue of all the superfluous wealth of advantages which could be amassed through obeying his duty, and if he always conceived of virtue in its complete purity and made it a principle of private and public instruction always to use this insight (a method of inculcating duties which has almost invariably been neglected), human morality would soon be improved. Historical experience has not proved the success of our ethical doctrines. The fault lies in the erroneous assumption that a motive derived from the idea of duty in itself is far too subtle for the common understanding, whereas a cruder motive based on advantages which can be expected either in this or in a future world from obedience to duty (without consideration of the latter itself as a motive) would act more forcibly upon the mind. Another fault is that it has hitherto been a principle of education and homiletics to place more stress on the quest for happiness than on worthiness of happiness, which is the highest postulate of reason. For *precepts* on how to be happy or at least how to avoid one's own disadvantage are not the same as *commandments*. They are never absolutely binding, for having first warned us, they leave us free to choose what we think best, provided that we are prepared to face the consequences. And any evils which might result from our failure to follow the advice we were given could not justifiably be regarded as penalties. For penalties apply only to a free will which violates the law. But nature and inclination cannot give laws to the free will. It is quite different with the idea of duty, for if we violate it, even without considering the disadvantages which might result, we feel the consequences directly, and appear despicable and culpable in our own eyes.

Here, then, is a clear proof that everything in morals which is true in theory must also be valid in practice. As a human being, a being subjected by his own reason to certain duties, each of us is therefore a *man of affairs* and since, as human beings, we never grow out of the school of wisdom, we cannot arrogantly and scornfully relegate the adherent of theory to the classroom and set ourselves up as better trained by experience in all that a man is and all that can be required of him. For all this experience will not in any way help us to escape the precepts of theory, but at most to learn how to apply it in better and more universal ways after we have assimilated it into our principles. But we are here concerned only with the latter, and not with any pragmatic abilities.

II. On the Relationship of Theory to Practice in Political Right

(*Against Hobbes*)[16]

Among all the contracts by which a large group of men unites to form a society (*pactum sociale*), the contract establishing a *civil constitution* (*pactum unionis civilis*) is of an exceptional nature. For while, so far as its execution is concerned, it has much in common with all others that are likewise directed towards a chosen end to be pursued by joint effort, it is essentially different from all others in the principle of its constitution (*constitutionis civilis*). In all social contracts, we find a union of many individuals for some common end which they all *share*. But a union as an end in itself which they all *ought to share* and which is thus an absolute and primary duty in all external relationships whatsoever among human beings (who cannot avoid mutually influencing one another), is only found in a society in so far as it constitutes a civil state, i.e., a commonwealth. And the end which is a duty in itself in such external relationships, and which is indeed the highest formal condition (*conditio sine qua non*) of all other external duties, is the *right* of men *under coercive public laws* by which each can be given what is due to him and secured against attack from any others. But the whole concept of an external right is derived entirely from the concept of *freedom* in the mutual external relationships of human beings, and has nothing to do with the end which all men have by nature (i.e., the aim of achieving happiness) or with the recognized means of attaining this end. And thus the latter end must on no account interfere as a determinant with the laws governing external right. *Right* is the restriction of each individual's freedom so that it harmonizes with the freedom of everyone else (in so far as this is possible within the terms of a general law). And *public right* is the distinctive quality of the *external laws* which make this constant harmony possible. Since every restriction of freedom through the arbitrary will of another party is termed *coercion*, it follows that a civil constitution is a relationship among *free* men who are subject to coercive laws, while they retain their freedom within the general union with their fellows. Such is the requirement of pure reason, which legislates *a priori*, regardless of all empirical ends (which can all be summed up under the general heading of happiness). Men have different views on the empirical end of happiness and what it consists of, so that as far as happiness is concerned, their will cannot be brought under any common principle nor thus under any external law harmonizing with the freedom of everyone.

The civil state, regarded purely as a lawful state, is based on the following *a priori* principles:

1. The *freedom* of every member of society as a *human being*.
2. The *equality* of each with all the others as a *subject*.
3. The *independence* of each member of a commonwealth as a *citizen*.

These principles are not so much laws given by an already established state, as laws by which a state can alone be established in accordance with pure rational principles of external human right. Thus:

1. Man's *freedom* as a human being, as a principle for the constitution of a commonwealth, can be expressed in the following formula. No one can compel me to be happy in accordance with his conception of the welfare of others, for each may seek his happiness in whatever way he sees fit, so long as he does not infringe upon the freedom of others to pursue a similar end which can be reconciled with the freedom of everyone else within a workable general law—i.e., he must accord to others the same right as he enjoys himself. A government might be established on the principle of benevolence towards the people, like that of a father towards his children. Under such a *paternal government* (*imperium paternale*), the subjects, as immature children who cannot distinguish what is truly useful or harmful to themselves, would be obliged to behave purely passively and to rely upon the judgment of the head of state as to how they *ought* to be happy, and upon his kindness in willing their happiness at all. Such a government is the greatest conceivable *despotism*, i.e., a constitution which suspends the entire freedom of its subjects, who thenceforth have no rights whatsoever. The only conceivable government for men who are capable of possessing rights, even if the ruler is benevolent, is not a *paternal* but a *patriotic* government (*imperium non paternale, sed patrioticum*). A *patriotic* attitude is one where everyone in the state, not excepting its head, regards the commonwealth as a maternal womb, or the land as the paternal ground from which he himself sprang and which he must leave to his descendants as a treasured pledge. Each regards himself as authorized to protect the rights of the commonwealth by laws of the general will, but not to submit it to his personal use at his own absolute pleasure. This right of freedom belongs to each member of the commonwealth as a human being, in so far as each is a being capable of possessing rights.

2. Man's *equality* as a subject might be formulated as follows. Each member of the commonwealth has rights of coercion in relation to all the others, except in relation to the head of state. For he alone is not a member of the commonwealth, but its creator or preserver, and he alone is authorized to coerce others without being subject to any coercive law himself . But all who are subject to laws are the subjects of a state, and are thus subject to the right of coercion along with all other members of the commonwealth; the only exception is a single person (in either the physical or the moral sense of the word), the head of state, through whom alone the rightful coercion of all others can be exercised. For if he too could be coerced, he would not be the head of state, and the hierarchy of subordination would ascend infinitely. But if there were two persons exempt from coercion, neither would be subject to coercive laws, and neither could do to the other anything contrary to right, which is impossible.

This uniform equality of human beings as subjects of a state is, however, perfectly consistent with the utmost inequality of the mass in the degree of its possessions, whether these take the form of physical or mental superiority over others, or of fortuitous external property and of particular rights (of which there may be many) with respect to others. Thus the welfare of the one depends very much on the will of the other (the poor depending on the rich), the one must obey the other (as the child its parents or the wife her husband), the one serves (the labourer) while the other pays, etc. Nevertheless, they are all equal as subjects *before the law*, which, as the pronouncement of the general will, can only be single in form, and which concerns the form of right and not the material or object in relation to which I possess rights. For no one can coerce anyone else other than through the public law and its executor, the head of state, while everyone else can resist the others in the same way and to the same degree. No one, however, can lose this authority to coerce others and to have rights towards them except through committing a crime. And no one can voluntarily renounce his rights by a contract or legal transaction to the effect that he has no rights but only duties, for such a contract would deprive him of the right to make a contract, and would thus invalidate the one he had already made.

From this idea of the equality of men as subjects in a commonwealth, there emerges this further formula: every member of the commonwealth must be entitled to reach any degree of rank which a subject can earn through his talent, his industry and his good fortune. And his fellow subjects may not stand in his way by *hereditary* prerogatives or privileges of rank and thereby hold him and his descendants back indefinitely.

All right consists solely in the restriction of the freedom of others, with the qualification that their freedom can coexist with my freedom within the terms of a general law; and public right in a commonwealth is simply a state of affairs regulated by a real legislation which conforms to this principle and is backed up by power, and under which a whole people live as subjects in a lawful state (*status iuridicus*). This is what we call a civil state, and it is characterized by equality in the effects and counter-effects of freely willed actions which limit one another in accordance with the general law of freedom. Thus the *birthright* of each individual in such a state (i.e., before he has performed any acts which can be judged in relation to right) is absolutely *equal* as regards his authority to coerce others to use their freedom in a way which harmonizes with his freedom. Since birth is not an act on the part of the one who is born, it cannot create any inequality in his legal position and cannot make him submit to any coercive laws except in so far as he is a subject, along with all the others, of the one supreme legislative power. Thus no member of the commonwealth can have a hereditary privilege as against his fellow subjects; and no one can hand down to his descendants the privileges attached to the rank he occupies in the commonwealth, nor act as if he were qualified as a ruler by birth and forcibly prevent others from reaching the higher levels of the hierarchy (which are *superior* and *inferior*, but never *imperans* and *subiectus*) through their own merit. He may hand down everything else, so long as it is material and not pertaining to his person, for it may be acquired and disposed of as property and may over a series of generations create considerable inequalities in wealth among the members of the commonwealth (the employee and the employer, the landowner and the agricultural servants, etc.). But he may not prevent his subordinates from raising themselves to his own level if they are able and entitled to do so by their talent, industry and good fortune. If this were not so, he would be allowed to practise coercion without himself being subject to coercive counter-measures from others, and would thus be more than their fellow-subject. No one who lives within the lawful state of a commonwealth can forfeit this equality other than through some crime of his own, but never by contract or through military force (*occupatio bellica*). For no legal transaction on his part or on that of anyone else can make him cease to be his own master. He cannot become like a domestic animal to be employed in any chosen capacity and retained therein without consent for any desired period, even with the reservation (which is at times sanctioned by religion, as among the Indians) that he may not be maimed or killed. He can be considered happy in any condition so long as he is aware that, if he does not reach the same level as others, the fault lies either with himself (i.e., lack of ability or serious endeavour) or with circumstances for which he cannot blame others, and not with the irresistible will of any outside party. For as far as right is concerned, his fellow-subjects have no advantage over him.[17]

3. The *independence* (*sibisufficientia*) of a member of the commonwealth as a *citizen*, i.e., as a co-legislator, may be defined as follows. In the question of actual legislation, all who are free and equal under existing public laws may be considered equal, but not as regards the right to make these laws. Those who are not entitled to this right are nonetheless obliged, as members of the commonwealth, to comply with these laws, and they thus likewise enjoy their protection (not as *citizens* but as co-beneficiaries of this protection). For all right depends on laws. But a public law which defines for everyone that which is permitted and prohibited by right, is the act of a public will, from which all right proceeds and which must not therefore itself be able to do an injustice to anyone. And this requires no less than the win of the entire people (since all men decide for all men and each decides for himself). For only towards oneself can one never act unjustly. But on the other hand, the will of another person cannot decide anything for someone without injustice, so that the law made by this other person would require a further law to limit his legislation. Thus an individual will cannot legislate for a commonwealth. For this requires freedom, equality and *unity* of the will of *all* the members. And the prerequisite for unity, since it necessitates a general vote (if freedom and equality are both present), is independence. The basic law, which can come only from the general, united will of the people, is called the *original contract*.

Anyone who has the right to vote on this legislation is a *citizen* (*citoyen*, i.e., citizen of a state, not *bourgeois* or citizen of a town). The only qualification required by a citizen (apart, of course, from being an adult male) is that he must be his *own master* (*sui iuris*), and must have some *property* (which can include any skill, trade, fine art or science) to support himself. In cases where he must earn his living from others, he must earn it only by *selling* that which is his,[18] and not by allowing others to make use of him; for he must in the true sense of the word *serve* no one but the commonwealth. In this respect, artisans and large or small landowners are all equal, and each is entitled to one vote only. As for landowners, we leave aside the question of how anyone can have rightfully acquired more land than he can cultivate with his own hands (for acquisition by military seizure is not primary acquisition), and how it came about that numerous people who might otherwise have acquired permanent property were thereby reduced to serving someone else in order to live at all. It would certainly conflict with the above principle of equality if a law were to grant them a privileged status so that their descendants would always remain feudal landowners, without their land being sold or divided by inheritance and thus made useful to more people; it would also be unjust if only those belonging to an arbitrarily selected class were allowed to acquire land, should the estates in fact be divided. The owner of a large estate keeps out as many smaller property owners (and their votes) as could otherwise occupy his territories. He does not vote on their behalf, and himself has only *one* vote. It should be left exclusively to the ability, industry and good fortune of each member of the commonwealth to enable each to acquire a part and all to acquire the whole, although this distinction cannot be observed within the general legislation itself. The number of those entitled to vote on matters of legislation must be calculated purely from the number of property owners, not from the size of their properties.

Those who possess this right to vote must agree *unanimously* to the law of public justice, or else a legal contention would arise between those who agree and those who disagree, and it would require yet another higher legal principle to resolve it. An entire people cannot, however, be expected to reach unanimity, but only to show a majority of votes (and not even of direct votes, but simply of the votes of those delegated in a large nation to represent the people). Thus the actual principle of being content with majority decisions must be accepted unanimously and embodied in a contract; and this itself must be the ultimate basis on which a civil constitution is established.

Conclusion

This, then, is an *original contract* by means of which a civil and thus completely lawful constitution and commonwealth can alone be established. But we need by no means assume that this contract (*contractus originarius* or *pactum sociale*), based on a coalition of the wills of all private individuals in a nation to form a common, public will for the purposes of rightful legislation, actually exists as *a fact*, for it cannot possibly be so. Such an assumption would mean that we would first have to prove from history that some nation, whose rights and obligations have been passed down to us, did in fact perform such an act, and handed down some authentic record or legal instrument, orally or in writing, before we could regard ourselves as bound by a pre-existing civil constitution. It is in fact merely an *idea* of reason, which nonetheless has undoubted practical reality; for it can oblige every legislator to frame his laws in such a way that they could have been produced by the united will of a whole nation, and to regard each subject, in so far as he can claim citizenship, as if he had consented within the general will. This is the test of the rightfulness of every public law. For if the law is such that a whole people could not *possibly* agree to it (for example, if it stated that a certain class of

subjects must be privileged as a hereditary *ruling class*), it is unjust; but if it is at least *possible* that a people could agree to it, it is our duty to consider the law as just, even if the people is at present in such a position or attitude of mind that it would probably refuse its consent if it were consulted.[19] But this restriction obviously applies only to the judgment of the legislator, not to that of the subject. Thus if a people, under some existing legislation, were asked to make a judgment which in all probability would prejudice its happiness, what should it do? Should the people not oppose the measure? The only possible answer is that they can do nothing but obey. For we are not concerned here with any happiness which the subject might expect to derive from the institutions or administration of the commonwealth, but primarily with the rights which would thereby be secured for everyone. And this is the highest principle from which all maxims relating to the commonwealth must begin, and which cannot be qualified by any other principles. No generally valid principle of legislation can be based on happiness. For both the current circumstances and the highly conflicting and variable illusions as to what happiness is (and no one can prescribe to others how they should attain it) make all fixed principles impossible, so that happiness alone can never be a suitable principle of legislation. The doctrine that *salus publica suprema civitatis lex est*[20] retains its value and authority undiminished; but the public welfare which demands *first* consideration lies precisely in that legal constitution which guarantees everyone his freedom within the law, so that each remains free to seek his happiness in whatever way he thinks best, so long as he does not violate the lawful freedom and rights of his fellow subjects at large. If the supreme power makes laws which are primarily directed towards happiness (the affluence of the citizens, increased population etc.), this cannot be regarded as the end for which a civil constitution was established, but only as a means of *securing the rightful state*, especially against external enemies of the people. The head of state must be authorized to judge for himself whether such measures are necessary for the commonwealth's prosperity, which is required to maintain its strength and stability both internally and against external enemies. The aim is not, as it were, to make the people happy against its will, but only to ensure its continued existence as a commonwealth.[21] The legislator may indeed err in judging whether or not the measures he adopts are *prudent*, but not in deciding whether or not the law harmonizes with the principle of right. For he has ready to hand as an infallible *a priori* standard the idea of an original contract, and he need not wait for experience to show whether the means are suitable, as would be necessary if they were based on the principle of happiness. For so long as it is not self-contradictory to say that an entire people could agree to such a law, however painful it might seem, then the law is in harmony with right. But if a public law is beyond reproach (i.e., *irreprehensible*) with respect to right, it carries with it the authority to coerce those to whom it applies, and conversely, it forbids them to resist the will of the legislator by violent means. In other words, the power of the state to put the law into effect is also *irresistible*, and no rightfully established commonwealth can exist without a force of this kind to suppress all internal resistance. For such resistance would be dictated by a maxim which, if it became general, would destroy the whole civil constitution and put an end to the only state in which men can possess rights.

It thus follows that all resistance against the supreme legislative power, all incitement of the subjects to violent expressions of discontent, all defiance which breaks out into rebellion, is the greatest and most punishable crime in a commonwealth, for it destroys its very foundations. This prohibition is *absolute*. And even if the power of the state or its agent, the head of state, has violated the original contract by authorizing the government to act tyrannically, and has thereby, in the eyes of the subject, forfeited the right to legislate, the subject is still not entitled to offer counter-resistance. The reason for this is that the people, under an existing civil constitution, has no longer any right to judge how the constitution should be administered. For if we suppose that it does have this right to judge and that it disagrees with the judgment of the actual head of state, who is to decide which side is right? Neither can act as judge of his own cause. Thus there would have to be another head above the head of state to mediate between the latter and the people, which is self-contradictory.—Nor can a right of necessity (*ius in casu necessitatis*) be invoked here as a means of removing the barriers which restrict the power of the people; for it is monstrous to suppose that we can have a right to do wrong in the direst (physical) distress.[22] For the head of state can just as readily claim that his severe treatment of his subjects is justified by their insubordination as the subjects can justify their rebellion by complaints about their unmerited suffering, and who is to decide? The decision must rest with whoever controls the ultimate enforcement of the public law, i.e., the head of state himself. Thus no one in the commonwealth can have a right to contest his authority.

Nonetheless, estimable men have declared that the subject is justified, under certain circumstances, in using force against his superiors. I need name only Achenwall,[23] who is extremely cautious, precise and restrained in his theories of natural right.[24] He says: "If the danger which threatens the commonwealth as a result of long endurance of injustices from the head of state is greater than the danger to be feared from taking up arms against him, the people may then resist him. It may use this right to abrogate its contract of subjection and to dethrone him as a tyrant." And he concludes: "The people, in dethroning its ruler, thus returns to the state of nature."

I well believe that neither Achenwall nor any others of the worthy men who have speculated along the same lines as he would ever have given their advice or agreement to such hazardous projects if the case had arisen. And it can scarcely be doubted that if the revolutions whereby Switzerland, the United Netherlands or even Great Britain won their much admired constitutions had failed, the readers of their history would regard the execution of their celebrated founders as no more than the deserved punishment of great political criminals. For the result usually affects our judgment of the rightfulness of an action, although the result is uncertain, whereas the principles of right are constant. But it is clear that these peoples have done the greatest degree of wrong in seeking their rights in this way, even if we admit that such a revolution did no injustice to a ruler who had violated a specific basic agreement with the people, such as the *Joyeuse Entree*.[25] For such procedures, if made into a maxim, make all lawful constitutions insecure and produce a state of complete lawlessness (*status naturalis*) where all rights cease at least to be effectual. In view of this tendency of so many right-thinking authors to plead on behalf of the people (and to its own detriment), I will only remark that such errors arise in part from the usual fallacy of allowing the principle of happiness to influence the judgment, wherever the principle of right is involved; and partly because these writers have assumed that the idea of an original contract (a basic postulate of reason) is something which must have taken place *in reality*, even where there is no document to show that any contract was actually submitted to the commonwealth, accepted by the head of state, and sanctioned by both parties. Such writers thus believe that the people retains the right to abrogate the original contract at its own discretion, if, in the opinion of the people, the contract has been severely violated.[26]

It is obvious from this that the principle of happiness (which is not in fact a definite principle at all) has ill effects in political right just as in morality, however good the intentions of those who teach it. The sovereign wants to make the people happy as he thinks best, and thus becomes a despot, while the people are unwilling to give up their universal human desire to seek happiness in their own way, and thus become rebels. If they had first of all asked what is lawful (in terms of *a priori* certainty, which no empiricist can upset), the idea of a social contract would retain its authority undiminished. But it would not exist as a fact (as Danton[27] would have it, declaring that since it does not actually exist, all property and all rights under the existing civil constitution are null and void), but only as a rational principle for judging any lawful public constitution whatsoever. And it would then be seen that, until the general will is there, the people has no coercive right against its ruler, since it can apply coercion legally only through him. But if the will is there, no force can be applied to the ruler by the people, otherwise the people would be the supreme ruler. Thus the people can never possess a right of coercion against the head of state, or be entitled to oppose him in word or deed.

We can see, furthermore, that this theory is adequately confirmed in practice. In the British constitution, of which the people are so proud that they hold it up as a model for the whole world, we find no mention of what the people are entitled to do if the monarch were to violate the contract of 1688.[28] Since there is no law to cover such a case, the people tacitly reserve the right to rebel against him if he should violate the contract. And it would be an obvious contradiction if the constitution included a law for such eventualities, entitling the people to overthrow the existing constitution, from which all particular laws are derived, if the contract were violated. For there would then have to be a *publicly constituted*[29] opposing power, hence a second head of state to protect the rights of the people against the first ruler, and then yet a third to decide which of the other two had right on his side. In fact, the leaders (or guardians—call them what you will) of the British people, fearing some such accusation if their plans did not succeed, *invented* the notion of a voluntary abdication by the monarch they forced out, rather than claim a right to depose him (which would have made the constitution self-contradictory).

While I trust that no one will accuse me of flattering monarchs too much by declaring them inviolable, I likewise hope that I shall be spared the reproach of claiming too much for the people if I maintain that the people too have inalienable rights against the head of state, even if these cannot be rights of coercion.

Hobbes is of the opposite opinion. According to him (*De Cive*, Chap. 7, § 14), the head of state has no contractual obligations towards the people; he can do no injustice to a citizen, but may act towards him as he pleases. This proposition would be perfectly correct if injustice were taken to mean any injury which gave the injured party a *coercive right* against the one who has done him injustice. But in its general form, the proposition is quite terrifying.

The non-resisting subject must be able to assume that his ruler has no *wish* to do him injustice. And everyone has his inalienable rights, which he cannot give up even if he wishes to, and about which he is entitled to make his own judgments. But if he assumes that the ruler's attitude is one of good will, any injustice which he believes he has suffered can only have resulted through error, or through ignorance of certain possible consequences of the laws which the supreme authority has made. Thus the citizen must, with the approval of the ruler, be entitled to make public his opinion on whatever of the ruler's measures seem to him to constitute an injustice against the commonwealth. For to assume that the head of state can neither make mistakes nor be ignorant of anything would be to imply that he receives divine inspiration and is more than a human being. Thus *freedom of the pen* is the only safeguard of the rights of the people, although it must not transcend the bounds of respect and devotion toward the existing constitution, which should itself create a liberal attitude of mind among the subjects. To try to deny the citizen this freedom does not only mean, as Hobbes maintains, that the subject can claim no rights against the supreme ruler. It also means withholding from the ruler all knowledge of those matters which, if he knew about them, he would himself rectify, so that he is thereby put into a self-stultifying position. For his will issues commands to his subjects (as citizens) only in so far as he represents the general will of the people. But to encourage the head of state to fear that independent and public thought might cause political unrest is tantamount to making him distrust his own power and feel hatred towards his people.

The general principle, however, according to which a people may judge negatively whatever it believes was *not decreed* in good will by the supreme legislation, can be summed up as follows: *Whatever a people cannot impose upon itself cannot be imposed upon it by the legislator either.*

For example, if we wish to discover whether a law which declares permanently valid an ecclesiastical constitution (itself formulated at some time in the past) can be regarded as emanating from the actual will or intention of the legislator, we must first ask whether a people is *authorized* to make a law for itself whereby certain accepted doctrines and outward forms of religion are declared permanent, and whether the people may thus prevent its own descendants from making further progress in religious understanding or from correcting any past mistakes. It is clear that any original contract of the people which established such a law would in itself be null and void, for it would conflict with the appointed aim and purpose of mankind. Thus a law of this kind cannot be regarded as the actual will of the monarch, to whom counter-representations may accordingly be made. In all cases, however, where the supreme legislation did nevertheless adopt such measures, it would be permissible to pass general and public judgments upon them, but never to offer any verbal or active resistance.

In every commonwealth, there must be *obedience* to generally valid coercive laws within the mechanism of the political constitution. There must also be a *spirit of freedom*, for in all matters concerning universal human duties, each individual requires to be convinced by reason that the coercion which prevails is lawful, otherwise he would be in contradiction with himself. Obedience without the spirit of freedom is the effective cause of all *secret societies*. For it is a natural vocation of man to communicate with his fellows, especially in matters affecting mankind as a whole. Thus secret societies would disappear if freedom of this kind were encouraged. And how else can the government itself acquire the knowledge it needs to further its own basic intention, if not by allowing the spirit of freedom, so admirable in its origins and effects, to make itself heard?

Nowhere does practice so readily bypass all pure principles of reason and treat theory so presumptuously as in the question of what is needed for a good political constitution. The reason for this is that a legal constitution of long standing gradually makes the people accustomed to judging both their happiness and their rights in terms of the peaceful *status quo*. Conversely, it does not encourage them to value the existing state of affairs in the light of those concepts of happiness and right which reason provides. It rather makes them prefer this passive state to the dangerous task of looking for a better one, thus bearing out the saying which Hippocrates told physicians to remember: *iudicium anceps, experimentum periculosum.*[30] Thus all constitutions which have lasted for a sufficiently long time, whatever their inadequacies and variations, produce the same result: the people remain content with what they have. If we therefore consider the *welfare of the people*, theory is not in fact valid, for everything depends upon practice derived from experience.

But reason provides a concept which we express by the words *political right*. And this concept has binding force for human beings who coexist in a state of antagonism produced by their natural freedom, so that it has an objective, practical reality, irrespective of the good or ill it may produce (for these can only be known by experience). Thus it is based on *a priori* principles, for experience cannot provide knowledge of what is right, and there is a *theory* of political right to which practice must conform before it can be valid.

The only objection which can be raised against this is that, although men have a mental notion of the rights to which they are entitled, their intractability is such that they are incapable and unworthy of being treated as their rights demand, so that they can and ought to be kept under control by a supreme power acting purely from expediency. But this counsel of desperation (*saito mortale*) means that, since there is no appeal to right but only to force, the people may themselves resort to force and thus make every legal constitution insecure. If there is nothing which commands immediate respect through reason, such as the basic rights of man, no influence can prevail upon man's arbitrary will and restrain his freedom. But if both benevolence and right speak out in loud tones, human nature will not prove too debased to listen to their voice with respect. *Tum pietate gravem meritisque si forte virum quem Conspexere, silent arrectisque auribus adstant* (Virgil).[31]

III. On the Relationship of Theory to Practice in International Right

Considered from a Universally Philanthropic, i.e., Cosmopolitan Point of View[32]

(Against Moses Mendelssohn)[33]

Is the human race as a whole likeable, or is it an object to be regarded with distaste? Must we simply wish it well (to avoid becoming misanthropists) without really expecting its efforts to succeed, and then take no further interest in it? In order to answer such questions, we must first answer the following one: Does man possess natural capacities which would indicate that the race will always progress and improve, so that the evils of the past and present will vanish in the future good? If this were the case, we could at least admire the human species for its constant advance towards the good; otherwise, we should have to hate or despise it, whatever objections might be raised by pretended philanthropists (whose feelings for mankind might at most amount to good will, but not to genuine pleasure).

For however hard we may try to awaken feelings of love in ourselves, we cannot avoid hating that which is and always will be evil, especially if it involves deliberate and general violation of the most sacred rights of man. Perhaps we may not wish to harm men, but shall not want to have any more to do with them than we can help.

Moses Mendelssohn was of the latter opinion (*Jerusalem* § II, pp. 44–7),[34] which he put forward in opposition to his friend Lessing's hypothesis of a divine education of mankind.[35] He regards it as sheer fantasy to say "that the whole of mankind here on earth must continually progress and become more perfect through the ages." He continues: "We see the human race as a whole moving slowly back and forth, and whenever it takes a few steps forward, it soon relapses twice as quickly into its former state." (This is truly the stone of Sisyphus;[36] if we adopt an attitude of this kind, as the Indians do, the earth must strike us as a place of atonement for old and forgotten sins.)" Man as an individual progresses; but mankind constantly fluctuates between fixed limits. Regarded as a whole, however, mankind maintains roughly the same level of morality, the same degree of religion and irreligion, of virtue and vice, of happiness (?) and misery." He introduces these assertions with the words (p. 46): "Do you presume to guess the plan of providence for mankind? Do not invent hypotheses" (he had earlier called these theories)j "just look around at what actually happens, and if you can briefly survey the history of all past ages, look at what has happened from time immemorial. All this is fact; it must have been intended and approved within the plan of higher wisdom, or at least adopted along with it."

I beg to differ. It is a sight fit for a god to watch a virtuous man grappling with adversity and evil temptations and yet managing to hold out against them. But it is a sight quite unfit not so much for a god, but even for the most ordinary, though right-thinking man, to see the human race advancing over a period of time towards virtue, and then quickly relapsing the whole way back into vice and misery. It may perhaps be moving and instructive to watch such a drama for a while; but the curtain must eventually descend. For in the long run, it becomes a farce. And even if the actors do not tire of it-for they are fools-the spectator does, for any single act will be enough for him if he can reasonably conclude from it that the never-ending play will go on in the same way for ever. If it is only a play, the retribution at the end can make up for the unpleasant sensations the spectator has felt. But in my opinion at least, it cannot be reconciled with the morality of a wise creator and ruler of the world if countless vices, even with intermingled virtues, are in actual fact allowed to go on accumulating.

I may thus be permitted to assume that, since the human race is constantly progressing in cultural matters (in keeping with its natural purpose), it is also engaged in progressive improvement in relation to the moral end of its existence. This progress may at times be *interrupted* but never *broken off*. I do not need to prove this assumption; it is up to the adversary to prove his case. I am a member of a series of human generations, and as such, I am not as good as I ought to be or could be according to the moral requirements of my nature. I base my argument upon my inborn duty of influencing

posterity in such a way that it will make constant progress (and I must thus assume that progress is possible), and that this duty may be rightfully handed down from one member of the series to the next. History may well give rise to endless doubts about my hopes, and if these doubts could be proved, they might persuade me to desist from an apparently futile task. But so long as they do not have the force of certainty, I cannot exchange my duty (as a *liquidum*)[37] for a rule of expediency which says that I ought not to attempt the impracticable (i.e., an *illiquidum*,[38] since it is purely hypothetical). And however uncertain I may be and may remain as to whether we can hope for anything better for mankind, this uncertainty cannot detract from the maxim I have adopted, or from the necessity of assuming for practical purposes that human progress is possible.

This hope for better times to come, without which an earnest desire to do something useful for the common good would never have inspired the human heart, has always influenced the activities of right-thinking men. And the worthy Mendelssohn must himself have reckoned on this, since he zealously endeavoured to promote the enlightenment and welfare of the nation to which he belonged. For he could not himself reasonably hope to do this unless others after him continued upon the same path. Confronted by the sorry spectacle not only of those evils which befall mankind from natural causes, but also of those which men inflict upon one another, our spirits can be raised by the prospect of future improvements. This, however, calls (or unselfish goodwill on our part, since we shall have been long dead and buried when the fruits we helped to sow are harvested. It is quite irrelevant whether any empirical evidence suggests that these plans, which are founded only on hope, may be unsuccessful. For the idea that something which has hitherto been unsuccessful will therefore never be successful does not justify anyone in abandoning even a pragmatic or technical aim (for example, that of flights with aerostatic balloons). This applies even more to moral aims, which, so long as it is not demonstrably impossible to fulfill them, amount to duties. Besides, various evidence suggests that in our age, as compared with all previous ages, the human race has made considerable moral progress, and short term hindrances prove nothing to the contrary. Moreover, it can be shown that the outcry about man's continually increasing decadence arises for the very reason that we can see further ahead, because we have reached a higher level of morality. We thus pass more severe judgments on what we are, comparing it with what we ought to be, so that our self-reproach increases in proportion to the number of stages of morality we have advanced through during the whole of known history.

If we now ask what means there are of maintaining and indeed accelerating this constant progress towards a better state, we soon realize that the success of this immeasurably long undertaking will depend not so much upon what *we* do (e.g., the education we impart to younger generations) and upon what methods *we* use to further it; it will rather depend upon what human *nature* may do in and through us, to *compel* us to follow a course which we would not readily adopt by choice. We must look to nature alone, or rather to *providence* (since it requires the highest wisdom to fulfill this purpose), for a successful outcome which will first affect the whole and then the individual parts. The schemes of men, on the other hand, begin with the parts, and frequently get no further than them. For the whole is too great for men to encompass; while they can reach it with their ideas, they cannot actively influence it, especially since their schemes conflict with one another to such an extent that they could hardly reach agreement of their own free volition.

On the one hand, universal violence and the distress it produces must eventually make a people decide to submit to the coercion which reason itself prescribes (i.e., the coercion of public law), and to enter into a *civil* constitution. And on the other hand, the distress produced by the constant wars in which the states try to subjugate or engulf each other must finally lead them, even against their will, to enter into a *cosmopolitan* constitution. Or if such a state of universal peace is in turn even more dangerous to freedom, for it may lead to the most fearful despotism (as has indeed occurred more than once with states which have grown too large), distress must force men to form a state which is not a cosmopolitan commonwealth under a single ruler, but a lawful *federation* under a commonly accepted *international right*.

The increasing culture of the states, along with their growing tendency to aggrandize themselves by cunning or violence at the expense of the others, must make wars more frequent. It must likewise cause increasingly high expenditure on standing armies, which must be kept in constant training and equipped with ever more numerous instruments of warfare. Meanwhile, the price of all necessities will steadily rise, while no one can hope for any proportionate increase in the corresponding metal currencies. No peace will last long enough for the resources saved during it to meet the expenditure of the next war, while the invention of a national debt, though ingenious, is an ultimately self-defeating expedient. Thus sheer exhaustion must eventually perform what goodwill ought to have done but failed to do: each state must be organized internally in such a way that the head of state, for whom the war actually costs nothing (for he wages it at the expense of others, i.e., the people), must no longer have the deciding vote on whether war is to be declared or not, for the people who pay for it must decide. (This, of course, necessarily presupposes that the idea of an original contract has already been realized.) For the people will not readily place itself in danger of personal want (which would not affect the head of state) out of a mere desire for aggrandizement, or because of some supposed and purely verbal offence. And thus posterity will not be oppressed by any burdens which it has not brought upon itself, and it will be able to make perpetual progress towards a morally superior state. This is not produced by any love on the part of earlier ages for later ones, but only by the love of each age for itself. Each commonwealth, unable to harm the others by force, must observe the laws on its own account, and it may reasonably hope that other similarly constituted bodies will help it to do so.

But this is no more than a personal opinion and hypothesis; it is uncertain, like all judgments which profess to define the appropriate natural cause of an intended effect which is not wholly within our control. And even as such, it does not offer the subject of an existing state any principle by which he could attain the desired effect by force (as has already been demonstrated); only the head of state, who is above coercion, can do so. In the normal order of things, it cannot be expected of human nature to desist voluntarily from using force, although it is not impossible where the circumstances are sufficiently pressing. Thus it is not inappropriate to say of man's moral hopes and desires that, since he is powerless to fulfill them himself, he may look to *providence* to create the circumstances in which they can be fulfilled. The end of *man* as an entire species, i.e., that of fulfilling his ultimate appointed purpose by freely exercising his own powers, will be brought by providence to a successful issue, even although the ends of *men* as individuals run in a diametrically opposite direction. For the very conflict of individual inclinations, which is the source of all evil, gives reason a free hand to master them all; it thus gives predominance not to evil, which destroys itself, but to good, which continues to maintain itself once it has been established.

Nowhere does human nature appear less admirable than in the relationships which exist between peoples. No state is for a moment secure from the others in its independence and its possessions. The will to subjugate the others or to grow at their expense is always present, and the production of armaments for defence, which often makes peace more oppressive and more destructive of internal welfare than war itself, can never be relaxed.

And there is no possible way of counteracting this except a state of international right, based upon enforceable public laws to which each state must submit (by analogy with a state of civil or political right among individual men). For a permanent universal peace by means of a so-called *European balance of power* is a pure illusion, like Swift's story of the house which the builder had constructed in such perfect harmony with all the laws of equilibrium that it collapsed as soon as a sparrow alighted on it.[39] But it might be objected that no states will ever submit to coercive laws of this kind, and that a proposal for a universal federation, to whose power all the individual states would voluntarily submit and whose laws they would all obey, may be all very well in the theory of the Abbe St Pierre[40] or of Rousseau, but that it does not apply in practice. For such proposals have always been ridiculed by great statesmen, and even more by heads of state, as pedantic, childish, and academic ideas.

For my own part, I put my trust in the theory of what the relationships between men and states *ought to be* according to the principle of right. It recommends to us earthly gods the maxim that we should proceed in our disputes in such a way that a universal federal state may be inaugurated, so that we should therefore assume that it *is possible* (*in praxi*). I likewise rely (*in subsidium*) upon the very nature of things to force men to do what they do not willingly choose (*fata volentem ducunt, nolentem trahunt*).[41] This involves human nature, which is still animated by respect for right and duty. I therefore cannot and will not see it as so deeply immersed in evil that practical moral reason will not triumph in the end, after many unsuccessful attempts, thereby showing that it is worthy of admiration after all. On the cosmopolitan level too, it thus remains true to say that whatever reason shows to be valid in theory, is also valid in practice.

Post-Reading Questions

1. How does Kant defend the value of theory in this essay?
2. Kant argues that the aim of morality is not to be happy but rather to become worthy of happiness. What does Kant mean by this?
3. How does Kant define "right"?
4. Could women and labourers be citizens in Kant's view? Why or why not?
5. What does Kant mean by the idea of "freedom of the pen"?

CASE STUDY
THE CANADIAN CHARTER OF RIGHTS AND FREEDOMS

Introduction

The Canadian Charter of Rights and Freedoms forms the first part of the 1982 Constitution Act, and replaces the earlier Canadian Bill of Rights. Its central purpose is to set out the core civil and political rights to which all Canadians are entitled, including the fundamental freedoms (e.g., freedom of conscience, religion, and association) and democratic rights (e.g., the rights to vote and to hold office) that are the hallmark of all contemporary liberal constitutions. In enumerating these rights and freedoms, the Charter also serves as an expression of the common political principles that are intended to bind the citizens of Canada, irrespective of their way of life. Legal cases in Canada in which the principles of the Charter have been invoked have contributed to a body of jurisprudence for interpreting the Charter's application in different contexts. Beyond our borders, the Charter has also been very influential in the drafting of bills of rights in other states, particularly other former British colonies (or commonwealth countries).

Insofar as the Charter enacts the spirit of Canada as a state, it very much resembles the idea of a commonwealth bound by a civil constitution envisioned by Kant in his 1793 essay "On the Common Saying: 'This May Be True in Theory, but It Does Not Apply in Practice.'" In this essay, Kant stresses the importance of the contract that creates a civil constitution, for only this kind of contract establishes a shared union governed by common ends. For Kant, a civil constitution establishes formal legal and political equality; crucially, it treats all as equals in the eyes of the law. This equality is compatible with economic inequality, but not with social inequality in the sense of hereditary privilege: all positions must be open to all in the state established by the civil constitution.

As might be expected, the nearly two centuries that separate Kant's outline of a civil constitution and Canada's Charter yield significant differences. Perhaps most notably, section 15 of the Charter, which guarantees equality rights to Canadians, is more far-reaching in its approach to equality among citizens: in particular, it includes minority language protections and equality rights for women, racial minorities, the disabled, and (through subsequent court challenges and jurisprudence) gays and lesbians.

A central challenge for any charter or bill of rights is that of balancing the rights and freedoms of all citizens, as these may sometimes be in tension with one another. For example, in a recent Supreme Court case (*R. v. N.S.*, 2012), justices were asked to consider whether a Muslim woman's request to wear a niqab (face veil or covering) when giving testimony at a trial would jeopardize the defendant's Charter-protected right to a fair trial. Kant of course could not have imagined a polity of such religious and cultural pluralism, nor the difficulty of accommodating such diversity by means of a single, common constitution. Nor would he necessarily have agreed that the laws that constitute the "public right" would need to acknowledge—much less explicitly accommodate—these social and cultural differences. For Kant, the civil law protects our external freedom in the commonwealth because it ensures that we are governed by rational laws rather than by arbitrary force or coercion. Our external freedom, and that of all other persons, is thereby protected by this arrangement: "*Right* is the restriction of each individual's freedom so that it harmonizes with the freedom of everyone else (in so far as this is possible within the terms of a general law). And *public right* is the distinctive quality of the *external laws* which make this constant harmony possible" (*On the Relationship of Theory to Practice in Political Right*).

Kant called his vision of the commonwealth "republican," though by this he did not mean that all persons living in the state are the authors of the laws. Unlike Canada's Charter, Kant believed that only some—namely, property-owning male citizens—are entitled to make the laws and to vote on legislation. However, all subjects of the civil state are nonetheless bound to obey the laws and, barring criminal actions, can expect protection from them.

The Canadian Charter of Rights and Freedoms

*The Constitution Act, 1982, being Schedule B to the Canada
Act 1982 (UK), 1982, c 11. http://publications.gc.ca/collections/
Collection/CH37-4-3-2002E.pdf*

Whereas Canada is founded upon principles that recognize the supremacy of God and the rule of law:

Guarantee of Rights and Freedoms

Rights and
freedoms in Canada

1. The Canadian Charter of Rights and Freedoms guarantees the rights and freedoms set out in it subject only to such reasonable limits prescribed by law as can be demonstrably justified in a free and democratic society.

Fundamental Freedoms

Fundamental
freedoms

2. Everyone has the following fundamental freedoms:
(a) freedom of conscience and religion;
(b) freedom of thought, belief, opinion, and expression, including freedom of the press and other media of communication;
(c) freedom of peaceful assembly; and
(d) freedom of association.

Democratic Rights

Democratic rights
of citizens

3. Every citizen of Canada has the right to vote in an election of members of the House of Commons or of a legislative assembly and to be qualified for membership therein.

Maximum duration
of legislative bodies

4.(1) No House of Commons and no legislative assembly shall continue for longer than five years from file date fixed for the return of the writs at a general election of its members.

Continuation
in special
circumstances

(2) In time of real or apprehended war, invasion or insurrection, a House of Commons may be continued by Parliament and a legislative assembly may be continued by the legislature beyond five years if such continuation is not opposed by the votes of more than one-third of the members of the House of Commons or the legislative assembly, as the case may be.

Annual sitting of
legislative bodies

5. There shall be a sitting of Parliament and of each legislature at least once every 12 months.

Mobility Rights

Mobility of citizens

6.(1) Every citizen of Canada has the right to enter, remain in and leave Canada.

Right to move and
gain livelihood

(2) Every citizen of Canada and every person who has the status of a permanent resident of Canada has the right
(a) to move to and take up residence in any province; and
(b) to pursue the gaining of a livelihood in any province.

Limitation

(3) The rights specified in subsection (2) are subject to
(a) any laws or practices of general application in force in a province other than those that discriminate among persons primarily on the basis of province of present or previous residence; and
(b) any laws providing for reasonable residency requirements as a qualification for the receipt of publicly provided social services.

Affirmative action programs

(4) Subsections (2) and (3) do not preclude any law, program or activity that has as its object the amelioration in a province of conditions of individuals in that province who are socially or economically disadvantaged if the rate of employment in that province is below the rate of employment in Canada.

Legal Rights

Life, liberty, and security of person

7. Everyone has the right to life, liberty, and security of the person and the right not to be deprived thereof except in accordance with the principles of fundamental justice.

Search or seizure

8. Everyone has the right to be secure against unreasonable search or seizure.

Detention or imprisonment

9. Everyone has the right not to be arbitrarily detained or imprisoned.

Arrest or detention

10. Everyone has the right on arrest or detention
(a) to be informed promptly of the reasons therefor;
(b) to retain and instruct counsel without delay and to be informed of that right; and
(c) to have the validity of the detention determined by way of *habeas corpus* and to be released if the detention is not lawful.

Proceedings in criminal and penal matters

11. Any persons charged with an offence has the right
(a) to be informed without unreasonable delay of the specific offence;
(b) to be tried within a reasonable time;
(c) not to be compelled to be a witness in proceedings against that person in respect of the offence;
(d) to be presumed innocent until proven guilty according to law in a fair and public hearing by an independent and impartial tribunal;
(e) not to be denied reasonable bail without just cause;
(f) except in the case of an offence under military law tried before a military tribunal, to the benefit of trial by jury where the maximum punishment for the offence is imprisonment for five years or a more severe punishment;
(g) not to be found guilty on account of any act or omission unless, at the time of the act or omission, it constituted an offence under Canadian or international law or was criminal according to the general principles of law recognized by the community of nations;
(h) if finally acquitted of the offence, not to be tried for it again and, if finally found guilty and punished for the offence, not to be tried or punished for it again; and
(i) if found guilty of the offence and if the punishment for the offence has been varied between the time of commission and the time of sentencing, to the benefit of the lesser punishment.

Treatment or punishment

12. Everyone has the right not to be subjected to any cruel and unusual treatment or punishment.

Self-crimination

13. A witness who testifies in any proceedings has the right not to have any incriminating evidence so given used to incriminate that witness in any other proceedings, except in a prosecution for perjury or for the giving of contradictory evidence.

Interpreter

14. A party or witness in any proceedings who does not understand or speak the language in which the proceedings are conducted or who is deaf has the right to the assistance of an interpreter.

Equality Rights

Equality before and under law and equal protection and benefit of law

15.(1) Every individual is equal before and under the law and has the right to the equal protection and equal benefit of the law without discrimination and, in particular, without discrimination based on race, national or ethnic origin, colour, religion, sex, age, or mental or physical disability.

Affirmative action programs

(2) Subsection (1) does not preclude any law, program or activity that has as its object the amelioration of conditions of disadvantaged individuals or groups including those that are disadvantaged because of race, national or ethnic origin, colour, religion, sex, age, or mental or physical disability.

Official Languages of Canada

Official languages of Canada

16.(1) English and French are the official languages of Canada and have equality of status and equal rights and privileges as to their use in all institutions of the Parliament and government of Canada.

Official languages of New Brunswick

(2) English and French are the official languages of New Brunswick and have equality of status and equal rights and privileges as to their use in all institutions of the legislature and government of New Brunswick.

Advancement of status and use

(3) Nothing in this Charter limits the authority of Parliament or a legislature to advance the equality of status or use of English and French.

English and French linguistic communities in New Brunswick

16.1(1) The English linguistic community and the French linguistic community in New Brunswick have equality of status and equal rights and privileges, including the right to distinct educational institutions and such distinct cultural institutions as are necessary for the preservation and promotion of those communities.

Role of the legislature and government of New Brunswick

(2) The role of the legislature and government of New Brunswick to preserve and promote the status, rights and privileges referred to in subsection (1) is affirmed.

Proceedings of Parliament

17.(1) Everyone has the right to use English or French in any debates and other proceedings of Parliament.

Proceedings of New Brunswick legislature

(2) Everyone has the right to use English or French in any debates and other proceedings of the legislature of New Brunswick.

Parliamentary statutes and records

18.(1) The statutes, records, and journals of Parliament shall be printed and published in English and French and both language versions are equally authoritative.

New Brunswick statutes and records

(2) The statutes, records, and journals of the legislature of New Brunswick shall be printed and published in English and French and both language versions are equally authoritative.

Proceedings in courts established by Parliament

19.(1) Either English or French may be used by any person in, or in any pleading in or process issuing from, any court established by Parliament.

Proceedings in New Brunswick courts	(2) Either English or French may be used by any person in, or in any pleading in or process issuing from, any court of New Brunswick.
Communications by public with federal institutions	20.(1) Any member of the public in Canada has the right to communicate with, and to receive available services from, any head or central office of an institution of the Parliament or government of Canada in English or French, and has the same right with respect to any other office of any such institution where (a) there is a significant demand for communications with and services from that office in such language; or (b) due to the nature of the office, it is reasonable that communications with and services from that office be available in both English and French.
Communications by public with New Brunswick institutions	(2) Any member of the public in New Brunswick has the right to communicate with, and to receive available services from, any office of an institution of the legislature or government of New Brunswick in English or French.
Continuation of existing constitutional provisions	21. Nothing in sections 16 to 20 abrogates or derogates from any right, privilege or obligation with respect to the English and French languages, or either of them, that exists or is continued by virtue of any other provision of the Constitution of Canada.
Rights and privileges preserved	22. Nothing in sections 16 to 20 abrogates or derogates from any legal or customary right or privilege acquired or enjoyed either before or after the coming into force of this Charter with respect to any language that is not English or French.

Minority Language Educational Rights

Language of instruction	23.(1) Citizens of Canada (a) whose first language learned and still understood is that of the English or French linguistic minority population of the province in which they reside, or (b) who have received their primary school instruction in Canada in English or French and reside in a province where the language in which they received that instruction is the language of the English or French linguistic minority population of the province, have the right to have their children receive primary and secondary school instruction in that language in that province.
Continuity of language instruction	(2) Citizens of Canada of whom any child has received or is receiving primary or secondary school instruction in English or French in Canada, have the right to have all their children receive primary and secondary school instruction in the same language.
Application where numbers warrant	(3) The right of citizens of Canada under subsections (1) and (2) to have their children receive primary and secondary school instruction in the language of the English or French linguistic minority population of a province (a) applies wherever in the province the number of children of citizens who have such a right is sufficient to warrant the provision to them out of public funds of minority language instruction; and (b) includes, where the number of those children so warrants, the right to have them receive that instruction in minority language educational facilities provided out of public funds.

Enforcement

Enforcement of guaranteed rights and freedoms	24.(1) Anyone whose rights or freedoms, as guaranteed by this Charter, have been infringed or denied may apply to a court of competent jurisdiction to obtain such remedy as the court considers appropriate and just in the circumstances.

Exclusion of evidence bringing administration of justice into disrepute

(2) Where, in proceedings under subsection (1), a court concludes that evidence was obtained in a manner that infringed or denied any rights or freedoms guaranteed by this Charter, the evidence shall be excluded if it is established that, having regard to all the circumstances, the admission of it in the proceedings would bring the administration of justice into disrepute.

General

Aboriginal rights and freedoms not affected by charter

25. The guarantee in this Charter of certain rights and freedoms shall not be construed so as to abrogate or derogate from any aboriginal, treaty or other rights or freedoms that pertain to the aboriginal peoples of Canada including
(a) any rights or freedoms that have been recognized by the Royal Proclamation of October 7, 1763; and
(b) any rights or freedoms that now exist by way of land claims agreements or may be so acquired.

Other rights and freedoms not affected by the Charter

26. The guarantee in this Charter of certain rights and freedoms shall not be construed as denying the existence of any other rights or freedoms that exist in Canada.

Multicultural heritage

27. This Charter shall be interpreted in a manner consistent with the preservation and enhancement of the multicultural heritage of Canadians.

Rights guaranteed equally to both sexes

28. Notwithstanding anything in this Charter, the rights and freedoms referred to in it are guaranteed equally to male and female persons.

Rights respecting certain schools preserved

29. Nothing in this Charter abrogates or derogates from any rights or privileges guaranteed by or under the Constitution of Canada in respect of denominational, separate or dissentient schools.

Application to territories and territorial authorities

30. A reference in this Charter to a province or to the legislative assembly or legislature of a province shall be deemed to include a reference to the Yukon Territory and the Northwest Territories, or to the appropriate legislative authority thereof, as the case may be.

Legislative power not extended

31. Nothing in this Charter extends the legislative powers of any body or authority.

Application of Charter

Application of Charter

32.(1) This Charter applies
(a) to the Parliament and government of Canada in respect of all matters within the authority of Parliament including all matters relating to the Yukon Territory and Northwest Territories; and
(b) to the legislature and government of each province in respect of all matters within the authority of the legislature of each province.

Exception

(2) Notwithstanding subsection (1), section 15 shall not have effect until three years after this section comes into force.

Exception where express declaration

33.(1) Parliament or the legislature of a province may expressly declare in an Act of Parliament or of the legislature, as the case may be, that the Act or a provision thereof shall operate notwithstanding a provision included in section 2 or sections 7 to 15 of this Charter.

Operation of
exception

(2) An Act or a provision of an Act in respect of which a declaration made under this section is in effect shall have such operation as it would have but for the provision of this Charter referred to in the declaration.

Five year limitation

(3) A declaration made under subsection (1) shall cease to have effect five years after it comes into force or on such earlier date as may be specified in the declaration.

Re-enactment

(4) Parliament or a legislature of a province may re-enact a declaration made under subsection (1).

Five year limitation

(5) Subsection (3) applies in respect of a re-enactment made under subsection (4).

Post-Case-Reading Questions

1. The Charter guarantees the fundamental rights and freedoms of Canadians, but states that these are subject to "reasonable limitations." What might be an example of a right or freedom that could reasonably be limited for the kinds of reasons suggested by Kant?
2. In what ways does the Charter vindicate Kant's insistence that "theory" and "practice" are complementary in matters of morality and politics?

Chapter VIII

John Stuart Mill

Introduction

John Stuart Mill is one of the paradigmatic figures of liberal theory and the most notable British philosopher in the nineteenth century. He was born in London in 1806. His father, James Mill, was a political philosopher, historian, and penal reformer. He was also, importantly, a close associate of Jeremy Bentham, the founder of utilitarianism—the moral theory that takes utility to be the ultimate measure of right in morality and politics. Both men had a lasting influence on the young Mill, with his father taking unusual steps to ensure a particularly extensive—and accelerated—education for his son. Starting at age three, Mill learned Greek, and thereafter was taught logic, mathematics, economics, Latin, and other classical subjects. But this rigid model of education, together with the social isolation imposed on him by his father, soon took its toll on the young man. The impact was severe, as he recounts in his *Autobiography*: he suffered a mental and emotional breakdown at the age of 20.

John Stuart Mill

photos.com/Thinkstock

With the help of poetry and romantic literature, which he credited with allowing him to explore the emotional realm that his education and upbringing had cut him off from, Mill gradually regained his mental health. The cultivation of affect, particularly empathy, thereafter became important to Mill; indeed, this aim inflects his philosophical project, as he explains in his memoir. Mill's newfound appreciation for feeling and romantic love eventually led him to a passionate but chaste affair with Harriet Taylor, whom he met in 1830. They formed a life-long relationship and intellectual collaboration that was central to the development of Mill's ideas, eventually marrying each other in 1851 (after Harriet became widowed).

Mill did not hold a university position, but instead worked for the British East India Company for 35 years. Despite this non-academic employment, Mill was a highly prolific writer, publishing books that are notably wide-ranging in their subject matter: *A System of Logic* (1843), *The Principles of Political Economy* (1848), *On Liberty* (1859), *Considerations on Representative Government* (1861), *Utilitarianism* (1861), as well as his *Autobiography* (1873) and *Three Essays on Religion* (1874), both published after his death.

Mill exhibited a keen awareness of social and political problems from an early age, and his activism sometimes caused him inconvenience: for example, he was arrested for distributing birth-control leaflets at the age of 17. A regular contributor to the *Westminster Review*, a radical publication founded by his father, in 1836 he founded the *London Review*. Mill also ran for Parliament and served one term as an MP in the 1860s. Mill's social and political sensitivity, guided by the principle of utility, turned him into a noted reformer. He passionately advocated on behalf of the marginalized and the oppressed, championing the rights of political prisoners, colonial people, workers, the poor, and women. Mill's progressive thinking led him to challenge the suspension of *habeas corpus*—the legal instrument that protects the individuals from the arbitrary treatment of the state—in Ireland and to argue for municipal reform, proportional representation, and women's suffrage.

Mill's moral and political philosophy was very much influenced by Jeremy Bentham's doctrine of utilitarianism. Reading Bentham's *Introduction to the Principles of Morals and Legislation* (1789) clarified Mill's own thinking with regard to ethics. Bentham claimed that human beings were driven to act by considerations of pain and pleasure: pain ought to be avoided and pleasure ought to be pursued. There is a slight leap here from a psychological fact—human beings avoid pain and seek pleasure—to the assertion of the overarching value of utility (happiness). Unlike the traditional views of morality as absolute rules written in heaven, or Kant's deontological morality that denounced the influence of any inclination in the consideration of moral actions, Bentham thought that the morality of our actions should be assessed in terms of their likely consequences—specifically, their utility. Before acting, he argued, we should consider calculating the utility that will result from our action. Stressing calculation of the utility of an act gave Bentham's version of utilitarianism a decisively quantitative character, however. This in turn made it vulnerable to criticism, for numerous issues of justice do not lend themselves well to empirical calculation.

Mill refined Bentham's utilitarianism, reducing the stress on quantitative calculation of action and instead emphasizing the quality of the happiness that is gained. Instead of simply counting each individual affected by an action as an equal unit to be tallied in either the "pain" or "pleasure" column to determine the balance of happiness, Mill devised a set of rules organized in a hierarchical manner to guide his moral judgment. This is why his version is called "rule utilitarian," as opposed to Bentham's "act-utilitarian" version. His distinctive approach also links utilitarian ethics to an ideal of the person as a "progressive being" who seeks to develop his or her faculties, as he asserts in "On Liberty". This explains why "it is better to be Socrates dissatisfied than a pig satisfied".[1]

Mill reinterpreted Bentham's "principle of utility," which requires us to minimize pain and maximize happiness, as "the greatest happiness principle." The utilitarian moral imperative thus becomes: act so as to bring about this state of maximum utility. This dictum might seem uncontroversial enough—for, who would oppose having more pleasure and less pain? But its revolutionary impact is made clear when we realize that Mill eschews reference to God (as the divine law-giver) and absolute moral rules in favour of secular norms. Significantly, the utilitarian principle of greatest happiness notably produces different answers (as compared with traditional moral theories) to such difficult moral issues such as euthanasia and animal rights. It should also lead us to conclude, Mill argued, that the subordination of women—fully half of the human population—is an unjustifiable wrong that ought to be remedied.

Like his teacher Bentham, Mill believed that democracy was the best form of government. But just as the principle of utility would not support unlimited individual freedoms, so would unbounded government authority be detrimental to the general happiness. In his celebrated essay "On Liberty"—excerpts of which appear below—Mill considers the limits that can and should be imposed on both the freedom of individuals and the legitimate political power of democratic governments. He tells us that, historically, liberty has been understood as protection against the tyranny of the political rulers whose power was regarded as necessary but also potentially dangerous. The question then becomes where the limit should be placed. In answering this question, Mill draws on utilitarian principles and states that insofar as the individual's action does not pose any threat to the public or harm anyone else, the state should not interfere (i.e., the principle of harm should prevail). The individual's own good, either physical or moral, is not enough reason to forbid an action. Mill also warns us that by liberty he does not mean abstract rights independent from utility, since utility remains the ultimate principle to which we should appeal in ethics and politics. Rather, the domain of human liberties, according to Mill, must include certain basic and practical liberties such as freedom of conscience, freedom of association, freedom of choice, and the pursuit of one's happiness. The fact that most of these rights have been enshrined in the constitutions of liberal democratic societies is a testament to Mill's lasting influence. In the second reading below—an excerpt from the essay "Utilitarianism"—Mill outlines the main ideas of utilitarianism and defends it against some common objections. Mill's arguments for the principle of utility remain highly relevant to discussions of ethics by contemporary utilitarian thinkers, as well as those of other moral philosophers. The case study for this chapter on Mill's thought raises the question of whether a law banning polygamy violates individual rights and freedoms—in this case, those of Canadian citizens as protected by the Charter.

Further Readings

Gray, J. (1996). *Mill on Liberty: A Defence*, 2nd edition. London: Routledge.

Riley, J. (2010). "Mill's Extraordinary Utilitarian Moral Theory," *Politics, Philosophy & Economics*, 9 (1): 67–116.

Ryan, A. (1970). *The Philosophy of John Stuart Mill*. London: Macmillan.

Ten, C.L. (1980). *Mill on Liberty*. Oxford: Clarendon. Available at www.victorianweb.org/philosophy/mill/ten/contents.html

Warburton, N. (2009). *Mill: A Very Short Introduction*. Oxford: Oxford University Press.

John Stuart Mill, *From* "On Liberty"

John Stuart Mill, "On Liberty," in On Liberty and Other Essays, *edited by John Gray (Oxford: Oxford University Press, 2008).*

Chapter 1 Introductory

The subject of this essay is not the so-called liberty of the will, so unfortunately opposed to the misnamed doctrine of philosophical necessity;[2] but civil, or social liberty: the nature and limits of the power which can be legitimately exercised by society over the individual. A question seldom stated, and hardly ever discussed, in general terms, but which profoundly influences the practical controversies of the age by its latent presence, and is likely soon to make itself recognized as the vital question of the future. It is so far from being new, that, in a certain sense, it has divided mankind, almost from the remotest ages; but in the stage of progress into which the more civilized portions of the species have now entered, it presents itself under new conditions, and requires a different and more fundamental treatment.

The struggle between liberty and authority is the most conspicuous feature in the portions of history with which we are earliest familiar, particularly in that of Greece, Rome, and England. But in old times this contest was between subjects, or some classes of subjects, and the government. By liberty, was meant protection against the tyranny of the political rulers. The rulers were conceived (except in some of the popular governments of Greece) as in a necessarily antagonistic position to the people whom they ruled. They consisted of a governing One, or a governing tribe or caste, who derived their authority from inheritance or conquest, who, at all events, did not hold it at the pleasure of the governed, and whose supremacy men did not venture, perhaps did not desire, to contest, whatever precautions might be taken against its oppressive exercise. Their power was regarded as necessary, but also as highly dangerous; as a weapon which they would attempt to use against their subjects, no less than against external enemies. To prevent the weaker members of the community from being preyed upon by innumerable vultures, it was needful that there should be an animal of prey stronger than the rest, commissioned to keep them down. But as the king of the vultures would be no less bent upon preying on the flock than any of the minor harpies, it was indispensable to be in a perpetual attitude of defence against his beak and claws. The aim, therefore, of patriots was to set limits to the power which the ruler should be suffered to exercise over the community; and this limitation was what they meant by liberty. It was attempted in two ways. First, by obtaining a recognition of certain immunities, called political liberties or rights, which it was to be regarded as a breach of duty in the ruler to infringe, and which, if he did infringe, specific resistance, or general rebellion, was held to be justifiable. A second, and generally a later expedient, was the establishment of constitutional checks, by which the consent of the community, or of a body of some sort, supposed to represent its interests, was made a necessary condition to some of the more important acts of the governing power. To the first of these modes of limitation, the ruling power, in most European countries, was compelled, more or less, to submit. It was not so with the second; and, to attain this, or when already in some degree possessed, to attain it more completely, became everywhere the principal object of the lovers of liberty. And so long as mankind were content to combat one enemy by another, and to be ruled by a master, on condition of being guaranteed more or less efficaciously against his tyranny, they did not carry their aspirations beyond this point.

A time, however, came, in the progress of human affairs, when men ceased to think it a necessity of nature that their governors should be an independent power, opposed in interest to themselves. It appeared to them much better that the various magistrates of the state should be their tenants or delegates, revocable at their pleasure. In that way alone, it seemed, could they have complete security that the powers of government would never be abused to their disadvantage. By degrees this

new demand for elective and temporary rulers became the prominent object of the exertions of the popular party, wherever any such party existed; and superseded, to a considerable extent, the previous efforts to limit the power of rulers. As the struggle proceeded for making the ruling power emanate from the periodical choice of the ruled, some persons began to think that too much importance had been attached to the limitation of the power itself. *That* (it might seem) was a resource against rulers whose interests were habitually opposed to those of the people. What was now wanted was, that the rulers should be identified with the people; that their interest and will should be the interest and will of the nation. The nation did not need to be protected against its own will. There was no fear of its tyrannizing over itself. Let the rulers be effectually responsible to it, promptly removable by it, and it could afford to trust them with power of which it could itself dictate the use to be made. Their power was but the nation's own power, concentrated, and in a form convenient for exercise. This mode of thought, or rather perhaps of feeling, was common among the last generation of European liberalism, in the Continental section of which it still apparently predominates. Those who admit any limit to what a government may do, except in the case of such governments as they think ought not to exist, stand out as brilliant exceptions among the political thinkers of the Continent. A similar tone of sentiment might by this time have been prevalent in our own country, if the circumstances which for a time encouraged it, had continued unaltered.

But, in political and philosophical theories, as well as in persons, success discloses faults and infirmities which failure might have concealed from observation. The notion, that the people have no need to limit their power over themselves, might seem axiomatic, when popular government was a thing only dreamed about, or read of as having existed at some distant period of the past. Neither was that notion necessarily disturbed by such temporary aberrations as those of the French Revolution, the worst of which were the work of a usurping few, and which, in any case, belonged, not to the permanent working of popular institutions, but to a sudden and convulsive outbreak against monarchical and aristocratic despotism. In time, however, a democratic republic came to occupy a large portion of the earth's surface,[3] and made itself felt as one of the most powerful members of the community of nations; and elective and responsible government became subject to the observations and criticisms which wait upon a great existing fact. It was now perceived that such phrases as "self-government," and "the power of the people over themselves," do not express the true state of the case. The "people" who exercise the power are not always the same people with those over whom it is exercised; and the "self-government" spoken of is not the government of each by himself, but of each by all the rest. The will of the people, moreover, practically means the will of the most numerous or the most active *part* of the people; the majority, or those who succeed in making themselves accepted as the majority; the people, consequently, *may* desire to oppress a part of their number; and precautions are as much needed against this as against any other abuse of power. The limitation, therefore, of the power of government over individuals loses none of its importance when the holders of power are regularly accountable to the community, that is, to the strongest party therein. This view of things, recommending itself equally to the intelligence of thinkers and to the inclination of those important classes in European society to whose real or supposed interests democracy is adverse, has had no difficulty in establishing itself; and in political speculations "the tyranny of the majority" is now generally included among the evils against which society requires to be on its guard.

Like other tyrannies, the tyranny of the majority was at first, and is still vulgarly, held in dread, chiefly as operating through the acts of the public authorities. But reflecting persons perceived that when society is itself the tyrant-society collectively, over the separate individuals who compose it—its means of tyrannizing are not restricted to the acts which it may do by the hands of its political functionaries. Society can and does execute its own mandates: and if it issues wrong mandates instead of right, or any mandates at all in things with which it ought not to meddle, it practises a social tyranny more formidable than many kinds of political oppression, since, though not usually upheld by such extreme penalties, it leaves fewer means of escape, penetrating much more deeply into the details of life, and enslaving the soul itself. Protection, therefore, against the tyranny of the magistrate is not enough: there needs protection also against the tyranny of the prevailing opinion and feeling; against the tendency of society to impose, by other means than civil penalties, its own ideas and practices as rules of conduct on those who dissent from them; to fetter the development, and, if possible, prevent the formation, of any individuality not in harmony with its ways, and compel all characters to fashion themselves upon the model of its own. There is a limit to the legitimate interference of collective opinion with individual independence: and to find that limit, and maintain it against encroachment, is as indispensable to a good condition of human affairs, as protection against political despotism.

But though this proposition is not likely to be contested in general terms, the practical question, where to place the limit—how to make the fitting adjustment between individual independence and social control—is a subject on which nearly everything remains to be done. All that makes existence valuable to anyone, depends on the enforcement of restraints upon the actions of other people. Some rules of conduct, therefore, must be imposed, by law in the first place, and by opinion on many things which are not fit subjects for the operation of law. What these rules should be, is the principal question in human affairs; but if we except a few of the most obvious cases, it is one of those which least progress has been made in resolving. No two ages, and scarcely any two countries, have decided it alike; and the decision of one age or country is a wonder to another. Yet the people of any given age and country no more suspect any difficulty in it, than if it were a subject on which mankind had always been agreed. The rules which obtain among themselves appear to them self-evident and self-justifying. This all but universal illusion is one of the examples of the magical influence of custom, which is not only, as the proverb says, a second nature, but is continually mistaken for the first. The effect of custom, in preventing any misgiving respecting the rules of conduct which mankind impose on one another, is all the more complete because the subject is one on which it is not generally considered necessary that reasons should be given, either by one person to others, or by each to himself. People are accustomed to believe, and have been encouraged in the belief by some who aspire to the character of philosophers, that their feelings, on subjects of this nature, are better than reasons, and render reasons unnecessary. The practical principle which guides them to their opinions on the regulation of human conduct, is the feeling in each person's mind that everybody should be required to act as he, and those with whom he sympathizes, would like them to act. No one, indeed, acknowledges to himself that his standard of judgment is his own liking; but an opinion on a point of conduct, not supported by reasons, can only count as one person's preference; and if the reasons, when given, are a mere appeal to a similar preference felt by other people, it is still only many people's liking instead of one. To an ordinary man, however, his own preference, thus supported, is not only a perfectly satisfactory reason, but the only one he generally has for any of his notions of morality, taste, or propriety, which are not expressly written in his religious creed; and his chief guide in the interpretation even of that. Men's opinions, accordingly, on what is laudable or blameable, are affected by all the multifarious causes which influence their wishes in regard to the conduct of others, and which are as numerous as those which determine their wishes on any other subject. Sometimes their reason—at other times their prejudices or superstitions: often their social affections, not seldom their antisocial ones, their envy or jealousy, their arrogance or contemptuousness: but most commonly, their desires or fears for themselves—their legitimate or illegitimate self-interest. Wherever there is an ascendant class, a large portion of the morality of the country emanates from its class interests, and its feelings of class superiority. The morality between Spartans and Helots,[4] between planters and negroes, between princes and subjects, between nobles and roturiers,[5] between men and women, has been for the most part the creation of these class interests and feelings: and the sentiments thus generated, react in turn upon the moral feelings of the members of the ascendant class, in their relations among themselves. Where, on the other hand, a class, formerly ascendant, has lost its ascendancy, or where its ascendancy is unpopular, the prevailing moral sentiments frequently bear the impress of an impatient dislike of superiority. Another grand determining principle of the rules of conduct, both in act and forbearance, which have been enforced by law or opinion, has been the servility of mankind towards the supposed preferences or aversions of their temporal masters, or of their gods. This servility, though essentially selfish, is not hypocrisy; it gives rise to perfectly genuine sentiments of abhorrence; it made men burn magicians and heretics. Among so many baser influences, the general and obvious interests of society have of course had a share, and a large one, in the direction of the moral sentiments: less, however, as a matter of reason, and on their own account, than as a consequence of the sympathies and antipathies which grew out of them: and sympathies and antipathies which had little or nothing to do with the interests of society, have made themselves felt in the establishment of moralities with quite as great force.

The likings and dislikings of society, or of some powerful portion of it, are thus the main thing which has practically determined the rules laid down for general observance, under the penalties of law or opinion. And in general, those who have been in advance of society in thought and feeling, have left this condition of things unassailed in principle, however they may have come into conflict with it in some of its details. They have occupied themselves rather in inquiring what things society ought to like or dislike, than in questioning whether its likings or dislikings should be a law to individuals. They preferred endeavouring to alter the feelings of mankind on the particular points on which they were themselves heretical, rather than make common cause in defence of freedom, with heretics generally. The only case in which the higher ground has been taken on principle and maintained with consistency, by any but an individual here and there, is that of religious belief: a case instructive in many ways, and not least so as forming a most striking instance of the fallibility of what is called the moral sense: for the *odium theologicum*, in a sincere bigot, is one of the most unequivocal cases of moral feeling. Those who first broke the yoke of what called itself the Universal Church,[6] were in general as little willing to permit difference of religious opinion as that church itself. But when the heat of the conflict was over, without giving a complete victory to any party, and each church or sect was reduced to limit its hopes to retaining possession of the ground it already occupied; minorities, seeing that they had no chance of becoming majorities, were under the necessity of pleading to those whom they could not convert, for permission to differ. It is accordingly on this battlefield, almost solely, that the rights of the individual against society have been asserted on broad grounds of principle, and the claim of society to exercise authority over dissentients, openly controverted. The great writers to whom the world owes what religious liberty it possesses, have mostly asserted freedom of conscience as an indefeasible right, and denied absolutely that a human being is accountable to others for his religious belief. Yet so natural to mankind is intolerance in whatever they really care about, that religious freedom has hardly anywhere been practically realized, except where religious indifference, which dislikes to have its peace disturbed by theological quarrels, has added its weight to the scale. In the minds of almost all religious persons, even in the most tolerant countries, the duty of toleration is admitted with tacit reserves. One person will bear with dissent in matters of church government, but not of dogma; another can tolerate everybody, short of a Papist or a Unitarian; another, every one who believes in revealed religion; a few extend their charity a little further, but stop at the belief in a God and in a future state. Wherever the sentiment of the majority is still genuine and intense, it is found to have abated little of its claim to be obeyed.

In England, from the peculiar circumstances of our political history, though the yoke of opinion is perhaps heavier, that of law is lighter, than in most other countries of Europe; and there is considerable jealousy of direct interference, by the legislative or the executive power, with private conduct; not so much from any just regard for the independence of the individual, as from the still subsisting habit of looking on the government as representing an opposite interest to the public. The majority have not yet learnt to feel the power of the government their power, or its opinions their opinions. When they do so, individual liberty will probably be as much exposed to invasion from the government, as it already is from public opinion. But, as yet, there is a considerable amount of feeling ready to be called forth against any attempt of the law to control individuals in things in which they have not hitherto been accustomed to be controlled by it; and this with very little discrimination as to whether the matter is, or is not, within the legitimate sphere of legal control; insomuch that the feeling, highly salutary on the whole, is perhaps quite as often misplaced as well grounded in the particular instances of its application. There is, in fact, no recognized principle by which the propriety or impropriety of government interference is customarily tested. People decide according to their personal preferences. Some, whenever they see any good to be done, or evil to be remedied, would willingly instigate the government to undertake the business; while others prefer to bear almost any amount of social evil, rather than add one to the departments of human interests amenable to governmental control. And men range themselves on one or the other side in any particular case, according to this general direction of their sentiments; or according to the degree of interest which they feel in the particular thing which it is proposed that the government should do, or according to the belief they entertain that the government would, or would not, do it in the manner they prefer; but very rarely on account of any opinion to which they consistently adhere, as to what things are fit to be done by a government. And it seems to me that in consequence of this absence of rule or principle, one side is at present as often wrong as the other; the interference of government is, with about equal frequency, improperly invoked and improperly condemned.

The object of this essay is to assert one very simple principle, as entitled to govern absolutely the dealings of society with the individual in the way of compulsion and control, whether the means used be physical force in the form of legal penalties, or the moral coercion of public opinion. That principle is, that the sole end for which mankind are warranted, individually or collectively, in interfering with the liberty of action of any of their number, is self-protection. That the only purpose for which power can be rightfully exercised over any member of a civilized community, against his will, is to prevent harm to others. His own good, either physical or moral, is not a sufficient warrant. He cannot rightfully be compelled to do or forbear because it will be better for him to do so, because it will make him happier, because, in the opinions of others, to do so would be wise, or even right. These are good reasons for remonstrating with him, or reasoning with him, or persuading him, or entreating him, but not for compelling him, or visiting him with any evil in case he do otherwise. To justify that, the conduct from which it is desired to deter him, must be calculated to produce evil to some one else. The only part of the conduct of anyone, for which he is amenable to society, is that which concerns others. In the part which merely concerns himself, his independence is, of right, absolute. Over himself, over his own body and mind, the individual is sovereign.

It is, perhaps, hardly necessary to say that this doctrine is meant to apply only to human beings in the maturity of their faculties. We are not speaking of children, or of young persons below the age which the law may fix as that of manhood or womanhood. Those who are still in a state to require being taken care of by others, must be protected against their own actions as well as against external injury. For the same reason, we may leave out of consideration those backward states of society in which the race itself may be considered as in its nonage. The early difficulties in the way of spontaneous progress are so great, that there is seldom any choice of means for overcoming them; and a ruler full of the spirit of improvement is warranted in the use of any expedients that will attain an end, perhaps otherwise unattainable. Despotism is a legitimate mode of government in dealing with barbarians, provided the end be their improvement, and the means justified by actually effecting that end. Liberty, as a principle, has no application to any state of things anterior to the time when mankind have become capable of being improved by free and equal discussion. Until then, there is nothing for them but implicit obedience to an Akbar or a Charlemagne,[7] if they are so fortunate as to find one. But as soon as mankind have attained the capacity of being guided to their own improvement by conviction or persuasion (a period long since reached in all nations with whom we need here concern ourselves), compulsion, either in the direct form or in that of pains and penalties for non-compliance, is no longer admissible as a means to their own good, and justifiable only for the security of others.

It is proper to state that I forgo any advantage which could be derived to my argument from the idea of abstract right, as a thing independent of utility. I regard utility as the ultimate appeal on all ethical questions; but it must be utility in the largest sense, grounded on the permanent interests of man[8] as a progressive being. Those interests, I contend, authorize the subjection of individual spontaneity to external control, only in respect to those actions of each, which concern the interest of other people. If anyone does an act hurtful to others, there is a prima facie case for punishing him, by law, or, where legal penalties are not safely applicable, by general disapprobation. There are also many positive acts for the benefit of others, which he may rightfully be compelled to perform; such as, to give evidence in a court of justice;

to bear his fair share in the common defence, or in any other joint work necessary to the interest of the society of which he enjoys the protection; and to perform certain acts of individual beneficence, such as saving a fellow creature's life, or interposing to protect the defenceless against ill-usage, things which whenever it is obviously a man's duty to do, he may rightfully be made responsible to society for not doing. A person may cause evil to others not only by his actions but by his inaction, and in either case he is justly accountable to them for the injury. The latter case, it is true, requires a much more cautious exercise of compulsion than the former. To make anyone answerable for doing evil to others, is the rule; to make him answerable for not preventing evil, is, comparatively speaking, the exception. Yet there are many cases clear enough and grave enough to justify that exception. In all things which regard the external relations of the individual, he is *de jure* amenable to those whose interests are concerned, and if need be, to society as their protector. There are often good reasons for not holding him to the responsibility; but these reasons must arise from the special expediencies of the case: either because it is a kind of case in which he is on the whole likely to act better, when left to his own discretion, than when controlled in any way in which society have it in their power to control him; or because the attempt to exercise control would produce other evils, greater than those which it would prevent. When such reasons as these preclude the enforcement of responsibility, the conscience of the agent himself should step into the vacant judgment seat, and protect those interests of others which have no external protection; judging himself all the more rigidly, because the case does not admit of his being made accountable to the judgment of his fellow creatures.

But there is a sphere of action in which society, as distinguished from the individual, has, if any, only an indirect interest; comprehending all that portion of a person's life and conduct which affects only himself, or if it also affects others, only with their free, voluntary, and undeceived consent and participation. When I say only himself, I mean directly, and in the first instance: for whatever affects himself, may affect others through himself; and the objection which may be grounded on this contingency will receive consideration in the sequel. This, then, is the appropriate region of human liberty. It comprises, first, the inward domain of consciousness; demanding liberty of conscience, in the most comprehensive sense; liberty of thought and feeling; absolute freedom of opinion and sentiment on all subjects, practical or speculative, scientific, moral, or theological. The liberty of expressing and publishing opinions may seem to fall under a different principle, since it belongs

to that part of the conduct of an individual which concerns other people; but, being almost of as much importance as the liberty of thought itself, and resting in great part on the same reasons, is practically inseparable from it. Secondly, the principle requires liberty of tastes and pursuits; of framing the plan of our life to suit our own character; of doing as we like, subject to such consequences as may follow: without impediment from our fellow creatures, so long as what we do does not harm them, even though they should think our conduct foolish, perverse, or wrong. Thirdly, from this liberty of each individual, follows the liberty, within the same limits, of combination among individuals; freedom to unite, for any purpose not involving harm to others: the persons combining being supposed to be of full age, and not forced or deceived.

No society in which these liberties are not, on the whole, respected, is free, whatever may be its form of government; and none is completely free in which they do not exist absolute and unqualified. The only freedom which deserves the name, is that of pursuing our own good in our own way, so long as we do not attempt to deprive others of theirs, or impede their efforts to obtain it. Each is the proper guardian of his own health, whether bodily, or mental and spiritual. Mankind are greater gainers by suffering each other to live as seems good to themselves, than by compelling each to live as seems good to the rest.

Though this doctrine is anything but new, and, to some persons, may have the air of a truism, there is no doctrine which stands more directly opposed to the general tendency of existing opinion and practice. Society has expended fully as much effort in the attempt (according to its lights) to compel people to conform to its notions of personal, as of social excellence. The ancient commonwealths thought themselves entitled to practise, and the ancient philosophers countenanced, the regulation of every part of private conduct by public authority, on the ground that the state had a deep interest in the whole bodily and mental discipline of every one of its citizens; a mode of thinking which may have been admissible in small republics surrounded by powerful enemies, in constant peril of being subverted by foreign attack or internal commotion, and to which even a short interval of relaxed energy and self-command might so easily be fatal, that they could not afford to wait for the salutary permanent effects of freedom. In the modern world, the greater size of political communities, and, above all, the separation between spiritual and temporal authority (which placed the direction of men's consciences in other hands than those which controlled their worldly affairs), prevented so great an interference by law in the details of private life; but the engines of moral repression have been wielded more strenuously against divergence from the reigning opinion in self-regarding, than even in social matters; religion, the most powerful of the elements which have entered into the formation of moral feeling, having almost always been governed either by the ambition of a hierarchy, seeking control over every department of human conduct, or by the spirit of Puritanism. And some of those modern reformers who have placed themselves in strongest opposition to the religions of the past, have been no way behind either churches or sects in their assertion of the right of spiritual domination: M. Comte,[9] in particular, whose social system, as unfolded in his *Système de Politique Positive*, aims at establishing (though by moral more than by legal appliances) a despotism of society over the individual, surpassing anything contemplated in the political ideal of the most rigid disciplinarian among the ancient philosophers.

Apart from the peculiar tenets of individual thinkers, there is also in the world at large an increasing inclination to stretch unduly the powers of society over the individual, both by the force of opinion and even by that of legislation: and as the tendency of all the changes taking place in the world is to strengthen society, and diminish the power of the individual, this encroachment is not one of the evils which tend spontaneously to disappear, but, on the contrary, to grow more and more formidable. The disposition of mankind, whether as rulers or as fellow citizens, to impose their own opinions and inclinations as a rule of conduct on others, is so energetically supported by some of the best and by some of the worst feelings incident to human nature, that it is hardly ever kept under restraint by anything but want of power; and as the power is not declining, but growing, unless a strong barrier of moral conviction can be raised against the mischief, we must expect, in the present circumstances of the world, to see it increase.

It will be convenient for the argument, if, instead of at once entering upon the general thesis, we confine ourselves in the first instance to a single branch of it, on which the principle here stated is, if not fully, yet to a certain point, recognized by the current opinions. This one branch is the liberty of thought: from which it is impossible to separate the cognate liberty of speaking and of writing. Although these liberties, to some considerable amount, form part of the political morality of all countries which profess religious toleration and free institutions, the grounds, both philosophical and practical, on which they rest, are perhaps not so familiar to the general mind, nor so thoroughly appreciated by many even of the leaders of opinion, as might have been expected. Those grounds, when rightly understood, are of much wider application than to only one division of the subject, and a thorough consideration of this part of the question will be found the best introduction to the remainder. Those to whom nothing which I am about to say will be new, may therefore, I hope, excuse me, if on a subject which for now three centuries has been so often discussed, I venture on one discussion more.

Chapter II Of the Liberty of Thought and Discussion

The time, it is to be hoped, is gone by, when any defence would be necessary of the "liberty of the press" as one of the securities against corrupt or tyrannical government. No argument, we may suppose, can now be needed, against permitting a legislature or an executive, not identified in interest with the people, to prescribe opinions to them, and determine what doctrines or what arguments they shall be allowed to hear. This aspect of the question, besides, has been so often and so triumphantly enforced by preceding writers, that it needs not be specially insisted on in this place. Though the law of England, on the subject of the press, is as servile to this day as it was in the time of the Tudors, there is little danger of its being actually put in force against political discussion, except during some temporary panic, when fear of insurrection drives ministers and judges from their propriety;[10] and, speaking generally, it is not, in constitutional countries, to be apprehended, that the government, whether completely responsible to the people or not, will often attempt to control the expression of opinion, except when in doing so it makes itself the organ of the general intolerance of the public. Let us suppose, therefore, that the government is entirely at one with the people, and never thinks of exerting any power of coercion unless in agreement with what it conceives to be their voice. But I deny the right of the people to exercise such coercion, either by themselves or by their government. The power itself is illegitimate. The best government has no more tide to it than the worst. It is as noxious, or more noxious, when exerted in accordance with public opinion, than when in opposition to it. If all mankind minus one, were of one opinion, and only one person were of the contrary opinion, mankind would be no more justified in silencing that one person, than he, if he had the power, would be justified in silencing mankind. Were an opinion a personal possession of no value except to the owner; if to be obstructed in the enjoyment of it were simply a private injury, it would make some difference whether the injury was inflicted only on a few persons or on many. But the peculiar evil of silencing the expression of an opinion is, that it is robbing the human race; posterity as well as the existing generation; those who dissent from the opinion, still more than those who hold it. If the opinion is right, they are deprived of the opportunity of exchanging error for truth: if wrong, they lose, what is almost as great a benefit, the clearer perception and livelier impression of truth, produced by its collision with error.

It is necessary to consider separately these two hypotheses, each of which has a distinct branch of the argument corresponding to it. We can never be sure that the opinion we are endeavouring to stifle is a false opinion; and if we were sure, stifling it would be an evil still.

First: the opinion which it is attempted to suppress by authority may possibly be true. Those who desire to suppress it, of course deny its truth; but they are not infallible. They have no authority to decide the question for all mankind, and exclude every other person from the means of judging. To refuse a hearing to an opinion, because they are sure that it is false, is to assume that *their* certainty is the same thing as *absolute* certainty. All silencing of discussion is an assumption of infallibility. Its condemnation may be allowed to rest on this common argument, not the worse for being common.

Unfortunately for the good sense of mankind, the tact of their fallibility is far from carrying the weight in their practical judgment, which is always allowed to it in theory; for while every-one well knows himself to be fallible, few think it necessary to take any precautions against their own fallibility, or admit the supposition that any opinion, of which they feel very certain, may be one of the examples of the error to which they acknowledge themselves to be liable. Absolute princes, or others who are accustomed to unlimited deference, usually feel this complete confidence in their own opinions on nearly all subjects. People more happily situated, who sometimes hear their opinions disputed, and are not wholly unused to be set right when they are wrong, place the same unbounded reliance only on such of their opinions as are shared by all who surround them, or to whom they habitually defer: for in proportion to a man's want of confidence in his own solitary judgment, does he usually repose, with implicit trust, on the infallibility of "the world" in general. And the world, to each individual, means the part of it with which he comes in contact; his party, his sect, his church, his class of society: the man may be called, by comparison, almost liberal and large-minded to whom it means anything so comprehensive as his own country or his own age. Nor is his faith in this collective authority at all shaken by his being aware that other ages, countries, sects, churches, classes, and parties have thought, and even now think, the exact reverse. He devolves upon his own world the responsibility of

being in the right against the dissentient worlds of other people; and it never troubles him that mere accident has decided which of these numerous worlds is the object of his reliance, and that the same causes which make him a Churchman in London, would have made him a Buddhist or a Confucian in Pekin. Yet it is as evident in itself, as any amount of argument can make it, that ages are no more infallible than individuals; every age having held many opinions which subsequent ages have deemed not only false but absurd; and it is as certain that many opinions, now general, will be rejected by future ages, as it is that many, once general, are rejected by the present.

The objection likely to be made to this argument would probably take some such form as the following. There is no greater assumption of infallibility in forbidding the propagation of error, than in any other thing which is done by public authority on its own judgment and responsibility. Judgment is given to men that they may use it. Because it may be used erroneously, are men to be told that they ought not to use it at all? To prohibit what they think pernicious, is not claiming exemption from error, but fulfilling the duty incumbent on them, although fallible, of acting on their conscientious conviction. If we were never to act on our opinions, because those opinions may be wrong, we should leave all our interests uncared for, and all our duties unperformed. An objection which applies to all conduct, can be no valid objection to any conduct in particular. It is the duty of governments, and of individuals, to form the truest opinions they can; to form them carefully, and never impose them upon others unless they are quite sure of being right. But when they are sure (such reasoners may say), it is not conscientiousness but cowardice to shrink from acting on their opinions, and allow doctrines which they honestly think dangerous to the welfare of mankind, either in this life or in another, to be scattered abroad without restraint, because other people, in less enlightened times, have persecuted opinions now believed to be true. Let us take care, it may be said, no to make the same mistake: but governments and nations have made mistakes in other things, which are not denied to be fit subjects for the exercise of authority: they have laid on bad taxes, made unjust wars. Ought we therefore to lay on no taxes, and, under whatever provocation, make no wars? Men, and governments, must act to the best of their ability. There is no such thing as absolute certainty, but there is assurance sufficient for the purposes of human life. We may, and must, assume our opinion to be true for the guidance of our own conduct: and it is assuming no more when we forbid bad men to pervert society by the propagation of opinions which we regard as false and pernicious.

I answer, that it is assuming very much more. There is the greatest difference between presuming an opinion to be true, because, with every opportunity for contesting it, it has not been refuted, and assuming its truth for the purpose of not permitting its refutation. Complete liberty of contradicting and disproving our opinion, is the very condition which justifies us in assuming its truth for purposes of action; and no other terms can a being with human faculties have any rational assurance of being right.

. . .

In the present age—which has been described as "destitute of faith, but terrified at scepticism"[11]—in which people feel sure, not so much that their opinions are true, as they should not know what to do without them—the claims of an opinion to be protected from public attack are rested not so much on its truth, as on its importance to society. There are, it is alleged, certain beliefs, so useful, not to say indispensable to well-being, that it is as much the duty of governments to uphold those beliefs, as to protect any other of the interests of society. In a case of such necessity, and so directly in the line of their duty, something less than infallibility may, it is maintained, warrant, and even bind, governments, to act on their own opinion, confirmed by the general opinion of mankind. It is also often argued, and still oftener thought, that none but bad men would desire to weaken these salutary beliefs; and there can be nothing wrong, it is thought, in restraining bad men, and prohibiting what only such men would wish to practise. This mode of thinking makes the justification of restraints on discussion not a question of the truth of doctrines, but of their usefulness; and flatters itself by that means to escape the responsibility of claiming to be an infallible judge of opinions. But those who thus satisfy themselves, do not perceive that the assumption of infallibility is merely shifted from one point to another. The usefulness of an opinion is itself matter of opinion: as disputable, as open to discussion, and requiring discussion as much, as the opinion itself. There is the same need of an infallible judge of opinions to decide an opinion to be noxious, as to decide it to be false, unless the opinion condemned has full opportunity of defending itself. And it will not do to say that the heretic may be allowed to maintain the utility or harmlessness of his opinion, though forbidden to maintain its truth. The truth of an opinion is part of its utility. If we would know whether or not it is desirable that a proposition should he believed, is it possible to exclude the consideration of whether or not it is true? In the opinion, not of bad men, but of the best men, no belief which is contrary to truth can be really useful: and can you prevent such men from urging that plea, when they are charged with culpability for denying some doctrine which they are told is useful, but which they believe to be false? Those who are on the side of received opinions, never fail to take all possible advantage of this plea; you do not find them handling the question of utility as if it could be completely abstracted from the truth: on the contrary, it is, above all, because their doctrine is the "truth," that the knowledge or the belief of it is held to be so indispensable. There can be no fair discussion of the question of usefulness, when an argument so vital may be employed on one side, but not on the other. And in point of fact, when law or public feeling do not permit the truth of an opinion to be disputed, they are just as little tolerant of a denial of its usefulness. The utmost they allow is an extenuation of its absolute necessity, or of the positive guilt of rejecting it.

. . .

Let us now pass to the second division of the argument, and dismissing the supposition that any of the received opinions may be false, let us assume them to be true, and examine into the worth of the manner in which they are likely to be held, when their truth is not freely and openly canvassed. However unwillingly a person who has a strong opinion may admit the possibility that his opinion may be false, he ought to be moved by the consideration that however true it may be, if it is not fully, frequently, and fearlessly discussed, it will be held as a dead dogma, not a living truth.

There is a class of persons (happily not quite so numerous as formerly) who think it enough if a person assents undoubtingly to what they think true, though he has no knowledge whatever of the grounds of the opinion, and could not make a tenable defence of it against the most superficial of objections. Such persons, if they can once get their creed taught from authority, naturally think that no good, and some harm, comes of its being allowed to be questioned. Where their influence prevails, they make it nearly impossible for the received opinion to be rejected wisely and considerately, though it may still be rejected rashly and ignorantly; for to shut out discussion entirely is seldom possible, and when it once gets in, beliefs not grounded on conviction are apt to give way before the slightest semblance of an argument. Waiving, however, this possibility—assuming that the true opinion abides in the mind, but abides as a prejudice, a belief independent of, and proof against, argument—this is not the way in which truth ought to be held by a rational being. This is not knowing the truth. Truth, thus held, is but one superstition the more, accidentally clinging to the words which enunciate a truth.

If the intellect and judgment of mankind ought to be cultivated, a thing which Protestants at least do not deny, on what can these faculties be more appropriately exercised by anyone, than on the things which concern him so much that it is considered necessary for him to hold opinions on them? If the cultivation of the understanding consists in one thing more than in another, it is surely in learning the grounds of one's own opinions. Whatever people believe, on subjects on which it is of the first importance to believe rightly, they ought to be able to defend against at least the common objections. But, some one may say, "Let them be *taught* the grounds of their opinions. It does not follow that opinions must be merely parroted because they are never heard controverted. Persons who learn geometry do not simply commit the theorems to memory, but understand and learn likewise the demonstrations; and it would be absurd to say that they remain ignorant of the grounds of geometrical truths, because they never hear anyone deny, and attempt to disprove them." Undoubtedly: and such teaching suffices on a subject like mathematics, where there is nothing at all to be said on the wrong side of the question. The peculiarity of the evidence of mathematical truths is, that all the argument is on one side. There are no objections, and no answers to objections. But on every subject on which difference of opinion is possible, the truth depends on a balance to be struck between two sets of conflicting reasons. Even in natural philosophy, there is always some other explanation possible of the same facts; some geocentric theory instead of heliocentric, some phlogiston instead of oxygen; and it has to be shown why that other theory cannot be the true one: and until this is shown, and until we know how it is shown, we do not understand the grounds of our opinion. But when we turn to subjects infinitely more complicated, to morals, religion, politics, social relations, and the business of life, three-fourths of the arguments for every disputed opinion consist in dispelling the appearances which favour some opinion different from it. The greatest orator, save one, of antiquity,[12] has left it on record that he always studied his adversary's case with as great, if not with still greater, intensity than even his own. What Cicero practised as the means of forensic success, requires to be imitated by all who study any subject in order to arrive at the truth. He who knows only his own side of the case, knows little of that. His reasons may be good, and no one may have been able to refute them. But if he is equally unable to refute the reasons on the opposite side; if he does not so much as know what they are, he has no ground for preferring either opinion. The rational position for him would be suspension of judgment, and unless he contents himself with that, he is either led by authority, or adopts, like the generality of the world, the side to which he feels most inclination. Nor

is it enough, that he should hear the arguments of adversaries from his own teachers, presented as they state them, and accompanied by what they offer as refutations. That is not the way to do justice to the arguments, or bring them into real contact with his own mind. He must be able to hear them from persons who actually believe them; who defend them in earnest, and do their very utmost for them. He must know them in their most plausible and persuasive form; he must feel the whole force of the difficulty which the true view of the subject has to encounter and dispose of; else he will never really possess himself of the portion of truth which meets and removes that difficulty. Ninety-nine in a hundred of what are called educated men are in this condition; even of those who can argue fluently for their opinions. Their conclusion may be true, but it might be false for anything they know: they have never thrown themselves into the mental position of those who think differently from them, and considered what such persons may have to say; and consequently they do not, in any proper sense of the word, know the doctrine which they themselves profess. They do not know those parts of it which explain and justify the remainder; the considerations which show that a fact which seemingly conflicts with another is reconcilable with it, or that, of two apparently strong reasons, one and not the other ought to be preferred. All that part of the truth which turns the scale, and decides the judgment of a completely informed mind, they are strangers to; nor is it ever really known, but to those who have attended equally and impartially to both sides, and endeavoured to see the reasons of both in the strongest light. So essential is this discipline to a real understanding of moral and human subjects, that if opponents of all important truths do not exist, it is indispensable to imagine them, and supply them with the strongest arguments which the most skilful devil's advocate can conjure up.

To abate the force of these considerations, an enemy of free discussion may be supposed to say, that there is no necessity for mankind in general to know and understand all that can be said against or for their opinions by philosophers and theologians. That it is not needful for common men to be able to expose all the misstatements or fallacies of an ingenious opponent. That it is enough if there is always somebody capable of answering them, so that nothing likely to mislead uninstructed persons remains unrefuted. That simple minds, having been taught the obvious grounds of the truths inculcated on them, may trust to authority for the rest, and being aware that they have neither knowledge nor talent to resolve every difficulty which can be raised, may repose in the assurance that all those which have been raised have been or can be answered, by those who are specially trained to the task.

. . .

It is illustrated in the experience of almost all ethical doctrines and religious creeds. They are all full of meaning and vitality to those who originate them, and to the direct disciples of the originators. Their meaning continues to be felt in undiminished strength, and is perhaps brought out into even fuller consciousness, so long as the struggle lasts to give the doctrine or creed an ascendancy over other creeds. At last it either prevails, and becomes the general opinion, or its progress stops; it keeps possession of the ground it has gained, but ceases to spread further. When either of these results has become apparent, controversy on the subject flags, and gradually dies away. The doctrine has taken its place, if not as a received opinion, as one of the admitted sects or divisions of opinion: those who hold it have generally inherited, not adopted it; and the conversion form one of these doctrines to another, being now an exceptional fact, occupies little place in the thoughts of their professors. Instead of being, as at first, constantly on the alert either to defend themselves against the world, or to bring the world over to them, they have subsided into acquiescence, and neither listen, when they can help it, to arguments against their creed, no trouble dissentients (if there be such) with arguments in its favour. From this time may usually be dated the decline in the living power of the doctrine. We often hear the teachers of all creeds lamenting the difficulty of keeping up in the minds of believers a lively apprehension of the truth which they nominally recognize, so that it may penetrate the feelings, and acquire a real mystery over the conduct. No such difficulty is complained of while the creed is still fighting for its existence: even the weaker combatants then know and feel what they are fighting for, and the difference between it and other doctrines; and in that period of every creed's existence, no a few persons may be found, who have realized its fundamental principles in all the forms of thought, have weighed and considered them in all their important bearings, and have experience the full effect on the character, which belief in that creed ought to produce in a mind thoroughly imbued with it. But when it has come to be an hereditary creed, and to be received passively, not actively—when the mind is no longer compelled, in the same degree as at first, to exercise its vital powers on the questions which its belief presents to it, there is a progressive tendency to forget all of the belief except the formularies, or to give it a dull and torpid assent, as if accepting it on trust dispensed with the necessity of realizing it in consciousness, or testing it by personal experience; until it almost ceases to connect itself at all with the inner life of the human being. Then are seen the cases, so frequent in this age of the world as almost to form the majority, in which the creed remains as it were outside the mind, encrusting and petrifying it against all other influences addressed to the higher parts of our nature; manifesting its power by not suffering any fresh and living convictions to get in, but itself doing nothing of the mind or heart, except standing sentinel over them to keep them vacant.

. . .

It still remains to speak of one of the principal causes which make diversity of opinion advantageous, and will continue to do so until mankind shall have entered a stage of intellectual advancement which at present seems at an incalculable distance. We have hitherto considered only two possibilities: that the received opinion may be false, and some other opinion, consequently, true; or that, the received opinion being true, a conflict with the opposite error is essential to a clear apprehension and deep feeling of its truth. But there is a commoner case than either of these; when the conflicting doctrines, instead of being one true and the other false, share the truth between them; and the nonconforming opinion is needed to supply the remainder of the truth, of which the received doctrine embodies only a part. Popular opinions, on subjects not palpable to sense, are often true, but seldom or never the whole truth. They are a part of the truth; sometimes a greater, sometimes a smaller part, but exaggerated, distorted, and disjoined from the truths by which they ought to be accompanied and limited. Heretical opinions, on the other hand, are generally some of these suppressed and neglected truths, bursting the bonds which kept them down, and either seeking reconciliation with the truth contained in the common opinion, or fronting it as enemies, and setting themselves up, with similar exclusiveness, as the whole truth. The latter case is hitherto the most frequent, as, in the human mind, one-sidedness has always been the rule, and many-sidedness the exception. Hence, even in revolutions of opinion, one part of the truth usually sets while another rises. Even progress, which ought to superadd, for the most part only substitutes, one partial and incomplete truth for another; improvement consisting chiefly in this, that the new fragment of truth is more wanted, more adapted to the needs of the time, than that which it displaces. Such being the partial character of prevailing opinions, even when resting on a true foundation, every opinion which embodies somewhat of the portion of truth which the common opinion omits, ought to be considered precious, with whatever amount of error and confusion that truth may be blended. No sober judge of human affairs will feel bound to be indignant because those who force on our notice truths which we should otherwise have overlooked, overlook some of those which we see. Rather, he will think that so long as popular truth is one-sided, it is more desirable than otherwise that unpopular truth should have one-sided asserters too; such being usually the most energetic, and the most likely to compel reluctant attention to the fragment of wisdom which they proclaim as if it were the whole.

. . .

We have now recognized the necessity to the mental well-being of mankind (on which all their other well-being depends) of freedom of opinion, and freedom of the expression of opinion, on four distinct grounds; which we will now briefly recapitulate.

First, if any opinion is compelled to silence, that opinion may, for aught we can certainly know, be true. To deny this is to assume our own infallibility.

Secondly, though the silenced opinion be an error, it may, and very commonly does, contain a portion of truth; and since the general or prevailing opinion on any subject is rarely or never the whole truth, it is only by the collision of adverse opinions that the remainder of the truth has any chance of being supplied.

Thirdly, even if the received opinion be not only true, but the whole truth; unless it is suffered to be, and actually is, vigorously and earnestly contested, it will, by most of those who receive it, be held in the manner of a prejudice, with little comprehension or feeling of its rational grounds. And not only this, but fourthly, the meaning of the doctrine itself will be in danger of being lost, or enfeebled, and deprived of its vital effect on the character and conduct: the dogma becoming a mere formal profession, inefficacious for good, but cumbering the ground, and preventing the growth of any real and heartfelt conviction, from reason or personal experience.

Before quitting the subject of freedom of opinion, it is fit to take some notice of those who say, that the free expression of all opinions should be permitted, on condition that the manner be temperate, and do not pass the bounds of fair discussion. Much might be said on the impossibility of fixing where these supposed bounds are to be placed; for if the test be offence to those whose opinion is attacked, I think experience testifies that this offence is given whenever the attack is telling and powerful, and that every opponent who pushes them hard, and whom they find it difficult to answer, appears to them, if he shows any strong feeling on the subject, an intemperate opponent. But this, though an important consideration in a practical point of view, merges in a more fundamental objection. Undoubtedly the manner of asserting an opinion, even though it be a true one, may be very objectionable, and may justly incur severe censure. But the principal offences of the kind are such as it is mostly impossible, unless by accidental self-betrayal, to bring home to conviction. The gravest of them is, to argue sophistically, to suppress facts or arguments, to misstate the elements of the case, or misrepresent the opposite opinion. But all this, even to the most aggravated degree, is so continually done in perfect good faith, by persons who are not considered, and in many other respects may not deserve to be considered, ignorant or incompetent, that it is rarely possible on adequate grounds conscientiously to stamp the misrepresentation as morally culpable; and still less could law presume to interfere with this kind of controversial misconduct. With regard to what is commonly meant by intemperate discussion, namely invective, sarcasm, personality, and the like, the denunciation of these weapons would deserve more sympathy if it were ever proposed to interdict them equally to both sides; but it is only desired to restrain the employment of them against the prevailing opinion: against the unprevailing they may not only be used without general disapproval, but will be likely to obtain for him who uses them the praise of honest zeal and righteous indignation. Yet whatever mischief arises from their use, is greatest when they are employed against the comparatively defenceless; and whatever unfair advantage can be derived by any opinion from this mode of asserting it, accrues almost exclusively to received opinions. The worst offence of this kind which can be committed by a polemic, is to stigmatize those who hold the contrary opinion as bad and immoral men. To calumny of this sort, those who hold any unpopular opinion are peculiarly exposed, because they are in general few and uninfluential, and nobody but themselves feels much interested in seeing justice done them; but this weapon is, from the nature of the case, denied to those who attack a prevailing opinion: they can neither use it with safety to themselves, nor, if they could, would it do anything but recoil on their own cause. In general, opinions contrary to those commonly received can only obtain a hearing by studied moderation of language, and the most cautious avoidance of unnecessary offence, from which they hardly ever deviate even in a slight degree without losing ground: while unmeasured vituperation employed on the side of the prevailing opinion, really does deter people from professing contrary opinions, and from listening to those who profess them. For the interest, therefore, of truth and justice, it is far more important to restrain this employment of vituperative language than the other; and, for example, if it were necessary to choose, there would be much more need to discourage offensive attacks on infidelity, than on religion. It is, however, obvious that law and authority have no business with restraining either, while opinion ought, in every instance, to determine its verdict by the circumstances of the individual case; condemning every one, on whichever side of the argument he places himself, in whose mode of advocacy either want of candour, or malignity, bigotry, or intolerance of feeling manifest themselves; but not inferring these vices from the side which a person takes, though it be the contrary side of the question to our own: and giving merited honour to every one, whatever opinion he may hold, who has calmness to see and honesty to state what his opponents and their opinions really are, exaggerating nothing to their discredit, keeping nothing back which tells, or can be supposed to tell, in their favour. This is the real morality of public discussion: and if often violated, I am happy to think that there are many controversialists who to a great extent observe it, and a still greater number who conscientiously strive towards it.

Chapter III Of Individuality, as One of the Elements of Well-Being

Such being the reasons which make it imperative that human beings should be free to form opinions, and to express their opinions without reserve; and such the baneful consequences to the intellectual, and through that to the moral nature of man, unless this liberty is either conceded, or asserted in spite of prohibition; let us next examine whether the same reasons do not require that men should be free to act upon their opinions—to carry these out in their lives, without hindrance, either physical or moral, from their fellow men, so long as it is at their own risk and peril. This last proviso is of course indispensable. No one pretends that actions should be as free as opinions. On the contrary, even opinions lose their immunity, when the circumstances in which they are expressed are such as to constitute their expression a positive instigation to some mischievous act. An opinion that corn-dealers are starvers of the poor, or that private property is robbery, ought to be unmolested when simply circulated through the press, but may justly incur punishment when delivered orally to an excited mob assembled before the house of a corn-dealer, or when handed about among the same mob in the form of a placard. Acts, of whatever kind, which, without justifiable cause, do harm to others, may be, and in the more important cases absolutely require to be, controlled by the unfavourable sentiments, and, when needful, by the active interference of mankind. The liberty of the individual must be thus far limited; he must not make

himself a nuisance to other people. But if he refrains from molesting others in what concerns them, and merely acts according to his own inclination and judgment in things which concern himself, the same reasons which show that opinion should be free, prove also that he should be allowed, without molestation, to carry his opinions into practice at his own cost. That mankind are not infallible; that their truths, for the most part, are only half-truths; that unity of opinion, unless resulting from the fullest and freest comparison of opposite opinions, is not desirable, and diversity not an evil, but a good, until mankind are much more capable than at present of recognizing all sides of the truth, are principles applicable to men's modes of action, not less than to their opinions. As it is useful that while mankind are imperfect there should be different opinions, so is it that there should be different experiments of living; that free scope should be given to varieties of character, short of injury to others; and that the worth of different modes of life should be proved practically, when anyone thinks fit to try them. It is desirable, in short, that in things which do not primarily concern others, individuality should assert itself. Where, not the person's own character, but the traditions or customs of other people are the rule of conduct, there is wanting one of the principal ingredients of human happiness, and quite the chief ingredient of individual and social progress.

In maintaining this principle, the greatest difficulty to be encountered does not lie in the appreciation of means towards an acknowledged end, but in the indifference of persons in general to the end itself. If it were felt that the free development of individuality is one of the leading essentials of well-being; that it is not only a coordinate element with all that is designated by the terms civilization, instruction, education, culture, but is itself a necessary part and condition of all those things; there would be no danger that liberty should be undervalued, and the adjustment of the boundaries between it and social control would present no extraordinary difficulty. But the evil is, that individual spontaneity is hardly recognized by the common modes of thinking, as having any intrinsic worth, or deserving any regard on its own account. The majority, being satisfied with the ways of mankind as they now are (for it is they who make them what they are), cannot comprehend why those ways should not be good enough for everybody; and what is more, spontaneity forms no part of the ideal of the majority of moral and social reformers, but is rather looked on with jealousy, as a troublesome and perhaps rebellious obstruction to the general acceptance of what these reformers, in their own judgment, think would be best for mankind. Few persons, out of Germany, even comprehend the meaning of the doctrine which Wilhelm von Humboldt, so eminent both as a savant and as a politician, made the text of a treatise—that "the end of man, or that which is prescribed by the eternal or immutable dictates of reason, and not suggested by vague and transient desires, is the highest and most harmonious development of his powers to a complete and consistent whole"; that, therefore, the object "toward which every human being must ceaselessly direct his efforts, and on which especially those who design to influence their fellow men must ever keep their eyes, is the individuality of power and development"; that for this there are two requisites, "freedom, and variety of situations"; and that from the union of these arise "individual vigour and manifold diversity," which combine themselves in "originality."[13]

. . .

He who lets the world, or his own portion of it, choose his plan of life for him, has no need of any other faculty than the ape-like one of imitation. He who chooses his plan for himself: employs all his faculties. He must use observation to see, reasoning and judgment to foresee, activity to gather materials for decision, discrimination to decide, and when he has decided, firmness and self-control to hold to his deliberate decision. And these qualities he requires and exercises exactly in proportion as the part of his conduct which he determines according to his own judgment and feelings is a large one. It is possible that he might be guided in some good path, and kept out of harm's way, without any of these things. But what will be his comparative worth as a human being? It really is of importance, not only what men do, but also what manner of men they are that do it. Among the works of man, which human life is rightly employed in perfecting and beautifying, the first in importance surely is man himself. Supposing it were possible to get houses built, corn grown, battles fought, causes tried, and even churches erected and prayers said, by machinery—by automatons in human form—it would be a considerable loss to exchange for these automatons even the men and women who at present inhabit the more civilized parts of the world, and who assuredly are but starved specimens of what nature can and will produce. Human nature is not a machine to be built after a model, and set to do exactly the work prescribed for it, but a tree, which requires to grow and develop itself on all sides, according to the tendency of the inward forces which make it a living thing.

. . .

In some early states of society, these forces might be, and were, too much ahead of the power which society then possessed of disciplining and controlling them.

There has been a time when the element of spontaneity and individuality was in excess, and the social principle had a hard struggle with it. The difficulty then was, to induce men of strong bodies or minds to pay obedience to any rules which required them to control their impulses. To overcome this difficulty, law and discipline, like the popes struggling against the emperors, asserted a power over the whole man, claiming to control all his life in order to control his character—which society had not found any other sufficient means of binding. But society has now fairly got the better of individuality; and the danger which threatens human nature is not the excess, but the deficiency, of personal impulses and preferences. Things are vastly changed, since the passions of those who were strong by station or by personal endowment were in a state of habitual rebellion against laws and ordinances, and required to be rigorously chained up to enable the persons within their reach to enjoy any particle of security. In our times, from the highest class of society down to the lowest, every one lives as under the eye of a hostile and dreaded censorship. Not only in what concerns others, but in what concerns only themselves, the individual or the family do not ask themselves what do I prefer? or, what would suit my character and disposition? or, what would allow the best and highest in me to have fair play, and enable it to grow and thrive? They ask themselves, what is suitable to my position? what is usually done by persons of my station and pecuniary circumstances? or (worse still) what is usually done by persons of a station and circumstances superior to mine? I do not mean that they choose what is customary, in preference to what suits their own inclination. It does not occur to them to have any inclination, except for what is customary. Thus the mind itself is bowed to the yoke: even in what people do for pleasure, conformity is the first thing thought of; they like in crowds; they exercise choice only among things commonly done: peculiarity of taste, eccentricity of conduct, are shunned equally with crimes: until by dint of not following their own nature, they have no nature to follow: their human capacities are withered and starved: they become incapable of any strong wishes or native pleasures, and are generally without either opinions or feelings of home growth, or properly their own. Now is this, or is it not, the desirable condition of human nature?

. . .

Chapter IV Of the Limits to the Authority of Society Over the Individual

What, then, is the rightful limit to the sovereignty of the individual over himself? Where does the authority of society begin? How much of human life should be assigned to individuality, and how much to society?

Each will receive its proper share, if each has that which more particularly concerns it. To individuality should belong the part of life in which it is chiefly the individual that is interested; to society, the part which chiefly interests society.

Though society is not founded on a contract, and though no good purpose is answered by inventing a contract in order to deduce social obligations from it, everyone who receives the protection of society owes a return for the benefit, and the fact of living in society renders it indispensable that each should be bound to observe a certain line of conduct towards the rest. This conduct consists, first, in not injuring the interests of one another; or rather certain interests, which, either by express legal provision or by tacit understanding, ought to be considered as rights; and secondly, in each person's bearing his share (to be fixed on some equitable principle) of the labours and sacrifices incurred for defending the society or its members from injury and molestation. These conditions society is justified in enforcing at all costs to those who endeavour to withhold fulfilment. Nor is this all that society may do. The acts of an individual may be hurtful to others, or wanting in due consideration for their welfare, without going the length of violating any of their constituted rights. The offender may then be justly punished by opinion, though not by law. As soon as any part of a person's conduct affects prejudicially the interests of others, society has jurisdiction over it, and the question whether the general welfare will or will not be promoted by interfering with it, becomes open to discussion. But there is no room for entertaining any such question when a person's conduct affects the interests of no persons besides himself, or needs not affect them unless they like (all the persons concerned being of full age, and the ordinary amount of understanding). In all such cases there should be perfect freedom, legal and social, to do the action and stand the consequences.

It would be a great misunderstanding of this doctrine to suppose that it is one of selfish indifference, which pretends that human beings have no business with each other's conduct in life, and that they should not concern themselves about the well-doing or well-being of one another, unless their own interest is involved. Instead of any diminution, there is need of a great increase of disinterested exertion to promote the good of others. But disinterested benevolence can find other instruments to persuade people to their good, than whips and scourges, either of the literal or the metaphorical sort. I am the last person to undervalue the self-regarding virtues; they are only second in importance, if even second, to the social.

It is equally the business of education to cultivate both. But even education works by conviction and persuasion as well as by compulsion, and it is by the former only that, when the period of education is past, the self-regarding virtues should be inculcated. Human beings owe to each other help to distinguish the better from the worse, and encouragement to choose the former and avoid the latter. They should be forever stimulating each other to increased exercise of their higher faculties, and increased direction of their feelings and aims towards wise instead of foolish, elevating instead of degrading, objects and contemplations. But neither one person, nor any number of persons, is warranted in saying to another human creature of ripe years, that he shall not do with his life for his own benefit what he chooses to do with it. He is the person most interested in his own well-being: the interest which any other person, except in cases of strong personal attachment, can have in it, is trifling, compared with that which he himself has; the interest which society has in him individually (except as to his conduct to others) is fractional, and altogether indirect: while, with respect to his own feelings and circumstances, the most ordinary man or woman has means of knowledge immeasurably surpassing those that can be possessed by anyone else. The interference of society to overrule his judgment and purposes in what only regards himself, must be grounded on general presumptions; which may be altogether wrong, and even if right, are as likely as not to be misapplied to individual cases, by persons no better acquainted with the circumstances of such cases than those are who look at them merely from without. In this department, therefore, of human affairs, Individuality has its proper field of action. In the conduct of human beings towards one another, it is necessary that general rules should for the most part be observed, in order that people may know what they have to expect; but in each person's own concerns, his individual spontaneity is entitled to free exercise. Considerations to aid his judgment, exhortations to strengthen his will, may be offered to him, even obtruded on him, by others; but he himself is the final judge. All errors which he is likely to commit against advice and warning, are far outweighed by the evil of allowing others to constrain him to what they deem his good.

I do not mean that the feelings with which a person is regarded by others, ought not to be in any way affected by his self-regarding qualities or deficiencies. This is neither possible nor desirable. If he is eminent in any of the qualities which conduce to his own good, he is, so far, a proper object of admiration. He is so much the nearer to the ideal perfection of human nature. If he is grossly deficient in those qualities, a sentiment the opposite of admiration will follow. There is a degree of folly, and a degree of what may be called (though the phrase is not unobjectionable) lowness or depravation of taste, which, though it cannot justify doing harm to the person who manifests it, renders him necessarily and properly a subject of distaste, or, in extreme cases, even of contempt: a person could not have the opposite qualities in due strength without entertaining these feelings. Though doing no wrong to anyone, a person may so act as to compel us to judge him, and feel to him, as a fool, or as a being of an inferior order: and since this judgment and feeling are a fact which he would prefer to avoid, it is doing him a service to warn him of it beforehand, as of any other disagreeable consequence to which he exposes himself. It would be well, indeed, if this good office were much more freely rendered than the common notions of politeness at present permit, and if one person could honestly point out to another that he thinks him in fault, without being considered unmannerly or presuming. We have a right, also, in various ways, to act upon our unfavourable opinion of anyone, not to the oppression of his individuality, but in the exercise of ours. We are not bound, for example, to seek his society; we have a right to avoid it (though not to parade the avoidance), for we have a right to choose the society most acceptable to us. We have a right, and it may be our duty, to caution others against him, if we think his example or conversation likely to have a pernicious effect on those with whom he associates. We may give others a preference over him in optional good offices, except those which tend to his improvement. In these various modes a person may suffer very severe penalties at the hands of others, for faults which directly concern only himself; but he suffers these penalties only in so far as they are the natural, and, as it were, the spontaneous consequences of the faults themselves, not because they are purposely inflicted on him for the sake of punishment. A person who shows rashness, obstinacy, self-conceit—who cannot live within moderate means—who cannot restrain himself from hurtful indulgences—who pursues animal pleasures at the expense of those of feeling and intellect—must expect to be lowered in the opinion of others, and to have a less share of their favourable sentiments; but of this he has no right to complain, unless he has merited their favour by special excellence in his social relations, and has thus established a title to their good offices, which is not affected by his demerits towards himself.

What I contend for is, that the inconveniences which are strictly inseparable from the unfavourable judgment of others, are the only ones to which a person should ever be subjected for that portion of his conduct and character which concerns his own good, but which does not affect the interests of others in their relations with him. Acts injurious to others require a totally different treatment. Encroachment on their rights; infliction on them of any loss or damage not justified by his own rights; falsehood or duplicity in dealing with them; unfair or ungenerous use of advantages over them; even selfish abstinence from defending them against injury—these are fit objects of moral reprobation, and, in grave cases, of moral retribution and punishment. And not only these acts, but the dispositions which lead to them, are properly immoral, and fit subjects of disapprobation which may rise to abhorrence. Cruelty of disposition; malice and ill nature; that most anti-social and odious of all passions, envy; dissimulation and insincerity; irascibility on insufficient cause, and resentment disproportioned to the provocation; the love of domineering over others; the desire to engross more than one's share of advantages (the πλεονεξία[14] of the Greeks); the pride which derives gratification from the abasement of others; the egotism which thinks self and its concerns more important than everything else, and decides all doubtful questions in its own favour;—these are moral vices, and constitute a bad and odious moral character: unlike the self-regarding faults previously mentioned, which are not properly immoralities, and to whatever pitch they may be carried, do not constitute wickedness. They may be proofs of any amount of folly, or want of personal dignity and self-respect; but they are only a subject of moral reprobation when they involve a breach of duty to others, for whose sake the individual is bound to have care for himself. What are called duties to ourselves are not socially obligatory, unless circumstances render them at the same time duties to others. The term duty to oneself, when it means anything more than prudence, means self-respect or self-development; and for none of these is anyone accountable to his fellow creatures, because for none of them is it for the good of mankind that he be held accountable to them.

The distinction between the loss of consideration which a person may rightly incur by defect of prudence or of personal dignity, and the reprobation which is due to him for an at fence against the rights of others, is not a merely nominal distinction. It makes a vast difference both in our feelings and in our conduct towards him, whether he displeases us in things in which we think we have a right to control him, or in things in which we know that we have not. If he displeases us, we may express our distaste, and we may stand aloof from a person as well as from a thing that displeases us; but we shall not therefore feel called on to make his life uncomfortable. We shall reflect that he already bears, or will bear, the whole penalty of his error; if he spoils his life by mismanagement, we shall not, for that reason, desire to spoil it any further: instead of wishing to punish him, we shall rather endeavour to alleviate his punishment, by showing him how he may avoid or cure the evils his conduct tends to bring upon him. He may be to us an object of pity, perhaps of dislike, but not of anger or resentment; we shall not treat him like an enemy of society: the worst we shall think ourselves justified in doing is leaving him to himself, if we do not interfere benevolently by showing interest or concern for him. It is far otherwise if he has infringed the rules necessary for the protection of his fellow creatures, individually or collectively. The evil consequences of his acts do not then fall on himself, but on others; and society, as the protector of all its members, must retaliate on him; must inflict pain on him for the express purpose of punishment, and must take care that it be sufficiently severe. In the one case, he is an offender at our bar, and we are called on not only to sit in judgment on him, but, in one shape or another, to execute our own sentence; in the other case, it is not our part to inflict any suffering on him, except what may incidentally follow from our using the same liberty in the regulation of our own affairs, which we allow to him in his.

The distinction here pointed out between the part of a person's life which concerns only himself, and that which concerns others, many persons will refuse to admit. How (it may be asked) can any part of the conduct of a member of society be a matter of indifference to the other members? No person is an entirely isolated being; it is impossible for a person to do anything seriously or permanently hurtful to himself, without mischief reaching at least to his near connexions, and often far beyond them. If he injures his property, he does harm to those who directly or indirectly derived support from it, and usually diminishes, by a greater or less amount, the general resources of the community. If he deteriorates his bodily or mental faculties, he not only brings evil upon all who depended on him for any portion of their happiness, but disqualifies himself for rendering the services which he owes to his fellow creatures generally; perhaps becomes a burthen on their affection or benevolence; and if such conduct were very frequent, hardly any offence that is committed would detract more from the general sum of good. Finally, if by his vices or follies a person does no direct harm to others, he is nevertheless (it may be said) injurious by his example; and ought to be compelled to control himself, for the sake of those whom the sight or knowledge of his conduct might corrupt or mislead.

And even (it will be added) if the consequences of misconduct could be confined to the vicious or thoughtless individual, ought society to abandon to their own guidance those who are manifestly unfit for it? If protection against themselves is confessedly due to children and persons under age, is not society equally bound to afford it to persons of mature years who are equally incapable of self-government? If gambling, or drunkenness, or incontinence, or idleness, or uncleanliness, are as injurious to happiness, and as great a hindrance to improvement, as many or most of the acts prohibited by law, why (it may be asked) should not law, so far as is consistent with practicability and social convenience, endeavour to repress these also? And as a supplement to the unavoidable imperfections of law, ought not opinion at least to organize a powerful police against these vices, and visit rigidly with social penalties those who are known to practise them? There is no question here (it may be said) about restricting individuality, or impeding the trial of new and original experiments in living. The only things it is sought to prevent are things which have been tried and condemned from the beginning of the world until now; things which experience has shown not to be useful or suitable to any person's individuality. There must be some length of time and amount of experience, after which a moral or prudential truth may be regarded as established: and it is merely desired to prevent generation after generation from falling over the same precipice which has been fatal to their predecessors.

I fully admit that the mischief which a person does to himself may seriously affect, both through their sympathies and their interests, those nearly connected with him, and in a minor degree, society at large. When, by conduct of this sort, a person is led to violate a distinct and assignable obligation to any other person or persons, the case is taken out of the self-regarding class, and becomes amenable to moral disapprobation in the proper sense of the term. If, for example, a man, through intemperance or extravagance, becomes unable to pay his debts, or, having undertaken the moral responsibility of a family, becomes from the same cause incapable of supporting or educating them, he is deservedly reprobated, and might be justly punished; but it is for the breach of duty to his family or creditors, not for the extravagance. If the resources which ought to have been devoted to them, had been diverted from them for the most prudent investment, the moral culpability would have been the same. George Barnwell[15] murdered his uncle to get money for his mistress, but if he had done it to set himself up in business, he would equally have been hanged. Again, in the frequent case of a man who causes grief to his family by addiction to bad habits, he deserves reproach for his unkindness or ingratitude; but so he may for cultivating habits not in themselves vicious, if they are painful to those with whom he passes his life, or who from personal ties are dependent on him for their comfort. Whoever fails in the consideration generally due to the interests and feelings of others, not being compelled by some more imperative duty, or justified by allowable self-preference, is a subject of moral disapprobation for that failure, but not for the cause of it, nor for the errors, merely personal to himself, which may have remotely led to it. In like manner, when a person disables himself, by conduct purely self-regarding, from the performance of some definite duty incumbent on him to the public, he is guilty of a social offence. No person ought to be punished simply for being drunk; but a soldier or a policeman should be punished for being drunk on duty. Whenever, in short, there is a definite damage, or a definite risk of damage, either to an individual or to the public, the case is taken out of the province of liberty, and placed in that of morality or law.

But with regard to the merely contingent, or, as it may be called, constructive injury which a person causes to society, by conduct which neither violates any specific duty to the public, nor occasions perceptible hurt to any assignable individual except himself; the inconvenience is one which society can afford to bear, for the sake of the greater good of human freedom. If grown persons are to be punished for not taking proper care of themselves, I would rather it were for their own sake, than under pretence of preventing them from impairing their capacity of rendering to society benefits which society does not pretend it has a right to exact. But I cannot consent to argue the point as if society had no means of bringing its weaker members up to its ordinary standard of rational conduct, except waiting till they do something irrational, and then punishing them, legally or morally, for it. Society has had absolute power over them during all the early portion of their existence: it has had the whole period of childhood and nonage in which to try whether it could make them capable of rational conduct in life. The existing generation is master both of the training and the entire circumstances of the generation to come; it cannot indeed make them perfectly wise and good, because it is itself so lamentably deficient in goodness and wisdom; and its best efforts are not always, in individual cases, its most successful ones; but it is perfectly well able to make the rising generation, as a whole, as good as, and a little better than, itself. If society lets any considerable number of its members grow up mere children, incapable of being acted on by rational consideration of distant motives, society has itself to blame for the consequences. Armed not only with all the powers of education, but with the ascendancy which the authority of a received opinion always exercises over the minds who are least fitted to judge for themselves; and aided by the *natural* penalties

which cannot be prevented from falling on those who incur the distaste or the contempt of those who know them; let not society pretend that it needs, besides all this, the power to issue commands and enforce obedience in the personal concerns of individuals, in which, on all principles of justice and policy, the decision ought to rest with those who are to abide the consequences. Nor is there anything which tends more to discredit and frustrate the better means of influencing conduct, than a resort to the worse. If there be among those whom it is attempted to coerce into prudence or temperance, any of the material of which vigorous and independent characters are made, they will infallibly rebel against the yoke. No such person will ever feel that others have a right to control him in his concerns, such as they have to prevent him from injuring them in theirs; and it easily, comes to be considered a mark of spirit and courage to fly ill the face of such usurped authority, and do with ostentation the exact opposite of what it enjoins; as in the fashion of grossness which succeeded, in the time of Charles II, to the fanatical moral intolerance of the Puritans. With respect to what is said of the necessity of protecting society from the bad example set to others by the vicious or the self-indulgent; it is true that bad example may have a pernicious effect, especially the example of doing wrong to others with impunity to the wrong-doer. But we are now speaking of conduct which, while it does no wrong to others, is supposed to do great harm to the agent himself: and I do not see how those who believe this, can think otherwise than that the example, on the whole, must be more salutary than hurtful, since, if it displays the misconduct, it displays also the painful or degrading consequences which, if the conduct is justly censured, must be supposed to be in all or most cases attendant on it.

But the strongest of all the arguments against the interference of the public with purely personal conduct, is that when it does interfere, the odds are that it interferes wrongly, and in the wrong place. On questions of social morality, of duty to others, the opinion of the public, that is, of an overruling majority, though often wrong, is likely to be still oftener right; because on such questions they are only required to judge of their own interests; of the manner in which some mode of conduct, if allowed to be practised, would affect themselves. But the opinion of a similar majority, imposed as a law on the minority, on questions of self-regarding conduct, is quite as likely to be wrong as right; for in these cases public opinion means, at the best, some people's opinion of what is good or bad for other people; while very often it does not even mean that; the public; with the most perfect indifference, passing over the pleasure or convenience of those whose conduct they censure, and considering only their own preference. There are many who consider as an injury to themselves any conduct which they have a distaste for, and resent it as an outrage to their feelings; as a religious bigot, when charged with disregarding the religious feelings of others, has been known to retort that they disregard his feelings, by persisting in their abominable worship or creed. But there is no parity between the feeling of a person for his own opinion, and the feeling of another who is offended at his holding it; no more than between the desire of a thief to take a purse, and the desire of the right owner to keep it. And a person's taste is as much his own peculiar concern as his opinion or his purse. It is easy for anyone to imagine an ideal public, which leaves the freedom and choice of individuals in all uncertain matters undisturbed, and only requires them to abstain from modes of conduct which universal experience has condemned. But where has there been seen a public which set any such limit to its censorship? or when does the public trouble itself about universal experience? In its interferences with personal conduct it is seldom drinking of anything but the enormity of acting or feeling differently from itself; and this standard of judgment, thinly disguised, is held up to mankind as the dictate of religion and philosophy, by nine-tenths of all moralists and speculative writers. These teach that things are right because they are right; because we feel them to be so. They tell us to search in our own minds and hearts for laws of conduct binding on ourselves and on all others. What can the poor public do but apply these instructions, and make their own personal feelings of good and evil, if they are tolerably unanimous in them, obligatory on all the world?

. . .

I cannot refrain from adding to these examples of the little account commonly made of human liberty, the language of downright persecution which breaks out from the press of this country, whenever it feels called on to notice the remarkable phenomenon of Mormonism. Much might be said on the unexpected and instructive fact, that an alleged new revelation, and a religion founded on it, the produce of palpable imposture, not even supported by the *prestige* of extraordinary qualities in its founder, is believed by hundreds of thousands, and has been made the foundation of a society, in the age of newspapers, railways, and the electric telegraph. What here concerns us is, that this religion, like other and better religions, has its martyrs; that its prophet and founder was, for his teaching, put to death by a mob; that others of its adherents lost their lives by the same lawless violence; that they were forcibly expelled, in a body, from the country in which they first grew up; while, now that

they have been chased into a solitary recess in the midst of a desert, many in this country openly declare that it would be right (only that it is not convenient) to send an expedition against them, and compel them by force to conform to the opinions of other people. The article of the Mormonite doctrine which is the chief provocative to the antipathy which thus breaks through the ordinary restraints of religious tolerance, is its sanction of polygamy; which, though permitted to Mohammedans, and Hindoos, and Chinese, seems to excite unquenchable animosity when practised by persons who speak English, and profess to be a kind of Christians. No one has a deeper disapprobation than I have of this Mormon institution; both for other reasons, and because, far from being in any way countenanced by the principle of liberty, it is a direct infraction of that principle, being a mere riveting of the chains of one-half of the community, and an emancipation of the other from reciprocity of obligation towards them. Still, it must be remembered that this relation is as much voluntary on the part of the women concerned in it, and who may be deemed the sufferers by it, as is the case with any other form of the marriage institution; and however surprising this fact may appear, it has its explanation in the common ideas and customs of the world, which teaching women to think marriage the one thing needful, make it intelligible that many a woman should prefer being one of several wives, to not being a wife at all. Other countries are not asked to recognize such unions, or release any portion of their inhabitants from their own laws on the score of Mormonite opinions. But when the dissentients have conceded to the hostile sentiments of others, far more than could justly be demanded; when they have left the countries to which their doctrines were unacceptable, and established themselves in a remote corner of the earth, which they have been the first to render habitable to human beings; it is difficult to see on what principles but those of tyranny they can be prevented from living there under what laws they please, provided they commit no aggression on other nations, and allow perfect freedom of departure to those who are dissatisfied with their ways. A recent writer, in some respects of considerable merit, proposes (to use his own words) not a crusade, but a *civilizade*, against this polygamous community, to put an end to what seems to him a retrograde step in civilization. It also appears so to me, but I am not aware that any community has a right to force another to be civilized. So long as the sufferers by the bad law do not invoke assistance from other communities, I cannot admit that persons entirely unconnected with them ought to step in and require that a condition of things with which all who are directly interested appear to be satisfied, should be put an end to because it is a scandal to persons some thousands of miles distant, who have no part or concern in it. Let them send missionaries, if they please, to preach against it; and let them, by any fair means (of which silencing the teachers is not one), oppose the progress of similar doctrines among their own people. If civilization has got the better of barbarism when barbarism had the world to itself, it is too much to profess to be afraid lest barbarism, after having been fairly got under, should revive and conquer civilization. A civilization that can thus succumb to its vanquished enemy, must first have become so degenerate, that neither its appointed priests and teachers, nor anybody else, has the capacity, or will take the trouble, to stand up for it. If this be so, the sooner such a civilization receives notice to quit, the better. It can only go from bad to worse, until destroyed and regenerated (like the Western Empire) by energetic barbarians.

Chapter V Applications

The principles asserted in these pages must be more generally admitted as the basis for discussion of details, before a consistent application of them to all the various departments of government and morals can be attempted with any prospect of advantage. The few observations I propose to make on questions of detail, are designed to illustrate the principles, rather than to follow them out to their consequences. I offer, not so much applications, as specimens of application; which may serve to bring into greater clearness the meaning and limit of the two maxims which together form the entire doctrine of this essay, and to assist the judgment in holding the balance between them, in the cases where it appears doubtful which of them is applicable to the case.

The maxims are, first, that the individual is not accountable to society for his actions, in so far as these concern the interests of no person but himself. Advice, instruction, persuasion, and avoidance by other people if thought necessary by them for their own good, are the only measures by which society can justifiably express its dislike or disapprobation of his conduct. Secondly, that for such actions as are prejudicial to the interests of others, the individual is accountable, and may be subjected either to social or to legal punishment, if society is of opinion that the one or the other is requisite for its protection.

In the first place, it must by no means be supposed, because damage, or probability of damage, to the interests of others, can alone justify the interference of society, that therefore it always does justify such interference. In many cases, an individual, in pursuing a legitimate object, necessarily and therefore legitimately causes pain

or loss to others, or intercepts a good which they had a reasonable hope of obtaining. Such oppositions of interest between individuals often arise from bad social institutions, but are unavoidable while those institutions last; and some would be unavoidable under any institutions. Whoever succeeds in an overcrowded profession, or in a competitive examination; whoever is preferred to another in any contest for an object which both desire, reaps benefit from the loss of others, from their wasted exertion and their disappointment. But it is, by common admission, better for the general interest of mankind, that persons should pursue their objects undeterred by this sort of consequences. In other words, society admits no right, either legal or moral, in the disappointed competitors, to immunity from this kind of suffering; and feels called on to interfere, only when means of success have been employed which it is contrary to the general interest to permit—namely, fraud or treachery, and force.

Again, trade is a social act. Whoever undertakes to sell any description of goods to the public, does what affects the interest of other persons, and of society in general; and thus his conduct, in principle, comes within the jurisdiction of society: accordingly, it was once held to be the duty of governments, in all cases which were considered of importance, to fix prices, and regulate the processes of manufacture. But it is now recognized, though not till after a long struggle, that both the cheapness and the good quality of commodities are most effectually provided for by leaving the producers and sellers perfectly free, under the sole check of equal freedom to the buyers for supplying themselves elsewhere. This is the so-called doctrine of free trade,[16] which rests on grounds different from, though equally solid with, the principle of individual liberty asserted in this essay. Restrictions on trade, or on production for purposes of trade, are indeed restraints; and all restraint, *qua* restraint, is an evil: but the restraints in question affect only that part of conduct which society is competent to restrain, and are wrong solely because they do not really produce the results which it is desired to produce by them. As the principle of individual liberty is not involved in the doctrine of free trade, so neither is it in most of the questions which arise respecting the limits of that doctrine; as for example, what amount of public control is admissible for the prevention of fraud by adulteration; how far sanitary precautions, or arrangements to protect workpeople employed in dangerous occupations, should be enforced on employers. Such questions involve considerations of liberty, only in so far as leaving people to themselves is always better, *caeteris paribus*, than controlling them: but that they may be legitimately controlled for these ends, is in principle undeniable. On the other hand, there are questions of liberty; such as the Maine Law . . . ; the prohibition of the importation of opium into China; the restriction of the sale of poisons; all cases, in short, where the object of the interference is to make it impossible or difficult to obtain a particular commodity. These interferences are objectionable, not as infringements on the liberty of the producer or seller, but on that of the buyer.

. . .

A further question is, whether the state, while it permits, should nevertheless indirectly discourage conduct which it deems contrary to the best interests of the agent; whether, for example, it should take measures to render the means of drunkenness more costly, or add to the difficulty of procuring them by limiting the number of the places of sale. On this as on most other practical questions, many distinctions require to be made. To tax stimulants for the sole purpose of making them more difficult to be obtained, is a measure differing only in degree from their entire prohibition; and would be justifiable only if that were justifiable. Every increase of cost is a prohibition, to those whose means do not come up to the augmented price; and to those who do, it is a penalty laid on them for gratifying a particular taste. Their choice of pleasures, and their mode of expending their income, after satisfying their legal and moral obligations to the state and to individuals, are their own concern, and must rest with their own judgment. These considerations may seem at first sight to condemn the selection of stimulants as special subjects of taxation for purposes of revenue. But it must be remembered that taxation for fiscal purposes is absolutely inevitable; that in most countries it is necessary that a considerable part of that taxation should be indirect; that the state, therefore, cannot help imposing penalties, which to some persons may be prohibitory, on the use of some articles of consumption. It is hence the duty of the state to consider, in the imposition of taxes, what commodities the consumers can best spare; and *a fortiori*, to select in preference those of which it deems the use, beyond a very moderate quantity, to be positively injurious. Taxation, therefore, of stimulants, up to the point which produces the largest amount of revenue (supposing that the state needs all the revenue which it yields) is not only admissible, but to be approved of.

The question of making the sale of these commodities a more or less exclusive privilege, must be answered differently, according to the purposes to which the restriction is intended to be subservient. All places of public resort require the restraint of a police, and places of this kind peculiarly, because offences against society are especially apt to originate there. It is, therefore, fit to confine the power of selling these commodities (at least for consumption on the spot) to persons of known or vouched-for respectability of conduct; to make such regulations respecting hours of opening and closing as may be requisite for public surveillance, and to withdraw the licence if breaches of the peace repeatedly take place through the connivance or incapacity of the keeper of the house, or if it becomes a rendezvous for concocting and preparing offences against the law. Any further restriction I do not conceive to be, in principle, justifiable. The limitation in number, for instance, of beer and spirit houses, for the express purpose of rendering them more difficult of access, and diminishing the occasions of temptation, not only exposes all to an inconvenience because there are some by whom the facility would be abused, but is suited only to a state of society in which the labouring classes are avowedly treated as children or savages, and placed under an education of restraint, to fit them for future admission to the privileges of freedom. This is not the principle on which the labouring classes are professedly governed in any free country; and no person who sets due value on freedom will give his adhesion to their being so governed, unless after all efforts have been exhausted to educate them for freedom and govern them as freemen, and it has been definitively proved that they can only be governed as children. The bare statement of the alternative shows the absurdity of supposing that such efforts have been made in any case which needs be considered here. It is only because the institutions of this country are a mass of inconsistencies, that things find admittance into our practice which belong to the system of despotic, or what is called paternal, government, while the general freedom of our institutions precludes the exercise of the amount of control necessary to render the restraint of any real efficacy as a moral education.

It was pointed out in an early part of this essay, that the liberty of the individual, in things wherein the individual is alone concerned, implies a corresponding liberty in any number of individuals to regulate by mutual agreement such things as regard them jointly, and regard no persons but themselves. This question presents no difficulty, so long as the will of all the persons implicated remains unaltered; but since that will may change, it is often necessary, even in things in which they alone are concerned, that they should enter into engagements with one another; and when they do, it is fit, as a general rule, that those engagements should be kept. Yet, in the laws, probably, of every country, this general rule has some exceptions. Not only persons are not held to engagements which violate the rights of third parties, but it is sometimes considered a sufficient reason for releasing them from an engagement, that it is injurious to themselves. In this and most other civilized countries, for example, an engagement by which a person should sell himself, or allow himself to be sold, as a slave, would be null and void; neither enforced by law nor by opinion. The ground for thus limiting his power of voluntarily disposing of his own lot in life, is apparent, and is very clearly seen in this extreme case. The reason for not interfering, unless for the sake of others, with a person's voluntary acts, is consideration for his liberty. His voluntary choice is evidence that what he so chooses is desirable, or at the least endurable, to him, and his good is on the whole best provided for by allowing him to take his own means of pursuing it. But by selling himself for a slave, he abdicates his liberty; he forgoes any future use of it beyond that single act. He therefore defeats, in his own case, the very purpose which is the justification of allowing him to dispose of himself. He is no longer free; but is thenceforth in a position which has no longer the presumption in its favour, that would be afforded by his voluntarily remaining in it. The principle of freedom cannot require that he should be free not to be free. It is not freedom, to be allowed to alienate his freedom.[17] These reasons, the force of which is so conspicuous in this peculiar case, are evidently of far wider application; yet a limit is everywhere set to them by the necessities of life, which continually require, not indeed that we should resign our freedom, but that we should consent to this and the other limitation of it. The principle, however, which demands uncontrolled freedom of action in all that concerns only the agents themselves, requires that those who have become bound to one another, in things which concern no third party, should be able to release one another from the engagement: and even without such voluntary release, there are perhaps no contracts or engagements, except those that relate to money or money's worth, of which one can venture to say that there ought to be no liberty whatever of retractation. Baron Wilhelm von Humboldt, in the excellent essay from which I have already quoted, states it as his conviction, that engagements which involve personal relations or services, should never be legally binding beyond a limited duration of time; and that the most important of these engagements, marriage, having the peculiarity that its objects are frustrated unless the feelings of both the parties are in harmony with it, should require nothing more than the declared will of either party to dissolve it. This subject is too important, and too complicated, to be discussed in a parenthesis, and I touch on it only so far as is necessary for purposes of illustration. If the conciseness and generality of Baron Humboldt's dissertation had not obliged him in this instance to content himself with enunciating his conclusion without discussing the premises, he would doubtless have recognized that the question cannot be decided on grounds so simple as those to which he confines himself. When a person, either by express promise or by conduct, has encouraged another to rely upon his continuing to act in a certain way—to build expectations and calculations, and stake any part of his plan of life upon that supposition—a new series of moral obligations arises on his part towards that person, which may possibly be overruled, but cannot be ignored. And again, if the relation between two contracting parties has been followed by consequences to others; if it has placed third parties in any peculiar position, or, as in the case of marriage, has even called third parties into existence, obligations arise on the part of both the contracting parties towards those third persons, the fulfilment of which, or at all events the mode of fulfilment, must be greatly affected by the continuance or disruption of the relation between the original parties to the contract. It does not follow, nor can I admit, that these obligations extend to requiring the fulfilment of the contract at all costs to the happiness of the reluctant party; but they are a necessary element in the question; and even if, as von Humboldt maintains, they ought to make no difference in the *legal* freedom of the parties to release themselves from the engagement (and I also hold that they ought not to make much difference), they necessarily make a great difference in the *moral* freedom. A person is bound to take all these circumstances into account, before resolving on a step which may affect such important interests of others; and if he does not allow proper weight to those interests, he is morally responsible for the wrong. I have made these obvious remarks for the better illustration of the general principle of liberty, and not because they are at all needed on the particular question, which, on the contrary, is usually discussed as if the interest of children was everything, and that of grown persons nothing.

. . .

The objections to government interference, when it is not such as to involve infringement of liberty, may be of three kinds.

The first is, when the thing to be done is likely to be better done by individuals than by the government. Speaking generally, there is no one so fit to conduct any business, or to determine how or by whom it shall be conducted, as those who are personally interested in it. This principle condemns the interferences, once so common, of the legislature, or the officers of government, with the ordinary processes of industry. But this part of the subject has been sufficiently enlarged upon by political economists, and is not particularly related to the principles of this essay.

The second objection is more nearly allied to our subject. In many cases, though individuals may not do the particular thing so well, on the average, as the officers of government, it is nevertheless desirable that it should be done by them, rather than by the government, as a means to their own mental education—a mode of strengthening their active faculties, exercising their judgment, and giving them a familiar knowledge of the subjects with which they are thus left to deal. This is a principal, though not the sole, recommendation of jury trial (in cases not political); of free and popular local and municipal institutions; of the conduct of industrial and philanthropic enterprises by voluntary associations. These are not questions of liberty, and are connected with that subject only by remote tendencies; but they are questions of development. It belongs to a different occasion from the present to dwell on these things as parts of national education; as being, in truth, the peculiar training of a citizen, the practical part of the political education of a free people, taking them out of the narrow circle of personal and family selfishness, and accustoming them to the comprehension of joint interests, the management of joint concerns—habituating them to act from public or semipublic motives, and guide their conduct by aims which unite instead of isolating them from one another. Without these habits and powers, a free constitution can neither be worked nor preserved; as is exemplified by the too-often transitory nature of political freedom in countries where it does not rest upon a sufficient basis of local liberties. The management of purely local business by the localities, and of the great enterprises of industry by the union of those who voluntarily supply the pecuniary means, is further recommended by all the advantages which have been set forth in this essay as belonging to individuality of development, and diversity of modes of action. Government operations tend to be everywhere alike. With individuals and voluntary associations, on the contrary, there are varied experiments, and endless diversity of experience. What the state can usefully do, is to make itself a central depository, and active circulator and diffuser, of the experience resulting from many trials. Its business is to enable each experimentalist to benefit by the experiments of others; instead of tolerating no experiments but its own.

The third, and most cogent reason for restricting the interference of government, is the great evil of adding unnecessarily to its power. Every function superadded to those already exercised by the government, causes its influence over hopes and fears to be more widely diffused, and converts, more and more, the active and ambitious part of the public into hangers-on of the government, or of some party which aims at becoming the government.

If the roads, the railways, the banks, the insurance offices, the great joint-stock companies, the universities, and the public charities, were all of them branches of the government; if, in addition, the municipal corporations and local boards, with all that now devolves on them, became departments of the central administration; if the employees of all these different enterprises were appointed and paid by the government, and looked to the government for every rise in life; not all the freedom of the press and popular constitution of the legislature would make this or any other country free otherwise than in name. And the evil would be greater, the more efficiently and scientifically the administrative machinery was constructed—the more skilful the arrangements for obtaining the best qualified hands and heads with which to work it. In England it has of late been proposed that all the members of the civil service of government should be selected by competitive examination, to obtain for those employments the most intelligent and instructed persons procurable; and much has been said and written for and against this proposal. One of the arguments most insisted on by its opponents, is that the occupation of a permanent official servant of the state does not hold out sufficient prospects of emolument and importance to attract the highest talents, which will always be able to find a more inviting career in the professions, or in the service of companies and other public bodies. One would not have been surprised if this argument had been used by the friends of the proposition, as an answer to its principal difficulty. Coming from the opponents it is strange enough. What is urged as an objection is the safety valve of the proposed system. If indeed all the high talent of the country *could* be drawn into the service of the government, a proposal tending to bring about that result might well inspire uneasiness. If every part of the business of society which required organized concert, or large and comprehensive views, were in the hands of the government, and if government offices were universally filled by the ablest men, all the enlarged culture and practised intelligence in the country, except the purely speculative, would be concentrated in a numerous bureaucracy, to whom alone the rest of the community would look for all things: the multitude for direction and dictation in all they had to do; the able and aspiring for personal advancement. To be admitted into the ranks of this bureaucracy, and when admitted, to rise therein, would be the sole objects of ambition. Under this regime, not only is the outside public ill-qualified, for want of practical experience, to criticize or check the mode of operation of the bureaucracy, but even if the accidents of despotic or the natural working of popular institutions occasionally raise to the summit a ruler or rulers of reforming inclinations, no reform can be effected which is contrary to the interest of the bureaucracy. Such is the melancholy condition of the Russian empire, as shown in the accounts of those who have had sufficient opportunity of observation. The czar himself is powerless against the bureaucratic body; he can send any one of them to Siberia, but he cannot govern without them, or against their will.[18] On every decree of his they have a tacit veto, by merely refraining from carrying it into effect. In countries of more advance civilization and of a more insurrectionary spirit, the public, accustomed to expect everything to be done for them by the state, or at least to do nothing for themselves without asking from the state not only leave to do it, but even how it is to be done, naturally hold the state responsible for all evil which befalls them, and when the evil exceeds their amount of patience, they rise against the government an make what is called a revolution; whereupon somebody else, with or without legitimate authority from the nation, vaults into the seat, issues his orders to the bureaucracy, and everything goes on much as it did before; the bureaucracy being unchanged, and nobody else being capable of taking their place.

. . .

John Stuart Mill, *From* "Utilitarianism"

John Stuart Mill, "Utilitarianism," in On Liberty and Other Essays, *edited by John Gray (Oxford: Oxford University Press, 2008).*

Chapter II What Utilitarianism Is

A passing remark is all that needs be given to the ignorant blunder of supposing that those who stand up for utility as the test of right and wrong, use the term in that restricted and merely colloquial sense in which utility is opposed to pleasure. An apology is due to the philosophical opponents of utilitarianism, for even the momentary appearance of confounding them with anyone capable of so absurd a misconception; which is the more extraordinary, inasmuch as the contrary accusation, of referring everything to pleasure, and that too in its grossest form, is another of the common charges against utilitarianism: and, as has been pointedly remarked by an able writer, the same sort of persons, and often the very same persons, denounce the theory "as impracticably dry when the word utility precedes the word pleasure, and as too practicably voluptuous when the word pleasure precedes the word utility." Those who know anything about the matter are aware that every writer, from Epicurus[19] to Bentham, who maintained the theory of utility, meant by it, not something to be contradistinguished from pleasure, but pleasure itself, together with exemption from pain; and instead of opposing the useful to the agreeable or the ornamental, have always declared that the useful means these, among other things. Yet the common herd, including the herd of writers, not only in newspapers and periodicals, but in books of weight and pretension, are perpetually falling into this shallow mistake. Having caught up the word utilitarian, while knowing nothing whatever about it but its sound, they habitually express by it the rejection, or the neglect, of pleasure in some of its forms; of beauty, or ornament, or of amusement. Nor is the term thus ignorantly misapplied solely in disparagement, but occasionally in compliment; as though it implied superiority to frivolity and the mere pleasures of the moment. And this perverted use is the only one in which the word is popularly known, and the one from which the new generation are acquiring their sole notion of its meaning. Those who introduced the word, but who had for many years discontinued it as a distinctive appellation may well feel themselves called upon to resume it, if by doing so they can hope to contribute anything towards rescuing it from this utter degradation.[20]

The creed which accepts as the foundation of morals—utility, or the greatest happiness principle—holds that actions are right in proportion as they tend to promote happiness, wrong as they tend to produce the reverse of happiness. By happiness is intended pleasure, and the absence of pain; by unhappiness, pain, and the privation of pleasure. To give a clear view of the moral standard set up by the theory, much more requires to be said; in particular what things it includes in the ideas of pain and pleasure; and to what extent this is left an open question. But these supplementary explanations do not affect the theory of life on which this theory of morality is grounded—namely, that pleasure, and freedom from pain, are the only things desirable as ends; and that all desirable things (which are as numerous in the utilitarian as in any other scheme) are desirable either for the pleasure inherent in themselves, or as means to the promotion of pleasure and the prevention of pain.

Now, such a theory of life excites in many minds, and among them in some of the most estimable in feeling the purpose, inveterate dislike. To suppose that life has (as they express it) no higher end than pleasure—no better and nobler object of desire and pursuit—they designate as utterly mean and grovelling; as a doctrine worthy only of swine, to whom the followers of Epicurus were, at a very early period, contemptuously likened; and modern holders of the doctrine are occasionally made the subject of equally polite comparisons by its German, French, and English assailants.

When thus attacked, the Epicureans have always answered, that it is not they, but their accusers, who represent human nature in a degrading light; since the accusation supposes human beings to be capable of no pleasures except those of which swine are capable. If this supposition were true, the charge could not be gainsaid, but would then be no longer an imputation; for if the sources of pleasure were precisely the same to human beings and to swine, the rule of life which is good enough for the one would be good enough for the other. The comparison of the Epicurean life to that of beasts is felt as degrading, precisely because a beast's pleasures do not satisfy a human being's conceptions of happiness. Human beings have faculties more elevated than the animal appetites, and when once made conscious of them, do not regard anything as happiness which does not include their gratification. I do not, indeed, consider the Epicureans to have been by any means faultless in drawing out their scheme of consequences from the utilitarian principle. To do this in any sufficient manner, many Stoic as well as Christian elements require to be included. But there is no known Epicurean theory of life which does not assign to the pleasures of the intellect, of the feelings and imagination, and of the moral sentiments, a much higher value as pleasures than to those of mere sensation. It must be admitted, however, that utilitarian writers in general have placed the superiority of mental over bodily pleasures chiefly in the greater permanency, safety, uncostliness, etc., of the former—that is, in their circumstantial advantages rather than in their intrinsic nature. And on all these points utilitarians have fully proved their case; but they might have taken the other, and, as it may be called, higher ground,

with entire consistency. It is quite compatible with the principle of utility to recognize the fact, that some *kinds* of pleasure are more desirable and more valuable than others. It would be absurd that while, in estimating all other things, quality is considered as well as quantity, the estimation of pleasures should be supposed to depend on quantity alone.

If I am asked, what I mean by difference of quality in pleasures, or what makes one pleasure more valuable than another, merely as a pleasure, except its being greater in amount, there is but one possible answer. Of two pleasures, if there be one to which all or almost all who have experience of both give a decided preference, irrespective of any feeling of moral obligation to prefer it, that is the more desirable pleasure. If one of the two is, by those who are competently acquainted with both, placed so far above the other that they prefer it, even though knowing it to be attended with a greater amount of discontent, and would not resign it for any quantity of the other pleasure which their nature is capable at; we are justified in ascribing to the preferred enjoyment a superiority in quality, so far outweighing quantity as to render it, in comparison, of small account.

Now it is an unquestionable fact that those who are equally acquainted with, and equally capable of appreciating and enjoying, both, do give a most marked preference to the manner of existence which employs their higher faculties. Few human creatures would consent to be changed into any of the lower animals, for a promise of the fullest allowance of a beast's pleasures; no intelligent human being would consent to be a fool, no instructed person would be an ignoramus, no person of feeling and conscience would be selfish and base, even though they should be persuaded that the fool, the dunce, or the rascal is better satisfied with his lot than they are with theirs. They would not resign what they possess more than he, for the most complete satisfaction of all the desires which they have in common with him. If they ever fancy they would, it is only in cases of unhappiness so extreme, that to escape from it they would exchange their lot for almost any other, however undesirable in their own eyes. A being of higher faculties requires more to make him happy, is capable probably of more acute suffering, and is certainly accessible to it at more points, than one of an inferior type; but in spite of these liabilities, he can never really wish to sink into what he feels to be a lower grade of existence. We may give what explanation we please of this unwillingness; we may attribute it to pride, a name which is given indiscriminately to some of the most and to some of the least estimable feelings of which mankind are capable; we may refer it to the love of liberty and personal independence, an appeal to which was with the Stoics one of the most effective means for the inculcation of it; to the love of power, or to the love of excitement, both of which do really enter into and contribute to it: but its most appropriate appellation is a sense of dignity, which all human beings possess in one form or other, and in some, though by no means in exact, proportion to their higher faculties, and which is so essential a part of the happiness of those in whom it is strong, that nothing which conflicts with it could be, otherwise than momentarily, an object of desire to them. Whoever supposes that this preference takes place at a sacrifice of happiness—that the superior being, in anything like equal circumstances, is not happier than the inferior—confounds the two very different ideas, of happiness, and content. It is indisputable that the being whose capacities of enjoyment are low, has the greatest chance of having them fully satisfied; and a highly endowed being will always feel that any happiness which he can look for, as the world is constituted, is imperfect. But he can learn to bear its imperfections, if they are at all bearable; and they will not make him envy the being who is indeed unconscious of the imperfections, but only because he feels not at all the good which those imperfections qualify. It is better to be a human being dissatisfied than a pig satisfied; better to be Socrates dissatisfied than a fool satisfied.[21] And if the fool, or the pig, is of a different opinion, it is because they only know their own side of the question. The other party to the comparison knows both sides.

It may be objected that many who are capable of the higher pleasures, occasionally, under the influence of temptation, postpone them to the lower. But this is quite compatible with a full appreciation of the intrinsic superiority of the higher. Men often, from infirmity of character, make their election for the nearer good, though they know it to be the less valuable; and this no less when the choice is between two bodily pleasures, than when it is between bodily and mental. They pursue sensual indulgences to the injury of health, though perfectly aware that health is the greater good. It may be further objected, that many who begin with youthful enthusiasm for everything noble, as they advance in years sink into indolence and selfishness. But I do not believe that those who undergo this very common change, voluntarily choose the lower description of pleasures in preference to the higher. I believe that before they devote themselves exclusively to the one, they have already become incapable of the other. Capacity for the nobler feelings is in most natures a very tender plant, easily killed, not only by hostile influences, but by mere want of sustenance; and in the majority of young persons it speedily dies away if the occupations to which their

position in life has devoted them, and the society into which it has thrown them, are not favourable to keeping that higher capacity in exercise. Men lose their high aspirations as they lose their intellectual tastes, because they have not time or opportunity for indulging them; and they addict themselves to inferior pleasures, not because they deliberately prefer them, but because they are either the only ones to which they have access, or the only ones which they are any longer capable of enjoying. It may be questioned whether anyone who has remained equally susceptible to both classes of pleasures, ever knowingly and calmly preferred the lower; though many, in all ages, have broken down in an ineffectual attempt to combine both.

From this verdict of the only competent judges, I apprehend there can be no appeal. On a question which is the best worth having of two pleasures, or which of two modes of existence is the most grateful to the feelings, apart from its moral attributes and from its consequences, the judgment of those who are qualified by knowledge of both, or, if they differ, that of the majority among them, must be admitted as final. And there needs be the less hesitation to accept this judgment respecting the quality of pleasures, since there is no other tribunal to be referred to even on the question of quantity. What means are there of determining which is the acutest of two pains, or the intensest of two pleasurable sensations, except the general suffrage of those who are familiar with both? Neither pains nor pleasures are homogeneous, and pain is always heterogeneous with pleasure. What is there to decide whether a particular pleasure is worth purchasing at the cost of a particular pain, except the feelings and judgment of the experienced? When, therefore, those feelings and judgment declare the pleasures derived from the higher faculties to be preferable *in kind*, apart from the question of intensity, to those of which the animal nature, disjoined from the higher faculties, is susceptible, they are entitled on this subject to the same regard.

I have dwelt on this point, as being a necessary part of a perfectly just conception of utility or happiness, considered as the directive rule of human conduct. But it is by no means an indispensable condition to the acceptance of the utilitarian standard; for that standard is not the agent's own greatest happiness, but the greatest amount of happiness altogether; and if it may possibly be doubted whether a noble character is always the happier for its nobleness, there can be no doubt that it makes other people happier, and that the world in general is immensely a gainer by it. Utilitarianism, therefore, could only attain its end by the general cultivation of nobleness of character, even if each individual were only benefited by the nobleness of others, and his own, so far as happiness is concerned, were a sheer deduction from the benefit. But the bare enunciation of such an absurdity as this last, renders refutation superfluous.

According to the greatest happiness principle, as above explained, the ultimate end, with reference to and for the sake of which all other things are desirable (whether we are considering our own good or that of other people), is an existence exempt as far as possible from pain, and as rich as possible in enjoyments, both in point of quantity and quality; the test of quality, and the rule for measuring it against quantity, being the preference felt by those who, in their opportunities of experience, to which must be added their habits of self-consciousness and self-observation, are best furnished with the means of comparison. This, being, according to the utilitarian opinion, the end of human action, is necessarily also the standard of morality; which may accordingly be defined, the rules and precepts for human conduct, by the observance of which an existence such as has been described might be, to the greatest extent possible, secured to all mankind; and not to them only, but, so far as the nature of things admits, to the whole sentient creation.

Against this doctrine, however, arises another class of objectors, who say that happiness, in any form, cannot be the rational purpose of human life and action; because, in the first place, it is unattainable: and they contemptuously ask, What right hast thou to be happy? A question which Mr Carlyle clenches by the addition, What right, a short time ago, hadst thou even *to be*?[22] Next, they say, that men can do *without* happiness; that all noble human beings have felt this, and could not have become noble but by learning the lesson of *Entsagen*, or renunciation; which lesson, thoroughly learnt and submitted to, they affirm to be the beginning and necessary condition of all virtue.

The first of these objections would go to the root of the matter were it well founded; for if no happiness is to be had at all by human beings, the attainment of it cannot be the end of morality, or of any rational conduct. Though, even in that case, something might still be said for the utilitarian theory; since utility includes not solely the pursuit of happiness, but the prevention or mitigation of unhappiness; and if the former aim be chimerical, there will be all the greater scope and more imperative need for the latter, so long at least as mankind think fit to live, and do not take refuge in the simultaneous act of suicide recommended under certain conditions by Novalis.[23] When, however, it is thus positively asserted to be impossible that human life should be happy, the assertion, if not something like a verbal quibble, is at least an exaggeration. If by happiness be meant a continuity

of highly pleasurable excitement, it is evident enough that this is impossible. A state of exalted pleasure lasts only moments, or in some cases, and with some intermissions, hours or days, and is the occasional brilliant flash of enjoyment, not its permanent and steady flame. Of this the philosophers who have taught that happiness is the end of life were as fully aware as those who taunt them. The happiness which they meant was not a life of rapture; but moments of such, in an existence made up of few and transitory pains, many and various pleasures, with a decided predominance of the active over the passive, and having as the foundation of the whole, not to expect more from life than it is capable of bestowing. A life thus composed, to those who have been fortunate enough to obtain it, has always appeared worthy of the name of happiness. And such an existence is even now the lot of many, during some considerable portion of their lives. The present wretched education, and wretched social arrangements, are the only real hindrance to its being attainable by almost all.

The objectors perhaps may doubt whether human beings, if taught to consider happiness as the end of life, would be satisfied with such a moderate share of it. But great numbers of mankind have been satisfied with much less. The main constituents of a satisfied life appear to be two, either of which by itself is often found sufficient for the purpose: tranquility, and excitement. With much tranquility, many find that they can be content with very little pleasure: with much excitement, many can reconcile themselves to a considerable quantity of pain. There is assuredly no inherent impossibility in enabling even the mass of mankind to unite both; since the two are so far from being incompatible that they are in natural alliance, the prolongation of either being a preparation for, and exciting a wish for, the other. It is only those in whom indolence amounts to a vice, that do not desire excitement after an interval of repose; it is only those in whom the need of excitement is a disease, that feel the tranquility which follows excitement dull and insipid, instead of pleasurable in direct proportion to the excitement which preceded it. When people who are tolerably fortunate in their outward lot do not find in life sufficient enjoyment to make it valuable to them, the cause generally is caring for nobody but themselves. To those who have neither public nor private affections, the excitements of life are much curtailed, and in any case dwindle in value as the time approaches when all selfish interests must be terminated by death: while those who leave after them objects of personal affection, and especially those who have also cultivated a fellow feeling with the collective interests of mankind, retain as lively an interest in life on the eve of death as in the vigour of youth and health. Next to selfishness, the principal cause which makes life unsatisfactory, is want of mental cultivation. A cultivated mind—I do not mean that of a philosopher, but any mind to which the fountains of knowledge have been opened, and which has been taught, in any tolerable degree, to exercise its faculties—finds sources of inexhaustible interest in all that surrounds it; in the objects of nature, the achievements of art, the imaginations of poetry, the incidents of history, the ways of mankind past and present, and their prospects in the future. It is possible, indeed, to become indifferent to all this, and that too without having exhausted a thousandth part of it; but only when one has had from the beginning no moral or human interest in these things, and has sought in them only the gratification of curiosity.

Now there is absolutely no reason in the nature of things why an amount of mental culture sufficient to give an intelligent interest in these objects of contemplation, should not be the inheritance of every one born in a civilized country. As little is there an inherent necessity that any human being could be a selfish egotist, devoid of every feeling or care but those which centre in his own miserable individuality. Something far superior to this is sufficiently common even now, to give ample earnest of what the human species may be made. Genuine private affections, and a sincere interest in the public good, are possible, though in unequal degrees, to every rightly brought-up human being. In a world in which there is so much to interest, so much to enjoy, and so much also to correct and improve, every one who has this moderate amount of moral and intellectual requisites is capable of an existence which may be called enviable; and unless such a person, through bad laws, or subjection to the will of others, is denied the liberty to use the sources of happiness within his reach, he will not fail to find this enviable existence, if he escape the positive evils of life, the great sources of physical and mental suffering—such as indigence, disease, and the unkindness, worthlessness or premature loss of objects of affection. The main stress of the problem lies, therefore, in the contest with these calamities, from which it is a rare good fortune entirely to escape; which, as things now are, cannot be obviated, and often cannot be in any material degree mitigated. Yet no one whose opinion deserves a moment's consideration can doubt that most of the great positive evils of the world are in themselves removable, and will, if human affairs continue to improve, be in the end reduced within narrow limits.[24] Poverty, in any sense implying suffering, may be completely extinguished by the wisdom of society, combined with the good sense and providence of individuals. Even that most intractable of enemies, disease, may be indefinitely reduced in

dimensions by good physical and moral education, and proper control of noxious influences; while the progress of science holds out a promise for the future of still more direct conquests over this detestable foe. And every advance in that direction relieves us from some, not only of the chances which cut short our own lives, but, what concerns us still more, which deprive us of those in whom our happiness is wrapped up. As for vicissitudes of fortune, and other disappointments connected with worldly circumstances, these are principally the effect either of gross imprudence, of ill-regulated desires, or of bad or imperfect social institutions. All the grand sources, in short, of human suffering are in a great degree, many of them almost entirely, conquerable by human care and effort; and though their removal is grievously slow—though a long succession of generations will perish in the breach before the conquest is completed, and this world becomes all that, if will and knowledge were not wanting, it might easily be made—yet every mind sufficiently intelligent and generous to bear a part, however small and inconspicuous, in the endeavour, will draw a noble enjoyment from the contest itself, which he would not for any bribe in the form of selfish indulgence consent to be without.

And this leads to the true estimation of what is said by the objectors concerning the possibility, and the obligation, of learning to do without happiness. Unquestionably it is possible to do without happiness; it is done involuntarily by nineteen twentieths of mankind, even in those parts of our present world which are least deep in barbarism; and it often has to be done voluntarily by the hero or the martyr, for the sake of something which he prizes more than his individual happiness. But this something, what is it, unless the happiness of others, or some of the requisites of happiness? It is noble to be capable of resigning entirely one's own portion of happiness, or chances of it: but, after all, this self-sacrifice must be for some end; it is not its own end; and if we are told that its end is not happiness, but virtue, which is better than happiness, I ask, would the sacrifice be made if the hero or martyr did not believe that it would earn for others immunity from similar sacrifices? Would it be made, if he thought that his renunciation of happiness for himself would produce no fruit for any of his fellow creatures, but to make their lot like his, and place them also in the condition of persons who have renounced happiness? All honour to those who can abnegate for themselves the personal enjoyment of life, when by such renunciation they contribute worthily to increase the amount of happiness in the world; but he who does it, or professes to do it, for any other purpose, is no more deserving of admiration than the ascetic mounted on his pillar. He may be an inspiriting proof of what men *can* do, but assuredly not an example of what they *should*.

Though it is only in a very imperfect state of the world's arrangements that anyone can best serve the happiness of others by the absolute sacrifice of his own, yet so long as the world is in that imperfect state, I fully acknowledge that the readiness to make such a sacrifice is the highest virtue which can be found in man. I will add, that in this condition of the world, paradoxical as the assertion may be, the conscious ability to do without happiness gives the best prospect of realizing such happiness as is attainable. For nothing except that consciousness can raise a person above the chances of life, by making him feel that, let fate and fortune do their worst, they have not power to subdue him: which, once felt, frees him from excess of anxiety concerning the evils of life, and enables him, like many a Stoic in the worst times of the Roman Empire, to cultivate in tranquillity the sources of satisfaction accessible to him, without concerning himself about the uncertainty of their duration, any more than about their inevitable end.

Meanwhile, let utilitarians never cease to claim the morality of self-devotion as a possession which belongs by as good a right to them, as either to the Stoic or to the Transcendentalist. The utilitarian morality does recognize in human beings the power of sacrificing their own greatest good for the good of others. It only refuses to admit that the sacrifice is itself a good. A sacrifice which does not increase, or tend to increase, the sum total of happiness, it considers as wasted. The only self-renunciation which it applauds, is devotion to the happiness, or to some of the means of happiness, of others; either of mankind collectively, or of individuals within the limits imposed by the collective interests of mankind.

I must again repeat, what the assailants of utilitarianism seldom have the justice to acknowledge, that the happiness which forms the utilitarian standard of what is right in conduct, is not the agent's own happiness, but that of all concerned. As between his own happiness and that of others, utilitarianism requires him to be as strictly impartial as a disinterested and benevolent spectator. In the golden rule of Jesus of Nazareth, we read the complete spirit of the ethics of utility. To do as one would be done by, and to love one's neighbour as oneself, constitute the ideal perfection of utilitarian morality. As the means of making the nearest approach to this ideal, utility would enjoin, first, that laws and social arrangements should place the happiness, or (as speaking practically it may be called) the interest, of every individual, as nearly as possible in harmony with the interest of the whole; and secondly, that education and opinion, which have so vast a power over human character, should so use that

power as to establish in the mind of every individual an indissoluble association between his own happiness and the good of the whole; especially between his own happiness and the practice of such modes of conduct, negative and positive, as regard for the universal happiness prescribes: so that not only he may be unable to conceive the possibility of happiness to himself, consistently with conduct opposed to the general good, but also that a direct impulse to promote the general good may be in every individual one of the habitual motives of action, and the sentiments connected therewith may fill a large and prominent place in every human being's sentient existence. If the impugners of the utilitarian morality represented it to their own minds in this its true character, I know not what recommendation possessed by any other morality they could possibly affirm to be wanting to it: what more beautiful or more exalted developments of human nature any other ethical system can be supposed to foster, or what springs of action, not accessible to the utilitarian, such systems rely on for giving effect to their mandates.

The objectors to utilitarianism cannot always be charged with representing it in a discreditable light. On the contrary, those among them who entertain anything like a just idea of its disinterested character, sometimes find fault with its standard as being too high for humanity. They say it is exacting too much to require that people shall always act from the inducement of promoting the general interests of society. But this is to mistake the very meaning of a standard of morals, and to confound the rule of action with the motive of it. It is the business of ethics to tell us what are our duties, or by what test we may know them; but no system of ethics requires that the sole motive of all we do shall be a feeling of duty; on the contrary, ninety-nine hundredths of all our actions are done from other motives, and rightly so done, if the rule of duty does not condemn them. It is the more unjust to utilitarianism that this particular misapprehension should be made a ground of objection to it, inasmuch as utilitarian moralists have gone beyond almost all others in affirming that the motive has nothing to do with the morality of the action, though much with the worth of the agent. He who saves a fellow creature from drowning does what is morally right, whether his motive be duty, or the hope of being paid for his trouble: he who betrays the friend that trusts him, is guilty of a crime, even if his object be to serve another friend to whom he is under greater obligations.[25] But to speak only of actions done from the motive of duty, and in direct obedience to principle: it is a misapprehension of the utilitarian mode of thought, to conceive it as implying that people should fix their minds upon so wide a generality as the world, or society at large. The great majority of good actions are intended, not for the benefit of the world, but for that of individuals, of which the good of the world is made up; and the thoughts of the most virtuous man need not on these occasions travel beyond the particular persons concerned, except so far as is necessary to assure himself that in benefiting them he is not violating the rights— that is, the legitimate and authorized expectations—of anyone else. The multiplication of happiness is, according to the utilitarian ethics, the object of virtue: the occasions on which any person (except one in a thousand) has it in his power to do this on an extended scale, in other words, to be a public benefactor, are but exceptional; and on these occasions alone is he called on to consider public utility; in every other case, private utility, the interest or happiness of some few persons, is all he has to attend to. Those alone the influence of whose actions extends to society in general, need concern themselves habitually about so large an object. In the case of abstinences indeed—of things which people forbear to do, from moral considerations, though the consequences in the particular case might be beneficial—it would be unworthy of an intelligent agent not to be consciously aware that the action is of a class which, if practised generally, would be generally injurious, and that this is the ground of the obligation to abstain from it. The amount of regard for the public interest implied in this recognition, is no greater than is demanded by every system of morals; for they all enjoin to abstain from whatever is manifestly pernicious to society.

The same considerations dispose of another reproach against the doctrine of utility, founded on a still grosser misconception of the purpose of a standard of morality, and of the very meaning of the words right and wrong. It is often affirmed that utilitarianism renders men cold and unsympathizing; that it chills their moral feelings towards individuals; that it makes them regard only the dry and hard consideration of the consequences of actions, not taking into their moral estimate the qualities from which those actions emanate. If the assertion means that they do not allow their judgment respecting the rightness or wrongness of an action to be influenced by their opinion of the qualities of the person who does it, this is a complaint not against utilitarianism, but against having any standard of morality at all; for certainly no known ethical standard decides an action to be good or bad because it is done by a good or a bad man, still less because done by an amiable, a brave, or a benevolent man, or the contrary. These considerations are relevant, not to the estimation of actions, but of persons; and there is nothing in the utilitarian theory inconsistent with the fact that there are other things which interest us

in persons besides the rightness and wrongness of their actions. The Stoics, indeed, with the paradoxical misuse of language which was part of their system, and by which they strove to raise themselves above all concern about anything but virtue, were fond of saying that he who has that has everything; that he, and only he, is rich, is beautiful, is a king. But no claim of this description is made for the virtuous man by the utilitarian doctrine. Utilitarians are quite aware that there are other desirable possessions and qualities besides virtue, and are perfectly willing to allow to all of them their full worth. They are also aware that a right action does not necessarily indicate a virtuous character, and that actions which are blameable often proceed from qualities entitled to praise. When this is apparent in any particular case, it modifies their estimation, not certainly of the act, but of the agent. I grant that they are, notwithstanding, of opinion, that in the long run the best proof of a good character is good actions; and resolutely refuse to consider any mental disposition as good, of which the predominant tendency is to produce bad conduct. This makes them unpopular with many people; but it is an unpopularity which they must share with every one who regards the distinction between right and wrong in a serious light; and the reproach is not one which a conscientious utilitarian need be anxious to repel.

If no more be meant by the objection than that many utilitarians look on the morality of actions, as measured by the utilitarian standard, with too exclusive a regard, and do not lay sufficient stress upon the other beauties of character which go towards making a human being lovable or admirable, this may be admitted. Utilitarians who have cultivated their moral feelings, but not their sympathies nor their artistic perceptions, do fall into this mistake; and so do as other moralists under the same conditions. What can be said in excuse for other moralists is equally available for them, namely, that if there is to be any error, it is better that it should be on that side. As a matter of fact, we may affirm that among utilitarians as among adherents of other systems, there is every imaginable degree of rigidity and of laxity in the application of their standard: some are even puritanically rigorous, while others are as indulgent as can possibly be desired by sinner or by sentimentalist. But on the whole, a doctrine which brings prominently forward the interest that mankind have in the repression and prevention of conduct which violates the moral law, is likely to be inferior to no other in turning the sanctions of opinion against such violations. It is true, the question, What does violate the moral law? is one on which those who recognize different standards of morality are likely now and then to differ. But difference of opinion on moral questions was not first introduced into the world by utilitarianism, while that doctrine does supply, if not always an easy, at all events a tangible and intelligible mode of deciding such differences.

It may not be superfluous to notice a few more of the common misapprehensions of utilitarian ethics, even those which are so obvious and gross that it might appear impossible for any person of candour and intelligence to fall into them: since persons, even of considerable mental endowments, often give themselves so little trouble to understand the bearings of any opinion against which they entertain a prejudice, and men are in general so little conscious of this voluntary ignorance as a defect, that the vulgarest misunderstandings of ethical doctrines are continually met with in the deliberate writings of persons of the greatest pretensions both to high principle and to philosophy. We not uncommonly hear the doctrine of utility inveighed against as a *godless* doctrine. If it be necessary to say anything at all against so mere an assumption, we may say that the question depends upon what idea we have formed of the moral character of the Deity. If it be a true belief that God desires, above all things, the happiness of his creatures, and that this was his purpose in their creation, utility is not only not a godless doctrine, but more profoundly religious than any other. If it be meant that utilitarianism does not recognize the revealed will of God as the supreme law of morals, I answer that a utilitarian who believes in the perfect goodness and wisdom of God necessarily believes that whatever God has thought fit to reveal on the subject of morals, must fulfil the requirements of utility in a supreme degree. But others besides utilitarians have been of opinion that the Christian revelation was intended, and is fitted, to inform the hearts and minds of mankind with a spirit which should enable them to find for themselves what is right, and incline them to do it when found, rather than to tell them, except in a very general way, what it is: and that we need a doctrine of ethics, carefully followed out, to *interpret* to us the will of God. Whether this opinion is correct or not, it is superfluous here to discuss; since whatever aid religion, either natural or revealed, can afford to ethical investigation, is as open to the utilitarian moralist as to any other. He can use it as the testimony of God to the usefulness or hurtfulness of any given course of action, by as good a right as others can use it for the indication of a transcendental law, having no connection with usefulness or with happiness.

Again, utility is often summarily stigmatized as an immoral doctrine by giving it the name of expediency, and taking advantage of the popular use of that term to contrast it with principle. But the expedient, in the sense in which it is opposed to the right, generally means that which is expedient for the particular interest of the agent himself; as when a minister sacrifices the interest of his country to keep himself in place. When it means anything better than this, it means that which is expedient for some immediate object, some temporary purpose, but which violates a rule whose observance is expedient in a much higher degree. The expedient, in this sense, instead of being the same thing with the useful, is a branch of the hurtful. Thus, it would often be expedient, for the purpose of getting over some momentary embarrassment, or attaining some object immediately useful to ourselves or others, to tell a lie. But inasmuch as the cultivation in ourselves of a sensitive feeling on the subject of veracity is one of the most useful, and the enfeeblement of that feeling one of the most hurtful, things to which our conduct can be instrumental; and inasmuch as any, even unintentional, deviation from truth does that much towards weakening the trustworthiness of human assertion, which is not only the principal support of all present social well-being, but the insufficiency of which does more than anyone thing that can be named to keep back civilization, virtue, everything on which human happiness on the largest scale depends; we feel that the violation, for a present advantage, of a rule of such transcendent expediency, is not expedient, and that he who, for the sake of a convenience to himself or to some other individual, does what depends on him to deprive mankind of the good, and inflict upon them the evil, involved in the greater or less reliance which they can place in each other's word, acts the part of one of their worst enemies. Yet that even this rule, sacred as it is, admits of possible exceptions, is acknowledged by all moralists; the chief of which is when the withholding of some fact (as of information from a malefactor, or of bad news from a person dangerously ill) would preserve some one (especially a person other than oneself) from great and unmerited evil, and when the withholding can only be effected by denial. But in order that the exception may not extend itself beyond the need, and may have the least possible effect in weakening reliance on veracity, it ought to be recognized, and, if possible, its limits defined; and if the principle of utility is good for anything, it must be good for weighing these conflicting utilities against one another, and marking out the region within which one or the other preponderates.

Again, defenders of utility often find themselves called upon to reply to such objects as this—that there is not time, previous to action, for calculating and weighing the effects of any line of conduct on the general happiness. This is exactly as if anyone were to say that it is impossible to guide our conduct by Christianity, because there is not time, on every occasion on which anything has to be done, to read through the Old and New Testaments. The answer to the objection is, that there has been ample time, namely, the whole past duration of the human species. During all that time mankind have been learning by experience the tendencies of actions; on which experience all the prudence as well as all the morality of life, is dependent. People talk as if the commencement of this course of experience had hitherto been put oft; and as if, at the moment when some man feels tempted to meddle with the property or life of another, he had to begin considering for the first time whether murder and theft are injurious to human happiness. Even then I do not think that he would find the question very puzzling; but, at all events, the matter is now done to his hand. It is truly a whimsical supposition that if mankind were agreed in considering utility to be the test of morality, they would remain without any agreement as to what *is* useful, and would take no measures for having their notions on the subject taught to the young, and enforced by law and opinion. There is no difficulty in proving any ethical standard whatever to work ill, if we suppose universal idiocy to be conjoined with it; but on any hypothesis short of that, mankind must by this time have acquired positive beliefs as to the effects of some actions on their happiness; and the beliefs which have thus come down are the rules of morality for the multitude, and for the philosopher until he has succeeded in finding better. That philosophers might easily do this, even now, on many subjects; that the received code of ethics is by no means of divine right; and that mankind have still much to learn as to the effects of actions on the general happiness, I admit, or rather, earnestly maintain. The corollaries from the principle of utility, like the precepts of every practical art, admit of indefinite improvement, and, in a progressive state of human mind, their improvement is perpetually going on. But to consider the rules of morality as improvable, is one thing; to pass over the intermediate generalizations entirely, and endeavour to test each individual action directly by the first principle, is another. It is a strange notion that the acknowledgement of a first principle is inconsistent with the admission of secondary ones. To inform a traveller respecting the place of his ultimate destination, is not to forbid the use of landmarks and direction posts on the way. The proposition that happiness is the end and aim of morality, does not mean that no road ought to be laid down to that goal, or that persons going thither should not be advised to take one direction rather than another. Men really ought to leave of talking a kind of nonsense on this subject, which they would neither talk nor listen to on other matters of practical concernment. Nobody argues that the art of navigation is not founded on astronomy, because sailors cannot wait to calculate the Nautical Almanac. Being rational creatures, they go to sea with it ready calculated; and all rational creatures go out upon the sea of life with their minds made up on the common questions of right and wrong, as well as on many of the far more difficult questions of wise and foolish. And this, as long as foresight is a human quality, it is to be presumed they will continue to do. Whatever we adopt as the fundamental principle of morality, we require subordinate principles to apply it by: the impossibility of doing without them, being common to all systems, can afford no argument against anyone in particular: but gravely to argue as if no such secondary principles could be had, and as if mankind had remained till now, and always must remain, without drawing any general conclusions from the experience of human life, is as high a pitch, I think, as absurdity has ever reached in philosophical controversy.

The remainder of the stock arguments against utilitarianism mostly consist in laying to its charge the common infirmities of human nature, and the general difficulties which embarrass conscientious persons in shaping their course through life. We are told that a utilitarian will be apt to make his own particular case an exception to moral rules, and, when under temptation, will see a utility in the breach of a rule, greater than he will see in its observance. But is utility the only creed which is able to furnish us with excuses for evil doing, and means of cheating our own conscience? They are afforded in abundance by all doctrines which recognize as a fact in morals the existence of conflicting considerations; which all doctrines do, that have been believed by sane persons. It is not the fault of any creed, but of the complicated nature of human affairs, that rules of conduct cannot be so framed as to require no exceptions, and that hardly any kind of action can safely be laid down as either always obligatory or always condemnable. There is no ethical creed which does not temper the rigidity of its laws, by giving a certain latitude, under the moral responsibility of the agent, for accommodation to peculiarities of circumstances; and under every creed, at the opening thus made, self-deception and dishonest casuistry get in. There exists no moral system under which there do not arise unequivocal cases of conflicting obligation. These are the real difficulties, the knotty points both in the theory of ethics, and in the conscientious guidance of personal conduct. They are overcome practically with greater or with less success according to the intellect and virtue of the individual; but it can hardly be pretended that anyone will be the less qualified for dealing with them, from possessing an ultimate standard to which conflicting rights and duties can be referred. If utility is the ultimate source of moral obligations, utility may be invoked to decide between them when their demands are incompatible. Though the application of the standard may be difficult, it is better than none at all; while in other systems, the moral laws all claiming independent authority, there is no common umpire entitled to interfere between them; their claims to precedence one over another rest on little better than sophistry, and unless determined, as they generally are, by the unacknowledged influence of considerations of utility, afford a free scope for the actions of personal desires and partialities. We must remember that only in these cases of conflict between secondary principles is it requisite that first principles should be appealed to. There is no case of moral obligation in which some secondary principle is not involved; and if only one, there can seldom be any real doubt which one it is in the mind of any person by whom the principle itself is recognized.

Post-Reading Questions

On Liberty

1. How does Mill defend the freedom of speech?
2. Is Mill right to argue that speech should be regulated (and punished) only when it is likely to cause very concrete harm?
3. Why is the cultivation of individuality so important, in Mill's estimation?
4. The kinds of liberties that Mill values—diversity of opinion and lifestyles—do not necessarily benefit all members of society. Given this, why does Mill not allow for some forms of state paternalism that might arguably increase the happiness of some?
5. Is the conception of harm at the heart of Mill's harm principle too weak? Would it still allow too many things that we might want, as a society, to prevent?

Utilitarianism

1. How does Mill respond to the criticism that we can't really know which actions will lead to the greatest happiness or pleasure?
2. Only the higher pleasures contribute to the greater good, in Mill's view. How does he respond to the objection that people will just opt for lower pleasures (such as getting drunk) over higher pleasures, thereby jeopardizing the goal of the greater good?

CASE STUDY
POLYGAMY IN CANADA

Introduction

This 2011 reference case considers whether or not Canada's law against polygamy—section 293 of the Criminal Code of Canada—is consistent with Canada's Charter of Rights and Freedoms. The Supreme Court of British Columbia initiated the challenge following failed attempts to charge members of the polygamous fundamentalist Mormon community of Bountiful, British Columbia, with offences related to sexual abuse and exploitation. Since defenders of the practice frequently cite religious freedom—a right protected by the Charter—as a reason to decriminalize plural marriage, it was felt that greater clarity was needed in order to ascertain whether the law against polygamy was indeed constitutional. The Court appointed counsel (*Amicus Curiae*) to argue the case against section 293's constitutionality, thereby testing the validity of the law and its capacity to withstand constitutional challenges. The Fundamentalist Church of Jesus Christ of Latter Day Saints (FLDS), the church of most of the Mormons in Canada who practice polygamy, were unsuccessful in their bid to receive party status in the case, but were still able to participate in the proceedings alongside a number of different advocacy groups on both sides of the issue.

The Court's decision criticized section 293 for being overly broad in scope and thereby criminalizing minors in polygamous unions, but nonetheless upheld the law against polygamy. Among the evidence considered was expert testimony attesting to the incompatibility of plural marriage with Canada's commitments—under both domestic and international law—to sexual equality and to the rights and welfare of children: generally married at a young age, girls in polygamous unions typically begin bearing children in their teens (with attendant health consequences). The Court also heard from women who had formerly been wives in polygamous Mormon marriages, and who, under the protection of anonymity, presented candid testimony of the harms that they experienced in these arrangements. More generally, the case considered the evolving status of the practice of polygamy in different cultural and religious traditions, chiefly in Mormonism but also in Islam. The history of the Mormons as a minority—and at times persecuted—religious community was also addressed.

In his decision, Chief Justice Robert J. Bauman repeatedly invoked the principle of harm, stating that Canada's law against plural marriage "seeks to protect against the many harms which are reasonably apprehended to arise out of the practice of polygamy." The religious freedom of Mormons and their status as a religious minority are significant considerations, he concluded, but do not offset the dangers that plural unions pose to children and women (and to society more generally). Yet while preventing abuse and other negative consequences features prominently in the Court's reasoning, it is by no means certain that Mill would support criminalization of the practice. Mill's staunch anti-paternalism and his belief in the importance of tolerating different ways of life (however foolish or ill-advised they may be) led him to reject widespread calls by Europeans for a ban against polygamy among American Mormons. This was despite his personal distaste for the practice, which in his view (as discussed in *On Liberty*) undermined the mutuality of marriage and reinforced women's subordination.

Whether Mill would support the ban on polygamy in Canada would likely pivot on whether the practice can be shown to involve coercion and harm. The Court's ruling in the British Columbia case does indeed cast doubt on the voluntariness of the practice of polygamy (for women)—a central criterion, for Mill, for state toleration. If polygamy does not involve force or overt harm, but simply entails cultural pressures that do not strictly prevent women from either choosing or exiting plural marriages, then it is likely that Mill would balk at the use of the state restrictions. For while Mill worried about what he called "the despotism of custom," ultimately he worried more about the use of state apparatus to enforce society's norms in cases lacking clear evidence of harm to others.

From Section 293 of the *Criminal Code of Canada*, 2011 BCSC 1588

Section 293 of the Criminal Code of Canada, *2011 BCSC 1588.*
www.courts.gov.bc.ca/jdb-txt/SC/11/15/2011BCSC1588.htm

I. Introduction

[1] By s. 293 of the Criminal Code of Canada, R.S.C. 1985, c. C-46, (initially in 1890 and periodically since then in successive revisions to the Code), Parliament has prohibited the practice of polygamy. British Columbia asks this Court to declare whether this prohibition is consistent with the freedoms guaranteed to all Canadians by the Canadian Charter of Rights and Freedoms, Part 1 of the Constitution Act, 1982, being Schedule B to the Canada Act, 1982 (U.K.), 1982, c. 11 [Charter].

[2] . . . the Attorney General for British Columbia has said in opening that the case against polygamy is all about harm. Absent harm, that party accepted that s. 293 would not survive scrutiny under the Charter.

[3] The challengers, led by the *Amicus Curiae*, counter (primarily) that this case is about a wholly unacceptable intrusion by the state into the most basic of rights guaranteed by the Charter—the freedom to practice one's religion, and to associate in family units with those whom one chooses.

. . .

[5] I have concluded that this case is essentially about harm; more specifically, Parliament's reasoned apprehension of harm arising out of the practice of polygamy. This includes harm to women, to children, to society, and to the institution of monogamous marriage.

[6] Based on the most comprehensive judicial record on the subject ever produced, I have concluded that the Attorneys General and their allied interested persons have demonstrated a very strong basis for a reasoned apprehension of harm to many in our society inherent in the practice of polygamy as I have defined it in these reasons.

[7] I turn to some of the harms that are reasonably apprehended to arise.

[8] Women in polygamous relationships are at an elevated risk of physical and psychological harm. They face higher rates of domestic violence and abuse, including sexual abuse. Competition for material and emotional access to a shared husband can lead to fractious co-wife relationships. These factors contribute to the higher rates of depressive disorders and other mental health issues that women in polygamous relationships face. They have more children, are more likely to die in childbirth and live shorter lives than their monogamous counterparts. They tend to have less autonomy, and report higher rates of marital dissatisfaction and lower levels of self-esteem. They also fare worse economically, as resources may be inequitably divided or simply insufficient.

[9] Children in polygamous families face higher infant mortality, even controlling for economic status and other relevant variables. They tend to suffer more emotional, behavioural, and physical problems, as well as lower educational achievement than children in monogamous families. These outcomes are likely the result of higher levels of conflict, emotional stress, and tension in polygamous families. . . . Rivalry and jealousy among co-wives can cause significant emotional problems for their children. The inability of fathers to give sufficient affection and disciplinary attention to all of their children can further reduce children's emotional security. Children are also at enhanced risk of psychological and physical abuse and neglect.

[10] Early marriage for girls is common, frequently to significantly older men. The resultant early sexual activity, pregnancies, and childbirth have negative health implications for girls, and also significantly limit their socio-economic development. Shortened inter-birth intervals pose a heightened risk of various problems for both mother and child.

[11] The sex ratio imbalance inherent in polygamy means that young men are forced out of polygamous communities to sustain the ability of senior men to accumulate more wives. These young men and boys often receive limited education as a result and must navigate their way outside their communities with few life skills and social support.

[12] Another significant harm to children is their exposure to, and potential internalization of, harmful gender stereotypes.

[13] Polygamy has negative impacts on society flowing from the high fertility rates, large family size, and poverty associated with the practice. It generates a

class of largely poor, unmarried men who are statistically predisposed to violence and other anti-social behaviour. Polygamy also institutionalizes gender inequality. Patriarchal hierarchy and authoritarian control are common features of polygamous communities. Individuals in polygynous societies tend to have fewer civil liberties than their counterparts in societies which prohibit the practice.

[14] Polygamy's harm to society includes the critical fact that a great many of its individual harms are not specific to any particular religious, cultural or regional context....

[15] I would answer the essential question before me: while s. 293 offends the freedom of religion of identifiable groups guaranteed by s. 2(a) of the Charter and the s. 7 liberty interests of children between 12 and 17 married into polygamy, the provision, save in its application to the latter group, is demonstrably justified in a free and democratic society. My reasons for that conclusion and the specific answers to the questions on the reference follow.

II. Course of Proceedings

A. The Reference Questions

[16] By Order in Council dated 22 October 2009, the Lieutenant Governor in Council referred two questions to this Court for hearing and consideration pursuant to the Constitutional Question Act, R.S.B.C. 1996, c. 68, s. 1 [CQA]:

 a) Is section 293 of the Criminal Code of Canada consistent with the Canadian Charter of Rights and Freedoms? If not, in what particular or particulars and to what extent?
 b) What are the necessary elements of the offence in section 293 of the Criminal Code of Canada? Without limiting this question, does section 293 require that the polygamy or conjugal union in question involved a minor, or occurred in a context of dependence, exploitation, abuse of authority, a gross imbalance of power, or undue influence?

[17] Section 293 provides: 293(1) Every one who
 (a) practises or enters into or in any manner agrees or consents to practise or enter into (i) any form of polygamy, or (ii) any kind of conjugal union with more than one person at the same time,
 whether or not it is by law recognized as a binding form of marriage; or
 (b) celebrates, assists or is a party to a rite, ceremony, contract or consent that purports to sanction

a relationship mentioned in subparagraph (a)(i) or (ii),
is guilty of an indictable offence and liable to imprisonment for a term not exceeding five years.

(2) Where an accused is charged with an offence under this section, no averment or proof of the method by which the alleged relationship was entered into, agreed to or consented to is necessary in the indictment or upon the trial of the accused, nor is it necessary on the trial to prove that the persons who are alleged to have entered into the relationship had or intended to have sexual intercourse.

B. The Participants

[18] The three parties to this reference are the Attorney General of British Columbia [AGBC], the Attorney General of Canada [AG Canada], and the *Amicus Curiae* [*Amicus*]. As both Attorneys General take the position that s. 293 is constitutionally sound, the Court appointed the *Amicus*, who is publically funded, to advance the case in opposition.

. . .

[21] Eleven such interested persons representing a range of different interests ultimately participated in these proceedings. They are:
 a) Beyond Borders: Ensuring Global Justice for Children [Beyond Borders], a Canadian-based volunteer organization without religious or political affiliation that advances the rights of children to be free from abuse and exploitation;
 b) the British Columbia Civil Liberties Association [Civil Liberties Association];
 c) the British Columbia Teachers' Federation [BCTF];
 d) the Canadian Association for Free Expression [CAFE];
 e) the Canadian Coalition for the Rights of Children [CCRC] jointly with the David Asper Centre for Constitutional Rights [Asper Centre] . . .;
 f) the Canadian Polyamory Advocacy Association . . .;
 g) the Christian Legal Fellowship, a national association of Christian legal professionals, law students, and interested persons who advocate for justice with compassion and support the use of moral and religious underpinnings to address social, legal and political issues in Canada;
 h) the Fundamentalist Church of Jesus Christ of Latter Day Saints [FLDS] and James Oler in his capacity as bishop of the FLDS;
 i) REAL Women of Canada [REAL Women], a

national non-profit organization dedicated to promoting equality for all women;

j) Stop Polygamy in Canada, an international group based in Alberta which provides information about polygamy in Canada; and

k) West Coast Legal Education and Action Fund [West Coast LEAF], an organization which promotes women's equality through equality rights litigation, law reform and public legal education.

[22] The Civil Liberties Association, CAFE, the Polyamory Advocacy Association and the FLDS argue against the constitutionality of s. 293. The remaining interested persons generally argue in support.

. . .

C. The Evidence

. . .

[28] Much of the evidence comprises affidavits and expert reports. Over 90 such are before me. In large measure, these were exchanged and filed with the Court in advance of the hearing according to a schedule directed by the Court . . . .

[29] The expert witnesses represent a broad range of disciplines including anthropology, psychology, sociology, law, economics, family demography, history, and theology. The calibre and breadth of knowledge of these experts is impressive. Some undertook original research specifically for this reference. Others are clinical experts who offer case study observations from their practices. Yet others have studied aspects of polygamy relevant to their particular disciplines for years.

[30] The lay witnesses are largely individuals who have lived—and in some cases continue to live—in polygamous families in both Canada and the United States. Most have experience with polygamy in the context of fundamentalist Mormonism, and they spoke of those experiences, both positive and negative. . . .

[31] Unusually, most of the FLDS's lay witnesses gave their evidence, both written and *viva voce*, under cover of anonymity pursuant to an order I granted earlier in the proceeding (indexed at 2010 BCSC 1351). Also somewhat unusually, the AGBC tendered the evidence of many of his lay witnesses by video affidavits which were played in Court during the hearing.

. . .

b) Polygamy in Canada
i) Bountiful

[702] I now turn to the Canadian experience with polygamy and it is overwhelmingly centred in the community of Bountiful.

[703] Speaking to the positive aspects of life in Bountiful, we heard evidence from a number of witnesses from the community who took advantage of the anonymity order I made earlier in these proceedings. Witnesses Nos. 2, 3, and 4, in particular, took the stand. They spoke to their early marriages (16 and 17 respectively in the case of No. 2 and No. 4, 15 in the case of No. 2's daughter); their desire for education, which they say is encouraged; and generally their satisfaction with life in Bountiful and the institution of plural marriage.

[704] Witness No. 1 described the benefits of having sister wives (at para. 8):

> I had five sister wives and I loved and still love all of them. Of course there were many children, and some of the ladies had to work outside of the home to help support our growing family. I was one of the working wives, and I will say that I appreciated more than I ever can express when my sister wife or wives would tend my toddlers, do my washing, and have a clean home and a delicious supper waiting when I returned from work. Just not having to wake my littlest children before I went to work was a great blessing. . . . It was a good life, especially since each of us had things we liked to do. . . .

[705] Witness No. 2, who is the second of her husband's two wives, described her relationship with her sister wife:

> A. My sister wife and I have lived—have lived at times in the same home. We've lived in different homes. We are now living again in the same home. I feel that we are both very committed in having a good relationship with each other, and conflict arises, yes, but I feel like that we can deal with it in a reasonable manner.

. . .

[706] There is a certain disconnect between their positivism and some aspects of these witnesses' realities. Witness No. 2 confirmed that no one from the community has graduated to become employed in any of a multitude of professional careers. Witness No. 3 is now attending summer sessions at Southern Utah University. She values education highly but admitted that because grades 11 and 12 at BESS are not certified, she did not receive her Dogwood diploma. Witness No. 4, with a calm that startled, related that she was born and raised in the FLDS in the United States and received an "assignment" by the Prophet to marry a Canadian stranger on a half-hour's notice. She was taken by car on an 18-hour drive north across the border with a false note from her parents listing the purpose of entry as visiting an aunt. The

whole process was repeated with a girl who became her 15 year-old junior wife some six months later.

[707] One theme that resonates in the evidence of the anonymous Bountiful witnesses is the stigma that attaches to their criminalized lifestyle and the insularity this breeds. As Witness No. 1 states (at paras. 11–12):

> I feel that the criminal prohibition against polygamy is totally unfair. We have been told many times that it isn't having multiple relationships with women that we are being prosecuted for, it is making a commitment to care of one another and any resulting children. We are being singled out and ridiculed for having children instead of aborting them, and taking care of them once we have them. We see instances around us in the greater community where 12 and 13 year old girls become pregnant and no media even considers it newsworthy, but let an FLDS girl have a baby at 16 and we have a whole inquiry upon us. It is hard to teach our children in school that Canada does not believe in discrimination and that all Canadians are free to believe whatever they wish when we are attacked for our beliefs. We are intelligent beings and even our little children know that there is no justice for us because we are those terrible FLDS people. We ladies cringe if one of our children has an accident. Woe betide the polygamist child who breaks his leg. Do we dare take him to the hospital? Will the cry of abuse be raised? What if we wait several hours hoping against hope that the leg is not broken and then take him in? Will the cry of neglect be cast at us?
>
> We are all affected by the stigma that is cast upon polygamists or at least upon FLDS polygamists. We hesitate to associate among the community at large unless of necessity. We are all weary of being everywhere misrepresented. We are all poorer; we have to pay so very much for lawyers. Perhaps we could send more children to university if all our money was not spent in legal fights. And there is always the very real fear in my mind that children could be taken away from their parents and that their father and maybe even their mother could end up in jail.

[708] Witness No. 6 is a man in his 40s who left the Bountiful community in the late 1980s. He offers this evidence about his experience (at paras. 6–13):

> I was born into a family with a father and many mothers in Bountiful. I grew up in a large home with 35 brothers and sisters, of whom 9 were my full biological siblings.
>
> The household was organized with everyone having a place and a role in the family. These roles were not only identified with the adults but

the children had important positions within the household.

> I attended the Bountiful school. In 1988, I decided to leave the community and strike out on my own. There were many reasons that I left the community but one of the main reasons was that I sought a less rigid lifestyle. I do not like to follow others. I prefer to make my own decisions and I did not want to follow the strict rules of the church.
>
> After leaving the Bountiful community I have kept in regular contact with many of my siblings still living in Bountiful. I also maintain a close relationship with my mother and I see her fairly regularly.
>
> . . .
>
> . . . I was taught that the marriage covenant was sacred and everlasting. I still believe that to be true.
>
> The FLDS is not my choice but I believe that religion is a personal choice. I believe that the only people who have the right to chose what goes on in Bountiful are the individuals who live there.
>
> . . .

[709] I will now concentrate on several aspects of the evidence led with respect to harm in connection with the community: teen pregnancy, the movement of young girls between the United States (largely Hildale/Colorado City) and Bountiful, and educational outcomes.

Young Mothers

[710] Among the most serious harms arguably associated with polygamy are the early sexualization of girls, early and frequent pregnancies, and marriage to older men. I have reviewed some of the expert evidence on these issues above. Does the evidence from Bountiful tend to confirm this to be the case?

[711] In early 2005, the British Columbia Vital Statistics Agency [BCVSA] conducted a review of teen pregnancy in Creston, the local health area incorporating Bountiful. As related in the affidavit of Dr. Perry Kendall, the Provincial Health Officer for British Columbia, that review indicated a higher than expected number of births to mothers between the ages of 14 and 18. . . .

[712] What that analysis revealed was that while Bountiful likely accounted for 8–24 per cent of the Creston area population, the five identified Bountiful families alone accounted for 38 per cent of the area's teen pregnancies. It also revealed a significant age gap between the mother and father in these pregnancies, with 28 per cent of the declared fathers being more than 10 years senior and roughly half being five years senior.

. . .

Conclusion

[1329] Having found s. 293 to infringe both s. 2(a) and s. 7 of the Charter, I advance to apply the *Oakes* test to each infringement.

a) Section 2(a)

[1330] To constitute a justifiable limit on a right or a freedom, the objective of the impugned measure must advance concerns that are pressing and substantial in a free and democratic society.

[1331] As I have concluded, s. 293 has as its objective the prevention of harm to women, to children and to society. The prevention of these collective harms associated with polygamy is clearly an objective that is pressing and substantial.

[1332] The positive side of the prohibition which I have discussed—the preservation of monogamous marriage—similarly represents a pressing and substantial objective for all of the reasons that have seen the ascendance of monogamous marriage as a norm in the West.

[1333] I reject the *Amicus'* concentration on, and rather dismissive critique of, the harms associated with the so-called "cruel arithmetic" of polygamy. The existence of these harms has been demonstrated by the defenders.

[1334] . . . the Court turns to determine whether there is a rational connection between the criminal prohibition of polygamy and Parliament's pressing and substantial objective.

[1335] Having found a reasoned apprehension that polygamy is associated with numerous harms, it follows that criminalizing the practice is one way of limiting those harms. . . .

[1336] The government need only show that "it is reasonable to suppose that the limit [on the right] may further the goal, not that it will do so" (*Hutterian Brethren* at para. 48). It is certainly reasonable to suppose that the limits on religious liberty that s. 293 imposes may further the objectives of the provision. The evidence that the incidence of polygamy would plausibly increase in a non-trivial way if not criminalized certainly makes this point.

[1337] The *Amicus* suggests that s. 293 has not been effective, and points to the miniscule number of prosecutions over the provision's 120 year history. The Supreme Court answered this submission in *R. v. Lucas*, [1998] 1 S.C.R. 439, where it rejected a similar argument with respect to s. 300 of the Criminal Code, the prohibition of defamatory libel (at 466):

> . . . However, it has been held that "[t]he paucity of prosecutions does not necessarily reflect on the

seriousness of the problem" . . . (*R. v. Laba*, [1994] 3 S.C.R. 965, at p. 1007. . .

[1338] The *Amicus* also maintains that s. 293 is not an effective deterrent since those who are religiously motivated to practice polygamy will do so regardless of its criminalization. Again, the Supreme Court answered this submission in *Malmo-Levine* (at paras. 177–78):

> This Court has exercised caution in accepting arguments about the alleged ineffectiveness of legal measures . . .
>
> Questions about which types of measures and associated sanctions are best able to deter conduct that Parliament considers undesirable is a matter of legitimate ongoing debate. *The so-called "ineffectiveness" is simply another way of characterizing the refusal of people in the appellants' position to comply with the law. It is difficult to see how that refusal can be elevated to a constitutional argument against validity based on the invocation of fundamental principles of justice. Indeed, it would be inconsistent with the rule of law to allow compliance with a criminal prohibition to be determined by each individual's personal discretion and taste.* [Emphasis added]

[1339] While the Supreme Court made these comments in the context of s. 7 of the Charter, in my view they have equal application to the rational connection analysis under s. 1.

[1340] As for the suggestion that a more focussed measure, rather than a general prohibition of polygamy, is more rationally connected to the objective, I have dealt with this submission in my discussion of the s. 7 claim. . . .

[1341] Moving to minimal impairment, it is my view that s. 293 minimally impairs religious freedom.

[1342] In addressing the harms reasonably believed to be associated with polygamy—inherently I add—Parliament is entitled to some deference. This is a complex social issue. Parliament is better positioned than the Court to choose among a range of alternatives to address the harms.

[1343] When one accepts that there is a reasoned apprehension that polygamy is inevitably associated with sundry harms, and that these harms are not simply isolated to criminal adherents like Warren Jeffs but inhere in the institution itself, the *Amicus'* complaint that there are less sweeping means of achieving the government's objective falls away. And it most certainly does when one considers the positive objective of the measure, the protection and preservation of monogamous marriage. For that, there can be no alternative to the outright prohibition of that which is fundamentally anathema to the institution. In the context of this objective, there is no such thing as so-called "good polygamy."

[1344] It is therefore my opinion that s. 293 is "carefully tailored so that rights are impaired no more than necessary" (*RJR-MacDonald*, at para. 160).

[1345] Finally, I find s. 293 to be proportional in its effects.

[1346] As Aharon Barak, former president of the Supreme Court of Israel, explained (in turn adopted by McLachlin C.J.C. in *Hutterarian Brethren*):

> . . . the test of proportionality (*stricto sensu*) examines whether realization of this proper objective is commensurate with the deleterious effect upon the human right . . . It requires placing colliding values and interests side by side and balancing them according to their weight.

[1347] I start with the deleterious effects.

[1348] I accept that for some, especially fundamentalist Mormons, the interference with a sincerely held belief represented by the prohibition in s. 293 is very significant. Still, I acknowledge the point made by the Attorneys General that some fundamentalist Mormons do choose to live monogamously without sacrificing their religious beliefs. And as we have seen, polygamy in Islam is not mandated, although it is permitted by the Qu-ran.

[1349] Further, I accept that the prohibition tends for some to encourage isolationism and insularity.

[1350] But, in my view, the salutary effects of the prohibition far outweigh the deleterious. The law seeks to advance the institution of monogamous marriage, a fundamental value in Western society from the earliest of times. It seeks to protect against the many harms which are reasonably apprehended to arise out of the practice of polygamy.

[1351] Finally, and not insignificantly, the prohibition is consistent with, and furthers, Canada's international human rights obligations. In my view, this adds very significant weight to the salutary effects side of the balance.

[1352] To the extent that s. 293 breaches the right guaranteed by s. 2(a) of the Charter, the Attorneys General have clearly met the burden of demonstrating that it is demonstrably justified in a free and democratic society.

b) Section 7

[1353] Laws which have been found to violate principles of fundamental justice are not easily saved by s. 1: *Charkaoui v. Canada (Citizenship and Immigration)*, 2007 SCC 9. As McLachlin C.J.C. explained "[t]he rights

protected by s. 7—life, liberty, and security of the person—are basic to our conception of a free and democratic society, and hence are not easily overridden by competing social interests" (at para. 66). Although she acknowledged that the task may not be impossible, it is nevertheless a hurdle that s. 293 is unable to overcome.

[1354] My conclusions with respect to pressing and substantial objective and rational connection in the context of the s. 2(a) infringement apply equally here.

[1355] However, it is at the minimum impairment stage that s. 293 fails the justification analysis, which is not surprising as its deficiency lies in its overbreadth.

[1356] In criminalizing "every one" in a prohibited union, s. 293 includes within its ambit young persons who are parties to such unions. This serious impairment of young persons" liberty interests does not advance the important objectives of s. 293. . . .

[1357] Accordingly, I find that to the extent s. 293 is contrary to the principles of fundamental justice guaranteed by s. 7 of the Charter by criminalizing young persons between the ages of 12 and 17 who marry into polygamy or a conjugal union with more than one person at the same time, the Attorneys General have not met the burden of demonstrating that this infringement is justified in a free and democratic society.

VIII. Disposition

[1358] It remains then to answer the questions posed on the reference.

> 1. Is Section 293 of the Criminal Code of Canada consistent with the Canadian Charter of Rights and Freedoms? If not, in what particular or particulars and to what extent?

[1359] . . . s. 293 is consistent with the Canadian Charter of Rights and Freedoms except to the extent that it includes within its terms, children between the ages of 12 and 17 who marry into polygamy or a conjugal union with more than one person at the same time.

[1360] For greater clarity. . . the inconsistency does not extend to persons who marry into polygamy before the age of 18 but are 18 years of age or older at the time of the laying of the information in respect of conduct that occurred at or after 18 years of age.

[1361] Granting a constitutional remedy in light of that conclusion is not within the terms of this reference. . . .

[1362] Alternatively, but to the same effect, I would read down "every one" in s. 293 to exclude the noted group of potential accused persons.

2. What are the necessary elements of the offence in s. 293 of the Criminal Code of Canada? . . . does s. 293 require that the polygamy or conjugal union in question involved a minor or occurred in a context of dependence, exploitation, abuse of authority, a gross imbalance of power, or undue influence?

[1363] . . . My conclusion (is) that the elements of the polygamy offence (s. 293(1)(a)(i)) and those of the conjugal union offence (s. 293(1)(a)(ii)) are the same:

1. an identified person, who
2. with the intent to do so,
3. practises, enters into, or in any manner agrees or consents to practice or enter into,

4. a marriage, whether or not it is by law recognized as a binding form of marriage, with more than one person at the same time.

[1364] Section 293 does not require that the polygamy or conjugal union in question involved a minor or occurred in a context of dependence, exploitation, abuse of authority, a gross imbalance of power or undue influence.

. . .

"The Honourable Chief Justice Bauman"

Post-Case-Reading Questions

1. Chief Justice Bauman concluded that the harm caused by polygamy is sufficient to warrant continued criminalization of the practice. What are the main dangers that he cites, and do you think they trigger Mill's "harm principle"?
2. Although s. 293 was found to infringe section 2 (a) of the Charter (freedom of religion, thought, association, belief, etc.), the decision found that the law banning polygamy sets a justifiable limit on that freedom (the *Oakes* test). Mill also allows limits to freedoms in a democratic society, but would he draw the line in the same place?

CHAPTER
IX

Karl Marx

Introduction

Karl Heinrich Marx was born in Trier, Prussia, in 1818. His father, a lawyer much influenced by the liberal ideas of the Enlightenment, was a Jew who converted to Christianity (Lutheranism) before Karl's birth. This was a pragmatic decision on the part of Karl's father, no doubt driven by his consideration of the restrictions on Jews during this period. The young Marx began his university education in 1835 at the University of Bonn, where he studied law. After an unsuccessful first year there, he transferred to the University of Berlin. Although still formally enrolled in law, Marx's interest in philosophy quickly began to deepen. Berlin was where Hegel held the chair in philosophy, and his system of absolute idealism dominated the intellectual scene.

Karl Marx

photos.com/Thinkstock

Abandoning the study of law by 1839, Marx wrote a philosophy thesis entitled "The Difference between the Democritean and Epicurean Philosophy of Nature," which he submitted to the University of Jena. In 1841, the university awarded him a doctorate for this work. Soon thereafter, Marx began to work as a political journalist in Cologne for the newspaper *Rheinische Zeitung* (*The Rhineland News*); he rose to editor before the Prussian government banned the publication in 1943. The same year, Marx married his childhood friend Jenny von Westphalen, a Prussian baroness to whom he had been engaged for six years. They moved to Paris, where Marx became the editor of a new journal, *Deutsch-Französische Jahrbücher*.

In Paris, Marx's writings soon earned him a reputation as a radical. There, he became acquainted with many revolutionaries and radical activists, among them Friedrich Engels. Their relationship was soon cemented into a lifelong friendship, as they recognized in each other a philosophical partner. Engels came from a wealthy Prussian family whose business was textile manufacturing, with an office in Manchester. In 1845 Marx was deported from Paris at the urging of the Prussian monarchy. With Engels' help, Marx moved with his family to England, where both he and Engels began working with several revolutionary organizations. As their influence grew, several of these groups joined to form an International

Communist League, with Engels as its first secretary. Both men were entrusted with writing a statement of principles for the League that could unite the working class around the world in the cause of revolution; this is the document known as *The Communist Manifesto*.

Marx was greatly influenced by Hegel's "dialectical" method of studying history, which viewed ideas, and human progress generally, as evolving by means of certain necessary processes of contradiction between opposing ideas—thesis and antithesis, culminating in a synthesis (though the process continues). However, Marx now jettisoned Hegel's emphasis on "the ideal" (in his dialectical method) and instead developed a materialist conception of history and progress, which focused on material matter and the processes related to these (such as the production of goods). This substitution came about as a result of the influence of another German philosopher, Ludwig Feuerbach. Feuerbach rejected Hegel's idealism and proposed a thesis of his own: reality was material. Marx married Hegel's dialectic view of history with Feuerbach's materialism to devise a new doctrine, "historical materialism." Historical materialism views the progress of humanity through the development of the material order. Accordingly, Marx detected several epochs in human history—starting with primitive communal society—each characterized by a particular mode of production with distinct features and tendencies.

Despite Marx's immense posthumous influence on the twentieth century, he lived much of his life in anonymity and struggled financially. His main income came from freelance writing that he did for different newspapers, but this did not provide for a steady income. From 1849 onward, however, his good friend Engels helped Marx and his family by providing a regular stipend. With his financial worries laid to rest, Marx was able to dedicate himself completely to writing his treatise on political economy, *Das Kapital* (*Capital*), the heady aim of which was to find the economic laws of societal transformation and change. He spent 10 hours every day in the Reading Room of the British Museum working on this massive project—his magnum opus—yet he only managed to finish and publish the first volume during his lifetime (in 1867). The second and third volumes were published by Engels following Marx's death in 1883; a fourth—unfinished—volume was never published in full.

The text we consider here, *The Communist Manifesto*, is a polemical work with particular political aims. The opening sentence of the document, which reads, "A spectre is haunting Europe—the spectre of Communism," signalled powerful and lasting changes in European and world history. The text is divided into four sections in which Marx provides the following: (1) a history of class struggle from the Middle Ages through the rise of the bourgeoisie to the present class situation of modern capitalist society, with a focus on the struggle between the bourgeoisie and the proletariat; (2) an account, and defence, of the relationship between the communist movement and the working class; (3) justification for why Marx and Engels' account of communism is superior to other socialist theories; and (4) an explanation of the international character of communism. Marx discovers the continuity of class struggle in all epochs up to his time and claims that such antagonisms provided the engine for the development of society, essentially propelling history forward. The text of *The Communist Manifesto* ends with as powerful a statement as it started with: "The proletarians have nothing to lose but their chains. They have a world to gain. Working men of all countries unite."

Further Readings

Elster, J. (1986). *An Introduction to Marx*. Cambridge: Cambridge University Press.

Gilbert, A. (1981). *Marx's Politics*. Rutgers: Rutgers University Press.

Miller, D. (1987). "Marx, Communism and Markets," *Political Theory* 15 (2): 182–204.

Wolff, J. (2002). *Why Read Marx Today?* New York and Oxford: Oxford University Press.

Wood, A. (2004). *Karl Marx*. Abingdon, U.K.: Taylor & Francis.

Karl Marx and Friedrich Engels, *The Communist Manifesto*

Karl Marx and Friedrich Engels, The Communist Manifesto
(New York: Oxford University Press, 2008).

A spectre is haunting Europe—the spectre of Communism. All the Powers of old Europe have entered into a holy alliance to exorcize this spectre: Pope and Czar, Metternich and Guizot, French Radicals and German police spies.

Where is the party in opposition that has not been decried as Communistic by its opponents in power? Where the opposition that has not hurled back the branding reproach of Communism, against the more advanced opposition parties, as well as against its reactionary adversaries?

Two things result from this fact:

I. Communism is already acknowledged by all European powers to be itself a power.

II. It is high time that Communists should openly, in the face of the whole world, publish their views, their aims, their tendencies, and meet this nursery tale of the spectre of Communism with a manifesto of the party itself.

To this end, Communists of various nationalities have assembled in London, and sketched the following manifesto, to be published in the English, French, German, Italian, Flemish, and Danish languages.

Chapter 1 Bourgeois and Proletarians[1]

The history of all hitherto existing society[2] is the history of class struggles.

Freeman and slave, patrician and plebeian, lord and serf, guild-master[3] and journeyman, in a word, oppressor and oppressed, stood in constant opposition to one another, carried on an uninterrupted, now hidden, now open fight, a fight that each time ended, either in a revolutionary reconstitution of society at large, or in the common ruin of the contending classes.

In the earlier epochs of history, we find almost everywhere a complicated arrangement of society into various orders, a manifold gradation of social rank. In ancient Rome we have patricians, knights, plebeians, slaves; in the Middle Ages, feudal lords, vassals, guild-masters, journeymen, serfs; in almost all of these classes, again, subordinate gradations.

The modern bourgeois society that has sprouted from the ruins of feudal society has not done away with class antagonisms. It has but established new classes, new conditions of oppression, new forms of struggle in place of the old ones.

Our epoch, the epoch of the bourgeoisie, possesses, however, this distinctive feature: it has simplified the class antagonisms. Society as a whole is more and more splitting up into two great hostile camps, into two great classes directly facing each other: bourgeoisie and proletariat.

From the serfs of the Middle Ages sprang the chartered burghers of the earliest towns. From these burgesses the first elements of the bourgeoisie were developed.

The discovery of America, the rounding of the Cape, opened up fresh ground for the rising bourgeoisie. The East-Indian and Chinese markets, the colonization of America, trade with the colonies, the increase in the means of exchange and in commodities generally, gave to commerce, to navigation, to industry, an impulse never before known, and thereby, to the revolutionary element in the tottering feudal society, a rapid development.

The previous feudal or guild organization of industry, under which industrial production was monopolized by closed guilds, now no longer sufficed for the growing wants of the new markets. The manufacturing system took its place. The guild-masters were pushed on one side by the manufacturing middle class; division of labour between the different corporate guilds vanished in the face of division of labour in each single workshop.

Meantime the markets kept ever growing, the demand ever rising. Even manufacture no longer sufficed. Thereupon, steam and machinery revolutionized industrial production. The place of manufacture was taken by the giant, modern industry, the place of the industrial middle class, by industrial millionaires, the leaders of whole industrial armies, the modern bourgeois.

Large-scale industry has established the world market, for which the discovery of America paved the way. This market has given an immense development to commerce, to navigation, to communication by land. This development has, in its turn, reacted on the extension of industry; and in proportion as industry, commerce, navigation, railways extended, in the same proportion the bourgeoisie developed, increased its capital, and pushed into the background every class handed down from the Middle Ages.

We see, therefore, how the modern bourgeoisie is itself the product of a long course of development, of a series of revolutions in the modes of production and of exchange.

Each step in the development of the bourgeoisie was accompanied by a corresponding political advance. An oppressed class under the sway of the feudal nobility, an armed and self-governing association in the medieval commune;[4] here independent urban republic, there taxable "third estate" of the monarchy, afterwards, in the period of manufacture proper, serving either the estate or the absolute monarchy as a counterpoise against the nobility, and, in fact, corner-stone of the great monarchies in general, the bourgeoisie has at last, since the establishment of modern industry and of the world market, conquered for itself, in the modern representative state, exclusive political sway. The executive of the modern state is but a committee for managing the common affairs of the whole bourgeoisie.

The bourgeoisie, historically, has played a most revolutionary part.

The bourgeoisie, wherever it has got the upper hand, has put an end to all feudal, patriarchal, idyllic relations. It has pitilessly torn asunder the motley feudal ties that bound man to his "natural superiors" and has left remaining no other nexus between man and man than naked self-interest, than callous "cash payment." It has drowned the most heavenly ecstasies of religious fervour, of chivalrous enthusiasm, of philistine sentimentalism, in the icy water of egotistical calculation. It has resolved personal worth into exchange value, and in place of the numberless indefeasible chartered freedoms, has set up that single, unconscionable freedom—free trade. In one word, for exploitation, veiled by religious and political illusions, it has substituted naked, shameless, direct, brutal exploitation.

The bourgeoisie has stripped of its halo every occupation hitherto honoured and looked up to with reverent awe. It has converted the physician, the lawyer, the priest, the poet, the man of science, into its paid wage-labourers.

The bourgeoisie has torn away from the family its sentimental veil, and has reduced the family relation to a mere money relation.

The bourgeoisie has disclosed how it came to pass that the brutal display of vigour in the Middle Ages, which reactionists so much admire, found its fitting complement in the most slothful indolence. It has been the first to show what man's activity can bring about. It has accomplished wonders far surpassing Egyptian pyramids, Roman aqueducts, and Gothic cathedrals; it has conducted expeditions that put in the shade all former Exoduses of nations and crusades.

The bourgeoisie cannot exist without constantly revolutionizing the instruments of production, and thereby the relations of production, and with them the whole relations of society. Conservation of the old modes of production in unaltered form, was, on the contrary, the first condition of existence for all earlier industrial classes. Constant revolutionizing of production, uninterrupted disturbance of all social conditions, everlasting uncertainty and agitation distinguish the bourgeois epoch from all earlier ones. All fixed, fast-frozen relations, with their train of ancient and venerable prejudices and opinions are swept away, all new-formed ones become antiquated before they can ossify. All that is solid melts into air, all that is holy is profaned, and man is at last compelled to face with sober senses, his real conditions of life, and his relations with his kind.

The need of a constantly expanding market for its products chases the bourgeoisie over the whole surface of the globe. It must nestle everywhere, settle everywhere, establish connexions everywhere.

The bourgeoisie has through its exploitation of the world market given a cosmopolitan character to production and consumption in every country. To the great chagrin of reactionists, it has drawn from under the feet of industry the national ground on which it stood. All old-established national industries have been destroyed or are daily being destroyed. They are dislodged by new industries, whose introduction becomes a life and death question for all civilized nations, by industries that no longer work up indigenous raw material, but raw material drawn from the remotest zones; industries whose products are consumed, not only at home, but in every quarter of the globe. In place of the old wants, satisfied by the productions of the country, we find new wants, requiring for their satisfaction the products of distant lands and climes. In place of the old local and national seclusion and self-sufficiency, we have intercourse in every direction, universal interdependence of nations. And as in material, so also in intellectual production. The intellectual creations of individual nations become common property. National one-sidedness and narrowmindedness become more and more impossible, and from the numerous national and local literatures, there arises a world literature.

The bourgeoisie, by the rapid improvement of all instruments of production, by the immensely facilitated means of communication, draws all, even the most barbarian, nations into civilization. The cheap prices of its commodities are the heavy artillery with which it batten down all Chinese walls, with which it forces the barbarians' intensely obstinate hatred of foreigners to capitulate. It compels all nations, on pain of extinction, to adopt the bourgeois mode of production; it compels them to introduce what it calls civilization into their midst, i.e., to become bourgeois themselves. In one word, it creates a world after its own image.

The bourgeoisie has subjected the country to the rule of the towns. It has created enormous cities, has greatly increased the urban population as compared with the rural, and has thus rescued a considerable part of the population from the idiocy of rural life. Just as it has made the country dependent on the towns, so it has made barbarian and semi-barbarian countries dependent on the civilized ones, nations of peasants on nations of bourgeois, the East on the West.

The bourgeoisie keeps more and more doing away with the scattered state of the population, of the means of production, and of property. It has agglomerated population, centralized means of production, and has concentrated property in a few hands. The necessary consequence of this was political centralization. Independent, or but loosely connected, provinces with separate interests, laws, governments, and systems of taxation, became lumped together into one nation, with one government, one code of laws, one national class interest, one frontier and one customs tariff.

The bourgeoisie, during its rule of scarce 100 years, has created more massive and more colossal productive forces than have all preceding generations together. Subjection of nature's forces to man, machinery, application of chemistry to industry and agriculture, steam navigation, railways, electric telegraphs, clearing of whole continents for cultivation, canalization of rivers, whole populations conjured out of the ground—what earlier century had even a presentiment that such productive forces slumbered in the lap of social labour?

We see then: the means of production and of exchange, on whose foundation the bourgeoisie built itself up, were generated in feudal society. At a certain stage in the development of these means of production and of exchange, the conditions under which feudal society produced and exchanged, the feudal organization of agriculture and manufacturing industry, in one word, the feudal relations of property became no longer compatible with the already developed productive forces; they hindered production rather than advancing it; they became so many fetters. They had to be burst asunder; they were burst asunder. Into their place stepped free competition, accompanied by a social and political constitution adapted to it, and by the economical and political sway of the bourgeois class.

A similar movement is going on before our own eyes. Modern bourgeois society with its relations of production, of exchange and of property, a society that has conjured up such gigantic means of production and of exchange, is like the sorcerer, who is no longer able to control the powers of the nether world whom he has called up by his spells. For many a decade past the history of industry and commerce is but the history of the revolt of modern productive forces against modern conditions of production, against the property relations that are the conditions for the existence of the bourgeoisie and of its rule. It is enough to mention the commercial crises that by their periodical return put on its trial, each time more threateningly, the existence of the entire bourgeois society. In these crises a great part not only of the existing products, but also of the previously created productive forces, are periodically destroyed. In these crises there breaks out a social epidemic that, in all earlier epochs, would have seemed an absurdity—the epidemic of over-production. Society suddenly finds itself put back into a state of momentary barbarism; it appears as if a famine, a universal war of devastation had cut off the supply of every means of subsistence; industry and commerce seem to be destroyed; and why? Because there is too much civilization, too much means of subsistence, too much industry, too much commerce. The productive forces at the disposal of society no longer tend to further the development of bourgeois civilization and the conditions of bourgeois property; on the contrary, they have become too powerful for these conditions, by which they are fettered, and so soon as they overcome these fetters, they bring disorder into the whole of bourgeois society, endanger the existence of bourgeois property. The conditions of bourgeois society are too narrow to comprise the wealth created by them. And how does the bourgeoisie get over these crises? On the one hand by enforced destruction of a mass of productive forces; on the other, by the conquest of new markets, and by the more thorough exploitation of the old ones. That is to say, by paving the way for more extensive and more destructive crises, and by diminishing the means whereby crises are prevented.

The weapons with which the bourgeoisie felled feudalism to the ground are now turned against the bourgeoisie itself.

But not only has the bourgeoisie forged the weapons that bring death to itself, it has also called into existence the men who are to wield those weapons—the modern workers—the proletarians.

In proportion as the bourgeoisie, i.e., capital, is developed, in the same proportion is the proletariat, the modern working class, developed—a class of labourers, who live only so long as they find work, and who find work only so long as their labour increases capital. These labourers, who must sell themselves piecemeal, are a commodity, like every other article of commerce, and are consequently exposed to all the vicissitudes of competition, to all the fluctuations of the market.

Owing to the extensive use of machinery and to division of labour, the work of the proletarians has lost all individual character, and, consequently, all charm for the workman. He becomes an appendage of the machine, and it is only the most simple, most monotonous, and most easily acquired knack, that is required of him. Hence, the cost of production of a workman is restricted, almost entirely, to the means of subsistence that he requires for his maintenance, and for the propagation of his race. But the price of a commodity, and therefore also of labour, is equal to its cost of production. In proportion, therefore, as the repulsiveness of the work increases, the wage decreases. Nay more, in proportion as the use of machinery and division of labour increases, in the same proportion the quantity of labour also increases, whether by prolongation of the working hours, by increase of the work exacted in a given time or by increased speed of the machinery, etc.

Modern industry has converted the little workshop of the patriarchal master into the great factory of the industrial capitalist. Masses of labourers, crowded into the factory, are organized like soldiers. As privates of the industrial army they are placed under the command of a perfect hierarchy of officers and sergeants. Not only are they slaves of the bourgeois class, and of the bourgeois state; they are daily and hourly enslaved by the machine, by the overlooker, and, above all, by the individual bourgeois manufacturer himself. The more openly this despotism proclaims gain to be its end and aim, the more petty, the more hateful and the more embittering it is.

The less the skill and exertion of strength implied in manual labour, in other words, the more modern industry becomes developed, the more is the labour of men superseded by that of women. Differences of age and sex have no longer any distinctive social validity for the working class. All are instruments of labour, more or less expensive to use, according to their age and sex.

No sooner is the exploitation of the labourer by the manufacturer, so far, at an end, that he receives his wages in cash, than he is set upon by the other portions of the bourgeoisie, the landlord, the shopkeeper, the pawnbroker, etc.

The former lower strata of the middle estate—the small tradespeople, shopkeepers, and rentiers, the handicraftsmen and peasants—all these sink gradually into the proletariat, partly because their diminutive capital does not suffice for the scale on which modern industry is carried on, and is swamped in the competition with the large capitalists, partly because their specialized skill is rendered worthless by new methods of production. Thus the proletariat is recruited from all classes of the population.

The proletariat goes through various stages of development. With its birth begins its struggle with the bourgeoisie. At first the contest is carried on by individual labourers, then by the workpeople of a factory, then by the operatives of one trade, in one locality, against the individual bourgeois who directly exploits them. They direct their attacks not only against the bourgeois conditions of production, they direct them against the instruments of production themselves; they destroy imported wares that compete with their labour, they smash to pieces machinery, they set factories ablaze, they seek to restore by force the vanished status of the workman of the Middle Ages.

At this stage the labourers still form a mass scattered over the whole country, and broken up by their mutual competition. If anywhere they unite to form more compact bodies, this is not yet the consequence of their own active union, but of the union of the bourgeoisie, which class, in order to attain its own political ends, is compelled to set the whole proletariat in motion, and is moreover yet, for a time, able to do so. At this stage, therefore, the proletarians do not fight their enemies, but the enemies of their enemies, the remnants of absolute monarchy, the landowners, the non-industrial bourgeois, the petty bourgeoisie. Thus the whole historical movement is concentrated in the hands of the bourgeoisie; every victory so obtained is a victory for the bourgeoisie.

But with the development of industry the proletariat not only increases in number; it becomes concentrated in greater masses, its strength grows, and it feels that strength more. The various interests and conditions of life within the ranks of the proletariat are more and more equalized in proportion as machinery obliterates all distinctions of labour, and nearly everywhere reduces wages to the same low level. The growing competition among the bourgeois, and the resulting commercial crises, make the wages of the workers ever more fluctuating. The unceasing improvement of machinery, ever more rapidly developing, makes their livelihood more and more precarious; the collisions between individual workmen and individual bourgeois take more and more the character of collisions between two classes. Thereupon the workers begin to form combinations against the bourgeois; they club together in order to keep up the rate of wages; they found permanent associations in order to make provision beforehand for these occasional revolts. Here and there the contest breaks out into riots.

Now and then the workers are victorious, but only for a time. The real fruit of their battles lies, not in the immediate result, but in the ever-expanding union of the workers. This union is helped on by the improved means of communication that are created by modern industry and that place the workers of different localities in contact with one another. It was just this contact that was needed to centralize the numerous local struggles, all of the same character, into one national struggle between classes. But every class struggle is a political struggle. And that union, to attain which the burghers of the Middle Ages, with their miserable highways, required centuries, the modern proletarians, thanks to railways, achieve in a few years.

This organization of the proletarians into a class, and consequently into a political party, is continually being upset again by the competition between the workers themselves. But it ever rises up again, stronger, firmer, mightier. It compels legislative recognition of particular interests of the workers, by taking advantage of the divisions among the bourgeoisie itself. Thus the Ten Hours bill in England was carried.[5]

Although collisions between the classes of the old society further, in many ways, the course of development of the proletariat. The bourgeoisie finds itself involved in a constant battle. At first with the aristocracy; later on, with those portions of the bourgeoisie itself, whose interests have become antagonistic to the progress of industry; at all times, with the bourgeoisie of foreign countries. In all these battles it sees itself compelled to appeal to the proletariat, to ask for its help, and thus, to drag it into the political arena. The bourgeoisie itself, therefore, supplies the proletariat with its own elements of education, in other words, it furnishes the proletariat with weapons for fighting the bourgeoisie.

Further, as we have already seen, entire sections of the ruling classes are, by the advance of industry, precipitated into the proletariat, or are at least threatened in their conditions of existence. These also supply the proletariat with a lot of elements of education.

Finally, in times when the class struggle nears the decisive hour, the process of dissolution going on within the ruling class, in fact within the whole range of old society, assumes such a violent, glaring character, that a small section of the ruling class cuts itself adrift, and joins the revolutionary class, the class that holds the future in its hands. Just as, therefore, at an earlier period, a section of the nobility went over to the bourgeoisie, so now a portion of the bourgeoisie goes over to the proletariat, and in particular, a portion of the bourgeois ideologists, who have raised themselves to the level of comprehending theoretically the historical movement as a whole.

Of all the classes that stand face to face with the bourgeoisie today, the proletariat alone is a really revolutionary class. The other classes decay and finally disappear in the face of modern industry; the proletariat is its special and essential product.

The middle estates, the small manufacturer, the shopkeeper, the artisan, the peasant, all these fight against the bourgeoisie, to save from extinction their existence as fractions of the middle class. They are therefore not revolutionary, but conservative. Nay more, they are reactionary, for they try to roll back the wheel of history. If by chance they are revolutionary, they are so only in view of their impending transfer into the proletariat, they thus defend not their present, but their future interests, they desert their own standpoint to place themselves at that of the proletariat.

The lumpenproletariat, that passively rotting mass thrown off by the lowest layers of old society, may, here and there, be swept into the movement by a proletarian revolution; its conditions of life, however, prepare it far more for the part of a bribed tool of reactionary intrigue.

In the conditions of the proletariat, those of old society at large are already virtually swamped. The proletarian is without property; his relation to his wife and children has no longer anything in common with the bourgeois family relations; modern industrial labour, modern subjection to capital, the same in England as in France, in America as in Germany, has stripped him of every trace of national character. Law, morality, religion, are to him so many bourgeois prejudices, behind which lurk in ambush just as many bourgeois interests.

All the preceding classes that got the upper hand sought to fortify their already acquired status by subjecting society at large to their conditions of appropriation. The proletarians cannot become masters of the productive forces of society, except by abolishing their own previous mode of appropriation, and thereby also every other previous mode of appropriation. They have nothing of their own to secure and to fortify; their mission is to destroy all previous securities for, and insurances of, individual property.

All previous historical movements were movements of minorities, or in the interest of minorities. The proletarian movement is the independent movement of the immense majority, in the interest of the immense majority. The proletariat, the lowest stratum of our present society, cannot stir, cannot raise itself up, without the whole superincumbent strata of official society being sprung into the air.

Though not in substance, yet in form, the struggle of the proletariat with the bourgeoisie is at first a national struggle. The proletariat of each country must, of course, first of all settle matters with its own bourgeoisie.

In depicting the most general phases of the development of the proletariat, we traced the more or less veiled civil war, raging within existing society, up to the point where that war breaks out into open revolution, and where the violent overthrow of the bourgeoisie lays the foundation for the sway of the proletariat.

Hitherto, every form of society has been based, as we have already seen, on the antagonism of oppressing and oppressed classes. But in order to oppress a class, certain conditions must be assured to it under which it can, at least, continue its slavish existence. The serf, in the period of serfdom, raised himself to membership in the commune, just as the petty bourgeois, under the yoke of feudal absolutism, managed to develop into a bourgeois. The modern labourer, on the contrary, instead of rising with the progress of industry, sinks deeper and deeper below the conditions of existence of his own class. He becomes a pauper, and pauperism develops more rapidly than population and wealth. And here it becomes evident, that the bourgeoisie is unfit any longer to be the ruling class in society, and to impose its conditions of existence upon society as an overriding law. It is unfit to rule because it is incompetent to assure an existence to its slave within his slavery, because it cannot help letting him sink into such a state, that it has to feed him, instead of being fed by him. Society can no longer live under this bourgeoisie, in other words, its existence is no longer compatible with society.

The essential condition for the existence, and for the sway of the bourgeois class, is the accumulation of wealth in the hands of private individuals, the formation and augmentation of capital; the condition for capital is wage labour. Wage labour rests exclusively on competition between the labourers. The advance of industry, whose involuntary promoter is the bourgeoisie, replaces the isolation of the labourers, due to competition, by their revolutionary combination, due to association. The development of modern industry, therefore, cuts from under its feet the very foundation on which the bourgeoisie produces and appropriates products. What the bourgeoisie, therefore, produces, above all, is its own grave-diggers. Its fall and the victory of the proletariat are equally inevitable.

Chapter II Proletarians and Communists

In what relation do the Communists stand to the proletarians as a whole?

The Communists do not form a separate party opposed to other working-class parties.

They have no interest separate and apart from those of the proletariat as a whole.

They do not set up any separate principles of their own, by which to shape and mould the proletarian movement.

The Communists are distinguished from the other working-class parties by this only: (1) In the national struggles of the proletarians of the different countries, they point out and bring to the front the common interests of the entire proletariat, independently of all nationality. (2) In the various stages of development which the struggle of the working class against the bourgeoisie has to pass through, they always and everywhere represent the interests of the movement as a whole.

The Communists, therefore, are on the one hand, practically, the most resolute section of the working-class parties of every country, that section which pushes forward all others; on the other hand, theoretically, they have over the great mass of the proletariat the advantage of clearly understanding the line of march, the conditions, and the ultimate general results of the proletarian movement.

The immediate aim of the Communists is the same as that of all the other proletarian parties: formation of the proletariat into a class, overthrow of the bourgeois supremacy, conquest of political power by the proletariat.

The theoretical conclusions of the Communists are in no way based on ideas or principles that have been invented, or discovered, by this or that would-be universal reformer.

They merely express, in general terms, actual relations springing from an existing class struggle, from a historical movement going on under our very eyes. The abolition of existing property relations is not at all a distinctive feature of Communism.

All property relations in the past were subject to constant historical replacement, constant historical change.

The French Revolution, for example, abolished feudal property in favour of bourgeois property.

The distinguishing feature of Communism is not the abolition of property generally, but the abolition of bourgeois property. But modern bourgeois private property is the final and most complete expression of the system of producing and appropriating products, that is based on class antagonisms, on the exploitation of some by others.

In this sense, the theory of the Communists may be summed up in the single sentence: abolition of private property.

We Communists have been reproached with the desire of abolishing the right of personally acquiring property as the fruit of a man's own labour, which property is alleged to be the ground work of all personal freedom, activity and independence.

Hard-won, self-acquired, self-earned property! Do you mean the property of the petty bourgeois and of the small peasant, a form of property that preceded the bourgeois form? There is no need to abolish that; the development of industry has to a great extent already destroyed it, and is still destroying it daily.

Or do you mean modern bourgeois private property?

But does wage labour create any property for the labourer? Not a bit. It creates capital, i.e., that kind of property which exploits wage labour, and which cannot increase except upon condition of begetting a new supply of wage labour for fresh exploitation. Property, in its present form, is based on the antagonism of capital and wage labour. Let us examine both sides of this antagonism.

To be a capitalist is to have not only a purely personal but a social *status* in production. Capital is a collective product, and only by the united action of many members, nay, in the last resort, only by the united action of all members of society, can it be set in motion.

Capital is, therefore, not a personal, it is a social power.

When, therefore, capital is converted into common property, into the property of all members of society, personal property is not thereby transformed into social property. It is only the social character of the property that is changed. It loses its class character.

Let us now take wage labour.

The average price of wage labour is the minimum wage, i.e., that quantum of the means of subsistence which is absolutely requisite to keep the labourer in bare existence as a labourer. What, therefore, the wage-labourer appropriates by means of his labour, merely suffices to prolong and reproduce a bare existence. We by no means intend to abolish this personal appropriation of the products of labour, an appropriation that is made for the maintenance and reproduction of human life, and that leaves no surplus wherewith to command the labour of others. All that we want to do away with is the miserable character of this appropriation, under which the labourer lives merely to increase capital, and is

allowed to live only in so far as the interest of the ruling class requires it.

In bourgeois society, living labour is but a means to increase accumulated labour. In Communist society, accumulated labour is but a means to widen, to enrich, to promote the existence of the labourer.

In bourgeois society, therefore, the past dominates the present; in Communist society, the present dominates the past. In bourgeois society capital is independent and has individuality, while the living person is dependent and has no individuality.

And the abolition of this state of things is called by the bourgeois, abolition of individuality and freedom! And rightly so. The abolition of bourgeois individuality, bourgeois independence, and bourgeois freedom is undoubtedly aimed at.

By freedom is meant, under the present bourgeois conditions of production, free trade, free selling and buying.

But if selling and buying disappears, free selling and buying disappears also. This talk about free selling and buying, and all the other "brave words" of our bourgeoisie about freedom in general, have a meaning, if any, only in contrast with restricted selling and buying, with the fettered traders of the Middle Ages, but have no meaning when opposed to the Communistic abolition of buying and selling, of the bourgeois conditions of production, and of the bourgeoisie itself.

You are horrified at our intending to do away with private property. But in your existing society, private property is already done away with for nine-tenths of the population; its existence is solely due to its non-existence in the hands of those nine-tenths. You reproach us, therefore, with intending to do away with a form of property the necessary condition for whose existence is the non-existence of any property for the immense majority of society.

In one word, you reproach us with intending to do away with your property. Precisely so; that is just what we intend.

From the moment when labour can no longer be converted into capital, money, or rent, into a social power capable of being monopolized, i.e., from the moment when individual property can no longer be transformed into bourgeois property, from that moment, you say, individuality vanishes.

You must, therefore, confess that by "individual" you mean no other person than the bourgeois, than the middle-class owner of property. This person must, indeed, be swept out of the way. Communism deprives no man of the power to appropriate the products of society;

all that it does is to deprive him of the power to subjugate the labour of others by means of such appropriation.

It has been objected that upon the abolition of private property all work will cease, and universal laziness will overtake us.

According to this, bourgeois society ought long ago to have gone to the dogs through sheer idleness; for those of its members who work, acquire nothing, and those who acquire anything, do not work. The whole of this objection is but another expression of the tautology: that there can no longer be any wage labour when there is no longer any capital.

All objections urged against the Communistic mode of producing and appropriating material products, have, in the same way, been urged against the Communistic modes of producing and appropriating intellectual products. Just as, to the bourgeois, the disappearance of class property is the disappearance of production itself, so the disappearance of class culture is to him identical with the disappearance of all culture.

That culture, the loss of which he laments, is, for the enormous majority, a mere training to act as a machine.

But don't wrangle with us so long as you apply, to the abolition of bourgeois property, the standard of your bourgeois notions of freedom, culture, law, etc. Your very ideas are but the outgrowth of the conditions of your bourgeois production and bourgeois property, just as your jurisprudence is but the will of your class made into a law for all, a will, whose essential content is determined by the material conditions of existence of your class.

The selfish conception that induces you to transform into eternal laws of nature and of reason, the social forms springing from your present mode of production and form of property—historical relations that rise and disappear in the progress of production—this conception you share with every ruling class that has disappeared. What you see clearly in the case of ancient property, what you admit in the case of feudal property, you are of course forbidden to admit in the case of your own bourgeois form of property.

Abolition of the family! Even the most radical flare up at this infamous proposal of the Communists.

On what foundation is the present family, the bourgeois family, based? On capital, on private gain. In its completely developed form this family exists only among the bourgeoisie. But this state of things finds its complement in the practical absence of the family among the proletarians, and in public prostitution.

The bourgeois family will vanish as a matter of course when its complement vanishes, and both will vanish with the vanishing of capital.

Do you charge us with wanting to stop the exploitation of children by their parents? To this crime we plead guilty.

But, you will say, we destroy the most hallowed of relations, when we replace home education by social.

And your education! Is not that also social, and determined by the social conditions under which you educate, by the intervention, direct or indirect, of society, by means of schools, etc.? The Communists have not invented the intervention of society in education; they do but seek to alter the character of that intervention, and to rescue education from the influence of the ruling class.

The bourgeois clap-trap about the family and education, about the hallowed co-relation of parent and child, becomes all the more disgusting, the more, by the action of modern industry, all family ties among the proletarians are torn asunder, and their children transformed into simple articles of commerce and instruments of labour.

But you Communists would introduce community of women, screams the whole bourgeoisie in chorus.

The bourgeois sees in his wife a mere instrument of production. He hears that the instruments of production are to be exploited in common, and, naturally, can come to no other conclusion than that the lot of being common to all will likewise fall to the women.

He has not even a suspicion that the real point aimed at is to do away with the status of women as mere instruments of production. For the rest, nothing is more ridiculous than the virtuous indignation of our bourgeois at the community of women which, they pretend, is to be openly and officially established by the Communists. The Communists have no need to introduce community of women; it has existed almost from time immemorial.

Our bourgeois, not content with having the wives and daughters of their proletarians at their disposal, not to speak of common prostitutes, take the greatest pleasure in seducing each other's wives.

Bourgeois marriage is in reality a system of wives in common and thus, at the most, what the Communists might possibly be reproached with, is that they desire to introduce, in substitution for a hypocritically concealed, an openly legalized community of women. For the rest, it is self-evident that the abolition of the present system of production must bring with it the abolition of the community of women springing from that system, i.e., of prostitution both public and private.

The Communists are further reproached with desiring to abolish countries and nationality.

The working men have no country. We cannot take from them what they have not got. Since the proletariat must first of all acquire political supremacy, must rise to be the national class, must constitute itself *the* nation, it is, so far, itself national, though not in the bourgeois sense of the word.

National differences and antagonisms between peoples are daily more and more vanishing, owing to the development of the bourgeoisie, to freedom of commerce, to the world market, to uniformity in the mode of production and in the conditions of life corresponding thereto.

The supremacy of the proletariat will cause them to vanish still faster. United action, of the leading civilized countries at least, is one of the first conditions for the emancipation of the proletariat.

In proportion as the exploitation of one individual by another is put an end to, the exploitation of one nation by another will also be put an end to. In proportion as the antagonism between classes within the nation vanishes, the hostility of one nation to another will come to an end.

The charges against Communism made from a religious, a philosophical, and, generally, from an ideological standpoint, are not deserving of serious examination.

Does it require deep intuition to comprehend that man's ideas, views, and conceptions, in one word, man's consciousness, changes with every change in the conditions of his existence, in his social relations and in his social life?

What else does the history of ideas prove, than that intellectual production changes in character in proportion as material production is changed? The ruling ideas of each age have ever been the ideas of its ruling class.

When people speak of ideas that revolutionize society, they do but express the fact, that within the old society, the elements of a new one have been created, and that the dissolution of the old ideas keeps even pace with the dissolution of the old conditions of existence.

When the ancient world was in its last throes, the ancient religions were overcome by Christianity. When Christian ideas succumbed in the eighteenth century to the ideas of the Enlightenment, feudal society fought its death battle with the then revolutionary bourgeoisie. The ideas of religious liberty and freedom of conscience, merely gave expression to the sway of free competition within the domain of knowledge.

"Undoubtedly," it will be said, "religious, moral, philosophical, political, juridical ideas, etc., have been modified in the course of historical development. But religion, morality, philosophy, political science, and law, constantly survived this change.

"There are, besides, eternal truths, such as freedom, justice, etc., that are common to all states of society. But Communism abolishes eternal truths, it abolishes all religion, and all morality, instead of constituting them on a new basis; it therefore acts in contradiction to all past historical experience."

What does this accusation reduce itself to? The history of all past society has consisted in the development of class antagonisms, antagonisms that assumed different forms at different epochs.

But whatever form they may have taken, one fact is common to all past ages, viz., the exploitation of one part of society by the other. No wonder, then, that the social consciousness of past ages, despite all the multiplicity and variety it displays, moves within certain common forms, in forms of consciousness which cannot completely vanish except with the total disappearance of class antagonisms.

The Communist revolution is the most radical rupture with traditional property relations; no wonder that its development involves the most radical rupture with traditional ideas.

But let us have done with the bourgeois objections to Communism.

We have seen above, that the first step in the revolution by the working class, is to raise the proletariat to the position of ruling class, to win the battle of democracy.

The proletariat will use its political supremacy to wrest, by degrees, all capital from the bourgeoisie, to centralize all instruments of production in the hands of the state, i.e., of the proletariat organized as the ruling class; and to increase the total of productive forces as rapidly as possible.

Of course, in the beginning, this cannot be effected except by means of despotic inroads on the rights of property, and on the conditions of bourgeois production; by means of measures, therefore, which appear economically insufficient and untenable, but which, in the course of the movement, outstrip themselves and are unavoidable as a means of entirely revolutionizing the mode of production.

These measures will of course be different in different countries.

Nevertheless, in the most advanced countries, the following will be pretty generally applicable:

1. Expropriation of property in land and application of all rents of land to public purposes.
2. A heavy progressive tax.
3. Abolition of all right of inheritance.
4. Confiscation of the property of all emigrants and rebels.
5. Centralization of credit in the hands of the state, by means of a national bank with state capital and an exclusive monopoly.

6. Centralization of transport in the hands of the state.

7. Extension of factories and instruments of production owned by the state; the bringing into cultivation of wastelands, and the improvement of the soil generally in accordance with a common plan.

8. Equal liability of all to labour. Establishment of industrial armies, especially for agriculture.

9. Combination of agriculture with industry, promotion of the gradual elimination of the contradictions between town and countryside.

10. Free education for all children in public schools. Abolition of children's factory labour in its present form. Combination of education with industrial production, etc., etc.

When, in the course of development, class distinctions have disappeared, and all production has been concentrated in the hands of associated individuals, the public power will lose its political character. Political power, properly so called, is merely the organized power of one class for oppressing another. If the proletariat during its contest with the bourgeoisie is compelled, by the force of circumstances, to organize itself as a class, if, by means of a revolution, it makes itself the ruling class, and, as such, sweeps away by force the old conditions of production, then it will, along with these conditions, have swept away the conditions for the existence of class antagonisms and of classes generally, and will thereby have abolished its own supremacy as a class.

In place of the old bourgeois society, with its classes and class antagonisms, we shall have an association, in which the free development of each is the condition for the free development of all.

Post-Reading Questions

1. Why, according to Marx and Engels, does private property adversely affect people's freedom?

2. Do you think private property negatively affects people's freedom and opportunities today?

3. Marx and Engels predicted that class struggle would intensify and escalate. Why?

4. Why is wage capitalism fundamentally exploitative, according to the authors of *The Communist Manifesto*?

5. What role do the ideals of freedom and self-development play in the humanist vision developed by Marx and Engels?

6. What is the relationship between the mode of production in society and people's consciousness, according to Marx and Engels? Why is this relationship so important, in their view?

CASE STUDY
THE WINNIPEG GENERAL STRIKE

Introduction

One of the key predictions of Karl Marx and Friedrich Engels' 1848 *Communist Manifesto* was that class antagonisms and struggles would intensify in newly industrializing societies and ultimately prepare the ground for communist revolution. Marx and Engels speculated that the cyclical crises of capitalism would generate increased trade union activity, and eventually lead to the radicalization of the proletariat. All of this may seem a rather distant and fanciful proposition. But while the rise of consumerist society has perhaps made social classes seem less starkly demarcated within industrialized countries today than in the nineteenth century, there have been times in Canada's recent past when explicit class struggle was very much in evidence. The Winnipeg General Strike of 1919, the largest general strike in Canada to date and possibly in North America, is a dramatic example of this.

Facing war-induced inflation and the loss of purchasing power, a cross-section of workers in Winnipeg petitioned the city council for wage increases. Unsuccessful in their efforts, the workers commenced a massive strike on 15 May 1919. City council retaliated four days later, declaring the strikers' actions illegal and firing them all. Yet in the days that followed, still more tradespeople joined in, and the focal issue quickly became the right of workers to engage in collective bargaining and strike actions. During a gathering of 25,000 strikers in the Market Square on 21 June 1919—known as Bloody Saturday—numerous strikers were injured, and two killed. Such was the scale and magnitude of the strike (at its height, estimated to include most of the workers of the city) that the federal government stepped in, led by Minister of Labour Gideon Decker Robertson. Considerable violence ensued when the army and local militia were brought in to subdue the strikers. However, the ultimate resolution of the strike in favour of the workers was widely viewed as a crucial success for trade unionism in Canada, and specifically for the rights to collective bargaining and strike action.

The rise of trade unionism in Canada might well be viewed as the result of Winnipeg workers' worsening conditions, and their growing awareness of themselves as a social class distinct from—and at odds with—the capitalist bourgeoisie. Class consciousness and class struggle, as Marx and Engels described these, were no doubt factors in the Winnipeg strike, and arguably many workers became radicalized through the experience of striking. But while solidarity among the city workers and their families meant that the strikers eventually prevailed, Marx and Engels would likely have viewed the victory as only a partial one. Both men warned of the dangers of a reformist socialist agenda in which better wages and work conditions would come to replace more important and far-reaching goals—in particular, the goal of dismantling capitalist relations of production and private ownership altogether.

While large-scale labour actions such as the Winnipeg General Strike and the Cape Breton coal mining strikes of the 1920s did not necessarily share many of the specific goals of communist revolution set out in the *Manifesto*, there is considerable common ground at the level of ideals. Workers' control of the means of production, the abolition of child labour, and the provision of free public education—key to the communist vision—were also important demands of Canada's earliest trade unions. But the Winnipeg strikers also strove to secure better wages for workers and to protect their rights to bargain collectively and, if necessary, to strike. These are causes echoed by many labour struggles in Canada today, as unions have faced increased restrictions on their collective bargaining powers and right to strike in recent years. The anti-capitalist sentiment among the Winnipeg strikers is also echoed in present-day politics, most notably in the "Occupy" movement that spread rapidly across the United States and Canada in 2011 and 2012.

Marx and Engels' historical predictions have fared less well: within countries of the industrialized global North, the gradual expansion and concentration of the proletariat has not come to pass. Nor has working-class consciousness and solidarity evolved in such a way as to trigger worldwide communist revolution, as these thinkers anticipated. In addition to the co-opting effect of what both men considered to be revisionist reforms, the impact of economic globalization has made for a much more complex tapestry of social classes than they could possibly have predicted. The dramatic loss of industrial sector jobs and rise of service economies in rich countries, the proliferation of export processing zones in the global South, and the introduction of new legal obstacles to union organizing are just a few of the challenges to solidarity on the part of the working classes and poor in advanced industrialized democracies like Canada.

J.M. Bumsted, "Deferring Expectations, 1919–1945"

J.M. Bumsted, "Deferring Expectations, 1919–1945," in A History of the Canadian Peoples, *3rd edition (Toronto: Oxford University Press, 2003).*

Most of the conditions and issues that initially produced labour unrest in Winnipeg in the spring of 1919 were traditional ones exacerbated by the war: workers sought recognition of union rights to organize, higher wages, and better working conditions. A walkout by workers in the city's metal trades and building industries was quickly joined by others (as many as 50,000) in a general sympathy strike. On 15 May the strikers voted to close down the city's services. Much of the rhetoric of the strike sounded extremely radical. Some labour leaders hoped to use the general strike as a weapon to bring capitalism to its knees. Many demobilized servicemen supported the strikers. Worried businessmen saw the general strike as a breakdown of public authority. Workers in other cities, such as Toronto and Vancouver, responded with declarations of support and threats of their own strikes. The Canadian government, represented locally by acting minister of justice Arthur Meighen (1874–1960), responded decisively. He supplemented the army with local militia, the Royal North West Mounted Police, and 1,800 special constables. The Canadian Naturalization Act was hastily amended in early June 1919 to allow for the instant deportation of any foreign-born radicals who advocated revolution or who belonged to "any organization entertaining or teaching disbelief in or opposition to organized government" (quoted in Avery, 1986: 222).

Meighen effectively broke the strike on 17 June when he ordered the arrest of 10 strike leaders on charges of sedition. On 21 June—"Black Saturday"—a public demonstration of strikers and returned soldiers, marching towards the Winnipeg city hall, was met by a charge of Mounties on horseback. The result was a violent melee that injured many, killed two strikers, and led to the arrest of a number of "foreign rioters." Black Saturday happened despite the best efforts of the strike leaders to prevent the demonstration from going forward. The Strike Committee subsequently agreed to call off the strike if a Royal Commission investigated it and its underlying causes. The Royal Commission, called by the province of Manitoba, found that much of the labour unrest in Winnipeg was justified and that the strike's principal goal was to effect the introduction of collective bargaining. On the other hand, the Manitoba Court of Queen's Bench convicted most of the arrested leaders (who were either British- or Canadian-born) on charges of sedition. The Department of Immigration held deportation hearings for the "foreigners" in camera. The use of the civil arm to suppress radicalism, long a part of the Canadian tradition, was given a new meaning in post-war Winnipeg. Perhaps most significantly, the strike and its handling by the government demonstrated the fragility of the post-war readjustment. The next decade would further emphasize the problems.

. . .

Despite the government's brutal suppression of the Winnipeg General Strike, industrial unrest remained high through 1925. The One Big Union, a radical and militant industrial union, flourished briefly in western Canada. In 1921 labour representatives sat in seven of nine provincial legislatures. In the federal election of that year, more than 30 labour candidates ran for office, although only four were actually elected. Labour unrest after Winnipeg was most prevalent in the geographical extremes of the country. There were a number of notable strikes in Cape Breton, Alberta, and British Columbia. In the coalfields, 22,000 miners were on strike....

How History Has Changed

The Winnipeg General Strike

The historical interpretation of the Winnipeg General Strike of 1919 illustrates several different ways in which history changes. In the case of the Winnipeg General Strike, not only has one of the contemporary interpretations of its origins and meaning come to dominate, but its very importance in the nation's history has altered over time.

In 1919, there were two competing interpretations of the Winnipeg General Strike, both of them extreme. A conspiratorial one, propounded by its opponents, saw the strike as a daring attempt to overthrow the existing industrial and political system. The strikers themselves insisted that the strike was a legitimate, peaceful demonstration by labour to demand the right to organize and earn a living wage. Neither of these interpretations gained dominance at the time, and the strike—after a brief period in the national eye—was remembered solely as a local issue for many years. Only J.S. Woodsworth's prominence in Ottawa kept it before the larger Canadian public in the 1930s and 1940s. Textbooks written in the 1940s made little or no mention of the strike. This limited profile began to change in 1950 with the publication of Donald C. Masters' *The Winnipeg General Strike*. The strike gained in importance during the expansion of Canadian textbook publishing in the 1960s, as authors discovered that it was one of Canada's most highly polarized historical events, ideal for "conflicting interpretations" approaches. The strike's historical importance also benefited from an increased popularity of history "from the bottom up" and from a new sympathy towards radical movements.

Since 1970 a number of serious, full-length academic studies have been published. Most have accepted the strikers' own interpretation, seeing the strikers as moderate gradualists, victimized by their opposition through the law and the courts. No one could be found to defend seriously the role or policy of the federal government in the strike, which was seen not as an incipient revolution but merely as a modest attempt to win collective bargaining. New studies have examined other aspects of the strike, such as the role of women, the role of the "alien" and racism, and socialist ideology, but the strikers' own interpretation has now been clearly established as the dominant one.

In recent years, a number of historians have endeavoured to expand the scope of labour unrest before, during, and after the Winnipeg General Strike both chronologically and regionally. They have documented the presence of thousands of local strikes beginning the years immediately before the war, and they have emphasized the number of sympathetic strikes in other urban centres in 1919. The result has been to render the situation in Winnipeg both more common and more general than was previously recognized.

Post-Case-Reading Questions

1. To what extent did the Winnipeg General Strike reflect the kind of class conflict that Marx and Engels describe in *The Communist Manifesto*?
2. What were the goals of the strikers in Winnipeg? How do these compare with the aims associated with communist revolution, as outlined by Marx and Engels?

CHAPTER

X

John Rawls

Introduction

John Rawls (1921–2002) is arguably the most important contemporary political philosopher in the English-
speaking world. Born in Baltimore, Maryland, into an
affluent family, Rawls was nonetheless made aware of social injustices from an early age by his mother, a women's
rights and social reformer. He attended public school until
age 14, at which time he was enrolled at a renowned pre-
paratory school in Connecticut (Kent). From there, Rawls
went to Princeton, where he intended to study the natural
sciences; he ended up switching to philosophy, obtaining
his AB (BA) in philosophy in 1943. Shortly after graduation, he joined the US Army in the Pacific as an infantry
soldier. The experience of World War II left a lasting impression on Rawls as a young man, particularly the horrific
aftermath of the bombing of Hiroshima in Japan. Much
later, he was to become a staunch critic of the Vietnam war.

© Gamma-Rapho via Getty Images

John Rawls

A year after the war ended, Rawls returned to Princeton, where he obtained a PhD
in moral philosophy in 1950. During his doctoral studies, he took courses not only in
philosophy but also in economics and American constitutional law and political thought,
and this shaped his thinking about problems of justice. After his doctorate, Rawls
taught for two years at Princeton, then received a Fulbright scholarship that took him
to Oxford University (1952–3). There, he was influenced by Sir Isaiah Berlin's thinking
on liberal theory, as well as by philosophers H.L.A. Hart and Stuart Hampshire. Upon
his return to the United States, Rawls held appointments at Cornell University and the
Massachusetts Institute of Technology, leaving for a position at Harvard in 1962. Rawls
remained at Harvard until his retirement in 1991, continuing to teach occasionally until he suffered a stroke in 1995. His professional accomplishments are many, including
serving as president of philosophical and legal theory societies and being awarded a
National Humanities Medal by the US government in 1999; more notably, he mentored a

generation of leading moral and political philosophers who studied at Harvard, including Thomas E. Hill, Joshua Cohen, Thomas Nagel, and Onora O'Neill. Rawls died of heart failure in November 2002.

It would be difficult to overstate the impact of Rawls' groundbreaking book *A Theory of Justice* (1971): much subsequent writing in social, moral, and political philosophy situates itself in relation to Rawls' pivotal theory. Indeed, this work is credited with reviving the discipline—in its Anglo-American analytic tradition—and becoming the anchor of contemporary political philosophy. The several thousand articles and books that have been written about *A Theory of Justice* since its publication testify to its enormous, and enduring, influence.

In the tradition of social contract theories, Rawls' *A Theory of Justice* presents a comprehensive account of what he calls "justice as fairness." The problem of the relationship between the ideals of liberty and equality finds an elegant solution in the liberal egalitarianism outlined in the book, which defends political liberty alongside extensive socio-economic equality. Using contractarian reasoning (echoing the social contract theorists), Rawls proposes that we see the principles of justice as those that free and rational individuals would choose to govern the terms of their political association. He calls this approach "justice as fairness." Rawls then invites us to imagine a hypothetical initial situation of negotiation and choice from which rational people might determine certain principles of justice. Rawls calls the antecedent part of the hypothetical situation the "original position," which has several features: (1) the participants in the original position are rational; (2) they are mutually disinterested in each other's affairs; (3) they have capacities both for a sense of justice and for a conception of the good; and (4) the participants negotiate behind a veil of ignorance. Participants' rationality, Rawls tells us, is "purposive" rationality, which guides us to use the most effective means to obtain a particular end. They are mutually disinterested in one another, not in the sense that they are amoral or asocial, but rather in the sense that each knows his or her own interest best and can thus advocate for his or her own interests. The veil of ignorance is a theoretical device that aims to ensure the impartiality of principles of justice by requiring that selected principles do not simply mirror our real-world interests (those based on wealth, social class, and even natural endowments). This is because these features of our lives are, according to Rawls, morally irrelevant and therefore should not shape the content of common principles of justice. The participants to this hypothetical choice situation know that they are free and equal; that they have the capacity to make and revise conceptions of the good; and that they have a moral personality or a sense of justice. They also know general facts about the economy and society (e.g., the fact that there are social classes). Rawls argues that the principles of justice we would choose under such conditions are ones that should shape the basic structure (i.e., core institutions and arrangements) of society; he does not intend for these principles to shape the private interactions of individuals with one another, however.

If Rawls is correct about the choice situation represented by the "original position," then we should arrive at the following two principles of justice: (1) "Each person is to have an equal right to the most extensive total system of equal basic liberties compatible with a similar system of liberty for all"; and (2) "Social and economic inequalities are to be arranged so that they are both: (a) to the greatest benefit of the least advantaged . . . and (b) attached to offices and positions open to all under conditions of fair equality of opportunity" (Rawls 1971, 302). The first principle refers to the political domain and to the freedoms associated with speech, conscience, and assembly; the second principle is concerned with the social and economic domains and the distribution of opportunities, income, and wealth. The first (liberty) principle has priority in the sense that it cannot be substituted for or superseded by distributions made possible by the second principle; that is, the principle of liberty is not to be subordinated to considerations of utility.

The case reading that follows, the Canada Health Act, provides an opportunity for readers to consider whether (and why) Rawlsian justice might require universal health care coverage.

Further Readings

Barry, B. (1989). *Theories of Justice*. Berkeley and Los Angeles: University of California Press.

Daniels, N. (ed.). (1989). *Reading Rawls*. Stanford: Stanford University Press.

Neal, P. (1990). "Justice as Fairness: Political not Metaphysical," *Political Theory* 18 (1): 24–50.

Okin, S. (1989). *Justice, Gender and the Family*. New York: Basic Books.

Sandel, M. (1998). *Liberalism and the Limits of Justice*. 2nd ed. Cambridge: Cambridge University Press.

John Rawls, From *A Theory of Justice*

John Rawls, A Theory of Justice *(Cambridge: Harvard University Press, 1971).*

Chapter I Justice as Fairness

. . .

2. The Subject of Justice

Many different kinds of things are said to be just and unjust: not only laws, institutions, and social systems, but also particular actions of many kinds, including decisions, judgments, and imputations. We also call the attitudes and impositions of persons, and persons themselves, just and unjust. Our topic, however, is that of social justice. For us the primary subject of justice is the basic structure of society, or more exactly, the way in which the major social institutions distribute fundamental rights and duties and determine the division of advantages from social co-operation. By major institutions I understand the political constitution and the principal economic and social arrangements. Thus the legal protection of freedom of thought and liberty of conscience, competitive markets, private property in the means of production, and the monogamous family are examples of major social institutions. Taken together as one scheme, the major institutions define men's rights and duties and influence their life-prospects, what they can expect to be and how well they can hope to do. The basic structure is the primary subject of justice because its effects are so profound and present from the start. The intuitive notion here is that this structure contains various social positions and that men born into different positions have different expectations of life determined, in part, by the political system as well as by economic and social circumstances. In this way the institutions of society favour certain starting places over others. These are especially deep inequalities. Not only are they pervasive, but they affect men's initial chances in life; yet they cannot possibly be justified by an appeal to the notions of merit or desert. It is these inequalities, presumably inevitable in the basic structure of any society, to which the principles of social justice must in the first instance apply. These principles, then, regulate the choice of a political constitution and the main elements of the economic and social system. The justice of a social scheme depends essentially on how fundamental rights and duties are assigned and on the economic opportunities and social conditions in the various sectors of society.

The scope of our inquiry is limited in two ways. First of all, I am concerned with a special case of the problem of justice. I shall not consider the justice of institutions and social practices generally, nor except in passing the justice of the law of nations and of relations between states (§ 58). Therefore, if one supposes that the concept of justice applies whenever there is an allotment of something rationally regarded as advantageous or disadvantageous, then we are interested in only one instance of its application. There is no reason to suppose ahead of time that the principles satisfactory for the basic structure hold for all cases. These principles may not work for the rules and practices of private associations or for those of less comprehensive social groups. They may be irrelevant for the various informal conventions and customs of everyday life; they may not elucidate the justice, or perhaps better, the fairness of voluntary cooperative arrangements or procedures for making contractual agreements. The conditions for the law of nations may require different principles arrived at in a somewhat different way. I shall be satisfied if it is possible to formulate a reasonable conception of justice for the basic structure of society conceived for the time being as a closed system isolated from other societies. The significance of this special case is obvious and needs no explanation. It is natural to conjecture that once we have a sound theory for this case, the remaining problems of justice will prove more tractable in the light of it. With suitable modifications such a theory should provide the key for some of these other questions.

The other limitation on our discussion is that for the most part I examine the principles of justice that would regulate a well-ordered society. Everyone is presumed to act justly and to do his part in upholding just institutions. Though justice may be, as Hume remarked, the cautious, jealous virtue, we can still ask what a perfectly just society would be like.[1] Thus I consider primarily what I call strict compliance as opposed to partial compliance theory (§§ 25, 39). The latter studies the principles that govern how we are to deal with injustice. It comprises such topics as the theory of punishment, the doctrine of just war, and the justification of the various ways of opposing unjust regimes, ranging from civil disobedience and militant resistance to revolution and rebellion. Also included here are questions of compensatory justice and of weighing one form of institutional injustice against another. Obviously the problems of partial compliance theory are the pressing and urgent matters. These are the things that we are faced with in everyday life. The reason for beginning with ideal theory is that it provides, I believe, the only basis for the systematic grasp of these more pressing problems. The discussion of civil disobedience, for example, depends upon it (§§ 55–59). At least, I shall assume that a deeper understanding can be gained in no other way, and that the nature and aims of a perfectly just society is the fundamental part of the theory of justice.

Now admittedly the concept of the basic structure is somewhat vague. It is not always clear which institutions or features thereof should be included. But it would be premature to worry about this matter here. I shall proceed by discussing principles which do apply to what is certainly a part of the basic structure as intuitively understood; I shall then try to extend the application of these principles so that they cover what would appear to be the main elements of this structure. Perhaps these principles will turn out to be perfectly general, although this is unlikely. It is sufficient that they apply to the most important cases of social justice. The point to keep in mind is that a conception of justice for the basic structure is worth having for its own sake. It should not be dismissed because its principles are not everywhere satisfactory.

. . .

3. The Main Idea of the Theory of Justice

My aim is to present a conception of justice which generalizes and carries to a higher level of abstraction the familiar theory of the social contract as found, say, in Locke, Rousseau, and Kant.[2] In order to do this we are not to think of the original contract as one to enter a particular society or to set up a particular form of government. Rather, the guiding idea is that the principles of justice for the basic structure of society are the object of the original agreement. They are the principles that free and rational persons concerned to further their own interests would accept in an initial position of equality as defining the fundamental terms of their association. These principles are to regulate all further agreements; they specify the kinds of social co-operation that can be entered into and the forms of government that can be established. This way of regarding the principles of justice I shall call justice as fairness.

Thus we are to imagine that those who engage in social co-operation choose together, in one joint act, the principles which are to assign basic rights and duties and to determine the division of social benefits. Men are to decide in advance how they are to regulate their claims against one another and what is to be the foundation charter of their society. Just as each person must decide by rational reflection what constitutes his good, that is, the system of ends which it is rational for him to pursue, so a group of persons must decide once and for all what is to count among them as just and unjust. The choice which rational men would make in this hypothetical situation of equal liberty, assuming for the present that this choice problem has a solution, determines the principles of justice.

In justice as fairness the original position of equality corresponds to the state of nature in the traditional theory of the social contract. This original position is not, of course, thought of as an actual historical state of affairs, much less as a primitive condition of culture. It is understood as a purely hypothetical situation characterized so as to lead to a certain conception of justice.[3] Among the essential features of this situation is that no one knows his place in society, his class position or social status, nor does any one know his fortune in the distribution of natural assets and abilities, his intelligence, strength, and the like. I shall even assume that the parties do not know their conceptions of the good or their special psychological propensities. The principles of justice are chosen behind a veil of ignorance. This ensures that no one is advantaged or disadvantaged in the choice of principles by the outcome of natural chance or the contingency of social circumstances. Since all are similarly situated and no one is able to design principles to favour his particular condition, the principles of justice are the result of a fair agreement or bargain. For given the circumstances of the original position, the symmetry of everyone's relations to each other, this initial situation is fair between individuals as moral persons, that is, as rational beings with their own ends and capable, I shall assume, of a sense of justice. The original position is, one might say, the appropriate initial status quo, and thus the fundamental agreements reached in it are fair. This explains the propriety of the name "justice as fairness": it conveys the idea that the principles of justice are agreed to in an initial situation that is fair. The name does not mean that the concepts of justice and fairness are the same, any more than the phrase "poetry as metaphor" means that that the concepts of poetry and metaphor are the same.

Justice as fairness begins, as I have said, with one of the most general of all choices which persons might make together, namely, with the choice of the first principles of a conception of justice which is to regulate all subsequent criticism and reform of institutions. Then, having chosen a conception of justice, we can suppose that they are to choose a constitution and a legislature to enact laws, and so on, all in accordance with the principles of justice initially agreed upon. Our social situation is just if it is such that by this sequence of hypothetical agreements we would have contracted into the general system of rules which defines it. Moreover, assuming that the original position does determine a set of principles (that is, that a particular conception of justice would be chosen), it will then be true that whenever social institutions satisfy these principles those engaged in them can say to one another that they are co-operating on terms to which they would agree if they were free and equal persons whose relations with respect to one another were fair. They could all view their arrangements as meeting the stipulations which they would acknowledge in an initial situation that embodies widely accepted and reasonable constraints on the choice of principles. The general recognition of this fact would provide the basis for a public acceptance of the corresponding principles of justice. No society can, of course, be a scheme of co-operation which men enter voluntarily in a literal sense; each person finds himself placed at birth in some particular position in some particular society, and the nature of this position materially affects his life prospects. Yet a society satisfying the principles of justice as fairness comes as close as a society can to being a voluntary scheme, for it meets the principles which free and equal persons would assent to under circumstances that are fair. In this sense its members are autonomous and the obligations they recognize self-imposed.

One feature of justice as fairness is to think of the parties in the initial situation as rational and mutually disinterested. This does not mean that the parties are egoists, that is, individuals with only certain kinds of interests, say in wealth, prestige, and domination. But they are conceived as not taking an interest in one another's interests. They are to presume that even their spiritual aims may be opposed, in the way that the aims of those of different religions may be opposed. Moreover, the concept of rationality must be interpreted as far as possible in the narrow sense, standard in economic theory, of taking the most effective means to given ends. I shall modify this concept to some extent, as explained later (§ 25), but one must try to avoid introducing into it any controversial ethical elements. The initial situation must be characterized by stipulations that are widely accepted.

In working out the conception of justice as fairness one main task clearly is to determine which principles of justice would be chosen in the original position. To do this we must describe this situation in some detail and formulate with care the problem of choice which it presents. These matters I shall take up in the immediately succeeding chapters. It may be observed, however, that once the principles of justice are thought of as arising from an original agreement in a situation of equality, it is an open question whether the principle of utility would be acknowledged. Offhand it hardly seems likely that persons who view themselves as equals, entitled to press their claims upon one another, would agree to a principle which may require lesser life prospects for some simply for the sake of a greater sum of advantages enjoyed by others. Since each desires to protect his interests, his capacity to advance his conception of the good, no one has a reason to acquiesce in an enduring loss for himself in order to bring about a greater net balance of satisfaction. In the absence of strong and lasting benevolent impulses, a rational man would not accept a basic structure merely because it maximized the algebraic sum of advantages irrespective of its permanent effects on his own basic rights and interests. Thus it seems that the principle of utility is incompatible with the conception of social co-operation among equals for mutual advantage. It appears to be inconsistent with the idea of reciprocity implicit in the notion of a well-ordered society. Or, at any rate, so I shall argue.

I shall maintain instead that the persons in the initial situation would choose two rather different principles: the first requires equality in the assignment of basic rights and duties, while the second holds that social and economic inequalities, for example inequalities of wealth and authority, are just only if they result in compensating benefits for everyone, and in particular for the least advantaged members of society. These principles rule out justifying institutions on the grounds that the hardships of some are offset by a greater good in the aggregate. It may be expedient but it is not just that some should have less in order that others may prosper. But there is no injustice in the greater benefits earned by a few provided that the situation of persons not so fortunate is thereby improved. The intuitive idea is that since everyone's well-being depends upon a scheme of co-operation without which no one could have a satisfactory life, the division of advantages should be such as to draw forth the willing co-operation of everyone taking part in it, including those less well situated. Yet this can be expected only if reasonable terms are proposed. The two principles mentioned seem to be a fair agreement on the basis of which those better endowed, or more fortunate in their social position, neither of which we could be said to deserve, could expect the willing co-operation of others when some workable scheme is a necessary condition of the welfare of all.[4] Once we decide to look for a conception of justice that nullifies the accidents of natural endowment and the contingencies of social circumstance as counters in quest for political and economic advantage, we are led to these principles. They express the result of leaving aside those aspects of the social world that seem arbitrary from a moral point of view.

The problem of the choice of principles, however, is extremely difficult. I do not expect the answer I shall suggest to be convincing to everyone. It is, therefore, worth noting from the outset that justice as fairness, like other contract views, consists of two parts: (1) an interpretation of the initial situation and of the problem of choice posed there, and (2) a set of principles which, it is argued, would be agreed to. One may accept the first part of the theory (or some variant thereof), but not the other, and conversely. The concept of the initial contractual situation may seem reasonable although the particular principles proposed are rejected. To be sure, I want to maintain that the most appropriate conception of this situation does lead to principles of justice contrary to utilitarianism and perfectionism, and therefore that the contract doctrine provides an alternative to these views. Still, one may dispute this contention even though one grants that the contractarian method is a useful way of studying ethical theories and of setting forth their underlying assumptions.

Justice as fairness is an example of what I have called a contract theory. Now there may be an objection to the term "contract" and related expressions, but I think it will serve reasonably well. Many words have misleading connotations which at first are likely to confuse. The terms "utility" and "utilitarianism" are surely no exception. They too have unfortunate suggestions which hostile critics have been willing to exploit; yet they are clear enough for those prepared to study utilitarian doctrine. The same should be true of the term "contract" applied to moral theories. As I have mentioned, to understand it one has to keep in mind that it implies a certain level of abstraction. In particular, the content of the relevant agreement is not to enter a given society or to adopt a given form of government, but to accept certain moral principles. Moreover, the undertakings referred to are purely hypothetical: a contract view holds that certain principles would be accepted in a well-defined initial situation.

The merit of the contract terminology is that it conveys the idea that principles of justice may be conceived as principles that would be chosen by rational persons, and that in this way conceptions of justice may be explained and justified. The theory of justice is a part, perhaps the most significant part, of the theory of rational choice. Furthermore, principles of justice deal with conflicting claims upon the advantages won by social co-operation; they apply to the relations among several persons or groups. The word "contract" suggests this plurality as well as the condition that the appropriate division of advantages must be in accordance with principles acceptable to all parties. The condition of publicity for principles of justice is also connoted by the contract phraseology. Thus, if these principles are the outcome of an agreement, citizens have a knowledge of the principles that others follow. It is characteristic of contract theories to stress the public nature of political principles. Finally there is the long tradition of the contract doctrine. Expressing the tie with this line of thought helps to define ideas and accords with natural piety. There are then several advantages in the use of the term "contract." With due precautions taken, it should not be misleading.

A final remark. Justice as fairness is not a complete contract theory. For it is clear that the contractarian idea can be extended to the choice of more or less an entire ethical system, that is, to a system including principles for all the virtues and not only for justice. Now for the most part I shall consider only principles of justice and others closely related to them; I make no attempt to discuss the virtues in a systematic way. Obviously if justice as fairness succeeds reasonably well, a next step would be to study the more general view suggested by the name "rightness as fairness." But even this wider theory fails to embrace all moral relationships, since it would seem to include only our relations with other persons and to leave out of account how we are to conduct ourselves toward animals and the rest of nature. I do not contend that the contract notion offers a way to approach these questions which are certainly of the first importance; and I shall have to put them aside. We must recognize the limited scope of justice as fairness and of the general type of view that it exemplifies. How far its conclusions must be revised once these other matters are understood cannot be decided in advance.

4. The Original Position and Justification

I have said that the original position is the appropriate initial status quo which insures that the fundamental agreements reached in it are fair. This fact yields the name "justice as fairness." It is clear, then, that I want to say that one conception of justice is more reasonable than another, or justifiable with respect to it, if rational persons in the initial situation would choose its principles over those of the other for the role of justice. Conceptions of justice are to be ranked by their acceptability to persons so circumstanced. Understood in this way the question of justification is settled by working out a problem of deliberation: we have to ascertain which principles it would be rational to adopt given the contractual situation. This connects the theory of justice with the theory of rational choice.

If this view of the problem of justification is to succeed, we must, of course, describe in some detail the nature of this choice problem. A problem of rational decision has a definite answer only if we know the beliefs and interests of the parties, their relations with respect to one another, the alternatives between which they are to choose, the procedure whereby they make up their minds, and so on. As the circumstances are presented in different ways, correspondingly different principles are accepted. The concept of the original position, as I shall refer to it, is that of the most philosophically favoured interpretation of this initial choice situation for the purposes of a theory of justice.

But how are we to decide what is the most favoured interpretation? I assume, for one thing, that there is a broad measure of agreement that principles of justice should be chosen under certain conditions. To justify a particular description of the initial situation one shows that it incorporates these commonly shared presumptions. One argues from widely accepted but weak premises to more specific conclusions. Each of the presumptions should by itself be natural and plausible; some of them may seem innocuous or even trivial. The aim of the contract approach is to establish that taken together they impose significant bounds on acceptable principles of justice. The ideal outcome would be that these conditions determine a unique set of principles; but I shall be satisfied if they suffice to rank the main traditional conceptions of social justice.

One should not be misled, then, by the somewhat unusual conditions which characterize the original position. The idea here is simply to make vivid to ourselves the restrictions that it seems reasonable to impose on arguments for principles of justice, and therefore on these principles themselves. Thus it seems reasonable and generally acceptable that no one should be advantaged or disadvantaged by natural fortune or social circumstances in the choice of principles. It also seems widely agreed that it should be impossible to tailor principles to the circumstances of one's own case. We should insure further that particular inclinations and aspirations, and persons' conceptions of their good do not affect the principles adopted. The aim is to rule out those principles that it would be rational to propose for acceptance, however little the chance of success, only if one knew certain things that are irrelevant from the standpoint of justice. For example, if a man knew that he was wealthy, he might find it rational to advance the principle that various taxes for welfare measures be counted unjust; if he knew that he was poor, he would most likely propose the contrary principle. To represent the desired restrictions one imagines a situation in which everyone is deprived of this sort of information. One excludes the knowledge of those contingencies which sets men at odds and allows them to be guided by their prejudices. In this manner the veil of ignorance is arrived at in a natural way. This concept should cause no difficulty if we keep in mind the constraints on arguments that it is meant to express. At any time we can enter the original position, so to speak, simply by following a certain procedure, namely, by arguing for principles of justice in accordance with these restrictions.

It seems reasonable to suppose that the parties in the original position are equal. That is, all have the same rights in the procedure for choosing principles; each can make proposals, submit reasons for their acceptance, and so on. Obviously the purpose of these conditions is to represent equality between human beings as moral persons, as creatures having a conception of their good and capable of a sense of justice. The basis of equality is taken to be similarity in these two respects. Systems of ends are not ranked in value; and each man is presumed to have the requisite ability to understand and to act upon whatever principles are adopted. Together with the veil of ignorance, these conditions define the principles of justice as those which rational persons concerned to advance their interests would consent to as equals when none are known to be advantaged or disadvantaged by social and natural contingencies.

There is, however, another side to justifying a particular description of the original position. This is to see if the principles which would be chosen match our considered convictions of justice or extend them in an acceptable way. We can note whether applying these principles would lead us to make the same judgments about the basic structure of society which we now make intuitively and in which we have the greatest confidence; or whether, in cases where our present judgments are in doubt and given with hesitation, these principles offer a resolution which we can affirm on reflection. There are questions which we feel sure must be answered in a certain way. For example, we are confident that religious intolerance and racial discrimination are unjust. We think that we have examined these things with care and have reached what we believe is an impartial judgment not likely to be distorted by an excessive attention to our own interests. These convictions are provisional fixed points which we presume any conception of justice must fit. But we have much less assurance as to what is the correct distribution of wealth and authority. Here we may be looking for a way to remove our doubts. We can check an interpretation of the initial situation, then, by the capacity of its principles to accommodate our firmest convictions and to provide guidance where guidance is needed.

In searching for the most favoured description of this situation we work from both ends. We begin by describing it so that it represents generally shared and preferably weak conditions. We then see if these conditions are strong enough to yield a significant set of principles. If not, we look for further premises equally reasonable. But if so, and these principles match our considered convictions of justice, then so far well and good. But presumably there will be discrepancies. In this case we have a choice. We can either modify the account of the initial situation or we can revise our existing judgments, for even the judgments we take provisionally as fixed points are liable to revision. By going back and forth, sometimes altering the conditions of the contractual circumstances, at others withdrawing our judgments and conforming them to principle, I assume that eventually we shall find a description of the initial situation that both expresses reasonable conditions and yields principles which match our considered judgments duly pruned and adjusted. This state of affairs I refer to as reflective equilibrium.[5] It is an equilibrium because at last our principles and judgments coincide; and it is reflective since we know to what principles our judgments conform and the premises of their derivation. At the moment everything is in order. But this equilibrium is not necessarily stable. It is liable

to be upset by further examination of the conditions which should be imposed on the contractual situation and by particular cases which may lead us to revise our judgments. Yet for the time being we have done what we can to render coherent and to justify our convictions of social justice. We have reached a conception of the original position.

I shall not, of course, actually work through this process. Still, we may think of the interpretation of the original position that I shall present as the result of such a hypothetical course of reflection. It represents the attempt to accommodate within one scheme both reasonable philosophical conditions on principles as well as our considered judgments of justice. In arriving at the favoured interpretation of the initial situation there is no point at which an appeal is made to self-evidence in the traditional sense either of general conceptions or particular convictions. I do not claim for the principles of justice proposed that they are necessary truths or derivable from such truths. A conception of justice cannot be deduced from self-evident premises or conditions on principles; instead, its justification is a matter of the mutual support of many considerations, of everything fitting together into one coherent view.

A final comment. We shall want to say that certain principles of justice are justified because they would be agreed to in an initial situation of equality. I have emphasized that this original position is purely hypothetical. It is natural to ask why, if this agreement is never actually entered into, we should take any interest in these principles, moral or otherwise. The answer is that the conditions embodied in the description of the original position are ones that we do in fact accept. Or if we do not, then perhaps we can be persuaded to do so by philosophical reflection. Each aspect of the contractual situation can be given supporting grounds. Thus what we shall do is to collect together into one conception a number of conditions on principles that we are ready upon due consideration to recognize as reasonable. These constraints express what we are prepared to regard as limits on fair terms of social co-operation. One way to look at the idea of the original position, therefore, is to see it as an expository device which sums up the meaning of these conditions and helps us to extract their consequences. On the other hand, this conception is also an intuitive notion that suggests its own elaboration, so that led on by it we are drawn to define more clearly the standpoint from which we can best interpret moral relationships. We need a conception that enables us to envision our objective from afar: the intuitive notion of the original position is to do this for us.[6]

. . .

Chapter II The Principles of Justice

. . .

II. *Two Principles of Justice*

I shall now state in a provisional form the two principles of justice that I believe would be chosen in the original position. In this section I wish to make only the most general comments, and therefore the first formulation of these principles is tentative. As we go on I shall run through several formulations and approximate step by step the final statement to be given much later. I believe that doing this allows the exposition to proceed in a natural way.

The first statement of the two principles reads as follows.

> First: each person is to have an equal right to the most extensive basic liberty compatible with a similar liberty for others.

> Second: social and economic inequalities are to be arranged so that they are both (a) reasonably expected to be to everyone's advantage, and (b) attached to positions and offices open to all.

There are two ambiguous phrases in the second principle, namely "everyone's advantage" and "open to all." Determining their sense more exactly will lead to a second formulation of the principle in § 13. The final version of the two principles is given in § 46; § 39 considers the rendering of the first principle.

By way of general comment, these principles primarily apply, as I have said, to the basic structure of society. They are to govern the assignment of rights and duties and to regulate the distribution of social and economic advantages. As their formulation suggests, these principles presuppose that the social structure can be divided into two more or less distinct parts, the first principle applying to the one, the second to the other. They distinguish between those aspects of the social system that define and secure the equal liberties of citizenship and those that specify and establish social and economic inequalities. The basic liberties of citizens are, roughly speaking, political liberty (the right to vote and to be eligible for public office) together with freedom of speech and assembly; liberty of conscience and freedom of thought; freedom of the person along with the right to hold (personal) property; and freedom from arbitrary arrest and seizure as defined by the concept of the rule of law. These liberties are all required to be equal by the first principle, since citizens of a just society are to have the same basic rights.

The second principle applies, in the first approximation, to the distribution of income and wealth and to the design of organizations that make use of differences in authority and responsibility, or chains of command. While the distribution of wealth and income need not be equal, it must be to everyone's advantage, and at the same time, positions of authority and offices of command must be accessible to all. One applies the second principle by holding positions open, and then, subject to this constraint, arranges social and economic inequalities so that everyone benefits.

These principles are to be arranged in a serial order with the first principle prior to the second. This ordering means that a departure from the institutions of equal liberty required by the first principle cannot be justified by, or compensated for, by greater social and economic advantages. The distribution of wealth and income, and the hierarchies of authority, must be consistent with both the liberties of equal citizenship and equality of opportunity.

It is clear that these principles are rather specific in their content, and their acceptance rests on certain assumptions that I must eventually try to explain and justify. A theory of justice depends upon a theory of society in ways that will become evident as we proceed. For the present, it should be observed that the two principles (and this holds for all formulations) are a special case of a more general conception of justice that can be expressed as follows.

> All social values—liberty and opportunity, income and wealth, and the bases of self-respect—are to be distributed equally unless an unequal distribution of any, or all, of these values is to everyone's advantage.

Injustice, then, is simply inequalities that are not to the benefit of all. Of course, this conception is extremely vague and requires interpretation.

As a first step, suppose that the basic structure of society distributes certain primary goods, that is, things that every rational man is presumed to want. These goods normally have a use whatever a person's rational plan of life. For simplicity, assume that the chief primary goods at the disposition of society are rights and liberties, powers and opportunities, income and wealth. . . . These are the social primary goods. Other primary goods such as health and vigor, intelligence and imagination, are natural goods; although their possession is influenced by the basic structure, they are not so directly under its control. Imagine, then, a hypothetical initial arrangement in which all the social primary goods are equally distributed: everyone has similar rights and duties, and income and wealth are evenly shared. This state of affairs provides a benchmark for judging improvements. If certain inequalities of wealth and organizational powers would make everyone better off than in this hypothetical starting situation, then they accord with the general conception.

Now it is possible, at least theoretically, that by giving up some of their fundamental liberties men are sufficiently compensated by the resulting social and economic gains. The general conception of justice imposes no restrictions on what sort of inequalities are permissible; it only requires that everyone's position be improved. We need not suppose anything so drastic as consenting to a condition of slavery. Imagine instead that men forgo certain political rights when the economic returns are significant and their capacity to influence the course of policy by the exercise of these rights would be marginal in any case. It is this kind of exchange which the two principles as stated rule out; being arranged in serial order they do not permit exchanges between basic liberties and economic and social gains. The serial ordering of principles expresses an underlying preference among primary social goods. When this preference is rational so likewise is the choice of these principles in this order.

In developing justice as fairness I shall, for the most part, leave aside the general conception of justice and examine instead the special case of the two principles in serial order. The advantage of this procedure is that from the first the matter of priorities is recognized and an effort made to find principles to deal with it. One is led to attend throughout to the conditions under which the acknowledgment of the absolute weight of liberty with respect to social and economic advantages, as defined by the lexical order of the two principles, would be reasonable. Offhand, this ranking appears extreme and too special a case to be of much interest; but there is more justification for it than would appear at first sight. Or at any rate, so I shall maintain (§ 82). Furthermore, the distinction between fundamental rights and liberties and economic and social benefits marks a difference among primary social goods that one should try to exploit. It suggests an important division in the social system. Of course, the distinctions drawn and the ordering proposed are bound to be at best only approximations. There are surely circumstances in which they fail. But it is essential to depict clearly the main lines of a reasonable conception of justice; and under many conditions anyway, the two principles in serial order may serve well enough. When necessary we can fall back on the more general conception.

The fact that the two principles apply to institutions has certain consequences. Several points illustrate this. First of all, the rights and liberties referred to by these principles are those which are defined by the public rules of the basic structure. Whether men are free is determined by the rights and duties established by the major institutions of society. Liberty is a certain pattern of social forms. The first principle simply requires that certain sorts of rules, those defining basic liberties, apply to everyone equally and that they allow the most extensive liberty compatible with a like liberty for all. The only reason for circumscribing the rights defining liberty and making men's freedom less extensive than it might otherwise be is that these equal rights as institutionally defined would interfere with one another.

Another thing to bear in mind is that when principles mention persons, or require that everyone gain from an inequality, the reference is to representative persons holding the various social positions, or offices, or whatever, established by the basic structure. Thus in applying the second principle I assume that it is possible to assign an expectation of well-being to representative individuals holding these positions. This expectation indicates their life prospects as viewed from their social station. In general, the expectations of representative persons depend upon the distribution of rights and duties throughout the basic structure. When this changes, expectations change. I assume, then, that expectations are connected: by raising the prospects of the representative man in one position we presumably increase or decrease the prospects of representative men in other positions. Since it applies to institutional forms, the second principle (or rather the first part of it) refers to the expectations of representative individuals. As I shall discuss below, neither principle applies to distributions of particular goods to particular individuals who may be identified by their proper names. The situation where someone is considering how to allocate certain commodities to needy persons who are known to him is not within the scope of the principles. They are meant to regulate basic institutional arrangements. We must not assume that there is much similarity from the standpoint of justice between an administrative allotment of goods to specific persons and the appropriate design of society. Our common sense intuitions for the former may be a poor guide to the latter.

Now the second principle insists that each person benefit from permissible inequalities in the basic structure. This means that it must be reasonable for each relevant representative man defined by this structure, when he views it as a going concern, to prefer his prospects with the inequality to his prospects without it. One is not allowed to justify differences in income or organizational powers on the ground that the disadvantages of those in one position are outweighed by the greater advantages of those in another. Much less can infringements of liberty be counterbalanced in this way. Applied to the basic structure, the principle of utility would have us maximize the sum of expectations of representative men (weighted by the number of persons they represent, on the classical view); and this would permit us to compensate for the losses of some by the gains of others. Instead, the two principles require that everyone benefit from economic and social inequalities. It is obvious, however, that there are indefinitely many ways in which all may be advantaged when the initial arrangement of equality is taken as a benchmark. How then are we to choose among these possibilities? The principles must be specified so that they yield a determinate conclusion. I now turn to this problem.

. . .

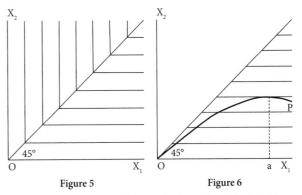

Figure 5   Figure 6

Source: Reprinted by permission of the publisher from *A Theory of Justice* by John Rawls, p. 76, Cambridge, MA: The Belknap Press of Harvard University Press, Copyright © 1971 by the President and Fellows of Harvard College.

13. Democratic Equality and the Difference Principle

The democratic interpretation, as the table suggests, is arrived at by combining the principle of fair equality of opportunity with the difference principle. This principle removes the indeterminateness of the principle of efficiency by singling out a particular position from which the social and economic inequalities of the basic structure are to be judged. Assuming the framework of institutions required by equal liberty and fair equality of opportunity, the higher expectations of those better situated are just if and only if they work as part of a scheme which improves the expectations of the least advantaged members of society. The intuitive idea is that the social order is not to establish and secure the more attractive prospects of those better off unless doing so is to the advantage of those less fortunate. (See the discussion of the difference principle that follows.)

The Difference Principle

Assume that indifference curves now represent distributions that are judged equally just. Then the difference principle is a strongly egalitarian conception in the sense that unless there is a distribution that makes both persons better off (limiting ourselves to the two-person case for simplicity), an equal distribution is to be preferred. The indifference curves take the form depicted in Figure 5. These curves are actually made up of vertical and straight lines that intersect at right angles at the 45° line (again supposing an interpersonal and cardinal interpretation of the axes). No matter how much either person's situation is improved, there is no gain from the standpoint of the difference principle unless the other gains also.

Suppose that x_1 is the most favoured representative man in the basic structure. As his expectations are increased so are the prospects of x_2, the least advantaged man. In Figure 6 let the curve OP represent the contribution to x_2's expectations made by the greater expectations of x_1. The point O, the origin, represents the hypothetical state in which all social primary goods are distributed equally. Now the OP curve is always below the 45° line, since x_1 is always better off. Thus the only relevant parts of the indifference curves are those below this line, and for this reason the upper left-hand part of Figure 6 is not drawn in. Clearly the difference principle is perfectly satisfied only when the OP curve is just tangent to the highest indifference curve that it touches. In Figure 6 this is at the point a.

Note that the contribution curve, the curve OP, supposes that the social co-operation defined by the basic structure is mutually advantageous. It is no longer a matter of shuffling about a fixed stock of goods. Also, nothing is lost if an accurate interpersonal comparison of benefits is impossible. It suffices that the least favoured person can be identified and his rational preference determined.

A view less egalitarian than the difference principle, and perhaps more plausible at first sight, is one in which the indifference lines for just distributions (or for all things considered) are smooth curves convex to the origin, as in Figure 7. The indifference curves for social welfare functions are often depicted in this fashion. This shape of the curves expresses the fact that as either person gains relative to the other, further benefits to him become less valuable from a social point of view.

A classical utilitarian, on the other hand, is indifferent as to how a constant sum of benefits is distributed. He appeals to equality only to break ties. If there are but two persons, then assuming an interpersonal cardinal interpretation of the axes, the utilitarian's indifference lines for distributions are straight lines perpendicular to the 45° line. Since, however, x_1 and x_2 are representative men, the gains to them have to be weighted by the number of persons they each represent. Since presumably x_2 represents rather more persons than x_1, the indifference lines become more horizontal, as seen in Figure 8. The ratio of

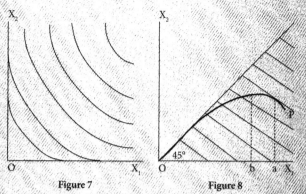

Figure 7   Figure 8

Reprinted by permission of the publisher from *A Theory of Justice* by John Rawls, p. 77, Cambridge, MA: The Belknap Press of Harvard University Press, Copyright © 1971 by the President and Fellows of Harvard College.

the number of advantaged to the number of disadvantaged defines the slope of these straight lines. Drawing the same contribution curve OP as before, we see that the best distribution from a utilitarian point of view is reached at the point which is beyond the point b where the OP curve reaches its maximum. Since the difference principle selects the point b and b is always to the left of a, utilitarianism allows, other things equal, larger inequalities.

To illustrate the difference principle, consider the distribution of income among social classes. Let us suppose that the various income groups correlate with representative individuals by reference to whose expectations we can judge the distribution. Now those starting out as members of the entrepreneurial class in property-owning democracy, say, have a better prospect than those who begin in the class of unskilled labourers. It seems likely that this will be true even when the social injustices which now exist are removed. What, then, can possibly justify this kind of initial inequality in life prospects? According to the difference principle, it is justifiable only if the difference in expectation is to the advantage of the representative man who is worse off, in this case the representative unskilled worker. The inequality in expectation is permissible only if lowering it would make the working class even more worse off. Supposedly, given the rider in the second principle concerning open positions, and the principle of liberty generally, the greater expectations allowed to entrepreneurs encourages them to do things which raise the long-term prospects of the labouring class. Their better prospects act as incentives so that the economic process is more efficient, innovation proceeds at a faster pace, and so on. Eventually the resulting material benefits spread throughout the system and to the least advantaged. I shall not consider how far these things are true. The point is that something of this kind must be argued if these inequalities are to be just by the difference principle.

I shall now make a few remarks about this principle. First of all, in applying it, one should distinguish between two cases. The first case is that in which the expectations of the least advantaged are indeed maximized (subject, of course, to the mentioned constraints). No changes in the expectations of those better off can improve the situation of those worst off. The best arrangement obtains, what I shall call a perfectly just scheme. The second case is that in which the expectations of all those better off at least contribute to the welfare of the more unfortunate. That is, if their expectations were decreased, the prospects of the least advantaged would likewise fall. Yet the maximum is not yet achieved. Even higher expectations for the more advantaged would raise the expectations of those in the lowest position. Such a scheme is, I shall say, just throughout, but not the best just arrangement. A scheme is unjust when the higher expectations, one or more of them, are excessive. If these expectations were decreased, the situation of the least favoured would be improved. How unjust an arrangement is depends on how excessive the higher expectations are and to what extent they depend upon the violation of the other principles of justice, for example, fair equality of opportunity; but I shall not attempt to measure in any exact way the degrees of injustice. The point to note here is that while the difference principle is, strictly speaking, a maximizing principle, there is a significant distinction between the cases that fall short of the best arrangement. A society should try to avoid the region where the marginal contributions of those better off are negative, since, other things equal, this seems a greater fault than falling short of the best scheme when these contributions are positive. The even larger difference between rich and poor makes the latter even worse off and this violates the principle of mutual advantage as well as democratic equality (§ 17).

A further point is this. We saw that the system of natural liberty and the liberal conception attempt to go beyond the principle of efficiency by moderating its scope of operation, by constraining it by certain background institutions and leaving the rest to pure procedural justice. The democratic conception holds that while pure procedural justice may be invoked to some extent at least, the way previous interpretations do this still leaves too much to social and natural contingency. But it should be noted that the difference principle is compatible with the principle of efficiency. For when the former is fully satisfied, it is indeed impossible to make any one representative man better off without making another worse off, namely, the least advantaged representative man whose expectations we are to maximize. Thus justice is defined so that it is consistent with efficiency, at least when the two principles are perfectly fulfilled. Of course, if the basic structure is unjust, these principles will authorize changes that may lower the expectations of some of those better off; and therefore the democratic conception is not consistent with the principle of efficiency if this principle is taken to mean that only changes which improve everyone's prospects are allowed. Justice is prior to efficiency and requires some changes that are not efficient in this sense. Consistency obtains only in the sense that a perfectly just scheme is also efficient.

Next, we may consider a certain complication regarding the meaning of the difference principle. It has been taken for granted that if the principle is satisfied, everyone is benefited. One obvious sense in which this is so is that each man's position is improved with respect to the initial arrangement of equality. But it is clear that nothing depends upon being able to identify this initial arrangement; indeed, how well off men are in this situation plays no essential role in applying the difference principle. We simply maximize the expectations of the least favoured position subject to the required constraints. As long as doing this is an improvement for everyone, as we assume it is, the estimated gains from the situation of hypothetical equality are irrelevant, if not largely impossible to ascertain anyway. There may be, however, a further sense in which everyone is advantaged when the difference principle is satisfied, at least if we make certain natural assumptions. Let us suppose that inequalities in expectations are chain-connected: that is, if an advantage has the effect of raising the expectations of the lowest position, it raises the expectations of all positions in between. For example, if the greater expectations for entrepreneurs benefit the unskilled worker, they also benefit the semi-skilled. Notice that chain connection says nothing about the case where the least advantaged do not gain, so that it does not mean that all effects move together. Assume further that expectations are close-knit: that is, it is impossible to raise or lower the expectation of any representative man without raising or lowering the expectation of every other representative man, especially that of the least advantaged. There is no loose-jointedness, so to speak, in the way expectations hang together. Now with these assumptions there is a sense in which everyone benefits when the difference principle is satisfied. For the representative man who is better off in any two-way comparison gains by the advantages offered him, and the man who is worse off gains from the contributions which these inequalities make. Of course, these conditions may not hold. But in this case those who are better off should not have a veto over the benefits available for the least favoured.

We are still to maximize the expectations of those most disadvantaged.

. . .

14. Fair Equality of Opportunity and Pure Procedural Justice

I should now like to comment upon the second part of the second principle, henceforth to be understood as the liberal principle of fair equality of opportunity. It must not then be confused with the notion of careers open to talents; nor must one forget that since it is tied in with the difference principle its consequences are quite distinct from the liberal interpretation of the two principles taken together. In particular, I shall try to show further on (§ 17) that this principle is not subject to the objection that it leads to a meritocratic society. Here I wish to consider a few other points, especially its relation to the idea of pure procedural justice.

First, though, I should note that the reasons for requiring open positions are not solely, or even primarily, those of efficiency. I have not maintained that offices must be open if in fact everyone is to benefit from an arrangement. For it may be possible to improve everyone's situation by assigning certain powers and benefits to positions despite the fact that certain groups are excluded from them. Although access is restricted, perhaps these offices can still attract superior talent and encourage better performance. But the principle of open positions forbids this. It expresses the conviction that if some places were not open on a basis fair to all, those kept out would be right in feeling unjustly treated even though they benefited from the greater efforts of those who were allowed to hold them. They would be justified in their complaint not only because they were excluded from certain external rewards of office such as wealth and privilege, but because they were debarred from experiencing the realization of self which comes from a skillful and devoted exercise of social duties. They would be deprived of one of the main forms of human good.

Now I have said that the basic structure is the primary subject of justice. This means, as we have seen, that the first distributive problem is the assignment of fundamental rights and duties and the regulation of social and economic inequalities and of the legitimate expectations founded on these. Of course, any ethical theory recognizes the importance of the basic structure as a subject of justice, but not all theories regard its importance in the same way. In justice as fairness society is interpreted as a cooperative venture for mutual advantage. The basic structure is a public system of rules defining a scheme of activities that leads men to act together so as to produce a greater sum of benefits and assigns to each certain recognized claims to a share in the proceeds. What a person does depends upon what the public rules say he will be entitled to, and what a person is entitled to depends on what he does. The distribution which results is arrived at by honouring the claims determined by what persons undertake to do in the light of these legitimate expectations.

These considerations suggest the idea of treating the question of distributive shares as a matter of pure procedural justice.[7] The intuitive idea is to design the social system so that the outcome is just whatever it happens to be, at least so long as it is within a certain range. The notion of pure procedural justice is best understood by a comparison with perfect and imperfect procedural justice. To illustrate the former, consider the simplest case of fair division. A number of men are to divide a cake: assuming that the fair division is an equal one, which procedure, if any, will give this outcome? Technicalities aside, the obvious solution is to have one man divide the cake and get the last piece, the others being allowed their pick before him. He will divide the cake equally, since in this way he assures for himself the largest share possible. This example illustrates the two characteristic features of perfect procedural justice. First, there is an independent criterion for what is a fair division, a criterion defined separately from and prior to the procedure which is to be followed. And second, it is possible to devise a procedure that is sure to give the desired outcome. Of course, certain assumptions are made here, such as that the man selected can divide the cake equally, wants as large a piece as he can get, and so on. But we can ignore these details. The essential thing is that there is an independent standard for deciding which outcome is just and a procedure guaranteed to lead to it. Pretty clearly, perfect procedural justice is rare, if not impossible, in cases of much practical interest.

Imperfect procedural justice is exemplified by a criminal trial. The desired outcome is that the defendant should be declared guilty if and only if he has committed the offense with which he is charged. The trial procedure is framed to search for and to establish the truth in this regard. But it seems impossible to design the legal rules so that they always lead to the correct result. The theory of trials examines which procedures and rules of evidence, and the like, are best calculated to advance this purpose consistent with the other ends of the law. Different arrangements for hearing cases may reasonably be expected in different circumstances to yield the right results, not always but at least most of the time. A trial, then, is an instance of imperfect procedural justice. Even though the law is carefully followed, and the proceedings fairly and properly conducted, it may reach the wrong outcome. An innocent man may be found guilty, a guilty man may be set free. In such cases we speak of a miscarriage of justice: the injustice springs from no human fault but from a fortuitous combination of circumstances which defeats the purpose of the legal rules. The characteristic mark of imperfect procedural justice is that while there is an independent criterion for the correct outcome, there is no feasible procedure which is sure to lead to it.

By contrast, pure procedural justice obtains when there is no independent criterion for the right result: instead there is a correct or fair procedure such that the outcome is likewise correct or fair, whatever it is, provided that the procedure has been properly followed. This situation is illustrated by gambling. If a number of persons engage in a series of fair bets, the distribution of cash after the last bet is fair, or at least not unfair, whatever this distribution is. I assume here that fair bets are those having a zero expectation of gain, that the bets are made voluntarily, that no one cheats, and so on. The betting procedure is fair and freely entered into under conditions that are fair. Thus the background circumstances define a fair procedure. Now any distribution of cash summing to the initial stock held by all individuals could result from a series of fair bets. In this sense all of these particular distributions are equally fair. A distinctive feature of pure procedural justice is that the procedure for determining the just result must actually be carried out; for in these cases there is no independent criterion by reference to which a definite outcome can be known to be just. Clearly we cannot say that a particular state of affairs is just because it could have been reached by following a fair procedure. This would permit far too much and would lead to absurdly unjust consequences. It would allow one to say that almost any distribution of goods is just, or fair, since it could have come about as a result of fair gambles. What makes the final outcome of betting fair, or not unfair, is that it is the one which has arisen after a series of fair gambles. A fair procedure translates its fairness to the outcome only when it is actually carried out.

In order, therefore, to apply the notion of pure procedural justice to distributive shares it is necessary to set up and to administer impartially a just system of institutions. Only against the background of a just basic structure, including a just political constitution and a just arrangement of economic and social institutions, can one say that the requisite just procedure exists. In Part Two I shall describe in some detail a basic structure that has the necessary features. Its various institutions are explained and connected with the two principles of justice. The intuitive idea is familiar. Suppose that law and government act effectively to keep markets competitive, resources fully employed, property and wealth (especially if private ownership of the means of production is allowed) widely distributed by the appropriate forms of taxation, or whatever, and to guarantee a reasonable social minimum. Assume also that there is fair equality of opportunity underwritten by education for all; and that the other equal liberties are secured. Then it would appear that the resulting distribution of income and the pattern of expectations will tend to satisfy the difference principle. In this complex of institutions, which we think of as establishing social justice in the modem state, the advantages of the better situated improve the condition of the least favoured. Or when they do not, they can be adjusted to do so, for example, by setting the social minimum at the appropriate level. As these institutions presently exist they are riddled with grave injustices. But there presumably are ways of running them compatible with their basic design and intention so that the difference principle is satisfied consistent with the demands of liberty and fair equality of opportunity. It is this fact which underlies our assurance that these arrangements can be made just.

It is evident that the role of the principle of fair opportunity is to insure that the system of co-operation is one of pure procedural justice. Unless it is satisfied, distributive justice could not be left to take care of itself, even within a restricted range. Now the great practical advantage of pure procedural justice is that it is no longer necessary in meeting the demands of justice to keep track of the endless variety of circumstances and the changing relative positions of particular persons. One avoids the problem of defining principles to cope with the enormous complexities which would arise if such details were relevant. It is a mistake to focus attention on the varying relative positions of individuals and to require that every change, considered as a single transaction viewed in isolation, be in itself just. It is the arrangement of the basic structure which is to be judged, and judged from a general point of view. Unless we are prepared to criticize it from the standpoint of a relevant representative man in some particular position, we have no complaint against it. Thus the acceptance of the two principles constitutes an understanding to discard as irrelevant as a matter of social justice much of the information and many of the complications of everyday life.

In pure procedural justice, then, distributions of advantages are not appraised in the first instance by confronting a stock of benefits available with given desires and needs of known individuals. The allotment of the items produced takes place in accordance with the public system of rules, and this system determines what is produced, how much is produced, and by what means. It also determines legitimate claims the honoring of which yields the resulting distribution. Thus in this kind of procedural justice the correctness of the distribution is founded on the justice of the scheme of co-operation from which it arises and on answering the claims of individuals engaged in it. A distribution cannot be judged in isolation from the system of which it is the outcome or from what individuals have done in good faith in the light of established expectations. If it is asked in the abstract whether one distribution of a given stock of things to definite individuals with known desires and preferences is better than another, then there is simply no answer to this question. The conception of the two principles does not interpret the primary problem of distributive justice as one of allocative justice.

By contrast the allocative conception of justice seems naturally to apply when a given collection of goods is to be divided among definite individuals with known desires and needs. The goods to be allotted are not produced by these individuals, nor do these individuals stand in any existing cooperative relations. Since there are no prior claims on the things to be distributed, it is natural to share them out according to desires and needs, or even to maximize the net balance of satisfaction. Justice becomes a kind of efficiency, unless equality is preferred. Suitably generalized, the allocative conception leads to the classical utilitarian view. For as we have seen, this doctrine assimilates justice to the benevolence of the impartial spectator and the latter in turn to the most efficient design of institutions to promote the greatest balance of satisfaction. As I observed earlier, on this conception society is thought of as so many separate individuals each defining a separate line along which rights and duties are to be assigned and scarce means of satisfaction allocated in accordance with rules so as to give the most complete fulfillment of desire. I shall put aside consideration of the other aspects of this notion until later. The point to note here is that utilitarianism does not interpret the basic structure as a scheme of pure procedural justice. For the utilitarian has, in principle anyway, an independent standard for judging all distributions, namely, whether they produce the greatest net balance of satisfaction. In his theory, institutions are more or less imperfect arrangements for bringing about this end. Thus given existing desires and preferences, and the natural continuations into the future which they allow, the statesman's aim is to set up those social schemes that will best approximate an already specified goal. Since these arrangements are subject to the unavoidable constraints and hindrances of everyday life, the basic structure is a case of imperfect procedural justice.

For the time being I shall suppose that the two parts of the second principle are lexically ordered. Thus we have one lexical ordering within another. But when necessary, this ordering can be modified in the light of the general conception of justice. The advantage of the special conception is that it has a definite shape and suggests certain questions for investigation, for example, under what conditions if any would the lexical ordering be chosen? Our inquiry is given a particular direction and is no longer confined to generalities. Of course, this conception of distributive shares is obviously a great simplification. It is designed to characterize in a clear way a basic structure that makes use of the idea of pure procedural justice. But all the same we should attempt to find simple concepts that can be assembled to give a reasonable conception of justice. The notions of the basic structure, of the veil of ignorance, of a lexical order, of the least favoured position, as well as of pure procedural justice are all examples of this. By themselves none of these could be expected to work, but properly put together they may serve well enough. It is too much to suppose that there exists for all or even most moral problems a reasonable solution. Perhaps only a few can be satisfactorily answered. In any case social wisdom consists in framing institutions so that intractable difficulties do not often arise and in accepting the need for clear and simple principles.

15. Primary Social Goods as the Basis of Expectations

So much, then, for a brief statement and explanation of the two principles of justice and of the procedural conception which they express. In later chapters I shall present further details by describing an arrangement of institutions that realizes this conception. At the moment, however, there are several preliminary matters that must be faced. I begin with a discussion of expectations and how they are to be estimated.

The significance of this question can be brought out by a comparison with utilitarianism. When applied to the basic structure the principle of utility requires us to maximize the algebraic sum of expectations taken over all relevant positions. (The classical principle weights these expectations by the number of persons in these positions, the average principle by the fraction of persons.) Leaving aside for the next section the question as to what defines a relevant position, it is clear that utilitarianism assumes some fairly accurate measure of these expectations. Not only is it necessary to have a cardinal measure for each representative individual but these measures must make sense in interpersonal comparisons. Some method of correlating the scales of different persons is presupposed if we are to say that the gains of some are to outweigh the losses of others. It is unreasonable to demand great precision, yet these estimates cannot be left to our unguided intuition. For judgments of a greater balance of interests leave too much room for conflicting claims. Moreover, these judgments may be based on ethical and other notions, not to mention bias and self-interest, which puts their validity in question. Simply because we do in fact make what we call interpersonal comparisons of well-being does not mean that we understand the basis of these comparisons or that we should accept them as sound. To settle these matters we need to give an account of these judgments, to set out the criteria that underlie them (§ 49). For questions of social justice we should try to find some objective grounds for these comparisons, ones that men can recognize and agree to. At the present time, there appears to be no satisfactory answer to these difficulties from a utilitarian point of view. Therefore it seems that, for the time being at least, the principle of utility makes such heavy demands on our ability to estimate the balance of advantages that it defines at best an ambiguous court of appeal for questions of justice.

I do not assume, though, that a satisfactory solution to these problems is impossible. While these difficulties are real, and the difference principle is framed to circumvent them, I do not wish to stress its relative merits on this score. For one thing, skepticism about interpersonal comparisons is often based on questionable views: for example, that the intensity of pleasure or of the enjoyment which indicates well-being is the intensity of pure sensation; and that while the intensity of such sensations can be experienced and known by the subject, it is impossible for others to know it or to infer it with reasonable certainty. Both these contentions seem wrong. Indeed, the second is simply part of a skepticism about the existence of other minds, unless it is shown why judgments of well-being present special problems which cannot be overcome.[8] I believe that the real difficulties with utilitarianism lie elsewhere. The main point is that even if interpersonal comparisons of satisfaction can be made, these comparisons must reflect values which it makes sense to pursue. It is irrational to advance one end rather than another simply because it can be more accurately estimated. The controversy about interpersonal comparisons tends to obscure the real question, namely, whether the total (or average) happiness is to be maximized in the first place.

The difference principle meets some of the difficulties in making interpersonal comparisons. This it does in two ways. First of all, as long as we can identify the least advantaged representative man, only ordinal judgments of well-being are required from then on. We know from what position the social system is to be judged. It does not matter how much worse off this representative individual is than the others. If positions can be ranked as better or worse, the lowest can be found. The further difficulties of cardinal measurement do not arise since no other interpersonal comparisons are necessary. And, of course, in maximizing with respect to the least favoured representative man, we need not go beyond ordinal judgments. If we can decide whether a change in the basic structure makes him better or worse off, we can determine his best situation. We do not have to know how much he prefers one situation to another. The difference principle, then, asks less of our judgments of welfare. We never have to calculate a sum of advantages involving a cardinal measure. While qualitative interpersonal comparisons are made in finding the bottom position, for the rest the ordinal judgments of one representative man suffice.

The difference principle also avoids difficulties by introducing a simplification for the basis of interpersonal comparisons. These comparisons are made in terms of expectations of primary social goods. In fact, I define these expectations simply as the index of these goods which a representative individual can look forward to. One man's expectations are greater than another's if this index for some one in his position is greater. Now primary goods, as I have already remarked, are things which it is supposed a rational man wants whatever else he wants. Regardless of what an individual's rational plans are in detail, it is assumed that there are various things which he would prefer more of rather than less. With more of these goods men can generally be assured of greater success in carrying out their intentions and in advancing their ends, whatever these ends may be. The primary social goods, to give them in broad categories, are rights and liberties, opportunities and powers, income and wealth. (A very important primary good is a sense of one's own worth; but for simplicity I leave this aside until much later, § 67.) It seems evident that in general these things fit the description of primary goods. They are social goods in view of their connection with the basic structure; liberties and powers are defined by the rules of major institutions and the distribution of income and wealth is regulated by them.

The theory of the good adopted to account for primary goods . . . is a familiar one going back to Aristotle, and something like it is accepted by philosophers so different in other respects as Kant and Sidgwick. It is not in dispute between the contract doctrine and utilitarianism. The main idea is that a person's good is determined by what is for him the most rational long-term plan of life given reasonably favourable circumstances. A man

is happy when he is more or less successfully in the way of carrying out this plan. To put it briefly, the good is the satisfaction of rational desire. We are to suppose, then, that each individual has a rational plan of life drawn up subject to the conditions that confront him. This plan is designed to permit the harmonious satisfaction of his interests. It schedules activities so that various desires can be fulfilled without interference. It is arrived at by rejecting other plans that are either less likely to succeed or do not provide for such an inclusive attainment of aims. Given the alternatives available, a rational plan is one which cannot be improved upon; there is no other plan which, taking everything into account, would be preferable.

Now the assumption is that though men's rational plans do have different final ends, they nevertheless all require for their execution certain primary goods, natural and social. Plans differ since individual abilities, circumstances, and wants differ; rational plans are adjusted to these contingencies. But whatever one's system of ends, primary goods are necessary means. Greater intelligence, wealth and opportunity, for example, allow a person to achieve ends he could not rationally contemplate otherwise. The expectations of representative men are, then, to be defined by the index of primary social goods available to them. While the persons in the original position do not know their conception of the good, they do know, I assume, that they prefer more rather than less primary goods. And this information is sufficient for them to know how to advance their interests in the initial situation.

Let us consider several difficulties. One problem clearly is the construction of the index itself. How are the different primary social goods to be weighed? Assuming that the two principles of justice are serially ordered, this problem is greatly simplified. The fundamental liberties are always equal, and there is fair equality of opportunity; one does not need to balance these liberties and rights against other values. The primary social goods that vary in their distribution are the powers and prerogatives of authority, and income and wealth. But the difficulties are not so great as they might seem at first because of the nature of the difference principle. The only index problem that concerns us is that for the least advantaged group. The primary goods enjoyed by other representative individuals are adjusted to raise this index, subject of course to the usual constraints. It is unnecessary to define weights for the more favoured positions in any detail, as long as we are sure that they are more favoured. But often this is easy since they frequently have more of every primary good, greater powers and wealth tending to go together. If we know how the distribution of goods to the more favoured affects the expectations of the most disfavoured, this is sufficient. The index problem largely reduces, then, to that of weighting primary goods for the least advantaged, for those with the least authority and the lowest income, since these also tend to be associated. We try to do this by taking up the standpoint of the representative individual from this group and asking which combination of primary social goods it would be rational for him to prefer. In doing this we admittedly rely upon our intuitive capacities. This cannot be avoided entirely, however. The aim is to replace moral judgments by those of rational prudence and to make the appeal to intuition more limited in scope, more sharply focused.

Another difficulty is this. It may be objected that expectations should not be defined as an index of primary goods anyway but rather as the satisfactions to be expected when plans are executed using these goods. After all, it is in the fulfillment of these plans that men gain happiness, and therefore the estimate of expectations should not be founded on the available means. Justice as fairness, however, takes a different view. For it does not look behind the use which persons make of the rights and opportunities available to them in order to measure, much less to maximize, the satisfactions they achieve. Nor does it try to evaluate the relative merits of different conceptions of the good. Instead, it is assumed that the members of society are rational persons able to adjust their conceptions of the good to their situation. There is no necessity to compare the worth of the conceptions of different persons once it is supposed they are compatible with the principles of justice. Everyone is assured an equal liberty to pursue whatever plan of life he pleases as long as it does not violate what justice demands. Men share in primary goods on the principle that some can have more if they are acquired in ways which improve the situation of those who have less. Once the whole arrangement is set up and going no questions are asked about the totals of satisfaction or perfection. Things work themselves out according to the principles that would be chosen in the original position. On this conception of social justice, then, expectations are defined as the index of primary goods that a representative man can reasonably look forward to. A person's prospects are improved when he can anticipate a preferred collection of these goods.

It is worth noting that this interpretation of expectations represents, in effect, an agreement to compare men's situations solely by reference to things which it is assumed they all prefer more of. This seems the most feasible way to establish a publicly recognized objective measure, that is, a common measure that reasonable persons can accept. Whereas there cannot be a similar agreement on how to estimate happiness as defined, say, by men's success in executing their rational plans, much less on the intrinsic value of these plans. Now founding expectations on primary goods is another simplifying device. I should like to comment in passing that this and other simplifications are accompanied by some sort of philosophical explanation, though this is not strictly necessary. Theoretical assumptions must, of course, do more than simplify; they must identify essential elements that explain the facts we want to understand. Similarly, the parts of a theory of justice must represent basic moral features of the social structure, and if it appears that some of these are being left aside, it is desirable to assure ourselves that such is not the case. I shall try to follow this rule. But even so, the soundness of the theory of justice is shown as much in its consequences as in the prima facie acceptability of its premises. Indeed, these cannot be usefully separated and therefore the discussion of institutional questions, particularly in Part Two, which may seem at first unphilosophical, is in fact unavoidable.

. . .

17. The Tendency to Equality

I wish to conclude this discussion of the two principles by explaining the sense in which they express an egalitarian conception of justice. Also I should like to forestall the objection to the principle of fair opportunity that it leads to a callous meritocratic society. In order to prepare the way for doing this, I note several aspects of the conception of justice that I have set out.

First we may observe that the difference principle gives some weight to the considerations singled out by the principle of redress. This is the principle that undeserved inequalities call for redress; and since inequalities of birth and natural endowment are undeserved, these inequalities are to be somehow compensated for.[9] Thus the principle holds that in order to treat all persons equally, to provide genuine equality of opportunity, society must give more attention to those with fewer native assets and to those born into the less favourable social positions. The idea is to redress the bias of contingencies in the direction of equality. In pursuit of this principle greater resources might be spent on the education of the less rather than the more intelligent, at least over a certain time of life, say the earlier years of school.

Now the principle of redress has not to my knowledge been proposed as the sole criterion of justice, as the single aim of the social order. It is plausible as most such principles are only as a prima facie principle, one that is to be weighed in the balance with others. For example, we are to weigh it against the principle to improve the average standard of life, or to advance the common good.[10] But whatever other principles we hold, the claims of redress are to be taken into account. It is thought to represent one of the elements in our conception of justice. Now the difference principle is not of course the principle of redress. It does not require society to try to even out handicaps as if all were expected to compete on a fair basis in the same race. But the difference principle would allocate resources in education, say, so as to improve the long-term expectation of the least favoured. If this end is attained by giving more attention to the better endowed, it is permissible; otherwise not. And in making this decision, the value of education should not be assessed solely in terms of economic efficiency and social welfare. Equally if not more important is the role of education in enabling a person to enjoy the culture of his society and to take part in its affairs, and in this way to provide for each individual a secure sense of his own worth.

Thus although the difference principle is not the same as that of redress, it does achieve some of the intent of the latter principle. It transforms the aims of the basic structure so that the total scheme of institutions no longer emphasizes social efficiency and technocratic values. We see then that the difference principle represents, in effect, an agreement to regard the distribution of natural talents as a common asset and to share in the benefits of this distribution whatever it turns out to be. Those who have been favoured by nature, whoever they are, may gain from their good fortune only on terms that improve the situation of those who have lost out. The naturally advantaged are not to gain merely because they are more gifted, but only to cover the costs of training and education and for using their endowments in ways that help the less fortunate as well. No one deserves his greater natural capacity nor merits a more favourable starting place in society. But it does not follow that one should eliminate these distinctions. There is another way to deal with them. The basic structure can be arranged so that these contingencies work for the good of the least fortunate. Thus we are led to the difference principle if we wish to set up the social system so that no one gains or loses from his arbitrary place in the distribution of natural assets or his initial position in society without giving or receiving compensating advantages in return.

In view of these remarks we may reject the contention that the ordering of institutions is always defective because the distribution of natural talents and the contingencies of social circumstance are unjust, and this injustice must inevitably carry over to human arrangements. Occasionally this reflection is offered as an excuse for ignoring injustice, as if the refusal to acquiesce

in injustice is on a par with being unable to accept death. The natural distribution is neither just nor unjust; nor is it unjust that persons are born into society at some particular position. These are simply natural facts. What is just and unjust is the way that institutions deal with these facts. Aristocratic and caste societies are unjust because they make these contingencies the ascriptive basis for belonging to more or less enclosed and privileged social classes. The basic structure of these societies incorporates the arbitrariness found in nature. But there is no necessity for men to resign themselves to these contingencies. The social system is not an unchangeable order beyond human control but a pattern of human action. In justice as fairness men agree to share one another's fate. In designing institutions they undertake to avail themselves of the accidents of nature and social circumstance only when doing so is for the common benefit. The two principles are a fair way of meeting the arbitrariness of fortune; and while no doubt imperfect in other ways, the institutions which satisfy these principles are just.

. . .

Chapter III The Original Position

. . .

24. The Veil of Ignorance

The idea of the original position is to set up a fair procedure so that any principles agreed to will be just. The aim is to use the notion of pure procedural justice as a basis of theory. Somehow we must nullify the effects of specific contingencies which put men at odds and tempt them to exploit social and natural circumstances to their own advantage. Now in order to do this I assume that the parties are situated behind a veil of ignorance. They do not know how the various alternatives will affect their own particular case and they are obliged to evaluate principles solely on the basis of general considerations.[11]

It is assumed, then, that the parties do not know certain kinds of particular facts. First of all, no one knows his place in society, his class position or social status; nor does he know his fortune in the distribution of natural assets and abilities, his intelligence and strength, and the like. Nor, again, does anyone know his conception of the good the particulars of his rational plan of life, or even the special features of his psychology such as his aversion to risk or liability to optimism or pessimism. More than this, I assume that the parties do not know the particular circumstances of their own society. That is, they do not know its economic or political situation, or the level of civilization and culture it has been able to achieve. The persons in the original position have no information as to which generation they belong. These broader restrictions on knowledge are appropriate in part because questions of social justice arise between generations as well as within them, for example, the question of the appropriate rate of capital saving and of the conservation of natural resources and the environment of nature. There is also, theoretically anyway, the question of a reasonable genetic policy. In these cases too, in order to carry through the idea of the original position, the parties must not know the contingencies that set them in opposition. They must choose principles the consequences of which they are prepared to live with whatever generation they turn out to belong to.

As far as possible, then, the only particular facts which the parties know is that their society is subject to the circumstances of justice and whatever this implies. It is taken for granted, however, that they know the general facts about human society. They understand political affairs and the principles of economic theory; they know the basis of social organization and the laws of human psychology. Indeed, the parties are presumed to know whatever general facts affect the choice of the principles of justice. There are no limitations on general information, that is, on general laws and theories, since conceptions of justice must be adjusted to the characteristics of the systems of social co-operation which they are to regulate, and there is no reason to rule out these facts. It is, for example, a consideration against a conception of justice that, in view of the laws of moral psychology, men would not acquire a desire to act upon it even when the institutions of their society satisfied it. For in this case there would be difficulty in securing the stability of social co-operation. It is an important feature of a conception of justice that it should generate its own support. That is, its principles should be such that when they are embodied in the basic structure of society men tend to acquire the corresponding sense of justice. Given the principles of moral learning, men develop a desire to act in accordance with its principles. In this case a conception of justice is stable. This kind of general information is admissible in the original position.

The notion of the veil of ignorance raises several difficulties. Some may object that the exclusion of nearly all particular information makes it difficult to grasp what is meant by the original position. Thus it may be helpful to observe that one or more persons can at any time enter this position, or perhaps, better, simulate the deliberations of this hypothetical situation, simply by reasoning in accordance with the appropriate restrictions. In arguing for a conception of justice we must be sure that it is among the permitted alternatives and satisfies the stipulated formal constraints. No considerations can be advanced in its favour unless they would be rational ones for us to urge were we to lack the kind of knowledge that is excluded. The evaluation of principles must proceed in terms of the general consequences of their public recognition and universal application, it being assumed that they will be complied with by everyone. To say that a certain conception of justice would be chosen in the original position is equivalent to saying that rational deliberation satisfying certain conditions and restrictions would reach a certain conclusion. If necessary, the argument to this result could be set out more formally. I shall, however, speak throughout in terms of the notion of the original position. It is more economical and suggestive, and brings out certain essential features that otherwise one might easily overlook.

These remarks show that the original position is not to be thought of as a general assembly which includes at one moment everyone who will live at some time; or, much less, as an assembly of everyone who could live at some time. It is not a gathering of all actual or possible persons. To conceive of the original position in either of these ways is to stretch fantasy too far; the conception would cease to be a natural guide to intuition. In any case, it is important that the original position be interpreted so that one can at any time adopt its perspective. It must make no difference when one takes up this viewpoint, or who does so: the restrictions must be such that the same principles are always chosen. The veil of ignorance is a key condition in meeting this requirement. It insures not only that the information available is relevant, but that it is at all times the same.

It may be protested that the condition of the veil of ignorance is irrational. Surely, some may object, principles should be chosen in the light of all the knowledge available. There are various replies to this contention. Here I shall sketch those which emphasize the simplifications that need to be made if one is to have any theory at all. (Those based on the Kantian interpretation of the original position are given later, §40.) To begin with, it is clear that since the differences among the parties are unknown to them, and everyone is equally rational and similarly situated, each is convinced by the same arguments. Therefore, we can view the choice in the original position from the standpoint of one person selected at random. If anyone after due reflection prefers a conception of justice to another, then they all do, and a unanimous agreement can be reached. We can, to make the circumstances more vivid, imagine that the parties are required to communicate with each other through a referee as intermediary, and that he is to announce which alternatives have been suggested and the reasons offered in their support. He forbids the attempt to form coalitions, and he informs the parties when they have come to an understanding. But such a referee is actually superfluous, assuming that the deliberations of the parties must be similar.

Thus there follows the very important consequence that the parties have no basis for bargaining in the usual sense. No one knows his situation in society nor his natural assets, and therefore no one is in a position to tailor principles to his advantage. We might imagine that one of the contractees threatens to hold out unless the others agree to principles favourable to him. But how does he know which principles are especially in his interests? The same holds for the formation of coalitions: if a group were to decide to band together to the disadvantage of the others, they would not know how to favour themselves in the choice of principles. Even if they could get everyone to agree to their proposal, they would have no assurance that it was to their advantage, since they cannot identify themselves either by name or description. The one case where this conclusion fails is that of saving. Since the persons in the original position know that they are contemporaries (taking the present time of entry interpretation), they can favour their generation by refusing to make any sacrifices at all for their successors; they simply acknowledge the principle that no one has a duty to save for posterity. Previous generations have saved or they have not; there is nothing the parties can now do to affect that. So in this instance the veil of ignorance fails to secure the desired result. Therefore I resolve the question of justice between generations in a different way by altering the motivation assumption. But with this adjustment no one is able to formulate principles especially designed to advance his own cause. Whatever his temporal position, each is forced to choose for everyone.[12]

The restrictions on particular information in the original position are, then, of fundamental importance. Without them we would not be able to work out any definite theory of justice at all. We would have to be content with a vague formula stating that justice is what would be agreed to without being able to say much, if anything, about the substance of the agreement itself. The formal constraints of the concept of right, those applying to principles directly, are not sufficient for our purpose. The veil of ignorance makes possible a unanimous choice of a particular conception of justice. Without these limitations on knowledge the bargaining problem of the original position would be hopelessly complicated. Even if theoretically a solution were to exist, we would not, at present anyway, be able to determine it.

The notion of the veil of ignorance is implicit, I think, in Kant's ethics (§40). Nevertheless the problem of defining the knowledge of the parties and of characterizing the alternatives open to them has often been passed over, even by contract theories. Sometimes the situation definitive of moral deliberation is presented in such an indeterminate way that one cannot ascertain how it will turn out. Thus Perry's doctrine is essentially contractarian: he holds that social and personal integration must proceed by entirely different principles, the latter by rational prudence, the former by the concurrence of persons of good will. He would appear to reject utilitarianism on much the same grounds suggested earlier: namely, that it improperly extends the principle of choice for one person to choices facing society. The right course of action is characterized as that which best advances social aims as these would be formulated by reflective agreement given that the parties have full knowledge of the circumstances and are moved by a benevolent concern for one another's interests. No effort is made, however, to specify in any precise way the possible outcomes of this sort of agreement. Indeed, without a far more elaborate account, no conclusions can be drawn.[13] I do not wish here to criticize others; rather, I want to explain the necessity for what may seem at times like so many irrelevant details.

Now the reasons for the veil of ignorance go beyond mere simplicity. We want to define the original position so that we get the desired solution. If a knowledge of particulars is allowed, then the outcome is biased by arbitrary contingencies. As already observed, to each according to his threat advantage is not a principle of justice. If the original position is to yield agreements that are just, the parties must be fairly situated and treated equally as moral persons. The arbitrariness of the world must be corrected for by adjusting the circumstances of the initial contractual situation. Moreover, if in choosing principles we required unanimity even when there is full information, only a few rather obvious cases could be decided. A conception of justice based on unanimity in these circumstances would indeed be weak and trivial. But once knowledge is excluded, the requirement of unanimity is not out of place and the fact that it can be satisfied is of great importance. It enables us to say of the preferred conception of justice that it represents a genuine reconciliation of interests.

A final comment. For the most part I shall suppose that the parties possess all general information. No general facts are closed to them. I do this mainly to avoid complications. Nevertheless a conception of justice is to be the public basis of the terms of social co-operation. Since common understanding necessitates certain bounds on the complexity of principles, there may likewise be limits on the use of theoretical knowledge in the original position. Now clearly it would be very difficult to classify and to grade for complexity the various sorts of general facts. I shall make no attempt to do this. We do however recognize an intricate theoretical construction when we meet one. Thus it seems reasonable to say that other things equal one conception of justice is to be preferred to another when it is founded upon markedly simpler general facts, and its choice does not depend upon elaborate calculations in the light of a vast array of theoretically defined possibilities. It is desirable that the grounds for a public conception of justice should be evident to everyone when circumstances permit. This consideration favours, I believe, the two principles of justice over the criterion of utility.

25. The Rationality of the Parties

I have assumed throughout that the persons in the original position are rational. In choosing between principles each tries as best he can to advance his interests. But I have also assumed that the parties do not know their conception of the good. This means that while they know that they have some rational plan of life, they do not know the details of this plan, the particular ends and interests which it is calculated to promote. How, then, can they decide which conceptions of justice are most to their advantage? Or must we suppose that they are reduced to mere guessing? To meet this difficulty, I postulate that they accept the account of the good touched upon in the preceding chapter: they assume that they would prefer more primary social goods rather than less. Of course, it may turn out, once the veil of ignorance is removed, that some of them for religious or other reasons may not, in fact, want more of these goods. But from the standpoint of the original position, it is rational for the parties to suppose that they do want a larger share, since in any case they are not compelled to accept more if they do not wish to, nor does a person suffer from a greater liberty. Thus even though the parties are deprived of information about their particular ends, they have enough knowledge to rank the alternatives. They know that in general they must try to protect their liberties, widen their opportunities, and enlarge their means for promoting their aims whatever these are. Guided by the theory of the good and the general facts of moral psychology, their deliberations are no longer guesswork. They can make a rational decision in the ordinary sense.

The concept of rationality invoked here, with the exception of one essential feature, is the standard one familiar in social theory.[14] Thus in the usual way, a rational person is thought to have a coherent set of preferences between the options open to him. He ranks these options according to how well they further his purposes; he follows the plan which will satisfy more of his desires rather

than less, and which has the greater chance of being successfully executed. The special assumption I make is that a rational individual does not suffer from envy. He is not ready to accept a loss for himself if only others have less as well. He is not downcast by the knowledge or perception that others have a larger index of primary social goods. Or at least this is true as long as the differences between himself and others do not exceed certain limits, and he does not believe that the existing inequalities are founded on injustice or are the result of letting chance work itself out for no compensating social purpose (§ 80).

The assumption that the parties are not moved by envy raises certain questions. Perhaps we should also assume that they are not liable to various other feelings such as shame and humiliation (§ 67). Now a satisfactory account of justice will eventually have to deal with these matters too, but for the present I shall leave these complications aside. Another objection to our procedure is that it is too unrealistic. Certainly men are afflicted with these feelings. How can a conception of justice ignore this fact? I shall meet this problem by dividing the argument for the principles of justice into two parts. In the first part, the principles are derived on the supposition that envy does not exist; while in the second, we consider whether the conception arrived at is feasible in view of the circumstances of human life.

One reason for this procedure is that envy tends to make everyone worse off. In this sense it is collectively disadvantageous. Presuming its absence amounts to supposing that in the choice of principles men should think of themselves as having their own plan of life which is sufficient for itself. They have a secure sense of their own worth so that they have no desire to abandon any of their aims provided others have less means to further theirs. I shall work out a conception of justice on this stipulation to see what happens. Later I shall try to show that when the principles adopted are put into practice, they lead to social arrangements in which envy and other destructive feelings are not likely to be strong. The conception of justice eliminates the conditions that give rise to disruptive attitudes. It is, therefore, inherently stable (§§ 80–81).

The assumption of mutually disinterested rationality, then, comes to this: the persons in the original position try to acknowledge principles which advance their system of ends as far as possible. They do this by attempting to win for themselves the highest index of primary social goods, since this enables them to promote their conception of the good most effectively whatever it turns out to be. The parties do not seek to confer benefits or to impose injuries on one another; they are not moved by affection or rancor. Nor do they try to gain relative to each other; they are not envious or vain. Put in terms of a game, we might say: they strive for as high an absolute score as possible. They do not wish a high or a low score for their opponents, nor do they seek to maximize or minimize the difference between their successes and those of others. The idea of a game does not really apply, since the parties are not concerned to win but to get as many points as possible judged by their own system of ends.

There is one further assumption to guarantee strict compliance. The parties are presumed to be capable of a sense of justice and this fact is public knowledge among them. This condition is to insure the integrity of the agreement made in the original position. It does not mean that in their deliberations the parties apply some particular conception of justice, for this would defeat the point of the motivation assumption. Rather, it means that the parties can rely on each other to understand and to act in accordance with whatever principles are finally agreed to. Once principles are acknowledged the parties can depend on one another to conform to them. In reaching an agreement, then, they know that their undertaking is not in vain: their capacity for a sense of justice insures that the principles chosen will be respected. It is essential to observe, however, that this assumption still permits the consideration of men's capacity to act on the various conceptions of justice. The general facts of human psychology and the principles of moral learning are relevant matters for the parties to examine. If a conception of justice is unlikely to generate its own support, or lacks stability, this fact must not be overlooked. For then a different conception of justice might be preferred. The assumption only says that the parties have a capacity for justice in a purely formal sense: taking everything relevant into account, including the general facts of moral psychology, the parties will adhere to the principles eventually chosen. They are rational in that they will not enter into agreements they know they cannot keep, or can do so only with great difficulty. Along with other considerations, they count the strains of commitment (§ 29). Thus in assessing conceptions of justice the persons in the original position are to assume that the one they adopt will be strictly complied with. The consequences of their agreement are to be worked out on this basis.

. . .

26. The Reasoning Leading to the Two Principles of Justice

In this and the next two sections I take up the choice between the two principles of justice and the principle of average utility. Determining the rational preference between these two options is perhaps the central problem in developing the conception of justice as fairness as a viable alternative to the utilitarian tradition. I shall begin in this section by presenting some intuitive remarks favouring the two principles. I shall also discuss briefly the qualitative structure of the argument that needs to be made if the case for these principles is to be conclusive.

It will be recalled that the general conception of justice as fairness requires that all primary social goods be distributed equally unless an unequal distribution would be to everyone's advantage. No restrictions are placed on exchanges of these goods and therefore a lesser liberty can be compensated for by greater social and economic benefits. Now looking at the situation from the standpoint of one person selected arbitrarily, there is no way for him to win special advantages for himself. Nor, on the other hand, are there grounds for his acquiescing in special disadvantages. Since it is not reasonable for him to expect more than an equal share in the division of social goods, and since it is not rational for him to agree to less, the sensible thing for him to do is to acknowledge as the first principle of justice one requiring an equal distribution. Indeed, this principle is so obvious that we would expect it to occur to anyone immediately.

Thus, the parties start with a principle establishing equal liberty for all, including equality of opportunity, as well as an equal distribution of income and wealth. But there is no reason why this acknowledgment should be final. If there are inequalities in the basic structure that work to make everyone better off in comparison with the benchmark of initial equality, why not permit them? The immediate gain which a greater equality might allow can be regarded as intelligently invested in view of its future return. If, for example, these inequalities set up various incentives which succeed in eliciting more productive efforts, a person in the original position may look upon them as necessary to cover the costs of training and to encourage effective performance. One might think that ideally individuals should want to serve one another. But since the parties are assumed not to take an interest in one another's interests, their acceptance of these inequalities is only the acceptance of the relations in which men stand in the circumstances of justice. They have no grounds for complaining of one another's motives. A person in the original position would, therefore, concede the justice of these inequalities. Indeed, it would be shortsighted of him not to do so. He would hesitate to agree to these regularities only if he would be dejected by the bare knowledge or perception that others were better situated; and I have assumed that the parties decide as if they are not moved by envy. In order to make the principle regulating inequalities determinate, one looks at the system from the standpoint of the least advantaged representative man. Inequalities are permissible when they maximize, or at least all contribute to, the long-term expectations of the least fortunate group in society.

Now this general conception imposes no constraints on what sorts of inequalities are allowed, whereas the special conception, by putting the two principles in serial order (with the necessary adjustments in meaning), forbids exchanges between basic liberties and economic and social benefits. I shall not try to justify this ordering here. From time to time in later chapters this problem will be considered (§§39, 82). But roughly, the idea underlying this ordering is that if the parties assume that their basic liberties can be effectively exercised, they will not exchange a lesser liberty for an improvement in economic well-being. It is only when social conditions do not allow the effective establishment of these rights that one can concede their limitation; and these restrictions can be granted only to the extent that they are necessary to prepare the way for a free society. The denial of equal liberty can be defended only if it is necessary to raise the level of civilization so that in due course these freedoms can be enjoyed. Thus in adopting a serial order we are in effect making a special assumption in the original position, namely, that the parties know that the conditions of their society, whatever they are, admit the effective realization of the equal liberties. The serial ordering of the two principles of justice eventually comes to be reasonable if the general conception is consistently followed. This lexical ranking is the long-run tendency of the general view. For the most part I shall assume that the requisite circumstances for the serial order obtain.

It seems clear from these remarks that the two principles are at least a plausible conception of justice. The question, though, it how one is to argue for them more systematically. Now there are several things to do. One can work out their consequences for institutions and note their implications for fundamental social policy. In this way they are tested by a comparison with our considered judgments of justice. Part II is devoted to this. But one can also try to find arguments in their favour that are decisive from the standpoint of the original position. In order to see how this might be done, it is useful as a heuristic device to think of the two principles as the maximin solution to the problem of social justice. There is an analogy between the two principles and the maximin rule for choice under uncertainty.[15] This is evident from the fact that the two principles are those a person would choose for the design of a society in which his enemy is to assign him his place. The maximin rule tells us to rank alternatives by their worst possible outcomes: we are to adopt the alternative the worst outcome of which is superior to the worst outcomes of the others.

The persons in the original position do not, of course, assume that their initial place in society is decided by a malevolent opponent. As I note below, they should not reason from false premises. The veil of ignorance does not violate this idea, since an absence of information is not misinformation. But that the two principles of justice would be chosen if the parties were forced to protect themselves against such a contingency explains the sense in which this conception is the maximin solution. And this analogy suggests that if the original position has been described so that it is rational for the parties to adopt the conservative attitude expressed by this rule, a conclusive argument can indeed be constructed for these principles. Clearly the maximin rule is not, in general, a suitable guide for choices under uncertainty. But it is attractive in situations marked by certain special features. My aim, then, is to show that a good cue can be made for the two principles based on the fact that the original position manifests these features to the fullest possible degree, carrying them to the limit, so to speak.

Consider the gain-and-loss table below. It represents the gains and losses for a situation which is not a game of strategy. There is no one playing against the person making the decision; instead he is faced with several possible circumstances which may or may not obtain. Which circumstances happen to exist does not depend upon what the person choosing decides or whether he announces his moves in advance. The numbers in the table are monetary values (in hundreds of dollars) in comparison with some initial situation. The gain (g) depends upon the individual's decision (d) and the circumstances (c). Thus $g = f(d, c)$. Assuming that there are three possible decisions and three possible circumstances, we might have this gain-and-loss table.

Decisions	Circumstances		
	C_1	C_2	C_3
d_1	−7	8	12
d_2	−8	7	14
d_3	5	6	8

The maximin rule requires that we make the third decision. For in this case the worst that can happen is that one gains five hundred dollars, which is better than the worst for the other actions. If we adopt one of these we may lose either eight or seven hundred dollars. Thus, the choice of d_3 maximizes $f(d, c)$ for that value of c, which for a given d, minimizes f. The term "maximin" means the *maximum minimorum*; and the rule directs our attention to the worst that can happen under any proposed course of action, and to decide in the light of that.

Now there appear to be three chief features of situations that give plausibility to this unusual rule.[16] First, since the rule takes no account of the likelihoods of the possible circumstances, there must be some reason for sharply discounting estimates of these probabilities. Offhand, the most natural rule of choice would seem to be to compute the expectation of monetary gain for each decision and then to adopt the course of action with the highest prospect. (This expectation is defined as follows: let us suppose that g_{ij} represent the numbers in the gain-and-loss table, where i is the row index and j is the column index; and let p_j, j = 1, 2, 3, be the likelihoods of the circumstances, with $\Sigma p_j = 1$. Then the expectation for the ith decision is equal to $\Sigma p_j g_{ij}$.) Thus it must be, for example, that the situation is one in which a knowledge of likelihoods is impossible, or at best extremely insecure. In this case it is unreasonable not to be skeptical of probabilistic calculations unless there is no other way out, particularly if the decision is a fundamental one that needs to be justified to others.

The second feature that suggests the maximin rule is the following: the person choosing has a conception of the good such that he cares very little, if anything, for what he might gain above the minimum stipend that he can, in fact, be sure of by following the maximin rule. It is not worthwhile for him to take a chance for the sake of a further advantage, especially when it may turn out that he loses much that is important to him. This last provision brings in the third feature, namely, that the rejected alternatives have outcomes that one can hardly accept. The situation involves grave risks. Of course these features work most effectively in combination. The paradigm situation for following the maximin rule is when all three features are realized to the highest degree. This rule does not, then, generally apply, nor of course is it self-evident. Rather, it is a maxim, a rule of thumb, that comes into its own in special circumstances. Its application depends upon the qualitative structure of the possible gains and losses in relation to one's conception of the good, all this against a background in which it is reasonable to discount conjectural estimates of likelihoods.

It should be noted, as the comments on the gain-and-loss table say, that the entries in the table represent monetary values and not utilities. This difference is significant since for one thing computing expectations on the basis of such objective values is not the same thing as computing expected utility and may lead to different results. The essential point though is that in justice as fairness the parties do not know their conception of the good and cannot estimate their utility in the ordinary sense. In any case, we want to go behind de facto preferences generated by given conditions. Therefore

expectations are based upon an index of primary goods and the parties make their choice accordingly. The entries in the example are in terms of money and not utility to indicate this aspect of the contract doctrine.

Now, as I have suggested, the original position has been defined so that it is a situation in which the maximin rule applies. In order to see this, let us review briefly the nature of this situation with these three special features in mind. To begin with, the veil of ignorance excludes all but the vaguest knowledge of likelihoods. The parties have no basis for determining the probable nature of their society, or their place in it. Thus they have strong reasons for being wary of probability calculations if any other course is open to them. They must also take into account the fact that their choice of principles should seem reasonable to others, in particular their descendants, whose rights will be deeply affected by it. There are further grounds for discounting that I shall mention as we go along. For the present it suffices to note that these considerations are strengthened by the fact that the parties know very little about the gain-and-loss table. Not only are they unable to conjecture the likelihoods of the various possible circumstances, they cannot say much about what the possible circumstances are, much less enumerate them and foresee the outcome of each alternative available. Those deciding are much more in the dark than the illustration by a numerical table suggests. It is for this reason that I have spoken of an analogy with the maximin rule.

Several kinds of arguments for the two principles of justice illustrate the second feature. Thus, if we can maintain that these principles provide a workable theory of social justice, and that they are compatible with reasonable demands of efficiency, then this conception guarantees a satisfactory minimum. There may be, on reflection, little reason for trying to do better. Thus much of the argument, especially in Part Two, is to show, by their application to the main questions of social justice, that the two principles are a satisfactory conception. These details have a philosophical purpose. Moreover, this line of thought is practically decisive if we can establish the priority of liberty, the lexical ordering of the two principles. For this priority implies that the persons in the original position have no desire to try for greater gains at the expense of the equal liberties. The minimum assured by the two principles in lexical order is not one that the parties wish to jeopardize for the sake of greater economic and social advantages. . . .

Finally, the third feature holds if we can assume that other conceptions of justice may lead to institutions that the parties would find intolerable. For example, it has sometimes been held that under some conditions the utility principle (in either form) justifies, if not slavery or serfdom, at any rate serious infractions of liberty for the sake of greater social benefits. We need not consider here the truth of this claim, or the likelihood that the requisite conditions obtain. For the moment, this contention is only to illustrate the way in which conceptions of justice may allow for outcomes which the parties may not be able to accept. And having the ready alternative of the two principles of justice which secure a satisfactory minimum, it seems unwise, if not irrational, for them to take a chance that these outcomes are not realized.

So much, then, for a brief sketch of the features of situations in which the maximin rule comes into its own and of the way in which the arguments for the two principles of justice can be subsumed under them. Thus if the list of traditional views (§ 21) represents the possible decisions, these principles would be selected by the rule. The original position clearly exhibits these special features to a very high degree in view of the fundamental character of the choice of a conception of justice. These remarks about the maximin rule are intended only to clarify the structure of the choice problem in the original position. They depict its qualitative anatomy. The arguments for the two principles will be presented more fully as we proceed.

. . .

Part Two Institutions

Chapter IV Equal Liberty

In . . . Part Two my aim is to illustrate the content of the principles of justice. I shall do this by describing a basic structure that satisfies these principles and by examining the duties and obligations to which they give rise. The main institutions of this structure are those of a constitutional democracy. I do not argue that these arrangements are the only ones that are just. Rather my intention is to show that the principles of justice, which so far have been discussed in abstraction from institutional forms, define a workable political conception, and are a reasonable approximation to and extension of our considered judgments. In this chapter I begin by setting out a four-stage sequence that clarifies how the principles for institutions are to be applied. Two parts of the basic structure are briefly described and the concept of liberty defined. After this, three problems of equal liberty are discussed: equal liberty of conscience, political justice and equal political rights, and equal liberty of the person and its relation to the rule of law. I then take up the meaning of the priority of liberty, and conclude with a brief account of the Kantian interpretation of the original position.

31. The Four-Stage Sequence

It is evident that some sort of framework is needed to simplify the application of the two principles of justice. For consider three kinds of judgments that a citizen has to make. First of all, he must judge the justice of legislation and social policies. But he also knows that his opinions will not always coincide with those of others, since men's judgments and beliefs are likely to differ especially when their interests are engaged. Therefore secondly, a citizen must decide which constitutional arrangements are just for reconciling conflicting opinions of justice. We may think of the political process as a machine which makes social decisions when the views of representatives and their constituents are fed into it. A citizen will regard some ways of designing this machine as more just than others. So a complete conception of justice is not only able to assess laws and policies but it can also rank procedures for selecting which political opinion is to be enacted into law. There is still a third problem. The citizen accepts a certain constitution as just, and he thinks that certain traditional procedures are appropriate, for example, the procedure of majority rule duly circumscribed. Yet since the political process is at best one of imperfect procedural justice, he must ascertain when the enactments of the majority are to be complied with and when they can be rejected as no longer binding. In short, he must be able to determine the grounds and limits of political duty and obligation. Thus a theory of justice has to deal with at least three types of questions, and this indicates that it may be useful to think of the principles as applied in a several-stage sequence.

At this point, then, I introduce an elaboration of the original position. So far I have supposed that once the principles of justice are chosen the parties return to their place in society and henceforth judge their claims on the social system by these principles. But if several intermediate stages are imagined to take place in a definite sequence, this sequence may give us a schema for sorting out the complications that must be faced. Each stage is to represent an appropriate point of view from which certain kinds of questions are considered.[17] Thus I suppose that after the parties have adopted the principles of justice in the original position, they move to a constitutional convention. Here they are to decide upon the justice of political forms and choose a constitution: they are delegates, so to speak, to such a convention. Subject to the constraints of the principles of justice already chosen, they are to design a system for the constitutional powers of government and the basic rights of citizens. It is at this stage that they weigh the justice of procedures for coping with diverse political views. Since the appropriate conception of justice has been agreed upon, the veil of ignorance is partially lifted. The persons in the convention have, of course, no information about particular individuals: they do not know their own social position, their place in the distribution of natural attributes, or their conception of the good. But in addition to an understanding of the principles of social theory, they now know the relevant general facts about their society, that is, its natural circumstances and resources, its level of economic advance and political culture, and so on. They are no longer limited to the information implicit in the circumstances of justice. Given their theoretical knowledge and the appropriate general facts about their society, they are to choose the most effective just constitution, the constitution that satisfies the principles of justice and is best calculated to lead to just and effective legislation.[18]

At this point we need to distinguish two problems. Ideally a just constitution would be a just procedure arranged to insure a just outcome. The procedure would be the political process governed by the constitution, the outcome the body of enacted legislation, while the principles of justice would define an independent criterion for both procedure and outcome. In pursuit of this ideal of perfect procedural justice (§14), the first problem is to design a just procedure. To do this the liberties of equal citizenship must be incorporated into and protected by the constitution. These liberties include those of liberty of conscience and freedom of thought, liberty of the person, and equal political rights. The political system, which I assume to be some form of constitutional democracy, would not be a just procedure if it did not embody these liberties.

Clearly any feasible political procedure may yield an unjust outcome. In fact, there is no scheme of procedural political rules which guarantees that unjust legislation will not be enacted. In the case of a constitutional regime, or indeed of any political form, the ideal of perfect procedural justice cannot be realized. The best attainable scheme is one of imperfect procedural justice. Nevertheless some schemes have a greater tendency than others to result in unjust laws. The second problem, then, is to select from among the procedural arrangements that are both just and feasible those which are most likely to lead to a just and effective legal order. Once again this is Bentham's problem of the artificial identification of interests, only here the rules (just procedure) are to be framed to give legislation (just outcome) likely to accord with the principles of justice rather than the principle of utility. To solve this problem intelligently requires a knowledge of the beliefs and interests that men in the system are liable to have and of the political tactics that they will find it rational to use given their circumstances. The delegates are assumed, then, to know these things.

Provided they have no information about particular individuals including themselves, the idea of the original position is not affected.

In framing a just constitution I assume that the two principles of justice already chosen define an independent standard of the desired outcome. If there is no such standard, the problem of constitutional design is not well posed, for this decision is made by running through the feasible just constitutions (given, say, by enumeration on the basis of social theory) looking for the one that in the existing circumstances will most probably result in effective and just social arrangements. Now at this point we come to the legislative stage, to take the next step in the sequence. The justice of laws and policies is to be assessed from this perspective. Proposed bills are judged from the position of a representative legislator who, as always, does not know the particulars about himself. Statutes must satisfy not only the principles of justice but whatever limits are laid down in the constitution. By moving back and forth between the stages of the constitutional convention and the legislature, the best constitution is found.

Now the question whether legislation is just or unjust, especially in connection with economic and social policies, is commonly subject to reasonable differences of opinion. In these cases judgment frequently depends upon speculative political and economic doctrines and upon social theory generally. Often the best that we can say of a law or policy is that it is at least not clearly unjust. The application of the difference principle in a precise way normally requires more information than we can expect to have and, in any case, more than the application of the first principle. It is often perfectly plain and evident when the equal liberties are violated. These violations are not only unjust but can be clearly seen to be unjust: the injustice is manifest in the public structure of institutions. But this state of affairs is comparatively rare with social and economic policies regulated by the difference principle.

I imagine then a division of labour between stages in which each deals with different questions of social justice. This division roughly corresponds to the two parts of the basic structure. The first principle of equal liberty is the primary standard for the constitutional convention. Its main requirements are that the fundamental liberties of the person and liberty of conscience and freedom of thought be protected and that the political process as a whole be a just procedure. Thus the constitution establishes a secure common status of equal citizenship and realizes political justice. The second principle comes into play at the stage of the legislature. It dictates that social and economic policies be aimed at maximizing the long-term expectations of the least advantaged under conditions of fair equality of opportunity, subject to the equal liberties being maintained. At this point the full range of general economic and social facts is brought to bear. The second part of the basic structure contains the distinctions and hierarchies of political, economic, and social forms which are necessary for efficient and mutually beneficial social co-operation. Thus the priority of the first principle of justice to the second is reflected in the priority of the constitutional convention to the legislative stage.

The last stage is that of the application of rules to particular cases by judges and administrators, and the following of rules by citizens generally. At this stage everyone has complete access to all the facts. No limits on knowledge remain since the full system of rules has now been adopted and applies to persons in virtue of their characteristics and circumstances. However, it is not from this standpoint that we are to decide the grounds and limits of political duty and obligation. This third type of problem belongs to partial compliance theory, and its principles are discussed from the point of view of the original position after those of ideal theory have been chosen (§ 39). Once these are on hand, we can view our particular situation from the perspective of the last stage, as for example in the cases of civil disobedience and conscientious refusal (§§ 57–59).

The availability of knowledge in the four-stage sequence is roughly as follows. Let us distinguish between three kinds of facts: the first principles of social theory (and other theories when relevant) and their consequences; general facts about society, such as its size and level of economic advance, its institutional structure and natural environment, and so on; and finally, particular facts about individuals such as their social position, natural attributes, and peculiar interests. In the original position the only particular facts known to the parties are those that can be inferred from the circumstances of justice. While they know the first principles of social theory, the course of history is closed to them; they have no information about how often society has taken this or that form, or which kinds of societies presently exist. In the next stages, however, the general facts about their society

are made available to them but not the particularities of their own condition. Limitations on knowledge can be relaxed since the principles of justice are already chosen. The flow of information is determined at each stage by what is required in order to apply these principles intelligently to the kind of question of justice at hand, while at the same time any knowledge that is likely to give rise to bias and distortion and to set men against one another is ruled out. The notion of the rational and impartial application of principles defines the kind of knowledge that is admissible. At the last stage, clearly, there are no reasons for the veil of ignorance in any form, and all restrictions are lifted.

It is essential to keep in mind that the four-stage sequence is a device for applying the principles of justice. This scheme is part of the theory of justice as fairness and not an account of how constitutional conventions and legislatures actually proceed. It sets out a series of points of view from which the different problems of justice are to be settled, each point of view inheriting the constraints adopted at the preceding stages. Thus a just constitution is one that rational delegates subject to the restrictions of the second stage would adopt for their society. And similarly just laws and policies are those that would be enacted at the legislative stage. Of course, this test is often indeterminate: it is not always clear which of several constitutions, or economic and social arrangements, would be chosen. But when this is so, justice is to that extent likewise indeterminate. Institutions within the permitted range are equally just, meaning that they could be chosen; they are compatible with all the constraints of the theory. Thus on many questions of social and economic policy we must fall back upon a notion of quasi-pure procedural justice: laws and policies are just provided that they lie within the allowed range, and the legislature, in ways authorized by a just constitution, has in fact enacted them. This indeterminacy in the theory of justice is not in itself a defect. It is what we should expect. Justice as fairness will prove a worthwhile theory if it defines the range of justice more in accordance with our considered judgments than do existing theories, and if it singles out with greater sharpness the graver wrongs a society should avoid.

Post-Reading Questions

1. What is the "difference principle"?
2. What is Rawls' notion of the "original position" and how does it function in his theory?
3. For Rawls, where one starts out in life (one's social class, wealth, etc.) should not determine one's access to the "primary goods" of life, such as rights, liberties, power, wealth, and opportunities. Is he right?
4. What are Rawls' two principles of justice, and do they seem likely to ensure a fair and just society?
5. In Rawls' theory, people don't "merit" their natural endowments or talents—that is, they don't deserve to be the exclusive beneficiaries of these. Why? Do you agree/disagree with Rawls?

CASE STUDY
UNIVERSAL HEALTHCARE IN CANADA

Introduction

The Canada Health Act, adopted by Parliament in 1984, expresses the conviction that a universal health care system is the most sensible and equitable one for citizens of a modern democracy. Access to insured health services—regardless of ability to pay—is critical to maintaining and improving the overall quality of health of all Canadians, according to the Act. By providing a publicly funded, universal health care system, Canada is in step with other advanced liberal democracies, all of which have comparable nation-wide systems (with the notable exceptions of the United States and South Africa).

Although Rawls himself did not address the issue of universal health care in any detail, other political philosophers have used some of Rawls' ideas to give philosophical justification for such a system—notably, for example, the philosopher Norman Daniels (*Just Health Care*, 1985). Several aspects of Rawls' thought as set out in his books *A Theory of Justice* (1971) and *Justice as Fairness: A Restatement* (2001) may be taken as supporting publicly funded and universally accessible medical care.

Using the device of the "original position," Rawls suggests that the fairest principles of justice are those that we would choose if we did not know the particulars of our personal social and economic situation. Uncertain of what the life lottery might hold for us, Rawls contends that we would prefer principles that did not penalize—or reward—individuals for their unchosen circumstances. The "difference principle" contained within the second principle of justice defended by Rawls is particularly relevant to the matter of health care, for it seeks to prohibit social and economic inequalities unless they are advantageous to what he called the "least well off" in society. This normative principle requires, in essence, that social and economic resources and opportunities be more equitably distributed to ensure that no one is unfairly disadvantaged by their starting circumstances in life (their family of origin, social class, disabilities, etc.).

Extending the logic of the difference principle to the realm of health, it is easy to see that the spirit of Rawls' conception of justice as fairness would require equitable access to a range of health care services, from life-saving treatments to preventative care. The principles of justice that Rawls identifies are to apply to what he calls "the basic structure of society," which includes the economy, the legal system, and the family. Applied to a society's system of health care, both the difference principle and the notion of fair equality of opportunity (both part of the second principle of justice) would seem to require that no citizen be deprived of essential medical care due to an inability to pay (or any other reason).

In recent years, considerable data has emerged in advanced industrialized societies in support of what is known as the "social determinants of health" thesis. According to data presented by proponents of this thesis, societies with a high degree of social and economic inequality have poorer health outcomes for society as a whole (i.e., not just for the poor), and lowered life expectancy rates as compared with countries with less inequality. While still considered controversial, these findings about the impact of inequality are defended by many medical sociologists, social epidemiologists, and public health specialists. Proponents of Rawls' theory are interested in any institutional arrangements that exacerbate inequality in society; hence the institutional arrangements surrounding healthcare are an important concern. Universal access to health care—both in terms of treatment or care and pharmaceuticals—could arguably help to offset the health-related effects of the economic inequality prevalent in market societies. Whether funded through a private insurance scheme (if truly accessible to all, irrespective of income) or through government revenue (typically generated by income tax, as is the case in most Canadian provinces), it is difficult to see how secure access to good quality health care would not be a vital component of a society constructed to reflect Rawls' idea of "justice as fairness." In the case reading provided below, legislators affirm the value of a federal system of health care, giving reasons that mesh with some of Rawls' thinking.

C-6 Canada Health Act (1985)

C-6 Canada Health Act (1985), R.S.C., 1985 (Ottawa: Minister of Justice).
http://laws-lois.justice.gc.ca/eng/acts/c-6

An Act relating to cash contributions by Canada and relating to criteria and conditions in respect of insured health services and extended health care services

Preamble

Whereas the Parliament of Canada recognizes:

—that it is not the intention of the Government of Canada that any of the powers, rights, privileges or authorities vested in Canada or the provinces under the provisions of the Constitution Act, 1867, or any amendments thereto, or otherwise, be by reason of this Act abrogated or derogated from or in any way impaired;

—that Canadians, through their system of insured health services, have made outstanding progress in treating sickness and alleviating the consequences of disease and disability among all income groups;

—that Canadians can achieve further improvements in their well-being through combining individual lifestyles that emphasize fitness, prevention of disease and health promotion with collective action against the social, environmental and occupational causes of disease, and that they desire a system of health services that will promote physical and mental health and protection against disease;

—that future improvements in health will require the cooperative partnership of governments, health professionals, voluntary organizations and individual Canadians;

—that continued access to quality health care

without financial or other barriers will be critical to maintaining and improving the health and well-being of Canadians;

And whereas the Parliament of Canada wishes to encourage the development of health services throughout Canada by assisting the provinces in meeting the costs thereof;

Now, therefore, Her Majesty, by and with the advice and consent of the Senate and House of Commons of Canada, enacts as follows:

SHORT TITLE

1. This Act may be cited as the Canada Health Act.

- 1984, c. 6, s. 1.

INTERPRETATION

2. In this Act,

"Act of 1977" [Repealed, 1995, c. 17, s. 34]

"cash contribution" means the cash contribution in respect of the Canada Health and Social Transfer that may be provided to a province under sections 24.2 and 24.21 of the *Federal-Provincial Fiscal Arrangements Act*;

"contribution" [Repealed, 1995, c. 17, s. 34]

"dentist" means a person lawfully entitled to practise dentistry in the place in which the practice is carried on by that person;

"extended health care services" means the following services, as more particularly defined in the regulations, provided for residents of a province, namely,

(*a*) nursing home intermediate care service,
(*b*) adult residential care service,
(*c*) home care service, and
(*d*) ambulatory health care service;

"extra-billing" means the billing for an insured health service rendered to an insured person by a medical practitioner or a dentist in an amount in addition to any amount paid or to be paid for that service by the health care insurance plan of a province;

"health care insurance plan" means, in relation to a province, a plan or plans established by the law of the province to provide for insured health services;

"health care practitioner" means a person lawfully entitled under the law of a province to provide health services in the place in which the services are provided by that person;

"hospital" includes any facility or portion thereof that provides hospital care, including acute, rehabilitative or chronic care, but does not include

(*a*) a hospital or institution primarily for the mentally disordered, or
(*b*) a facility or portion thereof that provides nursing home intermediate care service or adult residential care service, or comparable services for children;

"hospital services" means any of the following services provided to in-patients or out-patients at a hospital, if the services are medically necessary for the purpose of maintaining health, preventing disease or diagnosing or treating an injury, illness or disability, namely,

(*a*) accommodation and meals at the standard or public ward level and preferred accommodation if medically required,
(*b*) nursing service,
(*c*) laboratory, radiological and other diagnostic procedures, together with the necessary interpretations,
(*d*) drugs, biologicals and related preparations when administered in the hospital,
(*e*) use of operating room, case room and anaesthetic facilities, including necessary equipment and supplies,
(*f*) medical and surgical equipment and supplies,
(*g*) use of radiotherapy facilities,
(*h*) use of physiotherapy facilities, and
(*i*) services provided by persons who receive remuneration therefor from the hospital,

but does not include services that are excluded by the regulations;

"insured health services" means hospital services, physician services and surgical-dental services provided to insured persons, but does not include any health services that a person is entitled to and eligible for under any other Act of Parliament or under any Act of the legislature of a province that relates to workers' or workmen's compensation;

"insured person" means, in relation to a province, a resident of the province other than

(*a*) a member of the Canadian Forces,
(*b*) [Repealed, 2012, c. 19, s. 377]
(*c*) a person serving a term of imprisonment in a penitentiary as defined in the Penitentiary Act, or
(*d*) a resident of the province who has not

completed such minimum period of residence or waiting period, not exceeding three months, as may be required by the province for eligibility for or entitlement to insured health services;

"medical practitioner" means a person lawfully entitled to practise medicine in the place in which the practice is carried on by that person;

"Minister" means the Minister of Health;

"physician services" means any medically required services rendered by medical practitioners;

"resident" means, in relation to a province, a person lawfully entitled to be or to remain in Canada who makes his home and is ordinarily present in the province, but does not include a tourist, a transient or a visitor to the province;

"surgical-dental services" means any medically or dentally required surgical-dental procedures performed by a dentist in a hospital, where a hospital is required for the proper performance of the procedures;

"user charge" means any charge for an insured health service that is authorized or permitted by a provincial health care insurance plan that is not payable, directly or indirectly, by a provincial health care insurance plan, but does not include any charge imposed by extra-billing.

CANADIAN HEALTH CARE POLICY

3. It is hereby declared that the primary objective of Canadian health care policy is to protect, promote and restore the physical and mental well-being of residents of Canada and to facilitate reasonable access to health services without financial or other barriers.

PURPOSE

4. The purpose of this Act is to establish criteria and conditions in respect of insured health services and extended health care services provided under provincial law that must be met before a full cash contribution may be made.

CASH CONTRIBUTION

5. Subject to this Act, as part of the Canada Health Transfer, a full cash contribution is payable by Canada to each province for each fiscal year...

PROGRAM CRITERIA

7. In order that a province may qualify for a full cash contribution referred to in section 5 for a fiscal year, the health care insurance plan of the province must,

throughout the fiscal year, satisfy the criteria described in sections 8 to 12 respecting the following matters:

(*a*) public administration;
(*b*) comprehensiveness;
(*c*) universality;
(*d*) portability; and
(*e*) accessibility.

Public Administration

8. (1) In order to satisfy the criterion respecting public administration,

(*a*) the health care insurance plan of a province must be administered and operated on a non-profit basis by a public authority appointed or designated by the government of the province;
(*b*) the public authority must be responsible to the provincial government for that administration and operation; and
(*c*) the public authority must be subject to audit of its accounts and financial transactions by such authority as is charged by law with the audit of the accounts of the province.

Designation of Agency Permitted

(2) The criterion respecting public administration is not contravened by reason only that the public authority referred to in subsection (1) has the power to designate any agency

(*a*) to receive on its behalf any amounts payable under the provincial health care insurance plan; or
(*b*) to carry out on its behalf any responsibility in connection with the receipt or payment of accounts rendered for insured health services, if it is a condition of the designation that all those accounts are subject to assessment and approval by the public authority and that the public authority shall determine the amounts to be paid in respect thereof.

Comprehensiveness

9. In order to satisfy the criterion respecting comprehensiveness, the health care insurance plan of a province must insure all insured health services provided by hospitals, medical practitioners or dentists, and where the law of the province so permits, similar or additional services rendered by other health care practitioners.

Universality

10. In order to satisfy the criterion respecting universality, the health care insurance plan of a province must

entitle one hundred per cent of the insured persons of the province to the insured health services provided for by the plan on uniform terms and conditions.

Portability

11. (1) In order to satisfy the criterion respecting portability, the health care insurance plan of a province

(*a*) must not impose any minimum period of residence in the province, or waiting period, in excess of three months before residents of the province are eligible for or entitled to insured health services;

(*b*) must provide for and be administered and operated so as to provide for the payment of amounts for the cost of insured health services provided to insured persons while temporarily absent from the province on the basis that

(i) where the insured health services are provided in Canada, payment for health services is at the rate that is approved by the health care insurance plan of the province in which the services are provided, unless the provinces concerned agree to apportion the cost between them in a different manner, or

(ii) where the insured health services are provided out of Canada, payment is made on the basis of the amount that would have been paid by the province for similar services rendered in the province, with due regard, in the case of hospital services, to the size of the hospital, standards of service and other relevant factors; and

(*c*) must provide for and be administered and operated so as to provide for the payment, during any minimum period of residence, or any waiting period, imposed by the health care insurance plan of another province, of the cost of insured health services provided to persons who have ceased to be insured persons by reason of having become residents of that other province, on the same basis as though they had not ceased to be residents of the province.

Requirement for Consent for Elective Insured Health Services Permitted

(2) The criterion respecting portability is not contravened by a requirement of a provincial health care insurance plan that the prior consent of the public authority that administers and operates the plan must be obtained for elective insured health services provided to a resident of the province while temporarily absent from the province if the services in question were available on a substantially similar basis in the province.

Definition of "Elective Insured Health Services"

(3) For the purpose of subsection (2), "elective insured health services" means insured health services other than services that are provided in an emergency or in any other circumstance in which medical care is required without delay.

Accessibility

12. (1) In order to satisfy the criterion respecting accessibility, the health care insurance plan of a province

(*a*) must provide for insured health services on uniform terms and conditions and on a basis that does not impede or preclude, either directly or indirectly whether by charges made to insured persons or otherwise, reasonable access to those services by insured persons;

(*b*) must provide for payment for insured health services in accordance with a tariff or system of payment authorized by the law of the province;

(*c*) must provide for reasonable compensation for all insured health services rendered by medical practitioners or dentists; and

(*d*) must provide for the payment of amounts to hospitals, including hospitals owned or operated by Canada, in respect of the cost of insured health services.

Reasonable Compensation

(2) In respect of any province in which extra-billing is not permitted, paragraph (1)(c) shall be deemed to be complied with if the province has chosen to enter into, and has entered into, an agreement with the medical practitioners and dentists of the province that provides

(*a*) for negotiations relating to compensation for insured health services between the province and provincial organizations that represent practising medical practitioners or dentists in the province;

(*b*) for the settlement of disputes relating to compensation through, at the option of the appropriate provincial organizations referred to in paragraph (a), conciliation or binding arbitration by a panel that is equally representative of the provincial organizations and the province and that has an independent chairman; and

(*c*) that a decision of a panel referred to in paragraph (b) may not be altered except by an Act of the legislature of the province.

Post-Case-Reading Questions

1. How does the Canada Health Act justify the provision of universal health care for Canadians?
2. Which ideas found in Rawls' theory of justice as fairness are reflected in the text of the Canada Health Act?

Chapter

XI

Robert Nozick

Introduction

Robert Nozick was born in 1938 to Russian immigrant parents in Brooklyn, New York. He did his undergraduate studies at Columbia College, where he obtained a BA in 1959. Shortly thereafter, he went to Princeton, completing an MA in 1961 and a doctoral degree in 1963 for a thesis on rational decision theory. Although at Columbia College he was a left-wing student activist, at Princeton he read and was much influenced by the work of advocates of free market economics, such as Milton Freidman and F.A. Hayek.

After obtaining his PhD, Nozick taught at Princeton (1962–5), Harvard (1965–7), and Rockefeller (1967–9) universities, before finally returning to Harvard as a full professor in 1969 at the remarkably young age of 30. Already well known in academic philosophical circles, his influence spread still wider with his groundbreaking book *Anarchy, State, and Utopia*. Published in 1974 and awarded the National Book Award in Philosophy and Religion the following year, the book remains Nozick's best-known work.

Robert Nozick

Harvard Gazette file photo. Used with permission.

The character of a particular political theory of justice depends to a large degree upon what principle is given supremacy. Marxists, arguably, take equality to be the ultimate ideal, while liberal egalitarians like Rawls take both equality and liberty to be key values. In *Anarchy, State, and Utopia*, Nozick treats individual liberty as the fundamental organizing principle of human society. He starts by writing, "Individuals have rights, and there are things no person or group may do to them (without violating their rights)." Starting from Lockean ideas about natural rights to life and liberty, Nozick radicalizes their implication by suggesting that justice requires strict restraints on people's (and the state's) behaviour so as to protect these fundamental rights. Our core rights, in his view, are negative ones (freedom from interference) that in turn trigger "side-constraints" on the conduct of others. The central claim of the theory is as follows: if we assume that everyone is entitled to the goods they currently possess, then a "just distribution" is simply the distribution that results from people's free, unfettered transactions. The right to property, for Nozick, is therefore not justified by an argument for desert or need, but rather based on what people are rightfully entitled to through their free exchanges and transactions—including labour and inheritance. This is what he calls the "entitlement theory of justice."

Nozick argues that theories of justice based on "end-state principles," and which favour a specific pattern of the distribution of goods (such as socialism), coerce people in unacceptable ways, abridging their social and economic liberty. Socialists cannot justly forbid the inequalities that result from free transfers of resources, since this would amount to forbidding "capitalist acts between consenting adults" (*Anarchy, State, and Utopia*, p. 162). Thus, no distributive scheme can be continuously realized without ongoing and illegitimate interference with people's lives; even Rawls' moderate proposal for a liberal society with social welfare features violates people's liberty. This is because the free choice of people to interact with each other would upset the patterns of distribution stipulated by the favoured scheme. To revert to the preferred distributional arrangement, the state either has to stop people from interacting with one another in certain ways or has to forcibly take from some the resources they gained through free and uncoerced transfers of their own shares.

For Nozick, the scheme of negative rights (essentially, people's personal liberty) and their corresponding obligations determines the limits of government's legitimate authority. In his view, we are not entitled to any positive rights, meaning that we cannot expect the government or anyone else to secure goods or states of affairs that we want (or need). This then implies that the role of the government is minimal—what Nozick calls a "night watchman" state, whose operations are limited to protecting people against violence, thievery, and fraud, and enforcing contracts. It becomes clear that while Nozick started where Hobbes and Locke began, he deduces this minimal state without the device of a contract. Such a minimal state does not engage in road construction, school and hospital building, helping the poor, etc.—all things that rational choosers in the state of nature might elect to include in the social contract. In his view, the taxation required to finance such infrastructure amounts to a form of forced labour since it requires people to work for longer than they would otherwise need to do (in order to pay the tax).

Nozick's belief in the primacy of liberty and property rights can also explain his advocacy for euthanasia: in 1997 he took part in a friend-of-the-court brief along with John Rawls, Ronald Dworkin, Thomas Nagel, and Judith Jarvis Thompson, presenting a "philosopher's point of view" to the US Supreme Court on the individual's right to die.

While Nozick is best known for his political philosophy, he also made significant contributions to other philosophical fields: *Philosophical Explanation* (1981) advanced our knowledge in epistemology, *Examined Life* (1989) contributed to ethics, and *The Nature of Rationality* (1993) enhanced the debate in decision theory. In 1997 he published a collection of his essays entitled *Socratic Puzzles*, and in 2001 his book *Invariance* came out. In January of 2002 he lost his long battle with cancer and died in Cambridge, Massachusetts.

The case that follows excerpts from *Anarchy, State, and Utopia* is the case of *R. v. Oakes*, which provides an opportunity to consider whether limits on the freedom that each individual enjoys in a liberal democracy are legitimate, and if so, which ones are and are not. This case may be read as exploring Nozick's claim that the principle of freedom should be supreme among liberal ideals and must not be balanced against any other competing ideals (such as security).

Further Readings

Hailwood, S.A. (1996). *Exploring Nozick: Beyond Anarchy, State and Utopia*. Aldershot: Avebury.

Lacey, A.R. (2001). *Robert Nozick*. Princeton: Princeton University Press.

Paul, J. (1981). *Reading Nozick: Essays on Anarchy, State and Utopia*. Totowa, N.J.: Rowman and Littlefield.

Schmidtz, D. (ed.) (2002). *Robert Nozick: Contemporary Philosophy in Focus*. Cambridge: Cambridge University Press.

Wolff, J. (1991). *Robert Nozick: Property Justice and the Minimal State*. Palo Alto, CA.: Stanford University Press.

Robert Nozick, From *Anarchy, State, and Utopia*

Robert Nozick, Anarchy, State, and Utopia *(New York: Basic Books, 1974).*

Part I

Chapter II The State of Nature

Individuals in Locke's state of nature are in "a state of perfect freedom to order their actions and dispose of their possessions and persons as they think fit, within the bounds of the law of nature, without asking leave or dependency upon the will of any other man" (sect. 4).[1] The bounds of the law of nature require that "no one ought to harm another in his life, health, liberty, or possessions" (sect. 6). Some persons transgress these bounds, "invading others' rights and . . . doing hurt to one another," and in response people may defend themselves or others against such invaders of rights (chap. 3). The injured party and his agents may recover from the offender "so much as may make satisfaction for the harm he has suffered" (sect. 10); "everyone has a right to punish the transgressors of that law to such a degree as may hinder its violation" (sect. 7); each person may, and may only "retribute to [a criminal] so far as calm reason and conscience dictate, what is proportionate to his transgression, which is so much as may serve for reparation and restraint" (sect. 8).

. . .

Chapter III Moral Constraints and the State

The Minimal State and the Ultraminimal State

The night-watchman state of classical liberal theory, limited to the functions of protecting all its citizens against violence, theft, and fraud, and to the enforcement of contracts, and so on, appears to be redistributive.[2] We can imagine at least one social arrangement intermediate between the scheme of private protective associations and the night-watchman state. Since the night-watchman state is often called a minimal state, we shall call this other arrangement the *ultraminimal state*. An ultraminimal state maintains a monopoly over all use of force except that necessary in immediate self-defence, and so excludes private (or agency) retaliation for wrong and exaction of compensation; but it provides protection and enforcement services *only* to those who purchase its protection and enforcement policies. People who don't buy a protection contract from the monopoly don't get protected. The minimal (night-watchman) state is equivalent to the ultraminimal state conjoined with a (clearly redistributive) Friedmanesque voucher plan, financed from tax revenues.[3] Under this plan all people, or some (for example, those in need), are given tax-funded vouchers that can be used only for their purchase of a protection policy from the ultraminimal state.

. . .

Moral Constraints and Moral Goals

. . .

In contrast to incorporating rights into the state to be achieved, one might place them as side constraints upon the actions to be done: don't violate constraints C. The rights of others determine the constraints upon your actions. (A *goal-directed* view with constraints added would be: among those acts available to you that don't violate constraints C, act so as to maximize goal G. Here, the rights of others would constrain your goal-directed behaviour. I do not mean to imply that the correct moral view includes mandatory goals that must be pursued, even within the constraints.) This view differs from one that tries to build the side constraints *C into* the goal *G*. The side-constraint view forbids you to violate these moral constraints in the pursuit of your goals; whereas the view whose objective is to minimize the violation of these rights allows you to violate the rights (the constraints) in order to lessen their total violation in the society.[4]

. . .

Why Side Constraints?

Isn't it *irrational* to accept a side constraint *C*, rather than a view that directs minimizing the violations of *C*? (The latter view treats *C* as a condition rather than a constraint.) If non-violation of *C* is so important, shouldn't that be the goal? How can a concern for the non-violation of *C* lead to the refusal to violate *C* even when this would prevent other more extensive violations of *C*? What is the rationale for placing the non-violation of rights as a side constraint upon action instead of including it solely as a goal of one's actions?

Side constraints upon action reflect the underlying Kantian principle that individuals are ends and not merely means; they may not be sacrificed or used for the achieving of other ends without their consent. Individuals are inviolable. More should be said to illuminate this talk of ends and means. Consider a prime example of a means, a tool. There is no side constraint on how we may use a tool, other than the moral constraints on how we may use it upon others. There are procedures to be followed to preserve it for future use ("don't leave it out in the rain"), and there are more and less efficient ways of using it. But there is no limit on what we may do to it to best achieve our goals. Now imagine that there was an over-rideable constraint *C* on some tool's use. For example, the tool might have been lent to you only on the condition that *C* not be violated unless the gain from doing so was above a certain specified amount, or unless it was necessary to achieve a certain specified goal. Here the object is not *completely* your tool, for use according to your wish or whim. But it is a tool nevertheless, even with regard to the over-rideable constraint. If we add constraints on its use that may not be overridden, then the object may not be used as a tool *in those ways. In those respects*, it is not a tool at all. Can one add enough constraints so that an object cannot be used as a tool at all, in *any* respect?

Can behaviour toward a person be constrained so that he is not to be used for any end except as he chooses? This is an impossibly stringent condition if it requires everyone who provides us with a good to approve positively of every use to which we wish to put it. Even the requirement that he merely should not object to any use

we plan would seriously curtail bilateral exchange, not to mention sequences of such exchanges. It is sufficient that the other party stands to gain enough from the exchange so that he is willing to go through with it, even though he objects to one or more of the uses to which you shall put the good. Under such conditions, the other party is not being used solely as a means, in that respect. Another party, however, who would not choose to interact with you if he knew of the uses to which you *intend* to put his actions or good, *is* being used as a means, even if he receives enough to choose (in his ignorance) to interact with you. ("All along, you were just *using* me" can be said by someone who chose to interact only because he was ignorant of another's goals and of the uses to which he himself would be put.) Is it morally incumbent upon someone to reveal his intended uses of an interaction if he has good reason to believe the other would refuse to interact if he knew? Is he *using* the other person, if he does not reveal this? And what of the cases where the other does not choose to be of use at all? In getting pleasure from seeing an attractive person go by, does one use the other solely as a means?[5] Does someone so use an object of sexual fantasies? These and related questions raise very interesting issues for moral philosophy; but not, I think, for political philosophy.

Political philosophy is concerned only with *certain* ways that persons may not use others; primarily, physically aggressing against them. A specific side constraint upon action toward others expresses the fact that others may not be used in the specific ways the side constraint excludes. Side constraints express the inviolability of others, in the ways they specify. These modes of inviolability are expressed by the following injunction: "Don't use people in specified ways." An end-state view, on the other hand, would express the view that people are ends and not merely means (if it chooses to express this view at all), by a different injunction: "Minimize the use in specified ways of persons as means." Following this precept itself may involve using someone as a means in one of the ways specified. Had Kant held this view, he would have given the second formula of the categorical imperative as, "So act as to minimize the use of humanity simply as a means," rather than the one he actually used: "Act in such a way that you always treat humanity, whether in your own person or in the person of any other, never simply as a means, but always at the same time as an end."[6]

Side constraints express the inviolability of other persons. But why may not one violate persons for the greater social good? Individually, we each sometimes choose to undergo some pain or sacrifice for a greater benefit or to avoid a greater harm: we go to the dentist to avoid worse suffering later; we do some unpleasant work for its results; some persons diet to improve their health or looks; some save money to support themselves when they are older. In each case, some cost is borne for the sake of the greater overall good. Why not, *similarly*, hold that some persons have to bear some costs that benefit other persons more, for the sake of the overall social good? But there is no *social entity* with a good that undergoes some sacrifice for its own good. There are only individual people, different individual people, with their own individual lives. Using one of these people for the benefit of others, uses him and benefits the others. Nothing more. What happens is that something is done to him for the sake of others. Talk of an overall social good covers this up. (Intentionally?) To use a person in this way does not sufficiently respect and take account of the fact that he is a separate person,[7] that his is the only life he has. *He* does not get some overbalancing good from his sacrifice, and no one is entitled to force this upon him—least of all a state or government that claims his allegiance (as other individuals do not) and that therefore scrupulously must be *neutral* between its citizens.

. . .

Chapter V The State

The State

We set ourselves the task, in Chapter III, of showing that the dominant protective association within a territory satisfied two crucial necessary conditions for being a state: that it had the requisite sort of monopoly over the use of force in the territory, and that it protected the rights of everyone in the territory, even if this universal protection could be provided only in a "redistributive" fashion. These very crucial facets of the state constituted the subject of the individualist anarchists' condemnation of the state as immoral. We also set ourselves the task of showing that these monopoly and redistributive elements were themselves morally legitimate, of showing that the transition from a state of nature to an ultraminimal state (the monopoly element) was morally legitimate and violated no one's rights and that the transition from an ultraminimal to a minimal state (the "redistributive" element) also was morally legitimate and violated no one's rights.

A protective agency dominant in a territory does satisfy the two crucial necessary conditions for being a state. It is the only generally effective enforcer of a prohibition on others' using unreliable enforcement procedures (calling them as it sees them), and it oversees these procedures. And the agency protects those non-clients in its territory whom it prohibits from using self-help

enforcement procedures on its clients, in their dealings with its clients, even if such protection must be financed (in apparent redistributive fashion) by its clients. It is morally required to do this by the principle of compensation, which requires those who act in self-protection in order to increase their own security to compensate those they prohibit from doing risky acts which might actually have turned out to be harmless[8] for the disadvantages imposed upon them.

We noted in beginning Chapter III that whether the provision of protective services for some by others was "redistributive" would depend upon the reasons for it. We now see that such provision need not be redistributive since it can be justified on other than redistributive grounds, namely, those provided in the principle of compensation. (Recall that "redistributive" applies to reasons for a practice or institution, and only elliptically and derivatively to the institution itself.) To sharpen this point, we can imagine that protective agencies offer two types of protection policies: those protecting clients against risky private enforcement of justice and those not doing so but protecting only against theft, assault, and so forth (provided these are not done in the course of private enforcement of justice). Since it is only with regard to those with the first type of policy that others are prohibited from privately enforcing justice, only they will be required to compensate the persons prohibited private enforcement for the disadvantages imposed upon them. The holders of only the second type of policy will not have to pay for the protection of others, there being nothing they have to compensate these others for. Since the reasons for wanting to be protected against private enforcement of justice are compelling, almost all who purchase protection will purchase this type of protection, despite its extra costs, and therefore will be involved in providing protection for the independents.

We have discharged our task of explaining how a state would arise from a state of nature without anyone's rights being violated. The moral objections of the individualist anarchist to the minimal state are overcome. It is not an unjust imposition of a monopoly; the *de facto* monopoly grows by an invisible-hand process and *by morally permissible means*, without anyone's rights being violated and without any claims being made to a special right that others do not possess. And requiring the clients of the *de facto* monopoly to pay for the protection of those they prohibit from self-help enforcement against them, far from being immoral, is morally required by the principle of compensation adumbrated in Chapter IV.

We canvassed, in Chapter IV, the possibility of forbidding people to perform acts if they lack the means to compensate others for possible harmful consequences of these acts or if they lack liability insurance to cover these consequences. Were such prohibition legitimate, according to the principle of compensation the persons prohibited would have to be compensated for the disadvantages imposed upon them, and they could use the compensatory payments to purchase the liability insurance! Only those disadvantaged by the prohibition would be compensated: namely, those who lack other resources they can shift (without disadvantaging sacrifice) to purchase the liability insurance. When these people spend their compensatory payments for liability insurance, we have what amounts to public provision of special liability insurance. It is provided to those unable to afford it and covers only those risky actions which fall under the principle of compensation—those actions which are legitimately prohibited when uncovered (provided disadvantages are compensated for), actions whose prohibition would seriously disadvantage persons. Providing such insurance almost certainly would be the least expensive way to compensate people who present only normal danger to others for the disadvantages of the prohibition. Since they then would be insured against the eventuation of certain of their risks to others, these actions then would not be prohibited to them. Thus we see how, if it were legitimate to prohibit some actions to those uncovered by liability insurance, and were this done, another *apparent* redistributive aspect of the state would enter by solid libertarian moral principles! (The exclamation point stands for *my* surprise.)

Does the dominant protective agency in a given geographical territory constitute the *state* of that territory? We have seen in Chapter II how the notion of a monopoly on the use of force is difficult to state precisely so that it does not fall before obvious counterexamples. This notion, as usually explained, cannot be used with any confidence to answer our question. We should accept a decision yielded by the precise wording of a definition in some text only if that definition had been devised for application to cases as complicated as ours and had stood up to tests against a range of such cases. No classification, in passing, by accident can answer our question in any useful manner.

. . .

It is plausible to conclude that the dominant protective association in a territory is its state, only for a territory of some size containing more than a few people. We do not claim that each person who, under anarchy, retains a monopoly on the use of force on his quarter acre of property is its state; nor are the only three inhabitants of an island one square block in size. It would be futile, and would serve no useful purpose, to attempt to specify conditions on the size of population and territory

necessary for a state to exist. Also, we speak of cases where almost all of the people in the territory are clients of the dominant agency and where independents are in a subordinate power position in conflicts with the agency and its clients. (We have argued that this will occur.) Precisely what percentage must be clients and how subordinate the power position of the independents must be are more interesting questions, but concerning these I have nothing especially interesting to say.

One additional necessary condition for a state was extracted from the Weberian tradition by our discussion in Chapter II: namely, that it claim to be the sole authorizer of violence. The dominant protective association makes no such claim. Having described the position of the dominant protective association, and having seen how closely it fits anthropologists' notions, should we weaken the Weberian necessary condition so that it includes a *de facto* monopoly which is the territory's sole effective judge over the permissibility of violence, having a right (to be sure, one had by all) to make judgments on the matter and to act on correct ones? The case is very strong for doing so, and it is wholly desirable and appropriate. We therefore conclude that the protective association dominant in a territory, as described, *is* a state. However, to remind the reader of our slight weakening of the Weberian condition, we occasionally shall refer to the dominant protective agency as "a state-like entity," instead of simply as "a state."

. . .

Part II

Chapter VII Distributive Justice

The minimal state is the most extensive state that can be justified. Any state more extensive violates people's rights. Yet many persons have put forth reasons purporting to justify a mare extensive state. It *is* impossible within the compass of this book to examine all the reasons that have been put forth. Therefore, I shall focus upon those generally acknowledged to be most weighty and influential, to see precisely wherein they fail. In this chapter we consider the claim that a more extensive state is justified, because necessary (or the best instrument) to achieve distributive justice; in the next chapter we shall take up diverse other claims.

The term "distributive justice" is not a neutral one. Hearing the term "distribution," most people presume that some thing or mechanism uses some principle or criterion to give out a supply of things. Into this process of distributing shares some error may have crept. So it *is* an open question, at least, whether redistribution should take place; whether we should do again what has already been done once, though poorly. However, we are not in the position of children who have been given portions of pie by someone who now makes last minute adjustments to rectify careless cutting. There is no *central* distribution, no person or group entitled to control all the resources, jointly deciding how they are to be doled out. What each person gets, he gets from others who give to him in exchange for something, or as a gift. In a free society, diverse persons control different resources, and new holdings arise out of the voluntary exchanges and actions of persons. There is no more a distributing or distribution of shares than there is a distributing of mates in a society in which persons choose whom they shall marry. The total result is the product of many individual decisions which the different individuals involved are entitled to make. Some uses of the term "distribution," *it* is true, do not imply a previous distributing appropriately judged by some criterion (for example, "probability distribution"); nevertheless, despite the title of this chapter, it would be best to use a terminology that clearly is neutral. We shall speak of people's holdings; a principle of justice in holdings describes (part of) what justice tells us (requires) about holdings. I shall state first what I take to be the correct view about justice in holdings, and then turn to, the discussion of alternate views.[9]

Section 1

The Entitlement Theory

The subject of justice in holdings consists of three major topics. The first is the *original acquisition of holdings*, the appropriation of unheld things. This includes the issues of how unheld things may come to be held, the process, or processes, by which unheld things may come to be held, the things that may come to be held by these processes, the extent of what comes to be held by a particular process, and so on. We shall refer to the complicated truth about this topic, which we shall not formulate here, as the principle of justice in acquisition. The second topic concerns the *transfer of holdings* from one person to another. By what processes may a person transfer holdings to another? How may a person acquire a holding from another who holds it? Under this topic come general descriptions of voluntary exchange, and gift and (on the other hand) fraud, as well as reference to particular conventional details fixed upon in a given society. The complicated truth about this subject (with placeholders for conventional details) we shall call the principle of justice in transfer. (And we shall suppose it also includes principles governing how a person may divest himself of a holding, passing it into an unheld state.)

If the world were wholly just, the following inductive definition would exhaustively cover the subject of justice in holdings.

1. A person who acquires a holding in accordance with the principle of justice in acquisition is entitled to that holding.
2. A person who acquires a holding in accordance with the principle of justice in transfer, from someone else entitled to the holding, is entitled to the holding.
3. No one is entitled to a holding except by (repeated) applications of 1 and 2.

The complete principle of distributive justice would say simply that a distribution is just if everyone is entitled to the holdings they possess under the distribution.

A distribution is just if it arises from another just distribution by legitimate means. The legitimate means of moving from one distribution to another are specified by the principle of justice in transfer. The legitimate first "moves" are specified by the principle of justice in acquisition.[10] Whatever arises from a just situation by just steps is itself just. The means of change specified by the principle of justice in transfer preserve justice. As correct rules of inference are truth-preserving, and any conclusion deduced via repeated application of such rules from only true premises is itself true, so the means of transition from one situation to another specified by the principle of justice in transfer are justice-preserving, and any situation actually arising from repeated transitions in accordance with the principle from a just situation is itself just. The parallel between justice-preserving transformations and truth-preserving transformations illuminates where it fails as well as where it holds. That a conclusion could have been deduced by truth-preserving means from premises that are true suffices to show its truth. That from a just situation a situation *could* have arisen via justice-preserving means does *not* suffice to show its justice. The fact that a thief's victims voluntarily *could* have presented him with gifts does not entitle the thief to his ill-gotten gains. Justice in holdings is historical; it depends upon what actually has happened. We shall return to this point later.

Not all actual situations are generated in accordance with the two principles of justice in holdings: the principle of justice in acquisition and the principle of justice in transfer. Some people steal from others, or defraud them, or enslave them, seizing their product and preventing them from living as they choose, or forcibly exclude others from competing in exchanges. None of these are permissible modes of transition from one situation to another. And some persons acquire holdings by means not sanctioned by the principle of justice in acquisition. The existence of past injustice (previous violations of the first two principles of justice in holdings) raises the third major topic under justice in holdings: the rectification of injustice in holdings. If past injustice has shaped present holdings in various ways, some identifiable and some not, what now, if anything, ought to be done to rectify these injustices? What obligations do the performers of injustice have toward those whose position is worse than it would have been had justice not been done? Or, than it would have been had compensation been paid promptly? How, if at all, do things change if the beneficiaries and those made worse off are not the direct parties in the act of injustice, but, for example, their descendants? Is an injustice done to someone whose holding was itself based upon an unrectified injustice? How far back must one go in wiping clean the historical slate of injustices? What may victims of injustice permissibly do in order to rectify the injustices being done to them, including the many injustices done by persons acting through their government? I do not know of a thorough or theoretically sophisticated treatment of such issues.[11] Idealizing greatly, let us suppose theoretical investigation will produce a principle of rectification. This principle uses historical information about previous situations and injustices done in them (as defined by the first two principles of justice and rights against interference), and information about the actual course of events that flowed from these injustices, until the present, and it yields a description (or descriptions) of holdings in the society. The principle of rectification presumably will make use of its best estimate of subjunctive information about what would have occurred (or a probability distribution over what might have occurred, using the expected value) if the injustice had not taken place. If the actual description of holdings turns out not to be one of the descriptions yielded by the principle, then one of the descriptions yielded must be realized.[12]

The general outlines of the theory of justice in holdings are that the holdings of a person are just if he is entitled to them by the principles of justice in acquisition and transfer, or by the principle of rectification of injustice (as specified by the first two principles). If each person's holdings are just, then the total set (distribution) of holdings is just. To turn these general outlines into a specific theory we would have to specify the details of each of the three principles of justice in holdings: the principle of acquisition of holdings, the principle of transfer of holdings, and the principle of rectification of violations of the first two principles. I shall not attempt that task here. (Locke's principle of justice in acquisition is discussed below.)

Historical Principles and End-Result Principles

The general outlines of the entitlement theory illuminate the nature and defects of other conceptions of distributive justice. The entitlement theory of justice in distribution is *historical*; whether a distribution is just depends upon how it came about. In contrast, *current time-slice principles* of justice hold that the justice of a distribution *is* determined by how things are distributed (who has what) as judged by some *structural* principle(s) of just distribution. A utilitarian who judges between any two distributions by seeing which has the greater sum of utility and, if the sums tie, applies some fixed equality criterion to choose the more equal distribution, would hold a current time-slice principle of justice. As would someone who had a fixed schedule of trade-offs between the sum of happiness and equality. According to a current time-slice principle, all that needs to be looked at, in judging the justice of a distribution, is who ends up with what; in comparing any two distributions one need look only at the matrix presenting the distributions. No further information need be fed into a principle of justice. It is a consequence of such principles of justice that any two structurally identical distributions are equally just. (Two distributions are structurally identical if they present the same profile, but perhaps have different persons occupying the particular slots. My having ten and your having five, and my having five and your having ten are structurally identical distributions.) Welfare economics is the theory of current time-slice principles of justice. The subject is conceived as operating on matrices representing only current information about distribution. This, as well as some of the usual conditions (for example, the choice of distribution is invariant under relabeling of columns), guarantees that welfare economics will be a current time-slice theory, with all of its inadequacies.

Most persons do not accept current time-slice principles as constituting the whole story about distributive shares. They think it relevant in assessing the justice of a situation to consider not only the distribution it embodies, but also how that distribution came about. If some persons are in prison for murder or war crimes, we do not say that to assess the justice of the distribution in the society we must look only at what this person has, and that person has, and that person has, . . . at the current time. We think it relevant to ask whether someone did something so that he *deserved* to be punished, deserved to have a lower share. Most will agree to the relevance of further information with regard to punishments and penalties. Consider also desired things. One traditional socialist view is that workers are entitled to the product and full fruits of their labour; they have earned it; a distribution is unjust if it does not give the workers what they are entitled to. Such entitlements are based upon some past history. No socialist holding this view would find it comforting to be told that because the actual distribution *A* happens to coincide structurally with the one he desires *D*, *A* therefore is no less just than *D*; it differs only in that the "parasitic" owners of capital receive under *A* what the workers are entitled to under *D*, and the workers receive under *A* what the owners are entitled to under *D*, namely very little. This socialist rightly, in my view, holds onto the notions of earning, producing, entitlement, desert, and so forth, and he rejects current time-slice principles that look only to the structure of the resulting set of holdings. (The set of holdings resulting from what? Isn't it implausible that how holdings are produced and come to exist has no effect at all on who should hold what?) His mistake lies in his view of what entitlements arise out of what sorts of productive processes.

We construe the position we discuss too narrowly by speaking of *current* time-slice principles. Nothing is changed if structural principles operate upon a time sequence of current time-slice profiles and, for example, give someone more now to counterbalance the less he has had earlier. A utilitarian or an egalitarian or any mixture of the two over time will inherit the difficulties of his more myopic comrades. He is not helped by the fact that *some* of the information others consider relevant in assessing a distribution is reflected, unrecoverably, in past matrices. Henceforth, we shall refer to such unhistorical principles of distributive justice, including the current time-slice principles, as *end-result principles* or *end-state principles*.

In contrast to end-result principles of justice, *historical principles* of justice hold that past circumstances or actions of people can create differential entitlements or differential deserts to things. An injustice can be worked by moving from one distribution to another structurally identical one, for the second, in profile the same, may violate people's entitlements or deserts; it may not fit the actual history.

Patterning

The entitlement principles of justice in holdings that we have sketched are historical principles of justice. To better understand their precise character, we shall distinguish them from another subclass of the historical principles. Consider, as an example, the principle of distribution according to moral merit. This principle requires that total distributive shares vary directly with moral merit; no person should have a greater share than anyone whose moral merit is greater. (If moral merit could be not merely ordered but measured on an interval or ratio scale,

stronger principles could be formulated.) Or consider the principle that results by substituting "usefulness to society" for "moral merit" in the previous principle. Or instead of "distribute according to moral merit," or "distribute according to usefulness to society," we might consider "distribute according to the weighted sum of moral merit, usefulness to society, and need," with the weights of the different dimensions equal. Let us call a principle of distribution *patterned* if it specifies that a distribution is to vary along with some natural dimension, weighted sum of natural dimensions, or lexicographic ordering of natural dimensions. And let us say a distribution is patterned if it accords with some patterned principle. (I speak of natural dimensions, admittedly without a general criterion for them, because for any set of holdings some artificial dimensions can be gimmicked up to vary along with the distribution of the set.) The principle of distribution in accordance with moral merit is a patterned historical principle, which specifies a patterned distribution. "Distribute according to I.Q." is a patterned principle that looks to information not contained in distributional matrices. It is not historical, however, in that it does not look to any past actions creating differential entitlements to evaluate a distribution; it requires only distributional matrices whose columns are labelled by I.Q. scores. The distribution in a society, however, may be composed of such simple patterned distributions, without itself being simply patterned. Different sectors may operate different patterns, or some combination of patterns may operate in different proportions across a society. A distribution composed in this manner, from a small number of patterned distributions, we also shall term "patterned." And we extend the use of "pattern" to include the overall designs put forth by combinations of end-state principles.

Almost every suggested principle of distributive justice is patterned: to each according to his moral merit, or needs, or marginal product, or how hard he tries, or the weighted sum of the foregoing, and so on. The principle of entitlement we have sketched is *not* patterned.[13] There is no one natural dimension or weighted sum or combination of a small number of natural dimensions that yields the distributions generated in accordance with the principle of entitlement. The set of holdings that results when some persons receive their marginal products, others win at gambling, others receive a share of their mate's income, others receive gifts from foundations, others receive interest on loans, others receive gifts from admirers, others receive returns on investment, others make for themselves much of what they have, others find things, and so on, will not be patterned. Heavy strands of patterns will run through it; significant portions of the variance in holdings will be accounted for by pattern-variables. If most people most of the time choose to transfer some of their entitlements to others only in exchange for something from them, then a large part of what many people hold will vary with what they held that others wanted. More details are provided by the theory of marginal productivity. But gifts to relatives, charitable donations, bequests to children, and the like, are not best conceived, in the first instance, in this manner. Ignoring the strands of pattern, let us suppose for the moment that a distribution actually arrived at by the operation of the principle of entitlement is random with respect to any pattern. Though the resulting set of holdings will be unpatterned, it will not be incomprehensible, for it can be seen as arising from the operation of a small number of principles. These principles specify how an initial distribution may arise (the principle of acquisition of holdings) and how distributions may be transformed into others (the principle of transfer of holdings). The process whereby the set of holdings is generated will be intelligible, though the set of holdings itself that results from this process will be unpatterned.

The writings of F.A. Hayek focus less than is usually done upon what patterning distributive justice requires. Hayek argues that we cannot know enough about each person's situation to distribute to each according to his moral merit (but would justice demand we do so if we did have this knowledge?); and he goes on to say, "our objection is against all attempts to impress upon society a deliberately chosen pattern of distribution, whether it be an order of equality or of inequality."[14] However, Hayek concludes that in a free society there will be distribution in accordance with value rather than moral merit; that is, in accordance with the perceived value of a person's actions and services to others. Despite his rejection of a patterned conception of distributive justice, Hayek himself suggests a pattern he thinks justifiable: distribution in accordance with the perceived benefits given to others, leaving room for the complaint that a free society does not realize exactly this pattern. Stating this patterned strand of a free capitalist society more precisely, we get "To each according to how much he benefits others who have the resources for benefiting those who benefit them." This will seem arbitrary unless some acceptable initial set of holdings is specified, or unless it is held that the operation of the system over time washes out any significant effects from the initial set of holdings. As an example of the latter, if almost anyone would have bought a car from Henry Ford, the supposition that it was an arbitrary matter who held the money then (and so bought) would not place Henry Ford's earnings under a cloud. In any event, *his* coming to hold it is not

arbitrary. Distribution according to benefits to others *is* a major patterned strand in a free capitalist society, as Hayek correctly points out, but it is only a strand and does not constitute the whole pattern of a system of entitlements (namely, inheritance, gifts for arbitrary reasons, charity, and so on) or a standard that one should insist a society fit. Will people tolerate for long a system yielding distributions that they believe are unpatterned?[15] No doubt people will not long accept a distribution they believe is *unjust*. People want their society to be and to look just. But must the look of justice reside in a resulting pattern rather than in the underlying generating principles? We are in no position to conclude that the inhabitants of a society embodying an entitlement conception of justice in holdings will find it unacceptable. Still, it must be granted that were people's reasons for transferring some of their holdings to others always irrational or arbitrary, we would find this disturbing. (Suppose people always determined what holdings they would transfer, and to whom, by using a random device.) We feel more comfortable upholding the justice of an entitlement system if most of the transfers under it are done for reasons. This does not mean necessarily that all deserve what holdings they receive. It means only that there is a purpose or point to someone's transferring a holding to one person rather than to another; that usually we can see what the transferrer thinks he's gaining, what cause he thinks he's serving, what goals he thinks he's helping to achieve, and so forth. Since in a capitalist society people often transfer holdings to others in accordance with how much they perceive these others benefiting them, the fabric constituted by the individual transactions and transfers is largely reasonable and intelligible.[16] (Gifts to loved ones, bequests to children, charity to the needy also are non-arbitrary components of the fabric.) In stressing the large strand of distribution in accordance with benefit to others, Hayek shows the point of many transfers, and so shows that the system of transfer of entitlements is not just spinning its gears aimlessly. The system of entitlements is defensible when constituted by the individual aims of individual transactions. No overarching aim is needed, no distributional pattern is required.

To think that the task of a theory of distributive justice is to fill in the blank in "to each according to his _____" is to be predisposed to search for a pattern; and the separate treatment of "from each according to his _____" treats production and distribution as two separate and independent issues. On an entitlement view these are *not* two separate questions. Whoever makes something, having bought or contracted for all other held resources used in the process (transferring some of his holdings for these cooperating factors), is entitled to it. The situation is *not* one of something's getting made, and there being an open question of who is to get it. Things come into the world already attached to people having entitlements over them. From the point of view of the historical entitlement conception of justice in holdings, those who start afresh to complete "to each according to his _____" treat objects as *if* they appeared from nowhere, out of nothing. A complete theory of justice might cover this limit case as well; perhaps here is a use for the usual conceptions of distributive justice.[17]

So entrenched are maxims of the usual form that perhaps we should present the entitlement conception as a competitor. Ignoring acquisition and rectification, we might say:

> From each according to what he chooses to do,
> to each according to what he makes for himself
> (perhaps with the contracted aid of others) and
> what others choose to do for him and choose to
> give him of what they've been given previously
> (under this maxim) and haven't yet expended or
> transferred.

This, the discerning reader will have noticed, has its defects as a slogan. So as a summary and great simplification (and not as a maxim with any independent meaning) we have:

From each as they choose, to each as they are chosen.

How Liberty Upsets Patterns

It is not clear how those holding alternative conceptions of distributive justice can reject the entitlement conception of justice in holdings. For suppose a distribution favoured by one of these non-entitlement conceptions is realized. Let us suppose it is your favourite one and let us call this distribution D_1; perhaps everyone has an equal share, perhaps shares vary in accordance with some dimension you treasure. Now suppose that Wilt Chamberlain is greatly in demand by basketball teams, being a great gate attraction. (Also suppose contracts run only for a year, with players being free agents.) He signs the following sort of contract with a team: In each home game, 25 cents from the price of each ticket of admission goes to him. (We ignore the question of whether he is "gouging" the owners, letting them look out for themselves.) The season starts, and people cheerfully attend his team's games; they buy their tickets, each time dropping a separate 25 cents of their admission price into a special box with Chamberlain's name on it. They are excited about seeing him play; it is worth the total admission price to them. Let us suppose that in one season one million persons attend his home games, and Wilt Chamberlain winds up with $250,000, a much

larger sum than the average income and larger even than anyone else has. Is he entitled to this income? Is this new distribution D_2, unjust? If so why? There is *no* question about whether each of the people was entitled to the control over the resources they held in D_1; because that was the distribution (your favourite) that (for the purposes of argument) we assumed was acceptable. Each of these persons *chose* to give 25 cents of their money to Chamberlain. They could have spent it on going to the movies, or on candy bars, or on copies of *Dissent* magazine, or of *Monthly Review*. But they all, at least one million of them, converged on giving it to Wilt Chamberlain in exchange for watching him play basketball. If D_1 was a just distribution, and people voluntarily moved from it to D_2, transferring parts of their shares they were given under D_1 (what was it for if not to do something with?), isn't D_2 also just? If the people were entitled to dispose of the resources to which they were entitled (under D_1), didn't this include their being entitled to give it to, or exchange it with, Wilt Chamberlain? Can anyone else complain on grounds of justice? Each other person already has his legitimate share under D_1. Under D_1, there is nothing that anyone has that anyone else has a claim of justice against. After someone transfers something to Wilt Chamberlain, third parties *still* have their legitimate shares; *their* shares are not changed. By what process could such a transfer among two persons give rise to a legitimate claim of distributive justice on a portion of what was transferred, by a third party who had no claim of justice on any holding of the others *before* the transfer?[18] To cut off objections irrelevant here, we might imagine the exchanges occurring in a socialist society, after hours. After playing whatever basketball he does in his daily work, or doing whatever other daily work he does, Wilt Chamberlain decides to put in *overtime* to earn additional money. (First his work quota is set; he works time over that.) Or imagine it is a skilled juggler people like to see, who puts on shows after hours.

Why might someone work overtime in a society in which it is assumed their needs are satisfied? Perhaps because they care about things other than needs. I like to write in books that I read, and to have easy access to books for browsing at odd hours. It would be very pleasant and convenient to have the resources of Widener Library in my back yard. No society, I assume, will provide such resources close to each person who would like them as part of his regular allotment (under D_1). Thus, persons either must do without some extra things that they want, or be allowed to do something extra to get some of these things. On what basis could the inequalities that would eventuate be forbidden? Notice also that small factories would spring up in a socialist society, unless forbidden. I melt down some of my personal possessions (under D_1) and build a machine out of the material. I offer you, and others, a philosophy lecture once a week in exchange for your cranking the handle on my machine, whose products I exchange for yet other things, and so on. (The raw materials used by the machine are given to me by others who possess them under D_1, in exchange for hearing lectures.) Each person might participate to gain things over and above their allotment under D_1. Some persons even might want to leave their job in socialist industry and work full time in this private sector. I shall say something more about these issues in the next chapter. Here I wish merely to note how private property even in means of production would occur in a socialist society that did not forbid people to use as they wished some of the resources they are given under the socialist distribution D_1.[19] The socialist society would have to forbid capitalist acts between consenting adults.

The general point illustrated by the Wilt Chamberlain example and the example of the entrepreneur in a socialist society is that no end-state principle or distributional patterned principle of justice can be continuously realized without continuous interference with people's lives. Any favoured pattern would be transformed into one unfavoured by the principle, by people choosing to act in various ways; for example, by people exchanging goods and services with other people, or giving things to other people, things the transferrers are entitled to under the favoured distributional pattern. To maintain a pattern one must either continually interfere to stop people from transferring resources as they wish to; or continually (or periodically) interfere to take from some persons resources that others for some reason chose to transfer to them. (But if some time limit is to be set on how long people may keep resources others voluntarily transfer to them, why let them keep these resources for *any* period of time? Why not have immediate confiscation?) It might be objected that all persons voluntarily will choose to refrain from actions which would upset the pattern. This presupposes unrealistically (1) that all will most want to maintain the pattern (are those who don't, to be "reeducated" or forced to undergo "self-criticism"?), (2) that each can gather enough information about his own actions and the ongoing activities of others to discover which of his actions will upset the pattern, and (3) that diverse and far-flung persons can coordinate their actions to dovetail into the pattern. Compare the manner in which the market is neutral among persons' desires, as it reflects and transmits widely scattered information via prices, and coordinates persons' activities.

It puts things perhaps a bit too strongly to say that every patterned (or end-state) principle is liable to be thwarted by the voluntary actions of the individual parties transferring some of their shares they receive under the principle. For perhaps some *very* weak patterns are not so thwarted.[20] Any distributional pattern with any egalitarian component is overturnable by the voluntary actions of individual persons over time; as is every patterned condition with sufficient content so as actually to have been proposed as presenting the central core of distributive justice. Still, given the possibility that some weak conditions or patterns may not be unstable in this way, it would be better to formulate an explicit description of the kind of interesting and contentful patterns under discussion, and to prove a theorem about their instability. Since the weaker the patterning, the more likely it is that the entitlement system itself satisfies it, a plausible conjecture is that any patterning either is unstable or is satisfied by the entitlement system.

. . .

Redistribution and Property Rights

Apparently, patterned principles allow people to choose to expend upon themselves, but not upon others, those resources they are entitled to (or rather, receive) under some favoured distributional pattern D_1. For if each of several persons chooses to expend some of his D_1 resources upon one other person, then that other person will receive more than his D_1 share, disturbing the favoured distributional pattern. Maintaining a distributional pattern is individualism with a vengeance! Patterned distributional principles do not *give* people what entitlement principles do, only better distributed. For they do not give the right to choose what to do with what one has; they do not give the right to choose to pursue an end involving (intrinsically, or as a means) the enhancement of another's *position*. To such views, families are disturbing; for within a family occur transfers that upset the favoured distributional pattern. Either families themselves become units to which distribution takes place, the column occupiers (on what rationale?), or loving behaviour is forbidden. We should note in passing the ambivalent position of radicals toward the family. Its loving relationships are seen as a model to be emulated and extended across the whole society, at the same time that it is denounced as a suffocating institution to be broken and condemned as a focus of parochial concerns that interfere with achieving radical goals. Need we say that it is not appropriate to enforce across the wider society the relationships of love and care appropriate within a family, relationships which are voluntarily undertaken?[21] Incidentally, love is an interesting instance of another relationship that is historical, in that (like justice) it depends upon what actually occurred. An adult may come to love another because of the other's characteristics; but it is the other person, and not the characteristics, that is loved.[22] The love is not transferrable to someone else with the same characteristics, even to one who "scores" higher for these characteristics. And the love endures through changes of the characteristics that gave rise to it. One loves the particular person one actually encountered. Why love is historical, attaching to persons in this way and not to characteristics, is an interesting and puzzling question.

Proponents of patterned principles of distributive justice focus upon criteria for determining who is to receive holdings; they consider the reasons for which someone should have something, and also the total picture of holdings. Whether or not it is better to give than to receive, proponents of patterned principles ignore giving altogether. In considering the distribution of goods, income, and so forth, their theories are theories of recipient justice; they completely ignore any right a person might have to give something to someone. Even in exchanges where each party is simultaneously giver and recipient, patterned principles of justice focus only upon the recipient role and its supposed rights. Thus discussions tend to focus on whether people (should) have a right to inherit, rather than on whether people (should) have a right to bequeath or on whether persons who have a right to hold also have a right to choose that others hold in their place. I lack a good explanation of why the usual theories of distributive justice are so recipient oriented; ignoring givers and transferrers and their rights is of a piece with ignoring producers and their entitlements. But why is it *all* ignored?

Patterned principles of distributive justice necessitate *re*distributive activities. The likelihood is small that any actual freely-arrived-at set of holdings fits a given pattern; and the likelihood is nil that it will continue to fit the pattern as people exchange and give. From the point of view of an entitlement theory, redistribution is a serious matter indeed, involving, as it does, the violation of people's rights. (An exception is those takings that fall under the principle of the rectification of injustices.) From other points of view, also, it is serious.

Taxation of earnings from labour *is* on a par with forced labour.[23] Some persons find this claim obviously true: taking the earnings of *n* hours labour is like taking *n* hours from the person; it is like forcing the person to work *n* hours for another's purpose. Others find the claim absurd. But even these, *if* they object to forced labour, would oppose forcing unemployed hippies to work for the benefit of the needy.[24] And they would also object to forcing each person to work five extra hours each week for the benefit of the needy. But a system that takes five hours' wages in taxes does not seem to them like one that forces someone to work five hours, since it offers the person forced a wider range of choice in activities than does taxation in kind with the particular labour specified. (But we can imagine a gradation of systems of forced labour, from one that specifies a particular activity, to one that *gives* a choice among two activities, to . . . ; and so on up.) Furthermore, people envisage a system with something like a proportional tax on everything above the amount necessary for basic needs. Some think this does not force someone to work extra hours, since there is no fixed number of extra hours he is forced to work, and since he can avoid the tax entirely by earning only enough to cover his basic needs. This is a very uncharacteristic view of forcing for those who *also* think people are forced to do something *whenever* the alternatives they face are considerably worse. However, *neither* view is correct. The fact that others intentionally intervene, in violation of a side constraint against aggression, to threaten force to limit the alternatives, in this case to paying taxes or (presumably the worse alternative) bare subsistence, makes the taxation system one of forced labour and distinguishes it from other cases of limited choices which are not forcings.[25]

The man who chooses to work longer to gain an income more than sufficient for his basic needs prefers some extra goods or services to the leisure and activities he could perform during the possible nonworking hours; whereas the man who chooses not to work the extra time prefers the leisure activities to the extra goods or services he could acquire by working more. Given this, if it would be illegitimate for a tax system to seize some of a man's leisure (forced labour) for the purpose of serving the needy, how can it be legitimate for a tax system to seize some of a man's goods for that purpose? Why should we treat the man whose happiness requires certain material goods or services differently from the man whose preferences and desires make such goods unnecessary for his happiness? Why should the man who prefers seeing a movie (and who has to earn money for a ticket) be open to the required call to aid the needy, while the person who prefers looking at a sunset (and hence need earn no extra money) is not? Indeed, isn't it surprising that redistributionists choose to ignore the man whose pleasures are so easily attainable without extra labour, while adding yet another burden to the poor unfortunate who must work for his pleasures? If anything, one would have expected the reverse. Why is the person with the nonmaterial or non-consumption desire allowed to proceed unimpeded to his most favoured feasible alternative, whereas the man whose pleasures or desires involve material things and who must work for extra money (thereby serving whomever considers his activities valuable enough to pay him) is constrained in what he can realize? Perhaps there is no difference in principle. And perhaps some think the answer concerns merely administrative convenience. (These questions and issues will not disturb those who think that forced labour to serve the needy or to realize some favoured end-state pattern is acceptable.) In a fuller discussion we would have (and want) to extend our argument to include interest, entrepreneurial profits, and so on. Those who doubt that this extension can be carried through, and who draw the line here at taxation of income from labour, will have to state rather complicated patterned *historical* principles of distributive justice, since end-state principles would not distinguish *sources* of income in any way. It is enough for now to get away from end-state principles and to make clear how various patterned principles are dependent upon particular views about the sources or the illegitimacy or the lesser legitimacy of profits, interest, and so on; which particular views may well be mistaken.

What sort of right over others does a legally institutionalized end-state pattern give one? The central core of the notion of a property right in *X*, relative to which other parts of the notion are to be explained, is the right to determine what shall be done with *X*; the right to choose which of the constrained set of options concerning *X* shall be realized or attempted.[26] The constraints are set by other principles or laws operating in the society; in our theory, by the Lockean rights people possess (under the minimal state). My property rights in my knife allow me to leave it where I will, but not in your chest. I may choose which of the acceptable options involving the knife is to be realized. This notion of property helps us to understand why earlier theorists spoke of people as having property in themselves and their labour. They viewed each person as having a right to decide what would become of himself and what he would do, and as having a right to reap the benefits of what he did.

This right of selecting the alternative to be realized from the constrained set of alternatives may be held by an *individual* or by a *group* with some procedure for reaching a joint decision; or the right may be passed back and forth, so that one year I decide what's to become of *X*, and the next year you do (with the alternative of destruction, perhaps, being excluded). Or, during the same time period, some types of decisions about *X* may be made by me, and others by you. And so on. We lack an adequate, fruitful, analytical apparatus for classifying the *types* of constraints on the set of options among which choices are to be made, and the *types* of ways decision powers can be held, divided, and amalgamated. A *theory* of property would, among other things, contain such a classification of constraints and decision modes, and from a small number of principles would follow a host of interesting statements about the *consequences* and effects of certain combinations of constraints and modes of decision.

When end-result principles of distributive justice are built into the legal structure of a society, they (as do most patterned principles) give each citizen an enforceable claim to some portion of the total social product; that is, to some portion of the sum total of the individually and jointly made products. This total product is produced by individuals labouring, using means of production others have saved to bring into existence, by people organizing production or creating means to produce new things or things in a new way. It is on this batch of individual activities that patterned distributional principles give each individual an enforceable claim. Each person has a claim to the activities and the products of other persons, independently of whether the other persons enter into particular relationships that give rise to these claims, and independently of whether they voluntarily take these claims upon themselves, in charity or in exchange for something.

Whether it is done through taxation on wages or on wages over a certain amount, or through seizure of profits, or through there being a big *social pot* so that it's not clear what's coming from where and what's going where, patterned principles of distributive justice involve appropriating the actions of other persons. Seizing the results of someone's labour is equivalent to seizing hours from him and directing him to carry on various activities. If people force you to do certain work, or unrewarded work, for a certain period of time, they decide what you are to do and what purposes your work is to serve apart from your decisions. This process whereby they take this decision from you makes them a *part-owner* of you; it gives them a property right in you. Just as having such partial control and power of decision, by right, over an animal or inanimate object would be to have a property right in it.

End-state and most patterned principles of distributive justice institute (partial) ownership by others of people and their actions and labour. These principles involve a shift from the classical liberals' notion of self-ownership to a notion of (partial) property rights in *other* people.

Considerations such as these confront end-state and other patterned conceptions of justice with the question of whether the actions necessary to achieve the selected pattern don't themselves violate moral side constraints. Any view holding that there are moral side constraints on actions, that not all moral considerations can be built into end states that are to be achieved . . . must face the possibility that some of its goals are not achievable by any morally permissible available means. An entitlement theorist will face such conflicts in a society that deviates from the principles of justice for the generation of holdings, if and only if the only actions available to realize the principles themselves violate some moral constraints. Since deviation from the first two principles of justice (in acquisition and transfer) will involve other persons' direct and aggressive intervention to violate rights, and since moral constraints will not exclude defensive or retributive action in such cases, the entitlement theorist's problem rarely will be pressing. And whatever difficulties he has in applying the principle of rectification to persons who did not themselves violate the first two principles are difficulties in balancing the conflicting considerations so as correctly to formulate the complex principle of rectification itself; he will not violate moral side constraints by applying the principle. Proponents of patterned conceptions of justice, however, often will face head-on clashes (and poignant ones if they cherish each party to the clash) between moral side constraints on how individuals may be treated and their patterned conception of justice that presents an end state or other pattern that *must* be realized.

May a person emigrate from a nation that has institutionalized some end-state or patterned distributional principle? For some principles (for example, Hayek's) emigration presents no theoretical problem. But for others it is a tricky matter. Consider a nation having a compulsory scheme of minimal social provision to aid the neediest (or one organized so as to maximize the position of the worst-off group); no one may opt out of participating in it. (None may say, "Don't compel me to contribute to others and don't provide for me via this compulsory mechanism if I am in need.") Everyone above a certain level is forced to contribute to aid the needy. But if emigration from the country were allowed, anyone could choose to move to another country that did not have compulsory social provision but otherwise was (as much as possible) identical. In such a case, the person's *only* motive for leaving would be to avoid participating in the compulsory scheme of social provision. And if he does leave, the needy in his initial country will receive no (compelled) help from him. What rationale yields the result that the person be permitted to emigrate, yet forbidden to stay and opt out of the compulsory scheme of social provision? If providing for the needy is of overriding importance, this does militate against allowing internal opting out; but it also speaks against allowing external emigration. (Would it also support, to some extent, the kidnapping of persons living in a place without compulsory

social provision, who could be forced to make a contribution to the needy in your community?) Perhaps the crucial component of the position that allows emigration solely to avoid certain arrangements, while not allowing anyone internally to opt out of them, is a concern for fraternal feelings within the country. "We don't want anyone here who doesn't contribute, who doesn't care enough about the others to contribute." That concern, in this case, would have to be tied to the view that forced aiding tends to produce fraternal feelings between the aided and the aider (or perhaps merely to the view that the knowledge that someone or other voluntarily is not aiding produces unfraternal feelings).

Locke's Theory of Acquisition

Before we turn to consider other theories of justice in detail, we must introduce an additional bit of complexity into the structure of the entitlement theory. This is best approached by considering Locke's attempt to specify a principle of justice in acquisition. Locke views property rights in an unowned object as originating through someone's mixing his labour with it. This gives rise to many questions. What are the boundaries of what labour is mixed with? If a private astronaut clears a place on Mars, has he mixed his labour with (so that he comes to own) the whole planet, the whole uninhabited universe, or just a particular plot? Which plot does an act bring under ownership? The minimal (possibly disconnected) area such that an act decreases entropy in that area, and not elsewhere? Can virgin land (for the purposes of ecological investigation by high-flying airplane) come under ownership by a Lockean process? Building a fence around a territory presumably would make one the owner of only the fence (and the land immediately underneath it). Why does mixing one's labour with something make one the owner of it? Perhaps because one owns one's labour, and so one comes to own a previously unowned thing that becomes permeated with what one owns. Ownership seeps over into the rest. But why isn't mixing what I own with what I don't own a way of losing what I own rather than a way of gaining what I don't? If I own a can of tomato juice and spill it in the sea so that its molecules (made radioactive, so I can check this) mingle evenly throughout the sea, do I thereby come to own the sea, or have I foolishly dissipated my tomato juice? Perhaps the idea, instead, is that labouring on something improves it and makes it more valuable; and anyone is entitled to own a thing whose value he has created. (Reinforcing this, perhaps, is the view that labouring is unpleasant. If some people made things effortlessly, as the cartoon characters in *The Yellow Submarine* trail flowers in their wake, would they have lesser claim to their own products whose making didn't *cost* them anything?) Ignore the fact that labouring on something may make it less valuable (spraying pink enamel paint on a piece of driftwood that you have found). Why should one's entitlement extend to the whole object rather than just to the *added value* one's labour has produced? (Such reference to value might also serve to delimit the extent of ownership; for example, substitute "increases the value of" for "decreases entropy in" in the above entropy criterion.) No workable or coherent value-added property scheme has yet been devised, and any such scheme presumably would fall to objections (similar to those) that fell the theory of Henry George.

It will be implausible to view improving an object as giving full ownership to it, if the stock of unowned objects that might be improved is limited. For an object's coming under one person's ownership changes the situation of all others. Whereas previously they were at liberty (in Hohfeld's sense) to use the object, they now no longer are. This change in the situation of others (by removing their liberty to act on a previously unowned object) need not worsen their situation. If I appropriate a grain of sand from Coney Island, no one else may now do as they will with *that* grain of sand. But there are plenty of other grains of sand left for them to do the same with. Or if not grains of sand, then other things. Alternatively, the things I do with the grain of sand I appropriate might improve the position of others, counterbalancing their loss of the liberty to use that grain. The crucial point is whether appropriation of an unowned object worsens the situation of others.

Locke's proviso that there be "enough and as good left in common for others" (sect. 27) is meant to ensure that the situation of others is not worsened. (If this proviso is met is there any motivation for his further condition of non-waste?) It is often said that this proviso once held but now no longer does. But there appears to be an argument for the conclusion that if the proviso no longer holds, then it cannot ever have held so as to yield permanent and inheritable property rights. Consider the first person Z for whom there is not enough and as good left to appropriate. The last person Y to appropriate left Z without his previous liberty to act on an object, and so worsened Z's situation. So Y's appropriation is not allowed under Locke's proviso. Therefore the next to last person X to appropriate left Y in a worse position, for X's act ended permissible appropriation. Therefore X's appropriation wasn't permissible. But then the appropriator two from last, W, ended permissible appropriation and so, since it worsened X's position, W's appropriation wasn't permissible. And so on back to the first person A to appropriate a permanent property right.

This argument, however, proceeds too quickly. Someone may be made worse off by another's appropriation in two ways: first, by losing the opportunity to improve his situation by a particular appropriation or anyone; and second, by no longer being able to use freely (without appropriation) what he previously could. A *stringent* requirement that another not be made worse off by an appropriation would exclude the first way if nothing else counterbalances the diminution in opportunity, as well as the second. A *weaker* requirement would exclude the second way, though not the first. With the weaker requirement, we cannot *zip* back so quickly from Z to A, as in the above argument; for though person Z can no longer *appropriate*, there may remain some for him to *use* as before. In this case Y's appropriation would not violate the weaker Lockean condition. (With less remaining that people are at liberty to use, users might face more inconvenience, crowding, and so on; in that way the situation of others might be worsened, unless appropriation stopped far short of such a point.) It is arguable that no one legitimately can complain if the weaker provision is satisfied. However, since this is less clear than in the case of the more stringent proviso, Locke may have intended this stringent proviso by "enough and as good" remaining, and perhaps he meant the non-waste condition to delay the end point from which the argument zips back.

Is the situation of persons who are unable to appropriate (there being no more accessible and useful unowned objects) worsened by a system allowing appropriation and permanent property? Here enter the various familiar social considerations favouring private property: it increases the social product by putting means of production in the hands of those who can use them most efficiently (profitably); experimentation is encouraged, because with separate persons controlling resources, there is no one person or small group whom someone with a new idea must convince to try it out; private property enables people to decide on the pattern and types of risks they wish to bear, leading to specialized types of risk bearing; private property protects future persons by leading some to hold back resources from current consumption for future markets; it provides alternate sources of employment for unpopular persons who don't have to convince any one person or small group to hire them, and so on. These considerations enter a Lockean theory to support the claim that appropriation of private property satisfies the intent behind the "enough and as good left over" proviso, *not* as a utilitarian justification of property. They enter to rebut the claim that because the proviso is violated no natural right to private property can arise by a Lockean process.

The difficulty in working such an argument to show that the proviso is satisfied is in fixing the appropriate base line for comparison. Lockean appropriation makes people no worse off than they would be *how*?[27] This question of fixing the baseline needs more detailed investigation than we are able to give it here. It would be desirable to have an estimate of the general economic importance of original appropriation in order to see how much leeway there is for differing theories of appropriation and of the location of the baseline. Perhaps this importance can be measured by the percentage of all income that is based upon untransformed raw materials and given resources (rather than upon human actions), mainly rental income representing the unimproved value of land, and the price of raw material *in situ*, and by the percentage of current wealth which represents such income in the past.[28]

We should note that it is not only persons favouring *private* property who need a theory of how property rights legitimately originate. Those believing in collective property, for example those believing that a group of persons living in an area jointly own the territory, or its mineral resources, also must provide a theory of how such property rights arise; they must show why the persons living there have rights to determine what is done with the land and resources there that persons living elsewhere don't have (with regard to the same land and resources).

The Proviso

Whether or not Locke's particular theory of appropriation can be spelled out so as to handle various difficulties, I assume that any adequate theory of justice in acquisition will contain a proviso similar to the weaker of the ones we have attributed to Locke. A process normally giving rise to a permanent bequeathable property right in a previously unowned thing will not do so if the position of others no longer at liberty to use the thing is thereby worsened. It is important to specify *this* particular mode of worsening the situation of others, for the proviso does not encompass other modes. It does not include the worsening due to more limited opportunities to appropriate (the first way above, corresponding to the more stringent condition), and it does not include how I "worsen" a seller's position if I appropriate materials to make some of what he is selling, and then enter into competition with him. Someone whose appropriation otherwise would violate the proviso still may appropriate provided he compensates the others so that their situation is not thereby worsened; unless he does compensate these others, his appropriation will violate the proviso of the principle of justice in acquisition and will be an illegitimate one.[29] A theory of appropriation incorporating this Lockean proviso will handle correctly the cases (objections to the theory lacking the proviso) where someone appropriates the total supply of something necessary for life.[30]

A theory which includes this proviso in its principle of justice in acquisition must also contain a more complex principle of justice in transfer. Some reflection of the proviso about appropriation constrains later actions. If my appropriating all of a certain substance violates the Lockean proviso, then so does my appropriating some and purchasing all the rest from others who obtained it without otherwise violating the Lockean proviso. If the proviso excludes someone's appropriating all the drinkable water in the world, it also excludes his purchasing it all. (More weakly, and messily, it may exclude his charging certain prices for some of his supply.) This proviso (almost?) never will come into effect; the more someone acquires of a scarce substance which others want, the higher the price of the rest will go, and the more difficult it will become for him to acquire it all. But still, we can imagine, at least, that something like this occurs: someone makes simultaneous secret bids to the separate owners of a substance, each of whom sells assuming he can easily purchase more from the other owners; or some natural catastrophe destroys all of the supply of something except that in one person's possession. The total supply could not be permissibly appropriated by one person at the beginning. His later acquisition of it all does not show that the original appropriation violated the proviso (even by a reverse argument similar to the one above that tried to zip back from *Z* to *A*). Rather, it is the combination of the original appropriation *plus* all the later transfers and actions that violates the Lockean proviso.

Each owner's title to his holding includes the historical shadow of the Lockean proviso on appropriation. This excludes his transferring it into an agglomeration that does violate the Lockean proviso and excludes his using it in away, in coordination with others or independently of them, so as to violate the proviso by making the situation of others worse than their baseline situation. Once it is known that someone's ownership runs afoul of the Lockean proviso, there are stringent limits on what he may do with (what it is difficult any longer unreservedly to call) "his property." Thus a person may not appropriate the only water hole in a desert and charge what he will. Nor may he charge what he will if he possesses one, and unfortunately it happens that all the water holes in the desert dry up, except for his. This unfortunate circumstance, admittedly no fault of his, brings into operation the Lockean proviso and limits his property rights.[31] Similarly, an owner's property right in the only *island* in an area does not allow him to order a castaway from a shipwreck off his island as a trespasser, for this would violate the Lockean proviso.

Notice that the theory does not say that owners do have these rights, but that the rights are overridden to avoid some catastrophe. (Overridden rights do not disappear; they leave a trace of a sort absent in the cases under discussion.)[32] There is no such external (and *ad hoc*?) overriding. Considerations internal to the theory of property itself, to its theory of acquisition and appropriation, provide the means for handling such cases. The results, however, may be coextensive with some condition about catastrophe, since the baseline for comparison is so low as compared to the productiveness of a society with private appropriation that the question of the Lockean proviso being violated arises only in the case of catastrophe (or a desert-island situation).

The fact that someone owns the total supply of something necessary for others to stay alive does *not* entail that his (or anyone's) appropriation of anything left some people (immediately or later) in a situation worse than the baseline one. A medical researcher who synthesizes a new substance that effectively treats a certain disease and who refuses to sell except on his terms does not worsen the situation of others by depriving them of whatever he has appropriated. The others easily can possess the same materials he appropriated; the researcher's appropriation or purchase of chemicals didn't make those chemicals scarce in a way so as to violate the Lockean proviso. Nor would someone else's purchasing the total supply of the synthesized substance from the medical researcher. The fact that the medical researcher uses easily available chemicals to synthesize the drug no more violates the Lockean proviso than does the fact that the only surgeon able to perform a particular operation eats easily obtainable food in order to stay alive and to have the energy to work. This shows that the Lockean proviso is not an "end-state principle"; it focuses on a particular way that appropriative actions affect others, and not on the structure of the situation that results.[33]

Intermediate between someone who takes all of the public supply and someone who makes the total supply out of easily obtainable substances is someone who appropriates the total supply of something in a way that does not deprive the others of it. For example, someone finds a new substance in an out-of-the-way place. He discovers that it effectively treats a certain disease and appropriates the total supply. He does not worsen the situation of others; if he did not stumble upon the substance no one else would have, and the others would remain without it. However, as time passes, the likelihood increases that others would have come across the substance; upon this fact might be based a limit to his property right in the substance so that others are not below their baseline position; for example, its bequest might be limited. The theme of someone worsening another's situation by depriving him of something he otherwise would possess may also illuminate the example of patents. An inventor's patent does not deprive others of an object which would not exist if not for the inventor. Yet patents would have this effect on others who independently invent the object. Therefore, these independent inventors, upon whom the burden of proving independent discovery may rest, should not be excluded from utilizing their own invention as they wish (including selling it to others). Furthermore, a known inventor drastically lessens the chances of actual independent invention. For persons who know of an invention usually will not try to reinvent it, and the notion of independent discovery here would be murky at best. Yet we may assume that in the absence of the original invention, sometime later someone else would have come up with it. This suggests placing a time limit on patents, as a rough rule of thumb to approximate how long it would have taken, in the absence of knowledge of the invention, for independent discovery.

I believe that the free operation of a market system will not actually run afoul of the Lockean proviso. (Recall that crucial to our story in Part I of how a protective agency becomes dominant and a *de facto* monopoly is the fact that it wields force in situations of conflict, and is not merely in competition, with other agencies. A similar tale cannot be told about other businesses.) If this is correct, the proviso will not play a very important role in the activities of protective agencies and will not provide a significant opportunity for future state action. Indeed, were it not for the effects of previous *illegitimate* state action, people would not think the possibility of the proviso's being violated as of more interest than any other logical possibility. (Here I make an empirical historical claim; as does someone who disagrees with this.) This completes our indication of the complication in the entitlement theory introduced by the Lockean proviso.

Post-Reading Questions

1. In what way is taxation akin to forced labour, according to Nozick?
2. What moral constraints does Nozick think it is right to impose on the just acquisition and transfer of our "holdings" (or property)?
3. Should social and economic inequalities between people exist in a *just* society, according to Nozick? How much inequality in society would Nozick allow?
4. Are maximum individual liberty and a minimalist state essential requirements of justice, as Nozick argues? And are they *sufficient* conditions—why/why not?

CASE STUDY
LIBERTY AND ITS LIMITS: *R. v. OAKES*

Introduction

As a libertarian thinker, Robert Nozick argues that it is rational for people to seek to maximize their individual freedom within the political arrangements that bind them. Using "state-of-nature" reasoning, Nozick suggests in *Anarchy, State, and Utopia* that people would voluntarily enter into a political framework that is considerably more minimalist in scope and power than are today's liberal democratic states. Indeed, given the choice, he insists, we would be more likely to form or join mutual-protection associations or agencies with carefully defined and limited powers than we would be to accept contemporary governments with their far-reaching powers.

Nozick's view that large-scale modern states inevitably constrain the freedom of individuals in illegitimate ways finds justification in the Canadian Supreme Court case of *R. v. Oakes*. This case concerned David Oakes, who was charged with unlawful possession of a narcotic for the purpose of trafficking. The trial judge determined that it was beyond a reasonable doubt that the respondent was in possession of a narcotic. However, he challenged the constitutional validity of section 8 of the Narcotic Control Act, which entails that if the accused is found to be in possession of a narcotic, the accused is also presumed to be in possession for the purpose of trafficking—a much more serious charge. Section 8 also specifies that it is the burden of the accused to establish the contrary, or else be convicted of trafficking. As such, it imposes what is known as the "reverse onus" on the accused to prove the contrary of the charge—despite the fact that under Canadian criminal law it is usually the burden of the Crown to establish beyond reasonable doubt the charges against the accused. From a Nozickean point of view, this reverse onus is a highly unjust constraint on the liberty of the accused, because it requires a person to undertake special actions in order to secure his or her freedom.

Oakes's lawyer argued that the problem with the "reverse onus" as found in section 8 of the Narcotic Control Act is that it is inconsistent with the principle of presumption of innocence as guaranteed by section 11 (d) of the Charter of Rights and Freedoms. While section 1 of the Charter makes clear that Canadians' rights and freedoms are subject to reasonable legislative limitations, the case of *R. v. Oakes* raised the question of just where the boundaries for such limitations should fall. The Ontario Court of Appeal ruled that section 8 did indeed constitute a "reverse onus" clause and was therefore incompatible with section 11 (d) of the Charter. The Crown appealed this decision, and a constitutional question was then raised as to whether section 8 indeed violated the Charter or whether it was instead a reasonable limit prescribed by law and demonstrably justified in a free and democratic society (as required by section 1 of the Charter).

The Constitution Act of 1982 enshrined the Canadian Charter of Rights and Freedoms in the constitution. Section 1 of the Charter states that no right or freedom is absolute: "The Canadian Charter of Rights and Freedoms guarantees the rights and freedoms set out in it subject only to such *reasonable* limits prescribed by law as can be *demonstrably justified* in a free and democratic society." (emphasis added) This formulation leaves open the question of when a limit is reasonable and justified, however. In 1986, the Supreme Court of Canada had occasion to take on this issue, and what emerged was an important test (subsequently named the "Oakes test" by Chief Justice Dickson) for determining the reasonableness and justifiability of legislation (such as section 8) that effectively limits citizens' basic rights and freedoms. While Nozick and libertarians generally emphatically disagree with the expansive scope of government powers implicitly endorsed by the Charter, they would arguably applaud the spirit of the Oakes test, for it adds one safety check on what they would see as the illegitimate constraint of individual freedom by the state.

From *R. v. Oakes*, [1986] 1 S.C.R. 103

R. v. Oakes, *[1986] 1 S.C.R. 103.*
http://scc.lexum.org/decisia-scc-csc/scc-csc/scc-csc/en/117/1/document.do

[The majority decision was delivered by the Chief Justice C.J. Dickson.]

This appeal concerns the constitutionality of s. 8 of the Narcotic Control Act, R.S.C. 1970, c. N-1. The section provides, in brief, that if the Court finds the accused in possession of a narcotic, he is presumed to be in possession for the purpose of trafficking. Unless the accused can establish the contrary, he must be convicted of trafficking. The Ontario Court of Appeal held that this provision constitutes a "reverse onus" clause and is unconstitutional because it violates one of the core values of our criminal justice system, the presumption of innocence, now entrenched in s. 11(d) of the Canadian Charter of Rights and Freedoms. The Crown has appealed.

I. Statutory and Constitutional Provisions

Before reviewing the factual context, I will set out the relevant legislative and constitutional provisions:

Narcotic Control Act, R.S.C. 1970, c. N-1.

3. (1) Except as authorized by this Act or the regulations, no person shall have a narcotic in his possession.

(2) Every person who violates subsection (1) is guilty of an indictable offence and is liable

(*a*) upon summary conviction for a first offence, to a fine of one thousand dollars or to imprisonment for six months or to both fine and imprisonment, and for a subsequent offence, to a fine of two thousand dollars or to imprisonment for one year or to both fine and imprisonment; or

(*b*) upon conviction on indictment, to imprisonment for seven years.

4. (1) No person shall traffic in a narcotic or any substance represented or held out by him to be a narcotic.

(2) No person shall have in his possession a narcotic for the purpose of trafficking.

(3) Every person who violates subsection (1) or (2) is guilty of an indictable offence and is liable to imprisonment for life.

. . .

8. In any prosecution for a violation of subsection 4(2), if the accused does not plead guilty, the trial shall proceed as if it were a prosecution for an offence under section 3, and after the close of the case for the prosecution and after the accused has had an opportunity to make full answer and defence, the court shall make a finding as

to whether or not the accused was in possession of the narcotic contrary to section 3; if the court finds that the accused was not in possession of the narcotic contrary to section 3, he shall be acquitted but if the court finds that the accused was in possession of the narcotic contrary to section 3, he shall be given an opportunity of establishing that he was not in possession of the narcotic for the purpose of trafficking, and thereafter the prosecutor shall be given an opportunity of adducing evidence to establish that the accused was in possession of the narcotic for the purpose of trafficking; if the accused establishes that he was not in possession of the narcotic for the purpose of trafficking, he shall be acquitted of the offence as charged but he shall be convicted of an offence under section 3 and sentenced accordingly; and if the accused fails to establish that he was not in possession of the narcotic for the purpose of trafficking, he shall be convicted of the offence as charged and sentenced accordingly.

Canadian Charter of Rights and Freedoms
11. Any person charged with an offence has the right
. . .
> (d) to be presumed innocent until proven guilty according to law in a fair and public hearing by an independent and impartial tribunal.

II. Facts

The respondent, David Edwin Oakes, was charged with unlawful possession of a narcotic for the purpose of trafficking, contrary to s. 4(2) of the Narcotic Control Act. He elected trial by magistrate without a jury. At trial, the Crown adduced evidence to establish that Mr. Oakes was found in possession of eight one gram vials of *cannabis* resin in the form of hashish oil. Upon a further search conducted at the police station, $619.45 was located. Mr. Oakes told the police that he had bought ten vials of hashish oil for $150 for his own use, and that the $619.45 was from a workers' compensation cheque. He elected not to call evidence as to possession of the narcotic. Pursuant to the procedural provisions of s. 8 of the Narcotic Control Act, the trial judge proceeded to make a finding that it was beyond a reasonable doubt that Mr. Oakes was in possession of the narcotic.

Following this finding, Mr. Oakes brought a motion to challenge the constitutional validity of s. 8 of the Narcotic Control Act, which he maintained imposes a burden on an accused to prove that he or she was not in possession for the purpose of trafficking. He argued that s. 8 violates the presumption of innocence contained in s. 11(d) of the Charter.
. . .

IV. The Issues

The constitutional question in this appeal is stated as follows:

> Is s. 8 of the Narcotic Control Act inconsistent with s. 11(d) of the Canadian Charter of Rights and Freedoms and thus of no force and effect?

Two specific questions are raised by this general question: (1) does s. 8 of the Narcotic Control Act violate s. 11(d) of the Charter; and, (2) if it does, is s. 8 a reasonable limit prescribed by law as can be demonstrably justified in a free and democratic society for the purpose of s. 1 of the Charter? If the answer to (1) is affirmative and the answer to (2) negative, then the constitutional question must be answered in the affirmative.

. . .

To return to s. 8 of the Narcotic Control Act, it is my view that, upon a finding beyond a reasonable doubt of possession of a narcotic, the accused has the legal burden of proving on a balance of probabilities that he or she was not in possession of the narcotic for the purpose of trafficking. Once the basic fact of possession is proven, a mandatory presumption of law arises against the accused that he or she had the intention to traffic. Moreover, the accused will be found guilty of the offence of trafficking unless he or she can rebut this presumption on a balance of probabilities. . . .

. . .

I conclude that s. 8 of the Narcotic Control Act contains a reverse onus provision imposing a legal burden on an accused to prove on a balance of probabilities that he or she was not in possession of a narcotic for the purpose of trafficking. It is therefore necessary to determine whether s. 8 of the Narcotic Control Act offends the right to be "presumed innocent until proven guilty" as guaranteed by s. 11(d) of the Charter.

(b) The Presumption of Innocence and s. 11(d) of the Charter
Section 11(d) of the Charter constitutionally entrenches the presumption of innocence as part of the supreme law of Canada. For ease of reference, I set out this provision again:

> 11. Any person charged with an offence has the right
> . . .
> (d) to be presumed innocent until proven guilty according to law in a fair and public hearing by an independent and impartial tribunal.

To interpret the meaning of s. 11(d), it is important to adopt a purposive approach. As this Court stated in *R. v. Big M Drug Mart Ltd.* . . . :

The meaning of a right or freedom guaranteed by the Charter was to be ascertained by an analysis of the purpose of such a guarantee; it was to be understood, in other words, in the light of the interests it was meant to protect.

In my view this analysis is to be undertaken, and the purpose of the right or freedom in question is to be sought by reference to the character and the larger objects of the Charter itself, to the language chosen to articulate the specific right or freedom, to the historical origins of the concepts enshrined, and where applicable, to the meaning and purpose of the other specific rights and freedoms. . . .

To identify the underlying purpose of the Charter right in question, therefore, it is important to begin by understanding the cardinal values it embodies.

The presumption of innocence is a hallowed principle lying at the very heart of criminal law. Although protected expressly in s. 11(d) of the Charter, the presumption of innocence is referable and integral to the general protection of life, liberty and security of the person contained in s. 7 of the Charter (see *Re B.C. Motor Vehicle Act*. The presumption of innocence protects the fundamental liberty and human dignity of any and every person accused by the State of criminal conduct. An individual charged with a criminal offence faces grave social and personal consequences, including potential loss of physical liberty, subjection to social stigma and ostracism from the community, as well as other social, psychological and economic harms. In light of the gravity of these consequences, the presumption of innocence is crucial. It ensures that until the State proves an accused's guilt beyond all reasonable doubt, he or she is innocent. This is essential in a society committed to fairness and social justice. The presumption of innocence confirms our faith in humankind; it reflects our belief that individuals are decent and law-abiding members of the community until proven otherwise.

The presumption of innocence has enjoyed longstanding recognition at common law. . . .

Further evidence of the widespread acceptance of the principle of the presumption of innocence is its inclusion in the major international human rights documents. Article 11(I) of the Universal Declaration of Human Rights, adopted December 10, 1948 by the General Assembly of the United Nations, provides:

Article 11
I. Everyone charged with a penal offence has the right to be presumed innocent until proved guilty according to law in a public trial at which he has had all the guarantees necessary for his defence.

. . .

Canada acceded to this Covenant, and the Optional Protocol which sets up machinery for implementing the Covenant, on May 19, 1976. Both came into effect on August 19, 1976.

In light of the above, the right to be presumed innocent until proven guilty requires that s. 11(d) have, at a minimum, the following content. First, an individual must be proven guilty beyond a reasonable doubt. Second, it is the State which must bear the burden of proof. As Lamer J. stated in *Dubois v. The Queen* . . . :

Section 11(d) imposes upon the Crown the burden of proving the accused's guilt beyond a reasonable doubt as well as that of making out the case against the accused before he or she need respond, either by testifying or calling other evidence.

Third, criminal prosecutions must be carried out in accordance with lawful procedures and fairness. The latter part of s. 11(d), which requires the proof of guilt "according to law in a fair and public hearing by an independent and impartial tribunal", underlines the importance of this procedural requirement.

(c) Authorities on Reverse Onus Provisions and the Presumption of Innocence

Having considered the general meaning of the presumption of innocence, it is now, I think, desirable to review briefly the authorities on reverse onus clauses in Canada and other jurisdictions.

. . .

Canadian Charter Jurisprudence

In addition to the present case, there have been a number of other provincial appellate level judgments addressing the meaning of the presumption of innocence contained in s. 11(d). This jurisprudence provides a comprehensive and persuasive source of insight into the questions raised in this appeal. In particular, six appellate level courts, in addition to the Ontario Court of Appeal, have held that s. 8 of the Narcotic Control Act violates the Charter: *R. v. Carroll, supra; R. v. Cook, supra; R. v. O'Day, supra; R. v. Stanger, supra; R. v. Landry, supra; R. v. Stock* (1983) . . .

Following the decision of the Ontario Court of Appeal in the present case, the Prince Edward Island Supreme Court (*in banco*) rendered its decision in *R. v. Carroll, supra*. Writing for the majority, MacDonald J. held . . . :

Unless a provision falls within s. 1 of the Charter, there cannot be a requirement that an accused must prove an essential positive element of the Crown's case other than by raising a reasonable doubt. The presumption of innocence cannot be said to exist if by shifting the persuasive burden the court is required to convict even if a reasonable doubt may be said to exist.

In a concurring judgment, Mitchell J. commented at pp. 107–08:

> Section 11(d) gives an accused person the right to be presumed innocent until proven guilty. It follows that if an accused is to be presumed innocent until proven guilty, he must not be convicted unless and until the Crown has proven each and all of the elements necessary to constitute the crime.

Applying these legal conclusions to s. 8 of the Narcotic Control Act, the Court held that s. 11(d) had been violated. As Mitchell J. stated at p. 108:

> Under s. 8 an accused is not presumed innocent until proven guilty. He is only presumed innocent until found in possession. Once the Crown proves the accused had possession of the narcotic, he is presumed to be guilty of an intention to traffic until he proves otherwise.

The Nova Scotia Supreme Court, Appellate Division, also concluded that s. 8 is an unconstitutional violation of the s. 11(d) presumption of innocence in its decision in *R. v. Cook*, *supra*. After reviewing *R. v. Oakes*, *supra*, and *R. v. Carroll*, *supra*, Hart J.A. concluded . . . :

> Section 8 of the Narcotic Control Act is a piece of legislation that attempts to relieve the Crown of its normal burden of proof by use of what is known as a reverse onus. Different types of reverse onus have been known to the law and proof of a case with the aid of a reverse onus can in my opinion, fall into the wording of s. 11(d) of the Charter as being proof "according to law". . . . I know of no justification, however, for holding that it would be "according to law" to allow use of a reverse onus clause which permitted the Crown the assistance of a provision which relieved it from calling any probative evidence to establish one of the essential elements of an offence.

. . .

To summarize, the Canadian Charter jurisprudence on the presumption of innocence in s. 11(d) and reverse onus provisions appears to have solidly accorded a high degree of protection to the presumption of innocence. Any infringements of this right are permissible only when, in the words of s. 1 of the Charter, they are reasonable and demonstrably justified in a free and democratic society.

. . .

(d) Conclusion Regarding s. 11(d) of the Charter and s. 8 of the Narcotic Control Act

. . .

In general one must, I think, conclude that a provision which requires an accused to disprove on a balance of probabilities the existence of a presumed fact, which is an important element of the offence in question, violates the presumption of innocence in s. 11(d). If an accused bears the burden of disproving on a balance of probabilities an essential element of an offence, it would be possible for a conviction to occur despite the existence of a reasonable doubt. This would arise if the accused adduced sufficient evidence to raise a reasonable doubt as to his or her innocence but did not convince the jury on a balance of probabilities that the presumed fact was untrue.

The fact that the standard is only the civil one does not render a reverse onus clause constitutional. . . .

To return to s. 8 of the Narcotic Control Act, I am in no doubt whatsoever that it violates s. 11(d) of the Charter by requiring the accused to prove on a balance of probabilities that he was not in possession of the narcotic for the purpose of trafficking. Mr. Oakes is compelled by s. 8 to prove he is not guilty of the offence of trafficking. He is thus denied his right to be presumed innocent and subjected to the potential penalty of life imprisonment unless he can rebut the presumption. This is radically and fundamentally inconsistent with the societal values of human dignity and liberty which we espouse, and is directly contrary to the presumption of innocence enshrined in s. 11(d). Let us turn now to s. 1 of the Charter.

V. Is s. 8 of the Narcotic Control Act a Reasonable and Demonstrably Justified Limit Pursuant to s. 1 of the Charter?

The Crown submits that even if s. 8 of the Narcotic Control Act violates s. 11(d) of the Charter, it can still be upheld as a reasonable limit under s. 1 which, as has been mentioned, provides:

> 1. The Canadian Charter of Rights and Freedoms guarantees the rights and freedoms set out in it subject only to such reasonable limits prescribed by law as can be demonstrably justified in a free and democratic society.

The question whether the limit is "prescribed by law" is not contentious in the present case since s. 8 of the Narcotic Control Act is a duly enacted legislative provision. It is, however, necessary to determine if the limit on Mr. Oakes' right, as guaranteed by s. 11(d) of the Charter, is "reasonable" and "demonstrably justified in a free and democratic society" for the purpose of s. 1 of the Charter, and thereby saved from inconsistency with the constitution.

It is important to observe at the outset that s. 1 has two functions: first, it constitutionally guarantees the rights and freedoms set out in the provisions which follow; and, second, it states explicitly the exclusive justificatory criteria (outside of s. 33 of the Constitution Act, 1982) against which limitations on those rights and freedoms must be measured. Accordingly, any s. 1 inquiry must be premised on an understanding that the impugned limit violates constitutional rights and freedoms—rights and freedoms which are part of the supreme law of Canada. As Wilson J. stated in *Singh v. Minister of Employment and Immigration*, *supra*: ". . . it is important to remember that the courts are conducting this inquiry in light of a commitment to uphold the rights and freedoms set out in the other sections of the Charter."

A second contextual element of interpretation of s. 1 is provided by the words "free and democratic society." Inclusion of these words as the final standard of justification for limits on rights and freedoms refers the Court to the very purpose for which the Charter was originally entrenched in the constitution: Canadian society is to be free and democratic. The Court must be guided by the values and principles essential to a free and democratic society which I believe embody, to name but a few, respect for the inherent dignity of the human person, commitment to social justice and equality, accommodation of a wide variety of beliefs, respect for cultural and group identity, and faith in social and political institutions which enhance the participation of individuals and groups in society. The underlying values and principles of a free and democratic society are the genesis of the rights and freedoms guaranteed by the Charter and the ultimate standard against which a limit on a right or freedom must be shown, despite its effect, to be reasonable and demonstrably justified.

The rights and freedoms guaranteed by the Charter are not, however, absolute. It may become necessary to limit rights and freedoms in circumstances where their exercise would be inimical to the realization of collective goals of fundamental importance. For this reason, s. 1 provides criteria of justification for limits on the rights and freedoms guaranteed by the Charter. These criteria impose a stringent standard of justification, especially when understood in terms of the two contextual considerations discussed above, namely, the violation of a constitutionally guaranteed right or freedom and the fundamental principles of a free and democratic society.

The onus of proving that a limit on a right or freedom guaranteed by the Charter is reasonable and demonstrably justified in a free and democratic society rests upon the party seeking to uphold the limitation. It is clear from the text of s. 1 that limits on the rights and freedoms enumerated in the Charter are exceptions to their general guarantee. The presumption is that the rights and freedoms are guaranteed unless the party invoking s. 1 can bring itself within the exceptional criteria which justify their being limited. This is further substantiated by the use of the word "demonstrably" which clearly indicates that the onus of justification is on the party seeking to limit: *Hunter v. Southam Inc.*, *supra*.

The standard of proof under s. 1 is the civil standard, namely, proof by a preponderance of probability. The alternative criminal standard, proof beyond a reasonable doubt, would, in my view, be unduly onerous on the party seeking to limit. Concepts such as "reasonableness," "justifiability," and "free and democratic society" are simply not amenable to such a standard. Nevertheless, the preponderance of probability test must be applied rigorously. Indeed, the phrase "demonstrably justified" in s. 1 of the Charter supports this conclusion. . . .

Having regard to the fact that s. 1 is being invoked for the purpose of justifying a violation of the constitutional rights and freedoms the Charter was designed to protect, a very high degree of probability will be, in the words of Lord Denning, "commensurate with the occasion." Where evidence is required in order to prove the constituent elements of a s. 1 inquiry, and this will generally be the case, it should be cogent and persuasive and make clear to the Court the consequences of imposing or not imposing the limit. See: *Law Society of Upper Canada v. Skapinker*, *supra*, at p. 384; *Singh v. Minister of Employment and Immigration*, *supra*, at p. 217. A court will also need to know what alternative measures for implementing the objective were available to the legislators when they made their decisions. I should add, however, that there may be cases where certain elements of the s. 1 analysis are obvious or self-evident.

To establish that a limit is reasonable and demonstrably justified in a free and democratic society, two central criteria must be satisfied. First, the objective, which the measures responsible for a limit on a Charter right or freedom are designed to serve, must be "of sufficient importance to warrant overriding a constitutionally protected right or freedom": *R. v. Big M Drug Mart Ltd.*, *supra*, at p. 352. The standard must be high in order to ensure that objectives which are trivial or discordant with the principles integral to a free and democratic society do not gain s. 1 protection. It is necessary, at a minimum, that an objective relate to concerns which are pressing and substantial in a free and democratic society before it can be characterized as sufficiently important.

Second, once a sufficiently significant objective is recognized, then the party invoking s. 1 must show that the means chosen are reasonable and demonstrably justified. This involves "a form of proportionality test": *R. v. Big M Drug Mart Ltd.* Although the nature of the proportionality test will vary depending on the circumstances, in each case courts will be required to balance the interests of society with those of individuals and groups. There are, in my view, three important components of a proportionality test. First, the measures adopted must be carefully designed to achieve the objective in question. They must not be arbitrary, unfair or based on irrational considerations. In short, they must be rationally connected to the objective. Second, the means, even if rationally connected to the objective in this first sense, should impair "as little as possible" the right or freedom in question: *R. v. Big M Drug Mart Ltd.* Third, there must be a proportionality between the effects of the measures which are responsible for limiting the Charter right or freedom, and the objective which has been identified as of "sufficient importance".

With respect to the third component, it is clear that the general effect of any measure impugned under s. 1 will be the infringement of a right or freedom guaranteed by the Charter; this is the reason why resort to s. 1 is necessary. The inquiry into effects must, however, go further. A wide range of rights and freedoms are guaranteed by the Charter, and an almost infinite number of factual situations may arise in respect of these. Some limits on rights and freedoms protected by the Charter will be more serious than others in terms of the nature of the right or freedom violated, the extent of the violation, and the degree to which the measures which impose the limit trench upon the integral principles of a free and democratic society. Even if an objective is of sufficient importance, and the first two elements of the proportionality test are satisfied, it is still possible that, because of the severity of the deleterious effects of a measure on individuals or groups, the measure will not be justified by the purposes it is intended to serve. The more severe the deleterious effects of a measure, the more important the objective must be if the measure is to be reasonable and demonstrably justified in a free and democratic society.

Having outlined the general principles of a s. 1 inquiry, we must apply them to s. 8 of the Narcotic Control Act. Is the reverse onus provision in s. 8 a reasonable limit on the right to be presumed innocent until proven guilty beyond a reasonable doubt as can be demonstrably justified in a free and democratic society?

The starting point for formulating a response to this question is, as stated above, the nature of Parliament's interest or objective which accounts for the passage of s. 8 of the Narcotic Control Act. According to the Crown, s. 8 of the Narcotic Control Act is aimed at curbing drug trafficking by facilitating the conviction of drug traffickers. In my opinion, Parliament's concern that drug trafficking be decreased can be characterized as substantial and pressing. The problem of drug trafficking has been increasing since the 1950's at which time there was already considerable concern. . . .

The objective of protecting our society from the grave ills associated with drug trafficking, is, in my view, one of sufficient importance to warrant overriding a constitutionally protected right or freedom in certain cases. Moreover, the degree of seriousness of drug trafficking makes its acknowledgement as a sufficiently important objective for the purposes of s. 1, to a large extent, self-evident. The first criterion of a s. 1 inquiry, therefore, has been satisfied by the Crown.

The next stage of inquiry is a consideration of the means chosen by Parliament to achieve its objective. The means must be reasonable and demonstrably justified in a free and democratic society. As outlined above, this proportionality test should begin with a consideration of the rationality of the provision: is the reverse onus clause in s. 8 rationally related to the objective of curbing drug trafficking? At a minimum, this requires that s. 8 be internally rational; there must be a rational connection between the basic fact of possession and the presumed fact of possession for the purpose of trafficking. Otherwise, the reverse onus clause could give rise to unjustified and erroneous convictions for drug trafficking of persons guilty only of possession of narcotics.

In my view, s. 8 does not survive this rational connection test. As Martin J.A. of the Ontario Court of Appeal concluded, possession of a small or negligible quantity of narcotics does not support the inference of trafficking. In other words, it would be irrational to infer that a person had an intent to traffic on the basis of his or her possession of a very small quantity of narcotics. The presumption required under s. 8 of the Narcotic Control Act is over-inclusive and could lead to results in certain cases which would defy both rationality and fairness. In light of the seriousness of the offence in question, which carries with it the possibility of imprisonment for life, I am further convinced that the first component of the proportionality test has not been satisfied by the Crown.

Having concluded that s. 8 does not satisfy this first component of proportionality, it is unnecessary to consider the other two components.

VI. Conclusion

The Ontario Court of Appeal was correct in holding that s. 8 of the Narcotic Control Act violates the Canadian Charter of Rights and Freedoms and is therefore of no force or effect. Section 8 imposes a limit on the right guaranteed by s. 11(d) of the Charter which is not reasonable and is not demonstrably justified in a free and democratic society for the purpose of s. 1. Accordingly, the constitutional question is answered as follows:

Question:

Is s. 8 of the Narcotic Control Act inconsistent with s. 11(d) of the Canadian Charter of Rights and Freedoms and thus of no force and effect?

Answer: Yes.

I would, therefore, dismiss the appeal.

Post-Case-Reading Questions

1. Why did the Court conclude that the "reverse onus" created by section 8 of the Narcotic Control Act violated David Oakes' rights under the Charter?
2. What political values does the Oakes decision direct us to consider when interpreting the "limitations clause" (section 1) of the Charter?

CHAPTER XII

Susan Moller Okin

Introduction

Susan Moller Okin was born in Auckland, New Zealand, in 1946. She attended the University of Auckland, where she earned a bachelor's degree in 1967. She then attended Oxford University, obtaining an MA in philosophy in 1970, and in 1975 earned her PhD from the Government Department at Harvard University. Okin taught at the University of Auckland, Vassar College, and Brandeis and Harvard universities before finally joining Stanford's faculty in 1990. At Stanford, she became director of the Ethics in Society Program (1993–6) and was the Martha Sutton Weeks Professor of Ethics in Society. Okin's groundbreaking book, *Justice, Gender, and the Family* (1989) was awarded the Victoria Shuck Award for best book on women in politics from the American Political Science Association.

Susan Moller Okin

Linda A. Cicero/Stanford News Service. Used with permission.

At the time of her death in 2004 at the age of 57, Okin was a visiting fellow at the Radcliffe Institute for Advanced Study, at Harvard University.

Okin's early philosophical work addresses the absence of women's experiences and perspectives from Western political thought—both past and present—and particularly from theories of justice. Her book *Women in Western Political Thought* (1979) is a benchmark for research on the treatment of women—and sex and gender more generally—in mainstream political philosophy. The author of numerous scholarly articles on topics ranging from feminist ethics to injustices facing women in a global context, Okin also wrote the lead essay in the highly publicized—and controversial—volume, *Is Multiculturalism Bad for Women?* (1999).

In her later years, Okin turned her attention to the plight of women in the global South. Her interest grew out of concerns about women's economic exploitation and disempowerment—including their unpaid caring labour—as well as misgivings about cultural and religious justifications for gendered practices and arrangements that harm or disadvantage women. In the last few years of her life, she contributed to the work of the Global Fund for Women, a San Francisco–based grant-making foundation promoting women's economic security, health, education, and leadership; she travelled on behalf of the organization to

India and Brazil, where her conversations with activists reaffirmed her belief in the urgent need to secure greater economic and social equality for all women.

In *Justice, Gender, and the Family*, Okin observes that despite the recognition of women's equal rights and anti-discrimination laws, we have not achieved sexual equality in liberal democratic societies. She locates the problem with the concept of "gender" as the deeply entrenched institutionalization of sexual differences. As such, gender is socially constructed and not based on any unalterable a priori essence, which is why, according to Okin, most feminist theorists reject the associated biological determinism. She asks why, given the importance of the question "How *just* is gender?," so few theories of justice have addressed the concept of gender in their theorizing. One reason for this neglect, Okin suggested, is that most theorists simply assume the traditional, gender-structured family. Implicit in this assumption is the idea that the family is located in the private sphere and hence is non-political, which in turn rules out the application of principles of justice to the relation between the sexes (particularly within the household). Against this view, Okin insists that issues of justice and equity are very relevant to the construction and development of families, and that political philosophy and public policy alike need to accord serious attention to the gendered patterns of inequality within the household.

By attending to patterns of gender injustice, Okin argues, we can see that the continued tension between women's household and childcare work and their participation in paid work is discriminatory because it views women's different work patterns as based on relevant gender responsibilities and not the result of arbitrary treatment. These patterns also allow us to see the gendered inequalities in the law, which the case reading for this chapter explores. Any viable contemporary theory of justice has to include gender, according to Okin, not only because the exclusion of women renders such theories incomplete, but because women around the world still face very real injustices in public and (so-called) private life. Moreover, political philosophers striving to imagine a more just society surely cannot expect that social and political justice could be attained if one of the core institutions of society—the family—is not also just. Principles of justice, therefore, ought to be extended to the family because it is a school of justice; the family is where the subjects of theories of justice are nurtured and developed, and so is fundamental to the very foundation of society. Okin, thus, rejects the claim that the family is a private institution to which standards of justice should not apply.

Further Readings

Abbey, R. (2011). *The Return of Feminist Liberalism*. Durham, UK: Acumen Publishing.

McKinnon, C. (1989). *Toward a Feminist Theory of the State*. Cambridge, MA.: Harvard University Press.

Nussbaum, M. (1999). *Sex and Social Justice*. New York and Oxford: Oxford University Press.

Nussbaum, M. (2004). "On Hearing Women's Voices: A Reply to Susan Okin," *Philosophy and Public Affairs* 32 (2): 193–205.

Philips, A. (ed.) (1998). *Feminism and Politics*. New York and Oxford: Oxford University Press.

Satz, D. (2009). *Toward a Humanist Justice: The Political Philosophy of Susan Moller Okin*. New York and Oxford: Oxford University Press.

Susan Moller Okin, From *Justice, Gender, and the Family*

Susan Moller Okin, Justice, Gender, and the Family *(New York: Basic Books, 1989).*

Chapter 6 Justice from Sphere to Sphere

... Here, I shall lay out four major flaws in the dichotomy between "private" domestic life and "public" life in the marketplace or politics, as it is currently drawn or assumed in theories of justice. These constitute, in other words, four respects in which the personal is political.

First, what happens in domestic and personal life is not immune from the dynamic of *power*, which has typically been seen as the distinguishing feature of the political. Power within the family, whether that of husband over wife or of parent over child, has often not been recognized as such, either because it has been regarded as natural or because it is assumed that, in the family, altruism and the harmony of interests make power an insignificant factor. This seems to be tacitly assumed by most contemporary theorists of justice, given their neglect of intra-familial relations. But the notion that power in its crassest form, physical violence, is not a factor in family life is a myth that has been exposed during the last century and increasingly exposed in the last two decades. As has now become well known, wife abuse, though still seriously underreported, is not an uncommon phenomenon. According to a 1976 national survey, it is estimated that between 1.8 and 5.7 million women in the United States are beaten each year in their homes. A recent government study of marital violence in Kentucky found that 4 per cent of women living with a male partner had been kicked or bitten, struck with a fist or an object, beaten up, or either threatened or attacked with a knife or gun during the previous year. Nine per cent reported this degree of physical abuse at some time in the past from the man they lived with, and some estimates of actual incidence are far higher. Thirty per cent of all female murder victims in 1986 were killed by their husbands or boyfriends, compared with 6 per cent of male victims killed by wives or girlfriends.[1]

People are far more tolerant of physical abuse of a woman by a man when they believe she is his wife or girlfriend than otherwise. This is probably due in part to the fact that violence used to be a legally sanctioned part of male dominance in the patriarchal family. The privacy that early liberal theorists claimed for the "individuals" they wrote about was the power of patriarchs; it was taken for granted that husbands and fathers should have power over their wives and children, including the right to "chastise" them physically. Until recently, though in principle no longer legally sanctioned, violence within families was in practice ignored; the police and the courts were loath to "intervene" in ostensibly "private" familial disputes. In the late nineteenth and early twentieth centuries, child abuse was "discovered." And in the 1970s and 1980s, partly as a result of the feminist and children's rights movements that originated in the 1960s, wife abuse has been "discovered" and child abuse "rediscovered." Family violence is now much less sanctioned or ignored than in the past; it is becoming recognized as a serious problem that society must act on. There is now no doubt that family violence, as it affects both wives and children, is closely connected with differentials of power and dependency between the sexes. It is certainly impossible to claim, in the face of current evidence, that the family is private and nonpolitical because power is an insignificant factor in it. In addition to physical force, there are subtler, though no less important, modes of power that operate within families, some of which will be discussed in the next chapter. As feminists have pointed out, in many respects the notion that state intervention in the family should be minimized has often served to reinforce the power of its economically or physically more powerful members. The privacy of home can be a dangerous place, especially for women and children.[2]

The second problem with the public/domestic dichotomy is that, as feminist historians and lawyers have shown, to the extent that a more private, domestic sphere does exist, its very existence, the limits that define it, and the types of behaviour that are acceptable and not acceptable within it all result from political decisions.[3] If there *were* a clear sphere from which the state refrained from intruding, that sphere would have to be defined, and its definition would be a political issue. But in fact, the state has not just "kept out of" family life. In innumerable ways, the state determines and enforces the terms of marriage. For hundreds of years, the common law deprived women of their legal personhood upon marriage. It enforced the rights of husbands to their wives' property and even to their wives' bodies, and made it virtually impossible for women to divorce or even to live separately from their husbands. Long after married women gained rights over their own property and the possibility of divorce, as we have seen, marriage has remained a peculiar contract, a preformed status contract whose terms have been enforced in innumerable ways. Courts have refused to allow wives to trade or forgo their rights to support, but have also refused to "intrude" into the family to enforce any specific level of support; few jurisdictions recognize marital rape; and married women have been "compelled, by law, to perform housework without pay [and] the obligation cannot be altered."[4] In addition, until the "divorce revolution" of the last two decades, the terms of divorce strongly reinforced traditional sex roles within marriage, by means of rewards and punishments. As Lenore Weitzman wrote in 1985, "the common law assumption that the husband was the head of the family remained firmly embodied in statute and case law until the last decade."[5]

There is a whole other dimension, too, to the state's pervasive regulation of family life. Historically, the law closed off to women most means of making a living wage. Until very recently, women have been legally denied rights routinely exercised by men in the spheres of work, marketplace, and politics, on the grounds that the exercise of such rights would interfere with the performance of their domestic responsibilities. All of this obviously reinforced the patriarchal structure of marriage, but the myth of the separation of the public and the domestic, of the political from the personal, was sustained throughout. Even now that most of the explicit legal disabilities of women have been done away with, the state has a direct hand in regulating family life in such crucial areas as marriage, divorce, and child custody. Who can marry whom, who is legally the child of whom, on what grounds marriages can be dissolved, and whether both spouses or only one must consent to their dissolution, are all directly determined by legislation. In turn, such laws themselves and how they are applied can have a critical impact on how people live their domestic lives, and thence a cyclical effect on their entire lives.

As Frances Olsen has pointed out with great clarity and perceptiveness, the very notion that the state has the option to intervene or not to intervene in the family is not only mythical but meaningless. In many ways "the state is responsible for the background rules that affect people's domestic behaviours." The law does not on the one hand legitimize any and all kinds of behaviour within the family—murder being the most obvious

example. But neither does it regulate the behaviour of family members toward each other in the same way that it regulates the behaviour of strangers; for example, parents can "ground" their children as a means of discipline, or enlist the state's help in restraining children who run away. Children cannot sue their parents (as others could) for kidnapping them on such occasions and, as Olsen says, "the staunchest opponents of state intervention in the family will insist that the state reinforce parents' authority over their children." "Because the state is deeply implicated in the formation and functioning of families," she argues, "it is nonsense to talk about whether the state does or does not intervene in the family."[6] On the vital question of divorce, for example, would "nonintervention" mean allowing divorce, or not allowing it? Making a divorce difficult or easy to acquire? The issue is not whether, but *how* the state intervenes. The myth that state intervention in the family is an option allows those who support the status quo to call it "nonintervention" and to label policies that would alter it—such as the provision of shelters for battered wives—"intervention." This language takes the focus off more pertinent questions such as whether the policy in question is equitable or prevents harm to the vulnerable.[7] Chapter 8[8] suggests some ways in which the state and its laws, which cannot avoid playing a crucial role in marriage and the family, might do so in ways that are more just and equitable than they do at present.

The third reason it is invalid to assume a clear dichotomy between a non-political sphere of family life and a public or political sphere is that domestic life is where most of our early socialization takes place. Feminist scholarship has contributed much to our understanding of how we *become* our gendered selves. Psychoanalytic and other psychologically based theories have explained how gender is reproduced specifically through gendered parenting. One of the earliest of such theories of development (though still highly influential, on account of its persuasiveness) is that of Nancy Chodorow. She argues, building on object-relations theory, that a child's experience of individuation—separating from the caregiver with whom he or she is at first psychologically fused—is a very different experience for those of the same sex as the nurturer than it is for those of the other sex.[9] In a gender-structured society like ours, where primary nurturers are almost always mothers (and, if not, other females), this makes for a sexually differentiated developmental path for girls and for boys. The psychological task of identification with the same-sexed parent is very different for girls, for whom the mother (or female surrogate) is usually present, than for boys, for whom the parent to identify with is often absent for long periods of the day, engaged in tasks the child has no concrete knowledge of. Chodorow argues that, as a result, the personality characteristics in girls and women that make them more psychologically connected with others, more likely to choose nurturing and to be regarded as especially suited for it—and those in men that lead them to a greater need and capacity for individuation and orientation toward achieving "public" status—can be explained by the assignation of primary parenting within the existing gender structure. Thus mothering itself is "reproduced" in girls. Once we admit the idea that significant differences between women and men are *created* by the existing division of labour within the family, it becomes increasingly obvious just how political an institution the family is.

Moreover, the connections between domestic life and the rest of life are accentuated by the fact that the complete answer to the question of why women are primary parents cannot be arrived at by looking solely at the family and at the psychology of gender development. A large part of the answer is to be found in the sex segregation of the workplace, where the great majority of women are still concentrated in low-paid, dead-end occupations. This fact makes it economically "rational" in most two-parent families for the mother to be the primary child rearer, which continues the cycle of gender.

A fourth respect in which "the personal is political" and the public/domestic dichotomy breaks down is that the division of labour within most families raises psychological as well as practical barriers against women in all other spheres. In liberal democratic politics, as well as in most workplace situations, speech and argument are often recognized as crucial components of full participation. Michael Walzer, for example, writes: "Democracy is . . . *the political way* of allocating power. . . . What counts is argument among the citizens. Democracy puts a premium on speech, persuasion, rhetorical skill. Ideally, the citizen who makes the most persuasive argument . . . gets his way."[10] Women, however, are often handicapped by being deprived of any authority in their speech. As one recent feminist analysis has diagnosed the problem, it is not "that women have not learned how to be in authority," but rather "that authority currently is conceptualized so that female voices are excluded from it."[11] This results, to a large extent, from the fact that women's public and private personae are inextricably linked in the minds of many men and is exacerbated by the fact that women are often represented in token numbers, both in influential positions in the workplace and on authoritative political bodies. One example of this is the sex bias in the nation's courtrooms, which has been increasingly well documented during the last few years. It affects judicial attitudes toward women as defendants, plaintiffs, victims, and lawyers, with consequent effects on sentencing, treatment of domestic-violence and rape victims, alimony and child support awards, and damages awards.[12] Sometimes women in the public sphere are simply not seen or heard. Sometimes we are seen and heard only insofar as we make ourselves seem as much as possible like men. Sometimes we are silenced by being demeaned or sexually harassed. And sometimes what we say is silenced or distorted because we have projected onto us the personae of particularly important women (especially their mothers) in the intra-psychic lives of men.

All of these handicaps, which women carry with them from the sexual division of labour at home to the outside spheres of life, certainly do not make it easy for us to make transitions back and forth between them. Because of the past and present division of labour between the sexes, for women especially, the public and the domestic are in many ways *not* distinct, separate realms at all. The perception of a sharp dichotomy between them depends on the view of society from a traditional male perspective that tacitly assumes different natures and roles for men and women. It cannot, therefore, be maintained in a truly humanist theory of justice—one that will, for the first time, include all of us. As the next chapter will show further, specifically in the context of contemporary life in the United States, what have been presented as separate spheres are in fact closely linked parts in a cycle of inequality between the sexes.

Chapter 7 Vulnerability by Marriage

. . . [M]ajor contemporary theories of social justice pay little or no attention to the multiple inequalities between the sexes that exist in our society, or to the social construct of gender that gives rise to them. Neither mainstream theorists of social justice nor their critics (with rare exceptions) have paid much attention to the internal inequalities of the family. They have considered the family relevant for one or more of only three reasons. Some have seen the family as an impediment to equal opportunity. But the focus of such discussion has been on class differentials among families, not on sex differentials within them. While the concern that the family limits equality of opportunity is legitimate and serious, theorists who raise it have neglected the issue of gender and therefore ignored important aspects of the problem. Those who discuss the family without paying attention to the inequalities between the sexes are blind to the fact that the gendered family radically limits the equality of opportunity of women and girls of all classes—as well as that of poor and working-class children of both sexes. Nor do they see that the vulnerability of women that results from the patriarchal structure and practices of the family *exacerbates* the problem that the inequality of families poses for children's equality of opportunity. As I shall argue in this chapter, with the increasing prevalence of families headed by a single female, children suffer more and more from the economic vulnerability of women.

Second and third, theorists of justice and their critics have tended either to idealize the family as a social institution for which justice is not an appropriate virtue, or, more rarely, to see it as an important locus for the development of a sense of justice. I have disagreed strongly with those who, focusing on an idealized vision of the family, perceive it as governed by virtues nobler than justice and therefore not needing to be subjected to the tests of justice to which we subject other fundamental social institutions. While I strongly support the *hope* that families will live up to nobler virtues, such as generosity, I contend that in the real world, justice is a virtue of fundamental importance for families, as for other basic social institutions. An important sphere of distribution of many social goods, from the material to the intangible, the family has a history of distributing these goods in far from just ways. It is also, as some who have overlooked its internal justice have acknowledged, a sphere of life that is absolutely crucial to moral development. If justice cannot at least begin to be learned from our day-to-day experience within the family, it seems futile to expect that it can be developed anywhere else. Without just families, how can we expect to have a just society? In particular, if the relationship between a child's parents does not conform to basic standards of justice, how can we expect that child to grow up with a sense of justice?

It is not easy to think about marriage and the family in terms of justice. For one thing, we do not readily associate justice with intimacy, which is one reason some theorists idealize the family. For another, some of the issues that theories of justice are most concerned with, such as differences in standards of living, do not obviously apply among members of a family. Though it is certainly not the case in some countries, in the United States the members of a family, so long as they live together, usually share the same standard of living. As we shall see, however, the question of who earns the family's income, or how the earning of this income is shared, has a great deal to do with the distribution of power and influence within the family, including decisions on how to spend this income. It also affects the distribution of other benefits, including basic security. Here, I present and analyze the facts of contemporary gender-structured marriage in the light of theories about power and vulnerability and

the issues of justice they inevitably raise. I argue that marriage and the family, as currently practised in our society, are unjust institutions. They constitute the pivot of a societal system of gender that renders women vulnerable to dependency, exploitation, and abuse. When we look seriously at the distribution between husbands and wives of such critical social goods as work (paid and unpaid), power, prestige, self-esteem, opportunities for self-development, and both physical and economic security, we find socially constructed inequalities between them, right down the list.

The argument I shall make in this chapter depends to a large extent on contemporary empirical data, but also reflects the insights of two theorists, moral philosopher Robert Goodin and economist Albert O. Hirschman. Neither has used his argument to make a case about the injustice of the gender-structured family, but both establish convincing arguments about power and vulnerability that will be invaluable as we look at the data about contemporary marriage.

Goodin's recent book *Protecting the Vulnerable* discusses the significance of socially caused vulnerability for issues of justice. He argues that, over and above the general moral obligations that we owe to persons in general, "we bear special responsibilities for protecting those who are particularly vulnerable to us."[13] His major aim is to justify the obligations that welfare states place on citizens to contribute to the welfare of their more vulnerable fellow citizens. But his arguments can be employed to shed light on a number of other important social issues and institutions, including marriage and the family. Goodin's theory is particularly applicable to marriage because of its concern not only with the protection of the vulnerable but also with the moral status of vulnerability itself. Obviously, as he acknowledges, some cases of vulnerability have a large natural component—the vulnerability of infants, for example, although societies differ in how they allocate responsibility for protecting infants. Some instances of vulnerability that may at first appear "natural," such as those caused by illness, are in fact to a greater or lesser extent due to existing social arrangements.[14] And "some of the most important dependencies and vulnerabilities seem to be *almost wholly social in character*" (emphasis added).[15] Because asymmetric vulnerabilities create social obligations, which may fail to be fulfilled, and because they open up opportunities for exploitation, Goodin argues that insofar as they are alterable they are morally unacceptable and should be minimized. In this, he cites and follows the example of John Stuart Mill, who complained about the "great error of reformers and philanthropists [who] . . . nibble at the consequences of unjust power, instead of redressing the injustice itself."[16] As Goodin concludes, in the case of those vulnerabilities that are "created, shaped, or sustained by current social arrangements . . . [w]hile we should always strive to protect the vulnerable, we should also strive to reduce the latter sort of vulnerabilities insofar as they render the vulnerable liable to exploitation."[17]

One of the tests Goodin employs to distinguish such unacceptable relations of asymmetrical vulnerability from acceptable relations of mutual vulnerability or interdependence is to examine the respective capacities of the two parties to withdraw from the relationship. Even if there is some degree of inequality in a relationship, Goodin says, "as long as the subordinate party can withdraw without severe cost, the superordinate cannot exploit him."[18] As I shall argue, the differing respective potentials for satisfactory withdrawal from the relationship is one of the major elements making marriage, in its typical contemporary manifestations in the United States, a morally unacceptable relationship of vulnerability.

The idea that the mutuality or asymmetry of a relationship can be measured by the relative capacities of the parties to withdraw from it has been developed extensively by Albert O. Hirschman, in two books written many years apart. In his 1970 book entitled *Exit, Voice and Loyalty*, Hirschman makes a convincing connection between the influence of voice by members within groups or institutions and the feasibility of their exit from them. There is a complex relation, he argues, between voice and exit. On the one hand, if the exit option is readily available, this will "tend to *atrophy the development of the art of voice.*" Thus, for example, dissatisfied customers who can easily purchase equivalent goods from another firm are unlikely to expend their energies voicing complaints. On the other hand, the nonexistence or low feasibility of the exit option can impede the effectiveness of voice, since the *threat* of exit, whether explicit or implicit, is an important means of making one's voice influential. Thus "voice is not only handicapped when exit is possible, but also, though in a quite different way, when it is not." Because of this, for members' influence to be most effective, "there should be the possibility of exit, but exit should not be too easy or too attractive."[19] Hirschman concludes that institutions that deter exit by exacting a very high price for it, thereby rendering implausible the threat of exit, also repress the use and effectiveness of voice. Thus both potential modes of influence for combating deterioration are rendered ineffective.

Because the subjects of Hirschman's attention in *Exit, Voice and Loyalty* are groups with many members, his concern is with the power of the members vis-à-vis the institution, rather than with the power of the members relative to one another. But in the case of a two-member institution, such as marriage, special dynamics result from the fact that exit by one partner does not just weaken the institution, but rather results in its dissolution. Whether or not the other party wishes to exit, he or she is effectively expelled by the decision of the other to exit. Because of this, the *relative* potential of the exit option for the two parties is crucial for the relationship's power structure. Hirschman has made this argument, in the context of international relations, in a book published 25 years earlier, *National Power and the Structure of Foreign Trade.*[20] There he showed how state A can increase its power and influence by developing trading relations with state B, which is more dependent on the continuance of the trading relationship than A is. While both states gain something from the trade, the gain is far more significant in the one case than in the other. Thus the less dependent state's greater potential for exiting unharmed from the relationship gives it power or influence that can be used (through explicit or implicit threat or withdrawal) to make the more dependent state comply with its wishes. In addition, because of the extent of its dependence on trade with A, state B may alter its economic behaviour in such a way that it becomes even more dependent on its trade with A.[21] Power (which may or may not remain latent) is likely to result from dependencies that are entered into voluntarily by parties whose initial resources and options differ, and in such circumstances the asymmetric dependency may well increase in the course of the relationship.

How do these principles apply to marriage? Few people would disagree with the statement that marriage involves, in some respects, especially emotionally, *mutual* vulnerability and dependence. It is, clearly, also a relationship in which some aspects of unequal vulnerability are not determined along sex lines. For example, spouses may vary in the extent of their love for and emotional dependence on each other; it is certainly not the case that wives always love their husbands more than they are loved by them, or vice versa. Nevertheless, as we shall see, in crucial respects gender-structured marriage *involves women in a cycle of socially caused and distinctly asymmetric vulnerability*. The division of labour within marriage (except in rare cases) makes wives far more likely than husbands to be exploited both within the marital relationship and in the world of work outside the home. To a great extent and in numerous ways, contemporary women in our society are *made* vulnerable by marriage itself. They are first set up for vulnerability during their developing years by their personal (and socially reinforced) expectations that they will be the primary caretakers of children, and that in fulfilling this role they will need to try to attract and to keep the economic support of a man, to whose work life they will be expected to give priority. They are rendered vulnerable by the actual division of labour within almost all current marriages. They are disadvantaged at work by the fact that the world of wage work, including the professions, is still largely structured around the assumption that "workers" have wives at home. They are rendered far more vulnerable if they become the primary caretakers of children, and their vulnerability peaks if their marriages dissolve and they become single parents.

Part of the reason that many non-feminist social theorists have failed to recognize this pattern is that they confuse the socially caused (and therefore avoidable) vulnerability of women with the largely natural (and therefore largely unavoidable) vulnerability of children. This goes along with the usually unargued and certainly unfounded assumption that women are inevitably the primary caretakers of children. But as I shall show, women are made vulnerable, both economically and socially, by the interconnected traditions of female responsibility for rearing children and female subordination and dependence, of which both the history and the contemporary practices of marriage form a significant part.

It may be argued that it makes no sense to claim that something as ill-defined and variable as "modern marriage" is unjust, since marriages and families take so many forms, and not all marriages result in the dependence and vulnerability of their female members. There is some validity to this objection, and I shall try to counter it by making qualifications and pointing out exceptions to some of the general points I shall make. Part of the peculiarity of contemporary marriage comes from its very lack of definition. The fact that society seems no longer to have any consensual view of the norms and expectations of marriage is particularly apparent from the gulf that exists between the continued *perception* of most men and women that it is still the primary responsibility of husbands to "provide for" their wives by participating in wage work and of wives to perform a range of unpaid "services" for their husbands, and the *fact* that most women, including mothers of small children, are both in the labour force *and* performing the vast majority of household duties. In addition, the persistent perception of the male as provider is irreconcilable with both the prevalence of separation and divorce and the fact that, more and more, women and children are not being provided for after divorce. Between the expectations and the frequent outcome lies an abyss that not only is unjust in itself but radically affects the ways in which people behave within marriage. There is no way to alleviate the continuing inequality of women without more clearly defining

and also reforming marriage. It seems evident, both from the disagreements between traditionalists and feminists and from the discrepancy between people's expectations of marriage and what in fact often happens to those who enter into it that there exists no clear current consensus in this society about what marriage is or should be.

Marriage has a long history, and we live in its shadow. It is a clear case of Marx's notion that we make our history "under circumstances directly encountered, given and transmitted from the past."[22] Certainly, gender is central to the way most people think about marriage. A recent, detailed study of thousands of couples, of different types—married and unmarried, heterosexual, gay and lesbian—confirms the importance of gender to our concept of marriage. Philip Blumstein and Pepper Schwartz's findings in *American Couples* demonstrate how not only current family law but the traditional expectations of marriage influence the attitudes, expectations, and behaviour of married couples. By contrast, the lack of expectations about gender, and the lack of history of the institution of marriage, allow gay and lesbian couples more freedom in ordering their lives together and more chance to do so in an egalitarian manner. As the study concludes: "First, while the heterosexual model offers more stability and certainty, it inhibits change, innovation, and *choice* regarding roles and tasks. Second, the heterosexual model, which provides so much efficiency, is predicated on the man's being the dominant partner." The unmarried couples interviewed did not, in general, assume so readily that one partner would be the primary economic provider or that they would pool their income and assets. Homosexual couples, because of the absence of both marriage and the "gender factor," made even fewer such assumptions than did cohabiting heterosexual couples. They were almost unanimous, for example, in refusing to assign to either partner the role of homemaker. By contrast, many of the married respondents still enthusiastically subscribed to the traditional female/male separation of household work from wage work. While the authors also found the more egalitarian, two-paycheck marriage "emerging," they conclude that "the force of the previous tradition still guides the behaviour of most modern marriages."[23]

It is important to recollect, in this context, how recently white married women in the United States have begun to work outside the home in significant numbers. Black women have always worked, first as slaves, then mostly—until very recently—as domestic servants. But in 1860, only 15 per cent of all women were in the paid labour force and, right up to World War II, wage work for married women was strongly disapproved of. In 1890, only 5 per cent of married women were in the labour force, and by 1960 the rate of married women's labour force participation had still reached only 30 per cent. Moreover, wage work has a history of extreme segregation by sex that is closely related to the traditional female role within marriage. The largest category of women workers were domestic servants as late as 1950, since which time clerical workers have outnumbered them. Service (mostly no longer domestic) is still very predominantly female work. Even the female-dominated professions, such as nursing, grade-school teaching, and library work, have been "pink-collar labour ghettos [which] have historically discouraged high work ambitions that might detract from the pull of home and children." Like saleswomen and clerical workers, these female professionals "tend to arrive early in their 'careers' at a point above which they cannot expect to rise."[24] In sum, married women's wage work has a history of being exceptional, and women's wage work in general has been—as much of it still is—highly segregated and badly paid.

The traditional idea of sex-differentiated marital responsibility, with its provider-husband and domestic-wife roles, continues to be a strong influence on what men and women think and how they behave. Husbands, at least, tend to feel this way even when their wives *do* work outside the home; and when there is disagreement about whether the wife should work, it is more often the case that she wants to but that he does not want to "let" her. Thirty-four per cent of the husbands and 25 per cent of the wives surveyed by Blumstein and Schwartz did not think that couples should share the responsibility for earning a living. These percentages rise sharply when children are involved: 64 per cent of husbands and 60 per cent of wives did not think that the wife should be employed if a couple has small children.[25] Given the emphasis our society places on economic success, belief in the male provider role strongly reinforces the domination of men within marriage. Although, as we shall see, many wives actually work longer hours (counting paid and unpaid work) than their husbands, the fact that a husband's work is predominantly paid gives him not only status and prestige, both within and outside the marriage, but also a greater sense of entitlement. As a consequence, wives experiencing divorce, especially if they have been housewives and mothers throughout marriage, are likely to devalue their own contributions to the marriage and to discount their right to share its assets. "Many divorcing women still see the money their husbands have earned as 'his money.'"[26] In ongoing marriages too, it is not uncommon for husbands to use the fact that they are the primary breadwinners to enforce their views or wishes.[27] . . .

Exit, Threat of Exit, and Power in the Family

At the beginning of this chapter, I summarized Goodin's argument that socially created asymmetric vulnerability is morally unacceptable, and should be minimized. I also referred to Hirschman's arguments about the effects of persons' relative potentials for exit on their power or influence within relationships or groups. Neither of these theorists considers the institution of contemporary marriage an example of such power imbalance.[28] But the evidence presented here suggests that typical, contemporary, gender-structured marriage is an excellent example of socially created vulnerability, partly because the asymmetric dependency of wives on husbands affects their potential for satisfactory exit, and thereby influences the effectiveness of their voice within the marriage.

There has been virtual silence among theorists about the dimension of power in the family that accrues to the spouse who would lose less by exiting from the marriage—a dimension that those who study it seem loath to recognize, partly, no doubt, because it ill accords with society's beliefs about how intimate or romantic relationships are conducted. Three rare scholars who have explicitly applied the notion that potential for exit affects power of voice within marriage are Heer, critiquing Blood and Wolfe's distorted theory of family power, and Bergmann and Fuchs in their recent studies of women's continuing inequality.[29] All three make brief but succinct and lucid arguments that are clearly further validated by the evidence presented here—that marriage is a clear case of asymmetric vulnerability, in which not only power to make decisions but also power to prevent issues from becoming objects of decision is related to the spouses' relative opportunities to exit satisfactorily from the relationship. More typically, marriage is not treated as a situation to which the general theory of the effects of unequal dependency and potential for exit on power applies. Blood asserts, for example, that Heer's "exit" theory is rendered implausible by the fact that "*only* 37 per cent" of the couples questioned in a 1939 study of marital success or failure had ever contemplated separation or divorce.[30] Surely this is a remarkably high percentage, especially given the far lower divorce rate then than now.

Of course, the family and other personal relations are special cases of this theory, as of so many others. But the aspects of families that make them different from other institutions such as political parties, schools, and so on, to which theories about the effect of different potentials for exit on power have typically been applied, do not render these theories inapplicable to them. Families are typically held together by strong ties of loyalty, and separation or divorce represents a drastic "solution" to their conflicts. But, particularly now that one in two marriages is expected to end in divorce, it is simply un-realistic to suggest that the threat of exit is absent, especially at times of marital conflict, or that the different abilities of spouses implicitly or explicitly to call on this threat are not likely to affect power and influence in the relationship. Ending a marriage usually causes pain and dislocation for both adults as well as for any children involved. However, the argument presented in this chapter has demonstrated clearly that, in all the ways that are affected by economic deprivation, women and children are likely to suffer considerably more than men from marital dissolution. It is highly probable that most wives, well aware of this fact, take it into consideration in deciding how firm a stand to take on, or even whether to raise, important issues that are likely to be conflictual. We cannot adequately understand the distribution of power in the family without taking this factor into account, and the idea that marriage is a just relationship of mutual vulnerability cannot survive this analysis.

If we are to aim at making the family, our most fundamental social grouping, more just, we must work toward eradicating the socially created vulnerabilities of women that stem from the division of labour and the resultant division of power within it. As I shall argue in the final chapter, in order to do anything effective about the cycle of women's socially created vulnerability, we must take into account the current lack of clarity in law, public policy, and public opinion about *what marriage is*. Since evidently we do not all agree about what it is or should be, we must think in terms of building family and work institutions that enable people to structure their personal lives in different ways. If they are to avoid injustice to women and children, these institutions must encourage the avoidance of socially created vulnerabilities by facilitating and reinforcing the equal sharing of paid and unpaid work between men and women, and consequently the equalizing of their opportunities and obligations in general. They must also ensure that those who enter into relationships in which there is a division of labour that might render them vulnerable are fully protected against such vulnerability, both within the context of the ongoing relationship and in the event of its dissolution.

Post-Reading Questions

1. Why is an analysis of the power structures and dynamics within families and marriage so important, according to Okin?
2. How has the sharp conceptual distinction between the public and private realms hampered political philosophers in their thinking about justice?
3. What does Okin mean by her reference to the "socially created vulnerabilities" that women face?
4. What is the relationship between justice within the family and justice within society as a whole, according to Okin?

CASE STUDY
TAKING GENDER SERIOUSLY: *R. v. LAVALLEE*

Introduction

This case concerns Angelique Lyn Lavallee, who was charged with murder after shooting her common-law husband, Kevin Rust, in the back of the head. Tried in the criminal division of the Provincial Court, Lavallee's defence focused on her situation as a victim of domestic violence. Her claim was supported by the expert testimony of a psychologist, and she was subsequently acquitted. The Crown then appealed the case. The Manitoba Court of Appeal overturned the acquittal and ordered a new trial, taking issue with the admissibility of the expert testimony and the trial Judge's instruction to the jury on this matter.

Lavallee appealed the decision to the Supreme Court, which in turn took up the issues of the admissibility of expert testimony about battered women and the availability of self-defence as legal grounds for acquittal. Self-defence, which falls under section 34 (2) of the Criminal Code, legally requires that three conditions be met:

1. The accused's action is the result of believing that he or she is the victim of unlawful assault.
2. The accused must have a reasonable apprehension of death or grievous bodily harm.
3. The accused must reasonably believe that he or she could not otherwise preserve his or her person from grave harm.

Importantly, the accused's belief about each of these must be objectively reasonable. At the time of the shooting, Lavallee was not under immediate attack. Her case is therefore an important one, because it changed the way that claims of self-defence are adjudicated in cases of persons who are victims of domestic violence. Henceforth, the perception of the accused with respect to the immediacy of the threat (in cases of domestic violence) is deemed relevant.

To shed new light on the question of self-defence, however, the subjective aspect of the conditions for battered women needed to be introduced, which only expert testimony could establish. But in its appeal, the Crown argued that the expert testimony was not needed because it was unnecessary; all that mattered were the bare "facts" of the case. The Court of Appeal sided with the Crown when it accepted that "there was ample evidence for the jury to conclude that Rust abused the accused" and that the expert testimony based on out-of-court statements by the accused should not have been given the same weight as other evidence provided in the court. The Supreme Court thus needed to determine whether Lavallee's self-defence case could have been presented minus the expert testimony—whether, in other words, the expert testimony was superfluous, or warranted.

The feminist critique of gender as socially constructed helps to illuminate the Lavallee case, for it suggests that both the reasoning of the Court of Appeal and the narrow framework of self-defence it employed are fundamentally biased against women. The Supreme Court acknowledged this bias in its ruling. Moreover, it located this discriminatory attitude in the history of a legal system that accepted the notion that women were in essence the property of men—a view that grounded the latter's right to discipline their wives, historically speaking. Susan Okin's argument that seemingly fair and neutral laws frequently ignore the particular circumstances, vulnerabilities, and burdens of women is also relevant here. By failing to acknowledge the special situation faced by battered women, an apparently neutral criminal code—and specifically, laws concerning self-defence—systematically disadvantages women and so is unjust according to liberal justice.

The key matters to be decided in this case, according to the Supreme Court, pertained to the temporal element of self-defence—i.e., the question of whether the threat was imminent—and the gravity of the threat. The Court's decision raises questions about the imposition of an objective criterion of reasonableness on the subjective aspect of the threat, suggesting that it ignores the unique experience of battered women. The Court furthermore found that the "battered women syndrome" establishes that in such cases the issue is not what an outsider would have reasonably perceived but what the accused *herself* reasonably perceived, given her situation and past experiences. Those who work with survivors of domestic violence note that the imbalance of power and the periodic nature of the abuse contribute to the victim's perception of the risks she faces and what options are open to her. Setting these issues against the broader tapestry of a society still rife with sexual inequalities, Okin's analysis helps us to imagine what a gender-sensitive approach to legal reform of the Criminal Code might look like.

From *R. v. Lavallee*, [1990] 1 S.C.R. 852

R. v. Lavallee, *[1990] 1 S.C.R. 852.*
http://scc.lexum.org/decisia-scc-csc/scc-csc/scc-csc/en/item/599/index.do

. . .

[The judgment of Dickson C.J. and Lamer, Wilson, L'Heureux-Dubé, Gonthier, and Cory JJ. was delivered by Justice Wilson.]

The narrow issue raised on this appeal is the adequacy of a trial judge's instructions to the jury regarding expert evidence. The broader issue concerns the utility of expert evidence in assisting a jury confronted by a plea of self-defence to a murder charge by a common-law wife who had been battered by the deceased.

1. The Facts

The appellant, who was 22 years old at the time, had been living with Kevin Rust for some three to four years. Their residence was the scene of a boisterous party on August 30, 1986. In the early hours of August 31 after most of the guests had departed the appellant and Rust had an argument in the upstairs bedroom which was used by the appellant. Rust was killed by a single shot in the back of the head from a .303 calibre rifle fired by the appellant as he was leaving the room.

. . .

The relationship between the appellant and Rust was volatile and punctuated by frequent arguments and violence. They would apparently fight for two or three days at a time or several times a week. Considerable evidence was led at trial indicating that the appellant was frequently a victim of physical abuse at the hands of Rust. Between 1983 and 1986 the appellant made several trips to hospital for injuries including severe bruises, a fractured nose, multiple contusions and a black eye. One of the attending physicians, Dr. Dirks, testified that he disbelieved the appellant's explanation on one such occasion that she had sustained her injuries by falling from a horse.

A friend of the deceased, Robert Ezako, testified that he had witnessed several fights between the appellant and the deceased and that he had seen the appellant point a gun at the deceased twice and threaten to kill him if he ever touched her again. Under cross-examination

Ezako admitted to seeing or hearing the deceased beat up the appellant on several occasions and, during the preliminary inquiry, described her screaming during one such incident like "a pig being butchered." He also saw the appellant with a black eye on one occasion and doubted that it was the result of an accident as she and the deceased stated at the time. Another acquaintance of the couple recalled seeing the appellant with a split lip.

At one point on the night of his death Rust chased the appellant outside the house and a mutual friend, Norman Kolish, testified that the appellant pleaded with Rust to "leave me alone" and sought Kolish's protection by trying to hide behind him. A neighbour overheard Rust and the appellant arguing and described the tone of the former as "argumentative" and the latter as "scared." Later, between the first and second gunshot, he testified that he could hear that "somebody was beating up somebody" and the screams were female. Another neighbour testified to hearing noises like gunshots and then a woman's voice sounding upset saying "Fuck. He punched me in the face. He punched me in the face." He looked out the window and saw a woman matching the description of the appellant.

Three witnesses who attended the party testified to hearing sounds of yelling, pushing, shoving and thumping coming from upstairs prior to the gunshots. It is not disputed that two shots were fired by the appellant. The first one went through a window screen. It is not clear where Rust was at the time. The appellant in her statement says that he was upstairs, while another witness places him in the basement. The second shot was the fatal one. After the second shot was fired the appellant was seen visibly shaken and upset and was heard to say "Rooster [the deceased] was beating me so I shot him," and "You know how he treated me, you've got to help me." The arresting officer testified that en route to the police station the appellant made various comments in the police car, including "He said if I didn't kill him first he would kill me. I hope he lives. I really love him," and "He told me he was gonna kill me when everyone left."

The police officer who took the appellant's statement testified to seeing a red mark on her arm where she said the deceased had grabbed her. When the coroner who performed an autopsy on the deceased was shown pictures of the appellant (who had various bruises), he testified that it was "entirely possible" that bruises on the deceased's left hand were occasioned by an assault on the appellant. Another doctor noted an injury to the appellant's pinkie finger consistent with those sustained by the adoption of a defensive stance.

The expert evidence which forms the subject matter of the appeal came from Dr. Fred Shane, a psychiatrist with extensive professional experience in the treatment of battered wives. At the request of defence counsel Dr. Shane prepared a psychiatric assessment of the appellant. The substance of Dr. Shane's opinion was that the appellant had been terrorized by Rust to the point of feeling trapped, vulnerable, worthless and unable to escape the relationship despite the violence. At the same time, the continuing pattern of abuse put her life in danger. In Dr. Shane's opinion the appellant's shooting of the deceased was a final desperate act by a woman who sincerely believed that she would be killed that night:

> . . . I think she felt, she felt in the final tragic moment that her life was on the line, that unless she defended herself, unless she reacted in a violent way that she would die. I mean he made it very explicit to her, from what she told me and from the information I have from the material that you forwarded to me, that she had, I think, to defend herself against his violence.

Dr. Shane stated that his opinion was based on four hours of formal interviews with the appellant, a police report of the incident (including the appellant's statement), hospital reports documenting eight of her visits to emergency departments between 1983 and 1985, and an interview with the appellant's mother. In the course of his testimony Dr. Shane related many things told to him by the appellant for which there was no admissible evidence. They were not in the appellant's statement to the police and she did not testify at trial. For example, Dr. Shane mentioned several episodes of abuse described by the appellant for which there were no hospital reports. He also related the appellant's disclosure to him that she had lied to doctors about the cause of her injuries. Dr. Shane testified that such fabrication was typical of battered women. The appellant also recounted to Dr. Shane occasions on which Rust would allegedly beat her, then beg her forgiveness and ply her with flowers and temporary displays of kindness. Dr. Shane was aware of the incidents described by Ezako about the appellant's pointing a gun at Rust on two occasions and explained it as "an issue for trying to defend herself. She was afraid that she would be assaulted." The appellant denied to Dr. Shane that she had homicidal fantasies about Rust and mentioned that she had smoked some marijuana on the night in question. These facts were related by Dr. Shane in the course of his testimony.

The appellant was acquitted by a jury but the verdict was overturned by a majority of the Manitoba Court of Appeal and the case sent back for retrial.

2. Lower Court Judgments

Manitoba Queen's Bench (Scott A.C.J.Q.B.)

After Dr. Shane testified and was cross-examined Crown counsel brought an application to have the evidence of Dr. Shane withdrawn from the jury. The first reason he gave was that the jury was perfectly capable of deciding the issue on the admissible evidence and that expert evidence was therefore "unnecessary and superfluous." The second reason was that Dr. Shane's comment that he found the accused credible was "wholly improper" in light of her failure to testify as to the facts upon which Dr. Shane based his opinion. The trial judge denied the application stating that the Crown's concerns could be met through an appropriate charge to the jury. . . .

With respect to the appellant's out-of-court statements, the trial judge cautioned the jury that, "[a]s with the verbal testimony, you may accept all, part or none of the statements attributed to Lyn Lavallee and as with all evidence, the real question is whether the things reported to have been said are true." Later he introduced Dr. Shane's testimony as follows:

> As counsel put it yesterday, you cannot decide this case on things you didn't hear. You cannot decide this case on things the witnesses didn't see or hear.
>
> A somewhat different, though related, evidentiary caution has to be noted with respect to the expert opinion evidence of Dr. Shane. There were two matters in his evidence, two facts, two sources of information that he had reference to which are not evidence in this case and that is the suggestion that people had been smoking marijuana at the party and the confirmatory evidence, as he called it, received from the mother of Lyn Lavallee. These are not matters in evidence before you.
>
> For example, there is absolutely no evidence that anyone was smoking marijuana at this party

and you must not consider that it took place. There is no evidence from the mother of the accused before you. The extent to which this impacts on the weight of the opinion of Dr. Shane is a matter for you to decide. You must appraise the value of the resulting opinion in light of the fact that there is no evidence about these matters before you. . . .

. . . *In terms of the matters considered by Dr. Shane he is left, therefore, with the deceased's (sic) statement, some supplementary information from the police report and his interpretation of the hospital records.* [Emphasis added.]

If the premises upon which the information is substantially based has not been proven in evidence, it is up to you to conclude that it is not safe to attach a great deal of weight to the opinion. An opinion of an expert depends, to a large extent, on the validity of the facts assumed by the evidence by the expert. . . .

The trial judge then reviewed the evidence given by Dr. Shane regarding the appellant's emotional and mental state at the time of the killing. He reiterated Dr. Shane's opinion that the appellant's act was "a reflection of her catastrophic fear that she had to defend herself." He also drew attention to Dr. Shane's awareness that the appellant would occasionally be the aggressor despite her denial to him that she had homicidal fantasies . . . (*Manitoba Court of Appeal* (Monnin C.J.M., Philp and Huband JJ.) (1988). [Edited majority opinion is summarized.]

Writing for himself and Monnin C.J.M., Philp J.A. begins by observing . . . that there was "ample evidence for the jury to conclude that Rust abused the accused." He adds that it "was a reasonable inference for the jury to draw that the injuries resulted from Rust's violent and abusive behaviour, notwithstanding her explanations at the time to the contrary."

Turning to Dr. Shane's evidence, the majority comments that in the course of stating the factual basis of his opinions and conclusions, Dr. Shane referred to many facts, incidents and events which were not before the court in the form of admissible evidence. These included: the smoking of marijuana on the night of the shooting; the deterioration of the intimate relationship between the appellant and Rust (the appellant had told Shane that they were sleeping in separate bedrooms); a reference to an abortion the appellant had obtained, after which Rust allegedly threatened to tell her parents that she was a "baby killer"; incidents where Rust would allegedly beg forgiveness from the appellant after beating her up; the appellant's "incredible remorse" after killing Rust, and the appellant's denial to Dr. Shane that she harboured homicidal fantasies about Rust.

Philp J.A. then refers to the appellant's written statement to the police in which she professed her love for Rust and her hope that he wouldn't die. . . . [H]e pointed out "discrepancies and conflicts in the narrative of events in the accused's statement, and the evidence of witnesses who testified at her trial," particularly with respect to the location of Rust when the first shot was fired. With respect to the accused's unsworn statement he concludes, . . .

. . . in the circumstances of this case, where much of the factual basis for the plea of self-defence lay in the statement of the accused, the jury ought not to have been told to "give this evidence no more nor less weight than any other evidence heard by you"; . . .

The instructions of the trial judge to the jury with respect to the evidence of Dr. Shane are a more troubling matter. The problem presented by the accused's out of court statement and comments, in my view, comes to a head in that context.

Philp J.A. then turns to the judgment of Dickson J. (as he then was) in *R. v. Abbey*, a case from this Court dealing with the admissibility of expert evidence and the use to which it can be put. After quoting from the judgment, Philp J.A. states . . .:

Canadian authorities support the view that an expert can state to the court the basis for his opinion, and that it is desirable that he do so. In Abbey, Dickson, J., confirmed this approach and . . . cautioned: "Before any weight can be given to an expert's opinion, the facts upon which the opinion is based must be found to exist."

Referring back to the case at bar, Philp J.A. comments . . . that the record did not disclose "the full extent of these secondhand facts, or their importance in the formation of Dr. Shane's opinion; nor can one speculate what his opinion might have been had his inquiries been limited to the admissible evidence properly before the court."

In his assessment of the trial judge's charge to the jury, Philp J.A. remarks that the trial judge properly pointed out that there was no evidence about marijuana smoking on the night in question, nor was there any evidence before them from the mother of the appellant. Philp J.A. found this latter warning insufficient. While he considered the trial judge's general instructions regarding the weight that should be placed on expert evidence to be proper, he felt that they "did not go far enough in the circumstances of this case". He gives three reasons . . . :

Firstly, the comments, placed in juxtaposition to the trial judge's reference to the "two facts, two sources of information that (Dr. Shane) had reference to which are not evidence in this case . . .," lose their impact. The jury may well have concluded that the trial judge's warning related only to Dr. Shane's reference to the marijuana, and to the "confirmatory evidence" of the accused's mother.

Secondly, I think the trial judge was in error in telling the jury that the police report (presumably, the document referred to by Dr. Shane as the "police summary of the incident") was a matter left for Dr. Shane to consider. That document was not evidence before the court, nor do we know what facts it contained.

Finally, although the trial judge did not refer to Dr. Shane's interviews with the accused (and her mother) when he told the jury what matters were left for Dr. Shane to consider, the conclusion that the jury was to ignore facts related in these interviews unless they were otherwise established by admissible evidence (and to weigh Dr. Shane's opinion accordingly) is dispelled by the trial judge's later references to these interviews.

Philp J.A. then quotes the passages from the trial judge's charge in which he reviewed Dr. Shane's admission that he would have to reassess his position if what the appellant had told him was not true. Philp J.A. also draws attention to the remark by the trial judge that the Crown emphasized that Shane's opinion would stand or fall on the appellant's veracity. In Philp J.A.'s view, these aspects of the trial judge's instructions were also deficient . . . :

> With respect, those comments of the trial judge, so crucial to the plea of self-defence, amounted to a misdirection. The issue was not just the veracity of the accused (and at this point, a careful charge with respect to the accused's unsworn self-serving evidence would have been appropriate). The pivotal questions the jury had to decide were the extent to which Dr. Shane's opinion was based on facts not established by admissible evidence; and the weight to be accorded to his opinion.

Finally, Philp J.A. finds . . . that the trial judge's charge fell so short of the standard required in *Abbey* that a new trial was warranted:

> This was an unusual case. The accused shot Rust in the back of the head when he was leaving the bedroom. The accused says Rust loaded the rifle and handed it to her. Friends of the accused and Rust, including the couple who had planned to stay overnight, were present in another part of the residence. In these circumstances, absent the evidence of Dr. Shane, it is unlikely that the jury, properly instructed, would have accepted the accused's plea of self-defence. The accused did

not testify, and the foundation for her plea of self-defence was, in the main, her unsworn exculpatory evidence and the hearsay evidence related by Dr. Shane. Because Dr. Shane relied upon facts not in evidence, including those related to him in his lengthy interviews with the accused, the factual basis for his opinion should have been detailed in his evidence.

Philp J.A. concludes by suggesting to the Crown that they proceed with a charge of manslaughter rather than second degree murder since a properly instructed jury would, in his opinion, be unlikely to convict the appellant of the latter offence.

3. Relevant Legislation

Criminal Code, R.S.C., 1985, c. C-46:
> 34. . . .
> (2) Everyone who is unlawfully assaulted and who causes death or grievous bodily harm in repelling the assault is justified if
> (a) he causes it under reasonable apprehension of death or grievous bodily harm from the violence with which the assault was originally made or with which the assailant pursues his purposes, and
> (b) he believes on reasonable and probable grounds, that he cannot otherwise preserve himself from death or grievous bodily harm.

4. Issues on Appeal

It should be noted that two bases for ordering a new trial are implicit in the reasons of the majority of the Court of Appeal. In finding that "absent the evidence of Dr. Shane, it is unlikely that the jury, properly instructed, would have accepted the accused's plea of self-defence" the Court of Appeal suggests that the evidence of Dr. Shane ought to have been excluded entirely. The alternative ground for allowing the Crown's appeal was that Dr. Shane's testimony was properly admitted but the trial judge's instructions with respect to it were deficient. Thus, the issues before this Court are as follows:

1. Did the majority of the Manitoba Court of Appeal err in concluding that the jury should have considered the plea of self-defence absent the expert evidence of Dr. Shane?
2. Did the majority of the Manitoba Court of Appeal err in holding that the trial judge's charge to the jury with respect to Dr. Shane's expert evidence did not meet the requirements set out by this Court in *Abbey*, thus warranting a new trial?

5. Analysis

(i) Admissibility of Expert Evidence

In *Kelliher (Village of) v. Smith*, [1931], this Court adopted the principle that in order for expert evidence to be admissible "the subject-matter of the inquiry must be such that ordinary people are unlikely to form a correct judgment about it, if unassisted by persons with special knowledge". More recently, this Court addressed the admissibility of expert psychiatric evidence in criminal cases in *R. v. Abbey* . . . .

Where expert evidence is tendered in such fields as engineering or pathology, the paucity of the layperson's knowledge is uncontentious. The long-standing recognition that psychiatric or psychological testimony also falls within the realm of expert evidence is predicated on the realization that in some circumstances the average person may not have sufficient knowledge of or experience with human behaviour to draw an appropriate inference from the facts before him or her . . . .

The need for expert evidence in these areas can, however, be obfuscated by the belief that judges and juries are thoroughly knowledgeable about "human nature" and that no more is needed. They are, so to speak, their own experts on human behaviour. This, in effect, was the primary submission of the Crown to this Court.

The bare facts of this case, which I think are amply supported by the evidence, are that the appellant was repeatedly abused by the deceased but did not leave him (although she twice pointed a gun at him), and ultimately shot him in the back of the head as he was leaving her room. The Crown submits that these facts disclose all the information a jury needs in order to decide whether or not the appellant acted in self-defence. I have no hesitation in rejecting the Crown's submission.

Expert evidence on the psychological effect of battering on wives and common-law partners must, it seems to me, be both relevant and necessary in the context of the present case. How can the mental state of the appellant be appreciated without it? The average member of the public (or of the jury) can be forgiven for asking: Why would a woman put up with this kind of treatment? Why should she continue to live with such a man? How could she love a partner who beat her to the point of requiring hospitalization? We would expect the woman to pack her bags and go. Where is her self-respect? Why does she not cut loose and make a new life for herself? Such is the reaction of the average person confronted with the so-called "battered wife syndrome." We need help to understand it and help is available from trained professionals.

. . .

Fortunately, there has been a growing awareness in recent years that no man has a right to abuse any woman under any circumstances. Legislative initiatives designed to educate police, judicial officers and the public, as well as more aggressive investigation and charging policies all signal a concerted effort by the criminal justice system to take spousal abuse seriously. . . .

In *State v. Kelly* . . . the New Jersey Supreme Court . . . conclude[d] . . . that the battering relationship is "subject to a large group of myths and stereotypes." As such, it is "beyond the ken of the average juror and thus is suitable for explanation through expert testimony." I share that view.

(ii) The Relevance of Expert Testimony to the Elements of Self-Defence

In my view, there are two elements of the defence under s. 34(2) of the Code which merit scrutiny for present purposes. The first is the temporal connection in s. 34(2)(a) between the apprehension of death or grievous bodily harm and the act allegedly taken in self-defence. Was the appellant "under reasonable apprehension of death or grievous bodily harm" from Rust as he was walking out of the room? The second is the assessment in s. 34(2)(b) of the magnitude of the force used by the accused. Was the accused's belief that she could not "otherwise preserve herself from death or grievous bodily harm" except by shooting the deceased based "on reasonable grounds"?

The feature common to both s. 34(2)(a) and (b) is the imposition of an objective standard of reasonableness on the apprehension of death and the need to repel the assault with deadly force. In *Reilly v. The Queen*, [1984] . . . this Court considered the interaction of the objective and subjective components of s. 34(2) . . . .

If it strains credulity to imagine what the "ordinary man" would do in the position of a battered spouse, it is probably because men do not typically find themselves in that situation. Some women do, however. The definition of what is reasonable must be adapted to circumstances which are, by and large, foreign to the world inhabited by the hypothetical "reasonable man."

. . .

I turn now to a consideration of the specific components of self-defence under s. 34(2) of the Criminal Code.

A. Reasonable Apprehension of Death

Section 34(2)(a) requires that an accused who intentionally causes death or grievous bodily harm in repelling an assault is justified if he or she does so "under reasonable apprehension of death or grievous bodily harm." In the present case, the assault precipitating the appellant's alleged defensive act was Rust's threat to kill her when everyone else had gone.

It will be observed that s. 34(2)(a) does not actually stipulate that the accused apprehend <u>imminent</u> danger when he or she acts. Case law has, however, read that requirement into the defence. . . . The law of self-defence is designed to ensure that the use of defensive force is really necessary. It justifies the act because the defender reasonably believed that he or she had no alternative but to take the attacker's life. If there is a significant time interval between the original unlawful assault and the accused's response, one tends to suspect that the accused was motivated by revenge rather than self-defence. . . .

. . .

Given the relational context in which the violence occurs, the mental state of an accused at the critical moment she pulls the trigger cannot be understood except in terms of the cumulative effect of months or years of brutality. As Dr. Shane explained in his testimony, the deterioration of the relationship between the appellant and Rust in the period immediately preceding the killing led to feelings of escalating terror on the part of the appellant:

> But their relationship some weeks to months before was definitely escalating in terms of tension and in terms of the discordant quality about it. They were sleeping in separate bedrooms. Their intimate relationship was lacking and things were building and building and to a point, I think, where it built to that particular point where she couldn't—she felt so threatened and so overwhelmed that she had to—that she reacted in a violent way because of her fear of survival and also because, I think because of her, I guess, final sense that she was—that she had to defend herself and her own sense of violence towards this man who had really desecrated her and damaged her for so long.

Another aspect of the cyclical nature of the abuse is that it begets a degree of predictability to the violence that is absent in an isolated violent encounter between two strangers. This also means that it may in fact be possible for a battered spouse to accurately predict the onset of violence before the first blow is struck, even if an outsider to the relationship cannot. Indeed, it has been suggested that a battered woman's knowledge of her partner's violence is so heightened that she is able to anticipate the nature and extent (though not the onset) of the violence by his conduct beforehand. In her article "Potential Uses for Expert Testimony: Ideas Toward the Representation of Battered Women Who Kill" (1986), 9 *Women's Rights Law Reporter* 227, psychologist Julie Blackman describes this characteristic . . . :

Repeated instances of violence enable battered women to develop a continuum along which they can "rate" the tolerability or survivability of episodes of their partner's violence. Thus, signs of unusual violence are detected. For battered women, this response to the ongoing violence of their situations is a survival skill. Research shows that battered women who kill experience remarkably severe and frequent violence relative to battered women who do not kill. They know what sorts of danger are familiar and which are novel. They have had myriad opportunities to develop and hone their perceptions of their partner's violence. And, importantly, they can say what made the final episode of violence different from the others: they can name the features of the last battering that enabled them to know that this episode would result in life-threatening action by the abuser.

. . . Dr. Blackman relates the role of expert testimony in cases where a battered woman kills her batterer while he is sleeping (or not actively posing a threat to her) and pleads self-defence:

> Perhaps the single most important idea conveyed by expert testimony in such a case pertains to the notion that a battered woman, because of her extensive experience with her abuser's violence, can detect changes or signs of novelty in the pattern of normal violence that connote increased danger. Support for this assertion must come from the woman herself, in her spontaneous, self-initiated description of the events that precede her action against the abuser. Only then can testimony from an expert offer scientific support for the idea that such a danger detection process can occur and can be expected to be as accurate as the "reasonable man" standard would imply.

Of course, as Dr. Blackman points out, it is up to the jury to decide whether the distinction drawn between "typical" violence and the particular events the accused perceived as "life threatening" is compelling. According to the appellant's statement to police, Rust actually handed her a shotgun and warned her that if she did not kill him, he would kill her. I note in passing a remarkable observation made by Dr. Walker in her 1984 study *The Battered Woman Syndrome*. Writing about the 50 battered women she interviewed who had killed their partners, she comments:

> Most of the time the women killed the men with a gun; usually one of several that belonged to him. <u>Many of the men actually dared or demanded the woman use the gun on him first, or else he said he'd kill her with it.</u> [Emphasis added]

Where evidence exists that an accused is in a battering relationship, expert testimony can assist the jury in determining whether the accused had a "reasonable" apprehension of death when she acted by explaining the heightened sensitivity of a battered woman to her partner's acts. Without such testimony I am skeptical that the average fact-finder would be capable of appreciating why her subjective fear may have been reasonable in the context of the relationship. After all, the hypothetical "reasonable man" observing only the final incident may have been unlikely to recognize the batterer's threat as potentially lethal. Using the case at bar as an example the "reasonable man" might have thought, as the majority of the Court of Appeal seemed to, that it was unlikely that Rust would make good on his threat to kill the appellant that night because they had guests staying overnight.

The issue is not, however, what an outsider would have reasonably perceived but what the accused reasonably perceived, given her situation and her experience.

. . .The requirement imposed in *Whynot* that a battered woman wait until the physical assault is "underway" before her apprehensions can be validated in law would, in the words of an American court, be tantamount to sentencing her to "murder by installment": *State v. Gallegos*, (1986) . . . .

B. Lack of Alternatives to Self-Help

Section 34(2) requires an accused who pleads self-defence to believe "on reasonable grounds" that it is not possible to otherwise preserve him or herself from death or grievous bodily harm. The obvious question is if the violence was so intolerable, why did the appellant not leave her abuser long ago? This question does not really go to whether she had an alternative to killing the deceased at the critical moment. Rather, it plays on the popular myth already referred to that a woman who says she was battered yet stayed with her batterer was either not as badly beaten as she claimed or else she liked it. Nevertheless, to the extent that her failure to leave the abusive relationship earlier may be used in support of the proposition that she was free to leave at the final moment, expert testimony can provide useful insights. Dr. Shane attempted to explain in his testimony how and why, in the case at bar, the appellant remained with Rust:

> She had stayed in this relationship, I think, because of the strange, almost unbelievable, but yet it happens, relationship that sometimes develops between people who develop this very disturbed, I think, very disturbed quality of a

relationship. Trying to understand it, I think, isn't always easy and there's been a lot written about it recently, in the recent years, in psychiatric literature. But basically it involves two people who are involved in what appears to be an attachment which may have sexual or romantic or affectionate overtones.

> And the one individual, and it's usually the women in our society, but there have been occasions where it's been reversed, but what happens is the spouse who becomes battered, if you will, stays in the relationship probably because of a number of reasons.

> One is that the spouse gets beaten so badly—so badly—that he or she loses the motivation to react and becomes helpless and becomes powerless. And it's also been shown sometimes, you know, in—not that you can compare animals to human beings, but in laboratories, what you do if you shock an animal, after a while it can't respond to a threat of its life. It becomes just helpless and lies there in an amotivational state, if you will, where it feels there's no power and there's no energy to do anything.

> So in a sense it happens in human beings as well. It's almost like a concentration camp, if you will. You get paralyzed with fear.

> The other thing that happens often in these types of relationships with human beings is that the person who beats or assaults, who batters, often tries—he makes up and begs for forgiveness. And this individual, who basically has a very disturbed or damaged self-esteem, all of a sudden feels that he or she—we'll use women in this case because it's so much more common—the spouse feels that she again can do the spouse a favour and it can make her feel needed and boost her self-esteem for a while and make her feel worthwhile and the spouse says he'll forgive her and whatnot.

Apparently, another manifestation of this victimization is a reluctance to disclose to others the fact or extent of the beatings. For example, the hospital records indicate that on each occasion the appellant attended the emergency department to be treated for various injuries she explained the cause of those injuries as accidental. Both in its address to the jury and in its written submissions before this Court the Crown insisted that the appellant's injuries were as consistent with her explanations as with being battered and, therefore, in the words of Crown counsel at trial, "the myth is, in this particular case, that Miss Lavallee was a battered spouse." In his testimony Dr. Shane testified that the appellant admitted to him that she lied to hospital staff and others about the cause of her injuries. In Dr. Shane's opinion this was consistent with her overall feeling of being trapped and helpless . . . .

. . . A related theory used to explain the failure of women to leave battering relationships is described by psychologist and lawyer Charles Patrick Ewing in his book *Battered Women Who Kill* (1987). Ewing describes a phenomenon labelled "traumatic bonding" that has been observed between hostages and captors, battered children and their parents, concentration camp prisoners and guards, and batterers and their spouses. According to the research cited by Ewing there are two features common to the social structure in each of these apparently diverse relationships. At pp. 19–20, he states:

> The first of these common features is an imbalance of power "wherein the maltreated person perceives himself or herself to be subjugated or dominated by the other." The less powerful person in the relationship—whether battered woman, hostage, abused child, cult follower, or prisoner—becomes extremely dependent upon, and may even come to identify with, the more powerful person. In many cases, the result of such dependency and identification is that the less powerful, subjugated persons become "more negative in their self-appraisal, more incapable of fending for themselves, and thus more in need of the high power person." As this "cycle of dependency and lowered self-esteem" is repeated over time, the less powerful person develops a "strong affective bond" to the more powerful person in the abusive relationship.
>
> The second feature common to the relationships between battered woman and batterer, hostage and captor, battered child and abusive parent, cult follower and leader, and prisoner and guard is the periodic nature of the abuse. In each relationship, the less powerful person is subjected to intermittent periods of abuse, which alternate with periods during which the more powerful, abusive person treats the less powerful person in a "more normal and acceptable fashion."
>
> . . .
>
> Given the clear power differential between battered women and their batterers and the intermittent nature of physical and psychological abuse common to battering relationships, it seems fair to conclude . . . that many battered women are psychologically unable to leave their batterers because they have developed a traumatic bond with them. [Citations omitted]

This strong "affective bond" may be helpful in explaining not only why some battered women remain with their abusers but why they even profess to love them. Of course, as Dr. Ewing adds, environmental factors may also impair the woman's ability to leave—lack of job skills, the presence of children to care for, fear of retaliation by the man, etc.—may each have a role to play in some cases.

. . .

I emphasize at this juncture that it is not for the jury to pass judgment on the fact that an accused battered woman stayed in the relationship. Still less is it entitled to conclude that she forfeited her right to self-defence for having done so. I would also point out that traditional self-defence doctrine does not require a person to retreat from her home instead of defending herself. . . .

If, after hearing the evidence (including the expert testimony), the jury is satisfied that the accused had a reasonable apprehension of death or grievous bodily harm and felt incapable of escape, it must ask itself what the "reasonable person" would do in such a situation. The situation of the battered woman as described by Dr. Shane strikes me as somewhat analogous to that of a hostage. If the captor tells her that he will kill her in three days time, is it potentially reasonable for her to seize an opportunity presented on the first day to kill the captor or must she wait until he makes the attempt on the third day? I think the question the jury must ask itself is whether, given the history, circumstances and perceptions of the appellant, her belief that she could not preserve herself from being killed by Rust that night except by killing him first was reasonable. To the extent that expert evidence can assist the jury in making that determination, I would find such testimony to be both relevant and necessary.

In light of the foregoing discussion I would summarize as follows the principles upon which expert testimony is properly admitted in cases such as this:

1. Expert testimony is admissible to assist the fact-finder in drawing inferences in areas where the expert has relevant knowledge or experience beyond that of the lay person.
2. It is difficult for the lay person to comprehend the battered wife syndrome. It is commonly thought that battered women are not really beaten as badly as they claim, otherwise they would have left the relationship. Alternatively, some believe that women enjoy being beaten, that they have a masochist strain in them. Each of these stereotypes may adversely affect consideration of a battered woman's claim to have acted in self-defence in killing her mate.
3. Expert evidence can assist the jury in dispelling these myths.
4. Expert testimony relating to the ability of an accused to perceive danger from her mate may go to

the issue of whether she "reasonably apprehended" death or grievous bodily harm on a particular occasion.

5.   Expert testimony pertaining to why an accused remained in the battering relationship may be relevant in assessing the nature and extent of the alleged abuse.

6.   By providing an explanation as to why an accused did not flee when she perceived her life to be in danger, expert testimony may also assist the jury in assessing the reasonableness of her belief that killing her batterer was the only way to save her own life.

Quite apart from Dr. Shane's testimony there was ample evidence on which the trial judge could conclude that the appellant was battered repeatedly and brutally by Kevin Rust over the course of their relationship. The fact that she may have exhibited aggressive behaviour on occasion or tried (unsuccessfully) to leave does not detract from a finding of systematic and relentless abuse. In my view, the trial judge did not err in admitting Dr. Shane's expert testimony in order to assist the jury in determining whether the appellant had a reasonable apprehension of death or grievous bodily harm and believed on reasonable grounds that she had no alternative but to shoot Kevin Rust on the night in question.

Obviously the fact that the appellant was a battered woman does not entitle her to an acquittal. Battered women may well kill their partners other than in self-defence. The focus is not on who the woman is, but on what she did.

Post-Case-Reading Questions

1.   In what ways does the situation of Angelique Lavallee call to mind Susan Okin's warnings about women's vulnerability in marriage (and common-law relationships)?

2.   According to the lead justice in this decision (Bertha Wilson), the admission of expert testimony may be important in determining whether it is reasonable for a woman subjected to domestic violence to perceive an imminent threat in a given situation. Why?

CHAPTER
XIII

Charles Mills

Introduction

Born in London in 1951 to Jamaican parents, Charles W. Mills grew up in Jamaica and, briefly, the United States. His parents had moved to England in 1948 (meeting en route), his mother to pursue nursing, and his father to take up a job as a liaison officer for West Indian students in the British colonial office. In Jamaica, the Mills were a prominent middle-class family whose members held positions in academe (both teaching and administration), the civil service, law enforcement, social work, and diplomacy. Mills has reflected in an autobiographical essay that in the context of the colonial "colour pyramid" that characterized Jamaica in this period, his was considered a mixed-race family, with his light-skinned mother perceived as "Jamaican white," his father as black, and he and his brother as brown (or sometimes "red") and therefore "relatively privileged" vis à vis black Jamaicans. This

Charles Mills

Used by permission of Charles Mills.

contrasted with Mills' reception as a black man upon moving to Canada for his doctoral studies, and, subsequently, to the United States, where he has lived and taught since 1987. To Mills, who has written extensively on racial hierarchy and the social construction of race, this discrepancy is not surprising, but it is nonetheless instructive.

Mills was awarded a Commonwealth Fellowship in 1973 to pursue an MA in philosophy at the University of Toronto (his undergraduate degree, from the University of the West Indies, was in physics). Later, Mills returned to Toronto for a PhD, which he completed in 1985. Much of Mills' focus during this time was on Marxist theory, which he found helpful in illuminating contemporary structures of social class domination. His earliest writings as a young assistant professor at the University of Oklahoma and the University of Illinois at Chicago (UIC) were also in Marxist philosophy, focusing particularly on the concept of ideology. When he began to write on race in the mid-1990s, this conceptual framework remained important to his thinking. By the time he wrote his first (and still best-known) book, *The Racial Contract* (1997), however, Mills had expanded beyond a Marxist paradigm to include a radical rereading of social contract theory. In this book, which engages both historical and present-day liberal thought, Mills probes beneath the characterization of liberal society as founded upon a social contract based on principles of equality, mutuality and consent. The social contract that various liberal thinkers have articulated as the basis for political society, Mills argues, is actually undergirded by an exclusionary contract marked by racial domination. Inspired in part by Carole Pateman's feminist classic *The Sexual Contract* (1988), Mills draws attention to the racialized system of oppression that he argues informs liberal theory and practice.

Since 2007, Mills has been the John Evans Professor of Moral and Intellectual Philosophy at Northwestern University in Chicago. In addition to the influence of Marxist philosophy on his work, Mills' writings incorporate and extend the insights of critical race theory and feminist thought. He has continued to write on race as a system of social and political domination, using his critical reflections on the workings of racial supremacy to address a range of topics in social and political philosophy (e.g., multiculturalism and affirmative action), ethics, and epistemology. Since the publication of his influential *The Racial Contract*, Mills has written *Blackness Visible: Essays on Philosophy and Race* (1998), *From Class to Race: Essays in White Marxism and Black Radicalism* (2003), *The Contract and Domination* (2007)—co-authored with Carole Pateman—and, most recently, *Radical Theory, Caribbean Reality: Race, Class and Social Domination* (2010).

In the (excerpted) article by Mills below, "Racial Liberalism," he extends his notion of a racial contract at the heart of the social contract tradition to an analysis of liberalism as a legal and political system. Concepts that are central to liberalism—notions of personhood, rights, and duties—are, he contends, highly racialized, and not universal as is typically supposed. Mills argues that we cannot diminish the racial character of liberalism by either disavowing or rejecting racial thinking in the present. Instead, philosophers and others concerned about the racist legacy of the liberal tradition need to continue to explore the ways in which liberal theory and practice are inflected by racialized social, economic, and political structures and practices. Yet despite the fact that so much of liberal political philosophy today is preoccupied with issues of social justice, racial inequalities receive strikingly little attention by key liberal thinkers like John Rawls and Robert Nozick. Mills notes that by confining their analyses to the realm of ideal theory, many liberal philosophers are able to falsely suppose that liberal polities, insofar as they embody liberal principles and values, treat all citizens as equals. Shifting to the realm of non-ideal theory would, Mills suggests, allow us to see more clearly the social injustices caused by entrenched racial group privileges and hierarchies.

Following the reading, we will examine a Canadian Human Rights tribunal case initiated in 2012 by the First Nations Child and Family Caring Society of Canada, which claimed that the federal government funding formula for welfare services for children discriminates against First Nations children living on reserves. Reservation-based child welfare agencies receive significantly less funding per head than do agencies serving non–First Nations (and off-reserve Native) children. The latter are funded provincially, whereas the former are federally funded. Aboriginal advocates reject this discrepancy as unjust, and contend that the federal government is guilty of systematic race-based discrimination. Though the government claims (and is legally obliged) to treat all Canadian citizens equally, this case raises the question of whether the entitlements and benefits of citizenship are differentially allocated in ways that echo Mills' analysis of an implicit racial hierarchy.

Further Readings

Graham, K. (2002). "Race and the Limits of Liberalism," *Philosophy of the Social Sciences* 32 (2): 219–39.

Mills, C. (1997, 1999). *The Racial Contract*. Ithaca, NY.: Cornell University Press.

Mills, C. and C. Pateman (2007). *The Contract and Domination*. Cambridge, UK: Polity Press.

Charles Mills, *From* "Racial Liberalism"

Charles Mills, "Racial Liberalism," PMLA (Publications of the Modern Language Association of America), 123 (5), October 2008: 1380–97.

Liberalism is globally triumphant. The anti-feudal egalitarian ideology of individual rights and freedoms that emerges in the seventeenth and eighteenth centuries to oppose absolutism and ascriptive hierarchy has unquestionably become, whether in right- or left-wing versions, the dominant political outlook of the modern age. Normative justifications of the existing order as well as normative critiques overwhelmingly use a liberal framework. Debate typically centres on the comparative defensibility of "neoliberal" or free market conceptions versus social democratic or welfarist conceptions of liberalism. But liberalism itself is rarely challenged.

Within liberalism there are rival perspectives on the moral foundations of the state and the ultimate basis of people's rights. For a century and a half from the 1800s onward, the utilitarianism of Jeremy Bentham, James and John Stuart Mill, and Henry Sidgwick was most politically influential. But the World War II experience of the death camps and the global movement for postwar decolonization encouraged a return to a natural rights tradition that seemed to put individual personal protections on a more secure basis. Not social welfare but "natural," pre-social individual entitlements were judged to be the superior and infrangible foundation. Thus, it is the language of rights and duties—independent of social utility—most strongly associated with the earlier, rival social contract tradition of 1650–1800, particularly in John Locke's and Immanuel Kant's versions, that is now ubiquitous.[1] Unsurprisingly, then, especially with the revival of social contract theory stimulated by John Rawls' 1971 *A Theory of Justice*, contractarian (also called deontological) liberalism has now become hegemonic.

But in these myriad debates about and within liberalism, a key issue tends to be missed, to remain unacknowledged, even though—or perhaps precisely because—its implications for the rethinking of liberalism, and for the world order that liberalism has largely rationalized, would be far-ranging. Liberalism, I suggest, has historically been predominantly a racial liberalism (Stokes and Meléndez), in which conceptions of personhood and resulting schedules of rights, duties,

and government responsibilities have all been racialized. And the contract, correspondingly, has really been a racial one, an agreement among white contractors to subordinate and exploit non-white non-contractors for white benefit (Mills, *Racial Contract*). Insofar as moral debate in contemporary political theory ignores this history, it will only serve to perpetuate it.

Race and the Social Contract

Let me begin with some general points about the social contract. The concept is, of course, to be taken not literally but rather as an illuminating metaphor or thought experiment. We are asked to imagine the socio-political order (society, the state) as being self-consciously brought into existence through a "contract" among human beings in a pre-social, pre-political stage of humanity (the "state of nature"). The enduring appeal of the metaphor, despite its patent absurdity as a literal representation of the formation of socio-political systems, inheres in its capturing of two key insights. The first (against theological views of divine creation or secular conceptions of an organicist kind) is that society and the polity are artificial, human constructs. The second (against classical and medieval views of natural social hierarchy) is that human beings are naturally equal and that this equality in the state of nature should somehow translate into egalitarian socio-political institutions (Hampton, "Contractarian Explanation," "Contract," and "Feminist Contractarianism").

For the Lockean and Kantian contracts that (in conjunction and in competition) define the mainstream of the liberal tradition—but not for the Hobbesian contract—moral equality is foundational.[2] The social ontology is classically individualist, and it demands the creation of a polity that respects the equal personhood of individuals and (whether in stronger or weaker versions) their property rights. Basic moral entitlements for the citizenry are then juridically codified and enforced by an impartial state. Economic transactions are, correspondingly, ideally supposed to be non-exploitative, though there will, of course, be controversy about how this concept should be cashed out. So fairness in a broad sense is the overarching contract norm, as befits an apparatus ostensibly founded on principles antithetical to a non-individual-respecting, socially aggregating utilitarianism. The moral equality of people in the state of nature demands an equality of treatment (juridical, political, and economic) in the liberal polity they create. The state is not alien or antagonistic to us but the protector of our rights, whether as the constitutionalist Lockean sovereign or the Kantian *Rechtsstaat*. The good polity is the just polity, and the just polity is founded on safeguarding our interests as individuals.

But what if—not merely episodically and randomly but systematically and structurally—the personhood of some persons was historically disregarded and their rights disrespected? What if entitlements and justice were, correspondingly, so conceived of that the unequal treatment of these persons, or subpersons, was not seen as unequal, not flagged as an internal inconsistency, but accommodated by suitable discursive shifts and conceptual framings? And what if, after long political struggles, there developed at last a seeming equality that later turned out to be more nominal than substantive, so that justice and equal protection were still effectively denied even while being triumphantly proclaimed? It would mean that we would need to recognize the inadequacy of speaking in the abstract of liberalism and contractarianism. We would need to acknowledge that race had underpinned the liberal framework from the outset, refracting the sense of crucial terms, embedding a particular model of rights bearers, dictating a certain historical narrative, and providing an overall theoretical orientation for normative discussions. We would need to confront the fact that to understand the actual logic of these normative debates, both what is said and what is not said, we would have to understand not just the ideal, abstract social contract but also its incarnation in the United States (and arguably elsewhere) as a non-ideal, racial contract.

Consider the major divisions in the political philosophy of the last few decades. In *Liberalism and the Limits of Justice*, Michael Sandel makes the point that Rawls' *A Theory of Justice* is important because—apart from carrying the Kantianism-versus-utilitarianism dispute to a higher theoretical level—it was central to not one but two of the major political debates of the 1970s and 1980s (184–85), left or social democratic liberalism versus right or laissez-faire liberalism (Rawls versus Robert Nozick) and liberalism or contractarianism versus communitarianism (Rawls versus Michael Walzer, Alasdair MacIntyre, Charles Taylor, and Sandel himself). A third

major debate, initiated by Rawls' essays in the 1980s and culminating in *Political Liberalism* (1996), could be said to be the debate of the two decades after 1990 on comprehensive versus political liberalism. In their domination of the conceptual and theoretical landscape, these overarching frameworks tend to set the political agenda, establishing a hegemonic framing of key assumptions and jointly exhaustive alternatives. One locates oneself as a theorist by choosing one or the other of these primary alternatives and then taking up the corresponding sociopolitical and normative picture, adopting the defining terms, and making the argumentative moves characteristically associated with it. So though other theoretical and political alternatives are not logically excluded, they tend to be marginalized.

But there is another debate—one that has been going on for hundreds of years, if not always in the academy—which is, in a sense, orthogonal to all three of the foregoing and is arguably more pressing than any of them: the conflict between racial liberalism (generally known as just liberalism) and deracialized liberalism. Racial liberalism, or white liberalism, is the actual liberalism that has been historically dominant since modernity: a liberal theory whose terms originally restricted full personhood to whites (or, more accurate, white men) and relegated non-whites to an inferior category, so that its schedule of rights and prescriptions for justice were all colour-coded. Ascriptive hierarchy is abolished for white men but not white women (Pateman) and people of colour. So racism is not an anomaly in an unqualified liberal universalism but generally symbiotically related to a qualified and particularistic liberalism (Mehta; Sala-Molins). Though there have always been white liberals who have been antiracist and anti-imperialist, whose records should not be ignored (Pitts), they have been in the minority. Indeed, the most striking manifestation of this symbiotic rather than conflictual relation is that the two philosophers earlier demarcated as central to the liberal tradition, Locke and Kant, limited property rights, self-ownership, and personhood racially. Locke invested in African slavery, justified Native American expropriation, and helped write the Carolina constitution of 1669, which gave masters absolute power over their slaves (Tully; Arneil; Armitage; Bernasconi and Mann). Kant, the most important ethicist of the modern period and the famous theorist of personhood and respect, turns out to be one of the founders of modern scientific racism, and thus a pioneering theorist of subpersonhood and disrespect (Eze; Bernasconi, "Who" and "Kant"; Mills, "Kant's *Untermenschen*"). So the inferior treatment of people of colour is not at all incongruent with racialized liberal norms, since by those norms non-whites are less than full persons.

If this analysis is correct, such inequality, and its historic ramifications, is arguably more fundamental than all the other issues mentioned above, since in principle at least all parties to the many-sided political debate are supposed to be committed to the nonracial moral equality of all. Thus, the rethinking, purging, and deracializing of racial liberalism should be a priority for us—and in fact the struggles of people of colour for racial equality over the past few hundred years can in large measure be most illuminatingly seen as just such a project. As Michael Dawson writes in his comprehensive study of African American political ideologies, "The great majority of black theorists challenge liberalism as it has been practised within the United States, not some abstract ideal version of the ideology. . . . [T]here is no necessary contradiction between the liberal tradition in *theory* and black liberalism. The contradiction exists between black liberalism and how liberalism has come to be understood in practice within the American context" (13).

Yet the need for such a reconstruction has been neither acknowledged nor acted on. Rawls and Nozick may be in conflict over left-wing versus right-wing liberalism, but both offer us idealized views of the polity that ignore the racial subordination rationalized by racial liberalism. Rawls and Sandel may be in conflict over contractarian liberalism versus neo-Hegelian communitarianism, but neither confronts how the whiteness of the actual American contract and of the actual American community and its conception of the good affects justice and conceptions of the self. Late Rawls may be in conflict with early Rawls about political versus comprehensive liberalism, but neither addresses the question of the ways in which both versions have been shaped by race, whether through an "overlapping consensus" (among whites) or a "reflective equilibrium" (of whites). From the perspective of people of colour, these intramural and intrawhite debates all fail to deal with the simple overwhelming reality on which left and right, contractarian and communitarian, comprehensive or political liberal should theoretically be able to agree: that the centrality of racial exclusion and racial injustice demands a reconceptualization of the orthodox view of the polity and calls for radical rectification.

The "Whiteness" of Political Philosophy, Demographic and Conceptual

Political philosophers in general, and liberal contractarians in particular, need to take race seriously. Unfortunately, for a combination of reasons, both externalist and internalist, they have not done so. Demographically, philosophy is one of the very whitest of the humanities; only about 1 per cent of American philosophers are African American, and similar or even smaller numbers are Latino, Asian American, and Native American.[3] So while the past two decades have generated an impressive body of work on race, largely by philosophers of colour though with increasing white contributions, it has tended to be ghettoized and not taken up in what (by conventional criteria) are judged the trend-setting sectors of the profession: the prestige journals and graduate programs and the writings of the most prominent figures in the field. Basically, one can choose to do race or choose to do philosophy. A manifestation of this marginalization is that Brian Leiter's biennial online *Philosophical Gourmet Report*, an unofficial and controversial but widely consulted list of the top graduate programs in the field and top departments for particular areas of specialization, has no entry for issues of race in its most recent (2006) version. This is not a respectable philosophical subject. Nor do ads in *Jobs for Philosophers*, the profession's official newspaper of available employment, usually include race as a desired area of specialization in their job descriptions. So though Africana philosophy and critical race theory are formally recognized by the American Philosophical Association as legitimate research areas, which represents progress, they remain marginal in the field, far more so than issues of gender and feminism, a manifestation of the greater proportion of (white) women in the profession (about 20 per cent).[4]

Philosophers of colour are absent not just from the halls of academe but from the texts also. Introductions to political philosophy standardly exclude any discussion of race,[5] except, perhaps, for brief discussions of affirmative action. Historical anthologies of political philosophy will present a lineup of figures extending from ancient Greece to the contemporary world—from Plato to NATO, in one wit's formulation—but with no representation of non-white theorists. Almost to the point of parody, the Western political canon is limited to the thoughts of white men. Steven Cahn's *Classics of Political and Moral Philosophy* (2002), for example, a widely used Oxford anthology of more than twelve hundred pages, includes only one non-white thinker, Martin Luther King, Jr., and not even in the main text but in the appendixes.[6] So it is not merely that the pantheon is closed to non-white outsiders but that a particular misleading narrative of Western political philosophy—indeed, a particular misleading narrative of the West itself—is being inculcated in generations of students. The central debates in the field as presented—aristocracy versus democracy, absolutism versus liberalism, capitalism versus socialism, social democracy versus libertarianism, contractarianism versus communitarianism—exclude any reference to the modern global history of racism versus antiracism, of abolitionist, anti-imperialist, anti-colonialist, anti–jim crow, anti-apartheid struggles. Quobna Cugoano, Frederick Douglass, W.E.B. DuBois, Mahatma Gandhi, Aimé Césaire, C.L.R. James, Frantz Fanon, Steve Biko, Edward Said are all missing.[7] The political history of the West is sanitized, reconstructed as if white racial domination and the oppression of people of colour had not been central to that history. A white supremacy that was originally planetary, a racial political structure that was transnational, is whitewashed out of existence. One would never guess from reading such works that less than a century ago "the era of global white supremacy" was inspiring "a global struggle for racial equality" (Borstelmann 15, 21). One would never dream that the moral equality supposedly established by modernity was in actuality so racially restricted that at the 1919 post–World War I peace conference in Versailles, the Japanese delegation's proposal to insert a "racial equality" clause in the League of Nations' covenant was soundly defeated by the "Anglo-Saxon" nations (including, of course, the United States), which refused to accept such a principle (Lake and Reynolds, ch. 12).

Moreover, not just the political theorists of the struggle against racism and white supremacy are jim crowed but, even more remarkable, justice itself as a subject is jim crowed. Contemporary political philosophy, at least in the Anglo-American tradition, is focused almost exclusively on normative issues. Whereas the original contract theorists used the contract idea to address questions of our political obligation to the state, contemporary contract theorists, following Rawls, only use it to address questions of social justice. So how, one might ask, could white political philosophers possibly exclude race and racial justice as subjects, considering that racial *injustice* has been so central to the making of the modern world and to the creation of the United States in particular? The answer: through the simple expedient of concentrating on what has come to be called "ideal theory."

Ideal theory is not supposed to contrast with non-ideal theory as a moral outlook contrasts with an amoral, *realpolitik* outlook. Both ideal and non-ideal theory are concerned with justice, and so with the appeal to moral ideals. The contrast is that ideal theory asks what justice demands in a perfectly just society while non-ideal theory asks what justice demands in a society with a history of injustice. So non-ideal theory is concerned with corrective measures, with remedial or rectificatory justice (Roberts). Racial justice is preeminently a matter of non-ideal theory, of what corrective measures are called for to rectify a history of discrimination. By

the apparently innocuous methodological decision to focus on ideal theory, white political philosophers are immediately exempted from dealing with the legacy of white supremacy in our actual society. You do not need affirmative action—and you certainly do not need reparations—in a society where no race has been discriminated against in the first place. In fact, if the social constructionist position on race is correct and race is brought into existence through racializing processes linked with projects of exploitation (aboriginal expropriation, slavery, colonial rule), then a perfectly just society would be raceless! By a weird philosophical route, the "colour blindness" already endorsed by the white majority gains a perverse philosophical sanction. In a perfectly just society, race would not exist, so we do not (as white philosophers working in ideal theory) have to concern ourselves with matters of racial justice in our own society, where it does exist—just as the white citizenry increasingly insist that the surest way of bringing about a raceless society is to ignore race and that those (largely people of colour) who still claim to see race are themselves the real racists.

The absurd outcome is the marginalization of race in the work of white political philosophers across the spectrum, most strikingly in the Rawls industry. The person seen as the most important twentieth-century American political philosopher and theorist of social justice, and a fortiori the most important American contract theorist, had nothing to say about the remediation of racial injustice, central to American society and history. His five major books (excluding the lectures on the history of moral and political philosophy)—*A Theory of Justice, Political Liberalism, Collected Papers, The Law of Peoples*, and *Justice as Fairness: A Restatement*—together total over two thousand pages. If one were to add together all their sentences on race and racism, one might get half a dozen pages, if that much. Indeed, perhaps the single most remarkable indicator of the marginality of race in Rawls' thought is that even the phrase *affirmative action*—referring to the most important postwar measure of racial justice in the United States—never appears in his writing.

. . .

In sum, the seeming neutrality and universality of the mainstream contract is illusory. As it stands, it is really predicated on the white experience and generates, accordingly, a contractarian liberalism that is racially structured in its apparatus and assumptions. Deracializing this racial liberalism requires rethinking the actual contract and what social justice demands for its voiding. It forces us to move to non-ideal theory and to understand the role of race in the modernity for which the contract metaphor has seemed peculiarly appropriate.

Deracializing Racial Liberalism

My suggestion is, then, that if we are going to continue to work within contract theory, we need to use a contract that registers rather than obfuscates the non-ideal history of white oppression and racial exploitation: the domination contract (Mills, *Racial Contract*; Pateman and Mills, chs. 3, 4).

Adopting the Domination Contract as a Framework
Even in the liberal tradition, contract theory has long been criticized for its emphasis on agreement. David Hume pointed out long ago that force rather than popular consent was the origin of most governments; he concluded that the metaphor of the contract should be abandoned. Rousseau, on the other hand, had the brilliant idea of incorporating the radical critique of the contract into a subversive conception of the contract itself. In his *The Social Contract*, Rousseau maps an ideal polity. But unlike any of the other classic contract theorists, he earlier distinguished, in *Discourse on the Origins of Inequality*, a non-ideal, manifestly unjust polity that also rests on a contract but that "irreversibly destroyed natural freedom, forever fixed the Law of property and inequality, [and] transformed a skillful usurpation into an irrevocable right" (173). So this, for Rousseau, is the actual contract that creates political society and establishes the architecture of the world we live in: a class contract among the rich. Instead of including all persons as equal citizens, guaranteeing their rights and freedoms, this contract privileges the wealthy at the expense of the poor. It is an exclusionary contract, a contract of domination.

Rousseau can be seen as initiating an alternative, radical democratic strain in contract theory, one that seeks to expose the realities of domination behind the facade and ideology of liberal consensuality. He retains the two key insights captured by the contract metaphor, the constructed nature of the polity and the recognition of human moral equality, but he incorporates them into a more realistic narrative that shows how they are perverted. Some human beings come to dominate others, denying them the equality they enjoyed in the state of nature. Carole Pateman's *The Sexual Contract*, which analogously posits an intramale agreement to subordinate women, can be read as applying Rousseau's innovation to gender relations. Drawing on Rousseau and Pateman, I in turn sought in my *The Racial Contract* to develop a comparable concept of an intrawhite agreement that—through

European expansionism, colonialism, white settlement, slavery, apartheid, and jim crow—shapes the modern world. Whites contract to regard one another as moral equals who are superior to non-whites and who create, accordingly, governments, legal systems, and economic structures that privilege them at the expense of people of colour.

In all three cases, the contract is an exclusionary one among a minority of the population rather than a universal and inclusive one. As such, it acknowledges what we all know to be true, that real-life societies are structured through and through by hierarchies of privilege and power. The concept of a domination contract captures better as a metaphor the patterns of socio-political exclusion characterizing actual modern polities and puts us in a better position for dealing with the important normative questions of social justice. Rather than a fictitious universal inclusion and moral and political egalitarianism, this revisionist contract expresses the reality of group domination and social hierarchy. By contrast with an ideal-theory framework, the domination contract is firmly located on the terrain of non-ideal theory. Not only does it point us toward the structures of injustice that need to be eliminated, unlike the evasive ideal mainstream contract, but it also recognizes their link with group privilege and group causality. These structures did not just happen to come into existence; rather, they were brought into being and are maintained by the actions and inactions of those privileged by them.

The idealization that characterizes mainstream liberalism is descriptive as well as normative, extending to matters of fact as well as subvarieties of justice. It is not only that the focus is on a perfectly just society but also that the picture of our own society is carefully sanitized. The contract in its contemporary incarnation does not, of course, have the social-scientific pretensions—the contract as ur-sociology or anthropology—of (at least some variants of) the original. Yet I would claim that some of the key factual assumptions of the original contract still remain in modern versions. It is not—the standard reply—just a necessary disciplinary abstraction, one that goes with the conceptual territory of philosophy but rather, in the phrase of Onora O'Neill, an idealizing abstraction, one that abstracts away from social oppression (Mills, "Ideal Theory"). And in this case it is a white abstraction.

. . .

In the United States, these assumptions and conceptual devices—the state of nature as empty of aboriginal peoples, society as non-exploitative and consensually and cooperatively founded, the political state illuminatingly conceived of as arising through the actions of an invisible hand—are unavoidably an abstraction from the European and Euro-American experience of modernity. It is a distinctively white (not colourless) abstraction away from Native American expropriation and African slavery and from the role of the state in facilitating both. It is in effect—though at the rarefied and stratospheric level of philosophy—a conceptualization ultimately grounded in and apposite for the experience of white settlerdom. Making racial socio-political oppression methodologically central would put us on very different theoretical terrain from the start.

The domination contract, here as the racial contract, thus provides a way of translating into a mainstream liberal apparatus—social contract theory—the radical agenda and concerns of political progressives. It offers a competing metaphor that more accurately represents the creation and maintenance of the socio-political order. The white privilege that is systematically obfuscated in the mainstream contract is here nakedly revealed. And the biasing of liberal abstractions by the concrete interests of the privileged (here, whites) then becomes transparent. It is immediately made unmysterious why liberal norms and ideals that seem attractive in the abstract—freedom, equality, rights, justice—have proved unsatisfactory, refractory, in practice and failed to serve the interests of people of colour. But the appropriate reaction is not (or so I would claim anyway) to reject these liberal ideals but rather to reject the mystified individualist social ontology that blocks an understanding of the political forces determining the ideals' restricted and exclusionary application. The group ontology of the domination contract better maps the underlying metaphysics of the socio-political order.

If the actual contract has been a racial one, what are the implications for liberal theory, specifically for the desirable project of deracializing racial liberalism? What rethinkings and revisions of seemingly colourless, but actually white, contractarian liberalism would be necessary?

Recovering the Past: Factually, Conceptually, Theoretically

To begin with, it would be necessary to recover the past, not merely factually but conceptually and theoretically, in terms of how we conceive of and theorize the polity. The idealizing white cognitive patterns of racial liberalism manifest themselves in a whitewashing not merely of the facts but also of their organizing conceptual and theoretical political frameworks. The contractarian ideal is classically social transparency, in keeping with a Kantian tradition of a *Rechtsstaat* that scorns behind-the-scenes *realpolitik* for ethical transactions that can stand up to

the light of day. But the centrality of racial subordination to the creation of the modern world is too explosive to be subjected to such scrutiny and so has to be retroactively edited out of national (and Western) memory because of its contradiction of the overarching contract myth that the impartial state was consensually created by reciprocally respecting rights-bearing persons.

For the reality is, as David Theo Goldberg argues in his book *The Racial State*, that modern states in general are racialized: "race is integral to the emergence, development, and transformations (conceptually, philosophically, materially) of the modern nation-state" (4). What should have been a *Rechtsstaat* is actually a *Rassensstaat*, and the citizenry are demarcated in civic status by their racial membership. The modern world order, what Paul Keal calls "international society" (1), is created by European expansionism, and the conquest and expropriation of indigenous peoples is central to that process: "non-Europeans were progressively conceptualized in ways that dehumanized them and enabled their dispossession and subordination" (21). So race as a global structure of privilege and subordination, normative entitlement and normative exclusion, is inextricably tied up with the development of the modern societies for which the contract is supposed to be an appropriate metaphor, whether in the colonized world or the colonizing mother countries. A model predicated on the (past or present) universal inclusion of colourless atomic individuals will therefore get things fundamentally wrong from the start. Races in relations of domination and subordination centrally constitute the social ontology. In their failure to admit this historical truth, in their refusal to acknowledge (or even consider) the accuracy of the alternative political characterization of white supremacy, mainstream contractarians reject social transparency for a principled social opacity not merely at the perceptual but at the conceptual and theoretical levels.

. . .

The founding of the American New World, peculiar in comparison with the origins of the Old World European powers, cuts both ways for the contract image. The youth of the United States as a nation, its creation in the modern period, and the formal and extensively documented establishment of the Constitution and the other institutions of the new polity have made the social contract metaphor seem particularly apt here. Indeed, it might seem that it comes close to leaving the metaphoric for the literal, especially given that the terrain of this founding was conceptualized as a "wilderness," "Indian country," a "state of nature" only redeemed by a civilizing and Christianizing European presence. But if the general metaphor of a social contract comes closest to being non-metaphoric here, so does the competing metaphor of a racial contract, because of the explicit and formal dichotomy of Anglo racial exclusion, more clear-cut and uncompromising than racial exclusion in, say, the Iberian colonies of the Americas, where *mestizaje* was the norm. The opposition between white and non-white has been foundational to the workings of American social and political institutions (the United States Congress made whiteness a prerequisite for naturalization in 1790, and social and juridical whiteness has been crucial to moral, civic, and political status).

. . .

Nor has the racial progress of the last half century eliminated the racial nature of the polity. The civil rights victories of the 1950s and 1960s—*Brown v. Board of Education* in 1954, the 1964 Civil Rights Act, the 1965 Voting Rights Act, the 1967 decision in *Loving v. Virginia* that finally judged anti-miscegenation laws (still on the books in sixteen states) unconstitutional, the 1968 Fair Housing Act—raised hopes of a second Reconstruction more successful than the first one but have not lived up to their promise because de facto discrimination has survived the repeal of de jure discrimination, as whites have devised various new strategies for circumventing antidiscrimination law (where it still exists and is enforced any more). Thus, Eduardo Bonilla-Silva speaks sardonically of "colour-blind racism" and "racism without racists." The 2004 celebrations of the fiftieth anniversary of the *Brown* decision were rendered somewhat hollow by the reality that schools today are more segregated than they were at the time of the decision (Orfield and Eaton; Kozol). In 2008, the fortieth anniversary of the Fair Housing Act, residential segregation in big cities with large black populations is virtually unchanged (Massey and Denton; Massey). The failure of the 1965 Voting Rights Act to prevent widespread disenfranchisement of blacks has not merely local but sometimes national repercussions (e.g., black exclusion in Florida making the 2000 Republican victory possible), and the act has yet to produce black political representation in proportion to African Americans' numbers in the population. Affirmative action is basically dead, most whites regarding it as unfair "reverse discrimination." The disproportionately black and Latino "underclass" has been written off as an insoluble problem. Less than 7 per cent of the population nationally, black males are now one-third of those imprisoned. Some authors have argued despairingly that racism should be seen as a permanent feature of the United States (Bell), while others have suggested that substantive racial progress in United States history has been confined narrowly to three periods (the Revolutionary War, the Civil War, and the cold

war, requiring the triple condition of war mobilization, elite intervention, and an effective mass protest movement), an "unsteady march" always punctuated by periods of backlash and retreat, such as the one we are living in now (Klinkner and Smith). So though progress has been made in comparison with the past, the appropriate benchmark should not be the low bar of abolition and repeal of jim crow but the simple ideal of racial equality.

Unsurprisingly, then, people of colour, and black American intellectuals in particular, have historically had little difficulty in recognizing the centrality of race to the American polity and the racial nature of American liberalism. No material or ideological blinders have prevented blacks and other people of colour from seeing that the actual contract is most illuminatingly conceptualized as a racial one that systematically privileges whites at the expense of non-whites. "Indeed, with the exception of black conservatism, all black ideologies contest the view that democracy in America, while flawed, is fundamentally good. . . . A central theme within black political thought has been . . . to insist that the question of *racial* injustice is a central problematic in *American* political thought and practice, not a minor problem that can be dismissed in parentheses or footnotes" (Dawson 14).[8]

But such dismissal is (as earlier documented) what occurs descriptively and prescriptively in the racial liberalism of contemporary white contractarians. If the racial subordination of people of colour was obvious and matter-of-fact to racial liberalism in its original, overtly racist incarnation, it can no longer be admitted by racial liberalism in its present race-evading and calculatedly amnesiac incarnation. The atrocities of the past now being an embarrassment, they must be denied, minimized, or conceptually bypassed. A cultivated amnesia, a set of constructed deafnesses and blindnesses, characterizes racial liberalism: subjects one cannot raise, issues one cannot broach, topics one cannot explore. The contractarian ideal of social transparency about present and past would, if implemented, make it impossible to continue as before: one would see and know too much. Instead, the European colonizing powers and the white settler states they created are paradigms of what Stanley Cohen calls "states of denial," where the great crimes of native genocide and African slavery, and their embedding in the everyday life of the polity, are erased from national memory and consciousness: "Whole societies have unmentioned and unmentionable rules about what should not be openly talked about" (45). Rogers Smith's *Civic Ideals* documents the consistency with which theorists of American political culture, including such leading figures as Alexis de Tocqueville, Gunnar Myrdal, and Louis Hartz, have represented it as essentially egalitarian and inclusive, placing racism and racial oppression in the categories of the anomalous and deviant—a perfect correlate at the more empirical level of political science of the evasions of political philosophy.

The repudiation of racial liberalism will thus require more than a confrontation with the historical record. It will also require an acknowledgment at the conceptual and theoretical levels that this record shows that the workings of such a polity are not to be grasped with the orthodox categories of raceless liberal democracy. Rather, the conceptual innovation called for is a recognition of white supremacy as itself a political system—a "white republic" (Saxton), a "white-supremacist state" (Fredrickson), "a racial order" (King and Smith), a "racial polity" (Mills, "The Racial Polity")—and of races themselves as political entities and agents. Racial liberalism's facial racelessness is in fact its racedness; deracializing racial liberalism requires us to colour in the blanks.

. . .

Conclusion

Race and liberalism have been intertwined for hundreds of years, for the same developments of modernity that brought liberalism into existence as a supposedly general set of political norms also brought race into existence as a set of restrictions and entitlements governing the application of those norms. Political theorists, whether in political science or political philosophy, have a potentially valuable role to play in contributing to the dismantling of this pernicious symbiotic normative system. But such a dismantling cannot be achieved through a supposed colour blindness that is really a blindness to the historical and enduring whiteness of liberalism. Racial liberalism, established by the racial contract, must be recognized for what it is before the promise of a nonracial liberalism and a genuinely inclusive social contract can ever be fulfilled.

Works Cited

Ackerly, Brooke, et al. "Symposium: John Rawls and the Study of Justice: Legacies of Inquiry." *Perspectives on Politics* 4 (2006): 75–133.

Armitage, David. "John Locke, Carolina, and the *Two Treatises of Government*." *Political Theory* 32 (2004): 602–27.

Arneil, Barbara. *John Locke and America: The Defence of English Colonialism*. New York: Oxford UP, 1996.

Bell, Derrick. *Faces at the Bottom of the Well: The Permanence of Racism*. New York: Basic, 1992.

Bernasconi, Robert. "Kant as an Unfamiliar Source of Racism." *Philosophers on Race: Critical Essays.* Ed. Julie K. Ward and Tommy L. Lott. Malden: Blackwell, 2002.

———. "Who Invented the Concept of Race? Kant's Role in the Enlightenment Construction of Race." *Race.* Ed. R. Bernasconi. Malden: Blackwell, 2001.

Bernasconi, Robert, and Anika Maaza Mann. "The Contradictions of Racism: Locke, Slavery, and the *Two Treatises*." *Race and Racism in Modern Philosophy*. Ed. Andrew Valls. Ithaca: Cornell UP, 2005.

Bird, Colin. *An Introduction to Political Philosophy*. New York: Cambridge UP, 2006.

Bogues, Anthony. *Black Heretics, Black Prophets: Radical Political Intellectuals*. New York: Routledge, 2003.

Bonilla-Silva, Eduardo. *Racism without Racists: Color-Blind Racism and the Persistence of Racial Inequality in the United States*. 2nd ed. Lanham: Rowman, 2006.

Borstelmann, Thomas. *The Cold War and the Color Line: American Race Relations in the Global Arena*. Cambridge: Harvard UP, 2001.

Boxill, Bernard R. *Blacks and Social Justice*. Rev. ed. Lanham: Rowman, 1992.

Cahn, Steven M., ed. *Classics of Political and Moral Philosophy*. New York: Oxford UP, 2002.

Cohen, Stanley. *States of Denial: Knowing about Atrocities and Suffering*. Malden: Polity, 2001.

Dawson, Michael C. *Black Visions: The Roots of Contemporary African-American Political Ideologies*. Chicago: U of Chicago P, 2001.

Dred Scott v. Sandford. 60 US 393. Supreme Ct. of the US. 6 Mar. 1857.

Eze, Emmanuel Chukwudi. "The Color of Reason: The Idea of 'Race' in Kant's Anthropology." *Postcolonial African Philosophy: A Critical Reader*. Ed. Eze. Cambridge: Blackwell, 1997.

Fredrickson, George. *White Supremacy: A Comparative Study in American and South African History*. New York: Oxford UP, 1981.

Freeman, Samuel, ed. *The Cambridge Companion to Rawls*. New York: Cambridge UP, 2003.

Goldberg, David Theo. *The Racial State*. Malden: Blackwell, 2002.

Hampton, Jean. "Contract and Consent." *A Companion to Contemporary Political Philosophy*. Ed. Robert E. Goodin, Philip Pettit, and Thomas Pogge. Rev. 2nd ed. Vol. 2. Malden: Blackwell, 2007.

———. "The Contractarian Explanation of the State." *Midwest Studies in Philosophy: The Philosophy of the Human Sciences*. Ed. Peter A. French, Theodore E. Uehling, Jr., and Howard K. Wettstein. Notre Dame: U of Notre Dame P, 1990.

———. "Feminist Contractarianism." *A Mind of One's Own: Feminist Essays on Reason and Objectivity*. Ed. Louise M. Antony and Charlotte E. Witt. Rev. 2nd ed. Boulder: Westview, 2001.

Haney López, Ian F. *White by Law: The Legal Construction of Race*. New York: New York UP, 1996.

Harris, Cheryl I. "Whiteness as Property." *Harvard Law Review* 106 (1993): 1709–91.

Hobbes, Thomas. *Leviathan*. Ed. Richard Tuck. Rev. ed. New York: Cambridge UP, 1996.

Jacobson, Matthew Frye. *Whiteness of a Different Color: European Immigrants and the Alchemy of Race*. Cambridge: Harvard UP, 1998.

Keal, Paul. *European Conquest and the Rights of Indigenous Peoples: The Moral Backwardness of International Society*. New York: Cambridge UP, 2003.

King, Desmond. *Separate and Unequal: African Americans and the U.S. Federal Government*. Rev. ed. New York: Oxford UP, 2007.

King, Desmond S., and Rogers M. Smith. "Racial Orders in American Political Development." *American Political Science Review* 99 (2005): 75–91.

Klinkner, Philip A., and Rogers M. Smith. *The Unsteady March: The Rise and Decline of Racial Equality in America*. Chicago: U of Chicago P, 1999.

Kozol, Jonathan. *The Shame of the Nation: The Restoration of Apartheid Schooling in America*. New York: Crown, 2005.

Kymlicka, Will. *Contemporary Political Philosophy: An Introduction*. 2nd ed. New York: Oxford UP, 2001.

Lake, Marilyn, and Henry Reynolds. *Drawing the Global Colour Line: White Men's Countries and the International Challenge of Racial Equality*. New York: Cambridge UP, 2008.

Litwack, Leon F. *Trouble in Mind: Black Southerners in the Age of Jim Crow*. New York: Knopf, 1998.

Massey, Douglas S. *Categorically Unequal: The American Stratification System*. New York: Sage, 2007.

Massey, Douglas S., and Nancy A. Denton. *American Apartheid: Segregation and the Making of the Underclass*. Cambridge: Harvard UP, 1993.

McGary, Howard. *Race and Social Justice*. Malden: Blackwell, 1999.

Mehta, Uday Singh. *Liberalism and Empire: A Study in Nineteenth-Century British Liberal Thought*. Chicago: U of Chicago P, 1999.

Mills, Charles W. "'Ideal Theory' as Ideology." *Hypatia: A Journal of Feminist Philosophy* 20.3 (2005): 165–84.

———. "Kant's *Untermenschen*." *Race and Racism in Modern Philosophy*. Ed. Andrew Valls. Ithaca: Cornell UP, 2005.

———. *The Racial Contract*. Ithaca: Cornell UP, 1997.

———. "Racial Exploitation and the Wages of Whiteness." *The Changing Terrain of Race and Ethnicity*. Ed. Maria Krysan and Amanda E. Lewis. New York: Sage, 2004.

———. "The Racial Polity." *Blackness Visible: Essays on Philosophy and Race*. Ithaca: Cornell UP, 1998.

Mishel, Lawrence R., Jared Bernstein, and Sylvia Allegretto. *The State of Working America, 2006/2007*. Ithaca: ILR, 2006.

Nozick, Robert. *Anarchy, State, and Utopia*. New York: Basic, 1974.

Oliver, Melvin L., and Thomas M. Shapiro. *Black Wealth/White Wealth: A New Perspective on Racial Inequality*. 10th anniversary ed. New York: Routledge, 2006.

O'Neill, Onora. "Justice, Gender, and International Boundaries." *The Quality of Life*. Ed. Martha C. Nussbaum and Amartya Sen. New York: Clarendon, 1993.

Orfield, Gary, and Susan E. Eaton. *Dismantling Desegregation: The Quiet Reversal of* Brown v. Board of Education. New York: New, 1997.

Outlaw, Lucius T., Jr. *Critical Social Theory in the Interests of Black Folks*. Lanham: Rowman, 2005.

Pateman, Carole. *The Sexual Contract*. Stanford: Stanford UP, 1988.

Pateman, Carole, and Charles W. Mills. *Contract and Domination*. Malden: Polity, 2007.

Pitts, Jennifer. *A Turn to Empire: The Rise of Imperial Liberalism in Britain and France*. Princeton: Princeton UP, 2005.

Rawls, John. *Collected Papers*. Ed. Samuel Freeman. Cambridge: Harvard UP, 1999.

———. *Justice as Fairness: A Restatement*. Ed. Erin Kelly. Cambridge: Harvard UP, 2001.

———. *The Law of Peoples, with "The Idea of Public Reason Revisited."* Cambridge: Harvard UP, 1999.

———. *Political Liberalism*. Expanded paperback ed. New York: Columbia UP, 1996.

———. *A Theory of Justice*. Rev. ed. Cambridge: Harvard UP, 1999.

Roberts, Rodney C., ed. *Injustice and Rectification*. New York: Lang, 2002.

Robertson, Lindsay G. *Conquest by Law: How the Discovery of America Dispossessed Indigenous Peoples of Their Lands*. New York: Oxford UP, 2005.

Rousseau, Jean-Jacques. *Discourse on the Origin and the Foundations of Inequality among Men*, or *Second Discourse. Rousseau:* The Discourses *and Other Early Political Writings*. Ed. and trans. Victor Gourevitch. New York: Cambridge UP, 1997.

———. *Of the Social Contract. Rousseau:* The Social Contract *and Other Later Political Writings*. Ed. and trans. Victor Gourevitch. New York: Cambridge UP, 1997.

Sala-Molins, Louis. *Dark Side of the Light: Slavery and the French Enlightenment.* Trans. John Conteh-Morgan. Minneapolis: U of Minnesota P, 2006.

Sample, Ruth J. *Exploitation: What It Is and Why It's Wrong.* Lanham: Rowman, 2003.

Sandel, Michael J. *Liberalism and the Limits of Justice.* 2nd ed. New York: Cambridge UP, 1998.

Saxton, Alexander. *The Rise and Fall of the White Republic: Class Politics and Mass Culture in Nineteenth-Century America.* 1990. New York: Verso, 2003.

Shapiro, Thomas M. *The Hidden Cost of Being African American.* New York: Oxford UP, 2004.

Shelby, Tommie. *We Who Are Dark: Philosophical Foundations of Black Solidarity.* Cambridge: Harvard UP, 2005.

Shklar, Judith N. *American Citizenship: The Quest for Inclusion.* 1991. Cambridge: Harvard UP, 2001.

Simmons, A. John. *Political Philosophy.* New York: Oxford UP, 2007.

Smith, Rogers M. *Civic Ideals: Conflicting Visions of Citizenship in U.S. History.* New Haven: Yale UP, 1997.

Stokes, Curtis, and Theresa Meléndez, eds. *Racial Liberalism and the Politics of Urban America.* East Lansing: Michigan State UP, 2003.

Tully, James. *An Approach to Political Philosophy: Locke in Contexts.* New York: Cambridge UP, 1993.

Wertheimer, Alan. *Exploitation.* Princeton: Princeton UP, 1996.

Williams, Linda Faye. *The Constraint of Race: Legacies of White Skin Privilege in America.* University Park: Pennsylvania State UP, 2003.

Wolff, Jonathan. *An Introduction to Political Philosophy.* Rev. ed. New York: Oxford UP, 2006.

Yancy, George, ed. *African-American Philosophers: Seventeen Conversations.* New York: Routledge, 1998.

———. Introduction "Situated Black Women's Voices in/on the Profession of Philosophy." *Hypatia: A Journal of Feminist Philosophy* 23.2 (2008): 155–59.

———, ed. "Situated Voices: Black Women in/on the Profession of Philosophy." *Hypatia: A Journal of Feminist Philosophy* 23.2 (2008): 160–89.

Post-Reading Questions

1. What is "racial liberalism," according to Mills?
2. What are some of the concrete ways in which the social contract underlying liberal society is a racialized one, according to Mills?
3. Which concepts in liberal political philosophy are most in need of critical rethinking, from Mills' perspective?
4. What is Mills' critique of John Rawls' version of the social contract?

CASE STUDY
UNEQUAL FUNDING FOR FIRST NATIONS CHILDREN

Introduction

Child welfare services for First Nations children living on reserves in Canada receive 22 per cent less funding than do similar services for children who do not live on reserves, amounting to a difference of about $200 million a year. While child welfare services on First Nations reserves are funded by the federal government, provincial governments fund non-reserve child welfare services; the two use significantly different funding formulas, and Aboriginal child advocates say the federal government's formula is ultimately unfair and discriminatory. This discrepancy in funding has far-reaching consequences: lack of availability of adequate family support services contributes to the disproportionately large number of Aboriginal children in the child welfare care system in Canada.

Seeking to remedy this situation, the First Nations Child and Family Caring Society (FNCFCS) and the national organization the Assembly of First Nations (AFN), filed a human rights complaint in 2007 against the federal government. Their goals were twofold: to draw attention to what they argue is a long-standing inequality, and to seek formal redress through the Human Rights Tribunal. Opening arguments began in September 2009. The federal government sought to have the case dismissed multiple times on technical grounds, including arguing that the case falls outside of the Human Rights Commission's jurisdiction because the federal funding does not involve a good or service. This strategy initially succeeded when the tribunal chair dismissed the case on a preliminary motion; upon appeal, however, the Federal Court of Canada sided with the FNCFCS (April 2012) and ordered the tribunal to hear the case. The hearings then began in February 2013, but were temporarily suspended when an Access to Information request finally turned up thousands of pages of government documents that the FNCFCS had requested years earlier. The Justice Department sought a long adjournment in order to process additional documents that officials said might be relevant; however, this request, which the FNCFCS opposed, was subsequently denied, and the hearings resumed in July 2013.

From the standpoint of liberal political theory, the lower level of funding for children living on First Nations reserves is, at first glance, troubling: contemporary proponents of liberalism defend equitable treatment of citizens irrespective of race or ethnicity, and it is not clear what could warrant less funding for Aboriginal children's services. One of the government's key arguments, however, is that the difference in funding formulas for child welfare is an instance of different-but-equal treatment; government lawyers in the case have insisted that there is no relevant comparison group for indigenous children living on reserves, which is needed to prove discrimination in a Human Rights Tribunal case.

This case requires that we think about equality and what it demands in different contexts. For many, if not most, liberals, equality requires not only formal equality under the law but also substantively equal access to valuable social goods such as education, health care, and child welfare services. However, as Charles Mills argues, liberals' endorsement of an ostensibly race-blind principle of socio-political equality does not tell the full story: "Liberalism has historically been predominantly racial liberalism . . . in which conceptions of personhood and resulting schedules of rights, duties, and government responsibilities have all been racialized." Viewed critically, Mills contends, liberalism incorporates a "racial contract" that permits, and in some sense even requires, the subordination of non-white persons. Another way of viewing this contract is to say that it exists between a minority of privileged persons in society, and is "structured through and through by hierarchies of privilege and power." Indigenous peoples and persons of African descent are, in the North American context, the racialized groups whose domination lies at the core of the racial contract, Mills argues.

In Canada, there is a long history of discrimination and violence perpetrated by colonial settlers and their governments against First Nations peoples; this history has prompted high-level commissions, inquiries, and official apologies (to Aboriginal peoples). But many First Nations advocates say that their communities remain poorly treated by federal and provincial governments, and their representatives unjustly harassed when they protest. Activist Cindy Blackstock, the executive director of the FNCFCS, the group that filed the child welfare funding human rights claim, was, for example, the target of close monitoring by both the departments of Justice and Aboriginal Affairs. The Federal Privacy Commissioner found in 2013 that this monitoring of Blackstock's personal life was in violation of the federal Privacy Act, and ordered the departments to cease this activity and destroy personal information about Blackstock that did not relate to federal child welfare policies.

Historically, some of the injustices associated with racial hierarchies in the United States and Canada have been rendered invisible by a different-but-equal rationale. The case of the differential welfare funding for First Nations children in Canada, Aboriginal advocates say, is an example of this. A similar discrepancy exists in funding for the education of First Nations children in Canada, and future legal challenges to this inequity by Aboriginal groups are likely. When viewed in light of the metaphorical racial domination contract sketched by Mills, these inequalities suggest that liberalism, in both theory and practice, still has some distance to go before it accords substantive equality to all citizens. At the very least, the First Nations child welfare human rights case requires that the government of Canada explain how unequal funding is compatible with the principle of equal treatment of all Canadians.

Cindy Blackstock, *From* "The Canadian Human Rights Tribunal on First Nations Child Welfare"

Cindy Blackstock, "The Canadian Human Rights Tribunal on First Nations Child Welfare,"
Children and Youth Services Review, 33 (2011): 187–94.

. . .

1. Introduction

. . .

On February 26, 2007, the Assembly of First Nations [AFN], a political organization representing all First Nations in Canada, and the First Nations Child and Family Caring Society of Canada [the Caring Society], a national non-profit organization providing services to First Nations child welfare organizations, took the historic step of holding Canada accountable before the Canadian Human Rights Commission for its current treatment of over 160,000 First Nations children resident on reserve. The complaint alleges that the Government of Canada discriminates against First Nations children on reserves by providing them with less government child welfare funding, and therefore benefit, than other children in Canada (First Nations Child and Family Caring Society of Canada, 2009).

There are more First Nations children in child welfare care today than ever before and the over-representation of First Nations is unrelenting and staggering (Blackstock, 2003; Assembly of First Nations, 2007).

Overall, the estimated 27,000 First Nations children in child welfare care account for 30 to 40 per cent of all children in child welfare care even though they represent less than 5 per cent of the child population (Blackstock & Trocmé, 2005). Neglect, driven by structural risks such as poverty, poor housing, and substance misuse linked to colonialism (Blackstock & Trocmé), account for a substantial proportion of the over-representation (Blackstock & Trocmé, 2005; Blackstock, 2008). Culturally based and equitable programs targeted to poverty, poor housing, and substance misuse are needed to deal with this and other problems experienced by First Nations children and their families. Unfortunately, there is pervasive evidence that First Nations receive inequitable resources to prevent and respond to maltreatment as compared to other Canadians (McDonald & Ladd, 2000; Clarke, 2007; Auditor General of Canada, 2008; Standing Committee on Public Accounts, 2009).

This article presents the facts leading up to the filing of the human rights case, the process after the complaint was filed, and the implications for First Nations children, individuals from minority groups, and the moral fabric of the country if the Government of Canada wins the case.

1.1. Colonialism: the birthplace of First Nations child welfare

A confidential 1966 departmental report [Department of Indian and Northern Affairs, Canada] estimated that 75 per cent of the children in the schools [residential schools] were from homes which, by reason of overcrowding and parental neglect or indifference are considered unfit for school children.

Royal Commission on Aboriginal Peoples (1996), Chapter 10, p. 13

Canada is a federalist country composed of a national government, ten provincial governments, three territorial governments, and Aboriginal[9] governments. Canada is also one of the few countries in the world that continue to apply a race-based piece of legislation known as the Indian Act (1985). The Indian Act (1985) is the oldest piece of federal legislation in the country with the first rendition dating back to the time of confederation. Among other powers, the Indian Act (1985) gives the federal government responsibility for the definition and maintenance of Indians and lands reserved for Indians (Sinclair, Bala, Lilles, & Blackstock, 2004). What this means in practice is that the Government of Canada determines which indigenous peoples are recognized for the purposes of treaty making and treaty benefit. Those who meet certain blood quantum criteria designed by the federal government are recognized as eligible treaty holders and are therefore called "status Indians." Those who fall short of government blood quantum requirements are called "non-status Indians" for which Canada recognizes no land rights or treaty obligations. If Canada holds onto its current blood quantum method of classifying status versus non-status Indians, demographers predict that there will be no status Indians in 200 years effectively absolving Canada from any land obligations (Clatworthy, 2005). The Indian Act (1985) also defines the structure of First Nations governments, wills and estates, commercial enterprise, land and resource use, and the establishment of reserve boundaries. Basically, reserves are Crown lands set aside for the use of Indians, which means that First Nations peoples can live on reserves, but the Crown actually owns the land and strictly governs the use thereof. The various provisions of the Indian Act yield little opportunity for First Nations to generate revenue linked to land ownership or resource extraction contributing to widespread poverty amongst First Nations community members (National Council on Welfare, 2008).

A Royal Commission on Aboriginal Peoples [RCAP] was conducted in 1996 to direct Canada away from the Indian Act—14 years later most of the recommendations remain unimplemented. There is no sign that the Canadian government is interested in leaving the definition of who is indigenous in Canada to a matter of self-identity, as Australia and New Zealand did decades ago, and there has been little progress in resolving outstanding land and resource disputes (Blackstock, 2008).

The Indian Act (1985) also plays a significant role in the safety and well-being of First Nations children and families. Beginning in the 1870s the government of Canada began forcibly removing First Nations children aged 5–15 years old from their families and placing them in residential schools with a goal of assimilating them under the guise of Christian education objectives (Milloy, 1999). At the height of their operations in the 1940s approximately 8,900 children attended the schools (Milloy, 1999). Although the schools began closing in the 1950s, the last federally run school did not close until 1996 (Department of Indian and Northern Affairs Canada, 2003) and many children were placed in the schools as child welfare placements (Milloy, 1999). One study suggests that by the 1960s, child welfare placements accounted for over 80 per cent of residential school admissions in Saskatchewan (Caldwell, 1967). The harms to the Aboriginal children who attended residential schools included extremely high rates of death due to preventable causes of disease (Bryce, 1922), abuse, and negligence, as well as, prolific cultural and linguistic erosion (Royal Commission on Aboriginal Peoples, 1996; Milloy, 1999; Blackstock, 2003). In fact the harms were so egregious that in 2008, the prime minister of Canada issued a public apology for residential schools and launched a truth and reconciliation commission (Harper, 2008).

An amendment to the Indian Act in the 1950s allowed provincial/territorial child welfare and education statutes to apply on reserve (Sinclair et al., 2004), however, the federal government was expected to fund these services on reserves. The provinces began delivering child welfare services in the mid 1950s, but social workers who had little or no knowledge about colonization and residential schools often mistook symptoms of systemic discrimination as parental failure (Royal Commission on Aboriginal Peoples, 1996; Union of BC Indian Chiefs, 2002; Blackstock, 2003). As a result, First Nations children were removed in large numbers and placed in residential schools (Caldwell, 1967) or with non-Aboriginal families, often permanently (Royal Commission on Aboriginal Peoples, 1996). Johnston (1983) a researcher for the Canadian Council on Social Development termed this period of mass removals the "60s scoop." Today, many social workers in Canada understand that the "60s scoop" was poorly thought out and resulted in harm to Aboriginal families (Union of BC Indian Chiefs, 2002), but the reality is that the proportion of First Nations children in child welfare has reached record levels eclipsing both the "60s scoop" and residential schools (Blackstock, 2003).

In an effort to stem the tide of removals, First Nations mobilized and began establishing their own child welfare agencies in the 1970s. These agencies are located on reserve and are funded by the federal government (McKenzie & Flette, 2003). Although First Nations agencies are expected to deliver culturally based child welfare services comparable to what other children in similar circumstances receive (Department of Indian and Northern Affairs Canada, 2005), their ability to do so is substantially restricted. The agencies must wear the straitjackets of provincial legislation and federal government funding regimes that are often not culturally appropriate and are rarely grounded in research evidence relevant to First Nations (Blackstock, 2003). It would be reasonable for provincial and federal governments to impose child welfare policy and practice on First Nations child welfare agencies if they could muster evidence of the efficacy of their solutions, but in the vast majority of circumstances they have not. This wholesale imposition of provincial and federal child welfare systems creates an untenable situation that stifles innovation in a system that desperately needs it.

Despite all odds, First Nations agencies have created some space for culturally based practices and emerging evidence suggests that they are having a positive impact in keeping First Nations children safely in their communities and in developing award winning programs responsive to the needs of First Nations children (Blackstock, 2003; Loxley et al., 2005). First Nations, however, understand that much more needs to be done and are actively challenging the legislative and funding barriers that block progress including the inequitable level of federal child welfare funding on reserves (Assembly of First Nations, 2007).

1.2. Inequality as a risk factor for First Nations children

Circumstances are dire. Inadequate resources may force individual agencies (First Nations child and family service agencies) to close down if their mandates are withdrawn, or not extended, by the provinces. This would result in provinces taking over responsibility for child welfare, likely at a higher cost to Indian and Northern Affairs Canada (INAC) . . . in addition to escalating costs for INAC, culturally appropriate services would be compromised. This would be contrary to the United Nations Convention on the Rights of the Child which guarantees specific rights for children including the right to non-discrimination and the preservation of families and indigenous culture.

Department of Indian Affairs and Northern Development, n.d., pp. 1, 6

The confluence between provisions in the Indian Act giving the federal government responsibility for Indians and lands reserved for Indians and the provincial government's assertion of child welfare laws creates a jurisdictional quagmire that further erodes the safety and wellbeing of First Nations children. Provincial/territorial child welfare laws apply on and off reserve but the provinces/territories expect the federal government to fund the service for on-reserve children. If the federal government allocates funds at lower levels than other children receive through the province, the province/territory typically does not top up the funding levels resulting in a two-tiered child welfare system where First Nations children get less (Auditor General of Canada, 2008; First Nations Child and Family Caring Society of Canada, 2009).

First Nations children are being placed in out of home care at six to eight times the rate of other children (Auditor General of Canada, 2008; Standing Committee on Public Accounts, 2009). Research suggests that the over-representation of First Nations children in child welfare care cannot be accounted for by differences in substantiated child sexual, physical or emotional abuse reports between First Nations and other children (Blackstock, Trocmé, & Bennett, 2004; Trocmé, Knoke, & Blackstock, 2004; Trocmé et al., 2006). It is neglect that fuels the over-representation of First Nations children in child welfare and this form of maltreatment is highly associated with poverty (Blackstock et al., 2004; Trocmé et al., 2004; Blackstock & Trocmé, 2005; Trocmé et al., 2006). The good news is that these factors can be mediated by services. However, federal child welfare funding on reserves is inequitable and is particularly lacking with respect to the funding of services especially designed to keep First Nations children safely in their homes known as "least disruptive measures" (Assembly of First Nations, 2007; Blackstock, 2008).

The inequalities in First Nations child welfare funding on reserves are longstanding and well documented (Royal Commission on Aboriginal Peoples, 1996; McDonald & Ladd, 2000; Loxley et al., 2005; Amnesty International, 2006; Assembly of First Nations, 2007; Auditor General of Canada, 2008; Standing Committee on Public Accounts, 2009) as are the tragic consequences of First Nations children going into child welfare care due, in part, to inequitable services (Kimmelman, 1985; McDonald & Ladd, 2000; Blackstock & Trocmé, 2005; Amnesty International, 2006; Clarke, 2007; Auditor General of Canada, 2008; National Council on Welfare, 2008; Blackstock, 2008; Martin & Blackstock, 2009; Standing Committee on Public Accounts, 2009). Estimates are that First Nations children on reserves receive 22 per cent less per capita in child welfare funding than other children (McDonald & Ladd, 2000) and the funding shortfall is particularly acute with regard to services intended to keep children safely at home (Loxley et al., 2005; Auditor General of Canada, 2008; Standing Committee on Public Accounts, 2009).

This inequity is further amplified for First Nations children by shortfalls in education funding, housing, and publicly funded voluntary sector supports (RCAP, 1996; Assembly of First Nations, 2007; Blackstock, 2007; 2008; National Council on Welfare, 2008; Loppie-Reading & Wien, 2009). For example, the federal government shortchanges First Nations elementary and secondary school funding even though only one in four First Nations children finishes high school. Estimates are that federal funding for elementary schools on reserves falls short by 40 per cent, and the problem is even worse in secondary schools, where the federal government spends 70 per cent less on First Nations students than they do for other children (Matthew, 2000). The shortfall in publicly funded voluntary sector is even more acute. Whereas Canadians receive approximately 67 billion dollars in publicly funded services, which translates into $2400 per person delivered through voluntary sector organizations each year (Canadian Council on Social Development, 2003), many First Nations receive no publicly funded voluntary sector supports such as food banks, non-profit parenting support programs, domestic violence programs, and social housing (Nadjiwan & Blackstock, 2003).

First Nations worked with the Canadian government to develop two research-based solutions to the child welfare inequality over a ten-year period, [but] the federal government did not implement them . . . and the number of First Nations children entering child welfare care continues to grow (Blackstock, 2007; Auditor General of Canada, 2008). The federal government and the Assembly of First Nations commissioned McDonald and Ladd (2000) to author the first report known as the *Joint National Policy Review on First Nations Child and Family Services* [NPR]. McDonald and Ladd (2000) found that federal child welfare funding on reserves fell 22 per cent below what was provided to children off reserves funded by the provinces. They also found that an acute shortfall in services intended to keep children

safely at home known as "least disruptive measures" contributed to the number of First Nations children entering child welfare care increasing by a staggering 71 per cent between 1995 and 2001. The McDonald and Ladd (2000) report set out 17 recommendations for improvements to First Nations child welfare funding on reserves but the federal government failed to implement them in a timely fashion. By 2004, the federal government viewed the McDonald and Ladd (2000) report as dated and, along with the Assembly of First Nations, commissioned a second report to document a research based and detailed funding formula and policies for First Nations child welfare on reserves. This solution, known as the Wen:de solution (Blackstock, Prakash, Loxley, & Wien, 2005; Loxley et al., 2005), was developed by over 20 leading researchers representing disciplines as diverse as economics, child welfare, community development, law and sociology. The Wen:de solution suggested that, at minimum, the federal government should provide an additional 109 million per annum nationally (excluding the Province of Ontario and the Territories) using a funding formula and policies structured in specific ways to achieve a basic level of culturally based equity in child welfare services on reserves. After the Wen:de solution was released in 2005, the federal government publicly acknowledged the links between the funding inadequacies and the growing number of First Nations children in care, (Department of Indian Affairs and Northern Development Canada, 2006; Prentice, 2007) but was not disposed to fix the problem despite running a 22 billion dollar surplus budget in 2005 and more recently spending billions to stimulate the economy.

First Nations were confronted with a choice; continue to work with government and hope they redress the inequality voluntarily or consider legal options. After 10 years of negotiations that failed to achieve results, it was apparent that voluntary strategies aimed at convincing Canada to provide equitable and culturally based child welfare services to First Nations children were unlikely to succeed.

1.3. The Canadian human rights complaint
The Canadian Human Rights Act (1985) authorizes the Canadian Human Rights Commission [Commission] to receive, assess, and adjudicate human rights complaints (Canadian Human Rights Tribunal, n.d.). The Commission has the authority to make these determinations on its own or refer the matter to the Canadian Human Rights Tribunal [Tribunal] for a full hearing. Should the Commission or Tribunal find that a human rights violation has occurred, they have the power to order a remedy which is enforceable in Federal Court

(Canadian Human Rights Act, 1985). The First Nations Child and Family Caring Society (the Caring Society) and the Assembly of First Nations (AFN) chose the human rights complaint over other legal options as the Canadian Human Rights Act (1985) includes the power to order specific relief for the discrimination.

At the time the complaint was filed, the Government of Canada joined with four other countries, including Australia, New Zealand, and the United States, to oppose the United Nations Declaration on the Rights of Indigenous Peoples [Declaration] (Strahl, 2008)....

The United Nations General Assembly adopted the UN Declaration on the Rights of Indigenous Peoples in September of 2007. The vote was 143 Nation States in favour, 11 abstained and 4, including Canada, voted against (UN News Centre, 2007). Subsequent to the vote, Australia and New Zealand are now supporting the Declaration leaving only Canada and the USA as officially opposed. These results suggest that world opinion is running against the Canadian government's views on the rights of indigenous peoples.

The first step of the Commission's process is to offer mediation to the complainants (AFN and the Caring Society) and the respondent (Government of Canada). The Caring Society and AFN agreed while the Canadian government refused. The Commission then ordered an assessment of the complaint to determine whether or not the Commission would formally accept the case and, if so, to recommend a process to resolve the complaint. The assessment phase would last over a year, with the Government of Canada refusing mediation a second time, repeatedly raising technical objections, questioning the authority of the Commission to hear the complaint and even alleging procedural unfairness. In the end, the Commission's assessment report accepted the complaint and recommended that a full tribunal be held on the merits of the case. The Commission's assessment report also recommended that the Canadian Human Rights Commission appoint its own legal counsel to represent the public interests at the tribunal as the implications for human rights were so significant. What this means in practical terms is that the Canadian Human Rights Commission becomes a legal actor in all future legal proceedings.

When the assessment report, including all of its recommendations, was formally accepted by the Canadian Human Rights Commissioners in September of 2008 and the tribunal was ordered to proceed, the Canadian government appealed the decision to Federal Court in an effort to overturn the Commission's decision and dismiss the case on the basis of two arguments related to the jurisdiction of the Canadian Human Rights Act

(CHRA) (Abel, 2009; *Attorney General of Canada v. the First Nations Child, Family Caring Society of Canada, the Assembly of First Nations, the Canadian Human Rights Commission, the Chiefs of Ontario, & Amnesty International Canada*, 2009). The first argument deals with whether federal government funding falls within the scope of the CHRA and the second issue relates to whether or not there is a comparator group for First Nations children served by child welfare on reserve. The Canadian Human Rights Act (1985) has jurisdiction over cases alleging discrimination associated with a good, accommodation, or service. The federal government argues that their funding is not a good or an accommodation, nor is it a service, and thus the child welfare complaint falls outside of the jurisdiction of the CHRA. The funding is not a service argument basically suggests that even when a funder (in this case the Canadian government) knowingly provides a lesser level of funding for a statutory government services (such as child welfare) to any group on a discriminatory ground, they cannot be held accountable under the CHRA (Abel, 2009). This argument, if successful, sets a foundation for Canadian governments to discriminate with impunity so long as that discrimination is related to providing lesser levels of funding on a discriminatory ground rather than the direct purchase of fewer services. Clearly this could have broad and destructive consequences for a wide array of minority groups in Canada.

In the comparator argument, the federal government argues that the Canadian Human Rights Act (1985) requires the complainants to substantiate their discrimination claim by identifying a comparator group to First Nations children on reserve receiving child welfare services funded by the federal government (First Nations Child et al., 2010). The federal government wants to limit any comparator group analysis to First Nations children on reserve, implying that (1) it funds all First Nations children on reserves equally and thus there is no discrimination and (2) funding for non-Aboriginal child welfare is outside of the federal government's mandate and thus any comparisons to provincial child welfare funding for other children is irrelevant (First Nations Child et al., 2010).

. . .

The complainants argue that a comparator group is not required to prove a discrimination claim and, even if it was required, there are a number of relevant comparator groups (First Nations Child et al., 2010)....

More recently, the federal government has advanced the argument that their funding is equitable. This statement has been made in the Federal Court record and reiterated by counsel representing Canada in federal court on 14 September 2009, but the Government of Canada has provided no reliable independent evidence to support its equity assertion (Canadian Human Rights Tribunal, 2009).

Overall, Canada's arguments prioritize legal technicalities over the central question of whether or not First Nations children are receiving a lesser child welfare benefit because of federal government policies and practices. Canada's pattern of behaviour seems out of step with its international human rights obligations to prioritize the safety and well being and non-discrimination of children as set out in the Convention on the Rights of the Child and the Declaration on the Rights of Indigenous Peoples.

. . .

1.5. I am a witness campaign

. . .

Reconciliation means not saying sorry twice (Blackstock, 2008). A year after the prime minister apologized for the wrongs done to Aboriginal children during the residential school era (Harper, 2008), it is important to measure the sincerity of the apology against how the Canadian government is treating First Nations children today (First Nations Child and Family Caring Society of Canada, 2009). A public education and engagement movement called the "I am a witness campaign" was launched to educate and engage the public by inviting individuals and organizations to follow the tribunal. Being a witness means the person or organization commits to following the tribunal either in person or via the media/internet/social networking sites so that they can hear all the facts and make up their own mind about whether or not the Government of Canada is treating First Nations children fairly. The idea of engaging people in a process where they self-educate and make up their own minds versus asking people to support our position in the Tribunal outright respects the facility and dignity of each witness while also providing a framework for sustainable change in public opinion. If people learn on their own about the rights violation they are much more likely to act on that knowledge than having it spoon fed to them. There is no charge to being a witness and people of all ages can sign up. This ensures the active engagement of all Canadians, particularly children and young people, and those of low economic means who are much more likely to come into contact with the child welfare system (Blackstock & Trocmé, 2005). The campaign is promoted using social networking sites, a website, and personal presentations and appeals. Over 6,000 individuals and organizations registered as witnesses in its first 10 months of operation (First Nations Child and Family

Caring Society of Canada, 2009) making the Canadian Human Rights Tribunal on First Nations child welfare the most formally watched court case on children's rights in Canadian history.

The underlying strategy of the "I am a witness" campaign is rooted in a fundamental belief in the value of democracy in correcting government policies that are contrary to the public good. The hope is that growing public awareness will put increased levels of public pressure on the Canadian Government to treat First Nations children equitably. The efficacy of engaging Canadians in policy changes affecting First Nations children has been demonstrated by the passage of Jordan's Principle, a child first principle to resolving intergovernmental jurisdictional disputes regarding the access of public services by First Nations children (Blackstock (2009b)). First Nations children are routinely denied public services available to other children as the federal and provincial governments cannot agree on who should pay for services on reserve. Jordan's Principle is named after Jordan River Anderson, a First Nations child who tragically spent two years unnecessarily in hospital while governments argued over payment for his home care. If he was non-Aboriginal the province would have picked up the cost and the child would have gone home when doctors determined he was medically able to do so. Jordan's Principle says that when a government service is available to other children and a jurisdictional dispute erupts over services for a First Nations child, the government of first contact pays for the service and then resolves the billing issue later. Jordan's Principle passed unanimously through the Canadian House of Commons on 12 December 2007 due, in part, to the large number of people and organizations who had formally registered their support on a web-based joint declaration of support (Blackstock (2009b)).

The democratic assumptions and strategies invoked in the "I am a witness" campaign are very similar to those used for Jordan's Principle, and clearly the organizers are hoping for a similar success. There is every reason to believe that the new campaign will be as successful as Jordan's Principle since it provides a medium for public education and immediate, cost free engagement that results in meaningful impact.

1.6. The tribunal begins . . . will Canada turn the page on racial discrimination?

> At a time when federal leaders are meeting a few blocks away to discuss what issues matter the most to Canadians—this case calls them back to the conscience of the Nation. Great governments, and great leaders, are not measured by interests and

issues. They are measured by whether they stand on guard for the values that define our country the most—equality, freedom, justice, and an unwavering commitment to human rights. In this case, the federal government has relied on a series of legal technicalities to question the jurisdiction of the tribunal to hear the case. They might be successful. And if they are what happens to the First Nations children who are denied equitable treatment by another Canadian government? And what happens to our Canada if vulnerable children can be denied equitable government services simply because of their race or other discriminatory grounds?

Blackstock (2009c)

On 14 September 2009 the historic Canadian Human Rights Tribunal on First Nations child welfare began. An opening statement was made by the First Nations Child and Family Caring Society (Blackstock, 2009c), and motions were argued regarding whether or not Amnesty International Canada and the Chiefs of Ontario should be granted interested party status in the proceedings. The Caring Society, The Assembly of First Nations (AFN), and the Canadian Human Rights Commission (the Commission) supported both applications for interested party status and were keen to proceed with a witness testimony in November of 2009. The Government of Canada vigorously opposed either group being granted interested party status and they requested an adjournment of the proceedings until January 2010. The decision by the Tribunal was to grant interested party status to both Amnesty International and the Chiefs of Ontario and to begin evidentiary hearings on the facts in November of 2009 (First Nations Child and Family Caring Society of Canada, 2009).

There was a change of course in November of 2009, when a newly appointed Tribunal chair, Shirish Chotalia, vacated the dates of the hearing on the merits for reasons that are still not clearly understood by the Caring Society. The Canadian government then brought a motion to the Canadian Human Rights Tribunal to dismiss the tribunal on the legal loophole arguing funding is not a service (*Attorney General of Canada v. the First Nations Child, Family Caring Society of Canada, the Assembly of First Nations, the Canadian Human Rights Commission, the Chiefs of Ontario, & Amnesty International Canada*, 2009) after they tried, and failed, to get the Federal Court to derail the tribunal on substantially the same arguments (*Attorney General of Canada v. the First Nations Child and Family Caring Society of Canada and the Assembly of First Nations*, 24 November 2009). The Canadian Government appealed the Federal Court

decision and lost again (*Attorney General of Canada v. the First Nations Child et al.*, 2009) so the motion to dismiss at the tribunal, heard on 2 and 3 June 2010, was Canada's best option to avoid a hearing on the merits. The Tribunal Chair is expected to release her decision on Canada's motion to dismiss in 2010.

2. Conclusion

I felt ashamed by the lack of action on the part of the Federal Government and its focus on legal loopholes at the expense of the human dimension. They chose to dismiss the complaint rather than to address the real issue—the severe mistreatment of vulnerable First Nations children and families on reserves. I came to realize that the dynamics of what transpired in those two days is a microcosm of what has been going on in this country for centuries.

Gillian McCloskey, Associate Executive Director, Ontario Association of Social Workers reflection on her attendance at the Tribunal hearings on 2, 3 June 2010 on Canada's motion to dismiss the case. (McCloskey, 2010, pp. 1–2)

Canada's decision to prioritize its jurisdictional arguments before the interests of vulnerable children coupled with its efforts to avoid a hearing on the merits and keep the hearing out of the public eye raise important questions about its motivation. Among the various explanations for Canada's decision making and conduct, the fact that Canada appears to have a very weak case on the merits may be playing a role. Not only is the government facing an impressive list of expert witnesses and reports being put forward by the First Nations Child and Family Caring Society of Canada and the Assembly of First Nations, but they are also faced with having to explain why a host of provincial governments (Auditor General of Canada, 2008) and Canada's own documents and reports (Department of Indian Affairs and Northern Development Canada, 2006) confirm the inequality. Canada has also reported problems securing expert and lay witnesses to testify on its behalf. In fact, it is proposing only one expert witness from an accounting firm contracted to produce a report to refute the testimony of the five independent expert witnesses supporting the First Nations case. In addition, Canada has been unable to identify even one social work expert who is willing to testify on their behalf.

Canada may also be concerned that, if the Tribunal finds that federal funding is a service and has resulted in discrimination it would set an important, and expensive, precedent of equality in government services for children on reserves. It is, of course, unconscionable, if not illegal, for a country to use racial discrimination against children to reduce government costs or to rely on government funding shortfalls as a justification for failing to remedy it.

No matter what Canada's motivations for wanting to derail a hearing on the merits, it is clear that its various tactics have the effect of delaying the proceedings and, the remedy to the inequality, for tens of thousands of vulnerable children and their families.

The efficacy of Canada's legal tactics in the Canadian Human Rights Tribunal and federal court actions will be determined over time, but all Canadians should hope they are not successful. If the Canadian government wins this case on the service or comparator issue, they effectively immunize themselves from ever being held accountable for discriminatory funding practices for public services. This will substantially erode the democratic and equality principles that define the country. Moreover, another generation of First Nations children will grow up being discriminated against by the Canadian government in ways that directly imperil their safety and wellbeing. If First Nations children win, then the Canadian government will not be above its own human rights laws and for the first time in history, First Nations children will be treated equally—at least in this one program area.

The Canadian government is faced with a choice that will test the moral fabric of the nation. Does it choose to continue to perpetrate racial discrimination against First Nations children or not? No matter what their choice, the role of the international social work community is to make the Canadian government famous. Discrimination prospers in darkness and silence and wilts with light and voice.

References

Abel, L. (2009, June, 22). Interview with Cindy Blackstock, First Nations Child and Family Caring Society of Canada: Interview about a human rights case against the feds launched by the Caring Society. Narrator, Lisa Abel, CHUO radio.

Aboriginal Peoples Television Network and Canadian Human Rights Commission, Attorney General of Canada (representing the Minister of the Department of Indian Affairs and Northern Development Canada), First Nations Child and Family Caring Society of Canada, Assembly of First Nations, Chiefs of Ontario and Amnesty International, (2010). Federal Court of Canada: Notice of Application; Court File No. T-1008-10.

Amnesty International (2006). *It is a matter of rights: Improving the protection of economic, social and cultural rights in Canada.* Ottawa: Amnesty International Canada.

Assembly of First Nations, 2007 & Assembly of First Nations (2007). Leadership action plan on First Nations child welfare. Ottawa: Assembly of First Nations & Assembly of First Nations (2007). Reclaiming Our Nationhood; Strengthening Our Heritage: Report to the Royal Commission on Aboriginal Peoples. Ottawa: Assembly of First Nations.

Attorney General of Canada v. the First Nations Child and Family Caring Society of Canada and the Assembly of First Nations (November 24, 2009). Federal Court of Canada Order: Docket T-1753-08.

Attorney General of Canada v. the First Nations Child and Family Caring Society of Canada and the Assembly of First Nations (March 30, 2010). Federal Court of Canada: Order and reasons for Order: Docket T-1753-08; Citation: 2010 FC 243.

Attorney General of Canada v. the First Nations Child and Family Caring Society of Canada, the Assembly of First Nations, the Canadian Human Rights Commission, the Chiefs of Ontario and Amnesty International Canada (December 21, 2009). Notice of motion of the respondent for an order to dismiss the complaint. Filed with the Canadian Human Rights Tribunal on December 21, 2009.

Attorney General of Canada v. the First Nations Child and Family Caring Society of Canada, the Assembly of First Nations, the Canadian Human Rights Commission, the Chiefs of Ontario, and Amnesty International Canada (September 28, 2009). Statement of particulars of the respondent, the Attorney General of Canada, in response to the amended statement of particulars of the Commission. Filed with the Canadian Human Rights Tribunal on September 28, 2009.

Auditor General of Canada (2008). First Nations child and family services program—Indian and Northern Affairs Canada. 2008 May: Report of the Auditor General of Canada Retrieved October 4, 2009 from www.oag-bvg.gc.ca/internet/English/aud_ch_oag_200805_04_e_30700.html#hd3a

Blackstock, C. (2003). First Nations child and family services: Restoring peace and harmony in First Nations communities. In K. Kufeldt, & B. McKenzie (Eds.), *Child welfare: Connecting research policy and practice* (pp. 331–342). Waterloo, ON: Wilfred Laurier University Press.

Blackstock, C. (2007). Residential schools: Did they really close or just morph into child welfare? *Indigenous Law Journal*, 6(1), 71–78.

Blackstock, C. (2008). Reconciliation means not saying sorry twice: Lessons from child welfare. From truth to reconciliation: Transforming the legacy of residential schools. Ottawa: Aboriginal Healing Foundation.

Blackstock, C. (2009a). Canadian Human Rights Tribunal diary. Unpublished document. Ottawa: First Nations Child and Family Caring Society of Canada.

Blackstock, C. (2009b). Jordan's Principle: How one boy inspired a world of change. *Canadian supplement to the state of the world's children, 2009: Aboriginal children's health—leaving no child behind* (pp. 46–52). Toronto: UNICEF.

Blackstock, C. (2009(c)). Opening statement by Cindy Blackstock, PhD, executive director First Nations Child and Family Caring Society of Canada at the Canadian Human Rights Tribunal on First Nations child welfare. Retrieved October 4, 2009 at http://fnwitness.ca/docs/Opening_Statement_by_Cindy_Blackstock.pdf

Blackstock, C., Prakash, T., Loxley, J., & Wien, F. (2005). *Wen:de—We are coming to the light of day*. Ottawa: First Nations Child and Family Caring Society of Canada.

Blackstock, C., & Trocmé, N. (2005). Community based child welfare for Aboriginal children. In Michael Ungar (Ed.), *Handbook for working with children and youth: Pathways to resilience across cultures and contexts* (pp. 105–120). Thousand Oaks: Sage Publications.

Blackstock, C., Trocmé, N., & Bennett, M. (2004). Child welfare response to Aboriginal and Caucasian children in Canada: A comparative analysis. *Violence Against Women, 10*(8), 901–916.

Bryce, P.H. (1922). *The story of a national crime: An appeal for justice to the Indians of Canada*. Ottawa: James, Hope & Sons.

Caldwell, G. (1967). *Indian residential schools: A research study of the child care programs of nine residential schools in Saskatchewan*. Ottawa: The Canadian Welfare Council.

Canada (2009). *Convention on the Rights of the Child: Third and Fourth reports of Canada covering January 1998–December 2007*. Retrieved December 6, 2009 at http://rightsofchildren.ca/wp-content/uploads/canadas-third-and-fourth-report-on-crc.pdf

Canadian Council on Social Development (2003). *Funding Matters: The impact of Canada's new funding regime on non-profit and voluntary sector organizations*. Ottawa: Canadian Council on Social Development.

Canadian Human Rights Act (R.S., 1985, c. H-6). Retrieved October 3, 2009 at http://laws.justice.gc.ca/en/h-6/index.html

Canadian Human Rights Tribunal (n.d.). What happens next? A guide to the tribunal process. Ottawa: Canadian Human Rights Tribunal.

Canadian Human Rights Tribunal (2009). *Recording of proceedings First Nations Child and Family Caring Society of Canada and the Assembly of First Nations versus Attorney General of Canada (representing the Minister of Indian Affairs): September 14, 2009*. Ottawa: Canadian Human Rights Tribunal.

Clarke, S. (2007). Ending discrimination and protecting equality: A challenge to the INAC funding formula of First Nations child and family service agencies. *Indigenous Law Journal, 6*(1).

Clatworthy, S. (2005). *Indian registration, membership, and population change in First Nations communities. Department of Indian Affairs and Northern Development Canada: Strategic Research and Analysis Directorate*.

Department of Indian Affairs and Northern Development (n.d.) First Nations Child and Family Services (FNCFS) Q's and A's. Retrieved on July 10, 2010 from www.fnwitness.ca/docs/INAC-Access-to-Info-Q&A.pdf

Department of Indian and Northern Affairs Canada (2003). Backgrounder: The residential school system. Ottawa: Indian and Northern Affairs Canada. Retrieved October 8, 2009 at www.ainc-inac.gc.ca/ai/rqpi/nwz/2008/20080425a_is-eng.asp

Department of Indian and Northern Affairs Canada (2005). *First Nations child and family services national program manual*. Ottawa: Indian and Northern Affairs Canada.

Department of Indian Affairs and Northern Development Canada (2006). First Nations child and family services. Retrieved January 10, 2009 at www.ainc-inac.gc.ca/ai/mr/is/fncfseng.Asp

First Nations Child and Family Caring Society of Canada (2009). I am a witness. Retrieved October 4, 2009 at www.fnwitness.ca

First Nations Child and Family Caring Society of Canada, Assembly of First Nations and the Canadian Human Rights Commission v. the Attorney General of Canada (February 24, 2010). Submission of the First Nations Child and Family Caring Society of Canada for cross-examination of affidavits to be open to the public. Filed with the Canadian Human Rights Tribunal on February 24, 2010.

First Nations Child and Family Caring Society of Canada and Assembly of First Nations and Canadian

Human Rights Commission and Attorney General of Canada and Chiefs of Ontario and Amnesty International Canada (May 14, 2010). Submissions of the First Nations Child and Family Caring Society of Canada (respondent's motion to dismiss). Filed with the Canadian Human Rights Tribunal on May 14, 2010.

First Nations Child and Family Caring Society of Canada and Assembly of First Nations and Canadian Human Rights Commission and Attorney General of Canada and Chiefs of Ontario and Amnesty International Canada (May 21, 2010). Reply of the Attorney General of Canada (respondent's motion for an order to dismiss the complaint). Filed with the Canadian Human Rights Tribunal on May 21, 2010.

First Nations Child and Family Caring Society of Canada and Assembly of First Nations and Canadian Human Rights Commission and Attorney General of Canada and Chiefs of Ontario and Amnesty International (May 28, 2010). Ruling Canadian Human Rights Tribunal, Member Shirish P. Chotalia. Ottawa: Canadian Human Rights Tribunal.

Harper, S. (2008). Statement of Apology on behalf of Canadians for the Indian residential school system. Retrieved September 28, 2009 at www.ainc-inac.gc.ca/ai/rqpi/apo/index-eng.asp

Indian Act (R.S., 1985, c. I-5). Retrieved October 4, 2009 at http://laws.justice.gc.ca/en/I-5/

Johnston, P. (1983). *Native children and the child welfare system*. Ottawa: Canadian Council on Social Development.

Kimmelman, E. (1985). *No quiet place: Manitoba review on Indian and Métis adoptions and placements*. Winnipeg: Manitoba Ministry of Community Services.

Loppie-Reading, C., & Wien, F. (2009). *Health inequalities and social determinants of Aboriginal Peoples' health*. Prince George: National Collaborating Centre for Aboriginal Health.

Loxley, J., De Riviere, L., Prakash, T., Blackstock, C.,Wien, F., & Thomas Prokop, S. (2005). *Wen:de: The journey continues*. Ottawa: First Nations Child and Family Caring Society of Canada.

Martin, P. and Blackstock, C. (2009). Shortage of funds; surplus of suffering. Op. Ed. Toronto Star, November 23, 2009.

Mason, C. (2007). World briefing—Americas: Native Canadians file rights complaint over child welfare. New York Times. Retrieved December, 2009 at http://query.nytimes.com/gst/fullpage.html?res=9505E4DE113EF937A15751C0A9619C8B63

Matthew, M. (2000). *The cost of quality First Nations education*. West Vancouver: First Nations Education Steering Committee.

McCloskey, G. (2010). Social worker's reflections on being a witness at the Canadian Human Rights Tribunal hearing, June 2, 3, 2010 on the underfunding of child welfare services for First Nations children on reserves. Retrieved July 10, 2010 from www.oasw.org/en/membersite/pdfs/WitnessArticle-GMcCloskey-June2010.pdf

McDonald, R., & Ladd, P. (2000). *Joint national policy review of First Nations child and family services joint national policy review*. Ottawa, ON: Assembly of First Nations.

McKenzie, B., & Flette, E. (2003). Community building through block funding in Aboriginal child and family services. In Kathleen Kufeldt, & Brad McKenzie (Eds.), *Child welfare: Connecting research policy and practice* (pp. 343–354). Waterloo: Wilfred Laurier University Press.

Milloy, J. (1999). *A national crime: The Canadian government and the residential school system—1879 to 1986*. Winnipeg: University of Manitoba Press.

Monsebraaten, L. (2009). *Native children flooding into children's aid societies*. Toronto Star, November 22, 2009 (pp. 1).

Nadjiwan, S., & Blackstock, C. (2003). *Caring across the boundaries*. Ottawa: First Nations Child and Family Caring Society of Canada.

Nafe, S. (2010). Witness reflections. Retrieved July 10, 2010 from www.fnwitness.ca/witness-reflections.php

National Council on Welfare (2008). *First Nations, Métis and Inuit children and youth: Time to act*. Ottawa: National Council on Welfare.

Prentice, J. (2007). The Alberta partnership on child welfare on-reserve. Retrieved March 16, 2009 from www.ainc-inac.gc.ca/ai/mr/spch/2007/apcw-apr2707-eng.asp

Royal Commission on Aboriginal Peoples (1996). *Report of the Royal Commission on Aboriginal Peoples*. Ottawa, ON: Indian and Northern Affairs Canada.

Sinclair, M., Bala, N., Lilles, H., & Blackstock, C. (2004). Aboriginal child welfare. In N. Bala, M. Kim, Zaph J. Williams, R. Vogl, & J. Hornick (Eds.), *Canadian child welfare law: Children, families, and the state*, 2nd ed. Toronto: Thompson Educational Publishing.

Strahl, C. (2008). Speaking notes for the honorable Chuck Strahl, PC, MP, Minister of Indian Affairs and Northern Development and Interlocutor for Métis and Non-Status Indians. Retrieved October 3, 2009 at www.ainc-inac.gc.ca/ai/mr/spch/2008/may0108-eng.asp

Standing Committee on Public Accounts (2009). Chapter 4: First Nations child and family services program—Indian and Northern Affairs Canada of the May 2008 report of the Auditor General: Report of the Standing Committee on Public Accounts. Retrieved March 24, 2009 from www.fncaringsociety.com/docs/402_PACP_Rpt07-e.pdf

Trocmé, N., Knoke, D., & Blackstock, C. (2004). Pathways to the overrepresentation of Aboriginal children in Canada's child welfare system. *The Social Service Review, 78*(4), 577–601.

Trocmé, N., MacLaurin, B., Fallon, B., Knoke, D., Pitman, L., & McCormack, M. (2006). *Mesnnmimk Wasatek: Catching a drop of light: Understanding the over-representation of First Nations children in Canada's child welfare system: An analysis of the Canadian incidence study of reported child abuse and neglect (CIS-2003).* Ottawa: First Nations Child and Family Caring Society of Canada.

Union of BC Indian Chiefs (2002). *Calling forth our future: Options for the exercise of indigenous peoples authority in child welfare.* Vancouver: Union of BC Indian Chiefs.

UN News Centre (2007). United Nations adopts the Declaration on the Rights of Indigenous Peoples. Retrieved October 19, 2009 at www.un.org/apps/news/story.asp?NewsID=23794&Cr=indigenous&Cr1

Post-Case-Reading Questions

1. Why do First Nations advocates involved with the human rights complaint against the government think that the different funding formula for Aboriginal child welfare services constitutes discrimination?
2. What is the federal government's response to the charges of discrimination and injustice in this case?
3. What, if any, liberal principles or values do the two sides appeal to in making their case?

Chapter XIV

Martha Nussbaum

PHILOSOPHER: MARTHA NUSSBAUM

Introduction

Martha Craven Nussbaum is a distinguished contemporary American philosopher and public intellectual. Born in 1947 in New York City into an affluent family, she attended the Baldwin school, in Bryn Mawr, Pennsylvania, as a teenager. She later attended New York University, where she received a BA in theatre and classics in 1969. Moving on to Harvard University for her graduate studies in classics and philosophy for her graduate studies, Nussbaum obtained a PhD in 1975.

Nussbaum taught at Harvard, Brown, and Oxford universities before taking up her current position at the University of Chicago. As the Ernst Freund Distinguished Service Professor of Law and Ethics, she is jointly appointed to the Philosophy Department and Law School as well as an associate in Classics,

Martha Nussbaum

Used by permission of Martha Nussbaum.

Political Science and the Divinity School. These diverse affiliations reflect Nussbaum's unusually wide breadth as a scholar, as well as a public figure who has written on such issues as religious intolerance, patriotism, and the role of the humanities in liberal societies.

Nussbaum has made significant scholarly contributions to the fields of ethics, social and political philosophy, ancient philosophy, and feminism. Her work, in turn, is informed by the insights of key figures in these areas, particularly Aristotle, Kant, Mill, Rawls, and Catharine MacKinnon. Of special note is Nussbaum's development of the idea of "human capabilities," which evolved out of her work with the World Institute for Development Economics Research (WIDER) and her collaboration with the Nobel Prize–winning economist and philosopher Amartya Sen. Nussbaum distinguishes human capabilities from human rights, which aim at a similar end—the well-being of people—but which remain politically controversial and (Nussbaum contends) do not fully express the importance of particular human functionings. By contrast, a human capability approach focuses our attention on the actual well-being and flourishing of human beings, assessed in terms of what we are able to do and be. Nussbaum argues that this approach is more concrete and useful than that of human rights; after all, what would be the point of having a right to a good if one lacks the capacity to enjoy that good? As such, capabilities or "substantial freedoms"—what a person can do or be—are what is needed for citizens to benefit from having rights in the first place.

A key part of Nussbaum's version of the human capability approach is the list of basic capabilities that she has developed over the years. Currently that list includes (1) life; (2) bodily health; (3) bodily integrity; (4) senses, imagination, and thought; (5) emotions; (6) practical reason; (7) affiliation; (8) other species; (9) play; (10) control over one's environment. She argues that every person should have these capabilities, and when an individual is deprived of any of them there is injustice, since the person fails to achieve a good life; in this sense, the capabilities "exert a moral claim" on governments to help fulfill their citizens' capabilities. Along with Sen, Nussbaum urges that national and international public planning and policy-making should foster and promote the capabilities of citizens. Together, Nussbaum and Sen helped to found the Human Development and Capability Association in 2003, an organization that promotes the human capability approach in the theory and practice. Nussbaum's research on human capabilities also led to her extensive participation in WIDER, where she was a research advisor from 1986 to 1993.

Some of Nussbaum's many publications include *The Fragility of Goodness: Luck and Ethics in Greek Tragedy and Philosophy* (1986 and 2000), *Love's Knowledge* (1990), *The Therapy of Desire* (1994), *Cultivating Humanity: A Classical Defense of Reform in Liberal Education* (1997), *Sex and Social Justice* (1998), *Women and Human Development* (2000), *Upheavals of Thought: The Intelligence of Emotions* (2001), *Frontiers of Justice: Disability, Nationality, Species Membership* (2006), *The Clash Within: Democracy, Religious Violence, and India's Future* (2007), *Creating Capabilities: The Human Development Approach* (2011), *The New Religious Intolerance* (2012), and *Political Emotions: Why Love Matters for Justice* (2013). She has also edited 13 books and received more than 30 honorary degrees from universities around the world.

In the text included here, "Women and Cultural Universals," Nussbaum uses the list of capabilities to suggest that there are certain cultural and religious traditions that are incompatible with a commitment to the full human functioning of girls and women. Practices that entail permanently giving up a core capacity—like sexual functioning—are suspect from the vantage point of human capabilities and ought to be strongly discouraged (or in some cases, legally prohibited). The case that follows this centres on an Ontario government report from 2004 that assesses the prospect of making available shari'a law in family law arbitration in the province. Pairing these readings raises the question of whether shari'a might entail asymmetrical treatment for women in ways that would deny them access to the sort of full autonomy that Nussbaum thinks is central to the core human capabilities.

Further Readings

Alexander, J. (2008). *Capabilities and Social Justice: The Political Philosophy of Amartya Sen and Martha Nussbaum,* Farnham, UK and Burlington, VT: Ashgate Publishing.
Beck, S. (2009). "Martha Nussbaum and the Foundations of Ethics: Identity, Morality and Thought-Experiments," *South African Journal of Philosophy* 28 (3): 261–70.
Charlesworth, H. (2000). "Martha Nussbaum's Feminist Internationalism," *Ethics* 111 (1): 64–78.
Hunt, L. (2006). "Martha Nussbaum on the Emotions," *Ethics* 116 (3): 552–77.

Martha Nussbaum, "Women and Cultural Universals"

Martha Nussbaum, "Women and Cultural Universals," in Sex and Social Justice
(Oxford: Oxford University Press, 1999).

Women and Cultural Universals

We shall only solve our problems if we see them as human problems arising out of a special situation; and we shall not solve them if we see them as African problems, generated by our being somehow unlike others.

—Kwame Anthony Appiah, *Africa in the Philosophy of Cultures*

Being a woman is not yet a way of being a human being.

—Catharine MacKinnon

I. A Matter of Survival

"I may die, but still I cannot go out. If there's something in the house, we eat. Otherwise, we go to sleep." So Metha Bai, a young widow in Rajasthan, India, with two young children, described her plight as a member of a caste whose women are traditionally prohibited from working outside the home—even when, as here, survival itself is at issue. If she stays at home, she and her children may die. If she attempts to go out, her in-laws will beat her and abuse her children. For now, Metha Bai's father travels from 100 miles away to plow her small plot of land. But he is aging, and Metha Bai fears that she and her children will shortly die with him.[1]

In this case, as in many others throughout the world, cultural traditions pose obstacles to women's health and flourishing. Depressingly, many traditions portray women as less important than men, less deserving of basic life support or of fundamental rights that are strongly correlated with quality of life, such as the right to work and the right to political participation. Sometimes, as in the case of Metha Bai, the women themselves resist these traditions. Sometimes, on the other hand, the traditions have become so deeply internalized that they seem to record what is "right" and "natural," and women themselves endorse their own second-class status.

Such cases are hardly confined to non-Western or developing countries. As recently as 1873, the U.S. Supreme Court upheld a law that forbade women to practise law in the state of Illinois, on the grounds that "[t]he constitution of the family organization, which is founded in the divine ordinance, as well as in the nature of things, indicates the domestic sphere as that which properly belongs to the domain and functions of womanhood."[2] And in 1993, a woman who was threatened and grossly harassed by her male co-workers, after becoming the first woman to work in the heavy metal shop in the General Motors plant in Indiana, was described by a federal district judge as having provoked the men's conduct by her "unladylike" behaviour—behaviour that consisted in using a four-letter word a few times in a five-year period.[3] Clearly our own society still appeals to tradition in its own way to justify women's unequal treatment.

What should people concerned with justice say about this? And should they say anything at all? On the one hand, it seems impossible to deny that traditions, both Western and non-Western, perpetuate injustice against women in many fundamental ways, touching on some of the most central elements of a human being's quality of life—health, education, political liberty and participation, employment, self-respect, and life itself. On the other hand, hasty judgments that a tradition in some distant part of the world is morally retrograde are familiar legacies of colonialism and imperialism and are correctly regarded with suspicion by sensitive thinkers in the contemporary world. To say that a practice endorsed by tradition is bad is to risk erring by imposing one's own way on others, who surely have their own ideas of what is right and good. To say that a practice is all right whenever local tradition endorses it as right and good is to risk erring by withholding critical judgment where real evil and oppression are surely present. To avoid the whole issue because the matter of proper judgment is so fiendishly difficult is tempting but perhaps the worst option of all. It suggests the sort of moral collapse depicted by Dante when he describes the crowd of souls who mill around in the vestibule of hell, dragging their banner now one way, now another, never willing to set it down and take a definite stand on any moral or political question. Such people, he implies, are the most despicable of all. They cannot even get into hell because they have not been willing to stand for anything in life, one way or another. To express the spirit of this chapter very succinctly, it is better to risk being consigned by critics to the "hell" reserved for alleged Westernizers and imperialists—however unjustified such criticism would in fact be—than to stand around in the vestibule waiting for a time when everyone will like what we are going to say. And what we are going to say is: that there are universal obligations to protect human functioning and its dignity, and that the dignity of women is equal to that of men. If that involves assault on many local traditions, both Western and non-Western, so much the better, because any tradition that denies these things is unjust. Or, as a young Bangladeshi wife said when local religious leaders threatened to break the legs of women who went to the literacy classes conducted by a local NGO (nongovernmental organization), "We do not listen to the *mullahs* any more. They did not give us even a quarter kilo of rice."[4]

The situation of women in the contemporary world calls urgently for moral standtaking. Women, a majority of the world's population, receive only a small proportion of its opportunities and benefits. According to the *Human Development Report*, in no country in the world is women's quality of life equal to that of men, according to a complex measure that includes life expectancy, educational attainment, and GDP (gross domestic product) per capita.[5] Some countries have much larger gender disparities than others. (Among prosperous industrial countries, for example, Spain and Japan perform relatively poorly in this area; Sweden, Denmark, and New Zealand perform relatively well.[6]) If we now examine the Gender Empowerment Measure, which uses variables chosen explicitly to measure the relative empowerment of men and women in political and economic activity,[7] we find even more striking signs of gender disparity. Once again, the Scandinavian nations do well; Japan and Spain do relatively poorly.[8]

If we turn our attention to the developing countries we find uneven achievements but, in the aggregate, a distressing situation. On average, employment participation rates of women are only 50 per cent those of men (in South Asia 29 per cent; in the Arab states only 16 per cent).[9] Even when women are employed, their situation is undercut by pervasive wage discrimination and by long hours of unpaid household labour. (If women's unpaid housework were counted as productive output in national income accounts, global output would increase by 20–30 per cent.) Outside the home, women are generally employed in a restricted range of jobs offering low pay and low respect. The percentage of earned income that goes to women is rarely higher than 35 per

cent. In many nations it is far lower: in Iran, 16 per cent; Belize, 17 per cent; Algeria, 16 per cent; Iraq, 17 per cent; Pakistan, 19 per cent. (China at 38 per cent is higher than Japan at 33 per cent; highest in the world are Sweden at 45 per cent, Denmark at 42 per cent, and the extremely impoverished Rwanda at 41 per cent, Burundi at 42 per cent, and Mozambique at 42 per cent.) The situation of women in the workplace is frequently undermined by sex discrimination and sexual harassment.

Women are much less likely than men to be literate. In South Asia, female literacy rates average around 50 per cent those of males. In some countries the rate is still lower: in Nepal, 35 per cent; Sierra Leone, 37 per cent; Sudan, 27 per cent; Afghanistan, 32 per cent.[10] Two-thirds of the world's illiterate people are women. In higher education, women lag even further behind men in both developing and industrial nations.[11]

Although some countries allowed women the vote early in this century, some still have not done so. And there are many informal obstacles to women's effective participation in political life. Almost everywhere, they are under-represented in government: In 1980, they made up only around 10 per cent of the world's parliamentary representatives and less than 4 per cent of its cabinet officials.[12]

As Metha Bai's story indicates, employment outside the home has a close relationship to health and nutrition. So too, frequently, does political voice. And if we now turn to the very basic issue of health and survival, we find compelling evidence of discrimination against females in many nations of the world. It appears that when equal nutrition and health care are present women live, on average, slightly longer than men—even allowing for a modest level of maternal mortality. Thus, in Europe the female/male ratio in 1986 was 105/100, in North America 104.7/100.[13] But it may be objected that for several reasons it is inappropriate to compare these developed countries with countries in the developing world. Let us, therefore, with Jean Drèze and Amartya Sen, take as our baseline the ratio in sub-Saharan Africa, where there is great poverty but little evidence of gender discrimination in basic nutrition and health.[14] The female/male ratio in 1986 was 102.2/100. If we examine the sex ratio in various other countries and ask the question, "How many more women than are now in country C would be there if its sex ratio were the same as that of sub-Saharan Africa?," we get a number that Sen has graphically called the number of "missing women." The number of missing women in Southeast Asia is 2.4 million; in Latin America, 4.4; in North Africa, 2.4; in Iran, 1.4; in China, 44.0; in Bangladesh, 3.7; in India, 36.7; in Pakistan, 5.2.; in West Asia, 4.3. If we now consider the ratio of the number of missing women to the number of actual women in a country, we get, for Pakistan, 12.9 per cent; for India, 9.5 per cent; for Bangladesh, 8.7 per cent; for China, 8.6 per cent; for Iran, 8.5 per cent; for West Asia, 7.8 per cent; for North Africa, 3.9 per cent; for Latin America, 2.2 per cent; for Southeast Asia, 1.2 per cent. In India, not only is the mortality differential especially sharp among children (girls dying in far greater numbers than boys), the higher mortality rate of women compared to men applies to all age groups until the late thirties.[15]

Poverty alone does not cause women to die in greater numbers than men. This is abundantly clear from comparative regional studies in India, where some of the poorest regions, for example, Kerala, have the most equal sex ratio, and some far richer regions perform very poorly.[16] When there is scarcity, custom and political arrangement frequently decree who gets to eat the little there is and who gets taken to the doctor. And custom and political arrangement are always crucial in deciding who gets to perform wage labour outside the home, an important determinant of general status in the family and the community. As Sen has argued, a woman's perceived contribution to the well-being of the family unit is often determined by her ability to work outside, and this determines, in turn, her bargaining position within the family unit.[17] Custom and politics decree who gets access to the education that would open job opportunities and make political rights meaningful. Custom and politics decree who can go where in what clothing in what company. Custom and politics decree who gets to make what sorts of protests against ill treatment both inside and outside the family and whose voice of protest is likely to be heard.

Customs and political arrangements, in short, are important causes of women's misery and death. It seems incumbent on people interested in justice, and aware of the information about women's status that studies such as the *Human Development Reports* present, to ask about the relationship between culture and justice and between both of these and legal-political arrangements. It then seems incumbent on them to try to work out an account of the critical assessment of traditions and political arrangements that is neither do-gooder colonialism or an uncritical validation of the status quo.

One might suppose that any approach to the question of quality of life assessment in development economics would offer an account of the relationship between tradition and women's equality that would help us answer these questions. But in fact such an account is sorely lacking in the major theoretical approaches that, until recently, dominated the development scene. (Here I do not even include what has been the most common practical approach, which has been simply to ask about

GNP (gross national product) per capita. This crude approach does not even look at the distribution of wealth and income; far less does it ask about other constituents of life quality, for example, life expectancy, infant mortality, education, health, and the presence or absence of political liberties, that are not always well correlated with GNP per capita.[18] The failure to ask these questions is a particularly grave problem when it is women's quality of life we want to consider. For women have especially often been unable to enjoy or control the fruits of a nation's general prosperity.)

The leading economic approach to the family is the model proposed by Nobel Prize–winning economist Gary Becker. Becker assumes that the family's goal is the maximization of utility, construed as the satisfaction of preference or desire, and that the head of the household is a beneficent altruist who will adequately take thought for the interests of all family members.[19] In real life, however, the economy of the family is characterized by pervasive "cooperative conflicts," that is, situations in which the interests of members of a cooperative body split apart, and some individuals fare well at the expense of others.[20] Becker deserves great credit for putting these issues on the agenda of the profession in the first place. But his picture of male motivation does not fit the evidence, and in a way substantial enough to affect the model's predictive value—especially if one looks not only at women's stated satisfactions and preferences, which may be deformed by intimidation, lack of information, and habit,[21] but at their actual functioning.[22] Furthermore, the model prevents those who use it from even getting the information about individual family members on which a more adequate account might be based.[23]

Suppose we were to retain a utilitarian approach and yet to look at the satisfactions of all family members—assuming, as is standardly done in economics, that preferences and tastes are exogenous and independent of laws, traditions, and institutions rather than endogenously shaped by them. Such an approach—frequently used by governments polling citizens about well-being—has the advantage of assessing all individuals one by one. But the evidence of preference endogeneity is great, and especially great when we are dealing with people whose status has been persistently defined as second class in laws and institutions of various sorts. There are many reasons to think that women's perception even of their health status is shaped by traditional views, such as the view that female life is worth less than male life, that women are weaker than men, that women do not have equal rights, and so forth. In general, people frequently adjust their expectations to the low level of well-being they think they can actually attain.[24] This approach, then, cannot offer a useful account of the role of tradition in well-being, because it is bound by its very commitments to an uncritical validation of the status quo.

More promising than either Becker's model or the standard utilitarian approach is one suggested by John Rawls's liberalism, with its account of the just distribution of a small list of basic goods and resources.[25] This approach does enable us to criticize persistent inequalities, and it strongly criticizes the view that preferences are simply given rather than shaped by society's basic structure. But in one way the Rawlsian approach stops short. Rawls's list of "primary goods," although it includes some capacity-like items, such as liberty and opportunity, also includes thing-like items, particularly income and wealth, and it measures who is least well off simply in terms of the amount of these thing-like resources an individual can command. But people have varying needs for resources: a pregnant woman, for example, needs more calories than a nonpregnant woman, a child more protein than an adult. They also have different abilities to convert resources into functioning. A person in a wheelchair will need more resources to become mobile than a person with unimpaired limbs; a woman in a society that has defined employment outside the home as off limits to women needs more resources to become a productive worker than one who does not face such struggles. In short, the Rawlsian approach does not probe deeply enough to show us how resources do or do not go to work in making people able to function. Again, at least some of our questions about the relationship between tradition and quality of life cannot be productively addressed.

Workers on such issues have therefore increasingly converged on an approach that is now widely known as "the capabilities approach." This approach to quality-of-life measurement and the goals of public policy[26] holds that we should focus on the question: What are the people of the group or country in question actually able to do and to be? Unlike a focus on opulence (say, GNP per capita), this approach asks about the distribution of resources and opportunities. In principle, it asks how each and every individual is doing with respect to all the functions deemed important. Unlike Becker's approach, the capability approach considers people one by one, not as parts of an organic unit; it is very interested in seeing how a supposed organic unit such as the family has constructed unequal capabilities for various types of functioning. Unlike a standard utilitarian approach, the capability approach maintains that preferences are not always reliable indicators of life quality, as they may be deformed in various ways by oppression and deprivation. Unlike the type of liberal approach that focuses only on the distribution

of resources, the capability approach maintains that resources have no value in themselves, apart from their role in promoting human functioning. It therefore directs the planner to inquire into the varying needs individuals have for resources and their varying abilities to convert resources into functioning. In this way, it strongly invites a scrutiny of tradition as one of the primary sources of such unequal abilities.[27]

But the capabilities approach raises the question of cultural universalism, or, as it is often pejoratively called, "essentialism." Once we begin asking how people are actually functioning, we cannot avoid focusing on some components of lives and not others, some abilities to act and not others, seeing some capabilities and functions as more central, more at the core of human life, than others. We cannot avoid having an account, even if a partial and highly general account, of what functions of the human being are most worth the care and attention of public planning the world over. Such an account is bound to be controversial.

II. Anti-Universalist Conversations

The primary opponents of such an account of capability and functioning will be "antiessentialists" of various types, thinkers who urge us to begin not with sameness but with difference—both between women and men and across groups of women—and to seek norms defined relatively to a local context and locally held beliefs. This opposition takes many forms, and I shall be responding to several distinct objections. But I can begin to motivate the enterprise by telling several true stories of conversations that have taken place at the World Institute for Development Economics Research (WIDER), in which the anti-universalist position seemed to have alarming implications for women's lives.[28]

At a conference on "Value and Technology," an American economist who has long been a leftwing critic of neoclassical economics delivers a paper urging the preservation of traditional ways of life in a rural area of Orissa, India, now under threat of contamination from Western development projects. As evidence of the excellence of this rural way of life, he points to the fact that whereas we Westerners experience a sharp split between the values that prevail in the workplace and the values that prevail in the home, here, by contrast, exists what the economist calls "the embedded way of life," the same values obtaining in both places. His example: Just as in the home a menstruating woman is thought to pollute the kitchen and therefore may not enter it, so too in the workplace a menstruating woman is taken to pollute the loom and may not enter the room where looms are kept. Some feminists object that this example is repellant rather than admirable; for surely such practices both degrade the women in question and inhibit their freedom. The first economist's collaborator, an elegant French anthropologist (who would, I suspect, object violently to a purity check at the seminar room door), replies: Don't we realize that there is, in these matters, no privileged place to stand? This, after all, has been shown by both Derrida and Foucault. Doesn't he know that he is neglecting the otherness of Indian ideas by bringing his Western essentialist values into the picture?[29]

The same French anthropologist now delivers her paper. She expresses regret that the introduction of smallpox vaccination to India by the British eradicated the cult of Sittala Devi, the goddess to whom one used to pray to avert smallpox. Here, she says, is another example of Western neglect of difference. Someone (it might have been me) objects that it is surely better to be healthy rather than ill, to live rather than to die. The answer comes back; Western essentialist medicine conceives of things in terms of binary oppositions: life is opposed to death, health to disease.[30] But if we cast away this binary way of thinking, we will begin to comprehend the otherness of Indian traditions.

At this point Eric Hobsbawm, who has been listening to the proceedings in increasingly uneasy silence, rises to deliver a blistering indictment of the traditionalism and relativism that prevail in this group. He lists historical examples of ways in which appeals to tradition have been politically engineered to support oppression and violence.[31] His final example is that of National Socialism in Germany. In the confusion that ensues, most of the relativist social scientists—above all those from far away, who do not know who Hobsbawm is—demand that Hobsbawm be asked to leave the room. The radical American economist, disconcerted by this apparent tension between his relativism and his affiliation with the left, convinces them, with difficulty, to let Hobsbawm remain.

We shift now to another conference two years later, a philosophical conference on the quality of life.[32] Members of the quality-of-life project are speaking of choice as a basic good, and of the importance of expanding women's sphere of choices. We are challenged by the radical economist of my first story, who insists that contemporary anthropology has shown that non-Western people are not especially attached to freedom of choice. His example: A book on Japan has shown that Japanese males, when they get home from work, do not wish to choose what to eat for dinner, what to wear, and so on. They wish all these choices to be taken out of their hands

by their wives. A heated exchange follows about what this example really shows. I leave it to your imaginations to reconstruct it. In the end, the confidence of the radical economist is unshaken: We are victims of bad universalist thinking, who fail to respect "difference."[33]

The phenomenon is an odd one. For we see here highly intelligent people, people deeply committed to the good of women and men in developing countries, people who think of themselves as progressive and feminist and antiracist, people who correctly argue that the concept of development is an evaluative concept requiring normative argument[34]—effectively eschewing normative argument and taking up positions that converge, as Hobsbawm correctly saw, with the positions of reaction, oppression, and sexism. Under the banner of their fashionable opposition to universalism march ancient religious taboos, the luxury of the pampered husband, educational deprivation, unequal health care, and premature death.

Nor do these anti-universalists appear to have a very sophisticated conception of their own core notions, such as "culture," "custom," and "tradition." It verges on the absurd to treat India as a single culture, and a single visit to a single Orissan village as sufficient to reveal its traditions. India, like all extant societies, is a complex mixture of elements[35]: Hindu, Muslim, Parsi, Christian, Jewish, atheist; urban, suburban, rural; rich, poor, and middle class; high caste, low caste, and aspiring middle caste; female and male; rationalist and mystical. It is renowned for mystical religion but also for achievements in mathematics and for the invention of chess. It contains intense, often violent sectarianism, but it also contains Rabindranath Tagore's cosmopolitan humanism and Mahatma Gandhi's reinterpretation of Hinduism as a religion of universal nonviolence. Its traditions contain views of female whorishness and childishness that derive from the Laws of Manu[36]; but it also contains the sexual agency of Draupadi in the *Mahabharata*, who solved the problem of choice among Pandava husbands by taking all five, and the enlightened sensualism and female agency of the *Kama Sutra*, a sacred text that foreign readers wrongly interpret as pornographic. It contains women like Metha Bai, who are confined to the home; it also contains women like Amita Sen (mother of Amartya Sen), who fifty years ago was among the first middle-class Bengali women to dance in public, in Rabindranath Tagore's musical extravaganzas in Santiniketan. It contains artists who disdain the foreign, preferring, with the Marglins, the "embedded" way of life, and it also contains Satyajit Ray, that great Bengali artist and lover of local traditions, who could also write, "I never ceased to regret that while I had stood in the scorching summer sun in the wilds of Santiniketan sketching *simul* and *palash* in full bloom, *Citizen Kane* had come and gone, playing for just three days in the newest and biggest cinema in Calcutra."[37]

What, then, is "the culture" of a woman like Metha Bai? Is it bound to be that determined by the most prevalent customs in Rajasthan, the region of her marital home? Or, might she be permitted to consider with what traditions or groups she wishes to align herself, perhaps forming a community of solidarity with other widows and women, in pursuit of a better quality of life? What is "the culture" of Chinese working women who have recently been victims of the government's "women go home" policy, which appeals to Confucian traditions about woman's "nature"?[38] Must it be the one advocated by Confucius, or may they be permitted to form new alliances—with one another, and with other defenders of women's human rights? What is "the culture" of General Motors employee Mary Carr? Must it be the one that says women should be demure and polite, even in the face of gross insults, and that an "unladylike" woman deserves the harassment she gets? Or might she be allowed to consider what norms are appropriate to the situation of a woman working in a heavy metal shop, and to act accordingly? Real cultures contain plurality and conflict, tradition, and subversion. They borrow good things from wherever they find them, none too worried about purity. We would never tolerate a claim that women in our own society must embrace traditions that arose thousands of years ago—indeed, we are proud that we have no such traditions. Isn't it condescending, then, to treat Indian and Chinese women as bound by the past in ways that we are not?

Indeed, as Hobsbawm suggested, the vision of "culture" propounded by the Marglins, by stressing uniformity and homogeneity, may lie closer to artificial constructions by reactionary political forces than to any organic historical entity. Even to the extent to which it is historical, one might ask, exactly how does that contribute to make it worth preserving? Cultures are not museum pieces, to be preserved intact at all costs. There would appear, indeed, to be something condescending in preserving for contemplation a way of life that causes real pain to real people.

Let me now, nonetheless, describe the most cogent objections that might be raised by a relativist against a normative universalist project.

III. The Attack on Universalism

Many attacks on universalism suppose that any universalist project must rely on truths eternally fixed in the nature of things, outside human action and history. Because some people believe in such truths and some do not, the objector holds that a normative view so grounded is bound to be biased in favour of some religious/metaphysical conceptions and against others.[39]

But universalism does not require such metaphysical support.[40] For universal ideas of the human do arise within history and from human experience, and they can ground themselves in experience. Indeed, those who take all human norms to be the result of human interpretation can hardly deny that universal conceptions of the human are prominent and pervasive among such interpretations, hardly to be relegated to the dustbin of metaphysical history along with recondite theoretical entities such as phlogiston: As Aristotle so simply puts it, "One may observe in one's travels to distant countries the feelings of recognition and affiliation that link every human being to every other human being."[41] Kwame Anthony Appiah makes the same point, telling the story of his bicultural childhood. A child who visits one set of grandparents in Ghana and another in rural England, who has a Lebanese uncle and who later, as an adult, has nieces and nephews from more than seven different nations, finds, he argues, not unbridgeable alien "otherness," but a great deal of human commonality, and comes to see the world as a "network of points of affinity."[42] But such a metaphysically agnostic, experiential and historical universalism is still vulnerable to some, if not all, of the objections standardly brought against universalism.

Neglect of Historical and Cultural Differences
The opponent charges that any attempt to pick out some elements of human life as more fundamental than others, even without appeal to a transhistorical reality, is bound to be insufficiently respectful of actual historical and cultural differences. People, it is claimed, understand human life and humanness in widely different ways, and any attempt to produce a list of the most fundamental properties and functions of human beings is bound to enshrine certain understandings of the human and to demote others. Usually, the objector continues, this takes the form of enshrining the understanding of a dominant group at the expense of minority understandings. This type of objection, frequently made by feminists, can claim support from many historical examples in which the human has indeed been defined by focusing on actual characteristics of males.

It is far from clear what this objection shows. In particular it is far from clear that it supports the idea that we ought to base our ethical norms, instead, on the current preferences and the self-conceptions of people who are living what the objector herself claims to be lives of deprivation and oppression. But it does show at least that the project of choosing one picture of the human over another is fraught with difficulty, political as well as philosophical.

Neglect of Autonomy

A different objection is presented by liberal opponents of universalism. The objection is that by determining in advance what elements of human life have most importance, the universalist project fails to respect the right of people to choose a plan of life according to their own lights, determining what is central and what is not.[43] This way of proceeding is "imperialistic." Such evaluative choices must be left to each citizen. For this reason, politics must refuse itself a determinate theory of the human being and the human good.

Prejudicial Application

If we operate with a determinate conception of the human being that is meant to have some normative moral and political force, we must also, in applying it, ask which beings we take to fall under the concept. And here the objector notes that, all too easily—even if the conception itself is equitably and comprehensively designed—the powerless can be excluded. Aristotle himself, it is pointed out, held that women and slaves were not full-fledged human beings, and because his politics were based on his view of human functioning, the failure of these beings (in his view) to exhibit the desired mode of functioning contributed to their political exclusion and oppression.

It is, once again, hard to know what this objection is supposed to show. In particular, it is hard to know how, if at all, it is supposed to show that we would better off without such determinate universal concepts. For it could be plausibly argued that it would have been even easier to exclude women and slaves on a whim if one did not have such a concept to combat.[44] On the other hand, it does show that we need to think not only about getting the concept right but also about getting the right beings admitted under the concept.

Each of these objections has some merit. Many universal conceptions of the being have been insular in an arrogant way and neglectful of differences among cultures and ways of life. Some have been neglectful of choice and autonomy. And many have been prejudicially applied. But none of this shows that all such conceptions must fail in one or more of these ways. At this point, however, we need to examine a real proposal, both to display its merits and to argue that it can in fact answer these charges.

IV. A Conception of the Human Being: The Central Human Capabilities

The list of basic capabilities is generated by asking a question that from the start is evaluative: What activities[45] characteristically performed by human beings are so central that they seem definitive of a life that is truly human? In other words, what are the functions without which (meaning, without the availability of which) we would regard a life as not, or not fully, human?[46] We can get at this question better if we approach it via two somewhat more concrete questions that we often ask ourselves. First is a question about personal continuity. We ask ourselves which changes or transitions are compatible with the continued existence of that being as a member of the human kind and which are not. Some functions can fail to be present without threatening our sense that we still have a human being on our hands; the absence of others seems to signal the end of a human life. This question is asked regularly, when we attempt to make medical definitions of death in a situation in which some of the functions of life persist, or to decide, for others or (thinking ahead) for ourselves, whether a certain level of illness or impairment means the end of the life of the being in question.[47]

The other question is a question about kind inclusion. We recognize other humans as human across many differences of time and place, of custom and appearance. We often tell ourselves stories, on the other hand, about anthropomorphic creatures who do not get classified as human, on account of some feature of their form of life and functioning. On what do we base these inclusions and exclusions? In short, what do we believe must be there, if we are going to acknowledge that a given life is human?[48] The answer to these questions points us to a subset of common or characteristic human functions, informing us that these are likely to have a special importance for everything else we choose and do.

Note that the procedure through which this account of the human is derived is neither ahistorical nor a priori. It is the attempt to summarize empirical findings of a broad and ongoing cross-cultural inquiry. As such, it is both open-ended and humble; it can always be contested and remade. Nor does it claim to read facts of "human nature" from biological observation; it takes biology into account as a relatively constant element in human experience.[49] It is because the account is evaluative from the start that it is called a conception of the good.

It should also be stressed that, like John Rawls's account of primary goods in A Theory of Justice,[50] this list of good functions, which is in some ways more comprehensive than his own list, is proposed as the object of a specifically political consensus.[51] The political is not understood exactly as Rawls understands it because the nation state is not assumed to be the basic unit, and the account is meant to have broad [applicability] to cross-cultural deliberations. This means, given the current state of world politics, that many of the obligations to promote the adequate distribution of these goods must rest with individuals rather than with any political institution, and in that way its role becomes difficult to distinguish from the role of other norms and goals of the individual. Nonetheless, the point of the list is the same as that of Rawlsian primary goods: to put forward something that people from many different traditions, with many different fuller conceptions of the good, can agree on, as the necessary basis for pursuing their good life. That is why the list is deliberately rather general.[52] Each of its components can be more concretely specified in accordance with one's origins, religious beliefs, or tastes. In that sense, the consensus that it hopes to evoke has many of the features of the "overlapping consensus" described by Rawls.[53]

Having isolated some functions that seem central in defining the very presence of a human life, we do not rest content with mere bare humanness. We want to specify a life in which fully human functioning, or a kind of basic human flourishing, will be available. For we do not want politics to take mere survival as its goal; we want to describe a life in which the dignity of the human being is not violated by hunger or fear or the absence of opportunity. (The idea is very much Marx's idea, when he used an Aristotelian notion of functioning to describe the difference between a merely animal use of one's faculties and a "truly human use."[54]) The following list of central human functional capabilities is an attempt to specify this basic notion of the good: All citizens should have these capabilities, whatever else they have and pursue.[55] I introduce this as a list of capabilities rather than of actual functionings, because I shall argue that capability, not actual functioning, should be the goal of public policy.

Central Human Functional Capabilities

1. *Life*. Being able to live to the end of a human life of normal length[56]; not dying prematurely or before one's life is so reduced as to be not worth living
2. *Bodily health and integrity*. Being able to have good health, including reproductive health; being adequately nourished[57]; being able to have adequate shelter[58]
3. *Bodily integrity*. Being able to move freely from place to place; being able to be secure against violent assault, including sexual assault, marital rape, and domestic violence; having opportunities for sexual satisfaction and for choice in matters of reproduction
4. *Senses, imagination, thought*. Being able to use the senses; being able to imagine, to think, and to reason—and to do these things in a "truly human" way, a way informed and cultivated by an adequate education, including, but by no means limited to, literacy and basic mathematical and scientific training; being able to use imagination and thought in connection with experiencing and producing expressive works and events of one's own choice (religious, literary, musical, etc.); being able to use one's mind in ways protected by guarantees of freedom of expression with respect to both political and artistic speech and freedom of religious exercise; being able to have pleasurable experiences and to avoid nonbeneficial pain
5. *Emotions*. Being able to have attachments to things and persons outside ourselves; being able to love those who love and care for us; being able to grieve at their absence; in general, being able to love, to grieve, to experience longing, gratitude, and justified anger; not having one's emotional developing blighted by fear or anxiety. (Supporting this capability means supporting forms of human association that can be shown to be crucial in their development.[59])
6. *Practical reason*. Being able to form a conception of the good and to engage in critical reflection about the planning of one's own life. (This entails protection for the liberty of conscience.)
7. *Affiliation*. (a) Being able to live for and in relation to others, to recognize and show concern for other human beings, to engage in various forms of social interaction; being able to imagine the situation of another and to have compassion for that situation; having the capability for both justice and friendship. (Protecting this capability means, once again, protecting institutions that constitute such forms of affiliation, and also protecting the freedoms of assembly and political speech.) (b) Having the social bases of self-respect and nonhumiliation; being able to be treated as a dignified being whose worth is equal to that of others. (This entails provisions of non-discrimination.)
8. *Other species*. Being able to live with concern for and in relation to animals, plants, and the world of nature[60]
9. *Play*. Being able to laugh, to play, to enjoy recreational activities

10. *Control over one's environment.* (a) *Political*: being able to participate effectively in political choices that govern one's life; having the rights of political participation, free speech, and freedom of association (b) *Material*: being able to hold property (both land and movable goods); having the right to seek employment on an equal basis with others; having the freedom from unwarranted search and seizure.[61] In work, being able to work as a human being, exercising practical reason and entering into meaningful relationships of mutual recognition with other workers.

The "capabilities approach," as I conceive it,[62] claims that a life that lacks any one of these capabilities, no matter what else it has, will fall short of being a good human life. Thus it would be reasonable to take these things as a focus for concern, in assessing the quality of life in a country and asking about the role of public policy in meeting human needs. The list is certainly general—and this is deliberate, to leave room for plural specification and also for further negotiation. But like (and as a reasonable basis for) a set of constitutional guarantees, it offers real guidance to policymakers, and far more accurate guidance than that offered by the focus on utility, or even on resources.[63]

The list is, emphatically, a list of separate components. We cannot satisfy the need for one of them by giving a larger amount of another one. All are of central importance and all are distinct in quality. This limits the trade-offs that it will be reasonable to make and thus limits the applicability of quantitative cost-benefit analysis. At the same time, the items on the list are related to one another in many complex ways. Employment rights, for example, support health, and also freedom from domestic violence, by giving women a better bargaining position in the family. The liberties of speech and association turn up at several distinct points on the list, showing their fundamental role with respect to several distinct areas of human functioning.

V. Capability as Goal

The basic claim I wish to make—concurring with Amartya Sen—is that the central goal of public planning should be the *capabilities* of citizens to perform various important functions. The question that should be asked when assessing quality of life in a country—and of course this is a central part of assessing the quality of its political arrangements—is, How well have the people of the country been enabled to perform the central human functions? And, have they been put in a position of mere human subsistence with respect to the functions, or have they been enabled to live well? Politics, we argue (here concurring with Rawls), should focus on getting as many people as possible into a state of capability to function, with respect to the interlocking set of capabilities enumerated by that list.[64] Naturally, the determination of whether certain individuals and groups are across the threshold is only as precise a matter as the determination of the threshold. I have left things deliberately somewhat open-ended at this point, in keeping with the procedures of the *Human Development Report*, believing that the best way to work toward a more precise determination, at present, is to focus on comparative information and to allow citizens to judge for themselves whether their policymakers have done as well as they should have. Again, we will have to answer various questions about the costs we are willing to pay to get all citizens above the threshold, as opposed to leaving a small number below and allowing the rest a considerably above-threshold life quality. It seems likely, at any rate, that moving all citizens above a basic threshold of capability should be taken as a central social goal. When citizens are across the threshold, societies are to a great extent free to choose the other goals they wish to pursue. Some inequalities, however, will themselves count as capability failures. For example, inequalities based on hierarchies of gender or race will themselves be inadmissible on the grounds that they undermine self-respect and emotional development.

The basic intuition from which the capability approach starts, in the political arena, is that human capabilities exert a moral claim that they should be developed. Human beings are creatures such that, provided with the right educational and material support, they can become fully capable of the major human functions. That is, they are creatures with certain lower-level capabilities (which I call "basic capabilities"[65]) to perform the functions in question. When these capabilities are deprived of the nourishment that would transform them into the high-level capabilities that figure on my list, they are fruitless, cut off, in some way but a shadow of themselves. They are like actors who never get to go on the stage, or a person who sleeps all through life, or a musical score that is never performed. Their very being makes forward reference to functioning. Thus, if functioning never arrives on the scene they are hardly even what they are. This may sound like a metaphysical idea, and in a sense it is (in that it is an idea discussed in Aristotle's *Metaphysics*). But that does not mean it is not a basic and pervasive empirical idea, an idea that underwrites many of our daily practices and judgments in many times and places. Just as we hold that a child who dies before getting to maturity has died especially tragically—for her activities of growth and preparation for adult activity now have lost their point—so too with capability and functioning more generally: We believe that certain basic and central human endowments have a claim to be assisted in developing, and exert that claim on others, and especially, as Aristotle saw, on government. Without some such notion of the basic worth of human capacities, we have a hard time arguing for women's equality and for basic human rights. Think, for example, of the remark of Catharine MacKinnon that I quoted as my epigraph. If women were really just trees or turtles or filing cabinets, the fact that their current status in many parts of the world is not a fully human one would not be, as it is, a problem of justice. In thinking of political planning we begin, then, from a notion of the basic capabilities and their worth, thinking of them as claims to a chance for functioning, which give rise to correlated political duties.

I have spoken both of functioning and of capability. How are they related? Getting clear about this is crucial in defining the relation of the capabilities approach to liberalism. For if we were to take functioning itself as the goal of public policy, the liberal would rightly judge that we were precluding many choices that citizens may make in accordance with their own conceptions of the good. A deeply religious person may prefer not to be well nourished but to engage in strenuous fasting. Whether for religious or for other reasons, a person may prefer a celibate life to one containing sexual expression. A person may prefer to work with an intense dedication that precludes recreation and play. Am I saying that these are not fully human or flourishing lives? Does the approach instruct governments to nudge or push people into functioning of the requisite sort, no matter what they prefer?

Here we must answer: No, capability, not functioning, is the political goal. This is so because of the very great importance the approach attaches to practical reason, as a good that both suffuses all the other functions, making them human rather than animal,[66] and figures, itself, as a central function on the list. It is perfectly true that functionings, not simply capabilities, are what render a life fully human: If there were no functioning of any kind in a life, we could hardly applaud it, no matter what opportunities it contained. Nonetheless, for political purposes it is appropriate for us to shoot for capabilities, and those alone. Citizens must be left free to determine their course after that. The person with plenty of food may always choose to fast, but there is a great difference between fasting and starving, and it is this difference we wish to capture. Again, the person who has normal opportunities for sexual satisfaction can always choose a life of celibacy, and we say nothing against this. What we do speak against, for example, is the practice of female

genital mutilation, which deprives individuals of the opportunity to choose sexual functioning (and indeed, the opportunity to choose celibacy as well).[67] A person who has opportunities for play can always choose a workaholic life; again, there is a great difference between that chosen life and a life constrained by insufficient maximum-hour protections and/or the "double day" that makes women in many parts of the world unable to play.

The issue will be clearer if we recall that there are three different types of capabilities that figure in the analysis.[68] First, there are *basic capabilities*: the innate equipment of individuals that is the necessary basis for developing the more advanced capability. Most infants have from birth the basic capability for practical reason and imagination, though they cannot exercise such functions without a lot more development and education. Second, there are *internal capabilities*: states of the person herself that are, as far as the person herself is concerned, sufficient conditions for the exercise of the requisite functions. A woman who has not suffered genital mutilation has the internal capability for sexual pleasure; most adult human beings everywhere have the internal capability to use speech and thought in accordance with their own conscience. Finally, there are *combined capabilities*, which we define as internal capabilities *combined with* suitable external conditions for the exercise of the function. A woman who is not mutilated but is secluded and forbidden to leave the house has internal but not combined capabilities for sexual expression (and work and political participation). Citizens of repressive nondemocratic regimes have the internal but not the combined capability to exercise thought and speech in accordance with their conscience. The aim of public policy is the production of *combined capabilities*. This means promoting the states of the person by providing the necessary education and care; it also means preparing the environment so that it is favourable for the exercise of practical reason and the other major functions.[69]

This clarifies the position. The approach does not say that public policy should rest content with *internal capabilities* but remain indifferent to the struggles of individuals who have to try to exercise these in a hostile environment. In that sense, it is highly attentive to the goal of functioning, and instructs governments to keep it always in view. On the other hand, we are not pushing individuals into the function: Once the stage is fully set, the choice is up to them.

The approach is therefore very close to Rawls's approach using the notion of primary goods. We can see the list of capabilities as like a long list of opportunities for life functioning, such that it is always rational to want them whatever else one wants. If one ends up having a plan of life that does not make use of all of them, one has hardly been harmed by having the chance to choose a life that does. (Indeed, in the cases of fasting and celibacy it is the very availability of the alternative course that gives the choice its moral value.) The primary difference between this capabilities list and Rawls's list of primary goods is its length and definiteness, and in particular its determination to place on the list the social basis of several goods that Rawls has called "natural goods," such as "health and vigor, intelligence and imagination."[70] Since Rawls has been willing to put the basis of self-respect on his list, it is not at all clear why he has not made the same move with imagination and health.[71] Rawls's evident concern is that no society can guarantee health to its individuals—in that sense, saying that our goal is full combined capability may appear unreasonably idealistic. Some of the capabilities (e.g., some of the political liberties) can be fully guaranteed by society, but many others involve an element of chance and cannot be so guaranteed. We respond to this by saying that the list is an enumeration of political *goals* that should be useful as a benchmark for aspiration and comparison. Even though individuals with adequate health support often fall ill, it still makes sense to compare societies by asking about actual health capabilities, because we assume that the comparison will reflect the different inputs of human planning and can be adjusted to take account of more and less favourable natural situations.

Earlier versions of the list appeared to diverge from the approach of Rawlsian liberalism by not giving as central a place as Rawls does to the traditional political rights and liberties—although the need to incorporate them was stressed from the start.[72] This version of the list corrects that defect of emphasis. These political liberties have a central importance in making well-being human. A society that aims at well-being while overriding these has delivered to its members a merely animal level of satisfaction.[73] As Amartya Sen has recently written, "Political rights are important not only for the fulfillment of needs, they are crucial also for the formulation of needs. And this idea relates, in the end, to the respect that we each owe each other as fellow human beings."[74] This idea has recently been echoed by Rawls: Primary goods specify what citizens' needs are from the point of view of political justice.[75]

The capability view justifies its elaborate list by pointing out that choice is not pure spontaneity, flourishing independently of material and social conditions. If one cares about people's powers to choose a conception of the good, then one must care about the rest of the form of life that supports those powers, including its material conditions. Thus the approach claims that its more comprehensive concern with flourishing is perfectly consistent with the impetus behind the Rawlsian project, which has always insisted that we are not to rest content with merely formal equal liberty and opportunity but must pursue their fully equal worth by ensuring that unfavourable economic and social circumstances do not prevent people from availing themselves of liberties and opportunities that are formally open to them.

The guiding thought behind this Aristotelian enterprise is, at its heart, a profoundly liberal idea,[76] and one that lies at the heart of Rawls's project as well: the idea of the citizen as a free and dignified human being, a maker of choices. Politics has an urgent role to play here, getting citizens the tools they need, both to choose at all and to have a realistic option of exercising the most valuable functions. The choice of whether and how to use the tools, however, is left up to them, in the conviction that this is an essential aspect of respect for their freedom. They are seen not as passive recipients of social planning but as dignified beings who shape their own lives.[77]

Let us now return to the Marglins and to Metha Bai. What would this universalist approach have to say about these concrete cases? Notice how close the Marglin approach is, in its renunciation of critical normative argument, to the prevailing economic approaches of which it presents itself as a radical critique. A preference-based approach that gives priority to the preferences of dominant males in a traditional culture is likely to be especially subversive of the quality of life of women, who have been on the whole badly treated by prevailing traditional norms. And one can see this clearly in the Marglins' own examples. For menstruation taboos, even if endorsed by habit and custom, impose severe restrictions on women's power to form a plan of life and to execute the plan they have chosen.[78] They are members of the same family of traditional attitudes that make it difficult for women like Metha Bai to sustain the basic functions of life. Vulnerability to smallpox, even if someone other than an anthropologist should actually defend it as a good thing, is even more evidently a threat to human functioning. And the Japanese husband who allegedly renounces freedom of choice actually shows considerable attachment to it, in the ways that matter, by asking the woman to look after the boring details of life. What should concern us is whether the woman has a similar degree of freedom to plan her life and to execute her plan.

As for Metha Bai, the absence of freedom to choose employment outside the home is linked to other capability failures, in the areas of health, nutrition, mobility, education, and political voice. Unlike the type of liberal view that focuses on resources alone, my view enables us to focus directly on the obstacles to self-realization imposed by traditional norms and values and thus to justify special political action to remedy the unequal situation. No male of Metha Bai's caste would have to overcome threats of physical violence in order to go out of the house to work for life-sustaining food.

The capabilities approach insists that a woman's affiliation with a certain group or culture should not be taken as normative for her unless, on due consideration with all the capabilities at her disposal, she makes that norm her own. We should take care to extend to each individual full capabilities to pursue the items on the list—and then see whether they want to avail themselves of those opportunities. Usually they do, even when tradition says they should not. Martha Chen's work with widows like Metha Bai reveals that they are already deeply critical of the cultural norms that determine their life quality. One week at a widows' conference in Bangalore was sufficient to cause these formerly secluded widows to put on forbidden colors and to apply for loans; one elderly woman, "widowed" at the age of seven, danced for the first time in her life, whirling wildly in the center of the floor.[79] In other cases, especially when a woman must negotiate a relationship with a surviving husband, it takes longer for her real affiliations and preferences to emerge. Chen's related study of a rural literacy project in Bangladesh[80] shows that it took a good deal of time for women previously illiterate to figure out, in consultation with development workers, that literacy might offer something to their own concrete lives. Nonetheless, what we do not see in any of these cases is the fantasy that the Marglins describe, a cultural monolith univocally repudiating the outsider and clinging to an "embedded way of life." Why should women cling to a tradition, indeed, when it is usually not their voice that speaks or their interests that are served?

VI. Answering the Objections: Human Functioning and Pluralism

We still need to show that this approach has answers to the legitimate questions that confronted it. Concerning *neglect of historical and cultural difference*, we can begin by insisting that this normative conception of human capability is designed to make room for a reasonable pluralism in specification. The capabilities approach urges us to see common needs, problems, and capacities, but it also reminds us that each person and group faces these problems in a highly concrete context. The list claims to have identified in a very general way some components that are fundamental to any human life. But it makes room for differences of context in several ways. First, it is open ended and nonexhaustive. It does not say that these are the only important things, or that there is anything

unimportant (far less, bad) about things not on the list. It just says that this is a group of especially important functions on which we can agree to focus for political purposes.

Further, the list allows in its very design for the possibility of multiple specifications of each of the components. Good public reasoning about the list will retain a rich sensitivity to the concrete context, to the characters of the agents and their social situation. Sometimes what is a good way of promoting education in one part of the world will be completely ineffectual in another. Forms of affiliation that flourish in one community may prove impossible to sustain in another. Arriving at the best specification will most reasonably be done by a public dialogue with those who are most deeply immersed in those conditions. We should use the list to criticize injustice, but we should not say anything at all without rich and full information.

We see this, for example, in Martha Chen's account of the Bangladeshi literacy project.[81] An initial approach that simply offered the women adult literacy materials met with no response. It was only after a period of "participatory dialogue," during which the local women told their stories and the development workers gave them rich narrative information about the lives of women elsewhere, that a picture of literacy for these women in these circumstances began to emerge and to make sense. Given the opportunity, they made for themselves a concrete local specification of this vague end. And it was clearly no external imposition: The women's narratives express a joy in self-command and agency that seems to come from something very deep in themselves. Rohima, of the West Shanbandha women's group, comments:

> Even my mother said yesterday: "You did not use to visit others' homes, did not speak to others. How have you learnt to speak so many things?" I said: "Ma, how I have learnt I cannot say. Whenever I am alone I sit with the books." Mother asked: "What do you see in the books?" I said: "Ma, what valuable things there are in the books you will not understand because you cannot read and write." If somebody behaves badly with me, I go home and sit with the books. When I sit with the books my mind becomes better.[82]

The books had to have some relation to the women's concrete situation, but it was equally important that the development workers did not back off when they saw that the women's local traditions contained no history of female literacy.

We can say the same of the related value of autonomy. It would have been very wrong to assume, with the

Marglins, that these women did not want separateness and choice, that they really wanted to submerge their own aims in those of husband and family. This, again, emerges retrospectively, in their moving accounts of their newfound feeling of selfhood and mental awareness. "My mind was rusty," says one young wife, "and now it shines." On the other hand, it also would have done no good to go into that village and deliver a lecture on Kant—or on human capabilities! The universal value of practical reason and choice would have meant little in the abstract. To make sense, it had to become concretely situated in the stories they told about themselves and their lives.

If we turn to the difficult story of Metha Bai, something similar emerges. Metha Bai's is the story of age-old traditions regarding widowhood in India.[83] Any approach to her situation would have to be based on an understanding of these traditions and their special connection with issues of caste in an upwardly mobile Hindu family. Talk of "the right to work" would have been no use without a concrete local understanding. On the other hand, if the workers in the widows project had simply backed off, saying that the local values did not include a value of right to work for widows, they would have missed the depth at which Metha Bai herself longed for choice and autonomy, both as means to survival for herself and her children and as means to selfhood. These are typical examples of the fruitful ways in which an abstract value can be instantiated in a concrete situation, through rich local knowledge.

One further observation is in order. This objector is frequently worried about the way in which universalist projects may erode the values that hold communities together. We have already seen that traditional community values are not always so good for women. We can now add that universalist values build new types of community. All the women studied by Chen stressed the solidarity promoted by the literacy project, the comfort and pleasure they had in consulting with a group of women (some local, some from the development project) rather than each being isolated in the home. Mallika, a young widow in Dapunia, vigorously expresses this idea:

> The group helped us and taught us many things. I have learned how to live unitedly. Before if any rich person abused or criticized, we could not reply. But now if anybody says anything bad, we, the 17 members of the group, go together and ask that person why he or she passed this comment. This is another kind of help we have gotten. Before we did not know how to get together and help each other. . . . Each one was busy with their own worries and sorrows, always thinking about food

for their children and themselves. Now we, the 17 members of the group, have become very close to one another.[84]

This story is no isolated phenomenon. In women's groups I have visited in both India and China, the first benefit that is typically mentioned is that of affiliation and friendship with other women in pursuit of common goals. This shows us something highly pertinent to the Marglins' nostalgic tale of embeddedness. We do not have to choose between "the embedded life" of community and a deracinated type of individualism. Universal values build their own communities, communities of resourcefulness, friendship, and agency, embedded in the local scene but linked in complex ways to groups of women in other parts of the world. For these women the new community was a lot better than the one they had inhabited before.

The liberal charges the capability approach with *neglect of autonomy*, arguing that any such determinate conception removes from the citizens the chance to make their own choices about the good life. We have already said a good deal about this issue, but let us summarize, stressing three points. First, the list is a list of capabilities, not a list of actual functions, precisely because the conception is designed to leave room for choice. Government is not directed to push citizens into acting in certain valued ways; instead, it is directed to make sure that all human beings have the necessary resources and conditions for acting in those ways. By making opportunities available, government enhances, and does not remove, choice.[85] It will not always be easy to say at what point someone is really capable of making a choice, especially when there are traditional obstacles to functioning. Sometimes our best strategy may well be to look at actual functioning and infer negative capability (tentatively) from its absence.[86] But the conceptual distinction remains critical. Even in the rare case in which the approach will favour compulsory measures—particularly in primary and secondary education—it does so because of the huge role education plays in opening other choices in life.

Second, this respect for choice is built deeply into the list itself, in the role it gives to practical reasoning, to the political liberties, and also to employment, seen as a source of opportunity and empowerment. One of the most central capabilities promoted by the conception will be the capability of choosing itself.[87]

The examples we have considered show the truth of these claims. In the literacy project, a concern for autonomy was fundamental in the method of participatory dialogue itself, which constructed a situation free from intimidation and hierarchy in which the women's own concerns could gradually emerge and develop on the basis of the information they received. Their ex post facto satisfaction with their new situation, in which life choices were greatly enhanced, indicates, I believe, that the focus on a general capability goal was not a violation of their autonomy. (Rohima comments: "It is good now . . . As my knowledge and understanding are good now, I will be able to do many things gradually."[88]) Indeed, we can see in the project as a whole the construction of full autonomy out of a more inchoate sense of the self. Metha Bai already had a robust sense of her own interests and how they diverged from the expectations of those around her. But the widows project, which extended her thoughts by providing information and advice, was crucial to the further development of her own conception of life.

Finally, the capability view insists that choice is not pure spontaneity, flourishing independently of material and social conditions. If one cares about autonomy, then one must care about the rest of the form of life that supports it and the material conditions that enable one to live that form of life. Thus, the approach claims that its own comprehensive concern with flourishing is a better way of promoting choice than is the liberal's narrower concern with spontaneity alone, which sometimes tolerates situations in which individuals are cut off from the fully human use of their faculties.

We now face the objection about *prejudicial application*. Catharine MacKinnon once claimed that "being a woman is not yet a way of being a human being."[89] As this remark suggests, most traditional ways of categorizing and valuing women have not accorded them full membership in the human species, as that species is generally defined. If this is so, one might well ask, of what use is it to identify a set of central human capabilities? For the basic (lower-level) capacity to develop these can always be denied to women, even by those who grant their centrality—for example, by denying women "rational nature," or by asserting that they are connected to dangerous or unclean animality. Does this problem show that the human function idea is either hopelessly in league with patriarchy or, at best, impotent as a tool for justice?

I believe that it does not. For if we examine the history of these denials we see, I believe, the great power of the conception of the human as a source of moral claims. Acknowledging the other person as a member of the very same kind would have generated a sense of affiliation and a set of moral and educational duties. That is why, to those bent on shoring up their own power, the stratagem of splitting the other off from one's own species seems so urgent and so seductive. But to deny humanness to beings with whom one lives in conversation

and interaction is a fragile sort of self-deceptive stratagem, vulnerable to sustained and consistent reflection, and also to experiences that cut through self-deceptive rationalization. Any moral conception can be withheld, out of ambition or hatred or shame. But the conception of the human being, spelled out, as here, in a roughly determinate way, seems much harder to withhold than others that have been made the basis for ethics, such as "rational being" or "person."

VII. Women and Men: Two Norms or One?

But should there be a single norm of human functioning for men and women? One might grant that human capabilities cross cultures while still maintaining that in each culture a division of labour should be arranged along gender lines.

One such position, which I shall call Position A, assigns to both males and females the same general normative list of functions but suggests that males and females should exercise these functions in different spheres of life: men in the public sphere, for example, and women in the home. The second, which I shall call Position B, insists that the list of functions, even at a high level of generality, should be different: for men, citizenship and rational autonomy; for women, family love and care.

Position A is compatible with a serious interest in equality and in gender justice. For what it says, after all, is that males and females have the same basic needs for capability development and should get what they need. It is determined to ensure that both get to the higher (developed) level of capability with respect to all the central functions. It simply holds that this can (and perhaps should) be done in separate spheres. Is this any more problematic than to say that human functioning in India can, and even should, take a different concrete form from functioning in England? Or that some people can realize musical capacities by singing; others by playing the violin?

The trouble comes when we notice that Position A usually ends up endorsing a division of duties that is associated with traditional forms of hierarchy. Even Mill, who made so many fine arguments against women's subordination, did not sufficiently ask how the very perpetuation of separate spheres of responsibility might reinforce subordination. It is hard to find plausible reasons for perpetuating functional distinctions that coincide with traditional hierarchy. Even in the fourth century BCE, Plato was able to see that women's role in childbearing does not require, or even suggest, that women be confined to the home.[90] Advances in the control of reproduction are making this less and less plausible. The disability imposed by childbearing on a member of the labour force is to a large extent socially constructed, above all by the absence of support for child care, from the public sphere, from employers, and from male partners.

Sometimes clinging to traditional divisions is a prudent way of promoting social change. Neither Chen nor her colleagues proposed to jettison all gender divisions within the Bangladeshi villages. Instead, they found "female jobs" for the women that were somewhat more dignified and important than the old jobs, jobs that looked continuous with traditional female work but were outside the home and brought in wages. The "revolution" in women's quality of life never would have taken place but for the caution of the women, who at each stage gave the men of the village reason to believe that the transformations were not overwhelmingly threatening and were good for the well-being of the entire group. But such pragmatic decisions in the face of recalcitrant realities do not tell how things ought to be. And it is likely that women's subordination will not be adequately addressed as long as women are confined to a sphere traditionally devalued, linked with a low "perceived well-being contribution."[91] The *Human Development Report*'s Gender Empowerment Measure rightly focuses, therefore, on the ability of women to win entry into the traditional male spheres of politics and administration.

I turn, then, to Position B, which has been influentially defended by many philosophers, including Rousseau and some of his followers in today's world.[92] Insofar as B relies on the claim that there are two different sets of basic innate capacities, we should insist, with John Stuart Mill, that this claim has not been borne out by any responsible scientific evidence. Experiments that allegedly show strong gender divisions in basic (untrained) abilities have been shown to contain major scientific flaws; these flaws removed, the case for such differences is altogether inconclusive.[93] Experiments that cross-label babies as to sex have established that children are differentially handled, played with, and talked to straight from birth, in accordance with the handler's beliefs about the child's biological sex. It is therefore impossible at present to separate "nature" from "culture."[94] There may be innate differences between the sexes, but so far we are not in a position to know them—any more than we were when Mill first made that argument in 1869.[95]

Second, we should note that even what is claimed in this body of scientific material without substantiation usually does not amount to a difference in what I have been calling the central basic capabilities. What is alleged is usually a differential statistical distribution of some specific capacity for a high level of excellence, not for crossing a basic threshold, and excellence in some

very narrowly defined function (say, geometrical ability), rather than in one of our large-scale capabilities such as the capability to perform practical reasoning. Thus, even if the claim were true it would not be a claim about capabilities in our capacious sense; nor, because it is a statistical claim, would it have any implications for the ways in which individuals should be treated. The political consequences of such alleged sex differences in our scheme of things, even had they been established, would be nil.

But we can also criticize Position B in a different way, arguing that the differentiated conceptions of male and female functioning characteristically put forward by B are internally inadequate and fail to give us viable norms of human flourishing.[96]

What do we usually find, in the versions of B that our philosophical tradition bequeaths to us? (Rousseau's view is an instructive example). We have, on the one hand, males who are "autonomous," capable of practical reasoning, independent and self-sufficient, allegedly good at political deliberation. These males are brought up not to develop strong emotions of love and feelings of deep need that are associated with the awareness of one's own lack of self-sufficiency. For this reason they are not well equipped to care for the needs of their family members or, perhaps, even to notice those needs. On the other hand, we have females such as Rousseau's Sophie,[97] brought up to lack autonomy and self-respect, ill equipped to rely on her own practical reasoning, dependent on males, focused on pleasing others, and good at caring for others. Is either of these viable as a complete life for a human being?

It would seem not. The internal tensions in Rousseau's account are a good place to begin.[98] Rousseau places tremendous emphasis on compassion as a basic social motivation. He understands compassion to require fellow feeling and a keen responsiveness to the sufferings of others. And yet, in preparing Emile for autonomous citizenship, he ultimately gives emotional development short shrift, allocating caring and responsiveness to the female sphere alone. It appears likely that Emile will be not only an incomplete person but also a defective citizen, even by the standards of citizenship recognized by Rousseau himself.

With Sophie, things again go badly. Taught to care for others but not taught that her life is her own to plan, she lives under the sway of external influences and lacks self-government. As Rousseau himself shows in his fascinating narrative of the end of her life,[99] Sophie comes to a bad end through her lack of judgment. Moreover, in the process she proves to be a bad partner and deficient in love. For love, as we come to see, requires judgment and constancy. Thus each of them fails to live a complete human life, and each fails, too, to exemplify fully and well the very functions for which they were being trained, because those functions require support from other functions for which they were not trained. The text leads its thoughtful reader to the conclusion that the capabilities that have traditionally marked the separate male and female spheres are not separable from one another without a grave functional loss. Society cannot strive for completeness by simply adding one sphere to the other. It must strive to develop in each and every person the full range of the human capabilities.

This more inclusive notion of human functioning admits tragic conflict. For it insists on the separate value and the irreplaceable importance of a rich plurality of functions. And the world does not always guarantee that individuals will not be faced with painful choices among these functions, in which, in order to pursue one of them well they must neglect others (and thus, in many cases, subvert the one as well). But this shows once again, I believe, the tremendous importance of keeping some such list of the central functions before us as we assess the quality of life in the countries of the world and strive to raise it. For many such tragedies—like many cases of simple capability failure—result from unjust and unreflective social arrangements. One can try to construct a society in which the tragic choices that faced Emile and Sophie would not be necessary, in which both males and females could learn both to love and to reason.

In April 1994, Metha Bai went to Bangalore for the widows' conference. She met widows from all over India, and they spent a week discussing their common problems. During that week, Metha Bai began to smile a lot. She bought beads in the forbidden color of blue, and she seemed pleased with the way she looked. With advice from a local NGO involved in the conference, she applied for and obtained a loan that enabled her to pay off the mortgage on the small property she still owns. Although her economic situation is not secure and she still does not hold a job outside the home, she has managed to stave off hunger. Like many women all over the world, she is fighting for her life, with resilience and fortitude.

Women belong to cultures. But they do not choose to be born into any particular culture, and they do not really choose to endorse its norms as good for themselves, unless they do so in possession of further options and opportunities—including the opportunity to form communities of affiliation and empowerment with other women. The contingencies of where one is born, whose power one is afraid of, and what habits shape one's daily thought are chance events that should not be permitted to play the role they now play in pervasively shaping women's life chances. Beneath all these chance events are human powers, powers of choice and intelligent self-formation. Women in much of the world lack support for the most central human functions, and this denial of support is frequently caused by their being women. But women, unlike rocks and plants and even horses, have the potential to become capable of these human functions, given sufficient nutrition, education, and other support. That is why their unequal failure in capability is a problem of justice. It is up to all human beings to solve this problem. I claim that a conception of human functioning gives us valuable assistance as we undertake this task.

Post-Reading Questions

1. Nussbaum claims that the list of capabilities is cross-cultural and universal. In what sense is it so (according to Nussbaum)?
2. Women's capabilities are readily undercut by sexual discrimination in many societies, Nussbaum argues. What are some of the ways in which women's traditional roles and circumstances prevent them from fully developing certain core capabilities?
3. Governments should be required to support central human capabilities, in Nussbaum's view. What might this mean in terms of concrete policies and programs?
4. How does Nussbaum respond to the charge that her argument is ethnocentric and insufficiently sensitive to cultural differences, and is her reply convincing?

CASE STUDY
SHARI'A LAW IN ONTARIO

Introduction

In 2004, an Islamic organization in Ontario proposed to establish a shari'a court that would permit Muslims in the province who so wished to use Islamic religious principles in arbitrations in family law and inheritance cases. Practitioners of other religious faiths—notably Catholicism and Judaism—regularly made use of Ontario's Arbitration Act to employ alternative, faith-based tribunals to resolve disputes in the areas of divorce, child custody, and inheritance. Former Attorney General Marion Boyd was asked to review the issue and make recommendations on the matter. Her controversial report, *Dispute Resolution in Family Law: Protecting Choice, Promoting Inclusion*, endorsed voluntary religious arbitration in matters of family law; a multicultural society such as Canada could and should accommodate the alternative legal remedies favoured by some members of religious communities, it argued. The report was careful to address the risks of such accommodation, however, and proposed numerous safeguards for women and children in particular.

Following much public, domestic, and international media criticism of Boyd's recommendations, Premier Dalton McGuinty finally concluded in September 2005 that he would not act upon the recommendations contained in the report. Far from extending the practice of alternative family courts to the Muslim community, McGuinty announced that he intended to end the use of existing religious arbitration in the province altogether. While many hailed the decision as a victory for secularism and women's equality, others viewed it as a defeat for multiculturalism and religious toleration in the province.

Women's rights advocates were especially vocal opponents of the proposed use of shari'a: numerous women groups argued that shari'a law would ultimately entail an asymmetrical treatment of women that would deny them full autonomy and equality with men. Notably, the Canadian Council of Muslim Women warned that women would not get a fair deal if Islamic principles were used to guide family and inheritance decisions, even with the use of proposed safeguards. Their position is consistent with liberal feminist Martha Nussbaum's insistence that "equality of the sexes should be a prominent part of the public political culture, and . . . religions that dispute sex equality should not have the option of making law to that effect."[100] Nussbaum argues that institutions and practices which reinforce girls' and women's subordination—however subtely—make it harder for them to develop and exercise central human capabilities. A public commitment to these capabilities, Nussbaum insists, will require that a society's (or a religious group's) social and cultural norms and practices be critically examined, and where necessary, reformed or even restricted. Some feminist critics dispute Nussbaum's claim that the capabilities approach to justice is truly universal and cross-cultural in character and scope, however.

The liberal feminist position expressed by feminist criticis of the shari'a proposal in Ontario was prominently featured by the media, but this was by no means the only view expressed. Anti-racist and pro-multicultural feminists warned that preventing Muslim women from opting for alternative, faith-based arbitration reflected a paternalistic and even racist attitude that failed to treat them as the diverse and capable persons that they are. These political objections echoed the concerns of post-colonial feminist scholars like Sherene Razack, who drew attention to the portrayal of Muslim women (by the media and politicians) as wholly without agency and so as needing to be rescued from men in their communities. A similar cross-section of views was expressed in Quebec when that province's National Assembly unanimously approved a 2005 resolution opposing any plans for future Islamic tribunals to be established in Quebec or Canada.

Marion Boyd, *From* "Dispute Resolution in Family Law: Protecting Choice, Promoting Inclusion"

Marion Boyd, "Dispute Resolution in Family Law: Protecting Choice, Promoting Inclusion" (December 2004).
Report prepared for the Government of Ontario (excerpt from Executive Summary).
www.attorneygeneral.jus.gov.on.ca/english/about/pubs/boyd/executivesummary.pdf

Arbitration

Arbitration is a dispute resolution method in which people participate only by choice. . . . Religious arbitration can allow the people in dispute to select a shared set of values and rules that may be different than Ontario law. Use of the Arbitration Act by minority communities is a way of engaging with the broader community by formalizing a method of decision-making which currently occurs in an informal manner.

Family Law

Family law is an area of shared jurisdiction between the federal and provincial governments. Most family law disputes are resolved without court action, but increasingly alternative dispute resolution is used. Arbitration can only resolve disputes that the parties could agree about themselves; it cannot change a person's status by granting a divorce, or by concluding that they are a parent. Domestic contracts, such as separation agreements, are a common means of resolving family law disputes and the law has some built-in safeguards for these types of contracts. The Review heard concerns about polygamy and child abduction, but these issues are not affected by arbitration. Criminal law and child welfare law protect children from abuse, and people have a duty to report children in need of protection.

. . .

Personal Law

Personal law is the law that pertains to an individual's status and membership in a community or family group. Family and inheritance matters fall within a category of personal law that developed primarily from religious sources. Personal law has been used throughout history to allow groups to maintain their cultural identity, by allowing them to continue to control their definitions of family and community. In parts of Europe, the practice of applying the personal law of an individual's country of origin continues until today. For example, the citizenship laws of France and Germany mean that people may not be subject to the laws of their country of residence, but rather their country of origin.

Themes in the Submissions

There were a number of different themes expressed by those consulted, which were often contradictory. Some thought that arbitration should not be permitted in family law and inheritance cases because it would offend the Charter and perpetuate an imbalance of power in cases of abuse. Others argued that arbitration should be permitted because it is less costly and more effective. Still others submitted that religiously-based arbitration must be permitted because it is protected by freedom of religion, and is integral to a faithful person's life.

In fact, religious arbitration is already being conducted by several different faiths. Although some participants in the Review fear that the use of arbitration is the beginning of a process whose end goal is a separate political identity for Muslims in Canada, that has not been the experience of other groups who use arbitration. . . .

Summary of Recommendations

1. Arbitration should continue to be an alternative dispute resolution option that is available in family and inheritance law cases, subject to the further recommendations of this Review.
2. The Arbitration Act should continue to allow disputes to be arbitrated using religious law, if the safeguards currently prescribed and recommended by this Review are observed.

Legislative

3. Section 51 of the Family Law Act should be amended to add mediation agreements and arbitration agreements to the definition of "domestic contracts" to bring these agreements into the general protections of Part IV of the Act. Therefore these agreements would be required to be in writing, signed by the parties and witnessed.

4. When Part IV of the Family Law Act applies, a mediation agreement or arbitration agreement should be able to be set aside on the same grounds as other domestic contracts.

. . .

8. Section 33 (4) of Part III of the Family Law Act, permitting the Court to set aside a domestic contract or paternity agreement for provision of support, should be amended to permit a court to set aside an arbitral award on the same grounds (unconscionability, person owed support is receiving social assistance, or the support is in arrears).

9. The Arbitration Act should be amended to permit a court to set aside an arbitral award in a family or inheritance matter if:

(a) the award does not reflect the best interests of any children affected by it;

(b) a party to it did not have or waive independent legal advice;

(c) the parties do not have a copy of the arbitration agreement, and a written decision including reasons; or

(d) applicable, a party did not receive a statement of principles of faith-based arbitration.

The parties should not be able to waive this provision.

. . .

Regulatory

12. Regulations in the Arbitration Act or the Family Law Act should require that arbitration agreements of family law and inheritance cases must be in writing and must set out:

   • a detailed list of issues that are submitted to arbitration;
   • whether the arbitration is binding or advisory;
   • the form of law, if not Ontario law, which will be used to decide the dispute, and in the case of religious law, which form of the religious law;
   • if the arbitration is under religious law, an acknowledgement that the party has received and reviewed the statement of principles of faith-based arbitration prior to signing the agreement;
   • explicit details of any waiver of any rights or remedies under the Arbitration Act;
   • an explicit statement that judicial remedies under s. 46 and the right to fair and equal treatment under s. 19 of the Arbitration Act cannot be waived;
   • an explicit statement recognizing that judicial oversight of children's issues cannot be waived and that s. 33 (4) of the Family Law Act continues to apply; and
   • an explicit statement that s. 56 of the Family Law Act applies to the agreement and cannot be waived and therefore a party can apply to set the agreement aside for additional reasons including if it is not in the best interests of any children affected by the agreement, there was not full and frank financial disclosure, or a party did not understand the nature or consequences of the agreement.

13. Regulations in the Arbitration Act or the Family Law Act should require arbitration agreements in family law and inheritance cases to contain either a certificate of independent legal advice or an explicit waiver of independent legal advice.

. . .

15. Regulations under the Arbitration Act should define the concept of a fair and equal process in the context of family law or inheritance arbitrations.

16. Regulations in the Arbitration Act or the Family Law Act should require that arbitrators who apply religious law in family law and inheritance arbitrations develop a statement of principles of faith-based arbitration that explains the parties' rights and obligations and available processes under the particular form of religious law.

. . .

19. Regulations under the Arbitration Act or the Family Law Act should require mediators and arbitrators in family law and inheritance cases to certify that they have screened the parties separately for domestic violence, that they have reviewed the certificates of Independent Legal Advice or the waiver of Independent Legal Advice, and are satisfied that each party is entering into the arbitration voluntarily and with knowledge of the nature and consequences of the arbitration agreement.

. . .

Independent Legal Advice

21. The certificate of Independent Legal Advice in family law and inheritance cases should state that the party has received advice about the Ontario and Canadian law applicable to his or her fact situation, the law of arbitration, and the remedies available to both parties under Ontario family and arbitration law.

. . .

23. If religious law is chosen under the arbitration agreement in a family law or inheritance case, the Independent Legal Advice certificate should explicitly state that the lawyer reviewed the statement of principles of faith-based arbitration and the lawyer is satisfied that the person has sufficient information to understand the nature and consequences of choosing the religious law.

24. Waivers of Independent Legal Advice in family law and inheritance cases should state that the party has waived the right to receive advice about Canadian and Ontario family law and Ontario arbitration law, and if religious law is chosen should state that the party has received and reviewed the statement of principles of faith-based arbitration required by Recommendations 16 and 17.

Public Legal Education

25. The Government of Ontario should develop, in collaboration with community organizations and experts, a series of public education initiatives, aimed at creating awareness of the legal system, alternative dispute resolution options, and family law provisions.

26. The initiatives in Recommendation 25 should be linguistically and culturally designed to suit the diverse needs of different communities . . .

. . .

28. Public legal information programs funded by the government of Ontario should include an overview of the options for resolving a family law dispute, including the arbitration process.

29. Public legal information programs in family law funded by the government of Ontario should be available to all community members who wish to attend, whether or not they have a matter before the court.

. . .

Training and Education for Professionals

31. The Government of Ontario should work together with professional bodies to develop a standardized screening process for domestic violence for use in family law and inheritance mediations and arbitrations.

. . .

33. The Government of Ontario should work with voluntary professional associations for mediators and arbitrators to provide training on issues of power imbalance in family law and inheritance cases…

. . .

Oversight and Evaluation of Arbitrations

. . .

41. Arbitrators in family law and inheritance cases should be required to provide the Government of Ontario with summaries of each decision, free of identifying information, and the Government should make these summaries available upon request for research, evaluation and consumer protection purposes. If in the future arbitrators become a self-regulating profession, the inventory of summaries of decisions should be transferred to the regulatory body for that profession.

. . .

Post-Case-Reading Questions

1. What liberal feminist principles might support the prohibition of faith-based arbitration in family law in Canadian society?
2. What liberal values might, on the other hand, support the establishment of alternative religious arbitration in a multicultural country such as Canada?
3. Were the safeguards proposed by Marion Boyd in her report sufficient to assuage concerns about the pressures and disadvantages that Muslim women participating in these arbitrations might potentially face?

XV

Jürgen Habermas

PHILOSOPHER: JÜRGEN HABERMAS

Introduction

Jürgen Habermas is a contemporary German political philosopher, social theorist, and public intellectual. He is one of the
most widely read and influential philosophers of our time, owing to the interdisciplinary nature of his work and his active
interventions in public debates over many decades. Born into
a middle-class family in Düsseldorf in 1929, Habermas was,
like most teenagers in that time, recruited into the National
Socialist Youth Organization. His passive association with this
group was severed at the end of World War II, which brought
with it the revelation of Nazi genocide. As a young man, he took
up the study of philosophy and became interested in Martin
Heidegger's thought; however, he was later a prominent critic of
Heidegger's reluctance to acknowledge his Nazi past.

Jürgen Habermas

© INTERFOTO/Alamy

   In 1954, Habermas completed his doctorate in philosophy at the University of Bonn,
writing his thesis on the work of German idealist Friedrich Schelling. In 1956, he obtained
a research assistantship at the newly established Institute for Social Research at Frankfurt
University, working for one of the Institute's founders, Theodor Adorno. The work of Adorno
and that of his close associate, Max Horkheimer—key figures in the first generation of the
Frankfurt School of Critical Theory—was to have a lasting influence on Habermas's thinking. During this time, his writing had a decidedly Marxist tenor. Habermas remained at the
Institute until 1958, when he left for the University of Marburg, earning his Habilitation—
the highest German university degree—in 1961. He subsequently taught at Heidelberg until
1964, at which time he returned to the Goethe University in Frankfurt as a professor of
philosophy and sociology. From 1971 until 1983, he held the post of the director of the Max
Planck Institute in Starnberg, after which he returned to his professorship at Frankfurt,
staying until his retirement in 1994. Since his retirement, Habermas has been based in
Starnberg but has taught part-time in the United States, mainly in Chicago and New York.

   Habermas's social, political, and moral philosophy has generated a vast body of literature. His social theory finds its most articulate expression in the monumental two-volume
text, *The Theory of Communicative Action* (1981), in which he gives a typology of action:

(1) communicative action, which is aimed at mutual understanding, and (2) instrumental or strategic action, which is aimed at success or domination. Habermas argues that every speech act—a linguistic utterance that performs an act such as promising something—invariably entails a claim to validity. Interlocutors may engage in the process of giving and receiving reasons, resulting in socially coordinated action, or what he calls communicative action. According to thinkers of the Frankfurt School, the Enlightenment era wrongly ignored communicative action as a viable form of rationality, recognizing only instrumental rationality.

The theorization of the possibility—and importance—of free and uncoerced communication can be traced back to Habermas's first publication, *The Structural Transformation of the Public Sphere* (1962). In this text, he lays out the emergence of the liberal public sphere as the location of communicative rationality manifested in public debates over matters of common concern. As such, communicative rationality, according to Habermas, holds tremendous emancipatory promise.

In *Moral Consciousness and Communicative Action* (1983), Habermas applies the idea of communicative rationality to moral theory and conceives of "discourse ethics," which elevates communicative interaction to a higher level of evaluation by submitting the validity claims raised in communication to rigorous testing. Two principles, namely, the discourse principle (D) and the universalization principle (U),[1] are presented as the tests that any moral claim ought to pass in order to gain moral validity. These two principles require that moral claims be discursively produced, deliberated upon, and accepted.

Habermas's theory of deliberative democracy—as formulated in *Between Facts and Norms: Contribution to a Discourse Theory of Law and Democracy* (1992)—extends his work on communicative rationality, exploring its implication for political and legal theory. Indeed, deliberative democracy now comprises a distinct perspective or even "school" of political thought, with numerous contemporary political philosophers influenced by Habermas identifying as theorists of deliberative democracy.

The breadth and volume of Habermas's body of work are unusually large: working in (and across) several different academic disciplines, he has been writing and publishing for 50 years at an astonishing pace. His books have been translated into many languages, and their influence extends over to disciplines beyond philosophy. A few of his books include *Theory and Practice* (1963), *The Logic of Social Sciences* (1967), *Knowledge and Human Interest* (1968), *Legitimation Crisis* (1973), *Communication and the Evolution of Society* (1976), *The Philosophical Discourse of Modernity* (1985), *The Inclusion of the Other* (1998), *The Postnational Constellation* (2001), and *The Divided West* (2006).

In the reading that is included here, Habermas gives an outline of three political models of association: liberal, republican, and deliberative. He argues that the liberal model emphasizes individual rights at the expense of community rights, and republicans commit the reverse error. According to Habermas, we need instead to move beyond this dichotomy and to recognize the interdependence and critical importance of both private and public autonomy (what he calls the "co-originality" of both).

The case reading that follows this essay by Habermas concerns a (now defunct) federal funding initiative known as the "Court Challenges Program" which enabled Canadian citizens to bring forth litigation connected to the Charter of Rights and Freedoms. Groups seeking to test the Charter's protection of their equality rights—such as women and advocates for the disabled—used this program to expose deficiencies in government policies and programs. As such, it reflects the spirit of Habermas's ideal of a deliberative democracy in which citizens contribute to public debate about which constitutional norms and rights should prevail in a democratic society.

Further Readings

Dews, P. (ed.). (1999). *Habermas: A Critical Reader*. Oxford: Blackwell.

Finlayson, G. (2005). *Habermas: A Very Short Introduction*. Oxford: Oxford University Press.

Ingram, D. (1993). "The Limits and Possibilities of Communicative Ethics for Democratic Theory," *Political Theory* 21 (2): 294–321.

McCarthy, T. (1981). *The Critical Theory of Jürgen Habermas*. Cambridge: MIT Press.

Payrow Shabani, O. (2003). *Democracy, Power and Legitimacy: The Critical Theory of Jürgen Habermas*. Toronto: University of Toronto Press.

Rasmussen, D. (1991) *Reading Habermas*. Cambridge, MA and Oxford: Basil Blackwell.

Jürgen Habermas, "Three Normative Models of Democracy"

Jürgen Habermas, "Three Normative Models of Democracy,"
Constellations, *1 (1), 1994: 1–10.*

I would like to sketch a proceduralist view of democracy and deliberative politics which differs in relevant aspects from both the liberal and the republican paradigm. Let me (1) remind you [of] the opposite features of these two established models. I will then (2) introduce a new proceduralist conception by way of a critique of the "ethical overload" of the republican view. The last part of the paper further elaborates (3) the three normative models of democracy by comparing their corresponding images of state and society.

(1) The Two Received Views of Democratic Politics

According to the "liberal" or Lockean view, the democratic process accomplishes the task of programming the government in the interest of society, where the government is represented as an apparatus of public administration, and society as a market-structured network of interactions among private persons. Here politics (in the sense of the citizens' political will-formation) has the function of bundling together and pushing private interests against a government apparatus specializing in the administrative employment of political power for collective goals. On the "republican" view, however, politics involves more than this mediating function; it is rather constitutive for the processes of society as a whole. "Politics" is conceived as the reflective form of substantial ethical life, namely as the medium in which the members of somehow solitary communities become aware of their dependence on one another and, acting with full deliberation as citizens, further shape and develop existing relations of reciprocal recognition into an association of free and equal consociates under law. With this, the liberal architectonic of government and society undergoes an important change: in addition to the hierarchical regulations of the state and the decentralized regulations of the market, that is, besides administrative power and individual personal interests, *solidarity* and the orientation to the common good appear as a *third source* of social integration. In fact, this horizontal political will-formation aimed at mutual understanding or communicatively achieved consensus is even supposed to enjoy priority, both in a genetic and a normative sense. An autonomous basis in civil society, a basis independent of public administration and market-mediated private commerce, is assumed as a precondition for the praxis of civic self-determination. This basis preserves political communication from being swallowed up by the government apparatus or assimilated to market structures. In the republican conception, the political public sphere acquires, along with its base in civil society, a strategic significance. These competing approaches yield two contrasting images of the citizen.

According to the liberal view, the citizen's status is primarily determined according to negative rights they have vis-à-vis the state and other citizens. As bearers of these rights they enjoy the protection of the government, as long as they pursue their private interests within the boundaries drawn by legal statutes—and this includes protection against government interventions. Political rights, such as voting rights and free speech, not only have the same structure but also a similar meaning as civil rights that provide a space within which legal subjects are released from external compulsion. They give citizens the opportunity to assert their private interests in such a way that by means of elections, the composition of parliamentary bodies, and the formation of a government, these interests are finally aggregated into a political will that makes an impact on the administration.

According to the republican view, the status of citizens is not determined by the model of negative liberties to which these citizens can lay claim *as* private persons. Rather, political rights—pre-eminently rights of political participation and communication—are positive liberties. They guarantee not freedom from external compulsion but the possibility of participation in a common praxis, through the exercise of which citizens can first make themselves into what they want to be—politically autonomous authors of a community of free and equal persons. To this extent, the political process does not just serve to keep government activity under the surveillance of citizens who have already acquired a prior social autonomy in the exercise of their private rights and pre-political liberties. Just as little does it act as a hinge between state and society, for administrative authority is not at all an autochthonous authority; it is not something given. Rather, this authority emerges from the citizens' power produced communicatively in the praxis of self-legislation, and it finds its legitimation in the fact that it protects this praxis by institutionalizing public liberty. So, the state's *raison d'être* does not lie primarily in the protection of equal private rights but in the guarantee of an inclusive opinion- and will-formation in which free and equal citizens reach an understanding on which goals and norms lie in the equal interest of all.

The polemic against the classical concept of the legal person as bearer of private rights reveals a controversy about the concept of law itself. While in the liberal view the point of a legal order is to make it possible to determine in each case which individuals are entitled to which rights, in the republican view these "subjective" rights owe their existence to an "objective" legal order that both enables and guarantees the integrity of an autonomous life in common based on mutual respect:

> For republicans rights ultimately are nothing but determinations of the prevailing political will, while for liberals some rights are always grounded in a 'higher law' of (. . .) reason.[2]

Finally, the different ways of conceptualizing the role of citizen and of law express a deeper disagreement about the *nature of the political process*. In the liberal view, the political process of opinion- and will-formation in the public sphere and in parliament is determined by the competition of strategically acting collectivities trying to maintain or acquire positions of power. Success is measured by the citizens' approval, quantified as votes, of persons and programs. In their choices at the polls, voters give expression to their preferences. Their voting decisions have the same structure as the acts of choice made by participants in a market. They license access to the positions of power that political parties fight over in the same success-oriented attitude.

According to the republican view, the political opinion- and will-formation occurring in the public sphere and in parliament obeys not the structures of market processes but the obstinate structures of a public communication oriented to mutual understanding. For politics, in the sense of a praxis of civic self-legislation, the paradigm is not the market but dialogue. This dialogic conception imagines politics as contestation over questions of value and not simply questions of preference.

(2) Proceduralist vs. Communitarian Views of Politics

The republican model as compared to the liberal one has the advantage that it preserves the original meaning of democracy in terms of the institutionalization of a public use of reason jointly exercised by autonomous citizens. This model accounts for those communicative conditions that confer legitimating force on political opinion- and will-formation. These are precisely the conditions under which the political process can be presumed to generate reasonable results. A contest for power, if represented according to the liberal model of market competition, is determined by the rational choice of optimal strategies. Given an indissoluble pluralism of pre-political values and interests that are at best aggregated with equal weight in the political process, politics loses all reference to the normative core of a public use of reason. The republican trust in the force of political discourses stands in contrast to the liberal skepticism about reason. Such discourses are meant to allow one to discuss value orientations and interpretations of needs and wants, and then to change these in an *insightful way*.

But contemporary republicans tend to give this public communication a communitarian reading. It is precisely this move towards an *ethical constriction* of *political discourse* that I call into question. Politics may not be assimilated to a hermeneutical process of self-explication of a shared form of life or collective identity. Political questions may not be reduced to the type of ethical questions where we, as members of a community, ask ourselves who we are and who we would like to be. In its communitarian interpretation the republican model is too idealistic even within the limits of a purely normative analysis. On this reading, the democratic process is dependent on the virtues of citizens devoted to the public weal. This expectation of virtue already led Rousseau to split the citizen oriented to the common good from the private man, who cannot be ethically overburdened. The unanimity of the political legislature was supposed to be secured in advance by a substantive ethical consensus. In contrast, a discourse-theoretic interpretation insists on the fact that democratic will-formation does not draw its legitimating force from a previous convergence of settled ethical convictions, but from both the communicative presuppositions that allow the better arguments to come into play in various forms of deliberation, and from the procedures that secure fair bargaining processes. Discourse theory breaks with a purely ethical conception of civic autonomy.

According to the communitarian view, there is a necessary connection between the deliberative concept of democracy and the reference to a concrete, substantively integrated ethical community. Otherwise one could not explain, in this view, how the citizens' orientation to the common good would be at all possible. The individual, so the argument goes, can become aware of her co-membership in a collective form of life, and therewith become aware of a prior social bond, only in a practice exercised with others in common. The individual can get a clear sense of commonalities and differences, and hence a sense of who she is and who she would like to be, only in the public exchange with others who owe their identities to the same traditions and similar formation processes. This assimilation of political discourses to the clarification of a collective ethical self-understanding does not sit well with the function of the legislative processes they issue in. Legal statutes no doubt also contain teleological elements, but these involve more than just the hermeneutic explication of shared value orientations. By their very structure laws are determined by the question of which norms citizens want to adopt for regulating their living together. To be sure, discourses aimed at achieving self-understanding—discourses in which the participants want to get a clear understanding of themselves as members of a specific nation, as members of a locale or a state, as inhabitants of a region, etc.; in which they want to determine which traditions they will continue; in which they strive to determine how they will treat each other, and how they will treat minorities and marginal

groups; in short, discourses in which they want to get clear about the kind of society they want to live in—such discourses are also an important part of politics. But these questions are subordinate to moral questions and connected with pragmatic questions. Moral questions in the narrow sense of the Kantian tradition are questions of justice. The question having *priority* in legislative politics concerns how a matter can be regulated in the equal interest of all. The making of norms is primarily a justice issue and is gauged by principles that state what is equally good for all. And unlike ethical questions, questions of justice are not related from the outset to a specific collective and its form of life. The politically enacted law of a concrete legal community must, if it is to be legitimate, at least be compatible with moral tenets that claim universal validity going beyond the legal community.

Moreover, compromises make up the bulk of political processes. Under conditions of religious, or in any way cultural and societal pluralism, politically relevant goals are often selected by interests and value orientations that are by no means constitutive for the identity of the community at large, hence for the whole of an intersubjectively shared form of life. The political interests and values that stand in conflict with each other without prospects of consensus are in need of a balancing that cannot be achieved through ethical discourses—even if the outcomes of bargaining processes are subject to the proviso that they must not violate a culture's agreed-upon basic values. The required balance of competing interests comes about as a compromise between parties that may rely on mutual threats. A legitimate kind of bargaining certainly depends on a prior regulation of fair terms for achieving results, which are acceptable for all parties on the basis of their differing preferences. While debates on such regulations should assume the forms of practical discourse that neutralize power, bargaining itself well allows for strategic interactions. The deliberative mode of legislative practice is not just intended to ensure the ethical validity of laws. Rather, one can understand the complex validity claim of legal norms as the claim, on the one hand, to compromise competing interests in a manner compatible with the common good and, on the other hand, to bring universalistic principles of justice into the horizon of the specific form of life of a particular community.

In contrast to the ethical constriction of political discourse, the concept of deliberative politics acquires empirical reference only when we take account of the multiplicity of communicative forms of rational political will-formation. It is not discourse of an ethical type that could grant on its own the democratic genesis of law. Instead, deliberative politics should be conceived as a syndrome that depends on a network of fairly regulated bargaining processes and of various forms of argumentation, including pragmatic, ethical and moral discourses, each of which relies on different communicative presuppositions and procedures. In legislative politics the supply of information and the rational choice of strategies are interwoven with the balancing of interests, with the achievement of ethical self-understanding and the articulation of strong preferences, with moral justification and tests of legal coherence. Thus "dialogical" and "instrumental" politics, the two ideal-types which Frank Michelman has opposed in a polarizing fashion, do in fact interpenetrate in the medium of deliberations of various kinds.

(3) Three Images of State and Society

If we start from this proceduralist concept of deliberative politics, this reading of democracy has implications for the concept of society. Both the liberal and the republican model presuppose a view of society as centered in the state—be it the state as guardian of a market-society or the state as the self-conscious institutionalization of an ethical community.

According to the *liberal view*, the democratic process takes place exclusively in the form of compromises between competing interests. Fairness is supposed to be granted by the general and equal right to vote, the representative composition of parliamentary bodies, by decision rules, and so on. Such rules are ultimately justified in terms of liberal basic rights. According to the *republican view*, democratic will-formation takes place in the form of an ethical-political discourse; here deliberation can rely on a culturally established background consensus shared by the citizenry. Discourse theory takes elements from both sides and integrates these in the concept of an ideal procedure for deliberation and decision-making. Weaving together pragmatic considerations, compromises, discourses of self-understanding and justice, this democratic procedure grounds the presumption that reasonable or fair results are obtained. According to this proceduralist view, practical reason withdraws from universal human rights, or from the concrete ethical substance of a specific community, into the rules of discourse and forms of argumentation. In the final analysis, the normative content arises from the very structure of communicative actions. These descriptions of the democratic process set the stage for different conceptualizations of state and society.

According to the republican view, the citizens' political opinion- and will-formation forms the medium through which society constitutes itself as a political whole. Society is, from the very start, political society—*societas civilis*. Hence democracy becomes equivalent to the political self-organization of society as a whole. This leads to a polemic *understanding of politics directed against the state apparatus*. In Hannah Arendt's political writings one can see where republican argumentation directs its salvos: in opposition to the privatism of a depoliticized population and in opposition to the acquisition of legitimation through entrenched parties, the public sphere should be revitalized to the point where a regenerated citizenry can, in the forms of a decentralized self-governance, (once again) appropriate the power of pseudo-independent state agencies. From this perspective, society would finally develop into a political totality.

Whereas the separation of the state apparatus from society elicits a polemical reaction from the republican side, according to the liberal view it cannot be eliminated but only bridged by the democratic process. The regulated balancing of power and interests has need of constitutional channelling, of course. The democratic will-formation of self-interested citizens is laden with comparatively weak normative expectations. The constitution is supposed to tame the state apparatus through normative constraints (such as basic rights, separation of powers, etc.) and to force it, through the competition of political parties on the one hand and that between government and opposition on the other, to take adequate account of competing interests and value orientations. This *state-centered understanding of politics* can forego the unrealistic assumption of a citizenry capable of collective action. Its focus is not so much the input of a rational political will-formation but the output of sensible and effective administrative accomplishments. Liberal argumentation aims its salvos against the potential disturbance of an administrative power that interferes with the spontaneous forces of a self-regulating society. The liberal model hinges, not on the democratic self-determination of deliberating citizens, but on the legal institutionalization of an economic society that is supposed to guarantee an essentially non-political common good by the satisfaction of private preferences.

Discourse theory invests the democratic process with normative connotations stronger than those found in the liberal model but weaker than those of the republican model. Once again, it takes elements from both sides and fits them together in a new way. In agreement with republicanism, it gives center stage to the process of political opinion- and will-formation, but without understanding the constitution as something secondary; rather it conceives the principles of the constitutional state as a consistent answer to the question of how the demanding communicative forms of a democratic opinion- and will-formation can be institutionalized. Discourse theory has the success of deliberative politics depend not on a collectively acting citizenry but on the institutionalization of the corresponding procedures and conditions of communication. Proceduralized popular sovereignty and a political system tied in to the peripheral networks of the political public sphere go hand-in-hand with the image of a *decentred society*. This concept of democracy no longer needs to operate with the notion of a social whole centered in the state and imagined as a goal-oriented subject writ large. Just as little does it represent the whole in a system of constitutional norms mechanically regulating the interplay of powers and interests in accordance with the market model.

Discourse theory altogether jettisons certain premises of the *philosophy of consciousness*. These premises either invite us to ascribe the praxis of civic self-determination to one encompassing macro-subject or they have us apply the rule of law to many isolated private subjects. The former approach views the citizenry as a collective actor that reflects the whole and acts for it; in the latter, individual actors function as dependent variables in system processes that move along blindly. Discourse theory works instead with the *higher-level intersubjectivity* of communication processes that flow through both the parliamentary bodies and the informal networks of the public sphere. Within and outside the parliamentary complex, these subjectless forms of communication constitute arenas in which a more or less rational opinion- and will-formation can take place.

Informal public opinion-formation generates "influence"; influence is transformed into "communicative power" through the channels of political elections; and communicative power is . . . again transformed into "administrative power" through legislation. As in the liberal model, the boundaries between "state" and "society" are respected; but in this case, civil society provides the social basis of autonomous public spheres that remain as distinct from the economic system as from the administration. This understanding of democracy suggests a new balance between the three resources of money, administrative power, and solidarity, from which modern societies meet their needs for integration. The normative implications are obvious: the integrative force of "solidarity," which can no longer be drawn solely from sources of communicative action, should develop through widely expanded and differentiated public spheres as well as through legally institutionalized procedures of democratic deliberation and decision-making. It should gain the strength to hold its own against the two other mechanisms of social integration—money and administrative power.

This view has implications for how one understands (a) legitimation and (b) popular sovereignty.

(a) On the liberal view, democratic will-formation has the exclusive function of *legitimating* the exercise of political power. Election results are the licence to assume governmental power, whereas the government must justify the use of power to the public. On the republican view, democratic will-formation has the significantly stronger function of *constituting* society as a political community and keeping the memory of this founding act alive with each election. The government is not only empowered to exercise a largely open mandate, but also programmatically committed to carry out certain policies. It remains bound to a self-governing political community. Discourse theory brings a third idea into play: the procedures and communicative presuppositions of democratic opinion- and will-formation function as the most important sluices for the discursive rationalization of the decisions of an administration constrained by law and statute. Rationalization means more than mere legitimation but less than the constitution of political power. The power available to the administration changes its aggregate condition as soon as it emerges from a public use of reason and a communicative power which do not just monitor the exercise of political power in a belated manner but more or less program it as well. Notwithstanding this discursive rationalization, only the administrative system itself can "act." The administration is a subsystem specialized for collectively binding decisions, whereas the communicative structures of the public sphere comprise a far-flung network of sensors that in the first place react to the pressure of society-wide problematics and stimulate influential opinions. The public opinion that is worked up via democratic procedures into communicative power cannot "rule" of itself, but can only point the use of administrative power in specific directions.

(b) The concept of popular sovereignty stems from the republican appropriation and revaluation of the early modern notion of sovereignty initially associated with absolutist regimes. The state, which monopolizes all the means for a legitimate implementation of force, is seen as an overpowering concentrate of power—as the Leviathan. This idea was transferred by Rousseau to the will of the united people. He fused the strength of the Leviathan with the classical idea of the self-rule of free and equal citizens and combined it with his modern concept of autonomy. Despite this sublimation, the concept of sovereignty remained bound to the notion of an embodiment in the assembled, physically present people. According to the republican view, the people are the bearers of a sovereignty that in principle cannot be delegated: in their sovereign character the people cannot have others represent them. Liberalism opposes this with the more realistic view that in the constitutional state any authority originating from the people is exercised only "by means of elections and voting and by specific legislative, executive, and judicial organs."[3]

These two views would exhaust the alternatives only if we had to conceive state and society in terms of the whole and its parts—where the whole is constituted either by a sovereign citizenry or by a constitution. To the discourse theory of democracy corresponds, however, the image of a decentred society. To be sure, with the political public sphere the proceduralist model sets off an arena for the detection, identification, and interpretation of those problems that affect society as a whole. But the "self" of the self-organizing legal community here disappears in the subjectless forms of communication that regulate the flow of deliberations in such a way that their fallible results enjoy the presumption of rationality. This is not to denounce the intuition connected with the idea of popular sovereignty but to interpret it in intersubjective terms. Popular sovereignty, even if it becomes anonymous, retreats into democratic procedures and the legal implementation of their demanding communicative presuppositions only in order to make itself felt as communicatively generated power. Strictly speaking, this communicative power springs from the interactions between legally institutionalized will-formation and culturally mobilized publics. The latter for their part find a basis in the associations of a civil society quite distinct from both state and economy alike.

Read in procedural terms, the idea of popular sovereignty refers to a context that, while enabling the self-organization of a legal community, is not at the disposal of the citizens' will in any way. Deliberation is certainly supposed to provide the medium for a more or less conscious integration of the *legal community*; but this mode does not extend to the whole of society in which the political system is *embedded* as only one among several subsystems. Even in its own proceduralist self-understanding, deliberative politics remains a component of a complex society, which as a whole resists the normative approach practiced in legal theory. In this regard the discourse-theoretic reading of democracy has a point of contact with a detached sociological approach that considers the political system neither the peak nor the centre, nor even the formative model of society in general, but just one action system among others. On the other hand, politics must still be able to communicate, through the medium of law, with all the other legitimately ordered spheres of action, however these happen to be structured and steered.

Post-Reading Questions

1. What are the shortcomings of the liberal and republican models of political authority, according to Habermas?
2. In what ways does the deliberative model of democracy overcome the failings of liberal and republican political models?
3. Why is a state's constitution so important to Habermas's vision of a politics based on deliberative communication?
4. How is the legitimation of political power to be achieved, according to the third (deliberative) political model?

CASE STUDY
THE COURT CHALLENGES PROGRAM

Introduction

Between 1985 and 2006, the Court Challenges Program funded equality litigation in Canada. First established in 1978 by Trudeau's Liberal government as a funding source for minority language group legal action, it later became the primary source of support for groups seeking to challenge the Charter of Rights and Freedoms' fulfillment of their equality rights. Women's groups made frequent use of this funding program, applying to it for funds to defray litigation in connection with women's equality rights under the Charter. Specifically, these groups sought to determine whether the equality rights guaranteed by section 15 (1) of the Charter were indeed secure by testing them in a series of court cases.

The Court Challenges Program was defunded by Brian Mulroney's Progressive Conservative government in 1992, but subsequently resuscitated by Jean Chrétien's Liberal government two years later. It continued for several years, until Conservative prime minister Stephen Harper finally ended the program in 2006. In 2008, however, a smaller-scale version of the program (the Language Rights Support Program) was re-established, with the specific and narrower purpose of funding minority language litigation. Currently, then, no government funding is available for equality rights legal cases in Canada.

This federal program was highly unusual in that it provided financial support for groups who sought, in essence, to democratically challenge the government's effectiveness in protecting their social equality rights as guaranteed by the Charter. As a consequence, the Court Challenges Program arguably made a unique contribution to Canada's democratic culture in the years during which it operated. Jürgen Habermas has argued that the hallmark of a mature democracy is the availability of genuine opportunities for citizens to participate in public, democratic deliberation. At times, this participation may consist in challenging certain constitutional norms, or seeking adjudication on the relative weight accorded to two possibly conflicting legal norms. In other instances, as in the case of section 15 (1) equality litigation, democratic participation may consist in testing the sincerity of government's commitment to protecting citizens' rights. As Habermas writes in "Three Normative Models of Democracy," under the discourse-theoretic model of democracy, "democratic will formation does not draw its legitimating force from a previous convergence of settled ethical convictions, but from both the communicative presuppositions that allow the better arguments to come into play in various forms of deliberation, and from the procedures that secure fair bargaining processes."

To the extent that the Court Challenges Program made it possible for certain groups of citizens to press for clarification and assurance of their Charter rights in the public domain, it can be seen as supporting a broadly deliberative democratic model of political life. Substantively (i.e., not just formally) equal access to public deliberation is critical to Habermas's vision of a democracy inspired by discourse ethics. Moreover, his emphasis on fairness and compromise are arguably well served by programs that encourage the debate of constitutional norms in a transparent, democratic forum. Whether Supreme Court challenges are the best means of fostering such debate—as well as the public argumentation and bargaining that Habermas sees as central to the legitimacy of deliberative form of democracy—is, however, open to question.

Larissa Kloegman, "A Democratic Defence of the Court Challenges Program"

Larissa Kloegman, "A Democratic Defence of the Court Challenges Program,"
Constitutional Forum, 16 (3), 2007: 107–15.

The introduction of the Charter of Rights and Freedoms[4] has provided many historically disadvantaged groups with an opportunity to have their rights acknowledged in the policy process. Indeed the Charter places a legal obligation upon governments to ensure their legislative efforts respect the rights of historically disadvantaged groups. Some claim, however, that the Charter has produced activist judges who create rights for "special" interest groups rather than defer to Parliament. Others suggest Canada's parliamentary system is not, on its own, favourable to all Canadians, and many groups and individuals are forced to the courts to make their interests and concerns known to government policy makers and legislators. The Court Challenges Program (CCP) was at the centre of this debate. This modest, federally funded initiative contributed to the protection and promotion of Canada's official language minority groups (OLMGs) for almost 30 years, and provided assistance to groups seeking to assert their section 15 Charter rights for almost 20. The Court Challenges Program served as a last resort for many of Canada's most disadvantaged groups, but the Harper government recently took the position that the CCP was one of several "wasteful programs" not "providing good value for money."[5] Funding for the program was eliminated in 2006, silencing many of Canada's most vulnerable groups.

After a brief look at the history and importance of the Court Challenges Program, this article offers an explanation for its cancellation and a fresh perspective on why it is important to reinstate it. In essence, the Conservative government appears to have adopted the analytical lens of Ted Morton & Rainer Knopff's "Charter revolution" theory to judge the merits of the program.[6] Considered in this light, it should not be surprising that the CCP was deemed a nuisance and eliminated. Unfortunately for many groups including OLMGs in Alberta, this means that it is now more difficult for members of disadvantaged groups to hold governments to account for failing to respect their Charter rights in the policy process.

Although a centralization of political power in Canada has been occurring for decades, the current government is the most extreme expression of its concentration in the Prime Minister's Office (PMO). As a result, traditional access points to government are diminishing ever more rapidly, forcing Canadians to use the courts in a last attempt to contribute to policy and legislation. Unfortunately, as litigation is both timely and expensive, only the richest in society can afford to utilize this final resort without a litigation-support program such as the CCP. Indeed, without the program, Canada's most vulnerable groups will continue to be left out in the cold.

What Is the Court Challenges Program?

The Court Challenges Program was created in 1978 by the federal government under Pierre Trudeau to assist language minorities (francophones living outside Quebec and anglophones living inside Quebec) wishing to challenge provincial legislation that might violate the Constitution Act, 1867[7] or the Manitoba Act, 1870.[8]

When section 15 of the Charter came into effect in 1985, many organizations lobbied the Mulroney government for a program similar to that of the CCP. Rather than create a new program, Minister of Justice John Crosbie expanded the mandate of the Court Challenges Program to include support for litigation efforts under sections 15 and 28[9] of the Charter.[10] Crosbie contracted the Canadian Council on Social Development (CCSD) to administer the program and granted it $9 million over five years.[11] The program was renewed in 1990 with a five-year budget of $12 million. Nevertheless, the Mulroney government eliminated the funding for the CCP in 1992. Public outcry caused the cancellation of the CCP to become a major issue and promises of its reinstatement surfaced in the campaigns of both the Liberal and Progressive Conservative parties in the following federal election.

In 1994, the federal government resuscitated the Court Challenges Program of Canada, this time as a non-profit corporation with a three-year contract worth an annual $2.75 million. Since then, the program's funding has been twice renewed, most recently in 2004 when the CCP was guaranteed an annual budget of $2.85 million through 2009. In spite of the most recent agreement, on 25 September 2006 funding for the Court Challenges Program was eliminated.[12]

Response to the Decision to Eliminate the Program

As with the first cancellation, public response was swift. Soon after the September 2006 announcement, the Standing Committee on Canadian Heritage heard from 22 witnesses, 18 of whom supported the reinstatement of the funding for the program.[13] The committee tabled a report in February 2007 recommending continued funding for the CCP. In addition, Canada's Official Languages Commissioner, Graham Fraser, received 117 complaints between October 2006 and April 2007,[14] upon receipt of which he requested a moratorium on the cancellation. His request was denied. In his annual report tabled May 2007, the Commissioner openly criticized the Conservative government for cancelling the Court Challenges Program, reminding the committee that it is "well known for having helped numerous individuals and groups pursue their rights in provincial and federal courts."[15] When the Commissioner appeared before a Senate committee in June 2007, he stated: "the elimination of the Court Challenges Program in particular delivered a serious blow to Canadians' ability to defend their language rights."[16]

Some have speculated that the cancellation of the program was an ideological decision, perhaps connected to the opposition of core supporters of the Harper government to same-sex marriage rights. "In some critical way," Professor Margot Young claims, "cancellation of this program is payback for the role it played in the successful legal struggle over same-sex marriage. One has only to look at a few of the websites or newsletters of groups on the religious right to see the linkage made between the attainment of same-sex marriage and the Court Challenges Program."[17]

Others applauded the decision to cancel the program, suggesting that if the cause is significant enough, a group should be able to obtain its own funding to go to court rather than receive government assistance. Gwendolyn Landolt, national vice-president of REAL Women of Canada,[18] claims: "If you have the support of the public, you can go to court, as we've done

. . . simply because we've asked our members for the money and they've produced it. . . . Why can't other groups do it?"[19] Executive director of the Alberta-based Canadian Constitution Foundation[20] and critic of the CCP, John Carpay, adds to this sentiment: "I trust in the wisdom of Canadians and I trust in the compassion of Canadians to contribute to worthwhile court cases. Canadians know justice when they see it. What the Court Challenges Program is—or hopefully was—is an affront, a statement of disbelief and distrust in the wisdom and compassion of Canadians to give voluntarily to a just cause."[21]

The views of Ms. Landolt and Mr. Carpay may be defensible, but they are also easily refuted. Some disadvantaged groups simply do not have access to the funding needed to proceed to litigation when all other avenues of political influence have failed (these avenues will be discussed shortly). For example, it is unlikely that the members of the National Anti-Poverty Organization (NAPO) would be able to raise enough money to cover court costs from their members, let alone the cost of a solicitor.

One must also be careful in drawing a conclusion about the importance of a particular issue on the basis of the amount of financial support drawn from its community of supporters. This is a problematic assumption. To illustrate, while the situation in Vancouver's Downtown Eastside is a growing concern for all Canadians, local housing and poverty action groups do not attract substantial amounts of revenue from the public. Though the reasons for this are too varied and complex to discuss here, one certainly ought not assume that the shoestring budgets of these organizations are an indication that the public does not care about the plight of poor Canadians. It simply underlines the reality that not all groups and individuals are in a position to gather the funding needed to question government action or inaction.

Why Is the Court Challenges Program So Important?

In essence, the failure of Canada's governments to provide the public with adequate opportunity to contribute to policy making and legislation has provided an important rationale for the Court Challenges Program as an alternative for groups and individuals seeking equal opportunity to influence decision makers and legislators. A brief examination of the efforts of Alberta's French-language official language minority groups and of provincial resistance to the public use of French, will help to clarify the importance of the program.

Francophones in Alberta

The 2001 census shows the majority of Canada's OLMGs live in Quebec, followed by Ontario, New Brunswick, and, perhaps surprising to some, Alberta.[22] Indeed Franco-Albertans have been quietly contributing to the cultural landscape of the province for well over a century.

Edmund Aunger notes that Alberta has an "extensive body of language law buried in a century of statutory and regulatory provisions."[23] While laws to protect the use of the French language in Alberta's public institutions do exist, the provincial government introduced legislative measures to promote English as the exclusive public language of the province. Nevertheless, these efforts did not prevent Franco-Albertans from reminding the English-speaking majority in Alberta of their presence and their rights. An instructive example of the difficulty disadvantaged groups face in having their rights protected by the majority is the effort of an opposition member of Alberta's legislature to speak French in the Assembly in 1987. Known as "L'affaire Piquette," the Speaker refused to allow the member to use French in the legislature during question period, reinvigorating attention to the state of Canada's "other" official language in Alberta. Less than a year later, the Supreme Court of Canada ruled that official bilingualism, provided for in section 110 of the Northwest Territories Act,[24] applied to the Legislative Assembly of Alberta, thus protecting the use of *both* French and English in the legislature and the courts. Further, the government was obliged to publish its statutes in both official languages.

Alberta's response to the Supreme Court's ruling was to enact the Languages Act 1988[25] which states: "All Acts, Ordinances and regulations enacted before July 6, 1988 are declared valid notwithstanding that they were enacted, printed and published in English only."[26] The Act essentially removes the government's obligation to have bills and legislative Standing Orders, records, and journals printed in French, but it still permits the use of French in oral communication in both the legislature and the courts.[27] Enactment of the Languages Act exemplifies the unwillingness of the Alberta government to promote French in the province; thus, the survival of minority Francophone communities in Alberta, for example, may seem dependent on alternative means of redressing the government's lack of commitment to its legal obligations to its French-speakers.

The very cultural survival of many OLMG communities is dependent on the legislative cooperation of a province. As some provinces have been less than willing to support the needs and rights of these members of the electorate, many communities relied on the Court Challenges Program to help them challenge provincial legislation which they believe violates their right to live and prosper in the official language of their choice.

Supplementing Public Access to the Policy Process

Guy Matte, the most recent president of the Court Challenges Program notes: "[a] democratic system involves majority rule. We understand that, but defending minority rights is the reason why there has to be a charter to protect those rights from the whims of the majority. It's important to uphold these principles in Canada."[28] In essence, the rights of all Canadians must be recognized to ensure legislation does not discriminate against disadvantaged groups. At the root of this discussion, then, is the importance of ensuring all citizens have sufficient opportunity to influence the policy process.

This concern with equitable influence over the policy process has indeed led Canadians to question the adequacy of our voting system, in addition to the adequacy of other features of our political framework. For example, the ability of citizens to influence policy-making and legislation is clearly limited by Canada's "first past the post" (FPTP) electoral system which, combined with multiparty competition, ensures that national political parties can form governments with less than 50 per cent of the popular vote. To secure and maintain public support, governing parties tend to focus on issues which appeal to a majority of voters, thus facilitating the neglect of some members of society. This creates periphery groups whose concerns are less likely to be observed by a party seeking majority support.

Nevertheless, academics have identified the bureaucracy, Members of Parliament, and cabinet ministers as "access points" in Canada's parliamentary system of government. Through these access points, it is suggested, all members of society are provided with an opportunity to advance their interests and concerns by contributing to the shaping of public policy and legislation. However, over the last several decades Canada has developed an increasingly centralized form of governance, and the level of control sought by prime ministers has diminished these access points. As a result, Canadians are forced to assert their Charter rights through court challenges. Since litigation is both time-sensitive and expensive, only those with adequate resources are able to utilize the courts as a last resort.

The Bureaucracy

In his extensive research on pressure-group influence, Paul Pross has identified an ebb and flow to bureaucratic cooperation with interest groups.[29] The Trudeau era, reflecting the emergence of social movements during this time, "ushered in the age of public consultation with the slogan 'come work with me.'"[30] By contrast, the Mulroney period was one in which public access to the bureaucracy was more limited. Alexandra Dobrowolsky notes that as Mulroney dramatically reduced the bureaucracy, civil service "insiders"—once sympathetic to furthering the goals of the women's movement—began to fear retribution for talking with "special" interest groups.[31] As one member of the bureaucracy put it: "Mulroney ran the government with favouritism and retribution and if you weren't a really big time supporter, then you were an enemy."[32]

While the concentration of power under Jean Chrétien has been well documented,[33] Prime Minister Harper has gone even further to restrict the openness of the bureaucracy. In May 2007, for instance, Jeffrey Monaghan, an Environment Canada employee, was handcuffed in his office by the RCMP and taken away for questioning in regards to the leak of a document outlining Conservative plans to abandon the Kyoto Accord.[34] The concern raised by critics at the time was that the handcuffs were being used as a scare tactic to keep [the] rest of the bureaucracy in line.

Members of Parliament

If a group is able to persuade a Member of Parliament to raise a particular issue, there are two formal opportunities to introduce it into House of Commons proceedings: during question period or before parliamentary committee hearings. Since question period has become little more than a media spectacle, the larger part of any meaningful discussion in the House now takes place in parliamentary committee where strict party discipline does not always apply, and where the views of constituents can usually be expressed freely by MPs without interference or fear of repercussion. In 2002, when Stephen Harper was Leader of the Opposition, he co-authored a letter to the editor of the *Globe and Mail* stating: "Standing committees of the House should not simply be extensions of the Prime Minister's Office, and members of Parliament should choose their committee chairs by secret ballot and their own agenda, free from the Whip's direction."[35]

Once in office, however, Harper indicated a change of mind regarding the importance of independent parliamentary committees to the policy process. For example, in May 2007, shortly after several meetings were shut down or corrupted by filibuster, a 200-page manual for Conservative committee chairs was leaked to Don Martin of the *National Post*, who revealed it to the public. Intended to guide the control of committees, the manual "details how to unleash chaos while chairing parliamentary committees."[36] Martin suggests that the manual

"proves that the [committee] chairmen are under intense supervision from the powers above."[37] This view of the government was confirmed by Conservative House whip Jay Hill when he stated that committees "do not have the right to pick who the chair is . . . [T]he chair, by the rules, must be a government member and I'm not going to allow the opposition to determine who that is."[38]

Cabinet Ministers

Ministers of the Crown, particularly those in cabinet, have traditionally been considered the most effective and direct access point to influence public policy. As close advisors to the prime minister increasingly influence the policy process, ministers exercise less and less control over policy outputs. "The Prime Minister's Office and the Privy Council Office, in particular," Donald Savoie notes, "keep a watchful eye on ministers and departments. The centre of government, after all, now belongs to the prime minister, not to ministers."[39] Unfortunately, this means that public access to policy influence via contact with ministers is stifled in favour of more centralized control over the policy process.

Media

Prime ministers increasingly rely on the media and professionalized advice to provide instant answers and partisan-strategic information via polling, media-reported public opinion, and professional marketing advice. In April 2007, acting on Prime Minister Harper's claim that "the press gallery has taken the view that they are going to be the opposition to the government,"[40] the Conservative government unveiled a 17,000-square-foot, state-of-the-art media "war room" to provide instant-response capability for a pending election. Indeed, the Conservative government rigorously controls its image and messaging. Prime Minister Harper's turbulent relationship with the media may explain why, in August 2007, the PMO ordered that reporters be evicted from a hotel in Charlottetown where the Conservative caucus was holding its annual retreat. This change from the "freewheeling meetings" of the Tories when in opposition, Jane Taber and Gloria Galloway of the *Globe and Mail* note, is limiting the public's ability to interact with MPs: "In an effort to control the message, keep discipline and ensure that caucus members are all on the same page, access to MPs is being carefully controlled and monitored."[41]

While it is true that the media provides a quick response to government policies, the government's efforts to control media messaging nevertheless renders the democratic process of public input and consultation on government policy and legislation relatively impotent. As a result, groups and individuals are forced to use the courts to participate in government by challenging policy and legislation created with ever-diminishing public input. Since not all groups and individuals are similarly economically situated, groups and individuals have differing levels of access to the courts. Therefore, some members of society need assistance to access the courts as an alternative to traditional access points to policy influence. The Court Challenges Program helped groups that would otherwise be unable to access the policy process. In this sense, the program supplemented Canada's brokerage-style party system by including peripheral interests into the policy process via litigation, when access points failed to do so.

If the Court Challenges Program Provides Assistance to Disadvantaged Canadians, Why Is There So Much Opposition to It?

Controversy has always surrounded the Court Challenges Program. Concerns have been raised regarding the administration of the program, the distribution of funding, and the selection of groups to fund for litigation support. Concerns related to democracy, to questions of minority rights protection at the expense of the majority, to conflicting definitions of equality, and to the delineation of what constitutes a "clarification" of Charter rights, are among the significant concerns raised.

Yet one must wonder why the Court Challenges Program, in particular, was eliminated while federal funds remain intact for other programs designed to assist with court and procedural costs. Deep conservative opposition to the Charter in general, and to "special" interest groups and so-called judicial activism in particular, may be at the root of the program's latest cancellation.

The "Charter Revolution"

Before 1982, the Supreme Court of Canada engaged in judicial review of the Constitution mainly to settle disputes over the division of powers. In Ted Morton and Rainer Knopff's view, the introduction of the Charter facilitated a more activist Court, which has had a direct effect on the ability of Parliament to fulfill its obligations to the electorate. This so-called "Charter revolution," the argument goes, is supported by "special" interest groups which legitimize and encourage a political role for the courts. This in turn, effectively undermines the supremacy of Parliament, and as a result the wishes and needs of the majority are ignored if not undermined.[42] As Morton and Knopff put the point, since 1982 "judges have abandoned the [parliamentary] deference and self-restraint that characterized their pre-Charter jurisprudence and

become more active in the political process."[43]

In his book *Friends of the Court: the Privileging of Interest Group Litigants in Canada*, Ian Brodie, one of the most vocal opponents of the Court Challenges Program and a former student of Morton's, contends that activist courts have been able to silence criticism by allying themselves with rights-seeking groups—including gay rights activists, feminists, and sympathetic lawyers and professors—which assist the courts in interpreting constitutional law, and use the Charter to create progressive policy. "The Supreme Court," Brodie claims, "is well on the road to establishing itself as a legislative, rather than a judicial, institution."[44]

From Brodie's perspective, the Court Challenges Program supports this process. "The federal government tried to encourage interest group litigation through the CCP," Brodie claims, "and there are good reasons to think that it was successful."[45] He suggests that through outreach programs and litigation efforts, the program prompted many groups to utilize the courts to achieve their policy objectives. In so doing, the courts and their "friends" have taken over the role of legislators. Brodie observes: "The new judicial involvement in the policy process is sometimes a result of the state working through interest groups. The Court Challenges Program represents the embedded state at war with itself in court."[46] It is indeed worth noting that in February 2006, seven months before the elimination of the Court Challenges Program, Ian Brodie was appointed Prime Minister Harper's Chief of Staff.

Quelling the Revolution: Prime Minister Harper and the Anti-Court Party

William Christian states: "Harper genuinely believes the sovereignty of Parliament has been eroded and that it is undesirable that an unelected court of nine men and women should have the final say over many fundamental aspects of Canadian life."[47] If this is an accurate portrait of Harper's views of the judiciary, then the Conservative government's cancellation of the Court Challenges Program can be interpreted as an effort to stem government-supported litigation by "special" interest groups or "liberal" movements (such as the feminist or gay rights movement) that encourages the "activism" of the judiciary and the undermining of parliamentary supremacy. In this context, it should not be surprising that after cutting the program, the next step for Conservatives might perhaps be to focus efforts on the judicial interpreters of the Constitution.

Tasha Kheiriddin and Adam Daifallah argue that "Canadian conservatives need to demand real reform of the judicial appointments process,"[48] and have advised them to heed the advice of the Vice-President of the National Citizens Coalition who has said that conservatives must "create a climate where there are more conservative voters, to elect more conservative politicians, and thus appoint more conservative judges. They must also produce more conservative lawyers who become those judges."[49] Prime Minister Harper has not kept his animosity towards the courts a secret, nor has he been shy about his intentions to stack the courts with judges who will reflect his own conservative views and agenda. By muffling the judicial component of the Charter revolution, Prime Minister Harper has taken steps—such as changing the configuration of federal Judicial Advisory Committees—to consolidate an ideologically conservative direction in the courts. He has begun to disenfranchise supporters of the Charter, and since it is virtually impossible to throw out the entrenched law of the Constitution, Harper will instead likely systematically unravel the efforts of Charter supporters and their attempts to promote justice for *all* Canadians.

Conclusion

The litigation undertaken with the support of the Court Challenges Program illustrates that public input into policy-making and legislation can be pursued in conjunction with representative democracy as it functions in a parliamentary system. The program supplements Canada's democratic process by recognizing and advancing the rights of disadvantaged groups and individuals on the periphery of Canadian society.

The lens of the Charter revolution theory brings clarity to opposition to the program. Moreover, the removal of the financial support many "special" interest groups need to make use of what is perhaps the most effective tool available to achieve respect for minority rights—the courts—is further evidence of the tendency for power to be concentrated in the prime minister's office. As noted by Jeffery Simpson, Prime Minister Harper "centralizes everything through his office, giving ministers almost no margin for manoeuvre or initiative, tightly scripting every public event, controlling all messages to the public, running foreign policy by himself, and earning the reputation of a decisive but distant sun king of a leader."[50]

Ironically, Harper's centralizing tactics will continue to diminish traditional access points for public input in the policy process, exacerbating the need for disadvantaged groups to use the courts in a last attempt to contribute to policy and legislation.

While some have speculated that the elimination of the Court Challenges Program was linked to the issue of same-sex marriage, the Harper government's decision hurt many other groups as well. Members of Canada's multicultural society, persons with a disability, and OLMGs, to name a few, will also be less able to ensure public policy respects their rights as a result of the elimination of the program. As demonstrated in Alberta, for example, although there are constitutional guarantees for minority language protection, OLMGs cannot benefit from those protections without the cooperation of provincial governments willing to fully recognize them. When provinces fail to acknowledge minority language rights, the Court Challenges Program helped members of disadvantaged minority language groups hold provincial governments to constitutional guarantees which ensure they can live and prosper in the official language of their choice.

Though a concentration of power in the centre of government has been evolving over decades, the current government is the most extreme expression of its concentration in the PMO. As a result, most traditional public access points to the policy process have become ineffective. The increased use of a professionalized class of advisors has led to the exclusion of any "outside" input—including that of the prime minister's own cabinet not to mention MPs in the Conservative caucus—into the policy process. This development has forced many groups and individuals to rely on the courts as a last resort to influence public policy and ensure that their rights are protected. In this context, and not surprisingly, the Court Challenges Program was regarded as the proverbial thorn in the side of an increasingly centralized government not open to influence or criticism from the public. Unfortunately, as the program gave a voice to those who would otherwise have no opportunity to influence public policy, when the Harper government eliminated its funding, many of Canada's most disadvantaged groups were silenced.

Post-Case-Reading Questions

1. How does the author's argument for the democratic impact of the Court Challenges Program connect with Habermas's idea of deliberative politics?
2. If the rights protected by the Canadian Charter of Rights and Freedoms are guaranteed, why do they need to be "tested" at all? Which citizens might be inclined to test the Charter in this way?

Michel Foucault

Introduction

Twentieth-century French thinker Michel Foucault has had an enormous influence on a number of fields of academic study, including philosophy, political theory, anthropology, gender studies, literary theory, sociology, criminology, and the history and philosophy of science. His writing is highly original and sometimes difficult, with a sharp critical edge aimed at challenging the orthodoxy in many scientific disciplines—unusual for a philosopher. Since the 1980s, the impact of his work on the social and human sciences has been increasing. It is not surprising, then, that in 2007 he was the most cited author in scholarly publications, according to the Web of Science. Thanks to Foucault, phrases such as "normalizing discourse," "genealogical historiography," "disciplinary power," "power/knowledge regimes," and so on are now virtually a part of everyday academic vernacular.

Michel Foucault

© INTERFOTO/Alamy

Paul-Michel Foucault was born in Poitiers, France, in 1926, into an educated, middle-class family (his father was a surgeon). He studied at the local lycée as well as at the Jesuit Collège Saint-Stanislas, attaining his baccalauréat in 1943. He continued to study philosophy at his local lycée, leaving in 1945 for Paris. There, he enrolled at one of the country's top secondary schools, the Lycée Henri-IV, to prepare for the entrance exam to the École Normale Supérieure (ENS). Among his teachers at the lycée were Jean Hyppolite, a Hegel scholar and existentialist philosopher. In 1946, Foucault gained entry to the highly exclusive and competitive ENS to study philosophy and psychology, earning degrees in these disciplines in 1948 and 1949. At ENS, he studied with Marxist philosopher Louis Althusser and phenomenologist Maurice Merleau-Ponty, among others. He passed his agrégation (an examination demonstrating preparedness to teach in higher education in France) in 1951 and went on to earn a psychopathology diploma in 1952 from the Institut de Psychologie de Paris. By this time, he had already started to teach: as a tutor in psychology, and later philosophy, at ENS from 1951 to 1955, and as a philosophy lecturer at the University of Lille from 1953 to 1955. Foucault then moved to Uppsala, Sweden, to teach French language and culture, leaving in 1958 in part because he was denied a doctorate for the work he had submitted to Uppsala University. After brief stints at the French Institute in Warsaw and Hamburg, Foucault returned to France in 1960 to take up a position as an associate professor of psychology at the University of Clermont-Ferrand. That same year, he submitted his doctoral work on the history of madness (as well as a secondary thesis, a translation and discussion of Kant's *Anthropology*) to the Sorbonne, which awarded him a doctorate in 1961.

Upon his return to France, Foucault remained restless, travelling to Brazil for a lecture tour and making repeated trips to Tunisia. Finding himself very much drawn to the latter country, he accepted a position as a philosophy professor at the University of Tunis, staying two years. Shortly after the student movement in 1968 was over, Foucault accepted a position as professor of philosophy at the university at the centre of the student movement, the Experimental University Centre of Vincennes (later to become University of Paris VIII). While Foucault was active in leftist politics, and well known as an advocate of prisoners' rights and gay liberation, he nonetheless sought and achieved mainstream academic success. He was frequently sought out for high-profile (and often broadcasted) national and international lectures, and was elected in 1970 to the prestigious Collège de France as Professor of History of Systems of Thought. This position was his crowning professional achievement, and Foucault remained at the Collège until his death in 1984 at the age of 58, from AIDS-related complications.

Foucault's work is generally divided into three periods: (1) The archeological or structuralist phase of his work in the 1960s, when he aimed to expose the structural rules constitutive of disciplinary discourses in psychiatry, medicine, and human sciences (*The Birth of the Clinic* [1963], *The Order of Things* [1966], *The Archeology of Knowledge* [1969]); (2) The second period, roughly the 1970s, when he developed a genealogical method that exposes rational discursive practices by revealing the origin of their disciplinary power and control (*Discipline and Punish* [1975], *Language, Counter-memory, Practice* [1977], and *Power/Knowledge* [1980]); and (3) The late period, in the early 1980s, when Foucault's attention turned to ethics. The works in this period include *The History of Sexuality, Vol. I: An Introduction* (1976); *The History of Sexuality, Vol. II: The Use of Pleasure* (1984); and *The History of Sexuality, Vol. III: The Care of the Self* (1984). Foucault's intellectual interest in the ways by which particular individuals are made into certain kinds of "subjects"— such as prisoners, homosexuals, and mental patients—was intertwined with his own life experience. As an out gay man living at times in conservative settings, he was also prone to periods of acute depression marked by intermittent suicide attempts and psychiatric hospitalization. Moreover, Foucault's transgressive personal life—he actively explored sadomasochism, self-mutilation, the gay men's bathhouse scene, and drugs—informed and intersected with his insightful and sometimes controversial writing on power, sexuality, and what he called "subjugated knowledges."

The excerpts included here, from Foucault's *Lectures at the Collège de France*, address the themes of power and knowledge. The influence of the philosopher Friedrich Nietzsche on Foucault's thought is apparent, particularly Nietzsche's writing on genealogy and power. Drawn by Nietzsche's radicalism, Foucault goes further than him, declaring in his early book, *The Order of Things*, that "Man is dead." By "Man," Foucault is referring to the Cartesian subject whose rationality promised emancipation, but who can no longer plausibly be said to be the centre of knowledge. Knowledge, instead, is produced in the relations of power among and between subjects—another Nietzschean insight. And by "power," Foucault does not merely mean state power, but power as a network of relationships criss-crossing and intersecting in all directions and across all structures. Power and knowledge are, moreover, mutually constitutive of one another. This close connection implies that knowledge is never neutral—an insight that in turn lends itself to critical analysis of any claim to truth. To help concretize Foucault's insights in these lectures, the case of *Norberg v. Wynrib* is presented following the reading; this case, which highlights the issues of trust and consent in the context of the doctor–patient relationship, calls to mind Foucault's reflections on different forms of power and agency, as well as their inherent complexities.

Further Readings

Gutting, G. (2005). *Foucault: A Very Short Introduction*. Oxford: Oxford University Press.
Hoy, D. (ed.). (1986). *Foucault: A Critical Reader*. Oxford: Blackwell.
Kritzman, L.D. (ed.). (1998). *Michel Foucault: Politics, Philosophy and Culture*. London: Routledge.
McCarthy, T. (1990). "The Critique of Impure Reason: Foucault and the Frankfurt School," *Political Theory* 18 (3): 437–69.
McNay, L. (1994). *Foucault: A Critical Introduction*. New York: Continuum.
Smart, B. (ed.). (1998). *Michel Foucault: A Critical Assessment*. London: Routledge.

Michel Foucault, *From* "Two Lectures on Power"

Michel Foucault, "Two Lectures on Power." Republished as "Lecture One" (7 January 1976) and "Lecture Two" (14 January 1976), in Society Must Be Defended: Lectures at the Collège de France, *translated by David Macey (New York: Picador, 2003).*

ONE

7 January 1976

What is a lecture? ~ Subjugated knowledges. ~ Historical knowledge of struggles, genealogies, and scientific discourse. ~ Power, or what is at stake in genealogies. ~ Juridical and economic conceptions of power. ~ Power as repression and power as war. ~ Clausewitz's aphorism inverted.

. . .

So what was I going to say to you this year? That I've just about had enough; in other words, I'd like to bring to a close, to put an end to, up to a point, the series of research projects—well, yes, "research"—we all talk about it, but what does it actually mean?—that we've been working on for four or five years, or practically ever since I've been here, and I realize that there were more and more drawbacks, for both you and me. Lines of research that were very closely interrelated but that never added up to a coherent body of work, that had no continuity. Fragments of research, none of which was completed, and none of which was followed through; bits and pieces of research, and at the same time it was getting

very repetitive, always falling into the same rut, the same themes, the same concepts. A few remarks on the history of penal procedure; a few chapters on the evolution, the institutionalization of psychiatry in the nineteenth century; considerations on sophistry or Greek coins; an outline history of sexuality, or at least a history of knowledge about sexuality based upon seventeenth-century confessional practices, or controls on infantile sexuality in the eighteenth and nineteenth centuries; pinpointing the genesis of a theory and knowledge of anomalies, and of all the related techniques. We are making no progress, and it's all leading nowhere. It's all repetitive, and it doesn't add up. Basically, we keep saying the same thing, and there again, perhaps we're not saying anything at all. It's all getting into something of an inextricable tangle, and it's getting us nowhere, as they say.

I could tell you that these things were trails to be followed, that it didn't matter where they led, or even that the one thing that did matter was that they didn't lead anywhere, or at least not in some predetermined direction. I could say they were like an outline for something. It's up to you to go on with them or to go off on a tangent; and it's up to me to pursue them or give them a different configuration. And then, we—you or I—could see what could be done with these fragments. I felt a bit like a sperm whale that breaks the surface of the water, makes a little splash, and lets you believe, makes you believe, or want to believe, that down there where it can't be seen, down there where it is neither seen nor monitored by anyone, it is following a deep, coherent, and premeditated trajectory.

That is more or less the position we were in, as I see it: I don't know what it looked like from where you are sitting. After all, the fact that the work I described to you looked both fragmented, repetitive, and discontinuous was quite in keeping with what might be called a "feverish laziness." It's a character trait of people who love libraries, documents, references, dusty manuscripts, texts that have never been read, books which, no sooner printed, were closed and then slept on the shelves and were only taken down centuries later. All this quite suits the busy inertia of those who profess useless knowledge, a sort of sumptuary knowledge, the wealth of a parvenu—and, as you well know, its external signs are found at the foot of the page. It should appeal to all those who feel sympathetic to one of those secret societies, no doubt the oldest and the most characteristic in the West, one of those strangely indestructible secret societies that were, I think, unknown in antiquity and which were formed in the early Christian era, probably at the time of the first monasteries, on the fringes of invasions, fires, and forests. I am talking about the great, tender, and warm freemasonry of useless erudition.

Except that it was not just a liking for this freemasonry that led me to do what I've been doing. It seems to me that we could justify the work we've been doing, in a somewhat empirical and haphazard way on both my part and yours, by saying that it was quite in keeping with a certain period; with the very limited period we have been living through for the last ten or fifteen years, twenty at the most. I am talking about a period in which we can observe two phenomena which were, if not really important, rather interesting. On the one hand, this has been a period characterized by what we might call the efficacy of dispersed and discontinuous offensives. I am thinking of many things, of, for instance, the strange efficacy, when it came to jamming the workings of the psychiatric institution, of the discourse, the discourses—and they really were very localized—of anti-psychiatry. And you know perfectly well that they were not supported, are not supported, by any overall systematization, no matter what their points of reference were and are. I am thinking of the original reference to existential analysis,[1] and of contemporary references to, broadly speaking, Marxism or Reich's theories.[2] I am also thinking of the strange efficacy of the attacks that have

been made on, say, morality and the traditional sexual hierarchy; they too referred in only vague and distant terms to Reich or Marcuse.[3] I am also thinking of the efficacy of the attacks on the judiciary and penal apparatus, some of which were very distantly related to the general—and fairly dubious—notion of "class justice," while others were basically related, albeit almost as distantly, to an anarchist thematic. I am also thinking much more specifically of the efficacy of something—I hesitate to call it a book—like *Anti-Oedipus*,[4] which referred to, which refers to nothing but its own prodigious theoretical creativity—that book, that event, or that thing that succeeded, at the level of day-to-day practice, in introducing a note of hoarseness into the whisper that had been passing from couch to armchair without any interruption for such a long time.

So I would say: for the last ten or fifteen years, the immense and proliferating criticizability of things, institutions, practices, and discourses; a sort of general feeling that the ground was crumbling beneath our feet, especially in places where it seemed most familiar, most solid, and closest [nearest] to us, to our bodies, to our everyday gestures. But alongside this crumbling and the astonishing efficacy of discontinuous, particular, and local critiques, the facts were also revealing something that could not, perhaps, have been foreseen from the outset: what might be called the inhibiting effect specific to totalitarian theories, or at least—what I mean is—all-encompassing and global theories. Not that all-encompassing and global theories haven't, in fairly constant fashion, provided—and don't continue to provide—tools that can be used at the local level; Marxism and psychoanalysis are living proof that they can. But they have, I think, provided tools that can be used at the local level only when, and this is the real point, the theoretical unity of their discourse is, so to speak, suspended, or at least cut up, ripped up, torn to shreds, turned inside out, displaced, caricatured, dramatized, theatricalized, and so on. Or at least that the totalizing approach always has the effect of putting the brakes on. So that, if you like, is my first point, the first characteristic of what has been happening over the last fifteen years or so: the local character of the critique; this does not, I think, mean soft eclecticism, opportunism, or openness to any old theoretical undertaking, nor does it mean a sort of deliberate asceticism that boils down to losing as much theoretical weight as possible. I think that the essentially local character of the critique in fact indicates something resembling a sort of autonomous and non-centralized theoretical production, or in other words a theoretical production that does not need a visa from some common regime to establish its validity.

This brings us to a second feature of what has been happening for some time now. The point is this: It is what might be called "returns of knowledge" that makes this local critique possible. What I mean by "returns of knowledge" is this: While it is true that in recent years we have often encountered, at least at the superficial level, a whole thematic: "life, not knowledge," "the real, not erudition," "money, not books,"[5] it appears to me that beneath this whole thematic, through it and even within it, we have seen what might be called the insurrection of subjugated knowledges. When I say "subjugated knowledges," I mean two things. On the one hand, I am referring to historical contents that have been buried or masked in functional coherences or formal systematizations. To put it in concrete terms if you like, it was certainly not a semiology of life in the asylum or a sociology of delinquence that made an effective critique of the asylum or the prison possible; it really was the appearance of historical contents. Quite simply because historical contents alone allow us to see the dividing lines in the confrontations and struggles that functional arrangements or systematic organizations are designed to mask. Subjugated knowledges are, then, blocks of historical knowledges that were present in the functional and systematic ensembles, but which were masked, and the critique was able to reveal their existence by using, obviously enough, the tools of scholarship.

Second, I think subjugated knowledges should be understood as meaning something else and, in a sense, something quite different. When I say "subjugated knowledges" I am also referring to a whole series of knowledges that have been disqualified as non-conceptual knowledges, as insufficiently elaborated knowledges: naive knowledges, hierarchically inferior know ledges, knowledges that are below the required level of erudition or scientificity. And it is thanks to the reappearance of these knowledges from below, of these unqualified or even disqualified knowledges, it is thanks to the reappearance of these knowledges: the knowledge of the psychiatrized, the patient, the nurse, the doctor, that is parallel to, marginal to, medical knowledge, the knowledge of the delinquent, what I would call, if you like, what people know (and this is by no means the same thing as [common] knowledge or common sense but, on the contrary, a particular knowledge, a knowledge that is local, regional, or differential, incapable of unanimity and which derives its power solely from the fact that it is different from all the knowledges that surround it), it is the reappearance of what people know at a local level, of these disqualified knowledges, that made the critique possible.

You might object that there is something very paradoxical about grouping together and putting into the same category of "subjugated knowledges," on the one hand, historical, meticulous, precise, technical expertise and, on the other, these singular, local knowledges, the non-commonsensical knowledges that people have, and which have in a way been left to lie fallow, or even kept in the margins. Well, I think it is the coupling together of the buried scholarly knowledge and knowledges that were disqualified by the hierarchy of erudition and sciences that actually gave the discursive critique of the last fifteen years its essential strength. What was at stake in both cases, in both this scholarly knowledge and these disqualified knowledges, in these two forms of knowledge—the buried and the disqualified? A historical knowledge of struggles. Both the specialized domain of scholarship and the disqualified knowledge people have contained the memory of combats, the very memory that had until then been confined to the margins. And so we have the outline of what might be called a genealogy, or of multiple genealogical investigations. We have both a meticulous rediscovery of struggles and the raw memory of fights. These genealogies are a combination of erudite knowledge and what people know. They would not have been possible—they could not even have been attempted—were it not for one thing: the removal of the tyranny of overall discourses, with their hierarchies and all the privileges enjoyed by theoretical vanguards. If you like, we can give the name "genealogy" to this coupling together of scholarly erudition and local memories, which allows us to constitute a historical knowledge of struggles and to make use of that knowledge in contemporary tactics. That can, then, serve as a provisional definition of the genealogies I have been trying to trace with you over the last few years.

You can see that this activity, which we can describe as genealogical, is certainly not a matter of contrasting the abstract unity of theory with the concrete multiplicity of the facts. It is certainly not a matter of some form or other of scientism that disqualifies speculation by contrasting it with the rigor of well-established bodies of knowledge. It is therefore not an empiricism that runs through the genealogical project, nor does it lead to a positivism, in the normal sense of the word. It is a way of playing local, discontinuous, disqualified, or non-legitimized knowledges off against the unitary theoretical instance that claims to be able to filter them, organize them into a hierarchy, organize them in the name of a true body of knowledge, in the name of the rights of a science that is in the hands of the few. Genealogies are therefore not positivistic returns to a form of science that is more attentive or more accurate. Genealogies are, quite specifically, anti-sciences. It is not that they demand the lyrical right to be ignorant, and not that they reject knowledge, or invoke or celebrate some immediate experience that has yet to be captured by knowledge. That is not what they are about. They are about the insurrection of knowledges. Not so much against the contents, methods, or concepts of a science; this is above all, primarily, an insurrection against the centralizing power-effects that are bound up with the institutionalization and workings of any scientific discourse organized in a society such as ours. That this institutionalization of scientific discourse is embodied in a university or, in general terms, a pedagogical apparatus, that this institutionalization of scientific discourses is embodied in a theoretico-commercial network such as psychoanalysis, or in a political apparatus—with everything that implies—is largely irrelevant. Genealogy has to fight the power-effects characteristic of any discourse that is regarded as scientific.

To put it in more specific terms, or at least in terms that might mean more to you, let me say this: you know how many people have been asking themselves whether or not Marxism is a science for many years now, probably for more than a century. One might say that the same question has been asked, and is still being asked, of psychoanalysis or, worse still, of the semiology of literary texts. Genealogies' or genealogists' answer to the question "Is it a science or not?" is: "Turning Marxism, or psychoanalysis, or whatever else it is, into a science is precisely what we are criticizing you for. And if there is one objection to be made against Marxism, it's that it might well be a science." To put it in more—if not more sophisticated terms—[at least] milder terms, let me say this: even before we know to what extent something like Marxism or psychoanalysis is analogous to a scientific practice in its day-to-day operations, in its rules of construction, in the concepts it uses, we should be asking the question, asking ourselves about the aspiration to power that is inherent in the claim to being a science. The question or questions that have to be asked are: "What types of knowledge are you trying to disqualify when you say that you are a science? What speaking subject, what discursive subject, what subject of experience and knowledge are you trying to minorize when you begin to say: "I speak this discourse, I am speaking a scientific discourse, and I am a scientist." What theoretico-political vanguard are you trying to put on the throne in order to detach it from all the massive, circulating, and discontinuous forms that knowledge can take?" And I would say: "When I see you trying to prove that Marxism is a science, to tell the truth, I do not really see you trying to demonstrate once and for all that Marxism has a rational structure and that its propositions are therefore the products of verification procedures. I see you, first and foremost, doing something different. I see you connecting to Marxist discourse,

and I see you assigning to those who speak that discourse the power-effects that the West has, ever since the Middle Ages, ascribed to a science and reserved for those who speak a scientific discourse."

Compared to the attempt to inscribe knowledges in the power-hierarchy typical of science, genealogy is, then, a sort of attempt to desubjugate historical knowledges, to set them free, or in other words to enable them to oppose and struggle against the coercion of a unitary, formal, and scientific theoretical discourse. The project of these disorderly and tattered genealogies is to reactivate local knowledges—Deleuze would no doubt call them "minor"[6]—against the scientific hierarchicalization of knowledge and its intrinsic power-effects. To put it in a nutshell: Archaeology is the method specific to the analysis of local discursivities, and genealogy is the tactic which, once it has described these local discursivities, brings into play the desubjugated knowledges that have been released from them. That just about sums up the overall project.

So you can see that all the fragments of research, all the interconnected and interrupted things I have been repeating so stubbornly for four or five years now, might be regarded as elements of these genealogies, and that I am not the only one to have been doing this over the last fifteen years. Far from it. Question: So why not go on with such a theory of discontinuity, when it is so pretty and probably so hard to verify?[7] Why don't I go on, and why don't I take a quick look at something to do with psychiatry, with the theory of sexuality?

It's true that one could go on—and I will try to go on up to a point—were it not, perhaps, for a certain number of changes, and changes in the conjuncture. What I mean is that compared to the situation we had five, ten, or even fifteen years ago, things have, perhaps, changed; perhaps the battle no longer looks quite the same. Well, are we really still in the same relationship of force, and does it allow us to exploit the knowledges we have dug out of the sand, to exploit them as they stand, without their becoming subjugated once more? What strength do they have in themselves? And after all, once we have excavated our genealogical fragments, once we begin to exploit them and to put in circulation these elements of knowledge that we have been trying to dig out of the sand, isn't there a danger that they will be recoded, recolonized by these unitary discourses which, having first disqualified them and having then ignored them when they reappeared, may now be ready to reannex them and include them in their own discourses and their own power-knowledge effects? And if we try to protect the fragments we have dug up, don't we run the risk of building, with our own hands, a unitary discourse? That is what we are being invited to do, that is the trap that is being set for us by all those who say, "It's all very well, but where does it get us? Where does it lead us? What unity does it give us?" The temptation is, up to a point, to say: Right, let's continue, let's accumulate. After all, there is no danger at the moment that we will be colonized. I was saying a moment ago that these genealogical fragments might be in danger of being recoded, but we could throw down a challenge and say, "Just try it!" We could, for instance, say, Look: ever since the very beginnings of anti-psychiatry or of the genealogies of psychiatric institutions—and it has been going on for a good fifteen years now—has a single Marxist, psychoanalyst, or psychiatrist ever attempted to redo it in their own terms or demonstrated that these genealogies were wrong, badly elaborated, badly articulated, or ill-founded? The way things stand, the fragments of genealogy that have been done are in fact still there, surrounded by a wary silence. The only arguments that have been put forward against them are—at the very best—propositions like the one we recently heard from, I think it was M. Juquin:[8] "All this is very well. But the fact remains that Soviet psychiatry is the best in the world." My answer to that is: "Yes, of course, you're right. Soviet psychiatry is the best in the world. That's just what I hold against it." The silence, or rather the caution with which unitary theories avoid the genealogy of knowledges might therefore be one reason for going on. One could at any rate unearth more and more genealogical fragments, like so many traps, questions, challenges, or whatever you want to call them. Given that we are talking about a battle—the battle knowledges are waging against the power-effects of scientific discourse—it is probably overoptimistic to assume that our adversary's silence proves that he is afraid of us. The silence of an adversary—and this is a methodological principle or a tactical principle that must always be kept in mind—could just as easily be a sign that he is not afraid of us at all. And we must, I think, behave as though he really is not frightened of us. And I am not suggesting that we give all these scattered genealogies a continuous, solid theoretical basis—the last thing I want to do is give them, superimpose on them, a sort of theoretical crown that would unify them—but that we should try, in future lectures, probably beginning this year, to specify or identify what is at stake when knowledges begin to challenge, struggle against, and rise up against the [institution] and the power- and knowledge-effects of scientific discourse.

As you know, and as I scarcely need point out, what is at stake in all these genealogies is this: What is this power whose irruption, force, Impact, and absurdity have become palpably obvious over the last forty years, as a result of both the collapse of Nazism and the retreat of Stalinism? What is power? Or rather—given that the question "What is power?" is obviously a theoretical question that would provide an answer to everything, which is just what I don't want to do—the issue is to determine what are, in their mechanisms, effects, their relations, the various power-apparatuses that operate at various levels of society, in such very different domains and with so many different extensions? Roughly speaking, I think that what is at stake in all this is this: Can the analysis of power, or the analysis of powers, be in one way or another deduced from the economy?

This is why I ask the question, and this is what I mean by it. I certainly do not wish to erase the countless differences or huge differences or huge differences, but, despite and because of these differences, it seems to me that the juridical conception and, let's say, the liberal conception of political power—which we find in the philosophers of the eighteenth century—do have certain things in common, as does the Marxist conception, or at least a certain contemporary conception that passes for the Marxist conception. Their common feature is what I will call "economism" in the theory of power. What I mean to say is this: In the case of the classic juridical theory of power, power is regarded as a right which can be possessed in the way one possesses a commodity, and which can therefore be transferred or alienated, either completely or partly, through a juridical act or an act that founds a right—it does not matter which, for the moment—thanks to the surrender of something or thanks to a contract. Power is the concrete power that any individual can hold, and which he can surrender, either as a whole or in part, so as to constitute a power or a political sovereignty. In the body of theory to which I am referring, the constitution of political power is therefore constituted by this series, or is modeled on a juridical operation similar to an exchange of contracts. There is therefore an obvious analogy, and it runs through all these theories, between power and commodities, between power and wealth.

In the other case, and I am obviously thinking here of the general Marxist conception of power, there is obviously none of this. In this Marxist conception, you have something else that might be called the "economic functionality" of power. "Economic functionality" to the extent that the role of power is essentially both to perpetuate the relations of production and to reproduce a class domination that is made possible by the development of the productive forces and the ways they are appropriated. In this case, political power finds its historical raison d'être in the economy. Broadly speaking, we have, if you like, in one case a political power which finds its formal model in the process of exchange, in the economy of the circulation of goods; and in the other case, political power finds its historical raison d'être, the principle of its concrete form and of its actual workings in the economy.

The problem that is at issue in the research I am talking about can, I think, be broken down as follows. First: Is power always secondary to the economy? Are its finality and function always determined by the economy? Is power's raison d'être and purpose essentially to serve the economy? Is it designed to establish, solidify, perpetuate, and reproduce relations that are characteristic of the economy and essential to its workings? Second question: Is power modeled on the commodity? Is power something that can be possessed and acquired, that can be surrendered through a contract or by force, that can be alienated or recuperated, that circulates and fertilizes one region but avoids others? Or if we wish to analyze it, do we have to operate—on the contrary—with different instruments, even if power relations are deeply involved in and with economic relations, even if power relations and economic relations always constitute a sort of network or loop? If that is the case, the indissociability of the economy and politics is not a matter of functional subordination, nor of formal isomorphism. It is of a different order, and it is precisely that order that we have to isolate.

What tools are currently available for a noneconomic analysis of power? I think that we can say that we really do not have a lot. We have, first of all, the assertion that power is not something that is given, exchanged, or taken back, that it is something that is exercised and that it exists only in action. We also have the other assertion, that power is not primarily the perpetuation and renewal of economic relations, but that it is primarily, in itself, a relationship of force. Which raises some questions, or rather two questions. If power is exercised, what is the exercise of power? What does it consist of? What is its mechanism? We have here what I would call an off-the-cuff answer, or at least an immediate response, and it seems to me that this is, ultimately, the answer given by the concrete reality of many contemporary analyses: Power is essentially that which represses. Power is that which represses nature, instincts, a class, or individuals. And when we find contemporary discourse trotting out the definition that power is that which represses, contemporary discourse is not really saying anything new. Hegel was the first to say this, and then Freud and then Reich.[9] In any case, in today's vocabulary, being an organ of repression is almost power's Homeric epithet. So, must the analysis of power be primarily, essentially even, an analysis of the mechanisms of repression?

Second—second off-the-cuff answer, if you like—if power is indeed the implementation and deployment of a relationship of force, rather than analyzing it in terms of surrender, contract, and alienation, or rather than analyzing it in functional terms as the reproduction of the relations of production, shouldn't we be analyzing it first and foremost in terms of conflict, confrontation, and war? That would give us an alternative to the first hypothesis—which is that the mechanism of power is basically or essentially repression—or a second hypothesis: Power is war, the continuation of war by other means. At this point, we can invert Clausewitz's proposition[10] and say that politics is the continuation of war by other means. This would imply three things. First, that power relations, as they function in a society like ours, are essentially anchored in a certain relationship of force that was established in and through war at a given historical moment that can be historically specified. And while it is true that political power puts an end to war and establishes or attempts to establish the reign of peace in civil society, it certainly does not do so in order to suspend the effects of power or to neutralize the disequilibrium revealed by the last battle of the war. According to this hypothesis, the role of political power is perpetually to use a sort of silent war to reinscribe that relationship of force, and to reinscribe it in institutions, economic inequalities, language, and even the bodies of individuals. This is the initial meaning of our inversion of Clausewitz's aphorism—politics is the continuation of war by other means. Politics, in other words, sanctions and reproduces the disequilibrium of forces manifested in war. Inverting the proposition also means something else, namely that within this "civil peace," these political struggles, these clashes over or with power, these modifications of relations of force—the shifting balance, the reversals—in a political system, all these things must be interpreted as a continuation of war. And they are interpreted as so many episodes, fragmentations, and displacements of the war itself. We are always writing the history of the same war, even when we are writing the history of peace and its institutions.

Inverting Clausewitz's aphorism also has a third meaning: The final decision can come only from war, or in other words a trial by strength in which weapons are the final judges. It means that the last battle would put an end to politics, or in other words, that the last battle would at last—and I mean "at last"—suspend the exercise of power as continuous warfare.

So you see, once we try to get away from economistic schemata in our attempt to analyze power, we immediately find ourselves faced with two grand hypotheses; according to one, the mechanism of power is repression—for the sake of convenience, I will call this Reich's hypothesis, if you like—and according to the second, the basis of the power-relationship lies in a warlike clash between forces—for the sake of convenience, I will call this Nietzsche's hypothesis. The two hypotheses are not irreconcilable; on the contrary, there seems to be a fairly logical connection between the two. After all, isn't repression the political outcome of war, just as oppression was, in the classical theory of political right, the result of the abuse of sovereignty within the juridical domain?

We can, then, contrast two great systems for analyzing power. The first, which is the old theory you find in the philosophers of the seventeenth century, is articulated around power as a primal right that is surrendered, and which constitutes sovereignty, with the contract as the matrix of political power. And when the power that has been so constituted oversteps the limit, or oversteps the limits of the contract, there is a danger that it will become oppression. Power-contract, with oppression as the limit, or rather the transgression of the limit. And then we have the other system, which tries to analyze power not in terms of the contract-oppression schema, but in terms of the war-repression schema. At this point, repression is not what oppression was in relation to the contract, namely an abuse, but, on the contrary, simply the effect and the continuation of a relationship of domination. Repression is no more than the implementation, within a pseudopeace that is being undermined by a continuous war, of a perpetual relationship of force. So, two schemata for the analysis of power: the contract-oppression schema, which is, if you like, the juridical schema, and the war-repression or domination-repression schema, in which the pertinent opposition is not, as in the previous schema, that between the legitimate and the illegitimate, but that between struggle and submission.

It is obvious that everything I have said to you in previous years is inscribed within the struggle-repression schema. That is indeed the schema I was trying to apply. Now, as I tried to apply it, I was eventually forced to reconsider it; both because, in many respects, it is still insufficiently elaborated—I would even go so far as to say that it is not elaborated at all—and also because I think that the twin notions of "repression" and "war" have to be considerably modified and ultimately, perhaps, abandoned. At all events, we have to look very closely at these two notions of "repression" and "war"; if you like, we have to look a little more closely at the hypothesis that the mechanisms of power are essentially mechanisms of repression, and at the alternative hypothesis that what is rumbling away and what is at work beneath political power is essentially and above all a warlike relation.

Without wishing to boast, I think that I have in fact long been suspicious of this notion of "repression," and

I have attempted to show you, in relation to the genealogies I was talking about just now, in relation to the history of penal law, psychiatric power, controls on infantile sexuality, and so on, that the mechanisms at work in these power formations were something very different from—or at least much more than—repression. I cannot go any further without repeating some of this analysis of repression, without pulling together everything I have said about it, no doubt in a rambling sort of way. The next lecture, perhaps the next two lectures, will therefore be devoted to a critical re-examination of the notion of "repression," to trying to show how and why what is now the widespread notion of repression cannot provide an adequate description of the mechanisms and effects of power, cannot define them.[11]

Most of the next lecture will, however, be devoted to the other side of the question, or in other words the problem of war. I would like to try to see the extent to which the binary schema of war and struggle, of the clash between forces, can really be identified as the basis of civil society, as both the principle and motor of the exercise of political power. Are we really talking about war when we analyze the workings of power? Are the notions of "tactics," "strategy," and "relations of force" valid? To what extent are they valid? Is power quite simply a continuation of war by means other than weapons and battles? Does what has now become the commonplace theme, though it is a relatively recent theme, that power is responsible for defending civil society imply, yes or no, that the political structure of society is so organized that some can defend themselves against others, or can defend their domination against the rebellion of others, or quite simply defend their victory and perpetuate it by subjugating others?

The outline for this year's course will, then, be as follows: one or two lectures devoted to a re-examination of the notion of repression; then I will begin [to look at]—I may go on in the years to come, I've no idea—this problem of the war in civil society. I will begin by eliminating the very people who are said to be the theorists of the war in civil society, and who are in my view no such thing, namely Machiavelli and Hobbes. Then I will try to look again at the theory that war is the historical principle behind the workings of power, in the context of the race problem, as it was racial binarism that led the West to see for the first time that it was possible to analyze political power as war. And I will try to trace this down to the moment when race struggle and class struggle became, at the end of the nineteenth century, the two great schemata that were used to identify the phenomenon of war and the relationship of force within political society.

TWO

14 January 1976

> *War and power. ~ Philosophy and the limits of power. ~ Law and royal power. ~ Law, domination, and subjugation. ~ Analytics of power: questions of method. ~ Theory of sovereignty. ~ Disciplinary power. ~ Rule and norm.*

. . .

What I have been trying to look at since 1970–1971 is the "how" of power. Studying the "how of power," or in other words trying to understand its mechanisms by establishing two markers, or limits; on the one hand, the rules of right that formally delineate power, and on the other hand, at the opposite extreme, the other limit might be the truth-effects that power produces, that this power conducts and which, in their turn, reproduce that power. So we have the triangle: power, right, truth. In schematic terms, let us say that there is a traditional question, which is, I think, that of political philosophy. It can be formulated thus: How does the discourse of truth or, quite simply, philosophy—in the sense that philosophy is the discourse of truth par excellence—establish the limits of power's right? That is the traditional question. Now the question I would like to ask is a question from below, and it is a very factual question compared to that traditional, noble, and philosophical question. My problem is roughly this: What are the rules of right that power implements to produce discourses of truth? Or: What type of power is it that is capable of producing discourses of power that have, in a society like ours, such powerful effects?

What I mean is this: In a society such as ours—or in any society, come to that—[multiple] relations of power traverse, characterize, and constitute the social body; they are indissociable from a discourse of truth, and they can neither be established nor function unless a true discourse is produced, accumulated, put into circulation, and set to work. Power cannot be exercised unless a certain economy of discourses of truth functions in, on the basis of, and thanks to, that power. This is true of all societies, but I think that in our society, this relationship among power, right, and truth is organized in a very particular way.

In order to characterize not just the mechanism of the relationship between power, right, and truth itself but its intensity and constancy, let us say that we are obliged to produce the truth by the power that demands truth and needs it in order to function: we are forced to tell the truth, we are constrained, we are condemned to admit the truth or to discover it. Power constantly asks questions and questions us; it constantly investigates and records; it institutionalizes the search for the truth, professionalizes it, and rewards it. We have to produce the truth in the same way, really, that we have to produce wealth, and we have to produce the truth in order to be able to produce wealth. In a different sense, we are also subject to the truth in the sense that truth lays down the law: it is the discourse of truth that decides, at least in part; it conveys and propels truth-effects. After all, we are judged, condemned, forced to perform tasks, and destined to live and die in certain ways by discourses that are true, and which bring with them specific power-effects. So: rules of right, mechanisms of power, truth-effects. Or: rules of power, and the power of true discourses. That, roughly, is the very general domain I wanted to examine, and which I have been examining to some extent and with, as I am well aware, many digressions.

I would now like to say a few words about this domain. What general principle guided me, and what were the imperative commands, or the methodological precautions that I resolved to take? Where relations between right and power are concerned, the general principle is, it seems to me, that one fact must never be forgotten: In Western societies, the elaboration of juridical thought has essentially centred around royal power ever since the Middle Ages. The juridical edifice of our societies was elaborated at the demand of royal power, as well as for its benefit, and in order to serve as its instrument or its justification. In the West, right is the right of the royal command. Everyone is of course familiar with the famous, celebrated, repeated, and repetitive role played by jurists in the organization of royal power. It must not be forgotten that the reactivation of Roman law in the middle of the Middle Ages—and this was the great phenomenon that made it possible to reconstruct a juridical edifice that had collapsed after the fall of the Roman Empire—was one of the instruments that was used to constitute monarchical, authoritarian, administrative, and, ultimately, absolute power. The juridical edifice was, then, formed around the royal personage, at the demand of royal power, and for the benefit of royal power. When in later centuries this juridical edifice escaped from royal control, when it was turned against royal power, the issue at stake was always, and always would be, the limits of that power, the question of its prerogatives. In other words, I believe that the king was the central character in the entire Western juridical edifice. The general system, or at least the general organization of the Western juridical system, was all about the king: the king, his rights, his power, and the possible limits of his power. That, basically, is what the general system, or at least the general organization, of the Western juridical system is all about.

No matter whether the jurists were the king's servants or his adversaries, the great edifices of juridical thought and juridical knowledge were always about royal power.

It was all about royal power in two senses. Either it had to be demonstrated that royal power was invested in a juridical armature, that the monarch was indeed the living body of sovereignty, and that his power, even when absolute, was perfectly in keeping with a basic right; or it had to be demonstrated that the power of the sovereign had to be limited, that it had to submit to certain rules, and that, if that power were to retain its legitimacy, it had to be exercised within certain limits. From the Middle Ages onward, the essential role of the theory of right has been to establish the legitimacy of power; the major or central problem around which the theory of right is organized is the problem of sovereignty. To say that the problem of sovereignty is the central problem of right in Western societies means that the essential function of the technique and discourse of right is to dissolve the element of domination in power and to replace that domination, which has to be reduced or masked, with two things: the legitimate rights of the sovereign on the one hand, and the legal obligation to obey on the other. The system of right is completely centred on the king; it is, in other words, ultimately an elimination of domination and its consequences.

In previous years when we were talking about the various little things I have mentioned, the general project was, basically, to invert the general direction of the analysis that has, I think, been the entire discourse of right ever since the Middle Ages. I have been trying to do the opposite, or in other words to stress the fact of domination in all its brutality and its secrecy, and then to show not only that right is an instrument of that domination—that is self-evident—but also how, to what extent, and in what form right (and when I say right, I am not thinking just of the law, but of all the apparatuses, institutions, and rules that apply it) serves as a vehicle for and implements relations that are not relations of sovereignty, but relations of domination. And by domination I do not mean the brute fact of the domination of the one over the many, or of one group over another, but the multiple forms of domination that can be exercised in society; so, not the king in his central position, but subjects in their reciprocal relations; not sovereignty in its one edifice, but the multiple subjugations that take place and function within the social body.

The system of right and the judiciary field are permanent vehicles for relations of domination, and for polymorphous techniques of subjugation. Right must, I think, be viewed not in terms of a legitimacy that has to be established, but in terms of the procedures of subjugation it implements. As I see it, we have to bypass or get around the problem of sovereignty—which is central to the theory of right—and the obedience of individuals who submit to it, and to reveal the problem of domination and subjugation instead of sovereignty and subjugation. Having said that, a certain number of methodological precautions had to be taken in order to follow this line, which was an attempt to bypass or deviate from the general line of the juridical analysis.

Methodological precautions. Our object is not to analyze rule-governed and legitimate forms of power which have a single centre, or to look at what their general mechanisms or its overall effects might be. Our object is, on the contrary, to understand power by looking at its extremities, at its outer limits at the point where it becomes capillary; in other words, to understand power in its most regional forms and institutions, and especially at the points where this power transgresses the rules of right that organize and delineate it, oversteps those rules and is invested in institutions, is embodied in techniques and acquires the material means to intervene, sometimes in violent ways. We can take an example if you like: rather than trying to see where and how the power to punish finds its basis in the sovereignty, as described by philosophy, of either monarchical right or democratic right, I tried to look at how the power to punish was embodied in a certain number of local, regional, and material institutions, such as torture or imprisonment, and to look at the simultaneously institutional, physical, regulatory, and violent world of the actual apparatuses of punishment. I tried, in other words, to understand power by looking at its extremities, at where its exercise became less and less juridicial. That was my first precaution.

Second precaution: My goal was not to analyze power at the level of intentions or decisions, not to try to approach it from inside, and not to ask the question (which leads us, I think, into a labyrinth from which there is no way out): So who has power? What is going on in his head? And what is he trying to do, this man who has power? The goal was, on the contrary, to study power at the point where his intentions—if, that is, any intention is involved—are completely invested in real and effective practices; to study power by looking, as it were, at its external face, at the point where it relates directly and immediately to what we might, very provisionally, call its object, its target, its field of application, or, in other words, the places where it implants itself and produces its real effects. So the question is not: Why do some people want to be dominant? What do they want? What is their overall strategy? The question is this: What happens at the moment of, at the level of the procedure of subjugation, or in the continuous and uninterrupted processes that subjugate bodies, direct gestures, and regulate forms of behaviour? In other words, rather than asking ourselves what the sovereign looks like from on high, we should be trying to discover how multiple bodies, forces, energies, matters, desires, thoughts, and so on are gradually, progressively, actually and materially constituted as subjects, or as the subject. To grasp the material agency of subjugation insofar as it constitutes subjects would, if you like, be to do precisely the opposite of what Hobbes was trying to do in *Leviathan*.[12] Ultimately, I think that all jurists try to do the same thing, as their problem is to discover how a multiplicity of individuals and wills can be shaped into a single will or even a single body that is supposedly animated by a soul known as sovereignty. Remember the schema of *Leviathan*.[13] In this schema, the Leviathan, being an artificial man, is no more than the coagulation of a certain number of distinct individualities that find themselves united by a certain number of the State's constituent elements. But at the heart, or rather the head, of the State, there is something that constitutes it as such, and that something is sovereignty, which Hobbes specifically describes as the soul of the Leviathan. Well, rather than raising this problem of the central soul, I think we should be trying—and this is what I have been trying to do—to study the multiple peripheral bodies, the bodies that are constituted as subjects by power-effects.

Third methodological precaution: Do not regard power as a phenomenon of mass and homogeneous domination—the domination of one individual over others, of one group over others, or of one class over others; keep it clearly in mind that unless we are looking at it from a great height and from a very great distance, power is not something that is divided between those who have it and hold it exclusively, and those who do not have it and are subject to it. Power must, I think, be analyzed as something that circulates, or rather as something that functions only when it is part of a chain. It is never localized here or there, it is never in the hands of some, and it is never appropriated in the way that wealth or a commodity can be appropriated. Power functions. Power is exercised through networks, and individuals do not simply circulate in those networks; they are in a position to both submit to and exercise this power. They are never the inert or consenting targets of power; they are always its relays. In other words, power passes through individuals. It is not applied to them.

It is therefore, I think, a mistake to think of the individual as a sort of elementary nucleus, a primitive atom or some multiple, inert matter to which power is applied, or which is struck by a power that subordinates or destroys individuals. In actual fact, one of the first effects of power is that it allows bodies, gestures, discourses, and desires to be identified and constituted as something individual. The individual is not, in other words, power's opposite number; the individual is one of power's first effects. The individual is in fact a power-effect, and at the same time, and to the extent that he is a power-effect, the individual is a relay: power passes through the individuals it has constituted.

Fourth implication at the level of methodological precautions: When I say, "Power is exercised, circulates, and forms networks," this might be true up to a certain point. We can also say, "We all have some element of fascism inside our heads," or, at a more basic level still, "We all have some element of power in our bodies." And power does—at least to some extent—pass or migrate through our bodies. We can indeed say all that, but I do not think that we therefore have to conclude that power is the best-distributed thing, the most widely distributed thing, in the world, even though this is, up to a point, the case. Power is not distributed throughout the body in democratic or anarchic fashion. What I mean is this: it seems to me—and this will be our fourth methodological precaution—it is important not to, so to speak, deduce power by beginning at the centre and trying to see how far down it goes, or to what extent it is reproduced or renewed in the most atomistic elements of society. I think that, on the contrary—and this is a methodological precaution that has to be taken—we should make an ascending analysis of power, or in other words begin with its infinitesimal mechanisms, which have their own history, their own trajectory, their own techniques and tactics, and then look at how these mechanisms of power, which have their solidity and, in a sense, their own technology, have been and are invested, colonized, used, inflected, transformed, displaced, extended, and so on by increasingly general mechanisms and forms of overall domination. Overall domination is not something that is pluralized and then has repercussions down below. I think we have to analyze the way in which the phenomena, techniques, and procedures of power come into play at the lowest levels; we have to show, obviously, how these procedures are displaced, extended, and modified and, above all, how they are invested or annexed by global phenomena, and how more general powers or economic benefits can slip into the play of these technologies of power, which are at once relatively autonomous and infinitesimal.

To make things clearer, I will take the example of madness. We could say this, we could make the descending analysis we have to distrust. We could say that from the late sixteenth century or the seventeenth century onward, the bourgeoisie became the ruling class. Having said that, how can we deduce that the mad will be confined? You can certainly make that deduction; it is always easy, and that is precisely what I hold against it. It is in fact easy to show how, because the mad are obviously of no use to industrial production, they have to be got rid of. We could, if you like, say the same thing, not about the madman this time, but about infantile sexuality—and a number of people have done so: Wilhelm Reich[14] does so up to a point, and Reimut Reich certainly does so.[15] We could ask how the rule of the bourgeoisie allows us to understand the repression of infantile sexuality. Well, it's quite simple: from the seventeenth or eighteenth century onward, the human body essentially became a productive force, and all forms of expenditure that could not be reduced to these relations, or to the constitution of the productive forces, all forms of expenditure that could be shown to be unproductive, were banished, excluded, and repressed. Such deductions are always possible; they are both true and false. They are essentially too facile, because we can say precisely the opposite. We can deduce from the principle that the bourgeoisie became a ruling class that controlling sexuality, and infantile sexuality, is not absolutely desirable. We can reach the opposite conclusion and say that what is needed is a sexual apprenticeship, sexual training, sexual precocity, to the extent that the goal is to use sexuality to reproduce a labour force, and it is well known that, at least in the early nineteenth century, it was believed that the optimal labour force was an infinite labour force: the greater the labour force, the greater the capitalist system of production's ability to function fully and efficiently.

I think that we can deduce whatever we like from the general phenomenon of the domination of the bourgeois class. It seems to me that we should be doing quite the opposite, or in other words looking in historical terms, and from below, at how control mechanisms could come into play in terms of the exclusion of madness, or the repression and suppression of sexuality; at how these phenomena of repression or exclusion found their instruments and their logic, and met a certain number of needs at the actual level of the family and its immediate entourage, or in the cells or the lowest levels of society. We should be showing what their agents were, and we should be looking for those agents not in the bourgeoisie in general, but in the real agents that exist in the immediate entourage: the family, parents, doctors, the lowest levels of the police, and so on. And we should be looking at how, at a given moment, in a specific conjuncture and subject to a certain number of transformations, these power-mechanisms began to become economically profitable and politically useful. And I think we could easily succeed in demonstrating—and this is, after all,

what I have tried to do on a number of occasions in the past—that, basically, what the bourgeoisie needed, and the reason why the system ultimately proved to work to its advantage, was not that the mad had to be excluded or that childhood masturbation had to be controlled or forbidden—the bourgeois system can, I repeat, quite easily tolerate the opposite of this. What did prove to be in its interest, and what it did invest, was not the fact that they were excluded, but the technique and procedures of their exclusion. It was the mechanisms of exclusion, the surveillance apparatus, the medicalization of sexuality, madness, and delinquency, it was all that, or in other words the micromechanics of power that came at a certain moment to represent, to constitute the interest of the bourgeoisie. That is what the bourgeoisie was interested in.

To put it another way: to the extent that these notions of "the bourgeoisie" and "the interests of the bourgeoisie" probably have no content, or at least not in terms of the problems we have just raised, what we have to realize is precisely that there was no such thing as a bourgeoisie that thought that madness should be excluded or that infantile sexuality had to be repressed; but there were mechanisms to exclude madness and techniques to keep infantile sexuality under surveillance. At a given moment, and for reasons that have to be studied, they generated a certain economic profit, a certain political utility, and they were therefore colonized and supported by global mechanisms and, finally, by the entire system of the State. If we concentrate on the techniques of power and show the economic profit or political utility that can be derived from them, in a certain context and for certain reasons, then we can understand how these mechanisms actually and eventually became part of the whole. In other words, the bourgeoisie doesn't give a damn about the mad, but from the nineteenth century onward and subject to certain transformations, the procedures used to exclude the mad produced or generated a political profit, or even a certain economic utility. They consolidated the system and helped it to function as a whole. The bourgeoisie is not interested in the mad, but it is interested in power over the mad; the bourgeoisie is not interested in the sexuality of children, but it is interested in the system of power that controls the sexuality of children. The bourgeoisie does not give a damn about delinquents, or about how they are punished or rehabilitated, as that is of no great economic interest. On the other hand, the set of mechanisms whereby delinquents are controlled, kept track of, punished, and reformed does generate a bourgeois interest that functions within the economico-political system as a whole. That is the fourth precaution, the fourth methodological line I wanted to follow.

Fifth precaution: It is quite possible that ideological production did coexist with the great machineries of power. There was no doubt an ideology of education, an ideology of monarchical power, an ideology of parliamentary democracy, and so on. But I do not think that it is ideologies that are shaped at the base, at the point where the networks of power culminate. It is much less and much more than that. It is the actual instruments that form and accumulate knowledge, the observational methods, the recording techniques, the investigative research procedures, the verification mechanisms. That is, the delicate mechanisms of power cannot function unless knowledge, or rather knowledge apparatuses, are formed, organized, and put into circulation, and those apparatuses are not ideological trimmings or edifices.

To sum up these five methodological precautions, let me say that rather than orienting our research into power toward the juridical edifice of sovereignty, State apparatuses, and the ideologies that accompany them, I think we should orient our analysis of power toward material operations, forms of subjugation, and the connections among and the uses made of the local systems of subjugation on the one hand, and apparatuses of knowledge on the other.

In short, we have to abandon the model of Leviathan, that model of an artificial man who is at once an automaton, a fabricated man, but also a unitary man who contains all real individuals, whose body is made up of citizens but whose soul is sovereignty. We have to study power outside the model of Leviathan, outside the field delineated by juridical sovereignty and the institution of the State. We have to analyze it by beginning with the techniques and tactics of domination. That, I think, is the methodological line we have to follow, and which I have tried to follow in the different research projects we have undertaken in previous years on psychiatric power, infantile sexuality, the punitive system, and so on.

Now if we look at this domain and take these methodological precautions, I think that one massive historical fact emerges, and that it will help to provide us with an introduction to the problem I wish to talk about from now onward. The massive historical fact is this: The juridico-political theory of sovereignty—the theory we have to get away from if we want to analyze power—dates from the Middle Ages. It dates from the reactivation of Roman law and is constituted around the problem of the monarch and the monarchy. And I believe that, in historical terms, this theory of sovereignty—which is the great trap we are in danger of falling into when we try to analyze power—played four roles.

First, it referred to an actual power mechanism: that of the feudal monarchy. Second, it was used as an instrument to constitute and justify the great monarchical administrations. From the sixteenth and especially the seventeenth century onward, or at the time of the Wars of Religion, the theory of sovereignty then became a weapon that was in circulation on both sides, and it was used both to restrict and to strengthen royal power. You find it in the hands of Catholic monarchists and Protestant antimonarchists; you also find it in the hands of more or less liberal Protestant monarchists; you also find it in the hands of Catholics who advocate regicide or a change of dynasty. You find this theory of sovereignty being brought into play by aristocrats and *parlementaires*,[16] by the representatives of royal power and by the last feudalists. It was, in a word, the great instrument of the political and theoretical struggles that took place around systems of power in the sixteenth and seventeenth centuries. In the eighteenth century, finally, you find the same theory of sovereignty, the same reactivation of Roman law, in the work of Rousseau and his contemporaries, but it now played a fourth and different role; at this point in time, its role was to construct an alternative model to authoritarian or absolute monarchical administration: that of the parliamentary democracies. And it went on playing that role until the time of the Revolution.

It seems to me that if we look at these four roles, we find that, so long as feudal-type societies survived, the problems dealt with by the theory of sovereignty, or to which it referred, were actually coextensive with the general mechanics of power, or the way power was exercised from the highest to the lowest levels. In other words, the relationship of sovereignty, understood in both the broad and the narrow sense, was, in short, coextensive with the entire social body. And the way in which power was exercised could indeed be transcribed, at least in its essentials, in terms of the sovereign/subject relationship.

Now, an important phenomenon occurred in the seventeenth and eighteenth centuries: the appearance—one should say the invention—of a new mechanism of power which had very specific procedures, completely new instruments, and very different equipment. It was, I believe, absolutely incompatible with relations of sovereignty. This new mechanism of power applies primarily to bodies and what they do rather than to the land and what it produces. It was a mechanism of power that made it possible to extract time and labour, rather than commodities and wealth, from bodies. It was a type of power that was exercised through constant surveillance and not in discontinuous fashion through chronologically defined systems of taxation and obligation. It was a type of power that presupposed a closely meshed grid of material coercions rather than the physical existence of a sovereign, and it therefore defined a new economy of power based upon the principle that there had to be an increase both in the subjugated forces and in the force and efficacy of that which subjugated them.

It seems to me that this type of power is the exact, point-for-point opposite of the mechanics of power that the theory of sovereignty described or tried to transcribe. The theory of sovereignty is bound up with a form of power that is exercised over the land and the produce of the land, much more so than over bodies and what they do. [This theory] concerns power's displacement and appropriation not of time and labour, but of goods and wealth. This makes it possible to transcribe, into juridical terms, discontinuous obligations and tax records, but not to code continuous surveillance; it is a theory that makes it possible to found absolute power around and on the basis of the physical existence of the sovereign, but not continuous and permanent systems of surveillance. The theory of sovereignty is, if you like, a theory which can found absolute power on the absolute expenditure of power, but which cannot calculate power with minimum expenditure and maximum efficiency. This new type of power, which can therefore no longer be transcribed in terms of sovereignty, is, I believe, one of bourgeois society's great inventions. It was one of the basic tools for the establishment of industrial capitalism and the corresponding type of society. This non-sovereign power, which is foreign to the form of sovereignty, is "disciplinary" power. This power cannot be described or justified in terms of the theory of sovereignty. It is radically heterogeneous and should logically have led to the complete disappearance of the great juridical edifice of the theory of sovereignty. In fact, the theory of sovereignty not only continued to exist as, if you like, an ideology of right; it also continued to organize the juridical codes that nineteenth-century Europe adopted after the Napoleonic codes.[17] Why did the theory of sovereignty live on in this way as an ideology and as the organizing principle behind the great juridical codes?

I think there are two reasons. On the one hand, the theory of sovereignty was, in the seventeenth century and even the nineteenth century, a permanent critical instrument to be used against the monarchy and all the obstacles that stood in the way of the development of the disciplinary society. On the other hand, this theory, and the organization of a juridical code centred upon it, made it possible to superimpose on the mechanism of discipline a system of right that concealed its mechanisms and erased the element of domination and the techniques of domination involved in discipline, and which, finally, guaranteed that everyone could exercise his or her own sovereign rights thanks to the sovereignty of the State. In other words, juridical systems, no matter whether they were theories or codes, allowed the democratization of sovereignty, and the establishment of a public right articulated with collective sovereignty, at the very time when, to the extent that, and because the democratization of sovereignty was heavily ballasted by the mechanisms of disciplinary coercion. To put it in more condensed terms, one might say that once disciplinary constraints had to both function as mechanisms of domination and be concealed to the extent that they were the mode in which power was actually exercised, the theory of sovereignty had to find expression in the juridical apparatus and had to be reactivated or complemented by judicial codes.

From the nineteenth century until the present day, we have then in modern societies, on the one hand, a legislation, a discourse, and an organization of public right articulated around the principle of the sovereignty of the social body and the delegation of individual sovereignty to the State; and we also have a tight grid of disciplinary coercions that actually guarantees the cohesion of that social body. Now that grid cannot in any way be transcribed in right, even though the two necessarily go together. A right of sovereignty and a mechanics of discipline. It is, I think, between these two limits that power is exercised. The two limits are, however, of such a kind and so heterogeneous that we can never reduce one to the other. In modern societies, power is exercised through, on the basis of, and in the very play of the heterogeneity between a public right of sovereignty and a polymorphous mechanics of discipline. This is not to say that you have, on the one hand, a garrulous and explicit system of right, and on the other hand, obscure silent disciplines that operate down below, in the shadows, and which constitute the silent basement of the great mechanics of power. Disciplines in fact have their own discourse. They do, for the reasons I was telling you about a moment ago, create apparatuses of knowledge, knowledges and multiple fields of expertise. They are extraordinarily inventive when it comes to creating apparatuses to shape knowledge and expertise, and they do support a discourse, but it is a discourse that cannot be the discourse of right or a juridical discourse. The discourse of discipline is alien to that of the law; it is alien to the discourse that makes rules a product of the will of the sovereign. The discourse of disciplines is about a rule: not a juridical rule derived from sovereignty, but a discourse about a natural rule, or in other words a norm. Disciplines will define not a code of law, but a code of normalization, and they will necessarily refer to a theoretical horizon that is not the edifice of law, but the field of the human sciences. And the jurisprudence of these disciplines will be that of a clinical knowledge.

In short, what I have been trying to show over the last few years is certainly not how, as the front of the exact sciences advances, the uncertain, difficult, and confused domain of human behaviour is gradually annexed by science: the gradual constitution of the human sciences is not the result of an increased rationality on the part of the exact sciences. I think that the process that has made possible the discourse of the human sciences is the juxtaposition of, the confrontation between, two mechanisms and two types of discourse that are absolutely heterogeneous: on the one hand, the organization of right around sovereignty, and on the other, the mechanics of the coercions exercised by disciplines. In our day, it is the fact that power is exercised through both right and disciplines, that the techniques of discipline and discourses born of discipline are invading right, and that normalizing procedures are increasingly colonizing the procedures of the law, that might explain the overall workings of what I would call a "normalizing society."

To be more specific, what I mean is this: I think that normalization, that disciplinary normalizations, are increasingly in conflict with the juridical system of sovereignty; the incompatibility of the two is increasingly apparent; there is a greater and greater need for a sort of arbitrating discourse, for a sort of power and knowledge that has been rendered neutral because its scientificity has become sacred. And it is precisely in the expansion of medicine that we are seeing—I wouldn't call it a combination of, a reduction of—but a perpetual exchange or confrontation between the mechanics of discipline and the principle of right. The development of medicine, the general medicalization of behaviour, modes of conduct, discourses, desires, and so on, is taking place on the front where the heterogeneous layers of discipline and sovereignty meet.

That is why we now find ourselves in a situation where the only existing and apparently solid recourse we have against the usurpations of disciplinary mechanics and against the rise of a power that is bound up with scientific knowledge is precisely a recourse or a return to a right that is organized around sovereignty, or that is articulated on that old principle. Which means in concrete terms that when we want to make some objection against disciplines and all the knowledge-effects and power-effects that are bound up with them, what do we do in concrete terms? What do we do in real life? What do the Syndicat de la magistrature and other institutions like it do? What do we do? We obviously invoke right, the famous old formal, bourgeois right. And it is in reality the right of sovereignty. And I think that at this point we are in a sort of bottleneck, that we cannot go on working like this forever; having recourse to sovereignty against discipline will not enable us to limit the effects of disciplinary power.

Sovereignty and discipline, legislation, the right of sovereignty and disciplinary mechanics are in fact the two things that constitute—in an absolute sense—the general mechanisms of power in our society. Truth to tell, if we are to struggle against disciplines, or rather against disciplinary power, in our search for a non-disciplinary power, we should not be turning to the old right of sovereignty; we should be looking for a new right that is both anti-disciplinary and emancipated from the principle of sovereignty.

At this point we come back to the notion of "repression." I may talk to you about that next time, unless I have had enough of repeating things that have already been said, and move on immediately to other things to do with war. If I feel like it and if I can be bothered to, I will talk to you about the notion of "repression," which has, I think, the twofold disadvantage, in the use that is made of it, of making obscure reference to a certain theory of sovereignty—the theory of the sovereign rights of the individual—and of bringing into play, when it is used, a whole set of psychological references borrowed from the human sciences, or in other words from discourses and practices that relate to the disciplinary domain. I think that the notion of "repression" is still, whatever critical use we try to make of it, a juridico-disciplinary notion; and to that extent the critical use of the notion of "repression" is tainted, spoiled, and rotten from the outset because it implies both a juridical reference to sovereignty and a disciplinary reference to normalization. Next time, I will either talk to you about repression or move on to the problem of war.

Post-Reading Questions

1. Foucault distinguishes power from force and domination. Why does he do so, and what are the key differences between them?
2. By what processes and means does "normalization" create certain kinds of "subjects," according to Foucault?
3. What is "disciplinary power"?
4. What is a "discourse," in Foucault's use of the term?

CASE STUDY
POWER AND CONSENT: *NORBERG v. WYNRIB*

Introduction

This 1992 Supreme Court of Canada case concerns both the nature of the relationship between doctors and their patients, and the circumstances in which alleged consent can be used as a defence against a charge of sexual assault. Laura Norberg, the appellant, became addicted to painkillers after using them to cope with acute pain from a curable medical condition. She received prescriptions for painkillers, and eventually, the drugs themselves, from the respondent, Dr Wynrib, an elderly physician. Dr Wynrib explicitly suggested a quid pro quo arrangement to Norberg: sexual services in return for prescriptions and drugs. In his defence, the respondent claimed that the appellant had consented to this exchange, which lasted for over a year.

This cases raises, in the first instance, important and difficult questions about whether apparent consent can coexist with a charge of sexual assault, and just what the requirements of demonstrated consent are. It also raises questions about the nature and scope of fiduciary duty, which requires one to act in the best interests of another by virtue of one's legal role or position. In its ruling, the Supreme Court argued that the appellant's drug addiction "placed her in a vulnerable position and diminished her capacity to make a real choice." It further contends that "the type of relationship" in question is relevant to the determination of whether consent was indeed possible or valid. Characterizing the relationship between physicians and patients as one of inequality of power, the Court found that the respondent "abused his power over the appellant and exploited the information he obtained concerning her weakness to pursue his own interests" (the appellant had made clear her addiction to the painkillers and asked for his assistance to overcome it). Moreover, the ruling notes that the doctor–patient relationship has aspects that are fiduciary in nature, in which trust is of the utmost importance.

Michel Foucault's provocative writings on power similarly emphasize the importance of understanding the dynamic character of the relations of power that characterize key institutional and interpersonal relationships in society. The exercise of power over others, in Foucault's analysis, entails the capacity of a person to influence, shape, or coerce another agent; as he explains in "The Subject and Power," power "is a way in which certain actions modify others."[18] This is not in itself an unusual description of power relations, but the originality of Foucault's account lies in part in his claim that we must not see these relationships as a "zero-sum game" in which one individual yields all the power and another yields none. Unlike violence and domination, a power relationship is one in which both agents exercise agency; even for the person with less power, different responses or reactions are possible. Foucault's conception of power does not, by itself, allow us to decide what should have been done in this case. One the one hand, his writing suggests that subordination and harm can indeed result from unequal relationships, even when apparent consent is given. This would seem to give endorsement to the Court's ruling, which awarded punitive damages to Norberg. On the other hand, Foucault's account of power relations raises questions about the standards of consent applied in this ruling. Specifically, his perspective implicitly disputes the possibility of a power-free relationship, and therefore casts doubt on the Court's suggestion that consent can be rendered void merely as a consequence of unequal power.

From *Norberg v. Wynrib*, [1992] 2 S.C.R. 226

Norberg v. Wynrib, *[1992] 2 S.C.R. 226.*
http://scc.lexum.org/decisia-scc-csc/scc-csc/scc-csc/en/item/893/index.do

Appellant became addicted to painkillers, and to one addictive drug in particular. She obtained the drugs from various doctors and from her sister. Eventually she began seeing the respondent, an elderly medical practitioner and, using several pretexts, obtained prescriptions for painkillers from him. At some point during this period, respondent confronted appellant about her drug usage and she admitted that she was addicted. He then made suggestions of a sexual nature by pointing upstairs where his apartment was located. Appellant then obtained the drug from other doctors but, when they reduced her supply, sought out respondent and gave in to his demands. Several instances of fondling and simulated intercourse occurred over the course of more than a year. After a time, appellant told respondent that she needed help with her addiction. Respondent advised appellant to "just quit." Appellant became the subject of a criminal investigation and respondent ceased giving her prescriptions but continued to give her pills after her visits upstairs. After being charged with "double doctoring"—obtaining narcotic prescription drugs from a doctor without disclosing particulars of prescriptions from other doctors—appellant went to a rehabilitation centre on her own initiative.

Appellant sought general and punitive damages against the respondent on the grounds of sexual assault, negligence, breach of fiduciary duty and breach of contract. At trial, appellant admitted that respondent did

not at any time use physical force. She also testified that he did things for her, that she "played" on the fact that he liked her and that she knew throughout the relationship that he was lonely. The action was dismissed at trial and on appeal.

At issue here was whether appellant should be allowed to recover damages.

Held: The appeal should be allowed.

[Position I: The judgment of La Forest, Gonthier and Cory JJ., delivered by La Forest J.]

. . .

This case concerns the civil liability of a doctor who gave drugs to a chemically dependent woman patient in exchange for sexual contact. The central issue is whether the defence of consent can be raised against the intentional tort of battery in such circumstances. The case also raises the issue whether the action is barred by reason of illegality or immorality. . . .

Assault—The Nature of Consent

The alleged sexual assault in this case falls under the tort of battery. A battery is the intentional infliction of unlawful force on another person. Consent, express or implied, is a defence to battery. Failure to resist or protest is an indication of consent "if a reasonable person who is aware of the consequences and capable of protest or resistance would voice his objection": see Fleming, *The Law of Torts* (7th ed. 1987), at pp. 72–73. However, the consent must be genuine; it must not be obtained by force or threat of force or be given under the influence of drugs. Consent may also be vitiated by fraud or deceit as to the nature of the defendant's conduct. The courts below considered these to be the only factors that would vitiate consent.

In my view, this approach to consent in this kind of case is too limited. As Heuston and Buckley, *Salmond and Heuston on the Law of Torts* (19th ed. 1987), at pp. 564–65, put it: "A man cannot be said to be 'willing' unless he is in a position to choose freely; and freedom of choice predicates the absence from his mind of any feeling of constraint interfering with the freedom of his will." A "feeling of constraint" so as to "interfere with the freedom of a person's will" can arise in a number of situations not involving force, threats of force, fraud or incapacity. The concept of consent as it operates in tort law is based on a presumption of individual autonomy and free will. It is presumed that the individual has freedom to consent or not to consent. This presumption, however, is untenable in certain circumstances. A position of relative weakness can, in some circumstances, interfere with the freedom of a person's will. Our notion of consent must, therefore, be modified to appreciate the power relationship between the parties.

An assumption of individual autonomy and free will is not confined to tort law. It is also the underlying premise of contract law. The supposition of contract law is that two parties agree or consent to a particular course of action. However, contract law has evolved in such a way that it recognizes that contracting parties do not always have equality in their bargaining strength. The doctrines of duress, undue influence, and unconscionability have arisen to protect the vulnerable when they are in a relationship of unequal power. For reasons of public policy, the law will not always hold weaker parties to the bargains they make. Professor Klippert in his book *Unjust Enrichment* refers to the doctrines of duress, undue influence, and unconscionability as "justice factors." He lumps these together under the general term "coercion" and states, at p. 156, that "[i]n essence the common thread is an illegitimate use of power or unlawful pressure which vitiates a person's freedom of choice." In a situation where a plaintiff is induced to enter into an unconscionable transaction because of an inequitable disparity in bargaining strength, it cannot be said that the plaintiff's act is voluntary.

If the "justice factor" of unconscionability is used to address the issue of voluntariness in the law of contract, it seems reasonable that it be examined to address the issue of voluntariness in the law of tort. This provides insight into the issue of consent: for consent to be genuine, it must be voluntary. The factual context of each case must, of course, be evaluated to determine if there has been genuine consent. However, the principles that have been developed in the area of unconscionable transactions to negate the legal effectiveness of certain contracts provide a useful framework for this evaluation.

An unconscionable transaction arises in contract law where there is an overwhelming imbalance in the power relationship between the parties. In *Morrison v. Coast Finance Ltd.* (1965), Davey J.A. outlined the factors to be considered in a claim of unconscionability:

> . . . a plea that a bargain is unconscionable invokes relief against an unfair advantage gained by an unconscientious use of power by a stronger party against a weaker. On such a claim the material ingredients are proof of inequality in the position of the parties arising out of the ignorance, need or distress of the weaker, which left him in the power of the stronger, and proof of substantial unfairness of the bargain obtained by the stronger. On proof of those circumstances, it creates a presumption of fraud which the stronger must repel by proving that the bargain was fair, just and reasonable. . . .

In *Lloyds Bank Ltd. v. Bundy* (1975), Lord Denning M.R. took a wider approach and developed the general principle of "inequality of bargaining power":

> . . . I would suggest that through all these instances [i.e., duress of goods, unconscionable transactions, undue influence, undue pressure, salvage agreements] there runs a single thread. They rest on "inequality of bargaining power." By virtue of it, the English law gives relief to one who, without independent advice, enters into a contract upon terms which are very unfair or transfers property for a consideration which is grossly inadequate, when his bargaining power is grievously impaired by reason of his own needs or desires, or by his own ignorance or infirmity, coupled with undue influences or pressures brought to bear on him by or for the benefit of the other. When I use the word "undue" I do not mean to suggest that the principle depends on proof of any wrongdoing. The one who stipulates for an unfair advantage may be moved solely by his own self-interest, unconscious of the distress he is bringing to the other. I have also avoided any reference to the will of the one being "dominated" or "overcome" by the other. One who is in extreme need may knowingly consent to a most improvident bargain, solely to relieve the

straits in which he finds himself. Again, I do not mean to suggest that every transaction is saved by independent advice. But the absence of it may be fatal.

...

It may be argued that an unconscionable transaction does not, in fact, vitiate consent: the weaker party retains the power to give real consent but the law nevertheless provides relief on the basis of social policy. This may be more in line with Lord Denning's formulation of "inequality of bargaining power" in *Lloyds Bank Ltd. v. Bundy, supra*, when one takes into account his statement that it is not necessary to establish that the will of the weaker party was "dominated" or "overcome" by the other party. But whichever way one approaches the problem, the result is the same: on grounds of public policy, the legal effectiveness of certain types of contracts will be restricted or negated. In the same way, in certain situations, principles of public policy will negate the legal effectiveness of consent in the context of sexual assault. In particular, in certain circumstances, consent will be considered legally ineffective if it can be shown that there was such a disparity in the relative positions of the parties that the weaker party was not in a position to choose freely.

...

Sexual abuse is merely one particular way in which one person can assault another. It demands careful examination of the relationship between the parties to appreciate whether both had capacity to consent, understanding the nature and consequences of the conduct, and also *whether one of the parties had such a greater amount of power or control over the other as to be in a position to force compliance*. This is an examination to determine whether, in all the circumstances, force was applied by one person to another and whether any consent apparently given was genuine. [emphasis added in original]

...

It must be noted that in the law of contracts proof of an unconscionable transaction involves a two-step process: (1) proof of inequality in the positions of the parties, and (2) proof of an improvident bargain. Similarly, a two-step process is involved in determining whether or not there has been legally effective consent to a sexual assault. The first step is undoubtedly proof of an inequality between the parties which, as already noted, will ordinarily occur within the context of a special "power dependency" relationship. The second step, I suggest, is proof of exploitation. A consideration of the type of relationship at issue may provide a strong indication of

exploitation. Community standards of conduct may also be of some assistance ...

If the type of sexual relationship at issue is one that is sufficiently divergent from community standards of conduct, this may alert the court to the possibility of exploitation.

Application to this Case

The trial judge held that the appellant's implied consent to the sexual activity was voluntary. Dr Wynrib, he stated, exercised neither force nor threats of force and the appellant's capacity to consent was not impaired by her drug use. The Court of Appeal agreed that the appellant voluntarily engaged in the sexual encounters. However, it must be asked if the appellant was truly in a position to make a free choice. It seems clear to me that there was a marked inequality in the respective powers of the parties. The appellant was a young woman with limited education. More important, she was addicted to the heavy use of tranquilizers and painkillers. On this ground alone it can be said that there was an inequality in the position of the parties arising out of the appellant's need. The appellant's drug dependence diminished her ability to make a real choice. Although she did not wish to engage in sexual activity with Dr Wynrib, her reluctance was overwhelmed by the driving force of her addiction and the unsettling prospect of a painful, unsupervised chemical withdrawal. That the appellant's need for drugs placed her in a vulnerable position is evident from the comments of the trial judge ....

On the other side of the equation was an elderly, male professional—the appellant's doctor. An unequal distribution of power is frequently a part of the doctor–patient relationship. As it is stated in *The Final Report of the Task Force on Sexual Abuse of Patients*, An Independent Task Force Commissioned by The College of Physicians and Surgeons of Ontario (November 25, 1991) (Chair: Marilou McPhedran), at p. 11:

Patients seek the help of doctors when they are in a vulnerable state—when they are sick, when they are needy, when they are uncertain about what needs to be done.

The unequal distribution of power in the physician–patient relationship makes opportunities for sexual exploitation more possible than in other relationships. This vulnerability gives physicians the power to exact sexual compliance. Physical force or weapons are not necessary because the physician's power comes from having the knowledge and being trusted by patients.

In this case, Dr Wynrib knew that the appellant was vulnerable and driven by her compulsion for drugs. It is likely that he knew or at least strongly suspected that she was dependant upon Fiorinal before she admitted her addiction to him. It was he who ferreted out that she was addicted to drugs. As a doctor, the respondent knew how to assist the appellant medically and he knew (or should have known) that she could not "just quit" taking drugs without treatment. . . .

However, it must still be asked if there was exploitation. In my opinion there was. Dr Herbert of the Department of Family Practice, Faculty of Medicine, University of British Columbia, expressed the opinion that "a reasonable practitioner would have taken steps to attempt to help Ms Norberg end her addiction by, for example, suggesting drug counselling, or, at the very least, by discontinuing her prescriptions of Fiorinal." However, Dr Wynrib did not use his medical knowledge and expertise to address the appellant's addiction. Instead, he abused his power over her and exploited the information he obtained concerning her weakness to pursue his own personal interests. . . .

There is also a body of opinion which regards sexual contact in any doctor–patient relationship as exploitative. In the opinion of the Task Force on Sexual Abuse of Patients,

> Due to the position of power the physician brings to the doctor–patient relationship, there are NO circumstances—NONE—in which sexual activity between a physician and a patient is acceptable. Sexual activity between a patient and a doctor ALWAYS represents sexual abuse, regardless of what rationalization or belief system the doctor chooses to use to excuse it. Doctors need to recognize that they have power and status, and that there may be times when a patient will test the boundaries between them. It is ALWAYS the doctor's responsibility to know what is appropriate and never to cross the line into sexual activity.

. . .

To summarize, in my view, the defence of consent cannot succeed in the circumstances of this case. The appellant had a medical problem—an addiction to Fiorinal. Dr Wynrib had knowledge of the problem. As a doctor, he had knowledge of the proper medical treatment, and knew she was motivated by her craving for drugs. Instead of fulfilling his professional responsibility to treat the appellant, he used his power and expertise to his own advantage and to her detriment. In my opinion, the unequal power between the parties and the exploitative nature of the relationship removed the possibility of the appellant's providing meaningful consent to the sexual contact.

Ex Turpi Causa

In my opinion, the principle of *ex turpi causa non oritur actio* does not bar the appellant's recovery for damages. It is wise to recall the statement of Estey J. in *Canada Cement LaFarge Ltd. v. British Columbia Lightweight Aggregate Ltd.*, [1983], that "cases where a tort action has been defeated by the *ex turpi causa* maxim are exceedingly rare." In my view, this is not one of those "rare" cases. The respondent forced the sex-for-drugs transaction on the appellant by virtue of her weakness. He initiated the arrangement for his own sexual gratification and then impelled her to engage in it. She was unwilling to participate but did so because of her addiction to drugs. It was only because the respondent prolonged the appellant's chemical dependency that the illicit relationship was available to him. The respondent has been found liable in this appeal because he took advantage of the appellant's addiction. To apply the doctrine of *ex turpi causa* in this case would be to deny the appellant damages on the same basis that she succeeded in the tort action: because she acted out of her desperation for Fiorinal. Surely public policy would not countenance giving to the appellant with one hand and then taking away with the other.

. . .

In sum, I do not believe that it is in the public interest to absolve a doctor of civil liability where he deliberately abuses his position of power and influence by suggesting and pursuing a sex-for-drugs arrangement with a self-admitted drug addict. Accordingly, the *ex turpi causa* maxim does not operate in the circumstances of this case to bar relief.

Damages

The appellant asks for an award of damages which includes the following: (1) compensatory damages for wrongful supply of drugs and prolongation of addiction, (2) aggravated damages for the remorse, shame, damaged self-confidence and emotional harm caused by the continued supply of drugs and the sexual exploitation of the appellant, and (3) punitive damages for the respondent's breach of trust. The courts below were unwilling to award damages. Only Locke J.A., dissenting, would have awarded $1,000 nominal damages for the respondent's negligence which prolonged the appellant's chemical dependence. I am concerned here, however, with damages for the sexual assault, which I have held constitutes the tort of battery at common law.

I begin by noting that the battery is actionable without proof of damage. Moreover, liability is not confined to foreseeable consequences. Aggravated damages may be awarded if the battery has occurred in humiliating or undignified circumstances. These damages are not awarded in addition to general damages. Rather, general damages are assessed "taking into account any aggravating features of the case and to that extent increasing the amount awarded" . . . . These must be distinguished from punitive or exemplary damages [which] are awarded to punish the defendant and to make an example of him or her in order to deter others from committing the same tort. . . .

Although aggravated damages will frequently cover conduct which could also be the subject of punitive damages, as I noted, the two types of damages are distinguishable; punitive damages are designed to punish whereas aggravated damages are designed to compensate. . . .

An award of damages should reflect the nature of the assault. In *R. v. McCraw*, [1991] 3 S.C.R. 72, this Court noted that a sexual assault results in a greater impact on the complainant than a non-sexual assault. Given that one can obtain considerable damages for an assault of a non-sexual nature, the appellant, in my opinion, is entitled to significant aggravated damages for the indignity of the coerced sexual assault. . . .

In the present case, there were repeated sexual encounters over a substantial period of time with a person in a position of power. The respondent used his power as a doctor to take advantage of the fact that the appellant was addicted to drugs. There is some distinction between this case and the rape cases cited above in that the assault here was not physically violent. However, the respondent's conduct has caused the appellant humiliation and loss of dignity as is evident from her testimony. She testified at trial that she thinks about the events with Dr Wynrib on a daily basis and that she has felt a great deal of shame. In fact, she felt that she did not deserve to have her son because of what she had done with Dr Wynrib. In view of the circumstances, I would award general damages of $20,000.

. . .

The question that must be asked is whether the conduct of Dr Wynrib was such as to merit condemnation by the Court. It was not harsh, vindictive or malicious to use the terms cited in *Vorvis, supra*. However, it was reprehensible and it was of a type to offend the ordinary standards of decent conduct in the community. Further, the exchange of drugs for sex by a doctor in a position of power is conduct that cries out for deterrence. As is stated in *The Final Report of the Task Force on Sexual Abuse of Patients, supra*, at p. 80:

> The limited understanding of sexual abuse involving a breach of trust has been a major barrier to effective self-regulation. Both the actual harm and the risk of harm to other patients posed by a physician who chooses to abuse his position of power to sexually exploit and abuse are rarely identified; moreover, when harm and risk of harm are identified, both are profoundly underestimated.

An award of punitive damages is of importance to make it clear that this trend of underestimation cannot continue. Dr Wynrib's use of power to gain sexual favours in the context of a doctor–patient relationship is conduct that is offensive and reprehensible. In all the circumstances, I would award an additional $10,000 in punitive damages.

. . .

[Position II: The reasons of L'Heureux-Dubé and McLachlin JJ. were delivered by McLachlin J.]

I have had the advantage of reading the reasons of my colleagues Justice La Forest and Justice Sopinka. With respect, I do not find that the doctrines of tort or contract capture the essential nature of the wrong done to the plaintiff. Unquestionably, they do catch aspects of that wrong. But to look at the events which occurred over the course of the relationship between Dr Wynrib and Ms Norberg from the perspective of tort or contract is to view that relationship through lenses which distort more than they bring into focus. Only the principles applicable to fiduciary relationships and their breach encompass it in its totality. In my view, that doctrine is clearly applicable to the facts of this case on principles articulated by this Court in earlier cases. It alone encompasses the true relationship between the parties and the gravity of the wrong done by the defendant; accordingly, it should be applied.

. . .

The relationship of physician and patient can be conceptualized in a variety of ways. It can be viewed as a creature of contract, with the physician's failure to fulfil his or her obligations giving rise to an action for breach of contract. It undoubtedly gives rise to a duty of care, the breach of which constitutes the tort of negligence. In common with all members of society, the doctor owes the patient a duty not to touch him or her without his or her consent; if the doctor breaches this duty he or she will have committed the tort of battery. But perhaps the most fundamental characteristic of the doctor–patient relationship is its *fiduciary* nature. All the authorities agree that the relationship of physician to patient also falls into that special category of relationships which the law calls fiduciary.

The recent judgment of La Forest J. in *McInerney v. MacDonald*, [1992], a case recognizing a patient's right of access to her medical records, canvasses those authorities and confirms the fiduciary nature of the doctor-patient relationship. . . .

I think it is readily apparent that the doctor–patient relationship shares the peculiar hallmark of the fiduciary relationship—trust, the trust of a person with inferior power that another person who has assumed superior power and responsibility will exercise that power for his or her good and only for his or her good and in his or her best interests. Recognizing the fiduciary nature of the doctor–patient relationship provides the law with an analytic model by which physicians can be held to the high standards of dealing with their patients which the trust accorded them requires. . . .

The foundation and ambit of the fiduciary obligation are conceptually distinct from the foundation and ambit of contract and tort. Sometimes the doctrines may overlap in their application, but that does not destroy their conceptual and functional uniqueness. In negligence and contract the parties are taken to be independent and equal actors, concerned primarily with their own self-interest. Consequently, the law seeks a balance between enforcing obligations by awarding compensation when those obligations are breached, and preserving optimum freedom for those involved in the relationship in question. The essence of a fiduciary relationship, by contrast, is that one party exercises power on behalf of another and pledges himself or herself to act in the best interests of the other.

Frankel, in "Fiduciary Law" (1983), 71 *Calif. L. Rev.* 795, compares the fiduciary relationship with status and contract relationships, with both of which fiduciary relationships may overlap. Like a status relationship (the relationship of parent and child is perhaps the archetypical status relationship), the fiduciary relationship is characterized by dependency, but the scope of that dependency is usually not as all-encompassing and pervasive as that obtaining in a status relationship. The beneficiary entrusts the fiduciary with information or other sources of power over the beneficiary, but does so only within a circumscribed area, for example entrusting his or her lawyer with power over his or her legal affairs or his or her physician with power over his or her body. . . .

The fiduciary relationship has trust, not self-interest, at its core, and when breach occurs, the balance favours the person wronged. The freedom of the fiduciary is limited by the obligation he or she has undertaken—an obligation which "betokens loyalty, good faith and avoidance of a conflict of duty and self-interest": *Canadian Aero Service Ltd. v. O'Malley*, [1974] S.C.R. 592, at p. 606. To cast a fiduciary relationship in terms of contract or tort (whether negligence or battery) is to diminish this obligation. If a fiduciary relationship is shown to exist, then the proper legal analysis is one based squarely on the full and fair consequences of a breach of that relationship.

. . . So the question must be asked, did a fiduciary relationship exist between Dr Wynrib and Ms Norberg? And assuming that such a relationship did exist, is it properly described as fiduciary for the purposes relevant to this appeal?

Wilson J. in *Frame v. Smith*, attributed the following characteristics to a fiduciary relationship: "(1) [t]he fiduciary has scope for the exercise of some discretion or power; (2) the fiduciary can unilaterally exercise that power or discretion so as to affect the beneficiary's legal or practical interests; (3) the beneficiary is peculiarly vulnerable to or at the mercy of the fiduciary holding the discretion or power."

Dr Wynrib was in a position of power vis-à-vis the plaintiff; he had scope for the exercise of power and discretion with respect to her. He had the power to advise her, to treat her, to give her the drug or to refuse her the drug. He could unilaterally exercise that power or discretion in a way that affected her interests. And her status as a patient rendered her vulnerable and at his mercy, particularly in light of her addiction. So Wilson J.'s test appears to be met. All the classic characteristics of a fiduciary relationship were present. Dr Wynrib and Ms Norberg were on an unequal footing. He pledged himself—by the act of hanging out his shingle as a medical doctor and accepting her as his patient—to act in her best interests and not permit any conflict between his duty to act only in her best interests and his own interests—including his interest in sexual gratification—to arise. As a physician, he owed her the classic duties associated with a fiduciary relationship—the duties of "loyalty, good faith and avoidance of a conflict of duty and self-interest."

. . .

Why then have so many of the jurists who looked at this case declined to consider it as an example of breach of fiduciary duty? . . .

I would summarize the situation as follows: the trial judge appears to have found a duty of trust and confidence and abuse thereof. None of the appellate judges who have written on the case offers a convincing demonstration of why it is wrong to characterize the relationship between Dr Wynrib and Ms Norberg as a fiduciary relationship; indeed none of the judgments seriously discusses the legal requirements for establishing the existence of a fiduciary duty or its breach, much less considers the facts in relation to those requirements. While the majority of the Court of Appeal and Sopinka J. suggest that the fiduciary duties to which Dr Wynrib was subject go no further than his duties in tort or contract, they offer no basis for this suggestion in principle, policy or authority, appearing to rest their case on the assumption that the only additional duties which a fiduciary relationship could impose would be akin to the duty of confidence. This closed, commercial view of fiduciary obligations is neither defended nor reconciled with the authorities, including those of this Court. Nor can thorough consideration of the plaintiff's rights as the victim of a breach of fiduciary obligation be avoided, with respect, on the ground that it was not a live issue or argued; it has been a central issue since the trial judge found the relationship to be one of trust, it was alluded to by all the judgments below, and it was argued before us.

I proceed then to consider the matter on the footing that the essential elements of breach of a fiduciary relationship are made out. Dr Wynrib, in accepting Ms Norberg as his patient, pledged himself to act in her best interests and undertook a duty of loyalty, good faith and avoidance of conflict of interest. Theirs was, as the trial judge observed, a relationship of trust, obliging him to exercise his power—including the power to provide or refuse drugs—solely to her benefit. The doctor breached that relationship when he prescribed drugs which he knew she should not have, when he failed to advise her to obtain counselling when her addiction became or should have become apparent to him, and most notoriously, when he placed his own interest in obtaining sexual favours from Ms Norberg in conflict with and above her interest in obtaining treatment and becoming well.

But, it is said, there are a number of reasons why the doctrine of breach of fiduciary relationship cannot apply in this case. I turn then to these alleged conditions of defeasibility.

The first factor which is said to prevent application of the doctrine of breach of fiduciary duty is Ms Norberg's conduct. Two terms have been used to raise this consideration to the status of a legal or equitable bar—the equitable maxim that he who comes into equity must come with clean hands and the tort doctrine of *ex turpi causa non oritur actio*. For our purposes, one may think of the two respectively as the equitable and legal formulations of the same type of bar to recovery. The trial judge found that although Dr Wynrib was under a trust obligation to Ms Norberg, she was barred from claiming damages against him because of her "immoral" and "illegal" conduct. While he referred to the doctrine of *ex turpi*, there seems to be little doubt that in equity the appropriate term is "clean hands" and consequently that is the expression I will use.

The short answer to the arguments based on wrongful conduct of the plaintiff is that she did nothing wrong in the context of this relationship. She was not a sinner, but a sick person, suffering from an addiction which proved to be uncontrollable in the absence of a professional drug rehabilitation program. She went to Dr Wynrib for relief from that condition. She hoped he would give her relief by giving her the drug; "hustling" doctors for drugs is a recognized symptom of her illness: Wilford, *Drug Abuse, A Guide for the Primary Care Physician* (1981), at pp. 280–82. Such behaviour is commonly seen by family physicians. Patients may, as did Ms Norberg, feign physical problems which, if *bona fide*, would require analgesic relief. They may, as Ms Norberg also did, specify the drug they wish to receive. Once a physician has diagnosed a patient as an addict who is "hustling" him for drugs the recommended response is to "(1) maintain control of the doctor–patient relationship, (2) remain professional in the face of ploys for sympathy or guilt and (3) regard the drug seeker as a patient with a serious illness."

We do not know when Dr Wynrib first identified Ms Norberg as a person suffering from drug addiction; we do know that he confronted her with his knowledge in the first year of their doctor–patient relationship. But whenever he became aware of the true nature of her medical condition, at that point only one form of relief was appropriate: Dr Wynrib, if he were to discharge properly the trust relationship he had assumed, was obliged to refuse Ms Norberg further drugs and to refer her for professional addiction treatment. He did neither, but instead took advantage of her sickness to obtain sexual favours in exchange for the drugs she craved. While there is no doubt that he maintained control of the relationship following his realization, he did so not by retaining a professional attitude and treating Ms Norberg as the sufferer of a serious illness who needed his help, but by exploiting his knowledge, position and the power they gave him over her to coerce her to satisfy his sexual desires. A more grievous breach of the obligations, legal and ethical, which he owed her as his patient can scarcely be imagined.

The law might accuse Ms Norberg of "double doctoring" and moralists might accuse her of licentiousness; but she did no wrong because not she but the doctor was responsible for this conduct. He had the power to cure her of her addiction, as her successful treatment after leaving his "care" demonstrated; instead he chose to use his power to keep her in her addicted state and to use her for his own sexual purposes.

. . .

This brings us to a second objection to treating this case on the basis of breach of fiduciary duty—that nothing that the law would not otherwise accord flows from categorizing the duty as fiduciary; in short, that the fiduciary obligation adds nothing, except perhaps a duty of confidence and non-disclosure, to an action in tort or contract. This appears to have been the view of the majority of the Court of Appeal below, per McEachern C.J. Sopinka J. adopts that same view. Neither authority nor principle is offered in support of this proposition.

What is really at issue here is the scope of the fiduciary obligation. The majority in the Court of Appeal and Sopinka J. would confine it to matters akin to the duty not to disclose confidential information, the situation dealt with in *Lac Minerals Ltd.* If that restriction is accepted, then they are is right; there is little reason to refer to it in this case. But I do not think that narrow view of the scope of the fiduciary obligation is correct. Accepting Sopinka J.'s statement for the majority in *Lac Minerals Ltd.* . . . that fiduciary obligations "must be reserved for situations that are truly in need of the special protection that equity affords," I assert that the situation at issue in the present case is precisely one that is "truly in need of the special protection that equity affords." . . .

If we accept that the principles can apply in this case to protect the plaintiff's interest in receiving medical care free of exploitation at the hands of her physician, as I think we must, then the consequences are most significant. As we have just seen, the defences based on the alleged fault of the plaintiff, so pressing in tort, may carry little weight when raised against the beneficiary of a fiduciary relationship. This is because the fiduciary approach, unlike those based on tort or contract, is founded on the recognition of the power imbalance inherent in the relationship between fiduciary and beneficiary, and to giving redress where that power imbalance is abused. Another consequence that flows from considering the matter on the basis of breach of fiduciary obligation may be a more generous approach to remedies, as I will come to presently. Equity has always held trustees strictly accountable in a way the tort of negligence and contract have not. Foreseeability of loss is not a factor in equitable damages. Certain defences, such as mitigation, may not apply.

But the most significant consequence of applying the doctrine of fiduciary obligation to a person in the position of Dr Wynrib is this. Tort and contract can provide a remedy for a physician's failure to provide adequate treatment. But only with considerable difficulty can they be bent to accommodate the wrong of a physician's abusing his or her position to obtain sexual favours from his or her patient. The law has never recognized consensual sexual relations as capable of giving rise to an obligation in tort or in contract. My colleagues, with respect, strain to conclude the contrary. La Forest J. does so by using the contractual doctrine of relief from unconscionable transactions to negate the consent which the plaintiff, as found by the trial judge, undoubtedly gave. The problems inherent in this approach have already been noted. Sopinka J. . . . finds himself tacking damages for the sexual encounters onto the breach of the duty to treat on the ground that "[t]he sexual acts were causally connected to the failure to treat and must form part of the damage suffered by the appellant." But can damages flow from acts the law finds lawful simply on the ground they are "connected" to damages for an actionable wrong? And what of the patient whose medical needs are fully met but who is sexually exploited? On Sopinka J.'s reasoning she has no cause of action. These examples underline the importance of treating the consequences of this relationship on the footing of what it is—a fiduciary relationship—rather than forcing it into the ill-fitting moulds of contract and tort. Contrary to the conclusion of the court below, characterizing the duty as fiduciary *does* add something; indeed, without doing so the wrong done to the plaintiff can neither be fully comprehended in law nor adequately compensated in damages.

A third objection raised to viewing the relationship between Dr Wynrib and Ms Norberg as fiduciary is that it will open the floodgates to unfounded claims based on the abuse of real or perceived inequality of power. The spectre is conjured up of a host of actions based on exploitation—children suing parents, wives suing husbands, mistresses suing lovers, all for abuse of superior power. The answer to this objection lies in defining the ambit of the fiduciary obligation in a way that encompasses meritorious claims while excluding those without merit. The prospect of the law's recognizing meritorious claims by the powerless and exploited against the powerful and exploitive should not alone serve as a reason for denying just claims. This Court has an honourable tradition of recognizing new claims of the disempowered against the exploitive. . . .

The criteria for the imposition of a fiduciary duty already enunciated by this Court in cases such as *Frame, Lac Minerals and Guerin* provide a good starting point for the task of defining the general principles which determine whether such a relationship exists. As we have seen, an imbalance of power is not enough to establish a fiduciary relationship. It is a necessary but not sufficient condition. There must also be the potential for interference with a legal interest or a non-legal interest of "vital and substantial 'practical' interest." And I would add this. Inherent in the notion of fiduciary duty, inherent in the judgments of this Court in *Guerin* and *Canson*, is the requirement that the fiduciary have assumed or undertaken to "look after" the interest of the beneficiary. . . . It is not easy to bring relationships within this rubric. Generally people are deemed by the law to be motivated in their relationships by mutual self-interest. The duties of trust are special, confined to the exceptional case where one person assumes the power which would normally reside with the other and undertakes to exercise that power solely for the other's benefit. It is as though the fiduciary has taken the power which rightfully belongs to the beneficiary on the condition that the fiduciary exercise the power entrusted exclusively for the good of the beneficiary. Thus the trustee of an estate takes the financial power that would normally reside with the beneficiaries and must exercise those powers in their stead and for their exclusive benefit. Similarly, a physician takes the power which a patient normally has over her body, and which she cedes to him for purposes of treatment. The physician is pledged by the nature of his calling to use the power the patient cedes to him exclusively for her benefit. If he breaks that pledge, he is liable.

In summary, the constraints inherent in the principles governing fiduciary relationships belie the contention that the recognition of a fiduciary obligation in this case will open the floodgates to unmeritorious claims. Taking the case at its narrowest, it is concerned with a relationship which has long been recognized as fiduciary—the physician–patient relationship; it represents no extension of the law. Taking the case more broadly, with reference to the general principles governing fiduciary obligations, it is seen to fall within principles previously recognized by this Court, and again represents no innovation. In so far as application of those principles in this case might be argued to give encouragement to new categories of claims, the governing principles offer assurance against unlimited liability while at the same time promising a greater measure of justice for the exploited.

I conclude that the wrong suffered by the plaintiff falls to be considered under the rubric of breach of fiduciary duty. The duty is established, as is the breach. The plaintiff is entitled to succeed against Dr Wynrib and to recover the appropriate damages at equity.

Damages

. . .

The action for breach of a fiduciary relationship is also broader than the action for breach of contract, which is confined to failure to provide proper medical treatment and does not extend to procuring sexual relations through abuse of the physician's power. In so far as the action concerns medical malpractice, principles of assessment of damages in contract and tort may be of assistance, at least by analogy. In so far as it concerns wrongful sexual exploitation, we enter into the exclusive terrain of equity.

It therefore seems appropriate in this case to assess damages according to the principles which generally govern damages for breach of fiduciary duty, having regard to the admonition in *Canson* that the remedy awarded need not be confined to that given in previous situations if the requirements of fairness and justice demand more, and that reference to the principles of assessment in contract and tort maybe of assistance in so far as they are relevant.

As discussed in *Canson*, the goal of equity is to restore the plaintiff as fully as possible to the position he or she would have been in had the equitable breach not occurred. . . . This is not a case where the traditional equitable remedies of restitution and account are available. Restoration *in specie* is not possible. And the plaintiff's loss is not economic. Where these remedies are not available, equity awards compensation in their stead: see *Canson*, *supra* at pp. 574–75. In awarding damages the same generous, restorative remedial approach, which stems from the nature of the obligation in equity, applies. The fiduciary, being the person with the advantage of power, assumes full responsibility and cannot be heard to complain that the victim of his or her abuse cooperated in his or her defalcation or failed to take reasonable care for his or her own interests.

From the principles I turn to the facts. Dr Wynrib's breach of his duty to Ms Norberg caused the following losses or injuries to her: (1) prolongation of her addiction; and (2) sexual violation.

Ms Norberg's period of addiction was prolonged from the time he ought reasonably to have known that she was addicted to the time she left his care and sought help for her addiction on her own. That is a period of at least two and one-half years. The evidence establishes, and this is fully in accordance with the medical literature, that Ms Norberg's addiction to Fiorinal was a very traumatic and damaging experience. She was desperate for the drug, desperate enough to engage in sexual activity with Dr Wynrib which she clearly found repugnant and degrading. . . .

The evidence amply attests to the misery and desperation of Ms Norberg during the period during which her addiction was prolonged by Dr Wynrib's failure to offer the appropriate medical treatment. Part of this, her sexual degradation, must be discounted under this head, since I have considered it independently. Taking this into account, I would award an additional $20,000 for suffering and loss during the period of prolonged addiction for which Dr Wynrib was responsible.

Second, Ms Norberg suffered repeated sexual abuse at the hands of Dr Wynrib. As the trial judge found, she did not want to have sexual relations with Dr Wynrib. She submitted only because it was the only way to get the drug she desperately craved, and the deprivation of which plunged her into what was described by Dr Fleming of the Department of Psychiatry, Faculty of Medicine, U.B.C., as the "extremely unpleasant experience" of withdrawal. . . .

The evidence is clear that Ms Norberg found the sexual contact degrading and dehumanizing. She avoided it for as long as she could, leaving Dr Wynrib's care when he first suggested it. When desperation drove her back, she submitted only when her addiction rendered it absolutely necessary. The repeated sexual encounters caused her humiliation and robbed her of her dignity. The pain of those encounters will probably remain with her all her life; Ms Norberg testified that she thinks about the events daily, that her recollections are an unhappy reminder of her addiction and desperation. When her son was born, she felt that she did not deserve to have her baby because of what she had done with Dr Wynrib. While the sexual encounters lack the violence of rape, the pain may be just as great because of its insidious psychological overtones. The rape victim may not, although she unfortunately often does, feel guilt. Ms Norberg, however inevitable and excusable her participation in this activity, clearly does suffer guilt, even years after the events. The evidence suggests her self-esteem has been vitally and perhaps permanently damaged. These *sequelae*, as *The Final Report of the Task Force on Sexual Abuse of Patients* (at pp. 84–85) makes disturbingly clear, are all too typical of victims of sexual exploitation by physicians.

. . .

I would award $25,000 in damages for sexual exploitation.

Finally, this is in my opinion an appropriate case in which to make an award of punitive damages. In so far as reference to tort principles may be appropriate I note that punitive damages have been awarded in several sexual assault cases. . . .

Quite apart from analogies with tort, punitive (or exemplary) damages are available with respect to breaches of fiduciary duty, and in particular for breaches of the sort exemplified by this case. In *W. (B.) v. Mellor*, [1989] . . . a doctor was held to be in breach of his fiduciary duty when he engaged in an exploitive sexual relationship with his patient. McKenzie J. awarded the plaintiff $15,000 in punitive damages. . . .

I find Ellis's statement, found in his text *Fiduciary Duties in Canada*, at p. 20–24, as to the circumstances which will constitute the conditions precedent for awarding punitive damages for a breach of fiduciary duty both helpful and applicable to the facts of this case:

> Where the actions of the fiduciary are purposefully repugnant to the beneficiary's best interests, punitive damages are a logical award to be made by the Court. This award will be particularly applicable where the impugned activity is motivated by the fiduciary's self-interest.

I do not think it can be seriously questioned that Dr Wynrib's activities were both purposefully repugnant to Ms Norberg's best interests, and motivated entirely by his own self-interest.

Punitive damages are awarded, not for the purpose of compensating the victim for her loss, but with a view to punishing the wrongdoer and deterring both him and others from engaging in similar conduct in the future. Dr Wynrib's conduct is sufficiently reprehensible and offensive to common standards of decency to render him liable to such a punitive award. While, given his age, it is unlikely that such damages will have much utility in terms of specific deterrent effect, concerns for general deterrence militate in favour of their being granted. The Report of the Task Force of the Ontario College of Physicians and Surgeons makes it clear that the sexual exploitation of patients by physicians is more widespread than it is comfortable to contemplate. Its damaging effects extend not only to those persons who are directly harmed, but also to the image of the profession as a whole and the community's trust in physicians to act in our best interests. In this context punitive damages may serve to reinforce the high standard of conduct which the fiduciary relationship between physicians and patients demands be honoured. This is completely in keeping with the law's role in protecting beneficiaries and promoting fiduciary relationships through the strict regulation of the conduct of fiduciaries. . . . An award of punitive damages in the present case would signal the community's disapprobation of the sexual exploitation of vulnerable patients, and for that reason ought to be made.

. . .

. . . Most important in this case . . . is the need for deterrence. Dr Wynrib is not alone in breaching the trust of his patient through sexually exploiting her; physicians, and all those in positions of trust, must be warned that society will not condone abuse of the trust placed in them. I would award punitive damages against Dr Wynrib in the amount of $25,000.

. . .

[Position III: Judgment delivered by Sopinka J.]

I have had the advantage of reading the reasons of Justice La Forest. He disposes of this appeal on the basis of the battery claim. With respect, I cannot agree with his approach on the issue of consent. I am also of the view that this case is more appropriately resolved on the basis of the respondent's duty to treat the appellant arising out of the doctor–patient relationship.

. . .

Breach of Duty

This professional duty arises out of the relationship of doctor–patient which is essentially based on contract. Breach of the duty can be the subject of an action in either contract or negligence. While undoubtedly, as in the case of lawyer and client, this relationship in some of its aspects involves fiduciary duties, not all facets of the obligations are fiduciary in nature.

. . .

The breach of duty alleged here is the obligation of a physician to treat the patient in accordance with standards in the profession. . . .

. . .

In my opinion, whether the appellant relies on contract or negligence, the duty to treat was not vacated by consent. In contract this would require the abandonment of the contractual relationship between the parties. The authorities reviewed by Locke J.A. show that this requires the mutual consent of the parties supported by consideration. I am satisfied that there was no such consent in this case.

While the parties may very well have had a relationship independent of the doctor–patient relationship, the latter relationship continued and was not abandoned. After the addiction was admitted to him in late 1982, the respondent's conduct was consistent with the continuation of a doctor and patient relationship. He ordered a series of x-rays to be taken of various parts of the appellant's body. He accepted these x-ray reports in August and November of 1984. He made gynaecological referrals for the appellant and in due course Dr Gowd, a gynaecologist, reported to the respondent in this regard. The only conclusion to be drawn from the evidence is that the respondent continued to act as the appellant's general practitioner and the appellant continued to seek medical care from him in this capacity. Neither the parties nor the medical community had any reason to believe that the parties had mutually abandoned their contract. In fact, the conduct of both the appellant and the respondent reinforced the existence of their doctor and patient relationship.

Moreover, even if the contract was abandoned, that did not put an end to the duty. The respondent did not change his status as a physician; nor did the appellant change her status as one who was in need of and sought treatment. This relationship continued even if technically the contract between them was terminated by mutual consent. The duty is supportable independently of contract on the basis of this relationship. Duty arising out of relationship is, of course, the basis of the law of negligence.

. . .

While the appellant consented to the sexual encounters, she did not consent to the breach of duty that resulted in the continuation of her addiction and the sexual encounters. The fact that a patient acquiesces or agrees to a form of treatment does not absolve a physician from his or her duty if the treatment is not in accordance with medical standards. Otherwise, the patient would be required to know what the prescribed standard is. In the absence of a clear statement by the respondent to the appellant that he was no longer treating her as her physician and an unequivocal consent to the cessation of treatment, I conclude that the duty to treat the appellant continued until she attended at the rehabilitation centre on her own initiative and was treated.

. . .

Damages

The breach of duty found was that in lieu of striving to cure the appellant of her addiction, the respondent promoted it in return for sexual favours. The result was that the addiction was prolonged in lieu of treatment and the appellant was subjected to the respondent's sexual advances. The sexual acts were causally connected to the failure to treat and must form part of the damage suffered by the appellant. I would assess the damages for both these components in the amount awarded by my colleague, La Forest J. I would not, however, award punitive damages. These are inappropriate in this case inasmuch as the basis of liability is the breach of professional duty. While the sexual episodes are an element of damage, they are not the basis of liability. These sexual episodes are the basis of liability in the reasons of La Forest J. who found the respondent liable for acts of sexual assault deserving of punishment. In the view that I have taken, they are rather an element of damage for breach of duty, and an award that includes as a component aggravated damages is adequate compensation to the appellant. . . .

Post-Case-Reading Questions

1. Why did Laura Norberg's apparent consent to a sexual relationship with Dr Wynrib not negate the charge of sexual assault, in the opinion of the Court?
2. How might Foucault's assertion that a power relationship is not one of complete force or domination illuminate this legal case? Does it lend support to Norberg's charges of sexual exploitation and assault, or instead, to Wynrib's defence that he was innocent of these allegations?

CHAPTER
XVII

Will Kymlicka

PHILOSOPHER: WILL KYMLICKA

Introduction

Will Kymlicka is a Canadian philosopher credited with making the questions surrounding cultural minority rights and multiculturalism a focal point of debate in contemporary political thought. A liberal democratic theorist, Kymlicka has also written widely on issues of nationalism, immigration, democracy, citizenship, the welfare state, and, most recently, animal ethics.

Kymlicka was born in London, Ontario, to a Czech-Canadian father and an English-Canadian mother. He attended Queen's University, where he obtained a BA in philosophy and political science in 1984. He then attended Oxford University, where, after receiving another BA in philosophy, he earned his DPhil in 1987. Kymlicka currently holds the Canada Research Chair in Political Philosophy in the Department of Philosophy at Queen's University, where

Will Kymlicka

Used by permission of Will Kymlicka.

he has taught since 1998. He is also a recurrent visiting professor in the Nationalism Studies Program at the Central European University in Budapest. Kymlicka's many books include *Liberalism, Community and Culture* (1989), *Contemporary Political Philosophy* (1990, second ed. 2002), *Multicultural Citizenship* (1995), *Finding Our Way: Rethinking Ethnocultural Relations in Canada* (1998), *Politics in the Vernacular* (2001) *Multicultural Odysseys* (2007), and *Zoopolis: A Political Theory of Animal Rights* (2011, co-authored with Sue Donaldson). He has also edited or co-edited numerous scholarly volumes on issues ranging from language rights and citizenship to global ethics. It is a testament to the impact of Kymlicka's work that it has been translated into 30 languages. This prodigious scholarship has made Kymlicka the recipient of awards and distinctions in Canada and internationally.

In the 1990s, Kymlicka's ground-breaking work, *Multicultural Citizenship*, along with James Tully's *Strange Multiplicities* and Charles Taylor's "The Politics of Recognition" and *Reconciling the Solitudes*, catapulted the issues of multiculturalism and cultural minority rights into the mainstream of social and political philosophy. As a result, the "Canadian School" of political philosophy is now best associated with a focus on these themes. Inspired by the central place accorded to issues of national identity, language rights, and Aboriginal self-determination in public debate in Canada, these authors argued that some cultural claims and rights ought to be recognized and institutionalized in liberal democracies as a matter of justice. Their approach contrasted significantly with US-based scholarship on diversity and multiculturalism, in which race, rather than culture, has tended to figure prominently.[1]

In *Multicultural Citizenship*, Kymlicka argues that we need to supplement traditional human rights with a liberal theory of minority rights. To do so, he distinguishes "national minorities" from "ethnic minorities," which are in turn contrasted with "social movements." Based on these distinctions, liberal democracies may be characterized by multinational diversity—composed of several national groups—or polyethnic diversity—composed of several ethno-cultural groups—or both. He argues that liberal democracies have increasingly sought to accommodate cultural pluralism by acknowledging three forms of group differentiated rights: (1) self-government rights, (2) polyethnic rights, and (3) special representation rights. Kymlicka sought to show that liberal theory can accommodate minority rights by way of arguing that individual freedom is tied to membership in one's cultural group and that group-specific rights can promote equality between the minority and majority groups. The core argument of the book establishes a close connection between freedom and culture: for liberals, the most important value is individual freedom, which can be properly understood as the possibility of having and making choices. Genuine choice is made possible only within the context of what Kymlicka calls "societal culture."[2] To bolster his claim, he presents three further arguments: (1) *the equality argument*, which states that the accommodation of differences is the essence of true equality; (2) *the argument based on historical agreement*, which states that the rights of national minorities should be granted because they are the result of historical agreement (treaties) between minority and majority groups in a state; and (3) *the diversity argument*, which suggests that the value of cultural diversity contributes to the richness of people's lives.

By insisting that the enjoyment of individual rights requires a secure societal context, Kymlicka bridges an old divide between liberalism—which maintains the primacy of individual rights—and communitarianism—which holds that collective goods and rights are supreme. This context, which members of the majority culture already enjoy, includes such things as being able to access education and key public services in one's own language. Kymlicka warns, however, that the policies which can help construct such a secure societal context for some cultural minorities should not foster powers that enable group leaders to wield arbitrary control over their own members; rather, policies of multiculturalism are justified insofar as they aim to protect the language, identity, or common institutions of groups, thereby helping to foster their equality vis à vis the dominant society.

The legal recognition of the claims of some national and cultural groups in numerous liberal democracies underscores the relevance of the insights of multicultural theorists like Kymlicka (and those of thinkers and activists from minority communities). Kymlicka's writing on the philosophical issues surrounding cultural recognition and equality are complemented by his long-standing interest in the concrete policies of multiculturalism: he is, notably, the co-director of the Multiculturalism Policy Index project, which charts the development of multiculturalist policies in liberal democratic states. In the Canadian context, the normative and policy dimensions of claims for cultural recognition and equality are perhaps most evident in the case of Aboriginal peoples. In response to their claims, both the courts and the Crown have increasingly moved away from a model of compensatory justice aimed at greater integration to one that recognizes the importance of national cultures and the right of self-government. The case chosen here to represent this shift is that of the Maa-nulth Treaty process, which concluded in 2011. Within Kymlicka's framework, the First Nations of Maa-nulth would be considered a national minority group whose rights to self-government and their traditional territory should be recognized. Readers are invited to consider whether the treaty supplies the legal and political framework required for the Maa-nulth people to achieve a secure societal context (in Kymlicka's terms) and genuine self-determination into the future.

Further Readings

Dhamoon, Rita. (2009). *Identity/Difference Politics: How Difference Is Produced, and Why It Matters*. Vancouver: University of British Columbia Press.

Hooker, J. (2009). *Race and the Politics of Solidarity*. Oxford: Oxford University Press.

Kymlicka, W. (2003). "Multicultural State and Intercultural Citizens," in *Theory and Research in Education* (July 2003): 147–69.

Kymlicka, W. (2007). *Multicultural Odysseys: Navigating the New International Politics of Diversity*. Oxford: Oxford University Press.

Parekh, B. (2006). *Rethinking Multiculturalism: Cultural Diversity and Political Theory*, 2nd edition. Cambridge, Mass.: Harvard University Press.

Taylor, C. (1993). *Reconciling the Solitudes*. Kingston and Montreal: McGill-Queen's University Press.

Tully, J. (1995). *Strange Multiplicity*. Cambridge: Cambridge University Press.

Will Kymlicka, From *Multicultural Citizenship*

Will Kymlicka, Multicultural Citizenship *(Toronto: Oxford University Press, 1995).*

Chapter 1 Introduction

1. The Issues

Most countries today are culturally diverse. According to recent estimates, the world's 184 independent states contain over 600 living language groups, and 5,000 ethnic groups. In very few countries can the citizens be said to share the same language, or belong to the same ethnonational group.[3]

This diversity gives rise to a series of important and potentially divisive questions. Minorities and majorities increasingly clash over such issues as language rights, regional autonomy, political representation, education curriculum, land claims, immigration and naturalization policy, even national symbols, such as the choice of national anthem or public holidays. Finding morally defensible and politically viable answers to these issues is the greatest challenge facing democracies today. In Eastern Europe and the Third World, attempts to create liberal democratic institutions are being undermined by violent nationalist conflicts. In the West, volatile disputes over the rights of immigrants, indigenous peoples, and other cultural minorities are throwing into question many of the assumptions which have governed political

life for decades. Since the end of the Cold War, ethnocultural conflicts have become the most common source of political violence in the world, and they show no sign of abating.[4]

This book outlines a new approach to these problems. There are no simple answers or magic formulas to resolve all these questions. Some conflicts are intractable, even when the disputants are motivated by a sense of fairness and tolerance, which all too often is lacking. Moreover, every dispute has its own unique history and circumstances that need to be taken into account in devising a fair and workable solution. My aim is to step back and present a more general view of the landscape—to identify some key concepts and principles that need to be taken into account, and so clarify the basic building blocks for a liberal approach to minority rights.

The Western political tradition has been surprisingly silent on these issues. Most organized political communities throughout recorded history have been multiethnic, a testament to the ubiquity of both conquest and long-distance trade in human affairs. Yet most Western political theorists have operated with an idealized model of the polis in which fellow citizens share a common descent, language, and culture. Even when the theorists themselves lived in polyglot empires that governed numerous ethnic and linguistic groups, they have often written as if the culturally homogeneous city-states of Ancient Greece provided the essential or standard model of a political community.[5]

To achieve this ideal of a homogeneous polity, governments throughout history have pursued a variety of policies regarding cultural minorities. Some minorities were physically eliminated, either by mass expulsion (what we now call "ethnic cleansing") or by genocide. Other minorities were coercively assimilated, forced to adopt the language, religion, and customs of the majority. In yet other cases, minorities were treated as resident aliens, subjected to physical segregation and economic discrimination, and denied political rights.

Various efforts have been made historically to protect cultural minorities, and to regulate the potential conflicts between majority and minority cultures. Early in this century, bilateral treaties regulated the treatment of fellow nationals in other countries. For example, Germany agreed to accord certain rights and privileges to ethnic Poles residing within its borders, so long as Poland provided reciprocal rights to ethnic Germans in Poland. This treaty system was extended, and given a more multilateral basis, under the League of Nations.

However, these treaties were inadequate. For one thing, a minority was only ensured protection from discrimination and oppression if there was a "kin state" nearby which took an interest in it. Moreover, the treaties were destabilizing, because where such kin states did exist, they often used treaty provisions as grounds for invading or intervening in weaker countries. Thus Nazi Germany justified its invasion of Poland and Czechoslovakia on the grounds that these countries were violating the treaty rights of ethnic Germans on their soil.

After World War II, it was clear that a different approach to minority rights was needed. Many liberals hoped that the new emphasis on "human rights" would resolve minority conflicts. Rather than protecting vulnerable groups directly, through special rights for the members of designated groups, cultural minorities would be protected indirectly, by guaranteeing basic civil and political rights to all individuals regardless of group membership. Basic human rights such as freedom of speech, association, and conscience, while attributed to individuals, are typically exercised in community with others, and so provide protection for group life. Where these individual rights are firmly protected, liberals assumed, no further rights needed to be attributed to the members of specific ethnic or national minorities:

> the general tendency of the postwar movements for the promotion of human rights has been to subsume the problem of national minorities under the broader problem of ensuring basic individual rights to all human beings, without reference to membership in ethnic groups. The leading assumption has been that members of national minorities do not need, are not entitled to, or cannot be granted rights of a special character. The doctrine of human rights has been put forward as a substitute for the concept of minority rights, with the strong implication that minorities whose members enjoy individual equality of treatment cannot legitimately demand facilities for the maintenance of their ethnic particularism. (Claude 1955: 211)

Guided by this philosophy, the United Nations deleted all references to the rights of ethnic and national minorities in its Universal Declaration of Human Rights.

The shift from group-specific minority rights to universal human rights was embraced by many liberals, partly because it seemed a natural extension of the way religious minorities were protected. In the sixteenth century, European states were being torn apart by conflict between Catholics and Protestants over which religion should rule the land. These conflicts were finally resolved, not by granting special rights to particular religious minorities, but by separating church and state, and entrenching each's individual freedom of religion. Religious minorities are protected indirectly, by guaranteeing individual freedom of worship, so that people can freely associate with other co-religionists, without fear of state discrimination or disapproval.

Many post-war liberals have thought that religious tolerance based on the separation of church and state provides a model for dealing with ethnocultural differences as well. On this view, ethnic identity, like religion, is something which people should be free to express in their private life, but which is not the concern of the state. The state does not oppose the freedom of people to express their particular cultural attachments, but nor does it nurture such expression—rather, to adapt Nathan Glazer's phrase, it responds with "benign neglect" (Glazer 1975: 25; 1983: 124). The members of ethnic and national groups are protected against discrimination and prejudice, and they are free to try to maintain whatever part of their ethnic heritage or identity they wish, consistent with the rights of others. But their efforts are purely private, and it is not the place of public agencies to attach legal identities or disabilities to cultural membership or ethnic identity. This separation of state and ethnicity precludes any legal or governmental recognition of ethnic groups, or any use of ethnic criteria in the distribution of rights, resources, and duties.[6]

Many liberals, particularly on the left, have made an exception in the case of affirmative action for disadvantaged racial groups. But in a sense this is the exception that proves the rule. Affirmative action is generally defended as a temporary measure which is needed to move more rapidly towards a "colour-blind" society. It is intended to remedy years of discrimination, and thereby move us closer to the sort of society that would have existed had we observed the separation of state and ethnicity from the beginning. Thus the UN Convention on Racial Discrimination endorses affirmative action programmes only where they have this temporary and remedial character. Far from abandoning the ideal of state and ethnicity, affirmative action is one method of trying to achieve that ideal.

Some liberals, particularly on the right, think it is counterproductive to pursue a "colour-blind" society through policies that "count by race." Affirmative action, they argue, exacerbates the very problem it was intended to solve, by making people more conscious of group differences, and more resentful of other groups. This dispute amongst liberals over the need for remedial affirmative action programmes is a familiar one in many liberal democracies.[7]

But what most post-war liberals on both the right and left continue to reject is the idea of *permanent* differentiation in the rights or status of the members of certain groups. In particular, they reject the claim that group-specific rights are needed to accommodate enduring cultural differences, rather than remedy historical discrimination. As we will see in subsequent chapters, post-war liberals around the world have repeatedly opposed the idea that specific ethnic or national groups should be given a permanent political identity or constitutional status.[8]

However, it has become increasingly clear that minority rights cannot be subsumed under the category of human rights. Traditional human rights standards are simply unable to resolve some of the most important and controversial questions relating to cultural minorities: which languages should be recognized in the parliaments, bureaucracies, and courts? Should each ethnic or national group have publicly funded education in its mother tongue? Should internal boundaries (legislative districts, provinces, states) be drawn so that cultural minorities form a majority within a local region? Should governmental powers be devolved from the central level to more local or regional levels controlled by particular minorities, particularly on culturally sensitive issues of immigration, communication, and education? Should political offices be distributed in accordance with a

principle of national or ethnic proportionality? Should the traditional homelands of indigenous peoples be reserved for their benefit, and so protected from encroachment by settlers and resource developers? What are the responsibilities of minorities to integrate? What degree of cultural integration can be required of immigrants and refugees before they acquire citizenship?

The problem is not that traditional human rights doctrines give us the wrong answer to these questions. It is rather that they often give no answer at all. The right to free speech does not tell us what an appropriate language policy is; the right to vote does not tell us how political boundaries should be drawn, or how powers should be distributed between levels of government; the right to mobility does not tell us what an appropriate immigration and naturalization policy is. These questions have been left to the usual process of majoritarian decision making within each state. The result, I will argue, has been to render cultural minorities vulnerable to significant injustice at the hands of the majority, and to exacerbate ethnocultural conflict.

To resolve these questions fairly, we need to supplement traditional human rights principles with a theory of minority rights. The necessity for such a theory has become painfully clear in Eastern Europe and the former Soviet Union. Disputes over local autonomy, the drawing of boundaries, language rights, and naturalization policy have engulfed much of the region in violent conflict. There is little hope that stable peace will be restored, or that basic human rights will be respected, until these minority rights issues are resolved.

It is not surprising, therefore, that minority rights have returned to prominence in international relations. For example, the Conference on Security and Co-operation in Europe (CSCE) adopted a declaration on the Rights of National Minorities in 1991, and established a High Commissioner on National Minorities in 1993. The United Nations has been debating both a Declaration on the Rights of Persons Belonging to National or Ethnic, Religious and Linguistic Minorities (1993), and a Draft Universal Declaration on Indigenous Rights (1988). The Council of Europe adopted a declaration on minority language rights in 1992 (the European Charter for Regional or Minority Languages). Other examples could be given.[9]

However, these declarations remain controversial. Some were adopted hastily, to help prevent the escalation of conflict in Eastern Europe. As a result, they are quite vague, and often seem motivated more by the need to appease belligerent minorities than by any clear sense of what justice requires. Both the underlying justification for these rights, and their limits, remain unclear.

I believe it is legitimate, and indeed unavoidable, to supplement traditional human rights with minority rights. A comprehensive theory of justice in a multicultural state will include both universal rights, assigned to individuals regardless of group membership, and certain group-differentiated rights or "special status" for minority cultures.

Recognizing minority rights has obvious dangers. The language of minority rights has been used and abused not only by the Nazis, but also by apologists for racial segregation and apartheid. It has also been used by intolerant and belligerent nationalists and fundamentalists throughout the world to justify the domination of people outside their group, and the suppression of dissenters within the group. A liberal theory of minority rights, therefore, must explain how minority rights coexist with human rights, and how minority rights are limited by principles of individual liberty, democracy, and social justice. That is the aim of this book. . . .

Chapter II The Politics of Multiculturalism

. . .

2. Three Forms of Group-Differentiated Rights

Virtually all liberal democracies are either multinational or polyethnic, or both. The "challenge of multiculturalism" is to accommodate these national and ethnic differences in a stable and morally defensible way (Gutmann 1993). In this section, I will discuss some of the most important ways in which democracies have responded to the demands of national minorities and ethnic groups.

In all liberal democracies, one of the major mechanisms for accommodating cultural differences is the protection of the civil and political rights of individuals. It is impossible to overstate the importance of freedom of association, religion, speech, mobility, and political organization for protecting group difference. These rights enable individuals to form and maintain the various groups and associations which constitute civil society, to adapt these groups to changing circumstances, and to promote their views and interests to the wider population. The protection afforded by these common rights of citizenship is sufficient for many of the legitimate forms of diversity in society.

Various critics of liberalism—including some Marxists, communitarians, and feminists—have argued that the liberal focus on individual rights reflects an atomistic, materialistic, instrumental, or conflictual view of human relationships. I believe that this criticism is profoundly mistaken, and that individual rights can be and typically are used to sustain a wide range of social relationships. Indeed, the most basic liberal right—freedom of conscience—is primarily valuable for the protection it gives to intrinsically social (and non-instrumental) activities.[10]

However, it is increasingly accepted in many countries that some forms of cultural difference can only be accommodated through special legal or constitutional measures, above and beyond the common rights of citizenship. Some forms of group difference can only be accommodated if their members have certain group-specific rights—what Iris Young calls "differentiated citizenship" (I. Young 1989: 258).

For example, a recent government publication in Canada noted that:

> In the Canadian experience, it has not been enough to protect only universal individual rights. Here, the Constitution and ordinary laws also protect other rights accorded to individuals as members of certain communities. This accommodation of both types of rights makes our constitution unique and reflects the Canadian value of equality that accommodates difference. The fact that community rights exist alongside individual rights goes to the very heart of what Canada is all about. (Government of Canada 1991a: 3)

It is quite misleading to say that Canada is unique in combining universal individual rights and group-specific "community rights." Such a combination exists in many other federal systems in Europe, Asia, and Africa. As I noted earlier, even the constitution of the United States, which is often seen as a paradigm of individualism, allows for various group-specific rights, including the special status of American Indians and Puerto Ricans.

It is these special group-specific measures for accommodating national and ethnic differences that I will focus on. There are at least three forms of group-specific rights: (1) self-government rights; (2) polyethnic rights; and (3) special representation rights. I will say a few words about each, before considering some of the issues they raise for liberal-democratic theory in subsequent chapters.

1. Self-government rights. In most multination states, the component nations are inclined to demand some form of political autonomy or territorial jurisdiction, so as to ensure the full and free development of their cultures and the best interests of their people. At the extreme, nations may wish to secede, if they think their self-determination is impossible within the larger state.

The right of national groups to self-determination is given (limited) recognition in international law. According to the United Nations' Charter, "all peoples have the right to self-determination." However, the UN has not defined "peoples," and it has generally applied the principle of self-determination only to overseas colonies, not internal national minorities, even when the latter were subject to the same sort of colonization and conquest as the former. This limitation on self-determination to overseas colonies (known as the "salt-water thesis") is widely seen as arbitrary, and many national minorities insist that they too are "peoples" or "nations," and, as such, have the right of self-determination. They demand certain powers of self-government which they say were not relinquished by their (often involuntary) incorporation into a larger state.[11]

One mechanism for recognizing claims to self-government is federalism, which divides powers between the central government and regional subunits (provinces/states/cantons). Where national minorities are regionally concentrated, the boundaries of federal subunits can be drawn so that the national minority forms a majority in one of the subunits. Under these circumstances, federalism can provide extensive self-government for a national minority, guaranteeing its ability to make decisions in certain areas without being outvoted by the larger society.

For example, under the federal division of powers in Canada, the province of Quebec (which is 80 per cent francophone) has extensive jurisdiction over issues that are crucial to the survival of the French culture, including control over education, language, culture, as well as significant input into immigration policy. The other nine provinces also have these powers, but the major impetus behind the existing division of powers, and indeed behind the entire federal system, is the need to accommodate the Québécois. At the time of Confederation, most English Canadian leaders were in favour of a unitary state, like Britain, and agreed to a federal system primarily to accommodate French Canadians.

One difficulty in a federal system is maintaining the balance between centralization and decentralization. While most Quebecers want an even more decentralized division of powers, most English Canadians favour a stronger central government. One of the challenges facing Canada, therefore, is finding an acceptable form of "asymmetrical federalism" which grants Quebec powers not given to other provinces. Other federal states face a similar problem.[12]

Federalism is often used to accommodate national diversity, and so some commentators include the rights and powers attached to federal units amongst the "collective rights" of national minorities (e.g., F. Morton 1985: 77; Van Dyke 1982: 24–31). Of course, many federal systems arose for reasons quite unrelated to cultural diversity. Federalism is often simply a form of administrative

decentralization (as in Germany), or the result of historical accidents of colonization (as in Australia). There is no inherent connection between federalism and cultural diversity. But federalism is one common strategy of accommodating national minorities. It is not surprising that countries which are "a federation of peoples" should also form a political federation.[13]

In the United States, however, a deliberate decision was made not to use federalism to accommodate the self-government rights of national minorities. It would have been quite possible in the nineteenth century to create states dominated by the Navaho, for example, or by Chicanos, Puerto Ricans, and native Hawaiians. At the time these groups were incorporated into the United States, they formed majorities in their homelands. However, a deliberate decision was made not to accept any territory as a state unless these national groups were outnumbered. In some cases, this was achieved by drawing boundaries so that Indian tribes or Hispanic groups were outnumbered (Florida). In other cases, it was achieved by delaying statehood until anglophone settlers swamped the older inhabitants (e.g., Hawaii; the southwest). In cases where the national minority was not likely to be outnumbered, a new type of non-federal political unit was created, such as the "commonwealth" of Puerto Rico, or the "Protectorate" of Guam.[14]

As a result, none of the 50 states can be seen as ensuring self-government for a national minority, the way that Quebec ensures self-government for the Québécois. Self-government is instead achieved through political institutions located inside existing states (e.g., Indian reservations), or entirely outside the federal system (e.g., Puerto Rico, Guam). This has tended to make national minorities in the United States more vulnerable, since their self-government powers do not have the same constitutional protection as states' rights. On the other hand, it has provided greater flexibility in redefining those powers so as to suit the needs and interests of each minority. It is much easier to negotiate new self-government provisions for the Navaho or Puerto Ricans than to modify the powers of individual states.

Federalism can only serve as a mechanism for self-government if the national minority forms a majority in one of the federal subunits, as the Québécois do in Quebec. This is not true of most indigenous peoples in North America, who are fewer in number and whose communities are often dispersed across state/provincial lines. Moreover, with few exceptions (such as the Navaho), no redrawing of the boundaries of these federal subunits would create a state, province, or territory with an indigenous majority. It would have been possible to create a state or province dominated by an Indian tribe in the nineteenth century, but, given the massive influx of settlers since then, it is now virtually inconceivable.

One exception concerns the Inuit in the north of Canada, who wish to divide the Northwest Territories into two, so that they will form the majority in the eastern half (to be called "Nunavut"). This redrawing of federal boundaries is seen as essential to the implementation of the Inuit's right of self-government, and has recently been approved by the federal government.

For the other indigenous peoples in North America, however, self-government has been primarily tied to the system of reserved lands (known as tribal "reservations" in the United States, and band "reserves" in Canada). Substantial powers have been devolved from the federal government to the tribal/band councils which govern each reserve. Indian tribes/bands have been acquiring increasing control over health, education, family law, policing, criminal justice, and resource development. They are becoming, in effect, a third order of government, with a collection of powers that is carved out of both federal and state/provincial jurisdictions.[15] However, the administrative difficulties are daunting. Indian tribes/bands differ enormously in the sorts of powers they desire. Moreover, they are territorially located within existing states/provinces, and must co-ordinate their self-government with state/provincial agencies. The exact scope and mechanisms of indigenous self-government in Canada and the United States therefore remain unclear.

Similar systems of self-government exist, or are being sought, by many other indigenous peoples. A recent international declaration regarding the rights of indigenous peoples emphasizes the importance of political self-government. In many parts of the world, however, the hope for political powers is almost utopian, and the more immediate goal is simply to secure the existing land base from further erosion by settlers and resource developers. Indeed, a recent study showed that the single largest cause of ethnic conflict in the world today is the struggle by indigenous peoples for the protection of their land rights.[16]

Self-government claims, then, typically take the form of devolving political power to a political unit substantially controlled by the members of the national minority, and substantially corresponding to their historical homeland or territory. It is important to note that these claims are not seen as a temporary measure, nor as a remedy for a form of oppression that we might (and ought) someday to eliminate. On the contrary, these rights are often described as "inherent," and so permanent (which is one reason why national minorities seek to have them entrenched in the constitution).

2. Polyethnic rights. As I noted earlier, immigrant groups in the last thirty years have successfully challenged the "Anglo-conformity" model which assumed that they should abandon all aspects of their ethnic heritage and assimilate to existing cultural norms and customs. At first, this challenge simply took the form of demanding the right freely to express their particularity without fear of prejudice or discrimination in the mainstream society. It was the demand, as Walzer put it, that "politics be separated from nationality—as it was already separated from religion" (Walzer 1982: 6–11).

But the demands of ethnic groups have expanded in important directions. It became clear that positive steps were required to root out discrimination and prejudice, particularly against visible minorities. For this reason, anti-racism policies are considered part of the "multiculturalism" policy in Canada and Australia, as are changes to the education curriculum to recognize the history and contribution of minorities. However, these policies are primarily directed at ensuring the effective exercise of the common rights of citizenship, and so do not really qualify as group-differentiated citizenship rights.

Some ethnic groups and religious minorities have also demanded various forms of public funding of their cultural practices. This includes the funding of ethnic associations, magazines, and festivals. Given that most liberal states provide funding to the arts and museums, so as to preserve the richness and diversity of our cultural resources, funding for ethnic studies and ethnic associations can be seen as falling under this heading. Indeed, some people defend this funding simply as a way of ensuring that ethnic groups are not discriminated against in state funding of art and culture. Some people believe that public funding agencies have traditionally been biased in favour of European-derived forms of cultural expression, and programmes targeted at ethnic groups remedy this bias. A related demand—discussed at length in Chapter V—is for the provision of immigrant language education in schools.

Perhaps the most controversial demand of ethnic groups is for exemptions from laws and regulations that disadvantage them, given their religious practices. For example, Jews and Muslims in Britain have sought exemption from Sunday closing or animal slaughtering legislation; Sikh men in Canada have sought exemption from motorcycle helmet laws and from the official dress-codes of police forces, so that they can wear their turban; Orthodox Jews in the United States have sought the right to wear the yarmulka during military service; and Muslim girls in France have sought exemption from school dress-codes so that they can wear the *chador*.[17]

These group-specific measures—which I call "poly-ethnic rights"—are intended to help ethnic groups and religious minorities express their cultural particularity and pride without it hampering their success in the economic and political institutions of the dominant society. Like self-government rights, these polyethnic rights are not seen as temporary, because the cultural differences they protect are not something we seek to eliminate. But, . . . unlike self-government rights, polyethnic rights are usually intended to promote integration into the larger society, not self-government.

3. Special representation rights. While the traditional concern of national minorities and ethnic groups has been with either self-government or polyethnic rights, there has been increasing interest by these groups, as well as other non-ethnic social groups, in the idea of special representation rights.

Throughout the Western democracies, there is increasing concern that the political process is "unrepresentative," in the sense that it fails to reflect the diversity of the population. Legislatures in most of these countries are dominated by middle-class, able-bodied, white men. A more representative process, it is said, would include members of ethnic and racial minorities, women, the poor, the disabled, etc. The under-representation of historically disadvantaged groups is a general phenomenon. In the United States and Canada, women, racial minorities, and indigenous peoples all have under one-third of the seats they would have based on their demographic weight. People with disabilities and the economically disadvantaged are also significantly underrepresented.[18]

One way to reform the process is to make political parties more inclusive, by reducing the barriers which inhibit women, ethnic minorities, or the poor from becoming party candidates or party leaders; another way is to adopt some form of proportional representation, which has historically been associated with greater inclusiveness of candidates.

However, there is increasing interest in the idea that a certain number of seats in the legislature should be reserved for the members of disadvantaged or marginalized groups. During the debate in Canada over the Charlottetown Accord, for example, a number of recommendations were made for the guaranteed representation of women, ethnic minorities, official language minorities, and Aboriginals.

Group representation rights are often defended as a response to some systemic disadvantage or barrier in the political process which makes it impossible for the group's views and interests to be effectively represented. Insofar as these rights are seen as a response to oppression or systemic disadvantage, they are most plausibly seen as a temporary measure on the way to a society where the need for special representation no longer exists—a form of political "affirmative action." Society should seek to remove the oppression and disadvantage, thereby eliminating the need for these rights.

However, the issue of special representation rights for groups is complicated, because special representation is sometimes defended, not on grounds of oppression, but as a corollary of self-government. A minority's right to self-government would be severely weakened if some external body could unilaterally revise or revoke its powers, without consulting the minority or securing its consent. Hence it would seem to be a corollary of self-government that the national minority be guaranteed representation on any body which can interpret or modify its powers of self-government (e.g., the Supreme Court). Since the claims of self-government are seen as inherent and permanent, so too are the guarantees of representation which flow from it (unlike guarantees grounded on oppression).[19]

This is just a brief sketch of three mechanisms used to accommodate cultural differences, all of which will be examined in more detail in subsequent chapters. Virtually every modern democracy employs one or more of these mechanisms. Obviously, these three kinds of rights can overlap, in the sense that some groups can claim more than one kind of right. For example, indigenous groups may demand both special representation in the central government, in virtue of their disadvantaged position, and various powers of self-government, in virtue of their status as a "people" or "nation." But these rights need not go together. An oppressed group, like the disabled, may seek special representation, but have no basis for claiming either self-government or polyethnic rights. Conversely, an economically successful immigrant group may seek polyethnic rights, but have no basis for claiming either special representation or self-government, etc.

I have not yet said anything in defence of these rights. I will try to provide a (qualified) defence of them in Chapters V and VI. But we must first address certain confusions about the relationship between individual rights and collective rights, which is the subject of the next chapter. . . .

. . .

Chapter V Freedom and Culture

This book aims to develop a distinctively liberal approach to minority rights. This is not the same as developing the traditional liberal approach, for there is no single traditional approach. There has been a striking diversity of views within the liberal tradition, most of which have been shaped by historical contingencies and political exigencies. To identify a distinctly liberal approach, therefore, we need to start all over again. We need to lay out the basic principles of liberalism, and then see how they bear on the claims of ethnic and national minorities.

The basic principles of liberalism, of course, are principles of individual freedom. Liberals can only endorse minority rights insofar as they are consistent with respect for the freedom or autonomy of individuals. In this chapter, I will show that minority rights are not only consistent with individual freedom, but can actually promote it. I will defend the idea—common in earlier Liberal theorists—that "the cause of liberty" often "finds its basis in the autonomy of a national group" (Barker 1948: 248).

Of course, some ethnic and national groups are deeply illiberal, and seek to suppress rather than support the liberty of their members. Under these circumstances, acceding to the demands of minority groups may result in gross violations of the most basic liberties of individuals. But in other cases, respecting minority rights can enlarge the freedom of individuals, because freedom is intimately linked with and dependent on culture. My aim in this chapter is to trace this connection between freedom and culture.

I will begin by describing the sort of "culture" which I think is particularly relevant to individual freedom (s. 1). The modern world is divided into what I will call "societal cultures," whose practices and institutions cover the full range of human activities, encompassing both public and private life. These societal cultures are typically associated with national groups. I will then try to explain why individual freedom is intimately tied up with membership in these cultures. This will require a brief discussion of the conception of freedom which is central to the liberal tradition (s. 2). I will then show how this freedom is dependent on the presence of a societal culture (s. 3), and why it matters that national minorities have access to their own culture (s. 4). I will also discuss whether immigrant groups should be given the rights and resources necessary to sustain a distinct societal culture, and how liberals should respond to cultures which are illiberal (s. 5).

My aim is to show that the liberal value of freedom of choice has certain cultural preconditions, and hence that issues of cultural membership must be incorporated into liberal principles. This will set up the discussion in the next chapter about how group-differentiated rights for ethnic and national minorities fit within a larger theory of liberal justice.

I. Defining Cultures

As I noted in Chapter II, the term "culture" has been used to cover all manner of groups, from teenage gangs to global civilizations. The sort of culture that I will focus on, however, is a *societal* culture—that is, a culture which provides its members with meaningful ways of life across the full range of human activities, including social, educational, religious, recreational, and economic life, encompassing both public and private spheres. These cultures tend to be territorially concentrated, and based on a shared language.[20]

I have called these "societal cultures" to emphasize that they involve not just shared memories or values, but also common institutions and practices. Ronald Dworkin has said that the members of a culture have "a shared vocabulary of tradition and convention" (Dworkin 1985: 231). But that gives us an abstract or ethereal picture of cultures. In the case of a societal culture, this shared vocabulary is the everyday vocabulary of social life, embodied in practices covering most areas of human activity. And in the modern world, for a culture to be embodied in social life means that it must be institutionally embodied—in schools, media, economy, government, etc.

Such "societal cultures" did not always exist, and their creation is intimately linked with the process of modernization (Gellner 1983). Modernization involves the diffusion throughout a society of a common culture, including a standardized language, embodied in common economic, political, and educational institutions. This occurs for a variety of reasons. It is a functional requirement of a modern economy, with its need for a mobile, educated, and literate work-force. Second, it reflects the need for a high level of solidarity within modern democratic states. The sort of solidarity essential for a welfare state requires that citizens have a strong sense of common identity and common membership, so that they will make sacrifices for each other, and this common identity is assumed to require (or at least be facilitated by) a common language and history. Third, the diffusion of a common culture seems required by the modern commitment to equality of opportunity. The provision of standardized public education throughout a society, for example, has been seen as essential to ensure equality of opportunity for people from different classes, races, and regions of the society.

Most contemporary liberals write as if this process of building a common culture extends throughout the entire country, so that there is just one such culture in each country. For example, Dworkin suggests that the United States contains a single "cultural structure" based on a "shared language" (Dworkin 1985: 232–3; 1989: 488).

The claim that all Americans share a common culture based on the English language is clearly false. Yet there is a kernel of truth in it. The United States has integrated an extraordinary number of people from very different backgrounds into a common culture. The vast majority of Americans do in fact participate in the same societal culture, based on the English language. At other times and places, differences in ethnicity, race, region, class, gender, and religion were often assumed to preclude the possibility of a common culture. But in the United States and other modern societies, the common culture is capacious, integrating a rich array of groups.

If there is not a single culture in the United States, there is a dominant culture that incorporates most Americans, and those who fall outside it belong to a relatively small number of minority cultures. To understand the impressive integrative power of this common culture, but also its limits, it is worth examining how immigrants and national minorities relate to the dominant American culture.

When immigrants come to the United States, they bring their language and historical narratives with them. But they have left behind the set of institutionalized practices, conducted in their mother tongue, which actually provided culturally significant ways of life to people in their original homeland. They bring with them a "shared vocabulary of tradition and convention," but they have uprooted themselves from the social practices which this vocabulary originally referred to and made sense of.

Some immigrants might hope to re-create these practices in their entirety in their new country. But that is effectively impossible without significant government support, which is rarely if ever provided. On the contrary, . . . immigration policy in the United States is intended to integrate immigrants within the existing English-speaking culture. Immigrants come as individuals or families, rather than entire communities, and settle throughout the country, rather than forming "homelands." They are expected to learn the English language and American history, and to speak English in public life—e.g., at school, work, and when interacting with governments and other public agencies. (I discuss whether this is legitimate or not below.)

Immigrants are no longer expected to assimilate entirely to the norms and customs of the dominant culture, and indeed are encouraged to maintain some aspects of their ethnic particularity. But this commitment to "multiculturalism" or "polyethnicity" is a shift in *how* immigrants integrate into the dominant culture, not whether they integrate. The rejection of "Anglo-conformity" primarily has involved affirming the right of immigrants to maintain their ethnic heritage in the private sphere—at home, and in voluntary associations. To a lesser extent, it also involved reforming the public institutions of the dominant culture so as to provide some recognition or accommodation of their heritage. But it has not involved the establishment of distinct and institutionally complete societal cultures alongside the anglophone society. (By "institutionally complete," I mean containing a full range of social, educational, economic, and political institutions, encompassing both public and private life.)

Under these conditions, the immigrants' mother tongue is often spoken at home, and passed on to the children, but by the third generation English has become the mother tongue, and the original language is increasingly lost. This process is speeded up, of course, by the fact that public schooling is only provided in English. In fact, it is very difficult for languages to survive in modern industrialized societies unless they are used in public life. Given the spread of standardized education, the high demands for literacy in work, and widespread interaction with government agencies, any language which is not a public language becomes so marginalized that it is likely to survive only amongst a small elite, or in a ritualized form, not as a living and developing language underlying a flourishing culture.[21]

So while there are many aspects of their heritage that immigrants will maintain and cherish, this will take the form not of re-creating a separate societal culture, but rather of contributing new options and perspectives to the larger anglophone culture, making it richer and more diverse. For the third generation, if not sooner, learning the original mother tongue is not unlike learning a foreign language. Learning the old language may be rewarding as a hobby or business skill, but for the children of immigrants, it is the anglophone culture which defines their options, not the culture from which their parents uprooted themselves.[22]

The situation of national minorities in the United States—i.e., groups whose homeland has been incorporated through conquest, colonization, or federation—is very different. At the time of their incorporation, each group constituted an ongoing societal culture, separate from the anglophone culture. They did not have to re-create their culture in a new land, since their language and historical narratives were already embodied in a full set of social practices and institutions, encompassing all aspects of social life. These practices and institutions defined the range of socially meaningful options for their members.

These groups have fought to retain their existence as distinct societal cultures, although not all have been accorded the language and self-government rights necessary to do so. Indeed, some groups have faced enormous pressures to assimilate. In the case of many Indian tribes, for example, there have been prohibitions on the use of their mother tongue, and attempts to break open their lands for settlement so that they have become minorities in their historical homelands. Yet they have persisted, and their status as self-governing "domestic dependent nations" is now more firmly recognized. The determination they have shown in maintaining their existence as distinct cultures, despite these enormous economic and political pressures, shows the value they attach to retaining their cultural membership.

So the typical situation of immigrant groups and national minorities is very different. Of course, I have oversimplified the contrast. The extent to which immigrant groups have been allowed or encouraged to integrate varies considerably, as does the extent to which national minorities have been able to maintain a separate culture (see below.)

But, as a general rule, both in the United States and in other Western democracies, dominant cultures have had far less success accommodating national groups than ethnic groups. In multination states, national minorities have resisted integration into the common culture, and instead sought to protect their separate existence by consolidating their own societal cultures. American Indian tribes and Puerto Ricans, like the Aboriginal peoples and Québécois in Canada, are not just subgroups within a common culture, but genuinely distinct societal cultures.

In short, for a culture to survive and develop in the modern world, given the pressures towards the creation of a single common culture in each country, it must be a societal culture.[23] Given the enormous significance of social institutions in our lives, and in determining our options, any culture which is not a societal culture will be reduced to ever-decreasing marginalization. The capacity and motivation to form and maintain such a distinct culture is characteristic of "nations" or "peoples" (i.e., culturally distinct, geographically concentrated, and institutionally complete societies). Societal cultures, then, tend to be national cultures.

This connection is confirmed from another direction, by studies of nationalism. Most analysts of nationalism have concluded that the defining feature of nations is that they are "pervasive cultures," "encompassing cultures," or "organizational cultures" (e.g., A. Smith 1986: 2; Margalit and Raz 1990: 444; Tamir 1993; Poole 1993). In short, just as societal cultures are almost invariably national cultures, so nations are almost invariably societal cultures.

2. Liberalism and Individual Freedom

I believe that societal cultures are important to people's freedom, and that liberals should therefore take an interest in the viability of societal cultures. To show this, however, I need briefly to consider the nature of freedom, as it is conceived within the liberal tradition.[24]

The defining feature of liberalism is that describes certain fundamental freedoms to each individual. In particular, it grants people a very wide freedom of choice in terms of how they lead their lives. It allows people to choose a conception of the good life, and then allows them to reconsider that decision, and adopt a new and hopefully better plan of life.

Why should people be free to choose their own plan of life? After all, we know that some people will make imprudent decisions, wasting their time on hopeless or trivial pursuits. Why then should the government not intervene to protect us from making mistakes, and to compel us to lead the truly good life? There are a variety of reasons why this is not a good idea: governments may not be trustworthy; some individuals have idiosyncratic needs which are difficult for even a well-intentioned government to take into account; supporting controversial conceptions of the good may lead to civil strife. Moreover, paternalistic restrictions on liberty often simply do not work—lives do not go better by being led from the outside, in accordance with values the person does not endorse. Dworkin calls this the "endorsement constraint," and argues that "no component contributes to the value of a life without endorsement . . . it is implausible to think that someone can lead a better life against the grain of his profound ethical convictions than at peace with them" (Dworkin 1989: 486).[25]

However, the fact that we can get it wrong is important, because (paradoxically) it provides another argument for liberty. Since we can be wrong about the worth or value of what we are currently doing, and since no one wants to lead a life based on false beliefs about its worth, it is of fundamental importance that we be able rationally to assess our conceptions of the good in the light of new information or experiences, and to revise them if they are not worthy of our continued allegiance.[26]

This assumption that our beliefs about the good life are fallible and revisable is widely endorsed in the liberal tradition—from John Stuart Mill to the most prominent contemporary American liberals, such as John Rawls and Ronald Dworkin. (Because of their prominence, I will rely heavily on the works of Rawls and Dworkin in the rest of this chapter.) As Rawls puts it, individuals "do not view themselves as inevitably tied to the pursuit of the particular conception of the good and its final ends which they espouse at any given time." Instead, they are "capable of revising and changing this conception." They can "stand back" from their current ends to "survey and assess" their worthiness (Rawls 1980: 544; cf. Mill 1982: 122; Dworkin 1983).

So we have two preconditions for leading a good life. The first is that we lead our life from the inside, in accordance with our beliefs about what gives value to life. Individuals must therefore have the resources and liberties needed to lead their lives in accordance with their beliefs about value, without fear of discrimination or punishment. Hence the traditional liberal concern with individual privacy, and opposition to "the enforcement of morals." The second precondition is that we be free to question those beliefs, to examine them in light of whatever information, examples, and arguments our culture can provide. Individuals must therefore have the conditions necessary to acquire an awareness of different views about the good life, and an ability to examine these views intelligently. Hence the equally traditional liberal concern for education, and freedom of expression and association. These liberties enable us to judge what is valuable, and to learn about other ways of life.

It is important to stress that a liberal society is concerned with both of these preconditions, the second as much as the first. It is all too easy to reduce individual liberty to the freedom to pursue one's conception of the good. But in fact much of what is distinctive to a liberal state concerns the forming and revising of people's conceptions of the good, rather than the pursuit of those conceptions once chosen.

Consider the case of religion. A liberal society not only allows individuals the freedom to pursue their existing faith, but it also allows them to seek new adherents for their faith (proselytization is allowed), or to question the doctrine of their church (heresy is allowed), or to renounce their faith entirely and convert to another faith or to atheism (apostasy is allowed). It is quite conceivable to have the freedom to pursue one's current faith without having any of these latter freedoms. There are many examples of this within the Islamic world. Islam has a long tradition of tolerating other monotheistic religions, so that Christians and Jews can worship in peace. But proselytization, heresy, and apostasy are generally prohibited. This was true, for example, of the "millet system" of the Ottoman Empire, which I will look at in more depth in Chapter VIII. Indeed, some Islamic states have said the freedom of conscience guaranteed in the Universal Declaration of Human Rights should not include the freedom to change religion (Lerner 1991: 79–80). Similarly, the clause in the Egyptian constitution guaranteeing freedom of conscience has been interpreted so as to exclude freedom of apostasy (Peters and de Vries 1976: 23). In such a system, freedom of conscience means there is no forced conversion, but nor is there voluntary conversion.

A liberal society, by contrast, not only allows people to pursue their current way of life, but also gives them access to information about other ways of life (through freedom of expression), and indeed requires children to learn about other ways of life (through mandatory education), and makes it possible for people to engage in radical revision of their ends (including apostasy) without legal penalty. These aspects of a liberal society only make sense on the assumption that revising one's ends is possible, and sometimes desirable, because one's current ends are not always worthy of allegiance. A liberal society does not compel such questioning and revision, but it does make it a genuine possibility.

3. Societal Cultures as Context of Choice

I have just outlined what I take to be the predominant liberal conception of individual freedom. But how does this relate to membership in societal cultures? Put simply, freedom involves making choices amongst various options, and our societal culture not only provides these options, but also makes them meaningful to us.

People make choices about the social practices around them, based on their beliefs about the value of these practices (beliefs which, I have noted, may be wrong). And to have a belief about the value of a practice is, in the first instance, a matter of understanding the meanings attached to it by our culture.

I noted earlier that societal cultures involve "a shared vocabulary of tradition and convention" which underlies a full range of social practices and institutions (Dworkin 1985: 231). To understand the meaning of a social practice, therefore, requires understanding this "shared vocabulary"—that is, understanding the language and history which constitute that vocabulary. Whether or not a course of action has any significance for us depends on whether, and how, our language renders vivid to us the point of that activity. And the way in which language renders vivid these activities is shaped by our history, our "traditions and conventions." Understanding these cultural narratives is a precondition of making intelligent judgments about how to lead our lives. In this sense, our culture not only provides options, it also "provides the spectacles through which we identify experiences as valuable" (Dworkin 1985: 228).[27]

What follows from this? According to Dworkin, we must protect our societal culture from "structural debasement or decay" (1985: 230).[28] The survival of a culture is not guaranteed, and, where it is threatened with debasement or decay, we must act to protect it. Cultures are valuable, not in and of themselves, but because it is only through having access to a societal culture that people have access to a range of meaningful options. Dworkin concludes his discussion by saying "We inherited a cultural structure, and we have some duty, out of simple justice, to leave that structure at least as rich as we found it" (1985: 232–3).

In this passage and elsewhere, Dworkin talks about "cultural structures." This is a potentially misleading term, since it suggests an overly formal and rigid picture of what (as I discuss below) is a very diffuse and open-ended phenomenon. Cultures do not have fixed centres or precise boundaries. But his main point is, I think, sound enough. The availability of meaningful options depends on access to a societal culture, and on understanding the history and language of that culture—its "shared vocabulary of tradition and convention" (Dworkin 1985: 228, 231).[29]

This argument about the connection between individual choice and culture provides the first step towards a distinctively liberal defence of certain group-differentiated rights. For meaningful individual choice to be possible, individuals need not only access to information, the capacity to reflectively evaluate it, and freedom of expression and association. They also need access to a societal culture. Group-differentiated measures that secure and promote this access may, therefore, have a legitimate role to play in a liberal theory of justice.[30]

Of course, many details remain to be filled in, and many objections need to be answered. In particular, this connection between individual choice and societal cultures raises three obvious questions: (1) is individual choice tied to membership in one's *own* culture, or is it sufficient for people to have access to some or other culture? (2) if (as I will argue) people have a deep bond to their own culture, should immigrant groups be given the rights and resources necessary to recreate their own societal cultures? and (3) what if a culture is organized so as to preclude individual choice—for example, if it assigns people a specific role or way of life, and prohibits any questioning or revising of that role? I will start answering these questions in the rest of the chapter, although a full answer will only emerge in later chapters.

4. The Value of Cultural Membership

I have tried to show that people's capacity to make meaningful choices depends on access to a cultural structure. But why do the members of a national minority need access to their *own* culture?[31] Why not let minority cultures disintegrate, so long as we ensure their members have access to the majority culture (e.g., by teaching them the majority language and history)? This latter option would involve a cost to minorities, but governments could subsidize it. For example, governments could pay for the members of national minorities to learn about the majority language and history.

This sort of proposal treats the loss of one's culture as similar to the loss of one's job. Language training for members of a threatened culture would be like worker retraining programmes for employees of a dying industry. We do not feel obliged to keep uncompetitive industries afloat in perpetuity so long as we help employees to find employment elsewhere, so why feel obliged to protect minority cultures, so long as we help their members to find another culture?

This is an important question. It would be implausible to say that people are never able to switch cultures. After all, many immigrants function well in their new country (although others flounder, and many return home). Waldron thinks that these examples of successful "cosmopolitan" people who move between cultures disprove the claim that people are connected to their own culture in any deep way. Suppose, he says, that

> a freewheeling cosmopolitan life, lived in a kaleidoscope of cultures, is both possible and fulfilling. . . . Immediately, one argument for the protection of minority cultures is undercut. It can no longer be said that all people need their rootedness in the particular culture in which they and their ancestors were reared in the way that they need food, clothing, and shelter. . . . Such immersion may be something that particular people like and enjoy. But they can no longer claim that it is something they need. . . . The collapse of the Herderian argument based on distinctively human *need* seriously undercuts any claim that minority cultures might have to special support or assistance or to extraordinary provision or forbearance. At best, it leaves the right to culture roughly on the same footing as the right to religious freedom. (Waldron 1992a: 762)

Because people do not need their own culture, minority cultures can ("at best") claim the same negative rights as religious groups—that is, the right to non-interference, but not to state support.

I think Waldron is seriously overstating the case here. For one thing, he vastly overestimates the extent to which people do in fact move between cultures, because (as I discuss below) he assumes that cultures are based on ethnic descent. On his view, an Irish-American who eats Chinese food and reads her child *Grimms' Fairy-Tales* is thereby "living in a kaleidoscope of cultures" (e.g., Waldron 1992a: 754). But this is not moving between societal cultures. Rather it is enjoying the opportunities provided by the diverse societal culture which characterizes the anglophone society of the United States.

Of course, people do genuinely move between cultures. But this is rarer, and more difficult. In some cases, where the differences in social organization and technological development are vast, successful integration may be almost impossible for some members of the minority. (This seems to be true of the initial period of contact between European cultures and indigenous peoples in some parts of the world.)

But even where successful integration is possible, it is rarely easy. It is a costly process, and there is a legitimate question whether people should be required to pay those costs unless they voluntarily choose to do so. These costs vary, depending on the gradualness of the process, the age of the person, and the extent to which the two cultures are similar in language and history.[32] But even where the obstacles to integration are smallest, the desire of national minorities to retain their cultural membership remains very strong (just as the members of the majority culture typically value their cultural membership).

In this sense, the choice to leave one's culture can be seen as analogous to the choice to take a vow of perpetual poverty and enter a religious order. It is not impossible to live in poverty. But it does not follow that a liberal theory of justice should therefore view the desire for a level of material resources above bare subsistence simply as "something that particular people like and enjoy" but which "they no longer can claim is something that they need" (Waldron 1992a: 762). Liberals rightly assume that the desire for non-subsistence resources is so normal—and the costs of forgoing them so high for most people's way of life—that people cannot reasonably be *expected* to go without such resources, even if a few people voluntarily choose to do so. For the purposes of determining people's claims of justice, material resources are something that people can be assumed to want, whatever their particular conception of the good. Although a small number of people may choose to forgo non-subsistence resources, this is seen as forgoing something to which they are entitled.

Similarly, I believe that, in developing a theory of justice, we should treat access to one's culture as something that people can be expected to want, whatever their more particular conception of the good. Leaving one's culture, while possible, is best seen as renouncing something to which one is reasonably entitled. This is a claim, not about the limits of human possibility, but about reasonable expectations.

I think that most liberals have implicitly accepted this claim about people's legitimate expectation to remain in their culture. Consider Rawls' argument about why the right to emigrate does not make political authority voluntary:

> normally leaving one's country is a grave step: it involves leaving the society and culture in which we have been raised, the society and culture whose language we use in speech and thought to express and understand ourselves, our aims, goals, and values; the society and culture whose history, customs, and conventions we depend on to find our place in the social world. In large part, we affirm our society and culture, and have an intimate and inexpressible knowledge of it, even though much of it we may question, if not reject. The government's authority cannot, then, be freely accepted in the sense that the bonds of society and culture, of history and social place of origin, begin so early to shape our life and are normally so strong that the right of emigration (suitably qualified) does not suffice to make accepting its authority free, politically speaking, in the way that liberty of conscience suffices to make accepting ecclesiastical authority free. (Rawls 1993a: 222)

Because of these bonds to the "language we use in speech and thought to express and understand ourselves," cultural ties "are normally too strong to be given up, and this fact is not to be deplored." Hence, for the purposes of developing a theory of justice, we should assume that "people are born and are expected to lead a complete life" within the same "society and culture" (Rawls 1993a: 277).

I agree with Rawls' view about the difficulty of leaving one's culture.[33] Yet this argument has implications beyond those which he himself draws. Rawls presents this as an argument about the difficulty of leaving one's political community. But his argument does not rest on the value of specifically political ties (e.g., the bonds to one's government and fellow citizens). Rather it rests on the value of cultural ties (e.g., bonds to one's language and history). And cultural boundaries may not coincide with political boundaries. For example, someone leaving East Germany for West Germany in 1950 would not be breaking the ties of language and culture which Rawls emphasizes, even though she would be crossing state borders. But a francophone leaving Quebec City for Toronto, or a Puerto Rican leaving San Juan for Chicago, would be breaking those ties, even though she is remaining within the same country.

According to Rawls, then, the ties to one's culture are normally too strong to give up, and this is not to be regretted. We cannot be expected or required to make such a sacrifice, even if some people voluntarily do so. It is an interesting question why the bonds of language and culture are so strong for most people. It seems particularly puzzling that people would have a strong attachment to a liberalized culture. After all, as a culture is liberalized—and so allows members to question and reject traditional ways of life—the resulting cultural identity becomes both "thinner" and less distinctive. That is, as a culture becomes more liberal, the members are less and less likely to share the same substantive conception of the good life, and more and more likely to share basic values with people in other liberal cultures.

The Québécois provide a nice illustration of this process. Before the Quiet Revolution, the Québécois generally shared a rural, Catholic, conservative, and patriarchal conception of the good. Today, after a rapid period of liberalization, most people have abandoned this traditional way of life, and Québécois society now exhibits all the diversity that any modern society contains—e.g., atheists and Catholics, gays and heterosexuals, urban yuppies and rural fanners, socialists and conservatives, etc. To be a "Québécois" today, therefore, simply means being a participant in the francophone society of Quebec. And francophones in Quebec no more agree about conceptions of the good than anglophones in the United States. So being a "Québécois" seems to be a very thin form of identity.

Moreover, the process of liberalization has also meant that the Québécois have become much more like English Canadians in their basic values. Liberalization in Quebec over the last thirty years has been accompanied by a pronounced convergence in personal and political values between English- and French-speaking Canadians, so that it would now be "difficult to identify consistent differences in attitudes on issues such as moral values, prestige ranking of professions, role of the government, workers' rights, aboriginal rights, equality between the sexes and races, and conception of authority" (Dion 1992: 99; cf. Dion 1991: 301; Taylor 1991: 54).[34]

In short, liberalization in Quebec has meant both an increase in differences amongst the Québécois, in terms of their conceptions of the good, and a reduction in differences between the Québécois and the members of other liberal cultures. This is not unique to Quebec. The same process is at work throughout Europe. The modernization and liberalization of Western Europe has resulted both in fewer commonalities within each of the national cultures, and greater commonalities across these cultures. As Spain has liberalized, it has become both more pluralistic internally, and more like France or Germany in terms of its modern, secular, industrialized, democratic, and consumerist civilization.

This perhaps explains why so many theorists have assumed that liberalization and modernization would displace any strong sense of national identity. As cultures liberalize, people share less and less with their fellow members of the national group, in terms of traditional customs or conceptions of the good life, and become more and more like the members of other nations, in terms of sharing a common civilization. Why then would anyone feel strongly attached to their own nation? Such an attachment seems, to many commentators, like the "narcissism of minor differences" (Ignatieff 1993: 21; Dion 1991).

Yet the evidence is overwhelming that the members of liberal cultures *do* value their cultural membership. Far from displacing national identity, liberalization has in fact gone hand in hand with an increased sense of nationhood. Many of the liberal reformers in Quebec have been staunch nationalists, and the nationalist movement grew in strength throughout the Quiet Revolution and afterwards. The same combination of liberalization and a strengthened national identity can be found in many other countries. For example, in Belgium, the liberalization of Flemish society has been accompanied by a sharp rise in nationalist sentiment (Peterson 1975: 208). The fact that their culture has become tolerant and pluralistic has in no way diminished the pervasiveness or intensity of people's desire to live and work in their own culture. Indeed, Walker Connor goes so far as to suggest that few if any examples exist of recognized national groups in this century having voluntarily assimilated to another culture, even though many have had significant economic incentives and political pressures to do so (Connor 1972: 350–1; 1973: 20).

Why are the bonds of language and culture so strong for most people? Commentators offer a number of reasons. Margalit and Raz argue that membership in a societal culture (what they call a "pervasive culture") is crucial to people's well-being for two reasons. The first reason is the one I have discussed above—namely, that cultural membership provides meaningful options, in the sense that "familiarity with a culture determines the boundaries of the imaginable." Hence if a culture is decaying or discriminated against, "the options and opportunities open to its members will shrink, become less attractive, and their pursuit less likely to be successful" (Margalit and Raz 1990: 449).

But why cannot the members of a decaying culture simply integrate into another culture? According to Margalit and Raz, this is difficult, not only because it is "a very slow process indeed," but also because of the role of cultural membership in people's self-identity. Cultural membership has a "high social profile," in the sense that it affects how others perceive and respond to us, which in turn shapes our self-identity. Moreover, national identity is particularly suited to serving as the "primary foci of identification," because it is based on belonging, not accomplishment:

> Identification is more secure, less liable to be threatened, if it does not depend on accomplishment. Although accomplishments play their role in people's sense of their own identity, it would seem that at the most fundamental level our sense of our own identity depends on criteria of belonging rather than on those of accomplishment. Secure identification at that level is particularly important to one's well-being.

Hence cultural identity provides an "anchor for [people's] self-identification and the safety of effortless secure belonging." But this in turn means that people's self-respect is bound up with the esteem in which their national group is held. If a culture is not generally respected, then the dignity and self-respect of its members will also be threatened (Margalit and Raz 1990: 447–9). Similar arguments about the role of respect for national membership in supporting dignity and self-identity are given by Charles Taylor (1992a) and Yael Tamir (1993:41, 71–3).

Tamir also emphasizes the extent to which cultural membership adds an "additional meaning" to our actions, which become not only acts of individual accomplishment, but also "part of a continuous creative effort whereby culture is made and remade." And she argues that, where institutions are "informed by a culture [people] find understandable and meaningful," this "allows a certain degree of transparency that facilitates their participation in public affairs." This in turn promotes a sense of belonging and relationships of mutual recognition and mutual responsibility (Tamir 1993: 72, 85–6). Other commentators make the related point that the mutual intelligibility which comes from shared national identity promotes relationships of solidarity and trust (Miller 1993; Barry 1991: 174–5). James Nickel emphasizes the potential harm to valuable intergenerational bonds when parents are unable to pass on their culture to their children and grandchildren (Nickel 1995). Benedict Anderson emphasizes the way national identity enables us to transcend our mortality, by linking us to something whose existence seems to extend back into time immemorial, and forward into the indefinite future (Anderson 1983).

No doubt all of these factors play a role in explaining people's bond to their own culture. I suspect that the causes of this attachment lie deep in the human condition, tied up with the way humans as cultural creatures need to make sense of their world, and that a full explanation would involve aspects of psychology, sociology, linguistics, the philosophy of mind, and even neurology (Laponce 1987).

But whatever the explanation, this bond does seem to be a fact, and, like Rawls, I see no reason to regret it. I should emphasize, again, that I am only dealing with general trends. Some people seem most at home leading a truly cosmopolitan life, moving freely between different societal cultures. Others have difficulty making sense of the cultural meanings within their own culture. But most people, most of the time, have a deep bond to their own culture.

It may seem paradoxical for liberals like Rawls to claim that the bonds to one's culture are "normally too strong to be given up." What has happened to the much vaunted liberal freedom of choice? But Rawls' view is in fact common within the liberal tradition . . . . The freedom which liberals demand for individuals is not primarily the freedom to go beyond one's language and history, but rather the freedom to move around within one's societal culture, to distance oneself from particular cultural roles, to choose which features of the culture are most worth developing, and which are without value.

This may sound like a rather "communitarian" view of the self. I do not think this is an accurate label. One prominent theme in recent communitarian writing is the rejection of the liberal view about the importance of being free to revise one's ends. Communitarians deny that we can "stand apart" from (some of) our ends. According to Michael Sandel, a leading American communitarian, some of our ends are "constitutive" ends, in the sense that they define our sense of personal identity (Sandel 1982: 150–65; cf. MacIntyre 1981: ch. 15; Bell 1993: 24–54). It makes no sense, on his view, to say that my ends might not be worthy of my allegiance, for they define who I am. Whereas Rawls claims that individuals "do not regard themselves as inevitably bound to, or identical with, the pursuit of any particular complex of fundamental interests that they may have at any given moment"(1974: 641), Sandel responds that we are in fact "identical with" at least some of our final ends. Since these ends are constitutive of people's identity, there is no reason why the state should not reinforce people's allegiance to those ends, and limit their ability to question and revise these ends.

I believe that this communitarian conception of the self is mistaken. It is not easy or enjoyable to revise one's deepest ends, but it is possible, and sometimes a regrettable necessity. New experiences or circumstances may reveal that our earlier beliefs about the good are mistaken. No end is immune from such potential revision. As Dworkin puts it, it is true that "no one can put everything about himself in question all at once," but it "hardly follows that for each person there is some one connection or association so fundamental that it cannot be detached for inspection while holding others in place" (Dworkin 1989: 489).

Some people may think of themselves as being incapable of questioning or revising their ends, but in fact "our conceptions of the good may and often do change over time, usually slowly but sometimes rather suddenly," even for those people who think of themselves as having constitutive ends (Rawls 1985: 242). No matter how confident we are about our ends at a particular moment, new circumstances or experiences may arise, often in unpredictable ways, that cause us to re-evaluate them. There is no way to predict in advance when the need for such a reconsideration will arise. As I noted earlier, a liberal society does not compel people to revise their commitments—and many people will go years without having any reason to question their basic commitments—but it does recognize that the freedom of choice is not a one-shot affair, and that earlier choices sometimes need to be revisited.

Since our judgments about the good are fallible in this way, we have an interest, not only in pursuing our existing conception of the good, but also in being able to assess and potentially revise that conception. Our current ends are not always worthy of our continued allegiance, and exposure to other ways of life helps us make informed judgments about what is truly valuable.

The view I am defending is quite different, therefore, from the communitarian one, although both views claim that we have a deep bond to a particular sort of social group. The difference is partly a matter of scope. Communitarians typically talk about our attachment to subnational groups—churches, neighbourhoods, family, unions, etc.—rather than to the larger society which encompasses these subgroups. But this difference in scope reflects an even deeper divergence. Communitarians are looking for groups which are defined by a shared conception of the good. They seek to promote a "politics of the common good," in which groups can promote a shared conception of the good, even if this limits the ability of individual members to revise their ends. They believe that members have a "constitutive" bond to the group's, values, and so no harm is done by limiting individual rights in order to promote shared values.

As most communitarians admit, this "politics of the common good" cannot apply at the national level. As Sandel puts it, "the nation proved too vast a scale across which to cultivate the shared self-understandings necessary to community in the . . . constitutive sense" (Sandel 1984: 93; cf. MacIntyre 1981: 221; Miller 1988–9: 60–7). The members of a nation rarely share moral values or traditional ways of life. They share a language and history, but often disagree fundamentally about the ultimate ends in life. A common national identity, therefore, is not a useful basis for communitarian politics, which can only exist at a more local level.

The liberal view I am defending insists that people can stand back and assess moral values and traditional ways of life, and should be given not only the legal right to do so, but also the social conditions which enhance this capacity (e.g., a liberal education). So I object to communitarian politics at the subnational level. To inhibit people from questioning their inherited social roles can condemn them to unsatisfying, even oppressive, lives.[35] And at the national level, the very fact which makes national identity so inappropriate for communitarian politics—namely, that it does not rest on shared values—is precisely what makes it an appropriate basis for liberal politics. The national culture provides a meaningful context of choice for people, without limiting their ability to question and revise particular values or beliefs.

Put another way, the liberal ideal is a society of free and equal individuals. But what is the relevant "society"? For most people it seems to be their nation. The sort of freedom and equality they most value, and can make most use of, is freedom and equality within their own societal culture. And they are willing to forgo a wider freedom and equality to ensure the continued existence of their nation.

For example, few people favour a system of open borders, where people could freely cross borders and settle, work, and vote in whatever country they desired. Such a system would dramatically increase the domain within which people would be treated as free and equal citizens. Yet open borders would also make it more likely that people's own national community would be overrun by settlers from other cultures, and that they would be unable to ensure their survival as a distinct national culture. So we have a choice between, on the one hand, increased mobility and an expanded domain within which people are free and equal individuals, and, on the other hand, decreased mobility but a greater assurance that people can continue to be free and equal members of their own national culture. Most people in liberal democracies clearly favour the latter. They would rather be free and equal within their own nation, even if this means they have less freedom to work and vote elsewhere, than be free and equal citizens of the world, if this means they are less likely to be able to live and work in their own language and culture.

And most theorists in the liberal tradition have implicitly agreed with this. Few major liberal theorists have endorsed open borders, or even seriously considered it. They have generally accepted—indeed, simply taken for granted—that the sort of freedom and equality which matters most to people is freedom and equality within one's societal culture. Like Rawls, they assume that "people are born and are expected to lead a complete life" within the same "society and culture," and that this defines the scope within which people must be free and equal (Rawls 1993a: 277).[36]

In short, liberal theorists have generally, if implicitly, accepted that cultures or nations are basic units of liberal political theory. In this sense, as Yael Tamir puts it, "most liberals are liberal nationalists" (1993: 139)—that is, liberal goals are achieved in and through a liberalized societal culture or nation.

5. Hard Cases

So far, I have suggested that liberals should care about the viability of societal cultures, because they contribute to people's autonomy, and because people are deeply connected to their own culture. I have also argued that national minorities typically have the sort of societal culture that should be protected, while immigrants typically do not, since they instead integrate into, and thereby enrich, the culture of the larger society. This leaves a number of unresolved questions: (1) how should liberal states respond to societal cultures that are illiberal? (2) if people have such a deep bond with their own language and culture, why not allow immigrants to develop their own societal cultures? and (3) have some national minorities over time ceased to possess a societal culture? I will look at each in turn.

1. How should liberals respond to illiberal cultures? Some nations and nationalist movements are deeply illiberal. Some cultures, far from enabling autonomy, simply assign particular roles and duties to people, and prevent people from questioning or revising them. Other cultures allow this autonomy to some, while denying it to others, such as women, lower castes, or visible minorities. Clearly, these sorts of cultures do not promote liberal values.

This shows that liberals cannot endorse cultural membership uncritically. Indeed, if the liberal commitment to respecting national identity flows from its role in enabling autonomy, should we not encourage or compel the members of illiberal cultures to assimilate to more liberal cultures? But again this ignores the way people are bound to their own cultures. The aim of liberals should not be to dissolve non-liberal nations, but rather to seek to liberalize them. This may not always be possible. But it is worth remembering that all existing liberal nations had illiberal pasts, and their liberalization required a prolonged process of institutional reform. To assume that any culture is inherently illiberal, and incapable of reform, is ethnocentric and ahistorical.

Moreover, the liberality of a culture is a matter of degree. All cultures have illiberal strands, just as few cultures are entirely repressive of individual liberty. Indeed, it is quite misleading to talk of "liberal" and "illiberal" cultures, as if the world was divided into completely liberal societies on the one hand, and completely illiberal ones on the other. The task of liberal reform remains incomplete in every society, and it would be ludicrous to say that only purely liberal nations should be respected, while others should be assimilated.

So, as a general rule, liberals should not prevent illiberal nations from maintaining their societal culture, but should promote the liberalization of these cultures. The issue of how to promote liberalization, and more generally how liberal states should treat non-liberal minorities, is a large topic, which I pursue at length in Chapter VIII.

2. If people have a deep bond with their own culture, as I have suggested, should we not allow immigrants to re-create their own societal cultures (and thereby effectively become a national minority)? There is nothing incoherent or impossible about this proposal. After all, many existing nations were initially formed by uprooted settlers establishing colonies in a new land. This is true of the English and French nations in Canada and the United States.

But there are important differences between colonists and immigrants. As Steinberg notes of the English colonists in America, "it is not really correct to refer to the colonial settlers as "immigrants." They came not as migrants entering an alien society, forced to acquire a new national identity, but as a colonial vanguard that would create a new England in the image of the one they left behind." They distinguished themselves from the non-English colonials who "were typically regarded as aliens who were obliged to adapt to English rule in terms of both politics and culture" (Steinberg 1981: 7).[37] There was a fundamentally different set of expectations accompanying colonization and immigration—the former resulted from a deliberate policy aimed at the systematic re-creation of an entire society in a new land; the latter resulted from individual and familial choices to leave their society and join another existing society.

None the less, this just raises the question—should governments treat immigrants as if they were colonists? Why not encourage immigrants to settle together—even set aside homelands for them—and give them the resources and self-government powers necessary to re-create a societal culture based on their mother tongue? Some consideration was in fact given to allowing Pennsylvania to be a German-speaking state after the American Revolution. And even today we could imagine encouraging new immigrants from another country to settle as a "colony," and redistributing political boundaries and powers to enable them to exercise self-government.

I do not think that such a policy would be inherently unjust, although it is difficult to imagine any country actually adopting it. But nor is it unjust that the American government (and other Western democracies) have decided not to give immigrants the legal status and resources needed to become national minorities. After all, most immigrants (as distinct from refugees) choose to leave their own culture. They have uprooted themselves, and they know when they come that their success, and that of their children, depends on integrating into the institutions of English-speaking society.

The expectation of integration is not unjust, I believe, so long as immigrants had the option to stay in their original culture. Given the connection between choice and culture which I sketched earlier, people should be able to live and work in their own culture. But like any other right, this right can be waived, and immigration is one way of waiving one's right. In deciding to uproot themselves, immigrants voluntarily relinquish some of the rights that go along with their original national membership.[38]

For example, if a group of Americans decide to emigrate to Sweden, they have no right that the Swedish government provide them with institutions of self-government or public services in their mother tongue. One could argue that a government policy which enabled American immigrants to re-create their societal culture would benefit everyone, by enriching the whole society. But the immigrants have no *right* to such policies, for in choosing to leave the United States they relinquish the national rights that go with membership in their original culture. Similarly, Swedish immigrants to America have no basis for claiming the language rights or self-government rights needed to recreate their societal culture.

Moreover, on a practical level, most existing ethnic groups are too "dispersed, mixed, assimilated and integrated" to exercise self-government. They are not sufficiently "compact, self-conscious [and] culture-maintaining" to have the territorial and institutional prerequisites for self-government (Glazer 1983: 227, 283; cf. Oliver 1992). And to try to re-create these prerequisites amongst already-settled immigrants would probably require coercion of half-integrated immigrants.

This does not mean that voluntary immigrants have no claims regarding the expression of their identity. On the contrary, if we reject the option of enabling immigrants to re-create their societal culture, then we must address the issue of how to ensure that the mainstream culture is hospitable to immigrants, and to the expression of their ethnic differences. Integration is a two-way process—it requires the mainstream society to adapt itself to immigrants, just as immigrants must adapt to the mainstream (Parekh 1990).

Enabling integration requires, in the first place, strong efforts at fighting prejudice and discrimination. This involves not only the rigorous enforcement of anti-discrimination laws, but also changes to the way immigrants are portrayed in school textbooks, government documents, and the media. Moreover, enabling integration may require some modification of the institutions of the dominant culture in the form of group-specific polyethnic rights, such as the right of Jews and Muslims to exemptions from Sunday closing legislation, or the right of Sikhs to exemptions from motorcycle helmet laws. Without these exemptions, certain groups would be disadvantaged (often unintentionally) in the mainstream. Immigrants can rightfully insist on maintaining some of their heritage, and dominant institutions should be adapted to accommodate those differences.

In terms of linguistic integration, the goal of ensuring that immigrants learn English need not require the abandonment of the mother tongue. Indeed, there is strong evidence that immigrants are more likely to learn English if use of their mother tongue is not discouraged. ESL (English-as-a-second-language) programs, and public opinion generally, have historically treated the desire to retain and use one's mother tongue in private life, and to pass it on to one's children, as evidence of a failure of integration on the part of immigrants. Current policy has operated on the assumption that the ideal is to make immigrants and their children as close as possible to unilingual native-speakers of English (i.e., that learning English requires losing their mother tongue), rather than aiming to produce people who are fluently bilingual (i.e., that learning English involves gaining a language, in addition to one's mother tongue).

This is a deeply misguided policy. It is not only harmful to the immigrants and their families, cutting them off unnecessarily from their heritage. But it also deprives society of a valuable resource in an increasingly globalized economy. And, paradoxically, it has proven to be counter-productive even in terms of promoting integration. People learn English best when they view it as supplementing, rather than displacing, their mother tongue (Skutnabb-Kangas 1988).[39] Moreover, there is an undercurrent of racism in the traditional attitude towards immigrant languages. As Richard Ruiz puts it, "*Adding* a foreign language to English is associated with erudition, social and economic status and, perhaps, even patriotism . . . but *maintaining* a non-English language implies disadvantage, poverty, low achievement and dis-loyalty" (Ruiz 1983: 55).

So there are many ways that special efforts should be made to accommodate the cultural differences of immigrants. But all of these measures take the form of adapting the institutions and practices of the main-stream society so as to accommodate ethnic differences, not of setting up a separate societal culture based on the immigrants' mother tongue. Hence these claims are best met within the parameters of what I have been calling "polyethnic rights," not national rights.

Moreover, there is little evidence that immigrants are seeking national rights, rather than polyethnic rights. Some commentators interpreted the "ethnic revival" in the United States in the 1970s as a repudiation of inte-gration into the mainstream society. But, as I noted in Chapter IV, this is dubious. Ethnic groups were demand-ing increased recognition and visibility within the main-stream society, not national self-government. Gans calls this "symbolic ethnicity," to emphasize that it is almost entirely lacking in any real institutionalized corporate existence (Gans 1979). The fact is that "the institution-al cement" needed to have a distinct societal culture is almost entirely lacking in American immigrant groups (Steinberg 1981: 58; cf. Edwards 1985: 9–10; Fishman 1989: 666–8). This is not surprising, since "ethnicity can-not long survive the erosion of the material and insti-tutional underpinnings which was precipitated by the immigrant experience" (Steinberg 1981: 74).

The ethnic revival, in other words, involved a revi-sion in the terms of integration, not a rejection of integra-tion. The ethnic revival amongst German-Americans, for example, was not a revival of the idea that Pennsylvania should be a German-speaking state. The fact that such a proposal seems so ludicrous shows, I think, that the older American ethnic groups have long ago abandoned any interest in being treated as national minorities.[40] The ethnic revival aimed, in large part, to make the posses-sion of an ethnic identity an acceptable, even normal, part of life in the mainstream society. In this it was strik-ingly successful, which helps explain why the "revival" lost its political urgency (Fishman 1989: 678–80).

So far I have been talking about voluntary immi-grants. The case of refugees fleeing persecution is differ-ent, since they did not choose to give up their culture. Indeed, many refugees flee their homeland precisely to be able to continue practising their language and culture, which is being oppressed by the government (e.g., the Kurds). Since they have not relinquished the rights which go with membership in their original cul-ture, refugees arguably should, in principle, be able to re-create their societal culture in some other country, if

they so desire. But which country? The sad fact is that the national rights of refugees are, in the first instance, rights against their own government. If that government is violating their national rights, there is no mechanism for deciding which other country should redress that in-justice. And, unfortunately, it is likely that few countries would voluntarily accept any refugees if they were there-by committed to treating refugees as national minorities. Moreover, refugee groups, even more than immigrant groups, are typically too small and dispersed to re-form into self-governing communities.[41]

The best that refugees can realistically expect is to be treated as immigrants, with the corresponding poly-ethnic rights, and hope to return to their homeland as quickly as possible.[42] This means that long-term refugees suffer an injustice, since they did not voluntarily relin-quish their national rights. But this injustice was com-mitted by their home government, and it is not clear that we can realistically ask host governments to redress it.

The line between involuntary refugees and volun-tary immigrants is difficult to draw, especially in a world with massive injustice in the international distribution of resources, and with different levels of respect for hu-man rights. If a middle-class American chooses to emi-grate to Sweden, that is clearly voluntary, and very few of us would think that she had a claim of justice that the Swedish government provide her with free English-language services (or vice versa for a middle-class Swede emigrating to the United States). But if a peasant from Ethiopia emigrates to the United States, her decision is voluntary in a very limited sense, even if she was not subject to persecution in her homeland, since it may have been the only way to ensure a minimally decent life for herself or her children. Indeed, her plight may have been as dire as that of some political refugees. (This is reflected in the rise of the term "economic refugees.")

Under these conditions, we may be more sympa-thetic to demands for national rights. We may think that people should not have to give up their culture in order to avoid dire poverty. Moreover, the plight of the Ethiopian peasant is at least partly our responsibility. I believe that rich countries have obligations of interna-tional justice to redistribute resources to poor countries, and had we done so, perhaps she would not have faced this awful choice. Enabling immigrants from poor coun-tries to re-create their societal culture may be a way of compensating for our failure to provide them with a fair chance at a decent life in their own country.

Perhaps then my argument should be limited to what Rawls calls "ideal theory"—that is, what would the claims of immigrants be in a just world? I believe that if the international distribution of resources were just, then immigrants would have no plausible claim of justice for re-creating their societal culture in their new country. But the international distribution of resources is not just, and until that injustice is rectified, perhaps immigrants from poor countries have stronger claims. On the other hand, the only long-term solution is to remedy the unjust international distribution of resources. After all, treating Ethiopian immigrants to the United States as a national minority does nothing for the far greater number of Ethiopians condemned to abject poverty in Ethiopia. As with the case of refugees, it is not clear that treating economic refugees to a new country as a national minority provides an appropriate way to redress injustices that must ultimately be solved in the original homeland.

3. Have some national minorities lost their societal culture? I have just argued that ethnic groups lack the "institutional cement" needed to form or maintain a distinct societal culture. But haven't some national minorities also lost the societal integration and institutional life which constitute a societal culture? After all, societal cultures art not permanent and immutable. (If they were, group-specific rights would not be needed to protect them.) And given the coercive attempts to assimilate many national minorities—particularly indigenous peoples—it would not be surprising if there is very little left of some cultures. Some indigenous peoples have been decimated in size, denied the right to maintain their own institutions, and progressively demoralized.

Under these circumstances, would it not be better for the members of the national minority to integrate into the mainstream, rather than struggle in vain to preserve something that is already lost? This is a legitimate question, and it is worth noting that a few indigenous peoples have in fact chosen as a group to relinquish their national rights, and in effect to be treated as a disadvantaged ethnic or racial group.

In some circumstances this might be the most prudent course, and any system of group differentiated rights must leave this option open. While national minorities may have the right to maintain themselves as a distinct society, they are certainly under no duty to do so.[43] However, I believe that the decision about whether to integrate must be up to the members of the minority themselves. It is not for people outside the group to decide if and when the societal culture is too thin to warrant maintaining.

For one thing, majority cultures would have a perverse incentive to destroy the societal culture of national minorities, and then cite that destruction as a justification for compelling assimilation. We should not establish a system which enables majorities to profit from their own injustices. Moreover, weakened and oppressed cultures can regain and enhance their richness, if given the appropriate conditions. There is no reason to think that indigenous groups, for example, cannot become vibrant and diverse cultures, drawing on their cultural traditions while incorporating the best of the modern world, if given the requisite preconditions. It is the potentiality of societal cultures that matters, not just their current state, and it is even more difficult for outsiders to judge the potentiality of a culture than to judge its current state.[44]

In general, then, I believe that national minorities have societal cultures, and immigrant groups do not. There is of course no necessity about this. It is possible to settle immigrant groups collectively, and to empower them, so that they become in effect national minorities, just as it is possible to tear down and disperse national minorities so that they become indistinguishable from uprooted immigrants. The history of racism, ethnocentrism, cultural imperialism, segregation, ghettoization, and discrimination against both national minorities and immigrants has created groups whose status is riven with contradictions and complexities. Moreover, as I discussed in Chapter II, there are some ethnocultural groups, such as the African-Americans, that were never appropriately seen as immigrants or national minorities. There are many such hard cues and grey areas.[45]

By emphasizing the distinction between national minorities and ethnic groups, my aim is not to resolve all these hard cases. I do not think there is any magical formula that will cover them all. Some historic injustices may be intractable, and elude any theoretical solution. However, we can at least be clear about what the relevant interests are. What matters, from a liberal point of view, is that people have access to a societal culture which provides them with meaningful options encompassing the range of human activities. Throughout the world, many minority groups are denied this access. They are caught in a contradictory position, unable either to fully participate in the mainstream of society or to sustain their own distinct societal culture. Insofar as polyethnic rights for immigrants or self-government rights for national minorities help secure access to a societal culture, then they can contribute to individual freedom. Failure to recognize these rights will create new tragic cases of groups which are denied the sort of cultural context of choice that supports individual autonomy.

6. Individuating Cultures
So far I have been taking for granted that there are such things as "separate" and "distinct" cultures, and that it makes sense to ask whether there is one or two or more of them in a particular country. But is this realistic?

Some people deny that it is meaningful to talk about individuating cultures in this way. According to Jeremy Waldron, the project of individuating societal cultures presupposes that cultures are somehow isolated and impervious to external influences. Yet in reality, he notes, there is an enormous amount of interchange between them. Cultures have influenced each other so much, he says, that there is no meaningful way to say where one culture ends and another begins. Indeed, there are no such things as cultures, just innumerable cultural fragments from innumerable cultural sources, without any "structure" connecting them or underlying them.

Waldron accepts that the meaningfulness of options depends on the fact that they have cultural meanings. But he rejects the assumption that the options available to a particular individual must come from a *particular* culture. As he puts it,

> From the fact that each option must have a cultural meaning, it does not follow that there must be one cultural framework in which each available option is assigned a meaning. Meaningful options may come to us as items or fragments from a variety of cultural sources . . . . [The fact] that people need cultural materials does not show that what people need is "a rich and secure cultural structure." It shows the importance of access to a variety of stories and roles; but it does not . . . show the importance of something called membership in a culture. (Waldron 1992a; 783–4)

For example, Waldron notes the influence of the Bible, Roman mythology, and *Grimms' Fairy-Tales* on American culture, and says that these cannot plausibly be seen as part of a single "cultural structure," since they are

> drawn from a variety of disparate cultural sources: from first-century Palestine, from the heritage of Germanic folklore, and from the mythology of the Roman Republic . . . They are familiar to us because of the immense variety of cultural materials, various in their provenance as well as their character, that are in fact available to us. But neither their familiarity nor their availability constitute them as part of a single cultural matrix. Indeed, if we were to insist that they are all part of the same matrix because they are all available to us, we would trivialize the individuation of cultures beyond any sociological interest (1992a: 784–5)

Waldron raises an interesting point. On any liberal view, it is a good thing that cultures learn from each other. Liberals cannot endorse a notion of culture that sees the process of interacting with and learning from other cultures as a threat to "purity" or "integrity," rather than as

an opportunity for enrichment.[46] Liberals want a societal culture that is rich and diverse, and much of the richness of a culture comes from the way it has appropriated the fruits of other cultures. So we do not want to build closed walls around cultures, to cut them off from "the general movement of the world," as John Stuart Mill put it.[47]

According to Waldron, it is inconsistent to desire a richer and more diverse cultural life and yet insist on maintaining distinct cultures. This emphasis on individuating cultures thwarts the process of cultural enrichment and diversification, Waldron claims, since the only non-trivial way of individuating cultures is to define them in terms of a common ethnic source that precludes learning from other cultures. So if we want to increase the range of valuable options available to people, we would be better off abandoning the idea of separate cultures, and instead promoting a *mélange* of cultural meanings from different sources.

However, Waldron's conclusion is, I think, mistaken. It is true that the options available to the members of any modern society come from a variety of ethnic and historical sources. But what makes these options "available," or meaningful, to us? After all, there are limits on the "cultural materials" which people find meaningful. I have argued that options are available to us if they become part of the shared vocabulary of social life—i.e., embodied in the social practices, based on a shared language, that we are exposed to.[48] Indeed, I think Waldron's examples support this view. For surely one of the reasons why *Grimms' Fairy-Tales* are so much a part of our culture is precisely that they have been translated and widely distributed in English. Were *Grimms' Fairy-Tales* only available in the original language, as is the case with the folklore of many other world cultures, they would not be available to us. It is often possible to trace the path by which our culture incorporates the cultural materials of other nations. The works of other cultures may become available to us through translation, or through the influx of immigrants who bring certain cultural narratives with them as they integrate. That we learn in this way from other cultures, or that we borrow words from other languages, does not mean that we do not still belong to separate societal cultures, or speak different languages.

Waldron is worried that the desire of national minorities to maintain their separate cultures requires insulating them from the outside world. For example, he interprets defenders of self-government for indigenous peoples as concerned with preserving the "purity" and "authenticity" of their culture. No doubt this is the motivation of some minority leaders, just as it is the motivation of many majority groups who seek to protect the purity of their culture from external influence (e.g., the Iranian government seeking to avoid Western influence; the French government seeking to avoid foreign "contamination" of their language).

But there is no inherent connection between the desire to maintain a distinct societal culture and the desire for cultural isolation. In many cases, the aim of self-government is to enable smaller nations to interact with larger nations on a more equitable basis. It should be up to each culture to decide when and how they will adopt the achievement of the larger world. It is one thing to learn from the larger world; it is another thing to be swamped by it, and self-government rights may be needed for smaller nations to control the direction and rate of change.

For example, most indigenous peoples favour economic development "provided they can control its pace and enjoy some of its benefits" (Gurr 1993: 300). Indeed, it is often majority cultures which have insisted on the "purity" of minority cultures. For example, some governments have argued that land claims should only be given to indigenous groups which have maintained their "authentic culture." The Brazilian government has tried to reinterpret Indian land rights so that they only apply to "real Indians"—that is, those who have not adopted any of the conveniences or products of the industrialized world. The (intentional) result is that ultimately there will "be virtually no holders of Indian rights and coveted lands would become available" (da Cunha 1992: 284).[49]

This is not how most indigenous peoples themselves understand the function of their national rights; nor is it how they understand the nature of their cultural identity, which is dynamic, not static. While indigenous peoples do not want modernization forced upon them, they demand the right to decide for themselves what aspects of the outside world they will incorporate into their cultures, and many indigenous peoples have moved toward a more urbanized and agricultural lifestyle. And they demand the right to use their traditional resources in the process.

It is natural, and desirable, for cultures to change as a result of the choices of their members. We must, therefore, distinguish the existence of a culture from its "character" at any given moment.[50] The character of a culture can change dramatically, as the Quiet Revolution in Quebec shows. In the space of a decade, French Quebec changed from a religious and rural society to a secular and urban one. Indigenous groups are undergoing similar changes. And of course every nation in Western society has undergone the same transition, although perhaps not as quickly. The process of modernization does not change the fact that these nations still form separate societal cultures, with their own institutions, using their own languages.

It is right and proper that the character of a culture change as a result of the choices of its members. This is indeed why systems of internal restrictions are illegitimate from a liberal standpoint. People should be able to decide what is best from within their own culture, and to integrate into their culture whatever they find admirable in other cultures. This follows from the liberal belief in the fallibility and revisability of our conceptions of the good, which I discussed earlier in this chapter.

But this is different from the culture itself being threatened—that is, for the very survival of the culture as a distinct society to be in jeopardy—as a result of decisions made by people outside the culture. This can happen if the land, language rights, and political institutions of a national minority are taken away. The desire of national minorities to survive as a culturally distinct society is not necessarily a desire for cultural purity, but simply for the right to maintain one's membership in a distinct culture, and to continue developing that culture in the same (impure) way that the members of majority cultures are able to develop theirs. The desire to develop and enrich one's culture is consistent with, and indeed promoted by, interactions with other cultures, so long as this interaction is not conducted in circumstances of serious inequality in power.

So the unavoidable, and indeed desirable, fact of cultural interchange does not undermine the claim that there are distinct societal cultures.

7. Conclusion

In this chapter, I have tried to show that liberals should recognize the importance of people's membership in their own societal culture, because of the role it plays in enabling meaningful individual choice and in supporting self-identity. While the members of a (liberalized) nation no longer share moral values or traditional ways of life, they still have a deep attachment to their own language and culture. Indeed, it is precisely because national identity does not rest on shared values—as Tamir puts it, national identity lies "outside the normative sphere" (Tamir 1993: 90) —that it provides a secure foundation for individual autonomy and self-identity. Cultural membership provides us with an intelligible context of choice, and a secure sense of identity and belonging, that we call upon in confronting questions about personal values and projects. And the fact that national identity does not require shared values also explains why nations are appropriate units for liberal theory—national groupings provide a domain of freedom and equality, and a source of mutual recognition and trust, which can accommodate the inevitable disagreements and dissent about conceptions of the good in modern society.

Insofar as this is so, group-differentiated rights that protect minority cultures can be seen, not only as consistent with liberal values but as actually promoting them. This does not mean that every measure that contributes to the stability of minority cultures is justified. In some cases, measures to protect cultural membership may be unnecessary, or come at too high a price in terms of other liberal goals. If measures to protect minority cultures are either unnecessary or too costly, then a policy of "benign neglect" may be justified in certain circumstances. But I will argue in the next chapter that to insist on benign neglect in all circumstances is neither fair nor even possible, and that certain group-differentiated rights are required by the principles of liberal justice.

Chapter VI Justice and Minority Rights

. . .

1. The Equality Argument

Many defenders of group-specific rights for ethnic and national minorities insist that they are needed to ensure that all citizens are treated with genuine equality. On this view, "the accommodation of differences is the essence of true equality,"[51] and group-specific rights are needed to accommodate our differences. I think this argument is correct, within certain limits.

Proponents of "benign neglect" will respond that individual rights already allow for the accommodation of differences, and that true equality requires equal rights for each individual regardless of race or ethnicity.[52] . . . [T]his assumption that liberal equality precludes group-specific rights is relatively recent, and arose in part as an (over-)generalization of the racial desegregation movement in the United States. It has some superficial plausibility. In many cases, claims for group-specific rights are simply an attempt by one group to dominate and oppress another.

But some minority rights eliminate, rather than create, inequalities. Some groups are unfairly disadvantaged in the cultural market-place, and political recognition and support rectify this disadvantage. I will start with the case of national minorities. The viability of their societal cultures may be undermined by economic and political decisions made by the majority. They could be outbid or outvoted on resources and policies that are crucial to the survival of their societal cultures. The members of majority cultures do not face this problem. Given the importance of cultural membership, this is a significant

inequality which, if not addressed, becomes a serious injustice.

Group-differentiated rights—such as territorial autonomy, veto powers, guaranteed representation in central institutions, land claims, and language rights—can help rectify this disadvantage, by alleviating the vulnerability of minority cultures to majority decisions. These external protections ensure that members of the minority have the same opportunity to live and work in their own culture as members of the majority.

As I discussed in Chapter III, these rights may impose restrictions on the members of the larger society, by making it more costly for them to move into the territory of the minority (e.g., longer residency requirements, fewer government services in their language), or by giving minority members priority in the use of certain land and resources (e.g., indigenous hunting and fishing rights). But the sacrifice required of non-members by the existence of these rights is far less than the sacrifice members would face in the absence of such rights.

Where these rights are recognized, members of the majority who choose to enter the minority's homeland may have to forgo certain benefits they are accustomed to. This is a burden. But without such rights, the members of many minority cultures face the loss of their culture, a loss which we cannot reasonably ask people to accept.

Any plausible theory of justice should recognize the fairness of these external protections for national minorities. They are clearly justified, I believe, within a liberal egalitarian theory, such as Rawls' and Dworkin's, which emphasizes the importance of rectifying unchosen inequalities. Indeed inequalities in cultural membership are just the sort which Rawls says we should be concerned about, since their effects are "profound and pervasive and present from birth" (Rawls 1971: 96; cf. Dworkin 1981).[53]

This equality-based argument will only endorse special rights for national minorities if there is actually a disadvantage with respect to cultural membership, and if the rights actually serve to rectify the disadvantage. Hence the legitimate scope of these rights will vary with the circumstances. In North America, indigenous groups are more vulnerable to majority decisions than the Québécois or Puerto Ricans, and so their external protections will be more extensive. For example, restrictions on the sale of land which are necessary in the context of indigenous peoples are not necessary, and hence not justified, in the case of Quebec or Puerto Rico.[54]

At some point, demands for increased powers or resources will not be necessary to ensure the same opportunity to live and work in one's culture. Instead, there will simply be attempts to gain benefits denied to others, to have more resources to pursue one's way of life than others have. This was clearly the case with apartheid, where whites constituting under 20 per cent of the population controlled 87 per cent of the land mass of the country, and monopolized all the important levers of state power.

One could imagine a point where the amount of land reserved for indigenous peoples would not be necessary to provide reasonable external protections, but rather would simply provide unequal opportunities to them. Justice would then require that the holdings of indigenous peoples be subject to the same redistributive taxation as the wealth of other advantaged groups, so as to assist the less well off in society. In the real world, of course, most indigenous peoples are struggling to maintain the bare minimum of land needed to sustain the viability of their communities. But it is possible that their land holdings could exceed what justice allows.[55]

The legitimacy of certain measures may also depend on their timing. For example, many people have suggested that a new South African constitution should grant a veto power over certain important decisions to some or all of the major national groups. This sort of veto power is a familiar feature of various "consociational democracies" in Europe, and, as I discuss in the next chapter, under certain circumstances it can promote justice. But it would probably be unjust to give privileged groups a veto power before there has been a dramatic redistribution of wealth and opportunities (Adam 1979: 295). A veto power can promote justice if it helps protect a minority from unjust policies that favour the majority; but it is an obstacle to justice if it allows a privileged group the leverage to maintain its unjust advantages.

So the ideal of "benign neglect" is not in fact benign. It ignores the fact that the members of a national minority face a disadvantage which the members of the majority do not face. In any event, the idea that the government could be neutral with respect to ethnic and national groups is patently false. As I noted in Chapter V, one of the most important determinants of whether a culture survives is whether its language is the language of government—i.e., the language of public schooling, courts, legislatures, welfare agencies, health services, etc. When the government decides the language of public schooling, it is providing what is probably the most important form of support needed by societal cultures, since it guarantees the passing on of the language and its associated traditions and conventions to the next generation. Refusing to provide public schooling in a minority language, by contrast, is almost inevitably condemning that language to ever-increasing marginalization.

The government therefore cannot avoid deciding which societal cultures will be supported. And if it

supports the majority culture, by using the majority's language in schools and public agencies, it cannot refuse official recognition to minority languages on the ground that this violates "the separation of state and ethnicity." This shows that the analogy between religion and culture is mistaken. As I noted earlier, many liberals say that just as the state should not recognize, endorse, or support any particular church, so it should not recognize, endorse, or support any particular cultural group or identity (Ch. I, s. 1). But the analogy does not work. It is quite possible for a state not to have an established church. But the state cannot help but give at least partial establishment to a culture when it decides which language is to be used in public schooling, or in the provision of state services. The state can (and should) replace religious oaths in courts with secular oaths, but it cannot replace the use of English in courts with no language.

This is a significant embarrassment for the "benign neglect" view, and it is remarkable how rarely language rights are discussed in contemporary liberal theory.[56] As Brian Weinstein put it, political theorists have had a lot to say about "the language of politics"—that is, the symbols, metaphors, and rhetorical devices of political discourse—but have had virtually nothing to say about "the politics of language"—that is, the decisions about which languages to use in political, legal, and educational forums (Weinstein 1983: 7–13). Yet language rights are a fundamental cause of political conflict, even violence, throughout the world, including Canada, Belgium, Spain, Sri Lanka, the Baltics, Bulgaria, Turkey, and many other countries (Horowitz 1985: 219–24).

. . .

2. The Role of Historical Agreements

A second argument in defence of group-differentiated rights for national minorities is that they are the result of historical agreements, such as the treaty rights of indigenous peoples, or the agreement by which two or more peoples agreed to federate.

There are a variety of such agreements in Western democracies, although their provisions have often been ignored or repudiated. For example, the American government has unilaterally abrogated certain treaties with Indian tribes, and the Canadian government proposed in 1969 to extinguish all of its Indian treaties. The language rights guaranteed to Chicanos in the American southwest under the 1848 Treaty of Guadelupe Hidalgo were rescinded by the anglophone settlers as soon as they formed a majority. The language and land rights guaranteed to the Métis under the Manitoba Act of 1870 suffered the same fate in Canada. Yet many treaties and historical agreements between national groups continue to be recognized, and some have considerable legal force. For example, the 1840 Treaty of Waitangi signed by Maori chiefs and British colonists in New Zealand, declared a "simple nullity" in 1877, has re-emerged as a central legal and political document (Sharp 1990).

The importance of honouring historical agreements is emphasized by proponents of group-differentiated rights, but has had little success convincing opponents. Those people who think that group-differentiated rights are unfair have not been appeased by pointing to agreements that were made by previous generations in different circumstances, often undemocratically and in conditions of substantial inequality in bargaining power. Surely some historical agreements are out of date, while others are patently unfair, signed under duress or ignorance. Why should not governments do what principles of equality require now, rather than what outdated and often unprincipled agreements require?[57]

One answer is to reconsider an underlying assumption of the equality argument. The equality argument assumes that the state must treat its citizens with equal respect. But there is the prior question of determining which citizens should be governed by which states. For example, how did the American government acquire the legitimate authority to govern Puerto Rico or the Navaho? And how did the Canadian government acquire legitimate authority over the Québécois and the Métis?

As I noted in Chapter II, United Nations declarations state that all "peoples" are entitled to "self-determination"—i.e., an independent state. Obviously this principle is not reflected in all existing boundaries, and it would be destabilizing, and indeed impossible, to fulfil. Moreover, not all peoples want their own state. Hence it is not uncommon for two or more peoples to decide to form a federation. And if the two communities are of unequal size, it is not uncommon for the smaller culture to demand various group-differentiated rights as part of the terms of federation. Forming a federation is one way of exercising a people's right of self-determination, and the historical terms of federation reflect the group's judgment about how best to exercise that right.

For example, the group-differentiated rights accorded French Canadians in the original confederation agreement in 1867, and the group-differentiated rights accorded Indians under various treaties, reflect the terms under which these communities joined Canada. It can be argued that these agreements define the terms under which the Canadian state acquired authority over these groups. These communities could have exercised their self-determination in other ways, but chose to join Canada, because they were given certain promises. If the Canadian government reneges on these promises, then

it voids (morally, if not legally) the agreement which made those communities part of Canada.[58] Because these agreements define the terms under which various groups agreed to federate with Canada, the authority of the Canadian state over these groups flows from, but is also limited by, these agreements (Chartrand 1991; 1993: 240–1).

In short, the way in which a national minority was incorporated often gives rise to certain group-differentiated rights. If incorporation occurred through a voluntary federation, certain rights might be spelled out in the terms of federation (e.g., in treaties), and there are legal and moral arguments for respecting these agreements. If incorporation was involuntary (e.g., colonization), then the national minority might have a claim of self-determination under international law which can be exercised by renegotiating the terms of federation so as to make it a more voluntary federation (Macklem 1993; Danley 1991).

This historical argument may justify the same rights as the equality argument. Many of the group-differentiated rights which are the result of historical agreements can be seen as providing the sort of protection required by the equality argument. For example, the right to local autonomy for Indian tribes/bands could be justified on the equality argument, if it helps the larger state show equal concern for the members of Indian communities. Autonomy is also justified on the historical argument, insofar as Indian peoples never gave the federal government jurisdiction over certain issues.

. . .

3. The Value of Cultural Diversity

A third defence of group-differentiated rights for national minorities appeals to the value of cultural diversity. As I have discussed, liberals extol the virtue of having a diversity of lifestyles within a culture, so presumably they also endorse the additional diversity which comes from having two or more cultures in the same country. Surely intercultural diversity contributes to the richness of people's lives, as well as intracultural diversity (Schwartz 1986: ch. 1).

This argument is attractive to many people because it avoids relying solely on the interests of group members, and instead focuses on how the larger society also benefits from group-differentiated rights. As Richard Falk puts it, "societal diversity enhances the quality of life, by enriching our experience, expanding cultural resources." Hence protecting minority cultures "is increasingly recognized to be an expression of overall enlightened self-interest" (Falk 1988: 23). Whereas the first two arguments appeal to the *obligations* of the majority, this third argument appeals to the *interests* of the majority, and defends rights in terms of self-interest not justice.

Cultural diversity is said to be valuable, both in the quasi-aesthetic sense that it creates a more interesting world, and because other cultures contain alternative models of social organization that may be useful in adapting to new circumstances.[59] This latter point is often made with respect to indigenous peoples, whose traditional lifestyles provide a model of a sustainable relationship to the environment. As Western attitudes towards nature are increasingly recognized to be unsustainable and self-destructive, indigenous peoples "may provide models, inspiration, guidance in the essential work of world order redesign" (Falk 1988: 23; cf. Clay 1989: 233; O'Brien 1987: 358).

There is some truth in this argument about the value of cultural diversity. None the less, I think it is a mistake to put much weight on it as a defence of national rights. First, one of the basic reasons for valuing intracultural diversity has less application to intercultural diversity. The value of diversity within a culture is that it creates more options for each individual, and expands her range of choices. But protecting national minorities does not expand the range of choices open to members of the majority in the same way. As I explained last chapter, choosing to leave one's culture is qualitatively different from choosing to move around within one's culture. The former is a difficult and painful prospect for most people, and very few people in the mainstream choose to assimilate into a minority culture. Indeed, measures to protect national minorities may actually reduce diversity within the majority culture, compared with a situation where minorities, unable to maintain their own societal culture, are forced to integrate and add their distinctive contribution to the diversity of the mainstream culture. Having two or more cultures within a state does expand choices for each individual, but only to a limited degree, and it would be implausible to make this the primary justification for minority rights.

There are other aesthetic and educational benefits from cultural diversity, apart from the value of expanding individual choice. But it is not clear that any of these values by themselves can justify minority rights. One problem is that the benefits of diversity to the majority are spread thinly and widely, whereas the costs for particular members of the majority are sometimes quite high. Everyone may benefit, in a diffuse way, from having flourishing minority cultures in Quebec and Puerto Rico. But some members of the majority culture are asked to pay a significant price so that others can gain this diffuse benefit. For example, unilingual anglophones residing in Quebec or Puerto Rico are unlikely to get government

employment or publicly funded education in English—benefits which they would take for granted elsewhere. Similarly, non-Indians residing on Indian lands may be discriminated against in terms of their access to natural resources, or their right to vote in local elections. It is not clear that the diffuse benefits of diversity for society as a whole justify imposing these sorts of sacrifices on particular people. It seems to me that these sacrifices are only consistent with justice if they are needed, not to promote benefits to the members of the majority, but to prevent even greater sacrifices to the members of the national minority.

Moreover, there are many ways of promoting diversity, and it seems likely that protecting national minorities involves more cost to the majority than other possible ways. For example, a society could arguably gain more diversity at less cost by increasing immigration from a variety of countries than by protecting national minorities. The diversity argument cannot explain why we have an obligation to sustain the particular sort of diversity created by the presence of a viable, self-governing national minority.

There is one further problem with the diversity argument. Let us say that the aesthetic or educational value of diversity does justify imposing certain costs on people in the majority culture. Why then does the value of diversity not also justify imposing a duty on the members of the minority to maintain their traditional culture? If the benefits of cultural diversity to the larger society can justify restricting individual liberties or opportunities, why does it matter whether these restrictions are imposed on people inside or outside the group? I noted earlier that a liberal theory of minority rights can accept external protections, but not internal restrictions. It is difficult to see how the diversity argument can make this distinction. Because it appeals to the interests of the larger society, it cannot explain why minorities should be able to decide for themselves whether or how to maintain their culture.

So it seems to me that the diversity argument is insufficient, by itself, to justify the rights of national minorities. Protecting national minorities does provide benefits to the majority, and these are worth pointing out. But these diffuse benefits are better seen as a desirable by-product of national rights, rather than their primary justification. To date, most majority cultures have not seen it in their "enlightened self-interest" to maintain minority cultures. No doubt this is due in part to ethnocentric prejudice, but we must recognize the powerful interests that majority nations often have in rejecting self-government rights for national minorities—e.g., increased access to the minority's land and resources, increased individual mobility, political stability, etc. It is unlikely that majorities will accept national rights solely on the basis of self-interest, without some belief that they have an obligation of justice to accept them. Conversely, it is unlikely that majorities will accept their obligations of justice towards national minorities without a belief that they gain something in the process. The diversity argument works best, therefore, when it is combined with arguments of justice.

The diversity argument is more plausible as a defence of polyethnic rights for ethnic groups. Unlike national self-government, these rights do contribute directly to diversity within the majority culture. Moreover, they do not involve the same sort of restrictions on the mobility or economic opportunities of the majority. Indeed, certain polyethnic policies can be seen as natural extensions of state policies regarding the funding of the arts, museums, educational television, etc.[60] Yet here again the problem arises that there are many ways of promoting diversity. Teaching children to be bilingual promotes diversity, but this cannot explain why we should teach immigrant languages in particular. Hence the diversity argument supplements, but cannot replace, justice arguments based on equality or historical agreement. . . .

Chapter VIII Toleration and Its Limits

1. Liberalism and Tolerance

. . .

Liberalism and toleration are closely related, both historically and conceptually. The development of religious tolerance was one of the historical roots of liberalism. Religious tolerance in the West emerged out of the interminable Wars of Religion, and the recognition by both Catholics and Protestants that a stable constitutional order cannot rest on a shared religious faith. According to Rawls, liberals have simply extended the principle of tolerance to other controversial questions about the "meaning, value and purpose of human life" (Rawls 1987: 4; 1985: 249; 1993a: p. xxviii).

But if liberalism can indeed be seen as an extension of the principle of religious tolerance, it is important to recognize that religious tolerance in the West has taken a very specific form—namely, the idea of individual freedom of conscience. It is now a basic individual right to worship freely, to propagate one's religion, to change one's religion, or indeed to renounce religion altogether. To restrict an individual's exercise of these liberties is seen as a violation of a fundamental human right.

There are other forms of religious toleration which are not liberal. They are based on the idea that each religious group should be free to organize its community as it sees fit, including along non-liberal lines. In the "millet

system" of the Ottoman Empire, for example, Muslims, Christians, and Jews were all recognized as self-governing units (or "millets"), and allowed to impose restrictive religious laws on their own members.

Since the millet system has been cited as an important precedent and model for minority rights (Sigler 1983; Van Dyke 1985: 74–5; Thornberry 1991: 29), it is worth considering in more detail. The Ottoman Turks were Muslims who conquered much of the Middle East, North Africa, Greece, and Eastern Europe during the fourteenth and fifteenth centuries, thereby acquiring many Jewish and Christian subjects. For various theological and strategic reasons, the Ottomans allowed these minorities not only the freedom to practise their religion, but a more general freedom to govern themselves in purely internal matters, with their own legal codes and courts. For about five centuries, between 1456 and the collapse of the Empire in World War I, three non-Muslim minorities had official recognition as self-governing communities—the Greek Orthodox, the Armenian Orthodox, and the Jews—each of which was further subdivided into various local administrative units, usually based on ethnicity and language. Each millet was headed by the relevant church leader (the Chief Rabbi and the two Orthodox Patriarchs).

The legal traditions and practices of each religious group, particularly in matters of family status, were respected and enforced through the Empire. However, while the Christian and Jewish millets were free to run their internal affairs, their relations with the ruling Muslims were tightly regulated. For example, non-Muslims could not proselytize, and they could only build new churches under licence. There were limits on intermarriage, and non-Muslims had to pay special taxes, in lieu of military service. But within these limits, "they were to enjoy complete self-government, obeying their own laws and customs." Their collective freedom of worship was guaranteed, together with their possession of churches and monasteries, and they could run their own schools (see Runciman 1970: 27–35; Braude and Lewis 1982: 1–34).

This system was generally humane, tolerant of group differences, and remarkably stable. As Braude and Lewis note, "For nearly half a millennium, the Ottomans ruled an empire as diverse as any in history. Remarkably, this polyethnic and multireligious society worked. Muslims, Christians, and Jews worshipped and studied side by side, enriching their distinct cultures (Braude and Lewis 1982: 1).

But it was not a liberal society, for it did not recognize any principle of *individual* freedom of conscience. Since each religious community was self-governing, there was no external obstacle to basing this self-government on religious principles, including the enforcement of religious orthodoxy. Hence there was little or no scope for individual dissent within each religious community, and little or no freedom to change one's faith. While the Muslims did not try to suppress the Jews, or vice versa, they did suppress heretics within their own community. Heresy (questioning the orthodox interpretation of Muslim doctrine) and apostasy (abandoning one's religious faith) were punishable crimes within the Muslim community. Restrictions on individual freedom of conscience also existed in the Jewish and Christian communities.

The millet system was, in effect, a federation of theocracies. It was a deeply conservative and patriarchal society, antithetical to the ideals of personal liberty endorsed by liberals from Locke to Kant and Mill. The various millets differed in the extent of their enforcement of religious orthodoxy. There were many periods during the 500-year history of the millets in which liberal reformers within each community pushed for constitutional restrictions on the power of the millet's leaders. And in the second half of the nineteenth century, some of the millets adopted liberal constitutions, in effect convening a religious theocracy into a secular system of liberal-democratic self-government for the various national groups in the Empire. Liberal reformers sought to use the millets as the basis for a system of federal institutions which provided external protections for national minorities—by limiting the power of other groups over them—while still constitutionally respecting the civil and political rights of individual members.[61]

But, in general, there were significant restrictions on the freedom of individuals in the Ottoman Empire to question or reject church doctrine. The Ottomans accepted the principle of religious tolerance, where that is "understood to indicate the willingness of a dominant religion to coexist with others" (Braude and Lewis 1982: 3), but did not accept the quite separate principle of individual freedom of conscience.[62]

The Ottoman millet system is perhaps the most developed model of non-liberal religious tolerance, but variations on that model can be found in many other times and places. And, as I noted in Chapter III, this is the sort of system desired by some non-liberal minorities today. It is often demanded in the name of "tolerance." But it is not the sort of tolerance which liberals historically have endorsed. These groups do not want the state to protect each individual's right to freely express, question, and revise her religious beliefs. On the contrary, this is precisely what they object to. What they want is the power to restrict the religious freedom of their own members.[63]

So it is not enough to say that liberals believe in toleration. The question is, what sort of toleration? Historically, liberals have believed in a very specific notion of tolerance—one which involves freedom of individual conscience, not just collective worship. Liberal tolerance protects the right of individuals to dissent from their group, as well as the right of groups not to be persecuted by the state. It limits the power of illiberal groups to restrict the liberty of their own members, as well as the power of illiberal states to restrict the liberty of collective worship.

This shows, I think, that liberals have historically seen autonomy and tolerance as two sides of the same coin. What distinguishes *liberal* tolerance is precisely its commitment to autonomy—that is, the idea that individuals should be free to assess and potentially revise their existing ends (Mendus 1989: 56). . . .

3. Accommodating Non-liberal Minorities

Why is Rawls so reluctant to endorse autonomy as a general human interest? What is wrong with Mill's "comprehensive" liberalism? The problem, Rawls says, is that not everyone accepts this ideal of autonomy, and so appealing to it in political life would be "sectarian." The autonomy-based defence of individual rights invokes "ideals and values that are not generally . . . shared in a democratic society," and hence "cannot secure sufficient agreement." To base liberalism on a controversial value like autonomy would mean that liberalism "becomes but another sectarian doctrine" (Rawls 1987: 6, 24; 1985: 246).

This is a legitimate point, but Rawls overstates it, and draws the wrong conclusion from it. The idea that we have an interest in being able to assess and revise our inherited conceptions of the good is very widely shared in Western democratic societies.[64] There are some insulated minorities who reject this ideal, including some indigenous groups (the Pueblo), and religious sects (the Amish and Mennonites). These group pose a challenge for liberal democracies, since they often demand internal restrictions that conflict with individual civil rights. We cannot simply ignore this demand, or ignore the fact that they reject the idea of autonomy.

But Rawls' strategy is no solution to the questions raised by the existence of non-liberal minorities. His strategy is to continue to enforce individual rights, but to do so on the basis of a "political" rather than a "comprehensive" liberalism. This obviously does not satisfy the demands of non-liberal minorities. They want internal restrictions that take precedence over individual rights. Rawls' political liberalism is as hostile to that demand as Mill's comprehensive liberalism. The fact that

Rawls' theory is less comprehensive does not make his theory more sympathetic to the demands of non-liberal minorities.

How then should a liberal state treat non-liberal minorities? I have argued that any theory which does not accord substantial civil rights to the members of minority cultures is seriously deficient from a liberal point of view. Some critics claim that I am therefore "drawn down the path of interference" in many existing minority cultures—for example, that I am committed to imposing a liberal regime on the Pueblo Indians, and forcing them to respect the religious liberty of the Protestants on the reservation.[65]

But this conflates two distinct questions: (1) what sorts of minority claims are consistent with liberal principles? (2) should liberals impose their views on minorities which do not accept some or all of these liberal principles? The first is the question of *identifying* a defensible liberal theory of minority rights; the second is the question of *imposing* that liberal theory.

So far, I have focused on the first question—i.e., identifying a defensible liberal conception of minority rights. With respect to that question, I believe that the most defensible liberal theory is based on the value of autonomy, and that any form of group-differentiated rights that restricts the civil rights of group members is therefore inconsistent with liberal principles of freedom and equality. The millet system, or the Pueblo theocracy, are therefore seriously deficient from a liberal point of view.

But that does not mean that liberals can impose their principles on groups that do not share them. This is obvious enough, I think, if the illiberal group is another country. The Saudi Arabian government unjustly denies political rights to women or non-Muslims. But it does not follow that liberals outside Saudi Arabia should forcibly intervene to compel the Saudis to give everyone the vote. Similarly, the German government unjustly denies political rights to the children and grandchildren of Turkish "guest-workers," who were born on German soil and for whom Germany is the only home they know. But it does not follow that liberals outside Germany should use force to compel Germany to change its citizenship laws.

In these cases, the initial moral judgment is clear enough. From a liberal point of view, someone's rights are being unjustly denied by their own government. But what is not clear is the proper remedy—that is, what third party (if any) has the authority to intervene in order to force the government to respect those rights?

The same question arises when the illiberal group is a self-governing national minority within a single country. For example, the Pueblo tribal council violates the rights of its members by limiting freedom of conscience, and by employing sexually discriminatory membership rules.[66] But what third party (if any) has the authority to intervene forcibly to compel the Pueblo council to respect those rights?

Liberal principles tell us that individuals have certain claims which their government must respect, such as individual freedom of conscience. But having identified those claims, we now face the very different question of imposing liberalism. If a particular government fails to respect those claims, who has the authority to step in and force compliance? (Note that by "imposing" liberalism, I am referring to forcible intervention by a third party to compel respect for liberal rights. Non-coercive intervention by third parties is a different matter, which I discuss below.)

The attitude of liberals toward imposing liberalism has changed over the years. In the international context, liberals have become increasingly skeptical about using force to compel foreign states to obey liberal principles. Many nineteenth-century liberals, including John Stuart Mill, thought that liberal states were justified in colonizing foreign countries in order to teach them liberal principles. Contemporary liberals, however, have generally abandoned this doctrine as both imprudent and illegitimate, and sought instead to promote liberal values through education, persuasion, and financial incentives.[67]

In the case of national minorities, however, liberals have been much more willing to endorse coercive third-party intervention. For example, many American liberals assume that the American Supreme Court has the legitimate authority to overturn any decisions of the Pueblo tribal council which violate individual rights. American liberals often assume that to have a right means not only that legislators should respect one's claim when passing legislation, but also that there should be some system of judicial review to make sure that the legislature respects one's claim. Moreover, this judicial review should occur at a country-wide level. That is, in addition to the various state and tribal courts which review the laws of state and tribal governments, there should also be a Supreme Court to which all governments within the country are ultimately answerable. Many American liberals often talk as if it is part of the very meaning of "rights" that there should be a single court in each country with the authority to review the decisions of all governments within that country, to ensure that they respect liberal rights.

This is a very particularistic understanding of rights. In some liberal countries (e.g., Britain), there is a strong tradition of respecting individual rights, but there is no constitutional bill of rights, and no basis for courts to overturn parliamentary decisions which violate individual rights. (The same was true in Canada until 1982.) In other countries, there is judicial review, but it is decentralized—that is, political subunits have their own systems of judicial review, but there is no single constitutional bill of rights, and no single court, to which all levels of government are answerable. Indeed, this was true in the United States for a considerable period of time. Until the passage of the Fourteenth Amendment, state legislatures were answerable to state courts for the way they respected state constitutions, but were not answerable to the federal Supreme Court for respecting the federal Bill of Rights.

It is easy to see why American liberals are committed to giving the Supreme Court authority over the actions of state governments. Historically, this sort of federal judicial review, backed up by federal troops, was required to overturn the racist legislation of Southern states, which state courts had upheld. Given the central role federal courts have played in the struggle against racism, American liberals have developed a deep commitment to the principle of centralized judicial review, according to which a single body should have the authority to review and overturn the actions of all levels of government within each country, on the basis of a single bill of rights.

But should the same sort of centralized judicial review which applies to state governments also apply to self-governing national minorities, such as Indian tribal governments or the Commonwealth of Puerto Rico? Like state governments, tribal governments were not historically subject to the federal Bill of Rights. But many liberals have sought to change this, and so passed the 1968 Indian Civil Rights Act, which subjects Indian tribal governments to most aspects of the federal Bill of Rights. But even here, tribal governments are only answerable to tribal courts, not (except under special circumstances) to the federal courts. The Commonwealth of Puerto Rico has also become subject in recent years to the federal Bill of Rights, and to judicial review by federal courts, although how and why this occurred is far from clear.[68]

Contemporary liberals, then, have become more reluctant to impose liberalism on foreign countries, but more willing to impose liberalism on national minorities. This, I think, is inconsistent. Many of the reasons why we should be reluctant to impose liberalism on other countries are also reasons to be skeptical of imposing liberalism on national minorities within a country. Both foreign states and national minorities form distinct political communities, with their own claims to self-government. Attempts to impose liberal principles by force are often perceived, in both cases, as a form of aggression or paternalistic colonialism. And, as a result, these attempts often backfire. The plight of many former colonies in Africa shows that liberal institutions are likely to be unstable and transient when they have arisen as a result of external imposition, rather than internal political reform. In the end, liberal institutions can only really work if liberal beliefs lave been internalized by the members of the self-governing society, be it an independent country or a national minority.[69]

There are, of course, important differences between foreign states and national minorities. Yet in both cases I believe there is relatively little scope for legitimate coercive interference. Relations between majority and minority nations in a multination state should be determined by peaceful negotiation, not force (as with international relations). This means searching for some basis of agreement. The most secure basis would be agreement on fundamental principles. But if two national groups do not share basic principles, and cannot be persuaded to adopt the other's principles, they will have to rely on some other basis of accommodation, such as a *modus vivendi*.

The resulting agreement may well involve exempting the national minority from federal bills of rights and judicial review. And, as I have noted, contemporary liberal societies have in fact provided such exemptions for some national minorities. Moreover, these exemptions are often spelled out in the historical terms of federation by which a national minority entered the larger state. In cases where the national minority is illiberal, this means that the majority will be unable to prevent the violation of individual rights within the minority community. Liberals in the majority group have to learn to live with this, just as they must live with illiberal laws in other countries.

This does not mean that liberals should stand by and do nothing. A national minority which rules in an illiberal way acts unjustly. Liberals have a right, and a responsibility, to speak out against such injustice. Hence liberal reformers inside the culture should seek to promote their liberal principles, through reason or example, and liberals outside should lend their support to any efforts the group makes to liberalize their culture. Since the most enduring forms of liberalization are those that result from internal reform, the primary focus for liberals outside the group should be to provide this sort of support.

Moreover, there is an important difference between coercively imposing liberalism and offering various incentives for liberal reforms. Again, this is clear in the international context. For example, the desire of former Communist countries to enter the EC has provided leverage for Western democracies to push for liberal reforms in Eastern Europe. Membership in the EC is a powerful, but non-coercive, incentive for liberal reform. Similarly, many people thought that the negotiations over the North American Free Trade Agreement provided an opportunity to pressure the Mexican government into improving its human rights record. The Mexican desire for a continental free-trade agreement provided the United States and Canada with some leverage to push for liberal reforms within Mexico. Obviously, there are many analogous opportunities for a majority nation to encourage national minorities, in a non-coercive way, to liberalize their internal constitutions. Of course there are limits to the appropriate forms of pressure. For example, refusing to extend trade privileges is one thing, imposing a total embargo or blockade is quite another. The line between incentives and coercion is not a sharp one, and where exactly to draw it is a much-debated point in the international context (see Damrosch 1989).

Finally, liberals can push for the development and strengthening of international mechanisms for protecting human rights. Many Indian tribes have expressed a willingness to abide by international declarations of human rights, and to answer to international tribunals for complaints of rights violations within their community. Indeed, they have shown greater willingness to accept this kind of international review than many majority nations, which jealously guard their sovereignty in domestic affairs. Most Indian tribes do not oppose all forms of external review. What they object to is being subject to the constitution of their conquerors, which they had no role in drafting, and being answerable to federal courts, composed solely of non-Indian justices.

This shows, I think, that the standard assumption of American liberals that there must be one court within each country which is the ultimate defender of individual rights seems doubly mistaken, at least in the case of multination states. History has shown the value of holding governments accountable for respecting human rights. But in multination states, the appropriate forums for reviewing the actions of self-governing national minorities may skip the federal level, as it were. Many national minorities would endorse a system in which the decisions of self-governing national minorities are reviewed in the first instance by their own courts, and then by an international court. Federal courts, dominated by the majority nation, would have little or no authority to review and overturn these decisions.

These international mechanisms could arise at the regional as well as global level. For example, European countries have agreed to establish their own multilateral human rights tribunals. Perhaps the American government and Indian tribes could agree to establish a similar bilateral human rights tribunal, on which both sides are fairly represented. There are many ways to strengthen mechanisms for respecting individual rights in a consensual way, without simply imposing liberal values on national minorities.

This is not to say that federal intervention to protect liberal rights is never justified. Obviously intervention is justified in the case of gross and systematic violation of human rights, such as slavery or genocide or mass torture and expulsions, just as these are grounds for intervening in foreign countries. The exact point at which intervention in the internal affairs of a national minority is warranted is unclear, just as it is in the international context. I think a number of factors are potentially relevant here, including the severity of rights violations within the minority community, the degree of consensus within the community on the legitimacy of restricting individual rights, the ability of dissenting group members to leave the community if they so desire, and the existence of historical agreements with the national minority. For example, whether it is justified to intervene in the case of an Indian tribe that restricts freedom of conscience surely depends on whether it is governed by a tyrannical dictator who lacks popular support and prevents people leaving the community, or whether the tribal government has a broad base of support and religious dissidents are free to leave.[70]

Cases involving newly arriving immigrant groups are very different. In these cases, it is more legitimate to compel respect for liberal principles, for reasons discussed in Chapter V. I do not think it is wrong for liberal states to insist that immigration entails accepting the legitimacy of state enforcement of liberal principles so long as immigrants know this in advance, and none the less voluntarily choose to come.

A more complicated case involves long-standing ethnic groups or religious sects who have been allowed to maintain certain illiberal institutions for many years, even many generations. This would include the Amish and Mennonites who emigrated to the United States and Canada early in this century, as well as the Hasidic Jews in New York. For various reasons, when these immigrant groups arrived, they were given exemptions from the usual requirements regarding integration, and were allowed to maintain certain internal restrictions. We may now regret these historical exemptions, but they were granted, and we cannot entirely dismiss them, unless they are unconscionably unjust (e.g., if they guaranteed a minority the right to maintain slaves). Relying on certain tacit or explicit assurances about their right to maintain separate institutions, these groups have now built and maintained self-contained enclaves that depend on certain internal restrictions. Had those assurances not been given, these groups might well have emigrated to some other country. As I noted in Chapter VI, it is not clear how much weight, morally speaking, should be given to these sorts of historical arguments, but it seems that these groups do have a stronger claim to maintain internal restrictions than newly arriving immigrants.[71]

4. Conclusion

The legitimacy of imposing liberal principles on illiberal national groups depends on a number of factors. The question of how two cultures, or two countries, should resolve differences of fundamental principle is a very complicated one which would require a book of its own. My project in this book is primarily to figure out what liberalism's fundamental principles are. Most contemporary liberal theorists have argued that the citizens of a liberal society, motivated by liberal principles of justice, would not accord political significance to their cultural membership. I have argued that this is a mistake, and that liberal principles of justice are consistent with, and indeed require, certain forms of special status for national minorities. Of course, the members of some minority cultures reject liberalism. In these cases, members of the more liberal majority will have to sit down with the members of the national minority, and find a way of living together. Liberals have no automatic right to impose their views on non-liberal national minorities. But they do have the right, and indeed the responsibility, to identify what those views actually are. Relations between national groups should be determined by dialogue. But if liberal theory is to contribute anything to that dialogue, it is surely by spelling out the implications of the liberal principles of freedom and equality. That is not the first step down the path of interference. Rather, it is the first step in starting a dialogue.

It is important to put this issue in perspective. The question of how to deal with illiberal cultures does not just arise in the context of minority cultures. While there are some illiberal national minorities, there are also illiberal majority cultures and illiberal homogeneous nation-states. (Indeed, some national minorities in Africa and Eastern Europe are much more liberal than the majority cultures.) In all of these cases, liberals both within and outside the illiberal group face the question of what actions are legitimate in promoting their liberal ideals. Whatever answers are appropriate in these other cases are likely to be appropriate for minority cultures.

Moreover, it is important not to prejudge the illiberal nature of a particular minority culture.[72] The liberality of a culture is a matter of degree. As I noted in Chapter III, all cultures have illiberal strands, just as few cultures are entirely repressive of individual liberty. To talk as if the world was divided into completely liberal societies on the one hand, and completely illiberal ones on the other, inhibits a constructive dialogue between cultures (Parekh 1994; Modood 1993).

Even when minority leaders express a hostility to liberalism, it is important to remember the political context. These leaders may simply be responding to the fact that liberals have been resisting the minority's claims for self-government, or other external protections. If we examine the way that minority cultures actually treat their members, in terms of respect for civil liberties and tolerance of dissent, they are often just as liberal as the majority culture.

For example, when some indigenous leaders say that they value community rights above individual rights, what they often mean is that they attach profound importance to their recognition as a distinct culture and society with inherent rights of self-government.[73] They want to be recognized as a distinct national community, and, in that sense, demand a "community right," not just individual rights. They are not necessarily saying that they attach little or no weight to individual liberty within their community. Indeed, many observers have noted that indigenous cultures are often quite individualistic in their internal organization. Many indigenous cultures display a profound antipathy to the idea that one person can be another's master (e.g., de Onis 1992: 39). The claim that indigenous peoples favour collective rights over individual rights is often a claim about the importance of indigenous self-government *vis-à-vis* the larger society, not a claim about how that self-government should be exercised *vis-à-vis* community members.

I do not mean to deny the extent of illiberal practices in some cultures. This is a profound challenge to a liberal theory of minority rights. But the challenge is not unique to minority cultures. It also arises for liberals in responding to illiberal practices in majority cultures and ethnically homogeneous nation-states. Liberals need to think more deeply about how to promote the liberalization of societal cultures, and about the role of coercive and non-coercive third-party intervention in that process. Dismissing the idea of self-government for national minorities will not make that problem go away.

Works Cited

Ackerman, Bruce (1980), *Social Justice in the Liberal State* (Yale University Press, New Haven, Conn.).

Adam, Heribert (1979), "The Failure of Political Liberalism," in H. Adam and H. Giliomee (eds.), *Ethnic Power Mobilized: Can South Africa Change?* (Yale University Press, New Haven, Conn.), 258–85.

Ajzenstat, Janet (1984), "Liberalism and Assimilation: Lord Durham Revisited," in S. Brooks (ed.), *Political Thought in Canada: Contemporary Perspectives* (Irwin, Toronto), 239–57.

—— (1988), *The Political Thought of Lord Durham* (McGill-Queen's University Press, Kingston).

Aleinikoff, Alexander (1994), "Puerto Rico and the Constitution: Conundrums and Prospects," *Constitutional Commentary*, 11: 15–43.

Anderson, Benedict (1983), *Imagined Communities: Reflection on the Origin and Spread of Nationalism* (New Left Books, London).

Asch, Michael (1984), *Home and Native Land: Aboriginal Rights and the Canadian Constitution* (Methuen, Toronto).

Bader, Viet (1995), "Citizenship and Exclusion: Radical Democracy, Community and Justice," *Political Theory*, 23/2211–46.

Ball, Milner (1989), "Stories of Origin and Constitutional Possibilities," *Michigan Law Review*, 87: 2280–2319.

Barker, Ernest (1948), *National Character and the Factors in Its Formation* (Methuen, London).

Barry, Brain (1991), "Self-Government Revisited," in *Democracy and Power: Essays in Political Theory*, (Oxford University Press, Oxford), 156–86.

Barsh, Russel, and Henderson, J. (1980), *The Road: Indian Tribes and Political Liberty* (University of California Press, Berkeley, Calif.).

—— (1982), "Aboriginal Rights, Treaty Rights and Human Rights: Indian Tribes and Constitutional Renewal," *Journal of Canadian Studies*, 17: 55–81.

Bell, Daniel (1993), *Communitarianism and Its Critics* (Oxford University Press, Oxford).

Binder, Guyora (1993), "The Case for Self-Determination," *Stanford Journal of International Law*, 29: 223–70.

Black, Samuel (1992), "Revisionist Liberalism and the Decline of Culture," *Ethics*, 102/2: 244–67.

Bloed, Arie (1994), "The CSCE and the Protection of National Minorities," *CSCE ODHIR Bulletin*, 1/3: 1–4.

Braude, Benjamin, and Lewis, Bernard (1982), "Introduction," in B. Braude and B. Lewis (eds.), *Christians and Jews in Ottoman Empire: The Functioning of a Plural Society* (Holmes & Meir, New York), 1–34.

Brilmayer, Lea (1992), "Groups, Histories, and Inter-national Law," *Cornell International Law Journal*, 25/3: 555–63.

Brotz, H. (1980), "Multiculturalism in Canada: A Muddle," *Canadian Public Policy*, 6/1: 41–6.

Buchanan, Alan (1975), "Revisability and Rational Choice," *Canadian Journal of Philosophy*, 5: 395–408.

—— (1989), "Assessing the Communitarian Critique of Liberalism," *Ethics*, 99/4: 852–82.

—— (1991), *Secession: The Legitimacy of Political Divorce* (Westview Press, Boulder, Col.).

Cairns, Alan (1991), "Constitutional Change and the Three Equalities," in Ronald Watts and Douglas Brown (eds.), *Options for a New Canada* (University of Toronto Press, Toronto), 77–110.

Caney, Simon (1991), "Consequentialist Defenses of Liberal Neutrality," *Philosophical Quarterly*, 41/165: 457–77.

Capotorti, F. (1979), *Study on the Rights of Persons Belonging to Ethnic, Religious and Linguistic Minorities.* UN Doc. E/CN. 4/Sub.2/384 Rev. 1 (United Nations, New York).

Carens, Joseph (1987), "Aliens and Citizens: The Case for Open Borders," *Review of Politics*, 49/3: 251–73.

Cassidy, Frank, and Bish, Robert (1989), *Indian Government: Its Meaning in Practice* (Institute for Research on Public Policy, Halifax).

Castles, Stephen, and Miller, Mark (1993), *The Age of Migration: International Population Movements in the Modern Age* (Macmillan, Basingstoke).

Chaplin, Jonathan (1993), "How Much Cultural and Religious Pluralism Can Liberalism Tolerate?" in John Horton (ed.), *Liberalism, Multiculturalism and Toleration* (St Martin's Press, New York), 32–49.

Chartrand, Paul (1991), *Manitoba's Métis Settlement Scheme of 1870* (University of Saskatchewan Native Law Centre, Saskatoon).

—— (1993), "Aboriginal Self-Government: The Two Sides of Legitimacy," in Susan Phillips (ed.) *How Ottawa Spends: 1993-1994* (Carleton University Press, Ottawa), 231–56.

Clarke, F. (1934), *Quebec and South Africa: A Study in Cultural Adjustment* (Oxford University Press, London).

Claude, Inis (1955), *National Minorities: An International Problem* (Harvard University Press, Cambridge, Mass.).

Clay, Jason (1989), "Epilogue: The Ethnic Future of Nations," *Third World Quarterly*, 11/4: 223–33.

Clinton, Robert (1990), "The Rights of Indigenous Peoples as Collective Group Rights," *Arizona Law Review*, 32/4: 739–47.

Connor, Walker (1972), "Nation-Building or Nation-Destroying," *World Politics*, 24: 319–55.

Copp, David (1992), "The Concept of a Society," *Dialogue*, 31/2: 183–212.

Crawford, James (1988), "The Rights of Peoples," in James Crawford (ed.), *The Rights of Peoples* (Oxford University Press, Oxford), 159–75.

Crowe, Keith (1974), *A History of the Original Peoples of Northern Canada* (McGill-Queen's University Press, Montreal).

da Cunha, Manuela (1992), "Custom Is Not a Thing, It Is a Path: Reflections on the Brazilian Indian Case," in Abdullah Ahmed An-Na'aim (ed.), *Human Rights in Cross-Cultural Perspective* (University of Pennsylvania Press, Philadelphia).

Damrosch, Lori (1989), "Politics across Borders: Nonintervention and Nonforcible Influence over Domestic Affairs," *American Journal of International Law*, 83/1: 1–50.

Danley, John (1991), "Liberalism, Aboriginal Rights and Cultural Minorities," *Philosophy and Public Affairs*, 20/2: 168–85.

Davidson, Chandler (1992), "The Voting Rights Act: A Brief History," in B. Grofman and C. Davidson (eds.), *Controversies in Minority Voting: The Voting Rights Act in Perspective* (Brookings Institute, Washington, DC), 7–51.

Deganaar, J. (1987), "Nationalism, Liberalism, and Pluralism," in J. Butler (ed.), *Democratic Liberalism in South Africa: Its History and Prospect* (Wesleyan University Press, Middletown, Conn.), 236–398.

de Onis, Juan (1992), *The Green Cathedral: Sustainable Development of Amazonia* (Oxford University Press, New York).

Dion, Stéphane (1991), "Le Nationalisme dans la convergence culturelle," in R. Hudon and R. Pelletier (eds.), *L'Engagement intellectual: mélanges en l'honneur de Léon Dion* (Les Presses de l'Université Laval, Sainte-Foy), 291–311.

—— (1992), "Explaining Quebec Nationalism," in R. Kent Weaver (ed.), *The Collapse of Canada?* (Brookings Institute, Washington, DC).

Duchacek, I.D. (1977), "Federalist Responses to Ethnic Demands: An Overview," in Daniel Elazar (ed.), *Federalism and Political Integration* (Turtledove Publishing, Ramat Gan), 59–71.

Dworkin, Ronald (1981), "What Is Equality? Part II: Equality of Resources," *Philosophy and Public Affairs*, 10/4: 283–345.

—— (1983), "In Defense of Equality," *Social Philosophy and Policy*, 1/1: 24–40.

—— (1985), *A Matter of Principle* (Harvard University Press, London).

—— (1989), "Liberal Community," *California Law Review*, 77/3: 479–504.

—— (1990), "Foundations of Liberal Equality," in Grethe Petersen (ed.), *The Tanner Lectures on Human Values*, 11 (University of Utah Press, Salt Lake City): 1–119.

Edwards, John (1985), *Language, Society and Identity* (Blackwell, Oxford).

Elazar, Daniel (1987), *Exploring Federalism* (University of Alabama, Tuscaloosa, Ala.).

Elkins, David (1992), *Where Should the Majority Rule? Reflections on Non-territorial Provinces and Other Constitutional Proposals* (Centre for Constitutional Studies, University of Alberta, Edmonton).

Elton, G.R. (1984), "Introduction," in W.J. Shiels (ed.), *Persecution and Toleration*, Studies in Church History 21 (published for the Ecclesiastical History Society by Basil Blackwell, Oxford), pp. xiii–xv.

Falk, Richard (1988), "The Rights of Peoples (in Particular Indigenous Peoples)," in James Crawford (ed.), *The Rights of Peoples* (Oxford University Press, Oxford), 17–37.

Fishman, Joshua (1989), *Language and Ethnicity in Minority Sociolinguistic Perspective* (Multilingual Matters Ltd., Clevedon).

Fleras, Augie, and Elliot, Jean Leonard (1992), *The Nations Within: Aboriginal–State Relations in Canada, the United States and New Zealand* (Oxford University Press, Toronto).

Gagnon, Alain-G (1993), "The Political Uses of Federalism," in Michael Burgess and Alain-G. Gagnon (eds.), *Comparative Federalism and Federation: Competing Traditions and Future Directions* (University of Toronto Press, Toronto), 15–44.

—— and Garcea, Jospeh (1988), "Quebec and the Pursuit of Special Status," in R. D. Olling and M. W. Westmacott (eds.), *Perspectives on Canadian Federalism* (Prentice-Hall, Scarborough), 304–25.

Galeotti, Anna (1993), "Citizenship and Equality: The Place for Toleration," *Political Theory*, 21/4: 585–605.

Galston, William (1991), *Liberal Purposes: Good, Virtues, and Duties in the Liberal State* (Cambridge University Press, Cambridge).

—— (1995), "Two Concepts of Liberalism," forthcoming in *Ethics*, 105/3.

Gans, Herbert (1979), "Symbolic Ethnicity: The Future of Ethnic Groups and Cultures in America," *Ethnic and Racial Studies*, 2/1: 1–20.

Gellner, Ernest (1983), *Nations and Nationalism* (Blackwell, Oxford).

Glazer, Nathan (1975), *Affirmative Discrimination: Ethnic Inequality and Public Policy* (Basic Books, New York).

—— (1978), "Individual Rights against Group Rights," in A. Tay and E. Kamenka (eds.), *Human Rights* (Edward Arnold, London), 87–103.

—— (1983), *Ethnic Dilemmas: 1964–1982* (Harvard University Press, Cambridge, Mass.).

Gordon, Milton (1975), "Toward a General Theory of Racial and Ethnic Group Relations," in N. Glazer and D. Moynihan (eds.), *Ethnicity, Theory and Experience* (Harvard University Press, Cambridge, Mass.).

—— (1978), *Human Nature, Class, and Ethnicity* (Oxford University Press, New York).

—— (1981), "Models of Pluralism: The New American Dilemma," *Annals of the Academy of Political and Social Science*, 454: 178–88.

Government of Canada (1991*a*), *Shaping Canada's Future Together: Proposals* (Supply and Services, Ottawa).

—— (1991*b*), *Shared Values: The Canadian Identity* (Supply and Services, Ottawa).

Grand Council of the Crees of Quebec (1992), *Status and Rights of the James Bay Crees in the Context of Quebec's Succession from Canada* (submission to the United Nations Commission on Human Rights, 48th Session).

Green, Leslie (1994), "Internal Minorities and Their Rights," in Judith Baker (ed.), *Group Rights* (University of Toronto Press, Toronto), 100–117.

Gurr, Ted (1993), *Minorities at Risk: A Global View of Ethnopolitical Conflict* (Institute of Peace Press, Washington, DC).

Gutmann, Amy (1993), "The Challenge of Multiculturalism to Political Ethics," *Philosophy and Public Affairs*, 22/3: 171–206.

Hannum, Hurst (1990), *Autonomy, Sovereignty, and Self-Determination: The Adjudication of Conflicting Rights* (University of Pennsylvania Press, Philadelphia).

—— (ed.) (1993), *Basic Documents on Autonomy and Minority Rights* (Martinus Nijhoff, Boston).

Higham, John (1976), *Send These to Me* (Atheneum, New York).

Hindess, Barry (1993), "Multiculturalism and Citizenship," in Chandran Kukathas (ed.), *Multicultural Citizens: The Philosophy and Politics of Identity* (Centre for Independent Studies, St Leonards), 33–45.

Horowitz, D. L. (1985), *Ethnic Groups in Conflict* (University of California Press, Berkeley, Calif.).

Howse, Robert, and Knop, Karen (1993), "Federalism, Secession, and the Limits of Ethnic Accommodation: A Canadian Perspective," *New Europe Law Review*, 1/2: 269–320.

Hudson, James (1986), "The Philosophy of Immigration," *Journal of Libertarian Studies*, 8/1: 51–62.

Hurka, Thomas (1994), "Indirect Perfectionism: Kymlicka on Liberal Neutrality," *Journal of Political Philosophy*, forthcoming.

Ignatieff, Michael (1993), *Blood and Belonging: Journey into the New Nationalism* (Farrar, Straus & Giroux, New York).

Janzen, William (1990), *Limits of Liberty: The Experiences of Mennonite, Hutterite, and Doukhobour Communities in Canada* (University of Toronto Press, Toronto).

Johnson, Gerald (1973), *Our English Heritage* (Greenwood Press, Westport, Conn.).

Kallen, Evelyn (1987), "Ethnicity and Collective Rights in Canada," in L. Driedger (ed.), *Ethnic Canada* (Copp Clark, Toronto), 318–36.

Karmis, Dimitrios (1993), "Cultures autochtones et libéralisme au Canada: les vertus médiatrices du communautarisme liberal de Charles Taylor," *Canadian Journal of Political Science*, 26/1: 69–96.

Karpat, Kemal (1982), "Millets and Nationality: The Roots of the Incongruity of Nation and State in the Post-Ottoman Era," in Braude and Lewis (1982), 141–69.

King, Timothy (1983), "Immigration from Developing Countries: Some Philosophical Issues," *Ethics*, 93/3: 525–36.

Knopff, Rainer (1979), "Language and Culture in the Canadian Debate: The Battle of the White Papers," *Canadian Review of Studies in Nationalism*, 6/1 66–82.

—— (1982), "Liberal Democracy and the Challenge of Nationalism in Canadian Politics," *Canadian Review of Studies in Nationalism*, 9/1: 23–39.

Kukathas, Chandran (1991), *The Fraternal Conceit: Individualist versus Collectivist Ideas of Community* (Centre for Independent Studies, St. Leonard's).

—— (1992*a*), "Are There Any Cultural Rights?" *Political Theory*, 20/1: 105–39.

Kymlicka, Will (1989*a*), *Liberalism, Community, and Culture* (Oxford University Press, Oxford).

—— (1989*b*), "Liberal Individualism and Liberal Neutrality," *Ethics*, 99/4; 883–905.

—— (1990), *Contemporary Political Philosophy: An Introduction* (Oxford University Press, Oxford).

—— (1992*a*), "The Rights of Minority Cultures: Reply to Kukathas," *Political Theory*, 20/1: 140–6.

—— (1995b), "Dworkin on Freedom and Culture," in Justine Burley (ed.), *Reading Dworkin* (Blackwell, Oxford), forthcoming.

—— (1995c), "Concepts of Community and Social Justice," in Fen Hampson and Judith Reppy (eds.), *Global Environmental change and Social Justice*, forthcoming.

Laczko, Leslie (1994), "Canada's Pluralism in Comparative Perspective," *Ethnic and Racial Studies*, 17/1: 20–41.

Laforest, Guy (1991), "Libéralisme et nationalisme au Canada à l'heure de l'accord du Lac Meech," *Carrefour*, 13/2: 68–90.

Laponce, J. A. (1987), *Languages and Their Territories* (University of Toronto Press, Toronto).

Larmore, Charles (1987), *Patterns of Moral Complexity* (Cambridge University Press, Cambridge).

Lenihan, Donald (1991), "Liberalism and the Problem of Cultural Membership," *Canadian Journal of Law and Jurisprudence*, 4/2: 401–19.

Lerner, Natan (1991), *Group Rights and Discrimination in International Law* (Martinus Nijhoff, Dordrecht).

Long, J. A. (1991), "Federalism and Ethnic Self-Determination: Native Indians in Canada," *Journal of Commonwealth and Comparative Politics*, 29/2: 192–211.

Lyons, David (1981), "The New Indian Claims and Original Rights to Land," in J. Paul (ed.), *Reading Nozick: Essays on* Anarchy, State and Utopia (Rowman & Littlefield, Totowa, NJ).

MacDonald, Ian (1989), "Group Rights," *Philosophical Papers*, 28/2: 117–36.

—— (1992), "Liberalism, Community, and Culture," *University of Toronto Law Journal*, 42: 113–31.

McDonald, Michael (1991b), "Should Communities Have Rights? Reflections on Liberal Individualism," *Canadian Journal of Law and Jurisprudence*, 4/2: 217–37.

—— (1993), "Liberalism, Community, and Culture," *University of Toronto Law Journal*, 42: 113–31.

Macedo, Stephen (1995), "Liberal Civic Education and Religious Fundamentalism," forthcoming in *Ethics*, 105/3.

MacIntyre, Alasdair (1981), *After Virtue: A Study in Moral Theory* (Duckworth, London).

Macklem, Patrick (1993), "Distributing Sovereignty: Indian Nations and Equality of Peoples," *Stanford Law Review*, 45/5: 1311–67.

McNeill, William (1986), *Polyethnicity and National Unity in World History* (University of Toronto Press, Toronto).

McRae, Kenneth (1979), "The Plural Society and the Western Political Tradition," *Canadian Journal of Political Science*, 12/4: 675–88.

Majone, Giandomenico (1990), "Preservation of Cultural Diversity in a Federal System: The Role of the Regions," in Mark Tushnet (ed.), *Comparative Constitutional Federalism* (Greenwood Press, New York), 67–76.

Makinson, David (1988), "Rights of Peoples: Point of View of a Logician," in James Crawford (ed.), *The Rights of Peoples* (Oxford University Press, Oxford), 69–92.

Maré, Gerhard (1992), *Brothers Born of Warrior Blood: Politics and Ethnicity and South Africa* (Raven Press, Johannesburg).

Margalit, Avishai, and Halbertal, Moshe (1994), "Liberalism and the Right to Culture," *Social Research*, 61/3: 491–510.

—— and Raz, Joseph (1990), "National Self-Determination," *Journal of Philosophy*, 87/9: 439–61.

Mason, Andrew (1990), "Autonomy, Liberalism and State Neutrality," *Philosophical Quarterly*, 40/160: 433–52.

—— (1993), "Liberalism and the Value of Community," *Canadian Journal of Philosophy*, 23/2: 215–40.

Mendus, Susan (1989), *Toleration and the Limits of Liberalism* (Humanities Press, Atlantic Highlands, NJ).

Mill, J. S. (1972), *Considerations on Representative Government*, in *Utilitarianism, Liberty, Representative Government*, ed. H. Acton (J. M. Dent, London).

—— (1982), *On Liberty*, ed. G. Himmelfarb (Penguin, Harmondsworth).

Miller, David (1988–9), "In What Sense Must Socialism Be Communitarian?" *Social Philosophy and Policy*, 6/2: 51–73.

—— (1993), "In Defense of Nationality," *Journal of Applied Philosophy*, 10/1: 3–16.

Mills, Richard (1974), *The Colonization of Australia 1829–42: The Wakefield Experiment in Empire Building* (Sydney University Press, Sydney).

Minow, Martha (1990b), "Putting up and Putting down: Tolerance Reconsidered," in Mark Tushnet (ed.), *Comparative Constitutional Federalism* (Greenwood Press, New York), 77–113.

Modood, Tariq (1992), *Not Easy Being British: Colour, Culture and Citizenship* (Trentham Books, Stoke-on-Trent).

—— (1993), "Kymlicka on British Muslims" and "A Rejoinder," *Analyse und Kritik*, 15/1: 87–91; 97–9.

Moon, Donald (1993), *Constructing Community: Moral Pluralism and Tragic Conflicts* (Princeton University Press, Princeton, NJ).

Moore, Margaret (1993), *Foundations of Liberalism* (Oxford University Press, Oxford).

Morton, F. L. (1985), "Group Rights versus Individual Rights in the Charter: The Special Cases of Native and the Québécois," in N. Nevitte and A. Kornberg (eds.), *Minorities and the Canadian State* (Mosaic Press, Oakville): 71–85.

Mulgan, Richard (1989), *Maori, Pākehā and Democracy* (Oxford University Press, Auckland).

Nettheim, Garth (1988), "'Peoples' and 'Populations': Indigenous Peoples and the Rights of Peoples," in James Crawford (ed.), *The Rights of Peoples* (Oxford University Press, Oxford), 107–26.

Nickel, James (1990), "Rawls on Political Community and Principles of Justice," *Law and Philosophy*, 9:205–16.

—— (1995), "The Value of Cultural Belonging: Expanding Kymlicka's Theory," *Dialogue*, 33/4 635–42.

Nielsson, Gunnar (1985), "States and 'Nation-Groups': A Global Taxonomy," in Edward Tiryakian and Ronald Rogowski (eds.), *New Nationalisms of the Developed West* (Allen & Unwin, Boston), 27–56.

Nietschmann, Bernard (1987), "The Third World War," *Cultural Survival Quarterly*, 11/3: 297–326.

Normal, W. J. (1994), "Towards a Normative Theory of Federalism," in Judith Baker (ed.), *Group Rights* (University of Toronto Press, Toronto), 79–99.

O'Brian, Sharon (1987), "Cultural Rights in the United States: A Conflict of Values," *Law and Inequality Journal*, 5: 267–358.

Oliver, Michael (1992), "Laurendeau et Trudeau: leurs opinion sur le Canada," in R. Hudon and R. Pelletier (eds.), *L'Engagement intellectual: mélanges en l'honneur de Léon Dion* (Les Presses de l'Université Laval, Sainte-Foy).

Parekh, Bhikhu (1990), "The Rushdie Affair: Research Agenda for Political Philosophy," *Political Studies*, 38: 695–709.

—— (1991), "British Citizenship and Cultural Difference," in Geoff Andrews (ed.), *Citizenship* (Lawrence & Wishart, London), 183–204.

—— (1994), "Decolonizing Liberalism," in Aleksandras Shtromas (ed.), *The End of "Isms"? Reflections on the Fate of Ideological Politics after Communism's Collapse* (Blackwell, Oxford), 85–103.

Penz, Peter (1992), "Development Refugees and Distributive Justice: Indigenous Peoples, Land and the Developmentalist State," *Public Affairs Quarterly*, 6/1 105–31.

—— (1993), "Colonization of Tribal Lands in Bangladesh and Indonesia: State Rationales, Rights to Land, and Environmental Justices," in Michael

Howard (ed.), *Asia's Environmental Crisis* (Westview Press, Boulder, Col.), 37–72.

Peters, R. and de Vries, G. (1976), "Apostasy in Islam," *Die Welt des Islams*, 17: 1–25.

Peterson, William (1975), "On the Subnations of Europe," in N. Glazer and D. Moynihan (eds.), *Ethnicity: Theory and Experience* (Harvard University Press, Cambridge, Mass.), 117–208.

Phillips, D. Z. (1993), *Looking Backward: A Critical Appraisal of Communitarian Thought* (Princeton University Press, Princeton, NJ).

Pomerance, Michla (1982), *Self-Determination in Law and Practice: The New Doctrine in the United Nations* (Martinus Nijhoff Publishers, The Hague).

Poole, Ross (1993), "Nationalism and the Nation State in Late Modernity," *European Studies Journal*, 10/1: 161–74.

Porter, John (1975), "Ethnic Pluralism in Canadian Perspective," in N. Glazer and D. Moynihan (eds.), *Ethnicity, Theory and Experience* (Harvard University Press, Cambridge, Mass.), 267–304.

Poulter, Sebastian (1987), "Ethnic Minority Customs, English Law, and Human Rights," *International and Comparative Law Quarterly*, 36/3: 598–615.

Rawls, John (1971), *A Theory of Justice* (Oxford University Press, London).

—— (1974), "Reply to Alexander and Musgrave," *Quarterly Journal of Economics*, 88/4: 633–55.

—— (1975), "Fairness to Goodness," *Philosophical Review*, 84: 536–54.

—— (1980), "Kantian Constructivism I Moral Theory," *Journal of Philosophy*, 77/9: 515–72.

—— (1982b), "The Basic Liberties and Their Priority," in S. McMurrin (ed.), *The Tanner Lectures on Human Values*, iii (University of Utah Press, Salt Lake City), 1–87.

—— (1985), "Justice as Fairness: Political not Metaphysical," *Philosophy and Public Affairs*, 14/3: 223–51.

—— (1987), "The Idea of an Overlapping Consensus," *Oxford Journal of Legal Studies*, 7/1: 1–25.

—— (1988), "The Priority of Right and Ideas of the Good," *Philosophy and Public Affairs*, 17/4: 251–76.

—— (1989), "The Domain of the Political and Overlapping Consensus," *New York University Law Review*, 64/2: 233–55.

—— (1993a), *Political Liberalism* (Columbia University Press, New York).

Raz, Joseph (1986), *The Morality of Freedom* (Oxford University Press, Oxford).

Réaume, Denise (1991), "The Constitutional Protection of Language: Security or Survival?" in D.

Schneiderman (ed.), *Language and the State: The Law of Politics of Identity* (Les Éditions Yvon Blais, Cowansville), 37–57,

Resnik, Judith (1989), "Dependent Sovereigns: Indian Tribes, States, and the Federal Courts," *University of Chicago Law Review*, 56: 671–759.

Rorty, Richard (1991), *Objectivity, Relativism, and Truth: Philosophical Papers I* (Cambridge University Press, Cambridge).

Rosenfeld, Michel (1991), *Affirmative Action and Justice: A Philosophical and Constitutional Inquiry* (Yale University Press, New Haven, Conn.).

Royal Commission on Electoral Reform and Party Financing (1991), *Reforming Electoral Democracy: Final Report*, vols. i and ii (Supply and Services, Ottawa).

Ruiz, Richard (1993), "Ethnic Groups Interests and the Social Good: Law and Language," in Winston van Horner and Thomas Tonneson (eds.), *Ethnicity, Law and the Social Good* (University of Wisonsin System American Ethnic Studies Coordinating Committee, Madison, Wis.), 49–73.

Runciman, Steven (1970), *The Orthodox Churches and the Secular State* (Auckland University Press, Auckland).

Russell, John (1993), "Nationalistic Minorities and Liberal Traditions," in Philip Bryden et al. (eds.), *Protecting Rights and Liberties: Essays on the Charter and Canada's Political, Legal and Intellectual Life* (University of Toronto Press, Toronto), 205–41.

Sandel, Michael (1982), *Liberalism and the Limits of Justice* (Cambridge University Press, Cambridge).

—— (1984), "The Procedural Republic and the Unencumbered Self," *Political Theory*, 12/1: 81–96.

—— (1990), "Freedom of Conscience or Freedom of Choice," in James Hunter and O. Guinness (eds.), *Articles of Faith, Articles of Peace* (Brookings Institute, Washington, DC), 74–92.

Schwartz, Brian (1986), *First Principles, Second Thoughts: Aboriginal Peoples, Constitutional Reform and Canadian Statecraft* (Institute for Research on Public Policy, Montreal).

Sharp, Andrew (1990), *Justice and the Maori: Maori Claims in New Zealand, Political Argument in the 1980s* (Oxford University Press, Auckland).

Sigler, Jay (1983), *Minority Rights: A Comparative Analysis* (Greenwood, Westport, Conn.).

Skutnabb-Kangas, Tove (1988), "Multilingualism and the Education of Minority Children," in T. Skutnabb-Kangas and J. Cummings (eds.), *Minority Education: From Shame to Struggle* (Multilingual Matters Ltd., Clevedon), 9–44.

Smith, Anthony (1986), *The Ethnic Origins of Nations* (Blackwell, Oxford).

Sowell (1990), *Preferential Policies: An International Perspective* (Morrow, New York).

Stark, Andrew (1992), "English-Canadian Opposition to Quebec Nationalism," in R. Kent Weaver (ed.), *The Collapse of Canada?* (Brookings Institute, Washington, DC), 123–58.

Steinberg, Stephen (1981), *The Ethnic Myth: Race, Ethnicity, and Class in America* (Atheneum, New York).

Svensson, Frances (1979), "Liberal Democracy and Group Rights: The Legacy of Individualism and Its Impact on American Indian Tribes," *Political Studies*, 27/3: 421–39.

Tamir, Yael (1993), *Liberal Nationalism* (Princeton University Press, Princeton, NJ).

Taylor, Charles (1985), *Philosophy and the Human Sciences: Philosophical Papers 2* (Cambridge University Press, Cambridge).

—— (1991), "Shared and Divergent Values," in Ronald Watts and D. Brown (eds.), *Options for a New Canada* (University of Toronto Press, Toronto), 53–76.

—— (1992a), "The Politics of Recognition," in Amy Gutmann (ed.), *Multiculturalism and the "Politics of Recognition"* (Princeton University Press, Princeton, NJ), 25–73.

Thornberry, Patrick (1991), *International Law and the Rights of Minorities* (Oxford University Press, Oxford).

Todorov, Tzvetan (1993), *On Human Diversity: Nationalism, Racism and Exoticism in French Thought* (Harvard University Press, Cambridge, Mass.).

Tomasi, John (1991), "Individual Rights and Community Virtues," *Ethics*, 101/3: 521–36.

—— (1995), "Kymlicka, Liberalism, and Respect for Cultural Minorities," *Ethics*, 105/3: 580–603.

Tsosie, Rebecca (1994), "Separate Sovereigns, Civil Rights and the Sacred Text: The Legacy of Thurgoo Marshall's Indian Law Jurisprudence," *Arizona State Law Journal*, 26/2: 495–533.

Tully, James (1994), "Aboriginal Property and Western Theory: Recovering a Middle Ground," *Social Philosophy and Policy*, 11/2: 153–80.

Van Dyke, Vernon (1977), "The Individual, the State, and Ethnic Communities in Political Theory," *World Politics*, 29/3: 343–69.

—— (1982), "Collective Entities and Moral Rights: Problems in Liberal-Democratic Thought," *Journal of Politics*, 44: 21–40.

—— (1985), *Human Rights, Ethnicity and Discrimination* (Greenwood, Westport, Conn.).

Waldron, Jeremy (1989), "Autonomy and Perfectionism in Raz's *Morality of Freedom*," *Southern California Law Review*, 62/3–4: 1097–152.

——(1992*a*), "Minority Cultures and the Cosmopolitan Alternative," *University of Michigan Journal of Law Reform*, 25/3: 751–93.

—— (1992*b*), "Superseding Historic Injustice," *Ethics*, 103/1: 4–28.

Walzer, Michael (1977), *Just and Unjust Wars* (Basic Books, New York).

—— (1980), "The Moral Standing of States," *Philosophy and Public Affairs*, 9/2: 209–29.

—— (1982), "Pluralism in Political Perspective," in M. Walzer (ed.), *The Politics of Ethnicity* (Harvard University Press, Cambridge. Mass.), 1–28.

—— (1990), "The Communitarian Critique of Liberalism," *Political Theory*, 18/1: 6–23.

Weaver, Sally (1985), "Federal Difficulties with Aboriginal Rights in Canada," in M. Boldt and J. Long (eds.), *The Quest for Justice: Aboriginal Peoples and Aboriginal Rights* (University of Toronto Press, Toronto), 139–47.

Weinstein, Brian (1983), *The Civic Tongue: Political Consequences of Language Choices* (Longman, New York).

Williams, Melissa (1994), "Group Inequality and the Public Culture of Justice," in Judith Baker (ed.), *Group Rights* (University of Toronto Press, Toronto), 34–65.

Young, Iris Marion (1989), "Polity and Group Difference: A Critique of the Ideal of Universal Citizenship," *Ethics*, 99/2: 250–74.

Post-Reading Questions

1. Why is membership in a secure "societal culture" important for citizens in liberal democratic states, according to Kymlicka?
2. How do national minorities differ from ethnocultural minorities, and what different kinds of claims and rights are justified in their respective cases?
3. Where do aboriginal peoples, such as First Nations peoples in Canada, fit within Kymlicka's framework of multicultural rights?
4. What are group-differentiated rights and what arguments does Kymlicka give in support of them?

CASE STUDY
THE MAA-NULTH FIRST NATIONS FINAL AGREEMENT

Introduction

Modern-day treaties between Aboriginal peoples in Canada and provincial and federal governments constitute an important part of Canada's recognition of the First Nations. These treaties cover comprehensive rather than specific land claims, and pertain to areas of Canada that are not covered by existing historical treaties or legal mechanisms (specifically, the "Numbered Treaties" entered into between 1871 and 1923). Since 1975—the date of the first modern-day treaty, the James Bay and Northern Quebec Agreement—the federal government has settled numerous self-government and comprehensive claims with Aboriginal peoples in Canada. These treaties are often precipitated by disputes over land rights, and by the First Nations' desire to secure their self-government rights. All contemporary treaties are the product of years of political negotiations between First Nations representatives and provincial and federal government officials. Such negotiations usually result in settlements of land and capital transfers to the bands in question, and may stipulate rights to natural resources that are important to Aboriginal ways of life (chiefly, fishing, hunting, and the management of migratory birds). Finally, they set out the law-making and political authority that First Nations possess, and the self-governance processes that they observe with respect to their membership. As Will Kymlicka suggests in his theory of cultural group rights, indigenous peoples have a prima facie right to self-determination, a right that is recognized—if not always honoured in practice—by section 35 (1) of Canada's constitution.

The most recent landmark agreement of this kind, the Maa-nulth Final Agreement, came into effect on April 1, 2011. Negotiated among the Maa-nulth First Nations (a group of five First Nations numbering over 2,000 people) of Vancouver Island, the British Columbia provincial government, and the federal government, this agreement marks the first modern treaty achieved on Vancouver Island, home to more than 50 First Nations. Like other such treaties, this one is the culmination of many years of negotiations: the Maa-nulth First Nations first entered the treaty process in 1994. The specific terms of the treaty include land and capital transfers as well as recognition of the Maa-nulth First Nations' rights to natural resources. The land package consists of approximately 25,000 hectares, the vast majority of it former provincial Crown land, along with some former Indian reserve land and newly purchased private land. As for the capital component, $73.1 million will be provided to the five Maa-nulth First Nations over 10 years (minus outstanding loans). On top of this, resource revenue payments of between $600,000 and $1.8 million will be paid annually to the bands over the next 25 years (one tribe will receive additional funds). Also promised is continued, ongoing government funding for Maa-nulth First Nations for their community programs and services, as well as one-time funding to offset the cost of implementing the provisions of the new treaty.

The significance of the Maa-nulth agreement (and others of this sort) does not reduce to the land and capital transfers to First Nations peoples, however. Kymlicka's argument for the rights of national minorities to self-determination and (if they so choose) self-government goes some distance in explaining why formal legal recognition of their group rights is so important to Aboriginal peoples: without these rights and the self-governance structures that they make possible, such minorities do not have access to the institutions that enable and support the autonomy of their members. Liberal equality demands that long-standing national minorities in Canada—such as Aboriginal peoples and French Canadians—have access to important social, economic, and political institutions and opportunities in their own language and cultural context if they so wish. In the case of indigenous peoples, this equality rationale is further strengthened by the fact that treaties that were negotiated long ago between First Nations and colonial settlers have been violated by the federal government, and so on legal grounds, ought to be restored.

The self-governance rights of the Maa-nulth are clearly spelled out in this final agreement, thereby reinforcing the distinct position of First Nations peoples within the Canadian political landscape. As a result, the federal Indian Act will cease to apply to the Maa-nulth First Nations (except for the matter of determining Indian status), and certain powers previously held by the federal and provincial governments will soon transfer to these bands. In particular, the Maa-nulth will now decide on questions to do with their day-to-day governance, cultural preservation, and eventually, even taxation. Some of the traditional institutions of the nations in the agreement will take on greater significance as a consequence, including the Huu-ay-aht First Nation's system of governance, which combines the role of hereditary chiefs with that of elected council members.

As readers will see from the following selections from the Maa-nulth First Nations Final Agreement, the sovereignty of the First Nations is symbolically—and in many respects, practically—underscored by the language of the treaty. Using Kymlicka's framework for group-differentiated citizenship and multicultural rights, the Maa-nulth First Nations appear to have, after a long battle, finally secured formal legal and political recognition of their right to self-government within the Canadian political system.

From The Maa-nulth First Nations Final Agreement

The Maa-nulth First Nations Final Agreement (2009).
*http://www.aadnc-aandc.gc.ca/DAM/DAM-INTER-BC/STAGING/texte-text/mna_fa_*
mnafa_1335899212893_eng.pdf

PREAMBLE

A. The Maa-nulth First Nations assert that they have used, occupied, and governed their traditional territories from time immemorial;

B. The Maa-nulth First Nations have never entered into a treaty or land claims agreement with the Crown;

C. The Constitution Act, 1982 recognizes and affirms the existing aboriginal and treaty rights of the Aboriginal peoples of Canada, and the courts have stated that aboriginal rights include aboriginal title;

D. The Maa-nulth First Nations assert that they have an inherent right to self-government, and the Government of Canada has negotiated self-government in this Agreement based on its policy that the inherent right to self-government is an existing aboriginal right within section 35 of the Constitution Act, 1982;

E. The Maa-nulth First Nations' existing aboriginal rights are recognized and affirmed by the Constitution Act, 1982, and the Parties have negotiated this Agreement in accordance with the British Columbia treaty process to provide certainty in respect of those rights and to allow them to continue and to have effect and be exercised as set out in this Agreement;

F. Canada and British Columbia acknowledge the perspective of the Maa-nulth First Nations that harm and losses in relation to their aboriginal rights have occurred in the past and express regret if any actions or omissions of the Crown have contributed to that perspective, and the Parties rely on this Agreement to move them beyond the difficult circumstances of the past;

G. Canada and British Columbia acknowledge the aspirations of the Maa-nulth First Nations to preserve, promote and develop the culture, heritage, language and economies of the Maa-nulth First Nations;

H. Canada and British Columbia acknowledge the aspirations of the Maa-nulth First Nations and the Maa-nulth-aht to participate more fully in the economic, political, cultural and social life of British Columbia in a way that preserves and enhances the collective identity of the Maa-nulth-aht as the Maa-nulth First Nations and to evolve and flourish as self-sufficient and sustainable communities; and

I. The Parties are committed to the reconciliation of the prior presence of the Maa-nulth First Nations and the sovereignty of the Crown through the negotiation of this Agreement which will establish new government-to-government relationships based on mutual respect.

Now Therefore the Parties Agree as Follows:

Chapter 1: General Provisions

1.1.0 Nature of Agreement

1.1.1 This Agreement is a treaty and a land claims agreement within the meaning of sections 25 and 35 of the Constitution Act, 1982.

1.1.2 This Agreement is binding on the Parties and on all persons.

1.1.3 The Parties and all persons are entitled to rely on this Agreement.

1.1.4 Canada will recommend to Parliament that federal settlement legislation provides that this

Agreement is approved, given effect, declared valid and has the force of law.

1.1.5 British Columbia will recommend to the Legislature that provincial settlement legislation provides that this Agreement is approved, given effect, declared valid and has the force of law.

1.1.6 Ratification of this Agreement by the Parties in accordance with Chapter 28 Ratification is a condition precedent to the validity of this Agreement and, unless so ratified, this Agreement is of no force or effect.

. . .

1.3.0 Constitution of Canada

1.3.1 This Agreement does not alter the Constitution of Canada, including:

    a. the distribution of powers between Canada and British Columbia;

    b. the identity of Maa-nulth First Nations as aboriginal people of Canada within the meaning of the Constitution Act, 1982; and

    c. sections 25 and 35 of the Constitution Act, 1982.

1.3.2 The Canadian Charter of Rights and Freedoms applies to each Maa-nulth First Nation government in respect of all matters within its authority.

. . .

Chapter XIII: Governance

13.1.0 Maa-Nulth First Nation Governance

13.1.1 Each Maa-nulth First Nation has the right to self-government, and the authority to make laws, as set out in this Agreement.

13.1.2 Each Maa-nulth First Nation has a Maa-nulth First Nation government in accordance with its Maa-nulth First Nation constitution and this Agreement.

13.1.3 The rights, powers, privileges and authorities of each Maa-nulth First Nation will be exercised in accordance with:

    a. this Agreement;

    b. its Maa-nulth First Nation constitution; and

    c. Maa-nulth First Nation law enacted by its Maa-nulth First Nation government.

13.1.4 Each Maa-nulth First Nation will act through its Maa-nulth First Nation government in exercising its rights, powers, privileges and authorities, and in carrying out its duties, functions, and obligations.

13.2.0 Legal Status and Capacity

13.2.1 Each Maa-nulth First Nation is a separate and distinct legal entity with the capacity, rights, powers, and privileges of a natural person including the ability to:

    a. enter into contracts and agreements;

    b. acquire and hold property or an interest in property and sell or otherwise dispose of that property or interest;

    c. raise, spend, invest, and borrow money;

    d. sue and be sued; and

    e. do other things ancillary to the exercise of its rights, powers, and privileges.

13.3.0 Maa-nulth First Nation Constitutions

13.3.1 Each Maa-nulth First Nation will have a Maa-nulth First Nation constitution, consistent with this Agreement, which will provide:

    a. for a democratic Maa-nulth First Nation government, including its duties, composition, and membership;

    b. that its Maa-nulth First Nation government is democratically accountable to its Maa-nulth-aht and Maa-nulth First Nation citizens with elections at least every five years;

    c. for a process for removal of office holders of its Maa-nulth First Nation government;

    d. for a system of financial administration with standards comparable to those generally accepted for governments in Canada through which its Maa-nulth First Nation government is financially accountable to its Maa-nulth-aht and Maa-nulth First Nation citizens;

    e. for conflict of interest rules comparable to those generally accepted for governments in Canada;

    f. for recognition and protection of rights and freedoms of its Maa-nulth-aht and Maa-nulth First Nation citizens;

    g. that every Maa-nulth-aht of that Maa-nulth First Nation is entitled to be a Maa-nulth First Nation citizen of that Maa-nulth First Nation;

    h. that every registered Indian of the applicable Maa-nulth Indian band is entitled to be a Maa-nulth First Nation citizen of that Maa-nulth First Nation;

    i. the process for the enactment of laws by its Maa-nulth First Nation government;

    j. a process for challenging the validity of the Maa-nulth First Nation laws of its Maa-nulth First Nation government;

    k. that a Maa-nulth First Nation law of its Maa-nulth First Nation government which is inconsistent or in Conflict with its Maa-nulth First Nation constitution is, to the extent of the inconsistency or conflict, of no force or effect;

    l. for the establishment of the Maa-nulth First Nation public institutions of its Maa-nulth First Nation government;

m. for conditions under which that Maa-nulth First Nation may dispose of its lands or interests in lands;

n. for amendment of its Maa-nulth First Nation constitution;

o. that its Maa-nulth First Nation government will establish processes for appeal or review of administrative decisions made by that Maa-nulth First Nation government or its Maa-nulth First Nation public institutions; and

p. for other provisions as determined by that Maa-nulth First Nation.

13.3.2 At the discretion of each Maa-nulth First Nation, its Maa-nulth First Nation constitution may provide for the appointment of *Ha'wiih* (hereditary chiefs) into its governance structure, including:

a. the process for appointment of *Ha'wiih*;

b. the duties of *Ha'wiih*; and

c. other related matters.

13.3.3 If a Maa-nulth First Nation exercises its discretion under 13.3.2, it will provide in its Maa-nulth First Nation constitution that the majority of office holders within its Maa-nulth First Nation government are elected.

13.3.4 Each Maa-nulth First Nation represents and warrants to Canada and British Columbia that:

a. its Maa-nulth First Nation constitution was approved by at least 50 per cent of the eligible voters of that Maa-nulth First Nation who voted to approve its Maa-nulth First Nation constitution; and

b. as of the effective date, its Maa-nulth First Nation constitution approved in accordance with 13.3.4a. has not been amended.

13.3.5 Each Maa-nulth First Nation constitution will come into force and effect on the effective date.

13.4.0 *Appeal and Judicial Review of Administrative Decisions*

13.4.1 If the processes established under 13.3.1o. provide for a right of appeal to a court, the Supreme Court of British Columbia has jurisdiction to hear those appeals.

13.4.2 The Supreme Court of British Columbia has jurisdiction to hear applications for judicial review of administrative decisions taken by a Maa-nulth First Nation public institution or a Maa-nulth First Nation government under its applicable Maa-nulth First Nation law.

13.4.3 The Judicial Review Procedure Act applies to an application for judicial review under 13.4.2 as if the Maa-nulth First Nation law were an "enactment" within the meaning of that Act.

13.5.0 *Registry of Laws*

13.5.1 Each Maa-nulth First Nation government will:

a. maintain a public registry of its Maa-nulth First Nation laws in the English language and, at the discretion of that Maa-nulth First Nation government, in the Nuu-chah-nulth language, the English version of which is authoritative; and

b. provide British Columbia and, upon request, Canada with copies of its Maa-nulth First Nation laws after they are enacted.

13.6.0 *Individuals Who Are Non-Members*

13.6.1 Each Maa-nulth First Nation government will consult with non-members concerning decisions of that Maa-nulth First Nation government that directly and significantly affect those non-members.

13.6.2 Each Maa-nulth First Nation public institution will consult with non-members concerning decisions of that Maa-nulth First Nation public institution that directly and significantly affect those non-members.

13.6.3 In addition to the requirements to consult in 13.6.1 and 13.6.2, the applicable Maa-nulth First Nation government will ensure that non-members, or their representatives, have the ability to participate in discussions and vote on decisions of a Maa-nulth First Nation public institution established by that Maa-nulth First Nation government that directly and significantly affect non-members.

13.6.4 Notwithstanding 13.6.3, the Maa-nulth First Nation government may provide that a majority of the members of its Maa-nulth First Nation public institutions will be Maa-nulth First Nation citizens.

13.6.5 Each Maa-nulth First Nation government will establish the means of participation under 13.6.3 by Maa-nulth First Nation law at the same time that it establishes a Maa-nulth First Nation public institution whose activities may directly and significantly affect non-members.

13.6.6 Each Maa-nulth First Nation government will provide that non-members have access to the appeal and review procedures established under 13.3.1o. in respect of the activities that directly affect those non-members.

13.7.0 *Transition to Maa-nulth First Nation Government*

13.7.1 The chief or chief councillor and councillors of the band council of the applicable Maa-nulth Indian band under the Indian Act, on the day immediately before the effective date, are the members of the applicable Maa-nulth First Nation government from the effective date until the office holders elected in its first election take office.

13.7.2 The first elections for the office holders of each Maa-nulth First Nation government will be initiated no later than six months after the effective date and the office holders elected in the election will take office no later than one year after the effective date.

13.8.0 Transition

13.8.1 Before a Maa-nulth First Nation government makes a Maa-nulth First Nation law in respect of adoption, child protection, health, social development, child care, or kindergarten to grade 12 education, that Maa-nulth First Nation government will provide at least six months notice to Canada and British Columbia of its intention to exercise the law-making authority.

13.8.2 Notwithstanding 13.8.1, upon agreement by the applicable Maa-nulth First Nation government, Canada and British Columbia, that Maa-nulth First Nation government may exercise a law-making authority before the expiration of the six month notice period required in accordance with 13.8.1.

13.8.3 At the request of Canada or British Columbia made within three months of receiving notice under 13.8.1, that Maa-nulth First Nation government will Consult with Canada or British Columbia, as applicable, in respect of:

a. options to address the interests of the Maa-nulth First Nation government through methods other than the exercise of law-making authority by that Maa-nulth First Nation government;

b. the comparability of standards established under proposed Maa-nulth First Nation law to standards under provincial law;

c. immunity of individuals providing services or exercising authority under its Maa-nulth First Nation law;

d. readiness;

e. quality assurance; and

f. other matters agreed to by that Maa-nulth First Nation government and Canada or British Columbia, as applicable.

13.8.4 At the request of a Maa-nulth First Nation government, Canada or British Columbia, made within three months of Canada and British Columbia receiving notice under 13.8.1, that Maa-nulth First Nation government and Canada or British Columbia, as applicable, will discuss:

a. any transfer of cases and related documentation from Canada or British Columbia to the applicable Maa-nulth First Nation public institution or that Maa-nulth First Nations government, including any confidentiality and privacy considerations;

b. any transfer of assets from Canada or British Columbia to that Maa-nulth First Nation public institution or that Maa-nulth First Nation government;

c. any appropriate amendments to federal law or provincial law, including amendments to address duplicate licensing requirements; and

d. other matters agreed to by that Maa-nulth First Nation government and Canada or British Columbia, as applicable.

13.8.5 A Maa-nulth First Nation government, Canada or British Columbia, as applicable, may negotiate agreements regarding any of the matters described in 13.8.3 and 13.8.4, but such agreement is not a condition precedent to the exercise of law-making authority by a Maa-nulth First Nation government. . . .

13.9.0 Notification of Provincial Legislation

13.9.1 Subject to an agreement under 13.9.4, before legislation is introduced in the Legislative Assembly, or before a regulation is approved by the lieutenant-governor-in-council, British Columbia will notify each Maa-nulth First Nation government of the proposed legislation or regulation if:

a. this Agreement provides that Maa-nulth First Nation government law-making authority in respect of the subject matter of the legislation or regulation;

b. the legislation or regulation may affect the protections, immunities, limitations in respect of liability, remedies over or rights referred to in 13.35.8; or

c. the legislation or regulation may affect: i. the rights, powers or obligations; or ii. the protections, immunities or limitations in respect of liability, referred to in 13.26.2,

except where this cannot be done for reasons of emergency or confidentiality.

13.9.2 If British Columbia does not notify a Maa-nulth First Nation government under 13.9.1 for reasons of emergency or confidentiality, British Columbia will notify that Maa-nulth First Nation government that legislation has been introduced in the Legislative Assembly, or a regulation has been deposited with the Registrar of Regulations.

13.9.3 A notification under 13.9.1 or 13.9.2 will include:

a. the nature and purpose of the proposed legislation or regulation; and

b. the date the proposed legislation or regulation is anticipated to take effect, if it has not already done so.

13.9.4 Each Maa-nulth First Nation may enter into an agreement with British Columbia establishing alternatives to the obligations which would otherwise apply under 13.9.1 to 13.9.3 and 13.9.5.

13.9.5 Subject to 13.9.6 or an agreement contemplated by 13.9.4, if, within 30 days after notice is provided in accordance with 13.9.1 or 13.9.2, the Maa-nulth First Nation government makes a request to British Columbia, then British Columbia and the Maa-nulth First Nation government will discuss the effect of the legislation or regulation, if any, on:

a. a Maa-nulth First Nation law of that Maa-nulth First Nation government; or

b. a matter referred to in 13.9.1b. or 13.9.1c.,

and British Columbia will have due regard for any views of the Maa-nulth First Nation government provided during such discussions.

13.9.6 If British Columbia establishes a process providing for collective discussion with First Nation governments in British Columbia in relation to matters referred to in 13.9.5:

a. each Maa-nulth First Nation government will participate in that process; and

b. the process is deemed to satisfy British Columbia's obligation, in accordance with 13.9.5, for discussion in respect of a particular matter.

13.9.7 Unless British Columbia agrees otherwise, each Maa-nulth First Nation government will retain the information provided in accordance with 13.9.1 to 13.9.6 in strict confidence until such time, if ever, the draft legislation is given first reading in the Legislative Assembly or a regulation is deposited with the Registrar of Regulations, as applicable.

13.9.8 The Parties acknowledge that nothing in 13.9.1 to 13.9.6 will delay the enactment of a provincial law.

13.9.9 Notwithstanding any other provision of this Agreement, to the extent that provincial legislation or a regulation referred to in 13.9.1 affects the validity of an otherwise valid Maa-nulth First Nation law, the Maa-nulth First Nation law will be deemed to be valid for a period of six months after the coming into force of the provincial legislation or regulation.

13.10.0 Delegation

13.10.1 Any law-making authority of a Maa-nulth First Nation government under this Agreement may be delegated by a law of that Maa-nulth First Nation government to:

a. a Maa-nulth First Nation public institution established by a law of that Maa-nulth First Nation government;

b. another First Nation government in British Columbia;

c. a public institution established by one or more First Nation governments in British Columbia;

d. British Columbia;

e. Canada;

f. a local government; or

g. a legal entity as agreed to by the Parties,

if the delegation and the exercise of any law-making authority is in accordance with the terms of this Agreement and the applicable Maa-nulth First Nation constitution.

. . .

13.11.0 Maa-nulth First Nation Government

13.11.1 Each Maa-nulth First Nation government may make laws in respect of the election, administration, management, and operation of that Maa-nulth First Nation government, including:

a. the establishment of Maa-nulth First Nation public institutions, including their respective powers, duties, composition, and membership, but the registration or incorporation of Maa-nulth First Nation public institutions will be under federal law or provincial law;

b. the establishment of Maa-nulth First Nation corporations, but the registration or incorporation of Maa-nulth First Nation corporations will be under federal law or provincial law;

c. the powers, duties, responsibilities, remuneration, and indemnification of members, officials, employees and appointees of that Maa-nulth First Nation government or its Maa-nulth First Nation public institutions;

d. financial administration of that Maa-nulth First Nation government, its Maa-nulth First Nation public institutions and the applicable Maa-nulth First Nation; and

e. elections, by-elections and referenda.

13.11.2 For greater certainty, in accordance with 1.8.11, nothing in 13.11.1 confers authority on a Maa-nulth First Nation government to make laws in respect of labour relations or working conditions.

13.11.3 Each Maa-nulth First Nation government will make laws to provide the Maa-nulth-aht and Maa-nulth First Nation citizens of the applicable Maa-nulth First Nation with reasonable access to information in the custody or control of that Maa-nulth First Government and its Maa-nulth First Nation public institutions.

13.11.4 Each Maa-nulth First Nation government will make laws to provide persons other than the Maa-nulth-aht and Maa-nulth First Nation citizens of the applicable Maa-nulth First Nation with reasonable access to information in the custody or control of that Maa-nulth First Government and its Maa-nulth First Nation public institutions regarding matters that directly and significantly affect those persons.

13.11.5 Maa-nulth First Nation law under 13.11.1, 13.11.3, or 13.11.4 prevails to the extent of a Conflict with federal law or provincial law, except federal law or provincial law in relation to the protection of personal information prevails to the extent of a conflict with Maa-nulth First Nation law under 13.11.1, 13.11.3, or 13.11.4.

13.12.0 Maa-nulth First Nation Assets

13.12.1 Each Maa-nulth First Nation government may make laws in respect of the use, possession and management of assets owned by the applicable Maa-nulth First Nation, a Maa-nulth First Nation public institution or a Maa-nulth First Nation corporation of that Maa-nulth First Nation located off the Maa-nulth First Nation lands of that Maa-nulth First Nation.

13.12.2 Each Maa-nulth First Nation government may make laws in respect of the use, possession and management of assets owned by the applicable Maa-nulth First Nation, a Maa-nulth First Nation public institution or a Maa-nulth First Nation corporation of that Maa-nulth First Nation located on the Maa-nulth First Nation lands of that Maa-nulth First Nation.

13.12.3 For greater certainty, the law-making authority under 13.12.1 and 13.12.2 does not include the authority to make laws regarding creditor's rights and remedies.

13.12.4 Federal law or provincial law prevails to the extent of a Conflict with Maa-nulth First Nation law under 13.12.1.

13.12.5 Maa-nulth First Nation law under 13.12.2 prevails to the extent of a Conflict with federal law or provincial law.

13.13.0 Maa-nulth First Nation Citizenship

13.13.1 Each Maa-nulth First Nation government may make laws in respect of citizenship in the applicable Maa-nulth First Nation.

13.13.2 The conferring of Maa-nulth First Nation citizenship does not:

a. confer or deny rights of entry into Canada, Canadian citizenship, the right to be registered as an Indian under the Indian Act, or any of the rights or benefits under the Indian Act; or
b. except as described in this Agreement or in any federal law or provincial law, impose any obligation on Canada or British Columbia to provide rights or benefits.

13.13.3 Maa-nulth First Nation law under 13.13.1 prevails to the extent of a Conflict with federal law or provincial law.

13.14.0 Maa-nulth First Nation Lands

13.14.1 Each Maa-nulth First Nation government may make laws in respect of:

a. the use of the Maa-nulth First Nation lands of the applicable Maa-nulth First Nation, including management, planning, zoning and development;
b. the ownership and disposition of estates or interests in the Maa-nulth First Nation lands of that Maa-nulth First Nation owned by that Maa-nulth First Nation, its Maa-nulth First Nation corporations or a Maa-nulth First Nation public institution of that Maa-nulth First Nation government; and
c. expropriation for public purposes and public works by the Maa-nulth First Nation government of estates or interests in the Maa-nulth First Nation lands of that Maa-nulth First Nation other than:

i. estates or interests granted or continued on the effective date, or thereafter replaced in accordance with this Agreement, unless specifically provided for otherwise in this Agreement;
ii. estates or interests expropriated by a federal expropriating authority or a provincial expropriating authority or otherwise acquired by Canada or British Columbia; and
iii. any other interests upon which the Parties have agreed in this Agreement,

if the Maa-nulth First Nation government provides fair compensation to the owner of the estate or interest and the expropriation is of the smallest estate or interest necessary for the public purpose or public work.

13.14.2 Maa-nulth First Nation law under 13.14.1 prevails to the extent of a conflict with federal law or provincial law.

13.14.3 Maa-nulth First Nation law under 13.14.1b. in respect of estates or interests that are recognized under federal law or provincial law must be consistent with federal law or provincial law in respect of estates or interests in land.

13.14.4 Each Maa-nulth First Nation government will make laws that will take effect on the effective date governing the establishment, amendment, repeal and content of community plans for the Maa-nulth First Nation lands of the applicable Maa-nulth First Nation.

13.14.5 A Maa-nulth First Nation law made in accordance with 13.14.4 will require that the community plans include:

a. a statement of objectives and policies that will guide decisions on land use planning and management of the Maa-nulth First Nation lands of the applicable Maa-nulth First Nation; and

b. content similar to that required in the official community plans of local government.

13.14.6 Each Maa-nulth First Nation government may develop and adopt community plans on an incremental basis, provided that it will develop and adopt community plans for all Maa-nulth First Nation lands of the applicable Maa-nulth First Nation within 10 years of the effective date.

13.14.7 Any development or use of Maa-nulth First Nation lands approved by a Maa-nulth First Nation government will be in accordance with a community plan adopted by that Maa-nulth First Nation government in accordance with this Agreement or a development plan in place as of the effective date.

13.14.8 Each Maa-nulth First Nation government will consult with other organizations and authorities on the development, amendment and repeal of its community plans similar to the manner and extent as local governments are required to consult with other organizations and authorities in respect of development, amendment and repeal of official community plans.

. . .

Post-Case-Reading Questions

1. What normative principles and historical facts does the treaty allude to in proclaiming the self-government rights of the Maa-nulth First Nations, and how might these connect with Kymlicka's argument for national self-government rights?

2. What are some of the features of the envisioned Maa-nulth First Nations government, according to the treaty?

CHAPTER
XVIII

Charles Taylor

PHILOSOPHER: CHARLES TAYLOR

Introduction

Charles Taylor is Canada's best-known contemporary philosopher. Born in Montreal in 1931 into a politically minded family, he later attended McGill University and obtained a degree in history in 1952. Awarded a Rhodes scholarship to Oxford, he earned another BA, this one in politics, philosophy, and economics (1955). Taylor continued his graduate work at Oxford under the supervision of Sir Isaiah Berlin and G.E.M. Anscombe, earning his doctorate in 1961. In 1961, he became a professor of philosophy and political science at McGill, where he taught until he retired as professor emeritus in 1997. For part of this time (1976–81) he was also Chichele Professor of Social and Political Theory at Oxford University and a fellow of All Souls College. After his retirement from McGill, Taylor continued to teach as a visiting professor at Northwestern University for several years.

Charles Taylor

Taylor's designation as one of Canada's most prominent public intellectuals is a consequence of his many contributions to political debates surrounding bilingualism, federalism, nationalism (including Quebec independence), and more recently, religious pluralism. He was a contributor to the work of the Bélanger-Campeau Commission Report (1991) on the political and constitutional future of Quebec. Appointed to Quebec's *Conseil de la langue française* in the same year, Taylor became known as a vocal critic of the province's restrictive commercial sign laws. In 2007 he was appointed co-chair of the Quebec government's high profile Consultation Commission on Accommodation Practices Related to Cultural Differences. Taylor was also active in federal politics: he ran (unsuccessfully) as a New Democratic Party candidate in federal elections in the 1960s, once against Pierre Elliott Trudeau. Taylor became a Companion of the Order of Canada in 1995, and subsequently received the distinction of Grand Officer of the National Order of Quebec in 2000. He is also a fellow of the Royal Society of Canada, the British Academy, and the American Academy of Arts and Sciences. Finally, Taylor has also been the recipient of two prestigious international awards, the Templeton Prize and the Kyoto Prize (the "Japanese Nobel"), which include cash awards of $1.68 million USD and $500,000 USD respectively.

Taylor's philosophical corpus is broad in scope: he has made significant contributions to the philosophies of language, history, religion, and the social sciences. His two-volume *Philosophical Papers* (1982 and 1985) and *Philosophical Arguments* (1995) testify to this diversity of research interests. Taylor's work in social and political philosophy, however, is the central axis of his philosophy. In this field, Taylor draws on the philosophical heritage of Aristotle and Hegel to argue for the importance of community and social context in shaping our beliefs, ideals, and behaviour. Partly as a response to the individualism of some strands of liberalism—which he viewed as deeply flawed—Taylor developed a "communitarian" conception of both the person and socio-political life. This perspective takes as its starting point the belief that our identity—the self—is formed not in a vacuum, but in a concrete society. Against liberal philosophers such as Locke and Rawls, Taylor argues that the liberal view of the individual as a self-contained, asocial bearer of rights who has primacy over the community ignores the fact that individuals are always situated in a communal context, and so are constituted by its social and political institutions. Indeed, individuals' rights and choices only find meaning and expression against the background of the culture and society in which they find themselves, according to Taylor.

Concurrently, Taylor argues against liberals' prioritization of rights over the good (or over the question of what we value). According to liberals, each individual has certain inviolable rights that the state should protect, but when it comes to which version of the good life to pursue, the state ought to remain neutral, allowing individuals to choose their life projects autonomously. Yet such a preference for the priority of rights is itself a particular view of the good, Taylor argues. Moreover, the good cannot be contemplated abstractly, independent of the broader social context; when we acknowledge this context, we see that our understanding of "the good" closely corresponds to the common good, irreducible to the preferences of individuals. Hence the community's pursuit of its shared values is not constrained by the requirement of neutrality; instead, it is prior to, and so takes precedence over, individuals' rights and liberties. Taylor's thinking in the domain of social and political philosophy is laid out in a large body of work that includes *Hegel* (1975), *Hegel and Modern Society* (1979), *Sources of the Self* (1989), *The Malaise of Modernity* (1991), *Ethics of Authenticity* (1992), *Multiculturalism: Examining the Politics of Recognition* (1994), *Modern Social Imaginaries* (2003), and *A Secular Age* (2007).

Taylor's communitarian perspective is much in evidence in the text that follows, "Why Do Nations Have to Become States?" In this piece, Taylor asserts that "free people are self-governing people." The text was written in 1979—a year prior to the referendum on sovereignty-association in Quebec—and lays out a case for the province as a distinct society within a federalist Canada. Although he affirms that nations have to become states "as a condition of self-rule," Taylor goes on to say that this argument does not apply to minority nations coexisting within the boundary of a larger democratic state (such as Quebec within Canada). Hence Taylor advances a second argument about what makes the identity of modern persons: contrary to the liberal view that sees the individual citizen as a rational, autonomous rights-bearer, one's identity depends upon communities of identification. On Taylor's account of (nationalist) identity, what is most critical both to the individual as a full human subject and citizen and to collective or group identity, are language and culture. It is within the media of language and culture that identity is expressed and reproduced. This condition, in turn, imposes a corresponding duty on others to recognize and respect the linguistic and cultural identity of the community.

In 2007, the Government of Quebec asked Taylor and sociologist Gérard Bouchard to head up a commission investigating what would constitute "reasonable accommodation" of minority cultural and religious communities in Quebec. The year-long public inquiry culminated in a set of public policy recommendations aimed at fostering greater integration and accommodation of diverse groups. However, the report also bears the imprint of Taylor's insights into the nature of social identity—and specifically, the importance of religion and language to identity. An excerpt from the commission's report is included in this chapter, thereby helping us to reflect on Taylor's contributions to both philosophical thinking and public life.

Further Readings

Abbey, R. (2001). *Charles Taylor*. Princeton, NJ: Princeton University Press.
Abbey, R. (ed.). (2004). *Charles Taylor*. Cambridge: Cambridge University Press.
Aronovitch, H. (2005). "Trudeau or Taylor? The Central Question," *Critical Review of International Social and Political Philosophy* 8 (3): 309–25.
Redhead, M. (2002). *Charles Taylor: Thinking and Living Deep Diversity*. Lanham, MD: Rowman & Littlefield.
Tully, J. (ed.). (1994). *Philosophy in the Age of Pluralism: The Philosophy of Charles Taylor in Question*. Cambridge: Cambridge University Press.

Charles Taylor, "Why Do Nations Have to Become States?"

Charles Taylor, "Why Do Nations Have to Become States?," in Reconciling the Solitudes: Essays on Canadian Federalism and Nationalism *(Kingston and Montreal: McGill-Queen's University Press, 1993).*

Chapter Three: Why Do Nations Have to Become States?[1]

There are three major modes of political justification in the modern world: welfare, rights, and self-government. Nationalist modes of thought have become involved in all three and point towards the need for nations to become sovereign states.

The Rise of Nationalism

The initial locus of nationalism as a political justification was in the context of the aim of self-government. The notion that self-government is a good in itself, that men live a higher life who are part of a free or self-managing people, returns early in the modern world. I say "returns" because it was seen as an ideal that the ancients had lived by and that needed to be recovered. It returns first in Renaissance Italy; Machiavelli stands at the end of the first return of the tradition of civic humanism. We find it again in seventeenth-century England, and it becomes part of the mainstream of European thought in the eighteenth century, with the American and French revolutions. Both look back to republican Rome as their model for a free people. Freedom cannot simply be defined as independence for the individual relative to state interference; it is no longer enough to demand "laissez-faire, laissez-passer." Free people are self-governing people.

This had a natural link with the nascent nationalism. The ancient tradition of civic humanism stressed that self-government was only possible for a community where the members identified strongly with their public institutions, to use modern language, or where men loved the laws, to use the old terminology. Self-government was possible because men were willing to die for the *patria*, for the laws, because they devoted themselves to *res publica*. They had what Montesquieu called virtue. Men who were devoted above all to private goals, or spiritual goals that by-passed the fatherland, were fit politically to live in despotisms but not in a free state. Machiavelli and Rousseau both made this point.

Thus, in both the American and French revolutions, the term for those who were partisans of self-rule was "patriot." This expressed one link between self-government and love of the *patria*. The idea of a democratic regime where the people lacked such dedication was still foreign to eighteenth-century believers in self-government. But the term expresses the link with modern nationalism, for today it has above all a nationalist ring; we think ironically of patriotism as the motive that may have pushed many Germans to follow Hitler many Russians to condone Stalin, where the beneficiary of this sentiment is now as much despotism and tyranny as free states. So has the term evolved. Many people even think now of free governments and nationalist feeling as being enemies of one another—in the last analysis, incompatible.

The connection is clear historically. Nationalism did not arise out of the value of self-government. The causes of modern nationalism are very deep and have to do with the erosion of earlier communities and identifications: the withering away of local community, the decline of religious identifications which often by-passed nationality. Indeed, the very notion of a group identification founded on a relation to the supernatural is strange to many moderns in Atlantic civilization; and the local neighbourhood society cannot have the place it once had. But people need a group identification, and the obvious one to take the place of the earlier forms is the one that springs to the attention of the speaking animal, namely, nationality based on language.

But once nationalism arises, it cannot but take the place of patriotism in the aspiration to self-government. Civic humanism needs a strong identification with a community. But this is the form that community-identification takes among modern, emancipated people (emancipated from church, from locality, from hierarchical allegiances). So patriotism comes to mean nationalism. And the context in which nationalism comes first to count politically is that of the call for self-rule. What is demanded here is self-determination. People can only rule themselves if they are grouped in their *patriae*. Only those who form together a *patria* can achieve self-rule, not just any agglomeration of humans who happen to be contiguous with one another. So the ideal demands that *patriae* be given some sort of political personality.

I use the vague term "political personality," rather than saying bluntly that *patriae* ought to be sovereign states, because the eighteenth century already saw our modern dilemma. Its thinkers saw that the dose identification with fatherland and the demands of universal participation require a small face-to-face society; whereas modern nations are very large and are spread over vast areas. The solution, as propounded by Montesquieu and Rousseau and as adopted by the nascent United States, was federation—smaller societies joined in a larger union. Both of the political ideas that dispute for the soul

of contemporary Quebec were born in the eighteenth century, and from exactly the same source, the aspiration to self-government. This demands that the *patria* be given a political expression. This could be taken to mean independent statehood, sovereignty. But given the size and nature of modern nations, it could also require federation. Of course, these two solutions were not necessarily seen as alternatives. The nation could demand independence and then adopt a federal structure.

The paradigm case is, of course, the United States. The fathers of U.S. independence convinced themselves that they formed a nation, that they could justifiably secede from the English nation to which they had seen themselves until quite recently as belonging (notably when they had fought together against New France, for example, at Louisbourg). They felt justified in this, because they saw themselves as betrayed by their ex-compatriots, denied the rights of Englishmen, relegated to a dependent status. So the modern idea was born. Self-determination is the right of a nation, because it is the condition of self-rule of the people who form the nation. This, either because, since they form a nation, the only *patria* they can identify with is that nation, and hence this must have political expression; or as in the case of the United States because, since they form a dependent group which can only achieve self-rule by breaking away, freedom demands that they found a *patria* and hence become a nation.

So the first and most important reason why nations had to become states is that it was seen as a condition of self-rule. The demand for the self-determination of nations was thus part of the aspiration to self-government, to popular rule. It was a demand of the left in the nineteenth century. It spread out with the ideas that flowed from the French Revolution. The term "self-determination" was coined later; in the aftermath of World War I it came into its own. And in this age, the desire for it made sense because it was seen as the inevitable condition and concomitant of self-rule. The new nations were achieving self-determination by carving up what had been autocratic or at least authoritarian-ruled empires: Russia, Germany, Austria.

The second great wave of self-determination came after World War II and involved conferring statehood on the ex-colonies of European imperial states. Here, too, self-rule and self-determination were but two sides of the same coin. Or so it was thought. The regimes that now exist in many of the ex-colonies are indeed very far from the tradition of civic humanism and would shock our eighteenth-century forebears (as would many aspects of our own regimes, to say the truth). But even so, the link is not entirely broken. All modern regimes pay obeisance to the ideal of popular rule. All are supposed to be expressions of the popular will, however bogus. All require some formal expression of this through plebiscites or mass elections or other modes of ratification, for the ideal of self-determination is still conceptually inseparable from that of self-rule.

So nations have become states in order to rule themselves. But do they have to? Certainly they do if they are otherwise hopelessly dependent. If you are a colony, you have as a nation no choice. This paradigm predicament is clarified once and for all by the eighteenth-century Americans, and it is repeated endlessly in the period after 1945. This is why the rhetoric of independence slips naturally into the claim that one lives in a colonial predicament. We see this in the language of Quebec nationalists. It can be seen clearly in the terrorism of the Front de libération du Quebec (FLQ)—echoing the Algerian Front de libération national (FLN)—but it is also evident among the more sophisticated.[2] Of course, there is some historical truth here. Quebec was a colony. But are we Quebeckers "colonized" now? This would be the shortest way to demonstrate that we must become a sovereign state. Well, we obviously are not in some straightforward sense, not as the Thirteen Colonies were in 1776; nor as, say, India was in 1947.

But it is claimed that there are other forms of dependence, other relations which make it such that the only road to genuine self-rule lies through independence. In order to understand these, we have to look at the other ways in which modern nationalism has become intricated in our political arguments and justifications. Nationalism, I said earlier, is a modern form of group identification, one prevalent among emancipated peoples. But to probe deeper, we would have to say that this very idea of identification, of having an identity, is modern. We can speak anachronistically of the identity of medieval man. But this is anachronistic, because a medieval man did not have the question to which identity is the answer.

The question is "Who am I?" The answer points to certain values, certain allegiances, a certain community perhaps, outside of which I could not function as a fully human subject. Of course, I might be able to go on living as an organism outside any values, allegiance, or even community. But what is peculiar to a human subject is the ability to ask and answer questions about what really matters, what is of the highest value, what is truly significant, what is most moving, most beautiful, and so on. The conception of identity is the view that outside the horizon provided by some master value or some allegiance or some community membership, I would be crucially crippled, would become unable to ask and answer

these questions effectively, and would thus be unable to function as a full human subject.

The judgment about identity is a judgment about me in particular, or about some particular person or group. There is no claim that others will be unable to function outside my horizon. The horizon necessary for me is not essential for human beings as such. There are some things which we might judge universally necessary; for instance, a minimum of freedom from crying need or a minimum of love as children. We might argue that without these, no one could become a fully human subject. But the claim about identity is particularized. I may come to realize that belonging to a given culture is part of my identity, because outside of the reference points of this culture I could not begin to put to myself, let alone answer, those questions of ultimate significance that are peculiarly in the repertory of the human subject. Outside this culture, I would not know who I was as a human subject. So this culture helps to identify me.

We can see how the question about identity is a modern one; it belongs to modern, emancipated subjects. For our medieval forebears, there could not have been a question about the conditions of human subjecthood for the individual. In a sense, there were conditions for man as such, especially in his relationship to God, which he could turn his back on with eventually catastrophic results. These conditions were unrecognized or seen only distortedly by pagans and infidels. That was their great misfortune. There was no question of the conditions being different for them. The idea that this can be so is inseparable from modern emancipated humanism. Being human is not just a matter of occupying the rank assigned to humans in the cosmic order. Our humanity is something we each discover in ourselves. To be human is not to be discovered in the order of things in which people are set, but rather in the nature that people discover in themselves. Of course, emancipated humanism does not of itself lead to the notion of identity. It is a necessary but not sufficient condition. The first versions of emancipated humanism of the seventeenth century give us a picture of man as an atomic subject, fulfilling his purposes as a producer and setting up a political order as his instrument. There is as yet no place for the notion of identity, for the question of what horizon of meaning will be essential for this or that person's being human. The need for a horizon of meaning is ignored altogether. Hence, individual and national differences are of no moral relevance.

The sense of the importance of these differences comes in the Romantic period, and it comes with what I have called the question of identity. For each individual to discover in himself what his humanity consists in, he needs a horizon of meaning, which can only be provided by some allegiance, group membership, cultural tradition. He needs, in the broadest sense, a language in which to ask and answer the questions of ultimate significance. The Romantic subject can never be the atomic subject of seventeenth-century thought—of Hobbes and Locke, for instance. Even the most individualistic of Romantic aspirations, in seeing the need for a horizon of meaning, sees that humans are essentially social; for this horizon, "this language comes to us within a society. Romantic individualism involves the demand that we break away from group conformity, that we elaborate an original statement; but it has no place for the seventeenth-century myth of the state of nature, the view that we could see our original condition as one of solitary agents of choice.

Since the Romantic insight is that we need a language in the broadest sense in order to discover our humanity, and that this language is something we have access to through our community, it is natural that the community defined by natural language should become one of the most important poles of identification for the civilization that is heir of the Romantics. Romanticism is a deepening of the modern aspiration to what I have called emancipation, to finding one's human purposes in oneself, autonomously, and not in some cosmic and hierarchic order in which we fit. Hence nationalism, the singling out of linguistic nationality as the paradigm pole of self-identity, is part of this modern drive to emancipation. It connects naturally with the demand for self-rule.

At the same time, the Romantic conception of identity, and also therefore nationalism, comes to modify the other modes of political justification that belong to the modern aspiration to emancipation—in terms of welfare and rights. The modern notion of rights is of what has been called "subjective rights." We can speak of subjective rights when we couch our claims about how it is licit and illicit to act in terms of privileges that are seen to belong to subjects. This big change also comes (naturally) in the seventeenth century. Instead of saying, "It is the law of nature that no one ought to take innocent life," we now start to say, "We all have a right to life." This way of putting it makes the norms governing people's behaviour towards us appear as a privilege, as it were, that we own. The point of this semantic transposition of natural law is, first, that it accords us a certain autonomy in deciding how the norms should be applied to us (if I have a right to life, then presumably I can waive it, a possibility which was not allowed by traditional natural law and which the modern theorists felt they had to block by inventing the notion of an "inalienable right"); and, second, that it underscores the dignity of the person. The point of natural law is now seen to be respect for the integrity of human subjects, who are seen as having a certain dignity. Rights talk is plainly part of modern emancipated humanism.

The same is true of modern justifications of welfare. These arise with the principle that the political and other structures in which people are set have no inherent value. People are no longer to be seen as commanding allegiance because they represent the hierarchical order of things, for example, or the chain of being. They are only instruments set up by people to accomplish their purposes. People and their purposes become the only source of political value. Political structures and policies are to be judged instrumentally. The criterion of welfare is a natural extension of this way of thinking. It requires only that one define welfare as what fulfils human purposes. In the influential utilitarian mode of thought, which has been so important in our civilization since the eighteenth century, it is thought that these purposes can be defined more narrowly in terms of desire-fulfilment. But defined narrowly or broadly, the welfare criterion of justification looks to the effects on human welfare of any structures or policies. It is consequentialist, if not always utilitarian.

Romantic conceptions of identity involve transformations in both these modes of justification. The core of the modern conception of rights is that respect is owed the integrity of the human subject. This obviously entails that the human subject has a right to life, to liberty; on Lockeian assumptions, also to property. But if we add the Romantic understanding of identity, as essential to human subjecthood, then plainly there is something else here to which we have a right, namely, that the conditions of our identity be respected. If we take the nationalist thesis that these are primarily our belonging to a linguistically defined nation, we have the beginnings of another justification of the rights of nations to political expression, which does not pass through the aspiration to self-rule, or not necessarily so. A parallel point can be made about justifications in terms of welfare.

Expression, Realization, and Recognition

Here I want to explore the argument that springs from rights along with the Romantic premises of identity, because this is the richest and most important source of contemporary thought, feeling, and demands. This involves three key notions of post-Romantic thought: expression, realization, and recognition. With regard to the first of these, the conditions of my identity are a horizon of meaning, a language in the broad sense in which I can ask and answer questions of ultimate significance. These I have access to through a culture, that of my community. Thus, it is essential for me that this culture be a rich and healthy one, that it be a going concern. If one takes the nationalist line that this culture's health is synonymous with that of the natural language of my community, then this language must be a going concern.

But languages and cultures are going concerns only to the extent that they are continually re-created through expression, be it through works of art, public institutions, or just everyday exchange. Keeping a language healthy involves giving it scope for expression. So if we have a right that the conditions of our identity be respected, and if these conditions are primarily concerned with the health of our natural language, and if these depend on its expressive power and hence also opportunity, then we have a right that our language be accorded scope for expression. This is what lies behind one of the most insistent demands of our contemporary debate, for what are called collective language rights. These are demands for linguistic rights but not for those of an individual (for example, the right to speak to the public authorities in one's own language or to be tried in a language one can command). The demands are for the right of a community's language to receive the scope it needs to maintain or increase its expressive power, which in turn is seen as a common condition of the identity of all speakers of the language.

The need for expression shades over into the need for what I have called realization—the second important notion I mentioned above. A language gains expressive power in being used for the whole gamut of human purposes. This includes being used in public life, in the world of economic management, of technology, of learning, and so on. This in turn requires that the community speaking the language be achieving something of its own in these fields. If all the important realizations are brought about by another people, then the language of public life, of economic management, of technology, and the like will almost inevitably be a foreign one.

This conclusion is reinforced if we take account of another important dimension. The language/culture that defines our identity must be one that can command our allegiance. We have to see it as valuable. If it comes to be depreciated in our eyes and if it remains the indispensable pole of our identity, we are in a catastrophic position, one in which we cannot avoid depreciating ourselves, tied as we are to an impoverished culture. That many people in modern times have felt the pain of this kind of self-depreciation is undeniable, as is the fact that it has sometimes been the basis of catastrophic reactions, especially the attempt to compensate by hyperchauvinism. The argument between nationalists and anti-nationalists concerns only the remedy. For the latter, self-identification via the nation is contingent and avoidable, and consequently the pains of belonging to an impoverished culture can be overcome by cultivating individuals, if necessary in some other language, and breaking their identification with the nation. For nationalists, this identification is necessary and indispensable, and the remedy can therefore only be the promotion of the national culture.

If we take this nationalist line, we can see that the national community has an even more vital need for self-realization. It is not just that the language risks losing its expressive power if it is not involved in the achievements of technology, the economy, and so on; it is also that the community cannot be without achievements in these sectors, because these are the sectors that today's people value; and a community without realizations of this kind will inescapably come to depreciate itself and thus find its identity undermined. For contemporaries, the crucially prestigious sectors are artistic creation, technological innovation, economic productivity, and, of course, political self-rule itself.

But now we can see the basis of another justification for nations becoming states, which can disconnect itself altogether from the aspiration to republican self-rule, from the tradition of civic humanism. The argument could be that the condition of a peoples having its own realizations in the field of art or technology or the economy is that it become a sovereign state, perhaps because this is the only condition of its insulating itself from some powerful and pervasive foreign pressure. Or the argument could go more directly—that political self-rule is a crucial realization that is necessary in itself for self-respect. Note that this is crucially different from the argument for self-rule in the tradition of civic humanism, the argument that presided over the original demand for self-determination, for it is not necessarily crucial for this demand for realization that the self-rule be republican—that is, that it involve real free popular participation, argument, persuasion, and competition for rule among equals. It suffices that it be rule from within the community rather than outside. The rule of a charismatic dictator can also serve to prove to a people that it is capable of political success; and a despotic government may preside over great economic, technological, and artistic realizations. This is why many Western liberals have come to accept as a valid fulfilment of the demand for self-determination the establishing of despotic regimes in Third World ex-colonies; for these governments, however non-republican, are indigenous and thus can meet this need for indigenous realization. One can learn that black is beautiful under an indigenous dictatorship as one never could under semi-liberal colonial institutions; so runs the argument. Whether it does not involve an inescapably patronizing element is another issue.

This separation of self-determination from its republican roots has relevance to our country in a different way. The purely republican case for Quebec independence is surely very weak. All rhetoric about colonialism aside, it is clearly not the case that separate statehood is the essential precondition of self-rule as it was for the Thirteen Colonies. In a federally structured representative democracy, clearly we have self-rule. That is why we are capable of going about the political business of deciding among ourselves whether we will go independent or not—this, through the normal political process. This is not how things happen in a real colonial predicament.

But we can construct another argument for political sovereignty out of the need for realization. The argument could go that Quebec needs an independent political instrument in order to ensure participation in economic direction, a role in technology design and the like either because of the overwhelming force of the neighbouring Anglo-Saxon culture of 250 million, the richest and strongest economy in the world, or because of the greater political clout that the English-Canadian majority inevitably exercises in Canada; or for both reasons. In short, it could be argued that an independent political entity is necessary to insulate Quebec to some degree from forces that threaten to occupy the whole space of economic management and technological innovation, not to mention a good part of those of political organization and the formation of public bureaucracies.

Something like this has been an important argument of nationalists in Quebec. One of the most popular arguments among independentists is to the effect that the majority in federal Canada has favoured the economic development of Ontario over Quebec and that the requirements of economic realization must therefore include an independent Quebec government with the major responsibility for the economic management of the province's economy. The argument ramifies greatly. Its relevance is not only to what we have called realization. It is also an argument about welfare: provincial underdevelopment has meant the impoverishment of Québécois, it is claimed. But realization is also an important element in it. I am not concerned here to weigh the argument; I am simply recording it as the form that this mode of justification of sovereignty takes in the present Quebec debate.

Of course, political independence has a more direct relation to realization. Political sovereignty is itself a realization, one that puts a people on the map. This brings us to the third important notion mentioned above. I spoke above about a political status "insulating" Quebec from the invasive influence of North America. Independentists usually object to this kind of language; they protest that their intention is not to turn inward but to have access to the outside world, which they have been denied by being buried as a minority in federal Canada. They touch here on a very important point, which a study of the Romantic conception of identity can also clarify. Because the language/culture that we need for our identity is one that we always receive from others, from our surroundings, it becomes very important that we be recognized for what we are. If this is denied or set at naught by those who surround us, it is extremely difficult to maintain a horizon of meaning by which to identify ourselves.

This obviously applies to individuals growing up in a community and living their lives in it, but it also applies between communities. This is especially evident when we appreciate how important the self-respect of a culture is. It is gained through realization, but the value of realization depends to a great degree on the recognition of others, on how the people are seen internationally by the world at large. There is therefore among a small people, whose self-confidence has been shaken by living in the shadow of the contemporary world's most powerful language and culture and technology, a tremendous hunger for international recognition. This goes a long way to explain the impact of the famous "Quebec libre" speech of General de Gaulle in 1967, which was appreciated far beyond the ranks of independentists.

It can also provide us with another reason for demanding independence, because the formal trappings of sovereignty—the exchange of ambassadors, a seat in the United Nations, and so on—are the paramount form of international recognition today. That is what it means to be internationally recognized. This, incidentally, is why it is very hard to conceive of the independentist movement in Quebec willingly making a deal for a renewed federation short of sovereignty; for the legal status of sovereign country is essential to the goal they seek. This can be caricatured by their enemies as the desire on the part of an elite to ride around in limousines in foreign capitals and cut a figure at international conferences. But it also has a more serious side in the need for recognition, for an acceptance by the world community that one counts for something, has something to say to the world, and is among those addressed by others—the need to exist as a people on the world stage.

Why Nations Have to Become States

We are now in a position to sum up this rather rambling set of answers to the question "Why should nations become states?" (a) The first answer might be "Because sovereignty is the condition of republican self-rule." This is the answer we can retrospectively put in the mouth of the American independence leaders, except that they had to become a nation at the same time. They made a nation-state, but all in order to rule themselves. It is the answer of the peoples of Central Europe between the wars and of the colonies struggling for liberation after World War II. But it is hard to apply this to our situation. So we turn to (b), another set of arguments that applies to rights. We can argue (i) that the conditions of our identity are indispensable to our being full human subjects; (ii) that, for people today, a crucial pole of identification (in some cases, *the* crucial pole) is their language/culture and hence their linguistic community; thus (iii) the availability of our linguistic community as a viable pole of identification is indispensable to our being full human subjects. Now (iv) we have a right to demand that others respect whatever is indispensable to our being full human subjects (for example, life and liberty). Therefore (v) we have a right to demand that others respect the conditions of our linguistic community being a viable pole of identification.

The conditions mentioned in (v) can be spelled out to include the health and expressive power of our language, a certain realization in crucial sectors on the part of our linguistic community, and some degree of international recognition. These, with other premises, can be made the basis of language legislation such as we now have in Quebec (collective rights), and also of political independence as a matter of right because it is supposedly indispensable to realization and recognition.

What we think of this argument will depend partly on our detailed conception of the conditions mentioned in (v), which may be different from those adumbrated above. But it may also depend on what we think of premises (i), (ii), and (iv). Of these, (ii) is the only controversial one today. It simply states what follows from our definition of identity. One would only challenge this if one wanted to challenge all talk about identity. No doubt many philosophers would, but in fact it is hard to see how much of our modern self-understanding could get on without some concept of this kind. Point (iv) is similarly basic to political thought and argument in the twentieth century.

The big disagreements concern point (ii), whether to affirm or deny it, and if the former, what variant to affirm. Some espouse (ii) in a strong, exclusive form that makes the linguistic community the all-important overriding pole of identity while others see it is an extremely important basis of a modern identity but not the only one. For those such as classical Marxists, the ultimate identity is indeed that of a group, but not a national society; rather, it is the world community of liberated mankind. Proletarians have no country, as the *Communist Manifesto* assures us. Now, for anti-nationalists of either

individual or collectivist stripe, the above argument does not carry through. There is no justification for restrictive language legislation and no justification for sovereignty apart from (a)—its being indispensable for republican self-rule. Since this clearly does not apply to the Quebec-Canada case, the demand is rejected out of hand.

We can see the shape of the battle that is joined between those who affirm (ii) in its most uncompromising form and those who deny it in any form—a battle whose general lines are perhaps distressingly familiar to us. But what if you think, as I do, that neither of these is right? You may not accept that the most important pole of identification is the national one, that making it the only one is liable to stultify human development and justify repressive policies. At the same time, you may not accept that group identification is of no importance at all for our identity; on the contrary, you may think that it is very important for everyone and that in certain circumstances (when the culture is menaced) it can be truly vital. If you also think, as I do, that something like these circumstances have existed in Quebec during the last two centuries, you will have trouble aligning either with the ultranationalists or with the anti-nationalists. But you can be sure of one thing if you feel like this: the Canadian scene will be perennially frustrating for you, because the extreme positions always seem to win out here. That ultranationalism should win in Quebec is perhaps not too surprising. More surprising is the resistance to it.

What perhaps needs more comment is the antinationalist stand of the rest of Canada. I do not mean by this that there is not a lot of Canadian nationalism around, both healthy and unhealthy. I certainly do not mean to deny that there is a lot of linguistic and cultural narrowness and bigotry in English Canada. From the standpoint of Quebec, we are painfully aware of this. There has certainly been intolerance of the minority—and it is really this, more than anything else, that makes the cause of Canadian unity seem desperate in the long run. But English Canada has not been nationalist in the sense characterized here. The intolerance and bigotry, the suppression of French schools and the French language, were never carried out from a sense of a threatened identity. Indeed, since English Canadians share a language with our giant neighbour, they have rarely had any sense of how language can play a crucial role in identity.

Hence, when faced with the demands of French Canada for some recognition of its rights as a nation, where this took the form of the right of French speakers or the powers and jurisdictions of Quebec, the rest of Canada has generally been hostile and uncomprehending. When pushed to a justification of its refusal, it has generally taken up the language of antinationalism; indeed, it has often gone even further and rejected even (i), the whole language of identity. English Canadian spokespersons have taken refuge in the crassly philistine contention that language is just a medium of communication, that we should choose our media for greatest efficiency, and that English should therefore predominate; or else they have argued that a society needs a minimum degree of unity and this precludes allowing wide rights to all minority languages. French is assimilated, on this argument, with all the languages spoken by new Canadians, and this assimilation by itself shows a complete misunderstanding of the nationalist demands of French Canada and, latterly, Quebec.

Politically, our situation seems to be this: while the argument of (a) is generally understood to be irrelevant for Quebec (by all except the minority with an insatiable taste for self-dramatization), some form of the argument I tried to formulate in (b) is accepted by the vast majority of Quebecers. That is, even opponents of independence and of the Parti Québécois accept some moderate variant of (ii)—that language and the linguistic community form a crucial part of the horizon that defines their identity. They are not willing to sacrifice everything to it, as are the ultranationalists, but its place cannot be denied. A stand like this is almost inevitable on the part of a small people whose language and culture have been so beleaguered for so long. The alternative would have been a most stultifying fatalism.

It is because of this identification that one can speak of a French Canadian nation and, latterly, a Quebec nation. Nations exist not just where there is the objective fact of speaking the same language and sharing a common history, but where this is subjectively reflected in a peoples identifications. To parody Marxist jargon, nations cannot only be *an sich*, they must also be *für sich*. Hence, almost all Quebeckers support conclusion (v) in some form. Their argument is over what the conditions are for the linguistic community's being a viable pole of identification. Does this require sovereignty? Certainly it requires some kind of political personality for Quebec. This, argue federalists, Quebec already possesses as a province in the Canadian federation.

It seems that two things prevent this being a satisfactory answer for most Quebeckers. In the first place, it is not clear that the province has all the powers it would need to ensure the level of realization it aspires to; secondly, the French fact in Canada still lacks international recognition. Sovereignty association claims to fill these two lacunae. Whether it could really deliver as promised is a big question, but, on the face of it, at least it looks as if it could. A new form of Canadian federation could do so

too, one founded on a recognition of the duality that is basic to the country. A public acceptance that the country is the locus of two nations could allow the international recognition that has hitherto always been muted.

I cannot hide the fact that I consider the federal solution to be the preferable one. Sovereignty association seems to me near-disastrous for two reasons. First, there will in fact be too much divergence of interest (coupled with bad blood) for it to work. If it gets off the ground at all, it will start breaking up almost immediately, especially as the will to make it work is absent among ultranationalists in Quebec, for whom sovereignty association is only a stopgap measure to make separation less abrupt and traumatic, and thus to make it saleable to the majority in the province. Even if it does get off the drawing board, sovereignty association will almost surely end badly. In the second place, sovereignty association is the project of the ultranationalists. If it wins, their vision of Quebec will be correspondingly strengthened. But few things are more spiritually destructive to a community than when ultranationalism wins out and a full-blooded affirmation of (ii) in its most extreme variant is made the basis of its social life. Not only does this breed a willingness to sacrifice everything else on the altar of the nation, but nationalism itself becomes an obsession with power. As things stand, only a renewed federation based on duality can be a long-term alternative to separation; that is, no long-term solution will be viable which fails to come to terms with the place that variants of argument (b) have in Quebec. But such a solution would require that English Canada come to have some understanding for (b) and hence for Quebec.

I have been discussing why nations have to become states. We have seen that beyond the traditional justification (a), there is a possible complex of arguments adumbrated in (b) which can justify statehood. But whereas (a) seems to give sufficient grounds for demanding sovereignty, since this is the necessary condition of republican self-rule, the predicament defined by (b) is more complicated.

The requirements of expression, realization, and recognition may push us towards sovereignty as a solution. But there may also be good reasons pushing us the other way. The advantages of supranational collaboration are more and more evident to us. These are partly economic and technological, as has been stressed in the European Community and in some of the arguments for maintaining Canadian unity. But they are also spiritual, in opening not only a wider identification but also a plurality of poles of identification. This can help protect us from the stultifying, repressive obsession with the nation, which is one of the standing dangers in modern civilization.

That is why federation remains an important option, just as Montesquieu and Rousseau saw two centuries ago, when our modern ideal of self-rule began to establish itself. In the best of all worlds, nations would not have to become states. It should be one of their options (self-determination) but not the top option. A higher aspiration is supranational unity, following the best of the modern political tradition.

Post-Reading Questions

1. Why does contemporary nationalism not reduce to the simple desire for self-rule, according to Taylor?
2. What is the relationship between language and identity, in Taylor's estimation, and how might it justify language protection policies?
3. Why does *public* recognition of one's culture and language continue to be so important in the contemporary world?
4. Is political sovereignty the logical outcome of aspirations for cultural recognition and self-determination, or are there other alternatives, according to Taylor?

CASE STUDY
THE BOUCHARD-TAYLOR COMMISSION
ON REASONABLE ACCOMMODATION IN QUEBEC

Introduction

In February 2007, Quebec premier Jean Charest requested that the lieutenant governor of the province establish a commission to address the challenges of "reasonable accommodation" in the province. This request was widely understood to refer to the problems and issues arising from cultural and religious diversity in Quebec. The *Consultation Commission on Accommodation Practices Related to Cultural Differences* was thus formed, headed by two well-known academics: Gérard Bouchard, a noted historian, sociologist, and fiction writer; and Charles Taylor, a philosopher and public intellectual whose essay precedes this case reading. The commission sponsored a series of public hearings in which Quebec residents from different communities were invited to present their views and concerns on issues related to religious, linguistic, and cultural diversity in the province. Informally known as the Bouchard-Taylor Commission, or alternately the Commission on Reasonable Accommodation, the initiative was very much in the public eye.

The final report of the commission, "Building the Future: A Time for Reconciliation," was released in 2008 to much fanfare. Although moderate and balanced in tone, it managed nonetheless to spark considerable controversy in Quebec. Among its recommendations were proposals for greater funding for organizations that engage and inform the public on issues of diversity, and for the establishment of a para-governmental agency dedicated to overseeing "intercultural harmonization" practices in the province. Also proposed were various strategies for improving the integration of new immigrants to Quebec. These recommendations reflect the fact that much of the impetus for the commission's establishment came from reports (some true, some false) of cultural clashes between religiously devout newcomers, particularly Muslims, and native Québécois.

A number of the commission's recommendations relate to the promotion of a broad policy of "interculturalism" for Quebec. Interculturalism is advanced by the commission as a uniquely Québécois alternative to the perspective of multiculturalism. Because multiculturalism (according to the commissioners) seems to suggest a strict parity between all linguistic and cultural groups, Bouchard and Taylor argued that it is not an appropriate framework for the Quebec context—where the French language and culture is of central importance. As Charles Taylor writes in "Why Do Nations Have to Become States?," the preservation of language and culture lies at the heart of the struggle of "nations" like Quebec for recognition as a distinct society. Not surprisingly, the "ultranationalists" to which Taylor refers in his essay were not appeased by the commission's final recommendations, for these did not encourage steps toward greater sovereignty for the province. Federalists took comfort in the report's moderate tone, but some immigrant group advocates and religious minority communities balked at the rejection of the framework of multiculturalism and the commissioners' sympathetic discussion of French Quebecers' fear of newcomers. Despite Taylor's statement (in the previous essay) that "in the best of all worlds, nations would not have to become states," then, nationalist aspirations centring on language and culture continue to rub up against federalist sentiments in the aftermath of the commission's work.

Gérard Bouchard and Charles Taylor, *From* "Building the Future: A Time for Reconciliation"

Excerpt from Gérard Bouchard and Charles Taylor, "Building the Future: A Time for Reconciliation," Abridged Report (Quebec: Government of Quebec, 2007). http://red.pucp .edu.pe/wp-content/uploads/biblioteca/buildingthefutureGerardBouchardycharlestaylor.pdf

. . .

Section II: A Crisis of Perception

. . . [A]fter a year of research and consultation, we have come to the conclusion that the foundations of collective life in Quebec are not in a critical situation. If we can speak of an "accommodation crisis," it is essentially from the standpoint of perceptions. Indeed, our deliberations did not reveal to us a striking or sudden increase in the adjustments or accommodation that public institutions allow, nor did we observe that the normal operation of our institutions would have been disrupted by such requests. We did, of course, observe occasional friction points, doubts and dissatisfaction, but nothing that confirms that the overall situation might be uncontrollable, eloquently confirmed by the very small number of accommodation cases that end up before the courts.

Since the overall situation is not critical, how can we explain that the Quebec government deemed it necessary to establish a commission to examine the "problem" of accommodation? To answer this question, we must reconstruct the chain of events that led to what we are calling a crisis of perception. In this way, we can pinpoint the circumstantial causes that have encouraged a significant number of Quebecers to adopt a very negative judgment of accommodation practices, even to the extent of believing that they threaten social order and our most basic values.

A. The Chronology of Events
The history of public debate in Quebec on the question of reasonable accommodation can be divided into four periods. The number and type of cases and the intensity of public debate are the key criteria that define the periods. The chronology that we have established comprises

73 cases or incidents and covers roughly 22 years, from December 1985 to April 2008. . . .

1. Antecedents (from December 1985 to April 2002)
During this period, we noted 13 accommodation cases reported in the media. Our first observation is that all of the cases, with one exception, involved reasonable accommodation in the literal sense. In each case, legal or quasilegal bodies were involved, i.e. the Commission des droits de la personne et des droits de la jeunesse (CDPDJ), the Tribunal des droits de la personne du Québec, the Montréal Municipal Court, the Superior Court of Quebec, the Federal Court of Appeal, and the Supreme Court of Canada. Generally speaking, the public discovered during this period the new legal obligations stemming from changes in jurisprudence and the coming into force of the charters. In 1994, the wearing of the Muslim headscarf was the focus of debate that led the CDPDJ to formulate an opinion on the question in 1995. Aside from this topic, no striking controversy emerged concerning the very validity of accommodation practices.

2. The intensification of controversy (from May 2002 to February 2006)
This second period marks a turning point in debate on accommodation. It began with the announcement of the Superior Court of Quebec judgment concerning the wearing of the kirpan, which had a significant impact on public opinion. Debate surrounding the application of sharia, especially in Ontario, also largely fuelled the controversy. The events of September 11, 2001, were still very much on people's minds: a social context permeated by suspicion and insecurity developed. Certain accommodation cases led to legal escalation: the decisions of lower courts were appealed, occasionally before the Supreme Court. What began as local cases became veritable issues whose legal developments society monitored closely. Another novelty was the emergence of topics of dispute such as the debate on Christmas trees, which are not, in a literal sense, a form of reasonable accommodation.

3. A time of turmoil (from March 2006 to June 2007)
This third period is noteworthy for the proliferation of cases or affairs reported in the media. During this 15-month period alone, we noted roughly 40 cases, compared with 13 and 12 cases, respectively, during the two preceding periods. These figures reflect the much more active role that the media began to play in respect of the accommodation question. The term "accommodation" entered public discourse and from then on became a hackneyed expression. Debate was no longer confined to the question of minority religious practices but now encompassed the much broader question of the integration of immigrants and minorities. A phenomenon that had begun to emerge during the preceding period now became fully apparent: part of the population reacted to accommodation requests as though it felt wronged by what it perceived to be "privileges." In January 2007, the leader of the ADQ released a letter in which he denounced the political leaders' submission and the "old reflex of the minority" that encourages Quebecers to "give in" and "collectively fade into the background." Hérouxville's notorious life standards were adopted shortly thereafter.[3] The accommodation crisis reached its height in March 2007 in the weeks preceding the provincial election: accommodation had become a social issue on which politicians made almost daily pronouncements.

. . .

B. Facts and Perceptions
During the time of turmoil, many cases or affairs led a significant number of Quebecers to adopt a very negative perception of reasonable accommodation. These cases or affairs focused usually on accommodation or adjustments perceived as being illegitimate or a form of threat to Quebec society's values.

In order to clarify the situation, the commission mandated two researchers who devoted over four months to reconstructing as rigorously as possible the facts based on a sampling of 21 cases among those that received the broadest media coverage and that fuelled most extensively the controversy. The researchers questioned the interveners and witnesses and relied on the documentation available.

Our research reveals that in 6 of the 21 cases studied, there was no apparent distortion between the facts reconstructed and the public's general perception of these cases. However, we noted striking distortions in the other 15 cases. Thus, the negative perception of reasonable accommodation that spread in the public often centred on an erroneous or partial perception of practices in the field. Here are [some] examples that illustrate the extent of these distortions.

1. Prenatal classes at the CLSC de Parc-Extension
Widespread perception: Men who accompanied their spouses to prenatal classes offered by the CLSC de Parc-Extension were excluded from the courses at the request of Muslim women who were upset by their presence.

The reconstructed facts: During the day, the CLSC de Parc-Extension organizes support and information meetings adapted to its clientele in the neighbourhood, which is very poor and mainly comprises immigrants, who have difficulty consulting health services. Prenatal care is one of the topics broached at these meetings. This service is used, above all, by immigrant women, but men are not excluded from it. Evening prenatal courses for expectant mothers and their spouses are offered in the two other CLSCs affiliated with the Centre de santé et de services sociaux de la Montagne.

2. The "directive" from the Société de l'assurance automobile du Québec

Widespread perception: The management of the Société de l'assurance automobile du Québec (SAAQ) has ordered its female driving examiners to relinquish their place to a male colleague when Orthodox Jews take their driving test.

The reconstructed facts: An SAAQ "accommodation guide" indicates the internal directives concerning the "exemption from the wearing of headgear for religious or medical reasons when a photograph is taken." This guide also provides an example of accommodation related to the driving test, i.e., the case of a female Muslim client who wishes to take the practical test with a female driving examiner. The guide explains that the SAAQ can respond to such requests "if a female driving examiner is available at the time." Otherwise, "an accommodation appointment may be granted at a later date since the centre is not required to reschedule other clients or to upset the test schedule to acquiesce *immediately* to such a request when it is not possible to do so." The guide also specifies that "reasonable accommodation does not, therefore, apply when the request contradicts another right, e.g., the right to gender equality, the infringement of public order, or the safety of the premises and individuals."

3. The Mont-Saint-Grégoire sugarhouse

Widespread perception: Muslims arrived one morning at the sugarhouse and demanded that the menu be altered to conform to their religious standard. All of the other customers were therefore obliged to consume pea soup without ham and pork-free pork and beans. In the afternoon, the same Muslims entered the crowded dance hall and interrupted the festivities to recite their prayers. The customers in the dance hall were in a manner of speaking expelled from the sugarhouse.

The reconstructed facts: One week before the outing, a representative of Astrolabe, a Muslim association, met with the sugarhouse's owners to discuss certain changes to the menu, which would apply solely to the members of the group. The modified menu excluded pork meat but included halal sausage and salami provided and paid for by Astrolabe. This arrangement having been made, the association reserved one of the four dining rooms in the sugarhouse for its exclusive use. On the appointed day, after the meal, 40-odd members of the group moved several tables and chairs in the room reserved for them for a short prayer. The management of the sugarhouse wanted to free up the room as quickly as possible (business was brisk and nearly 300 customers were waiting to be seated) and proposed to those individuals who wished to pray that they use instead the dance hall, which was almost empty at that time. The dance hall can accommodate roughly 650 people and 30 customers were then in the room, some of them waiting to be seated in the dining room. Several young girls were dancing to popular music. The management of the sugarhouse interrupted the music so that the Muslim customers could say their prayers, which took less than 10 minutes. The music then resumed. According to the management, no one was expelled from or asked to leave the dance hall.

4. Certified kosher food

Widespread perception: In the food sector, many firms secretly modify their recipes and invest heavily to make their products conform to Orthodox Jewish religious standards, which occasions a substantial price increase that consumers assume unwittingly. In Quebec, the increase is on the order of several tens of millions of dollars and perhaps more each year. The companies and the rabbis share these revenues.

The reconstructed facts: No authoritative comprehensive study currently exists on the topic. However, we do have at our disposal testimony and partial but reliable overviews that clearly establish that (a) the interest that businesses display in kosher certification reflects marketing strategies that cover a portion of the United States; (b) the additional costs that consumers must assume are very minimal; (c) kosher certification may require companies to modify certain production procedures, e.g., additional washing, but not to modify the composition of their products; and (d) rabbis do not profit by certification.

. . .

C. Dissatisfaction with Accommodation

We have thus observed with respect to a majority of cases that aroused controversy significant distortions between facts and perceptions. Given this observation, we can only ask ourselves what form debate would have taken if the public had obtained complete, objective information. The most likely hypothesis is that an accommodation crisis would not have arisen. Two sources of distortions clearly contributed to the perception crisis:

the well-known phenomenon of the rumour and the media, which participants at the forums and hearings often criticized and several representatives of which engaged in fairly harsh self-criticism. However, we cannot explain by means of these factors alone Quebecers' astonishing reaction. With the help of debate on accommodation, Quebecers have engaged in self-examination and questioned themselves as never before perhaps since the Quiet Revolution. . . .

. . .

Section III: The State of Harmonization Practices

A. The Rationale for Reasonable Accommodation
. . . Our investigation reveals that in Quebec harmonization measures are now a part of the day-to-day life of public institutions such as health establishments, schools, and universities.

At the same time as this change, a new tradition has taken shape in the realm of law. The traditional conception of equality, based on the principle of uniform treatment, has given way to another conception that pays closer attention to differences. Little by little, the law has come to recognize that the rule of equality sometimes demands differential treatment. It is this conception that the legal provision of reasonable accommodation reflects. . . .

The adjustment of rules is thus intended to prevent individuals from being put at a disadvantage or excluded and their right to equality to thus be compromised. In these different situations, the duty of accommodation created by law does not require that a regulation or a statue be abrogated but only that its discriminatory effects be mitigated in respect of certain individuals by making provision for an exception to the rule or a specific adaptation of it. . . .

. . .

It is important to note that the duty of accommodation is not limitless. For the duty of accommodation to exist, discrimination as conceived by the charters must first be present. Section 10 of the Quebec Charter of Human Rights and Freedoms lists 13 grounds for discrimination that may justify an accommodation request. These grounds are mainly circumstantial, such as pregnancy or marital status, or permanent traits such as sex, skin colour, or a disability, or socio-cultural traits such as religion, language, and so on. This first criterion thus excludes from the realm of reasonable accommodation any request not based on a recognized discriminatory ground.

The realism of the request and the ability of the employer or the organization concerned to accommodate the individual are a second, highly restrictive constraint. Jurists use the expression undue hardship to indicate it. Indeed, according to tradition in the realm of labour law, a request may be rejected if it involves an unreasonable cost, upsets the organization's operation, infringes the rights of others or prejudices the maintenance of security and public order.

. . .

Section V: A Proposed Policy Respecting Harmonization Practices

. . .

A. Reasonable Accommodation and Concerted Adjustment
The field of harmonization practices is complex and there is more than one way to define and delineate it. We have decided to give priority to the framework for handling requests, which leads us to distinguish between the legal route and the citizen route. Under the legal route, requests must conform to formal codified procedures that the parties bring against each other and that ultimately determine a winner and a loser. Indeed, the courts impose decisions most of the time. The legal route is that of reasonable accommodation. Requests follow a much different route under the second path, which is less formal and relies on negotiation and the search for a compromise. Its objective is to find a solution that satisfies both parties and it corresponds to concerted adjustment.

Generally speaking, we strongly favour recourse to the citizen route and concerted adjustment, for several reasons: (a) it is good for citizens to learn to manage their differences and disagreements; (b) this path avoids congesting the courts; (c) the values underlying the citizen route (exchanges, negotiation, reciprocity, and so on) are the same ones that underpin interculturalism. In quantitative terms, we have noted, moreover, that most requests follow the citizen route and only a small number rely on the courts.

In some situations, the legal route may be the only solution, but it should be avoided as much as possible. To this end, it is in the interveners' interests to engage in negotiations that simultaneously emphasize a contextual, deliberative and reflexive approach. The contextual dimension takes into account the unique nature of individual situations. Through the deliberative dimension, the interveners engage in dialogue and the reflexive dimension allows them to engage in self-criticism and mend their ways when necessary.

. . .

B. Three Types of Guidelines
Undue hardship

. . .

. . . Accommodation or adjustment requests are thus limited by: (a) the institution's aims (provide care, educate, make a profit, and so on); (b) the financial cost and functional constraints; (c) other people's rights.

Moreover, as we saw in section IV, rights and freedoms themselves may be limited in the name of "regard for democratic values, public order and the general well-being of the citizens of Quebec" (Quebec Charter of Human Rights and Freedoms). Several statutes seek to promote or protect certain common public values, e.g., the Education Act, the Act Respecting Health Services and Social Services, and the Act Respecting Occupational Health and Safety. Obviously, harmonization practices may not contravene these statutes and must remain faithful to Quebec's common public values.

Ethical reference points

The negotiation process linked to accommodation or adjustment requests bring into play a second series of guidelines that fulfil an ethical role. While certain attitudes and behaviour foster the emergence of mutually satisfactory solutions, others may lead to withdrawal, inflexibility and, ultimately, to court action. Among the ethical reference points that should guide any negotiation, let us mention openness to the Other, reciprocity, mutual respect, the ability to listen, good faith, the ability to reach compromises, and a willingness to rely on discussion to resolve stalemates. The institution of a culture of compromise largely centres on all of these factors that foster the coordination of action and the peaceful, concerted resolution of disputes.

. . .

C. Two Controversial Questions
Two questions pertaining to harmonization practices have been keenly debated in recent months, concerning (a) the hierarchical ordering of rights and (b) the approach adopted by the courts to evaluate the applicants' religious beliefs. . . .

. . .

Section VII: An Evolving Quebec
A. Anxiety over Identity
. . .

French-speaking Quebec is a minority culture and needs a strong identity to allay its anxieties and behave like a serene majority. This is the first lesson that we should draw from recent events. The identity inherited from the French-Canadian past is perfectly legitimate

and it must survive, but it can no longer occupy alone the Quebec identity space. It must hinge on the other identities present, in a spirit of interculturalism, in order to prevent fragmentation and exclusion. All in all, it is a question of sustaining through symbols and imagination the common public culture, which is made up of universal values and rights, but without disfiguring it. Quebec must now apply itself to this difficult task.

. . .

C. Inequality and Discrimination
. . .

3. Racism and discrimination

Quebec has adopted tools to combat discrimination and racism. Mention should be made, among others, of the Quebec Charter of Human Rights and Freedoms, the Déclaration de 1986 sur les relations interethniques et interraciales, equal employment opportunity programs for disadvantaged groups, programs designed to foster the development of ethnic minorities, the adoption by many public institutions of anti-racist policies, the programs of the ministère de l'Immigration et des Communautés culturelles, the fight against racial profiling, and that the government is slated to announce in the spring of 2008 to more effectively combat racism and discrimination.

Tools to combat discrimination exist but they do not appear to be used as much as they should be in conjunction with concrete initiatives. An analysis of the findings of recent studies leads us to conclude that between 20 and 25 per cent of Quebecers claim to have been the victims of discrimination over the past three to five years, mainly in the workplace. This proportion doubles in racialized groups. During our consultations, we also heard about numerous cases of discrimination. Here are some examples: a young Muslim pharmacy student who wears a headscarf was refused for a training session by 50 pharmacists before she found an Arab pharmacist willing to accept her; a 17-year-old Muslim girl who also wears a headscarf is regularly insulted at school and in the street, but her mother has taught her never to respond, since she does not want to "instill hatred in her;" an immigrant woman who was at the top of her class at the Université de Montréal submitted 200 applications for a training session and received as many refusals; a newcomer, an engineer, managed several hundred employees in his country of origin but has been unable to find a job here (he has sent his curriculum vitae to 250 firms).

At the root of discrimination are stereotypes, which are both the cause and consequence of stigmatization. A number of Quebecers have a negative image of all ethnic minorities that they then attribute to individual members of the groups. . . .

. . .

D. Looking to the Future

As we can see, the debate on harmonization practices is linked to factors that are crucial to the future of Quebec society. This undoubtedly goes a long way to explaining why this debate reached such a level of intensity in 2006 and the first months of 2007. . . .

2. The edification of a common identity

To plan for its future, Quebec society must naturally rely on its own integration model. As we have seen, interculturalism fosters the edification of a common identity through interaction between citizens of all origins. Moreover, we believe that this process is solidly under way in at least eight avenues or spheres. Let us point out that, in keeping with the rule of law and the imperatives of pluralism, the identity that we are edifying must be able to develop as a citizen culture, i.e., all Quebecers must recognize themselves in it and achieve self-fulfilment through it. Below are the eight avenues to be emphasized.

1. French as the common public language. The intercultural approach would hardly have any meaning if Quebecers were unable to communicate with each other in the same language.
2. The development of a feeling of belonging to Quebec society through the schools, civic life, intercultural exchanges, knowledge of the territory, and so on.
3. The exploration and promotion of common values as rallying points, a source of solidarity and factors in the definition of a future or a horizon for Quebec, e.g., pluralism, equality (especially gender equality), secularism, non-discrimination, and non-violence.
4. The edification of a genuine national memory that takes into account ethnocultural diversity and makes Quebec's past accessible to citizens of all origins.
5. Contributions linked to artistic and literary creation, which foster the development of a common imagination sustained by cultural diversity.
6. Citizenship participation and societal choices that help to establish values and basic guidelines in policies and programs. Over time, these choices give rise to a political mentality and national traditions.
7. The associative idea that places intercultural exchanges in the realm of concrete, citizen action.

It encourages intercommunity initiatives and all forms of projects that assemble individuals from different ethnocultural milieus.

8. Symbols of collective life. Repeated interaction with institutions in Quebec society lead to the internalization of the attendant language, rituals, symbols and codes.

This list is not exhaustive. It can be enriched by other factors that contribute to the redefinition of a Quebec identity asserted in a spirit of respect for ethnocultural diversity and the pluralist philosophy that Quebec has adopted, without harming the French-Canadian heritage to which, precisely, this identity opens new horizons.

Section VIII: Priority Recommendations

Below is a summary of our priority recommendations. . . . Our recommendations follow five key themes:

1. . . . they call for a definition of new policies and programs pertaining to interculturalism (legislation, a declaration or a policy statement) and secularism (a proposed white paper).
2. Several recommendations are linked to the central theme of integration and focus primarily on: (a) recognition of immigrants' skills and diplomas; (b) francization programs; (c) the need for more sustained efforts to regionalize immigration; and (d) the need for enhanced coordination between government departments.
3. From the standpoint of intercultural practices and mutual understanding, our recommendations highlight: (a) the need for broader training of all government agents in public establishments, starting with the schools, because of the role they play in socialization; and (b) the need to further encourage community and intercommunity action projects.
4. In keeping with the harmonization policy formulated in our report, our recommendations are intended to foster the accountability of interveners in the citizen sphere (public and private agencies) by ensuring that they have received adequate training. We are asking the government to ensure that the practical knowledge acquired in institutions be recorded, promoted and disseminated in all of the milieus concerned.
5. Another priority field is the fight against inequality and discrimination. Our recommendations in this respect focus primarily on: (a) the underrepresentation of ethnic minorities in the public service;

(b) the urgency of combating the numerous forms of discrimination, Islamophobia, anti-Semitism and racism to which racialized groups are subject, especially Blacks; (c) the support to be offered immigrant women; (d) the need to increase the resources of the Commission des droits de la personne et des droits de la jeunesse; and (e) the strengthening of economic and social rights in the Quebec Charter.

Conclusion

The rationale underlying our report stems from three intersecting themes: (a) interculturalism; (b) open secularism; and (c) harmonization practices. For each of these themes, we have sought to find balanced positions. In the case of interculturalism, it is a question of reconciling the imperatives of pluralism stemming from the growing diversification of our society and the necessary integration of a small nation that constitutes a cultural minority in North America. The system centred on open secularism, as we have defined it, hinges on a delicate balance between its four main components, i.e., freedom of conscience, the equality of citizens, the reciprocal autonomy of Church and the State, and the neutrality of the State. The policy respecting harmonization practices takes into account both the desirable or necessary changes and respect for other people's rights and the smooth operation of institutions.

This general guideline, based on the search for balance, has a twofold advantage. First, it avoids radical solutions, which are always to be feared in the realm of intercultural relations. Second, it is in keeping with the procedures adopted by public and private institutions and agencies in Quebec. For these reasons, we believe that it is in Quebec society's interests to accept these moderate proposals, designed to ensure in the long run the fair treatment of all of the groups in question.

. . .

Post-Case-Reading Questions

1. Does the report see recent incidents of cultural and religious tension as stemming from deep and possibly unbridgeable differences among communities in Quebec?
2. Why does the report conclude that the challenges posed by cultural and religious accommodation in Quebec are not a matter that should be left strictly up to the courts and politicians?
3. How does the issue of race figure in the report's analysis and recommendations?

Endnotes

Chapter I | Plato

1. The Greek word is *dikastês*, a member of a jury panel. These were very large (500 in Socrates's trial) and they combined the duties of jury and judge, as they decided both the question of guilt and the penalty. Here Plato is obviously thinking of the act of judging, and the translation "judge" is unavoidable.

2. The phrase is used of Menelaus by Apollo, who is encouraging Hector to fight him, in *Iliad* 17, 588.

3. This is the first appearance of the rulers who are to be chosen from the guardians and further tested and educated (414a and Books VI and VII). There was an earlier mention of rulers at 389c, but there they were not said to be a special group of guardians, which they now become—in fact the most important group in the state. The rest of the guardians are now to be considered their helpers or auxiliaries and are to carry out their orders. We shall find later that only the rulers have knowledge, whereas the auxiliaries have only opinion or belief.

4. There is no doubt that the Greeks painted their statues, at times only certain parts of them.

5. The reference is obscure; it may be to an unknown saying or proverb, or may refer to a game like checkers, where the pieces on each side, or perhaps any cluster of pieces, was called a *polis* or city, while the separate pieces were called dogs.

6. The subject of marriage and children, here so lightly passed over, will be fully dealt with in the fifth book.

7. From *Odyssey* I, 351–2, but our texts read: "Men always praise that song most which is new to those who hear it." Plato is probably quoting from memory, or he may have had a different text.

8. The Hydra was a primeval monster with many heads. As soon as one head was cut off, two or three new heads grew in its place. The slaying of the Hydra was one of the labours of Heracles.

9. i.e., Apollo at Delphi: a rock in the sanctuary was said to be the navel of the earth.

10. The doctrine of the four cardinal virtues is often met with in Plato. It seems to be referred to here as well known. *Hosiotês* or piety is often a candidate for a place in the list.

11. The difference between moderation and justice seems clear in the Greek. The city is moderate if each group is satisfied with its position in the state, and they all agree as to who should rule. Justice is more positive; it implies that each group actually performs its function in the state. Moreover, those who are dissatisfied with their own are likely to interfere with the work which properly belongs to others.

12. Plato uses the word *aretê* in two somewhat different senses. It can refer to *the* quality, or combination of qualities, which makes a person, an animal, or even an object good at doing something that nothing else can do, or at least do

as well (above I, 353b ff., cp. 335b–c), and it is then best translated by excellence (cp. below 444a). Each of the virtues, however, is also an *aretê*, and it is then best translated "virtue." Of course, the two senses merge at times; we may note, however, that in this discussion Plato does not use the term to describe the individual virtues.

13. The reference seems to be to 432d–433a.

14. Plato here (442e–443e) seems to link his present more psychologically profound definition of justice and injustice as inner states of soul with the more external description of them in the first book. Clearly the unjust man who, in the argument with Thrasymachus, wanted to get the better of everybody (e.g., 349c) is here the man whose appetitive part is out of control and rebels against the ruling reason (442a). His antisocial conduct now follows from this.

15. The enumeration and description of the bad forms of governments and individual characters is not taken up again until the eighth book. The central books of the *Republic* are therefore formally a digression, but only formally, for they contain vitally important themes.

16. The expression "having wives and children in common" which Plato himself uses (cp. 423e–424a) obscures the fact that wives and husbands are treated on a footing of perfect equality; their "marriages" are purely temporary unions for the duration of certain festivals, and at the next festival they are likely to have other partners. Plato's system actually requires from his guardians, both male and female (and it only applies to them), a very high degree of continence. Except for those few festivals, there must be no sexual relations as long as they are of an age to have children.

17. A proverbial expression applied to those who neglect their proper tasks to follow some fascinating but vain hope of immediate gain. It also reminds one of I, 336e.

18. Adrasteia was a kind of Nemesis, a punisher of pride and proud words. The "bow to Adrasteia" is therefore a kind of apology for a bold statement to follow.

19. Plato is here adapting a phrase of Pindar, to us a fragment. The text is uncertain. As it stands in the text it means "They pluck from wisdom the unripe fruit of laughter," which does not seem to make much sense. The Pindaric phrase was "they pluck the unripe fruit of wisdom," i.e., their wisdom is not wisdom; it seems likely that Plato simply replaced *sophias* (of wisdom) by *geloiou* "they pluck the unripe fruit of laughter." As the original meant that their wisdom was no wisdom, the adaptation then means that their laughter is no true laughter, because what they laugh at is not laughable.

20. This sounds strange to us because we regard the practical and material world as more "true" and more real than theory; but to Plato, the unchanging Platonic Forms and such things as mathematical realities were not only more exact, but also more real and true than the world of phenomena.

As these are always changing no real knowledge of them is possible, but only opinion or belief.

21. It is important to remember in this context that the word *philosophos*, which was not in common use before this time, retained its etymological meaning as a lover of truth and wisdom rather than a philosopher in our more restricted sense. Plato does not mean that the world should be ruled by pale metaphysicians from the remoteness of their studies; he is maintaining that a statesman needs to be a thinker, a lover of truth, beauty, and the Good, with a highly developed sense of values. The rest of this book and the next two are largely devoted to explaining the character and necessary training of the Platonic *philosophos*, and this includes practical experience.

22. These shadows of themselves and each other are never mentioned again. A Platonic myth or parable, like a Homeric simile, is often elaborated in considerable detail. These contribute to the vividness of the picture but often have no other function, and it is a mistake to look for any symbolic meaning in them. It is the general picture that matters.

23. *Odyssey* II, 489–90, where Achilles says to Odysseus, on the latter's visit to the underworld, that he would rather be a servant to a poor man on earth than king among the dead.

24. Plato does indeed require his philosopher to go back into the cave to help those less fortunate than himself, but only as a duty, not because he loves his neighbour or gets any emotional satisfaction from helping him.

25. These images are called "divine" in comparison with the shadows in the cave, presumably because the real world is thought of as the work of the gods and in any case closer to "reality."

26. Dialectic does away with hypotheses in the sense that it goes behind them and no longer relies on them as unproved assumptions, for as the dialectician comes down the line again, after attaining the knowledge of the Good, what were unproved assumptions to the geometer, for example, can now be deduced from this knowledge and therefore cease to be hypotheses.

27. Before (i.e., at the end of Book VI, 511d–3) Plato called the highest mental process *noêsis*, which we translated as "understanding." Now he calls it *epistêmê* (knowledge), and he applies the term *noêsis* to both the higher sections—that is, to the whole intelligible world, which we here translate as "intelligence." The change is probably not careless but deliberate, and it illustrates his apparent dislike of a fixed technical vocabulary which he seems to have felt was at times an obstacle to understanding. At any rate he has just told us that we should not quarrel about words (533e).

Chapter II | Niccolò Machiavelli

1. By considering views actually held about them.
2. Medicine studies both health and disease, and a faculty (art or skill) can operate in opposite ways: a good mechanic can service or sabotage a machine.

3. i.e., We rule out the possibility that his health might make him walk unhealthily.
4. Not invariably, because individual words acquire specialized meanings.
5. Some editors reject the bracketed words.
6. A proportion of four terms; a continuous one has three terms of which the middle one is used twice.
7. The letters evidently represent the lines in a diagram, but below the "terms" seem to be represented merely by letters.
8. The one that represents just distribution.
9. 1132b21ff.
10. Citizens whose rights are equal either absolutely or relatively to their values as citizens.
11. Cf. a17 above.
12. *Logos* is the reading of nearly all the [manuscripts], whereas *nomos* (law) is what one would expect from the context; the translation attempts a compromise.
13. 1130a3f.
14. See note on 1133b23.
15. That natural laws are immutable.
16. For the rest of the paragraph the translation follows Bywater's text.
17. M. Ostwald (p. 132 of his translation of the *Ethics*, Indianapolis, 1962) rightly rejects the prevalent view that A. is contrasting official wholesale with official retail measures (the language here and at 1134b24–27 above clearly refers to local variations); but what truth, if any, underlies the generalization is still obscure.
18. When the agent is not aware of all the circumstances, as is explained below.
19. 1111a20ff.
20. They are *essentially* just only when performed from a just state of character.
21. The standard sedative in Greek medicine.
22. Because they think that justice consists in keeping certain rule of conduct.
23. Cf. Plato, *Republic* 334a.
24. To either flank—not to the rear, which would be too obvious (?).
25. Cf. note on a12 above.
26. They are species of the same genus.
27. Viz. legal justice; see below.
28. i.e., lays down general principles.
29. The circumstances of our actions are often too particular and complicated to be covered satisfactorily by any generalization.
30. Lesbian moulding was ogival, i.e. took the form of a double curve; its regularity was checked by a leaden rule bent to the required shape.

Chapter III | Aristotle

1. Another famous Machiavellian metaphor, implicit in his belief that the able ruler may be compared to a skilled physician who diagnoses illnesses before they have gone beyond the possibility of any cure.

2. King Louis XII took Milan in February 1499, driving Ludovico Sforza into exile in Germany, but Sforza returned a year later on 5 February 1500, only to be betrayed by his Swiss troops at the battle of Novara, where he was captured on 5 April 1500.

3. Machiavelli's use of the indefinite article "a" expresses his contempt for this ruler's ineptitude.

4. In 1511 Pope Julius II organized the Holy League to drive Louis XII and the French out of Italy. The League's members included most of the other European powers (hence, Machiavelli's characterization of it as "the whole world")—not only from Spain, Venice, and the Papal States but also (at least on paper) the England of Henry VIII and the Germany of Emperor Maximilian I. In April 1512 Louis XII won a pyrrhic victory over League forces at Ravenna, but was forced to withdraw from the peninsula.

5. Normandy was annexed to France in 1204; Gascony was taken back from the English in 1453; Burgundy was joined to France in 1477; and Brittany was added to the Kingdom of France in 1491 through the marriage of King Charles VIII to Anne of Brittany, who subsequently married King Louis XII.

6. Machiavelli generally refers to the Ottoman Empire and its ruler with a collective singular noun—"the Turk." By Greece he means the entire Balkan Peninsula, not the present European state. The Ottoman Turks crossed the Hellespont as early as 1354, and in 1453 Mohammed II conquered Constantinople, destroying the last vestiges of the ancient Byzantine Empire, a Christian state. The conquest of the Greek peninsula by the Turks was not completed until 1461.

7. Machiavelli employs the Latin term *compedes*—shackles or fetters.

8. In 211 BC the Romans supported a coalition of Greeks against Phillip V of Macedon. This Aetolian League opposed the Achaen League, allied with Macedon. The first war with Phillip V was won by him, and it was only in a second war, terminating in the Roman victory at the battle of Cynoscephalae (197 BC), that the Romans and their Greek allies defeated Macedon. But during the second war the Aetolian League shifted alliances and became the allies of Antiochus II of Syria against the Romans, while the Achaen League, once allied with Phillip V, now changed sides and supported Rome in the successful victory over Phillip V. The shifting alliances and frequent wars of classical antiquity were just as complex as the similar changes of alliances between Italian and European states in Italy during the fifteenth and sixteenth centuries.

9. Seven of Alexander the Great's best generals divided up his empire that stretched from Greece to Egypt, Syria, and Persia.

10. Machiavelli employs an Italian version (*sangiachie*) of the Turkish word, meaning an administrative district of a Turkish vilayet or province.

11. Machiavelli's term for oligarchy is *uno stato di pochi*.

12. After the end of the Peloponnesian War (431–404 BC) the victorious Spartans tore down the city walls defending Athens and established a government favourable to them known as the Thirty Tyrants, but a democratic government hostile to Sparta was re-established after 403 BC. After defeating the Thebans in 382 BC, the Spartans established a pro-Spartan oligarchy in the city that lasted three years, but through the efforts of Pelopidas and Epaminondas this oligarchy was eventually overthrown as well.

13. Capua was punished (not completely destroyed) in 211 BC for its support of Hannibal in the Second Punic War (218–201 BC) after Rome recaptured the city. Carthage was destroyed at the end of the third Punic War (149–146 BC) by Scipio Aemilianus in 146 BC. Numantia in Spain was destroyed by the same general in 133 BC.

14. Even though Titus Quinctius Flaminius, the conquering roman general who defeated Phillip V of Macedon at the battle of Cynoscephalae (197 BC), declared the independence of the Greek city-states in 196 BC, after a number of wars and uprisings against Roman influence, the Romans destroyed Greek independence after the battle of Leucopetra in 146 BC. After that date Greece effectively became a province of Rome, and in the process, Corinth, Thebes, and Euboea were badly damaged.

15. Florence purchased Pisa in 1405 from Gabriele Visconti and occupied the city in the following year, but the Pisans rebelled against Florentine control in 1494 when Charles VIII invaded Italy. Pisa was retaken by the Florentine republic only in 1509, during a military campaign in which Machiavelli played a political role.

16. Like many Renaissance thinkers, Machiavelli believed that history could instruct his contemporaries and that modern practice should follow the best procedures of the ancient world (almost always those of republican Rome).

17. Like Machiavelli, Baldesar Castiglione's *The Book of the Courtier* (1528)—the only Italian book to rival the audience of *The Prince* during the European Renaissance—employs the metaphor of the archer in discussing the doctrine of imitation: "and if, for all that, they are unable to attain to that perfection, such as it is, that I have tried to express, the one who comes the nearest to it will be the most perfect; as when many archers shoot at a target and none of them hits the bull's eye, the one who comes closest is surely better than all the rest" (*The Book of the Courtier*, trans. Charles Singleton (New York: Norton, 2002), 7).

18. It should be noted that Machiavelli mixes historical and literary figures somewhat indiscriminately here from his readings of the Old Testament, Livy, Plutarch, and Xenophon.

19. Machiavelli's metaphors describing the ideal prince's actions suggest an artistic quality to political action, by comparing the prince to an artist fashioning a work of art from a shapeless mass of inchoate material.

20. The Machiavellian formula for success requires a convergence of three qualities: *virtù* (virtue in the non-moral sense, implying ability, ingenuity, or skill); *fortuna* (Fortune, that is, the favour of the fickle classical goddess personified in Chapter XXV of *The Prince* as a woman,

and not merely temporary good luck); and *occasione* (the opportunity, recognized only by the quality of *virtù*).

21. Two other important terms in Machiavelli's often vague political vocabulary: *ordini* (institutions, laws, regulations) and *modi* (methods, procedures). The term *ordini* is particularly important in the *Discourses on Livy*, where the *virtù* of a single heroic figure is less important than how that hero's ability or skill in creating a state can be institutionalized in a long-lasting republican form of government. But in the *Discourses on Livy* the exceptional *virtù* of heroic figures is quite important for the foundation and for the redemption of republics and principalities. Instituting new *ordini e modi*, for Machiavelli, is the most difficult task of the statesman.

22. Machiavelli sometimes showed little sympathy for Savonarola, even though the friar's plan to institute a Grand Council of some 3,600 citizens in Florence would have been an extension of republican participation in the state's affairs. In a private letter to Ricciardo Becchi dated 8 March 1498, Machiavelli described on of Savonarola's impassioned sermons quite critically. However, he later also spoke of Savonarola with great respect in his discussion of politics and religion in the *Discourses on Livy* (I. II).

23. Machiavelli's source is the *History* (22.4) of Justin, a second- or third-century AD historian who wrote a Latin epitome (a summary or abridgement) of the *Historiae Philippicae* or *Philippic Histories* by Pompeius Trogus, a contemporary of Livy. Trogus' history in forty-four books focused upon the history of Macedon and suggested that the empires of the Parthians or the Macedonians were equally as important as that of Rome. As is frequently the case, Machiavelli's citations in Latin are slightly different from the Latin texts contemporary readers use today, since he employed manuscripts or editions different from our modern critical editions. Some scholars detect the influence of Polybius (7.8) here as well. Machiavelli says something similar about Walter, the Duke of Athens, a would-be tyrant of Florence expelled from the city in 1343 in his *Florentine Histories* (2.34): "nor did he lack anything as prince but the title" (*Florentine Histories*, trans. Laura F. Banfield and Harvey Mansfield (Princeton: Princeton University Press, 1988), 91).

24. Some scholars use this remark to argue for a dating of the *Discourses on Livy* as subsequent to 1513 and the composition of *The Prince*. Others have argued that the *Discourses on Livy* was begun first but was interrupted by Machiavelli to write *The Prince* because of the particular historical and political situation that existed at that date (a Medici pope, Leo X, in Rome, and Medici family members controlling the city of Florence at the same time).

25. The word *patria* is almost always associated by Machiavelli in his works with a city-state, not a "country" in our contemporary sense of the word. However, the word *patria* also implies a very strong moral and political pathos in Machiavelli's vocabulary, even if translating the word as "fatherland" conjures up rather sinister connotations. In a letter to Francesco Vettori dated 16 April 1527 Machiavelli declares that he loves his *patria* more than his soul.

26. Machiavelli's treatment of Agathocles seems to have come from Justin's epitome of Pompeius Trogus (see n. 23), but Diodorus Siculus and Polybius also mention him. Actually the western portion of Sicily remained under Carthaginian control.

27. In this important statement, Machiavelli separates *virtù* from the completely immoral actions of Agathocles, declaring that such misdeeds can only earn *dominio* (power) but not glory. Yet he has just completed the praise of Cesare Borgia, whose deed included all the kinds of evil actions typical of Agathocles. One explanation is that Machiavelli considered Borgia's cruelties necessary, whereas those of Agathocles were senselessly cruel and unnecessary. Another possible explanation for this apparent contradiction is that Machiavelli excused some evil means if the end was sufficiently noble. In the case of Borgia, Machiavelli felt that with the combination of papal power (Alexander VI) and Borgia's military prowess, a strong, central Italian state might be established that could protect Italy from foreign invasions. Subsequently, in 1513 when he composed *The Prince*, a similar situation existed, with a Medici pope in power and Medici princes (first Giuliano, Duke of Nemours, then Lorenzo, Duke of Urbino) in control of the city of Florence. Florence and a Medici pope might also form the nucleus of a central Italian state that could guarantee Italian independence. When this opportunity disappeared with the death of Leo X and that of Lorenzo, Duke of Urbino, by 1519, the practical goal of *The Prince* disappeared, probably explaining why Machiavelli did not publish the work during his lifetime.

28. On 1 October 1499, executed by his Florentine employers.

29. On 26 December 1501.

30. Since Fermo was then a free republic, Oliverotto was actually establishing a tyrannical government, not merely replacing another tyrant. Thus, it would have been sensible for him to remove any citizen with enough influence, power, or wealth to oppose his designs.

31. Strictly speaking, Giovanni Fogliani was Oliverotto's uncle, not his father, but he did serve as Oliverotto's father when the boy was young.

32. Machiavelli's entire discussion of cruelty focuses upon the practical and technical results of a cruel action, not its moral or ethical significance. But even for those readers of Machiavelli who believe him to be amoral or immoral, the sarcastic phrase "if it is permitted to speak well of evil" implicitly admits that there is a moral realm where such cruel actions may be condemned.

33. Renaissance medical theory (inherited from classical medical treatises and the practice of Hippocrates and Galen) held that the human body was governed by four different "humours": blood, black bile, yellow bile, and phlegm. In like manner, the body politic mimicked the human body in being dominated by various kinds of similar forces.

34. Machiavelli generally distinguishes between the members of a city-state who have rights and privileges and participate in the municipal government, on the one hand, an those people who live in the surrounding *dominio* (territory or dominion), and who have fewer, if any, rights of the citizen. Here he notes that even in a government controlled by a prince there can be active participation in the government by its citizens—what Machiavelli calls an *ordine civile* ("proper civil society")—without that government necessarily evolving into an absolute form.

35. In Chapters VI–VII (and subsequently in Chapters XII–XIII). [Eds note: Chapter VI, part of Chapter VII, and Chapter XII are excerpted in this volume.]

36. That of King Charles VIII of France in 1494–5.

37. In his *Mémoires* (7.4), the French historian Philippe de Commynes reports that the French army marked the houses in which they quartered their troops with chalk. The contemptuous tone of Machiavelli's phrase underscores his belief that Italian resistance to Charles was virtually non-existent.

38. The man in question is no doubt Brother Girolamo Savonarola, whose sermon of 1 November 1494 interpreted the successful French invasion as a divinely sent castigation of the sins of Italy, the Church, and Florence.

39. 14 September 1488.

40. Muzio Attendolo Sforza.

41. At this battle, also known as Agnadello (14 May 1509), Venice was soundly defeated by French troops.

42. Since the technical term for a day's battle is "una giornata" in the vocabulary of Machiavelli's day, his phrase could also be translated as "in a single battle." In the case of this battle, the combat did only last a single day.

43. This is a gross exaggeration, since Venice lost none of her extremely valuable overseas territories on which her commercial empire was really based. Venetian conquest of mainland territory had slowly taken place since the fourteenth century. Machiavelli must mean that in what he considers the eight-hundred-year history of Venice, this was the republic's worst military disaster.

44. Machiavelli here puns on the meaning of the word *condotta*, which is not only the past participle of the verb *condurre* (to conduct), but also, as a noun (*la condotta*), can refer to the contract by which a mercenary soldier is engaged by his employer. The term *condotta* also explains the origin of the Italian terms for such soldiers: *condottieri*—soldiers with a *condotta* or contract who fight for money.

45. The traditional advice-to-princes literature has a long history, stretching back to the classical antecedents of Plato, Artistotle, Cicero, and Xenophon, to medieval and Renaissance writers such as Dante, Aquinas, Marsilius of Padua, Egidio Colonna, Poggio Braccionlini, Giovanni Pontano, and Erasmus. The Latin chapter titles of *The Prince* often repeat some of the themes of this literature. Chapter XVII, for example, discusses a question often treated in other treatises on the ideal prince. Before Machiavelli, political theorists had argued that it was better to be loved than to be feared. Machiavelli, of course, argues the contrary.

46. This is an instance of Machiavelli's use of the term *virtù* where the translation must reflect its traditional moral value, since the context of the word, here coupled with vice, demands such a meaning.

47. Here the word *virtù* is used as an adverb, but it continues to retain the traditional moral connotation mentioned in the previous note.

48. Attributing Giuliano della Rovere's expenditure in his campaign to become Pope Julius II to generosity rather than simony is to take a generous view of this fascinating individual, obviously admired by Machiavelli for his resolution and bravery.

49. King Louis XII. Since he died on 31 December 1514, some scholars cite this sentence to argue that Machiavelli did not revise *The Prince* after this date.

50. Ferdinand I of Aragon and V of Castile and Leon.

51. Machiavelli's sources for the life of Julius Caesar are Cicero's *De Officiis* (I.14) and Suetonius' *Divus Iulius* (11–12).

52. The verb Machiavelli employs here is *racconiciare*—meaning literally to mend or to repair.

53. Pistoia was a Tuscan city subjugated to the Republic of Florence. It was torn by political strife between factions identified with the Panciatichi and the Cancellieri families. Machiavelli was sent there four times in 1501 by the Florentine government to deal with these political upheavals.

54. Virgil, *Aeneid*, I. 563–4.

55. It is clear from the context of this statement that by *fortuna* Machiavelli refers here not to the more philosophical concept of Fortune but to common-sense ideas of good and bad luck.

56. In 205 BC Quintius Pleminius took Locri (a Greek city in Calabria) back from Hannibal and pillaged it. He was eventually arrested after the Locrians complained to the Roman Senate about his behaviour, but Scipio, under whose command the man served, did nothing to stop him or to punish him. Machiavelli's source is Livy, 29.8–9.

57. Machiavelli provides another comparison of the qualities of Hannibal and Scipio in *Discourses on Livy* (3.21). His source is again Livy (28–9). Polybius' *Histories* (11.19) also makes a similar comparison, but there is some question about whether Machiavelli had access to his work.

58. Machiavelli's source is Cicero, *De Officiis* (1.11).

59. Machiavelli's sources are Ovid's *Fasti* (5.385–6) and Statius' *Achilleid* (2.381–452). Chiron is also mentioned as the mentor of Achilles in Dante's *Inferno* (12.71). Machiavelli emphasizes the dual nature of the centaur, wishing to buttress his argument that political action demands both bestial deeds and those more in keeping with humanity. Chiron was a centaur renowned for his wisdom, but other centaurs were famous for their lustfulness. In fact, one of the most famous episodes in classical mythology (and subsequent figurations in both classical and Renaissance or baroque art) was the battle between the Lapiths and the

centaurs, who arrived to celebrate a wedding and misbe-haved badly until they were driven away by Theseus and others. The theme usually symbolized the triumph of civilization over barbarism. Machiavelli intends to promote political action that admits both civilized and barbaric deeds.

60. Machiavelli found the reference to these two political symbols in Cicero, *De Officiis* (1.13). However, Cicero maintains that force and treachery are inhuman and contemptible.

61. In this chapter, Machiavelli employs the verb "to colour" to indicate disguising the truth. A contemporary equivalent might be "whitewash."

62. In spite of some English translations to the contrary, Machiavelli never said that "the ends justify the means." Here he simply says that ends ("the final result") matter when no other independent means of establishing a decision exist, "no tribunal to which to appeal." He believes that in political affairs there is rarely any such tribunal. In the *Discourses on Livy* (1.9) there is another important discussion of the relationship of means and ends: "It is truly appropriate that while the act accuses him, the result excuses him, and when the result is good, like that of Romulus, it will always excuse him, because one should reproach a man who is violent in order to ruin things, not one who is so in order to set them aright" (*Discourses on Livy*, trans. Julia and Peter Bondanella (Oxford: Oxford University Press, 2003), 45). Machiavelli seems willing to excuse some shocking acts (such as the murder of Remus by Romulus) if the deed is done for an extremely important and moral cause (in this case, the foundation of the city of Rome, and implicitly its empire). To justify such an action as the killing of a brother means to render such an action just, and Machiavelli certainly does not believe that what Romulus did was just. But he is willing, in this particular and limited case, to excuse what Romulus did, not because it was just but because excusing an action means to recognize that an action is wrong but was committed under extraordinary circumstances that attenuate its wrongness. Justification of immoral actions in general implies that no moral values exist; excusing an individual immoral action maintains a belief in a system of moral values, but finds an exception to such general rule in the practical conduct of an individual in a single case.

63. Most likely a reference to Ferdinand I of Aragon and V of Castile and Leon.

64. The Moorish kingdom in the south of Spain. Ferdinand began his attacks in 1481, and they terminated in the liberation of all of Spain from the Moors in 1492.

65. While Ferdinand liberated Granada with traditional forces, on 5 October 1495, he instituted a national army, and it was such an army of his own subjects that would win fame for Spanish arms in Europe during the sixteenth century.

66. In fact Ferdinand turned his wars against the Moors into a religious crusade against the infidel.

67. Both Jews and Moors (or *moriscos*) who were forcibly converted to Christianity were called "*Marranos*," a term

that might be best translated as "swine," since it makes a derogatory reference to the pigs that neither Jews nor Muslims would eat. The Spanish Inquisition began persecution of the *Marranos* in 1483 even before the conquest of Granada in 1492. Machiavelli combines this conquest and the 1492 expulsion of Jews from Spain with the expulsion of the *Marranos*, which took place a few years later in 1501–2. In addition to being driven into exile, the property of the exiles was confiscated and added to that of the Crown. A number of the Spanish Jews migrated to Italy, and Machiavelli no doubt met some of them.

68. Ferdinand occupied various cities in North Africa for a time—Oran in 1509, Bugia in 1510, Tripoli in 1511. This was done to prevent a staging of a counter-attack against southern Spain, but also for religious reasons.

69. Ferdinand divided the Kingdom of Naples with King Louis XII of France in 1503, taking the entire kingdom in 1505.

70. The word "lately" indicates that Machiavelli refers here to Spain's participation in the Holy Leagues in 1512, an alliance Pope Julius II organized against the French to defend, at least in theory, the unity of the Church. This word also convinces many scholars that this passage must have been written before 1513.

71. This ruler was famous for the severity and cruelty of his punishments.

72. Livy, 35.49. Machiavelli's Latin text differs slightly from the current critical editions.

73. In 1499.

74. Their defeat at the battle of Vailà or Agnadello in 1509 by the French and the troops in the League of Cambrai.

75. Machiavelli opposed the temporizing policies of his superior, Piero Soderini. In 1511–12, during the formation of the Holy League by Pope Julius II, Florence did not support her traditional ally France, and even tolerated a council being held in nearby Pisa set up to depose the Pope. But she also did not really support the Pope and the Spanish. The result was the sack of Prato in 1512 by a Spanish army, the downfall of Soderini's republican government, Machiavelli's dismissal from political office as Soderini's close confidant and assistant, and the return of the Medici to rule Florence in 1512.

76. Here the word *virtù* is given a literary and artistic twist.

77. Machiavelli again employs the word *arte* here. [Eds note: The explanatory note on this word belongs to a part of the text not reprinted here. A summary of that note is as follows: Machiavelli refers several times to the military profession as *arte*. In his time the word *arte* could be translated as "guild" and referred to one's trade or profession. But Machiavelli did not believe that the military should be a professional force; as such the word is translated as "art," which aligns with Machiavelli's exploration of warfare, translated as *The Art of War*.]

78. Here the term *stato* refers to the territory surrounding and including the city-state, and takes on a geographical as well as a political connotation.

79. The technical term for guild is *arte*. In the traditional

80. Machiavelli writes *tribù* (literally "tribes"), but he means neighbourhoods or *quartieri* into which cities like Florence are still divided today. Such districts usually depended upon the major church in that area.

81. Machiavelli's declaration seems based on his dilemma-like literary style (his habitual either/or construction), rather than any empirical evidence. Certainly he provides no historical evidence for asserting that men control one-half of their destiny.

82. Here Machiavelli writers *ordinate virtù*, combining two of his favourite political terms to indicate that the ability of the prince needs to be channelled into institutions that may stand up to Fortune's irrational force.

83. That is to say, the sudden shifts from good fortune to bad.

84. In 1506, Julius was forced to retake the city in 1512. Machiavelli witnessed his first triumphant procession through Bologna in 1506.

85. Here and elsewhere, when Machiavelli mentions the brevity of the lives of the popes, he means to underline the brevity of their tenure as popes, not their complete life-span.

86. Fortune and their means of procedure.

87. [1956] Que. Q.B. 447.

88. [1951] A.C. 66. 3

Chapter IV | Thomas Hobbes

1. Hobbes' earliest account of what constitutes a free or voluntary action (and why it makes no sense to argue about a free *will*) can be found in *Elements of Law (Human Nature)*, XII. 1–5. Its later continuation is in his controversy with bishop Bramhall (see the Molesworth edition of Hobbes' *English Works* (1839), iv. 229–78 and vol. V). His position is that it is nonsense to talk about a free *will*. But it is significant to talk about a free *action* when the action proceeds from the passions which are the will (fear, anger, love, and the like) and when the action itself is not constrained by external physical force. In *Leviathan* see VI. 53, XIV. 8, XXI. 1–4, et al.

2. See *De Divinatione*, ii. 119 (Loeb, p. 505). The quotation is much to Hobbes' taste: see XLVI. 11.

3. The examples that follow are drawn from theology. Hobbes argues seriously about such insignificant names in a number of places in *Leviathan*, for example VIII. 27, XXXIV. 2, and XLVI. 16–30. One of the instances he has already given, "incorporeal substance," IV. 21, is of major philosophical and religious interest and he returns to it frequently in his work, for example in *An Answer to Bishop Bramhall* (*English Works*, iv. 383–4).

4. Useless fires.

5. Paragraphs 1–3 of the chapter should be read in conjunction with *Elements of Law (Human Nature)*, XII.

6. See note to p. 9. [Note to p. 9: This is a key concept for Hobbes. In *De Corpore*, XV. 2 (first published in 1655) he defines endeavor (or *conatus*) as "*motion made in less space and time than can be given; that is less than can be determined or assigned by exposition or number; that is, motion made through the length of a point, and in an instant or point of time.*" See also *Elements of Law (Human Nature)*, VII. 1–2, *White's De Mundo Examined*, XIII. 2, and *Leviathan*, VI. 1–2. On the one hand Hobbes' concept is among the first stirrings of the idea that led Leibniz and Newton to the differential calculus. On the other hand, and in the context of the physiology and mechanistic psychology of *Leviathan*, it refers to motion too minute or too quick to be perceived: in modern terms something, for example, like the impulses along nerve fibres.]

7. Desire to rid the body of waste products, and to empty the bowels. "Excretion" and "exoneration" are nearly synonyms.

8. [This material is] of the utmost importance in understanding Hobbes' moral philosophy. [It] assert[s], in the light of the preceding and succeeding physiological accounts of aversions and desires, that what each individual calls good and evil when he or she is not a member of a civil society relates *only* to that individual's personal aversions and desires. Such is the "natural" condition of mankind. The matter had earlier been deployed in *Elements of Law (Human Nature)*, VII. But it is not the end of the story since the "natural" condition of mankind is, because of the formation of civil societies in which the individual is a citizen, not the *usual* condition. Summaries of Hobbes' completed thesis can be seen in XV. 40 and XLVI. 32.

9. Cf. VIII. 16. It is one of Hobbes' most challenging assertions that man is a restless, unsatisfiable creature whose search for power (in the special sense defined in X. 1 and used in XI. 2) ends only at death. Note that if life is the movement (see note to p. 7) which is desires, senses, imagination, etc., it is at first difficult to understand what "life" a soul could have apart from the body. Hobbes grasps the nettle in Ch. XXXVIII: the soul *is* life; resurrection is *of the body*.

10. This is literally true in view of Hobbes' earlier identification of imagination with decaying sense. See II. 2.

11. This paragraph, and the one following (which concludes with the most quoted sentence in all English philosophy), is the central statement of the first move in Hobbes' political theory: that unrestricted individual freedom (i.e. the right of nature) means the war of each against every man; cf. XXI. 8.

12. It is a bold or unworldly human being that cannot still recognize the fears Hobbes describes and the precautions he lists.

13. Hobbes may well be right, although his account, as he says, depends not upon what ever was actual, but on what, given human nature as it really is, *would* be actual in the absence of an effective sovereign power, and almost is actual in civil wars, when civil society breaks down. But there is a at least one ancient report, given by Sextus

Empiricus (second century AD). Having quoted Orpheus, "a theologian," to the effect that "There was a time when every man lived by devouring his fellow," Sextus continues with an account of how the state of war was deliberately contrived in the Persian Empire: "the shrewd Persians have a law that on the death of their kind they must practise lawlessness for the next five days . . . in order to learn by experience how great an evil lawlessness is . . . so that they may become more trusty guardians of their kings" (*Against the Professors*, ii. 33; Loeb, iv. 205–7). In more general terms the notion of a state of war, or something like it, where there is no law, is very ancient. See, for example, Cicero, *Pro Sestio*, 92 (Loeb, p. 159).

14. This fundamental law of nature, "seek peace" (as Hobbes paraphrases it), together with the second, that we should not seek to maintain our rights to all things, are different in kind from those laws that Hobbes derives from them in Ch. XV. The two fundamental laws are the conditions that reason shows to be necessary for avoiding the state of war. In both *Elements of Law (Human Nature)*, XIV. 14 and XV. 2, and *De Cive* (I. 15 and II. 1–3) Hobbes treats these two law separately from the derived laws, although in both *De Cive*, II. 3, and *Leviathan*, XIV. 5, there is an assumption that the second law can be derived from the first, and need not be regarded as an independent condition for the avoidance of the state of war. In *De Cive* (II. 1) Hobbes explains that "By right reason in the natural state of men, I understand not, as many do, an infallible faculty, but the act of reasoning, that is, the peculiar and true ratiocination of every man concerning those actions of his which may either redound to the damage, or benefit of his neighbours."

15. For the "Golden Rule," see Matthew 7:12, or Luke 6:31: "And as ye would that men should do to you, do ye also to them likewise." Hobbes sets this in a context in which others adopt toward me the same rule. The Gospels do not seem to expect such reciprocation, although turning the other cheek can certainly be associated with vaster benefits than merely avoiding a here-and-now state of war. The "law of all men" that Hobbes cites in Latin is the converse of the Golden Rule. It is "do not do to other what you would not wish to be done to you." See also XXVI. 13.

16. From his accounts of human physiology Hobbes asserts the generalization that, as a matter of fact, whatever a man does voluntarily (or "freely," see not to p. 29) will have as its object some good to himself. See *Elements of Law (Human Nature)*, VII, XII, and particularly XVI. 6: "For by necessity of nature every man doth in all his voluntary actions intend some good unto himself." And again, *De Cive*, I. 7: "every man is desirous of what is good for him, and shuns what is evil . . . and this he doth, by a certain impulsion of nature, no less than that whereby a stone moves downward." This is the position sometimes called "psychological egoism." See *Leviathan*, XV. 16, and my Introduction, pp. xxviii–xxxi.

17. The distinction can be found in Aquinas's *Summa Theologiae*, 1a2ae, quest. 114, a. 3. *Meritum congrui* is a

benefit in keeping with or in proportion to one's deserving; *meritum condigni* is a benefit without limit granted by someone else, for example by God placing one in a state of eternal bliss.

18. For a discussion of covenants see *Elements of Law (Human Nature)*, XV. 9–14. For a seventeenth-century claim to covenant with God, see the Scottish National Covenant of 1638, which speaks of Christians "who have renewed their Covenant with God" and calls upon God "to witness" the declaration. Hobbes seems to have less difficulty with the Old Testament covenant between God and the Jews: see XXXV. 2.

19. The paragraph is important when read in conjunction with §4 as it sets some limit to what a man grants to Leviathan, the state, when he agrees to restrict his freedom in order to avoid the state of war. See also XXVIII. 2.

20. Hobbes returns to the phrase or its like in XXVI. 4, XXX. 12, *et al*. It is originally drawn from Plato, *Republic*, I. 331e and 332c, and the idea is developed in Aristotle, *Nicomachean Ethics*, V. 1. See also Aquinas, *Summa Theologiae*, 2a2ae, quest. 58, a.1.

21. Hobbes alludes to Psalm 14: "The fool hath said in his heart, there is not God" (repeated in Psalm 53: 1).

22. Hobbes seems to be paraphrasing the somewhat enigmatic text of Matthew 11:12: "And from the days of John the Baptist until now the kingdom of heaven suffereth violence, and the violent take it by force."

23. Sire Edward Coke, 1552–1634, English lawyer. His *Institutes of Law*, published between 1628 and 1644, began with a commentary on a textbook on tenure by Sir Thomas Littlejohn. See also XXVI. 11 and 24.

24. In sections 6–8 Hobbes turns to what will be one of his primary concerns in the later Parts of *Leviathan*, namely, under what conditions, if any, can religious belief and concerns justify disobedience to a worldly sovereign power. Cf. §8 with Ch. XXXVIII.

25. Cf. *De Cive*, V.

26. Cf. Thucydides, *History*, i. 5, where Thucydides describes the plunder and piracy of ancient times—"it being a matter at that time nowhere in disgrace, but rather carrying with it something of glory."

27. Some of the material in this chapter is usefully augmented by reading *De Cive*, VI.

28. See note to p. 92 [note 25].

29. See note to p. 29 [note 8].

30. Essentially the same account of liberty reappears in David Hume's *Enquiry concerning Human Understanding* (1748), sect. VIII, pt. I: "By liberty, then, we can only mean *a power of acting or not acting, according to the determination of the will*; that is, if we choose to remain at rest, we may; if we choose to move, we also may."

31. The example is drawn from Aristotle's *Nicomachean Ethics*, iii. 1, although Aristotle is more cautious than Hobbes: "But with regard to the things that are done from fear of greater evils . . . it may be debated whether such actions are involuntary or voluntary. Something of the sort happens also with regards to the throwing of goods overboard

in a storm; for in the abstract no one throws goods away voluntarily, but on condition of its securing the safety of himself and his crew any sensible man does so. Such actions then, are mixed, but are more like voluntary actions . . . " (W.D. Ross's translation).

32. David Hume suggests that such necessity and liberty is a reason for holding God morally responsible for man's actions. [Hobbes' identification of moral laws with civil laws [and with law of nature] is a main theme of *Leviathan*: see XX. 16, XXVI, et al. See also *Elements of Law* (*De Corpore Politico*), XX. 10, and *De Cive*, VI. 9.]

33. This clause (and sections 11–15 in general, together with section 21) opens a wider scope for civil disobedience than a sovereign might approve.

34. In Quebec, students planning to enter university must complete two years of study at a CÉGEP—similar to a junior college—following their secondary school education.

Chapter V | John Locke

1. The lawful power of making laws to command whole politic societies of men, belonging so properly unto the same entire societies, that for any prince or potentate of what kind soever upon earth, to exercise the same of himself, and not by express commission immediately and personally received from God, or else by authority derived at the first from their consent, upon whose persons they impose laws, it is no better than mere tyranny. Laws they are not therefore which public approbation hath not made so. Hooker's *Eccl. Pol. L.* i. Sect. 10. Of this point therefore we are to note, that since men naturally have no full and perfect power to command whole politic multitudes of men, therefore utterly without our consent, we could in such sort be at no man's commandment living. And to be commanded we do consent, when that society, whereof we be a part, hath at any time before consented, without revoking the same after by the like universal agreement. Laws therefore human, of what kind so ever, are available by consent. Ibid.

2. Two foundations there are which bear up public societies; the one a natural inclination, whereby all men desire sociable life and fellowship; the other an order, expressly or secretly agreed upon, touching the manner of their union in living together: the latter is that which we call the law of a common-weal, the very soul of a politic body, the parts whereof are by law animated, held together, and set on work in such actions as the common good requireth. Laws politic, ordained for external order and regiment among men, are never framed as they should be, unless presuming the will of man to be inwardly obstinate, rebellious, and averse from all obedience to the sacred laws of his depraved mind, little better than a wild beast, they do accordingly provide, notwithstanding, so to frame his outward actions, that they be no hindrance unto the common good, for which societies are instituted. Unless they do this, they are not perfect. Hooker's *Eccl. Pol. L.* i. Sect. 10.

3. Human laws are measure in respect of men whose actions they must direct, howbeit such measures they are as have also their higher rules to be measured by, which rules are two, the law of God, and the law of nature; so that laws human must be made according to the general laws of nature, and without contradiction to any positive law of scripture, otherwise they are ill made. Hooker's *Eccl. Pol. L.* iii. Sect. 9. To constrain men to any thing inconvenient doth seem unreasonable. Ibid. l. i. Sect. 10.

4. Luke 22, 25.

5. 2 Tim. 2. 19.

6. Luke 22. 32.

7. Rom. 1.

8. Gal. 5.

9. Matth. 18. 20.

10. Exod. 22. 20, 21.

11. Deut. 2.

12. 1 Cor. 5.12, 13.

Chapter VI | Jean-Jacques Rousseau

1. *what is allowed by right:* in French "ce que le droit permet." The French *droit* can also mean law in the abstract, whereas English *right* and *law* are separate concepts, which often imposes a choice of not entirely equivalent terms in translating.

2. *its sovereign body:* in French "membre du souverain." *Souverain* being usually the equivalent of "monarch," the sense in which Rousseau habitually uses the word, to signify the supreme political authority, of whatever persons it is composed, blurs the distinction between monarchical and popular authority. In Geneva, Rousseau had been by right a member of the General Council ("Grand conseil"), also called the Sovereign Council, of 1,200 citizens and burgesses.

3. *Man was born free:* in French "L'homme est né libre," often translated and quoted as "Man is born free," which would be the equivalent of "L'homme naît libre." The past tense implies that natural liberty existed once; the present, that it exists for every man at birth, as in the Declaration of the Rights of Man in 1789, "Men are born and remain free, and with equal rights." In I. iv Rousseau writes, about the children of slaves: "they are born men and free," but IV. ii has: "each man having been born free."

4. *only through convention:* the argument here, taken largely from Locke (second *Treatise on Civil Government*, 1690, ch. vi), was directed at the defenders of monarchy, who often assimilated it to paternal power. Rousseau's case is made more fully in the *Discourse on Inequality* and Book I, ch. v of the Geneva MS of the *Contract*.

5. *for the benefit of the governed:* Hugo Grotius or de Groot (1583–1645), the creator in modern times of the Natural Law approach to political theory. Rousseau alludes here to his treatise *De iure belli ac pacis* (*On the Law of War and Peace*) (1625), I. iii. 8.

6. "Learned researches on political law are often no more than the history of former abuses, and it is misguided

diligence to take the trouble of studying them too deeply"—from the manuscript *Treatise on France's interests as regards her neighbours*, by the M. d'A. [*The M. d'A.*: the Marquis d'Argenson, political writer, minister, and brother of a more successful politician, the Comte d'Argenson; the passage quoted comes from his best-known work, usually known as "Considérations sur l'ancien gouvernement de la France," written before 1738.] This is exactly what Grotius did.

7. *Hobbes's view also*: Thomas Hobbes of Malmesbury, 1588–1679, perhaps the most formidable of the pro-monarchical predecessors of Rousseau, but despite the hostile comment here he saw absolute monarchy as being beneficial to its subjects, insofar as it protected them against civil war. Rousseau tacitly refers to Hobbes's position in I. iv (third paragraph).

8. *the Emperor Caligula*: Caius Caligula, emperor of Rome 37–41 CE, notorious for his cruelty and depravity. The opinion ascribed to him here by Philo of Alexandria (?–*c.* 54 CE), which must have been found by Rousseau in a 1668 translation of the *History of the Jews* by Flavius Josephus, was to the effect that those commanding all creatures in the world ought to be considered as being gods rather than men.

9. *Aristotle*: the reference is to Aristotle's *Politics*, I. 2.

10. See a short treatise by Plutarch, [*a short treatise by Plutarch*: the Greek moralist and biographer Plutarch. The work he refers to is set on Circe's island, where the sorceress had turned some of Odysseus' men into pigs (Homer, *Odyssey*, X)] entitled *That animals employ reason*.

11. *with whom they have been identified*: this alludes to arguments in Filmer's *Patriarcha*.

12. *with apparent irony*: "The stronger man's arguments are always the best" ("la raison du plus fort est toujours la meilleure") is a proverbial French expression used with irony by La Fontaine in a celebrated fable, *The Wolf and the Lamb* (*Fables*, 1668, I. x), to which Rousseau is probably alluding.

13. *"Obey the powers that be"*: this summarizes the opening of the thirteenth chapter of St Paul's Epistle to the Romans, which Rousseau quotes directly two lines later. The King James Bible has "there is no power but of God." Such authorities were much used in works by apologists of royal power, such as the *Politique tirée des propres paroles de l'Écriture Sainte* (*Politics taken from the very words of Holy Scripture*), 1709, by Louis XIV's bishop, Bossuet.

14. *agreed convention*: in French "les conventions"; other translations have "conventions" or "covenants." It is the idea of free consent that is essential here.

15. *to transfer*: in French the legal term "aliéner," which with its derivatives occurs often in the *Contract*. I avoid translating by *alienate* because of the more recent meanings that the word has acquired.

16. *subject to a king*: in these considerations Rousseau's target is the Natural Law school generally; here the reference is to Grotius's *De iure belli ac pacis*, I. iii, and soon after to both Grotius and Pufendorf, who argued that a man might sell himself in order to get his subsistence. This was denied by Montesquieu (*Spirit of Laws*, XV. ii).

17. *the cave of the Cyclops*: *Odyssey*, IX; Locke used the same example in the first *Treatise on Civil Government*, ch. xix.

18. *the so-called right of slavery*: the argument for slavery based on the right of war is made both by Grotius (*De iure belli ac pacis*, III. vii) and Hobbes in the *De cive* (*Of the Citizen*) (1642), ch. viii, which is followed by Pufendorf.

19. *not naturally enemies*: see Part I of the *Discourse on Inequality* for Rousseau's full description of the state of nature, which is in direct opposition to Hobbes's view that men's natural state is "the war of all against all."

20. *relationships between things*: i.e., between states, as is made clear two paragraphs later.

21. *the Establishments . . . the Peace of God*: the former were a compilation of edicts ascribed to Louis IX (1214–1270); the Peace, or Truce, of God refers to Church decrees, repeated at intervals in the tenth and eleventh centuries, proscribing feudal warfare on certain days.

22. *polity*: in French "politie," an archaic word for Rousseau, but one which he often uses in the sense of the political organization of society. He emphasized in a letter to his publisher Rey (23 December 1761) that it was not to be confused with *politique* "policy."

23. The Romans, who understood and observed the laws of war better than any other nation on earth, carried their scruples on this point so far that citizens were not allowed to serve as volunteers unless they committed themselves to fighting against the enemy, and an enemy specifically named. When the legion in which the younger Cato had fought his first campaign was disbanded, the elder Cato wrote to Popilius to say that if he wished his son to continue to serve with him he would have to take the military oath again, because, once the first oath had been cancelled, he could no longer bear arms against the enemy. And Cato also wrote to his son telling him to take care not to go into battle without taking the new oath. I know that the siege of Clusium and other particular incidents could be used against my argument, but for my part I am citing laws and customs. Of all peoples the Romans transgressed their laws least often, and their laws were the finest of all. [*The Romans . . . of all*: this note was added in 1782.]

24. *less to national powers than to their subjects*: I translate literally as regards *less . . . than* (in French: "moins des avertissements aux puissances qu'à leurs sujets"), but it may seem that the context calls for "notices given to national powers rather than their subjects."

25. *are based on reason*: the arguments also resemble those of Montesquieu, *Spirit of Laws*, X. iii, "The Right of Conquest."

26. *give itself to a king*: the reference is to *De iure belli ac pacis*, I. iii. 8, but the arguments in this paragraph are mainly directed against the concept of the "double contract" in Pufendorf (*De jure naturae et gentium*, VII. ii), which combines contract of "association," creating a society, with one of "submission," accepting a ruler.

27. *there has been unanimity:* Rousseau re-emphasizes this point in IV. ii.

28. *a point in the development of mankind:* the supposition recalls the passage from the state of nature to the social state, described in the later sections of Part I of the *Discourse on Inequality,* but in the *Contract* the historical aspect is virtually eliminated.

29. *Each of us . . . part of the whole:* in French "Chacun de nous met en commun sa personne et toute sa puissance sous la suprême direction de la volonté générale, et nous recevons en corps chaque membre comme partie indivisible du tout." The last words in the Geneva MS are "comme partie inaliénable du tout," "as an inalienable part of the whole." The formulation of the contract is the first passage in the work in which the term *volonté générale* appears.

30. The true sense of this word has almost disappeared in modern writers. Most of them take a town to be a city and a town-dweller to be a citizen. They are unaware that it is houses that make a town, but citizens who make the City. [*citizens who make the City:* Rousseau's use of *cité* here seems to be influenced by the word from which it is derived, Latin *civitas,* the place inhabited by *cives*; it meant "state" and later "township," implying a degree of local autonomy.] The same error once cost the Carthaginians dear. In my reading I have not seen the title of *cives* given to the subjects of any ruler, not even to the Macedonians in ancient times, nor to the English nowadays, although they are nearer to being free than any others. The French alone call themselves *citizens* as a matter of course, because they have no true idea of what it means, as can be seen from their dictionaries; otherwise, they would be guilty of treason in usurping it. Among them, the name expresses a virtue, not a right. Bodin, meaning to discuss our citizens and burgesses, made a sad blunder in taking the one for the other. [*taking the one for the other:* broadly, Genevan citizens (*citoyens*) were eligible for public office in the city and they and burgesses (*bourgeois*) could be members of the governing councils. Others, the "natives" and "inhabitants" (*natifs, habitants*) had official permission to dwell within the city but few or no political rights. The categories were based on parentage and place of birth. Rousseau was a *citoyen* by virtue of being born within the city walls of a father who was a *citoyen.* The error he complains of in Jean Bodin (to whom he probably owes the distinction between town and city that he elaborates here) is found in some but not all editions of his *Six Books of the Republic,* 1576, I. vi. The long, celebrated, and controversial article by d'Alembert to which Rousseau refers in the next sentence appeared in the seventh volume (1757) of Diderot and d'Alembert's *Encyclopédie*; it was in answer to it that Rousseau wrote his *Letter à M. d'Alembert sur les spectacles* (*Letter to M. d'Alembert on Theatre*), 1758.] M. d'Alembert did not make the same mistake in his article *Geneva,* where he correctly distinguished the four orders (or even five, if you count those who are simply foreigners) to which those living in our city belong, only two of them constituting the Republic. No other French author,

to my knowledge, has understood the true sense of the word *citizen.*

31. *the sovereign . . . the state:* this passage contains perhaps the clearest illustration of what Rousseau means by the key terms *sovereign* and *state,* both of which, for him, denote the association of citizens, not a person or body set over them and distinct from them.

32. *no kind of fundamental law . . . binding on the people as a body:* in the view of the chief legal officer of Geneva, the *Procureur général,* when arguing that the *Social Contract* should be condemned, Rousseau implied in this passage that a government could be removed and changed by its people; the book was therefore "destructive of every government."

33. *the sanctity of the contract:* in IV. viii, this is one of the articles of the civil religion.

34. *any form of guarantee to its subjects:* literally, "has no need of a guarantor in its relation to the subjects" ("n'a nul besoin de garant envers les sujets"), the meaning being clarified by what follows. The sentence is important because the idea of a guarantee against state power was a central issue in attacks on Rousseau made by liberals such as Benjamin Constant, in his *Principes de politique* (*Principles of Politics*), 1815.

35. *as we shall see later:* see II. iv, especially the last three paragraphs.

36. *forced to be free:* on this notorious remark, see the Introduction, p. xxi.

37. *will not depend on any person:* in French "le garantit de toute dépendance personnelle," i.e., he is answerable only to the law and the state, not to an individual having power over him, such as a king or nobleman.

38. *The Civil State:* it is interesting to compare what Rousseau says in this chapter with the description of the state of nature in the *Discourse on Inequality,* which has often been claimed to be inconsistent with it.

39. *Property:* more exactly "real estate" or "realty," the French *domaine réel* being a legal term. The discussion is more sophisticated than in the *Political Economy* (section III, beginning; see p. 25), where the emphasis is more on the individual owner.

40. *Nuñez Balboa:* Balboa (1475–1517), discoverer of the Pacific Ocean in 1513, is here taken as an example of the Spanish *conquistadores.* In Part II of *Emile* he is unfavourably compared to Emile on the grounds that Emile has a right to land because he has cultivated it.

41. *as we shall see in due course:* in II. iv.

42. Under a bad government, this equality is only apparent and illusory: it serves only to keep the poor wretched and preserve the usurpations of the rich. Laws in reality are always useful to those with possessions and detrimental to those who have nothing: whence it follows that the social state is advantageous to men only if all have a certain amount, and none too much.

43. *cannot be transferred:* in French "est inaliénable"; compare *transfer* for "aliéner" and the note.

44. *being only the exercise of the general will:* a different

definition of sovereignty is contained in the correspond-ing chapter (I. v) of the Geneva MS: "There is therefore in the state a common force which sustains it, a general will which directs this force, and it is the application of the one to the other which constitutes sovereignty." Rousseau adopts this definition later in the final version (II. iv, end of first paragraph).

45. *cannot be represented except by itself:* this is argued at length in III. xv.

46. *an individual's will:* as the end of the paragraph makes clear, the "individual" here is a monarch, the passage be-ing directed against the idea that the general will could be vested in any one person. A few lines later, although the words given to the "sovereign authority" ("le souverain") are "I . . . want," the reference must be to the people as sovereign.

47. *Our political theorists:* specialist opinion is divided con-cerning the identity of the thinkers meant here; Rousseau refers later in the chapter to the Natural Law school (Grotius etc.), but it seems likely that Montesquieu also is under attack, since his famous interpretation of the English constitution (*Spirit of Laws*, XI. vi) involves divid-ing political power into legislative, executive, and judicial.

48. *the idea associated with the word law:* see II. vi.

49. *his translator Barbeyrac:* the important translation of Grotius's *De iure belli ac pacis* by Jean Barbeyrac (1674–1744) appeared in 1724 under the title *Du droit de la guerre et de la paix*.

50. *is always in the right:* in French "la volonté générale est toujours droite," sometimes translated "is always right," which is misleading, because the English *right* can mean "correct," but the French "droite" lacks this sense. As the immediate sequel shows, Rousseau firmly denies that the general will always correctly knows its own good.

51. "Every interest," says the Marquis d'Argenson, "has a dif-ferent basis. Two individual interests agree when having a basis different from that of a third." He could have added that agreement between all interests is formed through their common basis, in contrast to the interest of each person. If there were no differing interests, we should scarcely be aware of the common interest, which would never meet any obstacle; everything would run by itself, and there would no longer be any skill in politics.

52. "In truth," says Machiavelli, "some divisions within states are harmful, and some are helpful. Those are harmful which are accompanied by parties and factions; helpful, those which subsist without organized parties or factions. The founder of a republic, being unable to prevent dis-sension within the state, must at least prevent the exis-tence of faction." (*History of Florence*, Bk. VII.) [*History of Florence*, Bk. VII: Rousseau quotes Machiavelli in Italian, here and later.]

53. *Lycurgus:* according to legendary tradition, Lycurgus gave laws to Sparta, whose customs were much admired by Rousseau; compare II. vii, etc.

54. *Solon, Numa, and Servius:* Solon, the historical legislator of Athens (640–548 BCE), is probably mentioned because of his division of the body of citizens into four classes according to wealth; Numa, the legendary second king of Rome (seventh century BCE), because he created nu-merous associations based on trade (in order, according to Plutarch, whom Rousseau seems to be following here, to reduce larger-scale civil conflict); and Servius Tullius, king of Rome in the sixth century BCE, because he orga-nized the *centuriae*, as Rousseau explains in detail later (IV. iv).

55. The attentive reader will not, I beg, be too hasty in accusing me of contradicting myself here. I have been unable to avoid it in the terms I use, given the poverty of the language; [*the poverty of the language:* Rousseau seems to mean that, since he has just said that the sovereign has absolute power over citizens, he might appear to contradict himself by mention-ing citizens' rights against the sovereign. Men in the social state, apparently, have something similar to natural rights, but no word for them is available. The idea is conveyed by a statement in the chapter's penultimate paragraph: "any man can make full use of that share of his goods and liberty that is left to him by these agreements."] but wait.

56. *for the community to use:* compare Locke, to whom Rousseau may be referring at the beginning of the para-graph: "though men when they enter into society give up the equality, liberty, and executive power they had in the state of nature . . . the power of the society or legislative constituted by them can never be supposed to extend far-ther than the common good" (second *Treatise on Civil Government*, IX. 131).

57. *not only in essence but also in respect of its object:* "in es-sence": because its source is everyone generally; "its ob-ject": what it is applied to, also everyone generally.

58. *the matter becomes contentious:* in French "contentieuse," which refers not merely to matters of dispute, but (as Rousseau indicates) specifically to those cases between private persons and public authorities which have not been envisaged in any relevant law.

59. *time to put mine:* see the discussion of government in Bk. III.

60. *has jurisdiction:* in French "connaît," which here has its le-gal sense (cp. English "take cognizance").

61. *preferable . . . to what it was before:* this passage adds to the description of the advantages of the social state found in I. viii.

62. *The Law:* see section I of the *Political Economy* for a sus-tained eulogy on the subject (p. 10), found also in the Geneva MS, I. vii.

63. *in metaphysical terms alone:* commentators agree that the target of this remark is Montesquieu's famous definition: "Laws in the broadest sense are the necessary relationships which derive from the nature of things" (*Spirit of Laws*, I. i). However, in the last two chapters of Book II, there seems to be at least some trace of Montesquieu's definition in the importance Rousseau gives to "relationships."

64. *I have already said:* see II. iv.

65. *to the legislative power:* this passage well illustrates a distinction that is fundamental in Rousseau's political

thought, that between sovereign and government (discussed at the beginning of III. i), which partly corresponds to the standard distinction between legislative and executive.

66. *any state ruled by laws*: cp. the definition at the beginning of section I of the *Political Economy*: "a lawful or popular government, that is to say a government which has as its object the good of the people".

67. By this word I do not refer only to aristocracies and democracies, but in general to any government directed by law, which is the general will. In order to be legitimate it is not necessary that the government should be indistinguishable from the sovereign, but that it should be the minister of the sovereign: then even a monarchy is a republic. This will be clarified in Book III.

68. A nation becomes famous only when its legislation is on the decline. It is not known during how many centuries Lycurgus's institutions ensured happiness for the Spartans before the rest of Greece took note of them.

69. *the argument put by Caligula*: see I. ii.

70. *his Statesman*: the dialogue also known as the *Politicus*.

71. *says Montesquieu*: in his *Considerations on the Greatness of the Romans and their Decadence* (1734), 1748 edition, ch. i.

72. Those who regard Calvin [*Calvin*: Jean Calvin was born in northern France, moving to Geneva in 1541 at the age of 32. The *Institution of the Christian Religion*, mentioned in Rousseau's note, was first published in 1536.] only as a theologian fail to recognize the extent of his genius. The wisdom of our edicts, to the drafting of which he contributed much, does him as much honour as the *Institutes*. Whatever changes time may bring in our religion, the memory of so great a man will always be blessed among us, so long as love of country and love of liberty are not extinct.

73. *combined in the same persons*: of the various *decemviri* (councils of ten) in Roman history, Rousseau is referring, here and in what follows, to the decemvirs who in 451 BCE were entrusted with absolute power and given the task of drawing up proposed laws, which when they were enacted as statutes by the *comitia centuriata* (see IV. iv) became the "Twelve Tables." The crisis he mentions occurred, according to legend, when a father killed his daughter in order to save her from one of the decemvirs; this supposedly brought about a revolution in which the decemvirs were overthrown.

74. *worth repeating*: see II. i; it is also repeated in III. xv.

75. *the fundamental rules of reasons of state*: in French "les règles fondamentales de la raison d'Etat." The last phrase would usually be translated as "reason of State" and denote political expediency in a bad sense, implying unscrupulousness, but such seems not to be the meaning here.

76. *attribute their own wisdom to the gods*: as his remarks in the next paragraph indicate, Rousseau has in mind instances such as Moses, bringing down from Mount Sinai the tablets on which was written the Decalogue, or Numa (mentioned in II. iii), said to have received counsel from the nymph Egeria.

77. "And in truth," says Machiavelli, "there was never an outstanding legislator, among any people, who did not resort to God, for otherwise his laws would not have been accepted. There are many advantages known to the prudent man, which have in themselves no self-evident reasons for making it possible to convince others of them." *Discourses on Livy*, Bk. I, ch. xi.

78. *the law of the child of Ishmael*: i.e., the religion of Muhammad.

79. *arrogant philosophers or blind partisanship*: an obvious reference to the "party" of the *philosophes* from whom Rousseau is distancing himself, most of them taking a destructively sceptical view of figures such as Moses or Muhammad.

80. *the same objective*: the allusion is not very clear, but what is meant is probably the idea in William Warburton's *The Divine Legation of Moses* (1737–41), well known in its time, that religion deterred wrongdoers by the belief in rewards and punishments after death.

81. *stronger than a large one*: Rousseau's views resemble Aristotle's (*Politics*, IV. iv), but his decided preference for small states was more certainly influenced by the example of the Greek city states, the early Roman republic, and Geneva. See also III. vi and xv.

82. *everything underneath*: in this passage, despite the suggestion in the term "satrapies" that the states in question are Oriental, Rousseau was no doubt criticizing the situation in France.

83. *other customary laws*: in French "d'autres coutumes," in the old sense of laws based on custom and codified; in France they varied greatly from region to region.

84. *particular subordination*: this is presumably the same as the dependence on persons mentioned in I. vii.

85. *civil liberty*: see I. viii.

86. If you wish to give the state cohesion, bring the limits of wealth and poverty as close together as possible: do not allow either extreme opulence or destitution. [*extreme opulence or destitution*: apart from Rousseau himself in the *Discourse on Inequality*, both Plato (*Laws*, Bk. V) and Aristotle (*Politics*, VI. x) advise against allowing excess of wealth and poverty.] Those two are inseparable by nature, and both are equally damaging to the common good; one produces the instruments of tyranny, and the other produces the tyrants. It is always between them that public liberty is traded, and one buying and the other selling.

87. Any branch of foreign trade, according to M. d'Argenson, brings only false advantages to the nation as a whole; it may enrich a few individuals, or even a few towns, but the nation in general gains nothing from it and the people does not benefit.

88. *each of these aims*: see Montesquieu, *Spirit of Laws*, XI. v, for an analogous list, the most interesting point of difference being that for Montesquieu the Romans' aim was expansion.

89. *which is moral*: the eighteenth-century French word *moral* used here can correspond approximately to English

psychological as well as to *moral*, which I retain because the ethical aspect is important in Rousseau's usage of the word.

90. *can belong to it alone:* see II. iv and vi.

91. *are called officers or kings:* in French "s'appellent *magistrats* ou *rois*." In eighteenth-century French *magistrat* could have the Latinate sense of "officer of government," but it tended to be applied to legal officials, including judges; Rousseau seems to exclude the legal aspect. To apply the term *kings* to members of a government is unusual, to say the least, and seems also to be based on Latin, the word *rex* (the origin of the French *roi*) meaning a ruler generally as well as a king.

92. Thus in Venice the College of Senators is given the name of Most Serene Ruler, even when the Doge is not present.

93. *the name of ruler:* on *prince*, see the note to the word *ruler*.

94. *is not a contract:* Rousseau is here arguing against a commonplace of seventeenth- and eighteenth-century contract theory, the concept of a pact of submission, which he criticizes in detail in III. xvi.

95. *ruler or principal officer:* in French "*prince ou magistrat*."

96. *the middle term being the government:* a geometric (or continuous) proportion is here a double ratio, e.g., A is to B as B is to C, A :B ::B : C, with B as the "middle term." If the middle term is identical in both single ratios, as in this example, the expression can be called "a three-term proportion," as Rousseau does later. The difficult eighteenth-century mathematical language in this chapter was elucidated by Marcel Françon in two articles on which editors and translators have since relied: "Le langage mathématique de J.-J. Rousseau," *Isis*, 40 (1949), 341–4; "Sur le language algébrique de Rousseau," *Annales de la société Jean-Jacques Rousseau*, 33 (1953–5), 243–6. See in English the notes in the edition of the *Contrat social* by Ronald Grimsley (Oxford, 1972), 155–7, which give more details than I can give here.

97. *the relationship becomes less:* to take one half and one twentieth as an example: the relation 1 : 20 is, for Rousseau, greater in mathematical terminology than 1 : 2, but in ordinary language there is less of a relationship between 1 and 20 than between 1 and 2.

98. *a moral agent:* in French "une penonne morale," one of the expressions conveying that a corporate entity, such as a government, can in various respects act like an individual, on which see Introduction.

99. *We have stated:* in the preceding chapter.

100. [Reference deleted for the purpose of this excerpt.]

101. *its rightfulness:* in French "rectitude," in Rousseau's sense (as shown in the sequel) of conformity to the general will.

102. *The Classification of Governments:* a standard element in political theory. Rousseau's division based on numbers resembles that of Aristotle, Machiavelli, and Hobbes rather than Montesquieu, who distinguishes between republic, monarchy, and despotism (*Spirit of Laws*, II. i). For Rousseau a republic is "any state ruled by laws" (II. vi), the people associated in the state retaining sovereign authority.

103. *is democracy:* as is often noted, this form of government by the people (criticized in the next chapter) is not what is usually meant nowadays by *democracy*, which corresponds more closely to the elective aristocracy mentioned by Rousseau in III. v.

104. *made virtue the principle of republics:* Montesquieu (*Spirit of Laws*, III. iii); although both writers make the same point about republics, *republic* for Montesquieu covered only aristocracy and democracy (ibid., I. ii), while for Rousseau it is, in this passage, "every properly constituted state."

105. The Count Palatine of Posen, the father of the present King of Poland and Duke of Lorraine. [*the present King of Poland and Duke of Lorraine*: Stanislas Lesczynski (1677–1766) was the titular king of Poland from 1704, but ruled only for short periods; in 1738 he became the sovereign duke of Lorraine. Rousseau may have found the quotation in his *Observations on the Government of Poland* (French edn. 1749).]

106. *"I prefer . . . servitude":* quoted by Rousseau in Latin: "Malo periculosam libertatem quam quietum servitium."

107. *priests, elders, senate, gerontes:* all these terms are etymologically connected with words meaning "old" (Greek *gerontes:* "elders," "chiefs").

108. It is clear that the world *optimates*, in antiquity, did not mean the best, but the most powerful. [*the most powerful:* Latin *optimates*, from *optimus* "best," is the term used by Cicero, etc., for "the aristocratic party" in Roman politics.]

109. *the worst of all forms of government:* Rousseau's long note to III. x, about Roman political history, says that "hereditary aristocracy is the worst of the legitimate kinds of administration." In the *Letters from the Mountains*, VI, summarizing *Contract* III. v, he makes a distinction: "The best form of government is aristocracy; the worst form of sovereignty is aristocracy."

110. *aristocracy in the true sense of the word:* here Rousseau is alluding to the Greek etymology, *aristoi* "the best," *-kratia* "power," "rule."

111. *the two powers:* the legislative and executive powers, as defined in III. i.

112. It is imperative that the manner of electing members of the government should be regulated by law; for if it is left to the wishes of the ruler, a hereditary aristocracy will be the inevitable result, as has happened in the republics of Venice and Berne. In Venice the state has long been non-existent; but in Berne it has been preserved by the extreme wisdom of the Senate: which makes it a very honourable but very dangerous exception.

113. *no longer available to the law:* cf. above, III. i, p. 95: "the dominant will of the ruling body is only, or should only be, the general will or the law, its power is only the public power concentrated in it, and as soon as it has the desire to do some absolute and independent act of its own, the cohesiveness of the whole begins to be weakened."

114. *fall on the wealthy:* however, in the passages of the *Politics* (IV. v–vii) to which Rousseau is presumably referring, Aristotle's assumption is that the rich are preferred in

oligarchy, a particular and inferior form of aristocracy, but in true aristocracy merit as well as wealth qualifies for rule.

115. *Monarchy:* Rousseau's pronounced dislike of monarchies is expressed with comparative restraint here; it is more overt in his unpublished works, e.g. the *Considerations on the Government of Poland*, ch. 8.

116. *the ruling body . . . executive power:* another reminder of the arguments advanced in III. i.

117. *is seen as:* in French "un être collectif représente un individu . . . un individu représente un être collectif," in which the sense of *représente* is obscure, as editors have noted; it cannot however mean *represent* in the sense of "act as representative for."

118. *drawing a great ship over the water:* Rousseau probably read the anecdote in Plutarch's *Life of Marcellus.*

119. *by Samuel . . . by Machiavelli:* 1 Samuel 8: 10–18; as regards Machiavelli, the reference is to *The Prince* generally. Rousseau's ensuing note argues against taking the conventional view of the book as a manual for cunning and unscrupulous rulers.

120. Machiavelli was a man of integrity and a good citizen; but as a servant of the Medici family he was forced, while his country was oppressed, to disguise his love of liberty. Simply by the choice of his execrable hero he revealed his secret purpose; and the difference between the maxims in his book on the Prince and hose in his *Discourses on Livy* and *History of Florence* demonstrates that he was a politician of great profundity, whose readers have hitherto been either superficial or corrupt. The Vatican has strictly banned his book: that was only to be expected; it is the Vatican that he most obviously describes.

121. *We have established:* in III. iii, final paragraph.

122. *immediate orders are therefore necessary:* on this important point Rousseau is following Montesquieu (*Spirit of Laws*, II. iv).

123. *others to act in his place:* probably a reference to what, in his *Judgement* on the Abbé de Saint-Pierre's *Polysynody*, Rousseau denounces as a "vizirate," when the vizir or minister serves his own interest instead of that of the king or the people.

124. *inferior to a republic:* this seems to be a momentary inconsistency in the use of terms, *republic* here meaning some form of democracy rather than, as is usual in the *Contract*, any state governed by laws (II. vi).

125. *a new epoch in the country's history:* this paragraph, added while the book was printing, was intended—so Rousseau says in the *Confessions*, Bk. XI—to flatter the Duc de Choiseul and thus facilitate the circulation of the book in France, but unfortunately produced the contrary effect.

126. *the choice of a good king:* the references to hereditary rule and regency in this paragraph make it clear that the main target is the French monarchical system (regency of Anne of Austria: 1643–61; of Philip of Orléans: 1715–23).

127. *your father wasn't a king:* this anecdote about Dionysius II, ruler of Syracuse in the fourth century BCE, is in Plutarch's *Sayings of Kings.*

128. *if someone else had been ruler:* Tacitus, *Histories*, I. xvi, quoted by Rousseau in the Latin.

129. *that I have already disproved:* see I. iii.

130. In his *Statesman.*

131. *as a punishment from Heaven:* perhaps no specific reference is intended here, but the idea is found in both Calvin (*Institution*, 1560 ed., IV. xx. 24) and Bossuet (*Politics*, IV. ii. 6).

132. *the English constitution . . . Poland:* on England, Rousseau must be following the famous analysis of the British constitution in Montesquieu, *Spirit of Laws*, XI. vi; on Poland, he himself gives an analysis in the *Considerations*, ch. 7.

133. *when discussing governments in general:* i.e. the answer will vary according to circumstances (III. iii. end).

134. *not mixed, but modified:* the meaning is somewhat clarified by Rousseau's remarks on the Roman tribunate (IV. v, second paragraph).

135. *commissions:* in French "tribunaux," which usually signifies courts of law, but here, presumably, committees assigned particular functions.

136. The gradual formation [*The gradual formation:* This note (like his note to the preceding chapter) was added while the book was in the press; the connection it makes between prosperity and liberty suggests that he was trying to adapt his argument in this chapter to the firm statement in II. xi that the greatest political good lies in liberty and equality.] and expansion of Venice in its lagoons provides a notable example of this evolution; and it is truly remarkable that, after more than twelve hundred years, the Venetians seem only to have reached the second stage, which began with the *Serrar di consiglio* in 1198. [*the Serrar di consiglio in 1198:* the Maggior Consiglio (Great Council) of 480 members elected by districts, dating from 1171, was "closed" in 1297 (not 1198) by constitutional measures which resulted in rule by an oligarchy formed by the city's great commercial families.] As for their former dukes, an object of reproach for the Venetians, it has been proved, whatever the *Squittinio della libertà veneta* [*the Squittinio della libertà veneta:* "The Squeaking of Venetian Liberty," the polemical tide of an anonymous pamphlet, 1612, arguing that the Holy Roman Emperor had the right to rule Venice.] may say, that they were not sovereigns.

An objection that is bound to be made is that the Roman Republic, so it will be said, followed exactly the opposite course, passing from monarchy to aristocracy and from aristocracy to democracy. [*from aristocracy to democracy:* because, in the common view, Rome after Romulus, its founder and first king, was a monarchy until the expulsion of the Tarquins, then, during what is known as the Republican period, an aristocracy governed by the patrician class, then (after the lengthy Conflict of the Orders, patricians against plebeians) a senatorial democracy, from about the beginning of the third century BCE. Rousseau's critique discounts the regal period, and argues that the Republic, having no definite form initially, became first a democracy, then a senatorial aristocracy, the civil wars in the first century BCE making it a monarchy under Julius Caesar and the first of the emperors, Augustus.] I am very far from sharing this view.

The government first established by Romulus was mixed, and it promptly degenerated into despotism. The state perished before its time for special reasons, as a new-born child can die before reaching maturity. The real date of the birth of the Republic was the expulsion of the Tarquins. But the Republic did not immediately acquire a fixed form, because in failing to abolish the patriciate the Romans had left half the job undone. The result was that a hereditary aristocracy, which is the worst of the legitimate kinds of administration, remained in conflict with a democracy, and the form of government stayed uncertain and ambiguous, to be fixed (as Machiavelli has shown) [*as Machiavelli has shown*: in the *Discourses*, I. iv.] only with the establishment of the tribunate; only then did a true government and a genuine democracy come into being. In reality the people was then not only sovereign, but also judge and minister of government; the Senate was no more than a subordinate body with the function of moderating or concentrating the government; and the consuls themselves, though they were patricians, and first ministers, and generals with absolute power when at war, were in Rome only the people's presidents.

Thenceforward it could be seen that the government, following its natural tendency, had a strong inclination to aristocracy. The patriciate ceased to exist almost of its own accord, and aristocracy was no longer confined to the patricians as in Venice or Genoa, but belonged to the senatorial body, which included both patricians and plebeians, and even to the tribunate when it began to usurp active powers: for words do not affect realities; and when the people has chiefs who govern for it, whatever name the chiefs bear, the government is still an aristocracy.

The abuse of aristocracy engendered the civil wars and the Triumvirate. Sulla, Julius Caesar and Augustus became, in the event, real monarchs; and finally, under the despotism of Tiberius, the state was dissolved. Roman history, therefore, does not contradict my principle, but confirms it.

137. *forced, but not obliged, to obey*: i.e. the moral obligation binding every citizen who accepts the social contract no longer exists.

138. *the general name of anarchy*: i.e. a government can remain, but there is no state in Rousseau's sense of a society controlled by the laws made by the people as sovereign.

139. *democracy . . . explanation*: the first two terms mean mob rule and rule by the few. The observations on the proper sense of *tyrant* may have been suggested by Machiavelli's analogous comments (*Discourses*, I. ii), in which he says that a monarchy degenerates into a tyranny, but without specifying further.

140. "For all those are considered and called tyrants who have perpetual power in a state that formerly had liberty" (Cornelius Nepos in his life of Miltiades, ch. viii).—It is true that Aristotle (*Nicomachean Ethics*, Book VIII, ch. x) distinguishes between the tyrant and the king, in that the first governs for his own benefit and the second only for the benefit of his subjects; but apart from the fact that all the Greek writers generally took the word *tyrant* in another sense, as is clear above all from Xenophon's *Hieron*, it would follow from Aristotle's distinction that, since the world began, not a single king has ever been known.

141. *the enforced labour of the corvée*: in French simply "les corvées" [the *corvée* was enforced labour, a spell of work imposed by the state on the unprivileged, often taking the form of the construction or repair of roads. Militias were raised by drawing lots, but the duty could be avoided by paying for a replacement.]. In the *Constitution for Corsica*, Rousseau admits that it was very unpopular in France, but says that in Switzerland no one complained of it.

142. *the Third Estate*: Rousseau chooses to consider only the representatives of the bourgeoisie, or Third Estate (*Tiers Etat*), as speaking for the people as a whole.

143. *it is nothing*: this attacks the view of English constitutional freedom accepted by many in France, notably Voltaire (e.g. in the *Letters Concerning the English Nation*, or *Philosophical Letters*, (1733–4) and Montesquieu, in a famous chapter (XI. vi) in the *Spirit of Laws*.

144. *the name of man was dishonourable*: Rousseau is alluding to feudal "homage" (from homme, "man"), according to which a lord's tenant or vassal bound himself to the lord's service.

145. *inconvenience is nothing*: cf. III. xii, end.

146. *the tribunes would not have dared to*: the lictors were attendants and escorts for state officials (magistrates); what Rousseau is referring to is perhaps that they are known to have acted sometimes as executioners.

147. In cold countries, to adopt the Orientals' love of comfort and luxury is willingly to accept their servitude; it means being under an even greater necessity of submitting to it.

148. *I have proved the contrary*: see I. ii, iv.

149. This is what I had intended to do in the sequel to this work [*the sequel to this work*: this must be the project mentioned in the Prefatory Note. In the summary of the *Social Contract* contained in *Émile*, Bk. V, Rousseau speaks of the possibility of leagues or confederacies, within which, he says, each state can be autonomous as regards its internal affairs.], when in discussing external relations I would have included federation—a totally new subject, the principles of which have not yet been established.

150. *from making a law to its execution*: editors connect this with a passage in Hobbes: "Those who met together with intention to erect a city, were almost in the very act of meeting, a democracy" (*De cive*, VII).

151. *the world's most fortunate nation*: those meant are generally assumed to be the power of the rural Swiss cantons.

152. *hard labour . . . a reformatory*: the Bernese form of punishment referred to was called *Schallenwerk*. Beaufort is put with Cromwell as being a leader of rebels in a civil war, the Fronde having been almost contemporaneous with the civil wars in England.

153. *the general will no longer the will of all*: the distinction is first made in II. iii (second paragraph). The passage that follows in IV. i, analyzing the interaction of particular and

general interests, may be compared with the remark in II. iv: "why is the happiness of each the constant wish of all, unless it is because there is no one who does not apply the word *each* to himself, and is not thinking of himself when he votes for all?"

154. *take great care to reserve to their members:* it is not entirely clear whether Rousseau means to approve of governments on this score, or to criticize them for it; a passage in the *Letters from the Mountains*, VII, suggests the latter, since in it Rousseau is critical of the fact that in Geneva the Petit Conseil (here equivalent to "government") does not allow the Conseil Général (the "sovereign") the right to express its opinions or to determine which questions it can discuss.

155. *the plebiscites of the people:* in French "les plébiscites du peuple," a slightly misleading phrase as regards Rome, since the plebeians, who passed plebiscites in their assemblies, were not the whole of the *populus*, "people," this including the patricians.

156. *Tacitus observes:* in the *Histories*, I. 85. The year in question is AD 69, when first Otho, then Vitellius, were briefly emperors.

157. *that he is not born a man:* a similar point is made in I. iv.

158. The assumption is always that the state in question is free; for apart from anything else, a man's family, his property, necessity, violence, or the lack of asylum, may make him continue to reside in a country against his will, and if so the fact of residence does not of itself entail consent to the contract, nor to any violation of it.

159. In Genoa the word *Libertas* is to be read at the entrances to prisons and on the chains of galley-slaves. This use of the slogan is telling and well-justified, for in reality it is only malefactors, at every level of society, who prevent the citizen from being free. In a country where every person of that kind was a galley-slave the citizens would enjoy the most perfect freedom.

160. *I have made sufficiently clear . . . I shall return to the subject later:* the references back are to various passages in III. x to xviii; and forward to IV. iii, iv.

161. *The Office of Censor:* the meaning here is wider than the modern sense of control of the media, and is closer to that of moral control over behaviour, exercised in Geneva and elsewhere by the religious authorities, a point not mentioned by Rousseau. Montesquieu (*Considerations*, VIII) had also expressed admiration for the Roman form of the institution.

162. *contrary to the usual opinion:* Rousseau's views on duels are to be found in the *Letter to d'Alembert* and *Julie*, Pt. I, Letter 57.

163. In this chapter I merely summarize what I have said at greater length in the *Letter to d'Alembert*.

164. In fact another island, which the delicacy of our language forbids me to name on this occasion. [*forbids me to name on this occasion:* the island of Chio. As pronounced in the eighteen century, its name would have offered an obvious play of words on *chier* "to shit."]

165. *Civil Religion:* on this extremely controversial chapter see Introduction. Although added at a late stage—it was not

in the version of the work sent by Rousseau to his publisher Rey late in 1760—its central argument, that states should have a civil religion, is found in a long and well-known letter to Voltaire, the "Letter on Providence" of 18 August 1756. The Geneva MS contains an untitled draft of the chapter.

166. *the same as Caligula's:* see I. ii.

167. *the Czars have gone to the same lengths:* this avoids the affirmation that the Czar is the head of the Russian Orthodox Church, which would not have been correct; Rousseau may be following Voltaire, *History of the Empire of Russia under Peter the Great*, Pt. I (1759), ch. x, on the changes carried out by Peter in 1721; "If the Czar did not make himself the head of the Russian church, as the kings of Great Britain are of the Anglican Church, he became in effect its absolute master."

168. *only its rulers:* in French "ses princes"; for the distinction between legislator and ruler see III. i.

169. It should be carefully noted that what binds the clergy into a single body is not so much formal assemblies, as in France, but the churches' communion. Communion and excommunication are the clergy's social pact: and thanks to this pact it will always be master of nations and kings. All the priests in communion together are fellow citizens, even if they come from opposite ends of the earth. The device is a political masterpiece. There was nothing like it among the pagan priests; and therefore they never formed a body of clergy.

170. *the reunion of the two heads of the eagle:* the phrase is puzzling. The two-headed eagle, an imperial emblem used by the House of Austria among others, denotes rule over east and west, as in the Roman Empire, but Rousseau's implication is that it denotes authority on both the secular and the religious domain.

171. *properly constituted:* Hobbes had stated (*De cive*, xviii, 28, end, to which Rousseau is presumably alluding) that in a Christian state the secular power should have both political and religious control.

172. For what Grotius approves of and what he condemns in Hobbes's *De cive*, see among other things a letter from him to his brother, 11 April 1643. [*a letter . . . April 1643:* Barbeyrac's preface to his translation of Grotius's *De iure belli ac pacis* quotes the letter, which says that according to Hobbes individuals should follow the religion approved in their country by the public authorities.] It is true that, inclined as he was to be indulgent, the learned writer appears to pardon Hobbes the good things in consideration of the bad; but not everyone is so forgiving.

173. *international law . . . treaties, etc.:* these subjects are presumably those that Rousseau had meant to discuss in the more general work which, in his Prefatory Note, he says he has abandoned.

Chapter VII | Immanuel Kant

1. Immanuel Kant, *Lectures on Ethics*. (Cambridge: Cambridge University Press, 1997), p. 125.

2. Immanuel Kant, *Groundwork of the Metaphysics of Morals*, translated & edited by M. Gregor and J. Timmermann. (Cambridge: Cambridge University Press, 1996), p. xviii.

3. *Über den Gemeinspruch*: "*Das mag in der Theorie richtig sein, taugt aber nicht für die Praxis*," *AA* VIII, 273–313. First published in *Berlinische Monatsschrift*, xxii (September 1793), 201–84. As we know from Kant's notes for the essay (*AA* XXIII, 125 ff.; cf. also Rudolf Reicke, *Lose Blätter aus Kants Nachlaß*, V (Königsberg, 18Sg), 148 f. and 179), he was attacking an essay by the eminent mathematician and writer Abraham Gotthelf Kistner (1719–1800), *Gedanken über das Unvermögen der Schriftsteller Empörungen zu bewirken* (*Thoughts on the inability of writers to produce rebellion*) (Göttingen, 1793), in which Kästner satirized the apparently useless activities of theorizing writers (cf. Dieter Henrich, (ed.), *Kant. Gentz. Rehberg. Über Theorie und Praxis* (Frankfurt/Main, 1967), p. 12). Kant also wished to show that the validity of a theory did not depend on its revolutionary consequences, thus dispelling ambiguities in the writing of his disciples. Cf. Henrich, *op. cit.* p. 12, who also refers to Johann Christian Gottlieb Schaumann (1768–1821), *Vermeil über Aufklärung, Freiheit und Gleichheit . . .* (*Essay on Enlightenment, Freedom arid Equality . . .*) (Halle, 1793).

4. *Anschauung* is the term Kant uses (Translator's note).

5. Possibly a reference to Edmund Burke's *Reflections on the Revolution in France* (1790); cf. the Everyman's Library Edition (London, 1910), pp. 55–6. It had been translated into German by Friedrich Gentz, as *Betrachtungen über die französische Revolution* (Berlin, 1793). Burke attacks those who theorise on politics without regard for experience. He uses the same quotation which Kant includes in this passage; cf. Paul Wittichen, "Kant und Burke," *Historische Zeitschrift*, XCII (1904), 254.

6. "Let him lord it there in his own court." Aeolus in Virgil, *Aneid I*, 140.

7. The terms *Staatsrecht* und *Völkerrecht* are two of the numerous compounds Kant forms out of the word *Recht*, which itself occurs again and again in his political writings. For the sake of consistency, it has been rendered throughout by the English "right," although it can often signify something more nearly equivalent to "law" or "justice." Kant himself twice supplies helpful definitions of the term in the works printed in this volume: cf. p. 73 and the section *Introduction to the Theory of Right*, pp. 132–5, for the relevant passages. For further remarks by Kant on the same topic cf. *AA* XXIII, 255–6. (Translator's note.)

8. [Kant's note] Cf. *Versuche über verschiedne Gegenstände aus der Moral und Literatur* (*Essays on Various Topics from Morality and Literature*), by C. Garve, Pt. I, pp. 111–16. I call this estimable writer's disagreements with my propositions *objections*, for they concern matters in which (as I hope) he wishes to reach agreement with me. They are Dot attacks, which are disparaging statements designed to provoke defence, for which I here find neither the space nor the inclination.

9. Christian Garve (1742–98), a well-known philosopher of the German Enlightenment, whose work Kant greatly esteemed on account of Garve's sincerity. In this essay, Kant is refuting Garve's views as expressed in *Versuche über verschiedne Gegenstände aus der Moral, der Literatur und dem gesellschaftlichen Leben*, I (Breslau, 1792), particularly 111–16. The passage is reprinted in Dieter Henrich (ed.), *Kant. Gentz. Rehberg. Über Theorie und Praxis* (Frankfurt/Main, 1967), pp. 134–8.

10. [Kant's note] Being worthy of happiness is that quality of a person which depends upon the subject's own individual free will and in accordance with which a universal reason, legislating both to nature and to the free will, would agree with all the aims of that person. It is thus entirely different from any aptitude for attaining happiness itself. For if a person's will does not harmonize with the only form of will which is fit to legislate universally to the reason, and thus cannot be contained within the latter (in other words, if his will conflicts with morality), he is not worthy of happiness and of that gift of attaining happiness with which nature endowed him.

11. [Kant's note] The necessity of assuming as the ultimate end of all things a *highest good* on earth, which it is possible to achieve with our collaboration, is not a necessity created by a lack of moral incentives, but by a lack of external circumstances within which an object appropriate to these incentives can alone be produced as an end in itself, as an *ultimate moral end*. For there can be no *will* without an end in view, although we must abstract from this end whenever the question of straightforward legal compulsion of our deeds arises, in which case the law alone becomes its determinant. But not every end is moral (that of personal happiness, for example, is not); the end must be an unselfish one. And the necessity of an ultimate end posited by pure reason and comprehending the totality of all ends within a single principle (i.e., a world in which the highest possible good can be realised with our collaboration) is a necessity experienced by the unselfish will as it *rises beyond* mere obedience to formal laws and creates as its own object the highest good. This idea of the totality of all ends is a peculiar kind of determinant for the will. For it basically implies that if we stand in a moral relationship to things in the world around us, we must everywhere obey the moral law; and to this is added the further duty of working with all our power to *ensure* that the state of affairs described (i.e., a world conforming to the highest moral ends) will actually exist. In all this, man may see himself as analogous to the divinity. For while the divinity has no subjective need of any external object, it cannot be conceived of as closed up within itself, but only as compelled by the very awareness of its own all-sufficiency to produce the highest good outside itself. In the case of the supreme being, this necessity (which corresponds to duty in man) can be envisaged *by us* only as a moral need. With man likewise, the motive provided by the idea of the highest possible earthly good, attainable through his collaboration,

is therefore not that of his own intended happiness, but only that of the idea as an end in itself and of obedience to it as a duty. For it does not hold out any prospect of happiness in the absolute sense, but only of a constant ratio between happiness and the worthiness of the subject, whatever the latter may be. But a determinant of the will which imposes this restriction both on itself and on its intention of becoming part of a whole such as we have described is *not selfish*.

12. [Kant's note] This is exactly what I myself insist upon. The incentive which men can have before they are given a specific goal (or end) can obviously be none other than the law itself, through the esteem which it inspires (irrespective of what ends one may have and seek to attain through obedience to the law). For the law, as the formal aspect of will, is all that remains if we discount the will's particular content (i.e., the goal, as Garve calls it).

13. "A matter of mere opportunity."

14. [Kant's note] Happiness embodies everything that nature has given us and nothing else. But virtue embodies that which no one but man can give or take away from himself. If it were replied that by deviating from the latter, man could at least incur blame and moral self-reproach, hence dissatisfaction and unhappiness, we might by all means agree. But only the virtuous man or one who is on the way to virtue is capable of this pure moral dissatisfaction, which comes not from any disadvantage resulting from his actions, but from their unlawfulness itself. His dissatisfaction is consequently not the cause but the effect of his being virtuous; and this unhappiness (if we choose to describe regrets over a crime as such) could not furnish a motive for being virtuous.

15. [Kant's note] Garve, in his notes to Cicero's *De Officiis*, 1783 edition, p. 6g, makes the following admission, which does credit to his own acuteness: "It is my innermost conviction that freedom will always remain unresolved and will never be explained." It is absolutely impossible to find a proof of its reality either in direct or indirect experience, and it cannot be accepted without any proof. Such a proof cannot be derived from purely theoretical considerations (for these would have to be sought in experience), nor therefore from purely practical propositions of reason, nor alternatively from practical propositions in the technical sense (for these too would have to be based on experience), but accordingly only from moral-practical ones. One must therefore wonder why Garve did not take refuge in the concept of freedom, at least in order to salvage the possibility of such imperatives.

16. Kant seeks here to refute Hobbes's political theory, which found its classic expression in the *Leviathan* (1651). The actual argument is explicitly directed against Hobbes's *De Cive* (1642).

17. [Kant's note] If we try to find a definite meaning for the word *gracious*, as distinct from kind, beneficent, protective etc., we see that it can be attributed only to a person to whom no *coercive rights* apply. Thus only the head of the *state's government*, who enacts and distributes all

benefits that are possible within the public laws (for the *sovereign* who provides them is, as it were, invisible, and is not an agent but the personified law itself), can be given the title of *gracious lord*, for he is the only individual to whom coercive rights do not apply. And even in an aristocratic government, as for example in Venice, the *senate* is the only "gracious lord." The nobles who belong to it, even including the *Doge* (for only the *plenary council* is the sovereign), are all subjects and equal to the others so far as the exercise of rights is concerned, for each subject has coercive rights towards every one of them. Princes (i.e., persons with a hereditary right to become rulers) are themselves called gracious lords only with future reference, an account of their claims to become rulers (i.e., by courtly etiquette, *par courtoisie*). But as owners of property, they are nonetheless fellow subjects of the others, and even the humblest of their servants must possess a right of coercion against them through the head of state. Thus there can be no more than one gracious lord in a state. And as for gracious (more correctly *distinguished*) ladies, they can be considered entitled to this appellation by their *rank* and their *sex* (thus only as opposed to the *male* sex), and this only by virtue of refinement of manners (known as gallantry) whereby the male sex imagines that it does itself greater honour by giving the fair sex precedence over itself.

18. [Kant's note] He who does a piece of work (*opus*) can sell it to someone else, just as if it were his own property. But guaranteeing one's labour (*praestatio operae*) is not the same as selling a commodity. The domestic servant, the shop assistant, the labourer, or even the barber, are merely labourers (*operarii*), not *artists* (*artifices*, in the wider sense) or members of the state, and are thus unqualified to be citizens. And although the man to whom I give my firewood to chop and the tailor to whom I give material to make into clothes both appear to have a similar relationship towards me, the former differs from the latter in the same way as the barber from the wig-maker (to whom I may in fact have given the requisite hair) or the labourer from the artist or tradesman, who does a piece of work which belongs to him until he is paid for it. For the latter, in pursuing his trade, exchanges his property with someone else (*opus*), while the former allows someone else to make use of him. But I do admit that it is somewhat difficult to define the qualifications which entitle anyone to claim the status of being his own master.

19. [Kant's note] If, for example, a war tax were proportionately imposed on all subjects, they could not claim, simply because it is oppressive, that it is unjust because the war is in their opinion unnecessary. For they are not entitled to judge this issue, since it is at least *possible* that the war is inevitable and the tax indispensable, so that the tax must be deemed rightful in the judgment of the subjects. But if certain estate owners were oppressed with levies for such a war, while others of the same class were exempted, it is easily seen that a whole people could never agree to a law of this kind, and it is entitled at least to make

representations against it, since an unequal distribution of burdens can never be considered just.

20. "The public welfare is the supreme law of the state."

21. [Kant's note] Measures of this kind might include certain restrictions on imports, so that the means of livelihood may be developed for the benefit of the subjects themselves and not as an advantage to foreigners or an encouragement for their industry. For without the prosperity of the people, the state would not have enough strength to resist external enemies or to preserve itself as a commonwealth.

22. [Kant's note] There is no *casus necessitatis* except where duties, i.e., an *absolute* duty and another which, however pressing, is nevertheless *relative*, come into conflict. For instance, it might be necessary for someone to betray someone else, even if their relationship were that of father and son, in order to preserve the state from catastrophe. This preservation of the state from evil is an absolute duty, while the preservation of the individual is merely a relative duty (i.e., it applies only if he is not guilty of a crime against the state). The first person might denounce the second to the authorities with the utmost unwillingness, compelled only by (moral) necessity. But if a person, in order to preserve his own life, pushes a shipwrecked fellow away from the plank he grasps, it would be quite false to say that (physical) necessity gives him a right to do so. For it is only a relative duty for me to preserve my own life (i.e., it applies only if I can do so without committing a crime). But it is an absolute duty not to take the life of another person who has not offended me and does not even make me risk my own life. Yet the teachers of general civil law are perfectly consistent in authorising such measures in cases of distress. For the authorities cannot combine a *penalty* with this prohibition, since this penalty would have to be death. But it would be a nonsensical law which threatened anyone with death if he did not voluntarily deliver himself up to death when in dangerous circumstances.

23. Gottfried Achenwall (1719–72), professor in Göttingen and the leading statistician of the age. His *Ius naturae in usum auditorium* was published in Göttingen, 1755–6 (7th ed. 1781). Kant used this work as a textbook for his lectures on Natural Law, held 12 times between 1767 and 1788. The use of textbooks for lectures was customary.

24. [Kant's note] Ius Naturae. Editio v. Pars posterior, §§203–206.

25. Charter granted to Brabant by Duke John III in 1354 in which the Duke undertook to maintain the integrity of the duchy and not to wage war, make treaties or impose taxes without consulting his subjects represented by the municipalities.

26. [Kant's note] Even if an actual contract of the people with the head of state has been violated, the people cannot reply immediately as a *commonwealth*, but only by forming factions. For the hitherto existing constitution has been destroyed by the people, but a new commonwealth has still to be organized. At this point, the state of anarchy supervenes, with all the terrors it may bring with it. And the wrong which is thereby done is done by each faction of the people to the others, as is clear from the case where the rebellious subjects ended up by trying to thrust upon each other a constitution which would have been far more oppressive than the one they abandoned. For they would have been devoured by ecclesiastics and aristocrats, instead of enjoying greater equality in the distribution of political burdens under a single head of state who ruled them all. [Editor's note: These remarks refer to the French Revolution.]

27. Georges Jacques Danton (1759–94), the French revolutionary leader.

28. This remark refers to the accession of William III of Orange and Mary to the British throne in 1688 (the Glorious Revolution). After James II had been overthrown, Parliament legislated for William's and Mary's accession, restricting the monarchy to the Protestant successors of James I.

29. [Kant's note] No right in a state can be tacitly and treacherously included by a secret reservation, and least of all a right which the people claim to be part of the constitution, for all laws within it must be thought of as arising out of a public will. Thus if the constitution allowed rebellion, it would have to declare this right publicly and make clear how it might be implemented.

30. "The judgment is uncertain, and experiments are dangerous."

31. "If they catch sight of a man respected for his virtue and services, they are silent and stand close with ears alert." Virgil, *Aeneid* I, 15 1–2.

32. [Kant's note] It is not immediately obvious how a universally *philanthropic* attitude can point the way to a cosmopolitan constitution, and this in turn to the establishment of *international justice* as the only state in which those capacities which make our species worthy of respect can be properly developed. But the conclusion of this essay will make this relationship clear.

33. Moses Mendelssohn (1729–86), a leading philosopher of the German Enlightenment. The reference is to Mendelssohn's essay "Über die Frage: was heist Aufklärung?" ("On the Question: What Is Enlightenment?"), *Berlinische Monatsschrift*, IV (9 September 1784), 193–200.

34. *Jerusalem, oder über religiöse Macht und Judentum* (Berlin, 1783), one of Mendelssohn's principal works.

35. Gotthold Ephraim Lessing (1729–81), the German writer and dramatist. These views are expressed in *Die Erziehung des Menschengeschlechts* (1780).

36. Sisyphus, a legendary Greek King of Corinth, was punished by the Gods for his misdeeds. His punishment involved continuously carrying a heavy stone to a mountain-top in Hades always to find that as soon as he reached the top the stone rolled down again (cf. Homer, *Odyssey* XI, 593–600).

37. "Something certain."

38. "Something uncertain."

39. I have been unable to trace this quotation.

40. The reference is to Rousseau's *Extrait du projet de paix perpétuelle* (1761).

41. Kant's quotation is in incorrect word order. It should run: *Ducunt volentem fata, nolentem trahunt* ("The fates lead him who is willing, but drag him who is unwilling"), Seneca, *Epistle* 107, II.

Chapter VIII | John Stuart Mill

1. John Stuart Mill, "Utilitarianism," in John Stuart Mill, *On Liberty and Other Essays* (Oxford: Oxford University Press), p. 140.
2. Mill here distinguishes his subject from that of determinism, which he had discussed in his *System of Logic*, bk. 6, ch. 2.
3. The United States of America.
4. Slaves in the Greek city-states of Sparta.
5. Plebeians, or common people.
6. The Roman Catholic Church.
7. Akbar (1542–1605) was a Mogul emperor in India, and Charlemagne (702–814) the first Holy Roman Emperor. Mill uses them as early examples of enlightened despotism.
8. In some editions, e.g., the Everyman edition, this phrase reads "the permanent interests of a man as a progressive being." However, this version is almost certainly mistaken, the "a" having crept into the text in a later, low-priced People's edition of *On Liberty*. See John Rawls, *A Theory of Justice*, 11th edn. (Cambridge, 1981), 209n., for a recognition of this error.
9. Auguste Comte (1798–1857) was the French founder of positivism. Mill criticizes his doctrine in *Auguste Comte and Positivism*, selections from which are to be found in the Everyman edition of *Utilitarianism, On Liberty, and Representative Government*, ed. H. B. Acton, 1972.
10. [Mill's note] These words had scarcely been written, when, as if to give them an emphatic contradiction, occurred the Government Press Prosecutions of 1858. That ill-judged interference with the liberty of public discussion has not, however, induced me to alter a single word in the text, nor has it at all weakened my conviction that, moments of panic excepted, the era of pains and penalties for political discussion has, in our own country, passed away. For, in the first place, the prosecutions were not persisted in; and, in the second, they were never, properly speaking, political prosecutions. The offence charged was not that of criticizing institutions, or the acts or persons of rulers, but of circulating what was deemed an immoral doctrine, the lawfulness of tyrannicide.

    If the arguments of the present chapter are of any validity, there ought to exist the fullest liberty of professing and discussing, as a matter of ethical conviction, any doctrine, however immoral it may be considered. It would, therefore, be irrelevant and out of place to examine here, whether the doctrine of tyrannicide deserves that tide. I shall content myself with saying that the subject has been at all times one of the open questions of morals; that the act of a private citizen in striking down a criminal, who, by raising himself above the law, has placed himself beyond the reach of legal punishment or control, has been accounted by whole nations, and by some of the best and wisest of men, not a crime, but an act of exalted virtue; and that, right or wrong, it is not of the nature of assassination, but of civil war. As such, I hold that the instigation to it, in a specific case, may be a proper subject of punishment, but only if an overt act has followed, and at least a probable connexion can be established between the act and the instigation. Even then, it is not a foreign government, but the very government assailed, which alone, in the exercise of self-defence, can legitimately punish attacks directed against its own existence.

11. The phrase comes from Thomas Carlyle. It was first published in Mill's periodical *The London and Westminster Review* (1838), and reprinted in Carlyle's *Critical and Miscellaneous Essays*, vi (London, l869), 46.
12. The Roman statesman Marcus Tullius Cicero (143–106 BCE). The greatest is presumably the Athenian orator Demosthenes (384–322 BCE).
13. [Mill's note] *The Sphere and Duties of Government*, from the German of Baron Wilhelm von Humboldt, pp. 11–13.
14. Which is to say covetousness or envy.
15. *The History of George Bramwell* was a melodramatic play by the playwright George Lillo.
16. Mill here clearly dissociates himself, and the principle of liberty he advocates, from any principle of *laissez-faire*, a principle he had defended earlier in his *Principles of Political Economy* (bk. 5, chs. 10 and 11) as merely a defeasible rule of thumb, or presumptive maxim.
17. Mill's argument here is not particularly strong, but is entirely consistent with his opposition to all other irrevocable contracts in which personal liberty is forfeited—such as the Victorian marriage contract.
18. Mill's fear of *pedantocracy* (a term apparently invented by Comte), of government by rule-bound bureaucrats or academics with spurious claims to special expertise, was shared by the Russian anarchist thinker Mikhail Bakunin, but there is no evidence of any mutual influence.
19. The Greek philosopher (342–270 BCE) who maintained that pleasure and the absence of pain alone had value. His followers, the Epicureans, are often regarded as exponents of a somewhat ascetic version of hedonism, akin to Mill's own views.
20. [Mill's note] The author of this essay has reason for believing himself to be the first person who brought the word utilitarian into use. He did not invent it, but adopted it from a passing expression in Mr Galt's *Annals of the Parish*. After using it as a designation for several years, he and others abandoned it from a growing dislike to anything resembling a badge or watchword of sectarian distinction. But as a name for one single opinion, not a set of opinions—to denote the recognition of utility as a standard, not any particular way of applying it—the term supplies a want in the language, and officers, in many cases, a convenient mode of avoiding tiresome circumlocution.
21. Mill's qualitative hedonism—the view that some pleasures are better than others, regardless of the quantity of satisfaction they give—is hard to distinguish from the

eudaimonism of Aristotle, in which human well-being consists in the fullest development of distinctively human powers. As in Aristotle, Mill implies that the higher pleasures are intellectual pleasures, but no argument is offered in support of this claim.

22. A reference to his contemporary, Thomas Carlyle, who had argued for the view Mill cites in his *Sartor Ruartus* (1836).

23. The German Romantic, whose thought had been discussed by Carlyle in his *Critical and Miscellaneous Essays* (1899).

24. This passage effectively brings out the centrality in Mill's thought of a dogmatic version of the theory of progress.

25. [Mill's note] An opponent, whose intellectual and moral fairness is a pleasure to acknowledge (the Rev. J. Llewellyn Davies), has objected to this passage, saying, "Surely the rightness or wrongness of saving, a man from drowning does depend very much upon the motive with which it is done. Suppose that a tyrant, when his enemy jumped into the sea to escape from him, saved him from drowning simply in order that he might inflict upon him more exquisite tortures, would it tend to clearness to speak of that rescue as 'a morally right action?' Or suppose again, according to one of the stock illustrations of ethical inquiries, that a man betrayed a trust received from a friend, because the discharge of it would fatally injure that friend himself or some one belonging to him, would utilitarianism compel one to call the betrayal 'a crime' as much as if it had been done from the meanest motive?"

I submit, that he who saves another from drowning in order to kill him by torture afterwards, does not differ only in motive from him who does the same thing from duty or benevolence; the act itself is different. The rescue of the man is, in the case supposed, only the necessary first step of an act far more atrocious than leaving him to drown would have been. Had Mr Davies said, "The rightness or wrongness of saving a man from drowning does depend very much"—not upon the motive, but—"upon the *intention*," no utilitarian would have differed from him. Mr Davies, by an oversight too common not to be quite venial, has in this case confounded the very different ideas of motive and intention. There is no point which utilitarian thinkers (and Bentham pre-eminently) have taken more pains to illustrate than this. The morality of the action depends entirely upon the intention—that is, upon what the agent *wills to do*. But the motive, that is, the feeling which makes him will so to do, when it makes no difference in the act, makes none in the morality: though it makes a great difference in our moral estimation of the agent, especially if it indicates a good or a bad habitual *disposition*—a bent of character from which useful, or from which hurtful actions are likely to arise.

Chapter IX | Karl Marx

All notes are by the Editor, except for those by Engels, which are indicated by square brackets at the end of the note.

1. By bourgeoisie is meant the class of modern capitalists, owners of the means of social production and employers of wage labour. By proletariat, the class of modern wage-labourers who, having no means of production of their own, are reduced to selling their labour power in order to live. [Note by Engels to the English edition of 1888.]

2. That is, all *written* history. In 1847, the pre-history of society, the social organization existing previous to recorded history, was all but unknown. Since then, Haxthausen discovered common ownership of land in Russia, Maurer proved it to be the social foundation from which all Teutonic races started in history, and by and by village communities were found to be, or to have been the primitive form of society everywhere from India to Ireland. The inner organization of this primitive Communistic society was laid bare, in its typical form, by Morgan's crowning discovery of the true nature of the *gens* and its relation to the *tribe*. With the dissolution of these primeval communities society begins to be differentiated into separate and finally antagonistic classes. I have attempted to retrace this process of dissolution in: *Der Ursprung Familie, des Privateigenthums und des Staats* (the Origin of the Family, Private Property and the State), 2nd edition, Stuttgart 1886. [Note by Engels to the English edition of 1888.]

3. That is, a full member of a guild, a master within, not a head of a guild. [Note by Engels to the English edition of 1888.]

4. "Commune" was the name taken, in France, by the nascent towns even before they had conquered from their feudal lords and masters local self-government and political rights as the "Third Estate." Generally speaking, for the economical development of the bourgeoisie, England is here taken as the typical country; for its political development, France. [Note by Engels to the English edition of 1888.)

This was the name given their urban communities by the townsmen of Italy and France, after they had purchased or wrested their initial rights of self-government from their feudal lords. [Note by Engels to the German edition of 1890.]

5. Limiting the working day for women and children to 10 hours, passed in 1847.

Chapter X | John Rawls

1. *An Enquiry Concerning the Principles of Morals*, sec. III, pt. I, par. 3, ed. L. A. Selby-Bigge, 2nd edition (Oxford, 1902), p. 184.

2. As the text suggests, I shall regard Locke's *Second Treatise of Government*, Rousseau's *The Social Contract*, and Kant's ethical works beginning with *The Foundations of the Metaphysics of Morals* as definitive of the contract tradition. For all of its greatness, Hobbes's *Leviathan* raises special problems. A general historical survey is provided by J.W. Gough, *The Social Contract*, 2nd ed. (Oxford, The Clarendon Press, 1957), and Otto Gierke, *Natural Law*

and the Theory of Society, trans. with an introduction by Ernest Barker (Cambridge, The University Press, 1934). A presentation of the contract view as primarily an ethical theory is to be found in G.R. Grice, *The Grounds of Moral Judgment* (Cambridge, The University Press, 1967). See also §19, note 30.

3. Kant is clear that the original agreement is hypothetical. See *The Metaphysics of Morals*, pt. I (*Rechtslehre*), especially §§47, 52; and pt. II of the essay "Concerning the Common Saying: This May Be True in Theory but It Does Not Apply in Practice," in *Kant's Political Writings*, ed. Hans Reiss and trans. by H.B. Nisbet (Cambridge, The University Press, 1970), pp. 73–87. See Georges Vlachos, *La Pensée politique de Kant*, (Paris, Presses Universitaires de France, 1962), pp. 326–335; and J.G. Murphy, *Kant: The Philosophy of Right* (London, Macmillan, 1970), pp. 109–112, 133–136, for a further discussion.

4. For the formulation of this intuitive idea I am indebted to Allan Gibbard.

5. The process of mutual adjustment of principles and considered judgments is not peculiar to moral philosophy. See Nelson Goodman, *Fact, Fiction, and Forecast* (Cambridge, Mass., Harvard University Press, 1955), pp. 65–68, for parallel remarks concerning the justification of the principles of deductive and inductive inference.

6. Henri Poincaré remarks: "Il nous faut une faculté qui nous fasse voir le but de loin, et, cette faculté, c'est l'intuition." *La Valeur de la science* (Paris, Flammarion, 1909), p. 27.

7. For a general discussion of procedural justice, see Brian Barry, *Political Argument* (London, Routledge and Kegan Paul, 1965), ch. VI. On the problem of fair division, see R.D. Luce and Howard Raiffa, *Games and Decisions* (New York, John Wiley and Sons, Inc., 1957), pp. 363–368; and Hugo Steinhaus, "The Problem of Fair Division," *Econometrica*, vol. 16 (1948).

8. See H.L.A. Hart, "Bentham." *Proceedings of the British Academy*, vol. 48 (London, 1962), pp. 340f, and Little, *Critique of Welfare Economics*, p. 54f.

9. See Herbert Spiegelberg, "A Defense of Human Equality," *Philosophical Review*, vol. 53 (1944), pp. 101, 113–123; and D.D. Raphael, "Justice and Liberty," *Proceedings of the Aristotelian Society*, vol. 51 (1950–1951), pp. 187f.

10. See, for example, Spiegelberg, pp. 120f.

11. The veil of ignorance is so natural a condition that something like it must have occurred to many. The closest explicit statement of it known to me is found in J.C. Harsanyi, "Cardinal Utility in Welfare Economics and in the Theory of Risk-Taking," *Journal of Political Economy*, vol. 61 (1953). Harsanyi uses it to develop a utilitarian theory, as I discuss below in §§27–28.

12. Rousseau, *The Social Contract*, bk. II. ch. IV, par. 5.

13. See R.B. Perry, *The General Theory of Value* (New York, Longmans, Green and Company, 1926), pp. 674–682.

14. For this notion of rationality, see the references to Sen and Arrow above, §23, note 9. The discussion in I.M.D. Little, *The Critique of Welfare Economics*, 2nd ed. (Oxford, Clarendon Press, 1957), ch. II, is also relevant here. For

rational choice under uncertainty, see below §26, note 18. H.A. Simon discusses the limitations of the classical conceptions of rationality and the need for a more realistic theory in "A Behavioral Model of Rational Choice," *Quarterly Journal of Economics*, vol. 69 (1955). See also his essay in *Surveys of Economic Theory*, vol. 3 (London, Macmillan, 1967). For philosophical discussions see Donald Davidson, "Actions, Reasons, and Causes," *Journal of Philosophy*, vol. 60 (1963); C.G. Hempel, *Aspects of Scientific Explanation* (New York, The Free Press, 1965), pp. 463–486; Jonathan Bennett, *Rationality* (London, Routledge and Kegan Paul, 1964), and J.D. Mabbott, "Reason and Desire," *Philosophy*, vol. 28 (1953).

15. An accessible discussion of this and other rules of choice under uncertainty can be found in W.J. Baumol, *Economic Theory and Operations Analysis*, 2nd ed. (Englewood Cliffs, N.J., Prentice-Hall Inc., 1965), ch. 24. Baumol gives a geometric interpretation of these rules, including the diagram used in §13 to illustrate the difference principle. See pp. 558–562. See also R.D. Luce and Howard Raiffa, *Games and Decisions* (New York, John Wiley and Sons, Inc., 1957), ch. XIII, for a fuller account.

16. Here I borrow from William Fellner, *Probability and Profit* (Homewood, Ill., R.D. Irwin, Inc., 1965), pp. 140–142, where these features are noted.

17. The idea of a four-stage sequence is suggested by the United States Constitution and its history. For some remarks as to how this sequence might be interpreted theoretically and related to procedural justice, see K.J. Arrow, *Social Choice and Individual Values*, 2nd ed. (New York, John Wiley and Sons, 1963), pp. 89–91.

18. It is important to distinguish the four-stage sequence and its conception of a constitutional convention from the kind of view of constitutional choice found in social theory and exemplified by J.M. Buchanan and Gordon Tullock, *The Calculus of Consent* (Ann Arbor, University of Michigan Press, 1963). The idea of the four-stage sequence is part of a moral theory, and does not belong to an account of the working of actual constitutions, except insofar as political agents are influenced by the conception of justice in question. In the contract doctrine, the principles of justice have already been agreed to, and our problem is to formulate a schema that will assist us in applying them. The aim is to characterize a just constitution and not to ascertain which sort of constitution would be adopted, or acquiesced in, under more or less realistic (though simplified) assumptions about political life, much less on individualistic assumptions of the kind characteristic of economic theory.

Chapter XI | Robert Nozick

1. John Locke, *Two Treatises of Government*, 2nd ed., ed. Peter Laslett (New York: Cambridge University Press, 1967). Unless otherwise specified, all references are to the *Second Treatise*.

2. Here and in the next section I draw upon and amplify

my discussion of these issues in footnote 4 of "On the Randian Argument," *The Personalist*, Spring 1971.

3. Milton Friedman, *Capitalism and Freedom* (Chicago: University of Chicago Press, 1962), chap. 6. Friedman's school vouchers, of course, allow a choice about who is to supply the product, and so differ from the protection vouchers imagined here.

4. Unfortunately, too few models of the structure of moral views have been specified heretofore, though there are surely other interesting structures. Hence an argument for a side-constraint structure that consists largely in arguing against an end-state maximization structure is inconclusive, for these alternatives are not exhaustive. . . . An array of structures must be precisely formulated and investigated; perhaps some novel structure then will seem most appropriate.

   The issue of whether a side-constraint view can be put in the form of the goal-without-side-constraint view is a tricky one. One might think, for example, that each person could distinguish in his goal between *his* violating rights and someone else's doing it. Give the former infinite (negative) weight in his goal, and no amount of stopping others from violating rights can outweigh his violating someone's rights. In addition to a component of a goal receiving infinite weight, indexical expressions also appear, for example, "*my* doing something." A careful statement delimiting "constraint views" would exclude these gimmicky ways of transforming side constraints into the form of an end-state view as sufficient to constitute a view as end state. Mathematical methods of transforming a constrained minimization problem into a sequence of unconstrained minimizations of an auxiliary function are presented in Anthony Fiacco and Garth McCormick, *Nonlinear Programming: Sequential Unconstrained Minimization Techniques* (New York: Wiley, 1968). The book is interesting both for its methods and for their limitations in illuminating our area of concern; note the way in which the penalty functions include the constraints, the variation in weights of penalty functions (sec. 7. I), and so on.

   The question of whether these side constraints are absolute, or whether they may be violated in order to avoid catastrophic moral horror, and if the latter, what the resulting structure might look like, is one I hope largely to avoid.

5. Which does which? Often a useful question to ask, as in the following:
   —"What is the difference between a Zen master and an analytic philosopher?"
   —"One talks riddles and the other riddles talks."

6. *Groundwork of the Metaphysic of Morals*. Translated by H. J. Paton, *The Moral Law* (London: Hutchinson, 1956), p. 96.

7. See John Rawls, *A Theory of Justice*, sects. 5, 6, 30.

8. Here, as at all other places in this essay, "harm" refers only to border crossings.

9. The reader who has looked ahead and seen that the second part of this chapter discusses Rawls' theory mistakenly may think that every remark or argument in the first part against alternative theories of justice is meant to apply to, or anticipate, a criticism of Rawls' theory. This is not so; there are other theories also worth criticizing.

10. Applications of the principle of justice in acquisition may also occur as part of the move from one distribution to another. You may find an unheld thing now and appropriate it. Acquisitions also are to be understood as included when, to simplify, I speak only of transitions by transfers.

11. See, however, the useful book by Boris Bittker, *The Case for Black Reparations* (New York: Random House, 1973).

12. If the principle of rectification of violations of the first two principles yields more than one description of holdings, then some choice must be made as to which of these is to be realized. Perhaps the sort of considerations about distributive justice and equality that I argue against play a legitimate role in *this* subsidiary choice. Similarly, there may be room for such considerations in deciding which otherwise arbitrary features a statute will embody, when such features are unavoidable because other considerations do not specify a precise line; yet a line must be drawn.

13. One might try to squeeze a patterned conception of distributive justice into the framework of the entitlement conception, by formulating a gimmicky obligatory "principle of transfer" that would lead to the pattern. For example, the principle that if one has more than the mean income one must transfer everything one holds above the mean to persons below the mean so as to bring them up to (but not over) the mean. We can formulate a criterion for a "principle of transfer" to rule out such obligatory transfers, or we can say that no correct principle of transfer, no principle of transfer in a free society will be like this. The former is probably the better course, though the latter also is true.

   Alternatively, one might think to make the entitlement conception instantiate a pattern, by using matrix entries that express the relative strength of a person's entitlements as measured by some real-valued function. But even if the limitation to natural dimensions failed to exclude this function, the resulting edifice would *not* capture our system of entitlements to *particular* things.

14. F.A. Hayek, *The Constitution of Liberty* (Chicago: University of Chicago Press, 1960), p. 87.

15. This question does not imply that they will tolerate any and every patterned distribution. In discussing Hayek's views, Irving Kristol has recently speculated that people will not long tolerate a system that yields distributions patterned in accordance with value rather than merit. ("'When Virtue Loses All Her Loveliness'—Some Reflections on Capitalism and 'The Free Society,'" *The Public Interest*, Fall 1970, pp. 3–15.) Kristol, following some remarks of Hayek's, equates the merit system with justice. Since some case can be made for the external standard of distribution in accordance with benefit to others, we ask about a weaker (and therefore more plausible) hypothesis.

16. We certainly benefit because great economic incentives

operate to get others to spend much time and energy to figure out how to serve us by providing things we will want to pay for. It is not mere paradox mongering to wonder whether capitalism should be criticized for most rewarding and hence encouraging, not individualists like Thoreau who go about their own lives, but people who are occupied with serving others and winning them as customers. But to defend capitalism one need not think businessmen are the finest human types. (I do not mean to join here the general maligning of businessmen, either.) Those who think the finest should acquire the most can try to convince their fellows to transfer resources in accordance with *that* principle.

17. Varying situations continuously from that limit situation to our own would force us to make explicit the underlying rationale of entitlements and to consider whether entitlement considerations lexicographically precede the considerations of the usual theories of distributive justice, so that the *slightest* strand of entitlement outweighs the considerations of the usual theories of distributive justice.

18. Might not a transfer have instrumental effects on a third party, changing his feasible options? (But what if the two parties to the transfer independently had used their holdings in this fashion?) I discuss this question below, but note here that this question concedes the point for distributions of ultimate intrinsic non-instrumental goods (pure utility experiences, so to speak) that are transferrable. It also might be objected that the transfer might make a third party more envious because it worsens his position relative to someone else. I find it incomprehensible how this can be thought to involve a claim of justice. . . .

Here and elsewhere in this chapter, a theory which incorporates elements of pure procedural justice might find what I say acceptable, *if* kept in its proper place; that is, if background institutions exist to ensure the satisfaction of certain conditions on distributive shares. But if these institutions are not themselves the sum or invisible-hand result of people's voluntary (nonaggressive) actions, the constraints they impose require justification. At no point does *our* argument assume any background institutions more extensive than those of the minimal night-watchman state, a state limited to protecting persons against murder, assault, theft, fraud, and so forth.

19. See the selection from John Henry MacKay's novel, *The Anarchists*, reprinted in Leonard Krimmerman and Lewis Perry, eds., *Patterns of Anarchy* (New York: Doubleday Anchor Books, 1966), in which an individualist anarchist presses upon a communist anarchist the following question: "Would you, in the system of society which you call 'free Communism' prevent individuals from exchanging their labour among themselves by means of their own medium of exchange? And further: Would you prevent them from occupying land for the purpose of personal use?" The novel continues: "[the] question was not to be escaped. If he answered 'Yes!' he admitted that society had the right of control over the individual and threw overboard the autonomy of the individual which he had always zealously defended; if on the other hand, he answered 'No!' he admitted the right of private property which he had just denied so emphatically. . . . Then he answered 'In Anarchy any number of men must have the right of forming a voluntary association, and so realizing their ideas in practice. Nor can I understand how anyone could justly be driven from the land and house which he uses and occupies . . . every serious man must declare himself: for Socialism, and thereby for force and against liberty, or for Anarchism, and thereby for liberty and against force.'" In contrast, we find Noam Chomsky writing, "Any consistent anarchist must oppose private ownership of the means of production," "the consistent anarchist then . . . will be a socialist . . . of a particular sort." Introduction to Daniel Guerin, *Anarchism: From Theory To Practice* (New York: Monthly Review Press, 1970), pages xiii, xv.

20. Is the patterned principle stable that requires merely that a distribution be Pareto-optimal? One person might give another a gift or bequest that the second could exchange with a third to their mutual benefit. Before the second makes this exchange, there is not Pareto-optimality. Is a stable pattern presented by a principle choosing that among the Pareto-optimal positions that satisfies some further condition C? It may seem that there cannot be a counterexample, for won't any voluntary exchange made away from a situation show that the first situation wasn't Pareto-optimal? (Ignore the implausibility of this last claim for the case of bequests.) But principles are to be satisfied over time, during which new possibilities arise. A distribution that at one time satisfies the criterion of Pareto-optimality might not do so when some new possibilities arise (Wilt Chamberlain grows up and starts playing basketball); and though people's activities will tend to move then to a new Pareto-optimal position, *this* new one need not satisfy the contentful condition C. Continual interference will be needed to insure the continual satisfaction of C. (The theoretical possibility of a pattern's being maintained by some invisible-hand process that brings it back to an equilibrium that fits the pattern when deviations occur should be investigated.)

21. One indication of the stringency of Rawls' difference principle, which we attend to in the second part of this chapter, is its inappropriateness as a governing principle even within a family of individuals who love one another. Should a family devote its resources to maximizing the position of its least well off and least talented child, holding back the other children or using resources for their education and development only if they will follow a policy through their lifetimes of maximizing the position of their least fortunate sibling? Surely not. How then can this even be considered as the appropriate policy for enforcement in the wider society? (I discuss below what I think would be Rawls' reply: that some principles apply at the macro level which do not apply to microsituations.)

22. See Gregory Vlastos, "The Individual as an Object of love in Plato" in his *Platonic Studies* (Princeton: Princeton University Press, 1973), pp. 3–34.

23. I am unsure as to whether the arguments I present be-
    low show that such taxation merely *is* forced labour; so
    that "is on a par with" means "is one kind of." Or alterna-
    tively, whether the arguments emphasize the great simi-
    larities between such taxation and forced labour, to show
    it is plausible and illuminating to view such taxation in
    the light of forced labour. This latter approach would re-
    mind one of how John Wisdom conceives of the *claims* of
    metaphysicians.

24. Nothing hangs on the fact that here and elsewhere I speak
    loosely of *needs*, since I go on, each time, to reject the cri-
    terion of justice which includes it. If, however, something
    did depend upon the notion, one would want to exam-
    ine it more carefully. For a skeptical view, see Kenneth
    Minogue, *The Liberal Mind*, (New York: Random House,
    1963), pp. 103–112.

25. Further details which this statement should include are
    contained in my essay "Coercion," in *Philosophy, Science,
    and Method*, ed. S. Morgenbesser, P. Suppes, and M. White
    (New York: St. Martin, 1969).

26. On the themes in this and the next paragraph, see the
    writings of Armen Alchian.

27. Compare this with Robert Paul Wolff's "A Refutation of
    Rawls' Theorem on Justice," *Journal of Philosophy*, March
    31, 1966, sect. 2. Wolff's criticism does not apply to Rawls'
    conception under which the baseline is fixed by the differ-
    ence principle.

28. I have not seen a precise estimate. David Friedman, *The
    Machinery of Freedom* (N.Y.: Harper & Row, 1973), pp.
    xiv, xv, discusses this issue and suggests 5 per cent of U.S.
    national income as an upper limit for the first two factors
    mentioned. However he does not attempt to estimate the
    percentage of current wealth which is based upon such
    income in the past. (The vague notion of "based upon"
    merely indicates a topic needing investigation.)

29. Fourier held that since the process of civilization had
    deprived the members of society of certain liberties (to
    gather, pasture, engage in the chase), a socially guaranteed
    minimum provision for persons was justified as compen-
    sation for the loss (Alexander Gray, *The Socialist Tradition*
    (New York: Harper & Row, 1968), p. 188). But this puts
    the point too strongly. This compensation would be due
    those persons, if any, for whom the process of civiliza-
    tion was a *net loss*, for whom the benefits of civilization
    did not counterbalance being deprived of these particular
    liberties.

30. For example, Rashdall's case of someone who comes upon
    the only water in the desert several miles ahead of others
    who also will come to it and appropriates it all. Hastings
    Rashdall, "The Philosophical Theory of Property," in
    Property, its Duties and Rights (London: MacMillan, 1915).

    We should note Ayn Rand's theory of property rights
    ("Man's Rights" in *The Virtue of Selfishness* (New York: New
    American Library, 1964), p. 94), wherein these follow from
    the right to life, since people need physical things to live.
    But a right to life is not a right to whatever one needs to
    live; other people may have rights over these other things

(see Chapter 3 of this book). At most, a right to life would
be a right to have or strive for whatever one needs to live,
provided that having it does not violate anyone else's rights.
With regard to material things, the question is whether
having it does violate any right of others. (Would appropriation of all unowned things do so? Would appropriating the water hole in Rashdall's example?) Since special
considerations (such as the Lockean proviso) may enter
with regard to material property, one *first* needs a theory of
property rights before one can apply any supposed right to
life (as amended above). Therefore the right to life cannot
provide the foundation for a theory of property rights.

31. The situation would be different if his water hole didn't
    dry up, due to special precautions he took to prevent this.
    Compare our discussion of the case in the text with Hayek,
    The Constitution of Liberty, p. 136; and also with Ronald
    Hamowy, "Hayek's Concept of Freedom; A Critique," *New
    Individualist Review*, April 1961, pp. 28–31.

32. I discuss overtiding and its moral traces in "Moral
    Complications and Moral Structures," *Natural Law
    Forum*, 1968, pp. 1–50.

33. Does the principle of compensation . . . introduce pattern-
    ing considerations? Though it requires compensation for
    the disadvantages imposed by those seeking security from
    risks, it is not a patterned principle. For it seeks to remove
    only those disadvantages which prohibitions inflict on
    those who might present risks to others, not all disadvan-
    tages. It specifies an obligation on those who impose the
    prohibition, which stems from their own particular acts,
    to remove a particular complaint those prohibited may
    make against them.

Chapter XII | Susan Moller Okin

1. *Report to the Nation on Crime and Justice*, 2nd ed.
   (Washington, D.C.: Government Printing Office, March
   1988), p. 33; *A Survey of Spousal Violence Against Women
   in Kentucky* (Washington, D.C.: Law Enforcement
   Assistance Administration, 1979), cited by Barbara
   Bergmann, *The Economic Emergence of Women* (New
   York: Basic Books, 1986), p. 205; *Age, Sex, Race and Ethnic
   Origin of Murder Victims, 1986*, U.S. Department of Justice
   Uniform Crime Reports (Washington, D.C.: Government
   Printing Office, July 1987), p. 11.

2. On the history of family violence and its connections
   with the traditional division of labour and dependence of
   wives, see Linda Gordon, *Heroes of Their Own Lives* (New
   York: Viking, 1988), esp. chaps. 8 and 9, and Elizabeth
   Pleck, *Domestic Tyranny* (New York: Oxford University
   Press, 1987), esp. chap. 10. On issues of power differentials
   and family privacy, see Gordon, *Heroes of Their Own Lives*,
   chap 9; Martha Minow, "We the Family: Constitutional
   Rights and American Families," *The American Journal of
   History* 74, no. 3 (1987); Susan Moller Okin, "Gender,
   the Public and the Private," in *Political Theory Today*,
   ed. David Held (Oxford: Polity Press, forthcoming); and
   Nikolas Rose, "Beyond the Public/Private Division: Law,

Power and the Family," *Journal of Law and Society* 14, no. 1 (1987).

3. See [Frances E.] Olsen, "The Myth of State Intervention [in the Family,]" [*University of Michigan Journal of Law Reform 18*(4) (1985)]; Minow, "We the Family"; and [Linda J.] Nicholson, *Gender and History: The Limits of Social Theory in the Age of the Family* (New York: Columbia University Press, 1986)], esp. introduction and part 3.

4. Sylvia Law and Nadine Taub, "Constitutional Considerations and the Married Woman's Obligation to Serve," unpublished ms. quoted in [Lenore] Weitzman, *The Marriage Contract*[: *Spouses, Lovers, and the Law* (New York: The Free Press, 1981)], p. 65; see also Weitzman, chap. 3 passim, on the wife's legal responsibility for domestic service and its consequences.

5. Lenore J. Weitzman, *The Divorce Revolution: The Unexpected Social and Economic Consequences for Women and Children in America* (New York: The Free Press, 1985), p. 2 and chap. 1 passim. See also Weitzman, *The Marriage Contract*, where she notes "the extent to which the traditional coverture-inspired model of marriage still persists despite major social and economic changes in the position of women in our society" (p. 6).

6. Olsen, "The Myth of State Intervention," p. 837.

7. Ibid., pp. 842, 861–64.

8. Chapter 8 not included in this excerpt. – Ed.

9. Nancy Chodorow, "Family Structure and Feminine Personality," in *Woman, Culture, and Society*, ed. M.Z. Rosaldo and Louise Lamphere (Stanford: Stanford University Press, 1974); idem, *The Reproduction of Mothering: Psychoanalysis and the Sociology of Gender* (Berkeley: University of California Press, 1978). For related arguments, see also Isaac Balbus, *Marxism and Domination* (Princeton: Princeton University Press, 1982); Dorothy Dinnerstein, *The Mermaid and the Minotaur: Sexual Arrangements and Human Malaise* (New York: Harper & Row, 1976).

10. [Michael] Walzer, *Spheres of Justice*[: *A Defense of Pluralism And Equality* (New York: Basic Books, 1983)], p. 304. Cf. Benjamin Barber, *Strong Democracy* (Berkeley: University of California Press, 1984), pp. 173–78. Though he starts by stating that "at the heart of strong democracy is talk," Barber's discussion is unusual in its emphasis on the fact that listening is just as important a part of "talk" as speaking, and that the "potential for empathy and affective expression" is as crucial as is eloquence or creativity. Thus Barber's approach is less biased in favour of traditionally masculine and away from traditionally feminine qualities than is usual in such discussions of political speech.

11. Kathleen Jones, "On Authority: Or, Why Women Are Not Entitled to Speak," in *Authority Revisited*, ed. J. Roland Pennock and John W. Chapman (New York: New York University Press, 1987).

12. Arizona, Massachusetts, New Jersey, New York, Rhode Island, and other states have established task forces to investigate and work toward elimination of sex and race bias in their courts. See, for example, Lynn Hecht Schafran and Norma J. Wikler, *Task Forces on Gender Bias in the Courts: A Manual for Action* (available from the Foundation for Women Judges, Washington, D.C.), and *Special Focus: Gender Bias in the Court System*, 1986 Annual Meeting of the American Bar Association, New York, August 10, 1986; also annual reports of the various state task forces.

13. Robert E. Goodin, *Protecting the Vulnerable: A Reanalysis of Our Social Responsibilities* (Chicago: University of Chicago Press, 1985), p. 109. He specifies, further: "Vulnerability amounts to one person's having the capacity to produce consequences of his actions and choices" (p. 114).

14. Ibid., p. 190. This is so in at least two respects: *who* becomes disabled by illness or accident is affected by social inequalities and working conditions, and the extent to which physical or mental disabilities render one vulnerable is partly a factor of social provisions (for example, wheelchair ramps) for the less able.

15. Ibid., p. 191.

16. John Stuart Mill, *Principles of Political Economy* (London: Parker and Son, 1848), bk. 5, chap. 11, sec. 9; cited by Goodin, *Protecting the Vulnerable*, p. 189.

17. Goodin, *Protecting the Vulnerable*, p. xi. This succinct statement of the position (argued in his chap. 7) is quoted from Goodin's synopsis.

18. Ibid., *Protecting the Vulnerable*, p. 197.

19. Albert O. Hirschman, *Exit, Voice and Loyalty: Responses to Decline in Firms, Organizations, and States* (Cambridge: Harvard University Press, 1970), pp. 43, 55, 83.

20. Albert O. Hirschman, *National Power and the Structure of Foreign Trade* (Berkeley: University of California Press, 1945; expanded ed. 1980). See pp. vi–viii of the expanded edition for a summary of the original argument, as well as some later reservations of the author about his failure to try to find a remedy for the asymmetrical dependency he had uncovered.

21. Ibid., *National Power*, p. 31.

22. Karl Marx, *The Eighteenth Brumaire of Louis Bonaparte*, in *Selected Works* (Moscow: Progress Publishers, 1969), vol. 2, p. 378.

23. Philip Blumstein and Pepper Schwartz, *American Couples* (New York: Morrow, 1983), pp. 324, 115.

24. Quotations are from Kathleen Gerson, *Hard Choices: How Women Decide About Work, Career, and Motherhood* (Berkeley: University of California Press, 1985), p. 209. For sources of this data, see also Jacob Mincer, "Labor Force Participation of Married Women: A Study of Labor Supply," in *Aspects of Labor Economics: A Conference of the Universities—National Bureau Committee for Economic Research* (Princeton: Princeton University Press, 1962), p. 64; Ruth Sidel, *Women and Children Last: The Plight of Poor Women in Affluent America* (New York: Viking, 1986), esp. pp. 50–56, 60; Suzanne M. Bianchi and Daphne Spain, *American Women in Transition* (New York: Russell Sage, 1986), p. 196. Gerson places "careers" in quotation

marks here because she and her respondents understand the word to mean "not mere labour force participation, but rather long-term, full-time attachment to paid work with the expectation, or at least the hope, of advancement over time" (p. 126*n*1). It does not imply any differentiation between manual and intellectual, or professional and nonprofessional work. I shall use *career* in this non-elitist sense.

25. Blumestein and Schwartz, *American Couples*, pp. 52, 118–125, 560*n*2. See also the Nye study cited there, which concludes that "both married men and married women still feel it is the husband's responsibility to provide for his wife." In Gerson's study, too, even among the non-traditional women, who placed great emphasis on self-sufficiency, "few expressed a willingness to provide full economic support for their partners or to indulge male partners who might prefer total domesticity to paid work" (*Hard Choices*, p. 113*n*4; see also pp. 174–5). Beliefs about the desirability of wives not working for wages are lagging behind actual social behaviour.

26. Lenore J. Weitzman, *The Divorce Revolution: The Unexpected Social and Economic Consequences for Women and Children in America* (New York: The Free Press, 1985), pp. 315–16.

27. Blumstein and Schwartz, *American Couples*, pp. 51–111 passim, esp. pp. 58–59, 82.

28. Goodin refers to marriage in the past as an institution of exploitation and domination but, because he thinks that the "traditional division of marital labour . . . is surely dead or dying," he concludes that "modern marriages relations . . . embody . . . a morally desirable sort of 'symmetry and complimentarity'" (*Protecting the Vulnerable*, pp. 72–79, 196). When Hirschman rarely and briefly refers to the family in the course of his arguments about the effect of exit potential on influence, what he says indicates that he is thinking almost entirely about families of origin, rather than families created by marriage (*Exit, Voice and Loyalty*, pp. 33, 76). In the only place where he exhibits any interest in the applicability of his argument to families by marriage, he briefly comments that the high costs (in energy and emotional expenditure as well as money) of obtaining a divorce may act as an incentive to the use of the voice option in resolving marital disputes (p. 79). However, in a recent paper, Hirschman argues that no-fault divorce law "undercuts the recourse to voice" in resolving marital difficulties. He suggests that those who framed the new laws "probably did not realize the extent to which the earlier obstacles to divorce indirectly encouraged attempts at mending the so easily frayed marital relationship and how much the new freedom to exit would torpedo such attempts." Citing Weitzman's work, he also makes brief reference to the differential impact of divorce on the two parties. "Exit and Voice: An Expanding Sphere of Influence," in A.O. Hirschman, ed., in *Rival Views of Market Society and Other Recent Essays*, (New York: Viking, 1986), pp. 96–98.

29. Bergman[n], *Economic Emergence*, pp. 269–70; [Victor] Fuchs, *Women's Quest [for Economic Equality* (Cambridge: Harvard University Press, 1988)], pp. 71–72; [David M.] Heer, "The Measurement and Bases of Family Power: An Overview," [*Marriage and Family Living 25*(2) (May, 1963),] p. 138.

30. [Robert O.] Blood, "The Measurement and Bases of Family Power: A Rejoinder," [*Marriage and Family Living 25*(4) (Nov., 1963),] p. 476*n*12 (emphasis added).

Chapter XIII | Charles Mills

1. Of the "big four" contract theorists (Thomas Hobbes, John Locke, Jean-Jacques Rousseau, Immanuel Kant), Locke and Kant are the most important for liberal theory. Hobbes' *Leviathan* conceptualizes morality and rights as conventional and argues for political absolutism, while the radical direct democracy of Rousseau's *Social Contract*, based on the "general will," represents more a challenge to than an endorsement of liberalism.

2. The Hobbesian model, non-liberal-democratic, is predicated on the approximate physical and mental (rather than moral) equality of self-seeking human beings in conflict with one another (the amoral state of nature as a state of war). So Hobbes' solution of a constitutionally unconstrained state—the absolutist sovereign—is obviously uncongenial to those seeking to use the contract model to critique absolutism.

3. For oral accounts of the African American experience in white philosophy, see Yancy, *African-American Philosophers*, and for the experience of black women in particular, Yancy, Introduction and "Situated." In the entire country, out of a total population of more than ten thousand professional philosophers, only about thirty black women practice philosophy. In October 2007, the Collegium of Black Women Philosophers was launched under the leadership of Kathryn Gines as an attempt to remedy this situation.

4. However, I would be remiss not to mention some positive recent developments, such as the online Symposia on Gender, Race, and Philosophy, hosted at MIT; the California Roundtable on Philosophy and Race; and SUNY Press's new book series Philosophy and Race.

5. See, e.g., Kymlicka; Bird; Wolff; Simmons.

6. Augustine is included in Cahn's anthology and, as a Berber, is a person of colour by contemporary standards, but since he wrote at a time when nobody was "raced," he does not count.

7. Bogues reclaims and reconstructs the work of some of the key figures in the diasporic black political tradition.

8. The very titles of recent works by black political philosophers show the centrality of race to their normative thinking: *Blacks and Social Justice* (Boxill), *Race and Social Justice* (McGary), *Critical Social Theory in the Interests of Black Folks* (Outlaw), *We Who are Dark* (Shelby).

9. Aboriginal means persons who are First Nations (also known as Indians), Métis, and Inuit.

Chapter XIV | Martha Nussbaum

I have discussed the capabilities approach in several other papers, to which I shall refer: "Nature, Function, and Capability: Aristotle on Political Distribution," *Oxford Studies in Ancient Philosophy* Supplementary Volume I (1988), 145–84, hereafter NFC; "Aristotelian Social Democracy," in *Liberalism and the Good*, ed. R.B. Douglass *et al.* (New York: Routledge, 1990), 203–52, hereafter ASD; "Non-Relative Virtues: An Aristotelian Approach," in *The Quality of Life*, ed. M. Nussbaum and A. Sen (Oxford: Clarendon Press, 1993), hereafter NRV; "Aristotle on Human Nature and the Foundations of Ethics," in *World, Mind and Ethics: Essays on the Ethical Philosophy of Bernard Williams*, ed. J.E.J. Altham and Ross Harrison (Cambridge: Cambridge University Press, 1995), 86–131, hereafter HN; "Human Functioning and Social Justice: In Defense of Aristotelian Essentialism," *Political Theory* 20 (1992), 202–46, hereafter HF; "Human Capabilities, Female Human Beings," in *Women, Culture, and Development*, ed. M. Nussbaum and J. Glover (Oxford: Clarendon Press, 1995), 61–104, hereafter HC; "The Good as Discipline, the Good as Freedom," in *The Ethics of Consumption and Global Stewardship*, ed. D. Crocker and T. Linden (Lanham, MD: Rowman and Littlefield, 1998), 312–41, hereafter GDGF; "Capabilities and Human Rights," *Fordham Law Review* 66 (1997), 273–300, hereafter CHR.

1. For this case and others like it, see Martha Chen, "A Matter of Survival: Women's Right to Employment in India and Bangladesh," in *Women, Culture, and Development* (hereafter WCD), ed. M. Nussbaum and J. Glover (Oxford: Clarendon Press, 1995), 37–57. See also M. Chen, *The Lives of Widows in Rural India* (forthcoming).

2. *Bradwell v. Illinois*, 83 U.S. (16 Wall.) 130 (1873).

3. *Carr v. Allison Gas Turbine Division, General Motors Corp.*, 32 F.3d 1007 (1994). Mary Carr won her case on appeal.

4. Martha Chen, *A Quiet Revolution: Women in Transition in Rural Bangladesh* (Cambridge, MA: Schenkman, 1983), 176.

5. *Human Development Report* (New York: United Nations Development Program, 1996) (hereafter *Report*); see also the 1995 *Report*, which focuses on gender. The countries in which women do best in life quality, according to the Gender Development Index (GDI), a measure using the same variables as the HDI (Human Development Index) but adjusted according to disparities between the sexes (see *Report*, 107, for the technical formulation) are, in order, Sweden, Canada, Norway, the United States, Finland, Iceland, Denmark, France, Australia, New Zealand, the Netherlands, Japan, Austria, the United Kingdom, and Belgium.

6. If we subtract the GDI rank from the HDI rank, we get −10 for Spain, −9 for Japan, 8 for Sweden, 10 for Denmark, and 4 for New Zealand.

7. These variables include percentage shares of administrative and managerial positions, percentage shares of professional and technical jobs, and percentage shares of parliamentary seats.

8. The ranking at the top: Norway, Sweden, Denmark, Finland, New Zealand, Canada, Germany, the Netherlands, the United States, Austria, Barbados, and Switzerland. Spain ranks 25; Japan, 37; France, 40; and Greece, 60.

9. These data are from the 1993 report; later reports disaggregate employment data into jobs of various specific kinds and no longer count unpaid agricultural labour as employment.

10. Again, these are 1993 data; the 1996 report gives the absolute percentages, which are, for these examples, Sierra Leone, 16.7 per cent; Afghanistan, 13.5 per cent; Sudan, 32 per cent; Nepal, 13 per cent. Nations in which the female literacy rate is strikingly out of step with the general level of economic development include Saudi Arabia, 47.6 per cent; Algeria, 45.8 per cent; Egypt, 37.0 per cent; Iraq, 42.3 per cent; Pakistan, 23.0 per cent; and India, 36.0 per cent. Striking progress in female literacy, on the other hand, if one can rely on the figures, has been made in Cuba, 94.6 per cent; Sri Lanka, 86.2 per cent; Philippines, 93.9 per cent; most of the former constituent states of the Soviet Union, in the 90s; Vietnam, 89.5 per cent; and China, 70.9 per cent. On the disparity of achievement between China and India, see Jean Drèze and Amartya Sen, *India: Economic Development and Social Opportunity* (Oxford: Clarendon Press, 1996).

11. Numbers of female students in tertiary education per 100,000 people: Hong Kong, 1,022; Barbados, 1,885; Republic of Korea, 2,866; Philippines, 3,140; Egypt, 499; China, 132; Iran, 764; Laos, 60; Pakistan, 149; Ethiopia, 24; and Rwanda, 19.

12. Countries where women hold a high percentage of parliamentary seats: Norway, 39.4 per cent; Sweden, 40.4 per cent; and Denmark, 33.0 per cent. Bangladesh at 10.6 per cent is ahead of the United States at 10.4 per cent, and India at 8.0 per cent is ahead of Japan at 6.7 per cent.

13. The statistics in this paragraph are taken from Jean Drèze and Amartya Sen, *Hunger and Public Action* (Oxford: Clarendon Press, 1989).

14. This is very likely due to the central role women play in productive economic activity. For a classic study of this issue, see Esther Boserup, *Women's Role in Economic Development* (New York: St. Martin's Press, 1970), 2nd ed. (Aldershot: Gower Publishing, 1986). For a set of valuable responses to Boserup's work, see *Persistent Inequalities*, ed. Irene Tinker (New York: Oxford University Press, 1990).

15. See Drèze and Sen, 52.

16. See Drèze and Sen, *India*.

17. See Sen, "Gender and Cooperative Conflicts," in Tinker, 123–49.

18. See Drèze and Sen, *India*, for graphic evidence of the relative independence of educational and health attainment from economic growth, in comparative regional studies.

19. Gary Becker, *A Treatise on the Family* (Cambridge, MA: Harvard University Press, 1981; 2nd ed. 1991).

20. See Sen, "Gender and Cooperative Conflicts"; Partha Dasgupta, *An Inquiry Into Well-Being and Destitution* (Oxford: Clarendon Press, 1993), chap. 11; on food

allocation, see Lincoln C. Chen, E. Huq, and S. D'Souza, "Sex Bias in the Family Allocation of Food and Health Care in Rural Bangladesh," *Population and Development Review 7* (1981), 55–70. Bargaining models of the family are now proliferating; for two valuable recent examples, see Shelly Lundberg and Robert A. Pollak, "Bargaining and Distribution in Marriage," *Journal of Economic Perspectives* 10 (1996), 139–58, and S. Lundberg, R. Pollak, and T.J. Wales, "Do Husbands and Wives Pool Their Resources? Evidence from the U.K. Child Benefit," *Journal of Human Resources* (forthcoming).

21. See, now, Gary Becker, "The Economic Way of Looking at Behaviour," the Nobel Address 1992, in *The Essence of Becker*, ed. Ramón Febrero and Pedro S. Schwartz (Stanford, CA: Hoover Institution Press, 1995), 647, on the role of childhood experiences in shaping preferences.

22. Sen, "Gender and Cooperative Conflicts," argues that Becker's account is much stronger as an account of actual preferences in the household than as an account of the real interests (life and death, good and bad health, good and bad nutrition) that underlie the preferences. (He provides evidence that people's perception of their health and nutritional status may be severely distorted by informational deficiencies.)

23. Becker now admits deficiencies in the model: "Many economists, including me, have excessively relied on altruism to tie together the interests of family members." Motives of "obligation, anger, and other attitudes usually neglected by theories of rational behaviour" should be added to the models. Becker, "The Economic Way of Looking at Behavior," 648. Elsewhere, Becker mentions guilt, affection, and fear—his example being a woman's habitual fear of physical abuse from men. Ibid., 647. It is unclear whether he still supports an organic one-actor model, with a more complicated motivational structure, or a "bargaining model," of the sort increasingly used by family economists. See Becker, *A Treatise on the Family*.

24. See Sen, "Gender and Cooperative Conflicts"; Jon Elster, *Sour Grapes* (Cambridge: Cambridge University Press, 1993).

25. See John Rawls, *A Theory of Justice* (hereafter TJ) (Cambridge, MA: Harvard University Press, 1970); *Political Liberalism* (hereafter PL) (New York: Columbia University Press, 1993, paper ed. 1996).

26. The "capabilities approach" was pioneered within economics by Amartya Sen and has been developed by both Sen and me in complementary but not identical ways. For an overview, see David Crocker, "Functioning and Capability: the Foundations of Sen's and Nussbaum's Development Ethic," in WCD, 152–98.

27. See Amartya Sen, "Equality of What?," in *Choice, Welfare, and Measurement* (Oxford: Basil Blackwell, 1982), 353–72; and Nussbaum, ASD.

28. Much of the material described in these examples is now published in *Dominating Knowledge: Development, Culture, and Resistance*, ed. Frédérique Apffel Marglin and Stephen A. Marglin (Oxford: Clarendon Press, 1990).

The issue of "embeddedness" and menstruation taboos is discussed in S.A. Marglin, "Losing Touch: The Cultural Conditions of Worker Accommodation and Resistance," 217–82, and related issues are discussed in S.A. Marglin, "Toward the Decolonization of the Mind," 1–28. On Sittala Devi, see F.A. Marglin, "Smallpox in Two Systems of Knowledge," 102–44; and for related arguments see Ashis Nandy and Shiv Visvanathan, "Modern Medicine and Its Non-Modern Critics," 144–84. I have in some cases combined two conversations into one; otherwise things happened as I describe them.

29. For Sen's own account of the plurality and internal diversity of Indian values, one that strongly emphasizes the presence of a rationalist and critical strand in Indian traditions, see M. Nussbaum and A. Sen, "Internal Criticism and Indian Relativist Traditions," in *Relativism: Interpretation and Confrontation*, ed. M. Krausz (Notre Dame: Notre Dame University Press, 1989), 299–325 (an essay originally presented at the same WIDER conference and refused publication by the Marglins in its proceedings); and A. Sen, "India and the West," *The New Republic* June 7, 1993. See also Bimal K. Matilal, *Perception* (Oxford: Clarendon Press, 1995) (a fundamental study of Indian traditions regarding knowledge and logic); and B.K. Matilal, "Ethical Relativism and the Confrontation of Cultures," in Krausz, ed., *Relativism*, 339–62.

30. S.A. Marglin, "Toward the Decolonization," 22–3, suggests that binary thinking is peculiarly Western. But such oppositions are pervasive in Indian, Chinese, and African traditions (see HC). To deny them to a culture is condescending: for how can one utter a definite idea without bounding off one thing against another?

31. See Eric Hobsbawm and Terence Ranger, eds., *The Invention of Tradition* (Cambridge: Cambridge University Press, 1983). In his *New Republic* piece, Sen makes a similar argument about contemporary India: The Western construction of India as mystical and "other" serves the purposes of the fundamentalist Bharatiya Janata Party (BJP), who are busy refashioning history to serve the ends of their own political power. An eloquent critique of the whole notion of the "other" and of the associated "nativism," where Africa is concerned, can be found in Kwame Anthony Appiah, *In My Father's House: Africa in the Philosophy of Cultures* (New York: Oxford University Press, 1991).

32. The proceedings of this conference are now published as M. Nussbaum and A. Sen, eds., *The Quality of Life* (Oxford: Clarendon Press, 1993).

33. Marglin has since published this point in "Toward the Decolonization." His reference is to Takeo Doi, *The Anatomy of Dependence* (Tokyo: Kodansha, 1971).

34. See S.A. Marglin, "Toward the Decolonization."

35. See Nussbaum and Sen, "Internal Criticism," and A. Sen, "Human Rights and Asian Values," *The New Republic*, July 10/17, 1997, 33–40.

36. See Roop Rekha Verma, "Femininity, Equality, and Personhood," in WCD.

37. Satyajit Ray, "Introduction," *Our Films, Their Films*

(Bombay: Orient Longman, 1976, reprinted New York: Hyperion, 1994), 5.

38. Personal communication, scholars in women's studies at the Chinese Academy of Social Sciences, June 1995.

39. Note that this objection itself seems to rely on some universal values such as fairness and freedom from bias.

40. See HF for a longer version of this discussion.

41. Aristotle, *Nicomachean Ethics* VIII.I. I discuss this passage in HN and NRV.

42. "If my sisters and I were 'children of two worlds,' no one bothered to tell us this; we lived in one world, in two 'extended' families divided by several thousand miles and an allegedly insuperable cultural distance that never, so far as I can recall, puzzled or perplexed us much." Appiah, vii–viii. Appiah's argument does not neglect distinctive features of concrete histories; indeed, one of its purposes is to demonstrate how varied, when concretely seen, histories really are. But his argument, like mine, seeks a subtle balance between perception of the particular and recognition of the common.

43. This point is made by the Marglins, as well as by liberal thinkers, but can they consistently make it while holding that freedom of choice is just a parochial Western value? It would appear not; on the other hand, F.A. Marglin (here differing, I believe, from S.A. Marglin) also held in oral remarks delivered at the 1986 conference that logical consistency is simply a parochial Western value.

44. See Noam Chomsky, in *Cartesian Linguistics* (New York: Harper and Row, 1966). Chomsky argues that Cartesian rationalism, with its insistence on innate essences, was politically more progressive, more hostile to slavery and imperialism, than empiricism, with its insistence that people were just what experience had made of them.

45. The use of this term does not imply that the functions all involve doing something especially "active." See here A. Sen, "Capability and Well-Being," in *The Quality of Life*, ed. M. Nussbaum and A. Sen (Oxford: Clarendon Press, 1993), 30–53. In Aristotelian terms, and in mine, being healthy, reflecting, and being pleased are all "activities."

46. For further discussion of this point, and for examples, see HN.

47. Could one cease to be one's individual self without ceasing to be human? Perhaps, in cases of profound personality or memory change, but I shall leave such cases to one side here. This is ruled out, I think, in Aristotle's conception but is possible in some other metaphysical conceptions.

48. See HN for a more extended account of this procedure and how it justifies.

49. Nor does it deny that experience of the body is shaped by culture. See NRV.

50. Rawls, TJ, 90–95, 396–7.

51. This was implicit in ASD but has become more prominent in recent essays. See A. Sen, "Freedoms and Needs," *New Republic*, January 10/17, 1994, 31–38; Nussbaum GDGF.

52. In ASD I call it "the thick vague theory of the good."

53. Rawls, PL. Note that the consensus is defined in terms of a normative notion of reasonableness. Thus, the failure of some real individuals to agree will not be fatal to the view.

54. On this relationship, see HN.

55. The current version of this list reflects changes suggested to me by discussions during my visits to women's development projects in India. These include a new emphasis on bodily integrity, on employment, on property rights, and on dignity and nonhumiliation.

56. Although "normal length" is clearly relative to current human possibilities and may need, for practical purposes, to be to some extent relativized to local conditions, it seems important to think of it—at least at a given time in history—in universal and comparative terms, as the *Human Development Report* does, to give rise to complaint in a country that has done well with some indicators of life quality but badly on life expectancy. And although some degree of relativity may be put down to the differential genetic possibilities of different groups (the "missing women" statistics, for example, allow that on the average women live somewhat longer than men), it is also important not to conclude prematurely that inequalities between groups—for example, the growing inequalities in life expectancy between blacks and whites in the United States—are simply genetic variation, not connected with social injustice.

57. The precise specification of these health rights is not easy, but the work currently being done on them in drafting new constitutions in South Africa and Eastern Europe gives reasons for hope that the combination of a general specification of such a right with a tradition of judicial interpretation will yield something practicable. It should be noticed that I speak of health, not just health care; and health itself interacts in complex ways with housing, with education, with dignity. Both health and nutrition are controversial as to whether the relevant level should be specified universally, or relatively to the local community and its traditions. For example, is low height associated with nutritional practices to be thought of as "stunting" or as felicitous adaptation to circumstances of scarcity? For an excellent summary of this debate, see S.R. Osmani, ed., *Nutrition and Poverty* (Oxford: Clarendon Press, WIDER series, 1990), especially the following papers: on the relativist side, T.N. Srinivasan, "Undernutrition: Concepts, Measurements, and Policy Implications," 97–120; on the universalist side, C. Gopalan, "Undernutrition: Measurement and Implications," 17–48; for a compelling adjudication of the debate, coming out on the universalist side, see Osmani, "On Some Controversies in the Measurement of Undernutrition," 121–61.

58. There is a growing literature on the importance of shelter for health; for example, that the provision of adequate housing is the single largest determinant of health status for HIV-infected persons. Housing rights are increasingly coming to be constitutionalized, at least in a negative form—giving squatters grounds for appeal, for example, against a landlord who would bulldoze their shanties. On this as a constitutional right, see proposed Articles 11, 12,

and 17 of the South African Constitution, in a draft put forward by the African National Congress (ANC) committee adviser Albie Sachs, where this is given as an example of a justiciable housing right.

59. Some form of intimate family love is central to child development, but this need not be the traditional Western nuclear family. In the development of citizens it is crucial that the family be an institution characterized by justice as well as love. See Susan Moller Okin, *Justice, Gender, and the Family* (New York: Basic Books, 1989).

60. In terms of cross-cultural discussion, this item has proven the most controversial and elusive on the list. It also properly raises the question whether the list ought to be anthropocentric at all, or whether we should seek to promote appropriate capabilities for all living things. I leave further argument on these questions for another occasion.

61. ASD argues that property rights are distinct from, for example, speech rights, in the sense that property is a tool of human functioning and not an end in itself. See also Nussbaum, CHR.

62. Sen has not endorsed any such specific list of the capabilities.

63. See Sen, "Gender Inequality and Theories of Justice," in WCD, 259–73; Becker, "The Economic Way of Looking at Behaviour."

64. With Sen, I hold that the capability set should be treated as an interlocking whole. For my comments on his arguments, see NFC.

65. See ibid., with reference to Aristotle.

66. See HN. This is the core of Marx's reading of Aristotle.

67. See chapter 4.

68. See NFC, referring to Aristotle's similar distinctions.

69. This distinction is related to Rawls's distinction between social and natural primary goods. Whereas he holds that only the social primary goods should be on the list, and not the natural (such as health, imagination), we say that *the social basis* of the natural primary goods should most emphatically be on the list.

70. TJ, 62.

71. Rawls comments that "although their possession is influenced by the basic structure, they are not so directly under its control." TJ, 62. This is of course true if we are thinking of health, but if we think of the social basis of health, it is not true. It seems to me that the case for putting these items on the political list is just as strong as the case for the social basis of self-respect. In "The Priority of Right and Ideas of the Good," *Philosophy and Public Affairs* 17 (1988), 251–76, Rawls suggests putting health on the list.

72. See ASD and GDGF.

73. See HN. For the relation of capabilities to human rights, see CHR.

74. Sen, "Freedoms and Needs," 38.

75. PL 187–8.

76. Though in one form Aristotle had it too. See also GDGF; and CHR.

77. Compare Sen, "Freedoms and Needs," 38: "The importance of political rights for the understanding of economic needs turns ultimately on seeing human beings as people with rights to exercise, not as parts of a 'stock' or a 'population' that passively exists and must be looked after. What matters, finally, is how we see each other."

78. Chapter 3 (in this volume) argues that religious norms should not be imposed without choice on individuals who may not have opted for that religious tradition. In that sense, any religiously based employment restriction is questionable.

79. Chen, *The Lives of Widows in Rural India*. Girls in some regions of India are betrothed at a very young age and at that point become members of their husband's family, although the marriage will not be consummated until puberty. Such a girl is treated as widowed even if the male dies before consummation.

80. Chen, *A Quiet Revolution*.

81. Ibid.

82. Ibid., 202. Married at age seven, abandoned by her husband many years later, Rohima lives with her brother. Four of her children have died; one son and one daughter survive. Her son gives her some financial support.

83. See the account of these in Chen, *The Lives of Widows*.

84. Chen, *A Quiet Revolution*, 216.

85. Sen has stressed this throughout his writing on the topic. For an overview, see "Capability and Well-Being." And for some complications, see GDGF.

86. This is the strategy used by Robert Erikson's Swedish team when studying inequalities in political participation. See Robert Erikson, "Descriptions of Inequality," in Nussbaum and Sen, eds., *The Quality of Life*.

87. Rawls proceeds in a similar way, insisting that satisfactions that are not the outgrowth of one's very own choices have no moral worth. He conceives of the "two moral powers" (analogous to our practical reasoning) and of sociability (corresponding to our affiliation) as built into the definition of the parties in the original position, and thus as necessary constraints on any outcome they will select. See ASD.

88. Chen, *A Quiet Revolution*, 199.

89. The remark was cited by Richard Rorty in "Feminism and Pragmatism," *Michigan Quarterly Review* 30 (1989), 263; it has since been confirmed and repeated by MacKinnon herself.

90. Plato, *Republic*, Book V. Although Plato's proposal is theoretical and utopian, it is closely based on observation of the functioning of women in Sparta. See S. Halliwell, *Plato: Republic V* (Warminster: Aris & Phillips, 1994).

91. See Sen, "Gender and Cooperative Conflicts."

92. On Rousseau, see Susan Moller Okin, *Women in Western Political Thought* (Princeton: Princeton University Press, 1979), and Jane Roland Martin, *Reclaiming a Conversation* (New Haven: Yale University Press, 1985). On some related recent arguments, for example, those of Allan Bloom, see Okin, *Justice*, chap. 1.

93. See the convincing summary in Anne Fausto-Sterling, *Myths of Gender*, 2nd ed. (New York: Basic Books, 1992).

94. Ibid.

95. John Stuart Mill, *The Subjection of Women* (1869), ed. Susan Moller Okin (Indianapolis, IN: Hackett, 1988).
96. Here I am in agreement with the general line of argument in Okin, *Women* and Martin, *Reclaiming*, and with the related arguments in Nancy Chodorow, *The Reproduction of Mothering* (Berkeley: University of California Press, 1978).
97. Jean-Jacques Rousseau, *Emile: or On Education*, trans. Allan Bloom (New York: Basic Books, 1979), Book V.
98. See Okin, *Women*; and Martin, *Reclaiming*.
99. See the discussion in Okin, *Women*.
100. Martha Nussbaum, *Sex and Social Justice* (Oxford: Oxford University Press, 1999), p. 21.

Chapter XV | Jürgen Habermas

1. (D): Only those action-norms are valid to which all possibly affected persons could agree as participants in rational discourses. (U): All affected can accept the consequences and the side effects its general observance can be anticipated to have for the satisfaction of everyone's interests. ("Discourse Ethics" in *Moral Consciousness and Communicative Action* [MIT Press, 1990]).
2. F.I. Michelman in *Florida Law Review* 41 (1989): 446 f.
3. Cf. *The Basic Law of the Federal Republic of Germany*, article 20, sec. 2.
4. Part I of *The Constitution Act, 1982*, being Schedule B to the *Canada Act 1982 (U.K.)*, 1982, c. 11 [*Charter*].
5. Treasury Board of Canada Secretariat, Press Release, "Canada's New Government cuts wasteful programs, refocuses spending on priorities, achieves major debt reduction as promised" (25 September 2006), online: Department of Finance, www.tbs-sct.gc.ca/media/nrcp/2006/0925_e.asp.
6. See: F.L. Morton & Rainer Knopff, *The Charter Revolution and the Court Party* (Peterborough: Broadview Press, 2000).
7. (U.K.), 30 & 31 Vict., c. 3, s. 91, reprinted in R.S.C. 1985, App. II, No. 5.
8. 33 Vict., c. 3 (Can.).
9. The program also included sections 2 and 27 when used in support of equality arguments under Section 15.
10. It is important to note that when the program was expanded to include equality rights, challenges could only be made against federal legislation, rather than against both levels of government (as is permitted by language challenges). When asked about the discrepancy, Noel Badiou, executive director of the CCP said it was not clear, but was likely a political decision. Email correspondence [26 June 2007].
11. Ian Brodie, *Friends of the Court: The Privileging of Interest Group Litigants in Canada* (Albany: State University Press, 2002) at 109. When John Crosbie was questioned 20 years later (in 2005) about why a Conservative government would expand such a program, he replied: "It was political correctness. If we had discontinued the program we would have received very bad publicity. It would have led

to the Liberal Party and opposition parties attacking on those grounds, saying we were not interested in human rights, and the institutions like *The Globe and Mail*, reinforcing our image as not being 'with it' on social issues. Because of that, I thought it was not worth it to quash the CCP when it was just beginning, in addition to which the *Charter* was new and needed to be tested to see what it really meant. But that time is long past." See Tasha Kheiriddin & Adam Daifallah, *Rescuing Canada's Right: Blueprint for a Conservative Revolution* (Mississauga: John Wiley & Sons Canada Ltd., 2005) at 104.
12. *Supra* note 5.
13. House of Commons, Standing Committee on Canadian Heritage, *Evidence*, No. 027 (6 December, 2006), online: http://cmte.parl.gc.ca/content/hoc/committee/391/chpc/evidence/ev2579520/chpcev27-e.pdf; House of Commons, Standing Committee on Canadian Heritage, *Evidence*, No. 028 (11 December, 2006), online: http://cmte.parl.gc.ca/content/hoc/committee/391/chpc/evidence/ev2600142/chpcev28-e.pdf; House of Commons, Standing Committee on Canadian Heritage, *Evidence*, No. 029 (13 December 2006), online: http://cmte.parl.gc.ca/content/hoc/committee/391/chpc/evidence/ev2608871/chpcev29-e.pdf; House of Commons, Standing Committee on Canadian Heritage, *Evidence*, No. 031 (1 February 2007), online: http://cmte.parl.gc.ca/content/hoc/committee/391/chpc/evidence/ev2654968/chpcev31-e.pdf.
14. Bill Curry, "Legal aid decision provokes backlash" *The Globe and Mail* (9 May 2007).
15. Commissioner of Official Languages, *Annual Report* (Ottawa: Public Works and Government Services Canada, 2007) at 6.
16. Senate, Standing Senate Committee on Official Languages, *Proceedings*, No. 16 (4 June 2007), online: www.parl.gc.ca/39/1/parlbus/commbus/ senate/com-e/o&-e/pdf/16 issue.pdf.
17. Margot Young, "Justice on the block: Cutting federal money for the Court Challenges Program hardest on those most in need of their constitutional rights" *Vancouver Sun* (12 October 2006).
18. REAL Women of Canada is an anti-feminist, non-partisan, non-denominational organization of independent women. Its mandate is "Women's Rights but not at the expense of human rights." See: <www.realwomenca.com>.
19. Standing Committee on Canadian Heritage, *Evidence*, No. 028 (11 December 2007), *supra* note 13 at 15.
20. The Canadian Constitution Foundation is a "registered charity, independent and non-partisan, with a unique charter which allows it to fund appropriate litigation." See: <www.canadianconstitutionfoundation.ca>.
21. *Supra* note 19 at 15.
22. Achieved by taking the total OLMG population in the province as a percentage of the total OLMG population in Canada. Quebec accounted for 37.1 per cent, while Ontario was 32.4 per cent, New Brunswick 15.7 per cent, followed by Alberta at 3.9 per cent of the total OLMG

population in Canada, and 9.2 per cent of the entire population of the province. Statistics Canada, *2001 Census of Population: Population by Mother Tongue, by Province and Territory*, E-STAT ed. (Ottawa: Statistics Canada, 2001), online: http://estat.statcan.ca/.

23. Edmund A. Aunger, "Legislating Language Use in Alberta: A Century of Incidental Provisions for a Fundamental Matter" (2004) 42 *Alberta Law Rev.* 463 at 497.

24. *Northwest Territories Act*, R.S.C. 1985, c. N-27.

25. *Languages Act*, R.S.A. 2000, c. L-6.

26. Ibid.

27. Kenneth Munro, "French Language and Educational Rights in Alberta: An Historical Perspective" in David Scheiderman, ed., *Language and the State: The Law and Politics of Identity* (Edmonton: Centre for Constitutional Studies, 1989) at 252.

28. Standing Committee on Canadian Heritage, *Evidence*, No. 031 (1 February 2007), *supra* note 13 at 1.

29. Paul Pross, *Group Politics and Public Policy*, 2nd ed. (Toronto: Oxford University Press, 1992) at 48. Pross has traced the history of the bureaucracy, and consequently, the development and progression of the pressure group as well. While he does not presume that pressure groups had influence on the organization of the bureaucracy, he does contend that the state of the bureaucracy has a direct influence on the organization and effectiveness of pressure groups.

30. Paul Pross, "An Unruly Messenger: Interest Groups and Bureaucracy in Canadian Democracy" (Paper presented to the Annual Meeting of the Institute of Public Administration of Canada, August 2006) [unpublished] at 6.

31. "Special" interest groups are considered by conservatives to be on the ideological left.

32. Alexandra Dobrowolsky "Of Special Interest: Interest, Identity, and Feminist Constitutional Activism in Canada" (1998) 31:4 *Canadian J. of Political Science* 707 at 732.

33. Donald Savoie, *Governing from the Centre: The Concentration of Power in Canadian Politics* (Toronto: University of Toronto Press, 1999); Jeffrey Simpson, *The Friendly Dictatorship* (Toronto: McClelland & Stewart Ltd., 2001).

34. "Leak plugged? Federal worker arrested for allegedly leaking environment docs" *Canadian Press* (9 May 2007), online: *Edmonton Sun* www.edmontonsun.com/news/canada/2007/05/09/4166826.html.

35. Bill Curry and Chuck Strahl, "Harper changes tune on appointments" *The Globe and Mail* (18 April 2006).

36. Don Martin, "Don Martin: Tories have book on political wrangling" *The National Post* (17 May 2007).

37. *Ibid.*

38. Murray Brewster, "Partisan political spat shuts down official languages committee" *CBC News Online* (15 May 2007).

39. Donald Savoie, "The Rise of Court Government in Canada" (1999) 32:4 *Canadian J. of Political Science* 635 at 643.

40. Alexander Panetta, "Harper says he'll avoid national media because they're biased against him" *Canadian Press* (24 May 2006).

41. Jane Taber and Gloria Galloway, "Journalists booted from Tory retreat" *Globe and Mail* (2 August 2007), online: *The Globe and Mail* www.theglobeandmail.com/servlet/story/rtgam.20070802.wtories02/bnstory/national/home.

42. *Supra* note 6.

43. Ibid. at 17.

44. *Supra* note 11 at 124.

45. Ian Brodie, "Interest Group Litigation and the Embedded State: Canada's Court Challenges Program" (2001) 34:2 *Canadian J. of Political Science* 357 at 371.

46. *Supra* note 11 at 122.

47. William Christian, "Court-challenge staff had to know the axe would fall" *Kitchener-Waterloo Record* (30 September 2006).

48. Kheiriddin & Daifallah, *supra* note 11 at 114.

49. Ibid.

50. Jeffery Simpson, "Canada goes greener: Farewell Kandahar, hello Kyoto" *The Economist* (December 2007) 47.

Chapter XVI | Michel Foucault

1. Michel Foucault is referring to the psychiatric movement (defined either as "anthropophenomenology" or *Daseinanalyse*) which derived new conceptual instruments from the philosophy of Husserl and Heidegger. Foucault examines this in his earliest writings. Cf. chapter 4 of *Maladie mentale et personalité* (Paris: PUF, 1954) ("La Maladie et l'existence"); the introduction to Ludwig Binswanger, *Le Rêve et l'existence* (Paris: Desclée de Brouwer) (reprinted in *Dits et écrits* vol. 1, pp. 65–119; English translation by Forrest Williams, "Dream, Imagination, and Existence," in Michel Foucault and Ludwig Binswanger, *Dream and Existence*, ed. Keith Holler [Atlantic Highlands, N.J.: Humanities Press]; "La Psychologie de 1850 à 1950," in A. Weber and D. Husiman, *Tableau de la philosophie contemporaine* (Paris: Fischbacher, 1954) (reprinted in *Dits et écrits* vol. 1, pp. 120–37); "La Recherche en psychologie," in J.E. Morrère, ed., *Des Chercheurs s'interrogent* (Paris: PUF, 1957) (reprinted in *Dits et écrits* vol. 1, pp. 137–58). Foucault returned to these topics in his last years; cf. *Colloqui con Foucault* (Salerno: 10/17 Cooperativa editrice, 1981) (French translation: "Entretien avec Michel Foucault," *Dits et écrits* vol. 4, pp. 41–95; English translation by James Goldstein and James Cascaito, *Remarks on Marx* [New York: Semiotext(e), 1991]).

2. See Wilhelm Reich, *Die Funktion des Orgasmus: zur Psychopathologie und zur Sociologie des Geschlechtslenens* (Vienna: Internationaler psychanalytischer Verlag, 1927) (French translation: *La Fonction de l'orgasme* [Paris: L'Arche, 1971]; English translation: *The Function of the Orgasm* [New York: Condor Books, 1983]); *Der Einbrach des Sexualmoral* (Berlin: Verlag fur Sexualpolitik, 1932) (French translation: *L'Irruption de la morale sexuelle*

[Paris: Payot, 1972]; English translation: *The Invasion of Compulsory Sex Morality* [New York: Farrar, Straus & Giroux, 1971]); *Charakteranalyse* (Vienna: Selbstverlag des Verfassers. 1933) (French translation: *L'Analyse caractérielle* [Paris: Payot, 1971]; English translation: *Character Analysis* [New York: Farrar, Straus & Giroux, 1972]); *Massenpsychologie des Faschismus: zur Sexualönomie der politischen Reaktion und zur proletarischen Sexualpolitik* (Copenhagen, Paris, and Zurich: Verlag fur Sexualpolitik, 1933) (French translation: *La Psychologie de masse du fascisme* [Paris: Payot, 1974]; English translation: *The Mass Psychology of Fascism* [New York: Simon and Schuster, 1970]); *Die Sexualität im Kulturkampf* (Copenhagen: Sexpol Verlag, 1936) (English translation: *The Sexual Revolution* [London: Vision Press, 1972]).

3. Michel Foucault is obviously referring here to Herbert Marcuse, *Eros and Civilizatino: A Philosophical Inquiry into Freud* (Boston: Beacon Press, 1955) (French translation: *Eros et civilisation* [Paris: Seuil, 1971]) and *One-Dimensional Man: Studies in the Ideology of Advanced Industrial Society* (Boston: Beacon Press, 1966) (French translation: *L'Homme unidimensionnel* [Paris: Seuil, 1970]).

4. Gilles Deleuze and Félix Guattari, *Anti-Oedipe* (Paris: Éditions de Minuit, 1972). It will be recalled that Foucault develops this interpretation of *Anti-Oedipe* as *livre evenement* in his preface to the English translation (English translation by Robert Hurley, Mark Seem, and Helen R. Lane. *Anti-Oedipus* [New York: Viking, 1983]). For the French version see *Dits et écrits* vol. 3, pp. 133–36.

5. In the manuscript, "travel" replaces "money."

6. The concepts of "minor" and "minority"—singular events rather than individual essences, individuation through "ecceity" rather than substantiality—were elaborated by Gilles Deleuze and Félix Guattari in their *Kafka, pour une littérature mineure* (Paris: Éditions de Minuit, 1975) (English translation by Reda Bensmaia, *Kafka: For a Minor Literature* [Minneapolis: University of Minnesota Press, 1986]), reworked by Deleuze in his article "Philosophie et minorite" (*Critique*, February 1978) and then further developed, notably in Gilles Deleuze and Félix Guattari, *Mille Plateaux; capitalisme et schizophrénie* (Paris: Éditions de Minuit, 1980) (English translation by Brian Massumi, *A Thousand Plateaus: Capitalism and Schizophrenia* [Minneapolis: University of Minnesota Press]). "Minority" also relates to the concept of "molecular" elaborated by Felix Guattari in *Psychoanalyse et transversalité, Essai d'analyse institutionelle* (Paris: Maspero, 1972). Its logic is that of "becoming" and "intensities."

7. Michel Foucault is referring to the debate about the concept of the episteme and the status of discontinuity that was opened up by the publication of *Les Mots el les choses: une archaeologie des sciences humaines* (Paris: Gallimard, 1966) (English translation: *The Order of Things* [London: Tavistock, 1970]). He replied to criticisms in a series of theoretical and methodological *mises au point*. See in particular "Réponse à une question," *Esprit*, May 1968,

reprinted in *Dits et écrits* vol. 1, pp. 673–95; "Réponse au Cercle d'épistemologie," *Cahiers pour l'analyse* 9 (1968), pp. 9–40, reprinted in *Dits et écrits* vol. 1, pp. 694–731; English translation: "On the Archaeology of the Science: Response to the Epistemology Circle," *Essential Works* vol. 2, pp. 297–353.

8. At that time, a *député* in the Parti Communiste Français.

9. Cf. G.W.F. Hegel, *Grundlinien der Philosophie des Rechtes* (Berlin, 1821), pp.182–340 (French translation: *Principes de la philosophie du droit* [Paris: Vrin, 1975]); *Hegel's Philosophy of Right*, translated with notes by T.M. Knox (Oxford: Clarendon Press, 1952); Sigmund Freud, "Das Unbewussten," in *Internationale Zeitschrifte fur ärtzliche Psychoanalyse*, vol. 3 (1915) (English translation: "The Unconscious," in *Pelican Freud Library, Vol. 11: On Metapsychology: The Theory of Psychoanalysis* [Harmondsworth: Penguin, 1984]); and *Die Zukunft einer Illusion* (Leipzig/Vienna/Zurich: Internationaler Psychoanalytischer Verlag, 1927) (French translation: *L'Avenir d'une illusion* [Paris: Denoël, 1932], reprinted Paris: PUF, 1995; English translation: *The Future of an Illusion*, in *The Pelican Freud Library, Vol. 12: Civilization, Society and Religion, Group Psychology, Civilization and Its Discontents and Other Works* [Harmondsworth: Penguin, 1985]; on Reich, cf. note 2 above.

10. Foucault alludes to the well-known formulation of Cad von Clausewitz's principle (*Vom Kriege* book 1, chap. 1, xxiv, in *Hinterlassene Werke*, bd. 1-2-3 [Berlin, 1832]): "War is a mere continuation of policy by other means. . . . War is not merely a political act, but also a truly political instrument, a continuation of political commerce, a carrying out of the same by other means." *On War*, edited with an introduction by Anatol Rapoport (Harmondsworth: Penguin, 1982) (French translation: *De la guerre* [Paris: Éditions de Minuit, 1955]).

11. This promise was not kept. A lecture on "repression" is, however, intercalated in the manuscript; it was presumably given at a foreign university. Foucault returns to this question in *La Volonté de savoir* (Paris: Gallimard, 1976) (English translation by Robert Hurley: *The History of Sexuality, Volume I: An Introduction* [Harmondsworth: Penguin, 1981]).

12. Thomas Hobbes, *Leviathan, or the Matter, Forme and Power of a Common-Wealth Ecclesiasticall and Civill* (London, 1651). The Latin translation of the text, which was in fact a new version, was published in Amsterdam in 1668.

13. Foucault is alluding to the famous frontispiece to the "Head" edition of *Leviathan* published by Andrew Crooke. It depicts the body of a state constituted by its subjects, with the head representing the sovereign, who holds a sword in one hand and a crosier in the other. The basic attributes of civil and ecclesiastical power are depicted below it.

14. Wilhelm Reich, *Der Einbruch der Sexualmoral*.

15. Reimut Reich, *Sexualität und Klassenkampf: zur Abwehr repressiver Ensublimierung* (Frankfurt am Main: Verlag

Neue Kritik, 1968) (French translation: *Sexualité et lutte de classe* [Paris: Maspero, 1969]).

16. The thirteen *parlements* of the Ancien Régime were high courts of appeal and had no legislative powers, though the parlement de Paris did attempt to usurp such powers. [Trans.]

17. The reference is to the "Napoleonic codes," or in other words the Code civil of 1804, the Code d'instruction criminelle of 1808, and the Code pénal of 1810.

18. Michel Foucault, "The Subject and Power," *Critical Inquiry*, 8 (4), 1982: 777–95, at p. 788.

Chapter XVII | Will Kymlicka

1. The comparatively sparse attention paid to race and racialized minorities by Canadian political philosophers, Kymlicka included, in discussions of diversity and multiculturalism has generated criticism by critical race theorists and scholars urging a more "intersectional" analysis of oppression.

2. He defines societal culture as the context of individuals' lives, which "provides its members with meaningful ways of life across a full range of human activities, including social, educational, religious, recreational and economic life, encompassing both public and private spheres. These cultures tend to be territorially concentrated, and based on a shared language" *MC*, p. 76.

3. For these estimates (and their imprecision), see Laczko 1994; Gurr 1993; Nielsson 1985. Iceland and the Koreas are commonly cited as two examples of countries which are more or less culturally homogeneous.

4. For surveys of minority rights claims worldwide, see Sigler 1983; Gurr 1993; Van Dyke 1977; Capotorti 1979; Hannum 1990.

5. On the assumption of cultural homogeneity in Western political thought, see McRae 1979; Van Dyke 1977; Walzer 1982: 1–3; McNeill 1986: 23. On the reality of cultural heterogeneity throughout history, and its causes, see McNeill 1986. On the ever-increasing scale of this diversity, see Castles and Miller 1993: 8.

6. For liberal endorsements of this position, see Glazer 1975: 220; 1978: 98; 1983: 124; Gordon 1975: 105; Porter 1975: 295; van den Berghe 1981*b*: 347; Ajzenstat 1984: 251–2; Rorty 1991: 209; Kukathas 1991: 22; Edwards 1985; Brotz 1980: 44.

7. For this debate, see Rosenfeld 1991; Sowell 1990.

8. For a variety of examples, see Barsh and Henderson 1980: 241–8; 1982: 69–70; Clinton 1990; Gordon 1975; 1978; 1981; Glazer 1975: 220; Van Dyke 1982: 28–30; Svensson 1979: 430–3; Adam 1979; Deganaar 1987; Knopff 1982: 29–39; Laforest 1991; Ajzenstat 1988: ch. 8; F. Morton 1985: 73–83; Schwartz 1986: ch. 1; Brotz 1980: 44–5; Asch 1984: 75–88, 100–4; Weaver 1985: 141–2; For more references and discussion, see Kymlicka 1989*a*: ch. 7; 1991.

9. For a summary of these developments, see Lerner 1991; Thornberry 1991; Bloed 1994; Hannum 1993.

10. On the importance of individual rights to the protection of groups, see Buchanan 1989; Walzer 1990; Macdonald 1989: 122–3; Tomasi 1991; Kymlicka 1990: chs. 4–6.

11. Some indigenous peoples have argued before the UN that they too have a right to self-determination under the UN Charter (see *Mikmaq Tribal Society v. Canada* (1984) UN Doc. E/CN.4/Sub.2/204; Grand Council of the Crees 1992). For discussions of the salt-water thesis, and the right of self-determination under international law, see Pomerance 1982; Thornberry 1991: 13–21, 214–18; Crawford 1988; Makinson 1988.

12. On English Canadian opposition to nationalist demands for decentralization, see Stark 1992. A certain amount of *de facto* asymmetry in powers has been a long-standing aspect of Canadian federalism. However, many Canadians are unwilling to recognize this asymmetry formally in the constitution (see Gagnon and Garcea 1988; Taylor 1991; Cairns 1991). This is one reason why the 1992 Charlottetown Accord was defeated in the national referendum. Some people have claimed that a federal system cannot survive if it accords special status, but this is refuted by the experience of many countries. For a survey of various forms of asymmetrical federalism, see Elazar 1987: 54–7.

13. In Germany, federalism was imposed by the Allies after World War II to help prevent the rise of nationalist or authoritarian movements. For helpful discussions of the relationship between federalism and cultural diversity, see Howse and Knop 1993; Minow 1990*b*; Majone 1990; Gagnon 1993; Long 1991; Duchacek 1977; Elkins 1992; Norman 1994.

14. Hence Nathan Glazer is quite wrong when he says that the division of the United States into federal units preceded its ethnic diversity (Glazer 1983 276–7). This is true of the original thirteen colonies, but decisions about the admission and boundaries of new states were made after the incorporation of national minorities, and these decisions were deliberately made so as to avoid creating states dominated by national minorities.

15. For a comparative review of these developments, see Fleras and Elliot 1992. A proposal to entrench Aboriginal self-government constitutionally as a third order of government in Canada was included in the 1992 Charlottetown Accord. This would have covered both the "ethnic government" exercised by band councils on Indian reserves, and the "public self-government" exercised by the Inuit majority within the new territory of Nunavut (see Asch 1984: ch. 7). For the relation of Indian self-government to federalism, see Resnik 1989; Cassidy and Bish 1989; Long 1991.

16. Gurr 1993: viii; cf. Nietschmann 1987.

17. For a discussion of these rights in the British context, see Parekh 1990: 705; 1991: 197–204; Modood 1992; Poulter 1987. In Canada, see E. Kallen 1987: 325–31. In the USA, see Minow 1990*b*; Sandel 1990. For the Muslim girls in France, see Galeotti 1993. It is sometimes said that these measures are purely "symbolic." But measures relating to employment are very material, affecting people's "life chances" not just their "lifestyles."

18. For statistics on the (under-)representation of blacks and Hispanics in the United States, see C. Davidson 1992: 46. For statistics on the representation of various social groups in Canada, see RCERPF 1991: 93–6 and 192.

19. While self-government may entail guaranteed representation on inter-governmental bodies which negotiate, interpret, and modify the division of powers, it may also entail *reduced* representation on federal bodies which legislate in areas of purely federal jurisdiction, insofar as the self-governing group is not governed by the decisions of these federal bodies. I discuss the relationship between self-government and representation in Ch. 7.

20. For an interesting exploration of the idea of a "society," and its requirements for a certain level of institutional completeness and intergenerational continuity, see Copp 1992.

21. e.g., American studies indicate "an almost complete breakdown in the transmission of non-English languages between the second and third generations" (Steinberg 1981: 45). One reason why languages which do not achieve the status of a public language are unlikely to survive is that people lack the opportunity or incentive to use and develop them in cognitively stimulating ways (Skutnabb-Kangas 1988).

22. As Clarke notes, language is sometime[s] a "technical accomplishment," and sometimes the "main support for a distinct cultural identity" (Clarke 1934: 20). Over time, the immigrant language shifts from the latter to the former. As the immigrants slowly lose their mother tongue, so at the same time, and as a consequence, the dominant language is (in a different sense) taken away from its original ethnic speakers. That is, as immigrants become members of the larger anglophone culture, the descendants of the original Anglo-Saxon settlers cease to have any exclusive or privileged say over the development and use of the English language. This helps explain why North American English has diverged from English in Britain, where Anglo-Saxons continue to be the overwhelming majority of the speakers of the language (Johnson 1973: 117).

23. In earlier times, cultures did not have to form societal culture to survive, since there were fewer society-wide institutions shaping people's options. (The language of public schools was not an issue when there were no public schools.) Indeed, the very idea of a "societal culture" is a modern one. In medieval times, the idea that the various economic classes or castes would share a common culture was unheard of. Thus Todorov is historically correct when he says that "Culture is not necessarily national (it is even only exceptionally so). It is first of all the property of a region, or of an even smaller geographical entity; it may also belong to a given layer of a population, excluding other groups from the same country; finally, it may also include a group of countries" (Todorov 1993: 387). However, as Todorov himself notes, there is a powerful tendency in the modern world for culture to become national in scope.

24. The following argument is presented in much more detail in Kymlicka 1989a: ch. 2–4; 1990: ch. 6.

25. Liberals often make an exception where individuals are particularly vulnerable to weakness of will (e.g., paternalistic legislation against addictive drugs). The connection between rational revisability, the endorsement constraint, and the liberal prohibition on state paternalism is quite complicated. For Rawls' discussion of perfectionism, see Rawls 1988: 260, 265. For Dworkin's account, see 1989: 486–7; 1990. For general discussions see Kymlicka 1989b; Waldron 1989; Moore 1993: ch. 6; Caney 1991; Mason 1990; McDonald 1992: 116–21; Hurka 1994.

26. Allen Buchanan calls this the "rational revisability" model of individual choice (Buchanan 1975). The claim that we have a basic interest in being able rationally to assess and revise our current ends is often phrased in terms of the value of "autonomy." This label may be misleading, since there are many other conceptions of autonomy. For example, on one account of autonomy, the exercise of choice is intrinsically valuable, because it reflects our rational nature (this view is ascribed to Kant). Another account of autonomy argues that nonconformist individuality is intrinsically valuable (this view is often ascribed to Mill). I am making the more modest claim that choice enables us to assess and learn what is good in life. It presupposes that we have an essential interest in identifying and revising those of our current beliefs about value which are mistaken. When I use the term autonomy, therefore, it is in this (relatively modest) sense of "rational revisability." I discuss these different conceptions of autonomy in Kymlicka 1989a: ch. 4; 1990: ch. 6.

27. I discuss this in greater length in Kymlicka 1989a: ch. 8; 1995b. Of course, the models we learn about in our culture are often closely related to the models in other cultures. For example, models derived from the Bible will be part of the structure of many cultures with a Christian influence. And there are international bodies, like the Catholic Church, which actively seek to ensure this commonality amongst models in different cultures. So in saying that we learn about conceptions of the good life through our culture, I do not mean to imply that the goods are therefore culture-specific, although some are.

28. In explaining his notion of the decay of a cultural structure, Dworkin says that "We are all beneficiaries or victims of what is done to the language we share. A language can diminish; some are richer and better than others" (1985: 229). This is misleading if he means that some languages are *inherently* richer than others. All human languages have an equal capacity for evolution and adaptation to meet the needs of their speakers (Edwards 1985: 19; Skutnabb-Kangas 1988: 12). However, the range of options available in one's language can clearly decay.

29. I should note that Dworkin made his brief comments about "cultural structures" in the context of an argument regarding public funding of the arts, and they were not intended to provide a comprehensive description or theory about the nature of cultures. However, since he is one of the few liberal theorists to address explicitly the question of the relationship between freedom and culture, I have tried to draw out

the implications of his view. See also his claim that people "need a common culture and particularly a common language even to have personalities, and culture and language are social phenomena. We can only have the thoughts, and ambitions, and convictions that are possible within the vocabulary that language and culture provide, so we are all, in a patent and deep way, the creatures of the community as a whole" (Dworkin 1989: 488; cf. Dworkin 1985: 228, and the discussion in Kymlicka 1995b).

30. In Rawls' terminology, we can say that access to such a culture is a "primary good"—i.e., a good which people need, regardless of their particular chosen way of life, since it provides the context within which they make those particular choices. I explore how this argument relates to Rawls' account of "primary goods" in more depth in Kymlicka 1989a: ch. 7. For related arguments about the dependence of freedom on culture, see Taylor 1985; Tamir 1993: chs. 1–2; Hargalit and Raz 1990.

31. I am trying to respond here to the cogent questions raised by Binder 1993: 253–5; Buchanan 1991: 54–5; Waldron 1992a; Tomasi 1995; Nickel 1995; Lenihan 1991; Margalit and Halbertal 1994, amongst others.

32. For a discussion of these costs, and the extent to which they vary between children and adults, see Nickel 1995.

33. It is worth remembering that, while many immigrants flourish in their new country, there is a selection factor at work. That is, those people who choose to uproot themselves are likely to be the people who have the weakest psychological bond to the old culture, and the strongest desire and determination to succeed elsewhere. We cannot assume a priori that they represent the norm in terms of cultural adaptability. As John Edwards notes, the ability to communicate does not only involve pragmatic language skills, but also the "inexpressible" knowledge of historical and cultural associations tied up with the language, and this may be difficult or impossible for immigrants to acquire fully: "the symbolic value of language, the historical and cultural associations which it accumulates, and the "natural semantics of remembering" all add to the basic message a rich underpinning of shared connotations . . . the ability to read between the lines, as it were, depends upon a cultural continuity in which the language is embedded, and which is not open to all. Only those who grow up within the community can, perhaps, participate fully in this expanded communicative interaction" (Edwards 1985: 17).

34. The only significant difference, Dion notes, concerns openness to immigration, a difference that is understandable in the light of francophone fears as a minority.

35. The danger of oppression reflects the fact that many traditional roles and practices were defined historically on the basis of sexist, racist, classist, and homophobic assumptions. Some social roles are so compromised by their unjust origins that they should be rejected entirely, not just gradually reformed (D. Phillips 1993). In some places, Sandel qualifies his idea of constitutive ends in a way that suggests that people can, after all, stand back and assess even their most deeply held ends. But once these qualifications are added in, it is no longer clear how Sandel's conception of the person differs from the liberal one he claims to be criticizing (see Kymlicka 1989a: chs. 2–4; 1990: ch. 5). In his more recent work, Rawls has attempted to accommodate the communitarian view, and defend liberalism without insisting on the rational revisability of our ends. I do not think his new defence works, and I explain why in Ch. 8.

36. Of course, once that national existence is not threatened, then people will favour increased mobility, since being able to move and work in other cultures is a valuable option for some people under some circumstances. For liberal defenders of open borders—all of whom see themselves as criticizing the orthodox liberal view—see Ackerman 1980: 89–95; Carens 1987; Hudson 1986; King 1983; Bader 1995.

37. As Higham puts it, "the English in all the colonies before the Revolution conceived of themselves as founders, settlers or planters—the formative population of those colonial societies—not as immigrants. Theirs was the polity, the language, the pattern of work and settlements, and many of the mental habits to which the immigrants would have to adjust" (Higham 1976: 6). There is surprisingly little written on the "theory of colonization," and how it differs from individual emigration. For one exception, see Mills 1974, esp. pp. 50, 117–20.

38. Of course, the children of immigrants do not consent, and it is not clear that parents should be able to waive their children's rights. For this reason, it is important that governments should strive to make the children of immigrants feel "at home" in the mainstream culture, to feel that it is "their" culture. Adult immigrants may be willing to accept a marginalized existence in their new country, neither integrated into the mainstream culture nor able to re-create their old culture. But this is not acceptable for children. It is they who would suffer most from the marginalization, since the parents at least had the benefit of being raised as full participants in a societal culture in their homeland, and can draw on this to add meaning to the practices they seek to maintain, in a diminished and fragmented way, in the new land. Children have the right to be raised as full participants in a societal culture which provides them with a diverse range of options, and parents cannot waive this right. For this reason, if we do not enable immigrants to re-create their old culture, then we must strenuously work to ensure that the children integrate into the mainstream.

39. Insofar as immigrant children are disadvantaged by the lack of bilingual education, this becomes an issue of basic fairness, since liberal theories of justice consider it a serious injustice to disadvantage people on the basis of unchosen factors like ethnicity, race, or class.

40. By contrast, the fact that Puerto Ricans continue to demand that Spanish be the official language of Puerto Rico shows that national minorities have not abandoned their national rights. See also the discussion of Hispanic groups in Ch. 2.

41. I should emphasize that I am talking here about the relatively small number of refugees who have resettled in Western countries. I am not talking about the very large refugee groups which have arisen in Asia or Africa when people flee into a neighbouring country to avoid war or famine. These groups may number in the hundreds of thousands or millions (e.g., in Pakistan, or Zaïre). But in the West, refugee groups tend to be small and dispersed.

42. Canada does make certain special allowances, beyond the usual polyethnic rights, for some refugees—e.g., the Doukhobours. The Doukhobours immigrated to Canada, not voluntarily as individuals, but *en masse* in order to preserve their culture, since they were being persecuted in Russia. Other groups, such as the Hutterites, came voluntarily, but only because of explicit promises from Canadian immigration officials that they would be able to settle as a group and maintain their own social institutions, such as schools. In neither of these cases can the group be said to have chosen to relinquish the claims that go with membership in their cultural community. The special arrangements regarding taxation, education, and military service for these groups reflect the fact that some groups fall in-between the category of national minority and voluntary immigrant, with an intermediate status that involves more than polyethnic rights but less than self-government. On the rights of these groups, see Janzen 1990.

43. Réaume 1991. This is one reason why I reject the claim that minority rights can be defended in terms of the intrinsic value of cultural diversity. This claim would not really defend the right to maintain one's culture—it would instead impose a *duty* to maintain one's culture (see Ch. 6, s. 3). The option for integration seems most relevant in the case of the outlying members of a national minority, who have, for whatever reason, dispersed from the major territorial concentration of the group (e.g., American Indians who have left the reservation for the city; French Canadians who live in western Canada).

44. Immigrant groups may also have this potentiality, given the appropriate conditions. But, if my earlier arguments were correct, immigrants have no claim of justice to those conditions, whereas national minorities do. Also, as I discuss in the next chapter, the value of cultural membership is not the only basis for national minorities to demand group-specific rights. In particular, national minorities may have historical rights that do not depend on the maintenance of a distinct societal culture.

45. Some of these groups have given rise to nationalist movements, even though they do not fit the usual pattern of "national" groups. Pre-existing societal cultures which have been incorporated into a larger state are the most common groups which see themselves as distinct "nations," and which have developed "nationalist" movements. But in some cases, an existing nation has undergone such a deep division, perhaps along racial or religious lines, that it has developed into two or more groups, each of which comes to see itself as a distinct nation or people, even though they continue to share a common language. If racial and religious differences and discrimination within a given societal culture become so entrenched that a common life comes to be seen as impossible, a sense of separate nationhood may develop within a subgroup of the larger society. And, over time, this subgroup may develop its own distinct "pervasive" or "societal" cultures (e.g., religious differences in the Punjab or Northern Ireland; racial differences in South Africa). Groups who share the same language, and who once shared many of the same institutions, may none the less come to feel incapable of sharing a common culture.

Such racial and religious differences account for most of the familiar cases of nationalist movements which are not based on language. But notice that such movements, from a liberal point of view, are either the cause or result of an injustice. To exclude people from participating in a public culture and institutions on the basis of race or religion is unjust. While the excluded group may go on to develop its own pervasive culture in response, this separate culture would not have developed were it not for the original injustice. Therefore, nationalist movements based on religion or race are evidence of an injustice, a failure to live up to liberal principles. Nationalist movements based on language, however, need not be grounded in injustice, and would persist even in an ideally just world. From a liberal point of view, language-based nationalism is maximally consistent with freedom and equality, since (unlike religious-based nationalism) it does not presuppose any shared conception of the good; and (unlike racially based nationalism) is not inherently exclusionary or discriminatory.

46. e.g., the idea that governments should preserve the "purity" of a language by preventing the adoption of foreign words is often illiberal. Many countries have adopted this aim, and established linguistic academies to try to enforce it (Edwards 1985: 27–34). This is a misguided policy, not only because it is futile to regulate word-choice in that way, but also because much of the pleasure and interest of a language comes from its diverse origins. However, this misguided attempt to preserve the purity of a language from foreign contamination is very different from the struggle to maintain the ability to use one's own (impure) language in public and private life, and not to be forced to use someone else's language. The people in France, Germany, and Spain who have been most concerned about preserving the purity of their language have no reason to worry about their ability to speak their own language. Conversely, many of the Puerto Ricans and Québécois who are concerned about maintaining their language rights have no interest in policing the adoption of foreign words.

47. As I noted earlier, Mill thought that the only or best way to ensure that smaller nations participate in the wider world is for them to assimilate to larger nations. The alternative for the members of small nations, he thought, is to

"sulk on his own rocks . . . revolving in his own little mental orbit, without participation or interest in the general movement of the world" (Mill 1972: 363–4). But isolation and assimilation are not the only options. One can enable smaller nations to participate in the larger world, but from a situation of equal power, where they can exercise some control over the rate and direction of cultural change.

48. While the members of a culture share the same language, it does not follow that all people who share the same language belong to the same culture. Not all anglophones in the world belong to the same culture. A culture, as I am defining it, involves a shared history as well as a common language, and their embodiment in particular societal practices and institutions. Hence English-speaking immigrants from Singapore, for example, must learn the "shared vocabulary of tradition and convention" which is used in American life. A common language, then, is necessary for a shared culture, but not sufficient. Of course, the idea of a "shared language" is itself slippery. For example, how do we distinguish different languages from different regional dialects of the same language? These judgments are somewhat arbitrary, and affected by political considerations. (Linguists like to say that a language is a dialect with an army.)

49. A similar problem arises with "ecocentric" arguments for preserving indigenous rights—i.e., the argument that Indian lands should be protected from external development because this is the best way to preserve the natural environment. This argument, which is popular amongst some First World environmentalists, has the result of limiting Indian claims to groups whose cultural practices and ethnic identity remain frozen in time. As da Cunha notes, many environmentalist discussions of Brazil have seen indigenous peoples as "part of the natural scenery." There has been a "naturalization" of indigenous groups, who are not seen as "agents with their own specific projects" (da Cunha 1992: 286–7; cf. Kymlicka 1995c). Hence environmentalists feel betrayed when indigenous peoples attempt to improve their standard of living by commercially exploiting their natural resources (e.g., by selling logging or mineral leases).

50. I explore this distinction in more depth in Kymlicka 1989a: ch. 8.

51. This phrase is from the judgment of the Canadian Supreme Court in explaining its interpretation of the equality guarantees under the Canadian Charter of Rights (Andrews v. Law Society of British Columbia 1 SCR 143; 56 DLR (4th) 1). See also Government of Canada 1991b: 10.

52. For examples of this view, see Knopff 1979; F. Morton 1985; Kukathas 1992a; Hindess 1993; Maré 1992: 107–10; Rawls 1975: 88, 93, and the references cited in Ch. 1 n.4.

53. I explored this relationship between national rights and liberal egalitarian justice in Kymlicka 1989a: ch. 9. For what it is worth, I continue to endorse the argument in that chapter, but I should have been clearer about its scope. I would now describe the argument in that chapter as an equality-based defence of certain external protections for national minorities. I did not use those terms at the time, in part because I did not have a very clear conception of the variety of rights, groups, and moral justifications that are involved in the debate.

54. I am here disagreeing with Tamir, who argues that the larger a national minority is, the more rights it should have (1993: 75). On my view, if a national group is large enough, it may have little need for group-differentiated rights, since it can ensure its survival and development through the usual operation of the economic marketplace and democratic decision making. (This might be true, for example, if a binational state contained two nations of roughly equal size and wealth.)

55. On the role of indigenous land claims in a liberal egalitarian framework, see Kymlicka 1995c; Penz 1992; 1993; Russell 1993; Tully 1994. It is important to note that the equality argument for land claims is not based on notions of compensatory justice. The compensatory argument says that because indigenous peoples were the legal owners of their traditional lands, and because their lands were taken away illegally, they should be compensated for this historical wrong. Since the debate over land claims is often couched in the language of compensatory justice, I should say a word about this. I take it as given that indigenous peoples have suffered terrible wrongs in being dispossessed of their lands, and that they should be compensated for this in some way. Moreover, I believe that indigenous peoples continue to have certain property rights under the common law (in former British colonies), wherever these have not been explicitly extinguished by legislation. (That is to say, the terra nullius doctrine is wrong in terms both of morality and the common law.) But it is a mistake, I think, to put too much weight on historical property rights. For one thing, these claims do not, by themselves, explain why indigenous peoples have rights of self-government. Many groups have been wrongfully dispossessed of property and other economic opportunities, including women, blacks, and Japanese immigrants in the United States and Canada during World War II. Each of these groups may be entitled to certain forms of compensatory justice, but this does not by itself explain or justify granting powers of self-government (rather than compensatory programmes to promote integration and equal opportunity within the mainstream). Suffering historical injustice is neither necessary nor sufficient for claiming self-government rights (see Ch. 2, s. 2).

Moreover, the idea of compensating for historical wrongs, taken to its logical conclusion, implies that all the land which was wrongly taken from indigenous peoples in the Americas or Australia or New Zealand should be returned to them. This would create massive unfairness, given that the original European settlers and later immigrants have now produced hundreds of millions of descendants, and this land is the only home they know. Changing circumstances often make it impossible and undesirable to compensate for certain historical wrongs. As Jeremy Waldron puts it, certain historical wrongs are "superseded" (Waldron 1992*b*). Also, the land held by some indigenous groups at the time of contact was itself the result of the conquest or coercion of other indigenous groups (Mulgan 1989: 30–1; Crowe 1974: 65–81). The compensatory argument would presumably require rectifying these pre-contract injustices as well. (For other difficulties with compensatory claims, see Brilmayer 1992.)

The equality argument does not try to turn back the historical clock, nor to restore groups to the situation they would have been in the absence of any historical injustice. (These compensatory aims actually fit more comfortably with Nozick's libertarian theory of entitlement than with a liberal egalitarian theory of distributive justice—see Lyons 1981.) The aim of the equality argument is to provide the sort of land base needed to sustain the viability of self-governing minority communities, and hence to prevent unfair disadvantages with respect to cultural membership now and in the future. In short, the equality argument situates land claims within a theory of distributive justice, rather than compensatory justice.

Waldron assumes that indigenous land claims are all based on claims for compensatory justice (Waldron 1992*b*). In fact, however, most indigenous groups focus, not on reclaiming all of what they had before European settlement, but on what they need now to sustain themselves as distinct societies (see the declaration of the World Council of Indigenous Peoples, quoted in Nettheim 1988: 115; Sharp 1990: 150–3). Historical factors are, of course, relevant in other ways. The "historical agreement" argument I discuss below is very much history-based.

56. The only attempt I know of to reconcile official languages with "benign neglect" is by Rainer Knopff. He argues that language has two functions: it can function as the vehicle for the transmission of a particular culture, but it can also function as "a culturally neutral, or utilitarian, means of communication which allows those of different cultures to participate in the same political community" (Knopff 1979: 67). By placing the emphasis on the utilitarian function, governments "can enact official languages without at the same time legislating official cultures . . . in enacting 'official languages,' one does not necessarily imply that the cultures which these languages transmit and represent thereby become 'official cultures'" (Knopff 1979: 67). Culture, Knopff argues, "remains a purely private affair" in Canada, for while English and French have official backing as the "utilitarian" languages, all languages compete on equal terms for "cultural" allegiance. It is the "task of the individual members of a culture to show the excellence of their product on the cultural marketplace, as it were. If they succeed, the language of that culture will become attractive to others . . . if [a] culture, and hence, language, cannot show itself to be worthy of choice in the light of standards of the good, then it deserves to disappear" (Knopff 1979: 70). This view of language as a "culturally neutral medium" has been thoroughly discredited in the literature. In any event, it is simply not true that teaching in the English language in public schools is totally divorced from the teaching of the history and customs of the anglophone society.

57. e.g., the Canadian government justified its proposal to eliminate the treaty rights of Indians on the grounds that "we can only be just in our time" (Trudeau 1969: 296). Trudeau was paraphrasing John F. Kennedy's famous quote about justice for blacks in the United States.

58. Chartrand argues that this is the current situation with respect to the Métis in Canada, who agreed to join Canada on the basis of promises made to them under the Manitoba Act 1870, which have since been broken (Chartrand 1993: 241).

59. These arguments parallel common arguments for the protection of endangered plant and animal species, which are seen as both enriching the world aesthetically, and as providing potential sources of valuable genetic material or other substances that might be of human benefit.

60. Many liberals defend state funding of the arts or museums on the ground that the state has a responsibility to ensure an adequate range of options for future generations, which the cultural market-place may fail to protect (Dworkin 1985: ch. 11; Raz 1986: 162; Black 1992; Kymlicka 1989*b*: 893–5). If we accept that active measures are justified to preserve the richness and diversity of our cultural resources, then programs such as the funding of ethnic festivals or immigrant language classes can be seen as falling under this heading. Indeed, as I noted in Chapter II, some people defend this funding simply as a way of ensuring that ethnic groups are not discriminated against in state funding of art and culture. (I should note that other liberals view any such state funding as illegitimate (e.g., Rawls 1971: 331–2; Waldron 1989).)

61. For a discussion of the attempts to reform the millets, inspired by Western liberalism, see Davidson 1982: 332; Braude and Lewis 1982: 18–23, 28–31; Karpat 1982: 159–63.

62. This system of toleration is, in one sense, the opposite of that in the West, since it unites, rather than separates, church and state. It is interesting to note that the two systems had similar historical origins. The Ottoman restrictions on the building and location of non-Muslim churches were similar to the system of "licensed coexistence" established under the Edict of Nantes (1598). Under that Edict, which ended the Wars of Religion[,] Protestants in France could only build new churches in certain locations, and only with a state licence. In the West, however, state-licensed coexistence between Protestants and Catholics gradually evolved into a system of individual freedom of conscience. This never occurred in the Ottoman Empire.

63. Interestingly, Rawls never considers this model of tolerance. He talks about "the principle of tolerance" as if there were just one, which he equates with the idea of freedom of conscience (e.g., Rawls 1987: 18, 23; **1989**: 251; 1982*b*: 25–6; 1985: 225). Yet the millet model is arguably the more natural form of religious tolerance. The historical record suggests that "in practice, religions

have usually felt most violently intolerant not of other religions but of dissenters within their own ranks" (Elton 1984: p. xiii).

64. See Nickel 1990: 214. Rawls' fear that the Millian conception of autonomy is not widely shared depends on conflating this conception of autonomy with the other, more controversial, conceptions discussed in Ch. 5 n. 7. It is important to note that while Mill's conception is "general," in applying to all areas of life, it is not "comprehensive," since it does not define a set of final ends or intrinsic goods to be pursued by each individual. Rather, it concerns the capacity by which we deliberate and assess our final ends.

65. This criticism has been raised by Kukathas 1992a; Chaplin 1993; McDonald 1993; Williams 1994, amongst others. The quotation is from Kukathas 1992a: 121.

66. If female members marry outside the tribe, their children are denied membership. But if men marry outside the tribe, the children are members. This discriminatory rule was upheld in *Santa Clara Pueblo v. Martinez* 436 US 49 (1978).

67. Some liberals hope that the United Nations will someday command the authority to intervene forcibly in foreign countries on behalf of human rights. But at present international intervention is largely limited to cases of gross violations of basic human rights—e.g., slavery, genocide, ethnic cleansing—and most contemporary liberals have accepted this. In any event, virtually everyone today agrees that only an internationally accepted body like the UN could have the authority to intervene forcibly. For example, a group of private citizens would have no legitimate authority to invade Saudi Arabia, even if they were motivated solely by a concern for human rights. Nor would a group of neighbouring states. No individual or state can simply declare itself the international protector of human rights, with the authority to forcibly intervene whenever and wherever it sees a government violating the rights of its citizens.

68. For the imposition of federal civil rights guarantees on Indian tribes, see Resnik 1989; Ball 1989; Tsosie 1994. For the imposition of both federal civil rights guarantees and federal court enforcement of them in Puerto Rico, see Aleinikoff 1994.

69. For a survey of the arguments against imposing liberalism on other countries, see Walzer 1977; 1980. I think that virtually all of Walzer's points also argue against imposing liberalism on national minorities, although Walzer himself does not always make this connection.

70. The ability of members to leave is a very important proviso. However, unlike some commentators (Svensson 1979: 437; Kukathas 1992a: 133), I do not think it is sufficient to justify internal restrictions, any more than racial segregation in the American South was made legitimate by the fact that blacks could move north (although some defenders of segregation did make this argument). Kukathas, for example, accords cultural groups very great powers over their own members (including the right to restrict their freedom of speech and association, or to discriminate in

the provision of services on the basis of gender or religious belief). Indeed, cultural minorities have virtually unlimited power over their own members, so long as individual members have a right to exit the community (Kukathas 1992a: 133). Kukathas thinks that this should be sufficient for liberals, for while it does not include any principle of respect for autonomy, it is a liberal theory "inasmuch as it does not sanction the forcible induction into or imprisoning of any individual in a cultural community" (1992a: 125). But this is too weak to count as a distinctly liberal theory. Very few conservatives, socialists, or communitarians would accept forcible induction into a community.

Kukathas later adds that individuals must have a "substantial" right of exit (1992a: 133), and that recognizing such a right will mean that "the ethical balance between individual and group has shifted irrevocably in the individual's direction" (1992a: 128, quoting Mulgan 1989: 64). The threat of exit, he thinks, will give individuals the *de facto* ability to question communal authority. But he has a dubious view of what gives individuals a "substantial" right to leave. He says that people have substantial freedom of exit even if they have been deprived of literacy, education, or the freedom to learn about the outside world, *so long as they have an open market society to enter into* (1992a: 134). In other words, one's freedom to leave is determined by the openness of the society one might enter, no matter how closed one's own community is. He seems to think that someone who has been denied an education (perhaps because she is female), and who is denied the right to associate with or speak to anyone outside her culture, none the less has a substantial freedom to leave, assuming she can enter a market society. Most liberals, I think, would argue that she does not have a substantial freedom to leave, since she lacks the preconditions for making a meaningful choice, and that any system of minority rights which gives cultural communities that much power over their individual members is seriously deficient from a liberal point of view. See also L. Green 1994; Kymlicka 1992a.

71. Some liberals have argued that tolerating these non-liberal groups can provide certain incidental benefits to the larger liberal society—e.g., a model of moral conviction that is difficult to sustain in modern societies (Macedo 1995; Galston 1995). I do not myself think this is an adequate reason for tolerating injustice.

72. Joseph Raz, for example, seems to assume that most indigenous cultures are inherently illiberal, and so incapable of liberalization. Speaking, *inter alia*, of indigenous communities which do not give their members the conditions of autonomous choice, he says we face the choice of "taking action to assimilate the minority group," or of accepting their illiberal ways. He says that the "break-up" of these communities is the "inevitable by-product" of attempts to liberalize their institutions (Raz 1986: 423–4). But he gives no reason for thinking that indigenous cultures are less capable of liberalizing than other cultures. As I noted in Ch. 5, it is important to remember that existing liberal

nations were all once quite illiberal. To assume that any culture which is now illiberal is therefore inherently illiberal, and incapable of reform, is ahistorical.

73. See e.g., the statement of the First Nations of Treaty 6 and 7, which said that applying the Canadian Charter to Aboriginal self-government "is a subjection of a value system based on individual rights. Our governments are based on the paramountcy of collective rights" (*Globe and Mail*, 24 Sept. 1992, p. A5).

Chapter XVIII | Charles Taylor

1. Taken from "Why Do Nations Have to Become States?" in *Philosophers Look at Canadian Confederation*, ed. Stanley G. French (Montreal: L'Association canadienne de philosophie, 1979).

2. For example, Jean-Pierre Charbonneau and Gilbert Paquette, "L'Acte de 1867, une constitution colonialiste," in *L'Option* (Montreal: Editions de l'homme, 1978), 125.

3. In January 2007, the town council of Herouxville approved a list of regulations drawn up by one of its counsellors. The list was directed at recent and prospective immigrants, particularly Muslims, and included prohibitions against actions already criminalized under Canadian law, such as stoning and burning women with acid. The list was widely condemned as racist, and quickly drew international notoriety. (Eds.)

Additional Credits

Index